COMPARATIVE DEFENSE POLICY

PART IV: FORCE POSTURE

PART V: WEAPONS ACQUISITION

PART VI: THE USE OF FORCE

CONTENTS

Manufactured in the United States of America

The Johns Hopkins University Press, Baltimore, Maryland 21218
The Johns Hopkins University Press Ltd., London

Library of Congress Catalog Card Number 73-19341
ISBN 0-8018-1581-9 (clothbound)
ISBN 0-8018-1597-5 (paperback)

Library of Congress Cataloging in Publication data
will be found on the last printed page of this book.

COMPARATIVE DEFENSE POLICY

Edited by

FRANK B. HORTON III
Associate Professor

ANTHONY C. ROGERSON
Assistant Professor

EDWARD L. WARNER III
Assistant Professor

With a Foreword by

RICHARD F. ROSSER
Professor and Head

Department of Political Science
United States Air Force Academy
Colorado

The views expressed herein are those of the authors and do not necessarily reflect the views of the United States Air Force or the Department of Defense, or the United Kingdom Ministry of Defense.

The Johns Hopkins University Press, Baltimore and London

FOREWORD: THE STUDY OF COMPARATIVE DEFENSE POLICY

COLONEL RICHARD F. ROSSER, USAF

Defense policy has become a major field of academic inquiry in recent years. It always has been a major concern of national decision-makers, whether labeled strategy, the use of force, or defensive posture; and whether referring to their own defense policy or that of their allies or enemies.

Yet most scholarly analysis of defense policy had concentrated on analyzing aspects of a single country's policy. Few attempts had been made to compare and contrast the defense policies of various countries. This fact partly was due to the newness of the field. Scholars continued to find gaps in their knowledge of a given country's defense policy, and were reluctant to attempt an international analysis until they had their own house in order. The absence of a comparative approach also reflected the particular orientation of many defense policy analysts; they were primarily interested in a particular country or area rather than in experimenting with conceptual approaches which might apply to a number of countries.

The Department of Political Science at the Air Force Academy also had tended to concentrate its research on the defense policy of one country, specifically the United States. Yet when the decision was made to prepare the third edition of *American Defense Policy*, edited by Lt. Col. Richard G. Head and Maj. Ervin J. Rokke (Baltimore: The Johns Hopkins Press, 1973), there was considerable interest among members of the Department in including materials about the defense policies of other countries. We believed that such analyses would foster greater insight into our own policy process and also contribute to the understanding of how other countries functioned in this area.

It soon was apparent that the whole field of defense policy deserved exploration using a comparative approach, and indeed could be the subject of a companion book to *American Defense Policy*. Three editors were chosen for *Comparative Defense Policy*: Major Frank B. Horton III; Squadron Leader Anthony C. Rogerson, the Royal Air Force Exchange Officer with the Department; and Major Edward L. Warner III.

In order to commission articles for the projected book and to stimulate conceptualization, we decided to organize a carefully structured conference to analyze the defense policies of a number of nations against a common conceptual framework. The Office of the Assistant Secretary of Defense for International Security Affairs provided a generous grant to make this conference possible.

The actual structuring of the conference remained a problem because so little conceptualization had been done about comparing defense policies. Therefore, we held a pre-conference planning meeting in April 1972, at the Air Force Academy, funded by the National Security Program of the Graduate School of Public Administration of New York University. Those in attendance quickly decided to narrow the scope of the conference to several specific facets of defense policy and to topics which could be researched. The topics chosen were four of the six general themes explored in this book: Military Profession (called Military Ideology at the conference); Military Doctrine; Force Posture; and Weapons Acquisition. Other topics, which would have lent themselves to comparative analysis, were postponed—perhaps for a later conference: The Recruitment Process, Military Education, Promotion Systems. Two topics not specifically addressed at the conference are covered in separate sections of this book, to provide a well-rounded treatment of the subject: Structure and Process, and The Use of Force.

We also decided at the pre-conference not to attempt a parallel examination of the same countries in relation to the four themes, but rather to examine a variety of nation-states within each theme in the hope that this would stimulate thinking among a broad range of scholars.

The conference itself, we believe, was a success. The contributors did an unusually good job with our comprehensive topic definition outlines; much of their work is included in this volume. The commentators also did an excellent job in summarizing, analyzing, and critiquing the papers on their panels. Their commentary, plus that given orally by them, the contributors, and the observers from the military and academic communities (summarized in the Conference Proceedings) was invaluable to the editors and writers of section introductions for this volume.

Finally, credit is due to our liaison in Washington, Major David P. Burke, for his help on the conference, and to the editors of *Comparative Defense Policy*, who did the major share of the work in developing the topic definitions and organizing the conference, in addition to working on the book itself.

The editors have contributed a most worthwhile intellectual endeavor. They have selected the best articles from the conference, plus outstanding articles and sections of books, to produce this work. The final selection of the book's topics and articles was based on Major Horton's experience in teaching comparative defense

policy in the spring of 1973 at the Air Force Academy. Having been tested in the classroom, the materials that follow should serve well, either organized by topic or by country, as a primary or supplemental text in courses on security or foreign policy, or international or comparative politics.

Much work remains to be done in the conceptual realm. However, we never expected to shape definitive models at the conference or in this book for comparing the topics discussed below. The essence of the exercise is to test the topic definitions used for their validity and, hopefully, to examine alternative models.

INTRODUCTION

FRANK B. HORTON III

WHY COMPARATIVE
DEFENSE POLICY?

The editors of this book became interested in the study of comparative defense policy for similar reasons. As students of international politics, we recognized a common failing of ethnocentricity among many students and practitioners of defense policy. This failing has often led to misperceptions of the policies and actions of other states and, at times, to poorly conceived reactions with serious consequences.[1] While clearer perceptions would not necessarily eliminate error or adverse outcomes in the international arena, they surely would tend to mitigate them.

As students of comparative politics, we pursued a field of inquiry that we felt might help to broaden the perspectives of defense policy students and practitioners and lead to more soundly based theory and policy.[2] A comparative approach would seem uniquely applicable to the study of defense policy. Nearly every country has to concern itself with the basic function of security and its mechanisms. In nearly every country those mechanisms and the issues with which they deal have an effect on and are affected by both international and domestic environments, including a uniquely broad set of participants in the policy process.

THE APPROACH

As Colonel Rosser pointed out in his Foreword, we cannot claim that a definitive comparative approach to defense policy has been set forth here—far from it. Yet the conference and

[1] For some examples that helped to motivate this book, see Richard A. Neustadt, *Alliance Politics* (New York: Columbia University Press, 1971).

[2] The application of comparative inquiry to foreign policy is already being pursued vigorously by many, including James N. Rosenau and Michael Brecher. Their work also served as a major inspiration for the present effort.

the course he mentions have helped us to narrow our focus in a manner that can prove useful to the teacher and student searching for a way to make the subject comprehensible, and to the researcher seeking a focal point for further work.

The first section of the book focuses on an important input factor in the policy equation; the second on the equation itself and the third through the sixth on selected significant outputs. Each section contains a short overview by the section editor, followed by a comparative article, then six or seven descriptive and explanatory articles covering one or more countries and their experience with the topic at hand. The countries covered in each section include the Soviet Union, China, Great Britain, France, India, and Israel; plus East and West Germany, Scandinavia (or Sweden alone), Japan, Pakistan, Egypt, and the United States, when interesting and instructive articles were available. The United States is not treated extensively; the reader is referred to the companion volume to this book, *American Defense Policy*, third edition, edited by Richard G. Head (one of the section editors for this volume) and Ervin J. Rokke (Baltimore, Md.: The Johns Hopkins Press, 1973). Each article is preceded by an introduction summarizing its main points and the highlights of the author's biography. Each section is concluded with a bibliography of further readings. The book ends with a Conclusion, a Bibliographic Essay, and an index.

The military profession—the subject of the first section—is a particularly useful starting point. The military is one of the most important actors in the defense policy process, and it is the primary instrument for execution of the outputs of that process. How the military is structured, recruited, and socialized; how it views itself, its tasks, and its environment; and how it is viewed and treated by society, provide important insights into the issues addressed in the rest of the book. Other inputs to the policy process are dealt

Major Frank B. Horton (USAF) is a 1962 West Point graduate. He received his MPA and PhD from Harvard University in 1966 and 1969 respectively. At the time of writing he was an Associate Professor in the Department of Political Science at the Air Force Academy. He has since been reassigned to Headquarters USAF. He has been consultant to many agencies, including the NSC staff, and has written on American foreign and defense policy.

The views expressed herein are those of the author and do not necessarily reflect the views of the United States Air Force or the Department of Defense.

with directly or indirectly as appropriate in the remaining sections of the book: domestic political context under Structure and Process; external environment under Military Doctrine; national wealth and will under Force Posture; economic autarky and industrial structure under Weapons Acquisition; and all of these under The Use of Force.

The second section, on structure and process, serves as the transition and explanatory link between the input and output sides of the equation. It contains articles that assess the military and other actors in the process, their interests, their relative power, and the action channels and issue areas within which they interact. It is perhaps the key section of the book.

The four output issue area sections are in logical but not necessarily real-world sequence. They are: military doctrine—the rationale for the rest (as often *ex post facto* as not); force posture—general force size and composition; weapons acquisition—how states obtain the hardware components of force posture (manpower acquisition, equally important, is touched on in the first section); and the use of force—offensive and defensive primarily (leaving compellence and deterrence for other texts).

The last section overlaps more than the others with foreign policy and international politics. Force use remains relevant to the study of comparative defense policy, however, as it reveals a great deal about the other sections: the military profession (Is it truly professional in the test of battle? Has the trauma of battle changed the profession?); structure and process (Do different actors get involved in this different kind of issue area? With different outcomes than one would have expected from the actors involved in other matters?); military doctrine (Did doctrine anticipate the manner in which force was ac-

tually used? If not, why not? If so, with what effect?); force posture (Was it adequate to the challenge? How did the battle alter the balance?); and even weapons acquisition (particularly if the conflict is protracted).

A number of other interesting observations that cross the topical lines drawn in this book derive from the attempt to answer certain questions, including "When does the military intervene in politics? What are the results?"; "Under what conditions does military doctrine precede force posture, and *vice versa*?"; "When does weapons acquisition drive force posture, and when the reverse?"; and "When does force use follow doctrine, and when not?"

While we will attempt to answer these and other questions as the book proceeds, the argument may be made that one might better get at them by organizing the articles in this book, or a course based on it, by country rather than by topic. Such an approach was used in an earlier version of a course on comparative defense policy at the Air Force Academy, with some success. This book has in fact been consciously designed so that it could be used to support a course so organized. As mentioned earlier, every section has an article on the Soviet Union, China, Great Britain, France, India, and Israel, facilitating grouping articles into six country blocks. The editors believe, however, that much would be lost with such an approach. Cross-national analysis has replaced a descriptive, country-by-country approach in recent texts and courses on comparative politics, with deeper insights accruing to the student. The reorganized course based on this book taught today at the Air Force Academy has provided the students with many insights into cause and effect that would not have been as readily grasped following the country-by-country sequence.

ACKNOWLEDGMENTS

There are many people the three editors must thank—more than would normally be the case, even for a long, edited book like this one. First of all, of course, are the individual section editors, all present or former members of the Department of Political Science at the Air Force Academy. Their biographical sketches appear at the bottom of the first page of the section introductions for which they are responsible. They all put in many long and thoughtful hours in the preparation of this manuscript. In addition, special thanks are due to Captain John Desiderio of the Department for his work in helping to get the final manuscript into shape and for proofing the book. Thanks also are due to Colonels Richard F. Rosser and Perry M. Smith, at the time of writing Professor and Head, and Deputy Head, respectively, of the Department, for their guidance and advice throughout the project. Many other members of the Department deserve special mention for assistance with the conference that produced many of the papers used in this book (these were mentioned by Colonel Rosser in his Foreword); for reading and reviewing the manuscript; for editorial assistance in final manuscript preparation; and many other tasks. They are: Lt. Colonels Richard J. Daleski, Richard L. Kuiper, and Chester Y. Williams, Dr. H. Eugene Bovis, Majors Kent E. Harbaugh, Russell R. MacDonald, Jr., Don L. Mansfield, Ervin J. Rokke, George M. Thompson, Jr., Captains Donald J. Alberts, James B. Christian, Deane C. Drury, John H. Garrison, Clifford A. Hickel, David C. Kozak, Harold W. Maynard, Douglas J. Murray; Lieutenants David K. Hall and Paul B. Williamson (USN). Our secretaries, as always, deserve our appreciation—Mrs. Nellie Dykes, Miss Jacqueline Mignolet, Mrs. Carol Rivard—and especially our principal secretary for the conference and the book, Miss Denise Pfalzgraf, without whose efforts both projects would have foundered. In addition, we would like to thank all the members of the newly formed Department of Political Science and Philosophy who helped in proofreading the manuscript.

Many people outside the Department of Political Science were also helpful. Professor Frank Trager, who arranged funding of the pre-conference planning meeting through the National Security Program at New York University, and Major David P. Burke, a former Department member now in the Office of the Joint Chiefs of Staff, who helped arrange funding of the final conference through the Office of the Secretary of Defense/International Security Affairs, deserve a special vote of thanks, as do those who attended the pre- and final conferences. Those present at the pre-conference were: Professor Graham Allison, Harvard University; Dr. Paul Hammond, the RAND Corporation; Professor Klaus Knorr, Princeton University; Professor Scott McNall, Arizona State University; Professor Sam Sarkesian, Loyola University of Chicago; and Professor Frank Trager, the director of the New York University program. Participants writing for the final conference were:

MILITARY IDEOLOGY PANEL

Lt. Colonel John C. M. Baynes (Ret.); Professor Stephen P. Cohen, University of Illinois; Professor John Erickson, University of Edinburgh (unable to attend); Professor Scott G. McNall, Arizona State University; Dr. Charles C. Moskos, Jr., Northwestern University; Dr. Amos Perlmutter, Smithsonian Institute; and Dr. William W. Whitson, the RAND Corporation.

MILITARY DOCTRINE PANEL

Professor Neville Brown, University of Birmingham; Mr. Michael I. Handel, Harvard University; Dr. Arnold Horelick, the RAND Corporation; Professor Edward A. Kolodziej, University of Illinois; Dr. Benjamin S. Lambeth, Harvard University; Professor Nils Ørvik, Queen's University; and Professor Ralph Powell, The American University.

FORCE POSTURE PANEL

Professor David Greenwood, King's College, Aberdeen; Professor Paul Y. Hammond, the RAND Coproration; Lt. Colonel Joseph Heinlein (USA), West Point; Professor Lorne J. Kavic, University of British Columbia; Professor Geoffrey Kemp, Tufts University; Major Edward L. Warner III, USAF Academy; and Professor Martin E. Weinstein, University of Illinois.

WEAPONS ACQUISITION PANEL

Dr. Arthur J. Alexander, the RAND Corporation; Professor Ian Bellany, University of Lancaster; Dr. James R. Blaker, the Pentagon (unable to attend); Mr. Frank E. C. Gregory, University of Southampton (unable to attend); Professor J. C. Hurewitz, Columbia University; Professor Harvey M. Sapolsky, Massachusetts Institute of Technology; and Mr. John Simpson, University of Southampton.

Those participating in both conferences, as Colonel Rosser has indicated, provided not only many of the papers in this volume but also much of the intellectual thrust behind the book, including contributing to its organization and to the content of the section introductions and the concluding essay.

The editors would like to add a special note of thanks to the students in the newly reactivated and restructured course in comparative defense policy taught by Major Horton during the spring of 1973. They were intimately aware of the direction the book was taking—organization, content, and conclusions—and they criticized it every step of the way. They also provided their own constructive views on sections to be included and their order, on articles to leave in and take out, and on conclusions that could be drawn from the material retained. If the book proves successful, especially as a text, they deserve much of the credit.

Finally, there are those outside the Department of Political Science who helped share the enormous administrative and editorial burden that preparation of this manuscript has entailed. We would like to thank the entire staff of The Johns Hopkins University Press for their efforts. Of particular note was Nancy Middleton Gallienne, our copy editor, who worked closely with us (and many times must have thought we were working against her) throughout the long and arduous process. At the Air Force Academy, the Printing Plant and the Graphics and Photographic Sections of the Division of Instructional Technology provided invaluable assistance. And last, but certainly not least, all three of the principal editors owe a debt of thanks to their wives for their support throughout the project, both moral and, many times during the project, substantive.

The principal editors take full responsibility for any shortcomings in the book. Also, to cite a phrase that bears repeating, the views expressed herein are those of the authors and do not necessarily reflect the views of the United States Air Force or the Department of Defense, or, in Squadron Leader Rogerson's case, of the United Kingdom Ministry of Defense.

PART ONE

THE MILITARY PROFESSION

INTRODUCTION

BARD E. O'NEILL

MILITARY PROFESSION
AND IDEOLOGY

Consideration of the military profession is a logical starting point for a volume that seeks to compare, at least in a preliminary way, a number of aspects of the defense policies of several nations. Although in general terms the military profession may be identified with the management of violence,[1] we will focus in this section on a narrower dimension—namely, the ideologies of military officers. By ideology I mean a system of separate but related attitudes, values, and principles.[2] Of particular interest are the ideological orientations of military officers toward the nature of man, international politics, the military profession, civil-military relations, and basic policy preferences. The latter will be of particular importance in explaining policy outcomes described in later sections of this volume.

IDEOLOGY AS AN INDEPENDENT
VARIABLE

While in part one military ideology is treated as a dependent variable, it may also be viewed as an independent variable that partially explains such things as structure and process, doctrine, force posture, weapons acquisition, and the use of force. When examining *structure and process*, for example, one deals with the role of the military as an interest group that competes with numerous rivals for national resources. To explain the demands the military makes and the strategy and tactics that it employs it is necessary to recognize the influence of ideological predis-

positions. An officer corps that viewed man as benign and international politics as beyond conflict would undoubtedly press its demands with much less vigor than one which saw man as evil and international relations as inherently marked by conflict.

Military ideology may also be an important determinant of doctrine. For instance, in his discussion of the importance of generations as an explanatory variable which, *inter alia*, accounts for the values and attitudes of segments of the Chinese People's Liberation Army (PLA), William Whitson also calls attention to the effect of orientations on *doctrine* when he suggests that successive generations of officers have tended to veer away from the concept of Maoist People's War.[3]

Military ideology can also be an important explanatory factor *vis-à-vis force posture, weapons acquisition*, and the *use of force*.[4] An officer corps that is primarily concerned with internal threats and that is substantially involved in politics is likely to differ in all three respects when compared to a military that is acutely and almost exclusively preoccupied with external enemies that possess modern equipment and large striking forces. One would not find it surprising if the former were to stress small, mobile forces, conventional weapons, and employment of resources against domestic threats, and if the latter emphasized more sophisticated forces, including air and naval units, which could be utilized within the framework of large scale conventional operations. The point is that military ideology, besides

---

[1]Samuel P. Huntington, *The Soldier and the State* (New York: Vintage Books, 1964), pp. 11–14; Janowitz, p. 4 of this volume [p. 19 of original article].

[2]Lawrence C. Mayer, *Comparative Political Inquiry* (Homewood, Illinois: The Dorsey Press, 1972), p. 226. Mayer points out that ideology can be used in two senses. In addition to the broad use of the term adopted above, ideology can refer to a comprehensive, consistent, and closed system of ideas and beliefs.

[3]See Whitson, p. 26 of this volume [p. 388 of original article].

[4]Whitson's article, for example, points out that the orientations of the ground forces of the PLA in China are related to the use of force and force posture. The orientations have precluded the acceptance of the long-range projection of military power delayed modernization and the development of other services, and led to the preference for conventional infantry supported by limited artillery and armor rather than the massed artillery and infantry-armor-artillery coordination. See Whitson, p. 33 [p. 405 of original article].

Captain Bard E. O'Neill (USAF), (Ph.D., Graduate School of International Studies, Denver University), is Assistant Professor of Political Science at the USAF Academy, where he specializes in comparative politics and Middle East-African studies.

The views expressed herein are those of the author and do not necessarily reflect the views of the United States Air Force or the Department of Defense.

being important per se, may also have a significant causal relationship to the other phenomena examined in this volume. With this in mind, let me turn directly to the determinants of military ideology.

MILITARY IDEOLOGY AS A DEPENDENT VARIABLE

General Theoretical Status

It should be noted at the outset that at the present time there is no theory of military ideology, a fact which is reflected in the wide diversity of approaches taken by the authors in this section. In other words, we have yet to arrive at a formula wherein causal variables with precise operational indicators are logically related by means of testable hypotheses to various classes of military ideologies.[5] Indeed, as the articles in this section demonstrate, we are still trying to identify those factors which may be useful in explaining the phenomenon of military ideology. The diverse approaches taken by the articles are summarized in the article introductions that follow.

Shared Explanations

Although the authors tend to stress different combinations of factors that account for ideological orientations, there is, nevertheless, an agreement that certain variables are particularly important. When explaining the acceptance or denial of civilian control, for example, almost

every writer considers both the effectiveness of civilian authorities and the content and processes of socialization as key factors. Of the two, the role of civilian politicians may be more important because, even in cases where socialization has emphasized civilian supremacy, the military has intervened (Pakistan). Other variables which may account for a willingness to accept civilian control are the use of the promotion process to reinforce civilian supremacy (Baynes, Cohen and Perlmutter), the increase in technical training (Erickson and Stupak), a strong personality as civilian leader (Perlmutter), external threats (Perlmutter), the overlap of generations (Baynes), the simultaneous development of military and political institutions (Baynes), success in war (Stupak), the willingness of civilian elites to satisfy requirements the military considers essential (Erickson), and the avoidance of independent military control over external assistance (Cohen).

In the absence of a formulation that suggests how these variables are to be weighted, mitigated or reinforced, and interrelated, we are left with what is at best a very loose synthesis.[6] Though much work needs to be done before we arrive at testable propositions which will yield probabilistic theory, the writers in this section are to be commended for taking the initial step in that direction while at the same time providing students with an appreciation of the military profession in several nations.

---

[5]On the requisites for probabilistic theory see Mayer, *op. cit.*, pp. 33–66.

[6]Mayer, *op. cit.*, pp. 62–64, and Eugene J. Meehan, *The Theory and Method of Political Analysis* (Homewood, Illinois: The Dorsey Press, 1965), pp. 132–34, characterize such a scheme as concatenated theory.

MILITARY ORGANIZATION

MORRIS JANOWITZ

*Professor Janowitz points out that because the content of military goals has
undergone significant change under the impact of technology and because
the range of political considerations which impinge on the military
has altered, the gap between military and civilian organization has closed
substantially. Specifically, he notes the following points of convergence:
(1) a greater reliance on persuasion and group consensus as a basis of
authority; (2) a narrowing skill differential between military and civilian
elites; (3) broader based recruitment patterns; (4) the association of
innovative perspectives and political skills with elite leadership roles; and
(5) the development of a political ethos. Nevertheless, Professor Janowitz
argues that fundamental organizational differences will remain between the
military and civilian sectors, since the military must maintain combat
readiness and the capability to support balance of power politics.*

*Morris Janowitz is Professor of Sociology at the University of Chicago, and
Chairman of the Inter-University Seminar on Armed Forces and Society.
Among his many writings are* The Professional Soldier *(1960) and* Sociology
and the Military Establishment *(1965). He is the editor of* The New Military
*(1964). He was also a member of the Social Science Advisory Board of the U.S.
Arms Control and Disarmament Agency in 1964.*

ORGANIZATION: CIVILIAN
VERSUS MILITARY

If an organizational perspective is applied to
the armed forces, it then becomes necessary to
contrast civilian and military organizations.
Many features and characteristics of military
organization, such as authoritarian and stratified
hierarchical structures, are, in fact, to be found
in varying degrees in civilian organizations.
Moreover, transformations in technology and in
military operations have brought about marked
changes in the inner format of the military establishment. Speier points out that civilian social scientists tend to exaggerate and distort the differences between military and civilian organization
and overlook what is common to large-scale
organization in general.[1]

The special characteristics of military organization derive from its goals, namely, the management of instruments of violence. However,

[1]Hans Speier, *The Social Order and the Risks of War*.
(New York: Geo. W. Stewart, 1952).

the content of military goals has undergone
tremendous changes under the impact of new
technology and as the range of political considerations which impinge on military operations
is altered. In general, the trend has been toward
narrowing the differences between military
organization and civilian organizations.

To analyze the contemporary military establishment in the United States as a social system,
it is therefore necessary to assume that it has
tended to display more and more of the characteristics typical of any large-scale, nonmilitary
bureaucracy. The decreasing difference is a result
of continuous technological change which vastly
expands the size of the military establishment,
increases its interdependence with civilian society, and alters its internal social structure. These
technological developments in war-making require more and more professionalization of military personnel. At the same time, the impact of
military technology during the past half-century
can be described in a series of propositions about
social change. Each of the conditions symbolized
by these propositions has had the effect of "civil-

*Reprinted with permission and with minor changes from "Military Organization," in Roger W. Little
(ed.),* Handbook of Military Institutions *(Beverly Hills, Calif.: Sage Publications, Inc., 1971),
pp. 13–51. Reprinted by permission of the publisher, Sage Publications, Inc., Beverly Hills, California.*

ianizing" military institutions and of blurring the distinction between the civilian and the military. Each of these trends has, of course, actual and potential built-in limitations:

1) A larger percentage of the national income of a modern nation is spent for the preparation, execution, and repair of the consequences of war. Thus there is a secular trend toward total popular involvement in the consequences of war and war policy, since the military establishment is responsible for the distribution of a progressively large share of available economic resources.

2) Military technology both vastly increases the destructiveness of warfare and widens the scope of automation in new weapons. It is commonplace that both of these trends tend to weaken the distinction between military roles and civilian roles as the destructiveness of war has increased. Weapons of mass destruction socialize danger to the point of equalizing the risks of warfare for both soldier and civilian.

3) The revolution in military technology means that the military mission of deterring violence becomes more and more central as compared with preparing to apply violence. This shift in mission tends to civilianize military thought and organization as military leaders concern themselves with broad ranges of political, social, and economic policies.

4) The complexity of the machinery of warfare and the requirements for research, development, and technical maintenance tend to weaken the organizational boundary between the military and the nonmilitary, since the maintenance and manning of new weapons require a greater reliance on civilian-oriented technicians. The countertrend, or at least limitation, is the greater effort by the military establishment to develop and train military officers with scientific and engineering backgrounds.

5) Given the "permanent" threat of war, it is well recognized that the tasks which military leaders perform tend to widen. Their technological knowledge, their direct and indirect power, and their heightened prestige result in their entrance, of necessity, into arenas that in the recent past have been reserved for civilians and professional politicians. The need that political and civilian leaders have for expert advice from professional soldiers about the strategic implications of technological change serves to mix the roles of the military and the civilian.

These propositions do not deny the crucial differences that persist between military and nonmilitary bureaucracies. The goals of an organization supply a meaningful basis for understanding differences in organizational behavior. The military establishment as a social system has unique characteristics because the possibility of hostilities is a permanent reality to its leadership. The fact that thermonuclear weapons alter the role of force in international relations does not deny this proposition. The consequences of preparation for future combat and the results of previous combat pervade the entire organization. The unique character of the military establishment derives from the requirement that its members are specialists in making use of violence and mass destruction.

Thus, the narrowing distinction between military and nonmilitary bureaucracies can never result in the elimination of fundamental organizational differences. Two pervasive requirements for combat set limits to these civilianizing tendencies.

First, while it is true that modern warfare exposes the civilian and the soldier to more equal risks, the distinction between military roles and civilian roles has not been eliminated. Traditional combat-ready military formations are maintained for limited warfare. The necessity for naval and air units to carry on the hazardous tasks of continuous and long-range reconnaissance and detection demands organizational forms that will bear the stamp of conventional formations. In the future, even with fully automated missile systems, conventional units must be maintained as auxiliary forces for the delivery of new types of weapons.

More important, no military system can rely on expectation of victory based on the initial exchange of firepower, whatever the form of the initial exchange may be. Subsequent exchanges will involve military personnel—again regardless of their armament—who are prepared to carry on the struggle as soldiers, that is, subject themselves to military authority and to continue to fight. The automation of war civilianized wide sectors of the military establishment; yet the need to maintain combat readiness and to develop centers of resistance after initial hostilities ensures the continued importance of military organization and authority.

Second, what about the consequences of the increased importance of deterrence as a military mission? Should one not expect that such a shift would also result in civilianizing the military establishment? If the military is forced to think about deterring wars rather than fighting them, the traditions of the "military mind" based on the inevitability of hostilities must change, and military authority must undergo transformation as well. There can be no doubt that this shift in mission is having important effects on military thought and organization. In fact, military pragmatism which questions the inevitability of total war is an important trend in modern society as the destructiveness of war forces military leaders to concern themselves with the political consequences of violence.

Again, there are limits to the consequences of this civilizing trend. The role of deterrence is not a uniquely new mission for the military establishment. Historically, the contribution of the military to the balance of power has not been made because of the civilian character of the military establishment. On the contrary, the balance of power formula operates, when it does, because the military establishment is prepared to fight.

With the increase in the importance of deterrence, military elites become more and more involved in diplomatic and political warfare, regardless of their preparation for such tasks. Yet the specific and unique contribution of the military to deterrence is the threat of violence which has currency, that is, it can be taken seriously because of the real possibility of violence. Old or new types of weapons do not alter this basic formula. In short, deterrence still requires organization prepared for combat. Moreover, the actuality and possibility of limited war permits the military to persist in maintaining conceptions of combat. These conceptions come to include a wide variety of functions with civilian and political components, but which are defined at least in part as military: guerrilla and counterguerrilla warfare, psychological warfare, military assistance and training, or even "nation-building."

These trends in self-concepts and roles are described and analyzed in *The Professional Soldier: A Social and Political Portrait* as they have affected the officer corps during the past half-century in the United States.[2] The military profession which has centered on the self-conception of the warrior types or the "heroic leader" requires the incorporation of new roles, namely, the "military manager" and the "military technologist." For the military establishment to accomplish its multiple goals, it must develop and maintain a balance between these different military types.

These basic changes in the military over the past fifty years can be summarized by a series of basic propositions on the transformation of military organization in response both to the changing technology of war and to the transformation of the societal context in which the armed forces operate.[3]

Changing organizational authority. There has been a change in the basis of authority and discipline in the military establishment, a shift from authoritarian domination to greater reliance on manipulation, persuasion, and group consensus. The organizational revolution which pervades contemporary society, and which implies management by means of persuasion, explanation, and expertise, is also to be found in the military.

Narrowing skill differential between military and civilian elites. The new tasks of the military require that the professional officer develop more and more skills and orientations common to civilian administrators and civilian leaders. The narrowing difference in skill between military and civilian society is an outgrowth of the increasing concentration of technical specialists in the military.

Shift in officer recruitment. The military elite has been undergoing a basic social transformation since the turn of the century. These elites have been shifting their recruitment from a narrow, relatively high social status base to a broader base more representative of the population as a whole.

Significance of career patterns. Prescribed careers performed with high competence lead to entrance into the professional elite, the highest point in the military hierarchy at which technical and routinized functions are performed. By contrast, entrance into the smaller group, the elite nucleus—where innovative perspectives, discretionary responsibility, and political skills are required—is assigned to persons with unconventional and adaptive careers.

Trends in political indoctrination. The growth of the military establishment into a vast managerial enterprise with increased political responsibilities has produced a strain on traditional military self-images and concepts of honor. The officer is less and less prepared to think of himself as merely a military technician. As a result, the profession, especially within its strategic leadership, has developed a more explicit political ethos.

Thus, in partial summary, since the turn of the century, the military establishment has been fusing with civilian enterprise. There has been a weakening of organizational boundaries. This organizational trend has been encountered in many other sectors of modern society, for example, the increased fusion of industrial and governmental agencies or of higher educational and business organizations. But this process of fusion of the military and civilian sectors had reached its systemic limits by the early 1960s.

This is not to postulate that there is a trend toward a return to a distinct, separate, and iso-

[2]Morris Janowitz, *The Professional Soldier: A Social and Political Portrait* (New York: Free Press, 1960).
[3]*Ibid.*, pp. 7–16, 21–36.

lated military establishment. The fusion of military and political goals alone makes this impossible. However, there is a trend in the military which seeks to strengthen its distinctive boundaries, jurisdictions, and competence while at the same time the military is deeply intertwined with the larger society. The increased political necessity for the military to act without unduly dislocating the civilian sector serves to make this a greater reality. Therefore, the notion of a completely voluntary military establishment becomes more and more a subject of popular discussion.

COMPARATIVE ANALYSIS: HISTORICAL

Analysis of contemporary American military institutions can be clarified both by comparison with previous historical periods and by cross-national contrasts with existing institutions. One such approach is to reexamine the models of ideal types of the past, present, or the hypothetical future which have been presented by historians and social scientists. In order to highlight the linkage of military organization to social structure in Western industrialized societies, it is relevant to speak of the development of the aristocratic-feudal model into either the democratic or totalitarian, and the contingency model of the garrison state.

Aristocratic-Feudal Model

The aristocratic-feudal model is a relevant base only if seen as describing the conditions of Western Europe, and not fully applicable to the historical emergence of the military in other parts of the world. The aristocratic-feudal model is a composite estimate of the armed forces among Western European powers before industrialism had its full impact. Under the aristocratic-feudal model, civilian and military elites were socially and functionally integrated. A narrow base of recruitment for both elites and a relatively monolithic power structure provided the civilian elite with a comprehensive basis for political control of the military. There was a rigid hierarchy in the aristocratic model which delineated both the source of authority and the prestige of any member of the military elite. The low specialization of the military profession made it possible for the political elite to supply the bulk of necessary leadership for the armed forces. Birth, family connections, and common values insured that the military embodied the ideology of dominant groups in society. Political control was civilian control because there was a unity of interest between aristocratic and military groups. The system was rooted in concepts of authority and land tenure which produced a relatively stable ruling

stratum. The military is responsible because it is part of the government. The officer fights because he feels that he is issuing orders.

Democratic Model

In contrast to the aristocratic-feudal model stands the democratic one. The democratic model is both a historical reality and an objective of political policy. Under the democratic model, the civilian and military elites are sharply differentiated. The civilian political elites exercise control over the military through a formal set of rules. These specify the functions of the military and the conditions under which the military may exercise its power. The military is professionals in the employment of the state. They are a small group and their careers are distinct from civilian careers. In fact, being a professional soldier is incompatible with any other significant social or political role. The military leaders obey the government because they believe it is their duty and their profession to fight. Professional ethics as well as democratic parliamentary institutions guarantee civilian political supremacy. The officer fights because of his career commitment.

Elements of the democratic model have been achieved only in certain Western industrialized countries, since it requires extremely viable parliamentary institutions and broad social consensus about the ends of government. The democratic model assumes that military leaders can be effectively motivated by professional codes of conduct and group loyalty. Paradoxically, certain types of officers with aristocratic backgrounds have made important contributions to the development of the democratic model.

Totalitarian Model

In the absence of a historical development toward the democratic model, the totalitarian model emerges in industrial societies as a replacement for the aristocratic-feudal one. The totalitarian model appearing in Germany and in Russia and, to a lesser degree, in Italy, did not arise from any natural or social unity of the existing political and military elites. On the contrary, a revolutionary political elite status, or a relatively low (middle-class) status based on a mass authoritarian political party, fashions a new type of control of the military elite. It may be forced into temporary alliance with the traditional military profession, but the revolutionary elites, bedecked with paramilitary symbols, are dedicated to reconstituting the military elites. Political control of the totalitarian variety is enforced by the secret police, by infiltrating party members into the military hierarchy, and by controlling the system of officer selection. Most important, the party develops and arms its own military units. Under party control of the totalitarian variety, the independence of the professional military is destroyed. The officer fights because he has no alternative.

Garrison State Model

The garrison state model, as offered by Harold D. Lasswell[4] results from the weakening of civil supremacy which can arise even in societies which have had an effective democratic political structure (also see Mills for an alternative formulation).[5] While the end result of the garrison state produces some patterns similar to the totalitarian model, the garrison state has a different natural history. It is, however, not the direct domination of politics by the military. Since modern industrial nations cannot be ruled merely by the political domination of a single small leadership bloc, the garrison state is not a throwback to a military dictatorship. It is the end result of the ascent to power of the military elite under conditions of prolonged international tensions. Internal freedom is hampered and the preparation for war becomes overriding. The garrison state is a new pattern of coalition in which military groups directly and indirectly wield unprecedented amounts of political and administrative power. The military retains its organizational independence, provided that it makes appropriate alliances with civil political factions. The officer fights for national survival and for glory.

The Military as a Modern Institution

In actual fact, and in a world perspective, the origins of the military in Western Europe and the United States derivatively represent one particular pattern of emergence and historical continuity. It was a pattern which generally linked the military to feudal institutions and to conservative traditions. The military emerged as a modern institution, in fact, as one of the first modern institutions in Western Europe, but it was a modern institution in a Western context.

From a historical point of view, the emergence of modern military institutions in Western Europe required that feudal military patterns be transformed, either by reformers from within or by the incorporation of new middle-class elements, so that complex technology could be made part of the apparatus of war-making. In Western Europe the concept of armed forces and society began to have fuller meaning as the military de-

veloped a separate bureaucratic organization. In this long-term development, which became intensified in the first half of the nineteenth century, a relatively common form of military profession and military organization was produced.

Because of the experiences of Western Europe, when scholars analyze the development of modern military institutions, it has been conventional to focus on the social origins of the officer corps. The historical emergence of the military establishment in Western Europe has been carefully documented by a decline in the concentration of officers from aristocratic and landed gentry background and growth in the infusion of middle-class patterns of recruitment.[6] The patterns and rates of change have varied from nation to nation, but there has been an overall uniformity in the long-term direction. But for Western Europe and for the United States, patterns of social recruitment are at best a partial indicator of patterns of civil-military relations. Even during the period of aristocratic dominance in the early nineteenth century the military profession was compatible with parliamentary institutions in Great Britain and with a nationalistic oligarchy in Prussia.

Middle-class elements entered a Prussian military which was predominantly recruited from landed higher and lower aristocratic groups, while the elite elements of the British armed forces were only slightly more distinct from their aristocratic counterparts. By contrast, the German system of education for its officer recruits served to differentiate them more from civilian institutions than did military education in Great Britain. What was important was that a political system emerged under the Prussian system in which the civilian political elites did not exercise control over the military through a set of formal rules. Instead, the policy was controlled by an oligarchy in which the military was an active and key element.

In the contemporary period, social recruitment supplies an even more partial index to patterns of armed forces and society in industrialized societies. Thus, for a variety of nations in Western Europe for which data are available—Great Britain, Germany, France, Norway, Sweden, and the Netherlands—the officer corps, and its elite members as well, continue to shift their recruitment from a narrow, relatively high social status to a broader base more representative of the population as a whole.

But this is not to say that the broadening of the base has taken place at a uniform rate in the

[4]Harold Lasswell, "The Garrison State," *American Journal of Sociology* 46 (January 1941): 455–68.
[5]C. Wright Mills, *The Power Elite* (New York: Oxford University Press, 1956).

[6]K. Demeter, *The German Officer Corps in Society and State* (New York: Frederick A. Praeger, 1965).

countries under investigation. Nor is it to imply that the consequences of this transformation have been similar in all of these countries. Thus, for example, there is reason to believe that the long-term shift toward a "middle-class" profession has taken place at a slower rate in England than in other countries. The top elite in the military has a greater concentration of upper-middle-class sons than in some other industrialized nations, as a result of the system of education and formal requirements for entrance. But this pattern of recruitment has not weakened civilian parliamentary controls.

In the current period, one sociological issue in Western Europe is the extent to which the military profession, that is, the officer class, is accessible to the sons of the working class. In England and in the Netherlands, the amount of such mobility from the lower classes into the officer corps is negligible, while in France it is more pronounced. In Norway, the figure reached 18.7% of the cadets for the period 1950–60, while for the United States in 1960 the percentage was over 30. The opening of the military to the working class represents general patterns of "democratization" and reflects the low prestige of the profession in industrial society. But the national differences derive in part from specific variations. In France this is the result of self-recruitment, especially recruitment of the sons of enlisted personnel into the officer ranks, and expresses a self-segregation trend in the military. To the contrary, in Norway it represents the desire for social mobility among working-class sons who are unable to enter a university career, and thereby serves to integrate the military with the civilian population.

Military Versus Civilian Control

In Western Europe or elsewhere, there is, of course, no guarantee that democratization of social origins (the broadening of the bases of recruitment) produces democratization of professional attitudes and a strengthening of the willingness to submit to civilian controls. In fact, there are clear-cut cases where the reverse may occur. Of significance are the process and content of professional socialization and the nature of the sociopolitical institutions for administering and controlling the military establishment and the organizational tasks of the military. In Western industrialized societies, as the military has become a bureaucratized and professionalized institution, the significance of social origins in fashioning military orientation declines.

In the evolution of professional military forms

throughout the world, Western concepts and practices had a profound effect. But because of different historical settings and because often the military experienced sharp discontinuities, the pattern of development was one that produced a more independent type of establishment with fewer and weaker linkages to the landed interest groups. Elements of European feudalism were developed in South America so that the linkages between landed interests and the military emerge. But even in Latin America, the military rapidly developed a more independent political base. Under the Ottoman Empire, the practices of recruitment and administration pushed early a "separate" establishment and placed it under centralized control. In this case also, the land tenure system did serve to strengthen relations between the military and traditional landed groups.

In parts of Asia and Africa, the military evolved as one governmental bureaucratic service, among others, but a most crucial one. This was in part the result of the colonial practices of the European powers, which destroyed traditional military forces linked to feudal-type ruling groups and which in turn created civil-service-type establishments under their control. As a result, in the new nations of Africa and Asia the military establishment is recruited from the middle and lower-middle classes, drawn mainly from rural areas of hinterlands. In comparison with Western European professional armies, there is a marked absence of a history of feudal domination. As a result, the military profession does not have strong allegiance to an integrated upper class which it accepts as its political leader, nor does it have a pervasive conservative outlook.

Militarism in the new nations of Africa and Asia is often reactive or unanticipated because of the weakness of civilian institutions and the breakdown of parliamentary forms of government. Military officers in these countries develop a sense of public service and national guardianship as a result of their military training and experience. Their politics are "supra-political" because they are suspicious of professional politicians and the bargaining process. A range of typologies of civil-military relations which help explain the process of social change and political development has been offered.[7] These typologies are designed to clarify the conditions under which militarism is restrained or developed in developing countries.

The power of the military in domestic politics

[7]Morris Janowitz, *The Role of the Military in Political Development of New Nations* (Chicago: University of Chicago Press, 1964).

and, derivatively, in international relations can be limited by an authoritarian regime based on personal and traditional power or it may be based on a newly developed personal autocracy. This is the (1) *authoritarian-personal* system of civil-military control and it is likely to be found in nations just beginning the process of modernization. The military can be excluded from domestic political influence by the power of a civilian single mass political party. When political power is lodged in a one-party state, under strong personal leadership without parliamentary institutions, it is possible to reduce old-fashioned militarism. This form of civil-military relations can be labeled (2) *a civilian mass party* system. In these states, both the civilian police and paramilitary institutions under the control of the mass party operate as counterweights to the military.

Militarism can be contained on the basis of (3) *a democratic competitive* system or a *semidemocratic* system. Competitive democratic systems have emerged mainly in industrialized societies where political power is exercised through a multiple-party and election system. Civilian political elites exclude the military from involvement in domestic partisan politics. Semicompetitive democratic patterns can be found in a few of the new nations because of powerful personal leadership of the chief executive and in part because colonial traditions have implanted a strong sense of self-restraint on the military. In these countries, there are competing civilian institutions and power groups, as well as a mass political party which dominates politics but permits a measure of political competition.

When the military expands its political activity and becomes a political bloc, the civilian leadership remains in power only because of the military passive assent or active assistance. The extent of political competition decreases, and it is appropriate to describe such a system as a (4) *civil military* coalition, because of the crucial role of the armed forces. Here the military serves as an active political bloc in its support of civilian parties and other bureaucratic power groups. The civilian group is in power because of the assistance of the military. The military may act as an informal, or even an explicit umpire between competing political parties and political groups. The military may, at this level, be forced to establish a caretaker government with a view to re-turning power to civilian political groups. Such alliances and caretaker governments can be unstable; they frequently lead to a wider level of involvement where the military sets itself up as the political ruling group. The result is a (5) *military oligarchy*, because, for a limited time at least, the political initiative passes to the military. When an actual takeover occurs and the military becomes the ruling group, civilian political activity is transformed, constricted, and repressed.

At each level of political intervention, and especially in the takeover of political power, the military operates as an incomplete agent of political change. In the new nations of Africa and Asia, military elites—because they are not linked to landed interest—are committed to an ideology of modernization. Lack of skills, both in economic management and in the arena of political negotiation, emerge as powerful barriers. In anticipating future developments, a variety of outcomes can be postulated in addition to the withdrawal of the military from the political arena under pressure because of administrative failure. One outcome is that the military seeks to transform itself into a quasi-political party undertaking for itself political functions or political activities. Another results when the military assumes leadership in the establishment of a political party in which its former personnel play a central role. A third development is the emergence of the army as an arbitrator between competing political groups. But the weight of evidence seems to indicate that the military per se is unable to supply essential political leadership, and effectiveness as a transitional government depends on its sensitivity and capacity to disengage itself or at least limit its involvement.

These forms of militarism must be distinguished from the intervention by the military in many South American countries where, in the past, it was much more designed and premeditated. Often coups represented power struggles between limited elite groups, and, in general, the military was not concerned with social and political change but rather with the maintenance of existing sociopolitical arrangements. More recently, military intervention in Latin American nations has been developing a posture of concern with social and political change, in the face of popular demands for such change.

THE RESHAPING OF THE SOVIET MILITARY COMMAND 1965–1970

JOHN ERICKSON

Professor Erickson discusses the process of "rejuvenation" in the Soviet military establishment, assesses the significance of key personnel changes, and examines the influence of the military on Soviet policies. The most salient aspects of the rejuvenation are the emergence of an officer-technician group within the military, the enhanced importance of logistics officers, a new law on military service that deals with age, limits rank and length of service, and the special attention lavished on the junior officers in 1969. As a result of these and other measures, the collective age of the military command has been reduced, the importance of education has been stressed, technocratization has continued and managerial elements have been introduced to the General Staff. In the realm of civil-military relations, Erickson points out that the General Staff retained a command function which is distinct among the world's armed forces and has acquired new competence in military-scientific affairs and the management apparatus acquired for this. He also notes that the military has given support for the party "line" and an increase of political agencies in the armed forces in return for party support for exercise and readiness patterns and defense preparations. Finally, he suggests the possibility of rationalizing the command structure through a separation of functions.

John Erickson is Professor of Politics at the University of Edinburgh, Scotland. He is the author or editor of several works on Soviet military affairs, including The Soviet High Command *(1962) and* Soviet Military Power *(1971), from which this excerpt is taken.*

INTRODUCTION

It was 'not by accident', to use a familiar Bolshevik phrase, that the effort to 'rejuvenate' and to reorganise the Soviet military command entered a new phase once Khrushchev was removed from the scene in October 1964. For a number of reasons, not least Khrushchev's own waywardness with the officer corps, the problem was becoming increasingly urgent and by the end of 1965 a general survey of the efficiency of all Soviet officers (up to the ranks of general and admiral) was completed, with every *fourth* officer recommended for promotion by the relevant reviewing boards.[1] Prosaic and bureaucratic though this may sound, the result was far from some routine change and its implications raise questions of major importance for the future of the entire Soviet military establishment. It is the purpose of this section to examine some of these implications—the process of 'rejuvenation' and restructuring in the officer corps as a whole, personnel changes in the operational commands, the General Staff, arms and services, the connection between particular appointments and shifts in operational concepts—while at the same time approaching the more fundamental question of who 'runs' the Soviet armed forces, or, to put it another way, which are the 'key' appointments, to whom and in what manner are they distributed, and finally in what sense can 'military influence' on Soviet policies be understood? If nothing else, such a line of enquiry can be used to guard against glib insertions about 'the Marshals', 'policy', the military 'role' and a military 'take-over'. In short, it is a particular manner of looking at the Soviet military system and an attempt to evaluate it on its own terms. The Soviet officer corps is demonstrably a subject in itself, requiring its own institutional and socio-

[1] See Col.-Gen. P. T. Lukashin (Deputy Chief Cadres/Personnel Administration) on selection, deployment and education of Soviet military cadres, *KVS*, 16 (August 1966).

Abridged, by permission, from Soviet Military Power *(Whitehall, London SW1A 2ET: Royal United Services Institute for Defence Studies, 1971), pp. 13–32.*

logical explanation,[2] but there is little point in delineating the scope and outcome of the 'debate' on military policy without some subsequent attempt to prescribe the position and influence of the men entrusted to implement these decisions.

Khrushchev had tackled both the 'rejuvenation' and restructuring of the Soviet command in his own way and after his own particular requirements. His 'demobilisation' of the elderly and unacceptable among Soviet officers in 1958–60 forced out 250,000 officers and his 'planned promotions' brought in 454 new generals in 1960. The new strategic missile command imposed a radical alteration on the structure of the Soviet forces, bringing engineer officers into greater prominence and contributing to the steady diversification of skills within the Soviet officer corps. Indeed, Khrushchev regarded the consolidation of a 'new' officer corps as a deliberate form of social engineering, designed among other things to promote political compliance and military utility in one swoop. The result (as with so many other of Khrushchev's schemes) was latterly both demoralisation and disorganisation; the pressure on the Soviet military cadres was very uneven and at the lower levels the speed of the turnover in men was dizzying, causing Marshal Malinovskii to complain at this cult of the 'new' when 'not even regimental commanders are assured of remaining in their positions', while at the higher levels the effect operated in reverse, inducing an unyielding conservatism.[3] In short, the 'new men' did not match the 'new look' in the organisation of Soviet strategic forces. The 'old guard' gave ground only slowly and reacted with predictable hostility to the massive military redundancies which made such inroads on the privileged and protected social position of the military in Soviet society.

Nor did the infusion of engineers and technicians into the Soviet armed forces, in particular into the élite arms of the strategic missile forces, the air defence command and the submarine branch of the navy, prove to be a totally unmixed blessing. These soldier-technicians with their special skills and higher education represented at once a challenge to the dominance of the 'traditional' officers and a break with the accepted image of the military commander; it was,

therefore, but a short step to question the nature of 'command' in modern war and thus to jeopardise the authority of the commander, who in an age of computers and nuclear weapons could no longer rely upon the simple military values of courage and 'selfless dedication'—even intuition was no substitute for technical skill and competence. On the other hand, the traditionalists were not slow to mount their own counter-attack against the encroachments of the technocrats; they pointed out that undue stress on 'theoretical training' could simply turn officers into *shkolasty*—bookworms—and that the technocrats showed a marked indifference to the political educational work conducted in the Soviet armed forces, insisting that their job was confined to 'the technological element' and ended with ensuring 'combat readiness'. As for the argument that the older and less competent barred the way to the young and the highly educated, this was also denied with some vehemence: on the contrary, there seemed to be a cult of youth and an excessive cultivation of educational qualification, which accounted for that rapid turnover about which Malinovskii complained in no uncertain terms. This initial eruption within the officer corps gradually subsided, though the flow of technical officers has not ceased as modernisation continues; if anything, the technocrat has tempered his criticism of the 'traditionalist' and has also come to want recognition as a 'commander' (a practical demonstration that an 'engineering philosophy' alone will not suffice to satisfy the needs of the armed forces). The officer-technocrat has similarly confined his pressure upon his traditionalist fellows to promoting modern techniques and technology, without seeking to reinterpret the *whole* system in terms of this self-same technology.[4]

It will be seen at once that the structural and the actuarial aspects of the Soviet military command are closely connected. Of all the privileges enjoyed by the Soviet military, perhaps none was greater than that of simply serving on in the armed forces, thus continuing those social and economic benefits which were of such account in a tightly constricted society; behind much of the hostility on the part of the traditionalists towards the technocrats lay the very real fear that they were becoming or might speedily become redundant, misgivings only deepened by Khrushchev's 'one-sidedness' which stressed the role of the strategic arms at the expense of the conventional forces. The debate over 'doctrines', therefore, must also be viewed in the light of these at-

[2]Such an explanation is attempted in my own study. 'The Soviet officer corps in the post-Stalin period (1954–69): intergroup mobility, vertical mobility and social stratification' (University of Glasgow SSRC project, *Social Structure and Social Mobility in the USSR*).

[3]See discussion in Roman Kolkowicz, *The Soviet Military and the Communist Party* (Princeton U.P., 1967), Ch. IX, pp. 309–21.

[4]*Ibid.*, pp. 319–20.

titudes and commitments. Yet this vested interest worked both ways, producing pressures at the upper and lower levels of the command. Military conservatism, the immobilism of 1948–52 and even Khrushchev's own personnel policy had all combined to give the Soviet officer corps a singular profile by the mid-60s: in 1945 this was the youngest officer corps in the world (particularly in its leading echelons), while in 1965 it had become indubitably the oldest. The Marshals and senior commanders in 1945 fell predominantly within the 41–48 age-bracket; in 1965 the senior officers represented on the 'Supreme Military Council'[5] (composed of *Politburo* members, together with senior officers down to Military District/Fleet command level and including the Military Council members of such echelons) were almost to a man aged over 60, an 'old boy net' in the literal sense.

Though 'rejuvenation' might be taken to mean simply lowering the average collective age of the command, the problem is considerably more complex than mere actuarial adjustment. In the first place, there is the problem of numbers as well as of categories. This can be approached by taking the figure for party membership in the armed forces as an approximate for officer strength (party membership or candidate membership and officer status being virtually synonymous): this would give a figure of some 20 per cent for officer strength out of a total manpower strength in the region of 3¼ million men (not including the para-military formations). There is, of course, the special problem of the configuration of the Soviet officer, the inflation of his role and functions—the absence of a large civilian component within the Soviet military establishment, the additives of the 'political officers', the performance of duties assigned in western armies to NCOs, all of which bears out this enlargement of the officer ratio.

In terms of profile, there are approximately five main groups which command attention: Groups I–III, representing the Front and Army commanders of the Second World War (now all aged over 60), Group IV—the most interesting—made up of officers who held wartime divisional or regimental commands (Colonel Tolubko, or Colonel Yakubovskii, for example) and Group V comprising the 'bulge' of colonels and junior generals whose wartime service was in the junior officer ranks or even as wartime NCOs. Group IV has undoubtedly the most significant 'spread',

straddling the 45–60 age-bracket and including officers implanted in the most senior command positions (such as Gorshkov, the Naval C-in-C, or Kutakhov, the Air Force C-in-C), together with those officers in 'top of the tree' or 'next to leading positions'—Ogarkov at the General Staff, Maryakhin at the head of Rear Services,* Kulikov as C-in-C GSFG—who will undoubtedly rise still further.† The upper edge of this group is formed by officers like Batitskii, C-in-C Air Defence Command (*PVO Strany*), who are on the mark of 60 (Batitskii was born in 1910), followed by a thicker stratum of officers in their late 50s—Yakubovskii was born in 1912, Tolubko in 1914—and the following stream of men in their late 40s, Kulikov (born 1922) or else Kutakhov who ended the war as commander of a Guards Aviation Regiment and was promoted to Marshal of Aviation in February 1969.

In addition to classifying the men it is also necessary to categorise their posts, or rather, to attempt some classification of 'key' posts and appointments, whether for their connotations of prestige (as 'jumping-off' posts for further advancement) or direct, possibly decisive, influence. Within that 'senior command triangle' with its base resting on the military district/fleet command and reaching to the top (Defence Minister, First Deputy Ministers and Deputy Ministers, Chief of the General Staff), it might be reckoned that there are some 3,000 appointments, taking into account the whole central administration as well as the staffs for arms and services. Out of this main body of senior commanders, some 300 can in turn be singled out as the incumbents of 'key' posts: the number takes account of the 'key' commands (the five branches of the Soviet armed forces), the position of the *first deputy* and *deputy* commanders (themselves identified by Soviet sources as a 'pool' of potential candidates for promotions), the occupants of 'key' military districts—Belorussia, Kiev, Volga, Far East—and the level of the 'technician colonel-generals'. Consider the command of the Kiev MD: this appears to be a post which is an indispensable 'jumping-off' position (witness Kulikov himself) or the Volga MD, a curious command at first sight but one which may house the 'alternative' command system in the event of nuclear attack (Ogarkov of the General Staff held this post prior to his promotion as First Deputy Chief/GS).

---

[5]This body is also referred to as the Higher Military Council or Main Military Council. (See Yu. P. Petrov, *Partiinoe stroitel'stvo v Sovetskoi Armii i Flote* Moscow, Voenizdat, 1964.)

Editor's Note—Maryakhin died unexpectedly in June 1972. He was succeeded by Army General S. K. Kurkotkin in August 1972.

†*Editor's Note*—Kulikov lived up to this expectation, being appointed as First Deputy Minister of Defense and Chief of the General Staff in September 1971.

There is also the important 'cycle' of command appointments, such as a military district command before taking the direction of a major military academy (for example, Losik from the Far East and thence the Armoured Forces Academy): the 'academy appointment' may not necessarily signify being 'kicked upstairs'.* Equally, it is impossible to dismiss the role of the 'Zakharov net', that is, Zakharov's own eminence as Chief of the General Staff and his influence—even patronage—in command appointments (again, Ogarkov serves as a good example). This list of singularities, however, would not be complete without reference to a new feature within the promotional pattern, the intrusion and assertiveness of the logistics officers, Maryakhin's domain, with something like a self-contained 'promotion line' (and a rapid one, at that) beginning to emerge within the whole system. In short, all rules have their exceptions.

The command changes also indicate much more complex shifts than simply redressing the balance of Khrushchev's latter days. To anticipate a specific argument, one of the more significant of the post-Khrushchev innovations has been the appointment of senior officers—Ogarkov, Alekseyev—to managerial and weapons programme co-ordination posts, even though such activity has not been given an institutional framework: it is this, among other things, which gives the present General Staff its singular prominence and importance, thus suffusing the influence of the technologists and engineers on an even wider scale and at the highest levels. In sum, an inspection of command changes provides some safeguard against sweeping conclusions drawn only from reviewing the abstractions of 'doctrinal debate' or simple contents analysis of Soviet pronouncements. Essentially the Soviet military system has eschewed the method of making either frequent or substantial institutional changes. It is not, therefore, institutional change but shifts in personnel—'key' officers who redefine the role and function of their positions—which must of necessity command close attention in order to make better sense of what is loosely called 'policy'.

'REJUVENATION AND RE-ORGANISATION': 1966–67 AND 1968–70

The senescence of senior officers, the plethora of colonels and the special problems of the contemporary junior officers formed the ungainly outlines of the profile of the command when the Brezhnev–Kosygin regime came to power. Obvious considerations of formal political decency and the 'settling-in' phase of the new leadership, professedly 'collective' in its style, reduced the scope for top-level changes. With Marshal Malinovskii's grip slackening (and ultimately loosed by his death in 1967), Grechko played an increasingly important part in what was a 'caretaker' military administration. Nevertheless, the appointment (indeed, the reappointment) of Marshal M. V. Zakharov (born in 1898) to the post of Chief of the General Staff was a step of considerable significance: this astonishingly energetic and vastly experienced officer speedily and unequivocally set the tone for the denunciation of 'hare-brained' military schemes—an obvious and sardonic reference to Khrushchev's military manias—and for the reinstatement of strict professionalism.[6]

These command changes, slow and selective as they were, went hand in hand with the implementation of a revised 'cadres policy' for the officer corps as a whole: indeed, a whole new manpower policy was also in the making, resulting finally in the updated 'Law on Universal Obligation for Military Service' which was promulgated in October 1967. By the end of 1965 the survey of the qualifications and record of all Soviet officers was complete, managed by Colonel-General Gusakovskii (Head of the Cadres Administration since 1963) but assisted latterly by a new First Deputy, Colonel-General P. T. Lukashin, who made it unpalatably plain that the 'good old days' of indefinite service were over—the traditional formula of 'combining old and young cadres' must no longer mean that 'officers who by virtue of their age are not able to pull their weight in operational units should retain their positions'. So often (according to Lukashin) these elderly men protected themselves by selecting elderly or incompetent deputy commanders, who would never outshine their superiors; equally bad was the practice of the commander using a competent deputy for his own purposes but deliberately holding such a deputy back from promotion for fear of losing these invaluable services. The

---

*Losik could well succeed Marshal A. Kh. Babadzhanyan as Head of the Soviet Armoured Forces, since the latter's recent appointment to this post ran wholly counter to the 'rejuvenation' principle: Babadzhanyan is in his mid-60s and his could be only a 'holding appointment' until a suitable candidate is prepared. Losik would also have held the principle 'prestige' posts and also has his wartime service as a tank officer to recommend him.

[6]See *KZ*, 4 February 1965.

deputy commander was henceforth to come into his own at the proper time. As for the older officer, the 'not so well trained' should be put on the reserve and the 'adequate' transferred to staff jobs, training establishments and military commissariats (administrative assignments).[7]

The autumn of 1967 brought further appointments which could be regarded as a 'balancing' process within the command group as a whole—naval and air promotions—and also in October the promulgation of the new law on military service, updating the existing Law of 1939 with its amendments enacted in 1940, 1941, 1943, and 1954. The new law set precise age-limits on service, limitations (and exceptions) which indicated the critical points in Soviet officer strength. The provisions of the new law relating to age, rank and length of service retained the age level of 60 for officers of 3-star rank (colonel-general, general, marshals and admirals) but stipulated transfer to the reserve (Class III) at this age: 1-star and 2-star generals would retire at the age of 55 as before, colonels at the age of 50 (an extension of 5 years): lieutenant-colonels were to retire at the age of 45, which left their position unaltered. Below the rank of lieutenant-colonel, however, there were some substantial changes in the direction of *extending* the period of service—majors for five more years (from 40 to 45), senior lieutenants and captains also for five more years (from 35 to 40), junior lieutenants and lieutenants for an additional ten (from 30 to 40). In addition, the 1967 Law authorised the mobilisation of reserve officers *under the age of* 30 for a further 2–3 years' service with the armed forces, even under peacetime conditions.[8]

General Shtemenko's own commentary on these new age/rank/length of service regulations emphasised that the revisions were designed to facilitate 'planned rejuvenation'—*planomernoe obnovlenie*—within the officer corps, as well as to prevent competent officers who were still 'relatively young' moving prematurely into the reserve (these were the regimental commanders simply pitched out in the piping days of Khrushchev's army—'too old at 35') and also to help to establish service in the armed forces as a viable profession.[9] This 'career-management' aspect was clearly causing the Soviet command concern: the provisions about junior officers implied that adequate enlistment had fallen off and it was not for nothing the 'junior officer' soon came to occupy a prominent place in the public preoccupations of the high command.

The 1967 Law also reduced the length of conscripted service, with the duration now fixed at two years, save for those joining the Navy or serving with the ships of the coastguard, which entailed three years: the call-up was fixed at 18, with two annual inductions in the middle and at the end of the calendar year and the grounds for deferment or exemption extended (except for deferment on educational grounds, which presently covers only those conscripts undergoing full-time or part-time education which must be a continuous course).* A much more radical innovation was contained in Articles 17–22 dealing with compulsory 'pre-military training' to be carried out in schools, factories and collective farms by instructors from the regular forces and in the free time of the pupils or young workers. Such a system had much to recommend it; the military instructional programme provided many surplus officers with jobs, the potential conscript could be given some rudimentary military training, the maintenance of the worker under instruction was not charged to the defence budget and, in addition, there is an inescapable element of 'social control' or 'youth control'.[10] Meanwhile *DOS AAF* carries on much more specialist training (radio operators, military technicians, specialists for civil defence units).

Meanwhile there were more promotions under the 'planned reconstruction' of the command. Admiral Gorshkov was promoted in October to Admiral of the Fleet of the Soviet Union: the artillery arm acquired a new Marshal (Kuleshov), as did the armoured forces (Babadzhanyan) and civil aviation (Loginov, who was colonel-general). These four appointments, which helped to distribute the honours and the status with some show of even-handedness, were accompanied by more shifts in the military district commands.

The invasion of Czechoslovakia produced one change at the top. General M. I. Kazakov, Chief of Staff/Warsaw Pact forces and *ex officio* First Deputy Chief/GS, was relieved of his duties on

[7] See Col.-Gen. Lukashin, *KVS loc. cit.* (1966).

[8] Text of draft law, *Izvestiya*, 13 October 1967 (supplement pp. 3–4): also *Pravda*, 13 October 1967, for Marshal Grechko's speech.

[9] See General S. M. Shtemenko, *Novyi zakon i voinskaya sluzhba* Moscow, Voenizdat, 1968, p. 30.

*This is to exclude previous deferment for evening course or correspondence course students, rather than 'day leave' students proper, thus closing an avenue of escape from military service.

[10] As one sample (among many) see report on effects of military training in a Minsk school: *Uchitel'skaya gazeta*, 4 September 1969.

7 August and replaced by General Shtemenko, who at once took charge of a 'signals and communications exercise' involving Soviet, Polish and East German troops, a move to set up the command-and-control system for a major military move. (Grechko and Yakubovskii met Marshal Koshevoi, C-in-C GSFG: Maryakhin* had already conferred with the East German and Polish heads of supply, Allenstein and Szczerba.) Kazakov ostensibly withdrew from his post on grounds of ill-health, though there have been no signs of his general retirement; Shtemenko does not appear to have participated specifically in his 'Warsaw Pact' capacity but rather as one of the few Soviet officers with the requisite experience of handling a senior operational staff. His role, as depicted by Mr. Malcolm Mackintosh, was to handle the 'high-level' operational staff' set up to mount the invasion;[11] only *after* the invasion did he take over specific Warsaw Pact duties, and it was not until February 1969 that formal acknowledgement of this was made. The invasion also added one more external 'Group of Forces' to the command set-up, Central Group in Czechoslovakia, which was formally established in January 1969 under the command of Lieutenant-General A. M. Mayorov (rapidly promoted to Colonel-General), a company commander in the war and a major-general in 1960, assigned subsequently to a divisional command: the First Deputy Commander, Lieutenant-General D. I. Litovtsev, was also the 'plenipotentiary' of the Soviet government in Czechoslovakia—an indication of special standing with the Party and the government.

Ogarkov's appointment as First Deputy Chief of the General Staff clearly demands some explanation. Since Povaly was already installed as head of the Operations Administration and remained there, Ogarkov scarcely replaced him, nor did he augment Povaly's functions in any discernible fashion. The basis of an explanation seems to lie rather in Ogarkov's background, training and experience in the engineering-technical side; his introduction to a senior post in the General Staff suggests that he was charged with the supervision and management of the military-scientific work controlled by the General Staff, or indeed the co-ordination of programmes involving the scientific–technical committees and research agencies, an 'inter-locking directorate'

related to military R&D. Ogarkov's duties are probably both managerial and entrepreneurial and perhaps the best institutional comparison is with Tukhachevskii's activity as *Nachal'nik vooruzheniya* in the early 1930s, where he acted as the 'overseer' of weapons programmes and weapons development.[12] The leading role which Ogarkov plays in the management and control of the weapons programme might also be guessed from his inclusion in the Soviet delegation to the SALT talks which first opened in Helsinki. There would appear to be much more to say both on the subject of Ogarkov and of the diversification of the General Staff's functions.

Inevitably the clashes with the Chinese on the Far Eastern frontiers impinged on the fortunes and commitments of the command, though the most spectacular moves involved the Ground Forces and the Navy. (Kutakhov himself went to the Far Eastern MD early in March, obviously to investigate the Ussuri incidents.) Amidst growing talk of 'preventive war' or 'pre-emptive strikes' against China, the Soviet command—with Zakharov in the lead—set about re-ordering Soviet defences in the Far East and along the length of the Sino–Soviet frontiers. In April–May the first moves began to show themselves with the assignment of Vice-Admiral Smirnov, chief of staff to Gorshkov in the big *SEVER* exercises in 1968 and head of the Operations Department/Main Naval Staff, to the command of the Pacific Fleet, replacing Admiral Amelko who moved back to Moscow as a deputy C-in-C of the Soviet Navy.

Of all branches of the Soviet armed forces, the naval leadership had shown the greatest stability, due in some measure to the relative youth of the senior command group as a whole. Gorshkov is the longest-serving C-in-C, having taken up his appointment in 1956: the Head of the Political Administration (Navy), Admiral V. M. Grishanov, has been in his post since 1958. In many important respects—homogeneity, professional skills, the combination of 'old and new cadres'—the naval command is the only true 'post-war command group emplaced within the Soviet system, due ironically enough to the persistent instability and the purges inflicted on the Navy in the period after the war. Command replacements in the Fleets (Northern, Baltic, Black Sea, and Pacific) have followed a fairly consistent pattern, though the period of service within given fleets has varied.

In the spring and summer of 1969 the naval

---

*Operation 'Niemen', opening on 24 July 1968, was a Rear Services exercise directed by General Maryakhin from Minsk: at the end of the month it was extended to East Germany and Poland.

[11]Malcolm Mackintosh, *The Evolution of the Warsaw Pact*, Adelphi Papers (No. 58), p. 15.

[12]Cf. Introduction to M. N. Tukhachevskii, *Izbrannye Proizvedeniya*. Vol. I. (Moscow: Voenizdat, 1964), pp. 3–27.

command enjoyed a series of 'upgrading' promotions: Lobov of the Northern Fleet (also a member of the Central Committee) was promoted to Admiral of the Fleet, an acknowledgement of the leading role of this naval command with its component of nuclear missile-launching submarines, and N. D. Sergeyev, Chief of the Naval Staff since 1964, was similarly elevated. This at least gave the naval command 'parity' in rank with its other partners in the Soviet strategic deterrent force.

The year 1969 was remarkable for the attention to the lower rungs of the ladder: in public announcement and acclaim, 1969 was 'the year of the junior officer', junior lieutenants, lieutenants and senior lieutenants in particular, upon whom the high command lavished obvious and special attention, while the military press carried extensive commentaries on their importance and value. *Molodoi Kommunist* published the results of an interesting (possibly a unique) sociological survey of lieutenants, based on a sampling of 1,000 young officers (750 married, 250 single, thus providing data on 'the social status and educational data' of these officers' wives).[13] The year also witnessed (or did not witness,) the singular 'non-event', the failure to convene the much-advertised Fifth All-Army Conference of Party Secretaries, announced as early as 27 November 1968 in *Krasnaya Zvezda*: since the assembly of the fifteen hundred or so party secretaries of military bodies is a rare but highly significant event, then the failure to carry through this assembly for all of Yepishev's exhortations meant that something had gone badly wrong. (It is not enough to explain this away by citing the trouble with the Chinese: once the incidents calmed down, the conference could well have gone ahead and it appears that the absence of unanimity over Czechoslovakia is much more accountable.)

The past year (1970) lacked the drama of 1969 and the focus, if indeed there was one, shifted steadily towards the 'institutional' consolidation of the military and the expansion of its influence. Both the Ground Forces and the Soviet Navy showed their paces in the two massive exercises, '*DVINA*' and '*OKEAN*' which were held between March–May 1970: '*DVINA*' was a full-scale test of the mobilisational and operational performance of the Ground Forces, played against a nuclear scenario,[14] while '*OKEAN*' also tested the naval forces even as the Soviet

Navy made a continuous impression with its growing number of ships on long distance patrol. Though not directly connected with command changes, there were two very significant developments in 1970 which deserve mention, if only to illuminate the background against which this 'command consolidation' took place. The first might best be described as the 'concordat' between Grechko and Brezhnev, which, for all the alarmist talk of a military 'take-over', brought the military to support the party's stance on strategic issues, on the expanded role of the political agencies in the armed forces and on the greater scope for 'political officers', while the party underwrote the military's interest in increased military training and in emphasising the 'defence requirement' when formulating internal policies. The very personification of that 'compact' was Brezhnev's appearance at the final parade of the '*DVINA*' manoeuvres. The second factor was the Soviet attainment of 'parity' in strategic weapons, an achievement which gave rise to the feeling that the worst days of 'inferiority' were over and to a sense of military 'muscle', available to be flexed if not actually used. The third component of this attitude was the effort to increase the efficiency of the management of strategic weapons programmes and the defence sector as a whole, a 'bigger bang for the same rouble.'

In the Far East Soviet forces were continually reinforced upwards to what looked like a theoretical force level of 35 divisions in the Far East and Mongolia, capable of further augmentation (an additional 25): in the European theatre, the Warsaw Pact was also 'rationalised' increasingly along the lines of an 'extra' Soviet military district and the Warsaw Pact forces ('grouped' into special East German, Czechoslovak, and Soviet contingents or other combinations) added to the Soviet forces simply as an additional 'high command' organisation. Both of these moves were reflected in the promotion patterns for 1970: Tolubko in the Far Eastern MD was raised in May 1960, to the rank of full General, thus raising the status of his command and Shtemenko of the Warsaw Pact command was removed in the late summer from his position in the Soviet General Staff, suggesting a revised arrangement for the Warsaw Pact command.

The third significant appointment passed barely without notice, though it may prove to have the greatest import of all: Colonel-General N. N. Alekseyev of the strategic deterrent forces, one of the leading Soviet delegates to the SALT talks along with Colonel-General Ogarkov, was promoted in the autumn to the rank of Deputy

---

[13] *Molodoi Kommunist* 9 (1969): 53–57. For an English version (and with differing data!) see 'Lieutenants' in *SMR* 10 (1969): 2–7.

[14] See *DVINA Voiskovye manevry . . . v marte* 1970 *goda* (Moscow: Voenizdat, 1970), 192 pp.

Defence Minister, an elevation which can only mean that Alekseyev has been put in charge of the co-ordination of strategic weapons programmes.

Five years and more of 'planned reconstruction' in the officer corps and the military command have produced varying results. 'Rejuvenation', or to use the Soviet formulation, the new principle of 'combining old and young cadres'— even *planomernoe obnovlenie*—reduced the collective age of the command and, in the persons of the newer commanders, brought in fresh professional skills. 'Technocratisation' has continued: at the end of 1969 Colonel-General Grigor'ev underlined the preponderance of engineer officers—'these personnel account for 80 per cent of our officer corps: the commander who is at the same time an engineer has become a central figure'. There are clear signs of the engineering and managerial element being introduced into the General Staff. The command changes as a whole reflect this dependence on professionalism, but at the same time the frequency of unfilled posts and the recourse to 'old cadres' suggests both a shortage of suitable candidates or a reluctance on the part of the very senior officers to rely on the untested young. The really interesting convergence will occur when the 50–55 year old *apparatchiki* on the Central Committee take over from the more elderly leaders: in not dissimilar style a comparable group in the military leadership—Group IV, the officers who achieved general's rank in the late 1950s—is making its own inroads into the highest command echelons. The forthcoming 24th Party Congress should show, in part, how far this convergence has progressed.

PERSONNEL, POLICIES, AND PREFERENCES

There is demonstrably much more to the reshaping of a command than a series of vertical moves along the promotion ladder. Committed as it was to the expansion and to the diversification of Soviet capabilities, the post-Khrushchev military leadership—which was essentially identical with that existing at the time of Khrushchev's dismissal, save for one or two adjustments*—embarked almost at once on a survey of the entire Soviet officer corps. The whole process of 'change' started up in 1965 against a tense and complicated background—the emphatic repudi-

ation of Khrushchev's ideas on military organisation, the revision of strategic doctrine and the denunciation of 'one-variant war', the realignment of personal loyalties and political affiliations, the preparations for changes in force structures, the refurbishing of the image of the officer, the insistence on professionalism and the encouragement of military expertise, and the recognition of a need to 'manage' a system increasingly impregnated with a complex technology. Continuity in personnel did not mean, however, continuity in policy. One of the first acts of the military leadership was to re-form the ranks of the 'military-industrial *apparat*' which Khrushchev had been at pains to break up, a process much assisted by the rapid re-centralisation of the defence industry agencies in March 1965. After an interval consistent only with minimum decency, Marshal Zakharov lashed out at Khrushchev for his wanton interference with military matters and set up professionalism as the hall-mark of the new look in military matters. To what extent, therefore, do the command changes represent particular preferences and priorities and in what manner do they correspond to modifications in operational requirements?

It was under the auspices of the 'old guard' that the military package was presented to the 'collective leadership' in 1965–66, a programme which was neither a simple reversal of Khrushchev's position—else the Ground Forces would have been reinstated without further ado—nor a surrender to the strident radicalism of the younger militants. The 'policy', in so far as it can be subsumed under a few heads, seemed to hinge on a recognition that nuclear war was (and is) a realistic likelihood, demanding both a revision of the 'inferior' strategic status of the Soviet Union and a purposeful investment in damage-limitation forces, together with stemming the complacency induced by Khrushchev's view that nuclear war would be an inconceivable act of insanity: in mid-1965 the military also managed to inject a greater sense of urgency into the civil defence preparations and a new centralised 'civil defence' organisation was set up to replace the local committees which had hitherto been responsible for such work (the new organisation came under Marshal Chuikov, so recently displaced as C-in-C of the Ground Forces).[15] With regard to Europe, while there was undoubted emphasis on preparation for

---

*Marshal M. V. Zakharov was reinstated as Chief of the General Staff after Biryuzov's death in October 1964 and General Yepishev was elected a full member of the Central Committee at the November (1964) Plenum.

[15]See V. I. Chuikov, *Grazhdanskaya oborona v raketno-yadernoi voine*. (2nd ed.) (Moscow: Atomizdat, 1969). (This edition mentions the Chinese nuclear threat.)

general war, there was also a recognition that there should be capabilities at any level of weapons. In the sense that there was a reversal of the Khrushchev line, it was focused on the contingency that 'deterrence' might fail and on making the requisite military provision for this contingency.

The appointment of Marshal Grechko, who had been *de facto* Defence Minister during Marshal Malinovskii's illness, confirmed that the search for diversification in Soviet capabilities would continue. Ambitious, hard-driving, experienced and intelligent, Grechko began his career with the Red Army as a cavalryman in 1919 (joining the 1st Cavalry Army, the 'old boy net' which dominated the Soviet command for many years) and by 1945 was an army commander, Kiev MD commander (1945–53), C-in-C GSFG (1953–57) and C-in-C Warsaw Pact Forces after 1960: he was fortunate also in enjoying the friendship of Khrushchev and a wartime association with Brezhnev.[16] While not espousing a fervid 'radicalism' in military affairs, Grechko had criticised sterile conservatism and on previous showing aligned himself with a 'firm' foreign policy and suspicion of *détente*. His administrative competence is not in doubt: in his various commands he pushed through a rigorous training programme and an insistence on 'readiness'—indeed, under Grechko, 'combat readiness' has been given a new meaning under an exercise pattern which carries a close connection with operational deployment and even 'mobilisation by manoeuvre' (as in the case of Czechoslovakia). 'Readiness' means what it implies and the large-scale exercise pattern is now presumably a permanent feature of Soviet military activity, with its risk of rapid escalation. Marshal Yakubovskii, First Deputy Defence Minister and C-in-C Warsaw Pact, evidently held pronounced views about the desirability of training and raising general purpose forces; but while a version of 'flexible response' (*gibkoe reagirovanie*) had impressed itself on the Soviet command, the general development remains one of preparation for nuclear warfare along the 'main axis' in the central battle area in Europe: on the flanks or in secondary theatres there could be non-nuclear operations (or even constraints on the use of nuclear weapons in the main battle area), hence the need to prepare for such eventualities.[17]

While the appointment in 1967 of two First Deputy Ministers (Yakubovskii and Sokolov) suggested a simple division of labour, with Sokolov being assigned as senior administrative officer to the Defence Ministry and Yakubovskii taking over the Warsaw Pact command, one of the firmest hands on the levers of power is that of the septuagenarian Chief of the General Staff, Marshal Zakharov, a senior officer of great energy and pervasive influence. He is likely to have lent his weight to the reorganisation of the capabilities of the general purpose forces; he quickly emerged as the spokesman for the priority of defence requirements in economic planning and as an advocate of the application of military expertise to defence planning as a whole. It is probable that the General Staff has also assumed certain 'command attributes' in the past five years, in the sense of furnishing direction and control for a situation—such as nuclear war— in which there would be no time to establish the *Stavka*-type centralised body for which Marshal Sokolovskii had earlier argued.[18] The lack of a formal Commander-in-Chief (though Grechko in 1967 did seem to propose that Brezhnev be given this appointment) would also strengthen the claim of the General Staff to a 'command-in-being' organisation: the command function of the Soviet General Staff thus sets it off distinctively from any other comparable body in any other of the world's armed forces. At present the General Staff appears to be 'holding the ring' in the absence of an agreed politico–military arrangement: a commentary in 1970 returned to the question of 'supreme command', suggesting that a political figure could be designated 'Supreme Commander', though he would be governed in his decisions by professional military opinion.

In the same fashion the absence of a new 'military–political organ' for co-ordination has affected the military–economic effort, the 'management' aspect: Ogarkov's appointment in 1968 for which there was no precedent, suggests a liaison between the General Staff (on the R & D side and concerning weapons development) with the 'defence industries committee' drawn together under K. N. Rudnev, L. V. Smirnov and V. N. Novikov, all experienced managers. The function of 'managing' the military–industrial and military R & D effort thus probably falls between several agencies, with the General Staff implanted at the centre.

[16]Cf. Marshal A. A. Grechko, *Bitva za Kavkaz*. Moscow, Voenizdat, 1969. Recounts Brezhnev's role.

[17]The relevant references are admirably laid out and analysed in Thomas W. Wolfe, *Soviet Power and Europe 1945–70*. Johns Hopkins Press, 1970, pp. 451–8.

[18]See also Marshal Sokolovskii and Major-General Cherednichenko in *KVS*, No. 7, April 1966, pp. 59–66, on 'contemporary military strategy'.

The recent appointment of Colonel-General N. N. Alekseyev to the post of Deputy Defence Minister with special responsibility for co-ordinating new weapons programmes would virtually close the circle and establish a revised institutional framework for military–industrial co-operation. Since both Alekseyev and Ogarkov were among the Soviet delegates to the SALT talks, they are obviously closely associated with long-term decisions on weapons development.

The 'operational' evolution of the General Staff is connected with the unresolved debate on 'supreme command': the General Staff has also acquired an enlarged competence in military-scientific affairs and the 'management apparatus' for this. In this operational context it is reasonable to suppose that Zakharov has a powerful voice in appointments (and will also have comparable influence on the choice of his successor). Ogarkov seems to have been advanced through the 'Zakharov net': the emplacement of younger MD commanders and the choice of commanders for Soviet Groups abroad would also come under Zakharov's scrutiny. The recent appointment of Babadzhanyan as Head of the Soviet Armoured Forces does nevertheless point towards an ingrained conservatism, keeping out Losik and the younger armour specialists. This post is particularly onerous, since with the exception of airborne formations, all Soviet divisions have a powerful component of armour; armour provides—in Marshal Yakubovskii's formulation—'one of the chief means of rapid exploitation of the deep strikes made by our missiles, air force and artillery'.[19] The conventional arms command has been as much reconstituted as 'rejuvenated': Pavlovskii is credited with the reorganisation of the Far Eastern frontier defences before taking over the Ground Forces, his chief of staff (Nikitin) is an experienced tank officer and in Sergei Stepanovich Maryakhin the Soviet command found another wartime tank officer, former commander of the Northern Group of Forces and of the Belorussian MD, selected in 1968 as head of Rear Services (Logistics).

The Rear Services are themselves relatively new as a centralised organisation, dating back to the spring of 1953: Marshal Bagramyan, who retired in 1968, took control in 1958. Logistics were in an earlier period roughly grafted on to the Soviet system—there were no true 'logistics officers' and 'rear services' posts in military staffs, these were at first filled from 'all-arms' officers until sufficient were turned out by the Military Academy of Rear Services and Transport. The 'intendancy services' were then unified into two basic branches, food supply and uniforms: advanced weapons introduced new categories of supply with special equipment and fuels required for missiles, while the advances in conventional fuel, protective clothing, food products—new rapid preparation, high-calorie foodstuffs, supervised by the technical committee of the *Upravlenie prodovol'-stvennogo snabzheniya*—improved methods of fuel supply and upgrading troop outfitting (improved uniforms in 1953, 1961 and 1969) threw logistics into its 'technical revolution'.[20] The post of 'chief of the rear' (*Nachal'nik tyla*) at MD, formation and unit level was transformed into that of 'deputy commander (Rear Services)', but this has tended to complicate the problem of 'command'. The logistics side of the Soviet command chain has now begun to carve out what looks like its own 'promotional pattern', which is a very new development and one likely to continue.

While the 'logistics empire' grows and is encouraged to grow, the new C-in-C of the Soviet Air Force, Kutakhov, has gone out of his way to stress the importance in the build-up of Soviet air-lift capabilities. Signs of vigorous interest in tactical aircraft were evident at the Domodedovo air show in 1967, with the appearance of a prototype vertical take-off aircraft, but while Vershinin, the ageing C-in-C, was an expert in fighter defences, the Soviet air force had considerable leeway to make up in its long-range air-lift and tactical lift capabilities, which seem to be a matter of some concern to Kutakhov. While emphasising the need for VTOL and STOL aircraft, as well as the requirement for all pilots to be able to land and take off from unsurfaced air strips or similar rough conditions, Kutakhov is at pains to emphasise the role of air transport.[21] Of the seven airborne divisions, three can be dropped simultaneously with their air-portable equipment, including artillery and light armoured vehicles: the 'airborne battle team'—'one of the most important elements of manoeuvre on the battlefield'—makes use of a growing number of helicopters. The 1970 *DVINA* exercises made extensive use of both air-borne and helicopter-borne forces.[22]

[19] For a good summary, see Col. Charles G. Fitzgerald, 'Armor: Soviet Arm of Decision?' *Military Review*, March 1969, pp. 35–46.

[20] Cf. *Tyl Sovetskoi Armii*. Moscow, Voenizdat, 1968, pp. 292–317.
[21] Marshal (Avn) Kutakhov, *KZ* (17 May 1969: KZ article).
[22] See *DVINA, op. cit.*

It is, nevertheless, consideration of and provision for general nuclear war which has formed the focus of the effort and the attention of the post-Khrushchev command. The 'first priority', according to Marshal Malinovskii in 1967, must be accorded to 'the strategic missile forces and atomic missile-launching submarines', a requirement which has remained unchanged. Strategic defence has also retained its priority as an element of the 'damage–limitation' requirement, though there seems to have been something of an internal battle for 'strategic defence' to maintain its equivalent value as part of the strategic arsenal. 'Rejuvenation' seems to have had little impact here: in the Strategic Missile Forces the ageing Marshal Krylov, C-in-C since 1963* and the spokesman for a hard line, presides over a command which is increasingly identified with the 'commander-engineer'.[23] For all the overt talk of 'balance', that which has been attained relates most closely to acquiring a more balanced posture for *general war*. The rest is a bonus, military spin-off either in the form of Soviet warships making their presence seen or off-shoots of the improvement in mobility of Soviet forces in the European theatre, that is, improved air-lift or logistical performance.

Viewed from the perspective (short as it is) of an established, senior command group pursuing its own prescribed military priorities, there is every reason for their hesitancy and circumspection in making significant changes, for 'filtering' the younger men through a series of test appointments and assignments. In so far as the 'new' men fit the overall development, they are judicious choices, bringing new skills to their assignments. In general, their single collective characteristic is that of *better professional education*. But the 'line' is still being held at the level of Deputy Defence Minister. To judge by the reaction of the senior leadership in 1968–69, they did discover the 'generation gap' and seemed to feel its greatest impact where it touched the specialised requirements of the armed forces. It is in the general areas of professionalism, specialist skills and updated tactical competences that the bulk of the command changes have exercised an effect: on the 'management' side there are signs that the military has produced a small but significant echelon of suitable senior officers, whose importance will continue to expand and who must play a growing part in long-term planning. The beneficiaries of the change, however, have been largely the 50–55 age-group, who must represent the next 'take-over' section. It remains to be seen to what degree they have been impressed with the idea of the flexibility of military power or whether—as seems most likely—they will continue to occupy themselves with the question of the relativism of military strength, working towards a 'balanced' structure in so far as it contributes to a better performance for general war. Since this question is by no means solved, this is to say that it must be inevitably the preoccupation of a 'rejuvenated' command, much as it has been the driving force behind the 'old guard'.

THE EVOLUTION OF 'THE MILITARY' AND THE SCOPE OF 'MILITARY INFLUENCE'

The 'old guard'—officers who held responsible military positions as much as a quarter of a century ago—have retained much of their grip on the Soviet military establishment. The overall effect of change within the command has been to bring in better-educated officers, with the younger group forming a highly educated professional elite and with education forming one of the mainsprings of mobility within the officer corps as a whole. There is still an understandable preference for men with wartime experience, and so far no substitute seems to have emerged for 'wartime experience' in an armed force which has not seen large-scale active service since 1945. At the same time, the demands of technology have built a whole new dimension into the command, the *tekhnary* with the logisticians forming a new but important sub-group; by and large, the 'technocratic' approach has been adopted, but this is by no means squared with what some mean by professional officer skills. Senior Soviet officers, Marshal Leonov (C-in-C, Signals Troops) for example, have stated that the shortening of the compulsory military service period has not lowered standards; with the better educational background of the average conscript, this is probably true and clearly the 'through-put' has been increased, but these are the least of the problems in the reorganised Soviet establishment.

Though not all the demands of the present senior leadership group for greater military authority to plan and to execute defence policies have been met, relations with the 'collective leadership' are reasonably good. The military lack any representation on the highest policy-

---

*Editor's Note—Krylov's death, in February 1972, was followed by the appointment of Army V. F. Tolubko in April 1972 as C-in-C of the Strategic Rocket Forces.

[23]See *Izvestiya*, 20 November 1969.

making body in the Soviet Union, but to offset this the Soviet Defence Minister is able to deal with the political leadership without resort to civilian intermediaries: the Brezhnev–Grechko relationship has not been without strain, but the general form of the 'compact' enjoining military support for the party's 'line' and for the proliferation of political agencies in the armed forces in return for the party underwriting the exercise and 'readiness' patterns, as well as emphasising the utility of defence preparations has endured and is likely to do so for some time.*

And with the military—either in an advisory or executive capacity—involved in a number of major policy decisions (the Middle East, Czechoslovakia, naval presence in the Indian Ocean, the SALT talks), then 'military influence' is inevitably displayed in a wider set of circumstances: in Sino–Soviet questions the military leadership and specialist advisers, with Zakharov in the foreground, would provide the 'Defence Committee' (or the Supreme Military Council, to use another of its varied names) with data on the Chinese military and would be responsible for estimates of the Chinese nuclear programme. It is reasonably clear that the advice tendered by Zakharov was in 1969 geared to restraining Soviet action, to consolidating and rationalising Soviet defences in the Far East and along the southern reaches of the Sino–Soviet border (hence the Central Asian MD) and to dismissing the notion of a 'preventive' strike against the Chinese nuclear installations. In short, the prevalence of 'military influence' has been promoted less by the soldiers pressing than by the politicians wavering.

There seems little likelihood (save in drastic circumstances) that this general arrangement will alter appreciably in the immediate future, though much of the current serious analysis of the evolution of *the central military-administrative system* suggests that somewhere in the recesses of the present machine some considerable thought is being given to organisation and structure, particularly the manner in which it can be rationalised by separating functions.[24] The persistence of a subdued but noticeable military grumbling suggests that there is recognition that in terms of institutional arrangement

things are by no means what they should be— the vacant post of Commander-in-Chief (*Glavnokomanduyushchyi*) and the absence of an effective body to co-ordinate the military and political aspects of strategy. There are signs of intense activity to 'manage' and to co-ordinate the military–industrial and the military–economic effort; one of the proposed solutions is to add 'military economists' to higher military staffs, to civilian planning organs and also to economic bodies within the state machine. The additional First Deputy Chief/General Staff, Ogarkov, and the appointment of Alekseyev show the same trend at a very high level. How long this process of 'personalising' solutions rather than giving them an institutional framework can continue is a matter for conjecture, but there are sufficient critical points in the system as a whole to justify (and to suggest) changes defined by separation of functions.

The other area of change (which will also affect 'military influence') will be more diffuse but perhaps even more decisive, involving the efforts paid to improving the 'military profession'—man-management and career-management. Military manpower in the sense of conscript masses is hardly decisive for the missile forces, the élite submarine arm of the Navy and the specialist arms of the Ground Forces. The 'advertising campaign' highlighting the military career is something new in the Soviet Union (and is to be distinguished from the technique of sheer exhortation): to the 'traditional' image of the armed forces has been added greater emphasis on the 'creativity' of such a career, indicating the military is now in full social competition with other career options. *Tvorchestvo*, 'creativity', the utility of the career and the scope for being an individual in the job (an inexact translation, but the flavours of the word are complex) and *prestizh* (social standing) are important in the choice of a career: in a survey of jobs and professions ranked by 'creativity', 'prestige' and payment the military came just over half-way along the scale (Point 55 out of an 80 Point scale). A survey of junior lieutenants showed that in the sample 17½ per cent were of 'peasant origin', the rest from factories or offices: in a much more detailed tabulation, only 4 per cent could be classed as coming from the land, with 27 per cent from factories and 26.8 per cent coming from educational institutes— 19.8 per cent of these officers had come from the ranks. Their motives for choosing the Army as their career were also classified, with the 'appeal of the military profession' accounting for well under half, followed by family tradition as

---

* *Editor's Note*—The Grechko–Brezhnev cooperative relationship was capped with Grechko's election to full Politburo membership in April 1973.

[24] Cf. A. Gromakov, 'Politika Kommunisticheskoi partii v oblasti voennogo stroitel'stva (1920–23 gg.), *VIZ*, No. 6, 1970, pp. 3–11 and V. Danilov, 'Stroitel'stvo tsentral'nogo voennogo apparata v 1921–1923 gg'. *VIZ*, No. 1, 1971, pp. 9–16.

a motive or 'advice to join' in the next two largest categories. Every *fourth* officer had a higher education: the majority (66 per cent) were married within one year of taking up their first posts after finishing military schools.[25]

One of the specific results of 'rejuvenation' over the past five years has been that the military–educational apparatus has been taken out of the hands of the 'old guard', a personnel change which will have important long-term effects. The educational requirement and commitment for the Soviet officer is increasing steadily, with a very onerous load for the 'commander-engineer', with more than 50 per cent of the Soviet officer corps now to be accounted as technicians or engineers of one type or another. The 'profile' of the officer corps is thus changing much more rapidly than its age-distribution, with its imbalances at the lower end and the top. (This says nothing of the problems of quality and quantity associated with Soviet NCOs.) The officer educational system consists presently of 120 military schools for various arms and services (3–5 years of military–technical education, passing out as lieutenant and with an engineering qualification) and 18 military academies with periods of study ranging from 2 to 6 years (2

[25]See *Molodoi Kommunist.* See also *Soviet Union,* No. 3, 1970 on the choice of careers: also *Sputnik,* No. 11, 1967, 'Portrait of a Generation', pp. 129–35. Also *Sotsialnye problemy truda i proizvodstva.* Moscow/Warsaw, 1969, Table p. 48.

years at the General Staff Academy), the duration of tuition and study being also expanded by the range of extra-mural or correspondence course work.

We thus arrive at a somewhat complex definition of 'rejuvenation' and its effects: there is, above all, the top echelon of leadership (Minister, First Deputy Minister and Deputy Minister) which is closely connected with the general evolution of the whole Soviet political élite, followed by the lowering of the 'average age' (for example, in MD commanders) and the senior officers as a whole, followed by the 'colonel-generals', whose specialist skills are quite as important as their age-levels in the several arms and services. As for the younger 'up-and-coming' officers in their early 40s, there is as much evidence to indicate militancy—mainly on the lines of their superiors not understanding the potentialities of technology—as to establish a strong apolitical sense (both of which attitudes have been resisted by the party, so there is proof that they exist).

In sum, the command has been re-shaped to embody a much greater degree of professionalism. At the same time, while this is no single feature of command changes, there is a dominant pragmatism at large within the military, which could lead to some sharp reappraisals of policy, or at least lay the professional and intellectual foundations for such change, some of which should become apparent by the mid-1970s.

ORGANIZATIONAL PERSPECTIVES AND DECISION-MAKING IN THE CHINESE COMMUNIST HIGH COMMAND

WILLIAM W. WHITSON

Dr. Whitson argues that it is misleading to portray the People's Liberation Army as a unitary institutional actor because the separate functions and various career opportunities open to the officer corps generate compromise, coalition, competition, and, at times, confusion. In analyzing the bureaucratic politics of the PLA, Whitson considers six major career channels (local forces, ground forces, the General Political Department, the General Rear Services Department, the Navy, and the Air Force) and five informal factors (military generations, field armies, military regions, the central elite, and personal relationships). Whitson suggests that among the informal factors military region is the most promising as a tool for prediction, because it is the focus for the practical expression of career equities in all career fields, of personal loyalties related to field army experience, of a more traditional Chinese administrative style, and of personal and family relationships. In short, he feels that each military region can be treated as a unitary, purposive actor.

William Whitson is Director of China Studies, the RAND Corporation. He is the editor of The Military and Politics in China in the 1970's *(1972) and the author of* The Chinese High Command, 1927–71 *(1973).*

For the sake of brevity and simplicity (if not for lack of hard data), the great majority of existing strategic analyses of the Far East begin with the fiction of "China" as a purposive actor, its collective behavior treated as if it were an individual possessing clear objectives, clear alternatives, and a set of rational criteria with which to choose among alternatives. Indeed, such a model of state behavior has been the traditional assumption for most international political analysis.[1] While it has served some purposes in the past—and will continue to do so in the future— this model clearly offers limited returns to research in Chinese decisionmaking; in fact, it constitutes an obstacle to such investigations because it tends to deny either the existence or the significance of controversy in the intranational decisionmaking process.

Students of international political behavior have been increasingly interested in two alternative models of decisionmaking. The first is based on the assumption that decisions and viewpoints within any government are structured by groups of organizations, members of which develop special interests and career investments in the survival and power of those organizations. Competition among these groups must inevitably invade the arena of national policy and may be expected to inject special interests into what might otherwise be "rational" choices.

The second model is what Allison calls the "bureaucratic politics model."[2] According to this model,

The decisions and actions of governments are essentially intra-national political outcomes: "outcomes" in the sense that what happens is not chosen as a solution to a problem but rather results from compromise, coalition, competition, and confusion among government officials who see different faces of an issue; "political" in the sense that the activity from which the outcomes emerge is best characterized as bargaining. . . . The actor is neither a unitary nation [Model I], nor a conglomerate of organizations [Model II], but rather a number of individual players [Model III]. Groups of these players constitute the agent for particular government decisions and actions. Players are men in jobs. . . . Answers to questions: "What is the issue?" and

[1] For some general comments on this model, see Graham Allison, "Conceptual Models and the Cuban Crisis," *American Political Science Review* 63, no. 3 (September 1969): 689–718.

[2] *Ibid.*, p. 690.

Reprinted with permission and with minor changes from Robert A. Scalapino (ed.), Elites in the People's Republic of China *(Seattle: University of Washington Press, 1972), pp. 381–415.*

"What must be done?" are colored by the position from which the questions are considered. For the factors which encourage organizational parochialism also influence the players who occupy positions on top of (or within) these organizations. . . . Thus propensities of perception stemming from position permit reliable prediction about a player's stances in many cases. . . . Government behavior can thus be understood . . . as outcomes of bargaining games. In contrast with Model I, the bureaucratic politics model sees no unitary actor but rather many actors as players, who focus not on a single strategic issue but on many diverse intra-national problems as well, in terms of no consistent set of strategic objectives but rather according to various conceptions of national, organizational and personal goals, making government decisions not by rational choice but by the pulling and hauling that is politics.[3]

MAJOR FORMAL AND INFORMAL GROUPINGS IN THE PEOPLE'S LIBERATION ARMY

Just as most of the literature about many national policies of Communist China portrays China as a unitary state, so literature about internal politics in China usually portrays the People's Liberation Army (PLA) as a unitary institutional actor. Terms such as "the army," "the PLA," and "the military" abound in both academic and government analyses. These terms do nothing to clarify the question of the high command's perceptions of their strategic problems. For, as in the larger sphere of national political analysis, "collective rationality" cannot be ascribed to a large group of men whose separate functions and career opportunities in any given case may be expected to generate compromise, coalition, competition, and confusion, to echo Allison's statement quoted above. For purposes of Model II speculation, we must, therefore, examine the less abstract groupings of senior leaders in the PLA.

At least six major career channels existed in the PLA before the Cultural Revolution: (1) local forces (militia and public security); (2) ground forces; (3) General Political Department; (4) General Rear Services Department; (5) navy; and (6) air force. These channels tended to be mutually exclusive; that is, between the ending of the Korean War in 1953 and the 1966 Cultural Revolution, officers generally did not move back and forth among these six career channels. By 1966, therefore, we could expect officers in each channel to have developed a distinctive set of organizational interests, values, attitudes, and goals. According to the fundamental premises of

[3]*Ibid.*, pp. 707–9.

Model II, each of these organizations would tend to encourage its members to behave in such a way as to enhance their own collective interests.

Five factors, however, which cut across career lines, tend to confuse each career group's definition of collective priority interests. The first, military generations, has divided the PLA leadership into eleven major groups of individuals who have shared distinctive political and military crises. The second, field armies, consists of five groupings based on the affiliation of individual officers with the field armies which conquered China during the 1945–50 Civil War. The third, military regions, has divided the PLA leadership into eleven geographic groupings, which remained remarkably stable between the ending of the Korean War and 1966. The fourth, the central elite, has constituted a special geographic and functional group, the majority located in Peking with a minority scattered around the country for brief periods. (In principle, any member of the central elite who spends more than two years in a regional locale must be expected to undergo a shift in perspectives that tends to conform to those of his military region.) The fifth factor, personal relationships, has distributed the PLA leadership into an infinite number of obscure loyalty groupings that generally lie beyond our analytical and data collection capability. Yet their importance for Model III analyses demands that we appreciate this factor as a major cause for error when we attempt to explain behavior within the high command.

We shall first consider each of the informal factors because they help provide an historical context within which current, formal organizational values and interests may be discussed more realistically. It has been principally these informal obstacles to collective, formal institutional perspectives which have generated individual differences in values, viewpoints, and goals among about 1,000 senior officers of the PLA, where each of these men acts as a player in a bargaining process in which his informal and formal organizational affiliations could be expected to influence his choice of the issues on which he might bargain, his perspectives toward such issues, and his ultimate bargaining behavior.

After discussing informal affiliations, this paper will identify probable, if not actual, differences in organizational viewpoints toward the following questions of continuing importance to the high command: (1) the priority of security values and goals; (2) the priority of perceived threats to those values and goals; (3) the "best" organization of available systems and resources for coping with perceived threats; and (4) the preferred strategy and tactics for deploying available resources.

INFORMAL FACTORS

Military Generations

If a military generation is defined as a group of officers who (regardless of age) *entered* the PLA at the same time and shared a given period of military professional and political experiences, the history of the Chinese Communist Party and the Red Army may be divided into eleven periods of major crises.[4] From the perspective of this study, the most important generations are the first four: first, before May 1928; second, from June 1928, to November 1931; third, December 1931–July 1937; and fourth, August 1937–December 1940. The first four military generations are the most important because these men occupy about 98 per cent of the 1,000 key military positions by which we may define the high command.

Among the six career channels enumerated above, how are these generations distributed? Within the ground forces, the majority of the military regional command and staff positions of significance are occupied by second- and third-generation officers with first-generation people found principally in Peking and fourth-generation people found principally at army (corps) and military district levels or below.

Although data on the other five career channels have not been assembled, a spot check of senior officer biographies in the General Rear Services, General Political Department, and so-called local forces suggests that these career channels have not offered younger men a relatively better rate of advancement than the ground forces. Only the air force and the navy seem to have provided such a preferred rate of advancement up to military regional level. At the national level (central elite), senior air force officers (all former army military officers) appear to be drawn principally from the second and third military generations, based on a preliminary survey of available biographies.

Since the bulk of the high command falls within the first four military generations, it is important to underline those aspects of experience which might be expected to distinguish one generation from the other. We should recognize that the time spread between the entry of the oldest member of the first generation into the Communist Party in 1923 and the entry of the youngest member of the fourth generation in late 1940 would be eighteen years. Quite apart from variations in generational experiences of the post–1940 period, it is argued that an officer's *earliest* experience profoundly directs, shapes, and dominates lifelong viewpoints toward such crucial questions as the role of the military in society, the authority of a field commander, the proper criteria for selecting future generals, the proper organization of military power, the most effective strategic and tactical techniques for applying military power, and all four contemporary questions raised at the beginning of this paper.[5]

Based on their collective experience, it seems likely that there is a broad generational viewpoint toward each of these questions. That viewpoint would be based principally on early military and political experience and education, later modified by other broad factors of developing personal ties, affiliation with a particular field army leadership, prolonged assignment to a particular military region, and, perhaps most important, long-term membership after 1953 in one of the six major career channels.

At the risk of oversimplifying differences, a summary judgment would propose that each successive generation, as a group, tended to veer progressively further away from the philosophy, style, and viewpoint of unconventional warfare, the so-called Maoist People's War. The first two generations were drawn predominantly from the poor central Yangtze Valley peasantry, and the second generation in particular had had minimal formal education, having spent their personal and professional formative years in a context of guerrilla warfare in which almost every political or military act aimed at the political mobilization of the masses. Already strongly tied to local customs and organized into local units (one county in Hupeh, for example, has produced approximately 150 second- and third-generation generals), these men may have abjured warlordism; but they probably acquired many of the politically myopic features of the warlord outlook: a strong

---

[4]Employing the three principal criteria of political crisis, military ethic (role of the military in society, authority of a commander, promotion criteria for younger officers), and military style (organization of military power, strategy, and tactics), it is possible to divide the PLA officer corps into eleven military generations, each characterized by one or more differences in their perceptions of the foregoing six factors of ethic and style. For a more detailed discussion of military generations in the PLA, see William W. Whitson, "The Concept of Military Generation: The Chinese Communist Case," in *Asian Survey* 8, no. 11 (November 1968): 921–47.

[5]For theoretical and factual evidence in support of this assumption, see Davis B. Bobrow, "Chinese Communist Response to Alternative U.S. Active and Passive Defense Postures" (paper delivered at conference in Oak Ridge, Tenn., December, 1965), pp. 31–32.

sense of local loyalty, reinforced by a traditional peasant (and Chinese) suspicion of "strangers," perhaps best stated by James E. Sheridan: " . . . a bandit became a warlord at the point where he acquired acknowledged control over a specific area and assumed the tasks of governing it."[6]

This sense of political role, rather than the performance of a primarily professional military function, should have been reinforced by the early experiences of the first two military generations. Furthermore, since their objective was clearly revolutionary, their style necessarily demanded assumption of control over all available resources, including ideology, in their desperate struggle against adverse odds. To label these men opportunists would be to miss the point that, in a struggle for survival, opportunism is the very essence of the struggle and "opportunist" is a compliment to the victor. In their early campaigns before November 1931, when the Central Kiangsi Soviet was formally established, the defensive strategy and the offensive guerrilla tactics of People's War were imposed by circumstances. These men at the outset thus tended to be local and regional (rather than national) in political perspective, political rather than military-professional in their sense of role, and oriented to the relatively independent strategic defense of a particular locale through offensive, small-unit, irregular tactics.

Conversely, the third and fourth generations entered the Red Army in a context of increasing division of labor between the military and the party. The party had grown to such an extent by late 1931 that it was possible to replace many military-political administrators in Kiangsi villages with party cadres, who were largely removed from military affairs. After November 1931, a variety of developments tended to instill new concepts that should have distinguished the military values of the third and especially the fourth generations from the first and especially the second: the establishment of professional military schools; an emphasis on conventional tactics and a more conventional defense of the entire "country" (that is, the Kiangsi Soviet before 1934 and much of North China after July 1937); and a greater emphasis on the professionalization of the officer corps under Russian auspices. The two later generations should have been less confident of the power of the untutored

masses as a military force, of their own skill as political manipulators (at which they have had considerably less experience than the first two generations), and of guerrilla warfare or, broadly, People's War for national defense. Furthermore, because of their entry into the Red Army during a period of great national crisis (after the Japanese invasion of Manchuria in September 1931), the third and fourth generations (the latter including a large number of students from North China) tended to be motivated by significantly different arguments for joining an army. Confronted by a foreign enemy and drawn from a wider, better-educated cross section of Chinese youth, these men might be expected to perceive their loyalties on a more national rather than a regional or local scale.

As suggested earlier, these broad comments about four major generations in the PLA high command could hardly establish more than a general foundation for differences in viewpoint toward contemporary problems of China's national security. After their first few years in service, later influences could be expected to alter generational stereotypes. Of these influences, the field army institutional evolution should have been of crucial importance.

The Field Armies

In 1954, with the reorganization of the PLA after the Korean War, all large organizations formerly labeled "field armies" were deactivated.[7] Thereafter, the three-division "army" (*chün*) became the principal ground force operational command, directly under the control of a military region headquarters. At the same time, air force and navy units were being organized under the local operational control of air defense districts and three major fleet headquarters. Between military regions, air defense districts, and fleet headquarters on the one hand, and the general staff in Peking on the other, there were no intervening levels of military bureaucracy.

Nevertheless, the senior officers who had led the earliest guerrilla units of the Red Army from their 1927 origins through the operations of the 1930's against the Nationalists and, after 1937, against the Japanese, then against the Nationalists, and finally against United Nations forces (from 1950 through 1953), had had careers marked by one unique and highly significant characteristic. Less than 15 per cent of the high command had served in more than one stream of

[6]*Chinese Warlord: The Career of Feng Yühsiang* (Stanford, Calif.: Stanford University Press, 1966), p. 19. For excellent discussions of the warlord outlook, see Hsi-sheng Chi, *The Chinese Warlord System: 1916 to 1928* (Washington, D.C.: Center for Research in Social Systems, 1969), Chap. iii; see also Sheridan, *Chinese Warlord*, esp. Chap. i, pp. 16 ff.

[7]For a more detailed discussion of field armies, see William W. Whitson, "The Field Army in Chinese Communist Military Politics," *CQ* 37 (January–March 1969): 1–30.

institutional evolution. That is, the five field armies which defeated the Nationalists between 1945 and 1949 had evolved through essentially independent processes of development over the previous twenty years. Among 85 per cent of 700 key military leaders analyzed, an officer who had first joined a unit, for example, from the Oyüwan Soviet (Central China) in 1928 had become a senior commander or commissar in the Second Field Army in 1949. An officer who had joined Ho Lung in central Hunan in 1928 had become a senior commander in the First Field Army by 1949.

Translated into American experience, the Chinese senior leadership would be comparable to an American leadership if the six American continental armies were being led by officers who had served together (and nowhere else) for forty years. Even if the continental armies were suddenly deactivated, we may imagine the strong informal bonds of shared victories and defeats which would remain active among former comrades, especially if deactivation did not actually remove leaders from the geographic locale which their old army had occupied.

Military Regions

The year 1954 brought a new geographic dimension to loyalties which had been founded informally on traditional generations and institutions (the field armies). Based on their own origins and operational areas, the various field armies became closely identified with particular military regions. In general, these relationships changed very little over those fifteen years. The relative stability of field army representation in thirteen military regions persisted between August 1966 and December 1967 in the midst of the Cultural Revolution, a year which brought the greatest number of personnel shifts in the entire post-1953 history of the PLA.

By October 1968, when all the revolutionary committees had been formed to replace the former party committees in each province in China, the distribution of power among field army representatives on revolutionary committees reflected the previous field army deployment patterns. With the exception of the First Field Army base where Ho Lung's former subordinates had suffered an unusual loss of status, other geographic power bases retained between 40 and 60 per cent of the representatives of any given field army elite. In other words, the informal loyalty groups which had emerged from field armies have apparently retained significance in the on-going intranational competition for status and influence.

The Central Elite

Just as the field armies acquired geographic power bases after 1949, so many field army senior leaders assumed posts of national importance in Peking. In one sense, such men at once represented military regional and old field army interest groups; in another sense, the senior figures in Peking were channels of communication and coercion from the center to their regional colleagues. However, the post-1945 process of central-regional negotiation, competition, and compromise over such matters as political and material resource allocations gradually brought an influx of regional figures into central positions. This process is reflected in an analysis of the make-up of three successive Central Committees over a twenty-four-year period, from 1945 to 1969.

Several interesting points emerge from such a study. First, the high command as a whole has moved from a status of 50 per cent representation on the Seventh Central Committee in 1945 through a loss of power on the Eighth Central Committee of 1956 (only 37 per cent) to an increase of power on the Ninth Central Committee elected in 1969 (65 per cent). Second, men whose careers had been built at the center, as contrasted with men whose careers had been built principally in "the provinces" (local soviets, border regions, or military regions) have suffered a persistent decline in relative representation from 52 per cent on the Seventh Central Committee to a maximum of 21 per cent on the Ninth Central Committee (only 27 full members out of a total of 170). Third, the accretion of power by the Second and Fourth Field Army representatives has brought them from a base of 11 per cent and 7 per cent, respectively, in 1945, to 22 per cent and 27 per cent in 1969. In effect, these two field army groups, backed up by their very powerful and wealthy military regional power bases, could dominate the Politburo and the Central Committee after 1969.

If these figures have any validity, they should suggest to aspiring career officers and party cadres that it pays to establish one's credentials at the regional level first before entering the vicious struggle for power and privilege in Peking. A reputation and a political foundation in a military region plus, of course, useful contacts within a particular career channel would appear to be an object lesson from the past twenty-four years of intranational conflict.

But given this process of gradual vertical movement along career channels and across geographic lines toward Peking, what effect may such a process have on the perspectives of any

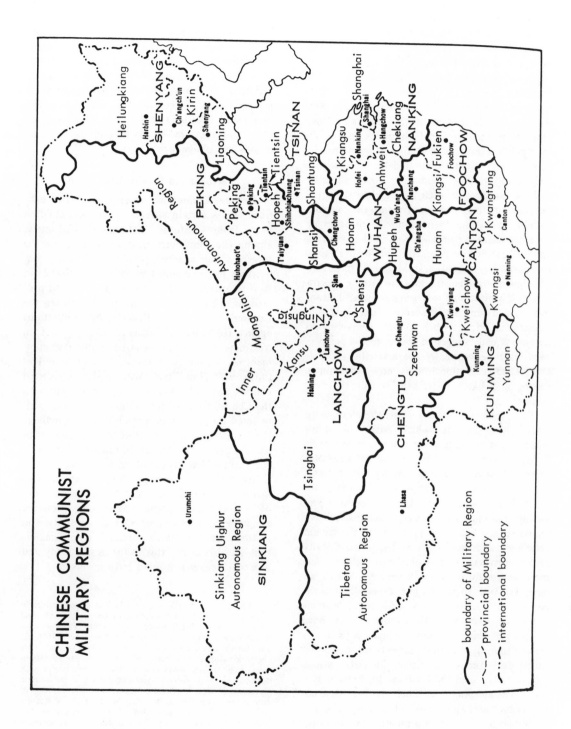

CHINESE COMMUNIST
MILITARY REGIONS

boundary of Military Region
provincial boundary
international boundary

Heilungkiang
Harbin ●
SHENYANG
Ch'angch'un ●
Kirin
Shenyang ●
Liaoning
PEKING
Peking
● Peking
Tientsin
Tientsin
Tientsin
Hopeh
Shihchiachuang
TSINAN
Shantung
Tsinan ●
Kiangsu
Nanking ●
Shanghai
Shanghai
Shanghai
Hangchow ●
Chekiang
NANKING
FOOCHOW
Fukien
Foochow ●
Taiyuan ●
Shansi
Chengchow ●
Honan
WUHAN
Hupeh
Wuch'ang ●
Anhwei
Hofei ●
Nanchang ●
Kiangsi
Ch'angsha ●
Hunan
CANTON
Kwangtung
Canton ●
Huhohaot'e ●
Shensi
Sian ●
Ningsia
Inner Mongolia
Autonomous Region
Kansu
Lanchow ●
LANCHOW
Hsining ●
Chengtu ●
CHENGTU
Szechwan
Kweiyang ●
Kweichow
Kwangsi
Nanning ●
Kunming ●
KUNMING
Yunnan
Urumchi ●
Sinkiang Uighur
Autonomous Region
SINKIANG
Tsinghai
Lhasa ●
Tibetan
Autonomous Region

29

given officer, already obligated to other sets and subsets of loyalties? Unquestionably, our hypotheses about Chinese high command perspectives must account for this process. Indeed, it is precisely because the outlook of the central elite *is* believed to be different from regional viewpoints that we must qualify our hypotheses when we speak of "the Chinese." Undoubtedly, military (and probably party) leaders at the center are under the greatest pressure to perceive their problems in terms of the national interest. Yet, they are also dependent on the continuing close support of their regional comrades to sustain their political leverage in Peking. It would not be easy, for example, for them to detach forces from their own military region for some allegedly national purpose if such a detachment would clearly erode their popularity within their region, thereby weakening their status in the eyes of their old regional comrades and, in the long run, imperiling their own political flexibility in Peking. As Allison has suggested, in Model III these central figures *must* engage in a bargaining process in which institutional and geographic affiliations and related military resources have real significance as intranational political resources. As we have already suggested above, such a perspective might be especially characteristic of first- and second-generation leaders, now dominant in Peking and likely to remain so for the next decade.

The problem for the analyst, therefore, is to assess the extent to which local obligations among central figures may impinge on their dialogue over national issues and produce outcomes which are "rational" principally in terms of the cross-purposes of local interests and goals, mutually balanced to maintain or reflect a prevailing intranational power relationship. We would suggest that the experience of the second generation and their relatively local, traditionally peasant perspectives, as contrasted with broader, more nationally oriented perspectives which we have ascribed to third- and especially fourth-generation leaders, would underscore a continuing concern for local loyalties among those second-generation leaders, whose arrivals in Peking during Cultural Revolution personnel shifts were the most recent. Indeed, various scholars have seen the Cultural Revolution as a sociopolitical trauma in which the near destruction of the party apparatus and the purge of many central leaders brought a dramatic shift of power over routine decisions and resource allocations toward regional authority at the expense of a confused central elite.[8]

While this trend may have been reversed after mid-1968, perhaps partly in the name of "war preparedness," the continuing absence of a national party machine suggests that the military region and its burdened but largely undamaged hierarchy through military district, armies, People's Armed Departments, and Public Security Bureaus have become and are likely to remain a locus of major political as well as military decisions. We must, therefore, assume that the perspectives of the central elite, now increasingly dominated by figures transferred from regional posts, strongly reflect their military regional origins and obligations.

Personal and Family Associations

Despite Communist assertions to the contrary and a certain success in weaning children away from Confucian notions of filial piety, among the four older generations that are the subject of this analysis, personal and family connections have remained of major significance in their approach to the jungle of political and professional career competition. Indeed, during the Cultural Revolution, Red Guard accusations against Ho Lung and others for their preferential treatment of relatives managed to side-step comment on the far more obvious role of Mao Tsetung's wife, Lin Piao's wife, and the assorted cousins and in-laws of various senior figures on the Central Cultural Revolution Group which attempted (largely unsuccessfully) to stage-manage the Cultural Revolution. Unfortunately, this critical dimension of Chinese intranational political competition has remained largely unresearched, if not disdained, among political analysts. This factor must weigh significantly on the decisions of senior figures about promotions, preferred assignments, preservation of local interests, and so forth. But the dearth of reliable data demands that we also ignore this factor in this study and accept whatever margin of error results.

---

[8]For judgments underscoring a revival of regionalism in China after the Cultural Revolution, see Leonard Schapiro and John W. Lewis, "The Roles of the Monolithic Party under a Totalitarian Leader," *CQ* 40 (October–December 1969): 62; and, for an excellent survey of factors which tended to erode the totalitarian unity of the central elite, see Michel Oksenberg, "The Institutionalization of the Chinese Communist Revolution: The Ladder of Success on the Eve of the Cultural Revolution," *CQ* 36 (October–December 1968): 61–92. For contrasting judgments (to the effect that the Cultural Revolution's politically centrifugal trends were only temporary), see Victor C. Falkenheim, "The Cultural Revolution in Kwangsi, Yunnan and Fukien," *Asian Survey* 9, no. 8 (August 1969): 580–97; and Gordon Bennett, "China's Continuing Revolution: Will It Be Permanent?" *Asian Survey* 10, no. 1 (January 1970): 2–17.

FORMAL CAREER INSTITUTIONS

Local Forces

A brief analysis of each so-called career channel in the Chinese armed forces should complete our analysis of major groups and organizations engaged in China's high-command intranational competition. Beginning at the lowest level, taking the most locally oriented forces within the military and paramilitary hierarchy of China, the militia has hardly been a career channel in the customary sense of the word.[9] However, it has acquired a set of functions under the leadership of aged or aging party and military leaders who have been released from service in the regular forces. By 1957, the militia and reserves were merged into a single organization under the local control of the party, aided by the PLA. For the vast majority of China's rural youth, the militia is the closest that they will ever get to a military organization.

In actual practice, the militia has fielded few effective units, has received minimal training, has been and remains responsive principally to military district and People's Armed Department (commune-level) control, and has performed only local guard and patrol duties which would not detract from their principal duties in agricultural production. Although the precise distribution of military generation and field army representatives within the militia is yet unresearched, it seems likely that overage officers and noncommissioned officers from local regular and public security ground force units have moved into the preferred senior posts of the militia "paper" units (regiment, battalion, and company). Thus, the collective loyalties and perspectives of these men are likely to echo those of units and senior leaders who have traditionally (since 1953) occupied relatively fixed garrison posts throughout China. Further, it seems likely that the majority of the senior figures in the militia organization are first- and second-generation PLA leaders.

These assumptions are approximately accurate, and, given a natural career interest in fostering the growth and power of their own organization, these men should have consistently favored People's War as a philosophy and should have argued for more resources with which to equip and train the militia. Despite China's claim to a strategy of People's War, the militia has received minimal attention since the late 1950s. Only since 1968 has it again received increased, though still marginal, attention, primarily in the name of war preparedness, local security, and population control and discipline.

Better trained and equipped than the militia, public security forces have been almost equally concerned with local security problems ranging from criminal investigations to local guard duty on railroads, at warehouses, and at party headquarters. Originally drawn from regular PLA units toward the end of the Civil War, public security forces were temporarily separated from PLA control between 1955 and 1962. Thereafter, they were gradually reassimilated by the PLA, the process being largely completed by late 1966. On the one hand, border defense forces probably have been under the direct control of military region headquarters since 1953. However, military internal security and municipal garrison forces have probably fallen under the control of military district headquarters (and now revolutionary and new provincial party committees).

On the basis of a cursory survey of key biographies, it appears that key leaders of public security forces have spent their lives as ground force commanders (or commissars) and today reflect approximately the same generational and field army distribution found in regular ground force units. However, there appears to have been minimal transfer back and forth from public security to regular forces. Thus, public security channels seem to have provided a career stream for officers, a stream tied very closely to the fate of local party and military leaders.

In consequence, we would expect that, like militia leaders, the top priority security values and goals of public security force commanders would be in consonance with local interests. Such local perspectives would be expected to identify internal (nonlocal) threats (from other Chinese) as the most significant. Indeed, these tendencies were criticized frequently during the Cultural Revolution, when "local forces" were under persistent Red Guard attack for simply performing their job of protecting local party leaders.[10]

---

[9]For a standard, though dated, reference on the militia, see Ting Li, *Militia of Communist China* (Hong Kong: URI, 1955). For updated analyses, see John Gittings, *The Role of the Chinese Army* (London and New York: Oxford University Press, 1967), Chap. x, and Samuel B. Griffith, *The Chinese People's Liberation Army* (New York: McGraw-Hill, 1967), Chap. xvi. For a remarkably perceptive comparison of the role of local military forces, see the excellent master's thesis by Michael M. Lent, "Local Military Control in Communist China, 1949-52 and 1967-68" (University of California, Berkeley, 1968).

[10]The literature of the Cultural Revolution, especially during 1967, is replete with criticism of the entire public security

Relatively immobile and rarely shifting from one district, not to mention one province, to another, these forces suffered a temporary eclipse during the Cultural Revolution but appear to be returning to many functions and posts of traditional responsibility.

From the viewpoint of organization and preferred strategic deployment of available military resources to cope with perceived threats, local forces and their leaders, armed with only light infantry weapons, minimal artillery, and very few vehicles, have probably retained a view of warfare only slightly more sophisticated than their country cousins, the militia. Consequently, we would expect them to be most concerned with local political and internal security problems, the impact of any national decisions (domestic or foreign) on such problems, and their ability either to mobilize or control the peasantry in the event of major crisis. At best, they would probably perceive their responsibility to be provincial (or at most military regional rather than national) and their "strategic" combat function to be either guerrilla command or light infantry conventional local defense.

From the viewpoint of political leverage, public security leaders had a voice at the national (Peking) level until 1962, when the gradual PLA assimilation of public security forces stripped those forces of top-level representation since, for most purposes, they fell under the control of military regions. A few forces remained under the minister of public security. However, Hsieh Fu-chih, the minister, eloquently expressed the situation when in 1967 he asserted that he really did not know his subordinates in the public security system sprawling across China nor could he evaluate their reliability.[11] In truth, their loyalties and career interests probably diminished substantially as they moved toward the State Council and Peking.

Ground Forces

The high command appears to be dominated by career ground force officers of the first three military generations.[12] Not only is the ground force hierarchy the dominant one among all career channels; all other career channels are also currently controlled by former ground force officers. This situation is least evident in the air force (see below) and the navy.

As noted earlier in the discussion of field armies and military regions, until the Cultural Revolution, army units rarely moved between provinces within a given military region and almost never between military regions. Possessing several basic military schools in which to train their officers, military region staffs probably could assume that they and their subordinates would spend the majority of their careers within the same military region. Only specialized training in artillery, communications, armor, airborne engineering, and political operations would normally require an officer's *temporary* absence from the military region, since he would attend a special school under national control. Certainly, among the four military generations with which we are most concerned, widespread shifts among military regions were unusual before the Cultural Revolution, and actually they were held to a minimum during the Cultural Revolution. A survey, for example, of officers assigned to revolutionary committees by September 1968, revealed that a maximum of 15 out of about 140 chairmen and vice-chairmen (including about eighty military officers) were newcomers to the military region. The remainder had served either at the same military region or at subordinate provincial levels before and during the Cultural Revolution.

Several implications follow from the Chinese Communist high command's "ground force syndrome" and from the relative immobility (after 1954) of ground force units and senior commanders. The ground force high command's priority of security values and goals has probably reflected the ambiguity of national versus local defense responsibilities, depending upon the military region. Military regional commanders and staffs most threatened by external military

---

apparatus in addition to the "local forces." For especially useful analyses of local force responses to central elite directives during the Cultural Revolution, including "fake power seizures," see Chalmers Johnson, "China: The Cultural Revolution in Structural Perspective," *Asian Survey* 8, no. 1 (January 1968): 1–15; Charles Neuhauser, "The Impact of the Cultural Revolution on the Chinese Communist Party Machine," *ibid.,* 8, no. 6 (June 1968): 465–88; and Jürgen Domes, "The Cultural Revolution and the Army," *ibid.,* 8, no. 5 (May 1968): 349–63.

[11]See *SCMP* 4023 (September 19, 1967): 21–22, for excerpts from Hsieh Fu-chih's speech of July 22, 1967, when he "noticed" that the Public Security Bureau, the Procuratorate, and the Courts of Justice (all ostensibly subordinate to Hsieh as minister of public security) had been deeply poisoned by Lo Jui-ch'ing and others.

[12]For general descriptions of the role of the ground forces up to 1966, see Gittings, *The Role of the Chinese Army*, and Griffith, *The Chinese People's Liberation Army*. For post-1966 roles, all previous references pertaining to the Cultural Revolution underline the expansion of power in the hands of ground force commanders at all levels. For a more recent analysis, Charles Neuhauser's "The Impact of the Cultural Revolution on the Chinese Communist Party Machine" is of special value, together with the excellent tabulation of key leader backgrounds in Richard Baum's "China: The Year of the Mangoes," *Asian Survey* 9, no. 1 (January 1969): 1–17.

forces (the six military regions stretching from Shenyang to Canton along China's east coast) have probably been most conscious of a dynamic priority relationship between internal and external security responsibilities. Further inland, seven other military regional commanders and staffs have probably been more intent on preserving internal stability, since external threats to them have been relatively minimal since 1950.

In all cases, however, it seems likely that the security values of these commanders and their staffs have ascribed primary importance to their own political survival within their military region, regardless of the temporary source of greater threat, internal political or external military. In brief, it would appear that a proprietary concern for their own status, their own resources, and their own political survival, especially among the now dominant first and second military generational leaders, would have linked their perspectives very closely with those of local force leaders.

As to their preferred organization of available resources, we have already noted the translation of field armies into a military regional organization during the 1950–54 period. It appears that the military regional headquarters gradually acquired powers over recruiting, logistics, personnel and unit assignments, operational planning, maneuvers, and, generally, military resource control that reflected a probable focus on the military region as a potentially self-contained theater of operations.

This is not to say that military regions have enjoyed equal power in their ability to negotiate with the central elite. In fact, a review of the Ninth Central Committee leadership would suggest that those military regions which traditionally controlled the greatest wealth and the most powerful ground forces emerged from the Cultural Revolution with the greatest political stature. Thus, in 1969 the commanders of the "top three" most powerful military regions (Shenyang, commanded by Ch'en Hsi-lien; Nanking, commanded by Hsü Shih-yu; and Canton, commanded by Huang Yung-sheng, now chief of general staff) were "elected" to membership on the Ninth Politburo. Although all military regional commanders were on the Ninth Central Committee, those three commanders would appear to have special powers, backed up by their dominant share of ground force units.

As to the dominant ground force leadership's preference for strategy and tactics, the following points seem worth noting.

1. The high command has failed to accent the long-range projection of military power, either through naval or strategic air forces. Instead, they have designed force levels best equipped to defend China against external ground threats on her borders and against internal threats. We spell out this point in greater detail under our discussion of the other career streams.

2. The modernization and professional development of the other services have probably been delayed by a general high command concern for a ground-oriented defense posture. Even ground force professionalization has proceeded fitfully, the majority of the regular ground units having experienced minimal combined arms maneuvers (with naval and air forces).

3. Indeed, the accent in the PLA during the past decade seems to have shifted away from massed artillery and infantry-armor-artillery coordination to a ground defense strategy oriented on separate military regions and a tactical scenario of infantry conventional combat supported by limited artillery and armored forces in selected areas. Apparently, in 1959 a decision was made to trade this delay in the modernization of PLA mobility, and fire support has been traded for greater resource allocations to the advanced weapons program, a bluff that the Russians called in the spring of 1969.

General Political Department

First organized in the late 1920s as a kind of institutional conscience to insure that commanders would not take advantage of their power to abuse either their authority or their peasant subordinates, the GPD ("the commissars") has evolved through forty years of political and military campaigning as an important career channel for military men with intramilitary political duties ranging from indoctrination of recruits to surveillance of senior officers whose behavior suggests unreliability.[13] Normally acting as secretary of the unit party committee, a political officer (or commissar at army level and above) had become a specialized careerist by 1950. In spite of the conventional belief that PLA officers were equally adept at either political or military tactics, a survey of about 800 high command biographies shows that only about 10 to 15 per cent had been worthy of high marks in both specialized fields. Indeed, by 1950 the majority

---

[13]For an excellent account of the role of the commissar in the Korean War, see Alexander George, *The Chinese Communist Army in Action* (New York: Columbia University Press, 1967). For an account of more recent commissar roles and conflicts with commanders, see Ellis Joffe, *Party and Army: Professionalism and Political Control in the Chinese Officer Corps* (Cambridge, Mass.: Harvard University Press, 1965).

of the first four generations had served either in a professional military command or staff role or in the military political sphere, with little concern for troop management.

As a consequence of their concern for civil-military relations, and especially the role of the peasant in providing combat service support to combat units, many commissars tended to acquire expertise at primitive logistical operations and moved, after 1949, into the new General Rear Services Department. Aside from this relatively more technical field, however, their concern with nontechnical subjects tended to bring them into conflict with commanders over priorities at various periods in the history of the PLA. During the Korean War their utility was challenged successively by United Nations forces, their own commanders, and finally their own troops. After the war, their status gradually declined to a point where, in 1960, 6,000 companies in the PLA did not have party branches, and commissars were denied jeeps to use on field maneuvers.[14]

From 1960 through the Cultural Revolution, the traditional competition between the commanders and commissars for power and control over resources waxed and waned. Although the entire senior staff of the GPD was finally purged in August 1967, probably much to the satisfaction of senior career commanders, their institutional function remained too important to be turned over to nonprofessionals. Furthermore, not all commissars have necessarily been primarily loyal to the GPD career channel. Biographic evidence suggests that, like the ground forces, commissar mobility between military regions and field army loyalty groups has been minimal. Thus, patterns of obligation have probably not been too different from those prevailing in the local and regular ground forces already discussed.

It was probably partly a consequence of those parochial loyalties that commissars suffered a notable decline in status during the Cultural Revolution. In addition to their temporary loss of their formal voice in Peking, they lost representation on the new (Ninth) Central Committee, as compared with prior representation on the Seventh and Eighth Committees. If we assume that men equally adept at command and commissar roles should be rated a commissar, they held 22 per cent of full memberships on the Seventh Central Committee (28 per cent held by commanders) and 19 per cent of Eighth Central Committee full

memberships (18 per cent held by commanders). In 1969, however, while still holding 21 per cent of the available full memberships, they had lost heavily to commanders, who now held 44 per cent of such memberships.

Although limited evidence exists to show that, at any given level of the military bureaucracy, commissars have traditionally been slightly older than commanders at the same level, it is likely that the generational distribution of commissars throughout all services is basically similar to that of the commanders. In general, commissars of the first four military generations have been better educated than commanders insofar as formal civil education is concerned. They have also had more experience with the Maoist concept of People's War, since they were normally charged with the training of militia, self-defense forces, and peasant mobilization, while commanders tended to focus their energies on the organization and training of regular forces.

Later generations of commissars, especially after 1946, shifted their functions away from mass mobilization and logistics because the entire PLA experienced a process of professionalization. Younger recruits into the GPD could thus expect to attend specialized political staff schools where they could study such technical subjects as intramilitary broadcasting, leaflet design and writing, mass warfare, stratagems, psychological warfare, and counterintelligence. All increasingly technical and complex, these subjects also tended to encourage a sense of professional status and expertise in younger commissars, who could prove their utility to contemporary commanders without threatening commander roles and specialization.[15] Thus, one former political officer told the author that his contemporaries (sixth generation) had little interest in leaving the professional military context, where their duties were clear, their status was coequal with commanders under most circumstances, and they did not have to worry about the risks of "politics" present in the civil community. Truly, the routine of military life had clipped the wings of potential revolutionary followers of Mao.

Despite the risk of being purged for excessive local loyalties, the fate of the GPD at the national level during the Cultural Revolution probably has encouraged commissars at the military regional level and below to remain sensitive to their status in the eyes of regional leaders. Indeed, just

[14]For this figure, see J. Chester Cheng (ed.), *The Politics of the Chinese Red Army* (Stanford, Calif.: Hoover Institution, 1966), Document No. 23.

[15]Many of these views about younger commissars in the General Political Department derive from interviews held with refugees, who were former political officers, in Hong Kong in 1968.

as the apex of a commander's career might be considered a post as deputy commander of a military region, so the commissar might be equally pleased with such a post as a cap to his career. In short, despite a tendency toward a broader, "national" commissar perspective due to the vaunted separate channel which the GPD has provided for the "Party within the army," the Cultural Revolution probably reinforced a practical concern for career equities and interests based on local and military regional ground rules of behavior and promotion. This judgment is speculative, however, since only limited evidence from interviewing can be adduced to support this thesis.

Nevertheless, by virtue of their collective knowledge of Maoist military principles, their long experience in applying those principles on the Chinese stage, their historic concern for the "correct" use of local military power to achieve local political objectives, the generally higher survival rate of local (military regional) commissars as contrasted with national-level commissars, and the post-Cultural Revolution shift of further nonmilitary administrative powers to military regional and provincial military district authorities during the 1970s, the General Political Department senior leaders are likely to share many of the viewpoints set forth below.

Possessing only limited representation in Peking, where a new GPD has been painfully emerging from the ashes of the Cultural Revolution, they are likely to emphasize the security of their own military region and subregional status, especially with respect to the new party organs that have been undergoing cautious revitalization since late 1968. Given the strong focus upon their own power status with respect to both local commanders and civil party figures, they are also likely to perceive radical Red Guard and other dispossessed groups as primary threats to their own status and to the stability of their local political sphere. Indeed, their professional experience with internal political mobilization has probably reinforced their focus on internal threats while encouraging commanders to shift *their* emphasis to real or imagined external threats, particularly in northeast China.

In the ongoing search for salience among a multiplicity of threats, commanders and commissars will probably continue to contend over the question of "correct" resource organization. However, the commanders will probably be glad to assign to commissars the responsibility of mobilizing the military potential of the peasant masses and the millions of disgraced Red Guards who have been sent into the countryside. To the extent that the General Political Department can mobilize the paramilitary strength of those people, the regular ground force commanders may be persuaded to return troops to professional routines. That such a process has already become a nationwide movement is suggested in the 1969 creation of youth companies which appear to be releasing regular soldiers from the menial tasks of farming on PLA-managed farms.

In consonance with the foregoing, the older (first four generations) leaders of the General Political Department will probably continue their historic preference for a strategy of local People's War, a strategy which affords them maximum opportunity to extend their own political power at the expense of both commanders and civil party competitors for local status and privilege. Thus, for different reasons, they are likely to share with many local and ground force professional commanders a preference for a defense decentralized among relatively independent military regions. Such a preference must be expected to clash with the tendency of coastal military regional commanders to look further outward rather than inward, as China's weapons technology promises a capability to project her military power beyond the Asian arena.

General Rear Services Department

There is some doubt about the career dimension of the GRSD channel, since schools seem to be quite limited in this field. However, given the existence of a Rear Service College in Peking and the increasing complexity of the logistical system and the defense mobilization base, over which the GRSD has acquired increasing responsibility, it seems likely that both the senior and the younger members of this corps of logisticians have gained a sense of professional self-awareness and an expertise that must have laid the foundation for routine selection and promotion procedures.[16]

We are not clear on the relationship between military production (advanced weapons, conventional weapons, and military research and development) and the General Rear Service Department elite. While the GRSD probably has responsibility for the procurement of military hardware and for its distribution, their control over the production of such hardware is probably

---

[16]It is very difficult to obtain reliable data on the role, strength, and status of the GRSD. Interviewing in Hong Kong has provided much of the information contained in this section. For an exceptionally useful treatment of military production economics, see Chu-yuan Ch'eng, "Growth and Structural Change in the Chinese Machine-Building Industry," *CQ 41* (January–March 1970): 26–57.

minimal. Thus, the GRSD is primarily concerned with distribution, not production, logistics.

Despite the evidence of their performance during the Cultural Revolution, there is great doubt that the available logistical system and its personnel could sustain a major campaign beyond China's borders or could even transfer resources in significant numbers from current locations to other areas inside of China. Despite the national performance of China's railroads during the Cultural Revolution, when more than a million Red Guards were shifted around the country to and from Peking, it appears likely that the high command has allocated key GRSD senior officers and matériel to local regions most likely to consume large quantities of ammunition and other resources in a war of defense.

The point of this surmise for our purposes is that many, perhaps most, GRSD senior officers probably share key military regional command perspectives about the priority of allocation of intranational and intramilitary regional resources. Yet, we must recognize that the planners of military production logistics perceive the national security problem in broader terms than local distribution of military consumables. Their concern with advanced weapons production as well as the less complex conventional weapons production cycle must reflect a national or central elite vision of priorities.

Thus, within the GRSD, as in the navy and air force, there is unquestionably a younger generation of technocrats who must seek the most efficient nationally (not locally) rationalized production of heavy military equipment. In so doing, they would probably oppose the apparent defense strategy of independent military regional theaters of operations and any tendency toward the creation of eleven separate tank, artillery, aircraft, and missile production centers. Since small arms and small arms ammunition seem to have been produced in excess to date, evidence should soon emerge pointing up a definite conflict between advocates of conventional heavy weapons production and those favoring more complex weapons systems. The victors in such a conflict would receive increased power over budgetary resources and strategic decisions. The conflict should divide less educated second-generation leaders from the more competent technocrats of the third and fourth military generations, men whose air force and naval colleagues probably share similar views. Furthermore, to the extent that defense industrial facilities are located in separate military regions (Szechwan, Lanchow, Sinkiang, and others), the hinterland

political parochialism of regional commanders and their staffs in those regions must be attenuated by the sense of national weapons priorities that probably influences their "captive" military industrialists.

We must therefore conclude that the GRSD, especially first- and second-generation senior leaders, probably retains a strong and pervasive element of localism in its collective outlook, in its selection of younger men for promotion, and in its preference for conventional weapons modernization. But the preferences of the more technically advanced services (air force and navy) have already begun to erode such a perspective in favor of viewpoints more generally associated with the central elite.

The Navy

Of the six career channels discussed in this paper, the navy is the smallest. By an accident of post-Civil War troop distribution (1949–50), most of the first appointees to the fleet headquarters along China's east coast came from the Fourth Field Army (in Canton, providing the South Sea Fleet's initial senior officers, and in Shenyang, providing North Sea Fleet leaders) and from the Third Field Army (in Nanking, Foochow, and Tsinan military regions, providing officers for the East Sea Fleet). Second- and third-generation army officers from the better educated Third and Fourth Field Armies soon assumed the responsibility of creating a new navy with the help of Russian advisers. In spite of some Cultural Revolution changes within the navy in Peking, the fleets remain dominated by the same generations that control the rest of the high command. However, younger men are obviously bringing new skills to the navy along with a new respect for "weapons over men," the antithesis of the Maoist military ethic.

As these young men advance, we may expect them to argue that the fleet, as an organization, must be conscious of a national orientation, consonant with a national mission of coast defense. Although the fleets have not received heavy budget allocations for a deep-sea navy, it must be anticipated that larger allocations will be forthcoming during the next decade or so. And they will be in response to a national and international perspective that the navy high command may be expected to sustain in opposition to more parochial local force, ground force, commissar, and rear service force viewpoints and interests.

That time is yet to come, however, even though the navy's political commissar won a seat on the Ninth Politburo. The navy's fate has been a hostage to a ground force viewpoint, which has presumably been responsible for a shortage of deep-draft vessels and an emphasis on many small, high-speed patrol boats and torpedo boats, designed for short-range coastal defense. Even China's submarines have remained within her coastal waters, and her few destroyers have never ventured into the game of flag-showing and international visits normally associated with a global power. At best, the navy seems to perceive its mission in Asian regional defensive rather than offensive terms.

On the intranational stage, its officers evidently rallied behind Peking in order to help stabilize some of the more chaotic situations that developed during the Cultural Revolution. In so doing, the navy probably expressed a sense of technical superiority over not only the ground forces but also over the peasant masses, from whom the navy has generally been remote. This Cultural Revolution behavior notwithstanding, the navy's future would not appear to be tied to its role on the intranational stage, but rather to its ability to demonstrate a need for its services (and improved equipment) along China's coasts against Asian regional enemies and across the Pacific and Indian oceans against China's global enemies. Thus, in contrast with the leaders of the ground forces, still preoccupied with limited projections of power internally to solve problems of internal stability, the navy's leaders may be expected to seek increasing support for naval modernization and nuclear weapons development in order to achieve strategic projections of power to cope with problems of external threats.

The Air Force

Boasting more than three thousand aircraft in their inventory by 1969, including over two thousand jet fighters, the air force leadership, like that of the navy, was shifted from the ground forces in 1949–50 to build a new air force with the help of Russian advisers. Although a few pilots had been trained during World War II, the majority of the top leaders of the air force are nonrated. Nevertheless, the experience gained against United Nations forces in Korea provided a new generation of rated leaders who gradually assumed command of operational units. Between 1953 and 1969, these younger leaders moved quickly into key positions in air armies and divisions. As a result, fourth-, fifth-, and sixth-generation air force members of military region and air defense district staffs tend to be among the youngest members of those staffs and, therefore, the entire high command. As suggested earlier, this fact would tend to create certain frictions between the air force and other career channels,

even if other factors did not help reinforce such frictions.[17]

The gradual spread of air bases around the east coast of China and then westward across her borders with Vietnam, Thailand, and Burma has reflected a primary concern with the mission of air defense against a conventional external threat. "Conventional" is stressed because the Chinese air force seems to have minimal defensive capability against nuclear-tipped missiles. Despite the obsolescing of many of their aircraft, the air force and its antiaircraft artillery and radars could probably give a creditable performance against manned fighter and bomber attacks. Thus, like the navy, the air force perspective seems to have been focused outward rather than inward.

The record would suggest that the air force has been more responsive to central elite directives than has the army, General Rear Services Department, General Political Department, or local troops. On the other hand, the probable subordination of air defense district commanders to military regional headquarters and the long-term garrisoning of air bases by the same air force units suggest that before 1968 unit commanders and air force deputy military regional commanders (air defense district commanders) probably established closer bonds with local ground force and party leaders than the navy did. Because of the importance of his air power for the coordinated defense of his military region, the military regional commander probably has enjoyed relatively direct, routine, and uninterrupted control over most available air force units within the region. Such relatively independent military regional control of jet fighters would be more likely than regional control of the more limited bomber and transport units. These units, and their bases, probably have been more directly responsive to the central elite.

Just as the majority of the air force leaders have been concerned with air defense, so their perspectives have probably not focused on problems of strategic (global) air power. Instead, strategic *Asian* threats have probably been the focus of the leaders and operational units. That focus should have taken priority over any problems of internal security and would thus join senior air force and navy commanders together in their search for solutions to a common problem, the external threat to China's borders and border military regions.

---

[17]For the most recent, unclassified treatment of the Chinese air force, see Richard M. Bueschel, *Chinese Communist Airpower* (New York: Praeger, 1968).

Looming on the horizon as a competitor for funds and resources devoted to modernization, the advanced weapons program has reached a stage in China where career equities within the high command have already been affected. Still a relatively small elite of military scientists and engineers plus a few unit commanders concerned with organization and training of missile units, since 1959 these men have played an increasingly significant role in the interelite process of negotiation and compromise over resources and rewards. The April 26, 1970, public announcement of China's successful satellite launch tended to confirm a time schedule predicted earlier by Robert McNamara and Melvin Laird, who anticipated Chinese possession of around twenty-five ICBMs by 1975.[18]

CONCLUSIONS

As we suggested at the outset, any attempt to predict Chinese behavior in terms of the rationality of "China" as a unitary, purposive actor must be challenged by the fact of controversy among contending domestic personalities and institutions. For the policymaker, however, it is not helpful to outline the basic viewpoints and interests that probably motivate separate interest groups within the Chinese military establishment. For, despite the existence of controversy, decisions *are* made in China, and their rationale, especially in the military sphere, usually seems to be discernible to foreign military observers, frequently on the spurious basis of professional insights.

It has not been the purpose of this chapter to deny the utility of such insights for describing or predicting Chinese military behavior. Indeed, an American air force planner must draw heavily on his own professional experience in seeking to understand his Chinese counterpart. Truly, in some measure, "an air force is an air force is an air force." But it is precisely the "Chineseness" of the People's Liberation Air Force that may be expected to confound the American planner when he might least expect aberrant behavior. And that Chinese quality in the behavior can be understood only to the extent that we appreciate the informal factors discussed above, that is, those factors which have constituted the unique experience of Chinese military leaders.

Among those factors (generations, field army affiliations, military regions, the central elite, and personal relationships), the phenomenon of the military region would appear to offer the greatest promise as a tool for prediction; the military region appears to have evolved into a *political* unit with remarkable staying power in the face of political instability. While regional and provincial political entities have enjoyed temporary ascendancy in the past, only the military region has enjoyed an unbroken record of institutional viability since 1954. As a focus for the practical expression of career equities in each of the six career fields, of personal loyalties stemming from field army experience, of a more traditional Chinese administrative-political style of "localism," and even of personal and family relationships, the military region provides the analyst with a unique qualitative aspect of the Chinese military-political scene. In oversimplified terms, prediction is likely to be more accurate if it is based on the comparative analysis of eleven military regions, each treated as a unitary, purposive actor, rather than on the analysis of China as one vast collectivity. This is only to say that Chinese military leaders, especially those generations at the top during the 1970s, are most likely to reach operational compromises among their many contradictory loyalties and interests through the focal institutional mechanism of the military region. It remains for research to discover greater refinements in the distinctive characteristics of each military regional elite.

[18]For these figures, see the *Washington Post*, April 26, 1970, p. 1.

BRITISH MILITARY IDEOLOGY

JOHN C. M. BAYNES

Utilizing, for the most part, an experiential approach, Lt.-Col. Baynes discusses the attitudes of British military officers between the ages of twenty-five and fifty-five. Although the officer corps has increasingly been drawn from a wider stratum of society, Baynes believes that tradition and loyalty remain strong because of the military's concurrent development with the monarchy, the overlapping of officer generations, and the stable political context in Britain. In terms of international orientations, he feels that while British officers accept conflict as inherent in the international system and view the Soviet Union as the principal threat, they are not inclined to risk intervention abroad due to the limited capability of the British military. Domestically, Baynes feels that the Ulster emergency has sensitized the officer corps to the possibility of and requirements for an internal police role should the parliamentary system be threatened. Finally, he foresees that the officer corps will come to view itself as the guardian of national virtue, will further decrease its ties with the upper classes, and will increase its links with the police.

Lt. Colonel Baynes has recently retired from the British Army. He holds an M.Sc. in Social Science from Edinburgh University and is the author of several books, including Morale: A Study of Men and Courage *(1967) and* The Soldier in Modern Society *(1972).*

"I never expect a soldier to think."
George Bernard Shaw. The Devil's Disciple, *Act. 3.*

INTRODUCTION

Any merit which this paper may possess springs from quarter of a century's personal involvement in the life of one of the British armed services, rather than from academic study. Like many who discover new fields of knowledge rather late in life, I thought, when I came across the social sciences in fairly recent years, that the key of understanding was suddenly in my hand. My delight in reports and surveys, and in the methods of compiling them, was for a time boundless. However, I have now become more cynical, and my eyes are no longer starry when I read books or essays full of tables and figures. For quantification of facts, if relevant, they are ideal; for recording opinions and attitudes, extremely suspect. My own view is that to comment usefully on an organisation one needs close and prolonged personal contact with it; a thorough knowledge of its history; and

carefully garnered data on indisputable facts (ages, sexes, places of birth, etc.) in that descending order of importance. That all this equipment is useless without an open mind is self-evident.

An open mind is especially necessary to detect change, and to accept that one's own careful observation and consequent theorising may be out of date. This possibility certainly affects my comments on the ideology of the British officer. I believe that what I have to say about officers who are now between 25 and 55—a generation's worth in short—is fairly accurate. But the young men just starting their careers now, who have grown up since that imprecise but recognisable point in the early sixties when many traditional standards were jettisoned, have different views than my generation.

It was my great good fortune to serve for twenty-six years in the British Army, until my retirement in April 1972. I followed my father

---

This is an original article written for this volume and the Conference on Comparative Defense Policy held at the Air Force Academy, February 7–9, 1973. Copyright reserved by the author.

into his regiment, The Cameronians (Scottish Rifles), and he in his turn had two uncles who were regular officers. As I write these words I look across the room at a portrait of an ancestor who served in the Coldstream Guards from 1809 to 1820, fighting as an ensign in the Peninsular War at the age of seventeen. His father had joined the Royal Horse Guards, The Blues, in 1777, "selling out" in 1788 on his marriage. Numerous other paternal relatives have served in various regiments over the past 200 years, as temporary officers at times of national crisis. My mother's grandfather was Chief-of-Staff to Napier at the Battle of Magdala, after making his name in the Indian Mutiny, and her brother ended a long military career as Inspector-General of Indian Cavalry. I give these details because I believe them to be important credentials for my comments on the ideology of the British officer.

Huntington points out that the military ethic "stresses the continuity and value of history."[1] Although the purely practical value of military history can be disputed, and I would only partly agree with that great Victorian officer and specialist on the American Civil War, Colonel G. F. R. Henderson, that: "In every respect, then, it is absolutely clear that a knowledge of military history is an essential ingredient in the making of a really useful officer . . . ,"[2] I certainly do believe in the need for historical knowledge to understand the social aspects of military affairs. I am also intensely aware of being a part of the procession of history described by E. H. Carr, which "winds along, swerving now to the right and now to the left, and sometimes doubling back on itself": I understand too his contention that the point in the procession at which I find myself determines my "angle of vision over the past."[3] Like a fish caught in a net by its gills, I cannot escape the closely enmeshed attitudes and beliefs which follow long service in a military environment, coupled with a family history of military involvement. Without some understanding of the long and complex history of the British armed forces, which in the case of the Navy and the Army span over three centuries at least, it is almost impossible to comprehend the ideology of the officer. It is sad that there is not room here to do more than stress two important aspects. The first is the very close link

between the development of the services with that of the constitutional monarchy; the two could be said to have grown up side by side. The second is what can be called the "overlapping" of generations. Because officers serve for long periods in their professional branches or regiments, overlapping each other in such a way as to mingle each generation with the next, the foundations of tradition are immensely strong.

THE STRATA FROM WHICH THE MILITARY OFFICER IS DRAWN

For information on the strata from which the military officers in Britain are drawn I rely heavily on a study by Wing Commander Peter Wright, of the Royal Air Force, which was carried out during a year's Defence Fellowship at Reading University 1968–69.[4] Wright personally conducted 249 interviews, of roughly one hour each, with officers of all three services holding commissions in the ranks of, or equivalent to, Captain, Major, and Lieutenant-Colonel. The sample was split, in accordance with the overall balance in the services concerned, between those holding "permanent regular" or "general list" commissions, and those on a "short service" or "supplementary list" engagement. It was also broken down by functions: roughly into fighting, communications, and administrative branches.

What came out clearly from Wright's study is that there is a wide variation in the strata of society from which British officers are drawn. His first table of particular interest is the one showing the schools at which his interview sample were educated. The "Top 28" schools referred to are the ones known in Britain as the "major public schools," though of course they are in reality private schools charging high fees, and so are not in any way public. For many years we have heard that they are on the way out, but they seem to survive, with full waiting lists. Attendance at the "Top 28" schools in 1969 was enjoyed by 16,625 pupils, representing 0.79% of the over-thirteen-year-old school population, and must be regarded as one of the indicators of the highest social standing in the country. Dartmouth, the Royal Naval College, took most of its entry up to 1948 at thirteen and fourteen years old on a fee-paying basis, and was equated at that time to a "Top 28" school. Now it only accepts young men on leaving school at eighteen, but many of the older officers among Wright's sample had been

---

[1]Samuel P. Huntington, *The Soldier and the State* (Cambridge, Mass.: Harvard University Press, 1957), p. 79.

[2]Colonel G. F. R. Henderson, *The Science of War* (Harlow, England: Longmans, 1905), p. 50.

[3]E. H. Carr, *What is History?* (London: Allen Lane, The Penguin Press, 1961), p. 36.

[4]Wing-Commander P. D. Wright, RAF, *The British Officer* (Defence Fellowship study, available from MOD Library, London).

through it in its earlier guise. The "other HMC schools" to which he refers are the rest of those, additional to the "Top 28," which belong to the body of some 209 independent schools controlled by the Head Masters' Conference. While many of them are given virtually the same social standing as the "Top 28," others bring with them that indefinable touch of unease which can be sensed in John Betjeman's poem "The City":

Young men who wear on office stools,
The ties of minor public schools, . . .[5]

but of course in national terms we are still talking of the "AB" or more affluent sections of the population. Attendance at a secondary grammar school, can, in Britain, indicate almost any social status. The spread could be right across the social spectrum, though the bulk of homes contributing entrance to these schools would probably be classified by advertisers in the categories B, C1, and C2. Finally, Wright's "other schools" include a miscellaneous selection from highly prestigious ones, several in other countries, to those at the bottom of the British rating, and this category is too wide to describe in any more detail.

The facts that stand out from a reading of Wright's table are these:

  a) A third of the middle piece officers in the British Army in 1969 (and it is probably little changed in 1972) come from the top group in the British "social-pecking" order, with a slightly smaller proportion in the Royal Navy.
  b) Over half the officers of the Royal Air Force come from a significantly lower social group, with a much smaller representation in the top elements.
  c) The army has the widest spread right across the different categories of school.

[5]John Betjeman, "The City" in *Collected Poems* (London: John Murray, 1958), p. 7.

We must also remember that although the social differences mentioned above are very real, they largely apply within a fairly narrow section of society. This is strongly brought out in Wright's table showing the occupation by social class of the fathers of officers in his sample. He uses the classification of occupations by social class employed by the British Registrar-General:

His own comments on the table are:

In general, of course, this demonstrates nothing more than would have been expected intuitively—that most of the fathers are to be found in the middle and upper classes; 72.5% of the fathers' occupations lie in the first two groups. However, two inter-service differences are worthy of note. The Army has about three times the percentage of the RN and the RAF in Group I—the imbalance is redressed almost completely for the RN and partially for the RAF when Group II is also included. And the RAF has about twice the proportion of the others in Group IIIB—the skilled blue-collar workers.

SELF AND OFFICIAL SELECTION PROCESSES IN OFFICER RECRUITING

It is tempting to claim that the fairly wide range of social origins among British officers reflects the *official* selection processes in use, while the continued presence of strong upper class elements in the seamen branch of the Royal Navy, especially among communications men, and in certain regiments of the Army, are the result of *self*-selection processes. It has the dangers of an oversimplification, but will serve as an introduction to this subject.

In all the British services the selection boards for officers bend over backwards to ignore social origins, and if anything they slightly favour the boy from a poor home to make up for what might be thought his possible disadvantages. In spite of this, boys from better-off homes still continue to produce better results in proportion to their

Schools of Interview Sample*

	RN		Army		RAF		Total	
	%	No.	%	No.	%	No.	%	No.
"Top 28" schools	7.3	6	32.5	27	3.6	3	14.4	36
Dartmouth	20.7	17	—	—	—	—	6.8	17
Other HMC schools	22.0	18	24.1	20	23.8	20	23.3	58
Secondary grammar schools	35.4	29	28.9	24	57.1	48	40.6	101
Other schools	14.6	12	14.5	12	15.5	13	14.9	37

*The percentages are of the total number of each service.

Father's Occupation by Social Class

		RN		Army		RAF		Total	
		%	No.	%	No.	%	No.	%	No.
I	Professional	8.5	7	27.7	23	10.7	9	15.7	39
II	Managerial and execu- tive	64.6	53	47.0	39	56.0	47	55.8	139
IIIA	Lower non- manual	8.5	7	6.0	5	8.3	7	7.6	19
IIIB	Skilled manual	11.0	9	8.4	7	20.2	17	13.3	33
IV	Semi-skilled manual	2.4	2	4.8	4	3.6	3	3.6	9
V	Unskilled manual	2.4	2	2.4	2	—	—	1.6	4
VI	Unclassified	2.4	2	3.6	3	1.2	1	2.4	6

numbers. Now that I am a civilian, I can point out that the British public schoolboy, while making no better a senior officer than his less fortunate contemporary, is certainly better in the junior ranks, though he tends to show early promise which is not fulfilled. Since the life at a public school has many similarities to service life this is not strange. The official Ministry of Defence policy is to open the field of selection for commissioned rank as wide as possible, and it is a policy which no one dares criticise. Given a reasonable level of academic ability, any fit young man can attempt to be commissioned. And even with low school qualifications he can join up in the ranks, and after a period of satisfactory service try for a commission.

The manner in which the self-selection process operates alongside the official one can best be demonstrated by reference to the Army. The vital factors here are the regiments of cavalry and infantry, and the people who run them. Particularly influential are Colonels of regiments, usually serving or retired general officers or other distinguished people, who still retain the right to accept or refuse candidates for their own regiments. Actually the refusal can be over-ruled by MOD, but what young officer is going to insist on joining a regiment which has turned him down? Most of the prestigious regiments have carefully maintained "Baby Books," in which they keep records of likely future officers, especially ones with regimental connections, from an early age. They also keep closely in touch with those of the "Top 28" schools from which their officers are traditionally found, and the links between them and these schools are numerous and strong. Once a young man is within striking age of joining he is interviewed

by the Colonel or his representative, and if he is accepted, he has nothing more to worry about, as long as he can pass the officer selection and training procedures.

Selection Boards and their methods are obviously a matter of considerable interest to social scientists of all persuasions; indeed from every aspect they provide excellent windows through which to examine the selector himself as well as his victim! Each service has its own board, but they are run in a similar manner, carrying out series of tests of the usual sort over a period of two or three days. As stressed already, every effort is made to ignore social origins in the search for qualities which would make a good officer, but the figures show that certain groups continue to do better than others. The annual "Westbury Analysis" (the Army Selection Board) for example, regularly reports the following trends:

a. A higher proportion of successful candidates come from the South of England (roughly below London) than the rest of the country, although this is an area occupied by only one-third of the population.

b. Candidates from the "Top 28" schools regularly do better than others.

c. Sons of commissioned officers are more likely to pass than others.

The data which can be obtained from analysis of candidates passing through selection boards, and their results, provide much the best information about the background of the modern officer. Attempts to draw conclusions from particulars of those men who go to the service academies are fraught with pitfalls. Not only has the Royal Air Force now turned to the universities to find its General List Officers, and has made Cranwell a post-graduate engineering college, but the Army has also carried out a major reorganisation in the past year, whereby the training centre for short service officers at Mons Officer Cadet School, Aldershot, has been incorporated into the Royal Military Academy, Sandhurst. So any examination of academy entry would first have to be annotated by endless references to dates, conditions, and so on. But much more difficult to spot, indeed impossible for anyone outside the organisation, would be the fact that during the 1960s the upper sections of the British population quietly dropped Sandhurst for any but their more academically backward sons. Almost imperceptibly the more prestigious regiments began to gather their best officers through the short service method of entry, converting to permanent regular after commissioning, or by direct entry from university. Of course they still had to accept some Sandhurst men, but it ceased to be their primary concern in their search for talent. And as the social "cachet" of Sandhurst disappeared, and its academic sterility became increasingly obvious in a period of vast university expansion, its intake became steadily more representative of the population at large but less so of the officer corps itself. Official spokesmen wishing to draw attention to the British Army's modern image can point to the fact that only 19% of Sandhurst entrants in 1967 were from "Top 28" schools, and 45.5% from secondary grammar schools, but this does not reflect the overall figure in the profession.

For a few years after the Second World War the British armed forces could pick and choose their officers from a large field. This applied not only to those who wished to be regular officers from the start, but also many temporary officers, undertaking National Service, who enjoyed the life and transferred to regular service. Things are different today, and even the much reduced modern forces have difficulty in finding enough young officers of the quality they want. The public schools are less insistent on playing games and instilling "Empire-building" virtues, and the urge among their output is toward a professional qualification following a period at university. The direct pursuit of money and personal advantage may also be out-doing ideas of public service. On the other hand, recent difficulties found by graduates in looking for jobs may now be bringing the services back slightly into favour at the universities, after a very lean period in the late 1960s.

CONTINUING POLITICAL INDOCTRINATION

The fundamental political stability of Great Britain since the Restoration of Charles II, in spite of all the wars and crises which have come to frighten each generation in turn, has meant that there has been no requirement for the overt indoctrination of military officers. They have been expected to give loyalty to the monarch and to refrain from personal dabbling in politics, though in fact they were able to be members of the House of Commons up until the end of the First World War, and sometimes found difficulty in avoiding the pitfalls of a dual role. But it is fair to say that they have neither required, nor would they have tolerated, any overt guidance towards any particular political belief, other than those expected of an English gentleman. This does not mean that there has not grown up an infinitely more effective, and to my mind desirable, method of keeping them on the right lines by what might almost be called "covert indoctrination." Nowhere could one find a more brilliant description of the traditional method, operated in its most polished form, than in the third volume of Osbert Sitwell's autobiography, *Great Morning*. I quote at length, because there are many facets of the passage which illuminate further areas of British military ideology with exquisite precision:

Having returned to England at the end of November 1912, I joined the Grenadier Guards and, a week later, was posted to the battalion stationed at the Tower of London. Towards this purpose, I had been obliged, directly I reached London, to present myself for an interview at the Regimental Orderly Room. From the distance of thirty years later, I can comprehend, what I did not altogether realise at the time, the extreme accomplishment of the group of persons forming this entity, and that the head of it was more expert than anyone I have ever met in wrapping himself round with an air of quasi-benevolent authority, and by this means obtaining an absolute and unquestioned obedience. And, since there have been modifications—for example, the chief would now be a young man, freshly versed in war, instead of being over sixty—let me give some account of this organisation, as it was; though it survives and can still be studied to this day [written in 1945].

The effective head, "the Lieutenant-Colonel," as he was known, of each of the four regiments of the Brigade as then constituted—Grenadiers, Coldstream, Scots Guards, Irish Guards—possessed as his headquarters or appropriate shrine a kind of small Greek temple in stucco, with fluted pillars and capitals of the Doric order, placed, as if for the sake of inviolability, behind the stout, spearlike iron railings of Birdcage

Walk. Besides being so important a military mandarin, the Lieutenant-Colonel was, as well . . . the improbable realisation of an ideal; an ideal cherished by a considerable number of contemporaries, including most officers and all the best tailors and haberdashers, hosiers, shoemakers and barbers in London, indeed in England. And this quality, or rather, the subconscious knowledge in the image that he embodied it, produced in him something of the genial, smiling impartiality of royal personages passing through the wards of a charitable institution. The English always put substance first, rather than its treatment; and just as roast beef is—or alas, was—their principal dish, so everything about him was immaculate, of the finest quality and cut; cloth, linen, and the man encased in them. Every pore of the skin, every hair of his grey moustache and eye-brows, was unemphatically—for emphasis would smack of ostentation—in its right place, and showed in miniature the same kind of order and beautiful military precision that the regimental parades exhibited on the grand scale. His manners, too, imbued though they were by their quality of rather impersonal affability—and though it was quite evident, as well, that the idol realised that affability was not his whole practice and that at times it was his duty to instil awe, were memorable in their perfection. At a single glance it might be deemed possible by the inexperienced, such was the apparent sincerity and straightforwardness of his self-presentation, to know all about him, even to write a testimonial, *strong sense of duty, hard-playing (golf, cricket, polo), generous, brave, fine shot, adequate rider, man of the world, C. of E. . . .* But where it would be easy for the young officer to go astray in the estimate he was making, would be if he were to dismiss the fine and benevolent old gentleman in front of him as at all remote, or out of touch with the true business of his regiment; for, as if the position he held bestowed upon him special powers of divination, he could, at one pounce, show himself singularly, surprisingly, frighteningly, well-informed.[6]

When I went to the Royal Military Academy, Sandhurst on its reopening in 1948 for the first post-war, long course of the traditional type, the influence there of the Brigade of Guards, and of the "quasi-benevolent authority" of men like Sitwell's "ideal," was particularly strong. It flourished in the inevitable conservative reaction which followed the war, and it printed itself firmly on at least fifteen years output of officers. Not until much more recently, when the flight from Sandhurst began among the brighter potential officers, as already described, has the young regular officer become accustomed to starting his career without his image of all that is admirable in military life being created by gleaming, immaculate Guards officers holding key positions on the Sandhurst staff, and perhaps more

important still, their supporting cohorts of immense, terrifying, and even more gleaming Warrant Officers and Sergeants. A few cadets used to resist the Guards-dominated "breaking-in," but most were delighted to succumb to it. It was the start of the process which has lead Corelli Barnett to write: "The way of life, manners and values of the British officer corps in the 1960s remain so strongly that of the rural upper class that in ten years of service grammar school boys became indistinguishable from the son of a landowner."[7] Once set on such a course, what officer needs overt indoctrination?

This traditional method of guidance operated in all the British forces, though especially perhaps in the Army and Royal Navy until quite recently. Although it has not yet disappeared, it has become less effective. The reason for its gradual weakening is the much eroded influence of men of the stamp of Sitwell's Regimental Lieutenant-Colonel. The change in civilian scales of value is behind this erosion. Even the sort of young man who still thinks of joining the army is today prouder of his school or university qualifications than he is of his tailor! Though the British upper classes are still a powerful and easily recognisable body, they no longer inspire the respect, almost reverence, which they were accorded even twenty years ago. In circles traditionally and bitterly opposed to them they are sometimes even ignored rather slanged. The result is that their children, though cherishing their wealth and status in private, mostly conceal obvious manifestations of upper class background in their day-to-day appearance and speech. And although older service officers still bear the stamp of their early training, the younger ones are beginning to be rather different. Out of uniform there are officers today among the younger element who eschew the tweed caps and "British Warm" overcoats which even a few years ago were such desired and obvious distinguishing marks.

PRESSURES ON OPINION FORMATION FROM THE PROMOTION SELECTION PROCESS

The ways in which the British armed forces employ the selection process for promotion to control the opinions of their officers is an extension of what I have earlier called "covert indoctrination." It would be useless to deny that strongly expressed opinions running contrary to

[6]Osbert Sitwell, *Great Morning* (New York: Macmillan, 1949), Reprint Society Edition, pp. 182–84.

[7]Corelli Barnett, *Britain and Her Army* (London: Allen Lane, The Penguin Press, 1970), p. 488.

those generally considered suitable in the profession are likely to hold back advancement, certainly into the higher ranks. As I see it, this is perfectly acceptable. It is essential that senior officers should have "sound" views reflecting, in broad terms, support of the Monarchy, the Constitution, and the Established Church. Most British citizens have no desire for Generals to show too much interest either in politics or unusual causes. The talents, interests, and driving force of men such as Orde Wingate of Chindit fame should undoubtedly be used up to a certain level of command in times of war and great stress. But nobody would want to see such a person in the position of Chief of the General Staff in peace time.

It is possible to check up on an officer's opinions, and so to cut him off at any level of the promotion race, because the whole of his career and development can be, and is, frequently examined by boards for appointments and promotion through reference to his annual *Confidential Report*. In all the British services a report consists of two or more parts. The first, which is the meat of it, is filled in by a commanding officer, after which it goes to one or two superior officers for comments and endorsement, and occasionally for alteration. Where the inter-service differences lie is in whether the officer sees his own report or not. Both the Royal Navy and the Royal Air Force use unseen reports, though each requires that officers should be notified of weaknesses which are considered to be within their power to rectify, and their reports have to be annotated to say that this has been done. The Army makes all officers read their own reports, apart from Major-Generals, who are reported on "unseen." (Above Major-General reports are not used.) The Army's use of open reports has the obvious danger of leading to over-generous assessments of an individual's abilities, while "unseen" reports in the other services have the occasional effect of enabling vindictive senior officers to write down subordinates in a way that they would not consider had they to actually face the individual across the table to justify what they had written. An army officer is recorded as saying: "Reports are always nicer than the truth." However, these reports are more subtle than appears on the surface. A man whose opinions are not approved of, in spite of consistent good work and blameless personal conduct, can be quietly shunted into a siding without any cause for complaint. The way in which this is put into effect is by the use of a wide range of gradings to provide a general assessment of the officer's qualities. The Army employs six gradings, starting with

"Outstanding." Below that each grade is lettered from 'A' to 'E'. 'A' is described as "Well above the average of his rank and service," and each letter has a similar sentence beside it, slightly less fulsome in each case. But the fact is, and everyone knows it, that although an 'A' grading looks splendid, and is adequate for normal promotion, it is just not good enough for access to the "General's Club." An 'A' at the important level of command of a battalion, or equivalent unit, is really the same as saying that a man's ceiling is full Colonel, or perhaps a Brigadier.

THE MILITARY'S ROLE IN BRITISH SOCIETY

In 1973 the British armed forces are both active and popular in a way which could hardly have been foreseen five years ago. 1968 was the year of which the late Mr. Gerry Reynolds reported to Parliament that: "British forces have not been in action anywhere in the world. No one has been killed or wounded in action anywhere in the world in the last twelve months—the first time this has happened in this century."[8] I can remember discussing the problem of keeping soldiers keen and interested during the long years which seemed then to be ahead with nothing warlike to occupy them. But at the end of 1969 the troubles in Ulster flared up again, and since then the Army has been back in the state of overstretch which it got to know so well during the years of closing-down the Empire.

The effects of the Ulster emergency are not yet fully clear, but they have changed certain attitudes which were previously common among the British people, especially its better educated sections. In particular, the over-optimistic have been reminded that human beings can still have deep, intractable differences to which no sensible remedy is of any application. Get the cleverest know-all in the Kingdom and ask him how he would solve the problem in Ulster, and in three minutes he will be throwing his hands out in despair. From this sense of hopelessness comes a realisation of the soldier's essential presence, and an admiration for the Army's conduct in such a difficult situation. A thirty-year-old Sergeant's words were reported in *The Times* recently. "One thing that Northern Ireland has certainly done is to give us a much better relationship with the British public. More often than not, when

---

[8]Report of Parliamentary proceedings in *The Times*, March 6, 1969.

people discover that you have been over there the instant reaction is pints all round."[9]

It is fair to say that a few years ago plenty of people could have been found to support the contention of Dr. Philip Abrams made early in 1969: "It is hard to think of a single military operation which the British armed forces could now undertake without incurring the ridicule or condemnation of some significant section of the British public."[10] Now that the Ulster problem has developed into something nearing civil war such attitudes have virtually disappeared.

It must be stressed that even in the pre-Ulster days any feelings of doubt about the usefulness of the services in British life were very far removed from evidence of strong or widespread antipathy. Such ill-will as did exist was directed more towards the Army than the Navy or RAF. The major reason for this must be the fact that there has been no conscription for over ten years. A certain type of person with intellectual leanings and an exaggerated faith in human rationality has always found soldiers and their doings distasteful: such people hate and mock all things military, and their outpourings were common in Britain of the 1960s. They helped to bring the military and other virtues into slight disrepute among many young people, but without causing any deep-seated anti-service sentiments in the population at large.

VIEWS OF BRITISH OFFICERS ON THE INTERNATIONAL SCENE

The Nature of International Politics

I take as my theme at this stage the generalisation that the British officer is pulled hard in two directions in his views on the nature of international politics. On one side he is conscious of belonging to a highly civilised nation which has voluntarily given up a great Empire in recent years, after surviving victoriously all the risks and dangers of the Second World War: in this respect he feels part of a generous and liberal tradition, and regards the world stage as one in which his country can play the part of the "moral broker." On the other side, he is only too conscious of the fact that God is on the side of the big battalions; of the immense influence of the

super powers; of the need for smaller nations to hold on tenaciously to every advantage they possess; and consequent on these considerations a sense approaching despair at the way Britain has not only lost power in the last fifty years, but seems to have deliberately jettisoned it. My own belief is that many officers went along with the "moral broker" line, which some worthy souls thought might do in place of a proper foreign policy, while the actual business of running down the Empire was in progress, but that as it becomes fully clear how much has been thrown away a sense of bitterness will tend to grow. I only hope it does not lead to frustration, but to determination and skill in maintaining and increasing our armed forces. The great danger on realising such loss of influence is to devote too much attention to past glories.

Conflict and Co-operation in the International System

It is unlikely that a person would take up the role of an officer in the all-voluntary armed forces without a sense of the strong possibility of conflict between the nations of the world: at the very least he would agree with Professor James Eayrs: "Military insurance is a prudent policy. The future's inscrutable, the states-system's malign, the international environment's hostile."[11] In fact it can probably be taken further still, and one can safely claim that the average officer believes strongly in the likelihood of co-operation. It might be said that the Royal Navy and Royal Air Force are especially conscious of the dangers of clashes with other nations, mainly because they have had less part to play in internal operations within the Empire since 1945 than the Army. Not being involved so deeply in minor security conflicts and combating subversion they concentrate on major external enemies to a greater extent.

Although a British officer sees conflict as the stronger element in the international system, he knows how important is co-operation. In fact it is the main lesson of British foreign and strategic history. Having never been strong enough to "go it alone," Britain has learnt to defend herself through alliances. The lessons learnt by Marlborough in the early years of the eighteenth century were well understood by his descendant, Churchill, who strove with the same energy to make and maintain the type of alliances which alone have preserved us down the centuries.

---

[9]C. Walker, article in *The Times* of April 12, 1972, in a series on "The Mood of Britain."

[10]Dr. P. Abrams, "Problems of Alienation" in John Erickson and N. Woolf (eds.), *Armed Forces and Society* (Edinburgh: Edinburgh University Press, 1970).

[11]J. Eayrs, "The Future Roles for the Armed Forces of Canada," *Foreign Policy Review* 28 (Toronto: CIIA, 1969).

PERCEPTIONS REGARDING SPECIFIC ENEMIES AND ALLIES

The British officer has one main enemy towards whom his attention is mainly turned, which of course is Soviet Russia. In each of the three services the angle of vision is slightly different.

The well-known build-up of Soviet sea-power in the past two decades, is undoubtedly the overriding source of worry for the Royal Navy today. The 1972 edition of *Jane's Fighting Ships* was rightly referred to in a review in *The Spectator* as "terrifying." It shows that USSR has 313 conventional and 95 nuclear submarines, compared with 133 American (41 of them strategic missile carriers). Raymond Blackburn, editor of *Jane's*, points out "that no other country in the world in this day and age of sophistication and inflation can possibly build as many submarines as the Soviet Navy has at the present time."[12] But worse still, there are few officers of the Royal Navy who could disagree with Blackburn's even more depressing suggestion that:

The stark truth is that the strength of the Royal Navy has fallen below the safety level required to protect the home islands, to guard the ocean trade routes for the world-deployed mercantile marine (still the largest in the world), to protect the vast commercial and financial interests overseas, and to meet NATO, ANZUK and other treaty commitments.

The thinking British naval officer cannot fail to be deeply concerned at the sorry state to which his nation has allowed its sea power to sink. One can only hope that he does not despair as he contemplates what can be done with such slender resources whenever the Russians decide to challenge our vital interests with their immense superiority.

For the soldier, particularly the member of the British Army of the Rhine (BAOR), similar fears and doubts must be prevalent when he first looks at figures of comparative strengths on the mainland of Europe, especially when the possibility of United States troop reductions in big numbers is mentioned. I think that a feeling of disbelief in the man's likelihood of success prevailed among British officers while Senator McGovern stalked the world headlines last year, and it stopped those who cared to ponder such matters as the balance of world power from scaring themselves to death. But the more realistic ones know that in respect of the big

U.S. presence in Europe the re-election of President Nixon has only temporarily staved off pressure for reductions, and that the free European nations must soon come to their senses and build their own proper combined defences. Since the majority of West Europeans clearly have little sense in this direction, what is it that prevents the British soldier from despairing too deeply of his future?

My belief is that although the British officer perceives the Russian threat as real, as likely to be used, and as dependent on military force, he cannot believe in an all-out war on the European continent. So what he does fear is something more insidious—being gradually squeezed to death after a period of "messing about." This obviously has a bearing on internal as well as external dangers, which will be discussed later. In respect of the external dangers, he sees his role as a member of NATO fulfilling the requirement described by General Sir John Hackett in a letter to *The Times* on 6 February 1968 "to maintain in being and suitably located a force sufficient in size, capability and readiness to make sure that the Soviet force, even though superior in strength to our own, would be unable to guide events in the sole interest of the U.S.S.R."[13] As long as he feels that this limited aim is being achieved I suspect that the British officer is not too worried.

For the airman, the external threat is of all too obvious a nature. Many of the officers in air stations around the British coast see Russian planes almost daily flying around our coasts, and they have no doubts about the readiness of those same cheerful Russian pilots, with whom they exchange waves and gestures in the morning sunlight, to move in and "mess us about" to the extreme if no RAF presence were detected.

Attitudes to Risk-taking and Military Intervention

When it comes to the taking of risks in international affairs it is safe to say that the British officer would react much along the lines described by Janowitz in his chapter on "The Logic of War" in *The Professional Soldier*, resembling his pre-Pearl Harbor Generals and Admirals who "had been inclined to avoid actual war because they felt they did not have adequate resources

[12]R. Blackburn, *Jane's Fighting Ships* (Marton: Sampson Law, 1972).

[13]General Hackett's letter caused quite a furor when printed, though largely an artificial one. He wrote it in his capacity as NATO Commander of NORTHAG after clearance with SACEUR. Because he was still a serving British General at the same time the inevitable braying about soldiers interfering in politics could be heard from various obvious sources.

at their disposal."[14] It is certainly difficult to think of any situation in the world where military leaders in Britain would recommend an overseas campaign. This is not so much due to any moral reservations about the use of force to settle such problems as can be solved by its application, but a realisation of the extreme difficulty in carrying out any such escapade successfully. The first consideration here is the tremendous strain which is being carried at this moment by the Army in Ulster. And although it does not affect the other services in quite such an obvious way, the Navy is heavily committed to patrolling the Ulster Coast, and transport element of the Royal Air Force is fully occupied flying military units backwards and forwards.

The British services are conscious of their high quality, and the good equipment with which they are provided, but nobody who has any interest in British defence can feel that there is much spare capacity for activities outside the straightforward defence of Europe, and the security of the homeland. The sense of running all operations on a shoe-string has eaten deep into the military mind in Britain. It has bred resourcefulness and an ability to react with extreme flexibility to numerous sudden demands, but it has also helped to develop an extreme distaste for becoming involved in anything other than essential activity.

If the country were militarily much stronger, I think that the approach of the average British officer to risk-taking and intervention in foreign affairs would be more belligerent. Throughout the years of our Imperial supremacy we found numerous excuses to interfere in what was going on around the world, often with considerable success. "Gunboat diplomacy" was after all a British invention. The best way of demonstrating reactions to intervention is by looking at specific cases that have occurred in the past twenty years.

An example of unsuccessful intervention was the Suez debacle in 1956. When that sorry affair was over, the bulk of British military opinion reflected the not particularly edifying reaction of a football crowd whose favourite team has been sent off the field by the referee—"We was robbed!" Most officers comforted themselves in a time of obvious national humiliation by saying that it was only because we were not allowed to go to the end of the Canal that we failed to bring peace and stability to the area. However, since that date, military opinion has generally

changed with regard to the Suez affair. It has gradually become clear that not only was the political motivation behind the attack on Suez extremely suspect, but that the military preparations made for it were incompetent as well. This incompetence sprang from lack of proper preparedness for such intervention, although we had for years maintained expensive bases in the Mediterranean in order to be able to intervene when required. Over the years it has, therefore, become fashionable in military circles in Britain to refer to Suez as an example of inefficiency which we must never again repeat.

Seven years after Suez, in 1964, came an intervention which serves as an example of the right way to do things. Although the area was one in which we had until recently had strong colonial interests, when we went to the aid of Malaysia, in what became known as the "confrontation" with Indonesia, we assisted an independent State under treaty obligations. It is not often realised what an extensive operation this was: 60,000 troops from Britain were involved at its height in 1965 along the borders of Borneo and Sarawak. This was the same size as the American force that in the same year was operating in Vietnam. Quietly but efficiently conducted, the intervention against Indonesia was an action on which the three services look back with pride and satisfaction. All were deeply involved in it, but the operations proved of little interest either in the United Kingdom, or around the world at large.

DOMESTIC OUTLOOK OF THE BRITISH OFFICER

Perceptions of the Current State of Affairs

The *Daily Telegraph* on 28 August 1972 carried a centre-page article by its defence correspondent which began: "The British public, normally dangerously complacent in defence matters, is showing increasing concern over internal security in the United Kingdom, with near-civil war in Northern Ireland, increasing violence in industrial disputes, intimidation of witnesses and workers, and general disregard by minority groups for the rule of law."[15]

This paragraph gives a summary of subjects which can be heard under discussion in any British gathering today, from a private home to a public meeting, but which would have been of little interest, to other than extremist groups, only five years ago. This is a profound change,

[14]Morris Janowitz, *The Professional Soldier* (New York: Free Press, 1960), p. 259.

[15]Brigadier W. F. K. Thompson, *The Daily Telegraph*, Aug. 28, 1972.

and one in which the military are deeply involved. The Ulster experience has opened many eyes to dangers previously unconnected with home affairs.

Now that these calamities are actually upon us, it is worth reflecting that they are perhaps less out of character than they seem. Corelli Barnett has written:

Since the early seventeenth century the English had nourished a deep suspicion of the state that had hardly diminished with the waiving of monarchial power. As foreigners noted, the English were anarchical and quarrelsome, renowned for their love of liberty. "Liberty" put another way, meant dislike of being organised; a dislike vividly manifested by the extraordinary illogic and localism of English institutions in the eighteenth century.[16]

Perhaps the apparent cohesion of British life during the past hundred years has been less typical than the troubled times we may be entering now. Even the cohesion we look back on is probably more apparent than real, as each generation has had its own crop of fears and alarms. But even if this is so, one can at least state that present preoccupation with internal violence within Britain is out of character with her experience of the twenty-five years following the Second World War. (The first fifteen of these, the prosperous 1950s, will probably become in time a target for nostalgia to equal Edwardian days!)

Although its troubles are old enough in all conscience, the violence which has beset Ulster since late 1969 has had unusual facets, two of which are of relevance to this paper:

a. *Use of the Army in a police role.* Although tradition says that the Army must never be used in a police role, it has had to be so employed in Ulster, and has done the job with skill. It has developed great expertise in gathering intelligence, to some extent built on previous colonial experience, and has developed many new internal security techniques.

b. *Internal morale in the Army.* Although fighting within their own country, and enduring astonishing and incessant abuse from people of their own tongue, the morale of the Army is extremely high, and its conduct and discipline remain exemplary.

To each generation of soldiers its own period of active service is of special importance. I remain a Malaya man, while others vary from Second World War (a few left serving) to Borneo, Aden, or what-have-you men. But the current crop of officers are being moulded into followers of the Northern Ireland creed. The mantle of high priest to their sect has passed after a brief spell on the shoulders of Major-General Tony Farrer-Hockley[17] to those of one Brigadier Frank Kitson, author of a book published in 1971 called *Low Intensity Operations.* Though it would be unfortunate to call it "the Bible" of the Ulster sect, in view of the religious nature of the troubles, it has become something of the sort. It has also caused a stir in other British circles, and deserves careful attention.

Kitson's book has the subtitle *Subversion, Insurgency, and Peace-keeping,* and the Foreward to it is by General Sir Michael Carver, Chief of the General Staff. Carver's seal of approval has exacerbated the annoyance caused among some "liberals" by Kitson's very mild suggestions that the Army could, under very grave circumstances, be used within Britain to deal with a major breakdown of law and order.

In a country in one of whose provinces the Army has been occupied for three years in a violent conflict, verging on civil war, one might not expect such suggestions to cause offence. But it did, and the "liberal" conscience was of course the victim. Since this issue is one of crucial importance to an understanding of the way in which the outlook of the British officer may be moving, it deserves careful attention.

The liberal objection to Kitson's suggestions appeared at its most coherent in skilfully written reviews. The most important of these appeared in *The Times Literary Supplement* on 11 February 1972. It ends by commenting that the book "reflects the limitations of current British military thought on this difficult and complex subject." What it fails to do, here itself reflecting the woolliness of the British intellectual approach to the study of war, is to accept Kitson's book for what it is. First, that it is a book with a limited aim, clearly stated in the introduction, which is to "draw attention to the steps which should be taken now in order to make the Army ready to deal with subversion, insurrection, and peace-keeping operations during the second half of the 1970s."[18] Second, the review gives the impres-

---

[16]Corelli Barnett, *The Collapse of British Power* (London: Eyre Methuen, 1972), p. 93.

[17]Major-General A. H. Farrer-Hockley has written extensively on military matters. He is now commanding a Division in BAOR.

[18]Frank Kitson, *Low Intensity Operations* (London: Faber, 1971), p. 2.

sion of being written by someone unaware that
Kitson has spent most of his life *doing* the things
he writes about, culminating with a recent tour
in command of a brigade in Northern Ireland.
When faced with savagery on the scale seen
recently in Belfast, Londonderry, and other
places in that forlorn land, the soldier has to
tackle the job in hand, without too much ques-
tioning of academic principles. Guidance is
needed, and he can get from Kitson practical
advice, clearly presented, in which the virtues of
humanity and discipline are not forgotten. But
the liberal intellectual, who naturally keeps well
clear of the trouble spots, still refuses to accept
reality, and tries to preserve his own faith in the
rational human mind. It is not to be wondered at
that British soldiers today are starting to develop
their own approach to matters that they have
previously eschewed.

Turning to the practical side of the Ulster
scene, over two hundred British soldiers have
been murdered in Ireland in the past two years.
Although troubles flared up in 1969, casualties
among the military were very slight until 1971.
It is reported that news coverage of events in
Ulster by foreign press and TV reporters is often
slanted against the British troops, though on
home media they are generally given fair and
accurate coverage. The reason for this is that
nobody can study the Ulster situation in an attempt to search for the truth, as opposed to making a good story to please a particular faction in
a distant land, without coming to the conclusion
that the only hope in that miserable, strife-torn
province lies in the calm discipline of the British
soldier.

It never ceases to astonish me that the Army
has kept its discipline so superbly in Northern
Ireland. The IRA are guerrillas of a toughness
and intensity that would make Uruguayan Tupa-
maros look like amateurs. The Protestant and
Catholic communities have been reared on well
over three centuries of bitter hatred which has
created outbursts of violence times without
number. Through the mean, ugly streets of
Belfast or Londonderry walks the British soldier,
risking the all too frequent and well-aimed
sniper's bullet, or the screaming abuse of a mob
of teenagers, or, even harder to stomach, perhaps, that of an apparently civilised young
woman with small children at her side. Amidst
it all he remains the rock of sanity; the good-
humoured, cheerful British figure who represents not only the best in his nation, but the eter-
nal argument for the military virtues as the antidote to bitterness, chaos, and anarchy.

THE DESIRED SHAPE OF THE
POLITICAL SYSTEM AND SOCIETY

Although I am sure that most British service
officers vote for the Conservative party at elections, within the current structure of political
parties I doubt if their feelings run particularly
deep. They are prepared to serve under any party
in power which accepts the sovereignty of the
Queen, the rule of law, and the importance of
traditional British freedom. Funnily enough, the
Labour party has thrown up a number of men
who have been conspicuously successful at
handling the military when in defence ministerial
posts. Lord Shinwell, one time pacifist, and Mr.
Gerry Reynolds, who died in 1970, spring immediately to mind. Of course the military life has
a great deal in common with the Socialist ideal.
Many socialist principles are echoed in the services: reward of merit, without monetary considerations; the career open to talent; the group
before self; the striving after common goals;
comradeship, etc. Although Conservative officers and Labour politicians regard each other
with deep suspicion from their normally distant,
entrenched positions, when they are forced to
meet and work together they often do so more
happily than expected. Throwing light on this
aspect of British life was a recent television
portrait of Mr. Michael Foot, a well-known
Labour MP with a reputation for being well to
the left of his party—and also an incessant critic
of defence expenditure. During the programme
Foot spoke eloquently of the wonderful atmosphere in Britain during the time of the Second
World War: the willingness to share hardships,
and the sense of national cohesion. Without taking the point too far, I would say that Foot's
image of the ideal Great Britain is remarkably
similar to that of the average service officer, and
I suspect that both would sacrifice a very great
deal to see the whole country united in its striving after one goal.

Alas, such wishes are the stuff of dreams, except when wars of survival unite a nation. The
nuclear stalemate has probably done away with
those wars for the developed nations, and "the
disintegrating society" is likely to be our play-
ground of the future, rather than the unified.
What is the role of the military under such conditions? It is likely to be much the same as it is
now in purely strategic terms. But in social terms
it is probably going to change quite significantly.

The Role of the Military in Society

My belief is that we will see in the future a
stronger sense among service officers of being

guardians of the nation's virtue; that the bonds between a traditional upper class and the military will grow steadily weaker; that links with the police will grow stronger; and finally, that European integration will have little effect on these processes.

When writing of the sense of guarding the national virtue I must make it very clear that there is no hint intended of anything remotely connected with a "coup d'état." Only in the most bizarre and unlikely circumstances, far beyond the range of the unpleasant possibilities actually foreseen in coming years, would such a thing be conceivable. Apart from an acute awareness of what Professor Abrams has called "the almost insurmountable contradiction rooted in the very idea of military government,"[19] the concept of orderly rule by an elected parliament is itself the cornerstone of such national virtue as Britain possesses. The military sense of guardianship I see taking the form of a strengthening of a sense of superiority, which has already been heightened in recent years by the declining standards of everyday life, based on the basic military qualities of discipline and cleanliness. The shoddier his surroundings, the more aware the serviceman must become of his own uniqueness, and the need to preserve his standards.

The RAF is ahead of the other services in respect of the social composition of its officer corps, and is more in tune with future patterns than either the Army or the Royal Navy. Although I demonstrated earlier the strong links still remaining between these two services and the "Top 28" schools, the trend is steadily towards a more middle-class officer corps, and not upper-middle so much as "middle" middle. Already the flow of blue-blood into the forces has almost dried up, except for a few of the more expensive regiments, as the competitive modern age allows less time for anything outside money-making to those who want to stay rich. (And when it comes to matters like wealth the English upper classes have never had much doubt about putting substance before the image.)

At one time it was difficult for the services and the police to work closely together because of the social variations in their officer corps. Today police officers and military officers are getting near to each other on a social plane, and co-operation is much easier. I believe it will be-come greater in the future, and that there will be a considerable link-up in the intelligence field. Commenting on the general inadequacy of current co-ordination between police and military, a former Chief Superintendent of Police wrote recently to *The Daily Telegraph*: "The permanent pooling of police and military traditions in peace-keeping and counter-subversion would improve strategic readiness for national emergencies, obviating a need for a 'third force,' and rendering unlikely the Army duplicating, still less usurping, the role of police Special Branch in monitoring subversive suspects."[20]

Such views are certainly not likely to be popular in liberal circles in Britain, where it is preferred to ignore the existence of "subversive suspects." Nor is there as yet much evidence of even a move towards the type of co-operation described above, outside Ulster. I am certain, however, that it will come, and events such as the massacre of the Israelis at the Olympic Games may well spark off reactions which less publicised events nearer home have failed to motivate. Thus we see a staid journal such as *The Economist* publishing an article in September 1972 on "The Anti-Terrorist," which starts with a general comment that "the things that will have to be done to beat terrorism are going to need a system of international co-operation beyond anything that has been devised yet," and continues to discuss possible action nearer home:

But in Britain there may well be an argument for bringing in a specially skilled section of the army—perhaps the Special Air Service—to form a new British counter-terrorist force.

It will be objected that this would confuse the roles of police and army, and that in the past Special Branch and MI5 have been able to cope pretty effectively with extremist movements within England.... And the Munich tragedy showed clearly enough that men who will have to deal with terrorism need a very high standard of marksmanship, quick reflexes, and the training to mount a surprise commando-type operation. These talents may be available within the police, but this is not the way in which the British police is accustomed to operating. It may be necessary for all British security and intelligence services to get into harness to deal with the urban guerrilla—which means forming sections of the Home Office and the Foreign Office, and maybe the Ministry of Defence as well.[21]

[19] P. Abrams, "Restoring Order: Some Early European Cases," in Morris Janowitz and J. Van Doorne (eds.), *On Military Intervention*, (Rotterdam: University of Rotterdam Press, 1971), p. 54.

[20] J. H. Waghorn, letter to the Editor of *The Daily Telegraph*, published September 8, 1972.
[21] *The Economist*, September 16, 1972, p. 16.

The Economist's practical views on what needs to be done in Britain are more important than its vaguely expressed desire for international co-operation. Although such co-operation is something the British are good at, as witness the reliance on allies which has been a principal factor in all our wars, as well as our active paid-up membership of many Treaty organisations, it is not a good foundation on which to build a structure for the armed forces. Although British society wants its military members to be able to work with those of other, friendly nations, it also wants them to be available in the last resort for home defence. Since organised military forces are intricately bound up with matters of national sovereignty and identity, it seems to me unlikely that we can ever expect to see meaningful international collaboration except at the highest headquarters. Below the Army Group level it is hard to believe in integration. Nor would it be desirable to waste time and resources attempting the creation of unworkable formations and units. I agree with Kitson "that whatever does evolve in Europe will take a long time to come about and that so far as the 1970s are concerned, Britain is still going to be concerned with defending her own national interests."[22] This is what both British society and the military themselves want the forces to be doing: integration is a goal which requires a slow, cautious approach, and does not yet come into focus as a matter of pressing importance.

[22] Frank Kitson, *op. cit.*, p. 23.

THE MILITARY'S IDEOLOGICAL CHALLENGE TO CIVILIAN AUTHORITY IN POST-WORLD WAR II FRANCE

RONALD J. STUPAK

Professor Stupak assesses the nature of and reasons for the evolution of a comprehensive ideology by the French Army which openly challenged the civilian, democratic ethic of both the Fourth and Fifth Republics. He points out that as a result of its defeats in 1870, 1940, and 1954, the Army became convinced that it had been undermined by a corrupt and decadent government. After the Indochina defeat and during the Algerian insurgency, the alienation of the Army from the government increased and led one segment of the officer corps, the armée militante, *to develop a systematic ideology that stressed,* inter alia, *the duty of the West, with France as its leader, to resist communism. In the wake of the downfall of the Fourth Republic, the demands of the* armée militante *to influence the formulation of policy culminated in an abortive coup in April 1961. Stupak attributes the failure of the coup to the opposition of the Air Force and the Navy (especially the technicians), to civilian resistance and to General de Gaulle's successful efforts in strengthening government institutions.*

Ronald J. Stupak is an Associate Professor of Political Science at Miami University, Oxford, Ohio, is the author of The Shaping of Foreign Policy *(1969), and is co-editor of* Readings in National Security Policy *(1963).*

Why did the French Army, which once took pride in being above politics, gradually become so deeply involved in political action—especially since the end of the Second World War—as to be found by 1958 openly antagonistic to the political leadership of the Fourth Republic and largely instrumental in effecting a profound change in the French governmental structure? This article will seek to answer this basic question and examine, more broadly, a major problem of French civil-military relations, namely, the evolution of a comprehensive political ideology by the French Army which openly challenged the civilian, democratic political ethic of both the Fourth and Fifth Republics. The nature and ramifications of this ideological confrontation will be probed in the light of the environment of postwar France, including the interrelationships of such factors as colonial defeats, weak civilian governments, and the communist threat. In addition, we will look at the military elements which did not join the "ideological militants" in the hope of discerning some of the factors that helped to create a balancing force within the professional officer corps.

And finally, the patterns of French economic, political and social responses will be scrutinized in order to demonstrate why this challenge to French democracy did not succeed.

The adjustment in civil-military relations will then be analyzed to determine the probability of such a confrontation arising in France's immediate future, or in that of other democratic industrial societies. The description and analysis of this ideological confrontation between the civilians and the Army in France is of significance to all advanced industrial nations because it demonstrates under what conditions the professional military ethic can be galvanized into a political instrument that attempts to be the arbiter of the political values of the whole society. Hence, any enlightenment on the French problem may help other nations at a corresponding stage of development to perceive under what circumstances a similar ideological challenge from the military professionals might erupt. In addition, the manner in which the de Gaulle government has attempted to neutralize this threat may serve as a model adaptable to other nations.

Reprinted by permission and with minor changes from Orbis *12, no. 2 (Summer 1968): 582–604. Reprinted by permission of the editors of* Orbis, *a Quarterly Journal of World Affairs. Copyright © by the Foreign Policy Research Institute.*

HISTORICAL BACKGROUND OF FRENCH CIVIL-MILITARY RELATIONS

The ideological challenge by the French Army to the constituted civilian authorities in the post-World War II era was no sudden eruption. The tendency since 1870 has been for the French Army to intrude more and more into the political decision-making process. The relationship between civilians and military has been characterized by a series of invasions by each side into what the other considers to be its autonomous sphere of action. Therefore, several major historical incidents and social-psychological phenomena should be examined in order to discern the trends that led to the postwar confrontation.

Prior to 1870 the French Army was truly non-political. It was the neutral agent of the government and obeyed the orders of its constitutional chief.[1] However, the Army had amassed a superiority complex dating back to the Napoleonic victories. With civilian support, it continued to focus the many-sided talents of the French nation on conquest and military glory. This preoccupation with conquest led to a psychological problem for the Army since it was never again able to repeat the great victories of the Napoleonic era.[2]

As the years passed and the Army experienced a continuous pattern of defeats and empty victories, it began to acquire an inferiority complex and to formulate a metaphysics of military conflict serving to explain its defeats in 1870, 1940, and 1954. The basic causes of its humiliations were seen to be that the politicians had "stabbed it in the back" on the home front, and that the liberal, democratic political environment in France had become weak, corrupt and decadent.[3]

During these years of continuous disappointments, however, the Army found professional pride in military victories in Indochina and particularly in North Africa. In these areas it found an outlet for its nationalist ambitions in conquest, administration, and the extension of French grandeur. Since actual combat was relatively rare, it was principally occupied in administrative duties, supervision of territories, construction and engineering, and pacification. Hence, the Army

acquired psychological, paternalistic and political interests in the French Empire.[4] When the decolonialization process began to decimate the French Empire after World War II, the Army viewed this as an institutional affront to its heroic past.

The Dreyfus Affair in the 1890s brought into question the relationship of a democratic state to its army. Senior army officers resented civilian prying into the administration of the Army and demanded the right to make their own rules and to manage their own affairs. In essence, "the proposition that Army justice and civilian justice were two separate things whose standards were not interchangeable was upheld with the passion of hysteria."[5] Thus, the attempt by civilians to thrust liberal democratic values into the military sphere set loose a chain of civil-military tensions that have had permanent repercussions.

First, the Army began to espouse even more strongly its conservative principles of honor, courage and duty against the crass, decadent values of republican France. Second, suspicion about the Army's desire to enter the political arena forced the politicians to keep the military under close supervision. Third, civilian republicans made a determined effort to break down the tight, isolated professionalism of the Army by insuring the promotion of republican-minded officers. Fourth, the efforts of civilians to interject democratic values into the Army caused the professional military to turn in upon itself, resulting in its greater isolation from civilian life and in a purge of officers suspected of being susceptible to republican values.[6]

Related to the tensions of the Dreyfus Affair was the wide cleavage between the socialist workers and the French Army which developed because liberal republican governments, over the years, had used the Army for such internal security functions as crushing the Paris Commune of 1870 and the general strikes of the early 1900s. To the socialists, the French Army became identified as the repressive symbol of capitalism, while, to the Army, the socialists with their internationalist slogans became identified as the subverters of the French national will. As time passed and the socialists became more powerful in the French governmental structure, the French Army became firmly convinced that the republican politicians were traitors to the "true" national heritage of France.[7]

---

[1]Guy Chapman, "The French Army and Politics," in Michael Howard (ed.), Soldiers and Governments (London: Eyre Spottiswoodie, 1957), pp. 56–57.

[2]John Terraine, "The Army in Modern France," History Today (November 1961): 734; "Fall of the Dinosaurs," The Economist (April 29, 1961): 419.

[3]Paul-Marie de la Gorce, The French Army: A Military-Political History (New York: George Braziller, 1963), pp. 400–32.

[4]Terraine, op. cit., p. 735.

[5]Ibid., p. 738.

[6]De la Gorce, op. cit., pp. 48–61.

[7]Edward Behr, "The French Army as a Political and Social Factor," International Affairs (October 1959): 438; de la Gorce, op. cit., pp. 123–24, 137.

Many of these tensions between the civilians and the military were submerged in the struggle for survival in World War I. However, during the interwar period this cohesion was shattered by several factors: Disillusionment with the war made French intellectuals critical of war and military life in general. In the flush of victory civilians tended to forget about the Army and this, in turn, produced a renewed sense of isolation and uselessness among the military. Many high-ranking officers lapsed into a complacency and strategic rigidity that disgusted junior officers. Then, as the economic and political dislocations of the 1930s unfolded, many French Army officers began to exhibit fascist tendencies. Moreover, the rise of revolutionary communism in the international sphere and of the Popular Front on the national level made the French military bitterly hostile to the French working class and to the French Republic; "Loyalty to France but not to the Republic" became the motto of an officer corps which viewed itself as the embodiment of the true national will of France.[8] Hence, during the 1930s the traditional, professional habit of obedience to constituted civilian authority began to erode.

It was also during the 1930s that Charles de Gaulle and others began to question the defensive strategy of the Army General Staff. De Gaulle opted for an offensive strategy based on mobile, armored divisions.[9] Consequently, when the Germans swept easily into France in 1940, many junior officers acquired a distaste for defensive tactics and a distrust of their general officers.

As the catastrophe of 1940 reached its climax, General Petain made the political decision to sign an armistice with Nazi Germany. The politicians accepted Petain's leadership "without demur, [and] indeed gladly threw their responsibility on to his shoulders."[10] In the face of external pressures, the politicians showed themselves weak and hesitant; even worse, they allowed the military to make the final political decision calling for an armistice.[11]

The collapse of the Third Republic in 1940 may have been predictable. What was not predictable was the phenomenon that accompanied the collapse: the appearance on foreign soil of an almost unknown general who, in defiance of the constituted authority of the nation, proclaimed that France had lost a battle but might yet bring honor to its national heritage by winning the war. The rebirth of the French national will personally embodied in General de Gaulle was founded on an act of military insubordination—the venerable Petain was not only his military superior but also Head of State—and it set Frenchmen against Frenchmen.[12]

The crisis of conscience this deed posed for all who wore the uniform of a French officer was traumatic. Many junior officers debated in their minds whose orders they should obey, Petain's or de Gaulle's. "Where does duty lie?" became a moral matter for the individual soldier to decide.[13] The echo of 1940 was to ring clear years later in the Generals' Revolt in Algeria in April 1961.

THE IDEOLOGICAL CHALLENGE TO CIVILIAN AUTHORITY IN POSTWAR FRANCE

At the end of the war, the French Army was divided and frustrated, yet fortified by the belief that the politicians had betrayed it in 1940. Most officers based their future actions on three conclusions. First, the 1940 defeat was caused by the incompetence of a General Staff still fighting World War I; hence, a new strategy had to be constructed. Second, had the government chosen to escape to Africa in order to continue the war, it could have saved the Army and the independence of the country. This theory, expounded by General de Gaulle, pointed up the vital need to hold North Africa, without which there could be no defense of France or Western Europe: were the tricolor to be lowered in Algeria, the red flag would soon fly in Paris.[14] Third, a good Frenchman must be prepared to disobey the government if it once again appears that corrupt politicians are on the verge of abandoning the empire or the national heritage.[15] Before the Army was able to formulate a new doctrine to reunite the fragmented military, however, a rash of national and international tensions brought it into open conflict with the civilians.

Immediately after the war, the Army saw itself faced with two immediate dangers—the Communist Party in France and the communist Ho Chi Minh in Indochina. These challenges were

---

[8]De la Gorce, op. cit., pp. 180–252; Behr, op. cit., p. 439.

[9]Charles de Gaulle, The Army of the Future (Philadelphia: Lippincott, 1941), p. 79.

[10]Chapman, op. cit., p. 69.

[11]Richard D. Challener, "The Third Republic and the Generals: The Gravediggers," in Harry L. Coles, (ed.), Total War and Cold War (Columbus: Ohio State University Press, 1963), p. 104.

[12]Terraine, op. cit., p. 740.

[13]Chapman, op. cit., p. 70.

[14]Jacques Soustelle, "France Looks at Her Alliances," Foreign Affairs (October 1956): 129.

[15]David Schoenbrun, "De Gaulle Faces an Anguished Army," New York Times Magazine (February 14, 1960): 90.

seen as the culmination of a long series of episodes which, since the Russian Revolution of 1917 and the Popular Front of the 1930s, had pushed the Army into direct opposition to international communism.

When the Army went off to fight communist guerrillas in Indochina, it found that the war was being fought increasingly against well-armed and well-trained fanatical nationalists. For over seven years, it fought this dirty, politicized war in a climate of general indifference or even open hostility on the part of the civilians in metropolitan France. This unfortunate situation arose for several reasons: (1) Since the French expeditionary force was confined to regulars, the nation was not seriously involved.[16] (2) Since in the latter stages U.S. aid paid the cost of the war, there was not even the sense of financial involvement for most Frenchmen. (3) The politicians of the Fourth Republic seemed neither capable of defining, nor willing to define, the ultimate objectives of the war. (4) Certain sections of the Left carried their anti-militarism to great lengths, such as extending guarantees to blood donors that plasma would not be used for wounded soldiers "suppressing the nationalists" in Indochina.[17]

The Army, which every year for almost nine years suffered casualties among its officers equal to the size of the graduating class from St. Cyr (the West Point of France), felt isolated and neglected.[18] This sense of alienation cemented the Regular Army officers into a band of brothers separated from the French nation as a whole. Thus, after the defeat at Dien Bien Phu, the colonial officers swore that it had been caused by the communists, the Leftists, and corrupt politicians in Paris.[19] Again the Army had been "stabbed in the back." In effect, army officers emerged from this traumatic defeat with three fixed ideas: resentment against the civilian government in Paris which had betrayed the true national will; a crude conception of a world in permanent struggle between Christian good and communist evil; and an admiration for communist techniques coupled with an intense hatred for communist ideology.[20] The Indochinese con-

flict left the French Army imbued with a sense of neglect, of failure, and most importantly, of mission.

In the postwar years, the Army became disgusted with the repeated collapse of French cabinets and the inability of a democratic, parliamentary republic to design a consistent policy in colonial affairs. The civilian leaders of the Fourth Republic were not able to cope with the military mystique because they lacked clear-cut objectives of their own.[21] In addition, the Army, observing the almost total indifference of the French people to the demise of the Fourth Republic in 1958, came to believe that it had better qualifications and a better right to define the policy of France than did the political authorities in Paris.

This weakness of the civilian governments and the inexorable decolonialization process in the postwar period had caused France to give up Madagascar, Morocco, Tunisia, and the Indochinese states. At this point, the Army had had its fill of the fumbling, compromise and complexity of international politics. It wanted and needed certainty and simplicity. Furthermore, since it began to equate colonial nationalism with communism, it felt sure that the Fourth Republic had sacrificed these lost segments of the French Empire to totalitarian domination.[22]

The French Army was also influenced in its actions by the French nation's close ties to the United States. Humiliated by France's dependence, it felt that Washington had actively contributed to its defeat in Indochina so that the United States itself could establish a foothold there. It also believed that the United States had forced France to accept German rearmament; that the United States had tried to obliterate the French officer corps by forcing France to integrate its military forces into the European Defense Community; and that the United States was anti-French in UN colonial debates while being overly complacent in its dealings with Egypt and the Arab League. When France was forced to withdraw from Suez in 1956, French Army officers were convinced that the French politicians were at the mercy of U.S. pressures.

On the other hand, the army officers' relations with U.S. military personnel in NATO seemed to have caused them to misinterpret completely U.S. intentions and policies toward France, communism, and international affairs in

[16]Behr, op. cit., p. 44. Note some of the articles being written on the growing professionalism of U.S. military personnel in the Viet Nam struggle: e.g., Robert Lee Sherrod, "Notes on a Monstrous War," Life (January 27, 1967): 20–29.

[17]"France Française," The Spectator (April 28, 1961): 587.

[18]Schoenbrun, op. cit., p. 92.

[19]Edgar S. Furniss, Jr., De Gaulle and the French Army (New York: Twentieth Century Fund, 1964), pp. 22–23.

[20]"The French Army," The Economist (January 30, 1960): 432–33.

[21]"France's Frustrated Army," The Economist (February 22, 1958): 675.

[22]Raoul Girardet, "Civil and Military Power in the Fourth Republic," in Samuel P. Huntington, (ed.), Changing Patterns of Military Politics (New York: The Free Press of Glencoe, 1962), pp. 129–30.

general. Thus, whether encouraged by the Central Intelligence Agency or not, General Challe, leader of the Generals' Revolt of April 1961, appeared convinced that a number of American interests would be advanced by a French victory in Algeria. His reasoning seemed to go as follows: Since the United States opposed communism, wished to get France back into effective NATO membership, and wanted to recapture its international prestige after the abortive invasion of Cuba, American leaders would necessarily have to back the French generals in their efforts to save Algeria from communist domination and in their parallel efforts to remove the major stumbling block to the attainment of this objective and an integrated NATO—General Charles de Gaulle.[23]

As the disappointments mounted in the postwar period and the politicalization of the Army became more widespread, the military became more fragmented. To make it even worse, this new fragmentation was superimposed upon the Vichy-de Gaulle split. The junior officers, especially the "hard bitten colonels," distrusted and disliked the "politicans' soldiers" who, as high ranking officers, owed their position and promotion to influential political groups and party programs.[24]

In addition, three distinct groups began to appear in the military officer corps and further splintered the professional military body. These groups were designated the *armée traditionelle*, which continued to obey all constituted authority; the *armée des techniciens*, which showed increasing interest in both a stable political system and a modernization of the armed forces that would include a French independent nuclear force; and the *armée militante*, which had been doing the actual fighting in the colonial wars along "conventional patterns" and had been losing approximately 300 officers in action each year since 1945.[25]

The *armée militante*, composed of officers who were defending their nation's empire in Indochina and Algeria, found that the nation had deserted them. Feeling isolated from fellow army officers and other branches of the service, they began to think of themselves as an "elite within an elite." The camaraderie these colonels and captains developed in fighting the colonial wars far from Paris gave them a feeling of purity and

power since they had not been tainted by corrupt politicians. In essence, the hierarchical command structure of the professional military came under challenge from an informal political nucleus of army officers who had served as leaders of the Foreign Legion and the paratroopers in Indochina and Algeria.[26] It was this colonial elite that arose as the prime mover in the threats to the democratic political ethic in 1958 and 1961. In looking for a moral justification for the type of war it had been sent to fight, this group formulated an ideology that became the starting point in the politicalization of the Army's cadres.

General de Gaulle added fuel to this fire of discontent. He expressed his contempt for politicians, political parties and the parliamentary system with such violence that he undermined the army officers' respect for any republican state. Furthermore, he explained his actions of 1940 in the following manner: Petain was the legal head of the French government; however, he was not the legitimate heir of the French national will. De Gaulle, while not the legal head of the French government, nevertheless was the legitimate embodiment of the French national heritage; hence, he had the right to lead the French nation and the duty to disobey the "illegitimate" Petain.[27] This doctrine, in effect, twisted the minds and tore the consciences of a whole generation of French officers.

Ultimately, Algeria became the issue upon which all the abovementioned perplexities intersected. The persistence of the political and military deadlock in Algeria had gradually come to dominate the French political arena at the expense of every other problem. So weak were the institutions of the Fourth Republic that the Army by 1958 had begun to assume nearly full power in Algeria. With its wealth of manpower, it supplied teachers, doctors and builders for its "experiment in social engineering."[28]

Meanwhile, fear that the Army would become the arbiter in all political crises forced the Fourth Republic to continue its "blind alley" policy in Algeria. The consequence was that the Army took full control of the situation, became convinced that it could govern a country more effectively than could the civilians, and saw its work in Algeria as a humanitarian effort against totalitarian, communist domination—an undertaking that could not be abandoned by orders from weak politicians. Thus, Algeria became an "absolute"

[23]Furniss, *op. cit.*, pp. 54–55; also see Andrew Tully, *CIA: The Inside Story* (New York: Crest Books, 1963), pp. 43–54.

[24]David Thompson, "The French Army in Revolt," *The Nation* (June 21, 1958): 556.

[25]Walter Kerr, "The French Army in Trouble," *Foreign Affairs* (October 1961): 742.

[26]Jean Planchais, "The French Army: A Close-Up," *New York Times Magazine* (February 18, 1962): 109; Paul Johnson, "The Colonels' Conspiracy," *New Statesman* (July 5, 1958): 4.

[27]Schoenbrun, *op. cit.*, pp. 90–94.

[28]Furniss, *op. cit.*, p. 23.

which the Army felt it could not surrender. This was passionately expressed by General Zeller at his trial after the Generals' Revolt of 1961:

France has need of Algeria. Without her . . . France faces, on the one hand, a political decline in the European and Atlantic framework, a menace on the south shore of the Mediterranean, a loss of economic advantages. Algeria wishes still . . . (at this point, General Zeller became faint and could not continue).[29]

Service in Algeria not only gave the Army a sense of power and a fortified sense of mission, it also brought to a head all the tensions that had troubled civil-military relations in France since the end of the Second World War. Appropriately then, it was from Algeria that the French Army unleashed its ideological challenges of May 13, 1958 and April 22, 1961.

THE *ARMÉE MILITANTE'S* COMPREHENSIVE IDEOLOGICAL DOCTRINE

Following the debacle of 1940 and the rescue of France by the Anglo-American invasion force, the colonial combat in Indochina and Algeria served to reinforce traditional military views regarding the decadence of the society at home. The colonial army's isolation and alienation was particularly dangerous because of the other ideas accompanying it. "The Army believed that it epitomized the best national virtues. It simultaneously believed that it represented the nation."[30] It was convinced that its colonial mission was vital and that military failures were the consequence of political and social defects in the French democratic system. Driven to the conclusion that French society had to be reshaped, it became thoroughly politicalized.

As colonial officers began to analyze the French defeat in Indochina, they became more and more certain that they had been "stabbed in the back." Moreover, the lessons from Southeast Asia reinforced their sense of mission in Algeria: it was their duty to save the West from the evils of communism. This dedication was strengthened by a comprehensive ideological construct known as "revolutionary warfare."

The exponents of this doctrine took many of their principles from the communist literature of Lenin and Mao Tse-tung.[31] Roger Trinquier has described the basic foundation of this construct:

"Warfare is now an interlocking system of actions—political, economic, psychological, military—that aims at the overthrow of the established authority in a country and its replacement by another regime."[32] Thus, the colonial struggles were seen as only a segment of the permanent conflict with the communists. And since war had been transformed from an occasional physical confrontation to a permanent war of ideas, the character of the military man must change also: he must be able to expound and put into practice a coherent strategic doctrine. Moreover, in this "total war," according to the *armée militante*, the political system of France had to be reconstructed in order to withstand the thrusts of international communist subversion.

Because of the lack of stable political leadership in Paris during the chaotic years of the Fourth Republic, the French military had to make many political decisions at every level, especially in Algeria. Therefore, it took the opportunity to apply its "revolutionary war" concepts in Algeria, employing terror, torture, and the building of "parallel hierarchies" in order to defeat the FLN.[33] The military became confident that it could enter into the political system of the French nation and restructure it.[34] Increasingly, the young officers came to favor a type of national socialism that would impose equity, clarity and decisiveness of policy through efficient technical means rather than political bargaining.[35] The militants in the Army eventually concluded that the Army should dominate not only Algeria, but also Paris.

The doctrine of "revolutionary war" contained the following postulates: First, the West and Christianity were seen to be locked in a permanent struggle against international communism directed by the Soviet Union. The Marxist-Leninist concept sees conflict as a permanent state and believes that it will remain so until the advent of a classless society. To this end, the communists wage war in all domains of man's activity, the spiritual, the intellectual and the material.[36]

This leads logically to the second tenet—universal war. War is universal because the com-

[29]*Le Procès des Generaux Challe et Zeller* (Paris: Nouvelles Editions Latines, 1961), p. 50. (My translation.)

[30]Furniss, *op. cit.*, p. 2.

[31]J. R. Tournoux, "A Proletarian Army," *The Reporter* (February 18, 1960): 19–20.

[32]Roger Trinquier, *Modern Warfare* (New York: Praeger, 1962), p. 6.

[33]*Ibid.* This is the theme of the entire book.

[34]Furniss, *op. cit.*, p. 36.

[35]George A. Kelly, "Algeria, the Army, and the Fifth Republic (1959–1961): A Scenario of Civil-Military Conflict," *Political Science Quarterly* (September 1964): 349.

[36]Tournoux, *op. cit.*, p. 20. For an in-depth analysis of the doctrine of "revolutionary war," consult the *Revue de Défense Nationale* (1955 to 1959) for articles by Colonel Lacheroy, Major Hogard, and Colonel Nemo.

munist conspiracy has agents spread throughout the world; wherever there is a communist agent, the revolutionary war is already being fought. Furthermore, since the communists use many indirect tactics, such as infiltration, subversion and propaganda, as well as direct assaults on weak positions, the West, under French direction, must be prepared to repulse the communists on every level. To accomplish this, the Army must have the absolute support of the civilian population.

Third, the Army adjudged any tactic to be operational if it allowed the Christian West to repel the evils of communism. This led it to undertake terror, propaganda and torture in Algeria to suppress the Moslems in order to save the country from communist domination. Since the growth of nationalism in an underdeveloped country, in whatever form or context, could lead, in the Army's twisted outlook, to that country becoming a communist satellite, any means could be justified to prevent such a catastrophe from occurring.

Fourth, since the Army saw itself as the embodiment of the national will, it believed that any persons or groups disagreeing with its ideological interpretation of the national and international scenes were necessarily traitors or communist agents. It felt that it had to have the power to make its voice heard at all levels, to carry out its national defense mission, and to look after the nation's destiny.

Fifth, many officers who were imbued with the concept of "revolutionary war" believed that the whole French political system had to be reshaped in order to give consistency and coherence to the French response. This threat to the French democratic tradition was clearly expressed by Colonel Lacheroy during a speech to the Ecole Militaire soon after the fall of the Fourth Republic in May 1958: "General de Gaulle has not understood the significance of the 13 May Revolution. Nor have the French. It destroyed the system—the system none of us wants anymore. . . ."[37]

When the Fourth Republic fell due to military pressures, the army militants were ready with their own program: First, Algeria, as an "absolute" and not just another issue in France's spectrum of international problems, had to remain French in order to provide concrete proof that the Army could rule efficiently and that it could win in an ideological conflict with the communists. The Army also continued to see Algeria as the key to the defense of Western Europe. If the communists controlled it, they would be able to infiltrate Europe through its soft underbelly in the Middle East and North Africa.

Second, the distinguished military records of colonial officers placed them in key staff assignments or in command of such crack units as the paratroops. In this way, the concepts of "revolutionary war" came to be taught at the military schools and in basic training programs for recruits. The Army unleashed a political and strategic indoctrination program among air force and army officers, conscripts, and senior civil servants in the defense ministry. It attempted to inculcate the values of order, duty and discipline into the Frenchman's mind in preference to the democratic values of individualism and freedom.

Third, even though the majority of army officers had no intention of assuming complete power in France, they nevertheless demanded the right to influence the formulation of governmental policy. An interesting distinction was drawn between "petty politics," in which the Army would be neutral, and "grand politics," which were to be formulated only in conjunction with the Army. Of course, the Army itself was to determine what constituted "grand politics." Thus, the Army demanded a "blanket veto" over policy formulations on almost every level.[38]

Fourth, in articles and other papers written after the events of May 13, 1958, army officers denounced the old notion of passive obedience. They asserted that they could no longer abide by the traditional concept of the Army as a blind, inert tool in the hands of a corrupt government or by the principles of complete nonintervention in politics. As Girardet intimates, the Army came to believe that obedience was revocable and conditional.[39] Hence, it began to act as if, on the political plane, it had a veto power over the life and death of each government.

Fifth, the ideological doctrine of "revolutionary war" was formulated under the direction of six or seven colonels, all of whom had seen continuous service in Indochina and Algeria. Their experiences had bred in them an irreconcilable antipathy toward democratic institutions and politically appointed generals. Since they constituted a tightly knit, informal organization within the Army, they broke down the formal chain of command structure within the military hierarchy.[40]

Finally, the militant theoreticians sought acceptance for their ideological doctrine in order to

---

[37]Quoted in Johnson, op. cit., p. 4.

[38]Bernard E. Brown, "The Army and Politics in France," Journal of Politics (May 1961): 276.
[39]Girardet, op. cit., pp. 142–43.
[40]Johnson, op. cit., pp. 4–5.

justify their existence. They feared that there would be little place for the colonial fighters in the French Army of the future, for it likely would be a nuclear army. Darsie Gillie claims that there was "significant symbolism" in the explosion of the last French experimental bombs in the Sahara, in the midst of the 1961 mutiny against the Fifth Republic.[41]

The colonial militants of the French Army clearly had launched a direct ideological attack against the democratic ethic and political systems of the Fourth and Fifth Republics.

THE MILITARY "BALANCERS"

The ideological challenge of the *armée militante* met resistance within the military establishment.[42] Despite the number of officers who paid tribute to the rebellious generals at their trials following the abortive April 1961 coup,[43] there were fragmented military elements which, along with nonmilitary forces, helped to save the French political system.

The behavior of the Air Force has been cited as one of the major reasons why the revolt of April 1961 failed. The Air Force was much less restive than the army militants. Much more democratically recruited than the Army, it suffered less from social and intellectual inbreeding. And because it was not so closely involved in the Algerian operations, fewer of its officers were frustrated or ideologically indoctrinated. Indeed, thanks to de Gaulle's enthusiasm for an independent nuclear striking force, it had an organizational stake in helping to preserve the Fifth Republic.

The Navy, little inclined to disobey General de Gaulle, tended to represent the traditionalist elements in the military. Generally conservative, naval officers (who had shown just as little inclination to disobey Marshal Petain) stressed the principles of obedience, duty, and noninvolvement in politics.[44] They supported de Gaulle because he was the legally constituted authority of the French government.

Long before the Generals' Revolt of 1961, disputes had arisen in the military between the growing school of nuclear strategists (e.g., Generals Charles Ailleret and Paul Stehlin) and the Algerian "revolutionary war" specialists, who competed over resources, strategies and political preferences.[45] In effect a split developed between the *armée des techniciens* and the *armée militante*. Since General de Gaulle was the fervent ally of the nuclear strategists, they formed the core of the government's support in April 1961. The military Gaullists, though relatively small in number, had been continuous admirers of the General from the days of Liberation. When the Fifth Republic was threatened, this group allied itself with civilian groups to protect the established order.[46]

The concept of "reflective" or conditional obedience formulated by the "revolutionary war" exponents affected other segments of the military. "Conditionalist" officers did not automatically carry out the tasks assigned to them by the leaders of the April 1961 revolt.[47] *Attentisme* (wait-and-see-ism) penetrated the military hierarchies in Algeria and metropolitan France; they wanted to wait and see how the revolt was progressing before taking action. During their pause, de Gaulle was able to take the offensive, and the *attentisme* group switched to de Gaulle's side.

Conscripts, who made up about two-thirds of the French soldiers in Algeria during the first half of 1961, had little in common with the regulars. They did not share the frustrations or the passions of the officers who had been fighting and losing campaigns for twenty years. Since the draftees represented a broad segment of French opinion and since most Frenchmen were becoming disgusted with the Army's actions in Algeria, it was not surprising that the conscripts obeyed civilian leaders at home rather than their military officers.[48] Their compliance with de Gaulle's call of April 20, 1961, ordering them to disobey rebellious officers, was a key factor in preventing the latter from accomplishing their mission.

Even the "unity of the Army" proposition, which the militants stressed as crucial to their ability to move swiftly in overthrowing the civilian government, began to work against them. As soon as some units obeyed de Gaulle's orders, turning from passivity to pro-government actions, the "unity of the Army" factor began to work in favor of the government instead of the generals. The fact that "the Army doesn't fire on the Army" was accepted by all segments of the military establishment, thus creating an action vacuum.[49] De Gaulle was then able to take the initiative and fill the vacuum on his terms.

[41]Darsie Gillie, "The General and the Generals," *The Spectator* (April 29, 1961): 589.

[42]Kelly, *op. cit.*, p. 357.

[43]Maurice Garcon, editor, *Le Procés d'Edmond Jouhaud* (Paris: Editions Albin Michel, 1962), *passim*.

[44]Planchais, *op. cit.*, p. 109.

[45]Kelly, *op. cit.*, p. 345.

[46]*Ibid.*, p. 350.

[47]*Ibid.*, pp. 358–59.

[48]Kerr, *op. cit.*, p. 94.

[49]"Charles and the Kingmakers," *The Economist* (April 29, 1961): 452.

There were other reasons why certain military officers refused to take an active part in the 1961 revolt: They believed that the revolt was poorly planned; the Foreign Legion should not have been used in what should have been strictly a French affair; the Army was being used simply as an instrument to protect the interests of the French settlers in Algeria; French Algeria was clearly such a hopeless cause that it was not worth jeopardizing the existence of the military establishment for; the leaders of the revolt had the objective of disrupting the French political system and not just winning in Algeria. Finally, certain segments of the military were jealous of, as well as displeased with, the prestige and power possessed by the informal clique of colonial officers.[50]

CIVILIAN RESISTANCE TO THE *ARMÉE MILITANTE*

When the challenge of April 1961 exploded, civilian leaders refused to sit back apathetically and watch the Fifth Republic crumble. On the day of the April revolt, trade unionists, businessmen, editors and columnists, and members of parliament quickly threw their support to President de Gaulle and the democratic political system. Volunteers gathered at the Ministry of the Interior, and the government hastily enrolled the most reliable elements into a militia to defend Paris against the threatened paratroop drop.[51]

However, long before this crisis erupted General de Gaulle had laid the foundation for a quick and decisive response. His leadership was essential to the defense of civilian government. The General did not want to isolate the Army from the decision-making process since he had a high place for it in his conception of the state. It was to be an obedient army, a disciplined instrument of governmental policy. Therefore, after April 1958 he sought to fashion this instrument circumspectly, by persuasion and gradual maneuver, seeking to avoid a clash, in order to establish his authority and the stability of the Fifth Republic. When the 1961 revolt erupted, he was able to castigate the generals in Algeria as despicable insurgents while making quick decisions which prepared metropolitan France for their thrust. Through his efforts to assimilate the Army into the governmental process and to strengthen the civilian governmental institutions, especially the

executive, de Gaulle emerged as the key reason for the collapse of the militants' ideological challenge.

Furthermore, the excesses of the French Army in Algeria assailed the conscience of the French people; they were appalled at the Army's techniques in fighting the war.[52] Two major opinion-making groups—the intellectuals and religious leaders—reacted by launching a direct attack on the militants' ideological construct, sense of mission, and moral justification for their actions in Algeria.

The protest of the intellectuals was an open "declaration of war" denouncing the Army's ideological explanations for the atrocities it was committing. The intellectuals' major contentions were contained in a manifesto entitled "Declaration of the Right of Refusing to Serve in the Algerian War," signed by 121 writers, artists and university teachers and issued in August 1960. It read in part as follows:

It is a protest on the part of men whose honor and whose clear conception of truth have been affronted. . . . What is citizenship if, under certain circumstances, it becomes shameful submission? Are there not cases where the refusal to serve is a sacred duty, where "treason" means a courageous respect for what is free? And when, according to the will of those who use it as an instrument of racial or ideological domination, the army declares itself in overt or hidden revolt against democratic institutions, does not revolt against the army take on another meaning?[53]

This "Manifesto of the 121" was widely circulated. It helped to increase desertions from the Army; awakened many people to the moral battle being waged between "fascism" and democracy; gave the Army reason to dread the intellectuals' influence; and helped to bring pressures on General de Gaulle to end the Algerian war by negotiation.[54]

Also, a group of Catholic priests serving in Algeria wrote a collective letter to their superiors in France protesting the torture of Moslem suspects by young, susceptible conscripts and warning that the war was corrupting the souls of young French recruits. This was followed by a decree in which a college of bishops, archbishops and cardinals condemned the use of torture by the French Army and encouraged disobedience on the part of those ordered to perform such inhuman outrages. A congress of Protestant clergymen announced their support of conscien-

[50]Kerr, *op. cit.*, p. 93; Kelly, *op. cit.*, p. 358; de la Gorce, *op. cit.*, p. 545.
[51]Edmond Taylor, "The Rebellion that Failed," *The Reporter* (May 11, 1961): 18; Gillie, *op. cit.*, p. 589.

[52]Furniss, *op. cit.*, p. 32.
[53]Quoted in Joseph Barry, "The Moral Crisis," *Commentary* (January 1961): 23.
[54]*Ibid.*, pp. 24–27.

tious objectors.[55] By these and similar actions, churchmen and intellectuals scored the militants' ideology and stirred the democratic conscience of French citizens.

Three other factors helped the Fifth Republic to withstand the military's assault: First, the Constitution of the Fifth Republic had strengthened the executive at the expense of parliament. Thus, in April 1961 de Gaulle in the National Assembly was able to invoke "the almost unlimited powers the new constitution bestows upon the president in a national emergency" under the provisions of Article 16.[56] De Gaulle gave his order countermanding those of the rebellious officers as a "directive from the President in his role as commander in chief."[57] Thus, the constitutionally strengthened Fifth Republic allowed President de Gaulle to act with supreme authority against the *armée militante*.

Second, the communists remained quiescent during the early years of the Fifth Republic, making it impossible for the Army to scare the French people into calling for its assistance in preventing a communist takeover.

Third, the United States and France's other allies firmly supported de Gaulle against the rebellious generals. This disrupted the insurgent generals' strategy since they had expected the support of the United States in the Algerian venture. It also tended to reinforce the legitimacy of de Gaulle and his government.

HOW DE GAULLE BLUNTED THE MILITARY CHALLENGE

When General de Gaulle came to power in 1958, he instituted procedures designed to weaken the political power of the Army's militants and to channel the activities of the military establishment toward the goals of governmental policy. Basically, he attempted to create a countervailing military doctrine more closely coordinated with his philosophical conception of France's national destiny and used this doctrine to integrate military officers more fully into a modernization program for France and for the armed forces.

He first sought to weaken the militants' strength in Algeria and to destroy the Army's "veto" over France's constitutional decision-making process. In an effort to break down the separateness of the politically undisciplined paratroop units which considered themselves an

army apart, an elite within the military elite, he issued the same camouflaged fatigues and colorful berets to all units serving in Algeria and assigned more conscripts to the paratroop units.[58] He had loyal commanders pushed forward into key command and staff positions, especially among pilots, tank specialists and technicians who would be enthusiastic about modernization plans. In this connection, de Gaulle's distaste for military integration within NATO was in part a psychological tactic, since he was sure that a national force obsessed for years with colonial warfare and convinced of its patriotic mission in Algeria could not simply be brought back to Western Europe and turned into a "stateless" army.[59]

As mentioned earlier, the Constitution of the Fifth Republic had strengthened the executive office of the Presidency (Articles 15 and 16) to insure the stability of the regime and presidential direction of civil-military relations.[60] On February 20, 1960, de Gaulle ordered civilian authorities to take over from the Army "the attributions which are its normal prerogative" in the governing of the Algerian departments.[61]

Also important among General de Gaulle's initial efforts to weaken the militants were his abolition of the psychological bureau in Algeria and the decentralization of all psychological war services; and his positive attempts to limit the scope of the psychological war specialists by inducing them to comply with new definitions.[62] In taking this latter step, he gave evidence that he recognized the importance and role of psychological warfare but desired to keep it within precise boundaries.

Yet in his earliest actions de Gaulle clearly attempted to avoid both a massive purge of the officer corps and a direct confrontation with the ideological militants. Rather, he tried to move cautiously in order to rally the support of the Army and civilians around his conception of the nation's *grandeur* and his vision of France's future.

In the wake of the Generals' Revolt, de Gaulle proceeded to accelerate the pace and magnitude of his efforts to make the Army more obedient to governmental policy. He severed the "Algerian albatross" from the Fifth Republic's neck; restructured the judiciary to include such organizations as the Court of State Security in order to

[55]*Ibid.*, p. 24; also see Furniss, *op. cit.*, p. 112.
[56]Taylor, *op. cit.*, p. 18.
[57]*Ibid.*, p. 19.

[58]Planchais, *op. cit.*, p. 109.
[59]"In Search of Status," *The Economist* (February 6, 1960): 531–32.
[60]Taylor, *op. cit.*, pp. 18–19.
[61]Kelly, *op. cit.*, pp. 355–56.
[62]*Ibid.*, pp. 353–54, 356.

expedite the process of trying and sentencing insurgent officers; instituted a long-term punishment system to control all future rebellious actions against the state; and began to identify the military more closely with the nation in matters of educating the youth and formulating the strategic nuclear doctrines for national defense.[63] He restructured the military commands and their missions, and reassigned the major part of the Army to metropolitan France in order to reduce its isolation from the homeland and assist French officers to find their place once more in French society.[64] In addition, under the Fifth Republic conscripts came to constitute about 75 per cent of the Army's manpower, apparently to ensure that a wholly professional defense force did not once again become the instrument for a powerful minority in the Army or on the political Right.[65]

De Gaulle's two major strategies for closing the gap between the nation and the Army were the *force de frappe* and the Gaullist vision of France's renewed greatness. The French President was determined to equip his military forces with their own nuclear deterrent and appropriate means of delivery. The *force de frappe* and the modernization it entailed were viewed by de Gaulle as the best way not only to rebuild and remodel the French Army but also to fracture the hold the ideological militants had on the military chain of command.[66]

At the same time, de Gaulle began to exert more French independence from alleged U.S. domination, while increasing France's role as the leader in the construction of a new, powerful Europe. By offering the professional military man a sufficiently dazzling prospect of new vistas of power and prestige in France and Europe, he hoped to take his mind off the colonial defeats.[67]

Over the past ten years, the military officer has acquired a material interest in the new military doctrine, a psychological outlet in the renewed national mission of extending France's *grandeur* throughout the world, and a professional respect for the stability and efficiency identified with the political system of the Fifth Republic. Thus, de Gaulle's major achievement has been to give the military a sense of status and direction within a civilian-controlled government,

and an opportunity to act as that government's pillar and guardian.

ON CIVIL-MILITARY RELATIONS IN OTHER DEMOCRATIC INDUSTRIAL SOCIETIES

The French experience since World War II has relevance to the civil-military relations of many advanced, democratic industrial societies. Since the primary challenge between nations in the present era seems to be less in direct military confrontations and more in a continuous ideological battle for the minds of men between "communism" and "democracy," military establishments in democracies may feel that they must play a larger role in the policy-making process. Military officers may seek to displace the politicians and civilian statesmen whom they accuse of losing the struggle or of being ignorant of the total ideological war unleashed by international communism.

The elimination of "final" military solutions due to the nuclear "balance of terror" may cause the military in democratic states to become impatient with limited war stalemates of the Korean type and protracted, inconclusive guerrilla conflicts of the Viet Nam type. The military's perception of civilian unwillingness to use "full" military force to "win" may lead the military to intervene in the political process in order to inject a "win-philosophy" and greater patriotism and discipline into the nation. Moreover, the impact of "internationalism," as exemplified by NATO, the Common Market and the United Nations, may eventually force military establishments to bring greater political pressure to bear in order to protect the nation-state's identity and to head off any state policies that might diminish their professional prerogatives and position.

In recent years the line between strategic and political questions has become increasingly ambiguous, a fact that has led to thrusts and counterthrusts on the part of civilians and the military into what each considers to be its autonomous sphere. Imbalances in the civil-military equilibrium will have to be constantly readjusted. An excellent example of this ambiguity is the debate that took place before the Test Ban Treaty was ratified by the United States in 1963. It was extremely difficult to separate the treaty's political aspects from its military ones. Hence, some military men sounded like politicians, while certain politicians sounded like military strategists.

Since the end of World War II, most democratic countries have not been able to forge a

[63]Général d'Armée le Puloch, "Avenir de l'Armée de Terre," *Revue de Défense Nationale* (June 1964): 947–60.

[64]Kerr, *op. cit.*, p. 93.

[65]"The French Army," *Survival* (March–April 1964): 67–68.

[66]Furniss, *op. cit., passim.*

[67]Pierre Rouside, "La France et l'O.T.A.N.," *Revue de Défense Nationale* (May 1964): 802–15.

military doctrine that could find full support from their military establishments. This state of affairs has automatically made military officers part of the political policy-making process and has led to political battles over the strategic doctrines of, and the resource allocations to, the various military services. These officers, in uniform and in retirement, have sought to impose their views regarding military strategy and doctrine and even domestic policy on civilian leaders, quite often through "client" congressmen. There has also been direct competition from the military establishment vis-à-vis civilian agencies for prestigious assignments—for example, in U.S. foreign aid missions.

The military's penchant for such values as efficiency, stability and predictability will no doubt continue to conflict with the democratic values of open discussion, freedom and individualism. This conflict will become dangerous if a parliamentary political system fails to function properly, for the military may enter the political arena to give direction and stability to the government. If social reforms come with revolutionary speed, the military may again feel it has to bring this "unstable process" to a halt in order to ensure a more orderly transformation of society. Thus, it appears that a democratic system wishing to avoid military intervention or takeover must have at the minimum a combination of a strong executive structure, a tradition of military subordination to civilian leaders, and a capable, professional civilian bureaucracy which can provide the nation with stability and direction.

THE BUNDESWEHR AND THE NATIONAL PEOPLE'S ARMY

M. DONALD HANCOCK

*In his comparative analysis of civil-military relations in the Federal
Republic of Germany and the German Democratic Republic, Professor
Hancock points out that civilian control has been effectuated in both cases,
albeit by different methods that are derived from contrasting class and
value systems. In the FRG it is rooted in principles of cabinet-level leadership
and indirect parliamentary scrutiny, while in the GDR it is based on party
dominance and multiple personal links between the party and military
commands. Unlike the GDR, there are no party-military ties in the FRG. On
the other hand, individual officers in the FRG are legally guaranteed access
to political information, the right to vote, and the privilege of competing for
public office should they choose to do so. In spite of the pluralism produced
by the latter, there have been no challenges to civilian supremacy. Finally,
Hancock suggests that the fact that socialization in the GDR military is
centralized, whereas in the FRG it is discontinuous, may account, at least in
part, for the fact that the East German Army has approached the nation-in-arms
ideal of civic and national consciousness more closely than the West German
Army.*

*M. Donald Hancock is Associate Professor of Government at the University
of Texas. He is author of* Sweden: The Politics of Postindustrial Change
(1972), and is co-editor of American Foreign Policy in International
Perspective *(1971).*

CIVIL-MILITARY RELATIONS

Least ambiguous in the political consequences
of German rearmament has been the effect of
system change on authority relations between
civilian and military leaders. The demand for effective political control over those assigned to
bear arms—first police units and later the two
armies—was shared by domestic and occupation
spokesmen in both Germanies. The form and
substance of civilian control in the two states
have differed, however, in accordance with contrasting class and value systems. These differences are rooted in the disintegration of the
wartime coalition in 1945 onward when the Soviet Union and the three Western powers proceeded to fashion counter political systems
after their own images.

The initial step in this process was the replacement of the Nazi elite with political leaders
and administrators whom Allied officials could
trust or at least tolerate. Even before the formal
end of hostilities the Soviet Union instigated
measures to recruit a dependable administrative
elite that would displace the crumbling structures
of the Third Reich. Leading these efforts was a
group of "old Communists" under the direction
of Walter Ulbricht, son of a Saxon tailor and a
founding member of the German Communist
Party (KPD) in 1919, who were flown by Soviet
officials from Moscow to the outskirts of Berlin
in late April 1945. Their assignment was to form
an anti-fascist administrative cadre in the capital
among former Communists, Social Democrats,
and members of the progressive center parties
of the Weimar era.[1] Once this immediate task
was accomplished, Ulbricht and his associates
turned their attention to the refounding of the
KPD and a wholesale purge of Nazi leaders
throughout the Soviet zone. By the middle of

[1]A first-hand account of the Ulbricht mission is provided
by Wolfgang Leonhard, *Die Revolution entlässt ihre Kinder*
(Berlin: Kippenheuer & Witsch, 1955).

Excerpted with permission from The Bundeswehr and the National People's Army: A Comparative Study of German Civil-Military Polity, *Monograph No. 2, 1972–73 (Denver: The Social Science
Foundation and Graduate School of International Studies, University of Denver, 1973), pp. 7–16, 31–44.*

1947 the KPD had consolidated its control of the political-administrative apparatus through its dominance of the Anti-Fascist Democratic Bloc and its fusion with the Social Democratic Party (SPD) to form the Socialist Unity Party (SED).

American, British, and French occupation forces made a less deliberate effort to displace the Nazi leadership with a specified group of their choosing, but the consequence of their denazification efforts was nevertheless the emergence of elite strata that mirrored their own basic values. With the death or arrest of most of the leading Nazi officials in the three Western zones, an alternative elite was recruited whose members, as Edinger has demonstrated, "had belonged neither to the Nazi elite nor to the counterelite, who had neither been strong opponents nor strong supporters of the totalitarian regime, neither strongly involved in running that regime nor in fighting it."[2] Yet they constituted a counter elite of another sort. Since the Western Allies actively sought out or at least tacitly endorsed political and administrative leaders with whom they shared basic value affinities, the evolving elite strata displayed markedly different characteristics from those of the Soviet zone elite. Thus men as diverse in foreign policy priorities and political skills as Konrad Adenauer, head of the Christian Democratic Union (CDU), and Kurt Schumacher, chairman of the West German SPD, assumed leadership positions whose positive support of pluralist democracy and ideological anti-Communism corresponded to the Allies' own synthesis of positive and negative values. Embodying a set of action orientations that were largely antithetical to those of their counterparts in the Soviet zone, members of the West German elite consolidated their authority over administrative-political structures in parallel steps with the KPD-SED in the East.

Reinforcing the authoritative status of these opposing elite groups was socioeconomic and political transformation imposed by the occupation powers under terms of the Potsdam Agreement. The socialization of financial and productive resources in the initial postwar years provided the SED elite with the instrumental means to embark on the gradual transition to socialism after 1949 under the constitution of the German Democratic Republic.[3] Conversely the democratization of political structures and the preservation of a capitalist economic system in the Western zones legitimized the authority of libertarian elites who sought with the formation of the Federal Republic of Germany to avoid the weaknesses of Weimar without embarking on revolutionary socioeconomic change.

When domestic and international policy considerations prompted German rearmament, differences in basic elite values and strategies of system change proved decisive in structuring civil-military relations in the two systems. The first moves occurred in the East where Soviet officials authorized the successive expansion of armed police units to increase domestic security during the formative "anti-fascist democratic" phase from 1945 to 1949. The German People's Police (DVP) was founded in June 1945, followed by the German Border Police (DGP) in November 1946 and the Garrisoned People's Police (KVP) in July 1948. Responding to these initiatives and pressure from the Western powers (particularly the United States) to rearm in the wake of the Korean War, the Adenauer government declared its willingness in 1950 to participate in a European army. Theodor Blank, a CDU member of parliament and a former trade union official, was appointed in October 1950 as the chancellor's representative to confer with the occupation forces on questions concerning the increase of allied troops. As a first step toward augmenting Western security, German officials established a Federal Border Guard (BGS) in March 1951. By the middle of the decade rearmament culminated in the creation of full-fledged armed forces in both states.[4]

In undertaking these separate rearmament measures, leaders in the Federal Republic adopted a constitutional formula of civilian control which embodies twin principles of cabinet-level leadership and indirect parliamentary

[2]Lewis J. Edinger, "Post-Totalitarian Elites in the German Federal Republic," *American Political Science Review* 54 (1960): 72.

[3]An authoritative East German account of this process is Stefan Doernberg, *Kurze Geschichte der DDR* (Berlin: Dietz Verlag, 1964). See also Ernst Deuerlein, *DDR, Geschichte und Bestandsaufnahme* (Munich: Deutscher Taschenbuch Verlag, 1966).

[4]The most comprehensive accounts of West and East German rearmament are Gerhard Wettig, *Entmilitarisierung und Wiederbewaffnung in Deutschland 1943-1955* (Munich: R. Oldenbourg Verlag, 1967) and Thomas M. Forster (pseud.), *NVA, Die Armee der Sowjetzone* (3rd ed., rev. Cologne: Markus-Verlag GMBH, 1966/67). Other useful sources include Hans Speier, "German Rearmament and the Old Military Elite," *World Politics* 6, no. 2 (January 1964): 147–68; Hans Meier-Welcker, *Deutsches Heerwesen im Wandel der Zeit* (Frankfurt am Main: Bernard & Graefe, 1956); Karl W. Deutsch and Lewis J. Edinger, *Germany Rejoins the Powers* (Stanford University Press, 1959); Karl Bauer, *Zehn Jahre nach Korea. Ein Beitrag zur Wehrpolitik in der Bundesrepublik Deutschland* (Boppard am Rhein: Harald Boldt Verlag, 1961); and Helmut Bohn, *Die Aufrüstung in der sowjetischen Besatzungszone Deutschlands* (Bonn: Deutscher Bundes-Verlag, 1960).

scrutiny whereas the SED elite sought to insure political primacy in the form of explicit party dominance. Despite intense controversy between the CDU and the SPD over West German rearmament, spokesmen for both parties espoused similar views on the control issue.[5] Adenauer spoke for all the major parties in the Federal Republic when he declared in a parliamentary debate in 1954: "In Germany . . . the army will be subordinate to the law that will be passed by the Bundestag. All those who exercise political responsibility in Germany will jointly supervise the implementation of that law. In the present era the army no longer occupies the central position that it had in the old form of society and government. The officer corps is no exclusive association that pursues its own political ambitions and in critical historical moments holds the fate of the nation in its hands. . . . The army [fulfills] important functions in democratic society, but . . . does not rule it."[6] For SED officials, on the other hand, political control was ideologically equivalent to class rule. In the tradition of orthodox principles of Marxism-Leninism, Minister of Defense Heinz Hoffmann has justified party control of the East German armed forces in the following terms: "The socialist army, which is created from the people and for the people, is a genuine people's army. The *leadership of the party of the working class* secures its character as a people's army. The total creation, training and education of the socialist armed forces, development of Marxist-Leninist military science, and deployment of all units of the armed forces in battle occur under the leadership of the communist and workers' parties. Leadership through the party is the major source of the strength and invincibility of all socialist armies."[7]

Institutionalized authority patterns directly reflect these contrasting political-ideological perspectives. In the Federal Republic the CDU-led majority sponsored a series of constitutional amendments and parliamentary bills between early 1952 and mid-1957 that (1) unified command authority over the new Bundeswehr and vested it in peacetime in the hands of the civilian Minister of Defense (who would relinquish command to the Federal Chancellor in case of war); (2) established a parliamentary Defense Committee to oversee the defense establishment; and (3) created in response to SPD initiatives the office of a military ombudsman to serve as an independent guardian of civil liberties within the armed forces. An important adjunct of formal-legalistic devices to maximize civilian control was the establishment of a personnel committee in 1955 to review the political qualifications of the initial volunteers for the West German officer corps. In addition to possessing the requisite military skills, only those generals and colonels who could demonstrate their loyalty to liberal democratic tenets were accepted for positions of leadership.[8] The effect of these multiple measures was a defense establishment that is subordinate through a mixed civilian-military bureaucracy in the Ministry of Defense to cabinet officials who are politically accountable to a majority in the Bundestag. The leadership cadre of the Bundeswehr, in contrast to many politically ambivalent officers in the Weimar Reichswehr, was composed of men who professed positive support for pluralist democracy and hence could be expected to refrain from overt steps to dictate or veto public policy.

A redefinition of structured authority relations occurred repeatedly in East Germany from the appearance of the People's Police to the creation of the NVA. During the initial phase of covert remilitarization, formal command over both the DVP and the KVP was vested first in the Central Administration for Training (HVS) and after 1949 in the Ministry of Interior. The KVP assumed autonomous ministerial status under Willi Stoph in June 1955 and was officially designated the Ministry of National Defense on January 18, 1956, when the Volkskammer (People's Chamber) endorsed the "Law on the Creation of the National People's Army." As in the Federal Republic, the Minister of Defense in the DDR serves as civilian commander-in-chief of the armed forces. He is technically accountable, as a member of the Ministerial Council, to both the Volkskammer and the DDR's plural executive organ, the State Council. Politically, neither successive administrative reorganizations nor the constitutional blueprint of authority relations has affected the primacy of SED control.

---

[5]For the views of the major combatants in the CDU-SPD conflict, see Konrad Adenauer, *Memoirs 1945–53* (Chicago: Henry Regnery Company, 1966); Adenauer, *Erinnerungen 1953–1955* (Stuttgart: Deutsche Verlags-Anstalt, 1966); and Lewis J. Edinger, *Kurt Schumacher: A Study in Personality and Political Behavior* (Stanford: Stanford University Press, 1965).

[6]*Stenographische Berichte des deutschen Bundestages, II Wahlperiode, 61. Tagnung*, December 15, 1954, p. 3134.

[7]Heinz Hoffmann, *Die marxistisch-leninistische Lehre vom Krieg und von den Streitkräften* (Berlin: Deutscher Militärverlag, 1962), p. 98.

[8]The personnel committee sought to determine such loyalty on the basis of the candidates' views toward the attempt by Wehrmacht officers to assassinate Hilter on July 20, 1944.

From the first chief of the HVS, Wilhelm Zaisser, to the present Minister of Defense, Hoffmann, the leaders of the East German armed forces have been members of the inner party elite. On the executive level, the Defense Minister's civilian superior—the chairman of the State Council, first Ulbricht and now Erich Honecker—is First Secretary of the SED. Within the NVA itself, as discussed below, the SED has cultivated strong bonds of partisan allegiance through deliberate programs of officer selection, recruitment to party membership, and civic education.

MILITARY ELITE PROFILES

Within differing frameworks of authority relations, patterns of officer recruitment have largely determined the course of working civil-military relations in both German states. These patterns predictably vary in accordance with the selection criteria of contrasting elite strata in the two republics, but the outcome in both cases has been to facilitate civilian control over the military.

Differences in the social and political characteristics of the two officer corps are significant in their own right as one index of the degree of divergence between the Federal Republic and the DDR. For purposes of comparison, data on the birth, social origins, non-military education, and anti-Nazi records have been compiled for the top leadership of the Bundeswehr and the NVA for 1957, 1962, and 1967.

On a descriptive level, the West German emphasis on military competence in officer recruitment and the East German insistence on the "class principle" of socialist consciousness have yielded sharply contrasting military elite profiles. All of the members of the formal West German elite for whom data are available in the three sample years had served in the Reichswehr and/or Wehrmacht as professional officers (compared to 61.7 per cent of the entire officer corps in 1964), whereas more than one of three NVA leaders claimed no previous military experience whatsoever. This contrast is revealed in the differing age structures of the two military elites, with the fewer number of professional officers from previous German armies in the NVA command accounting in part for the greater prevalence of elite incumbents who were born after 1910. More importantly, differences in recruitment criteria have resulted in contrasting patterns of social origins as well as educational and political credentials among leading officials in the Bundeswehr and the NVA.

That the West German military elite has been recruited exclusively among experienced officers from past political epochs means that members of the Bundeswehr elite have been drawn primarily from the professional and upper-middle social classes that contributed the bulk of the German officer corps from the mid-nineteenth century onward.[9] In contrast, only a fourth (in 1957) to just over a tenth (in 1967) of the NVA leadership had similar upper middle class origins; between a half and nearly two thirds claimed a working class background. These differences in social origins are reflected in the fact that virtually all leading West German officers had advanced to a secondary level of education or beyond in all three sample years while fewer than a quarter of their counterparts in the NVA had progressed beyond primary school.

A difference in kind between the NVA and the Bundeswehr leadership is the former's open partisan allegiance, a characteristic that follows from the multiple personal links between the SED and the military command. While a few members of the formal West German military elite were active opponents of the Nazi regime—including two Inspectors-General of the Bundeswehr, Adolf Heusinger and Ulrich de Maizière—fully nine out of eleven NVA elite incumbents in 1957 claimed anti-Nazi records. Most of these were trusted partisans such as Stoph and Hoffman who joined the KPD prior to 1933, engaged in illegal underground activity or emigrated during the years of National Socialist rule, and assumed positions of leadership early in the rearmament program. A smaller group of antifascists were professional officers or non-commissioned officers in the Wehrmacht who were taken prisoner or deserted on the Eastern front and were resocialized to Communist norms in the Soviet Union. Prominent examples were Vincenz Müller, the NVA's first chief of staff, and Hermann Reutzsch, who was commander of the Fifth Military District (Neubrandenburg) from 1956 to 1960.

By the early 1960s the relative percentage of NVA elite incumbents with wartime anti-Nazi records began to decline. One reason was that some of the old Communists (e.g., Stoph) assumed other positions of political responsibility. A second is that many former Soviet POWs re-

---

[9]On the recruitment of German officers in the past see Karl Demeter's authoritative study, *Das deutsche Offizierkorps in Gesellschaft und Staat 1650-1945* (4th ed., rev. Frankfurt am Main: Bernard & Graefer Verlag, 1965), and Gordon Craig, *The Politics of the Prussian Army 1840-1945* (Oxford: At the Clarendon Press, 1955).

tired from active service once they had completed their assignment of imparting military skills to the new army. The most important factor of change, however, is the gradual displacement of both groups since the early 1960s by members of an ascending military elite composed of younger professional officers who combine qualities of expert military training and impeccable party credentials. In 1965 more than 96 per cent of all NVA officers were members of the SED—providing, in the view of the Ministry of National Defense, "a persuasive expression of both the political-ideological unity of the officer corps and its inseparable link with the SED."[10]

No equivalent party-military ties exist in the Federal Republic. Individual officers and recruits in the Bundeswehr are legally guaranteed access to political information and the right to vote, and professional soldiers may compete for public office if they take a temporary leave-of-absence.[11] Any attempt to cultivate overt party links with the Bundeswehr, on the other hand, would be considered a direct violation of the constitutional and political principles governing civil-military relations in the Federal Republic.

By yielding military leadership profiles that are largely congruent with the sociopolitical characteristics of other strategic leaders, recruitment practices in the Bundeswehr and the NVA have contributed to elite consensus on the primacy of civilian control in both systems. A community of values endorsing prescribed civil-military relations as well as the goals of public policy is explicit in the DDR where the NVA leadership comprises part of the new political class that has assumed power since 1945 as the advocate of a Marxist-Leninist vision of collectivist transformation. Far less political conformity characterizes the pluralist West German elites, even though both military and civilian leaders manifest broadly similar social characteristics as representatives of the professional and upper middle classes.[12] Nevertheless, the absence of

efforts by Bundeswehr personnel to violate established constitutional channels of civil-military relations indicates elite agreement on the principle of civilian ascendancy. In individual cases West German officers have occasionally voiced their disapproval of public policy—most dramatically Heinz Trettner who resigned as Inspector-General in 1966 because of his opposition to ministerial sanction of unionization within the armed forces. At no time, however, has the Bundeswehr leadership issued a direct challenge to civilian authority. Nor have postwar military leaders sought, in the tradition of Quartermaster-General Hans von Seeckt during the Weimar era, to insulate the Bundeswehr from executive supervision.[13] In their day-to-day behavior West German officers act on a professional commitment to the defense of established society and political institutions that corresponds functionally to the explicit ideological affirmation of socialist achievements among leaders of the NVA.

Working civil-military relations therefore reveal that both the Federal Republic and the DDR have in fact broken with the historical German tradition of military irresponsibility. This does not mean that military spokesmen refrain from attempts to influence government policy, for at least Bundeswehr officials engage in lobbying activities on behalf of competing military priorities in the Defense Ministry and during deliberations of the parliamentary Defense Committee. In the larger context of who wields ultimate authority over military activities, however, both German states appear to have achieved the objective of civilian control that escaped would-be reformers at critical junctures in the past—the DDR by politicizing the military, the Federal Republic by civilizing it.

GOALS OF CIVIC EDUCATION

Few postwar reforms in the Federal Republic have elicited such extended debate as the Bundeswehr's formulation of *Innere Führung*. A major reason can be discerned in its elusive elaboration by Graf von Baudissin, one of the chief architects of the principles of *Innere*

[10]Ministerium für Nationale Verteidigung, "Angaben zur sozialen Charakteristik des Offizierkorps der NVA" (typed communication to the author), p. 6.

[11]By the late 1960s relatively few soldiers had taken advantage of this opportunity. No members of the Bundeswehr elite had competed for public office, although a reserve officer was elected to the Bundestag in 1965. Most political activity has been restricted to the local or state level.

[12]According to the findings of Karl Deutsch *et al.*, 43 per cent and 29 per cent of a sample of West German leaders in 1964 claimed middle and upper class origins, respectively, and 66 per cent had advanced to the university level in their studies. Ludz' data on social background characteristics of the members of the SED's Central Committee reveal, in contrast, that 50 per cent of the East German elite in 1963 claimed lower class backgrounds and 24 per cent had attended a uni-

versity. These percentages are calculated from Karl W. Deutsch, Lewis J. Edinger, Roy C. Macridis, and Richard L. Merritt, *French and German Elite Responses, 1964: Code Book and Data*, Appendix II (New Haven: Yale University, Political Science Research Library, 1966), and Ludz, *Parteielite im Wandel, op. cit.*

[13]Hans Meier-Welcker, *Seeckt* (Frankfurt am Main: Bernard & Graefer Verlag, 1965), and Craig, *Politics of the Prussian Army, op. cit.*

Führung during the initial phase of West German rearmament: "Henceforth the German soldier must be conscious of the fact that he does not defend one sort of political system or another but a concept of life. Not national interests alone but decisive questions of human existence are at stake. . . . "[14] Authors of the Bundeswehr's basic handbook have attempted to translate such abstract generalizations into more concrete terms as follows: *Innere Führung* rests on a democratic ideal of the individual soldier as a "co-responsible citizen" who personally experiences "the values, worth defending, of our way of life."[15] Such a soldier is expected to affirm civic liberties and express personal judgments on important political events, exercising during his military service his constitutional rights as a citizen to participate fully in the electoral process. The military purpose of this citizenship ideal is to insure that each member of the Bundeswehr knows "for what he may have to fight."[16] In the official view of the Bundeswehr: "Military performance will be correspondingly higher the freer man feels himself, the more willingly he accepts his role, the more incisively he accepts the hardships of training, and the more conscious he is in his spiritual defense."[17]

Given the deliberate emphasis on creating a nonpartisan army within the prevailing legal framework of civil-military relations in the Federal Republic, Bundeswehr officials have been necessarily vague in elaborating these positive principles of *Innere Führung*. Instead, they have concentrated on depicting the "nature, methods, dangers, and weaknesses of communism . . . " as a necessary adjunct of psychological defense—so that each soldier "will be in the position to see through the intentions and maneuvers of communist tactics. . . . "[18]

The tenets of socialist education in the NVA are largely a reverse image of those underlying *Innere Führung* in the Bundeswehr. They include education to class consciousness in the spirit of orthodox Marxism-Leninism, knowledge of the "revolutionary tradition of the international working-class movement, . . . " and awareness of the soldiers' collective responsibility to fulfill their class mission "in the class struggle between socialism and imperialism."[19] Specific operational goals of socialist education in the NVA are defined as teaching devotion to the "socialist fatherland" and unquestioned loyalty to both the Soviet Union and other "brother armies" in the Warsaw Pact. Like principles of psychological defense in the Bundeswehr, civic-military education in the NVA also stresses negative values as a means to enhance defense preparedness. The most important of these, stated in unsubtle terms, is "hatred against the enemies of the people."[20]

Thus the ideal NVA soldier is considered a militant socialist who "views it as an honor to risk his talents, knowledge, and life for the [DDR], who knows precisely who his friends and enemies are and how he must behave as a true revolutionary and a German patriot in a defensive situation. . . . "[21] He must also, in the words of Defense Minister Hoffmann, submit himself wholly to the "iron discipline" of the socialist military organization. "Without discipline there can be no united will and no united action. Unless military commands are carried out without question, there can be no victory."[22]

REALITY AND CONTRASTS

The extent to which parallel programs of civil-military education in the Bundeswehr and the NVA have approached in the practice the ideal of a nation-in-arms polity remains an open question. Behavioral effects have differed over time in both armed forces, largely as a consequence of changes in the broader sociopolitical environments of the two German states.

Within the Bundeswehr the abstract nature of *Innere Führung* and citizen-in-uniform norms has invited confusion from the initial stages of rearmament. At the height of the Cold War negative values of anti-Communism largely sufficed to engender a sense of political awareness (if not military zeal) among West German officers and to a lesser extent among recruits, but the positive imperatives of *Innere Führung* which were enunciated by von Baudissin and other ministry officials remained subject to

---

[14]Wolf Graf von Baudissin, "The New German Army," *Foreign Affairs* 34, no. 1 (October 1955): 4.
[15]Hans Edgar Jahn, Kurt Neher and Herbert Pfeill (eds.), *Wissenswertes über die Bundeswehr* (Frankfurt am Main: Verlag Soldat und Technik, 1960), p. 9.
[16]*Ibid*.
[17]*Ibid*., p. 10.
[18]*Ibid*., pp. 12–13.

[19]Heinz Hoffmann, "Sozialistische Militärmacht und Frieden. Gedanken zum Militarprogramm der befreiten Arbeiterklasse," in W. I. Lenins Ruf: "An alle!" (Berline: Dietz Verlag, 1967), p. 53.
[20]*Ibid*.
[21]Statement by Waldemar Verner, an admiral in the East German navy and Deputy Minister of National Defense, quoted in "FDJ-Wahlen—Startbahn für kämpferische Jugendarbeit 1962," in *Volksarmee*, 1962/65.
[22]Hoffmann, "Sozialistische Militärmacht und Frieden," *op. cit*.

contradictory expectations. Conceding that the Bundeswehr could not function as a "school of the nation," the SPD military expert Fritz Erler nevertheless argued that training in civic-military norms was essential to enhance the solidarity of primary groups within the new army.[23] At the same time, as numerous military and political leaders tirelessly maintained, the quest for an army composed of citizens in uniform was not intended to countervene the functional requirement of military efficiency. Balancing the opposing claims of citizen and soldier, however, would require a "spiritual elasticity" that makes the outward conformity of *Kadavergehorsam* in earlier German armies appear "relatively simple and unproblematic."[24]

As events proved, the synthesis has been achieved only imperfectly. Too many recruits joined the Bundeswehr who lacked elementary knowledge of civic rights and principles of political behavior. Too few professional junior officers were available who were sufficiently knowledgeable to act on the positive values of formal civic-military norms in the day-to-day task of military leadership. The result was a persisting tension between the theoretical ideal of civic consciousness and the reality of widespread political apathy and reliance by many junior officers on traditional forms of military discipline to enforce troop conformity.

With the decline in overt East-West tension since the mid-1960s, the problematics of civic-military education in the Bundeswehr have only increased in complexity. The shortage of qualified junior officers continues; anti-Communism no longer provides a sufficient impulse for political cohesion and high morale in the armed forces; and an increasing number of critically conscious West German youth have either refused military service altogether or deliberately flaunt military authority if they do join the Bundeswehr. Under the Brandt coalition government, Defense Minister Helmut Schmidt responded to the intensified crisis of *Innere Führung* by initiating extensive discussions within the Bundeswehr on sources of officer discontent—which resulted in the publication in 1970 of a range of reform proposals to improve conditions of professional service[25] and appointed a

group of eight young officers in 1971 to redefine principles of civic-military education in more comprehensible and practical terms.[26]

Whether such efforts will enhance the prospects that tenets of *Innere Führung* can transcend abstraction in the daily lives of military personnel is uncertain. Despite its commitment to comprehensive civic-military education, the Bundeswehr exercises no monopoly as an agent of socialization. As Schmidt has observed: "Every company of the Bundeswehr resembles a one-room village school made up of everyone from laggards to university students. But it is inconceivable that the army can accomplish in 15 or 18 months what the school failed to do in 8 or 10 years."[27] Accordingly the effectiveness of the Bundeswehr's role as an instrument of civic education—promoting domestic civic-military objectives associated with a nation-in-arms polity—will remain in large measure dependent on simultaneous efforts throughout the West German sociopolitical system to redefine civic responsibility and authority relations.

The practical effect of civic-military education has also fluctuated in the DDR, although in reverse sequence with comparable efforts in the Bundeswehr. Throughout the 1950s widespread public resistance to the forced pace of system transformation meant that East German officials encountered considerable difficulty in cultivating socialist consciousness in the armed forces. A former NVA officer reported in 1960 that "our army personnel are exposed to a certain extent to bourgeois ideology to which they often capitulate, . . . "[28] and Honecker complained publicly about "officers here and there who do not always see in recruits their class comrades and equal fighters for the cause of socialism and peace. . . . "[29] One result of ideological dissonance was the high rate of desertion to the Federal Republic among officers and recruits during the 1950s and early 1960s.[30]

With the progressive consolidation of the DDR after the sector border was secured in Berlin in 1961, overt resistance to the dissemination of official civil-military norms in the NVA has perceptibly declined. The physical closure of the East German system has prompted a pragmatic accommodation to the existing regime, while the centralized coordination of most

[23]Fritz Erler, "Die deutschen Soldaten," *Der Monat* 7, no. 83 (August 1955), p. 418.

[24]F. R. Allemann, "Was ist eine demokratische Armee?" *Der Monat* 7, no. 81 (June 1955), p. 195.

[25]Press and Information Office of the German Federal Government, *White Paper 1970 on the Security of the Federal Republic of Germany and on the State of the German Federal Armed Forces* (Bonn: Bundesministerium der Verteidigung, 1970).

[26]"Bundeswehr: Einklassige Dorfschule," *Der Spiegel* 26, no. 15 (April 3, 1972), pp. 50, 52, 54, 57.

[27]*Ibid.*, p. 50.

[28]*Rheinischer Merkur*, September 30, 1960.

[29]Quoted in Bohn, *op. cit.*, p. 153.

[30]According to West German sources, over 17,000 military personnel left the DDR between 1953 and August 13, 1961.

agents of political socialization in the hands of the SED increases the probability that NVA civic-military education efforts will contribute to both a growing sense of positive identification with socialist principles and a separate East German identity among the nation's youth. Given the absence of apparent conflict within the armed forces over the goals and practice of socialist education, the NVA thus appears—at least superficially—to have approached the nation-in-arms ideal of civic and national consciousness more closely than the Bundeswehr.

THE PRIMACY OF POLITICS

The military's role in the Federal and Democratic republics emerges as an important if limited factor in postwar German politics. As instruments of national security both armies help shield competitive models of system change. Simultaneously the Bundeswehr and to a lesser extent the NVA provide bargaining leverage for West and East German leaders to promote alliance policies favorable to their respective national interests. The domestic achievements of the two armed forces as agents of civic-military education are mixed, with ambiguity and in the implementation of proclaimed nation-in-arms objectives in the Bundeswehr contrasting with greater apparent effectiveness in the NVA.

In performing each of these functions both German armies are subordinate to the dictates of domestic civilian leadership as well as supranational military command. The East German formula of politicized control differs in kind from West German reliance on consitutional guarantees and an implicit community of values between civilian and military elites to maintain civilian ascendancy. Despite these differences the effect in both states is to insure military accountability—thereby all but eliminating the possibility that either army could become an independent political force in the tradition of the Prussian officer corps and the Reichswehr.

Such a projection by no means excludes modifications in the future performance of the Bundeswehr and the NVA. Qualitative change in the professional competence of the two officer corps or in civic consciousness and military morale among recruits inevitably would affect the capacity of the armies to contribute to the pursuit of national policy objectives. Alternatively, agreement on the mutual reduction of forces in NATO and the Warsaw Pact could curtail the foreign policy functions performed by the armies in their different alliance systems. In that case a conceivable consequence would be the increased domestic importance of the armed forces (possibly as volunteer armies) as channels of educational and social mobility

Thus, in postwar retrospect, the Bundeswehr and the NVA have played a crucial supportive role in the internal consolidation of the Federal Republic and the DDR and their emergence as subjects of international politics. Yet the primary impulse for divergent patterns of system change has been consistently derived from the civilian rather than the specialized military sector. As both German states increasingly confront multiple pressures of postindustrial modernization and regional-international interdependence, clues must accordingly be sought in the larger sociopolitical systems of the two Germanies for appraising the prospects of future transformation.

MILITARY IDEOLOGY: SOUTH ASIA

STEPHEN P. COHEN

Professor Cohen discusses the ethos of military organization in South Asia. He points out that the officer corps in Pakistan, India, and Bangladesh have a pessimistic view of the nature of politics and man, and believe that war is inevitable, albeit not desirable. In his analysis of the attitudinal differences and similarities among the three military organizations, Cohen examines social origins and recruitment patterns of the officer corps, the internal military environment, the domestic political and social contexts, and the impact of external political and military factors. Cohen argues that social and economic constraints have resulted in limited ambitions on the part of South Asian military organizations. Their instinct is to survive and conserve what they have. He notes the professional growth of the Indian and Pakistani military and suggests that such growth is now self-sustaining. Moreover, Cohen believes that a greater sense of realism about the use of military force will preclude the South Asian military organizations from waging war against one another.

Stephen P. Cohen is an Associate Professor of Political Science and Asian Studies at the University of Illinois. He has extensive experience in the study of Indian security policy, including research appointments at the American Institute of Indian Studies and a number of research trips to the United Kingdom and South Asia. Cohen is the author of The Indian Army: Its Contribution to the Development of a Nation *(1971), and numerous articles.*

INTRODUCTION

India and Pakistan each maintain comprehensive military organizations, with a full range of equipment, services, and branches. Of equal importance, they are expected to fight, unlike the military of so many other Third World nations which tend to be decorative.

The military of South Asia share some characteristics with other systems—their interest in technology, their pessimistic view of the nature of politics and man, and their belief in the inevitability although not necessarily the desirability of war. They share with each other some features which derive from the South Asian environment and their common inheritance from the colonial British Indian Army. These include an elite-mass structure, similar training systems, a limited number of personal ties with each other, and the compulsions of geography and regional political marginality. Finally, the South Asian armies do differ from each other in a few respects, especially their resource bases and the somewhat dissimilar ways in which subregional political cultures flourish.

We shall examine below the variables which account for these differences and similarities.

SOCIAL ORIGINS AND RECRUITMENT

The South Asian subcontinent is no less heterogeneous than all of Europe. This is true whether one considers religious, ethnic, linguistic, or racial diversity. This heterogeneity is further complicated by relatively underdeveloped communications systems and the existence of numerous regional and subregional social systems. Finally, the range of economic disparity within each region as well as between regions is fully comparable to all of Europe. This very diversity is one of the main characteristics of the political culture of South Asia, and one of the prime tasks of any political or administrative elite in the region is coping with it.

This is an original article written for this volume and the Conference on Comparative Defense Policy held at the Air Force Academy, February 7-9, 1973. Copyright reserved by the author. Research for this paper was made possible by support from the American Institute of Indian Studies and the University of Illinois at Urbana.

The military of South Asia, perhaps more than any other institution, have controlled diversity by exploiting it. What has often been regarded as a handicap has here at least been bent to the requirements of the modern state. The critical element remains the officer corps: no matter how diverse the military may be, it will function if the officer corps is recruited from a common base (as in the case of the British) or undergoes certain common experiences (especially training) so that diverse origins can be bridged.

Regionalism and the Officer Corps

As long as military power in South Asia was concentrated in the hands of the British the problem of regional origins of the officer corps was not crucial: until the very transfer of power most officers were themselves British, and certainly all officers in crucial senior positions were. Yet the British had not ignored India's regional diversity in structuring the Indian Army. They solved the problem by dividing it. From the late Eighteenth Century onward the structure which obtains in the present armies of South Asia was laid down.[1] The officer corps was in effect divided into two cadres: King's Commissioned Officers who were virtually all British until the 1920s and 1930s, and "Viceroy's Commissioned Officers." The VCO was a genuine innovation in military organization. The rank was more important than the noncommissioned officer.[2] The British were reluctant to give KCOs to Indians, but readily promoted the ablest men of each unit to VCO. Since all Indian Army units were organized along "class" lines, this meant that regional elites (if they were recruited to the Army) had a chance to become VCOs.[3]

In varying degrees, the same set of relationships exists in the three major South Asian states. In terms of diversity of the officer corps and the other ranks India is at one end of the scale, Bangladesh at the other. In Bangladesh all officers are drawn from East Bengal, and virtually all are Bengali Muslims.[4] They come from virtually identical social backgrounds, the upper class of Bangladesh, and share many political and social attitudes. But they all speak Bengali, as do the soldiers of the Bangladesh Army, and Bengali theoretically could replace English as the medium for the military and even as the basis for recruitment examinations.

Pakistan presently is considerably more homogeneous than it was when it incorporated several thousands of Bengali officers and jawans, but it still does not yet fully reflect the heterogeneous character of Pakistan. One region of Pakistan, the Punjab, now provides 50% of the officer corps of the army. Six districts of the Punjab provide over 70% of the jawans.[5] In brief, the Punjab dominates the Pakistan military now as it did before the civil war. The consequences of that domination were momentous for the events of 1971, and may still be politically important in the future.

Finally, India presents a case of even greater diversity. As in Pakistan, the Punjab dominates, due partly to the predilections of the British for recruitment from that province and partly because of the strong interest of Punjabis in the martial arts. Precise figures are not available, but as of the mid-1950s a third of the cadets in the National Defense Academy were of Punjabi origin, while Delhi—adjacent to the Punjab and virtually a cultural extension of it—provided 15%. Madya Pradesh, Madras (now Tamilnad), Mysore, and Kerala supplied less than 5% each, and West Bengal and Andhra Pradesh supplied less than 1% in some years.[6]

However, while the Punjab may dominate in numerical terms, it does not overwhelm as it does in Pakistan. Bengalis, Tamils, Maharashtrians (especially from Bombay), and Malayalees, have provided considerable numbers of officers, and individuals from the major urban centers in all regions of India, have provided candidates for the officer cadre in substantial numbers. They may not be areas with strong local martial traditions, but the educational requirements for an officer have changed greatly, and these regions have large numbers of educated youth. This is especially true in the technical branches of the Army

---

[1]Stephen Cohen, *The Indian Army* (Berkeley: University of California Press, 1971), Chapters 1, 2.

[2]The practice of maintaining two officer cadres was and is highly functional. The British officer provided the link between units which came from very different regions of India, the VCO the link within the unit between the Western culture of the British officer and the indigenous culture of the Indian soldier, the *jawan*.

[3]"Class," in South Asian military terminology, refers to a particular caste, ethnic, or cultural group recruited to the army. It does not refer to class in the sense of social level for which we will use the term "social class."

[4]An indeterminate number of so-called "Biharis," East Bengalis who were Urdu-speaking immigrant groups from

India, may be among the "Bengali" officers trapped in West Pakistan, but it is doubtful that many will return to Bangladesh or find positions in the military.

[5]Dilip Mukerjee, *Zulfikar Ali Bhutto: Quest for Power* (Delhi: Vikas, 1972), p. 168.

[6]Cohen, *op. cit.*, pp. 182–85. While they may not be a reliable source for regional composition, casualty figures for Indian officers during the 1971 war do seem to reflect a gradual diffusion and dispersion of the recruitment base. See Lok Sabha, "Answer to Unstarred Question No. 2219," April 7, 1972.

and the two technologically based services, the Air Force and Navy.[7]

Social Class

There is a narrower range of social class differences than regional origins among the officer corps of South Asia. To some extent, the three states can be considered together, although there may be some significant differences between India on the one hand, and Pakistan and Bangladesh on the other.

Because of their common roots in the British Indian Army, the three officer corps still perform a social role of considerable political significance. The role is that of a skilled professional elite; its political significance is twofold. First, the function of the officer corps is indispensable to the existence of the state; and second, the officer corps reflects the aspirations and interests of a Westernized, secular, social elite. Despite a debate which began well before 1947, no attempt has been made to radically alter the life-style of the officer or to snap the close link between the English-speaking, Westernized elites of India and Pakistan, and probably, Bangladesh. As long as English is the medium of instruction as well as the medium of recruitment, the officer corps in all three states will necessarily be drawn from a narrow sliver of their respective societies. These officers, by virtue of their role in their government, the power that they command, and the generally high status accorded to them, constitute an important component of the national elites of the three states.

However, it would be inaccurate to conclude that the recruiting base of the officer corps has remained unchanged. Although the data are not precise the status of the officer seems to have declined for some segments of South Asian society. Several factors are responsible. In India, the pay schedule for the lower rungs of the officer corps has remained virtually unchanged since 1939, while the value of the rupee has declined by over 80%. Since 1962 the life of an officer has become much more difficult, involving long periods of isolation at remote mountain postings, two major wars, and a series of difficult counterinsurgency struggles in Nagaland and elsewhere.[8] In Pakistan, the prestige of the military was diminished greatly by the losses of 1965 and 1971; only in Bangladesh can the military be said to have gained much in social status. These factors, coupled with the virtual doubling in size of the military of India and Pakistan, may have had the effect of hastening the process of shifting the social base of the officer corps. The officer corps is still limited to English-speaking Indians and Pakistanis, but they now tend to come from ambitious, mobile, middle-class families, rather than the old elites. Additionally, new routes of entry into the officer corps, especially in India, add to its social diversity. A substantial number of officers are now promoted from the ranks. In Bangladesh, some guerrilla leaders were taken into the officer cadre. It is significant, however, that when an individual is promoted up from the ranks, he also undergoes a change in status. In India, at least, he will not command troops that he once served with as a jawan.

Ideology

The area in which there was the greatest break with tradition, and also the area in which there was and is the greatest difference between the officer corps of the successor states was that of their ideological environment. Under the British, young Indian officers were—literally—not permitted to hold any ideology, whether political or religious. Those that did either held their beliefs to themselves or were removed from the officer corps.[9]

However, India and Pakistan were founded upon certain ideological assumptions, and their professional soldiers were expected to hold beliefs which conformed to stated objectives and principles of state. In India this meant an adjustment to a secular democracy; in Pakistan it meant some form of Islamic government. In India, secularism is perhaps the only basis upon which minority social and religious groups can establish a harmonious relationship with the dominant Hindu majority. In Pakistan, the meaning of an Islamic state was never fully clarified. The only point of agreement, especially between the East and West wings, was that it meant a separate identity from that of India.[10] However, in the West, there was a stronger interest in the notion of an Islamic state, a region in which Muslims could live according to their religious principles. In East Bengal, however, there was greater concern in the problem of eliminating Hindu influence in commerce, land ownership, education, and cultural life. East and

---

[7]The diversity becomes apparent upon an examination of the names which appear in the various Indian military journals and magazines, or in accounts of the recent war with Pakistan. See Bhargave, G.S., *Their Finest Hour* (Delhi: Vikas, 1972).

[8]Their social status and attractiveness as a profession are problems which several Indian officers have written about at length. See various recent issues of the United Service Institution of India *Journal*.

[9]Cohen, *op. cit.*, pp. 134–35.

[10]Philip Oldenberg, "Politics in Bangladesh: Notes on Past Perceptions and Current Realities" (Center for Asian Studies, University of Illinois, mimeo., 1972).

West Pakistan achieved independence simultaneously, but their interests and objectives were not entirely congruent. This difference in approach was to permeate the officer corps as well and became of profound importance when the military undertook the reconstruction of Pakistani politics.

The Pakistan Army, dominated by West Pakistanis, sought to establish an identity based upon the assumptions and beliefs which were prevalent in the West. From the beginning the military claimed a special position in the new state of Pakistan; it stressed that the virtues of Pakistan were its virtues, that they reflected the Islamic character of Pakistan. In numerous publications as well as in the military schools of Pakistan, the history of Pakistan was traced to Muslim dominance in South Asia and Pakistanis were portrayed as the natural conquerors of the region by virtue of their purer religion and their martial characteristics.[11] The history of the Pakistan Army was the history of the Punjabi and the frontier Muslim; since there were hardly any other Muslims in the Army, this seemed entirely natural.

These assumptions led to the grotesquely inflated belief of the martial superiority of Pakistan over "Hindu India." Pakistan Army officers, especially those from West Pakistan, literally fantasized about their army's superiority on a man-to-man basis.[12] The worth of one Pakistani soldier was variously rated at five, ten, and fifteen Hindus.

This developed into a fatal linkage of region, religion, and martial character. Those who held such beliefs felt quite sincerely that martial traditions—usually found in particular regions of South Asia—were of prime importance in estimating military worth; religion could enhance (as in the case of the Muslim) or corrupt (as in the case of the Hindu) a genuine martial race or class. These beliefs were applied to the Bengalis of Pakistan as well as the Bengalis, Tamils, etc., of India. This disdain towards Bengalis was ex-

pressed in many ways; personal insults, slow recruitment of Bengali officers and jawans, a lack of trust, and a reluctance to promote them to higher command or critical military positions.

The Indians had no such difficulty in adjusting to the secular democratic ideology of the Indian Republic. Because of the relatively high educational requirements for an officer, many minority groups such as Christians, Parsees, and even Jews have found their way into the officer cadre in substantial numbers. While an attempt has been made to praise and encourage the individual castes and classes which find a place as jawans, the officer corps is treated very much as is the civil service. It is not to be the repository of any special ideology as much as it is to be a neutral, technically skilled professional body of men. In fact, the demands for social relevance and utility which are now often placed upon the civil service are less often made of the military which has been able to protect its isolation.

As we have noted, some of the differences in recruitment patterns between the two successor officer corps can be of great political importance. India and Pakistan were both based upon heterogeneous social systems. In addition, both were dominated by officers from the Punjab. However, it is not until this domination coincides with exclusivist racial and religious ideologies which seriously threaten non-Punjabi groups that conflict develops. This happened in Pakistan, and was a major factor in that nation's tragic dissolution. All three systems still face the problem of utilizing the officer cadre as a vehicle for social mobility. This is strongly resisted by senior officers, who themselves tend to recruit and promote in their own image. Their problem is that the elites which provided manpower for the officer corps are neither interested in nor capable of doing so. Sooner or later they will have to face the problem of reconstructing an officer corps which does not so sharply symbolize class differences. This process is well under way in the services and branches organized around a particular technology or weapons system, and will be hastened as the infantry component declines still further.[13]

THE INTERNAL MILITARY ENVIRONMENT

In view of the great heterogeneity of South Asian society the military organizations of the re-

---

[11]Fazal Muqeem Khan, *The Story of the Pakistan Army* (Karachi: Oxford University Press, 1963), prologue. For a quite different emphasis on the origins of "Pakistan" stressing the existence of a separate East Bengali identity long before the Muslim invasions from the West, see Kamruddin Ahmad, *The Social History of East Pakistan* (Dacca: Pioneer Press, 1967).

[12]This distortion of reality has often been dismissed as typical Punjabi bravado. The actions of the (West) Pakistanis in East Bengal during 1971 indicate that it was much more than that, as do reports of the difficulty of many West Pakistanis in accepting the reality of their military positions vis-à-vis the Indians. For an example of this frame of mind, see the semi-authoritative account of the 1965 war: Brig. Gulzar Ahmed, *Pakistan Meets Indian Challenge* (Rawalpindi: Al Mukhtar Publ., n.d., probably 1967).

[13]One responsible observer places it around 35% of the army. K. Subrahmanyam, "Indian Defense Recruitment Policy" (mimeo., Institute of Defense Studies and Analyses, New Delhi, 1972).

gion have had to involve themselves with social and cultural change as well as military education and professionalization. This process of accommodation and education is particularly visible in the expansion of entry routes into the officer corps in India but less so in Pakistan, where entry was controlled and restricted for political reasons.

Entry and Professional Training

Under the British, only Indian Army commissioned officers were fully trained in India before World War II, and this process did not begin until 1932. Thus, the senior officers of all Indian and Pakistani services were until recently primarily trained abroad.[14] Since independence, however, many new routes of entry into the officer corps have been opened up, both diversifying and expanding the annual number of new commissioned officers. Since the regional and class origins of the officer corps have become an important political concern, steps have also been taken to assure the representative distribution of new officers.

The various schools and academies constitute a comprehensive military education system. In a transitional society such as India, these institutions must also perform the task of easing the process of social change and adjustment for the overwhelming number of cadets who do not come from elite families. The military academies thus not only inculcate the principles of military honor and leadership, they teach a system of conduct appropriate to a fledgling member of an all-Indian institution.

In sum, the military education systems of South Asia must carry more than a military burden, for they involve themselves with the complicated process of cultural adjustment. This is also another reason why the military education system, at least in India, extends well beyond the basic military academies and schools.

Because of educational and language deficiencies the South Asian practice has been to spread military education throughout an officer's career, sending him for higher military training only when he is ready for it.[15] Most of the higher military education systems of South Asia are primarily technical in nature, and quite comparable to similar systems in Western military organiza-

tions. However, the Indian military education system is distinguished by features with important political and military implications—the joint service approach, inter-service cooperation, and strong civilian participation. As a result it has been eminently successful in contributing to both civilian control over the military in India and in furthering service cooperation by the creation of another inter-service tie.

With a much smaller military establishment, and one dominated by the army, Pakistan never developed as extensive nor as diverse a military education system as India. Further, there has never been as strong a commitment to representative recruitment of officers in Pakistan as in India, and the military education system was developed in part with the purpose of maintaining an imbalance between East and West Pakistani officers.[16] Finally, because Pakistani politics was dominated by the Army for so many years, the Indian inter-service institutions have virtually no counterpart in Pakistan.

Political Indoctrination

The overt attempt to inculcate specific political beliefs or ideologies is conspicuous by its absence in the armies of South Asia. This is not to say that the military do not have political beliefs, nor that they may be strongly held, but only that India, Pakistan, and probably Bangladesh will continue the British practice of prohibiting explicitly political discussions within the officer corps. Only the most generalized kind of political instruction and history is provided the jawans of each nation; officers receive the same kind of instruction, although on a more sophisticated level, but it is orientated primarily towards the history of the state and its relations with other states. The military do not believe that their soldiers need to be politically motivated to fight well; only the most generalized form of nationalism is taught.[17] They placed their faith in discipline, honor and obedience, and purely military skills, although this approach has been challenged on two fronts.

The first is the role of Islam in the fighting ethos of the Pakistani soldier. Because the Pakistani military was and is entirely Muslim it could turn to Islamic theories of the state and the role of the military in defending the state against

---

[14]For a discussion of these foreign-trained officers see Cohen, *op. cit.*, pp. 114 ff. The Indian Army is entirely India-trained now (except for officers who have taken advanced courses abroad).

[15]For discussions of this system see the annual *Report* of the Ministry of Defense. Also, A. L. Venkateshwaran, *Defence Organization in India* (Delhi: Publications Division, 1967).

[16]See the disingenuous account in Mohammad Ayub Khan, *Friends Not Masters* (Karachi: Oxford University Press, 1967), p. 27.

[17]Numerous articles in the United Service Institution *Journal* make this point. See, for example, Capt. M. K. Roy, "Educational Co-efficients for a Military Officer in the 'Eighties," Jan.-Mar. 1971, and Maj. Gen. P. S. Bhagat, *Forging the Shield* (Calcutta: Statesman Press, 1965).

non-Muslim threats. Generally, the leadership of
the Pakistan military has chosen not to emphasize the theory of *jehad*, or holy war, except as a
battle cry for jawans. Islam failed to provide clear
guidelines for the construction of a Pakistani
state, and that was one of the factors which led
the military to intervene in politics; they apparently saw no pressing need to utilize Islam for
their own purposes when it had not succeeded
elsewhere. This reluctance to turn the Pakistani
military into a quasi-religious organization was
reinforced by the relatively secular origins of the
senior Pakistani military leadership.

The second challenge to an apolitical military
came from China, and was directed against India.
After the 1962 debacle many Indian civilians and
some officers felt that the proper response to the
Chinese threat included an expansion of political
indoctrination programs. A "people's army," emphasizing militant nationalism, or even a return
to Hinduism as the basis for the fighting ethos
were both suggested—and both rejected. The
military argued that the few cases of Indian prisoners speaking favorably about their Chinese
captors was not symptomatic of a general weakening of morals but only the temporary failure of
a proven military training system.[18] Their solution to the problem was military, not political,
and reflected their conservative approach to military organization.

Although explicit political indoctrination is
rarely encountered in the military of South Asia,
several important "purely" military values and
beliefs are inculcated, and these have had important political and economic consequences in both
India and Pakistan. One of these is the British-
derived theory of civilian control. This theory
ostensibly sets the limits of civilian and military
authority, but it has also provided a justification
for the military take-over in Pakistan as well as
the expansion of civilian authority in India.

A second important military belief, common
to the military of all three major South Asian
states, is the pronounced preference for modern
technology and a desire to keep up not only with
neighboring military establishments, but with
nonregional, especially Western, armies, air
forces, and navies. The military of South Asia
crave "modernity," by which they often mean
technology. This predilection towards the most
modern equipment available partly reflects the
fact that the officer corps is drawn from the educated, Westernized middle and upper classes of
South Asia. However, it also reflects the bitter
historical experience of South Asian armies,

which have many times had to fight with inferior,
obsolete, or inadequate equipment. Not only does
this increase the chance of defeat, the officer
corps regard it as a betrayal on the part of political leadership. Finally, they are sensitive to international military judgements. Unlike most
national elites the military feel that they must be
judged by foreign as well as domestic criteria,
and while they acknowledge that they draw a
disproportionate amount of resources from India,
Pakistan, and Bangladesh, they will argue that
comparatively speaking other nations spend
more on their military.[19]

Another strand of South Asian military
thought in South Asia should be noted here, for
it tends to provide a balance to the interest in
technological sophistication described above. Because of the complex relationship between army
and society in South Asia, and because of the
comparatively low level of modern equipment
available to the military, there has always been
an emphasis on "man management" and organization. This has been necessary to maintain a
balance between groups and social classes within
the military, and also to provide something of a
substitute for inferior equipment. Although the
terminology is different, it is a military ethos
which parallels the P.L.A.'s emphasis on man
over machine.

Informal Associations and Promotion Procedures

The difference between Indian and Pakistani
professional career patterns is due to the factor of
civilian influence. Although officers from the
Punjab are disproportionately recruited in both
India and Pakistan they have had a much greater
political impact in the latter nation. The importance of Punjabis acting as an informal association has actually increased since 1971, for the
common threat of Bengal separatism no longer
binds the four regions of West Pakistan together.
Various published reports indicate that President
Z. A. Bhutto has tried to balance Punjabi officers
with non-Punjabis in an effort to anticipate and
forestall any future Punjabi-dominated coup.[20]

Regionalism among the officer corps exists in
India as it exists within various political parties
and civil services, but it has never reached a
flash point. There are, allegedly, cliques of
Bengali and South Indian officers in the Army,
Navy, and Air Force, but there is no evidence to

---

[18]Bhagat, *ibid.*

[19]Brig. N. B. Grant, "Short Term Cheapness Is Not Long
Term Economy," U.S.I. *Journal* (July-Sept. 1970). Elements
of the Bangladesh military wish to build up at least a small
but modern air force, navy and armored ground forces.

[20]Mukerjee, *ibid.*

indicate that such informal groups influence promotions or political and military attitudes, nor is there any such evidence with regard to the large Punjabi contingent. A more important basis for association is the common experience which officers undergo in the various service academies, or their shared tie to a particular regiment or command.

At the senior levels of the Indian military such informal ties, if they are of any significance, may not survive the civilian-dominated promotion procedure. India is a clear example of the use of promotion policy (and post-service appointments) to both control and shape the attitudes and actions of the officer corps. Further, the whole pyramid of the officer corps in all three services is shaped by civilians, who thus determine the number of officers at each rank, as well as their identity at the senior levels.[21]

Promotion up to the rank of lieutenant-colonel or equivalent is usually automatic; after that grade the procedure is by selection, but there is a tenure and age limit for each rank.[22] By extending these limits, by participation in the selection process (only at the higest grades), or by offering lucrative post-service appointments the civilian-dominated Ministry of Defense can and does obtain a high degree of obedience from the officer corps. Senior officers who conform can expect to receive positions in the diplomatic service, become administrators of public sector corporations, or find employment in the vast and expanding network of government defense production facilities. The effectiveness of this control process is made evident by the very small number of retired senior officers who have consistently spoken out against the government or who have entered politics. Another measure of strong civilian control are the very few examples of "leaks" by officers in serving positions; rules concerning the illegal dissemination of information outside the government are strictly obeyed, and the dominant ethos among the military, even dissidents, is to settle differences within the government.[23]

THE INTERNAL SOCIAL AND POLITICAL ENVIRONMENT

The military of South Asia interact with their social and political environment in a variety of important ways. They are dependent upon it for a stream of (volunteer) manpower, for military equipment (or for the foreign exchange to purchase such equipment abroad), for operating funds, and for political direction. So, in fact, are all military organizations, the difference being that in South Asia this dependency is further heightened by the special characteristics of local social and economic systems and political traditions.

Poverty, Heterogeneity, and the Military

Armies based upon poor societies face certain problems which are not encountered in richer societies. This is true whether the political context is colonial, revolutionary, or national.

In South Asia poverty has always conditioned the organizational format of the military, including its manpower supply, the attitude of the officer corps, and the attitude of the society towards the military itself. This desperate poverty, combined with social heterogeneity, has always meant that there has been a ready supply of volunteers for at least the lower ranking positions of the military. Only when the recruiting base was restricted to a few castes or groups has there been a danger of manpower shortage.

To make themselves competitive in the job market the armies of South Asia need only pay approximately $20 per month for recruits. Even then they come in large numbers and are eager to join. But the benefits of the military go beyond pay. The military retains something of its closed, caste-like identity, and it is not uncommon to encounter families with their third or fourth generation serving in the army.[24] Joining the military also means joining the government and additional security and prestige for the jawan's family. For most South Asian peasants the military is perceived as a highly desirable career: it is often a step up in status, not a step down. This desirability is heightened in those regions which are traditional recruiting grounds. Even in the Punjab, which is the most prosperous region in both India and Pakistan, families often send one or more sons into the military to maintain the historical tie.

If extreme poverty solves the manpower problem for the lower ranks of the military, it complicates it for recruitment to the higher. As the armies of South Asia grow in technical complex-

[21]Inder Malhotra, "Too Little Room at the Top," *The Statesman* (New Delhi), July 24, 1972, and subsequent letters on August 14, 1972.

[22]See Venkateshwaran, *op. cit.*, for details.

[23]One other important feature of this system is that officers who have strongly disagreed with the government, in both India and Pakistan, are not harassed after their retirement. Even the Presidents of Pakistan, Generals Mirza, Ayub, and Yahya have received relatively gentle treatment after their involuntary fall from power.

[24]See Cohen, *op. cit.*, pp. 187 ff.

ity they require larger numbers of officers, non-coms, and jawans with higher educational qualifications. Here the military must compete with an expanding public and private corporate sector and it often fails to compete successfully. There have been chronic shortages of medical and engineering personnel in both states for a number of years; India at least has had to resort to a limited conscription system for skilled personnel. As we have noted, the difficult working conditions for the military have made it less attractive to the upper classes and castes, and the prestige of a military career has declined in precisely those groups with the required educational and technical skills. This shortage has led to demands for increased pay and pension benefits to make the military more competitive.

Poverty also has an impact upon the kind and quantity of weapons available to the military. We shall deal with the weapons acquisition process from the point of view of the military in greater detail, but some general comments are appropriate here.

There is a mixture of pride and anguish in South Asia concerning the military's voracious appetite for modern weapons. For many, the military symbolize the emergence of these nations as modern, contemporary, efficient and powerful. The flypast, military parades and naval visits have all become ceremonial events which generate great popular acclaim. This is no less true of Bangladesh than India and Pakistan. The enthusiasm for these activities reflects the gradual militarization of civilian society, and both political elites and the military themselves are eager to exploit the armed forces to gain popular acclaim.

However, there has always been a strong undercurrent of criticism of military expenditures as being nonproductive even when they are acknowledged to be necessary. As an alternative to a large military establishment based upon a heavy, costly and modern weapons system, there is a long subcontinental tradition of arguing for a military based upon alternative structures. One such alternative, which has not found favor within the military, has been that of a "people's army," in which patriotism, zeal, equalitarianism and large numbers replace conventional military structures.[25]

Another alternative, which has been seriously considered within the military, is that of a small,

well-equipped strike force, backed up by a larger militia. In this context the Israeli example has been carefully studied in India, Pakistan, and Bangladesh. However, it also requires external military assistance, which in turn presupposes either substantial diversion of foreign exchange or a foreign political tie. In the final analysis the structures of the South Asian military reflect a compromise between the military's strong interest in modern technology and the obvious limitations of financial and technical resources. The military, especially the army, have quite "modern" sectors with relatively up-to-date equipment, especially in armored units. As for the rest, they must get along with older, more obsolete equipment, hoping to bridge the gap with discipline, organization, and a very high standard of training.

The Military, Social Disorder, and Social Change

Although the military of South Asia are entirely dependent upon their supporting societies for manpower, equipment and financial support, they have been reluctant to consider the use of the military to change or develop those societies. Although there is a long tradition of "aid to the civil"—the use of the military to restore law and order or to assist in disaster relief—these are tasks which are approached with caution and reluctance.[26] In India a systematic attempt has been made to relieve the military of aid to the civil activities. Most of the Indian states as well as the Union Government maintain armed police and paramilitary units to deal with internal disorder; the number of civic disorders in recent years has increased, but the overall trend is a decrease in the use of the Indian Army to contain them.[27] Flood, famine, and other disaster activities continue as before. Indian officers have always returned to their cantonments with relief, preferring to emphasize preparations for military training.

In sharp contrast, the Pakistan Army had been deeply involved in aid to the civil activities from its inception.[28] Further, these activities have been more "political." Making a virtue out of

---

[25]Advocates of this model spoke out as early as the 1920s. In some ways the Indian National Army of World War II, a rebel force of Indians who fought the British under Japanese tutelage, was such a people's army. In it efforts were made to break down the religious, caste and social differences so pronounced in the Indian Army.

[26]Aid to the civil is a procedure in which the military are formally requested by civilian officials to assist them. They remain under civilian direction (unless martial law is imposed), and the operation is usually of brief duration and terminated when civilians wish.

[27]Each year's aid to the civil operations are duly reported in the Ministry of Defense *Report*.

[28]Fazal Muqeem Khan, Chapter XIV, "Nation Building Activities," and Raymond A. Moore, "The Army as a Vehicle for Social Change in Pakistan," *Journal of Developing Areas* (October 1967).

necessity, the Pakistanis developed various professional justifications for increased involvement in civilian matters and ultimately embraced the notion of civic action.[29] The old British Indian Army engaged in civic action when it developed close ties with various sectors of Indian society, especially those that constituted its recruitment base. Subsequently, these activities were carried to greater lengths in Pakistan than in India. Although the leadership of the Pakistan military sought to remain aloof from a dangerous thicket of social and economic problems, it was forced to deal with them in part because of the breakdown of civilian and administrative elites. The "aid to the civil" programs described above became civic action programs as the military's own prestige and reputation were increasingly involved. As William Gutteridge notes, the strength of the Pakistan Army was derived from a policy of exclusiveness, detachment, and separateness; unlike an army within a nation-at-arms (as in Israel) or an army committed to civic action programs (as in China) it achieved its social and political purpose by leadership rather than permeation.[30] Yet, it was committed to the reformation of Pakistan, especially after it seized power, and the pages of the Pakistani professional military journal were filled with articles describing various ways in which the Pakistan Army could become a true "people's army".[31]

While a true civic action program could be carried out in large parts of West Pakistan where the claim to be a people's army bore some relationship to reality, there was only a limited opportunity in the East where the need for civic action and aid to the civic programs was greatest. The obstacles in the East were two-fold: the highly unrepresentative nature of the military, especially the officer corps, and Bengali elite perception of the military, especially its dominant Punjabi contingent, as discriminatory and racist to a degree that recalled the colonial situation. The Pakistan military entered a situation for which it was unprepared by its social composition, training, and experience. Their very com

petence as professional soldiers led them to the tragic assumption that they could succeed in the task of restructuring Pakistani politics through constitutional reform at the center and civic action programs in the countryside. They were wrong, although had they not expanded their internal role Pakistan might have disintegrated earlier than 1971.

Events in Pakistan were observed closely by the Indian military. They have stubbornly (and at times bitterly) resisted an increased civic action role, except in the special situation found in Nagaland and neighboring hill areas.[32] A senior Indian general recently expressed the view of most of his colleagues when he stated that the prime function of the military in peacetime was to prepare for war, not to undertake "civil responsibilities or engage in civil works." He noted that the defeat of the Pakistanis was due to such "civil involvement" and expressed his wish that any civilians in India who had been considering an increase in the military's civic role ponder the fate of the Pakistanis.[33]

The Political and Administrative Environment

For purposes of political direction and financial support the military officer corps in India, and Bangladesh (and apparently now Pakistan as well) look to their political and administrative masters. Their relationship with civilian authorities is if anything more subordinate than their British predecessors, and is quite comparable to the pattern which obtains in many states with tight civilian control over the military.

Firstly, this relationship is based on a theory of civilian control which is accepted by both sides. In its briefest form this theory states that there are two separate spheres of activity: civilian and military, and that they are and should be separate. The military and their civilian opposites each have their own responsibilities, including the obligation not to intervene in matters which do not properly concern them. The duties of civilians include diplomacy, the setting of broad strategic objectives for the military, and providing the resources for the military to fight with;

[29]Civic action technically refers to any action which makes the soldier a "brother" of the population, as well as its protector. It can range from basic military courtesy and discipline up to formal projects. See Edward G. Lansdale, "Civic Action Helps Counter the Guerilla Threat," *Army Information Digest* 18 (June 1962): 52.

[30]*Military Institutions and Power in the New States* (New York: Praeger, 1965), pp. 55–56.

[31]The *Pakistan Army Journal* is not publicly available but copies can be seen at least at the U.S.I. of Great Britain. Some typical articles have been titled: "A Plea for a People's Army," "Afro-Asian Revolutionary Warfare and Our Military Thought," "The Effectiveness of Guerrilla War," and "A New Look at Infiltration."

[32]In September 1972, Nagaland was officially declared to be once again under civilian authority and the military have no special legal position in the state. A classic counterinsurgency war has been waged there and in the nearby Mizo hill tracts. Both of these insurgencies apparently received assistance from outside power; one of the first joint undertakings between Bangladesh and India was the destruction of guerrilla bases located in each other's territory.

[33]Lieut. Gen. G. G. Beweer, *Times of India* (Bombay) (September 10, 1972), Beweer is to be the new Chief of Army Staff for India.

the responsibility of the military is to fight when and where they are told to fight, to offer advice and information, but to refrain from intervention in political matters. In brief, the prevalent model of civil-military relations is based on "objective" control: the military are to retain their identity, function, and role.

Obviously, this 'theory' does not provide a guide to all or even most situations when 'political' and 'military' interact, nor does it indicate what purely political or military are. Each South Asian system has worked out its own civil-military relationship within the broad outlines of the theory described above; in practice, they have been quite different.

The political environment of the officer corps has been most restrictive and powerful in India. Civilians have taken the initiative in determining the "proper" role of the military and have built upon old institutions and created new ones to enforce their will. These range from stringent financial controls to various downward adjustments in the symbolic and ritual status of the armed forces, especially the Indian Army. These restrictions and sanctions are balanced by a system of rewards and honors (also controlled by civilians) which can be distributed among cooperative officers.

This system of civilian control has remained stable despite several crises. It rests not only upon the presence of strong political leadership but the continued existence of a highly qualified and self-confident civilian bureaucracy. The focal point of civilian control is the Ministry of Defense, but other ministries are involved in the process. These include the Home Ministry (which has played a major role in intelligence operations) and the Finance Ministry (which has a virtual veto over the military budget process). These ministries have a very long tradition of participation in the defense policy process, both in operational and structual problems.[34]

Although it shared a theory of civilian control with India, pre-civil war Pakistan was in effect a military-dominated state for a number of years. Even before the coup of 1958, the military exercised great political power and was virtually autonomous in defense matters.

While the Indians were attempting to imitate the pattern of civil-military relations found in Britain (and which was modestly established in

British India itself), the Pakistanis moved backward in time. The Commander-in-Chief had no serious civilian supervision over either budget or operations. The power of the Pakistani military—especially the Army—proliferated rapidly in what they regarded as a vacuum of leadership. Apparently with reluctance (but certainly not with any anticipation of failure) Ayub led the military into an alliance with the civilian bureaucracy, and then discarding the bureaucracy, into open military rule in 1958. The calculations which brought the military to this point in Pakistan and sustained it are worth examining, because they point out the important role of civilian authority and competence (or at least the military's *perception* of civilian competence).

Ayub and his colleagues fully subscribed to the British-originated theory of separate spheres of military and political authority. Each has its own task, neither should interfere in the duties of the other. However, the military regarded political disorder in Pakistan as directly affecting their own organizational integrity. Religious riots had their echoes within the ranks, and frequent aid to the civil operations, especially in East Pakistan, were harming both the military's defense capabilities and its reputation.[35]

A second calculation was the impact on the army itself were Pakistani politics to be democtratized. Politicians in East Pakistan not only demanded democracy but they wanted parliamentary democracy and the election of public officials on the basis of one-man one-vote. Over the years the special East Pakistani perspective on the military and foreign policy became known, and to the very end remained unacceptable to the army. By 1970, the Awami League had called for the abolition of "all-Pakistan services" and their replacement by federal services recruited from all parts of Pakistan on the basis of proportional representation.[36] This included the military: the federating units were to have their own militia or para-military forces for local defense. Since another part of the platform called for the withdrawal from SEATO, CENTO and the establishment of friendly relations with neighboring countries via a policy of non-alignment, such limited defense forces would be sufficient. Finally, they would be financed out of the revenues which were to be raised by each of the federating units. This included foreign exchange—and most of it was earned by East Pakistan.

[34]For a full discussion of the Indian defense policy process, and the role of military and civilian within it, see Stephen Cohen, *The Indian Security Policy-Making Process* (New York: Columbia University, Southern Asian Institute mimeo, 1970), an excerpt of which appears on pp. 156–68 of this volume.

[35]See Cohen, "Arms and Politics in Pakistan," *India Quarterly* (Oct.-Dec. 1964): 409.

[36]Documentation is in: Government of India, *Bangladesh Documents*, Publications Division, 1971.

If these steps had been implemented Pakistan might have survived, but the Pakistan military would not have. To my knowledge, no national army has ever voluntarily agreed to its own partition when it thought that there were alternatives. While the West would have retained its recruiting base, it would have lost much of the revenue which permitted it to maintain a substantial air force and armored corps. Self-interest appeared to be congruent with national interest, and in retrospect it is not surprising that the military chose to institute a reign of terror in East Pakistan rather than acquiesce to the Awami League's demands. Professional soldiers were not ready to admit defeat in both the immediate tactical situation of the Bengal revolt and in the longer struggle they had carried on to reform and reshape Pakistani politics.

A third calculation was the army's judgment that it could effectively reform Pakistani politics without becoming too deeply involved in the day-to-day governance of the country. If the "real" representatives of the people could be given power, the military could return to its normal duties. This calculation proved to be the most erroneous of all.

The military was never able to adjust and reconcile competing interests and objectives of the major groups of Pakistan; nor could it devise a system of politics which performed the same function without threatening the military's own values and objectives, as the election of a predominantly East Pakistani government might have done. For the Pakistani officer corps, politics turned out to be a tar baby; the military could neither impose a quick "fix" on the political system nor perform vital political functions themselves.

In the final analysis the tragic destruction of a united Pakistan was the result of both civilian and military actions. Even though the Pakistani case was touted in the West as an ideal model of enlightened military rule, one should not have expected much from a military organization with such limited political expertise, and a very narrow social and geographical base. The shortcomings of the military were well known to politicians in both the East and West, but they were themselves unable to either influence or supplant the military for any length of time. Pakistan deteriorated as a working political system not only (or even primarily) because of the objective economic, social, and cultural differences between East and West, but because its politicians, civil servants and military were unable to accommodate their own interests to those objective differences. Too often a series of strong men considered elections to be a dangerous concession to the whim of the people. In this the military played a key role. Their distrust of dissent, their narrow regional origins, and their inflated professional requirements led them—unnecessarily—to their fatal political role.

Ironically, the Pakistani experience greatly strengthened civilian control in India. After the 1958 coup, Nehru took special steps to ensure the domination of civilian over military; after the failure of Ayub's regime the Indian military itself certainly realized the pitfalls of intervention in politics, not the least of which was the deterioration of the military itself as a fighting organization.

It is also apparent that these events were observed in Pakistan itself, as indicated by the subsequent developments in Pakistan and Bangladesh. It is premature to state that military rule can be avoided in either state, but the efforts to prevent its return can be briefly described.

With the loss of East Pakistan and the development of a military stalemate in the West, the military leadership of Pakistan was plunged into disgrace. Senior officers who were not fully associated with Yahya Khan, the chief of the Junta, attempted to recruit Zulfikar Ali Bhutto as a political figurehead. He has apparently outmaneuvered them and imposed his own energetic form of leadership upon what remains of Pakistan.[37] Bhutto's main task was to impose his will upon the military itself, for even after defeat they constituted the only substantial institution remaining intact in Pakistan.

Characteristically, Bhutto attacked the problem directly. In a series of public statements he stressed the link between "civilization," civilized government, and civilian control over the military. As he proceeded to purge the officer corps, he justified his actions on the grounds that some officers were not reconciled to their new role under civil dominance, and stated his belief that the Pakistan military had become too unrepresentative. Yet, while he has tried to limit the role of the military in politics, he has also made a special point of praising their professional competence and honor.

For Bhutto, the presence of large numbers of troops and officers in Indian hands has been fortuitous; while there has been some pressure from families and friends for their return, their absence has enabled him to raise several new divisions from scratch and to fill their ranks with politically reliable soldiers and officers. Simultaneously, tribunals are being held to look into

---

[37]Mukerjee, *op. cit.*, provides an authoritative account.

the causes of the 1971 military debacle and may further lower the prestige and power of the generals associated with that defeat.

At this point it is not clear whether Bhutto's objective is to establish civilian control over the military by confining it to the cantonments of Pakistan and filling its officer corps with apoliticals or whether he intended to establish "subjective" control: bringing the military and society closer together. The latter would involve more representative recruitment, and an insistence upon conformity of the officers with civilian political values. One suspects that a mixed strategy is being planned: civilian authority is to be emphasized and civilian decisions are not to be challenged, but the many links between West Pakistani society and the military are not to be overlooked. If he retains power, Bhutto will probably create an officer corps which is *pro forma* apolitical but whose key positions are manned by officers that he can trust.

Because of their experience in undivided Pakistan, the political and administrative elites of Bangladesh are acutely sensitive to any potential threat of military domination.[38] Such a threat could have come from two directions; the growth in political power of the various regional Mukti Bahinis which fought during the civil war, or by the actions of the Bengali contingent of the Pakistan armed forces which had defected to the Bangladesh government. Neither threat has materialized. The intervention of Indian government in East Bengal terminated the growth of the Bahinis before most of them developed strong local roots. A few remain, but they are gradually developing into regional political parties. The fledgling Bangladesh Army is very small, and its officers are quite junior in experience and rank. Those few Bengali officers who did reach general rank have been trapped in West Pakistan, and the present heads of the Bangladesh Army, Navy, and Air Force have only been promoted to Colonel or equivalent.

The Bangladesh government has taken a number of other steps to institutionalize civilian control. They have abandoned the Pakistani "commander-in-chief" system in favor of a staff system along Indian lines. Bangladesh has also instituted the Indian pattern of financial and publicity control over the military, and has restricted the contacts of the military with the public and press. These and other actions coupled with a strong and decisive political leadership should ensure civilian control in Bangladesh for some

time. On their part, the Bangladesh military seem quite content with this arrangement.

THE EXTERNAL ENVIRONMENT OF THE SOUTH ASIAN MILITARY

Each South Asian military establishment is part of the environment of every other establishment in the region. When we discuss the attitudes and beliefs of a particular officer corps, we are also describing part of the environment of the other officer corps.

The External Environment and Domestic Political Intervention

The officer corps of both India and Pakistan have had wide and varied contacts abroad. The Indian Army was associated with a number of UN operations in Korea, the Congo, and the Middle East, and individual Indian officers have performed important tasks for the UN. India has helped to train several foreign armies and air forces, most notably Ethiopia and Nepal, and its military schools train a number of foreign officers within India. The Indian military have engaged in occasional Commonwealth military exchange programs and the IAF was involved in joint air defense planning with Commonwealth and American air forces after the 1962 conflict with China. When India began to receive military assistance and initiated large scale purchases of weapons her officers came into contact with the military of the United States, Great Britain, and eventually, the Soviet Union. Some Indian officers have been trained abroad in the use of foreign equipment.

The Pakistanis have had an equally wide range of foreign contacts. Through SEATO and CENTO many officers received training in the United States and Great Britain and participated in exchange and training programs with Jordan, Turkey, and Iran. At various times these CENTO allies and the United States have provided quantities of weapons for Pakistan, sometimes covertly and illegally, and the U.S. maintained a large military training mission in Pakistan for many years. Finally, the Pakistan military has developed ties with the Chinese military in part because of Chinese deliveries of weapons and military equipment.

The effect of these foreign contacts on domestic politics is difficult to measure, but some tentative conclusions can be noted. It is doubtful that they have profoundly influenced the values or attitudes of the military of India or Pakistan. Foreign governments probably flatter themselves when they worry about their impact on the politi-

---

[38]The following is based largely upon discussions in Bangladesh in August 1972.

cal attitudes of the South Asian military or the "threat" of the impact of competing governments. This appears to be true at least for India, whose officers are under tight political control. In retrospect it was probably true for pre-civil war Pakistan as well. The most important difference between India and Pakistan has not been in the number of foreign ties, nor in the "winning" or "losing" of support for particular foreign governments among the officer corps, but in the attitude of the military toward the initiation and perpetuation of such ties.

With a few exceptions the Indian military's contacts with other states and military systems have been initiated by civilians, run under civilian supervision, and terminated when civilians wished them to end.[39] Strong political guidance has always been present, and there is no more sensitive issue in the Indian parliament than the possibility of an unsupervised foreign contact with the Indian military. This extraordinary control stems both from a fear of foreign influence growing within the Indian military and, as we shall discuss below, from the compulsions of a policy of nonalignment. Indian officers are quite restrained in their contact with foreign visitors. Even military assistance groups located in India have been denied all but the most necessary contact with their Indian counterparts.

In contrast, the Pakistan military, especially the army, has not only had extensive direct foreign contacts, it has often initiated them. Long before the coup of 1958 the Pakistani military had felt confident enough of its autonomy and independence from civilian control to initiate contacts with various foreign governments. The timing of one contact was crucial: it came at the precise moment that the first democratically elected government of Pakistan was being dismissed by the then Governor-General, and signalled a period of bureaucratic-military rule. From that point onward, the American military tie played a vital role in Pakistani politics, and the military controlled that tie. The special relationship of the Pakistan military to the United States indicated their independence not only in internal military matters but in foreign and alliance policy. As long as the military was able to determine defense requirements they felt justified in expanding their own political power in the face of what was thought to be political incompetence or indifference to military needs. Presently their special ties to foreign states and military establishments have been interrupted at least temporarily by President Bhutto; if he is to restore civilian rule and retain power he must gain control over these foreign military links. If he can effectively manage these relationships, and guarantee a supply of weapons and equipment, it is doubtful that the military will raise many objections to their loss of power.

The Officer Corps and the Regional and International Environments

The members of the various officer corps in South Asia do not differ greatly from each other or from professional colleagues in other states in terms of their general view of international politics or the role of force in the world. Like most soldiers, they tend to have a pessimistic view of the nature of man, and have a belief in the inevitability of conflict and war. Also, like most professionals, they do not particularly anticipate or desire war except as a last resort. This is so even though the military of South Asia spend most of their time analyzing past wars and preparing for future ones. They have had an active military past. In 1947 they engaged in a struggle for control over Kashmir; in 1962 the Indian Army fought a limited but desperate war with China; full-scale war raged in 1965 and again in 1971, during the struggle over Bangladesh. The rate of arms acquisition in both India and Pakistan indicates that the expectation is for more, not less, war.

All of this was important in shaping the attitudes within the Indian and Pakistani military. Before independence the Indian Army had been used primarily for internal security duties, or as an imperial expeditionary force. The expectation of the British, as well as many Indians and Pakistanis, was that the successor states would maintain very low arms levels and perhaps a joint command structure. The high frequency and intensity of warfare has ruled this out. It has meant that the officer corps of India and Pakistan view themselves as professional soldiers, comparable to the officer corps of other modern outward-facing armies. The threat of future conflict continually brings them back to this model. Like most professionals, the military of South Asia tend to have a relatively objective view of each other.[40] Although the individual ties between Indian and Pakistani officers are now very few in number, the two armies do have much in com-

[39]The exceptions include B. M. Kaul, a distant relative of late Jawaharlal Nehru. Kaul was highly atypical in his close political ties with Nehru and other Indian politicians, his idealism, and his sense of destiny and mission. At various times he approached American officials directly.

[40]With the exception of the Pakistani view of India as a nonmartial state described above.

mon due to their shared origins. Finally, the officers of South Asia have an instrumental view of nonregional foreign powers. While their social origins and personal inclinations may be Western, they have long since learned the importance of good relations with various Communist states and other Third World military establishments.

Where the South Asian military do differ, of course, is in their view of each other's objectives and interests and those of states which form part of the South Asian balance of influence. Here there is a substantial difference between the Indian and Pakistani military: Indian officers have always had two main enemies, Pakistan and China, while Pakistan has only one serious military threat, India.

For the officer corps of India and Pakistan, conflict with each other has always carried with it some special characteristics and special problems. Cynical observers have termed the relationship a communal conflict with armor, but it is more than that. Ethnic, cultural, and organizational similarities have made it something of a fraternal struggle. As in such a struggle there are similarities and differences and, above all, a common historical legacy. Part of the legacy is remembered with affection and warmth, but parts are tinged with bitterness and hatred, and have provided the grounds for substantial mistrust. Communal considerations do, of course, complicate this attraction-repulsion relationship. Before the 1971 civil war, Pakistan had a substantial Hindu minority living in East Pakistan, and India's Muslim population alone is now larger than the entire population of West Pakistan. These minorities once constituted a hostage to the good conduct of the two military organizations and placed limits on the overt use of religion as a wartime rallying cry.

Other than the complications brought about by these historic ties between India and Pakistan, the approach of both military establishments to each other, and the approach of the Indians to their long land frontier with the Chinese is quite conventional in military terms. A combination of terrain, weapons technology and military tradition have created what are essentially two relatively modern World War II armies on the Western border between India and Pakistan. The Indians are severely limited in the resources they can apply to the Himalayan border with China, and these resources appear to be deployed in conventional ways. The philosophy of the Indian military at least is to rely upon standard, traditional methods of organization and combat, emphasizing training and discipline, rather than innovation. The Pakistanis did make an ill-fated attempt at sponsoring insurrectionary warfare, and it is doubtful that the experiment will be repeated.

The Compulsions of Nonalignment

A final factor shaping the attitudes of the military of South Asia is the dependent position of the subcontinent in the international system and the severe restrictions on the maneuverability of India and Pakistan.

South Asia has never been an area of overwhelming interest for any of the superpowers or China.[41] The major external powers have viewed the region in terms of their relationship with each other. Geography, resources, poverty, and military utility, all combine to make the region marginal and peripheral for them. This has become especially true since the decline of the Cold War era when the superpowers thought the region was worth keeping out of each other's camp, and Pakistan played a limited intelligence role for the United States.

From the 1950s for India, and from 1961 onward for Pakistan, and from 1971 for Bangladesh, the military of South Asia have become instruments of a reactive foreign policy which recognizes the marginal role of the region. This has variously been termed nonalignment or bi-alignment, but whatever the label it is a policy which whether Indian, Pakistani, or Bangladesh shares some vital assumptions. Briefly, these are: that the major threat comes from the immediate region; that each regional power lacks the resources to adequately defend itself and simultaneously fulfill economic objectives; that external ties must be developed to overcome such deficiencies, and finally, that because of the peripheral nature of the region, no outside power can be fully trusted to fulfil any but the most trivial commitments. This approach was pioneered and developed by the Indians, but the supreme compliment by imitation can be observed in Pakistan and Bangladesh.

This situation has had a profound effect upon the military of South Asia. By social class, education, language, military tradition, and technological interests they might be predisposed to political and military ties with various Western nations. Yet, they have long since bent any

[41]William J. Barads, *India, Pakistan and the Great Powers* (New York: Praeger, 1972). For an informed Indian view see Bhabani Sen Gupta, *The Fulcrum of Asia* (New York: Pegasus, 1970), and Pran Chopra, *The Indo-Soviet Treaty* (New Delhi: S. Chand, 1972), and for Bhutto's current outlook, Mukerjee Dilip, *Zulfikar Ali Bhutto*, (New Delhi: Vikas, 1972). For Bangladesh, "nonalignment" will necessarily include a strong tie to India, but also ties with outside powers to prevent Indian domination.

such personal predilection to political and strategic compulsions. Pakistanis and Indians learned to deal with American sources when the British were unable to meet their requirements, and have since adjusted to Soviet, Chinese, and various East and West European sources of equipment. The military of these two nations, and one must now add that of Bangladesh, are required to balance off a variety of foreign sources and develop a flexibility which makes it impossible to maintain any lingering overt political preference for the West.

CONCLUSION

In concluding this essay about three military establishments which still carry within them so much of their past, it is fitting to invoke a favorite military metaphor of the nineteenth century. This metaphor viewed the officer corps as the "brain" of an army, while the infantry constituted its heart, artillery the muscle, signals the nerves, and so forth.

But the metaphor is incomplete in at least one important way: a brain, by itself, can do nothing, but an officer corps can literally recreate or renew damaged or destroyed parts of an army, or even devise totally new parts to meet new circumstances. This is one of the most important characteristics of the officer corps of South Asia; they have several times been asked to create an organization *de novo*, or adjust to radically changing political or military circumstances. This explains much of their interest in internal matters and organizational integrity, especially in Pakistan (and we judge in the future, Bangladesh). They take their military role seriously, are attentive to an international standard of military excellence, and are painfully aware of the limitations on their own development placed by the social and economic patterns of their supportive societies.

Because of these social and economic constraints (and in India, Bangladesh, and now Pakistan, political and administrative constraints), the military of South Asia tend to have limited ambitions. Their instinct is to survive, to retain what they have, to change, but change only very gradually. This explains their successes and their failures. Where they have completely broken away from tradition and past methods, they have often met with disaster: the Pakistani experiments with guerrilla warfare, the Indian strategy of playing a game of bluff against the Chinese in 1962—without having the resources to see the game to the end. Their successes, however, are no less remarkable. The fact is that the military of India and Pakistan have achieved increasing levels of professional competence through the years; their growth is now self-sustaining, and political compulsions will dictate that the military remain isolated from foreign military influence. Along with increasing professionalism has come a greater sense of realism concerning the limitations on the use of military power in what are essentially political disputes.

Future wars between the nations of South Asia remain a likely possibility, and conflict stemming from both internal instability and extra-regional pressure seems to be an increasing probability. However, it is doubtful that the military themselves will precipitate involvement unless their own professional integrity is threatened.

THE MILITARY AND POLITICS IN ISRAEL

AMOS PERLMUTTER

Professor Perlmutter's discussion of civil-military relations in Israel stresses the depoliticization and nationalization of the Army (Zahal), civilian supremacy, the role of the defense minister as the final arbiter in civil-military conflicts, the control of the defense minister over the integration, morale and professional standards of the officer corps, and the centralized aspects of defense decisionmaking. The role of David Ben Gurion as the architect of Israeli civil-military relations is viewed as crucial. Perlmutter argues that because Zahal is a citizen army and reserve organization, military service is brief, the officers are permanently integrated with society, and the possibility of the officer corps becoming ideologically or politically independent is minimal. He then points out that such military-societal linkages are reinforced by the role of the military as an important instrument of political socialization and by the diffusion of military elites among the industrial technocrats and bureaucratic elites in Israel.

Amos Perlmutter has taught at several institutions such as MIT, Harvard, and the American University, and has written numerous books and articles, including Egypt the Praetorian State *(1973), and* Military and Politics in Israel *(1969) from which this excerpt is taken.*

THE ERA OF TRANSITION

In June 1947 Ben Gurion, the head of the Jewish Agency, took over the defence portfolio. He set out to accomplish two tasks: (1) the reorganization of Haganah, to make it responsible *only* to national authorities; and (2) the rapid and intensive mobilization of men and resources, so that Yishuv would have an army ready to meet the expected Arab invasion.

By October 1947, only six months after Ben Gurion had taken charge of defence matters, Haganah's budget had risen to £3.3 million,[1] the highest in Haganah history. Under his direction the Palmach was strengthened and enlarged; the scope of Haganah's purchasing operation in Europe was widened; a group of former Jewish partisans was organized in France; Jewish volunteers were recruited in the United States; the Jewish Brigade and Haganah were mobilized to bring trained men and volunteers to Palestine; and all the financial resources of World Zionism were invested in the task of arming and training an independent Jewish military force in Palestine. Thus on May 1948 the United Nations assigned date for British departure from Palestine, Ben Gurion had an army ready to command.

In order to accomplish the above, Ben Gurion had to unify the autonomous and semi-autonomous military structures which had previously been responsible for those functions. The task was monumental but he proved equal to it. He moved toward unification in stages, gradually achieving his objective by transferring all military functions to the Provisional Government under his authority. In the process, he abolished Haganah's headquarters, its general staff, and the parity system by which promotions were determined. The rivalries between the various military organizations in Palestine complicated his task and he found opposition coming from all directions. The NMO refused to accept the authority of the Provisional Government and the Palmach persisted in operating its own general staff, even though it acknowledged the authority of the Provisional Government and its defence minister.

---

[1] Ben Zion Dinour *et al.* (eds.), *Sepher Toldot Ha-Haganah (History of the Haganah)* (Heb.), Vol. II, Part III (Tel Aviv: Ma'arachot, 1964), p. 44.

Excerpted with permission from The Military and Politics in Israel *(New York: Praeger Publishers, 1967), pp. 49–79. Reprinted by permission of Praeger Publishers, Inc., New York, and Frank Cass and Co., Ltd., London.*

CIVIL-MILITARY RELATIONS: THE ISRAELI FORMULA

The transformation of Israel's voluntary, semi-professional, and highly politicized security organizations into a unified, compulsory, professional, and depoliticized army was accomplished by the determination and skill of David Ben Gurion. As Premier and Defence Minister from 1947 to 1963 (interrupted for 15 months between 1953 and 1955), Ben Gurion stamped his indelible mark on Israel's army and Defence Ministry. More than any other factors, his personality and nationalist vision shaped the course of civil–military relations in the new state of Israel.

In April 1948, the Provisional Government's defence portfolio was formally instituted as the Ministry of Defence in the government of Israel. In assuming responsibility for defence, Ben Gurion recalls that "I made it clear to the Provisional Government when it delegated the defence portfolio to me . . . that I would accept the ministry only under the following conditions: (1) The army that will be formed [Zahal] and all its branches be subordinated to the government of the people and only to *that* government. (2) All persons acting on behalf of the army or the Haganah will act only according to a clearly defined function established by the government of the people. The procedures which prevailed in the Haganah could not and will not prevail when the army of the state of Israel will be established."[2]

The following are the unwritten but firmly institutionalized concepts and procedures initiated by the first defence minister of Israel:

1. The nationalization, formalization, and depoliticization of the army.

2. The supremacy of civilian authorities in determining the issues of war and peace in Israel.

3. The defence minister as the final arbiter of conflicts between civilians and the military.

4. The direct and permanent control of the defence minister over the integrity, the morale, and the professional standards of the officer corps.

5. A highly centralized decisionmaking process in matters of defence and related foreign policy issues limited to a small and highly cohesive group of civilian and military selected and dominated by the defence minister.

As Defence Minister, Ben Gurion set out to accomplish the following: (1) To consolidate all offices and functions related to security held previously by independent or autonomous political or military structures by centralizing authority in his hands. (2) To define and separate the functions of chief of staff and "head of war" previously fused in the office of the head of Haganah.

At the helm of the Defence Ministry, Ben Gurion assumed the policy-making function of "head of war" while Zahal's chief of staff was delegated the operational function of maintaining and training the army—the instrument of war. The chief of staff, although clearly subordinate to the defence minister, was allowed considerable independence and autonomy on purely military matters. A parallel office of director general was created in the Defence Ministry to administer the support function of supplying and arming the military. The director general was independent of the army and directly subordinate to the defence minister. The appointment of Zahal's chief of staff and the director general of the Ministry was ultimately the responsibility of the defence minister.

Although the formal organization of the defence establishment determined the basic operational ground rules, personalities played at least an equal role in influencing the development of institutional practices and procedures.

Having assumed the position of head of war, Ben Gurion created an *ad hoc* kitchen cabinet to advise him, which was composed of one or two favourite cabinet members, Mapai's "army specialists," several senior civil servants, Zahal's chief of staff, the chief of intelligence, and a few selected senior officers and personal advisers. The members of the group met only at Ben Gurion's request and their individual or collective influence varied according to circumstances and force of personality; unswerving loyalty to Ben Gurion was the common bond between them. The group advised not only on questions of military strategy and doctrine but on foreign policy issues as well. This *ad hoc* cabinet was vested with responsibility for making major decisions concerning Israel's security and the army's future. Cabinet ministers, while exempted from the actual decisionmaking process, were nevertheless expected to approve and defend these policies at home and abroad.

Among those around Ben Gurion were Shaul Avigor, the former Head of Haganah, Iser Arel, the Chief of Intelligence and Espionage, *Ha-Mosad* (not to be confused with Zahal's Intelligence Division, *Aman*), and other *ad hoc* "security experts."

The type of authority which Ben Gurion exer-

---

[2]Ben Gurion, Preface, *op. cit.*, p. 54. (Ben Gurion's italics.)

cised in relation to his subordinates would be defined by Weber as charismatic authority. Weber's biographer, Bendix, has characterized this as "domination on the basis of leadership, the extraordinary power of a person and the identification of followers with that person."[3] Such authority is legitimatized by the creation of disciples, which is not easy to do, especially in a democratic society like Israel. But two disciples emerged and became dominant figures in their own right. They were General Moshe Dayan, Zahal's Chief of Staff from 1953 to 1957, and Shimon Peres, who was Director General from 1953 to 1959 and Deputy Defence Minister from 1959 to 1965.

In prestige and importance, the Defence Ministry has always ranked second to Zahal. The army fell heir to the reputation and role of its predecessor, Haganah, while the Defence Ministry was relegated to the unglamorous task of quarter-mastership. Zahal officers have traditionally regarded the Ministry as a cluster of "clerks and merchants."

While Zahal received the best of intellectual and organizational attention, the Ministry of Defence was neglected. In its early days, the Ministry was run by prominent politicians and technocrats such as Levi Eshkol (its first Director General and now the Prime Minister), Pinhas Sapir (its second Director General, formerly Minister of Finance and now Secretary General of Israel Labour Party, M'ai), Israel Galeeli (First Deputy Minister of Defence, now Minister of Information), Shaul Avigor (Head of Haganah), and others. When it became apparent to these politicians that the Defence Ministry was dominated by Ben Gurion, they saw little opportunity to further their own ambitions and left. Galeeli was phased out, but continued to serve occasionally on an ad hoc basis, over a dispute with Ben Gurion on the relationships between the minister and Zahal. According to Ben Gurion, Galeeli agreed with him that the Palmach headquarters should be abolished and that its battalions could be directly under the chief command (Zahal's general staff), but that he, Galeeli, would be the intermediary between the defence minister (Ben Gurion) and Zahal's chief of staff. In the end Ben Gurion prevailed

and Galeeli did resign; and the office of Head of Haganah was finally abolished by Ben Gurion.[4]

Although Ben Gurion is frequently given credit for having strengthened the civilian arm of defence, he actually boosted the role of Zahal as against the Ministry. As Minister of Defence, he institutionalized the primacy of the army in the Ministry, primarily for personal and political reasons. He established a special type of relationship with the army's high command and during Dayan's tenure as Chief of Staff was on especially close terms with the senior officers who were moulded in the Ben Gurion–Dayan image. In contrast to his intense interest in military affairs, Ben Gurion generally left the administration of the Defence Ministry to its directors except where high-level political decisions were involved.

Officially, the army was responsible to the government of Israel—a coalition composed of Mapai and the small Socialist, religious, and liberal parties. In reality, however, neither Mapai nor Mapai ministers in the cabinet had very much influence over the army. The smaller parties in the coalition were rarely consulted on army or defence matters. The Knesset's Defence and Foreign Affairs Committee was a docile and pro forma group. From outside the government, the United Labour Party still exercised some influence on military decisions because of its strong historical involvement with defence. Galeeli, Allon, and former Palmach commanders were consulted on defence matters, but beyond this their influence declined. The kibbutz movement still conducted defence seminars (organized by former Palmach officers) and offered criticism, but to little effect.

For all practical purposes, the army fell solely under the jurisdiction of Ben Gurion in his dual role of Prime Minister and Minister of Defence. He exercised control over the defence establishment by assuming the responsibility for making the final decision on foreign policy matters relating to war and peace and by his power to appoint and promote top-level army officers. In this sense, he acted more as supreme commander than as defence minister.

Ben Gurion viewed Israel as a state with its back to the sea, surrounded by hostile Arab governments. In these circumstances, the fate

---

[3]See Reinhard Bendix, Max Weber: An Intellectual Portrait (Garden City: Doubleday, 1960), p. 302. On charismatic authority, explanation, and controversy, see recent literature on newly emerging political systems and their problems which has given a widespread use to the sociological term charisma which its originator, Max Weber, never anticipated.

[4]This new information relating only Ben Gurion's point of view is found in his serialized memoirs beginning in Ma-Ariv (April 30, 1968). See Ben Gurion, "From the Diary," op. cit., pp. 25–26. The basic points introduced here have already been made by Ben Gurion in preface, History of the War.

of the nation rested on the ability of the army to defend it and the political wisdom of the man responsible for the conduct of foreign policy.

In order to keep the army from engaging in party politics and to make Zahal more professional, Ben Gurion assumed power to approve all appointments and promotions from chief of staff down to lieutenant-colonel. The outgoing chief of staff had considerable influence on the choice of a successor. Before acting on his recommendation, however, Ben Gurion usually consulted some of his chief informal advisers. When it came to determining the appointment or promotion of other senior officers, Ben Gurion relied heavily on the recommendations of the chief of staff and members of the high command, and he and Dayan worked especially well together for Dayan was a loyal Ben Gurionite, dedicated to the same principles as his chief.[5] In this way Ben Gurion did leave the high command considerable political leverage over security and promotions policy.

Ben Gurion used his appointive powers to assure that the army maintained a youthful leadership. He believed that an army composed mainly of reserves should be geared to handle rapid shifts in rank to allow for the emergence of new talent.[6] As this would suggest, promotions at levels below the high command were based primarily on merit and, on the whole, a suitably apolitical and professional atmosphere was maintained. As will be shown, however, not even Ben Gurion's considerable efforts could entirely prevent a powerful army high command system from intervening in politics.

Under General Dayan, the powers and prestige of Zahal's chief of staff and the high command far outweighed those of the director general of the Ministry. This did not occur because of strong personalities in Zahal and weak ones in the Defence Ministry, nor because of Ben Gurion's propensity to favour the army over the Ministry. It resulted from Zahal's superior prestige, cohesion, and purpose. The Defence Ministry was a relative newcomer which had not yet distinguished itself nor could it share with Zahal the credit for liberating the nation in 1948.

The army was actually the first bureaucratic structure to be successfully transformed from an autonomous pre-independence organization into a truly national institution subordinate to the government. This was achieved by taking the army out of politics.

Ben Gurion banned political groups from operating actively within Zahal and replaced the political parity system with a merit system for determining appointments and promotions. His objective was clear: the removal of the left from the positions of influence they had secured in the defence establishment. In doing so, Ben Gurion frustrated the ambitions of many Palmach commanders and ideologues. They eventually made a mass exodus from the army and were followed by many ranking politicians who resigned from the Defence Ministry.

The problem was how to thwart the formation of a leftist people's army or the creation of a professional clique divorced from the nation and its ideals. Ben Gurion succeeded in averting these extremes by establishing an army whose ideological and moral values were democratic and egalitarian and not collectivist—a Socialist people's army—or professionalist, operating outside the context of Israel's goals and social values.

The dissolution of Palmach's general staff and the NMO was no small task. Throughout 1948–49, a controversy raged in the councils of the HOL, in the cabinet, in Zahal's high command, and among the public over the future of Palmach in Zahal. The question was also reflected in the parliamentary debates on the Defence Service Bill, the Veteran's Law, and the Military Jurisdiction Law.

Ben Gurion, supported by Avigor and Generals Dori (Zahal's first Chief of Staff), and Yadin (its second Chief of Staff), advocated the creation of a professional regular army with a vast and permanent reserve system, while former Palmach commanders and ideologues, led by Sadeh, Allon, and Galeeli, promoted the formation of a people's army, very much like Palmach, based on small and highly mobile units, whose backbone remains the collective agricultural system, but especially maintaining the high command close to Palmach.

The transformation of Haganah into Zahal was made relatively easy because of the war. "Due to the urgent matters of war and the declaration of independence," writes Ben Gurion, "no final decision concerning the organization of Zahal took place in the meetings of the Provisional Government. . . . So the decision of the

---

[5]Interviews during the summer of 1967 with most members of Dayan's former General Staff (1953–58), have convinced me of Dayan's clear understanding of the line between military and civilian responsibilities.

[6]Between 1948 and 1967 Israel had seven chiefs of staff, and all but two were under 40 years old when appointed. Among senior officers, mobility was similar to that of the junior officers and the average ages proportionately low: 40 to 44 for brigadier-generals, 35 to 40 for colonels, and 30 to 35 for lieutenant-colonels.

Provisional Government and the organization of Zahal [on the final authority of the defence minister in matters of defence] did not prevail due to the divisions within the military forces."[7] National unity against the Arab invaders prevailed over particular and politically interested groups.

The integration of the formerly autonomous military organizations into Zahal could have been accomplished only with their co-operation. Because Zahal's new general staff was a carry-over from Haganah's general staff, the co-operation between Palmach's Southern Command and Zahal's headquarters was understandably smooth. Generals Yadin and Laskov later testified to this in the midst of the Palmach challenge to Ben Gurion's leadership. The war eased the integration of autonomous military units by uniting them under one command. But the key to the accomplishment of this formidable task was the persistent, stubborn, and autocratic personality—Ben Gurion. From 1947 to his last day as Defence Minister in 1963, Zahal was his chief concern.

Ben Gurion's efforts to dissolve and remove the extrapolitical and the ideological aspects inherited by Zahal from Haganah, Palmach, and the NMO, ran into formidable opposition. Even those officers who favoured depoliticization of the army were reluctant to abandon the Haganah and Palmach legacies. A group of Palmach officers, including their most prominent officer and former commander, Yigal Allon, resigned from the army as soon as the armistice with the Arabs at Rhodes (1949) was concluded.

These officers, on the whole, argued that the professionalization of the army and the "isolation" of its officer corps would undermine the pioneer-egalitarian spirit of the kibbutz and Palmach, and that it could also undermine the commitment to service of Israeli society. This group generally advocated extrapolitical functions for the army and especially for its officer corps. Ben Gurion and other senior officers strongly believed that the army's primary task was on the battlefield; they envisioned a small, but highly professional, army. Ben Gurion probably overreacted to the NMO and Palmach controversies, for in the end even he could not accept such a narrow role for the Israeli army.

It was hope that dedication to professional skills in a stable society would decrease the extra-curricular and political activities of the professionals. And indeed, the functional proliferation of the Israeli army has not only reduced

but, in some ways, extinguished the political concern in dedicated officers. The military was limited to its function—protecting the state from external aggression and war.

A comprehensive study of political articulation and commitment, and political interventionist tendencies (and we clearly separate the two) of Zahal's officer corps is not yet available. Political articulation is correlated to the educational level of the officers and Israeli officers born in the Arab countries with low education are low in political consciousness. The better trained and educated are politically articulate but also highly professional. Politically conscious to a high degree are young officers from the kibbutzim, especially from Mapam Socialist collectives.

On the whole, the social isolation (not to be confused with a societal isolation) of professional officers and their apolitical attitudes has been greater than among the Haganah–Palmach and the 1948–50 Zahal officer corps. However, this type of corporate and professional separatism is the hallmark of the professional soldier. Because Zahal is a people's army and a reserve organization, its barracks life is short, the officers are permanently integrated with society, and the chances of officers becoming ideologically or professionally independent are minimal. In Israel, the chance of a particularly long military career is remote because the officer corps is continuously rotated and thus is kept young.

The kibbutzim encourage their young men to volunteer for training as pilots, paratroopers, or other élite military occupations. One of Ben Gurion's major efforts, after 1956, was to direct kibbutz-born inductees to join these élite corps; the experience of Sinai had proven to him that a high proportion of able and valiant leaders had come from the agrarian collective settlements.[8] This was reaffirmed in 1967. While the collective settlements are no more than 4% of Israel's population, 25% of the total killed and wounded Zahal officers were from the kibbutzim.

The training of young officers (ages 17–19) emphasizes their role as leaders and socializers. The fraternity type and the small group are still the models for Israeli army units. Many of Palmach's leadership training principles have been included in the army's officer training programme and, as in the Palmach, the *mem-mem* (platoon leader) is to serve as a model for the new recruits, most of whom have immigrated to

---

[7]Ben Gurion, Preface, *op. cit.*, p. 54.

[8]For an interesting study of the role of the kibbutz born in Zahal, see Yehudah Amir, "Sons of Kibbutzim in Zahal," *Megamot* (Heb.) 15, no. 2–3 (August 1967): 250–58.

Israel since 1948. The career of a junior officer is totally dependent upon achievement, and leadership ability is the key to promotion. Only a small number of men elect the army as a career. After a few years' service, the junior officer is considered ready to pursue further education or to assume junior management positions in industry and government.

Prior to 1962 most senior officers had originally served in the Palmach, the Haganah, or the British army, but since then they have been joined by men who were junior officers during the Sinai Campaign.

. The senior officers provided a valuable core of leadership in the early phases of political modernization but few, if any, leaders with political interventionist inclinations have emerged from the present senior officer group.

The most significant change in political institutions and practices in the new state was the growing formalization and bureaucratization: voluntary civil action gave way to formal compulsory service. The creation of Zahal from the Haganah illustrates how a colonizing movement and a society of social mission, predominantly maintained with primary, non-formalized groups, were transformed into formal bureaucratic structures.

S. N. Eisenstadt holds that "All this did not give rise to a pure Weberian type of neutral bureaucracy. The non-bureaucratic elements existed not only on the top, directive levels . . . but became strongly interwoven also at other levels."[9] The organization of Zahal corroborates all aspects of this change: from voluntary to compulsory social and political action; from non-formal to formal organization; and intervention of non-bureaucratic elements at all levels.

The process by which Yishuv institutions and structures were politically demobilized deserves attention both for historical and analytical reasons. Although this is not the place to deal with the subject in depth, it is noteworthy in view of Zahal's distinction as the first structure to be successfully institutionalized and bureaucratized.

In Israel, the demobilization of a number of institutions and structures was correlated with the dictates of political power. The power of most Yishuv organizations derived from the voluntary groups which supported them. The political task of the government, the bureaucracy and the army, therefore, was to nationalize and formalize these institutions, structures, and procedures.

To politically disarm these structures required, of course, a monumental effort. The philosophy inherent in the policies of the Yishuv and Socialist-Zionism was Revolutionary Constructivism—a doctrine of accumulating political, social, and economic power under the Mandatory—which led to the establishment of powerful and interested political and economic structures to fulfill their goals.

Zahal was the first to be nationalized and formalized. In fact, it was to become the model of a demobilized, institutional, and bureaucratic structure in Israel. Had the army remained politically autonomous—styling itself along the mobilizing principles of UKM—it would have become a political instrument of the small, but militant, pioneer élite based in the agricultural settlements and in the kibbutzim.[10]

And yet, the process of formalization in the army after the integration of Palmach–NMO into Zahal could not proceed without the legacy of the past. The tasks of modernization, rapid integration of immigrants, and functional proliferation imposed upon Zahal a new role—the maker of citizens, the inculcator of civic and nationalist culture. Here the traditions of Haganah and Palmach were again of great service—not as a component for the accumulation of political, social, and economic power but as an instrument of the state advancing the aims of national integration, political mobilization, and economic modernization.

Ben Gurion established the HOL to strengthen the state, not particularist interests. He argued that the leadership of the HOL,

---

[9]Eisenstadt, "Israel," op. cit., p. 427.

[10]The processes by which the Yishuv's institutional and social structures were depoliticized should be of interest to scholars concerned with political development and modernization. Israel could serve as an excellent case study and model for analysing the elements and parameters of political and social mobilization. The Israelis refer to the processes of national integration since 1948 as *Mamlachtiout. Mamlacha* means kingdom and the analogy is taken from the Biblical reign of the Judges when the twelve divided tribes were finally united in the first Jewish kingdom. *Mamlachtiout* means the process of ingathering the Jews, political and social mobilization by the government, bureaucratization, formalization, and the integration of the immigrants. The conceptual framework for the study of *mamlachtiout*, or political integration, was laid by Eisenstadt in *Israeli Society* (New York: Basic Books, 1968), and *Absorption of Immigrants, op. cit.,* also in his "Patterns of Leadership and Social Homogeneity in Israel," *International Social Science Bulletin* 8 (Fall 1959): 36–53. The concept of political integration is closely linked in sociological literature with the concepts of political and social mobilization and modernization. The process of making a nation or a people "whole" or "entire," is found in the literature associated with the transfer of "old social, economic and psychological commitments" to "new patterns of socialization and behavior" (Karl W. Deutsch, "Social Mobilization and Political Development," *The American Political Science Review* 55, no. 3 (September 1961): 494).

caught up in its socialistic preconceptions, was arresting the processes of modernization so vital to the future of Israel. He also felt that Mapai had lost its erstwhile vision. Thus he was determined to turn the institutions of the new state—the government, and especially Zahal—into carriers of the lost vision which he sought to restore within new political procedures and institutions.

"The primary function of the ZHL has been to safeguard the state," Ben Gurion wrote. "However, this is not its sole function. The army must also serve as *an educational and pioneering centre* for Israeli youth—for both those born here and newcomers. It is the duty of the army to educate a pioneer generation, healthy in body and spirit, courageous and loyal, which will unite the broken tribes and diasporas to prepare itself to fulfil the historical tasks of the State of Israel through self-realization."

In 1949 these statements sounded more like prophecy than statesmanship. Time has vindicated Ben Gurion's vision of the army as a citizens' academy, the inculcator of public spirit.

ZAHAL'S ROLE EXPANSION

Zahal's extra-military functions—those activities not directly related to warfare—are a critical aspect of civil–military relations in Israel. In developing states, breakdowns in modernization, an uneven development in social and political mobilization, or inadequate integration have often created situations where the army must assume the tasks of managing and directing economic, agricultural, and educational enterprises. In such situations the army usually intervenes because of the absence, impotence, or indifference of other élites.[11] In Israel, however, there was *no* such modernization breakdown. The task of modernizing and integrating fell upon civilian organizations and the army simply complemented their work.

In Israel there is a reasonable and well-established reciprocity between the civilian stratification, economic, and political systems and the social and stratification systems of the army. In other words, the *exchange* of goods, services, and skills between these two sectors and the revolution in modern military doctrines has

closed the gap between these two sectors. This is so for the following reasons:

a) The rate of technological change has accelerated and a wider diversity of skill is required to maintain the military establishment.

b) The diversification and specialization of military technology have lengthened the time of formal training required for mastery of military technology, with the result that the temporary citizen army becomes less important and the completely professional army more vital.

c) The complexity of the machinery of warfare and the requirement for research, development, and technical maintenance tend to weaken the line of organization between the military and the nonmilitary. The result is that the differentiation between the soldier and the civilian is seriously weakened.[12] In all these trends, the model of the professional soldier is being changed by "civilianizing" the military élite to a greater extent than the civilian élite is militarized.

Zahal's participation in nation-building was dictated by Israel's special needs:

The involvement of Zahal in functions which are not purely military is no function of any particular ideology. It is not the desire on the part of Zahal to be an innovator but a condition of Israeli reality. The circumstances surrounding Israel demand a *pioneer army*; an army not bound by routine military functions but an army fulfilling nation-building functions. The army in a state of ingathering the immigrants must participate in this effort.[13]

Ben Gurion assigned Zahal many of the functions which had formerly been performed exclusively by the pioneers. In taking on these tasks, the army assumed the pioneer image as well. Thus the *esprit de corps* of Zahal was nourished by the pioneer legacy of the past.

In the realm of education, the argument for assigning Zahal the mission of ingathering and integrating Israel's mass immigration—between 1948 and 1955—was that it could penetrate areas either neglected or impenetrable by civilian authorities and other national institutions. The postwar immigrants lacked the political dedication, intellectual commitments, and organizational genius, characteristic of those who came prior to independence and consequently required more intensive indoctrination and orientation.

---

[11]See Moshe Lissak, "Modernization and Role Expansion of the Military in Developing Countries: A Comparative Analysis," *Comparative Studies in Society and History* 9, no. 3 (April 1967): 233–55. I am grateful to Professor Lissak for ideas, advice, and help in developing the theme of this chapter.

[12]See Morris Janowitz, *The Professional Soldier* (New York: Free Press, 1960), pp. 347–442; Janowitz and Roger Little, *Sociology and the Military Establishment* (New York: Russell Sage, rev. ed. 1965), pp. 9–26.

[13]*Bamachane* (Zahal's weekly) (February 15, 1951), p. 16.

During this same period, the Defence Ministry expanded military-related industries which had been pioneered by the Haganah before and during the War of Liberation. Shimon Peres (1953–65) guided the Ministry into the areas of applied military science and technology. Under his administration, the Defence Ministry took over the armaments industry, expanded the aviation industry, established the electronics industry, and forged ahead on nuclear research and development. Zahal officers and veterans play a key role in the management of all such enterprises and a special relationship between the Ministry and Zahal has developed as a result of this exchange of services.

The Defence Ministry and Zahal also cooperate with the civilian sectors of Israeli society in training manpower to meet the increasingly exacting requirements of new science and technology. Here the Defence Ministry, Zahal, and the civilian sector have formed an exchange system whereby each sector prepares manpower for the other.[14]

Education

Zahal's educational activities can be broken down into two main types. The first embraces information, indoctrination, and entertainment programmes aimed at strengthening the civic and national consciousness of the recruits. The second category encompasses efforts to raise the level of manpower prior to induction and to ready soldiers and officers for smooth integration into society upon completion of military service.

In 1952, a military specialization programme was proposed to complement the humanities, science, and agriculture programmes already existing in the high schools. This effort was to be tied in with the formation of a military academy, connected with Israel's foremost high schools, the *Reali* Gymnasium in Haifa and the *Herzelia* Gymnasium in Tel-Aviv.

Supporters of the proposal, led by General Yadin—then Commander in Chief—argued that the function of Israeli high schools was not only to train future scientists but also officers; that the training of officers was a civic function in Israel; and that military education at this level would raise the standards of Zahal's officer corps.[15] The proposal's critics—mainly senior

high school teachers and members of the left kibbutz movement—argued that such a system would foster the growth of an army élite, a special class of officers, which would be contrary to the ideals of Israel. The controversy was resolved by compromise: the proposal for a military specialization programme in high school was dropped but a military academy was established in conjunction with the *Reali* School so that future cadets might "mix" with "civilians."

The flood of immigrants coming into Israel from the East had a great impact on the social and educational structure of the post-1950 army. The level of educational attainment of its officers was of special concern to the army. To close the educational gap within officer groups and between officers and conscripts, Zahal provided special schools to teach Hebrew and related subjects to newcomers. Women have figured prominently in this effort as teachers.

The army also moved into areas which were largely neglected by civilian authorities. This includes education among the lower classes and in geographically remote territories. Special attention was given to the educationally deprived, the high-school drop-outs, and the late developers, by establishing a special army educational centre—Camp Marcus, on Mt. Carmel, which was built in 1948, and trained 4,830 soldiers between 1948 and 1950.[16] The drive to eliminate illiteracy in the army began in 1955. Elementary education—compulsory in Israel—was adopted by the army and was provided to 6,500 soldiers in 1966.[17]

Nahal

A no less important function of the army is played by Zahal's special army unit, the *Nahal* (Fighting Youth Movement) whose erstwhile leaders were former members of Palmach. The men in Nahal carry on the tradition of farmer-soldiers, working in border kibbutzim while serving in the army. Some kibbutzim are Nahal creations (Nahal-Oz, Almagor, and others) and frequently the servicemen remain in the border collective settlements (usually on the most sensitive spots at the Syrian or Egyptian borders) they have helped establish after discharge from the service. The Nahal currently plays a key role in settling the Israeli occupied territories in the Golan Heights (Nahal Golan) and in Northern Sinai (Nahal Sinai), Beisan Valley (Nahal Regev). Nahal also conducts special courses for

---

[14]This has also been true of the American army since World War II, where most electronics, radio, and television technicians receive their training.

[15]On the controversy and the views of General Yadin and others, see *Bamachane* (February 28, 1952), pp. 3, 16. Also consult *Ha-Aretz* during the same period.

[16]"Camp Marcus," *Bamachane* (July 20, 1950): 7–8.

[17]*Bamachane* (October 29, 1967): 10.

agricultural instructors who are to assume leadership positions in new immigrant settlements.[18]

The Nahal programme, like Palmach, is composed of volunteers recruited mainly from the collective and co-operative agricultural settlements and from the pioneer Socialist youth movements in the cities. In purpose, ideology, and structure, the Nahal is modelled after the Palmach.

Like the Palmach, the Nahal conceives itself as the élite of the pioneer groups. The Nahal, however, does not serve as the reservoir *par excellence* of Zahal's officer cadre as was the case with Palmach. The chances that Nahal recruits will continue their careers as agricultural settlers are far greater than the possibility that they will become officers.[19]

Nahal does not play in Zahal the role that Palmach played in the Haganah. Nahal was created in the spirit of the old agricultural pioneer settlements (before 1948) which regarded the kibbutz as an instrument to conquer the land. While the kibbutz and the Palmach movement served as the chief political and social mobilizers in Israel, Nahal and its kibbutzim are only one aspect of Zahal's role expansion. On the other hand, as Zahal's chief export to African nations, Nahal enhances the influence of Zahal in foreign affairs and has become a major supplier of military aid.[20]

Defence Industries

The Defence Ministry adopted the Haganah tradition of self-sufficiency in weapon-making, relying as little as possible on foreign weapons suppliers. This policy necessitated the formation of a sizeable industrial and scientific research complex which has developed weapons and techniques of warfare unique to the Israelis.[21]

The munitions industry originally developed as a branch of Haganah. Under the Defence Ministry it has grown from a small-scale arms manufacturing operation into a highly complex electronics industry. The Ministry is engaged in both the production and purchase of weapons. These two functions have strengthened the Ministry's leverage with respect to the development and supervision of aircraft and electronics corporations, which are estimated to employ more than 20,000 people.

The army developed special technical schools and courses, designed to create a technologically skilled cadre to fill industrial manpower needs. The army also set up a special office (in connection with the Defence Ministry) for career counselling and occupational placement of skilled servicemen and officers. This is to facilitate the absorption of army veterans into civilian society.

In 1966 the Air Force Technical High School was opened. The Air Force had been training technicians and laboratory men since its formation in 1948, and the opening of its own school attracted Air Force volunteers and guaranteed them a career after their service was completed.

The Defence Ministry's "invasion" into areas of technological modernization and private industry, especially electronics, and its control over industrial-scientific corporations connected with military functions, has been justified by the argument that only the Ministry could do the job. When Israel gained independence, its industries were small, with little capital to invest, and poor administrative talent. The Ministry, on the other hand, was financially and administratively capable of maintaining munitions, aircraft, and electronic industries even at high cost and loss. Critics of the Ministry claim that it has an efficient administration and that, being subject to civil service regulations, it is uneconomical for the Ministry to control all its extended functions.

Since the 1967 war the Defence Ministry expanded its electronics, aircraft, and missile industries. This is also a considerable contribution to economic growth and industrial modernization and proliferation in Israel. The slow and poor response of the private and some of the public sector to the orders of the Ministry again indicates the extraordinary role of the Ministry's advocates on the contribution of the military–industrial complex to economic modernization in Israel and above all the creation of greater capabilities for weapon autarchy on the part of Israel.

Control over Science

In Israel, science has always been closely tied to security. As early as 1947, the Haganah

---

[18] *Bamachane* (May 5, 1955). In 1966 the Nahal organized its first industrial cadre to work in the newly built Negev city, Arad. On the relations between the army and the Youth Movement, see *Etzioni*, "Israeli Army," *op. cit.*, pp. 6–7.

[19] On Nahal's training programme and participants, see Irving Heymount, "The Israeli Nahal Program," *The Middle East Journal* 21, no. 3 (Summer 1967): 319–24.

[20] A list of Nahal programmes in Asian, African, and Latin American countries is found in Heymount, *ibid.*, p. 314. See also I. Oron (ed.), *Middle East Record 1960* (London: Weidenfeld and Nicolson, 1962), pp. 302–03, 306–15; and *Middle East Record 1961* (Tel-Aviv: Israel Oriental Society, 1967), pp. 333–44.

[21] On defence industries and their relation to Israel's economy, see Sir Leon Bagrit, "The Modernization of Israel," *Ha-Boker* (April 4, 1965); Zeev Shiff, "Controversies in the Defence System," *Ha-Aretz* (August 12, December 14, December 21, 1966); Philip Offer, "Between the Army and the Civilians," *Ha-Aretz* (November 20, 1963); General Chaim Hertzog, "Industry and Security," *Ha-Aretz* (March 25, 1966); Y. Elitzur, "Invaders to the Civilian Industries," *Ma-Ariv* (January 4, 1963).

organized the Hemed (scientific branch of Zahal) which enlisted Israel's best scientists. The scientific army was inherited by Zahal but has since been incorporated into the Ministry of Defence. In this manner the production of nuclear weapons has been separated from the military proper.

In the area of nuclear technology and the application of atomic and nuclear energy to both peaceful and military uses, the Defence Ministry is the supreme authority. Israel's nuclear reactors and missile factories are subject to the Ministry's control and supervision.[22] Shimon Peres' greatest achievement was the development of the nuclear reactor at Dimona which greatly enhanced both his and the Ministry's reputation.

Zahal willingly surrendered the munitions industries and nuclear research and development to its civilian counterpart because they detracted from the army's efficiency and mobility. The fewer bureaucratic structures, argue Zahal senior officers, the more flexible the army.

Military and Society

Changes in the structure of the army élite in Israel have produced a remarkable change in its ideology. No longer does it entertain the political expectations of the Palmach or the NMO. It acts as one élite among others—an élite whose organizational tasks have been recruited to nation-building, economic modernization, and national integration.

The military élites have been diffused among the industrial-technocrats and bureaucratic élites of Israel. A tacit but highly institutionalized pattern has been established between the army and society. For the benefit of a vigorous and mobile army, officer turnover in Zahal is rapid; the society then absorbs the much-needed retired young officers.

The high requirements for efficiency and merit in Zahal naturally make Zahal's veterans a most desirable element in civic society. Zahal's

graduates are achievement-orientated, and are pragmatic, experienced managers. The highly nepotistic Histadrut enterprises; the politically appointed senior civil servants; the government-dominated "private" co-operatives; and the politically orientated kibbutzim, all compete for the politically "neutral" and administration-orientated Zahal officers. Thus a Zahal officer develops an *alternative* career while still serving in the army.

Senior officers may take a leave of absence with the army's encouragement to study economic-administrative skills. The majority concentrate on economics, business administration, or operations research, either in Israel or abroad (Great Britain, France, United States), others prepare for a law or university career.

It is impossible for a student of the military and society in Israel not to observe the close interplay between the two. No simple cry of an industrial–military complex could dismiss the subject. Nor could the pioneer legacy explain all the motives behind Zahal's role expansion. The organizational, administrative, and human resources of Zahal have been successfully exploited by Israeli society for its own expansion, industrial growth, and modernization. It is equally true that Zahal successfully exploits its image as heir to the pioneer and its high prestige, both of which raise the status of its officers in the eyes of the public.

Role expansion represents the equilibrium achieved by Zahal between its strictly professional functions and the voluntaristic legacy of its pioneer forerunners. The transfer of the functions of a mission-oriented community to a military apparatus and its bureaucratic structures and the interplay of two opposing orientations— professional versus voluntaristic attitudes— shaped this army in a way which could not have been predicted by either orientation. Zahal's role since independence has been charted along these patterns, neither of which has gained ascendancy over, nor excluded, the other. A typology of officers in Zahal could be established according to these orientations but would, of course, be beyond the scope of this study.

---

[22]The Atomic Energy Commission and its directors are employees of the Defence Ministry.

BIBLIOGRAPHY: THE MILITARY PROFESSION

Abdel-Malek, Anouar. *Egypt: Military Society*. New York: Vintage Books, 1968.

*Abrahamsson, Bengt. *Military Professionalism and Political Power*. Beverly Hills: Sage, 1972.

Allon, Yigal. *The Making of Israel's Army*. New York: Universe Books, 1970.

Al-Qazzaz, Ayad. "Army and Society in Israel." *Pacific Sociological Review* 16, no. 2 (April 1973): 143–65.

*Ambler, John Steward. *Soldiers Against the State: The French Army in Politics*. Garden City, New York: Doubleday, 1968.

Andreski, Stanislav. *Military Organization and Society*. Berkeley: Univ. of California Press, 1968.

Astiz, Carlos A. "The Argentine Armed Forces: Their Role and Political Involvement." *The Western Political Quarterly* 22, no. 4 (December 1969): 862–78.

Barnett, Correlli. *Britain and Her Army, 1509–1970*. New York: William Morrow, 1970.

Baynes, J. C. M. *The Soldier in Modern Society*. London: Eyre Methuen, 1972.

*Beeri, Eliezer. *Army Officers in Arab Politics and Society*. New York: Frederick A. Praeger, 1970.

*Bienen, Henry (ed.). *The Military Intervenes*. New York: Russell Sage Foundation, 1968.

———. *The Military and Modernization*. Chicago: Aldine-Atherton, 1971.

Brill, William H. *Military Intervention in Bolivia*. Political Studies Series #3. Washington, D.C.: Institute for the Comparative Study of Political Systems, 1967.

Brvenner, William. "A Comparison of Professional Military Educational Systems." *Air University Review* 62, no. 3 (March–April 1971): 53–62.

Buck, James H. "The Japanese Self-Defense Forces." *Asian Survey* 7, no. 9 (September 1967): 597–613.

Challener, Richard D. *The French Theory of the Nation in Arms, 1866–1939*. New York: Russell & Russell, 1965.

Chang, David W. "The Military and Nation-Building in Korea, Burma and Pakistan." *Asian Survey* 9, no. 11 (November 1969): 818–30.

Chang, Parris H. "Regional Military Power: The Aftermath of the Cultural Revolution." *Asian Survey* 12, no. 12 (December 1972): 999–1013.

*Cohen, Stephen P. *The Indian Army*. Berkeley: University of California Press, 1971.

———. "The Untouchable Soldier: Caste, Politics and the Indian Army." *Journal of Asian Studies* 28 (May 1969): 453–68.

Craig, Gordon A. *The Politics of the Prussian Army, 1640–1945*. London: Oxford University Press, 1955.

Crouch, Harold. "Military Politics under Indonesia's New Order." *Pacific Affairs* 45 (Summer 1972): 206–19.

Daalder, H. *The Role of the Military in the Emerging Countries*. The Hague: Mouton, 1969.

DuBois, Victor D. *Military Rule and Its Repercussions in West Africa*. VDB-6-69. Hanover, New Hampshire: American University Field Staff, 1969.

Dupree, Louis. *The Military Is Dead! Long Live the Military!* LD-1-69. Hanover, New Hampshire: American University Field Staff, 1969.

Eayrs, James. "Future Roles for the Armed Forces of Canada." *Behind the Headlines* 28, nos. 1–2 (April 1969): 1–16.

Einaudi, Luigi R. *Revolution from Within? Military Rule in Peru Since 1968*, P-4676. Santa Monica, California: The RAND Corp., July 1971.

Einaudi, Luigi R., and Stepan, Alfred C. *Latin American Institutional Development: Changing Military Perspectives in Peru and Brazil*, R-586-005. Santa Monica, California: The RAND Corp., April 1971.

Erickson, John. "The Army, the Party and the People." *RUSI Journal* 115 (December 1970): 27–31, 45–47.

*———. *The Soviet High Command, 1918–1941*. London: MacMillan, 1962.

———. "Toward a 'New' Soviet High Command." *RUSI Journal* 114 (September 1969): 37–44.

Feit, Edward. *The Armed Bureaucrats*. Boston: Houghton Mifflin, 1973.

———. "Military Coups and Political Development: Some Lessons from Ghana and Nigeria." *World Politics* 20 (January 1968): 179–93.

———. "Pen, Sword and People: Military Regimes in the Formation of Political Institutions." *World Politics* 25, no. 2 (January 1973): 251–73.

———. "The Rule of the 'Iron Surgeons': Military Government in Spain and Ghana." *Comparative Politics* 1 (July 1969): 485–97.

Forster, Thomas M. *The East German Army*. London: George Allen and Unwin, 1967.

Forstmeier, Friedrich. "The Image of the German Officer." *RUSI Journal* 114 (December 1969): 52–55.

Fraser, Angus. *The Proper Role of the Military in Chinese Society*. P-629. Washington, D.C.: Institute for Defense Analysis, March 1970.

Garner, Maurice A. "Changing Recruitment Patterns and Organizational Ideology: The Case of a British Military Academy." *Administrative Science Quarterly* 17, no. 4 (December 1972): 499–507.

———. "Some Implications of the British Experience with an All-Volunteer Army." *Pacific Sociological Review* 16, no. 2 (April 1973): 177–91.

*Gittings, John. *The Role of the Chinese Army*. New York: Oxford University Press, 1967.

Goerlitz, Walter. *History of the German General Staff, 1657–1945*. New York: Frederick A. Praeger, 1953.

Goldwert, Marvin. *Democracy, Militarism, and Nationalism in Argentina, 1930–1966*. Austin: University of Texas Press, 1972.

* = particularly recommended.

Gregory, Ann. "Dimensions of Factionalism in the Indonesian Military." Mimeo. Paper presented at the Sixty-sixth Annual Meeting of the American Political Science Association. Los Angeles, September 1970.

Griffith, Samuel B. *The Chinese People's Liberation Army.* New York: McGraw-Hill Book, 1967.

Grkovic, George. "Soviet Universal Military Services." *U.S. Naval Institute Proceedings* (April 1969): 55–63.

Gutteridge, William F. *Military Institutions and Power in the New States.* New York: Frederick A. Praeger, 1965.

Hanning, Hugh. "Defence and British Public Opinion." *Brassey's Annual: Defense and the Armed Forces (1970).* Edited by J. L. Moulton. New York: Frederick A. Praeger, 1970, pp. 108–18.

———. *Defence and Development.* London, RUSI, March 1970.

Hansen, Roy A. "Public Orientations to the Military in Chile." *Pacific Sociological Review* 16, no. 2 (April 1973): 192–208.

Hauser, William L. "The British Army at the End of Empire." *Military Review* 52, no. 9 (1972): 3–15.

*———. *The American Army in Crisis.* Baltimore: The Johns Hopkins Press, 1973.

———. "The French Army After Algeria." *Military Review* 52, no. 8 (August 1972): 3–12.

Heiman, Leo. "The Russification of Soviet Armed Forces." *Ukrainian Quarterly* 24 (Spring 1968): 38–48.

Heymont, Irving. "The Israeli NAHAL Program." *Middle East Journal* 21 (Summer 1967): 314–24.

"How Unification Worked for Canada." *Armed Forces Journal International* 110, no. 8 (April 1973): 38–39.

*Huntington, Samuel P. *The Soldier and the State: The Theory and Politics of Civil-Military Relations.* New York: Vintage Books, 1964.

*———. (ed.). *Changing Patterns of Military Politics.* New York: The Free Press of Glencoe, 1962.

Hurewitz, J. C. "The Beginnings of Military Modernization in the Middle East: A Comparative Analysis." *The Middle East Journal* 22 (1968): 144–58.

Hyman, Elizabeth. "Soldiers in Politics: New Insights on Latin American Armed Forces." *Political Science Quarterly* 87, no. 3 (September 1972): 401–18.

*Janowitz, Morris. *The Military in the Political Development of New Nations.* Chicago: University of Chicago Press, 1964.

———. (ed.). *The New Military: Changing Patterns of Organization.* New York: Russell Sage Foundation, 1964.

*———. *The Professional Soldier.* New York: The Free Press, 1971.

———. "The Decline of the Mass Army." *Military Review* (February 1972): 10–16.

Janowitz, Morris, and Little, Roger W. *Sociology and the Military Establishment.* New York: Russell Sage Foundation, 1965.

*Janowitz, Morris, and Van Doorn, Jacques (eds.). *On Military Ideology.* Rotterdam: Rotterdam University Press, 1971.

*———. *On Military Intervention.* Rotterdam: Rotterdam University Press, 1971.

Joffe, Ellis. *Party and Army: Professionalism and Political Control in the Chinese Officer Corps, 1949-1964.* Cambridge, Massachusetts: Harvard University Press, 1971.

Johnson, John J. *The Role of the Military in Underdeveloped Countries.* Princeton, New Jersey: Princeton University Press, 1962.

———. *The Military and Society in Latin America.* Stanford, California: Stanford University Press, 1964.

Jones, Alvin G. "Training and Doctrine in the British Army Since 1945." *The Theory and Practice of War.* Edited by Michael Howard. London: Cassell, 1969, pp. 313–33.

Kelly, George A. *Lost Soldiers: The French Army and Empire in Crisis, 1947-1962.* Cambridge, Massachusetts: MIT Press, 1965.

Kie-Chang, John. "The Political Role of the Korean Military." *Studies in Asia* (1967): 71–86.

Kim, Se-Jin. *The Politics of Military Revolution in Korea.* Chapel Hill, North Carolina: University of North Carolina Press, 1971.

Koch, H. W. "Brothers in Arms." *RUSI Journal* 112 (August 1967): 261–64.

Koh, B. C. "North Korea: Profile of a Garrison State." *Problems of Communism* 18 (Jan./Feb. 1969): 18–27.

*Kolkowitz, Roman. *The Soviet Military and the Communist Party.* Princeton, New Jersey: Princeton University Press, 1967.

Kourvetaris, George A. "Professional Self-Images and Political Perspectives in the Greek Military." *American Sociological Review* 36, no. 6 (December 1971): 1043–57.

Kourvetaris, George A., and Dobratz, Betty A. "Social Recruitment and Political Orientations of the Officer Corps in a Comparative Perspective." *Pacific Sociological Review* 16, no. 2 (April 1973): 228–54.

*Lang, Kurt. *Military Institutions and the Sociology of War.* Beverly Hills, California: Sage Publications, 1972.

Lee, J. M. *African Armies and Civil Order.* New York: Frederick A. Praeger, 1969.

Lefeyer, Ernest W. *Speak and Scepter.* Washington, D.C.: The Brookings Institution, 1970.

Lemarchand, Rene. "Civil-Military Relations in Former Belgian Africa." Mimeo. Paper delivered at the 1972 Annual APSA Meeting, Washington, D.C., September 1972.

Lissak, Moshe. "Center and Periphery in Developing Countries and Prototypes of Military Elites." *Studies in Comparative International Development* 5 (1964–70): 144–50.

*Little, Roger W. (ed.). *Handbook of Military Institutions.* Beverly Hills, California: Sage Publications, 1971.

* = particularly recommended.

Lovell, John D., et al. "Recruitment Patterns in the Republic of Korea Military Establishment." *Journal of Comparative Administration* 1 (February 1970): 428–54.

Luckham, A. Robin. "Institutional Transfer and Breakdown in a New Nation: The Nigerian Military." *Administrative Science Quarterly* 16 (December 1971): 387–405.

*———. *The Nigerian Military: A Sociological Analysis of Authority and Revolt 1960–1967*. Cambridge University Press, 1971.

McGaurr, Darcy. *Conscription and Australian Military Capability*. Canberra Paper No. 11. Canberra: Australian National University Press, 1971.

McNall, Scott G. "Latin American Armies: An Analysis of the Socio-Economic Factors Contributing to their Dominance." *Proceedings of the Conference on Comparative Defense Policy*. USAF Academy, Colorado: Department of Political Science, 1973.

Mackintosh, Malcolm. *Juggernaut: A History of the Soviet Armed Forces*. London: Secker and Warburg, 1967.

Marshall, S. L. A. "The Army of Israel." *Military Review* 48 (April 1968): 3–9.

Matsueda, Tsukasa, and Moore, George E. "Japan's Shifting Attitudes Toward the Military." *Asian Survey* 7, no. 9 (September 1967): 614–25.

Mazrui, Ali A., and Rothschild, Ronald. "The Soldier and the State in East Africa." *The Western Political Quarterly* 20, no. 1 (March 1967): 82–96.

Menard, Orville D. *The Army and the Fifth Republic*. Lincoln: University of Nebraska Press, 1967.

Menaul, S. W. B. (ed.). *Recruiting for the Armed Forces of the 1970's*. London: RUSI, October 1969.

Miewald, Robert D. "Weberian Bureaucracy and the Military Model." *Public Administration Review* 30, no. 2 (March/April 1970): 129–33.

Miller, Norman N. *Military Coup in Uganda*. NMM-3-71. Hanover, New Hampshire. American University Field Staff, 1971.

Miners, N. J. *The Nigerian Army 1956–1966*. London: Methuen, 1971.

Moskos, Charles C. "Military Ideology: Discussion." *Proceedings of the Conference on Comparative Defense Policy*. USAF Academy, Colorado: Department of Political Science, 1973.

Needler, Martin C. *Anatomy of a Coup d'Etat: Ecuador 1963*. Spec. Art. Series #1. Washington, D.C.: Institute for the Comparative Study of Political Systems, 1964.

———. "Political Development and Military Intervention in Latin America." *The American Political Science Review* 60 (Sept. 1966): 616–26.

———. "The Causality of the Latin American Coup d'Etat." Mimeo. A paper presented to the Annual American Political Science Association Meeting, Washington, D.C., September 1972.

Nelsen, Harvey. "Military Forces in the Cultural Revolution." *China Quarterly*, no. 51 (July/Sept. 1972): 444–74.

Nordlinger, Eric A. "Soldiers in Mufti: The Impact of Military Rule Upon Economic and Social Change in the Non-Western States." *The American Political Science Review* 69, no. 4 (December 1970): 1131–48.

Nun, Jose. "The Middle-Class Military Coup." *The Politics of Conformity in Latin America*. Edited by Claudio Veliz. London: Oxford University Press, 1967, pp. 66–118.

Ozbudun, Ergun. *The Role of the Military in Recent Turkish Politics*. Occ. Paper 14. Cambridge, Massachusetts: Harvard University Center for International Affairs, 1966.

Paget, Roger K. "The Military in Indonesian Politics." *Pacific Affairs* 40 (Fall/Winter 1967/68): 294–314.

Parrish, Michael. "The New Soviet High Command." *Military Review* 49 (February 1969): 22–27.

———. *The Soviet Armed Forces: Books in English, 1950–1967*. Stanford, California: Hoover Institution Press, 1970.

Partridge, P. H. *Educating for The Profession of Arms*. Canberra Paper No. 5. Canberra, Australia: Australian University Press, 1969.

Patch, Richard W. *Bolivia's Nationalism and the Military*. RWD-1-69. Hanover, New Hampshire: American University Field Staff, 1969.

Payne, Arnold. *The Peruvian Coup d'Etat of 1962*. Political Studies Series #5. Washington, D.C.: Institute for the Comparative Study of Political Systems, 1968.

Payne, Stanley G. *Politics and the Military in Modern Spain*. Stanford, California: Stanford University Press, 1967.

Perlmutter, Amos. "From Obscurity to Rule: The Syrian Army and the Ba'th Party." *The Western Political Quarterly* 22, no. 4 (December 1969): 827–45.

*———. *Military and Politics in Israel: Nation-Building and Role Expansion*. New York: Frederick A. Praeger, 1969, pp. 606–43.

———. "The Praetorian State and the Praetorian Army." *Comparative Politics* (April 1969): 382–83.

———. "The Arab Military Elite." *World Politics* 22, no. 2 (January 1970): 269–300.

*———. *Military Ideology*. Cambridge, Mass.: Harvard University Press; forthcoming.

Pinckney, Robert. *Ghana under Military Rule: 1966–1969*. London: Methuen, 1972.

Potash, Robert A. *The Army and Politics in Argentina: 1928–1945*. Stanford, California: Stanford University Press, 1969.

Powell, Ralph. "Soldiers in the Chinese Society." *Asian Survey* 11, no. 8 (August 1971): 743–60.

*Preston, Adrian. "The Profession of Arms in Post-war Canada, 1945–1970." *World Politics* 23 (January 1971): 189–214.

Price, Robert M. "Military Officers and Political Leadership: The Ghanaian Case." *Comparative Politics* 3 (April 1971): 361–79.

Putnam, Robert D. "Toward Explaining Military Intervention in Latin American Politics." *World Politics* 20, no. 1 (October 1967): 83–110.

Pye, Lucian W. *Guerrilla Communism in Malaya: Its Social and Political Meaning.* Princeton, N.J.: Princeton University Press, 1956.

————. "Armies in The Process of Political Development," *Aspects of Political Development.* Boston: Little, Brown, 1966.

Quandt, William B. *Algerian Military Development: The Professionalization of a Guerrilla Army,* P-4792. Santa Monica, Calif.: The RAND Corporation, March 1972.

Ralston, David B. *Soldiers and States: Civil-Military Relations in Modern Europe.* Boston: D. C. Heath, 1966.

Rogerson, Anthony C. "Service Academy Education—British Developments." Mimeo. Paper presented to Annual Meeting of the International Studies Association, New York, April 1973.

Rosenbaum, H. Jon. "Brazil's Military Regime." *Current History* 58 (February 1970): 73–78.

Sampson, Allan. "Army and Islam in Indonesia." *Pacific Affairs* 54 (Winter 71/72): 545–65.

Schroeder, Rudolf. "The People's Army." *Survival* 13, no. 10 (October 1971): 346–48.

Secher, H. P. "Controlling the New German Military Elite." *Proceedings of The American Philosophical Society* 109 (1965): 63–84.

Sheikh, Ahmed. "The International Soldier." *Military Review* 50 (June 1970): 80–90.

Shinka, L. K. "Compulsory Military Training." *U. S. I. Journal* 97 (April/June 1967): 114–26.

Sims, Stephen A. "The New Role of the Military." *Problems of Communism* 18 (Nov./Dec. 1969): 26–32.

Steiner, Henry J., and Trubek, David M. "Brazil: All Power to the Generals." *Foreign Affairs* 49 (April 1971): 474–79.

*Stepan, Alfred. *The Military in Politics: Changing Patterns in Brazil.* Princeton, N.J.: Princeton University Press, 1971.

Stern, Frederick. *The Citizen Army.* New York: St. Martin's Press, 1957.

Susskind, Harold A. "Turkey's Professional Military Education." *Air University Review* 23 (May/June 1972): 50–54.

"The Swedish Army: Motivating the Conscript." *Armed Forces Journal International* 110, no. 6 (February 1972): 36–38.

Taylor, Philip B. *The Venezuelan Golpe de Estado of 1958.* Political Studies Series #4. Washington, D.C.: Institute for Comparative Study of Political Systems, 1968.

*Vagts, Alfred. *A History of Militarism, Civilian & Military.* London: Hollis and Carter, 1959.

Vandevater, E. *NATO's Men on Horseback.* P-2841-1. Santa Monica, Calif.: The RAND Corporation, February 1964.

*Van Doorn, Jacques (ed.). *Armed Forces and Society.* The Hague: Mouton, 1968.

————. *Military Profession and Military Regimes.* The Hague: Mouton, 1969.

*Van Gils, M. R. (ed.). *The Perceived Role of the Military.* Rotterdam: Rotterdam University Press, 1971.

Waldman, Eric. *The Goose Step is Verboten.* New York: The Free Press, 1964.

Weaver, Jerry L. "Political Style of the Guatemalan Military Elite." *Studies in Comparative International Development* 5 (1969–70): 63–81.

Weiker, Walter F. *The Turkish Revolution, 1960–1961: Aspects of Military Politics.* Washington, D.C.: The Brookings Institution, 1963.

Welch, Claude E. *Soldier and State in Africa.* Evanston, Ill.: Northwestern University Press, 1970.

Wesson, Robert G. "The Military in Soviet Society." *The Russian Review* 30, no. 2 (April 1971): 139–146.

Wheeler-Bennett, J. W. *The Nemesis of Power: The German Army in Politics 1918–1945.* New York: St. Martin's Press, 1967.

Whitson, William W. "The Concept of Military Generation: The Chinese Communist Case." *Asian Survey* 8, no. 11 (November 1968): 921–47.

————. "The Field Army in Chinese Communist Military Politics." *Studies in Comparative Communism* 37 (Jan./Mar. 1969): 1–30.

————. "The Military Ideology of the Chinese High Command." *Proceedings of the Conference on Comparative Defense Policy.* USAF Academy, Colorado: Department of Political Science, 1973.

*Whitson, William W., with Chen-Hsia Huang. *The Chinese High Command: A History of Communist Military Politics, 1927–71.* New York: Frederick A. Praeger, 1973.

Withers, Glenn A. "Has Conscription A Future?" *Australian Quarterly* 44 (March 1972): 12–21.

*Wolfe, J. N., and Erickson, John (eds.). *The Armed Services and Society.* Edinburgh: Edinburgh University Press, 1970.

Wyckoff, Theodore. "The Brazilian Military Oligarchy: Political Attitudes and Motivations." Mimeo. Delivered to the 1971 Annual Meeting of the American Political Science Association, Chicago, 1971.

Young, Peter. *The British Army, 1642–1970.* London: William Kinder, 1967.

* = particularly recommended.

PART TWO

STRUCTURE AND PROCESS

INTRODUCTION

EDWARD L. WARNER III

The term "defense policy" refers to the variety of activities which a state undertakes to protect and promote its national security. These actions are, for the most part, directly associated with the development, maintenance and employment of national military capabilities. Undertakings in this area are the products of governmental deliberation, decision and execution. Policymaking on security issues involves its own characteristic sets of individual and group participants and is marked by distinctive patterns of policy formulation, political bargaining, and implementation.

BUREAUCRATIC POLITICS[1]

Defense policymaking tends to be a relatively closed process. Decisions associated with the elaboration of a state's military doctrine or the development of its force posture are generally taken within the executive branch of government behind a screen of security classification restrictions. The major decisions are made by members of the highest national political leadership. Although these leaders are independent decision-makers, without affiliation with the large governmental bureaucracies, the selection and implementation of the courses of action they choose are strongly influenced by the political maneuvering and routine operation of large bureaucratic institutions.

Several governmental bureaucracies have important stakes in the defense policy process. The most prominent of these are the departments or ministries whose functional responsibilities lie in the defense, foreign policy, budgetary, and intelligence fields. In most socialist states, these agencies are joined by those state-controlled scientific institutions and industrial production ministries involved in weapons research, development, and production. (Similar constituencies are also present in nonsocialist systems but generally are located within the private sector of the economy.)

These defense-related bureaucracies are normally composed of a number of functionally specialized suborganizations. The military establishment usually includes a number of separate military services and a variety of staff organizations with responsibilities for military planning, intelligence, logistics support, and, frequently, weapons development. Similarly the finance and foreign policy bureaucracies routinely possess components which concentrate upon the defense policy aspects within their broader fields of competence.

All major state bureaucracies are officially subordinate to the national political leadership. They tend to operate, however, as a loose alliance of quasi-sovereign entities with their own distinctive organizational interests and an abiding commitment to protect and, when possible, to advance these parochial interests in the national policy arena. Organizational belief systems typically include shared images of both the domestic and international political environment and a number of policy convictions and goal

[1]"Bureaucratic politics" refers to a recently emergent approach for the study of American foreign and defense policy. While its roots are traceable to a variety of sources, the most important recent books in the field are Graham T. Allison, *Essence of Decision: Explaining the Cuban Missile Crisis* (Boston: Little Brown, 1971) and Morton H. Halperin, *Bureaucratic Politics and Foreign Policy* (Washington, D.C.: The Brookings Institution, 1973). The discussion that follows seeks to condense a number of the major points from these and many other works in this field. For a selected anthology of such materials see Part III, "American Defense Policymaking" in Richard G. Head and Ervin J. Rokke (eds.), *American Defense Policy*, third edition (Baltimore: The Johns Hopkins Press, 1973), pp. 266–495.

Major Edward L. Warner III (USAF) (Ph.D. candidate, Princeton University) is currently working in the national security community in Washington, D.C., following a tour of duty in the Political Science Department at the Air Force Academy. His field of interest is Comparative and International Politics, with particular emphasis on Soviet military affairs.

The views expressed herein are those of the author and do not necessarily reflect the views of the United States Air Force or the Department of Defense.

preferences. These preferences are likely to reflect intense concerns about the status of assigned responsibilities (roles and missions), the acquisition of capability resources (budgeting support, manpower, and equipment), the protection of organizational autonomy, and the maintenance of high morale among assigned personnel.[2] These concerns are frequently expressed as a series of avoidance imperatives: avoid encroachment on functional territory, avoid reductions in authorizations, avoid the loss of autonomy, and avoid a decline in morale.[3]

The members of large government agencies are likely to display the prevailing bureaucratic world-view. Their trained outlooks reflect the specialized responsibilities, distinctive skills, and specialized operations associated with their organizations. Individuals acquire these bureaucratic biases because of selective recruitment, common training and indoctrination, shared career experiences, internal and group pressures for conformity with organizational tenets, and as a result of individual responses to institutional incentives (pay, promotion, and prestige) that encourage partisan support.

The leading representatives of those government agencies with major defense responsibilities are central figures in the development and execution of national security policy. Their varying institutional outlooks and competitive attempts to promote these points of view contribute to the substantial political conflict which usually accompanies defense policymaking. This conflict is aggravated by the complexity of national security problems. Such issues present a variety of faces which is often perceived quite differently by the parties involved. These problems are compounded by the absence of established criteria for the comparison and evaluation of alternative policy goals or courses of action.[4] In these circumstances, significant bargaining and maneuver are likely to accompany defense policy decisions. Nevertheless, the competitive drives for organizational advantage tend to be mitigated by what Warner Schilling has called "the strain toward agreement"[5]—the pressures on all participants to adopt compromises which produce at least the appearance of policy agreement.

ORGANIZATIONAL PROCESS[6]

The impacts of institutional setting and decisional processes upon defense policy are not solely confined to the parochial conflicts which commonly accompany these issues. From the acquisition of weaponry to the employment of military force, defense policy actions are the products of complex bureaucratic organizations. They reflect the standardized routines which shape the policy processes within and among government agencies.

Bureaucracies operate in accordance with established routines. A variety of standard operating procedures (SOP's) are developed to guide organizational responses to problems. These procedures establish the action channels for policy search and deliberation and form the basis for activities which bureaucracies can undertake. When a policy problem arises, SOP's are likely to play important roles in determining who participates in the policy debate, what information and policy options are available for consideration, and, eventually, how selected courses of action are carried out. Thus these routines play important roles in framing policy conflicts. This, in turn, can make the definitions of these procedural matters the objects of considerable maneuver and struggle.

The existence of these organizational routines tends to inhibit policy flexibility. Bureaucratic organizations are prone to respond to requests for policy advice and directives to act by recommending and implementing activities drawn from their preexisting repertories of contingency plans. When innovation is attempted, it is likely to involve only minor modification of the programmed routines.

ADDITIONAL CONSIDERATIONS

Bureaucratic politics and organizational processes are not the only domestic factors that influence the development of national defense policies. Important decisions on defense matters are made by the national political leadership. These choices often reflect the personal biases and preferences of individual leaders as well as political concerns which reach beyond the competing claims of the major government bureaucracies.

Whatever the bureaucratic constraints, individual leaders can make a difference. National political executives enjoy considerable latitude in

[2]Morton H. Halperin, "Why Bureaucrats Play Games," *Foreign Policy* 2 (Spring, 1971): 76–88.

[3]Allison, *op. cit.*, p. 82.

[4]Warner Schilling, "The Politics of National Defense: Fiscal 1950," in W. Schilling, P. Y. Hammond, and G. H. Snyder, *Strategy, Politics and Defense Budgets* (New York: Columbia University Press, 1962), pp. 11–13.

[5]*Ibid.*, p. 23.

[6]The section is largely based on Allison's model or paradigm of the same name. See Allison, *op. cit.*, pp. 67–100.

the routine management of defense matters. They are capable of leading public and specialized opinion on security policy matters in most situations, including the initiation of major military undertakings. Political leaders must be careful, however, to avoid arousing substantial opposition to their defense policies. Dramatic military policy failures or excessive defense expenditures can erode support from specialized elites and the general public. Such loss of support can jeopardize the success of other political undertakings and even threaten the leader's tenure in office.

THE SUBSEQUENT ESSAYS

The articles within this section employ diverse perspectives to discuss the structure and process of defense policymaking. Samuel Huntington's theoretical overview[7] emphasizes the political conflicts associated with the development of military policy. He speaks of the "two worlds" of defense policy to indicate that military policy is simultaneously affected by events in the international and domestic political environments. Huntington also notes that the various elements of military policy—defense budgeting, the assignment of roles and missions, weapons acquisition, etc., grouped as "strategic" or "structural"—are each characterized by their own distinctive policymaking processes. This process pluralism often contributes to inconsistencies in goals and actions among the various elements of military policy.

Within the national case studies, Parris Chang, Stephen Cohen, Michael Brecher, and Ernst Gohlert survey the broad contours of policymaking in China, India, Israel, and West Germany. Chang's description of the role of the People's Liberation Army (PLA) in Chinese politics[8] complements William Whitson's earlier article on the composition of the PLA[9] and the studies of Chinese military doctrine,[10] force posture,[11] and weapons acquisition[12] which follow. All of these essays on China stress the importance of institutional factors, in particular the differences in perspective between the Chinese

military services and among the commanders of the eleven military regions. The general background presented in Cohen's article[13] serves as a useful basis for the discussions of Indian military ideology,[14] force posture,[15] and weapons acquisition[16] elsewhere in this volume. Brecher's essay on high policymaking in Israel[17] demonstrates the crucial impact of personality and individual style in shaping the different relationships among political and military leaders within a common institutional setting. Gohlert discusses the organizational strategy employed by Chancellor Willy Brandt for the formulation of West German defense policy.[18]

The remaining articles in this section focus upon national policymaking structures and processes by reference to specific policy issues. Thomas Wolfe provides important information on the individual and institutional participants involved in the development of Soviet military policy in his discussion of the internal practices associated with Soviet participation in the bilateral Strategic Arms Limitation Talks with the United States.[19] Other essays on the composition of the Soviet military establishment,[20] as well as the military doctrine,[21] the strategic force posture,[22] and the aircraft acquisition process[23] of the Soviet Union discuss the specific activities of many of the policymaking participants identified by Wolfe. Lawrence Scheinman[24] emphasizes the dominance of a limited number of bureaucratic groups and the largely passive roles played by the political parties and the National Assembly in his description of the French nuclear weapons program during the Fourth Republic. Richard Neustadt discusses the defense policymaking processes in the United States and the

---

[7]Samuel P. Huntington, "The Two Worlds of Military Policy," pp. 107–13.

[8]Parris H. Chang, "Mao Tse-tung and His Generals: Some Observations on Military Intervention in Chinese Politics," pp. 121–27.

[9]William W. Whitson, "Organizational Perspectives and Decisionmaking in the Chinese High Command," pp. 24–38.

[10]Harry Harding, "The Making of Chinese Military Policy," pp. 216–32.

[11]Joseph J. Heinlein, "China's Force Posture: Factors in the Policy Process," pp. 326–39.

[12]James Blaker, "Weapons Acquisition: China," pp. 444–52.

[13]Stephen Cohen, "The Security Policymaking Process in India," pp. 156–68.

[14]Stephen Cohen, "Military Ideology: South Asia," pp. 73–87.

[15]Lorne Kavic, "Force Posture: India and Pakistan," pp. 376–90.

[16]Wayne Wilcox, "Indian Defense Industry: Technology and Resources," pp. 479–81.

[17]Michael Brecher, "Formulation of High Policy Decisions: Israel," pp. 169–85.

[18]Ernst W. Gohlert, "An Organizational Perspective on German National Security Policy," pp. 146–55.

[19]Thomas W. Wolfe, "Soviet Interests in SALT: Institutional and Bureaucratic Considerations," pp. 113–20.

[20]John Erickson, "The Reshaping of the Soviet Military Command 1965–70," pp. 11–23.

[21]Benjamin Lambeth, "The Sources of Soviet Military Doctrine," pp. 200–15.

[22]Edward L. Warner, "Soviet Strategic Force Posture: Some Alternative Explanations," pp. 310–25.

[23]Arthur Alexander, "Weapons Acquisition in the Soviet Union, United States and France," pp. 426–43.

[24]Lawrence Scheinman, "The Security Policymaking Process in the Fourth Republic," pp. 140–45.

United Kingdom[25] from a unique perspective. He examines several misperceptions held by American and British officials about the workings of each other's governments, which contributed to the deterioration of their alliance relationship during the Suez Crisis of 1956 and the Skybolt Affair of 1962.

[25]Richard A. Neustadt, "London and Washington: Misperceptions Between Allies," pp. 000–00.

Through the examination of defense policy formulation in several countries, the reader should emerge with an important basis for understanding many of the case studies on specific policy activities contained within this volume and a greater sensitivity to the importance of an organizational setting and the political dynamics associated with the development of national security policy.

THE TWO WORLDS OF MILITARY POLICY

SAMUEL P. HUNTINGTON

Professor Huntington calls attention to the combination of domestic and foreign political considerations which shape a state's defense policy, differentiating between the strategic and structural aspects of such policies. Huntington defines strategic military policy decisions as those said to be made primarily with regard to the international environment and covering such matters as the size and composition of the state's armed forces as well as their geographic deployment and actual use. Structural defense policy decisions, in contrast, are identified as those with predominantly domestic political content and include questions of the size and distribution of the defense budget, military personnel policies (pay, recruitment and retention), supply, and the organizational format of the defense establishment. Huntington emphasizes the interrelationships between these matters and distinguishes between periods of policy equilibrium and disequilibrium defined in terms of the presence or absence of a general consensus among relevant groups and policy continuity regarding the overall shape of a state's defense policy.

Samuel P. Huntington is the Frank G. Thompson Professor of Government at Harvard University and Associate Director of the Harvard Center of International Affairs. He is the author of The Soldier and the State *(1957),* The Common Defense *(1961), and* Political Order in Changing Societies *(1968); and coauthor, with Z. Brzezinski, of* Political Power: USA/USSR *(1964); and is an editor of the quarterly journal,* Foreign Policy.

The most distinctive, the most fascinating, and the most troublesome aspect of military policy is its Janus-like quality. Indeed, military policy not only faces in two directions, it exists in two worlds. One is international politics, the world of the balance of power, wars and alliances, the subtle and the brutal uses of force and diplomacy to influence the behavior of other states. The principal currency of this world is actual or potential military strength: battalions, weapons, and warships. The other world is domestic politics, the world of interest groups, political parties, social classes, with their conflicting interests and goals. The

Reprinted by permission and with minor changes from The Common Defense *(New York: Columbia University Press, 1961), pp. 1–12.*

currency here is the resources of society: men, money, material. Any major decision in military policy influences and is influenced by both worlds. A decision made in terms of one currency is always payable in the other. The rate of exchange, however, is usually in doubt. Who knows the difference in international influence between a military budget of $35 billion and one of $40 billion? What will the commitment of six divisions to a nasty limited war cost in men, material, and domestic well-being? The uncertainty of the rate of exchange lies at the root of many of the dilemmas of military policy-making.

Military policy cuts clearly across the usual distinction between foreign policy and domestic policy. Domestic policy consists of those activities of a government which affect significantly the allocation of values among groups in society, while foreign policy consists of those activities of a government which affect significantly the allocation of values between it and other governments. The categories are not mutually exclusive. Foreign aid programs impose demands on the domestic economy; agricultural surpluses have implications for foreign affairs. Domestic politics serves as a constraint on the formulation of policies which are primarily responses to the external environment and have their principal impact on that environment. Conversely, international politics serves as a constraint on the formulation of policies which are primarily responses to the domestic environment and have their principal impact on that environment. With military policy, however, it is almost impossible to say which is the primary focus and which the constraint. It is neither primarily foreign nor primarily domestic. Instead it consists of those elements of both foreign and domestic policy which directly affect the armed forces. A commercial treaty and a collective security treaty are both foreign policy. A shift from excise taxes to income taxes and an across-the-board cut in governmental expenditures are both fiscal policy. The collective security treaty and the expenditures decision, however, are also military policy. The former directly affects the responsibilities of the armed forces, the latter their size and readiness.

THE COMPETITION OF PURPOSES

People sometimes argue that military policy involves the determination of the military programs and actions required to implement a given set of national goals. National policy or foreign policy or national security policy, they say, is decided first, and military policy then follows, subordinate to the more "ultimate" goals of higher policy. This image is a logical construct of what people think military policy ought to be. It is an image, however, which has little basis in fact. The crux of military policy, to be sure, is the relation of force to national purposes. But it is always national purposes in the plural, national purposes which are continually conflicting, often being compromised, and seldom being realized. Military policy is not the result of deductions from a clear statement of national objective. It is the product of the competition of purposes within individuals and groups and among individuals and groups. It is the result of politics not logic, more an arena than a unity. It is where a nation and its government come to grips with fundamental conflicts between those purposes which relate to the achievement of values in the world of international politics—conquest, influence, power, territory, trade, wealth, empire, and security—and those which relate to the achievement of values in the domestic world—economic prosperity, individual freedom and welfare, inexpensive government, low taxation, economic stability, social welfare. The competition between the external goals of the government as a collective entity in a world of other governments and the domestic goals of the government and other groups in society is the heart of military policy.

Broad goals, such as security, welfare, inexpensive government, are accepted as legitimate by most groups in society. But legitimacy does not necessarily imply compatibility. The realization of any one goal normally limits realization of the others. Because they are all legitimate they are all articulated, but also because they are legitimate the tendency of democratic politics is to obscure and to moderate the conflict among them. The latent conflict exists nonetheless, and it may well crystallize into actual conflict over specific issues, when, for instance, a government has to choose between balancing its budget and increasing its military security. In addition to general goals, particular groups participating in the policy process have their own specific, limited goals. The competition of purposes is not just among the broad goals of policy but also among the specific goals of these particular groups and between specific goals and broad goals. The fascination of military policy stems in large part from the intensity, complexity, and importance of the competing purposes which enter into its formation.

STRATEGY AND STRUCTURE

Military policy can be roughly divided into strategy and structure. Decisions made in the categories or currency of international politics may be described as *strategic* in character. Strategy concerns the units and uses of force. More precisely, strategic decisions may be subdivided into two broad divisions: (1) program decisions concerning the strength of the military forces, their composition and readiness, and the number, type, and rate of development of their weapons; and (2) use decisions concerning the deployment, commitment, and employment of military force, and manifested in military alliances, war plans, declarations of war, force movements, and the like. A strategic concept identifies a particular need and implicitly or explicitly prescribes decisions on the uses, strengths, and weapons of the armed services. *Structural* decisions, on the other hand, are made in the currency of domestic politics. They deal with the procurement, allocation, and organization of the men, money, and material which go into the strategic units and uses of force. Among the more important types of structural decisions are: (1) budget decisions concerning the size and distribution of funds made available to the armed forces; (2) personnel decisions concerning the number, procurement; retention, pay, and working conditions of members of the military services; (3) material decisions concerning the amount, procurement, and distribution of supplies to the armed forces; and (4) organizational decisions concerning the methods and forms by which the military services are organized and administered.[1]

The categories of decision—strategic and structural—are not independent of the purposes of decision. In general, when the goal of policy is related to the external environment, the decision is made in terms of the strategic categories. When the policy goal is domestic, it is made in terms of structural categories. Conversely, since any major issue in military policy inevitably has both strategic and structural implications, *how* the issue is defined for decision may well influence *what* the decision is. If another government becomes more and more powerful and unfriendly, the reaction may be to augment the military forces (the decision is made first in strategic terms) and then to increase the military budget, and perhaps as a result to multiply taxes and governmental borrowing or to reduce other programs. On the other hand, if the goal of policy is less governmental interference in the economy, the first step is a structural decision to reduce the military budget, and only later are decisions made to reduce force levels and perhaps foreign policy commitments. A category of decision, however, cannot simply be equated with any one particular purpose of decision. Military budgets go up as well as down, and, indeed, during a period of war mobilization budgets may be increased before strategy is formulated and before it is entirely clear how and for what the money will be spent.

In practice no sharp line exists between the strategic and structural elements in a military policy decision. This is particularly true of the overall magnitude of the military effort. This is determined by many strategic and structural decisions on force levels, budgets, personnel, and by other decisions which are not directly part of military policy at all. The determination of the resources available to the government and the allocation of those resources to military, domestic, and foreign purposes is, indeed, the crux of national policy. The determination of the magnitude of the military effort combines strategy and structure and also transcends them.

The various elements of military policy may conflict with each other or be compatible with each other. Obviously, a major action in any one area of strategy or structure implies demands upon the other areas. A decision to defend a certain territory with ground forces, for instance, is a strategic action on the use of force. It implies certain actions to insure that the forces and weapons necessary for the mission are in existence. These actions, in turn, may imply decisions on the budget (increasing ground force expenditures either by raising the total military budget or reallocating resources from other forces), on personnel (conscription or higher pay may be necessary to get the additional men required), on material (changes in procurement

---

[1]My distinction between strategy and structure parallels that drawn by Charles H. Donnelly in his annual surveys of *United States Defense Policies* (H. Doc. 436, 85C2; H. Doc. 227, 86C1; H. Doc. 432, 86C2), between "strategic policies," and organization, manpower, budgetary, fiscal, and procurement policies. See also Paul H. Nitze's distinction between action policy and declaratory policy, "Atoms, Strategy and Policy," *Foreign Affairs 34* (Jan. 1956): 187–88, and Roger Hilsman's categories of crisis policy, program policy, and anticipatory policy, "The Foreign Policy Consensus: An Interim Research Report," *Jour. of Conflict Resolution* 8 (Dec. 1959): 376–77. The distinction between strategy and structure in military *policy*, of course, should not be confused with the traditional distinction between strategy and tactics in military *science*.

and base construction policies), and possibly on organization (enhancing the position of the ground forces in the overall defense organization). The failure to undertake any one of these structural actions may, at the extreme, negate the strategic decision or, at the least, create imbalances and contradictions in military policy. A decision to build a long-range missile within three years, for instance, is strategic. A decision to have it built by the Army in a government arsenal instead of a private company under contract with the Air Force is structural. But if it is technically or administratively impossible for the arsenal to construct the missile within the specified time limit while the private company could do so, the decision on structure will reverse the decision on strategy.

The more numerous the loci of decision-making, the more likely are there to be disharmonies among the various elements of military policy. In the American system of government, decisions on strategy are largely executive decisions, decisions on structure normally require both executive and legislative action. Within strategy and structure the decision-making process tends to be still further fragmented. One group of agencies is concerned with budgetary decisions; another with matters of organization; yet a third with personnel policy. Decisions on weapons may be made by one group and decisions on missions by another. To some extent each element of military policy is the product of a distinctive policy-making process. Many agencies, of course, play a role in shaping all or most of the components of military policy, but the broad scope of these agencies frequently hampers them in getting their views to prevail within any specific decision-making process. The likelihood of conflict is further increased by the different roles which individuals and groups play in making different types of decisions. A budgetary official with the power to grant or withhold funds may be on the periphery of the process of force level determination. Military men who decide upon the weapons they need may appear as claimants before civilians to get the money to procure the weapons. A politically appointed executive official, like the Secretary of Defense, who has much influence on the overall size of the military forces, may have little influence over their commitments and use. Each process of decision is unique, and even if the actors in the several processes are the same, their roles in those processes may vary considerably. The different processes necessarily produce policies embodying different and often conflicting goals.

The formulation of military policy is often discussed in terms of the contrasting roles and functions of civilian and military groups. Actually, the civil-military distinction is not very meaningful as far as policy is concerned. Rarely, if ever, does one find all the civilians ranged against all the military. Much more important is the distinction between the tendencies to think in terms of domestic goals and structural categories, on the one hand, and external goals and strategic categories, on the other. Both tendencies undoubtedly exist in some degree in almost all persons participating in the military policy-making process. Nonetheless, some individuals and groups tend to emphasize domestic goals and the structural categories, and other individuals and groups foreign goals and the strategic categories. The former may include budgetary officials throughout the government, some congressmen, many politically appointed civilian officials, and some high-ranking military officers. The latter group is more likely to include middle-ranking officials in the State Department and the military services, many congressmen, and some politically appointed executive officials. The clash between these two groups comes to a head in determining the magnitude of the military effort. The crucial differences over policy usually involve differences over concerns and values stemming from organizational and political position rather than from roles and occupations reflecting personal career lines and social background. Often the military are caught between a civilian State Department which expands their commitments and a civilian Budget Bureau which limits their resources. The relations of the military to these two agencies are two key foci of civil-military relations. Yet the conflicts involved are not fundamentally civil-military ones. They are between civilian-defined external policy goals and civilian-defined internal policy goals.

EQUILIBRIUM AND DISEQUILIBRIUM

The history of military policy, like that of other areas of public policy, can be divided into phases of controversy and change (or disequilibrium) and phases of harmony and stability (or equilibrium). Military policy is in equilibrium when: (1) no sharp conflicts exist among the dominant goals of domestic policy, military policy, and foreign policy; and (2) no major changes in policy are taking place. An existing policy equilibrium may be disturbed by a drastic change in either its external or domestic environment. When one environment is upset, disequilibrium ensues until that environment again becomes stabilized and the process of adjustment produces a new policy balance. A change in the external environment, for instance, such as a fundamental shift in the balance of power, the rise of new and threatening states, the decline of old and established empires, the acquisition or loss of territory, tends to produce changes in foreign policy which, in turn, disrupt the existing relation between foreign policy and military policy. Either military strategy and military structure adjust to accommodate these changes or continuing disharmony develops between foreign policy and military policy. The satisfactory adjustment of military policy to the external changes, in turn, may then force other changes in domestic policy or produce continuing disharmonies between domestic policies and military policy. Conversely, a major shift in the domestic condition of a country—the rise of new industries, the change from a predominantly rural to a predominantly urban society, a shift in government from absolute monarchy to democracy—may produce changes in domestic policies requiring adjustments in military policy and foreign policy. The adjustments may take years to work themselves out, and disequilibrium may continue for decades with foreign policy, domestic policy, and strategy and structure embodying competing values and purposes.

Policy reflects the power, interests, and attitudes of the public and private individuals and groups concerned with it and affected by it. A change in policy requires either a change in the attitudes of the groups which influence policy or a change in the groups themselves. A policy equilibrium, on the other hand, means that a stable and reasonably harmonious pattern of relationships exists among these groups. Needless to say, policies are never completely static, nor intergroup relationships completely harmonious. Equilibrium simply means relative stability and harmony as contrasted with the change and conflict characteristic of disequilibrium.

During a period of disequilibrium, more groups become concerned with the policy area. The area receives more time and energy of general policy-makers (Congress and the President) and assumes a larger role in public discussion and partisan debate than it does during periods of stability. The number of alternative future courses of action increases. The gap between what significant groups consider to be the felt needs requiring governmental action and the existing patterns of action widen noticeably. Maladjustments between various component elements of policy appear to increase. Disharmonies and fissions develop. Changes in policy are more fre-

quent and more fundamental. During periods of equilibrium, on the other hand, the importance of the policy area appears to subside. The groups actively concerned with the policy decrease in number. Policy, in a sense, settles into a routine. The major choices have been made. The doors which were open have been closed, and the general course has been set. A balance exists among the goals and interests of the narrowed range of groups with continuing concerns in the area. Alterations in policy are few and of less significance. Balance, order, stability, consensus, and habit replace uncertainty, conflict, choice, change, and creativity.

In practice no sharp line divides equilibrium from disequilibrium. Over a period of time, however, it is possible to distinguish a rise and fall in the importance of any area of public policy and a corresponding expansion and contraction of the process through which it is made. Policy on the force levels of the Army, for instance, was in disequilibrium during the twenty years from 1790 to 1809: Congress changed the authorized unit strength of the Army eleven times during this period, and personnel strength fluctuated from a little more than 700 to a little less than 7,000. During the twenty years from 1878 to 1897 on the other hand, a stable equilibrium prevailed: the authorized unit strength of the Army remained constant at 25 regiments of infantry, 10 of cavalry, and 5 of artillery, and its personnel strength varied from a high of 28,265 to a low of 25,652. Stability and balance involved consensus and consistency. In 1801 the Jeffersonians reduced the Army by 30 percent. Democrats and Republicans, however, succeeded each other in office in the 1880s with no appreciable effect upon its force levels.

A classic case of prolonged disequilibrium between foreign policy and military policy occurred in France during the 1920s and 1930s. French foreign policy was concerned primarily with the problem of a resurgent Germany. Shortly after World War I the French negotiated alliances with the new states of eastern Europe, Poland and the Little Entente (Czechoslovakia, Yugoslavia, and Rumania) in particular, which implied that France would come to their aid if they were attacked by Germany. To fulfill this commitment, France would have to be able to launch or to threaten to launch an offensive against Germany if the latter menaced France's eastern allies. Hence, presumably France should have a professional, mobile army capable of quickly carrying out this mission. French military policy, however, did not correspond to these foreign policy needs. Instead it reflected the military experience of World War I and the ideologies and viewpoints of domestic political groups. The former bred the conviction within the French military establishment that the defensive was the superior form of warfare. The latter held that a democratic society was incompatible with a professional elite force and required universal short-term military service.

France built the Maginot Line and until 1935 maintained universal military service for one year. Instead of a ready professional force, French military strength consisted of large numbers of recently trained reserves. Military action of any sort required extensive mobilization, and offensive military action seemed "adventurous" when the elaborate strong points of the Maginot Line existed to protect France against invasion. For a decade or more French military policy and foreign policy were reasonably stable. But stability alone did not mean equilibrium. Foreign policy commitments, strategic programs, and manpower policies were fundamentally out of balance. The consequences of this lack of consensus were painfully obvious when the Germans remilitarized the Rhineland in 1936. The leaders of the French government asked the advice of the military chiefs on sending an expeditionary force into Germany. "Our military system," General Gamelin replied, "does not give us this possibility." The active units are but "the nucleus of the mobilized national army." Any rapid military operation in the Rhineland "even in a more or less symbolic form is fantastic." A significant military counterthrust would require the mobilization of a million reservists. To "chase three regiments of the Wehrmacht," in the words of the postwar Commission of Inquiry of the National Assembly, "it would have been necessary to put all the French army on a war footing."[2]

The lack of balance and harmony between French foreign policy and French military policy was not unnoticed during the interwar years. Many political leaders (including Paul Reynaud) and many military men (including Charles De Gaulle) pointed it out. But the conflicting goals and the system of decision-making made it impossible to bridge the gap. The requisite political strength did not exist to give France either the "army of her policy," as Reynaud wanted, or the "policy of her army," which some of the Rightists wanted. Changes in the attitudes or the power of either group were impossible, and the result was not equilibrium but conflict and stalemate.

The history of American military policy traditionally has been written in terms of the classic cycle of war and peace. During peace, the familiar story goes, America tends to neglect its military establishment: the armed services are starved for money and men and reduced to a small corps of regulars who struggle to keep alive military knowledge and the military spirit in an apathetic and indifferent country. As crises loom in the distance, the military warn the country of the need to rearm. The civilians, however, are slow to respond until war or national emergency is present or imminent. At this point the peacetime dike stopping the flood of military preparation gives way, the martial spirit seizes the populace, and the country rushes headlong into rearmament and the enthusiastic and successful prosecution of a war. Once the conflict is over, however, the country just as enthusiastically demobilizes, is outwitted at the peace conference, forgets the lessons of its prewar unpreparedness, and once again lets its military might decay.

There are substantial elements of truth in this picture. Military policy, however, is shaped by more than the cycle of war and peace. Only fundamental and permanent changes in a government's environment produce fundamental and permanent changes in its military policy. Wars may or may not involve such changes. If a war results in a marked extension of a state's territory and responsibilities, inevitably this is reflected in its military policy. It is the result of the war, however, rather than the war itself which produces the changes. On the other hand, a war which does not markedly alter the antebellum environment has little effect on military policy no matter how serious a conflict it may be. In such cases the war simply marks a temporary change in the environment of policy and produces only temporary changes in policy. After the war the prewar equilibrium is reestablished. The American Civil War was the biggest war of the century between 1815 and 1914 and yet it produced few significant changes in American military policy. But the Spanish-American War, a little war if not a splendid one, was associated with basic changes in military policy because it was part of a fundamental shift in the international position of the United States. The study of military policy and the study of war are two distinct although related pursuits.

This theory does not presuppose a mechanical or deterministic alternation of equilibrium and disequilibrium. It simply holds that at any given time military policy is a response to both its external and internal environments. If these environments are stable, a policy equilibrium *may* emerge; if not, disequilibrium prevails. The

[2]Richard D. Challener, *The French Theory of the Nation in Arms, 1866–1939* (New York: 1955), pp. 264–65.

period of each may be long or short and bears no necessary fixed relationship to the other. Rapid changes in the environments might make disequilibrium rather than its opposite the rule in military policy. The theory assumes only that policy must be related to these environments, not that it moves through any necessary progression of phases.

SOVIET INTERESTS IN SALT: INSTITUTIONAL AND BUREAUCRATIC CONSIDERATIONS

THOMAS W. WOLFE

After briefly outlining the unitary command and bureaucratic models for the analysis of the Soviet political process, Dr. Wolfe discusses the roles of a number of individuals and institutions apparently involved in the development of Soviet policy in the bilateral American-Soviet Strategic Arms Limitation Talks. He inventories and assesses the interests and types of participation of the various bureaucratic groups which include the Ministry of Foreign Affairs, the scientific intelligentsia, the military, and the defense industrial producers.

Thomas W. Wolfe is a Senior Staff Member of the RAND Corporation's Social Science Department and a Professorial Lecturer at George Washington University. He has published numerous articles on Soviet military and foreign policy and is the author of Soviet Strategy at the Crossroads *(1964) and* Soviet Power and Europe, 1945–1970 *(1970).*

MODELS OF THE SOVIET POLICYMAKING PROCESS

In order to properly understand the influence of institutional and bureaucratic factors upon Soviet policy toward the Strategic Arms Limitation Talks (SALT) or upon Soviet security policy generally, one would have to know a good deal more about the structure and process of policymaking in the Soviet system than is, I am afraid, generally known. Nevertheless, this article examines the subject, beginning with a few remarks on the two most frequently used analytical models of the Soviet policymaking process.[1]

The first, one might call it the unitary command model, has a lineage which goes back to the totalitarianism of the Stalinist period. It rests on the basic assumption that an authoritarian leadership with highly centralized machinery of planning and control at its disposal is in a position to make up its mind according to its own calculation of preferred policy alternatives, and to dictate its decisions to all subordinate echelons of Party and State for implementation. Viewed in terms of this model, the Soviet policymaking process is seen as the work of a fully informed, unitary leadership which is always the master

---

[1] For more detailed discussion, see the author's *Policymaking in the Soviet Union: A Statement with Supplementary Comments*, P-4131 (Santa Monica, Calif.: The RAND Corporation, June 1969).

Excerpted by permission and with minor changes from Soviet Interests in SALT: Political, Economic, Bureaucratic and Strategic Contributions and Impediments to Arms Control, *P-4702 (Santa Monica, Calif.: The RAND Corporation, September 1971), pp. 13–30. This article should not be interpreted as reflecting the views of the RAND Corporation or the official opinion or policy of any of its governmental or private research sponsors. The article from which this excerpt is taken was prepared for presentation at the International Arms Control Symposium in Philadelphia on October 15, 1971.*

and never the captive of the overlapping bureaucracies over which it presides,[2] and which, within the parameters of opportunity and constraint which confront any government, will make rational policy choices best suited to serve its perceived interests.

In recent years, a new paradigm or model has come to be favored by some Western scholars looking to the concepts of comparative systems analysis and the theory of complex organizations for better ways to interpret the processes of change, diversification and interest-group politics at work within the formal structure of Soviet institutions.

The basic assumption upon which this second or bureaucratic model rests is that no single centralized leadership entity—even in a highly authoritarian or totalitarian system—has the time or information at its disposal to make all of the important decisions for the system. Since the top leadership cannot master all the details and complexities of the issues with which it deals, it must depend on inputs of information and technical judgment flowing upward from subordinate organizations. These organizations in turn operate according to the "laws" and habits of bureaucracies in general: they have their own axes to grind, constituencies to please, traditional claims on the budget, commitments to programs already laid down; they tend to apply old routines to new problems, to pursue such interests as self-preservation and growth along with their assigned tasks, and so on. As centers of partial power in the system, the various bureaucracies have a claim to be heard; the way they marshal their arguments and the skill of their advocacy can help to shape the issues as they are presented to the top leadership, so that in a sense the policy options open to it are already somewhat circumscribed before they become a matter of decision.

Besides emphasizing the effect of bureaucratic phenomena upon Soviet policymaking, this model also views the top leadership itself as a far from homogeneous group prepared to speak with a single voice on the issues which come before it. Rather, the ruling oligarchy is presumed to have many differing alignments of interest and ties with various competing pressure groups; it is seen to engage in internal political maneuvering and to strike committee compromises which may tend to water down its decisions or even rob them of logical consistency upon occasion.

With respect to our subject, each of the foregoing models would seem to have rather different implications for the Soviet approach to SALT. If the first case applies, for example, one should expect the top Soviet leadership to have gone into the SALT talks with its "single" mind made up, that is to say—without differing essentially as to what Soviet objectives should be. Moreover, the leadership should have faced no real impediments from within the Soviet bureaucratic structure to working out any agreements it might see fit with the United States. On the other hand, if the second case applies, there may have been not only competing policy preferences within the top leadership itself, but bureaucratic phenomena and the influence of pressure groups within the system may have made it difficult to arrive at a coordinated position on agreements with the United States.

Which of these cases more closely approximates Soviet reality is open to argument. I am inclined, with certain reservations,[3] toward the second, both on the basis of some evidence—to be taken up later in this paper[4]—that formulation of a SALT position has been a discordant issue within the Soviet establishment, and on more general grounds relating to the role and relative influence of various interest groups on Soviet policy. Let me pursue the latter question a bit further here.

For both doctrinal and practical reasons, Soviet leaders have customarily denied the existence of interest groups in the Soviet Union. Doctrinally, it runs against the Marxist-Leninist grain for the Soviet leaders to admit that rival interests may arise within a supposedly classless

---

[2]Although the tendency of bureaucracies to look out for their own interests is recognized by this model, it is assumed that in the Soviet case the political leaders from Stalin onward have successfully managed to ensure compliance from their administrative bureaucracies and to prevent the formation of lower-level power centers in the system.

[3]My reservations toward the "pure" bureaucratic model in the Soviet case stem from two points. First, the power of bureaucracies lies more in their ability to obstruct innovation than to take initiatives, and since the Soviet system has shown a capacity for policy initiatives from the central leadership, the latter presumably has found ways to impose its will upon the system's administrative machinery. Second, the dual character of Soviet bureaucracy—a government machine to administer the country's affairs and a Party apparatus to give directions and check on performance, with all these divided functions coalescing in a small coterie of leaders at the top—tends to smudge the features of the pure bureaucratic model. As one observer has put it, the Soviet administrative system tends to work precisely because it violates many of the principles of a classical bureaucracy. See Jerry F. Hough, *The Soviet Prefects: The Local Party Organs in Industrial Decision-Making* (Cambridge, Mass.: Harvard University Press, 1969), p. 3.

[4]Evidence is presented in the author's *Soviet Interests in SALT: Political, Economic, Bureaucratic and Strategic Contributions and Impediments to Arms Control*, P-4702 (Santa Monica, Calif.: The RAND Corporation, September 1971), pp. 34, 35.

society.[5] In practical terms, they have sought to suppress the emergence of autonomous groups of any kind that might develop a life of their own and challenge the leadership monopoly of the Party. Nevertheless, a kind of creeping pluralism seems to have spread within the system, and the leaders themselves appear to have tacitly recognized this not only by acting as arbiters among various institutional and interest groups, but also by occasionally championing the cause of one group at the expense of another.[6]

For our purposes, several broad groups which have interests of one kind or another in Soviet defense policy and SALT may be discussed briefly here. They include the foreign affairs intelligentsia, the scientific intelligentsia, the military, and that portion of the R&D and industrial establishment best described perhaps as the military-industrial complex: each of these in turn embraces a variety of subgroups.

THE FOREIGN AFFAIRS INTELLIGENTSIA

As treated here, this group is understood to exclude the political chieftains who preside over Soviet affairs at the Politburo level; rather, it is made up primarily of those elements of Party-government officialdom professionally concerned with foreign policy and related matters, and lodged bureaucratically in such places as the Ministry of Foreign Affairs, the apparatus of the Party Secretariat and Central Committee, the intelligence services, and various schools for diplomatic training.[7] This group also includes specialists to be found in certain academic institutes which do research in foreign policy and arms control fields, such as the recently founded Institute of the U.S.A. and the older Institute of World Economics and International Relations, both of which come under the aegis of the USSR Academy of Sciences.

The extent to which the foreign affairs intelligentsia may influence policy, as distinct from the part it plays in running the day-to-day business of Soviet diplomacy, is difficult to ascertain. In the past, under both Stalin and Khrushchev, the professional voice of the Ministry of Foreign Affairs apparently carried little policy weight, as epitomized by Khrushchev's remark that "Gromyko only says what we tell him to. . . . If he doesn't, we'll fire him and get someone who does."[8] Under the present regime, neither Brezhnev nor Kosygin has stepped into Khrushchev's shoes as the preeminent spokesman of Soviet foreign policy, and Gromyko is no longer treated disparagingly, which suggests that his stature and that of the professionals who support him has grown.[9]

With respect to SALT, no single viewpoint can be attributed to a group as diverse as the foreign affairs intelligentsia. However, one might suppose that its general orientation lies in the direction of keeping the negotiations going and exploring the opportunities they present for diplomatic gains. The merging of foreign policy interests, such as Soviet-US relations, with defense considerations is probably of concern to this group, but its competence in the defense field and its direct influence upon military policy decisions would appear to be rather limited. The apparent compartmentalization between the diplomatic and defense personnel in the Soviet SALT delegation, for example, seems to suggest that the integration of foreign and defense policy issues occurs at the upper reaches of the governing apparatus, possibly through *ad hoc* bodies set up for the purpose, rather than at routine working levels of the bureaucracy.[10]

The policy role of the academic specialists within the foreign affairs intelligentsia merits

[5]Although the Soviet system does not sanction the politics of "social bargaining," the existence of differing "social groups" which share a particular "community of goals and interests" is sometimes recognized. See G. V. Osipov, ed., *Sotsiologii v SSSR* [Sociology in the USSR] (Moscow: Izdatel' stvo "Mysl'," 1966), II: 487.

[6]Or, conversely, some leaders have courted particular groups to strengthen their own hand in elite politics, a case in point being the support of the military solicited by Khrushchev in 1957 to help repel the challenge of the so-called "anti-Party group."

[7]For a good description of the Soviet foreign policy elites, see Jan F. Triska and David D. Finley, *Soviet Foreign Policy* (New York: The Macmillan Co., 1968), pp. 75–106.

[8]Averell Harriman, "My Alarming Interview with Khrushchev," *Life*, (July 13, 1959): 33. A discussion of the generally subordinate policy role of the Foreign Ministry under Stalin may be found in Robert M. Slusser, "The Role of the Foreign Ministry," in Ivo J. Lederer, ed., *Russian Foreign Policy* (New Haven, Conn.: Yale University Press, 1962), pp. 211–39.

[9]An index of Gromyko's improved stature is provided by comparing the frequency with which he participated in top-level diplomatic talks with important foreign leaders under the Khrushchev and Brezhnev-Kosygin regimes. During the 1961–63 period, his participation was slightly below 60 percent. In the first two years of the successor regime, the figure went above 85 percent. This comparison is drawn from a dissertation by Jon D. Glassman, *Soviet Foreign Policy Decision-Making* (New York: Columbia University Press 1968), p. 135. [*Editor's Note*: Gromyko's move to full Politburo membership in April 1973 further demonstrates the growth in his personal importance and necessarily that of the Ministry of Foreign Affairs as well.]

[10]For what it is worth, a member of the Institute of World Economics and International Relations stated in a recent interview that *ad hoc* bodies are frequently convened to recommend resolution of knotty issues involving foreign policy and defense interests. The Soviet scholar in question also implied that an important mediating role in ironing out such issues before they reach the Politburo's agenda is played by the professional staff of the Central Committee.

some additional comment. In the past couple of years, a number of these men have made scholarly visits to the United States, and at least one of them—G. A. Arbatov, director of the Institute of the U.S.A.—has been reputed to have the ear of Brezhnev, Kosygin and other highly placed leaders. Since the published material of Arbatov's institute has tended to reflect a more sophisticated analysis of the factors shaping American foreign policy than the "primitive sloganeering" of other Soviet media,[11] the question arises: How may Soviet policy be affected by the addition of this new analytical source to the previously existing information-gathering and analysis networks serving the Soviet leadership? The question is not easily answered, for it immediately raises others: How much access to the political summit do the academic specialists really enjoy, and is their advice treated as a serious input to decisionmaking? Perhaps, as one observer has put it, the most to be expected from the analytical contributions of the new breed of Soviet researchers is some dilution of the "ideological self-deception" to which the Soviet leadership may be prone.[12]

THE SCIENTIFIC INTELLIGENTSIA

From the early days of the Soviet state, the scientific intelligentsia has been treated as a relatively favored group because of the need for its expertise to modernize the society and create the scientific-technological base for Soviet military-industrial power. At the same time, however, successive Soviet regimes have sought to prevent the scientific elite from jelling into a cohesive institutional force that might challenge the decisionmaking prerogatives of the political leadership.

Thus, while senior Soviet scientists have been invited periodically to high policy councils as individual consultants on problems in their own fields of competence, they have been neither expected nor entitled to argue a case or to voice political judgments.[13] Similarly, despite its high prestige and importance as a national resource, the Soviet Academy of Sciences has been hedged around with restrictions designed to keep it from

serving as a significant vehicle for policy lobbying by the scientific community.[14] Another factor which has tended to discourage potential lobbying by the scientific intelligentsia is the rather large proportion of this group whose activities are wholly or in part associated with the defense sector of the Soviet research and development establishment.[15] Scientists working in this sector have access to better research facilities and conditions than their counterparts in the civilian sector of the economy, but a side effect of these advantages is the constraint imposed upon expression of any disagreement with official policy.

Despite the various conditions which have acted to muffle potential dissent from Soviet scientists and to insulate them from the policy-making process, developments of the past few years suggest that trouble may be brewing for the Brezhnev-Kosygin regime within the scientific intelligentsia. The clandestine Sakharov "manifesto" of 1968[16] and subsequent petitions by this eminent physicist and a few other Soviet scientists may be symptomatic of more widespread restiveness among the scientific elite, posing for the regime the delicate problem of how to deal with critics whose professed aim is to improve the Soviet system from within.

So far as SALT is concerned, Sakharov may have had some influence on the Soviet position. His manifesto made a strong case against ABM defenses; indeed, in terms of traditional Soviet strategic policy and doctrine favoring such defenses, his argument amounted to heresy. Although no public debate over the merits of ABM ensued in the Soviet Union, it is notable that the Soviet side of SALT reportedly shifted later to a position which "concentrated on the need to

---

[11] For an analysis of the published output of Arbatov's institute during a six-month period in 1970, see Merle Fainsod, "Through Soviet Eyes," *Problems of Communism* (November–December 1970): 59–64.

[12] Zbigniew Brzezinski, "Know Thy Enemy," *Newsweek* (August 30, 1971): 40.

[13] *Cf.* Alexander Dallin *et al.*, *The Soviet Union, Arms Control, and Disarmament*, (New York: School of International Affairs, Columbia University, 1964), p. 62.

[14] The creation of various bodies for the control of scientific activity, such as the State Committee for the Coordination of Scientific Research and its successors, while aimed toward improvement of the national research effort, also has had the effect of reducing the autonomy and potential policy leverage of the Academy of Sciences.

[15] Reliable figures are not available on the number of Soviet scientific professional personnel associated with defense R&D. The total number of scientific professionals given by both Soviet and Western sources is, however, in fairly close agreement. For example, the figure of 660,000 for 1966 is given by Nikolai D. Tiamshanskii, *Ekonomika i organizatsiia nauchno-issledovatel'skikh rabot v mashinostroenii* [Economics and Organization of Scientific-Research Work in Machine Building] (Leningrad, 1967), p. 6. This compares with a figure of 670,000 for 1966 in E. Zaleski *et al.*, *Science Policy in the USSR* (Paris: OECD, 1969), p. 137. If Western estimates that 60–75 percent of total R&D expenditures in the USSR are in the defense sector can be roughly correlated with personnel involved, then the number of scientific professionals associated with defense R&D might be on the order of 400,000–500,000.

[16] Andrei Sakharov, *Progress, Coexistence, and Intellectual Freedom* (New York: W. W. Norton, 1968). This document has been circulated clandestinely via *samizdat* in the Soviet Union, but has not been published there.

curb rival anti-missile systems"[17]—a shift which may have been at least indirectly attributable to the man who is sometimes known as the father of the Soviet hydrogen bomb.

Whether or not the regime in fact was responsive to Sakharov's lobbying against ABM, there are some indications that its SALT position may be under general question within the Soviet scientific community. As pointed out recently by two American analysts, the regime has made very little use of scientists as propaganda spokesmen on matters relating to SALT.[18] This is in distinct contrast with the substantial propaganda role Soviet scientists had been called upon to play in the past on other disarmament issues, suggesting perhaps that a critical attitude among the scientific elite toward the regime's approach to SALT may have counselled against repeating the past practice.

It must be emphasized, of course, that signs of latent dissatisfaction among Soviet scientists do not necessarily mean that the Brezhnev-Kosygin regime has a scientific revolt on its hands. The dissidents may represent only a bold minority, and the bulk of the scientific intelligentsia may have a vested interest in maintaining a status quo which gives high priority to defense-related research and development activity. Indeed, many scientists may side with other groups inclined to argue against tampering with the country's security by diverting Soviet technology from the very field in which it has competed most successfully with the West. With regard to the SALT talks, if this conception of the national interest were to be widely held within the scientific elite, one might expect its members to favor a policy designed to steer clear of agreements of the kind that could have the effect of terminating Soviet efforts to overtake the United States in areas of military technology where the USSR still lags behind, such as MIRV, certain fields of electronics, data handling, and so on.

THE MILITARY

Like each previous Soviet regime, the present leadership has faced the problem of staking out the "permissible" limits of military influence on Soviet policy. In part, this problem arises be-cause the military establishment, with its innate tendencies toward professional autonomy, is potentially the most potent interest group in the society. True, the military establishment is not without its fair share of divergent internal alignments—among the services, between the professional officer corps and political officers, between a new class of military technicians and traditional line officers, and so on. However, these differing interest alignments tend to be overshadowed by strong binding elements of discipline, duty and patriotism which give the Soviet military community a greater cohesiveness and sense of purpose than most other segments of the society, with the exception of the Party *apparat* itself.

In general, without dwelling on the details of political-military relations under the Brezhnev-Kosygin regime, it can be said that the "permissible" sphere of military influence has grown, though I don't subscribe to the view advanced by an occasional newspaper columnist that there has been a major shift of political power to the marshals.[19] So far as the formal indices of power standing are concerned, no military men have been taken into the Politburo—where Marshal Zhukov was the only professional soldier admitted in recent times*—and the proportion of symbolic military representation on lesser Party bodies such as the Central Committee and Central Auditing Commission had remained about the same under the Brezhnev-Kosygin regime as before.[20]

However, despite the unchanged formal footing of the military leaders at the summit of the Soviet policymaking structure, they have acquired greater prestige and influence under the present regime. The reasons for this are complex and cannot be explored here,[21] but the

---

[17]Chalmers M. Roberts, "Third Round of SALT Winds Up in Helsinki," *Washington Post* (December 19, 1970). [*Editor's Note:* Subsequently, the shift of the Soviet position led to the ABM Treaty, signed in May, 1972.]

[18]Matthew P. Gallagher and Karl F. Spielmann, Jr., *The Public Understanding of SALT in the Soviet Union: A Study of Soviet Propaganda Policy and the Awareness Levels of Selected Population Groups* (Arlington, Va.: Institute for Defense Analyses, March 1971), 1:26.

[19]See the author's article, "Are the Generals Taking Over?" *Problems of Communism* (July–October 1969): 106–10.

*[*Editor's Note:*] This significant step was taken, however, with the elevation of Defense Minister A. A. Grechko to full membership in the Politburo in April, 1973.

[20]In fact, the military representation on the Central Committee (full and candidate members) declined slightly at the two Party Congresses held under the Brezhnev-Kosygin regime, to about 8.5 percent from the 10 percent elected at the 22nd Party Congress in 1961. On the other hand, the actual number of military men made full members of the Central Committee (i.e., with voting rights) increased from 14 at the 22nd Party Congress to 20 at the 24th Party Congress.

[21]Several categories of reasons might be briefly mentioned. (1) Internal elite politics. The Brezhnev-Kosygin regime owed some debt to the military for "cooperating" in Khrushchev's ouster. No single collective leader had, initially at least, the personal prestige to flout professional military opinion as Khrushchev had done, etc. (2) Greater dependence on the instrumental role of the military in support of Soviet policy interests, cases in point being the Czechoslovak intervention, the border crises with China, the expansion of the Soviet presence in the Middle East and Mediterranean. (3) The "successes" scored by the military, notably the well-executed

effect has been, by all accounts, to give the Ministry of Defense, headed by Marshal Grechko, and the General Staff, under Marshal Zakharov, and his successor, General Kulikov, both enlarged professional scope in managing the Soviet defense effort and more opportunity for bringing military advice and expertise to bear in the policy councils of the regime.[22]

The internal channels of communication and the organizational arrangements through which the professional military voice reaches the top leadership are not well understood, but they apparently include the Higher Military Council, a policy-recommending body which brings together leading political and military officials,[23] and, as some analysts have suggested, a committee or commission of military and industrial officials to deal with defense production issues.[24] A high-level supervisory function over military R&D and procurement also rests with D. F. Ustinov, a member of the Party Secretariat, but the agency through which he exercises this function is not known. Besides military access to the top leadership through intermediary bodies, direct consultation between the Politburo and military leaders has been a customary practice in the past and presumably continues.[25] An indication that military authorities may have been seeking additional institutional arrangements to provide a top-level link between themselves and the political leadership came to the surface in 1967, when the military press dwelt briefly on the need for peacetime creation of a single "supreme military-political organ."[26] However, this theme was soon dropped, without it being made known whether or not such an organ had been set up.

Coming now to the question of military influence on Soviet SALT policy, one finds the military leadership in the somewhat ambivalent position of having to support the negotiations while also being concerned lest the talks lead to agreements which might adversely affect the Soviet military posture. This is not, of course, an unfamiliar dilemma for the Soviet military, nor one peculiar to the Soviet side of the arms control negotiating table.

Precisely how hard the Soviet military leaders have dragged their feet with respect to SALT is difficult to gauge, but that they have done so seems hardly disputable. As noted later in this paper, there was clearly reluctance on the part of the military toward entering the talks at all,[27] and since they began in late 1969 the subject has been studiously avoided in the public statements of virtually every prominent figure in the Soviet military hierarchy.[28]

Although Soviet military leaders have shied away from discussion of the effects of SALT upon the Soviet military posture, they obviously have a close interest in this question. Some measure of the professional military attention given the negotiations may be found in the composition of the Soviet SALT delegation itself, one-third of which is made up of military men.[29] The two most prominent military delegates are Colonel General N. V. Ogarkov, a first deputy chief of the General Staff, and Colonel General N. N. Alekseyev, also of the General Staff. Both of these men hold important posts having to do with weapons research and selection; they can be presumed to serve not only as informed ad-

---

handling of the military phase of the Czechoslovak episode and the effect of the strategic buildup in boosting the USSR to full strategic equality with the United States. (4) Finally, the increasing complexity and the cost of maintaining modern military power, calling for encouragement of innovation and efficiency in the management of military affairs, and thus putting a higher premium on professional expertise.

[22] For an informed analysis of some of the trends which have enlarged the professional role of the Soviet military, see the study by David Holloway, cited in footnote 2 above.

[23] The current status of the Higher Military Council [*Vysshii Voennyi Sovet*] is somewhat obscure. Khrushchev chaired this body in his time, but both Brezhnev and Kosygin have been mentioned as succeeding to the role. For background discussion of this institution, see the author's *The Soviet Military Scene: Institutional and Defense Policy Considerations*, RM–4913–PR (Santa Monica, Calif., The RAND Corporation, June 1966), pp. 11–12. See also Roman Kolkowicz, *The Soviet Military and the Communist Party*, (Princeton, N.J.: Princeton University Press, 1967), pp. 58–77, 124–43.

[24] See Holloway, *op. cit.*, p. 6; Andrew Sheren, "Structure and Organization of Defense-Related Industries," in *Economic Performance and the Military Burden in the Soviet Union* (Washington, D.C.: Joint Economic Committee, Congress of the United States, 1970), p. 124.

[25] Both Khrushchev and the late Marshal R. Ya. Malinovskii, Minister of Defense under Khrushchev, gave public accounts of this practice in the early sixties. See N. S. Khrushchev, *O vneshnei politike Sovetskogo Soiuza: 1960* [The Foreign Policy of the Soviet Union: 1960] (Moscow: 1961), I: 34; *Krasnaia zvezda* (April 17, 1964).

[26] See Major General V. Zemskov, "For the Theoretical Seminar: An Important Factor for Victory in War," *Krasnaia zvezda* (January 5, 1967).

[27] See the author's *Soviet Interests in SALT*, P-4702 (Santa Monica, Calif.: The RAND Corporation 1971), pp. 34, 35. See also Gallagher and Spielmann, *op cit.*, pp. 20–25.

[28] A conspicuous example was the report delivered by Marshal Grechko at the 24th Party Congress, in which he repeatedly accused "US ruling circles" of such nefarious activities as "stepping up preparations for war against the Soviet Union" without once paying even lip service to the strategic arms negotiations. *Pravda* (April 3, 1971).

[29] The original Soviet SALT delegation numbered 24 (6 delegates and 18 advisers), of whom 8 were military (2 delegates, 6 advisers). This compared with a US delegation of 24, of whom 5 were military officers (1 delegate, 4 advisers). The US delegation also included 5 civilians currently or formerly associated with the Defense Department. How many of the Soviet civilians were in a comparable category is not known. Some changes have occurred in both delegations in the course of the negotiations, but the military-civilian ratio has remained about the same.

visers on these matters to the chairman of the Soviet delegation, Deputy Foreign Minister V. S. Semyonov, but also as watchdogs of the corporate interests of the Soviet military. Whether any of the military men on the delegation are institutional representatives of the Strategic Rocket Forces and the ABM component of the PVO (Air Defense), the two military entities most immediately concerned with strategic arms, cannot be ascertained from the information publicly available, but presumably these institutions are represented. The defense industry sector appears to have a representative in the person of P. S. Pleshakov, deputy minister of radio industry.

Unfortunately, the confidential nature of the SALT proceedings permits little insight into the negotiating role of the Soviet military representatives or the influence they have had on substantive issues. Some inkling of this can be gathered, however, in a few instances. One example is the FBS (Forward-Based Systems) issue. The Soviet military press in the spring of 1970 zeroed in on the theme that so-called "tactical" aircraft based in the NATO area were "intended mainly to accomplish strategic tasks through direct nuclear strikes against targets in the Soviet Union."[30] Subsequently, it became known through comment in both the American and Soviet press that the Soviet Union had begun at about the same time to insist in SALT that forward-based US tactical aircraft must be included in any limitation on strategic offensive weapons, on the grounds that such aircraft gave the United States "unilateral military advantages."[31] The inference is that urging from Soviet military quarters may have led to adoption of a stiff position on the FBS issue, even though this tended to muddy negotiations on intercontinental delivery systems.

So far as one can judge, to sum up, the Soviet marshals probably are not in a position to call the tune in the SALT talks. However, they may be able to exert a generally conservative influence on the negotiations, as a result of which the political leadership may tend to avoid proposals that might seem to give away military advantage for the sake of improving the negotiating climate.

THE SOVIET "MILITARY-INDUSTRIAL COMPLEX"

Soviet commentators habitually deny that there is any counterpart in the USSR to what is known in the United States as the "military-industrial complex."[32] However, the institutional anatomy of such a complex is certainly visible in the Soviet Union, even though its inner workings are seldom open to scrutiny. It has two major segments—the producers of arms, or what Soviet sources customarily refer to as the "defense industry sector" of the economy, and the users, that is, the military establishment itself. These two bureaucracies and their numerous subgroups, which are knit together in a basic supplier-customer relationship, and whose activities are overseen by various coordinating and controlling agencies at the upper levels of the Party government hierarchy, constitute the visible anatomy of the Soviet military-industrial complex.

A detailed description of this complex is not feasible here,[33] but a few words on the makeup of its industrial side may be worthwhile in terms of attempting to assess its influence. Eight All-Union ministries comprise the core of the "defence industry sector," which is responsible for the production of most military goods in the USSR, although several other industrial ministries also contribute to military production.[34] Conversely, some plants in the defense industries also manufacture a variety of products for the civilian economy, an effort which, as noted previously,[35] is currently receiving increased attention.

---

[32]Soviet assertions that the USSR has no military-industrial complex rest on the fiction that the absence of the profit motive in the Soviet system makes such a complex impossible by definition. See, for example, Colonel General K. Skorobogatkin, "In the Interests of Aggression and Profits," *Krasnaia zvezda* (December 28, 1969).

[33]For useful treatment of the subject, see: Sheren, *loc. cit.*, William T. Lee, "Soviet Military Industrial Complex," *Armed Forces Management* (May 1970): 25–35; Richard Armstrong, "Military-Industrial Complex—Russian Style," *Fortune* (August 1, 1969): 85–126.

[34]Sheren, *loc. cit.*, p. 123, identifies the eight industrial ministries of the defense sector as follows. Given in parentheses are abbreviations of the Russian designations of the ministries and the name of the responsible minister. Defense Industry (MOP—S. A. Zverev); Aviation Industry (MAP—P. V. Dementev); Shipbuilding Industry (MSP—B. E. Butoma); Electronics Industry (MEP—A. I. Shokin); Radio Industry (MR—V. P. Kalmykov); General Machine Building (MOM—S. A. Afanasev); Medium Machine Building (MSM—E. P. Slavskii); Machine Building (MM—V. V. Bakhirev). In addition to the ministries listed, others which contribute to military production include the ministries of instrument manufacturing, tractor and agricultural machinery building, chemical industry, and automobile industry.

[35]See page 11 of Wolfe, *op. cit.*, fn 13. Following Brezhnev's call at the 24th Party Congress for increased defense industry support of the civilian economy, Soviet officials announced plans for greater output of civilian goods by the defense sector.

---

[30]Colonel V. Aleksandrov, "For Carrying Out An Aggressive Policy: Attack Aviation of the USA," *Krasnaia zvezda* (May 13, 1970). See also Gallagher and Spielmann, *op. cit.*, p. 24.

[31]See Hedrick Smith, "After the Helsinki Arms Talks, New Complications," *New York Times* (December 24, 1970); V. Shestov, "What Is Behind the Propaganda Screen?" *Pravda* (February 3, 1971).

The defense industry bureaucracy has at least two notable features which bear on its potential as an interest group. The first is its continuity, both organizationally and in terms of key personnel. Since the late thirties when a separate cluster of defense industries and their supporting R&D institutions was established,[36] these industries have tended to keep their centralized or "vertical" organizational structure intact throughout various industrial shakeups, including the economic decentralization of the 1957–65 period. As a result, though growth and change have occurred in the defense sector,[37] basic enterprise groupings and lines of ministerial authority have remained relatively more stable than in other economic sectors. As for personnel, essentially the same set of major executives has administered the defense-related industries for many years; the collective experience of the eight incumbent ministers (named in footnote 34), for example, totals more than 200 years, so one may assume these are men who know their way around within the Soviet bureaucratic world and how to manipulate it to serve their institutional interests.

A second pertinent feature of the defense industry sector is its symbiotic relationship with the military establishment. In the Soviet Union, not only production of military goods, but the bulk of military R&D is carried out in institutions under the jurisdiction of the defense-related industrial ministries.[38] At the upper levels of the military establishment and the defense industries, the close link between military requirements and their fulfillment by the R&D and production programs of the defense industry sector apparently

has led to a mutual interest in preserving arrangements which have enabled the Soviet Union to compete successfully against the West in the field of military technology.

But this community of interest has operated at sub-levels of the interlocking military-industrial bureaucracies also. A network of ties too intricate to trace here has emerged between weapons design-production groups in industry and their immediate customers in the military establishment. One result is the formation of what might be called informal subgroup "alliances" devoted to promoting particular weapons categories, for example, between working elements of the Ministry of General Machine Building, which is believed to be responsible for design and production of strategic ballistic missiles,[39] and military representatives of the Strategic Rocket Forces.

How the various weapons procurement subgroups may be able to influence the Soviet SALT position is a highly speculative question. The groups concerned with offensive and defensive strategic systems have the most at stake in SALT, and may conceivably find their interests undercut by nonstrategic alliance groups hoping to capture more defense resources for their purposes. Some mediation of these competing claims presumably occurs within the General Staff and other Ministry of Defense agencies, but other regulatory bodies involving such key figures as D. F. Ustinov probably enter the picture before final judgments are made, lest the military agencies become both judges and advocates of their own projects. Finally, however, while the various alliance groups within the military-industrial complex may compete for priority among themselves, and perhaps seek their own power-wielding champions at higher rungs of the organizational ladder, they can also be expected to find common cause in resisting outside efforts to divert military-industrial resources to the civilian sector.

This included oil drilling equipment, tractors, machine tools, transport equipment, automation devices, and optical instruments. See S. A. Zverev, "The Potentialities of the Sector." *Izvestiia* (July 7, 1971).

[36] A Soviet account of the creation of a separate defense industry complex in the 1937–38 period may be found in an article of reminiscences by Marshal M. V. Zakharov, "On the Eve of World War II: May 1938–September 1939," *Novaia i Noveishaia Istoriia* [New and Newest History] 5 (September–October 1970): 3–27.

[37] Sheren, *loc. cit.*, p. 126.

[38] Scientific research institutes (NII), general design buros (OKB), and some plant facilities for experimental production comprise the R&D network within the defense industry sector, with cross ties at all levels with military representatives of the Ministry of Defense. See Sheren, *loc. cit.*, pp. 30, 35.

[39] Sheren, *loc. cit.*, p. 130. Similar alliances might be expected between subgroups in the Air Forces and Aviation Industry, the Ground Forces and the Ministry of Defense Industry, and so on. The Ministry of Defense Industry, incidentally, is the oldest of the various defense industries, and has traditionally been the chief producer of conventional ground weapons.

MAO TSE-TUNG AND HIS GENERALS:
SOME OBSERVATIONS ON MILITARY INTERVENTION IN CHINESE POLITICS

PARRIS H. CHANG

Professor Chang discusses the role of the People's Liberation Army in Chinese politics over the past decade, noting in particular fluctuations in military participation within the most important government and party bodies since the Cultural Revolution. He describes the apparent operations of the central policymaking bodies concerned with Chinese defense policy and the role of the PLA within them. Chang also examines the probable roles of leading military figures in the succession struggle which is likely to occur following the death of Mao.

Dr. Chang, an Associate Professor of Political Science at Pennsylvania State University, is the author of numerous articles on Chinese military affairs. This chapter is drawn from a larger study on military intervention in Chinese politics since the 1960s which is in progress.

I

One very conspicuous characteristic of Chinese politics since the 1960s has been the increasing participation of the People's Liberation Army (PLA) in China's political process. It is true that the PLA had been heavily politicized and had performed various nonmilitary functions in China's polity prior to the 1960s. Yet the new political roles assumed by the PLA since the 1960s are decidedly more important, and its intervention in Chinese politics has introduced a new power equation into the Chinese political system.

Whereas the PLA acted more or less like a pressure group "lobbying" the leadership of the Chinese Communist Party (CCP) to protect and enhance its corporate interests in the 1950s, the PLA-CCP relationship underwent subtle but significant qualitative changes in the first half of the 1960s. The PLA, under Lin Piao's stewardship, was transformed into the CCP's competitive institution as it became the object of national emulation after 1963 and rivaled the party in prestige and political/ideological correctness. It also became Mao's instrument of power and was used by Mao first to apply pressure on, and, then, attack the party bureaucracy. In the initial stages of the Great Proletarian Cultural Revolution (GPCR) in the spring and summer of 1966,

the PLA was virtually a "veto group"; it directly participated in the resolution of political conflicts at the highest level, and its support for the Maoist faction resulted in the defeat and displacement of anti-Maoist party leaders.[1]

The PLA intervention in the political process can be viewed as the "socialization of political conflict," in which the politically weak mobilized new participants and expanded the arena of political conflict so as to redress the balance of forces.[2] In the wake of the collapse of Mao's utopian Great Leap and commune programs in the early 1960s, Mao was opposed and politically eclipsed by other party leaders who controlled the party machinery. To overcome the opposition within the party and to project his will, Mao was compelled to go outside the party organizations to recruit support from other groups.[3]

---

[1] For a somewhat more detailed treatment of PLA's political roles, see Parris H. Chang, "The Changing Patterns of Military Participation in Chinese Politics," *Orbis* 16, no. 3 (Fall 1972): 780–802.

[2] This concept is adopted from E. E. Schattschnider, *The Semisovereign People: A Realist's View of Democracy in America* (New York: Holt, Rinehart & Winston, 1961). Several scholars of Chinese politics, e.g., Professor Tang Tsou of the University of Chicago and Professor Richard Baum of the University of California at Los Angeles, have applied the similar concept to analyzing Chinese politics since the Great Proletarian Cultural Revolution.

[3] This tactic has been used over and over again by Mao. See Parris H. Chang, "Research Notes on the Changing Loci

---

This is an updated and substantially revised version, for this publication, of "Mao Tse-tung and His Generals," which originally appeared in the Military Review *(September 1973).*

Hence, he turned to the PLA, coopted it, and changed its political roles in the system.

In this regard, it is important to remember that the initial expansion of PLA's political power falls into the category of what Morris Janowitz calls "reactive militarism."[4] That is, the PLA has gained new political power, not through a premeditated coup ("designed militarism" by Janowitz's definition) as the military has done in many other political systems, but through circumstances largely not of its own making. Granted that some PLA leaders may have actually contemplated from the outset the military intervention to enhance their own personal power, it still remains true that the expansion of PLA's political power had been a direct result of the pressure of party leaders, especially Mao, and of severe political turmoil and the virtual paralysis of party/government authorities.

What is most striking of the PLA intervention in Chinese politics is that the scope, objective and domain of the intervention have been structured largely by the civilian leaders, and by Mao in particular.[5] It was the civilian party leadership headed by Mao that expanded or contracted the political roles of the PLA, in response to political exigencies both before and during the GPCR. It is often overlooked that, in the initial stages of the GPCR, the Maoist leadership placed major reliance on the spontaneous forces of the "revolutionary left" (the Red Guards and rebels) and that it did not intend to involve the PLA extensively in the GPCR. Only when this strategy proved unworkable in the face of strong resistance by conservative power holders in Peking and the provinces was it that Mao and his supporters reversed the PLA's "nonintervention" stand, and pushed the PLA into the arena of GPCR to support the "revolutionary left" in January 1967.

The PLA's direct, extensive involvement in the GPCR after January 1967 soon led to the PLA supplantation of civilian party/government authorities in most provinces and takeover of various political and economic functions previously performed by party and governmental organizations. From the spring of 1967 onward,

and for more than a year, a military government existed in most provinces as local PLA leaders enforced a direct military rule through the mechanism of a "Military Control Committee." The assumption of such important political functions by the PLA, it should be pointed out again, was not the result of the PLA's own initiative. What happened was that the leftists' assaults on the provincial authorities in their attempts at "seizure of power from below" (in emulation of the 1871 "Paris Commune") paralyzed the party and government machinery and severely disrupted public order, and the Maoist leadership was compelled to move the PLA into the power vacuum to maintain law and order, hence political power devolved into the hands of local PLA leaders.

In the course of PLA intervention in Chinese politics since the early 1960s, Mao has used the PLA as his political instrument and attempted to set limits on its power and authority. Indeed, the PLA has depended upon the civilian leadership headed by Mao for sanctioning the expansion of its political roles and functions. However, the political control over the PLA by the party leadership has been weakened considerably over time. The virtual destruction of civilian party and government authorities after January 1967 left the system with only one organizational hierarchy capable of exercising effective authority—the PLA—and severely undermined the capability of the party leadership in Peking to control its actions.

After the July 1967 Wuhan Incident and the ensuing conservative military "backlash" against Mao's radical goals of the GPCR, the Maoist leadership was compelled to grant the PLA the power to use naked force (a power previously denied) to restore order. This new power, authorized in a central directive on 5 September 1967, was to make the PLA the controlling political force in the provinces. The PLA leaders, to the sorrow and dismay of Maoists, soon took advantage of their enhanced power to crack down the "revolutionary left" and, effectively, closed the Red Guard episode.

II

It seems clear that, whereas Mao succeeded in securing PLA intervention on his side to defeat his opponents (e.g., Liu Shao-ch'i) within the party and was largely able to determine the scope and objectives of the intervention up to the summer of 1967, thereafter the PLA intervention has assumed a logic and purposes of its own and become less amenable to political control by the

of Decision in the CCP," *The China Quarterly* (October–December 1970): especially 173–74, and Richard Baum "Elite Behavior Under Conditions of Stress," *Elites in the People's Republic of China*, edited by Robert A. Scalapino (Seattle, Wash.: University of Washington Press, 1972), pp. 550–52.

[4]Morris Janowitz, *The Military in the Political Development of New Nations: An Essay in Comparative Analysis* (Chicago: University of Chicago Press, 1964), p. 16.

[5]I am grateful to Professor Tang Tsou for this point.

civilian party leadership. Not unlike the genie released from the bottle, many PLA leaders have refused to give up their political roles and "return to the barracks" after the sweet taste of power. Despite the apparent desire of Mao to circumvent PLA's political roles and to bring the PLA under party control, the political prominence of the PLA continued into the seventies. Thus, when the 29 provincial-level party committees were reconstituted in August 1971 (more than two years after the Ninth Party Congress which politically symbolized the return of political normalcy), PLA commanders or professional military political commissars still headed 21 of them; and, among the 158 ranking provincial officials (first party secretaries, second secretaries, secretaries and deputy secretaries), 95, or 60 percent, of them were PLA men.

There seems to be no question that the role of the PLA was the basic cause of the conflict between Lin Piao and Mao and that Mao perceived Lin's enhanced power position as threatening his own. Lin and his supporters had greatly benefited from PLA's rise to unprecedented political prominence. Not only had Lin replaced Liu Shao-ch'i as Mao's successor and become the sole vice chairman of the party, but he had also placed many of his followers from the Fourth Field Army in key positions and substantially expanded his base of power. For example, Lin promoted a fellow Fourth Field Army leader, Huang Yung-sheng, Commander of the Canton Military Region (MR), to the post of the PLA Chief of Staff in March, 1968, bypassing many equally, if not better, qualified men, including several incumbent deputy chiefs of staff. In addition, Lin put his followers from the Fourth Field Army and his wife in control of the "Administrative Unit" of the Military Affairs Commission (MAC), the regime's supreme military decision-making body. Moreover, Lin also replaced more than 300 senior military officials at various levels with his own men and made considerable inroads into the power base of other military factions.

When the Ninth Party Congress was convened in April, 1969, Lin's men packed the meeting. He was the featured speaker, delivering the political report to the Congress, and the Congress adopted a new Party Constitution containing an unprecedented provision which saluted Lin Piao and sanctioned his succession to Mao:

Comrade Lin Piao has consistently held high the great red banner of Mao Tse-tung thought and has most loyally and resolutely carried out and defended Comrade Mao Tse-tung's proletarian revolutionary line. Comrade Lin Piao is Comrade Mao Tse-tung's close comrade-in-arms and successor.

In the newly elected Central Committee (CC), approximately 46 percent or 127 of the 279 members were career soldiers, and, in the 25-member Politburo, 13 were military representatives. In these two highest decision-making bodies of the party, Lin's supporters constituted the largest and most influential group. In the post Congress period, the military continued to dominate the party, and under his stewardship, Lin managed to place the army in control of nearly every aspect of life in China, defying the "unified leadership" of the party.

This situation was not anticipated nor desired by Mao, for it was contrary to his dictum that the party must direct the "gun," and the "gun" should not be allowed to command the party. Given the increasingly strong position of the military and Lin Piao in China's post-GPCR politics, a suspicious Mao apparently viewed the whole situation with grave apprehension. When the party's CC met in a plenary session at Lushan in late August to early September 1970 to consider, among other things, a draft of the new state constitution, Lin Piao spoke in favor of retaining the post of head of state (to which Lin may have aspired), in disagreement with Mao who wanted to abolish the post. Mao's distrust of Lin was strengthened and he apparently made a decision shortly thereafter to curtail Lin Piao's power and to reassert the party's control over the military. In December 1970, Mao called an enlarged Politburo session at Pei-tai-ho and subjected Lin Piao and his five top aides, Huang Yung-sheng, Wu Fa-hsien, Li Tso-p'eng, Yeh Ch'un, and Ch'iu Hui-tso (all of them members of the Politburo and of Administrative Unit of MAC), to severe criticism. Following the meeting, at the end of January 1971, Mao reshuffled the commanding officers of the Peking Military Region and the Peking Garrison, replacing Lin Piao's men there, and transferred troop units considered loyal to Lin out of the Peking area.[6]

In fact, these maneuvers have been detailed vividly in a secret party document titled "Chung-fa 1972 (12)." In Mao's own words, he adopted three measures after the Lushan conference:

One was to throw stones, one was to mix in sand, and the third was to dig up the cornerstone. I criti-

---

[6]For an excellent analysis of the causes of the Mao-Lin conflict and its development, see Ying-mao Kau, "Editor's Introduction," *Chinese Law and Government* 5, no. 3/4 (Fall/Winter 1972–73): 3–30.

cized the material Ch'en Po-ta had used to deceive many people, and I commented on reports of the Thirty-Eighth Army and of the Tsinan Military District on opposing arrogance and complacency. I also made critical comments on a document of the long forum of the Military Affairs Commission, which didn't criticize Ch'en at all. My method was to get hold of these stones and make critical comments, and then let everyone discuss them—this was throwing stones. When dirt is too tightly packed, no air can get through; but if a little sand is mixed in, air can circulate. Not enough people had been mixed into the "Administrative Unit" of the Military Affairs Commission, so I added a few more men—this is called mixing in sand. Reorganizing the Peking Military Region is called digging up the cornerstone.[7]

The intention and implications of Mao's moves were not lost on Lin Piao and his top aides. And soon thereafter, according to another secret CCP document "Chung-fa 1972 (4)," Lin Piao and his cohorts went into action to prepare a coup against Mao to which they gave the code name "571 Project."[8] In fact, the Maoist determination to destroy Lin Piao is so obvious, judging from Mao's own remarks contained in the Number 12 document, that it seems highly questionable that Lin Piao could have escaped his political doom. Hence, whether or not Lin did plan to assassinate Mao is largely a moot question.

III

Amid efforts to expose and repudiate Lin's crimes since the fall of 1971, the Chinese leadership has also renewed an intensive nationwide campaign to downgrade the role of the PLA and reassert party control over all the spheres of Chinese life. The arrogance and complacency of PLA men and their tendency as leaders in the various party and government organizations to ignore the principle of democratic centralism and to rule by fiat have been singled out for attack. The role of the PLA cadres has been subjected to mounting criticism and close scrutiny by their civilian colleagues.

Also, in the wake of Lin Piao's demise, many of Lin's followers have been removed from positions of power. In the PLA's central headquarters, for example, the PLA Chief of Staff Huang Yung-sheng, the Air Force Commander Wu Fa-hsien, the Navy's First Political Commissar Li Tso-p'eng, the Logistics Department

head Ch'iu Hui-tso, among others, have been dismissed from their respective posts and dropped from the reshuffled Politburo announced after the Tenth Party Congress in late August 1973. In the provinces, a large number of PLA leaders who have close ties with Lin and his Fourth Field Army System have also been dismissed. These dismissals include commanders of Sinkiang and Chengtu Military Regions (MR), of Chekiang and Kiangsi Military Districts (MD), and Political Commissars of Wuhan and Foochow MR's, and Chekiang, Hunan, Kiangsi and Kweichow MD's. In the new Central Committee elected by the Tenth Party Congress, most of Lin Piao's supporters have failed to win reelection, and the total representation of the PLA has decreased from 46% in the Ninth CC to approximately 30% now (60 of the 195 regular members and 38 of the 124 alternate members). In the 25-man Politburo (21 regulars and 4 alternates), the military men have been reduced from 13 to 7, although two of them are also vice-chairmen of the Party and members of the nine-man Politburo Standing Committee.

Several other new developments in personnel changes also deserve close attention. Since the beginning of 1972, and particularly during the later part of 1972, veteran party officials have increasingly been rehabilitated and appointed to the posts of provincial party secretaries to replace PLA men in the provincial party committees. Thus, in contrast with the overwhelming representation of the PLA men (60%) in the provincial party committees in August 1971, the ratio of PLA men as of July 1973 was slightly lower than civilian cadres—among the approximately 163 party secretaries (including every rank) who are in good standing, 80 (or 49 percent) are of civilian backgrounds, 77 (or 47 percent) are PLA men, while the backgrounds of the remaining six are obscure. The replacement of PLA men by veteran party officials—e.g., the transfer of T'an Ch'i-lung from Fukien to Chekiang as the top official there, in place of the purged military figure Nan P'ing, the promotion of Saifudin to succeed Lung Shu-chin as the First Secretary of Sinkiang, Hua Kuo-feng's return from Peking to Hunan to resume his responsibility as first secretary, and the appointment of Chao Tzu-yang, Lin Li-ming and Chiao Lin-yi as party secretaries of Kwangtung (Chiao has also replaced General Huang Jung-lai as first secretary of Canton)—is undoubtedly designed by the current central leadership to counterbalance the influence of PLA men in provincial politics.

Furthermore, PLA officers of non-Lin Piao factions have been assigned to various local

---

[7] The text of the document is translated into English in *ibid.*, pp. 31–42. The quoted passage is based on *ibid.*, p. 38, with minor corrections in translation.

[8] *Ibid.*, pp. 43–57.

party/government and PLA organizations to strengthen the anti-Lin forces there and to change the balance of power among rival groups. The appointment of a First Field Army leader Yang Yung, dismissed as Commander of Peking MR during the GPCR, as the Commander of Sinkiang MR, the transfer of the Second Field Army figures, Ch'en Tsai-tao and Chung Han-hua, former Commander and Political Commissar of Wuhan MR respectively, and the principal figures of the 1967 Wuhan Incident, to the Foochow and Canton MRs (the strongholds of Lin's Fourth Field Army) and the promotion of Chen Chang-feng (Mao's former bodyguard) to the posts of Commander and a provincial party secretary in Kiangsi are a few indications of this emerging trend.

The old field army affiliations and personal ties continue to be salient elements of factional cleavages within the Chinese leadership,[9] as the leaders themselves appear to think and act in terms of them.

In this regard, the Chinese Communists are not unlike non-Communist Chinese political figures, e.g., Yuan Shih-k'ai, who excelled in the tactics of "divide and rule, check and balance." Interestingly enough, Lin Piao actually accused Mao and his group precisely of that: "Today, they use this group to attack that group; tomorrow they use that group to attack this group . . . they manufacture contradictions and splits in order to attain their goals of divide and rule, destroying each group in turn and maintaining their ruling position."[10]

Mao's operational method of "divide and rule, check and balance," although enabling him to retain and maximize control of the factions in the leadership, may prove to be dysfunctional for the system in the long run. Yuan Shih-k'ai's relationship with the Pei-yang Army leaders provides a lesson. For rivalry and division encouraged and fostered by Mao's manipulative approach will most likely outlast Mao to plague the future leadership. Without an arbiter of Mao's authority and stature, the future Chinese leadership probably will experience more conflicts and instability than it has thus far.

In addition to its historical field army factional cleavages, the PLA is by no means united in its views and preferences. Like the military establishment in other polities, the PLA also has its interservice rivalry among its various service arms, conflicts among its old and young officers, and among different groupings holding diverse strategic preferences and priorities. The bitter debate in 1965 between the advocates of the "people's war strategy" (articulated by Lin Piao) and of the "forward strategy" (argued by then PLA Chief of Staff Lo Jui-ch'ing) with regard to China's response to the escalated war in Indochina is a celebrated case and has received much analysis by Western scholars.[11]

Different services of the PLA have also differed on domestic political issues as well as on strategic/foreign policy options. On the domestic scene, the ground army appears to be more conservative politically, favors decentralization of power and opposes the radical goals of the GPCR, while the navy and air force tend to support centralization of control and the GPCR. On the issue of strategy, the ground force leans to a more conventional type warfare, while the technically oriented units such as navy and air force stress a modern, tactical warfare.[12] The conflicting preferences of various services and branches of the PLA may have underlaid a public debate over development of steel or electronics industry in 1971.[13] It seems that the Chinese conventional ground forces, in view of their weaponry and equipment, would stand to benefit more from a large-scale investment in and development of the steel industry, while the technically oriented air force, navy and missile units, given the requirement of their sophisticated weapons, would be the chief beneficiaries from the development of electronics industry.[14]

[11]See Harry Harding, Jr., and Melvin Gurtov, *The Purge of Lo Jui-ch'ing: The Politics of Chinese Strategic Planning,* R-548-PR (Santa Monica, Calif.: The RAND Corporation, February 1971), and Uri Raanan, "Peking's Foreign Policy 'Debate,' 1965-1966," and Donald Zagoria, "The Strategic Debate in Peking," in Tang Tsou (ed.), *China in Crisis,* Vol. II (China's Policies in Asia and America's Alternatives) (Chicago: University of Chicago Press, 1968) pp. 23-71, 237-68.

[12]Allen S. Whiting, "China: The Struggle for Power," *The New Republic* (Dec. 4, 1971), and Harry Harding, Jr., "The Making of Chinese Military Policy," in William Whitson (ed.), *The Military and Political Power in China in the 1970's* (New York: Praeger, 1972), pp. 361-85.

[13]See, for example, *Jen-min Jih-pao* (People's Daily), August 17, 1971.

[14]The subsequent decision to stress steel over electronics may have been related to an assessment of external threat. As long as the main threat is defined to come from north, i.e., the Soviets, ground forces have to be relied upon heavily and they will have top priority for new equipment; but if the threat is thought to come from east and south, the U.S., the air force and navy will play a more active role in China's defense. In this connection, we can speculate that the air force and navy have resisted the "opening" to the U.S., while the ground forces supported the move.

[9]See William Whitson and Chen-hsia Huang, *The Chinese High Command: A History of Communist Military Politics, 1927-71* (New York: Praeger Publishers, 1972), for the history and development of the five "Field Army Systems" as corporate factional groups in the Chinese leadership.

[10]Quoted in "Chung-fa 1972 (4)," *Chinese Law and Government, op. cit.,* p. 54.

In this connection, it is perhaps pertinent to discuss procedures of conflict resolution and locus of decision in the Chinese high command. In structural terms, prior to 1969 the Politburo was the regime's highest decision-making body, and important measures were brought to it for decision.[15] Even so, already in the early 1960s political power in China had become diffused (and more so since the GPCR), and often effective decisions were made elsewhere outside the Politburo (e.g., by some "ad-hoc" bodies) and were then approved by the Politburo or its Standing Committee in a *pro forma* manner.[16] Due to growing dissension at the top, and as different leaders attempted to enlist "outside" support to change the equilibrium in their favor, the arena of political conflict had been steadily expanded and a significant number of political actors below the Politburo level were drawn into participation, for example, through the Central Work Conferences, in the decision-making process and the resolution of conflicts.[17]

Military leaders, both at the center and provinces (and a few of them were then not members of the CC), took part in these Central Work Conferences. Their participation enabled them to articulate their views and aggregate their corporate interests, for although many issues deliberated therein were nonmilitary in appearance (e.g., national economy, allocation of resources), decisions on these matters frequently had direct implications for the military establishment.

[15]The 1956 Party Constitution approved by the Eighth Party Congress prescribed that the Politburo and its Standing Committee directed the Secretariat to attend to the daily work of the Party, government, and armed forces; the 1969 and 1973 Party Constitutions have entrusted this power only to the chairman, the vice-chairman (now the five vice-chairmen) and the Standing Committee of the Politburo, and not to the Politburo itself.

[16]Two examples can be cited to illustrate this point. A 5-man "CC Financial and Economic Group" said to have been set up in 1962 and headed by Ch'en Yun to take charge of the regime's over-all financial and economic policies, made certain important proposals which were approved by a politburo meeting convened and chaired by Liu Shao-ch'i in 1962; see "The Crimes of Liu Shao-ch'i," *Shou-tu hung-wei-ping* (Peking: Propaganda Department of the Revolutionary Rebel Headquarters of Capital Universities and Colleges Red Guard), Nos. 31 and 32 (22 February 1967). The 5-man "Cultural Revolution Group" headed by P'eng Chen put forth the "February Outline Report" which also obtained Liu's approval at a Politburo Standing Committee meeting on 5 February 1966; see *Counter-Revolutionary Revisionist P'eng Chen's Towering Crimes of Opposing the Party, Socialism and the Thought of Mao Tse-tung* (Peking: Liaison Centre for Thorough Criticism of Liu-Teng-Tao, Tungfang hung Commune, China University of Science and Technology, Red Guard Congress), 10 June 1967, in *Survey of China Mainland Magazines*, No. 640 (13 January 1969), pp. 6–7.

[17]For a detailed analysis of the Central Work Conferences and the policy-making process of China in the 1950s and 1960s, see Parris H. Chang, "Research Notes on the Changing Loci of Decision in the CCP," *op. cit.*, pp. 169–94.

With respect to deliberation and decision of military and national security policy, the locus of effective authority lies in the Military Affairs Committee (MAC). Headed by Mao since 1935, and including the top officials of central PLA headquarters, service arms, and selected regional-provincial PLA leaders, the MAC is unquestionably the regime's topmost military decision-making organ. It makes decisions on overall policy for the armed forces and national security affairs. Concrete policy proposals, plans and "position papers" are believed to be routinely originated within a secretarial body attached to the MAC—its Staff Office (headed by PLA Chief of Staff Lo Jui-ch'ing who was concurrently the MAC Secretary-general until his purge in late 1965) or, after 1968, its "Administrative Unit." This secretarial body, under the stewardship of the senior MAC Vice-chairman (P'eng Teh-huai up to 1959, Lin Piao up to 1971, and Yeh Chien-ying since), attends to day-to-day business and is charged with coordinating and supervising the implementation of military-national security measures within China's huge military establishment. When the top MAC leaders are in essential agreement, policy decisions are enacted by the small MAC Standing Committee which had only eight members, including Mao and Lin, on the eve of the GPCR. On controversial issues, the Chinese leaders have resorted to enlarged sessions of the MAC, in which regional PLA leaders who are not MAC members also take part, to build up consensus and settle differences, as was the case with the dispute over China's response to the escalation of the Vietnamese War in the summer of 1965, and possibly over the steel vs. electronics controversy in 1971. Actions decided by the MAC may be further reviewed and approved by the Politburo or its Standing Committee, depending on the issues and the circumstances. A major issue, if it involves allocation of resources or foreign affairs, may be brought to the Central Work Conference for deliberation, so that necessary coordination can be worked out with civilian Party officials in charge of other areas.

IV

It remains to assess the role of the PLA in China's polity, and its prospects in the post-Mao era. In spite of the adverse effect of the Lin Piao purge, and the efforts by the civilian Party officials to curb the military influence, the PLA is still a formidable political force to be reckoned with in China's political system. To be sure, the military representation in the new Politburo and CC has declined somewhat in comparison with the Ninth CC. Nonetheless the PLA leaders who hold key positions in the regime's administrative apparatus (e.g., the seat of First Party Secretary in 18 provinces is occupied by a PLA man) which must implement central directives continue to be represented in the CC, and these and other PLA leaders are in a strategic position to block the implementation of central directives, if these directives were inimical to their interests and imposed against their will.

It is also true that, despite interservice rivalry and conflicting interests within the military establishment, the PLA as a whole has a common interest in enhancing its prestige and status in society, in receiving greater defense allocations and in increasing its role and influence in the political system, and that they can be expected to close ranks to fight against attempts by other groups to encroach upon their prerogatives. Furthermore, as the image of the Chinese leadership has been tarnished, and the ability of the regime to elicit compliance from the population by persuasion has diminished as a result of the social, political upheaval since the GPCR, China's rulers will have to continue to rely on coercive means of control, and those who command the instruments of coercion will perforce remain a dominant political force in China.

At present, China is on the threshold of an important transitional period. As long as Mao remains on the scene, he may, by the sheer weight of his personal authority, and through manipulation of rival political groups, using divide and rule tactics, keep the military in check. When Mao finally departs (he will be eighty in December 1973), his exit is likely to generate a succession crisis and may lead to further expansion of the military's political role. Undoubtedly, the succession to Mao was a major problem preoccupying the minds of the delegates to the Tenth Party Congress in August 1973, and the Congress has made an arrangement designed to effect an orderly transition after Mao. Instead of naming an individual future successor as the Ninth Party Congress did in 1969, the Tenth Party Congress has endorsed a coalition type of leadership under Premier Chou En-lai to forestall a successional crisis and to guide China smoothly into the post-Mao era. In fact, the new Politburo Standing Committee, full Politburo and CC that emerged from the Congress contain rival political groups holding conflicting views and interests, and the new leadership is a shaky coalition at best. Despite his enormous charisma, and great political and administrative talent, Premier Chou clearly lacks the kind of power and authority Mao has wielded, and after Mao's passing Chou may not

be able to hold the pieces together. Even if the coalition or collective leadership under Chou works in the short run, Chou, at seventy-five, is not likely to be around too long, and an intensive struggle for succession will eventually ensue.

In such a struggle, not only is the military going to be actively involved, but several military leaders are likely to seek the top leadership position. As of now, three Politburo members, Li Teh-sheng, Ch'en Hsi-lien and Hsu Shih-yu appear to be the stronger contenders. Li Teh-sheng, newly elevated to the vice-chairman of the Party, controls the party machinery in the PLA as Director of the PLA General Political Department, and at the same time officiates as First Party Secretary of Anhwei. Ch'en is Commander of Mukden Military Region, which encompasses the whole of Manchuria, and is concurrently First Party Secretary of Liaoning; he has under his command more than half a million troops and the industrial might of Manchuria. Hsu, Commander of Nanking MR, which has jurisdiction over Kiangsu, Chekiang and Anhwei provinces, is also First Party Secretary of Kiangsu; he has close to 300,000 soldiers and the rich resources of the three East China provinces behind him.

To have a fair chance of success in the post-Mao struggle for power, the serious contenders must have a military, territorial or important organizational base of power. Due to their present positions, the military men named above have considerable advantage in a struggle for succession. Even should they not become "candidates" for the national leadership, they undoubtedly will play the role of "king-vetoers" to deny the leadership post to those they oppose, or act as "king-makers" and play an important role in determining China's future leader.

The nature of future contenders for national power, furthermore, may serve to prolong and intensify the forthcoming succession crisis which in turn may deepen the military involvement and expand the military influence in the regime's political affairs. Men in Mao's peer group, like Chou En-lai, Teng Hsiao-p'ing, and P'eng Chen, have had distinguished revolutionary careers; each, in his own right, has had great stature and has been a *national* leader of long standing. On the other hand, none of the future contenders possess such credentials and appear to lack the high personal and intellectual qualities of the older generation of CCP leaders. While the younger leaders are not exactly faceless and some of them have indeed been ranking regional party/military figures for more than a decade (e.g., Ch'en Hsi-lien and Hsu Shih-yu), they are by no means household names—they are probably better known to "China-watchers" outside China than to the rank-and-file of the CCP, let alone to the Chinese masses. As they differ so very little in terms of their careers, accomplishments, and seniority, each will probably feel that he is equally deserving and has an equal right to aspire to the supreme leadership position. Should someone come to the top momentarily, he will have extreme difficulty consolidating his position, as his peers are unlikely to be deterred from attempts to unseat and replace him.

To conclude: Mao's succession problem is far from settled, and political uncertainty and instability lie ahead. In such a situation, the political influence of the military in China is bound to increase further. Not only will the military, as a group, actively participate in the resolution of political conflicts, in decision-making processes and have a deciding voice in shaping the policy priorities of the regime, but some of its leaders who have formidable military, territorial and economic bases of power and hold interlocking Party-government-military leadership positions will also contend for China's supreme leadership position.

LONDON AND WASHINGTON: MISPERCEPTIONS BETWEEN ALLIES

RICHARD E. NEUSTADT

This article highlights important aspects of the defense policymaking processes of Great Britain and the United States by examining their views of one another during the course of the Suez and Skybolt crises in their normally cooperative alliance relationship. It identifies a number of crucial misperceptions that contributed to these disagreements which arose when key individuals on both sides failed to comprehend adequately the political and bureaucratic characteristics of the government machinery of their ally. Professor Neustadt focuses upon their mutual misinterpretations regarding the nature of political accountability, standard operating procedures and the various interests and relationships among key political actors within each system. He thus provides us a compelling reason for the study of comparative defense policy and policy processes.

Richard E. Neustadt is a Professor of Government and Associate Dean of the John F. Kennedy School of Government, Harvard University. He has written extensively on the politics of the American executive branch and is the author of Presidential Power *(1960),* Alliance Politics *(1970), and numerous articles.*

INTRODUCTION

Misunderstandings regarding the inner politics of other governments can play an important role in shaping the relationships among states. A variety of misperceptions of this nature on the part of both British and American leaders contributed significantly to the strains in the Anglo-American alliance which accompanied the Suez Crisis of 1956, a strategic issue, and the Skybolt Affair of 1962, basically a structural issue, with strategic overtones. Following brief summaries

Extracted by permission and with editorial modifications and deletions from Alliance Politics *(New York: Columbia University Press, 1970), pp. 11–29, 32–55, and 76–114. Copyright © 1970 Richard E. Neustadt.*

of these two crises, a series of instances are examined in which men in London and Washington contributed to these difficulties by failing to take into account critical nuances about the operation of their ally's internal political machine.

TWO CRISES: SUEZ AND SKYBOLT

The Suez Crisis

On July 26, 1956, Nasser nationalized the Suez Canal. (The last British troops had left their base two weeks before.) Nasser gave as his reason American abandonment of Aswan and his need for compensating funds from Canal revenues. That reason may or may not have been real. Within a week the British Cabinet, Eden in the van, had privately decided to restore Western control of the Canal by force, unless negotiation would suffice to do it, in the process squelching Nasser once and for all: invasion would serve to unseat him. That resolve, though unannounced because contingent, seemed to square with current sentiment in the House of Commons and the country.

The French were partners in the military planning, eager partners, indeed champing at the bit. The government of Guy Mollet, six months in office, had convinced itself of two things: first, that its survival and indeed that of the Fourth Republic, turned on the forceable repression of the rebellion in Algeria; second, that the rebels were dependent on Nasser's support. Israeli plans were also being instigated by the French, contingent on British support.

Eden felt that Eisenhower would not really interfere, surely he could not help but draw a parallel between the two Canals, Suez and Panama. Americans might need the precedent of intervention in Suez; this should keep them quiet.

In secrecy a diplomatic "cover story" was prepared: Israel would attack Egypt on the Sinai Peninsula, with France and Britain intervening to protect the Canal. Their ultimatum would demand that both belligerents withdraw from its vicinity: Egypt would refuse: they then would occupy the area by force to save world commerce. Washington naturally was told nothing.

On October 29, the day Israel marched, Washington was giving what attention it could spare from our election to events in Hungary, seeking by all means at its disposal to keep world attention riveted upon them without seeming to exploit them for itself. Within hours of the Israeli attack Eisenhower was reading press cables of the British/French ultimatum, not alone to Israel but also to Egypt. By all accounts, his anger was profound: "They did not tell me." The sentiment apparently was shared by his associates, aghast at the *lèse majesté*—not least by Dulles.

Worse was to come. On October 31, the British bombed Egyptian airfields while Israeli columns raced across Sinai. Then "nothing happened," no invasion followed: the Canal remained in Egypt's hands and ships were sunk to block it. Eisenhower is said to have been astounded: waywardness was bad enough; incompetence required punishment.

By November 5, Israel and Egypt were no longer fighting. Only on that day did the first allied troops appear at the Canal, ostensibly to separate the combatants. By then the only fire to be ceased was theirs against Egyptians. Hence punishment: our Secretary of the Treasury, George Humphrey, strong in government and close to Eisenhower, gave the British Treasury a virtual ultimatum: as Londoners recall it, he posed the simple choice of an immediate cease-fire or war on the pound, with not a dollar to be had for oil supplies. Unless they heeded the UN, he now would block their path to dollars from the International Monetary Fund, put off their hopes of credit from our Export-Import Bank, and make no effort to align our central bankers behind sterling.

Reluctantly, the British did as they were told. In a painful morning Cabinet on November 6, they opted for cease-fire. This would leave their forces one-third of the way down the Canal. Two or five or six days more (estimates differed, but their Chiefs of Staff said five or six) would see them in possession of the whole. The French were horrified but helpless: allied forces had British commanders, and British troops were in the van on the road south. The French were too entangled to proceed alone. So they, too, acquiesced. As others have noted, the Entente-Cordiale died then and there.

On November 17, Foreign Secretary Lloyd visited Dulles in the hospital. Their interchange has been reported widely. In one version, Dulles asked him, "Why did you stop?" Lloyd countered, "Why didn't you give us a wink?" Dulles replied, "Oh, I couldn't do that." This often has been cited as a nasty sort of joke. Far from it, I take Dulles to have been entirely serious. His words go to the heart of the case.

The Skybolt Affair

In March 1960, Prime Minister Macmillan met Eisenhower at Camp David. There the PM asked for and received assurance that the US would endeavor to develop an air-to-surface missile, carried by a bomber for release upon a target

800 miles away. Macmillan also was assured that if we found it technically feasible to make, we would produce it for ourselves and he could then place orders for the RAF. This was the Skybolt missile, so called by our Air Force. With Skybolt, the RAF Bomber Command would double its prospective life of proclaimed usefulness as a strategic deterrent. Throughout the 1960's bombers, then, could carry on as symbols of Great Britain's nuclear independence. And London would not have to pay for anything except its missiles as an add-on to our orders after we brought Skybolt to the production stage.

At the same time that he struck this advantageous bargain, Macmillan pledged to Eisenhower something we were eager to acquire, a European base for nuclear submarines. Macmillan offered, we accepted, Holy Loch in Scotland as our base.

However, before the end of August 1962, Secretary of Defense McNamara's technical and budgetary aides were urging him to do what Budget Bureau sources had proposed for a year before, namely to cancel Skybolt. By now they could present him a full argument on grounds of cost-effectiveness: development was slow, expensive, and unpromising. We had alternatives: for the short term we could use another air-to-surface missile with a simpler guidance system and a shorter range, the Hound Dog; in the longer term, the mission of defense-suppression that we envisioned for Skybolt would be moot, as Minuteman took over from manned bombers. As for deterrence (Britain's intended use of Skybolt) Minuteman could meet our needs in combination with Polaris. On November 7 McNamara saw the President, together with the Secretary of State, Dean Rusk, and Kennedy's Assistant, McGeorge Bundy. On his showing they agreed that Skybolt ought to go, and also that the British must be warned without delay.

McNamara lost no time in summoning the British Ambassador, Sir David Ormsby Gore. Then, by prearrangement, after Embassy dispatches had reached London, McNamara telephoned to the British Secretary of Defense Thorneycroft. In neither case could McNamara say to them definitively that Skybolt would be stopped. But what he could do was make plain to them his own strong disposition. Gore apparently expressed himself appalled. Thorneycroft's response was relatively calm: if Skybolt's cancellation were to follow then the British must go on to something else. He is said to have dropped the word "Polaris," among others, and hung up the telephone. Thorneycroft's claim soothed McNamara, who assumed thereafter

that the British chaps were working on their problem. However, despite Thorneycroft's calm, the news was hardly welcome, least of all to the PM, and it went nowhere else.

On December 11, McNamara went to London to offer the much shorter range Hound Dog missile as a substitute for Skybolt. What ensued was "a Pinero drama of misunderstanding," as Arthur Schlesinger described it in *A Thousand Days*.[1] The reasons are not far to seek: Thorneycroft was waiting for an offer of Polaris; McNamara was expecting him to ask for it. What McNamara offered was a crushing disappointment, and offensive to boot. How, as Henry Brandon notes, could Englishmen base "independence" upon something labeled Hound Dog?

The crisis finally came to a head at a meeting between Kennedy and Macmillan at Nassau beginning on 19 December. The President proposed an earlier idea: Polaris tied to NATO. Macmillan responded with an eloquent soliloquy. Its point was buried in a reference to the Queen's prerogative of using British weapons independently at moments of supreme emergency. On this the two sides built a compromise, the so-called Nassau Agreement.

By that Agreement, reached after two days of bargaining, the British were to get from us Polaris missiles; they would build the needed submarines, also the nuclear warheads, with our technical assistance under previous agreements. They pledged this weaponry to NATO from the outset, in a multinational force—to which we also would contribute—under integrated command. The pledge was permanent, an irreversible commitment. But it contained an emergency escape clause. In a time of supreme peril to Great Britain, these submarines could be withdrawn, temporarily of course, for independent use by HMG. Integration thus was married to a form of independence.

The postscript occurred on January 14, 1963, when President de Gaulle held a press conference. In well-rehearsed responses to set questions he announced that France would veto British membership in the EEC and also that he had no interest in the Nassau offer to France also. France would build her own deterrent for herself: true independence.

LONDON AND WASHINGTON

"London" and "Washington" are shorthand terms for vast machines of government, which

---

[1] Arthur Schlesinger, *A Thousand Days* (Boston: Houghton Mifflin, 1965), p. 861.

labeled "A" and "B" we would be less likely to personify. These are not "friendly" in the sense of human individuals, nor is my inquiry addressed to human friendship. We deal here with the friendship of machines. Before I turn to differences in their internal workings, let me give you a quick sketch of the working parts. Then you can more readily observe the shades of difference, part by part.

Some Basic Concepts

These machines are not manlike, although men are in them. Each machine is a complex array of mutually dependent, institutionalized "positions." These are known to us as public offices, elective or appointive as the case may be. Each position is linked to many others along lines of set procedure for getting things done. These procedural lines are known to us by such catch phrases as budgetary process, legislative programming, nominating process, cable traffic. However known, these lines are "action channels," regularized means of moving to decision, taking action or avoiding it.

Each position and each channel has a history, reflecting a succession of laws, customs, precedents, and past incumbents. These frame the work requirements for every new incumbent.

In each position sits a man discharging it as best he can in light of its requirements and his ambitions as he sees them—brains and temperament allowing—in short, by his totality of human "interests." That totality emphatically includes his sense of duty, and loyalties: personal, political, programmatic. He is no *homo economicus*.

For action purposes, each man is linked to many other men, although in no sense equally to all, by the procedural channels running past or through their jobs as well as his. Precisely how their work relates to his for given purposes defines the link in given situations. Our Secretaries of State and Treasury, for instance, are linked differently when diplomatic action calls for words as against money.

A man may have another link to colleagues. Depending on procedures for selection and advancement, his future may be governed by their judgment.

For want of better words, the moves toward action in a government machine—from positions, through channels—can be termed a "game," the men becoming "players." The game they play is known as governing their country. Their object is public authority wielded (or withheld) for substantive purposes. They play for "stakes" deriving from their interests. It is sometimes fun

but not a sport; nor on the evidence before you do they take it so. I urge you not to do so either.

A player's stakes blend personal with substantive concerns. For every player, any move toward action brings an element of personal challenge wrapped in a substantive guise. Of these his stakes are made. The substance is important, never doubt it, for that is what the game is all about. But so is the personal element. It makes no difference whether the move is of his own making or arises from sources outside his control. Either way, involvement of his job in some degree involves himself. Attached to his position are assorted expectations in the minds of his associates, evoked by its requirements and his career. Attached to his position also are his expectations of himself. Both sorts of expectations are reflected in his interests. He is man-in-office, with a record to defend and a future to advance, not least in history. The personal is tightly interwoven with the institutional. It is a rare player who can keep the two distinct, much less view both apart from substance. None was so rare in the cases before you.

Accordingly, this is a game in which the stakes rise high. Whether they are high or low for any given player depends upon the expectations centering on him. These can change as rapidly as the surrounding circumstances alter in the eyes of other players. Hence the stakes are subject to quick change. Stakes can be far lower than were Dulles's when he withdrew our offer on Aswan. Stakes can rise as fast as his did at the moment the Canal was seized "because" of that withdrawal. And stakes can rise as high as Eden's on the eve of the Suez intervention. In public life, there is nothing higher than that: the prize of office and the fruits of policy, along with the verdict of history. What matters more to a man than his head when he identifies it with the public good?

The working parts as here described are common to both Washington and London. Moreover these machines, the British and American, have common origins: the British Constitution and English common law. They also share the hallmarks of "democracy," as understood on our side of the globe. Both governments are constitutional in character, representative in form, limited in scope, confined by guarantees of private right, hence private property, and legitimatized by the symbols of popular sovereignty. Finally, they share a working language (more or less), a source of endless trouble in their dealings with each other.

Accordingly, the game of governance as played in both machines is broadly speaking the same game. Action channels and positions in the one bear a family resemblance to those in the other. But resemblance is deceptive. Only in an overview are these machines alike. Only in the broad are their games the same. Details diverge. The players in our cases ran afoul of the details.

Most statesmen on both sides can catalogue gross differences: presidential versus cabinet government, federalism versus centralism, factionalism versus party discipline, a written Constitution versus parliamentary self-restraint, all in the context of a newly populated continent versus a long-settled island. But these were known to everyone in 1956 and 1962 as well as now. Why then the misperceptions of our crises?

Misperceptions in these crises were occasioned not by the gross differences but rather by small shadings—sometimes hidden, often subtle—in their application to positions and to channels, thus to players and to stakes of human interest. We were tripped up by nuances.

As between London and Washington the differences that count lurk at this lower level of nuance, of fine detail.

Suez and Skybolt

What are the "little" differences between these two machines? Or rather, more precisely, what were they in the time span of our crises? Both machines evolve and change with time. Answers for the middle fifties and the early sixties will be wrong, to some degree, a decade hence. Still, we learn a lot by looking at the past decade. As of then, what were the nuances?

By way of answer, let us move back through our crises, taking note of things these players stumbled over when they looked across the water at each other. Thus we can at once uncover differences and register the difficulties of these men. I offer you a series of instances, subsumed under four categories. These are broad categories, by no means mutually exclusive, and meant to be suggestive, not definitive. They help, however, to illuminate small differences. I think that you will find them much more useful for the purpose than formal institutional divisions.

The first category is political accountability; it deals with stakes of players stemming from the press of party politics on their positions. This is a heavy weight in topmost places, British and American alike. The second category is SOPs, standard operating procedures; it deals with stakes of players stemming from the twists and turns in action channels as these flow through, or around, their positions. Relative relationships to given channels confer relative advantages on men in jobs. The third category is job-to-job

relationships; it deals with stakes of players stemming from the links between their own positions and assorted others as personified in given individuals. The fourth category is on-the-job perspectives; it deals with stakes of players stemming from the substance in a governmental action seen—as they are bound to see—by light of their positions. This, of course, is light strained through the fixed ideas they may have brought to office from their schooling and experience.

My stress is upon *stakes*. For this there is good reason. Paranoid behavior follows misperceived constraints. At every turning point in Suez and in Skybolt, constraints were but the passive voice of stakes.

Political Accountability

Looking for shades of difference in our two machines, we begin with political accountability. Consider this instance taken from the Suez story.

In September and October 1956, Dulles and his President seem to have drawn much comfort from the rising press and parliamentary opposition Eden was encountering at home. This they counted on to reinforce their own foot-dragging against British intervention by armed force. I have suggested that our men may have analogized to their experience in 1954 when Democratic leaders in Congress stood against our intervention at the time of Dien Bien Phu. If so, the analogy was faulty.

In modern British practice, a Prime Minister whose party has a good working majority in Commons, as Eden's did, need heed the Opposition party and the press only if and as their views are strongly shared in Cabinet and his own back benches. Cabinet dissension means much; especially in context of back-bench dissension. But opposition from the Opposition counts next to nothing. For Eisenhower during 1954, plagued by McCarthyites and Brickerites in Republican ranks, the Minority Leader of the Senate, Lyndon Johnson, was a power to be reckoned with—also a helping hand. Not so Hugh Gaitskell in the reckoning of Eden.

Americans have been brought up on Bagehot, read at first or second hand, which is a pity. For *The English Constitution* shows us Westminster and Whitehall of the 1860s, a time when party discipline was relatively lax, when Independent Members lived up to the name, when Governments were actually dependent upon changeable majorities in Commons. Ninety years later all was different.

Nowadays when lines are drawn in Commons for and against the Government, its MPs rarely nerve themselves to vote in dangerous numbers against their own front bench. For if they are ambitious they can have no place to go except toward that bench themselves; no one can help them get there save the men who sit there. And if they find contentment in remaining where they are, their safest course is to appear consistent, which usually means following their leaders. Those who nominate MPs seem to admire that; so, apparently, do most constituents.

In the days of Eden's premiership—also Macmillan's for the Skybolt case—Tories held a comfortable majority of seats in Commons. No Minister was worried about losing votes of confidence. No one thought the Opposition capable of drawing a majority out of desertions from Conservative ranks. That sort of thing occurred only in textbooks. By all accounts available to me, what worried modern Ministers was not desertions but abstentions. The Tories had been traumatized in 1940 when abstentions on their own side yielded Neville Chamberlain so relatively narrow a majority as to impair beyond recall the public image of his Government. He went. By this route Tory Premiers ever since have feared to go.

Yet in 1956, so far as back-bench sentiment among Conservatives was organized against the Government, it was to Eden's right, not to his left, hard line not soft line, centered in the "Suez Group," so-called, which had emerged two years before out of antipathy to the Egyptian course that he, as Foreign Secretary, had set for Churchill's Government.

Eisenhower and Dulles were correct in thinking Suez posed a parliamentary threat to Eden's premiership. But it was the sort of threat to spur him on, not slow him down. So, I think, it did.

Standard Operating Procedures

Turning from nuances in political accountability we come to my second category, operating procedures. What shades of difference here are illustrated by our crises? Let me give you three instances, two British, one American, drawn from Skybolt and Suez combined.

First, early in November 1962, Kennedy and his associates agreed that since our Skybolt cancellation would create a British problem, London should be warned in time to seize it, to resolve it, and to tell us what was wanted. Our men conceived correctly that the problem was important, running to the heart of British defense policy and also to the heart of party politics: the independent nuclear deterrent. We also thought the Tories had a firm hold on their own machine, with Commons in the pocket of the Cabinet. Macmillan and his colleagues, being clever

chaps, would know a thorny problem when they saw it, and would grasp it. In this we made an error opposite to Dulles's concerning Parliament. We did not overrate the Opposition or back benchers, but we underrated the collegiality of the front bench. We misread the inner character of Cabinet procedure.

London was proceeding with a "Government Decision," an official Cabinet action, taken two years earlier. This constituted a commitment to the independent nuclear deterrent, premised on the Camp David Agreement for Skybolt. Macmillan's heart was set on the deterrent. That two-year-old decision assured it to him. Cabinet action committed permanent officials, civil and military alike. It also committed the Conservative majority in Commons. His deterrent was safe at least until the next General Election; and no doubt he meant to make it an election issue. Washington's warning put this whole structure in doubt. Our warning posed an "iffy" question. To raise it with his colleagues was to risk their commitment. Any substitute for Skybolt on its present terms would cost *new* money, funds not previously earmarked. Whence was it to come? From social services? Or aircraft carriers? Besides, Polaris in particular was hated by the Air Force and unwanted by the Navy. Faced thus might the Cabinet undo its decision? The Prime Minister wanted none of that.

Reportedly, Macmillan never let the "iffy" question near his Cabinet. Sensible Prime Ministers do not take such things there. Instead he acted as though Britain had no problem, as though what was "iffy" ran the other way, a matter of our honor not his need: would Kennedy repudiate an Eisenhower agreement? In short, Macmillan stood upon the status quo, and clung to it determinedly until he got to Nassau in December. Then, when he was forced to shift his ground and managed to make good with the Americans, he put before the Cabinet his Polaris deal by cable, asking prompt response since Kennedy was waiting. His Foreign and Defence Secretaries were with him when he cabled. The Cabinet acceded, cost and Service anguish notwithstanding. What else could they have done?

As for Macmillan's Defence Secretary, Thorneycroft, the man to whom our warning was addressed, when he received it he had reasons of his own for keeping just as quiet as his Prime Minister. He too was wedded to a nuclear deterrent. He may well have preferred Polaris to Skybolt. But our warning gave him no option to say so: advocacy in advance of cancellation from our side—accompanied by a compensatory offer—would make him seem a traitor to his Air Force and Macmillan. While Thorneycroft waited for our cancellation he apparently said nothing in his Ministry. When we made no compensatory offer, he embraced the status quo and brandished it in public against us.

Our men conceived their warning as a means to mobilize the British. It had an opposite effect. Immobility resulted. The reasons are not far to seek. They go to the heart of government by colleagues.

The Cabinet governs through assertion of two strong conventions. One I mentioned earlier: its hold upon MPs. The other is its hold on permanent officials, who will do as they are told provided that the telling comes in proper form from their own Minister (within his jurisdiction) or from Cabinet, as the last stage of committee work in which they have engaged. While effectively asserted, these conventions offer Cabinet members an unlimited power. But by definition it adheres to them collectively. Agreement or at least show of solidarity is needed to induce it. Nothing risks back-bench acquiescence more than front-bench disarray. Nothing risks bureaucratic acquiescence more than a failure of form. For those two conventions are in essence tacit treaties. MPs surrender judgment to a leadership committee in return for governance reflective of their interests, political and other; hence the stress on solidarity. Bureaucrats exchange obedience for consultation, for assurance of a hearing; hence the stress on form.

As instruments of power, British Cabinets approximate our Presidency and Congress combined, along with heads of federal agencies, state governors and legislatures, mayors of major cities, and the Supreme Court. Besides, front benches are informally the counterparts of presidential nominating conventions. Yet for this very reason the exercise of power is a sticky business, as sticky to Englishmen as to Americans. Where we have public struggles by avowedly independent institutions, they have private struggles by ostensibly united Ministries and Ministers. Very frequently our struggles approach stalemate. So do theirs. But unlike us they need to keep such things from public sight, lest solidarity and form be compromised. This inhibition makes their system all the stickier.

In Cabinet, changing course is hard, and hazardous. To quote the private comment of a very close observer: "The obverse of our show of monolithic unity behind a Government position when we have one is slowness, ponderousness, deviousness, in approaching a position, getting it taken, getting a 'sense of the meeting.' Nothing in our system is harder to do, especially if press leaks are at risk."

Those who would innovate proceed at risk. Timing has inordinate importance. Especially is this the case for a Prime Minister who knows his mind but is uncertain of his colleagues. For the ranks of bureaucrats are theirs, not his. Officials serve departments headed by his colleagues. And the loyalties of back-benchers do not run to him alone. He has to take his colleagues into camp before he can command their troops. Should he remain uncertain he is well advised to wait, and meanwhile steer the settled course. Macmillan waited. This was not hard to do: one thing a PM can control himself is the Cabinet agenda.

Second, the same procedural constraints lay back of a misreading from our side during the Suez crisis. Another Prime Minister who knew his mind was Eden after Egypt seized the Canal. Far from waiting, he then rounded up his colleagues, voiced their common shock, enhanced their anger by his own, and gained assent to a contingent use of force. That assent gave him the leeway to prepare for the contingency. He did so in selective consultation with a shifting set of colleagues and a narrow band of permanent officials, mostly military. His secretiveness increased as Dulles's initiative to defuse the crisis—and Nasser's prudence—made the contingency harder to reach.

Thereby Eden skated on thin ice, right to the edges both of solidarity and of form. The record does not show that he slipped over either edge. The colleagues whose portfolios or party standing gave them "need to know" were kept sufficiently informed so none could claim he lacked a voice. The senior permanent official in the Foreign Office, also the Cabinet Secretary, and of course the Chiefs of Staff, were in the know. Every other departmental civil servant was excluded. This cost Eden dear when his finances struck a snag they could have spotted in advance. But keeping them in ignorance was well within his rights, so long as their masters—his colleagues—concurred, which they did.

Yet, despite its very different look, Eden's conduct speaks to the same order of constraints as does Macmillan's six years later. A governmental course was set by the initial Cabinet action, Eden in the van. Were it to be reversed he must again be in the van; he scarcely could afford "repudiation." But neither could he afford to show "weakness." Besides, he *wanted* use of force. He wanted it so much that he embraced Franco-Israeli plans. Rejection for the sake of "honor" might have given him safe grounds on which to seek reversal from his colleagues: rather spare Wogs than connive with Frogs (to say nothing of Israelis). Who could have thought this weakness?

Instead he chose to help those planners manufacture a contingency in substitution for the ones Egyptian caution and our strictures were removing from sight. Then, at another moment of collegial anger, this time against Dulles, he sought Cabinet assent to switch contingencies. He got it. With it he gained cover for all subsequent secretive undertakings.

Eden managed to make Cabinet power serve his purpose, but the very way he did it left him vulnerable when his use of force, once under way, encountered our man Humphrey. At the crucial Cabinet meeting where our "ultimatum" was discussed, its nature left no room for failing to consult the Treasury and none for failing to respect the Chiefs of Staff. The latter judged—quite wrongly, it appears—that five or six more days were needed to complete their operation. Chancellor Macmillan, briefed at last by his officials, judged the pound could not survive that long without help from the IMF, where Humphrey had a veto. Caught between the two, Eden cracked.

Evidently this astonished Dulles, judging by his alleged remark to Britain's Foreign Secretary Selwyn Lloyd: "Why did you stop?" In light of the estimates of field commanders at the time and commentators since, that question echoes down the years. It seems two days at most, not five or six, could have sufficed to secure the Canal, and in these days Macmillan could have been at Humphrey constantly, or Eden at Eisenhower, promising and warning. Meanwhile, even a hint of Humphrey's threat could have served to keep officials in line, also Tories, to say nothing of men-on-the-streets; anti-Americanism would have been a tonic.

Yet Eden's vulnerability at this juncture—health aside—shows how thin was the ice on which he previously had skated. His colleagues had assented to the use of force, but not to consequences such as these, and their assent had been obtained by means which left most of them uncommitted in detail, hence free to disengage. The scheme was his and Lloyd's, not theirs; so were the plots and plans. This had made it easier to gain their acquiescence. Now it made it harder to keep them up to scratch. Macmillan, once so keen for force, could now reverse himself on departmental grounds with no embarrassment.

The Chiefs of Staff, meanwhile, had planned the war according to their lights, and now were executing it according to their fashion. Civilian meddling in the Cabinet's name they had to tolerate, but not meddling from the PM alone. They served the Queen, which is to say the Government, not him; and "she" was scarcely proof against the possibility that if pushed very hard

they might resign. This was no Government of National Coalition but a Tory Cabinet with a war contested by the Opposition. Eden's colleagues had no stomach for a contest also with their military advisers. This logic had sufficed to keep the seaborne landings sacrosanct in Musketeer. Now it sufficed again. The Chiefs of Staff presumably were only doing what professionals so placed will often do: padding numbers in the search for a safe answer. Never mind.

Eden could not make the Chiefs assure him a quick finish. At most he might have asked them for another estimate, while calling on the Chancellor for still another day. But if Macmillan refused it, as apparently he did, and if most other seniors fell away, what then? Then only by a show of will which mesmerized his colleagues, casting all the fear of party-gods into them, could Eden have gone on. Some men might have accomplished that. Not Eden. He had used up the advantages of office. He also had used up himself. Physically and emotionally he was drained. His plight speaks to the exercise of power inside a collegium.

An American Administration is a collegial body of a sort and in a way, but certainly not of this sort, nor precisely in this way. Behind the Dulles inquiry "Why did you stop?" lie procedures of a presidential system where one man's word suffices, at the least, to buy a few days' time from his subordinates. Eden, *in extremis*, lacked subordinates; he had Colleagues.

Still, our President confronts procedural constraints of other sorts which can be almost equally compelling. These are no better understood by Englishmen than Cabinet conventions are by us. By way of illustration, here is a third instance, this one drawn from Skybolt.

In November 1962, Macmillan, then Prime Minister, waited on events with confidence, apparently, that President Kennedy was under no compulsion to upset the status quo. Our Chiefs of Staff were known to favor Skybolt. There was no outcry against it in Congress or the press. No doubt its development was costly, far exceeding estimates, but this had happened on both sides of the Atlantic with new weapons ever since the war. Besides, the Americans knew as well as he that British entry to the Common Market now hung in the balance and that this was not a time to trouble other waters: they wanted Britain in the EEC as much as he did, if not more.

Why then would we insist on making trouble? Macmillan evidently saw no reason unless Kennedy were out to do him harm. This, I am told, he discounted.

Such reasoning was logical except in one particular. It left out of account our budgetary process. For Kennedy was under a compulsion, or at least a strong temptation, created by the politics of American-style budgeting.

The Kennedy Administration stood to save $2.5 billion in three years, provided Skybolt could be stopped once and for all. But presidential wishes would not guarantee the saving. Congress must acquiesce. The weapon had good friends there: key committee members in both Houses who owed no thanks to the President for their seniority. How best to curb their friendship? By way of answer McNamara invoked a standard tactic which he probably regretted not having employed the year before on the B-70. This tactic was to take the weapon out of Kennedy's next Annual Budget, which in any case was sure to show a deficit. If Skybolt's friends then sought congressional action to finance it, the onus of "new" cost would fall on them in context of that deficit.

Annual Budgets go to Congress in January. Were Skybolt to be kept out of the next one, it must be cancelled by December. If it remained in being it would have to be budgeted. The President would then have lost his chance to shift the onus. For the Annual Budget was *his* presentation. Skybolt's presence there would carry his endorsement, which its friends could cite against a later cancellation. To deny them that advantage he must cancel now. Otherwise they might succeed in financing the weapon for another fiscal year. By then sunk costs would be so high that friends could make a most compelling case for its completion and production. In prospect there went the whole $2.5 billion. Kennedy could best belie that prospect by immediate cancellation. So McNamara evidently told him. The argument apparently convinced not only Kennedy but also Rusk, the Secretary of State.

Actually, there might have been a way at once to defer cancellation and to guarantee the saving. A President can "impound" funds voted by Congress and refuse to spend them. McNamara surely knew of this device. Indeed he had just used it to deny the Air Force funds appropriated despite him for the B-70. But for that very reason he reportedly did not wish to employ it soon again against the Air Force, especially not in context of embarrassment for Britain. Evidently neither did Kennedy.

To London all of this was quite incomprehensible. There are no close counterparts in British practice. Even the terms mean different things. There, Treasury officials oversee the spending of departments, and Department Heads appeal against the Chancellor in Cabinet. The outcome is definitive. A British budget is not even couched in spending terms. What Parliament receives and votes under that label are measures to raise revenue, covering the Cabinet's expenditure decisions. Kennedy's particular temptation literally could not arise. If a Prime Minister were comparably tempted, his tactics would be set by Cabinet tempers, not by Parliamentary timetables.

Moreover, no Prime Minister had yet encountered McNamara's stakes in "cost effectiveness," or had been exposed to comparable analyses at home. The notion that a weapons system should be dropped because some abstruse calculation showed its whole cost relative to benefit, in dollar terms, higher than that of a presumptive substitute was quite as strange to English politicians of the time as to our Military Services. McNamara sought to teach our Services a lesson, which no doubt enhanced his interest in the Skybolt cancellation. But London could not know this, for his methods were not practiced there. The warning he conveyed there fit into no context of experience.

Job-to-Job Relations

Let me turn now from these matters of procedure to a closely connected category for distinguishing small differences between London and Washington. This is the category of job-to-job relations. We deal here with relations among players whose positions are linked—of necessity, not choice—by action channels or promotion systems. Dulles and Humphrey are, of course, a case in point. But more illuminating, I believe, are several other instances. I offer you three, two British, one American, again drawn from both crises.

The first of these instances concerns Macmillan as Chancellor of the Exchequer, in relation to Eden as Prime Minister. In late September 1956, before Macmillan came home to report Ike's doggishness, he had spent time in Washington. This lent credence to his word. He had been there as Chancellor on Treasury business, a meeting of the IMF, which brought him into contact with his opposite number, Humphrey. Macmillan also saw Dulles at least once and paid a courtesy call on his friend in the White House. Humphrey then was only on the fringes of our Suez policy. Dulles and Eisenhower, on the other hand, were in the midst of it. They were its architects. Yet, after seeing them, Macmillan left there with those doggish notions firmly in his head. How could they have allowed him to depart in such a fashion?

Presumably they did so because they did not perceive him as the key to British conduct. They evidently saw him as a Humphrey in reverse, the Cabinet money-man, powerful of course, disposed to war—they knew that—but not a man-in-charge. Lloyd and Eden, not Macmillan, were their opposite numbers. What they may have told the Chancellor I do not know. What they forbore to emphasize sufficiently is obvious.

Events would show that Eisenhower meant what he previously had written London, namely that he must dispute the use of force save as a last resort if Cairo ran amok. Eden was arranging now for Tel Aviv to do so. Eisenhower and Dulles, knowing nothing of this, could not have told Macmillan that these two were not the same. But what they could have done, presumably, was convey their own fixity of purpose. This they plainly failed to do.

Why so? Personalities perhaps afford a partial answer. Eisenhower and Macmillan both were men of private charm, and fond of one another. Imprecision is commonplace when such as these engage in casual conversation. Yet these two often had done business with each other in the past, no lack of clarity about it. Had the President perceived the Chancellor as crucial to our case, they might have talked more pointedly of Suez, less of politics, than it appears they did. Presumably he did not see him so.

As Chancellor, Macmillan did indeed become the key we were to turn much later in the day, when Humphrey's threat invoked his ministerial brief. But in advance of events which brought us to that pass, his Treasury position was the least of his importance. What made Macmillan crucial while he visited in Washington was rather his own standing among leaders of his party as one of the two most likely to succeed to Eden's Premiership, whenever Eden—not a well man—chose or had to go. Macmillan's star just then was on the rise. He long had seemed a trifle radical for Tory leadership, but his hard line on Egypt pleased the Right. Beyond this, Eden personally seems to have viewed Macmillan's rival, R. A. Butler, as unworthy of promotion. Like Churchill before him (and Macmillan after), Eden evidently never forgave Butler for his faithfulness to Neville Chamberlain in 1938: of such stuff Ministers were to be made, but not Prime Ministers. When Eden went, he would be the first to give the Queen advice on his successor. While these two remained foremost in the race there could be little doubt how his advice would run.

The Chancellor who came to Cabinet fresh from Washington thus had a special hold on the Prime Minister. It evidently was maintained. Even though Macmillan may have been the man, above all, whose defection at the last caused Eden to call off his war, when the time came for

him to go Macmillan did succeed him. By all accounts the Queen then chose as Eden wanted. And this suggests that had Macmillan come from Washington in sober mood, cautious not ebullient, Eden might have drawn back from his deal, or at least viewed its timing implications with a care these evidently never got.

For an American, the mutual relations of Macmillan and Eden—and Butler—hold the fascination of a mystery. We have no close counterparts. These men had lived in intimacy, power intertwined, on one front bench or other, governing or opposing, for almost a generation. So they would go on until each was ennobled or deceased. Not even senior Senators on our side have to live so; each by his seniority acquires a committee which becomes a piece of power all his own. As for our Cabinet Members, these are like ships passing in the night: cleared from different ports and headed toward oblivion. So far as I can find, Eden and Macmillan did not relish one another. Their relationship was less friendly than systemic. So for their relations with "Rab" Butler, who served each, in turn, as colleague and lieutenant without ever lessening their grudge against him. Among Ministers on our side, such long-lived relations are almost unthinkable because there hardly ever is occasion for them. Grudges abound in Washington, but those who hold them go their separate ways in four years or in eight. And Presidents have neither need nor scope to choose their own successors out of their own Cabinets. If Eisenhower failed to see Macmillan as a key, this scarcely is surprising.

Now let me shift the scene from 1956 to 1962. My next two instances are drawn from Skybolt. These I shall treat together, since in many ways they are each other's mirror image. I refer on the one hand to McNamara as our Secretary of Defense in his relations with his President and Services, and with the State Department, and on the other hand to Thorneycroft as British Defence Secretary in his comparable relations on home grounds.

In November 1962, while these two entertained false hopes of one another's plans, each evidently took for granted that the other's terms of reference were akin to his. Each erred accordingly. Despite identical titles and commensurate jurisdictions, their positions were more unlike than they realized.

Thorneycroft apparently viewed McNamara with confidence as a successful British Secretary of Defence, a man who could carry his colleagues in Cabinet. McNamara seems to have viewed Thorneycroft with hope as an effective American Secretary of Defense, a man who could enforce his will upon the Chiefs of Staff. Thorneycroft had grounds for confidence. On taking office in September he had visited the States, felt McNamara's force, and seen the President's delight in him. McNamara, in turn, had grounds for hope. That visit reportedly showed Thorneycroft to be far quicker on the uptake than his predecessor.

Thus, when Thorneycroft heard McNamara's warning about Skybolt he seems to have assumed his caller meant to cancel and would bring it off. In this he was quite right. A man who could do that surely could offer him a satisfactory substitute. In this he was quite wrong. When McNamara heard Thorneycroft say something of Polaris he seems to have assumed that his respondent would look into it and ask for it. In this he too was wrong.

I already have told you why Thorneycroft forbore to take initiative within his Ministry. He was too weakly placed to rile his Services. He was also too weakly placed in Cabinet, since the PM much preferred the status quo. Thorneycroft had just climbed back into the Cabinet by Macmillan's grace. He had no strength to muster there except what he could glean from his portfolio. These weaknesses were reciprocal.

McNamara suffered no such weaknesses. He had his Chiefs off balance. He had White House backing. And he also had the friendship of the Secretary of State, who saw things much as he did in those days. Besides, they were drawn close by shared relief in the successful outcome of the Cuban missile crisis. Within the Executive Branch, at least, McNamara never had been stronger.

It is easy to see why McNamara's hopes for Thorneycroft were disappointed, but why the disappointment in reverse? What falsified the latter's confidence in McNamara? Apparently the answer lies in a weak spot amidst his strengths which Thorneycroft seems never to have noticed: McNamara could carry his colleagues but not Rusk's subordinates, not without a fight. Presumably he could have won the fight, but not without a cost. The cost would have included inconvenience for himself, embarrassment for Rusk, and possibly a strain in their relations.

For McNamara to accompany the Skybolt cancellation with an offer of Polaris as a substitute for Britain would entangle budgetary action, where the lead was his, with diplomatic action, where the lead was Rusk's. And it would be done over the dead bodies of the Europeanists in Rusk's Department (to say nothing of his own). For reasons I already have explained, their opposition could not help but be intense. Were McNamara to accompany his cancellation with an offer, he must first take the initiative to draw that opposition from Rusk's men and to defeat it on Rusk's own terrain.

The fact that the initiative was McNamara's would cause extra trouble. In the eyes of State Department staffers he then would be a poacher on "their" ground, a grabber of the lead which was their Secretary's, not his. What they saw would not matter in the end, provided Rusk and Kennedy saw differently. But what they said would only make it harder for those two to give the victory to McNamara. Whereas if the initiative were Thorneycroft's, not his, that difficulty scarcely could arise.

As Thorneycroft did not dare to be called traitor by his Air Force, so McNamara did not care to be called poacher in the State Department. Their risks were not commensurate. Thorneycroft might have lost his job. McNamara almost surely could have won his fight. But their side-stepping followed the same logic. Each thought he would be taken off his own hook by the other's initiative. Each lived in happy ignorance of what the other thought. Each waited for the other: Thorneycroft for McNamara's offer, McNamara for Thorneycroft's request. Each, of course, was disappointed.

Although unfortunate, their ignorance is understandable. How could McNamara grasp the inhibitions of a Thorneycroft, his presumed opposite number? McNamara's predecessors might have done so. To be cheese in a sandwich between Chief of Government and Chiefs of Staff was not for them an unfamiliar role. Possibly the McNamara of 1967 might have empathized with Thorneycroft. Not so in 1962; McNamara then had nothing comparable in his experience.

Harder still became the task of empathizing in reverse. How could Thorneycroft have grasped the inhibitions of a McNamara who to him seemed immeasurably strong? British officialdom, at least in civil service ranks, lies down when it is told to do so by its Ministers. The Foreign Office may dispute a Defence project heatedly, but let the Foreign Secretary take his colleague's side and that is usually the end of it (assuming Cabinet concurrence). Not so with us, especially not in Rusk's tenure of office, and in his case least of all on European questions. There, officials with good causes, deeply felt, would never cease to press them on him, around him, or over his head, seeking allies anywhere and everywhere in other agencies, the Services, the White House staff, the press corps, Congress, foreign embassies, or the Eastern Establishment (bulwark of bipartisanship). Had McNamara taken up his fight and won it, that would not have made an end of it. The skirmishing would have gone on, guerrilla-style, for years. Apparently he was aware of that. But this remains for Englishmen among the most incomprehensible of features in our system. Thorneycroft could not have been expected to conceive that mighty McNamara, scourge of his own Services, would hesitate to tackle a few Foreign Office types.

Role Perspectives

This double instance of misreading by these Defense Ministers, each of the other, can be used to illustrate more than the subtleties attendant on relations among men in jobs. There also is wrapped up in it an illustration of the fourth and final category I have offered you: the category of perspectives molded by such jobs. Some transatlantic differences attendant on this category have been mentioned in my crisis summaries, most notably, perhaps, the relative significance of the Suez Canal in Eden's eyes and Eisenhower's. But nothing serves so well to show what lies behind this category as the different shades of meaning McNamara and Thorneycroft, respectively, attached to national defense.

In 1962 "defense" for McNamara seems to have remained real, hence technical. Limited wars were likely in our future. Nuclear war might be averted by deterrence of the Russians. They alone, besides ourselves, had intercontinental nuclear capability. Deterrence turned upon their understanding of our power to strike back if they struck first. Their understanding turned upon our weaponry—its character, emplacement, and control. These turned upon technology.

For Thorneycroft, however, by 1962 "defence" apparently had come to be symbolic, hence political. Three medium-sized H-bombs could obliterate his island. Were these to be deterred, *our* weaponry must do it. He had neither funds nor space to replicate our forces, and his own made little difference independently of ours. Now that our deterrent had been brought into the missile age, he could not even offer us the time advantage once possessed by British bombers. Britain still was an "unsinkable aircraft carrier," but aircraft were no longer indispensable to our deterrent. The RAF, even when armed with Skybolt, would impress the Russians only if they thought it might be used without us to strike them. The Navy, even if provided with Polaris, would be in the same situation. But British Ministers and Services had no intention of striking independently. To strike first was to invite the end of Britain. As for a second strike, they long since had tied all their plans to ours. Whether Skybolt or Polaris, whether aircraft or

submarines, their independent nuclear deterrent was strategically irrelevant: independent it would not deter; dependent it would be superfluous. But by no means was it irrelevant politically.

In terms both of diplomacy and of internal politics, "nuclear independence" mattered much to British Ministers. So it was in Macmillan's time (and so it remains in Harold Wilson's). What mattered was the symbol. A nuclear strike force "made in Britain" and controlled there symbolized the British role in nuclear development, a comforting reminder of past greatness and a hint of future services to Europe. It also kept Great Britain in the "Nuclear Club," a haughty circle, and assured her right to claim a place in talks on the great questions of the day, not least on the defense of Europe. Further, it kept alive the "special" character of her "relationship" with us: command-control arrangements between the RAF and USAF were the most concrete links left among the many forged by World War II. Finally, Britain's nuclear force was now an issue in home politics, attacked by Labour and defended by the Tories who perceived in its defense a hold on "jingo" sentiments among the working class. This Tory vision evidently had some substance: Harold Wilson hastened to adopt Macmillan's weapons as his own, hence neutralize the issue, after Labour entered office two years later.

In the words of an official on our side, nuclear weapons had become by 1962 "the most expensive status symbols since colonies." The British were as much committed to the one as ever to the other, none more so than Thorneycroft. He had a special vision topping all the rest. He personally seems to have conceived their nuclear force as trading-stock for a deal with de Gaulle. His colleagues had not bought this vision from him at the time, but he just then was trying hard to sell it. No wonder that, as Arthur Schlesinger records, Thorneycroft and McNamara spoke in different languages when finally they met one another face to face.

Conclusion

I have dug a series of instances out of the Suez and Skybolt crises and have used them to illustrate four categories equally descriptive of the British and American machines. I have done it to make plain important nuances of difference, subtle yet not slight, between those two machines. No wonder that in these same instances officials on one side misread the other side and acted in a fashion to exacerbate relations. The nuances encountered in these instances do not exhaust, by any means, the total of small shadings one discovers when one crosses the Atlantic. But these suffice, I trust, to make the point. When those officials tried to read each other right, theirs was a hard task.

Still, if we would influence an ally, inducing its machine to act as we would like, accurate perception (and commensurate response) become incumbent on American officials, with respect not only to the British but to governments where differences are greater and our knowledge less. What shall we need to make a better job of it than our men managed in the crises now before you? Or possibly does this ask more than we have reason to expect from our machine and from our intellectual resources? May it be that in these crises our men suffered not avoidable mistakes but rather limitations native to relations between governments?

THE NUCLEAR POLICYMAKING PROCESS IN THE FOURTH REPUBLIC

LAWRENCE SCHEINMAN

Professor Scheinman writes of the dominance of technocratic administrators in the development of French atomic policy between 1945 and 1960 in the period of the French Fourth Republic. He attributes the ability of these bureaucrats to shape the French nuclear program to a combination of a succession of weak unstable coalition governments and widespread apathy among the many political parties within the National Assembly. This article has general application to the understanding of defense policy processes in weak coalition governments.

Lawrence Scheinman is a Professor of Government at Cornell University. He is the author of Atomic Energy Policy in France Under the Fourth Republic *(1965), from which this article is excerpted; coauthor of* International Law and Political Crisis *(1968);* Euratom: Nuclear Integration in Europe *(1967);* Nuclear Safeguards, the Peaceful Atom and the IAFA *(1969); and numerous monographs and articles.*

The growth and development of French atomic policy during the Fourth Republic was conditioned by capacity and characterized by continuity. The atomic program underwent steady growth which at most times was geared to the technical, financial and material resources available to the CEA. On some projects, such as the nuclear submarine, policy outdistanced capacity and resulted in failure. In general, however, policy and capacity were in step and combined to produce substantial results—prototype electricity production reactors and the atomic bomb.

The continuity of French atomic policy during the Fourth Republic leads to the question of the nature of the policy-making process itself. An examination of the evolution of such policy between 1945 and 1960 has shown that French atomic policy, both in its civil and military perspective, was molded, guided and developed by a small group of persons operating through informal channels of communication outside the

Excerpted by permission and with minor changes from "Conclusion," Atomic Energy Policy in France Under the Fourth Republic *(Princeton, N.J.: Princeton University Press, 1965), pp. 203-15. Copyright ©1965 by Princeton University Press.*

mainstream of political activity. The formal policy-making institutions, in other words, played a relatively minor, and in the case of the Parliament, even a nebulous role in the formulation of French atomic policy. The small cadre of individuals which shaped atomic policy was drawn from administrative, executive, military and legislative sources in roughly that order of importance. It was largely through their efforts, and because of the general course of external affairs, that the final decision to enter the nuclear club imposed itself on the responsible political authorities.

The development of public policy through informal channels of communication which exist beneath the veneer of formal political institutions is not unusual. The uniqueness of the present case derives from the nature of the policy issue involved. Decisions of such importance as national security or the future defensive posture of the nation, both of which are implicitly bound up with atomic policy, are not as a matter of course shuttled among middle-range politically unaccountable officials. Given the tremendous implications of nuclear power, it is quite evident that nuclear policy falls into that category of issues which deserve and are usually given the highest priority and the most careful consideration by responsible political leadership. It is this consideration which was lacking through a good part of the Fourth Republic.

The similarities which may appear to exist between the French experience on the one hand and that of the United States and Great Britain on the other, are more apparent than real and will be treated below. It is submitted that the French experience has a number of unique qualities which result more from the nature of the political system of the Fourth Republic than from any other single factor. And it is to that political system that we once again turn our attention.

In the Fourth Republic, the legislature, and certain elements of the administration, exercised substantial influence—if not control—over many policy areas. French cabinets, initially weakened by their coalition nature, were condemned to negotiate from a position of weakness and consequently were often unable effectively to promulgate positive policy measures. One highly regarded scholar has stated that ministerial instability "renders the ministers impotent and therefore ineffective as representatives of the deputies' will, leaving the bureaucracy as the principal source of policy making. . . ."[1]

The nature of French politics made it difficult for governments to adopt and pursue positive atomic policy, especially insofar as military matters were concerned. In its initial stages, atomic energy was too insignificant in comparison with economic, agricultural or educational issues to engage the interest of the government. When, in the mid-1950s, the military implications of the existence of an atomic complex on French soil no longer could be realistically disregarded, no government was prepared to take the responsibility for defining what this policy should be. Governments of the period were composed of political groups which were either ideologically and electorally committed to a position which precluded them from publicly supporting a military atomic policy or, if favorable in principle, generally unwilling to support a policy which would require vast sums of money to activate. The Gaullists were an exception to this general rule, and they consistently lobbied both in the government and Parliament for a definitive and positive military atomic policy. At the time, however, they did not hold so commanding a position in French politics that they could successfully force the issue. Coalition cabinets, formed between members of those political groups which dominated politics in the Fourth Republic, led to a situation in which policies of drift and noncommitment were the most rational ones to pursue. Indeed, it may generally be said that during most of the life of the Fourth Republic, the political executive did not have an atomic policy but was guided by M. Queuille's formula of postponing any decision which threatened the cohesiveness of the coalition. Quite simply, government coalitions could not reach consensus.

The failure of the government to define and promulgate a military atomic policy denied Parliament the opportunity of critically assessing the development of such policy. At no time during the Fourth Republic was there an organized debate on the relationship of French atomic development to its military implications. Even the 1956 debate on the Euratom proposal did not directly broach this problem. The tenor of the arguments presented by those desirous of retaining freedom to engage in a weapons program, however, gave evidence of tacit approval for a positive military atomic policy on the part of a number of parliamentary groups. Furthermore, it is highly probable that by 1958 Parliament, if given the opportunity, would have sanctioned a military atomic program. Nevertheless, except for the Pisani Resolution, introduced in the Council of the Republic in June 1956, there was no concerted effort of any parliamentary group

[1] Philip Williams, *Politics in Post-War France*, 2d ed. (London: Longmans, Green, 1958), p. 405.

to precipitate a debate on military atomic policy by use of written or oral questions with debate or through the use of the interpellation. The number of parliamentarians who did utilize the question device in order to clarify atomic military policy were few in number, one of the most prominent being M. Michel Debré.

The general apathy of the legislature with regard to military policy extended to civil atomic programs as well. This is evidenced by the nature and paucity of the debates on the Five-Year Plans of 1952 and 1957. The former debate turned on the problem of communists in the CEA; that of 1957 was lost in the shadow of the ratification debate on the Rome Treaties which preoccupied the parliamentarians.

Parliamentary apathy also reflects the general lack of interest of the political parties in atomic policy. Again, the Gaullists represented an exception to the general rule, and all the Gaullists who held cabinet posts—General Koenig, M. Palewski and M. Chaban-Delmas—were instrumental in moving atomic policy closer to the bomb. The Radicals also contributed to this trend, but as a group they were clearly divided on the issue of the bomb. MM. Gaillard and Bourgès-Maunoury represented that wing of the Party which favored military atomic policy, and they were probably joined in this view by the Mendesists, judging by Mendès-France's favorable attitude in 1954 and his generally nationalist position. M. Faure and his supporters represented a more pacifist attitude. Aside from these two political parties, however, public support for a military atomic policy came from a few isolated deputies such as Pierre André.

Thus, it cannot be said that the traditional formal government institutions, *qua* institutions, were instrumental in or crucial to the elaboration of atomic policy. The political executive did not supply initiative and direction, and the legislature did not serve as a forum in which a dialogue on atomic policy could develop. Despite this void in political leadership, there did exist an atomic policy in the Fourth Republic which unfolded progressively until it publicly manifested itself in the Sahara Desert in February 1960. As we have maintained, this policy evolved through the efforts of administrative, political and military personnel operating outside the public political forum in what, for the sake of convenience, we might call a political subsystem.

The focal point of these activities was the Commissariat à l'Energie Atomique, and thus it is important to understand the nature of this institution. Legally insulated from the ministries and from the permanent civil service, responsible only to the Prime Minister who was vested with authority and control over the CEA, that agency occupied a crucial position in the atomic sphere. The ministerial instability prevalent in the Fourth Republic enhanced the power and autonomy of the CEA in the same manner that the traditional administrative structure gained flexibility under these circumstances. The scientific and administrative leadership of the CEA capitalized on its legal position and on the political setting to firmly establish that organization as the focal point for the conception as well as for the execution of atomic policy. Parliamentary apathy only served to reinforce the position of the CEA, and the result was that initiative and guidance on atomic policy matters flowed upward from the CEA to the political executive. More often than not, the latter granted the support necessary to the elaboration of programs to which the Commissariat had assigned priority. In keeping with the tradition of administrative caution, however, the CEA never went too far too fast—it always sought to acquire at least a modicum of support among members of the political hierarchy. As events during the Faure administration in 1955 indicated, positive support was not always forthcoming. Yet this did not result in a change of policy—or even a breach of continuity—and with the exception of the Gaillard government in 1958, no government in the Fourth Republic appeared strong enough to bear the responsibility for making a final determination one way or the other on a military atomic program for France. The lack of positive support only delayed the final result; it did not affect the nature of policy itself.

Apart from the CEA, after 1954, military atomic policy was developed with the almost continuous support of the Minister of National Defense, Gaullist members of the different governments and a number of Radicals. In addition there was the core of military officers who favored an atomic weapons program and who, from time to time, held important positions in the Ministry of National Defense. This group's consensus on military policy received further support from members of Parliament, many of whom held positions on the parliamentary committees of Finance and National Defense in both chambers. Other groups may have participated in the atomic policy process, but the most effective were those enumerated above.

By mid-1957, the consensus which had been reached among the groups most interested in a military orientation extended far into the public arena, and by 1958, even members of the Socialist Party, such as M. Montalat, were speaking openly in favor of an atomic bomb for France. Clearly, however, by this time political and public opinion rather than conditioning the direction of policy, could do little more than give moral support to a government willing to accept the responsibility for a final decision.

The Euratom Treaty case is instructive on several points. Euratom represents the only policy measure dealing with atomic energy, during the Fourth Republic, where it may fairly be said that the initiative came from the political executive. Atomic energy was only a secondary factor; the primary objective was the continuation of the drive toward a united Europe. Matters were complicated by the existence of the Monnet Action Committee which spearheaded the drive for European integration in the mid-1950s, and counted M. Mollet and several members of his cabinet among its adherents. In a sense, what was involved here was a conflict between what might be termed two political subsystems centering on different policy issues. The case involved a confrontation of value priorities between the political and administrative leadership: atomic integration and the renunciation of atomic weapons on the one hand, atomic independence and freedom to pursue a military atomic program on the other. The eventual result was a diluted form of integration coupled with military atomic freedom.

Because Euratom brought atomic policy questions onto the open political stage, the arena of debate became wider, with various forces picking up adherents so that a general debate on policy began to develop. For the pro-Euratom forces, the main priority was integration, not renunciation, and for the Commissariat administration and its supporters, military freedom was the basic priority, not total defeat of atomic cooperation in the cadre of the Six. In this sense, the value priorities were more complementary than may at first appear to be the case. Despite the polemics over the Euratom project, the resolution of the issues involved took place at the secondary levels of the political system. The political executive, the CEA administration and key Gaullist and Radical ministers, managed to effect a compromise in advance of public debate, so that Prime Minister Mollet did not, in the end, find it necessary to use the confidence weapon. In this instance the atomic policy forum was broader than that usually experienced during the Fourth Republic. The Euratom case both highlighted the division of forces over the nuclear armaments question and pointed up the role and effectiveness of these groups.

Two general conclusions may be drawn from

this study: that French atomic policy, rather than developing through the institutional channels of the political executive and the legislature, evolved as a result of consensus-building between interested parties holding a variety of effective governmental posts, and that the focal point of policy leadership was the continuous administration of the Commissariat à l'Energie Atomique. The executive was not a source of atomic policy but a medium through which the crucial actors sought and gained support for their policies. Final authority, of course, rested with the responsible political authorities, and to the extent that their official imprimaturs were necessary for policy to be fully elaborated, they were essential elements in the policy-making process. Governments, however, were not strong enough to underwrite a military atomic policy or courageous enough to stop the trend toward a French atomic bomb which originated as early as 1952. It is vain to argue that Mendès-France, or Faure or Mollet, adopted one position or another; in truth, each of them reserved decision for a future government while France steadily progressed toward the atomic bomb under the tutelage of the military atomic cadre discussed above. The central role of the CEA derived not only from its position as France's atomic agency but also from the continuity in its leadership and the dual role played by its administrative head who served in a political capacity also as delegate of the government. Similarly, the legislature was neither a source of policy nor an element of control over policy. Atomic policy, then, developed outside the mainstream of politics and its formulation and elaboration were dealt with at a secondary level of government where the participants were relatively unaffected by the irresolute political system which prevailed above.

Considered in the general framework of French politics, this study lends support to the proposition that ministerial instability enhances the influence and policy-making role of administrative or technocratic services. The *immobilisme* of governments, to which administrative influence is in great part attributed, is evident in the matter of atomic policy development. Whether the overriding importance of more immediate problems than atomic energy or the unsteady nature of political coalitions are raised as an explanation, it would seem clear that in the Fourth Republic, French atomic destiny was not molded by the responsible political authorities.

It may be argued with some justification that whatever the effect of the peculiarities of the political system on the development of nuclear policy, the French experience has a good deal in common with that of the other nuclear nations. It is certainly true, for example, that the initial impulse to action for military applications of nuclear power in France, Great Britain and the United States came from scientific sources. However, French scientists were, on the whole, much less disposed to lobby for a nuclear weapons program than were their American and British counterparts. The role of American scientists in initiating the atomic bomb project and in later nuclear programs is well known.[2] It is also a matter of record that British scientists were among the first to express an interest in the military potential of the atom in the early days of the war, and that British scientists also strongly urged their government to continue atomic research, including the production of plutonium, at the close of the war.[3] The interest of French scientists in the military applications of atomic power was short-lived in comparison with the sustained interest eventually exhibited by several groups of American and British scientists, especially after the Cold War crystallized and the Soviet Union entered the nuclear club. The French scientific community was by no means monolithic, but the weight of scientific thinking tended toward the peaceful uses of atomic energy—even after France advanced to the point where it was possible to take the option for a military nuclear program. The conspicuous absence of Francis Perrin, High Commissioner of the CEA, from the testing grounds of the first French nuclear device in February 1960 bears witness to this attitude.

Of course, as this study shows, interest in atomic weapons for France was not lacking. The role played by scientists of the United States and Great Britain in generating interest in nuclear weapons was taken in France by what we may call the administrator-technicians or technocrats. For our purposes, this term is intended to apply largely to the French Polytechnicien, the individual possessing scientific and technical knowledge, trained for leadership, and endowed with administrative skill and *esprit*. It was the *anciens Polytechniciens* ·such as M. Guillaumat, Administrator-General of the CEA, and M. Taranger, Industrial Director of the CEA, who fulfilled, in France, the role attributed to elements of the scientific community in the United

States and Great Britain. To be sure, a relationship of reciprocal support existed between the administrative-technocratic leadership of the CEA and both political and military groups, but it was the Commissariat cadre which provided the element of continuous advice and support for a military atomic program and which assured continuity in French nuclear progress, even in the face of disinterested or unsympathetic political leadership.

There is little basis upon which to equate technocrats in one system with scientists in another beyond the proposition that both belong to the category of non-political participants in the political process. In the present situation, however, the technocrat, unlike the scientist, is more than a consultant or advisor. He also occupies an authoritative position in the political hierarchy and while often as limited as the scientist in determining the broad lines of policy, his participation at the executory level enables him to emphasize certain policy features over others. This may be particularly evident when the administrative-technocratic institution enjoys a considerable degree of autonomy as does the CEA. Technocrats and scientists also hold comparable positions on the ground that technologically advanced nations, interested in maintaining and improving their condition, are bound to place considerable weight on the advice of such persons, regardless of the nature of the political system. This has been the experience of Western democratic nations as much as it has become somewhat characteristic of the totalitarian system of the Soviet Union. Distinctions aside, however, of the three Western nuclear nations under consideration, France under the Fourth Republic would appear to represent the most striking example of minimal political leadership and maximum technocratic direction in the orientation of atomic policy.

Another similarity between France, Great Britain and the United States is that in all three countries the decision to undertake an atomic weapons program preceded public debate on this issue. Again, the analogy has only limited application, for both the American and British programs were conceived in time of war, when in the interest of national security even minimal public discussion and debate could not be held. Nor were the implications of atomic power as clear in the early and mid-1940s as they were later. France, however, undertook a comparable program in time of peace. Moreover, in France, the opportunity to come to grips with the issue of atomic weapons was presented when the National Assembly considered the Euratom pro-

[2] For the postwar experience of American scientists see, Robert Gilpin, *American Scientists and Nuclear Weapons Policy* (Princeton, N.J.: Princeton University Press, 1962).

[3] Alfred Goldberg, "The Atomic Origins of the British Nuclear Deterrent," *International Affairs* 40, no. 3 (July, 1964): 417; Harvey A. DeWeerd, Richard Rosecrance (ed.), "British-American Collaboration on the A-Bomb in World War II," in *The Dispersion of Nuclear Weapons* (New York: Columbia University Press, 1964), pp. 29–47.

posal. As we have seen, this debate only went so far as to prevent the foreclosure of France's atomic future by assuring that France would remain free of juridical and material restraints which might prevent her from pursuing a nuclear weapons program should she eventually determine to do so. The question of what atomic policy should be was bypassed by both the parliamentarians and the government.

In the United States, a Joint Committee on Atomic Energy was established in 1946, and its extensive power over the atomic development of the nation thus brought atomic energy under Congressional control. This committee not only brought atomic energy problems into the political marketplace but also has exercised its mandate with considerable vigilance.[4] In the Fourth Republic, Parliament had little more than a passing acquaintance with nuclear problems or nuclear programs. In Great Britain, the Parliament was excluded from the atomic policy dialogue for a number of years after the war, but this would appear to reflect the nature of the British political system where command, control and continuity emanate from the top leadership in the cabinet. It was the latter which made the unequivocal decision to enter Great Britain in the nuclear club.[5]

This last comment marks the crucial difference between the British and American programs and the evolution of the French program. In the former two cases, the decision to embark on a nuclear weapons program was taken, after some urging by scientists, by the responsible political authorities as a matter of positive public policy. The British and American decisions were unqualified and clear political acts from which flowed the executory action of the responsible military, political, administrative and scientific agencies. Within the broad limits set by those decisions, middle-range advisory and executory groups could and did exercise a considerable amount of influence. In France, the situation was reversed. The action of responsible political leadership was the last in a long chain of events— a response to protracted internal pressure combined with the force of the external military and political environment. Guidance and direction for nuclear policy came not from the French government or the French Parliament, but from a small, dedicated group of administrator-technocrats, politicians and military officers whose activities centered on and emanated from the CEA. This group exhorted successive governments at least to prepare the groundwork for an eventual decision to create an atomic arsenal, and their persuasiveness increased in direct proportion to the decline of French influence and prestige in the international environment. Whatever the similarities between France and its nuclear allies in terms of the role of the administrative, technocratic or scientific bureaucracies in the policymaking process, the French case must be distinguished on the ground that the ultimate decisions were reached in noticeably different ways.

[4]Harold P. Green and Alan Rosenthal, *Government of the Atom* (New York: Atherton Press, 1963).
[5]Goldberg, *International Affairs* 40, no. 3 (July 1964): 420.

AN ORGANIZATIONAL PERSPECTIVE ON GERMAN NATIONAL SECURITY POLICY

ERNST W. GOHLERT

Professor Gohlert describes the organizational mechanisms that have been developed under Chancellor Willy Brandt for the formulation of West German defense policy. This institutional format is examined with respect to the distribution of decisionmaking responsibility and the various staffing and coordination procedures which are employed. Gohlert identifies the semi-independent status of the German Cabinet Minister as an important factor which encourages collegiality within the national security policy process of the Federal Republic.

Ernst W. Gohlert, an Assistant Professor of Political Science at Eastern Washington State College, is engaged in continuing research on West German defense policy.

We know a great deal about German national security *policy*. Journalistic and scholarly literature is replete with analyses of German *Sicherheitspolitik*, past, present, and future. German government publications afford ample access to official statements on foreign policy and national security goals. For instance, only a small investment of time and effort will afford insight into recent security policy, with its emphasis on military balance, detente, i.e., *Ostpolitik*, and disarmament or arms limitation.[1] Learning about German security *policy* seemingly presents no major hurdles. This is important. But it is equally important or more so to understand the workings of the political-bureaucratic fountains, which dispense policy, because of the broader implications for Germany's strategic position and her internal political evolution. Here lies the crux of the matter. Our knowledge of the Federal Republic's national security policy remains fragmentary and incomplete, insofar as we know nothing or very little about the mechanisms and personalities involved in its formulation.[2] This is the kind of information—in the case of Germany—which is either unavailable or incomplete. Without a claim to comprehensiveness, this paper represents a modest attempt to examine selected aspects of German national security organization. Who is responsible for national security decisionmaking? What is the role of staff in this process? And what are the organizational mechanisms employed to coordinate policy implementation?

These introductory observations apply by-and-large also to the United States, except that a great deal of research has been done on American national security *organization* as well as the policy it has produced. For this reason alone, it is useful and interesting to attempt a comparison of organizational responses to common problems. However, there are other reasons why such a comparison may serve heuristic functions. As a junior partner of the United States, German national security organization evolved in the shadow of U.S. influence. It would indeed be difficult to probe the consequences of this influence, without taking the American experience in national security organization into account. Furthermore, a comparison is also of interest to American students of national security because

---

[1] Cf. Willy Brandt, "Venturing More Democracy," *The Bulletin* Supplement (November 4, 1969): 10; Helmut Schmidt, "Serving NATO's Twin Policies of Security, Detente," *The Bulletin* 19 (February 16, 1971): 33–34; Helmut Schmidt, "Important to Keep a Balance While Reducing Forces," *The Bulletin* 20 (February 22, 1972): 45–46; Helmut Schmidt, "We Can Win Detente Only if We Keep our Guard Up," *The Bulletin* 20 (July 11, 1972): 184; Germany, Bundesminister für innerdeutsche Beziehungen, *Bericht der Bundesregierung und Materialien zur Lage der Nation 1971* (February 1971): 44; Germany, Presse und Informationsamt, *Jahresbericht der Bundesregierung 1971* (1972): 150; Germany, Federal Ministry of Defense, *White Paper 1971/1972, The Security of the Federal Republic of Germany and the Development of the Federal Armed Forces*, Bonn (December 1971): 3–11.

[2] Cf. Thomas Ellwein, "Probleme der Regierungsorganisation in Bonn," *Politische Vierteljahresschrift* 2 (1968): 234–54.

---

it places "the shoe on the other foot," with its beneficial antidote to ethnocentrism. The scope of this paper does not permit a review of all major aspects of current American national security arrangements, nor will a complete analytical description of the German security system be attempted here.[3] Instead, I propose to deal selectively with the three questions concerning key organizational issues—decisionmaking reponsibility, staff, and coordination—as they apply to the German national security bureaucracy, with American experience providing a comparative background.

Before proceeding, it may be helpful to outline the argument that provides the structure for the following discussion. The premise is this: German organizational responses in the area of national security organization are a function of significant factors in the international and domestic environments, specifically the American influence and Germany's constitutional context and styles of leadership. I maintain that these forces helped to shape Chancellor Brandt's organizational strategy, which is characterized by adaptation and fluidity. Adaptation here means almost imitation of institutional forms and practices germane to the United States. And fluidity pertains to undefined or ill-defined relations among various components of the German national security system. Furthermore, I contend that adaptation or imitation was not a matter of choice but of perceived necessity. German national security organization was locked into a pattern dictated in its main outlines by key foreign policy decisions in the early Adenauer years, particularly the decision to rearm Germany within the framework of the Western Alliance. Affinity of threat perception reflected in the alliance was also conducive to organizational responses in national security matters not unlike those of the United States. In effect, organizational strategies for national security from Adenauer to Brandt are a melange of responses to international and domestic requirements plus the political personalities at the top. This is what the following discussion of decisionmaking responsibility, staff, and coordination will reflect. But first a brief description of the German national security machinery is in order.

BRANDT'S APPARAT

Richard Neustadt cautioned against the confusion of nomenclature with functions. For instance, the American and the British Cabinet share the same title and certain structural characteristics, but they do not necessarily perform the same functions. There is a difference between form and function.[4] This warning may well be heeded in comparing German national security arrangements with their American counterpart. Also, in the case of Germany, we should not attribute organizational similarities automatically to the centrifugal pull of U.S. influence. Frequently, the domestic context has as much or more impact on organization.

The Brandt government leans toward the collegial as opposed to the hierarchical principle of organization. Nonetheless, the national security system has its pecking order, its top and bottom. Sitting on top is the Federal Chancellery or *Bundeskanzleramt* (BKA), the organizational equivalent of the Executive Office. The BKA is the chief staff agency with many important functions, including advising the Chancellor, coordinating the ministries, and serving as the government's secretariat.[5] There are five major sections with domestic and foreign jurisdictions.[6] Section II deals exclusively with foreign and national security affairs and Section V is responsible for planning. Each section has its own director, who reports to the BKA Chief.[7] This important position has been held by several well-known individuals, including Dr. Globke under Adenauer, and Professor Ehmke under Brandt. These men are not unlike a Sherman Adams or a John Ehrlichman. The top leadership in the BKA includes also a parliamentary state secretary—this position has been adopted from the British system—and more importantly, a state secretary, who is responsible for foreign affairs. In the Brandt government this position has been held by Egon Bahr, Brandt's version of Henry Kissinger. The most recent addition to the BKA is a crisis team or *Krisenstab*.[8]

Report," presented to the International Studies Association Convention, San Francisco, Calfiornia, March 22, 1973.

[4]Richard E. Neustadt, "White House and Whitehall," *Public Interest* 2 (1966): 50–69.

[5]Germany, Der Chef des Bundeskanzleramtes, *Organisation, Personalstruktur und Unterbringung des Bundeskanzleramtes* (8 März 1970): 1. I am grateful to Herrn Wambach from the *Bundeskanzleramt* for making this document available to me.

[6]These sections are: I—Justice and Administration; II—Foreign Affairs, Inter-German Affairs, and National Security; III—Domestic Policy; IV—Economic, Fiscal, and Social Policy; V—Planning (Germany, Bundeskanzleramt, *Organisation*, September 1972). Cf. also organizational chart.

[7]Traditionally the BKA chief held the position of state secretary. However, under Chancellors Erhard and Brandt, the BKA chief was designated as Minister for Special Affairs.

[8]The crisis team or *Krisenstab* is lodged in Section I—Justice and Administration. The reason for this arrangement is not readily apparent.

[3]A more comprehensive treatment of German national security organization can be found in my paper: "German National Security Organization and Process: A Preliminary

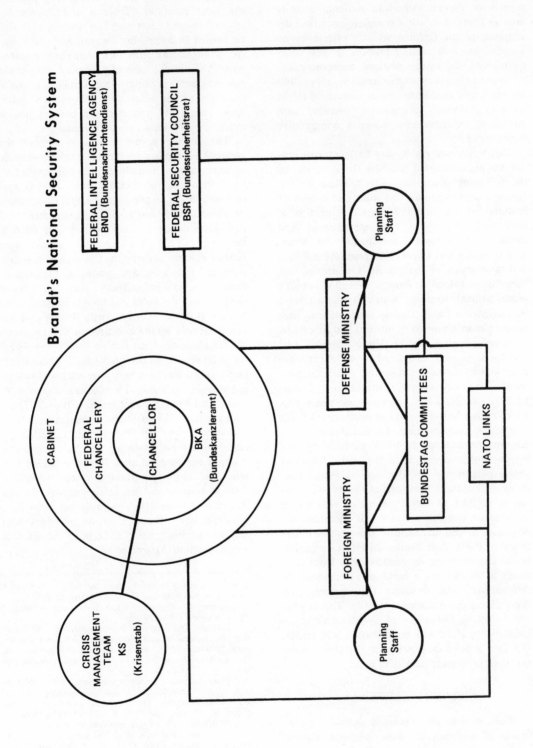

Brandt's National Security System

The national security center consists of the Chancellor, the BKA, and the Cabinet, which is composed of some fifteen ministries with both line and staff responsibilities.[9] The Foreign and Defense Ministries stand out because of their politico-military orientation. Their staff functions are concentrated in the area of planning. The Foreign Ministry in particular has a planning staff very similar to the State Department's Planning and Coordinating Staff.[10] On the operational side, both the Foreign and Defense Ministries serve as conduits to the periphery of the national security system. In point of fact, they provide most of the contacts with parliamentary committees on foreign and military affairs as well as the policy and planning units in the North Atlantic Treaty Organization.

Somewhere between the center, i.e., the Chancellor, the BKA, the Cabinet, and the periphery, lies the intelligence community, represented by the Federal Intelligence Agency, the *Bundesnachrichtendienst* (BND). The BND leads a buffered existence similar to the American Central Intelligence Agency. Its main channel into the national security process is an interministerial committee, the Federal Security Council or *Bundessicherheitsrat* (BsR). This organ was intended to operate like the American National Security Council.[11] However, there are important differences in terms of both structure and function, which reflect the influence of the constitutional context. Particulars will concern us later in the discussion, suffice it to point here to the fact that the BsR is an integral part of the Cabinet and not of the Chancellor's staff, i.e., the BKA. The significance of its locale is modified somewhat due to the supervising role of the BKA. The BsR also provides an access point for the military, which is represented by the Chief of Staff, who speaks for the Federal Armed Forces Defense Council, the *Militaerischer Fuehrungsrat* (MFR). The MFR is the German Joint Chiefs of Staff.

Major structural-functional resemblances with the American national security system are apparent. They are particularly pronounced with respect to staff—the BKA—and planning. The creation of the Foreign Ministry's Planning Staff was a direct response to NATO's Atlantic Policy Planning Group (APAG), which in turn received its stimulus from the State Department's Policy Planning Council. The Germans followed the American lead in these organizational matters partially out of necessity and partially because they decided to turn American experience to their own advantage.[12] It became increasingly necessary to dovetail German foreign and security organization with their American counterparts in order to make orderly management of mutual security affairs possible.[13]

Aside from the similarities, we need to become aware of the extent to which Brandt's security organization represents a pronounced shift away from Adenauer's personalized security arrangements and toward the highly institutionalized process that features many of the sophisticated techniques and procedures associated with the American system. From simulation, game theory, decision trees, and other methodologies to computers and McNamara-type managers, the German national security system has the makings of a stream-lined, up-to-date organization. Although the shift from a personal approach in security matters to an institutional pattern occurred gradually, most of the organizational reforms came to fruition under the Brandt government in 1969.

BRANDT'S ORGANIZATIONAL STRATEGY

Chancellor Adenauer's predilection for authoritarian leadership was generally known. His organizational strategy aimed at maximum personal influence and control. This is the major reason for his dislike of highly institutionalized processes.[14] How does Chancellor Brandt's strategy compare? If a Brandt strategy exists, on whom does it focus—the Chancellor, the Cabinet, or someone else? What kind of staff structure exists in the interest of a coherent foreign policy and national security process? How do the staff agents relate to the principal

[9]The size of the Cabinet has varied from 13 members, including the Chancellor, in Adenauer's first government, to 22 ministers under Erhard in 1964. (Arndt Merkel, "The Cabinet Reform," *International Journal of Politics* 2-3 [Summer/Fall 1972]: 10-11.) Currently, there are 15 ministers in Brandt's Cabinet, not counting the Chancellor and two ministers without portfolio. ("Chancellor Willy Brandt and his New Cabinet," *The Bulletin* 29 [December 19, 1972]: 340-45.)

[10]The State Department's Policy Planning Council was renamed Planning and Coordinating Staff in 1969. I. M. Destler, *Presidents, Bureaucrats, and Foreign Policy: The Politics of Organizational Reform* (Princeton, N.J.: Princeton University Press, 1972), p. 214.

[11]Germany, Deutscher Bundestag, *Stenographische Berichte*, 62. Sitzung (1954), 3221. Prior to 1969 the BsR was known as the *Bundesverteidigungsrat* (BvR).

[12]Cf. Wilhelm G. Grewe, "Planung in der Aussenpolitik," *Europa-Archiv* 19 (1965): 725-40.

[13]A concrete example of the need for mutual coordination and corresponding organizational mechanisms is cited by W. W. Rostow, "The Planning of Foreign Policy," *The Dimensions of Diplomacy* (Baltimore: The Johns Hopkins Press, 1964), pp. 47-48.

[14]Cf. my comments in "German National Security Organization . . . ," pp. 1-7.

and to each other in order to produce maximum bargaining advantage for the latter? These are questions which I. M. Destler raised with reference to the American national security context.[15] They are helpful guides here as well, because answers or even partial answers to these questions will provide insight into the issue of decisionmaking responsibility in the German national security system.

There is ample evidence that Chancellor Brandt has an organizational strategy for his foreign and domestic government. His conception of this strategy is not always clear to the observer nor does it appear to be fully applied. Brandt's "coherent concept of government," *kohaerentes Regierungsrezept*, has several components.[16] The overall goal is the achievement of major domestic and foreign priorities, which the Social Democratic Party considers to be long overdue. This means *detente* or *Ostpolitik* in the foreign realm. It means also a governmental apparatus characterized by system, coordination and integration, highly qualified staffs, and long-term planning.[17] One of the most important elements in Brandt's strategy is the coalescence of the Chancellor's control in domestic and foreign policy with the Cabinet's role as coordinating device. The Federal Chancellery (BKA) serves as intermediary in this situation. A move in this direction requires *distance* from Adenauer's "Chancellor Democracy." Consequently, Brandt's intent is not to produce a version of "presidential government." Instead, decisionmaking responsibility in national security matters and in the government as a whole, follows from the collegial principle, which rests on various interrelated centers of power. This strategy is at the same time facilitated and complicated by the Basic Law, Germany's Constitution. In order to gain insight into Brandt's organizational strategy with respect to the issue of decisionmaking responsibility in national security affairs, we need to examine Article 65 of the Basic Law and the actual relationship between the national security components.

Article 65 of the Basic Law accounts for important parameters concerning national security organization. Jurisdictional lines are drawn between the Chancellor, the Cabinet, and the individual ministers. The Chancellor is responsible for establishing the general political guidelines of his government. This is the "Chancellor Principle." The Cabinet is in charge of the overall government program. And the individual ministers control the affairs of their departments.[18] The ambiguity inherent in the Chancellor, Cabinet, and departmental principles offers both advantages and disadvantages. It means flexibility and fluidity on the one hand, and potential obstruction of the Chancellor's will on the other. A strong Chancellor like Adenauer was generally able to overcome the ministerial demands for independence, seemingly sanctioned by Article 65. Other Chancellors, particularly Erhard, were less successful and lost. One of the main advantages of these constitutional principles, from the standpoint of national security organization, is the legitimization of institutional integration. It should not be presumed that Article 65 represents a checks and balances type arrangement superimposed by the Allies—although it may partially have this effect—rather, these provisions of the German Constitution have a venerable tradition dating from Germany's first constitution, the 1871 *Reichsverfassung*. The principles enshrined in Article 65 reached the Basic Law *via* Articles 55–57 of the Weimar Constitution.

The primary instrument of Brandt's organizational strategy is the Federal Chancellery (BKA). Consequently, the relationship between the various national security components is affected by their position vis-à-vis the BKA. The impression that Brandt turned initially to his staff for all or most of the necessary support functions is reinforced by the BKA's subsequent rise to a super-staff under its chief, Professor Ehmke. The pivotal power of the BKA is dependent on its relationship to the Chancellor. For instance, the influence of Ehmke and Bahr, Brandt's state secretary and foreign policy advisor, derives directly from their personal relationship with Brandt. With only a few exceptions, the BKA leadership from Globke to Ehmke and Bahr, has served the Chancellor as confidant and advisor.[19] The BKA derives status from this special relationship, which translates into potential bargaining advantage. Whether this influence is used in the Chancellor's interest is a separate question. The relationship between the BKA and other national security components, therefore, is more than *primus inter pares*. This is evident in the ties between the BKA and the Cabinet.

[15]Destler, *Presidents, Bureaucrats, and Foreign Policy*, pp. 88–94.

[16]Germany, Der Chef des Bundeskanzleramtes, *Organisation, . . .*, p. 3.

[17]*Ibid.*

[18]Cf. the Basic Law in Peter H. Merkl, *The Origin of the West German Republic* (New York: Oxford University Press, 1963), pp. 213–48.

[19]Cf. Germany, Bundeskanzleramt, *Die Leiter des Bundeskanzleramtes seit Bestehen der Bundesregierung* (13. September 1972); Rolf Zundel, "Auf Normalmass gestutzt," *Die Zeit* (March 26, 1971): 4; Alfred Grosser, *Deutschland Bilanz: Geschichte Deutschlands seit 1945* (Munich: Carl Hanser Verlag, 1972), pp. 188–89.

The BKA has two masters, the Chancellor and the Cabinet. On its face such an arrangement suggests problems. And, indeed, many of the difficulties with Brandt's organizational strategy can be traced to conflicting jurisdictional lines. According to the Cabinet by-laws, the BKA is responsible for the conduct of Cabinet affairs, including the supervision of the legislative process, clearances for high-ranking appointments, relations with the rest of the government, and preparation of all Cabinet meetings.[20] It is clear that the BKA is not only the Chancellor's principal staff and "agent of coordination"[21] but performs in similar capacities for the Cabinet.[22] A concrete illustration of the Chancellor-BKA-Cabinet relationship is the "early-stage coordination" system, a planning program implemented by the BKA in cooperation with individual ministries at the behest of the Chancellor and the Cabinet. The operational problems encountered by the BKA speak of suspicion, jealousy, and mistrust focused on the BKA.[23]

The unequal relationship between the BKA and other components of the security system is put to the test in its contacts with the Foreign and Defense Ministries. The underlying fundamental issue concerns the role of staff. From the standpoint of organizational strategy, however, it raises the question of who should be "the primary foreign affairs official."[24] This question is currently the basis of widespread criticism of the Nixon NSC system.[25] In the German system, the official relations between the BKA and the Foreign and Defense Ministries are centered in Cabinet meetings and frequent situation meetings. There are two types of situation meetings. One includes a small group of officials from the BKA, the Foreign Ministry, and the Press and

Information Office, who deal with current foreign policy and national security matters. The larger situation meeting, composed of additional representatives from the Defense and Interior Ministries, and the Federal Intelligence Agency (BND), is concerned with long-range security and other programs.[26] The participants are comparable to the American Senior Review Group, in that position papers or programs presented by subordinated staff units are reviewed before they reach the Chancellor and the Cabinet.[27] Difficulties already referred to, tend to surface in the situation meetings. For instance, the BKA is confronted by the fact that its special relationship with the Chancellor does not necessarily produce sufficient political capital to overcome the power of the Foreign and Defense Ministries. The ministers of these departments lord over large bureaucracies, which amounts to considerable bargaining advantage for them. And their cooperation is essential to the functioning of the national security machinery. Consequently, the usefulness of the BKA, as far as the Chancellor's own bargaining advantage is concerned, comes to a grinding halt when faced by ministerial opposition.[28] As a matter of necessity, therefore, decisionmaking responsibility is shared in the German national security system by the Chancellor, his BKA, and the major department heads, specifically the Foreign and Defense Ministers.

The characteristics of the relationship between the BKA and the major ministries apply in essence also to the BKA's organizational ties with the Federal Security Council (BsR). This is not surprising because the BsR is a special interministerial Cabinet committee. Chaired by the Chancellor, the BsR is responsible for planning, coordinating, and implementing national security policy.[29] The other permanent members are the Ministers of Foreign Affairs, Defense, Interior, Finance, Economics, and Transport, and Telecommunications, plus the Chief of the intelligence community and the Chief of Staff. The BKA Chief participates in all Council meetings. His staff draws up the agenda which requires the approval of the Chancellor. All business has to be cleared by the BKA Chief before it can be brought before the Council. An official from the

[20]These provisions are contained in Articles 7, 15, 20, and 21 of the Cabinet's By-Laws. See Günther Behrendt, *Das Bundeskanzleramt* (Frankfurt: Athenäum Verlag, 1967), pp. 50–53.

[21]Destler, *Presidents, Bureaucrats, and Foreign Policy*, p. 259.

[22]Rolf Zundel, "Bonn, Adenauer-Allee Nr. 141," *Die Zeit* (September 4, 1970): 44; and Reimut Jochimsen, "Establishing and Developing an Integrated Project Planning and Coordination System for the West German Federal Government," *International Journal of Politics* 2 no. 2–3 (Summer/Fall 1972): 55.

[23]Zundel, "Auf Normalmass gestutzt," p. 4; Zundel, "Bonn, Adenauer-Allee Nr. 141," p. 44; Anon., "Der Macher," *Der Spiegel* (February 1971): 36; Claus Grossner, "Wenn Zukunft verplant wird," *Die Zeit* (April 9, 1971): 8.

[24]Destler, *Presidents, Bureaucrats, and Foreign Policy*, p. 93.

[25]*Ibid.* See also John P. Leacacos, "Kissinger's Apparat." *Foreign Policy* (Winter 1971/1972): 3–27; Hendrick Smith, "Foreign Policy: At Center, Kissinger, Exercising Control for the President," *The New York Times* (January 18–24, 1971): 6–8 (special publication of a collection of articles from *The New York Times*); Charles W. Yost, "Charles Yost: On Affairs of State," *The New York Times* (May 30, 1971).

[26]Günter Diehl, *Denken und Handeln: Planung in der Aussenpolitik* (Freudenstadt: Eurobuch-Verlag August Lutzeyer, 1970), p. 53.

[27]*Ibid.*

[28]This is even more so the case because most German governments are coalitions of two or more political parties. Cf. also the sources cited in footnote 23.

[29]Germany, Federal Ministry of Defense, *White Paper 1970 on the Security of the Federal Republic of Germany and on the State of the German Federal Armed Forces*, Bonn (1970), p. 171.

BKA who heads an inter-ministerial secretariat serves as the Council's executive secretary. The responsibilities of the Federal Security Council are comparable to the "integration of domestic, foreign, and military policies relating to national security"[30] assigned to the American National Security Council. However, the inclusive nature of the German Security Council makes it more into a smaller Cabinet, which in effect heightens the importance of the entire Cabinet and, consequently, leads to a game plan different from its American counterpart. Brandt's organizational strategy unfolds against the ministerial background, by virtue of Article 65 of the Basic Law, rather than in an extraministerial context, similar to the situation of the presidential staff. Finally, it should be emphasized not to accept at face value the apparent dominance of the BKA in its relations with the Security Council. Here the constraints are like those noted with reference to the BKA and the situation meetings. They derive from the same sources of ministerial power, which places the relevance of Article 65 clearly into relief. American presidents may incur major political risks if they decide to ignore or to bypass major departments, such as State, but there is nothing unconstitutional about this approach. After all, the President is the chief foreign policy decisionmaker. The Chancellor's position is not as clear cut. He is restrained by the Basic Law on this matter, which legitimizes the power of the Cabinet. In the last analysis, decisionmaking responsibility for national security affairs is relatively dispersed in comparison with the American national security system.

BRANDT'S NATIONAL SECURITY STAFF

The indispensability of staff is implied in the preceding discussion; it is underscored by its major functions in two key areas—planning and coordination. The former includes broad, long-term analysis of all major problems confronted by the political leadership, as opposed to the day-to-day operational duties of line officials. Coordination involves supervision of line agencies and officials to assure harmonious interaction in pursuit of established priorities and purposes.[31] Destler identifies two types of staff, the "planning staff," à la the State Department's Policy Planning Council, and the "general substantive staff," e.g., the NSC staff and the Office

of International Security Affairs (ISA), in the Defense Department.[32] All staffs have one common problem, "building sufficient bargaining advantage to give them policy impact."[33] There are two ways to overcome this problem: one, "a close relationship to the boss and the boss's interests"; two, "a regular role in important policy-making processes."[34] This typology provides a useful comparative context for the analysis of problem areas concerning German national security staffs. A brief discussion of the types of staff in the German system will precede an analysis of the particularly problematic staff position held by Brandt's BKA chief.

First, both types of staff discussed by Destler are also part of the German national security structure. The planning staffs of the Foreign and Defense Ministries have been previously referred to. The Foreign Ministry's planning staff does not rank with the planning unit in the BKA, but it has considerably more prestige and influence than the newly created Planning and Coordinating Staff of the State Department.[35] The relative high standing of the German Foreign Policy Planning Staff derives from the status of the Foreign Minister. Given the relative dispersion of decisionmaking responsibility, it stands to reason that the Foreign Ministry's staff derives bargaining advantage from its boss. The planning staff in particular enjoys a fairly close relationship with the Foreign Minister, to whose office it is attached.[36] In addition, the minister allows his planning unit to play an important role by channeling their work to the highest decisionmaking levels.[37]

The Federal Chancellery (BKA) is the "general substantive staff" of the German national security system. The multi-purpose and *ad hoc* nature of the BKA allows it to service the Chancellor's and the Cabinet's daily business, providing information and analysis, coordinating and managing the "general policy formulation process."[38] Aside from the planning staffs of the Foreign and Defense Ministries, most of the national security staff is comprised of the BKA[39] and the Federal Security Council (BsR). These staffs are

---

[30]U.S., Office of the Federal Register, *United States Government Organizational Manual—1970/71*, Revised July 1, 1970, p. 60.

[31]Destler, *Presidents, Bureaucrats, and Foreign Policy*, pp. 222–23.

[32]*Ibid.*, pp. 224–28.

[33]*Ibid.*, p. 234.

[34]*Ibid.*, p. 235.

[35]Cf. footnote 10.

[36]Diehl, *Denken und Handeln*, pp. 21–24.

[37]*Ibid.*

[38]These functions are attributed by Destler to the "general substantive staff." (Destler, *Presidents, Bureaucrats, and Foreign Policy*, pp. 230–33.)

[39]The entire BKA staff consists of approximately 400 employees. See Werner Kaltefleiter, "From the Chancellor Principle to the Cabinet Principle," *International Journal of Politics* 2 no. 2–3 (Summer/Fall 1972): 7.

comparable to the NSC staff. However, jurisdictional lines are even less clearly defined than in the American system. The state secretary, currently Egon Bahr, holds a position similar to that of the American Special Assistant for National Security Affairs. Yet his influence does not compare to Kissinger's. He is the Chancellor's foreign policy and national security advisor and trouble shooter, but he does not control the national security machinery in the sense of leading an elaborate committee structure. State Secretary Bahr is not even a regular member of the Federal Security Council; he stands overshadowed by Professor Ehmke, the BKA chief.[40] A closer examination of the chief's position will prove interesting and instructive.

Until 1964 two state secretaries provided the leadership in the BKA. One of the secretaries served as the official head of the organization with the title of Chief of the Federal Chancellery. Chancellor Erhard changed this arrangement when he nominated Ludger Westrick, his confidant and former state secretary in the Economics Ministry, to the position of Federal Minister for Special Affairs and Chief of the Federal Chancellery.[41] This precedent was followed by Chancellor Brandt in 1969, with the appointment of Professor Ehmke as minister and BKA chief. In effect, this situation is analogous to a recommendation repeatedly made for the American system, namely the proposal for the creation of a "First Secretary of the Government," who would head a "super-cabinet."[42] The wisdom of American presidents not to heed this advice is borne out by the German experience.

To begin with, a German state secretary is a politicized civil servant, with a superior. A German minister, on the other hand, is not a civil servant but a politician without a boss.[43] The minister is a permanent member of the Cabinet; he sits as the Chancellor's colleague, not as his subordinate.[44] In his capacity as BKA chief, he is bound by the Chancellor's instructions. In his role as minister, he is a relatively free agent with full voting powers in the Cabinet. This situation may lead first to personal conflict for the individual; second, if the conflict is resolved in favor of his responsibilities as head of the Chancellery, a violation of the Constitution may occur, because the Chancellor will in effect have a dual vote in the Cabinet; third, if he decides to act as an independent agent, he will be unable to lead the Chancellor's staff. There are other problems stemming from the fact that the BKA chief, in his capacity as minister, is equal to other Cabinet members, who regard his status in conjunction with his special relationship to the Chancellor as a major threat to their own power. Furthermore, elevation from state secretary to minister created a gulf between the BKA chief and the state secretary in the Chancellery, with whom he needs to work very closely. In other words, as pointed out by Eschenburg, the shift from state secretary to minister alleviated *distance* where it is necessary and increased it where it is undesirable and harmful.[45]

The problem inherent in the position of the BKA chief helps to explain why Chancellor Brandt's organizational strategy ran into serious difficulties. Brandt found himself confronted by a growing organizational bottleneck. The BKA chief is neither able to capitalize on his close relationship with the boss, because of insufficient cooperation from the operating agencies, nor is he able to play a full role in the policymaking process. Strengthening the BKA with a ministerial appointment proved to be counterproductive.

Nevertheless, this does not mean that the entire national security organization is ineffective. Obviously, the foreign policy and national security staff has something to do with the success of *Ostpolitik*.[46] Perhaps the best indication that these difficulties have been recognized by Brandt and others is the fact that significant changes in personnel have recently been implemented. Professor Ehmke is no longer the head of the Chancellery. Ehmke's prominent political profile and the BKA's reputation as a super-ministry acquired during his tenure, reduced his political value for the Chancellor, and accounts for the transfer to the Ministry of Research and Technology.[47] The most important change, however, is the redesignation of the BKA chief as state secretary. This position was filled after the 1972 election by Horst Grabert, a former senator from Berlin.[48]

[40] C. L. Sulzberger, "A Shrewdness of Kissingers: I," *The New York Times* (December 24, 1972): 9.

[41] The official reason given for this arrangement was a provision in the civil service law which requires retirement at the age of 65. Westrick had reached this age. For an excellent discussion of this issue, see Theodore Eschenburg, *Zur Politischen Praxis in der Bundesrepublik*, II (Munich: R. Piper and Co. Verlag, 1966), pp. 148–53.

[42] Henry M. Jackson (ed.), *The National Security Council: Jackson Subcommittee Papers on Policy-Making at the Presidential Level* (New York: Frederick A. Praeger), pp. 19–23.

[43] Eschenburg, *Zur Politischen Praxis in der Bundesrepublik*, p. 149.

[44] *Ibid.*, p. 151.

[45] *Ibid.*, p. 153.

[46] Bahr has been instrumental in negotiating the recent treaties with Moscow, Warsaw, and East Berlin.

[47] Carl-Christian Kaiser, "Die Konflikte sind eingebaut," *Die Zeit* (December 26, 1972): 3.

[48] *Ibid.*

COORDINATION OF NATIONAL SECURITY AFFAIRS UNDER BRANDT

"The Federal Government has to coordinate the ministries in such a way that the various parts of the governmental apparatus constitute an integrated whole. The primary political task of the government is to bring about this kind of coordination."[49] "Coordination means the intimate link between the Chancellor and the overall effectiveness of the organization."[50] Adolf Hüttl's view of coordination relates closely to the issues of decisionmaking responsibility and staff, and it coincides with Destler's emphasis on "bargaining advantage."[51] In a sense, the entire preceding discussion bears on the subject of coordination. However, the focus is now on the major coordination *mechanisms* and the problems which they entail.

We know already that the Chancellor's key "agents of coordination" in national security affairs are found in the BKA—specifically its chief and the state secretary—and in the Foreign and Defense Ministries. The primary instruments for coordination are the BKA, the Cabinet, the Federal Security Council (BsR), and the situation meetings. Beginning with the Kennedy administration, the White House Staff emerged as the main coordination device of the American national security system. This development has occurred largely at the expense of other organizations with considerable coordination potential, e.g., the State Department. Brandt's approach to coordination parallels the recent American experience in that the Federal Chancellery appears to be the logical institutional device to bring about the kind of integration and overall effectiveness discussed by Hüttl. Brandt seized upon the BKA as a tool which could help him overcome "negative coordination"—coordination "by isolating and protecting the vital interests of each individual department"[52]—and produce instead "positive coordination"—coordination motivated by common goals.[53] Brandt's organizational strategy calls for a staff which will not only strengthen his own position as Chancellor, but will also be capable of reinforcing and constantly supporting the coordinating role of the Cabinet. This approach is very much in keeping with

Article 65 of the Basic Law and the by-laws of the Cabinet, which designate the BKA as the Cabinet's official secretariat.

The necessity of staff, particularly from the standpoint of coordination, is difficult to deny. The problem, as both the German and American experience shows, is the tendency for the servant to look more and more like the master. Or, more appropriately, it raises once more the issue of who the proper "agent of coordination" should be. A strong NSC staff or a strong BKA tends to smother other coordination devices as a matter of course. This is counter-productive because coordination without or against the operating departments is no coordination at all. This realization leads Destler and others to advocate strategies for national security organization which center on the Secretary of State. But, a strategy which ignores the coordination potential of this position is more likely to occur in the American than in the German system. The reason for this lies again in the provisions of Article 65, which legitimizes the semi-independent status of the Cabinet. As a consequence, Professor Ehmke discovered relatively early in the game that more power on his part does not automatically translate into bargaining advantage in his dealings with the ministers. Ehmke even devised methods of bypassing the ministers by going directly to the state secretaries and by establishing *ad hoc* Cabinet committees designed to impose discipline on their members.[54] Judging by the frequent opposition to the BKA, these attempts have been less than successful.[55]

The Cabinet continues to be the weakest link in the governmental chain.[56] This is the case despite the concerted efforts of Brandt's government to increase the Cabinet's self-esteem and importance. The reasons for failure are implicit in the preceding discussion about the role played by the BKA and the parochialism and selfish orientation of the various ministries. As far as the Cabinet is concerned, "negative coordination" seems to occur more often than not.[57] The Federal Security Council, being a special Cabinet committee, does not remain unaffected by these circumstances. The BsR is specifically charged with the "coordination of national defense."[58]

---

[49] Adolf Hüttl, "Koordinierungsprobleme der Bundesregierung," *Der Staat* Nr. 1 (1967): 10.

[50] *Ibid.*, p. 15.

[51] A term used by Destler throughout his book.

[52] Jochimsen, "Establishing and Developing an Integrated Project . . . ," p. 54. Cf. also Zundel, "Bonn, Adenauer-Allee Nr. 141," p. 44.

[53] Jochimsen, "Establishing and Developing an Integrated Project . . . . ," p. 55.

[54] Anon., "Der Macher," p. 36.

[55] The state secretaries have little to gain from cooperation with the BKA. Their professional advancement is dependent on their bosses, the ministers.

[56] Hüttl, "Koordinierungsprobleme der Bundesregierung," p. 13.

[57] Jochimsen, "Establishing and Developing an Integrated Project . . . ," p. 53.

[58] Germany, Deutscher Bundestag, *Stenographische Berichte*, 102. Sitzung, (1967), 4751.

But the afflictions of the Cabinet as a decision-making and coordinating body and the extent to which the BsR is actually an instrument of the BKA chief, prevent alleviation of the negative BKA syndrome of generating frequent opposition rather than cooperation.

Finally, a brief evaluation of the situation meetings presents a more encouraging picture. According to Gunter Diehl, the former director of the Foreign Ministry's planning staff, the situation meetings have developed into "important leadership instruments for the Chancellor."[59] Diehl believes that these frequent conferences between the national security-oriented ministries and the intelligence community have had a salutary effect on national security organization.[60] The partial explanation for this estimate may lie in the less obtrusive role of the BKA in these meetings.

CONCLUSION

Although this paper is concerned with the issues of decisionmaking responsibility, staff, and coordination in the German national security context, some observations reaching beyond the immediate concerns are in order. What are the implications of this analysis for Germany's stra-

tegic position and her internal political evolution?

In comparing Adenauer's and Brandt's organizational strategies for national security, we noted a pronounced shift from an *ad hoc*, personal approach in the case of Adenauer to a systematic, institutional pattern under Brandt. The growing institutionalization of German national security processes is an expression of self-assertion and independence. It reflects the search for a stable organizational base, relatively free from external manipulation. The same features—self-assertion, independence, and search for stability—characterize Germany's strategic position today.

Brandt's organizational strategy displays also adaptability with reference to the American influence and fluidity resulting largely from the German constitutional context. The lessons inherent in the evolution of the national security machinery proscribed by Brandt's strategy are not conclusive. For whatever additional reasons adaptation to the American security organization may have occurred, Germany's future national security system is not likely to become a carbon copy of its U.S. counterpart. Instead, we are more likely to encounter a German national security organization structured in accordance with the specific needs of *German* security, namely, a European peace system and improved inter-German relations. Furthermore, the "Cabinet Principle" will remain a prominent element of national security strategy and organization.

---

[59]Diehl, *Denken und Handeln*, pp. 53–54.
[60]*Ibid.*, p. 54.

THE SECURITY POLICY-MAKING PROCESS IN INDIA

STEPHEN P. COHEN

Professor Cohen provides a comprehensive survey of the numerous governmental and public groups active in the formulation of Indian defense policy. He emphasizes the relatively closed nature of the Indian security policy process and the dominance of civilian government bureaucrats over the military professionals and the public at large. Cohen also notes the emergence of growing interest and expertise regarding military policy matters outside of the government and speculates about the future impact of this development.

For a biography of Stephen P. Cohen, see his article "Military Ideology: South Asia" in the MILITARY PROFESSION *section of this book.*

INTRODUCTION

Security policy-making in present-day India is an ongoing process. In this study, special attention is given to the origin of ideas and issues, the role of various groups concerned with security policy, and the relation of security policy to other policy areas.[1] It identifies important participants in the formulation of security policy and describes their particular functions.

THE SECURITY POLICY-MAKING PROCESS

The security policy-making process may be defined as the subsystem of the political system in which political and administrative actors influence the organization and utilization of the armed forces in the name of the state. Security policy-making may be visualized as separate only if we remember that there are crucial overlaps between the defense, foreign policy, and domestic policy processes. There is a gradation of in-

terest and influence in defense matters. Those at the periphery of the security policy-making process have only marginal or intermittent interest and influence; those at the center have continuing interest and/or great influence. Generally, interest and influence are linked, but on certain issues (and especially during periods of crisis) the relationship is unpredictable, as those with hitherto low interest gain considerable influence over security matters. This happened before the 1962 war with China, when several Congress politicians exercised a veto and allegedly refused to permit the trade of territory between India and China.[2] It is also true that interest does not necessarily indicate influence on security policy, particularly for politicians.

In comparative terms the Indian defense policy process is considerably more "closed" than its American counterpart, and perhaps even more so than the British, after which it is in part modeled. It is closed in the dual sense that there are relatively few groups involved in policy-making, compared with the American process, and information about the process is extraordi-

[1] For some of the intellectual foundations of this approach, see Gabriel Almond, *The American People and Foreign Policy* (New York: Praeger, 1960); James N. Rosenau, ed., *Domestic Sources of Foreign Policy* (New York: The Free Press, 1967); Samuel P. Huntington, *The Common Defense* (New York: Columbia University Press, 1961), and the excerpt from Huntington above, pp. 107-13.

[2] T. J. S. George, *Krishna Menon*, paperback ed. (Bombay: Jaico, 1966), pp. 300-1; Michael Brecher, *India and World Politics: Krishna Menon's View of the World* (London: Oxford University Press, 1968), p. 169.

Excerpted by permission and with minor changes from "The Indian Security Policy-Making Process," in India and Japan: The Emerging Balance of Power in Asia and Opportunities for Arms Control, 1970–75, *ACDA/IR-170, Vol. III (New York: South Asian Institute/East Asia Institute, Columbia University, April 1971). Although based on a work prepared for the United States Arms Control and Disarmament Agency, the views set forth here are those of the author and do not necessarily reflect the views of the United States Arms Control and Disarmament Agency or any other agency of the United States government.*

narily difficult to obtain, whether one is at the center of decision-making or on its periphery.[3]

Although there is relatively little data about the workings of the key bureaucracies—the three armed services and the Defense, External Affairs, and Finance Ministries—it is important to note their role in the process, particularly the kinds of interests and approaches each bureaucracy represents, and their respective power in various facets of security policy-making.

The Ministry of Defense

The Ministry of Defense occupies a powerful and central position in the security policy-making process.[4] It has little operational authority, except in the growing defense industrial sector, but it can veto or modify matters brought to it for approval by the three services. The services are completely dependent upon the Ministry of Defense for policy guidance, although the ministry is not particularly well equipped or staffed to deal with strategic or tactical problems. The Ministry of Defense is the government's private and public spokesman on defense matters; private in that it represents the interests of the military in interministerial disputes (especially with Finance and Home) and public, since it carefully regulates the flow of fact and information about the govenment's military and defense activities.

Although the Ministry of Defense is a relatively new creation, considerable power is due both to the development of new responsibilities and to the slow acquisition of tasks previously handled elsewhere. Before independence, the military functioned under the leadership of the commander-in-chief of the Indian Army, who had a place on the Viceroy's Executive Council. After independence, this place was taken by a civilian Minister of Defense, the post of Commander-in-Chief was abolished, and the three service chiefs were placed under the authority of the minister.[5] As an Indian observer com-

ments, the ministry developed haltingly and even apologetically, but "with time have come confidence and a sense of authority, and its role has increased from merely obtaining policy decisions of the Government and coordination to becoming the Government itself."[6] The function of the Ministry of Defense is now nothing less than "the defense of India and every part thereof, including preparation for defense and all such acts as may be conducive in times of war to its prosecution, and after its termination to effective demobilization."[7]

The ministry has three major tasks: the approval or ratification of service-originated proposals (including their financial implications), the making of policy decisions concerning the location and operation of defense industries, and the clarification or alteration of defense policy requests from the public, especially from Parliament.

The great power of the Ministry of Defense lies in its central position in the policy-making process: it controls information, it can often veto or modify decisions and suggestions formulated in the military, and, often as important, it can decide what is and is not "policy," and hence a matter subject to Ministry or Cabinet review. It has total authority over the expanding defense industry. The military has no legal or administrative control over armaments plants (when on occasion a military officer heads a Defense Ministry establishment, he reports to the ministry, not to his own service).

Since V. K. Krishna Menon's tenure as Minister of Defense (1957–62), the ministry has been led by a powerful politician close to the prime minister. Even before Menon, when its political leadership was relatively weak, the ministry was controlled by very powerful and senior Indian Civil Service (ICS) officers, who were instrumental in bringing the ministry through its first critical years.[8] Through the years the ministry's politicians and administrators have tended to

---

[3]This is a universal complaint of politicians and the press, although in fairness to the government it should be noted that the demand for data is not very strong and many M.P.s take no advantage of the opportunities open to them to visit defense establishments. This is discussed in greater detail later.

[4]There is, remarkably, no good description of the actual operation of a Union ministry although for the Ministry of Defense. A. L. Venkateswaran, *Defense Organisation in India* (New Delhi: Publications Division, 1967) is very useful. It was designed not only to inform the general public about defense matters but to serve as a handbook on the ministry for its new members and those who must deal with it.

[5]For a history, see Venkateswaran, *Defense Organisation in India*, especially pp. 120ff. The author describes the process by which the Ministry of Defense acquired control over the location and movement of important files, interposing itself

between the military, political leadership, and other ministries, most notably Finance. When read carefully, the story of a brilliant bureaucratic coup emerges.

[6]Maharaj K. Chopra, *India: The Search for Power* (Bombay: Lalvani, 1969), p. 224. Chopra is the Military Correspondent of the *Indian Express*, a frequent contributor to Indian and foreign journals, and an ex-Air Force officer.

[7]Ministry of Defense, *Report, 1968–69* (New Delhi: Ministry of Defense, 1969), Appendix A., p. 197.

[8]A brief account of the various ministers is in S. S. Khera, *India's Defense Problem* (Bombay: Orient Longmans, 1968), pp. 66ff. The recent move of Y. B. Chavan from the Defense Ministry to the Finance Ministry in June 1970 and his replacement by Jagjivan Ram, marked the first substantial exception to this generalization. The subsequent departure from Defense of the top civil servant further weakened the power of the ministry.

view defense problems from a civilian perspective; the Ministry of Defense is, and has been, an important instrument for controlling the military and its power has grown in direct proportion as it has been able to carry out this function.

Defense Ministry personnel perceive their role in part as that of checking the excesses of the military, balancing and coordinating the requests of the three services (and between important branches of individual services), and prodding the military to hasten their transformation from a colonial-style organization to one that more closely reflects the aspiration and values of a free India. To this end, they have created numerous all-service training and education establishments to blot out parochial loyalties.[9] The ministry's greatest successes are in the numerous interservice institutions and the extensive defense production empire that it controls. Other than this, its power is bureaucratic: it can, and does, mediate when conflicts arise within the military and between the military and other ministries, especially Finance. It also serves as the government's spokesman on security matters. The military never makes any policy statements and its public statements require prior Defense Ministry approval.[10]

Because of the ministry's central position in the bureaucratic network, the very small number of gazetted Defense Ministry personnel makes (or contributes to) a large number of very important decisions. All important service proposals, especially those dealing with organization, equipment, and manpower, must be passed upon by Defense personnel before they are dealt with by Finance if there are any fiscal implications. This means that relatively young Indian Administrative Service (IAS) officers with little defense experience can judge or at least annotate decisions.[11] It is therefore important to take a brief look at the composition of the Defense Ministry's bureaucracy.

Considering its responsibilities, the Ministry's Class I cadre is incredibly small. The minister receives direct advice from only the eight officers

of the rank of Joint Secretary or above in the Defense Ministry.[12] There are only an additional eight such officers in the Defense Production and Supply branch of the Defense Ministry. The total of all gazetted officers in the ministry is eighty-five.[13] By comparison, the External Affairs Ministry is almost as large with seventy-four, seventeen at Joint Secretary level or above. Clearly, the personnel limitations of the Ministry of Defense prevent it from effectively administering the many bureaucracies and establishments for which it has policy responsibility without drawing upon the military for administrative manpower.

The civilian personnel are not specially selected or trained for dealing with security policy, which adds to the difficulty of the ministry's task. As of February 1969 only one civilian who had completed a course at India's premier defense training institution, the National Defense College, was working in the Defense Ministry and "no other out of scores who had graduated from the N.D.C. has been brought to the Ministry."[14] Further, training within the ministry is likely to be skimpy: K. Subrahmanyam notes that, of the fourteen officers at Joint Secretary and above, only four have risen from the rank of Deputy Secretary, the rest having entered directly at the level of Joint Secretary. Since their tenure is for only five years, he adds, "It is quite obvious that in the first two to three years, these officers who are generalists would be acquiring knowledge about a field to which they had hitherto been complete strangers and would be in a position to contribute to policy-making only in the second half of their tenure in the Ministry of Defense."[15]

The ministry's combination of great power and relatively low expertise has inevitably caused great concern in the military. One retired officer has characterized the "civilian defense official of India" as "one who can talk about and pronounce judgement upon the knottiest professional problem with nonprofessional competence but professional air."[16]

The political leadership of the Ministry of Defense after independence was either uninformed about security matters or politically

---

[9]These include the National Defense Academy (an interservice officer training institution, India's tri-service West Point), and the National Defense College (an interservice civil and military school for advanced political, diplomatic, and economic studies).

[10]Even visits to service installations or forward areas are ultimately processed through the Ministry of Defense. Defense is also responsible for replying to all parliamentary questions, although it may consult with individual services.

[11]There are striking parallels between this situation and one of the causes of the notorious dispute between Kitchener and Curzon in 1905. See Stephen P. Cohen, "Issue, Role and Personality: The Kitchener-Curzon Dispute," *Comparative Studies in Society and History* 10, no. 3 (April 1968): 337-55.

[12]Delhi Telephone Directory (June 1969).

[13]Adding in the officers of the Ministry of Finance (Defense), 126.

[14]K. Subrahmanyam, "Understanding Defense Issues," *Hindustan Times* (Feb. 16, 1969). The author is a senior member of the Defense cadre on deputation as director of the Institute for Defense Studies and Analyses, New Delhi.

[15]*Ibid.* See also Subrahmanyam, "The Process of Decision Making," *Overseas Hindustan Times* (Aug. 2, 1969).

[16]Chopra, *India: The Search for Power*, p. 245.

obscure. Before Menon, all ministers were political lightweights and only one had any substantial interest in security policy. Menon's appointment began a new pattern; he and his successors (Y. B. Chavan and Sd. Swaran Singh) brought considerable personal competence and political power to the ministry. Their lack of experience in security matters has not necessarily made them dependent upon the defense bureaucracy; Menon and Chavan undertook personal crash courses in security affairs, and Swaran Singh had served for several years as Minister of External Affairs.

The Defense Ministry is also the single important source of information about security matters. All publicity for all the services, the defense production establishment, and several paramilitary operations emanates from the ministry-controlled Directorate of Public Relations. In a unique arrangement, its officers are not deputed from Information and Broadcasting (as in other ministries) but formally join the Ministry of Defense. Except for an occasional parliamentary report, the bulk of information about India's military operations comes through the Defense Ministry in its annual report, publications, and statements in Parliament by its political heads. Compared with other nations, "leaks" from the military and the ministry to the press are few and far between; in part, this is due to an intense security-consciousness, but the major reason is a rather strict line laid down by the ministry with regard to the rules of the game in internicine service quarrels and ministry-military conflict. Even retired officers have been criticized for speaking out, less for revealing alleged secrets than for breaking time-honored tradition of keeping conflict within the bureaucratic framework.

The Indian Military

Constitutionally, the Indian armed forces are responsible to the President of India in his role as Commander-in-Chief. In fact, the President has never exercised any direct control over the Defense Ministry. The military are charged with operational authority, not policy-making, an important distinction in Indian bureaucratic language, and one that the Ministry of Defense has taken upon itself to interpret. Thus "policy" matters must be referred to the Ministry of Defense by the military, and the ministry has a large voice in determining what is and what is not policy.

The military is responsive to demands from a variety of sources: foreign military pressures, especially Pakistan and China, Finance and Defense pressures to reduce expenditures or to account for used funds and internal organizational requirements, especially in matters of pay, recruitment, status, promotion, and postservice benefits.

The personnel requirements of the three services give rise to the military's special public, the castes and regions that have traditionally supplied large numbers of recruits and contain many ex-servicemen. This public transmits its demands and concerns to the military directly through the military's own recruiting network and its personal ties to the major recruiting areas, and indirectly through politicians and such interest groups as the Indian Ex-Servicemen's League. These demands are purely organizational; strategic issues are ignored by this particular public.[17]

Securing information concerning the intentions and capability of enemy military forces is a major task of the military. There have been recent major changes in the methods of information gathering. Before 1963 "foreign" intelligence was handled by the Home Ministry; the military held responsibility only for tactical intelligence. Since then, the military's intelligence apparatus has been strengthened but it is still not known precisely what responsibilities it must share in this area with External Affairs, Defense, and the Home Ministry. For example, border security is still partially a Home Ministry responsibility, and groups such as the Indo-Tibetan Force and Border Security Force report to the Home Ministry, although they may be under local military operational control.[18]

The role of the Home Ministry in security matters is maintained for two reasons: many of the potential subversive forces that threaten India can operate with some ease within the borders, and keeping the responsibility for their surveillance in the Home Ministry excludes the military from establishing a significant domestic intelligence operation. No doubt, there is serious difficulty in coordinating intelligence with operations in areas such as Nagaland. The military also shares intelligence-gathering responsibility with the Ministry of Defense.

Since the 1962 war with China, the military has operated with increasing autonomy in matters related to potential or actual military threats. This change was precipitated by Krishna

---

[17]There is no equivalent of the American Legion in India, or of the Air Force Association, Navy League, etc. None of the services has a "captive" public pressure group at its command.

[18]See Khera, *India's Defense Problem*, p. 214; Subrahmanyam, "Process of Decision Making"; and Lt. Col. J. S. Bindra, "The Intelligence Problem," *United Service Institution of India Journal* 98, no. 411 (April–June 1969): 133–37.

Menon's decision to involve the Ministry of Defense in the detailed placement of troops in Ladakh and the North-East Frontier Agency (NEFA) in 1962.[19] While it can be argued that the hopscotch nonwar that preceded hostilities was essentially a political action and that the disadvantageous position in which the Indian Army found itself was simply part of the political price, the military viewed the situation quite differently. Its view of civil-military relations was that, when war was imminent, political should yield to military control. Menon's strategic games proved to be so calamitous that the military was able to reassert its control over the placement of troops on the borders; the military now determines the placement of all troops and the strategic and tactical decisions are largely made by the military (the use of airpower against foreign targets is probably an exception), while responsibilities for the structural and organizational foundations are shared with the Defense and Finance Ministries.

Most of the important decisions concerning Indian defense involve the Indian Army, the premier service in age, size, and prestige. If we judge from the character of the strategic threats to India, it is unlikely that the army's preeminent position will be significantly reduced in the years to come. Further, since the cost of their weapons system is extraordinarily large by Indian standards, the growth of the air force and the navy will be limited, despite recent arms purchases from the USSR. The army's formal role in the defense policy process is much greater than its share of the budget would suggest.[20] Legally, the army is treated on a par with the other two services but its formal powers are greatly exceeded by the influence it derives from its traditional authority.

The Commanders-in-Chief of the Army, Navy, and Air Force were restyled Chiefs of the Army (Navy or Air Force) Staff in 1955; but before that, in 1948, it was determined that they would sit as equals on the Joint Chiefs of Staff Committee (JCS) and that the chairmanship of that committee would rotate among the three services according to seniority.[21] Thus the army

chief has served as chief of the JCS only four times, and some army chiefs have never held that position. The rotation is inflexible, and attempts allegedly made by General J. N. Chaudhuri to create a fourth member of the JCS as chairman were unsuccessful.[22]

This system, which enhances the status of the Chiefs of the Air Force and Navy beyond their actual power, is reinforced by the multiplication of committees under the Defense Minister. Each chief sits on three separate committees: the JCS, the Defense Minister's Committee (which also includes the Minister and Deputy Minister, Defense Secretary, Financial and Scientific Advisers), and the individual Service Committee in which each chief meets separately with the minister and his civilian advisers on matters limited to the individual service.

The chiefs do not meet with any civilian politicians other than the Defense Minister, who is their formal link to the Prime Minister, the Cabinet, and Parliament. If there is a powerful Defense Minister or Defense Secretary, the policy-making role of the chiefs can be severely circumscribed, especially in peacetime. The system of committee control was not dismantled during the two major military conflicts of 1962 and 1965, but the military's greater expertise and information about the battlefield helped to decentralize authority to each service. It was not decentralized enough for many in the military, however, who have bitterly complained about the referral of allegedly tactical decisions all the way to the Cabinet.[23]

Finance, External Affairs, and Other Participants

Several other ministries and branches of government have subsidiary roles in the security policy-making process. These include the Ministry of External Affairs (coordination of foreign relations, especially with India's immediate neighbors, but also with likely sources of arms aid), Home Ministry (coordination of intelligence), Finance Ministry (funding the military, as well as the Defense Ministry), Ministry of

[19]For important accounts of this conflict, see Brig. J. P. Dalvi, *Himalayan Blunder* (Bombay: Thackers, 1969), and Lt. Gen. B. M. Kaul, *The Untold Story* (Bombay: Allied, 1967).

[20]The 1969–70 budget estimates (gross expenditures) for the three services are: Army, $1 billion; Navy, $60 million; and Air Force, $260 million. Government of India, *Defense Services Estimates, 1969–70* (New Delhi: Government of India Press, 1969), p. 5. Rs 7.5 $1.

[21]"It was clear [in 1947] that for a balanced expansion of the three services they could no longer continue to be under the Army Chief. . . . The Government of India decided that the

two younger services too should have independent Chiefs. . . . The three Chiefs are directly responsible to the Defense Minister for the administration of their services and are also collectively the professional military advisers to the Government." Venkateswaran, *Defense Organisation in India.* p. 139.

[22]See an article allegedly inspired by Chaudhuri, "Need to Streamline Defense Planning," *Times of India* (Oct. 15, 1963), Chaudhuri has recently urged the creation of a Chief of Defense Staff or permanent chairman of the Chiefs of Staff Committee. See his *Arms, Aims, and Aspects* (Bombay: Manaktalas, 1966), p. 30.

[23]See Dalvi, *The Himalayan Blunder*, and Kaul, *The Untold Story*, for many examples in 1962.

Information and Broadcasting (public relations), Ministry of Labor (welfare of exservicemen), Ministry of Industrial Development (development of defense-related industries), Ministry of Works, Housing, and Supply (procurement of stores, disposal of surplus war material), the Cabinet Secretariat, the Prime Minister's Secretariat, the Planning Commission and Parliament. A number of interservice and interministry coordinating committees have also been created but they do not appear to be policy-*making* bodies. The function of these committees, as well as the cabinet and Parliament, is to ratify decisions made within the bureaucracies.

Ministry of Finance. The influence of the Ministry of Finance in security policy-making is confined exclusively to fiscal management, although it does represent the popular notion that the defense budget is too large and that unnecessary expenditures can be trimmed. The Finance Ministry exerts its influence in two ways: first, in discussions about the over-all shape of the budget, and presumably in negotiations concerning the limits to be placed upon defense spending; second, through the functioning of the Finance Adviser (Defense). This remarkable position, held by a senior civil service officer with Finance experience, is a branch of the Finance Ministry but is physically (and in part administratively) located in the Defense Ministry. The Finance Adviser "is responsible for preparing the Defense Estimates in close consultation with the Defense Ministry in all stages," and he can report to both the ministers of Finance and Defense.[24]

As a general rule, Finance appears to approach defense matters with a single-minded devotion to economy and reduction of expenditure, an approach that has led to great bitterness within the military and the Defense Ministry.[25] In recent years an attempt has been made to change the entire process of budget making by instituting a variety of planning and control techniques derived from a study of the McNamara reforms in the Pentagon. Politicians of all parties have begun to prod the Defense Ministry to increase its efforts along these lines.[26] It can be expected that the process begun in 1963 of increasing Defense control over the budgetary process will continue, especially

if the Finance Ministry is placed under the control of a politician who is sympathetic to the ambitions and goals of the prime minister.

Ministry of External Affairs (MEA).[27] The role of the External Affairs ministry in the security policy process is in the area of strategy, rather than structure. In this sphere MEA has always had two important advantages that have enhanced its power. First, its minister has often been the Prime Minister or a close confidant of the Prime Minister. Second, the MEA bureaucracy is highly skilled and considerably more expert than that of many other ministries. Specialization in foreign affairs has been encouraged by the establishment of a small, well-trained Indian Foreign Service cadre.

"External Affairs," as mandated to the ministry, includes not only relations with India's immediate neighbors but also with Sikkim, Bhutan, and Nagaland, all areas of considerable operational interest to the military. In these areas, MEA has a veto over major policy decisions and maintains separate lines of communication and authority back to Delhi.[28] It has had more than a veto in the area of arms control policy for many years. Until 1964, MEA was the only ministry with any competence in this policy area. It has long been involved in international arms control conferences and contains a number of experts on the legal and political aspects of disarmament.

Although it is a highly competent ministry, MEA is neither the focal point nor the originator of security policy. Like most bureaucracies, the Ministry of External Affairs has difficulty dealing with crises and demands that confront it on short notice and there are special circumstances that make it difficult for MEA to initiate policy. During its years under Nehru's personal leadership, there were clear and firm lines of policy for the bureaucracy to follow. With Nehru's death and a far more complicated international environment, maintaining consistency in policy has become more difficult and problems that could formerly be handled at lower levels must now be referred up the bureaucratic ladder to higher officials. Policy-planning cells have been developed in MEA (and in Defense) but it is doubtful that their impact will be any greater than their prototype, the Policy Planning Staff of the U.S. State Department. In addition, the high priority

---

[24] Venkateswaran, *Defense Organisation in India*, p. 125.

[25] See Khera, *India's Defense Problem*, p. 246. An apocryphal story is that of the battalion commander in Punjab called by the Controller of Defense Accounts to account for his unusual expenditure of small arms ammunition in Sept. 1965.

[26] See the Public Accounts Committee (1968–69), *Sixty-Ninth Report* (New Delhi: Lok Sabha Secretariat, 1969), Chap. 1.

[27] For an excellent description of the foreign policy processes see J. Bandyopadhyaya. *The Making of India's Foreign Policy* (Bombay: Allied, 1970).

[28] Bandyopadhyaya notes, however, that MEA has been very slow to establish institutions which would enable it to better supervise the military aspects of foreign policy (pp. 179ff.).

work of answering parliamentary questions has dramatically increased in recent years for MEA, as it has for other important ministries, further occupying the MEA bureaucracy.

The Cabinet. The role of the Cabinet in the security policy-making process is to ratify and legitimize decisions made elsewhere rather than actually initiate policy. The Cabinet routinely accepts the suggestions of the Prime Minister and the concerned cabinet minister after a minimum amount of debate.[29] Higher security policy is made in consultation between the Prime Minister and the Defense Minister, with other ministers consulted as required before formal cabinet meetings. During periods of crisis, the Defense Committee of the Cabinet performs this ratificatory function and is empowered to act on behalf of the full Cabinet. The significant difference between the full Cabinet and the smaller Defense Committee of the Cabinet is that the three service chiefs are authorized to attend meetings of the Committee and "give on-the-spot military appreciation or clarification on the various points that may be raised during discussion."[30] The Chiefs are not members of this Committee and have no formal role in cabinet decision-making.

Within the Cabinet Secretariat, two very small groups deal with security affairs. The Military Wing of the Secretariat, consisting of six officers of colonel and brigadier rank, serves as the secretariat for the Joint Chiefs of Staff. An even smaller Intelligence Wing doubles as the secretariat for the interministry Joint Intelligence Committee. The reason for locating these groups in the Cabinet Secretariat is uncertain; neither the Cabinet nor the Defense Committee of the Cabinet requires their full-time services and they are too small to contribute effectively to the operation of the Joint Chiefs Committee or the Joint Intelligence Committee.[31]

Public Opinion and Security Policy: The Influential and the Interested

There are other groups involved in the security policy-making process that are not part of the government structure but represent public interest in various aspects of India's defense structure and security policy. These groups include the press, political parties, and several research institutions. Although this public has maintained considerable interest in security

matters, its influence has not been very great in policy decisions. The several exceptions to this lack of influence are in policy areas that affect civilian India such as recruitment and defense production.

The low strike record of the defense industries is unparalleled in Indian labor, largely because of the close cooperation between the leadership of the defense workers union and the Ministry of Defense and the military. Labor leaders in the defense production industries—even those with Communist sympathies—are sensitive to the demands of national security, and some claim that they have tried to separate defense matters from "politics." This may be due in part to a basic sympathy with the policies of the Union government, but also perhaps also to a realization that harassment in this sector would lead to strong governmental counterpressures.

The political leadership of those regions and castes that have traditionally supplied military recruits have also worked closely with the government. However, as the recruitment base has broadened, politicians from all areas have begun to demonstrate a greater interest in recruitment policy.

The role of public groups in security policy decision making is perceived differently by those who are in formal governmental positions of decision-making and those who represent public interest in security policy but have no authority in that area.

Members of the press, politicians, and security-conscious citizens resent their own lack of influence and information and criticize the government bureaucrats for the elitist and manipulative style of controlling information and ignoring criticism.[32] Their desire to have a greater say in security matters is tempered, however, by their belief that security matters should be kept secretive and that they are highly technical and therefore can only be understood thoroughly by those with military experience.

Those persons with direct authority for security policy-making have an elitist view of their responsibilities and often discount efforts by politicians and the press to influence policy. Like their counterparts elsewhere, they tend to regard such issues as nuclear weapons acquisition, foreign policy, and security policy as properly above day-to-day public debate. Questions in parliament require them to re-examine policy continually, but rarely if ever lead to its change.

---

[29] Brecher, chaps. 13, 16, and 17, and interviews with several politicians of ministerial rank, 1968–69.

[30] Venkateswaran, *Defense Organisation in India*, p. 90.

[31] K. Subrahmanyam, "The Process of Decision Making," *Overseas Hindustan Times* (Aug. 2, 1969).

[32] For a vigorous statement of this view, see Nirad C. Chaudhuri, *The Continent of Circe* (Bombay: Jaico paperbacks, 1968), chap. 14.

Senior members of the Defense and External Affairs Ministries generally regard public opinion that does not coincide with their own judgements as misguided. They are greatly concerned by the possibility that during periods of military crisis, when there is need for unanimity, there could be sharp differences between public opinion and government policy on critical issues.[33]

Security Policy Interest Groups. The political parties are the most significant group interested in security policy, although their influence is more potential than actual. This influence is often passive: the government and defense bureaucracies anticipate demands that might be placed upon them and either act in such a way as to satisfy demands or attempt to change the minds of those who might make such demands.

Of the political parties, many speak with more passion than knowledge, for the level of security expertise among party leaders (with some exceptions) is relatively low. Only three parties have any significant numbers of members with sustained interests in security affairs, although the level of interest and expertise in all parties is growing more rapidly now than at any time since independence.

The three parties that have taken a sustained interest in security policy are the Congress, Jan Sangh, and Swatantra. Leaders of these parties not only speak in parliamentary debates on security matters—as do the leaders of other important parties—but they speak with some experience and expertise, and their party organizations have made a special attempt to educate their membership on security issues.

Before the division of the Indian National Congress in 1969–70, some of the most interesting and important debates on security affairs were held *within* the party, usually between Cabinet members and those in the organization or parliamentary backbenchers. These debates made the all-India Congress Committee sessions of more than casual interest, for in this forum government leaders were severely tested by members of their own party. There was added interest in these debates when Cabinet members were challenged by Congressmen who themselves had once held important portfolios, or who were prime material for executive positions. However, once in such a position dissenters

rarely spoke out—especially on security affairs—because of the convention of ministerial silence on policy matters under Cabinet consideration. This convention did not always extend to those in parliamentary party leadership positions, and party whips and secretaries often spoke their mind freely.

When the Congress party divided, it was not along neat ideological, geographical, or political lines. In some ways the two successor Congress parties each reflected the diversity and complexity of the old Congress; in each there was considerable diversity of opinion on security matters. However, the 1971 elections virtually destroyed the power of the "Organization" or "Old" Congress, and under Mrs. Gandhi's leadership the "New" Congress has achieved the dominant position of the undivided party. Within the present Congress Party there are divergent views about such matters as recruitment, nuclear weapons development, policy toward Pakistan, and military and political ties with external powers.

Of the other opposition parties only Swatantra and Jan Sangh have had any sustained interest in security policy. This interest derives largely from the character of the party leadership of Swatantra and the ideological interests of Jan Sangh. Swatantra has always had a large number of former civil servants in its leadership, as well as a significant number of retired generals.[34] While there are important disagreements within this leadership on some security issues (most notably the bomb), there has always been a high level of interest and information.[35] Jan Sangh's interest in defense policy derives from its vision of a greater, more powerful India in addition to its militant organizational inclinations.[36] It is doubtful that these two parties have had an influence on policy in proportion to their considerable interest. Their personal and ideological overlap with the ruling Congress party (even before the split) is very small.

This is not true of the ideological overlap between Congress and the two socialist parties, the Praja Socialist Party (PSP) and the Samyukta Socialist Party (SSP). Indeed, there has always

---

[33]A Deputy Secretary in the Defense Ministry writes in the official guide to the ministry: "No responsible Government can allow itself to be swept away by public opinion, which cannot always be as fully informed, as Government can be, of the undercurrents of events and their implications. In such circumstances, public opinion cannot be allowed to be the over-riding factor in the interest of the State itself." Venkateswaran, *Defense Organisation in India*, p. 88.

[34]The retired generals are less influential in their capacity as public critics than one might expect. A few have taken to journalism and politics, and some are free-lance critics, such as General K. M. Cariappa. They have not done well in politics, however, except in areas that provide large numbers of soldiers for the army.

[35]Swatantra, alone of all the parties, seems to have picked up the remnants of the defunct Liberal movement.

[36]See J. A. Curran, Jr., *Militant Hinduism in Indian Politics: A Study of the R.S.S.* (New York: Institute for Pacific Relations, 1951), and the pages of *Organiser*, the Jan Sangh Weekly.

been a considerable exchange of individuals and ideas between them.[37] Although small in size the PSP, especially, has always presented itself as the authentic conscience of the Congress Party, and it has probably had a disproportionate influence on members of the Congress party in government. The same can be said of a few independent MPs and many Gandhians in and out of Congress.[38]

In most cases the "influence" that we have described amounts to being listened to by the government, and often does not involve any substantial change of policy. With very few exceptions, even those MPs and politicians who are relatively well informed on defense matters know very little, compared with many U.S. Congressmen or informed British MPs.

Since 1963, and especially since 1965, "public opinion" has become increasingly institutionalized and, where not subject to government pressures, can be expected to be more influential. Each major political party has designated one or more MPs as its specialists on defense in Parliament. They are briefed by the military and government and are given limited access to classified data. Many of India's major newspapers and news agencies have designated one reporter as a Defense Correspondent and the Ministry of Defense has run orientation courses for accredited Indian "war correspondents," who will be granted special battlefield access. There are only a small number of these political and journalistic defense experts, however, and their military expertise is not thorough.[39]

Another recent development in informing public opinion has been the creation, in New Delhi, of the Institute for Defense Studies and Analyses (IDSA).[40] It has begun to generate large quantities of data, interpretation, and analysis via a journal, several newsletters, original papers, seminars, and conferences. Within a period of

three years it has significantly raised the quality of public debate on defense and security matters.

All of the above efforts are dependent upon the goodwill of the Government of India, particularly the Ministry of Defense. There are limits to the ability of an official bureaucracy to cooperate in arming critics with information.[41] Outside of Defense-supported or encouraged endeavors, there are few substantial focal points of criticism or analysis. India's premier academic institution devoted to international affairs has never taken any interest in security matters, and the Indian Council of World Affairs has only sponsored an occasional lecture in the area, despite the fact that its director, H. N. Kunzru, was once deeply involved in military studies. A few independent institutes have produced occasional papers on security matters but these have had little or no impact on either policy or public opinion.[42]

Specific Interests of the Security-Conscious Public. Indian politicians have been consistently interested in a narrow range of security issues. One recurring issue is the policy of recruitment of the officer corps and other ranks. Their demands fall into two categories: (1) attempts to secure or retain a special place in the military for constituents; and (2) attempts to equalize recruitment (if necessary, through compulsion or national service), so that all classes, castes, and regions are equally represented in the military, especially the army, with its allegedly feudal and antidemocratic composition.[43]

A second major concern of Indian politicians is the location and operation of defense installa-

---

[37]See Thomas A. Rusch, "Indian Socialists and the Nuclear Non-Proliferation Treaty," *Journal of Asian Studies* (Aug. 1969): 755–70.

[38]The most notable being Acharya Kripalani and J. P. Narayan.

[39]Some exceptions are three retired officers, Maj. Gen. D. K. Palit, now the military correspondent of the *Hindustan Times*; Wing-Commander M. K. Chopra of the *Indian Express*; and Gen. J. N. Chaudhuri, who wrote an anonymous column for the *Statesman* while on active service. Some papers (e.g., the *Hindu*) have not been able to obtain a suitable military correspondent; many rely upon their political or diplomatic correspondents for military analysis. Girilal Jain, Dilip Mukerjee (both of the *Times of India*), S. Mulgaokar, G. S. Bhargava, Pran Chopra, and B. G. Verghese are among the distinguished senior journalists with defense expertise.

[40]Its budget is derived entirely from the Ministry of Defense, although the ministry does not exercise direct control over the Institute. It is largely independent of the ministry but its director is on deputation from Defense.

[41]One important limit is the extreme permeability of Indian politics. By any standards it is an open system, and it is easy for foreign nations to gain access to informed Indian public opinion. Not only do major powers maintain information and propaganda services but there are many personal contacts with Indian opinion leaders. Most of these contacts are mutually useful, but both the disparity in resources and ideological considerations tend to make some segments of Indian opinion relatively dependent. This is true not only of the Communist Party of India (CPI) and avowedly pro-West parties such as Swatantra, but also of individuals and factions in many other parties and in the press and even the bureaucracies. To permit and encourage free public debate on such sensitive issues as defense policy also means that the viewpoints of various foreign powers will enter the debate through Indian spokesmen, as well as through normal channels of diplomatic intercourse. For a general statement of this phenomenon, see Andrew M. Scott, *The Revolution in Statecraft: Informal Penetration* (New York: Random House, 1965).

[42]The Institute of Political and Social Studies (Calcutta) has published several papers and volumes, including K. K. Sinha, ed., *Problems of Defense of South and East Asia* (Bombay: Manaktalas, 1969). There are very small defense study groups affiliated with Allahabad and Poona Universities.

[43]See Stephen P. Cohen, "The Untouchable Soldier: Caste, Politics, and the Indian Army," *Journal of Asian Studies* (May 1969): 453–68, and "The Indian Military and Social Change," *Institute for Defense Studies and Analyses Journal* 2, no. 1 (July 1969): 12–29.

tions; cantonments and defense factories are no less desirable in India than in the United States and MPs and state political leaders often lobby the government to secure their fair share of these political plums.[44]

A third issue has been the reaction of the government to real or alleged incursions upon Indian territory by Chinese or Pakistani forces. Indian politicians are very sensitive to the permeability of Indian society, and even minor transgressions are laden with important symbolic overtones. Regardless of particular circumstances, all frontiers must be equally well defended and all foreign troops must be expelled from Indian territory. This sentiment is especially strong among MPs and politicians from states with long and difficult frontiers—they are among the most interested in defense affairs. Because of traditional recruitment patterns, their constituents are well represented in the Indian Army. This is especially true of the states of Punjab, Harayana, Rajasthan, Uttar Pradesh, Himachal Pradesh, and Jammu and Kashmir.

There are several historical and structural reasons for this limited public interest in security affairs. Recruitment to the military had always been confined to a rather narrow spectrum of castes and regions, although World War II temporarily expanded the base. There was virtually no interchange between political and military careers in British India, and there is very little today. Soldiers are recruited from rural India and tend to make the military a profession, as do officers. Recent changes in the length of tour of duty and in the nature of the officer corps may gradually change the composition of the recruitment base, but the impact will not be felt for years.

Of greater significance is the lack of any "military-industrial" complex. Important decisions concerning weapons choice, strategy, and organization are all made within the bureaucracies; Parliament's only influence over these decisions is the ability to ratify them. Further, most important defense industries are run by the government itself and there is no incentive for those who run these plants to lobby politicians or use the press to further their objectives. A limited amount of bargaining and negotiation has taken place, involving the press and political parties, when the government has purchased weapons from abroad. This lobbying has apparently declined as the United States has withdrawn from the position of arms supplier and the Soviet Union has filled many of India's requests. With the exception of the bomb issue, there are no "great debates" over strategic options, weapons systems, or defense organization in India.

Government Response to Public Interest. Recognizing the volatility of even elite public opinion on security matters, the Ministry of Defense has made a limited effort to increase the size and quality of the security-conscious public since 1963. The then Defense Minister, Y. B. Chavan, greatly improved press coverage of defense matters and revised the ministry's information policy.[45] Visits by politicians, journalists, and even scholars to cantonments and militarily sensitive border areas have actually been encouraged by the Ministry, via its Directorate of Public Information. Other steps taken to improve the quality of public debate on defense matters have been described above. Thus, even though they tightly control the flow of information about defense, and can always resort to the plea of 'national security' to silence critics, both politicians and bureaucrats associated with the security policy process remain concerned about public pressure. One improbable form of pressure is that Parliament will enact legislation, perhaps in a snap vote, not required or requested by the government. This has never happened in the past, although there have been occasions that have required the direct intervention of the prime minister to quash popular resolutions.[46] However, defense matters are still regarded as so sensitive by MPs of all parties that is more likely that the government itself would use specific security issues to built support among wavering MPs and parties. A clear-cut military defeat could force security policies to a Parliamentary vote, but the result of such a vote is highly unpredictable.

A less tangible but very important form of influence is the desire on the part of those in the bureaucracy and government to have popular approval of their actions in such a vital area as security policy. India's defense is seen as resting ultimately upon the will of the population to resist and to make sacrifices willingly, so that in security matters the government often goes out of its way to meet criticism before it reaches the

---

[44]The location of the MIG factories seems to correlate fairly closely with considerations of political, as well as strategic, advantages.

[45]The change in policy was dramatically reflected in the greatly expanded Ministry of Defense *Reports.*

[46]One dramatic case was Nehru's intervention to sidetrack a resolution urging compulsory universal military training, shortly after the Chinese attacked India. See *Lok Sabha Debates,* 3rd Series 9, no. 7 (Nov. 15, 1962): cols. 1827ff.

floor of Parliament or the pages of the daily press. This new willingness to deal sympathetically with press and parliamentary criticism may be temporary but it has affected the structure and quality of public opinion on security matters.

CONCLUSIONS

1. In a decision-making system of any complexity, different kinds of issues tend to be handled in different places in the process. As we have indicated above, *strategic* decisions (war vs. peace, relative threats from China vs. Pakistan) are handled at the highest (cabinet and ministerial) level. Since 1965 *tactical* deployment of the military has apparently become the province of the services themselves, although such decisions may have strategic and political implications. *Structural* decisions are the most bureaucratized in the Indian system, and depend less on individual personalities than on service, role, and institutional interests. These decisions rarely involve the public or press, and only on occasion appear in Parliament; they are usually formulated and processed within the three services and the Defense and Finance ministries. Of these structural decisions, weapons choices are of prime importance, for they often are laden with strategic, economic, and political implications. They are also the decisions most vulnerable to outside influence, and have a direct and immediate effect on India's relations with her neighbors and potential arms suppliers.

2. The imagery of hugeness associated with India (the world's largest democracy and second largest nation) is not usually extended to her defense establishment, but *India maintains the world's fourth largest army, as well as substantial air and sea forces.* The process by which the size, shape, and use of these military forces are determined has evolved largely during the past twenty years. It has been dominated by men trained in the British Indian bureaucratic tradition but is now being slowly transformed by the emergence of new issues and new interests that substantially affect India's national purpose and existence.

3. Compared with those of other democratic systems, India's security policy-making processes are relatively closed and are dominated by bureaucratic elites. Unlike many other issue areas, however, security policy involves several different bureaucracies. Moreover, elected public officials who, though they may play only a small role in policy formulation, must continually be ratifying and legitimizing the policy product of the bureaucracies.

4. The key bureaucracy is the Ministry of Defense, and within it a relatively small group of professional civil servants who control the channels of communication and decision-making. Although their average experience in defense matters is very limited, civil servants in the Ministry of Defense have managed to increase their power over the years. This power is based on doctrines of civilian control, strict financial checks upon military spending and the collaboration of civilian politicians responsible for defense. In addition, the Ministry has direct responsibility for the expanding state armaments industry and regulates the flow of news and information concerning its own activities and those of the three armed services. The Ministry of Defense also has a veto over all service-originated proposals that involve policy matters or new expenditures and usually interprets such proposals for civilian political leadership. In summary, its power is bureaucratic and relatively invisible to the public eye.

5. Although the three services must operate within the narrow limits set for them by the Ministry of Defense, their freedom of movement within those limits can be substantial. This is especially true of the Indian Army, one of the most efficient and well-disciplined military forces in the Third World. Since its humiliation in 1962 the Army has demonstrated its capacity to regroup and reorganize and has achieved high levels of competence and efficiency. It has obtained relative freedom over its own tactical disposition in the battlefield and prides itself upon its independence from meddling civilian hands. The army's tactical freedom of maneuver has not been accompanied by any great expansion of its voice in decision making and its leadership is still subordinate (and seems content to remain subordinate) to civilian political and bureaucratic elites.

6. The External Affairs and Finance Ministries play important roles in determining strategic and structural security policy, respectively. When security and foreign policy overlap, or defense involves extraordinary expenditures, these two bureaucracies have at least a veto over policy. Other ministries and agencies participate in the security policy process on an intermittent basis as their special interests or areas of competence overlap or collide with those of the military and the Ministry of Defense.

7. The security-conscious public in India plays a limited role in the daily policy-making effort but has the potential for greater influence. This can come through parliamentary pressure, defense-oriented interest groups and the inter-

change of personnel and ideas between the broader defense-attentive public and the government and security bureaucracies. Since 1969, each new security crisis has increased the size of this defense-interested segment of Indian public opinion, although it is still largely confined to urban (and especially northern) India. The defense-interested elite is evenly distributed through all national political parties, the national (especially English-language) press, and a few interest groups, such as defense workers, military families, and retired service personnel. The concern of most of these interest groups has always been with structural and organizational defense problems, not strategic security issues.

8. There are only a few strategic analysts in India and they are a very recent phenomenon. Recognizing the superficiality and meagerness of much of the criticism of security matters, the Government of India has relaxed its information policy and recently established the Institute of Defense Studies and Analyses. The dual purpose of the institute is to conduct independent studies of critical security problems and to inform and educate Indian public opinion through a variety of publications, journals, and seminars.

9. Generally, debates in the public domain, including Parliament, have had little impact on government policy. At best, difficult parliamentary questions may embarrass the government or force it to clarify or expound on a particular policy or increase the flow of data and information, but they do not lead to changes in basic policy. However, as the volume and intensity of public discussion on security issues increase, one can expect that the government will increasingly take public opinion into account in the formulation and execution of policy if only to forestall or reduce potential criticism. This anticipatory policy modification will increase as present and future Indian governments are forced to rely upon new political groups to maintain themselves in power. Security issues are unlikely to bring down any government but they can be used to embarrass or pressure the party in power.

[*Editor's Note*: The following two paragraphs are based upon material not included in this excerpt.]

10. Decisions on the acquisition of conventional weapons systems are of great importance because of their strategic, economic, and political significance and because of their vulnerability to outside influence. Such decisions are among the most highly bureaucratized in the entire security policy-making process. The availability of weapons systems at acceptable terms from external suppliers is an important determinant of the priority accorded to a particular defense need and to strategic or tactical theories that call attention to such a need. A key issue in determining the source of support, and the degree of self-sufficiency deemed necessary, for the development of a weapons system is whether that system will be useful in defense against Pakistan, against China, in building a broader strategic role for India in Asia, or in some combination of these security concerns. A further reason for the importance attached to conventional arms acquisition by Indians is its value as a symbol of political support between supplier and recipient. This is seen to be one of the few effective sources of leverage India has in influencing great power military support levels for Pakistan and, at some later date perhaps, China.

11. Major new policy challenges frequently stimulate important changes in decision-making processes. The effect of China's nuclear explosion on Indian security policy-making has been twofold. First, it has brought about changes in procedures and policy assumptions. The concentration of foreign and defense policy-making in the hands of the prime minister and a few close advisors, the sense that a technological military threat from China was remote, the moralistic image of a nonaligned India, and the lack of interest in a nuclear-based defense system are all either under serious challenge in India today or are already vestiges of the past. Second, the Chinese nuclear capability, by focusing public attention on strategic, political, economic, scientific, and international problems affecting the interests of important groups not previously concerned with security issues, has brought those groups into the security policy-making process. A new generation of politicians has focused on this issue, challenging the inactivity and conservatism of their elders. The Indian scientific community has become very much involved in nuclear defense issues, and the growth in size and prestige of the Indian Atomic Energy Commission has brought about an institutional base from which a nuclear weapons program can be mounted. The Indian Army sees the significance of nuclear weapons for its interests in terms of tactical uses along the northern frontiers. Though the conventional wisdom suggests that the Himalayas provide inappropriate terrain for the use of tactical nuclear weapons, this view is now being challenged within the military. Increasing concern with this issue could well bring the army into a much more active role in the debate over the nuclear issue.

POSTSCRIPT, 1973

The Indian security policy-making process today is essentially identical to that described above. This is so despite the severe strains of major domestic political developments and the protracted struggle in East Bengal, which culminated in large-scale warfare between India and Pakistan in December 1971.

Within the Union Cabinet there is probably more defense expertise—politically close to the Prime Minister—than at any time since Independence. Two ex-defense ministers, Swaran Singh and Y. B. Chavan, sit as ministers of External Affairs and Finance, respectively, while a third political ally of Mrs. Gandhi (Jagjivan Ram) retains the defense portfolio. No serious disagreement has arisen within this group either over budgetary matters or strategic questions.

In 1962 and 1965 Indian military action was characterized by hesitancy, confusion, and a lack of firm political guidance. Partly due to the homogeneity of views within the Cabinet, and partly due to the military's stress on relative autonomy and interservice coordination, there was little or none of this in 1971—in many ways a textbook example of successful political-military coordination.[47] However, future conflicts in South Asia may not provide the time for adequate planning and coordination, nor may the tactical military situation be so favorable.[48]

Public interest in security matters has continued to grow rapidly. Books dealing with military and security problems have become a minor growth industry, non-governmental experts have increased from tens to hundreds, and now include substantial numbers of journalists, scholars, and members of public and private research institutes. Even within the Indian government expertise may be more widespread: at least the Planning Commission is now permitted to play some limited role in commenting on the defense budget (previously, planning was carried out with virtually no consideration of the effect of defense spending).

As in other nations the expansion of information and expertise about security affairs may not be accompanied by an expansion of popular or even elite participation. The dispersal of knowledge may well inform and stabilize public opinion, and provide at least the illusion of participation. But those who have only recently perfected and mastered the security policy processes are not likely to share that power. And, as long as decisions appear to be made sensibly, few members of the public—even the elite public—are likely to press for such a share.

---

[47] For a summary see Mohammed Ayoob and K. Subrahmanyam, *The Liberation War* (New Delhi: S. Chand, 1972), pp. 241–43, 273ff.

[48] D. K. Palit, a retired general and presently the military correspondent of the *Hindustan Times*, argues that India will have to adjust to the prospect of sharp, limited conflicts, ridding itself of a World War II total war mentality. See his "Strategic Concepts: Old and New," Institute of Defense Studies and Analyses *Journal* 4, no. 3 (Jan. 1972): 302–26.

FORMULATION OF HIGH POLICY DECISIONS: ISRAEL

MICHAEL BRECHER

The policy-making practices employed within a given institutional setting can vary significantly as a result of differences in the personalities and working styles of those individuals who occupy the crucial leadership roles. Professor Brecher examines the various relationships that existed among Israel's prime-ministers, defense ministers, and foreign ministers, and the manners in which they worked with their bureaucratic and other agencies in the development of Israeli foreign and military policy between 1948 and 1968.

Michael Brecher is a professor of political science at McGill University in Montreal, Canada. A noted student of Asian politics and international relations, Brecher is the author of numerous books and articles including Nehru: A Political Biography *(1959),* The New States of Asia *(1963),* India and World Politics *(1968),* A Framework for Research on Foreign Policy Behavior *(1969),* The Foreign Policy System of Israel *(1972), and* Decisions in Israel's Foreign Policy *(forthcoming, 1974).*

TYPES OF DECISIONS

Foreign *Relations* have long been an object of historical inquiry. Foreign *Policy*, by contrast, has emerged only recently as a branch of social science. In the past fifteen years models, frameworks, approaches, theories, and hypotheses have proliferated. Yet it is a commentary on the state of the field that many books which are devoted to the analysis of foreign policy do not contain a single explicit reference to the meaning of *decision*, the motor force of state behaviour in international systems. The concept of decision is assumed but not defined; or it is used as a synonym for policy and is not regarded as essential to the inquiry.[1]

It is important, therefore, to define and to classify foreign policy decisions: three universal indicators will be combined—a *time continuum*, a spectrum of *initiation-reaction*, and a *scale of importance*.

A foreign policy decision may be defined as the selection, among perceived alternatives, of one option leading to a course of action in the international system. A decision is made by an individual or individuals or a group authorized by

the political system to act within a prescribed sphere of external behaviour.

Foreign policy decisions occur at precise points in time; that is to say (in the Israeli system), the Foreign Minister or the Prime Minister or both, or the Cabinet or its Ministerial Committee on Defence, or on rare occasions the *Knesset*, or a Foreign Office committee or official(s) select option X at point Y in time, which leads to a course of action towards another state or states, an international organization, etc. The time span, however, between stimulus and decision, whether self- or externally-induced, and the selection of option X may extend from a day or less to many months (1—d days). And within the gestation period the number of pre-decisional stages may be one, a few, or many.

There is conspicuous variety, too, in the initiation-reaction mix. Virtually all decisions contain both types of stimuli, but the proportions vary from almost total initiative to almost total reaction. Furthermore, there appears to be *a meaningful correlation between these two spectra—time span and initiation-reaction—and the importance of foreign policy decisions*. They may be scaled into three categories:

Strategic decisions are irrevocable policy acts, measured by significance for a foreign policy system as a whole. 'Significance' refers to the number of environmental components which receive feedback from the decision, the intensity

---

[1]For a survey of selected literature on foreign policy decisions see the author's *The Foreign Policy System of Israel* (New Haven, Conn.: Yale University Press, 1972), p. 373, note 1, and Appendix E.

---

of those consequences, and the length of time in which the 'fall out' from the decision affects the behaviour of decision-makers or institutions; that is, the scope and duration of impact. The time dimension in this context may extend from the immediate future to many years.

Tactical decisions are indissolubly linked to strategic (high-policy) decisions and are almost always of lesser significance. They may precede, and serve as pre-decisional stages for, a strategic decision: for example, the Sinai Campaign (alignment with France—20 September 1956— preparatory to launching the Campaign—29 October); and the Six Day War (mobilization of reserves, delay in military action, and formation of the National Unity Government—16 May–1 June 1967—and the decision to go to war—4 June). They may also follow strategic decisions, from which they logically derive and *without which they could not have occurred*: for example, Jerusalem (the annexation of East Jerusalem in June 1967, more than 17 years after the decision to make the city Israel's capital); and Reparations (acceptance of direct negotiations with Bonn—in January 1951—after the strategic decision to seek and accept German Reparations—in January 1950—could not be fulfilled through an indirect approach to the four Occupying Powers).

The continuous flow of day-to-day foreign policy choices to execute strategic and tactical decisions may be designated *implementing* decisions. They comprise the bulk of behaviour-creating choices in the on-going process of action-reaction-interaction which, in its totality, constitutes foreign policy for any designated period.[2]

The evidence from Israeli foreign policy indicates that *implementing* choices are characterized by *the highest proportion of reactive stimulus and the briefest time span* between inducement and decision. *Strategic* decisions reveal *much greater initiative and a much longer time span*. And *tactical* decisions reveal *variety in both source of stimulus and time span*. This emerges from the graphical representation of selected Israeli decisions shown in Figs. 1–3.

Implementing Decisions: (Fig. 1)

1. To send a complaint to the UN Security Council following a *Feda'iyun* raid.
2. To send a representative to a specific international conference.
3. To reply or not to reply to a letter to the editor of the *New York Times* critical of Israel—and if affirmative, in what form.
4. To criticize the Government of India for discourtesy to President Shazar while en route to Nepal for a state visit in 1966.

---

[2]A somewhat similar fourfold typology of decisions, though not focusing on *foreign* policy, is to be found in David Braybrooke and Charles E. Lindblom, *A Strategy of Decision: Policy Evaluation as a Social Process* (New York: The Free Press, 1963), pp. 61–79.

IMPLEMENTING DECISIONS

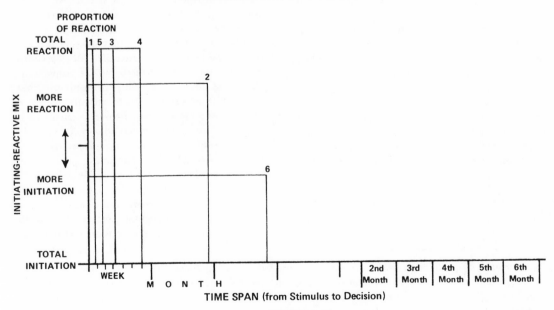

FIGURE 1

TACTICAL DECISIONS

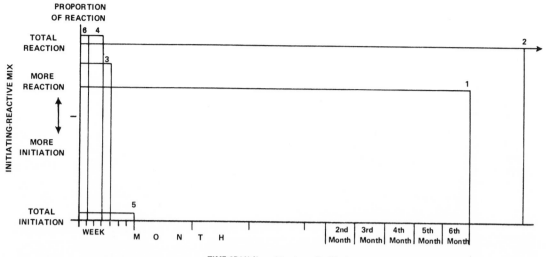

FIGURE 2

Tactical Decisions: (Fig. 2)

5. To protest or not to protest to the Government of Ghana for the expulsion of an Israeli diplomat from a social gathering during an OAU summit meeting in Accra in 1965.
6. To invite a foreign leader to visit Israel during a projected tour of Arab states.

Tactical Decisions: (Fig. 2)

1. To delay active pursuit of diplomatic relations with Peking until after the Geneva Conference on Indochina. The decision was taken by the Ministerial Committee on Foreign Affairs and Defence in May 1954, after six months of gestation. There was some Israeli initiative, but it was more reactive.
2. To shift the diversion point for Israel's National Water Carrier Project, from Gesher B'not Ya'acov, in the Israel-Syria Demilitarized Zone, to Eshed Kinrot, at the northwestern corner of Lake Tiberias (Kinneret, Sea of Galilee). The decision, wholly reactive, was taken in November 1958, after five years of persistent US and UN (and Syria's) opposition to the Gesher B'not Ya'acov site.
3. To approve sanctions against Rhodesia when it proclaimed UDI in November 1965. It was primarily reactive and was taken within three days of that proclamation.
4. To delay a military response to Nasser's closure of the Tiran Straits. The decision was taken on 28 May 1967 by the Cabinet following the Foreign Minister's three-day visit to Paris, London, and Washington.

5. To integrate East Jerusalem into Jerusalem. The decision, entirely at Israel's initiative, was taken on 18 June 1967, a little less than two weeks after the Six Day War.
6. To reject United States proposals for a Jordan–Israel settlement, as announced by Secretary of State Rogers. The decision, entirely reactive, was taken by the Cabinet on 22 December 1969, within a day of their publication.

Strategic Decisions: (Fig. 3)

1. To make Jerusalem the seat of Government. Despite overwhelming Israeli public opinion in favour, the decision was taken only on 11 December 1949—18 months after the declaration of independence. A UN General Assembly Resolution on the 9th, reaffirming a *corpus separatum* over the City, was necessary to trigger the more reactive-induced decision.
2. To seek reparations from Germany. Five years passed after the first pre-decisional act in 1945; and the decision process took almost four months. The dire economic conditions shaped the decision.
3. To support United Nations actions in Korea. The decision, entirely reactive, was taken on 2 July 1950, seven days after the outbreak of war between North and South Korea.
4. To embark on the Sinai Campaign. It was in gestation for at least ten months, from January to October 1956 and, while reactive to *Feda'iyun* raids, was primarily an initiative of Israeli leaders.

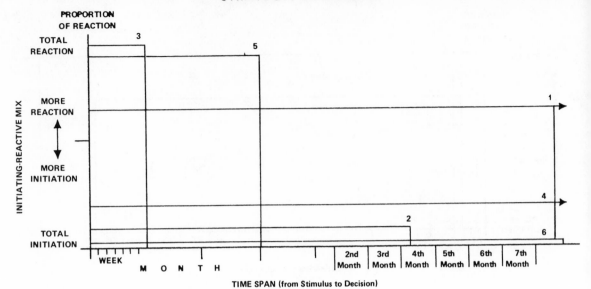

FIGURE 3

5. To act on 5 June 1967. The decision took three weeks and was entirely a reaction to UAR actions from 14 May onwards.
6. To create an Israeli presence in Africa. An entirely Israeli initiative, though set against the stimulus of the Arab blockade, it took some years to crystallize.[3]

It is not the purpose of this inquiry to explore *all* Israeli foreign policy decisions. We shall begin with a comparative analysis of *ministerial* roles and relationships—of Prime Minister–Defense Minister and Foreign Minister—during the period 1948–68, with a focus on the pairs of persons who held these posts. This will be followed by a probe into the relationships between the two crucial bureaucratic structures—Foreign Office and Defence Ministry—and, in that connection, the roles of the Defence Minister when he was not Prime Minister at the same time.

PRIME MINISTER–DEFENCE MINISTER AND FOREIGN MINISTER: ROLES AND RELATIONSHIPS

There were four pairs of persons at the summit of decision-making during Israel's first twenty years of independence: Ben Gurion as Prime Minister–Defence Minister had two

Foreign Ministers, Sharett (1948–56) and Meir (1956–63); and Eshkol as Prime Minister–Defence Minister worked with Meir (1963–66) and Eban (1966–68).[4] Both Meir and Eban readily accepted the primacy of the Head of Government in the formulation of foreign policy, a striking feature of democratic states in the post-Second World War era; Sharett as Foreign Minister did so in theory but less so in practice. This was not without consequence for decision-making. Nor was the diversity in *status-influence* among the four pairs.

The *Eshkol–Meir* relationship was the closest approximation to equals for, although the higher *authority* of the Prime Minister was acknowledged, they were of the same generation and rank of *Yishuv* and *Mapai* leaders, with many years of competent ministerial service and membership in all the key decision-making structures—Cabinet, Ministerial Committee on (Foreign Affairs and) Defence, *Sareinu* (Our Ministers), *Havereinu* (Our Comrades, that is, the senior leaders of *Mapai*), and the *Mapai* Leadership Bureau.

---

[3]The most important strategic-level decisions (and some tactical-level ones) are analysed in Brecher, *Decisions in Israel's Foreign Policy* (New Haven: Yale University Press, 1974).

[4]Sharett was also Prime Minister—but he was Foreign Minister at the same time. His key decision-making colleague in foreign and security policy from January 1954 to February 1955 was Defence Minister Lavon; that relationship will be examined in the following section.

The pair became a trio in 1967 with the appointment of Dayan as Defence Minister. From 1969 onwards a new pair of persons functioned at the formal summit—Mrs. Meir as Prime Minister and Eban as Foreign Minister.

The greatest gap in status and influence was evident in the *Ben Gurion–Meir* period: as long as he was Prime Minister, BG was the towering political figure whose decisions, though challenged, were rarely set aside. The 'BG Complex' strengthened the institutional gap—much more for Meir than for Sharett.

The gap between *Eshkol and Eban* was also marked but for other reasons. Eban's superior knowledge and skill in foreign affairs was recognized and valued by the Prime Minister. But Eban was the supreme technician of the Gromyko–Couve de Murville–Rusk type, without an independent power base in the political system. Eshkol was Ben Gurion's (initially-chosen) successor and the senior leader of *Mapai*, the pre-eminent party within the government coalition.

The *Ben Gurion–Sharett* relationship was the most complex—and significant—for decision-making. They were undoubtedly unequal in both status and influence. Yet Sharett was a political leader before independence, much more so than the other two Foreign Ministers, and he had a reputation as *the* foreign affairs expert of the *Yishuv*. His selection as Foreign Minister in 1948 was viewed as natural by the entire *Yishuv*. And he perceived his expertise as vastly superior to that of Ben Gurion, with a consequent 'right' to primacy in this sphere of public policy—though he understood and accepted the Prime Minister's ultimate *authority*. Not by accident was the Ben Gurion–Sharett relationship the most vibrant and tense, culminating in the rupture of 1956.

Measured along a simple ordinal scale, from greatest to least gap in status-influence, within the formulation pyramid, the ranking of Prime Minister-Foreign Minister relationship is:

1. Ben Gurion–Meir
2. Eshkol-Eban
3. Ben Gurion–Sharett
4. Eshkol–Meir

We may begin with the first in time and in impact upon Israel's foreign policy.

Ben Gurion and Sharett

Israel's charismatic leader had a clear and forceful image of the Prime Minister's proper role in the formulation of foreign policy. In his published oral memoirs he declared:[5]

I would say quite openly that an Israeli Prime Minister must also be his own Foreign Minister. Foreign affairs, like defence, is one of the key spheres of government, and, like defence, can be affected by a right or wrong decision at the lowest level, which is not the case with other ministries. . . . Because of this, I was naturally interested in all that went on in the Foreign Ministry. I would read all the important diplomatic cables each morning and would make whatever suggestions I thought fit. If foreign governments took any action or made statements or decided policy which affected Israel, I considered it my duty and my responsibility to *decide* on our reaction. Matters of vital issue would of course come before the Cabinet for their decision. But I would make my position known between Cabinets. If it differed from that of the Foreign Minister, he could either accept my line or bring it before the Government.

The nature of his relationship with Sharett in the policy process was stated at length by Ben Gurion to this writer with typical candour:[6]

Day-to-day issues I left to Sharett. I relied on him: he knew the details and he was honest. He always kept me informed. When there were differences of opinion, he accepted my view. Sometimes he opposed me in Cabinet discussion.

Until Sharett became Prime Minister he never made major decisions alone. After he became Prime Minister [and BG returned to the Cabinet as Defence Minister, in February 1955], I told him I would never act without his agreement.

Sharett perceived his relationship with Ben Gurion in the policy process very differently. He had wide latitude and discretion in making (tactical and implementing) decisions, he remarked in 1960, four years after his resignation from the government: 'Of course, I consulted the Prime Minister on basic [i.e. strategic] issues, by phone or in person.' Usually the matter was settled to their mutual satisfaction—and he modified or altered BG's view not infrequently during these discussions. In case of deadlock, and where Sharett felt strongly, he took the issue to the Cabinet. There the proposed action—retaliation—was sometimes overruled. 'Ben Gurion was not pleased on those occasions', when Sharett succeeding in mobilizing a doveish majority.

It was in that context that Sharett assessed Ben Gurion's capability in foreign affairs:

He lacks skill and subtlety. He does not think through all the consequences and implications of an act or statement. For example, his remark that 'Israel is part of Europe'—a brainwave of Shimon Peres— contradicts Israel's image as part of Asia and undermines her position in Afro-Asia.

Ben Gurion relies on his own judgement much more than on any advisers. He is surrounded by little men unworthy of his trust.

His mind is a powerful searchlight that is always focused on a specific object, with the result that the area surrounding it recedes even more into obscurity.

[5]Pearlman, *Ben Gurion Looks Back* (London: Weidenfeld & Nicolson, 1965), pp. 127–28 (emphasis added).

[6]Interview, July 1966.

He is interested in only a few broad themes and areas: the permanent irritant—Russia; the permanent challenge—America; the long-time friend—France. He is not, however, well-informed about foreign affairs generally.[7]

Ben Gurion was continuously involved in foreign policy but, by his own admission, with unequal emphasis on issue-areas: 'The things I thought about most concerned Security. Other

[7]The Sharett assessment of Ben Gurion and their relationship as Prime Minister and Foreign Minister is based upon an interview in Jerusalem, July 1960.

areas of interest were Education, development of the Negev, and population dispersal. I didn't take a special interest in economic matters (and that included foreign economic issues). I left these to Eshkol and Kaplan. I never went to meetings of the Economic Committee of the Government.' BG's involvement in the formulation of foreign policy can indeed best be portrayed in terms of a series of concentric circles (Fig. 4), stemming from the core of security and the unshakeable conviction that foreign policy must be subordinate to security needs—certainly for Israel.

BEN GURION'S FOREIGN POLICY CONCERNS

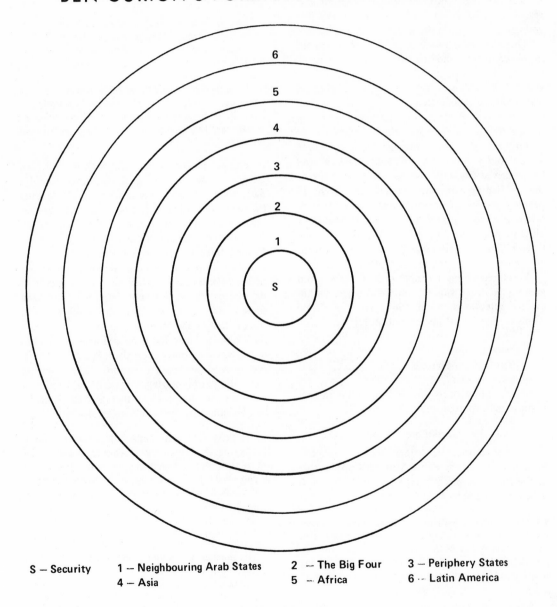

S — Security   1 — Neighbouring Arab States   2 — The Big Four   3 — Periphery States
4 — Asia   5 — Africa   6 — Latin America

FIGURE 4

The innermost circle (1), where his interest was intense and permanent, comprises all issues concerning Israel's neighbours, that is, borders, armistice violations, boycott, refugees, UN discussions on the Palestine question, the military and economic capability of Arab states, inter-Arab relations, contacts with Arab representatives, and, at decisive points, the Jordan waters question. The second circle consists of all the larger political issues affecting relations with the Big Four: potential sources of arms and economic aid—the United States, France, Britain, and Germany—and the Soviet Union, because of Israel's commitment to three million Jews and Moscow's role as patron of the Arab states. Circle 3 comprises relations with the 'periphery states'—Turkey, Iran, Ethiopia, and Cyprus, those countries just beyond 'the Arab fence'—and the horn of Africa. Those three circles must be set apart from all others in Ben Gurion's hierarchy of foreign policy interests; even among these one must distinguish between his obsession with 'the Arabs', his active involvement in the basic policy decisions with the four key states for Israel's survival, and his more subdued but natural interest in the periphery as a derivative of the first circle.

To these must be added any major issue concerning American Jewry, including relations with 'the Presidents' Club' (heads of major Jewish organizations in the US), Goldmann, the American Jewish Committee, and the leaders of religious groups. There was also for BG a set of circles of qualitatively lesser interest: Asia, partly due to his fascination for Oriental civilizations and Buddhism; then Africa, low on the scale despite its diplomatic importance to Israel and the challenge of underdevelopment; and finally, Latin America.[8]

Ben Gurion's sources of information on foreign affairs were varied: cables from Israel's diplomatic missions, which he received three or four times a day and read, except for those on consular affairs; reports and letters from senior ambassadors, notably those in Washington, New York (UN), Paris, London, Rome, and perhaps one or two others; appreciation reports from the intelligence bureaus of the Army, the General Security Service, the Police, and the Foreign Office; occasional newspapers and journals, including the *Economist*, the *New Statesman*,

New York Times, *The Times*, and the *Jewish Chronicle;* and face-to-face discussions with visitors from abroad, returning Israeli diplomats, Foreign Ministry officials, or anyone he cared to call.

Ben Gurion's participation in the policy process was of four kinds:

1. Consultations with the Foreign Minister, usually two or three times a week.
2. Response to a Foreign Office initiative, that is, a request, usually conveyed through the Foreign Minister's political secretary, for the Prime Minister's views or directive on a specific matter.
3. Response to a particular Israeli action or a development abroad, derived from the cables.
4. The Prime Minister's own initiative. He wrote drafts of letters or messages to heads of government, if he saw fit.

There were, of course, the institutional forums for discussion on foreign policy—the Cabinet, its Ministerial Committee on (Foreign Affairs and) Defence, *Sareinu*, and *Havereinu*. But the principal continuous link with the Foreign Office and, therefore, with day-to-day implementing decisions was through the political secretaries of the Prime Minister and Foreign Minister. From 1952 to 1963 it was, essentially, Navon's telephone.

Ben Gurion did not conceal his disdain for the ritual and formal aspects of diplomacy. Nor did he have great respect for the Foreign Service Technical Élite, with few exceptions. Their expertise was used to the minimum necessary for his knowledge about an important policy issue. As many remarked, BG rarely sought advice. To the extent that he did so, it came from a 'kitchen cabinet' on defence policy. This comprised a few Cabinet colleagues, varying over time, *Mapai*'s defence specialists, a few senior civil servants from the Ministry of Defence, *Tzahal*'s Chief of Staff, Director of Intelligence and a few other officers, and the Head of the Security Service.

Within the Foreign Ministry, Sharett's pattern of decisionmaking was akin to a university seminar, with participants persuading one another by rational discourse: the *Hanhalah*[9] was an active and vibrant discussion group during Sharett's period in office. His concept of *ee-hizdahut* (non-identification) was tested in this forum during the first year of independence. And it was there that Sharett's perception and advocacy on a myriad of issues were debated with his 'brains trust'—people like Eytan (director-general

---

[8]This construct is based upon insights gained from discussions in 1960 with members of Ben Gurion's staff, notably Y. Navon (Political Secretary, 1952–63), S. Peres (Director-General, Defence Ministry, 1953–59, and Deputy Defence Minister, 1959–65), and T. Kollek (Director-General, Prime Minister's Office, 1952–65).

[9]The *Hanhalah* or Directorate of the Foreign Ministry comprises the Director-General, Assistant Directors-General, and Advisers—Legal and Political.

throughout his tenure and beyond), Rosenne (legal adviser for all but one of the first twenty years), Shiloah (initiator of the Periphery Doctrine and, to many, the 'éminence grise' of the Ministry), Rafael, Kohn, and a few others. The 'Anglo-Saxon' group in the Foreign Office exerted predominant influence in the Sharett years, even more than later.

Sharett was preoccupied with language: his critics termed it concern with style at the expense of substance. Sharett's failures in diplomacy were the result of vanity—both personal and (his perception of) national pride. A notable example was his misjudgement of the significance of Communist China and exaggeration of the possible alienation of the United States when, by procrastination, he nullified a Peking initiative for diplomatic relations in 1955.[10]

Sharett achieved much in the realm of diplomacy during the early years. More than any other individual, he secured the support of the United Nations, the super powers, and public opinion on three crucial occasions: the Partition Resolution of November 1947; recognition by Moscow and Washington in May 1948; and admission to the UN—while other states were still excluded—in May 1949. In essence, this assured Israel's legitimacy in the global system, thereby easing the task of *Tzahal* and the Prime Minister–Defence Minister. Sharett was also the principal architect of the Foreign Office. And through non-identification he was able to retain the continued support of America and the Soviet Union for a brief period—until the Korean War created the problem of necessary choice for the new state.

Despite these achievements, Sharett was compelled to resign as Foreign Minister in June 1956. It was the most important schism in terms of policy and process, for it symbolized the triumph of the 'Ben Gurionist' image and its derivatives—retaliation and rigidity: that image has enjoyed predominance in the high policy élite ever since.[11]

The split occurred over two interrelated issues—the relationship between the Defence Ministry and the Foreign Office, and the activist versus diplomatic approach to the pursuit of Israel's external aims. The conflict may also be viewed in a framework of differentiation of function and time sequence. Ben Gurion was responsible for all policies directly related to the confrontation with Israel's Arab enemies. And Sharett had jurisdiction over Israel's normal diplomacy—relations with the UN and individual states, including the super powers. From 1949 to 1953 the emphasis was on the diplomatic field: thus Sharett played a prominent and highly acclaimed role. As the security situation deteriorated, from 1954 onward, in the perception of BG, Dayan, and the *Tzahal* leadership generally, the clash between the two approaches increased in intensity. Stressing his diplomatic, moderate line, Sharett succeeded on at least four occasions in frustrating the BG–Dayan demand for retaliation. Concerned about the possible long-term implications for Security, Ben Gurion decided in 1956 that Sharett was a serious liability in the preservation of Israel's vital interests. The timing of Ben Gurion's action appears, in retrospect, to have been linked to the Sinai Campaign, then in the planning stage: he was concerned lest Sharett jeopardize this crucial decision by mobilizing a slim Cabinet majority against it.

Ben Gurion and Meir

The choice of Golda Meir to succeed Sharett in June 1956 reflected the victory of 'Ben Gurionism' and its policy consequence: the road to the Sinai Campaign was now open. Indeed the consensus then and later was that Ben Gurion wanted—and found—a Foreign Minister who would carry out his directives without dissent. This was assured for various reasons. First, Mrs. Meir, at the time, admired Ben Gurion as the 'Father of the Nation,' who could do virtually no wrong. Moreover, as revealed by the analysis of élite images, she genuinely shared his image of 'the Arabs' and the need for a tough policy—retaliation—towards Israel's neighbours. And thirdly, she accepted the post with hesitation—some said, trepidation—because of lack of self-confidence. As she herself remarked after leaving that portfolio ten years later, 'I wept to the *Haverim* not to impose the Foreign Minister's post on me.'[12]

The result was a fundamentally different role-relationship between the Prime Minister–Defence Minister and the Foreign Minister in the policy process. Mrs. Meir's subordinate role in decision-making was further emphasized by the fact that, as her official biographer acknowledged in 1962—while she was still Foreign Minister: 'At no stage did Ben-Gurion relinquish the direction of foreign policy nor was he likely to do so whoever his foreign minister might be.'[13] The

---

[10] For an analysis of this important issue see the author's *Decisions in Israel's Foreign Policy* (New Haven: Yale University Press, 1974), Chap. 4.

[11] Sharett's departure from the government is analyzed in *The Foreign Policy System of Israel*, pp. 387–91.

[12] Interview, Aug. 1966.

[13] Syrkin, M., *Golda Meir: Woman with a Cause* (New York: G. P. Putnam's Sons, 1963).

most conspicuous effect was greater harmony in the decision process. There was no longer any personal rivalry or basic differences on perceptions and policy. Mrs. Meir readily accepted the qualitative primacy of defence considerations and yielded to BG's prophetic wisdom in this sphere. This was apparent during the two major crises over arms and Germany in 1957–8 and 1959: she strongly opposed any relations with Germany; but there is no evidence that she challenged Ben Gurion in this matter, certainly not in the Cabinet discussions.[14]

This change was reflected in a different pattern of consultation: Sharett preferred to take disagreements to the Cabinet for decisions, while Meir settled her differences with Ben Gurion in private or in the pre-Cabinet *Sareinu* discussions. Further, Meir exercised less discretion than did Sharett in tactical and implementing decisions; she tended to the safe side in deciding whether or not to bring a matter to the Prime Minister's attention. It was expressed, too, in a different approach to decision-making within the Foreign Office. Discussions at *Hanhalah* meetings were *ad hoc*, with very little preparation—'freeflowing and not focused', as one participant remarked. 'Mrs. Meir', said another, 'wanted to deal with the practical and operative end of policy,' whereas Sharett always began with an analytic presentation. And unlike Sharett—or Eban—she did very little drafting.[15]

The 'absolute harmony' between Ben Gurion and Meir gave way within a year to friction. It was partly personal—the clash between Meir and Peres, then Director-General of the Defence Ministry—and partly institutional, that is, the jurisdictional conflict between the Foreign Office and the Defence Establishment. The core was Peres' alleged interference in foreign policy issues, especially over arms deals with Germany and France in the late 1950s. As one senior official remarked, 'Ben Gurion didn't back him but he didn't block him either'.[16] Tension was heightened by the Lavon Affair, with Meir increasingly critical of Ben Gurion's obsessive behaviour. There was, too, a growing divergence in outlook, with Peres and Dayan urging a primary orienta-

tion to Europe, and especially France, while Meir inclined to view the United States as Israel's most reliable ally.

There is a consensus that the Foreign Office role in strategic- and tactical-level decision-making declined under Mrs. Meir. Sharett, surveying the change in 1960, remarked that the Foreign Ministry became 'a mere instrument of Ben Gurion. He alone makes major policy decisions; Golda merely executes them. She acts at the will of Ben Gurion; she does not take initiatives in foreign affairs.' The decision-making role of the Foreign Office since 1956, he concluded, was confined to minor technical matters.[17] A dozen senior Foreign Ministry officials at the time agreed with this assessment.[18]

Mrs. Meir thought seriously of resigning after the 1959 *Knesset* elections but, as with Sharett in 1955, she was persuaded by Ben Gurion to remain in office. Her major achievement as Foreign Minister was Israel's conspicuous and successful 'presence' in Africa and the development of Israel's technical assistance programme in the Third World generally.

Eshkol and Meir

Eshkol's succession to Ben Gurion in June 1963 marked the great divide in Israel's leadership: it was a change from charisma to competence, from vision to solidity. Nowhere was the contrast more striking than in their approach to decision-making, in foreign as in domestic policy. With the coming of Eshkol to the prime ministership, a new equilibrium emerged at the summit of foreign policy decision-making. As the Director-General of the Prime Minister's Office remarked: 'Ben Gurion considered himself, and was considered, a towering figure—a man apart from his colleagues. Eshkol was more dependent on Mrs. Meir, for party reasons. Moreover, at the beginning he had no knowledge of, or pretensions about, foreign policy.'[19]

Consultation was continuous: a regular one-hour weekly meeting between the Prime Minister and the Foreign Minister on Sunday at 4 P.M., with the PM's political secretary present; regular consultation between their political secretaries—'many times daily by telephone'—and between the Directors-General of the two ministries. Eshkol also activated the Ministerial Committee on Defence, still another forum for consultation. Mrs. Meir's pattern of consultation outside the Foreign Office extended beyond the regular and *ad hoc*

[14]These two issues are analyzed in *The Foreign Policy System of Israel*, pp. 415–26. These cases also illuminate all three levels of the rivalry-co-operation nexus—inter-personal, inter-bureaucratic, and inter-party—which manifest themselves in the Cabinet, its Ministerial Committee on Defence, and on rare, dramatic occasions on the floor of the *Knesset* as well.

[15]Interviews with various participants in meetings of the Foreign Office *Hanhalah* while Mrs. Meir was Foreign Minister.

[16]Interview with Ya'acov Herzog, April 1966.

[17]Interview, July 1960.

[18]Interviews in Jerusalem, 1960, 1965–66, and 1968.

[19]Interview with Herzog, April 1966.

sessions with the Prime Minister. There were frequent meetings with other ministers. And finally, the FM periodically consulted, i.e., reported to, the *Knesset* Committee on Foreign Affairs and Security.

The Prime Minister did not read Foreign Office cables except those concerned with his special interest—foreign economic policy: his political secretary read the important ones to him and provided a summary of others. Unlike Ben Gurion, Eshkol relied very heavily on his staff, notably Herzog and Yafeh, for information and advice about foreign affairs. Yet, ironically, Eshkol was more involved in foreign policy than was BG. 'On the one hand, Eshkol makes fewer decisions; on the other, his range of interests is broader. He does not have Ben Gurion's absolute concentration in a few areas.'[20] Thus, while Mrs. Meir had a more harmonious relationship with Eshkol, she had less freedom of action as Foreign Minister than with Ben Gurion. Relations with 'the Arabs' were at the core of Eshkol's interests, as with his predecessors, followed by the United States and France. He attached more importance than did BG to improved relations with the Soviet Union, and to Diaspora Jewry as well. Over the years he was involved in many strategic-level decisions. He played a vital, sometimes decisive, role in the following: the Jordan Waters issue (in 1954–55, 1961, and 1966); the Common Market (1960 ff.); diplomatic relations with West Germany (1965); and the Six Day War (1967).

Eshkol and Eban

The departure of Mrs. Meir from the Foreign Office at the beginning of 1966 altered the role-relationship at the summit once more. Eban is much more the diplomat than the politician. Even more than Foreign Minister Meir with BG and Eshkol, he accepts the Prime Minister's higher authority in all policy. He has been the supreme advocate for Israel abroad and he has executed basic decisions. But with few exceptions (like the 'Middle East Tashkent' proposal soon after he assumed office) he did not initiate strategic-level decisions. This had the advantage of harmony—the result of acquiescence—but the disadvantage of inadequate dialogue and dissent. Yet Eshkol greatly respected his knowledge, his vast experience in diplomacy, and his qualities: Eban filled a genuine void and thereby exerted influence, for Eshkol never felt at ease in this sphere.

Some of Eban's attitudes to decision-making emerged in a 1970 interview:[21]

Q. You are faced, very often, with the need to make decisions. Do you have your own technique of decision-making?
A. We have a tradition of intuitive decisions, and many decisions concerning security matters are reached by the image of reality to which we wish to respond, I prefer using intuition combined with an attempt to analyse. Usually, the decisions which perhaps could be reflected upon later were those which were taken without an effort at analysis. . . .

One should engage in an exercise which includes all the given points and all possible results. We sometimes botched these steps. At times, perhaps, we were caught by surprise. Sometimes there were reactions which were not anticipated, and if there were a little more time they could have been taken into account. Whether one calls this an exercise or a war game, it is [nonetheless] a certain process in which people sit down and say: if this decision is taken, these are the likely consequences.

DEFENCE MINISTRY AND FOREIGN MINISTRY

The relationship between Prime Minister-Defence Minister and Foreign Minister in the formulation of Israeli high policy had a deeper *institutional* base, namely, between the Defence Ministry and the Foreign Office. One reason was that, with two brief exceptions (1954–55 and 1967–68), the Prime Minister held the Defence portfolio as well—for eighteen of Israel's first twenty years. More fundamentally, the pervasive character of the security problem since independence has compelled the meshing of the Defence and Foreign ministries in the policy process. Indeed, given its wide-ranging activities and responsibilities, the Defence Ministry has maintained a close relationship with all major branches of the bureaucracy:

> with Foreign Affairs over all matters relating to Arab hostility and the impact of the conflict abroad;
> with Finance, because of the very large share of the Budget allocated to Defence;
> with Commerce and Industry regarding military imports, purchases and sales;
> with Labour about the optimum use of manpower;
> with Education concerning instructional programmes in *Tzahal* and *Gadna*; and
> with Agriculture over the *Nahal* programme.

Thus, while Ben Gurion and others did not regard as imperative or inevitable the holding of the Defence portfolio by the Prime Minister, the De-

---

[20] Interview with Yahil, July 1966.

[21] Interview with Eli Eyal on the *Galei Tzahal* (Army) radio station. Reprinted in *Bamahane* (Tel Aviv), 3 Feb. 1970.

fence Ministry has always been the pivotal bureaucratic structure. And the Prime Minister is
best equipped by his status and authority to co-
ordinate the various liaison relationships spilling
over from the needs of defence in a state under
permanent siege.

While the intensity has varied over time, friction and rivalry between the two ministries has
been permanent: everyone affirmed this reality
about the key bureaucratic relationship in the
policy process—during interviews in 1960, 1965-
66, 1968, and 1969-70. A major expression of
that conflict in the early years was over decision-
making control on armistice affairs. Ben Gurion
perceived this solely as an extension of Israel's
struggle for security against the persistent Arab
assault. Sharett insisted that the Mixed Armistice
Commissions with Egypt, Jordan, and Syria were
Israel's only legitimate and regular avenue of
contact with her neighbours, the most important
aspect of her *foreign* affairs; and further, that the
MAC and UNTSO were the institutional presence of the UN in the Arab–Israel conflict, once
more, in the realm of foreign affairs. During the
first five years decisions relating to armistice
violations were taken by the Defence Ministry
with Foreign Office liaison. In 1954, as Prime
Minister–Foreign Minister, Sharett succeeded
in regaining formal control of this sphere.

The decision process before the Sinai Campaign (1956) involved continuous consultation
among five or six people—the Prime Minister,
who was at the same time Minister of Defence,
the Foreign Minister, the Chief of Staff, the
Director-General of the Foreign Ministry, the
Head of the Staff Duties Branch of the General
Staff (who acted for the Chief of Staff in the latter's absence), and the Director of Armistice Affairs. Not all the above persons were concerned in
every case. While a serious incident would inevitably involve Ministers directly, decisions
were more frequently taken at the official level,
the Ministers being informed through their
private secretaries.

A typical case would begin with the receipt of
reports of an incident at GHQ. In the context of
the General Armistice Agreements these reports
ran along two parallel channels: firstly, from the
front line unit involved through the operations
reporting system to the Head of the Staff Duties
Branch and the Chief-of-Staff; secondly, from the
Israel Delegation to the Mixed Armistice Commission concerned to the GSO, Armistice. The
Chief-of-Staff would then report to the Prime
Minister and Minister of Defence. The GSO,
Armistice would inform the Director of Armistice
Affairs in the Ministry for Foreign Affairs, who

would in turn inform the Director-General of
the Ministry for Foreign Affairs and the Minister
for Foreign Affairs. At the same time the COS
(or the Chief-of-Staff Duties Branch at GHQ)
would get in direct contact with the Director of
Armistice Affairs, or vice versa. The whole process of reporting and consultation was conducted
by telephone and, in general, only a few minutes
elapsed between the start of an incident and the
decision how to react to it on the General Armistice Agreement level.

The basis of the system was speed and flexibility of communication, both up and down and
laterally, the mutual trust and confidence of the
persons involved at all levels, and a practical
routine of co-operation. 'Things worked in a
pragmatic way.' Within the Foreign Office the
Director of Armistice Affairs was responsible to
the Director-General. From the outset he would
report an incident to the Director-General or, in
his absence, to the Foreign Minister. He would
also contact the Defence Minister immediately
through his political or military secretary, and the
Ramatkal—Chief-of-Staff—through his military
assistant, a middle-ranking *Tzahal* officer who,
since 1958, was the representative of the General
Staff in the Foreign Office. The lines of communication were flexible, though these four components were almost always involved in the
decision process.[22] (See Fig. 5.)

Friction between the two ministries from 1957
to 1963 existed on four levels, intertwined and
mutually aggravating. There was, first, a deep
clash of *personality*—between the sentimental,
intuitive, and extroverted Mrs. Meir and the
rational, intellectual, and secretive Shimon
Peres. Foreign Minister Meir was almost 60
when the friction came into the open; Peres was
not yet 35. Yet that *generation gap* was related to
the struggle between the 'old guard' (the *vatikim*
or veterans) and the young men (the *tze'irim*) for
control of *Mapai*: Mrs. Meir and Peres were
performing crucial roles in this contest, still unresolved in 1973. As Ben Gurion moved towards
the end of an illustrious career, that battle for
control became accentuated by rivalry for the
inheritance of BG, the 'Father of the Nation'.

The 'old guard'—Meir, Aranne, Eshkol, etc.—
was not only old. It remained (emotionally) committed to socialism. And as the winds of change
swept over Israel, they clung to their ideological
roots. The young men—Dayan, Peres, etc.—were
not only younger. They were technocrats, ad-

[22]Based upon interview with M. R. Kidron, a former
Director of Armistic Affairs, June 1966 and correspondence,
June 1970.

DECISION-MAKING ON ARMISTICE VIOLATIONS

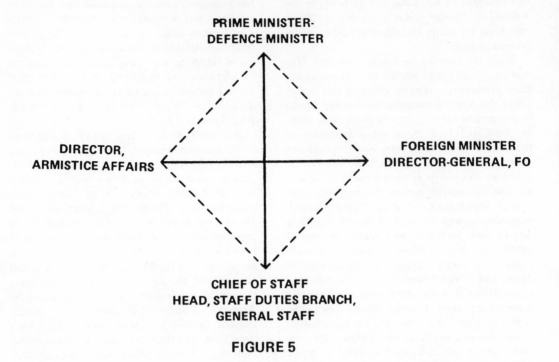

**PRIME MINISTER-
DEFENCE MINISTER**

**DIRECTOR,
ARMISTICE AFFAIRS**

**FOREIGN MINISTER
DIRECTOR-GENERAL, FO**

**CHIEF OF STAFF
HEAD, STAFF DUTIES BRANCH,
GENERAL STAFF**

FIGURE 5

mirers of science and technology, disdainful of ideologies. They were (and are) pragmatic activists. They are, indeed, more genuine Ben Gurionists: he too had contempt for doctrine and wanted Israel to move from the Age of Ideology to the Nuclear Age or, more correctly, the Age of Scientific Excellence. To all these factors was added a renewed and more intense conflict over the appropriate *jurisdiction* of the Defence and Foreign ministries in the policy process.

While the clashes of personality and of the generations were present, as well as rivalry within *Mapai*, the core of the dispute was *status*— Peres was a junior minister—and *institutional interests.*

Friction between the two ministries over the years was readily acknowledged by Peres. His analysis of the reasons was trenchant:

1. The institutions were not developed in accordance with given plans. Jurisdiction was not decided 'before the father died and the children grew up'. All accepted Ben Gurion as the central figure—but were jealous of each other. The personality of Ben Gurion—it overshadowed all the others; they grew but they were overshadowed.
2. The lack of equilibrium between the two institutions in the national mind. The Army has the love and affection of the nation in much greater proportion— the army uniform has a much higher status than the

ambassador's suit. The Army's status is somewhat reduced [1966] but it is still the most beloved institution.
3. Clash of personality.
4. Lack of national tradition in thinking on foreign affairs. Most parties have an ideological approach to foreign policy questions; the leaders are more interested in the internal aspects of party politics. Very few thought beyond that.
5. A natural institutional friction.
6. The Army contempt for the Foreign Office verbal approach to national problems.
7. Sharett was a Weizmannist.
8. The Foreign Office is the institution which represents national prudence; the Defence Ministry is the institution that represents national achievements. In Israel our achievements were so outstanding that it became the preferred guide to policy.

Of his specific clash with Mrs. Meir he perceived two causes: personal friction—'the difference between the generations, among others'; and her feeling that he had created a parallel Foreign Office. In his defence he remarked that all defence ministries have their own networks and are deeply involved in foreign affairs, a natural extension from security affairs.[23]

During Eshkol's tenure as Prime Minister-Defence Minister, the relationship with the For-

---

[23]Interview, June 1966.

eign Office in policy formulation was one of harmony, both with Meir and Eban as his Foreign Ministers. The policy process became much more complex in the last eighteen months of Eshkol's prime ministership—with the return of Dayan to the centre of decision-making as Defence Minister. For the first time a tripartite *institutional* relationship existed—Prime Minister's Office, Foreign Ministry, and Defence Ministry. This was further complicated by the upsurge of Dayan's charismatic influence, the decline of Eshkol's prestige due to alleged weakness during the May–June 1967 crisis, and Foreign Minister Eban's lack of a political base in *Mapai* and in the country. And the clash between Defence Ministry and Foreign Office, symbolized by the personalities, images, and behaviour of Dayan and Eban, continued into 1973.

The extent of institutional competition or co-operation was not unrelated to the occupancy of ministerial posts. Tension was greatest in the 1954–56 period, at first within a complex triangular personal relationship—Sharett as PM and FM, Lavon as DM, and Ben Gurion as the ultimate wielder of decision-making power—and later with BG as Defence Minister and Sharett as Foreign Minister. Their two contrasting images of 'the Arabs', which extended to the technical elites of the Foreign Office and Defence Ministry, and their personality differences reached a point of irreconcilability under the impact of mounting Arab guerrilla attacks on Israel during the year before the Sinai Campaign. Harmony was at its peak in the 1965–67 period, with Eshkol as PM–DM and Meir as FM, followed by Eban. Ben Gurionist domination of the Defence Establishment passed with the departure of BG, Dayan, and Peres (1963–65). Yet there is no mechanical relationship of degree of harmony or tension between DM and FM (and their ministries) and the formulation process affecting strategic-level decisions: for example, harmony in the autumn of 1956 led to decisive formulation (the Sinai Campaign); harmony between Prime Minister–Defence Minister and Foreign Minister in May 1967 did not. Other variables in the formulation process were no less important in determining the outcome.

CABINET AND ITS DEFENCE COMMITTEE

Cabinet involvement in the foreign policy process was continuous and often intense. Thus Ben Gurion recalled: 'Foreign affairs were discussed almost every week in the Cabinet. It was the first and main topic: there was a report by

the Foreign Minister followed by discussion. I cannot remember a single meeting at which foreign affairs were not discussed.'[24] The three Foreign Ministers and other Cabinet members concurred.[25] This practice had been institutionalized in the Jewish Agency Executive before independence. It also derived from the authority vested in the government to make foreign policy, as provided in the 1948 Law and Administration Ordinance and the Transition Law of 1949. Moreover, every minister has had the right from the outset to request the Government Secretary to place a foreign policy issue on the agenda of a Cabinet meeting. It may also come before the Cabinet if the Prime Minister or the Foreign Minister considers government approval of a proposed course of action necessary or desirable.

While authority to make strategic-level decisions in foreign policy has always rested with the government, influence was not evenly distributed among its members.[26] The role of Cabinet, as distinct from individuals or groups within it, varied over time. In part, it depended on the presence or absence of a ministerial Committee dealing with foreign affairs and/or defence. These stages of Cabinet and Committee involvement in the decision process may be delineated as follows:

1948–end of 1953: The Prime Minister-Defence Minister and the Foreign Minister constituted a duumvirate, that is, when they agreed, Cabinet approval was assured. Basic disagreements were rare during that period and were contained within the framework of their pre-Cabinet and inter-Cabinet meeting discussions, oral and written. There was no Ministerial Committee at the time. And the Cabinet had virtually no influence on foreign or defence policy decisions. The consensus about this period was aptly summed up by Ben Gurion's political secretary for more than a decade: 'The Cabinet had the feeling that foreign policy was in good hands. They discussed these matters certainly, but when the Prime Minister and Foreign Minister agreed, they could get anything through the Cabinet.'[27]

1954–mid-1956: The Cabinet emerged as an important decision-making organ in both foreign and defence policy, for various reasons. Throughout 1954 Ben Gurion was in 'retirement', and Sharett, then Prime Minister and Foreign Minis-

[24]Interview, July 1966.
[25]Interviews in 1960 (Sharett) and in 1965–66, 1968, and 1969–70 (all others).
[26]This point is elaborated at length in *The Foreign Policy System of Israel*, pp. 211–21.
[27]Interview with Navon, Dec. 1965.

ter, brought all foreign policy issues of substance before the Cabinet. While security matters were under Lavon as Defence Minister, and Ben Gurion's influence was felt through Dayan as Chief-of-Staff and Peres as Director-General of Defence, Sharett was able, through Cabinet support, to withstand the pressure for retaliation; in the process, the Cabinet acquired influence over strategic-level decisions.

Nor did this wane with the return of Ben Gurion in February 1955. By that time the basic clash between BG and Sharett over retaliation had come into the open; and Sharett appealed to the Cabinet over the head of the Prime Minister. Both men acknowledged this, as did other ministers; and sometimes the Prime Minister was overruled—by a narrow 7–6 majority, comprising two or three *Mapai* ministers and those from the NRP, then known as the *Mizrahi* and *Ha-po'el Ha-mizrahi*, and the Progressives or Independent Liberals. One such occasion was the BG–Dayan-sponsored proposal in October–December 1955 to occupy Sharm-el-Sheikh.[28] Thus the Cabinet played a crucial role in decision-making, even though Sharett recalled later to the author that he 'did not divulge everything about foreign policy' to his ministerial colleagues.

The Ministerial Committee on Foreign Affairs and Defence existed during that second phase but it was utterly without influence, according to Eshkol, Meir, and Ben Gurion himself. 'I don't remember when it started to function', BG told this writer. 'I don't remember even sitting on this Committee [he didn't, except briefly in 1955]. For a long time it didn't exist. It was not important, because foreign affairs were discussed in the Cabinet.'[29] This was also true for security decisions by and large, because BG was always concerned lest *Tzahal* become a victim of political pressures—and 'the sons of all are in the army'.

Mid-1956—end of 1961: With the departure of Sharett in June 1956, Ben Gurion's dominance over security and foreign policy was unchallenged—as the decision to embark on the Sinai Campaign revealed.[30] And the Ministerial Committee on Foreign Affairs and Defence remained a nonentity. Yet Ben Gurion's prerogatives were severely tested in the two Cabinet crises over arms and Germany in 1957–58 and 1959. The place of Cabinet in the decision process during that phase and even earlier was well portrayed by the Director-General of the Prime Minister's

Office at the time, Teddy Kollek.[31] Cabinet meetings begin with a report on foreign affairs by the Foreign Minister; in her [Mrs. Meir's] absence, the Director-General of the Foreign Office or the Prime Minister reports. Thus major issues are placed before the Cabinet—at the regular weekly meeting on Sunday morning—'where a principle is involved, in the view of the Prime Minister and/or Foreign Minister; where no principle is at stake, according to them, they settle it between themselves'.

At the same time, 'the coalition character of the Government inhibits complete reports and full discussion'—for two reasons: 'because of concern that there might be leaks [as there were during one of the crises over German arms] and because a large part of Israeli foreign policy comes under the category "secret" and therefore does not go to the Cabinet, matters like contacts with the Arabs and relations with the "Periphery" states'. Yet 'the Prime Minister was certainly not given *carte blanche* to decide foreign policy before 1956 and, even since then, does not have full freedom of action.'

Residual authority over matters to be placed before the Cabinet lay with the Prime Minister–Defence Minister; that is, the decision to seek—or to dispense with—Cabinet approval on a security issue was at his discretion except for matters which are formally specified in law as falling within the jurisdiction of 'the Government'. Indeed, the Defence Minister need not consult—let alone secure the approval of—his cabinet colleagues for such a major decision as mobilization of the reserves, though he must notify the *Knesset* Committee on Foreign Affairs and Security of this act within ten days; and that Committee may confirm or modify the order, withhold confirmation, or refer it to the plenary *Knesset*—but this is *legal authority* only.

1962–mid-1963: The arms deals with Germany caused great turmoil within the coalition Cabinets and led to the resignation of the seventh and eighth governments, in December 1957 and July 1959, respectively: the controversy centred on control over security decisions; and Ben Gurion was accused of authoritarianism in this sphere. This dispute reached its zenith in 1961, when the Lavon affair broke through the surface of Israeli politics. Ben Gurion resigned on 31 January, and the Cabinet crisis was not resolved until the formation of the tenth government on 2 November. During the prolonged negotiations the lesser parties—*Ahdut Ha'avodah*, the Progressives, and *Mapam*—tried to wrest conces-

[28]Dayan, M. *Diary of the Sinai Campaign* (Jerusalem: Steimatsky, 1965), pp. 12–15.
[29]Interview, July 1966.
[30]This is explored at length in chapter 6 of the author's *Decisions in Israel's Foreign Policy*.

[31]Interview, July 1960.

sions from *Mapai*, notably the yielding of its monopoly over the 'big three' portfolios, Defence, Finance, and Foreign Affairs, and the introduction of institutional controls over military-security policy.

The outcome was a modest innovation, the creation of a Ministerial Committee on Defence—as the price of *Ahdut Ha'avodah's* return to the coalition: it came into existence on 2 November 1961 and consisted of Eshkol (Finance), Meir (Foreign Affairs), Dayan (Agriculture), Allon (Labour), and Shapira (Interior), under the chairmanship of Ben Gurion, Prime Minister and Defence Minister. The *Mapai* majority was overwhelming—four, with one each from *Ahdut Ha'avodah* and the NRP. Yet its powers were restricted to advice, because of BG's firm opposition to interference in the critical area of military-security matters and to the curtailment of the Cabinet's decision-making authority. Thus the Committee was granted the right to *request* information and, at its initiative or that of the Cabinet or the Prime Minister, to *discuss* all aspects of military affairs, from military planning and operations to arms purchases and weapons development. Its power to *investigate* was limited to officers and Defence Ministry officials whom the Minister of Defence authorized to appear. And it was not given any policy-making authority. In short, Ben Gurion's paramountcy was barely dented, and the role of Cabinet slightly enhanced by its new—subordinate—pressure group.

Mid-1963–1968: During Ben Gurion's last eighteen months in office the new Ministerial Committee on Defence was not encouraged—or even permitted—to become a major influence on decision-making, although its members were given full access to information in the security field and expressed views on a wide range of issues. The change came with Eshkol's succession in June 1963 and, especially, in January 1966, when the membership was increased from six to ten. Eshkol himself termed it 'a miniature Cabinet' whose decisions, in effect, were final, 'like a War Cabinet.'[32] And Mrs. Meir referred to it as 'a powerful small Cabinet responsible for decisions on security'.[33] So it continued until the crisis of May–June 1967, when the Cabinet as a whole re-emerged as the principal decision-making organ on strategic- and tactical-level issues of foreign and security policy. Even before then, however, as Mrs. Meir remarked while still Foreign Minister, 'on basic issues the Cabi-

net makes decisions, for example, the votes on *apartheid*. And before every General Assembly there are at least two or three issues which the Cabinet has to decide.'

These were *foreign policy* decisions. Indeed, one of the curious results of the enhancement of the Ministerial Committee on Defence under Eshkol was that, from mid-1963 to mid-1967 foreign policy issues received two hearings at the summit of government, one in the Ministerial Committee and one in the Cabinet, while security matters were discussed once, in the Committee. With the further expansion of the Committee to 15 in May 1967, however, it became almost indistinguishable from the Cabinet of 22. And with a weaker head of government as a result of that crisis, along with a strong, competing Defence Minister, the Cabinet's decision-making power finally coincided with its authority. It continued in this role during the political struggle after the Six Day War.

OTHERS: *HAVEREINU* ET AL.

To the question, 'did the *Knesset* Committee on Foreign Affairs and Security exercise any influence on your thinking and decisions', Ben Gurion replied:[34]

Oh, yes. It was very important. There were two opposition groups—the Left on policy towards Russia, the Right on Israel's boundaries. Discussion was very serious. There was no demagoguery. It was very different from *Knesset* debates.

The most active participants were Bernstein [General Zionists], Harari [Progressives], Hazan [*Mapam*], Allon and Galili [*Ahdut Ha'avodah*]. There were none from the religious parties—Shapira being in the Cabinet; but Unna spoke.

Yet a distinction was drawn by BG between the Committee's influence on his *thinking* and on his *decisions*: on the latter it was marginal. Eshkol echoed this view: 'We look upon it as an important Committee. They [its members] demand their rights. It has representatives from the opposition parties too; that compels them to be listened to—and to be responsible.'[35]

The consensus of members, observers, officials, and ministers is that the *Knesset* Committee was, for the most part, a consumer of information on foreign and security policy and only occasionally a decision-making organ. It is best described as an institutional pressure on policy within the formal framework of Israel's political

---

[32]Interview, July 1966.
[33]Interview, Aug. 1966.

[34]Interview, July 1966.
[35]Interview, Aug. 1966.

system. That role was strengthened by its permissive links to parties and their leaders: this applied to the Cabinet as well. Ministers were forbidden to discuss security matters with others (as are members of the *Knesset* Committee) except with the leaders of their parties if they are not members of the Cabinet. Thus, Barzilai and Bentov of *Mapam* consulted party leaders Ya'ari and Hazan before indicating their view in the Cabinet on the proposed Sinai Campaign in 1956. And later, under Eshkol, Independent Liberal Minister Kol told the Prime Minister he was sharing his knowledge on foreign and security matters with Rosen and Harari. In this way, three political structures—Cabinet, *Knesset* Committee, and party leadership bureaus—have been intermeshed in the policy process.

The reality of *Havereinu* (Our Comrades) is beyond doubt; but its precise role in the policy process is difficult to assess. To Ben Gurion, *Havereinu* and *Sareinu* (Our Ministers) were virtually the same, and *Sareinu* met every Thursday afternoon to synchronize views in order to avoid dissension within *Mapai* ranks at Cabinet meetings on the following Sunday. They discussed all major questions of foreign policy and defence, he added. Ben Gurion's political secretary, Navon, differentiated the two party organs and contributed further details about their composition, role, influence, and antecedents. '*Havereinu* is the most powerful decision-making

organ within *Mapai*. Its basic membership was about ten [the head of *Mapai*'s *Knesset* faction was included]; but there was also a floating membership of up to ten persons, who were invited for special discussions, people like Sharett [when not in office], Avigur, branch leaders in Tel Aviv and Haifa, etc.' Navon agreed that, in its very function—to assure a *Mapai* consensus in a coalition government—nonministers were given access to Cabinet discussion; in fact, they helped to make Cabinet decisions—in advance, an intriguing variation on Cabinet practice.[36]

Havereinu's antecedent in the policy process was the Political Committee of *Mapai*. According to Navon, it was a body of twenty-three, which existed in the early years, 'certainly from 1952 to 1956'. Although short-lived, this party organ was more important than *Havereinu* in this sphere. 'Foreign policy issues were debated there', said Navon. Ben Gurion concurred. And Sharett used to take his differences with BG to the Political Committee—which he took into his confidence 'up to a point'. Then, after his resignation, the Committee 'withered'.

Under Eshkol, various structures of decision-making were activated and/or enlarged. The Ministerial Committee on Defence was increased to ten at the beginning of 1966 and fifteen in

---

[36]Interview, Dec. 1965.

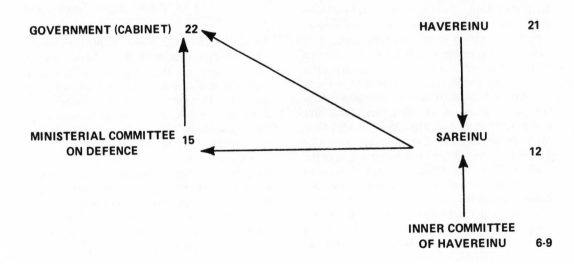

HIGH-POLICY DECISION-MAKING UNDER ESHKOL

GOVERNMENT (CABINET)   22   **HAVEREINU   21**

MINISTERIAL COMMITTEE   15
ON DEFENCE   **SAREINU**
                                              12

INNER COMMITTEE
OF HAVEREINU   6-9

FIGURE 6

June 1967. *Sareinu* comprised all ministers from the Alignment (12) and continued to meet every week before Cabinet sessions. *Havereinu*, too, was larger, with twenty-one—the twelve Alignment ministers, the Secretaries-General of the two parties and of the *Histadrut*, and half a dozen invitees. Because of its size, Eshkol formed an *Inner Committee of Havereinu*, a small group of *Mapai* and *Ahdut* leaders, varying from six to nine depending upon the issue, which met once or twice a week.[37] Thus, at the close of Israel's second decade there was a complex decision-making apparatus in foreign and security policy, with two informally linked hierarchies: In reality, power lay with the Inner Committee of *Havereinu*, modified by non-alignment members of the Ministerial Committee on Defence. When the

alignment leaders were agreed on a policy issue, approval was assured, for they commanded a majority in the Ministerial Committee and the Cabinet.

In summary, there is a *complex process of formulating high policy* in Israel, with multiple forces enmeshed in the struggle to influence and to make basic decisions on foreign and security policy: institutional (Cabinet, Ministerial Committee on Defence, Defence Ministry, Foreign Office, *Knesset, Knesset* Committee on Foreign Affairs and Security, *Havereinu, Sareinu*, parties and the political committees); ideological; personal (Ben Gurion and the dissident Leftists); and the communications media (the publication of secret documents). The Cabinet is, however, the ultimate arena for strategic-level decision-making in policy issues involving party, personal and institutional conflicts.

[37]Interview, Aug. 1966.

BIBLIOGRAPHY: STRUCTURE AND PROCESS

*Allison, Graham T. *Essence of Decision*. Boston: Little, Brown, 1971.

*Almond, Gabriel, and Powell, G. Bingham. *Comparative Politics: A Developmental Approach*. Boston: Little, Brown, 1966.

Aspaturian, Vernon V., "The Soviet Military-Industrial Complex—Does It Exist?" *Journal of International Affairs* 26, no. 1 (1972): 1–28.

Bayne, E. A. *Israel's Decision Makers, Factors Affecting Israel's Foreign Policy in the Crisis of 1967*, EAB-5-67. Hanover, N.H.: American Universities Field Staff, July 1967.

*Brecher, Michael. *The Foreign Policy System of Israel*. New Haven, Conn.: Yale University Press, 1972.

*Brecher, Michael; Steinberg, B.; Stern, Janice. "A Framework for Research on Foreign Policy Behavior." *Journal of Conflict Resolution* 13 (March 1969): 75–101.

Brzezinski, Zbigniew, and Huntington, Samuel P. *Political Power: USA/USSR*. New York: The Viking Press, 1965.

Byers, R. B. "Perceptions of Parliamentary Surveillance of the Executive: The Case of Canadian Defence Policy." *Canadian Journal of Political Science* 5 (June 1972): 234–50.

Caldwell, Lawrence T. "The Defense Voice in the Foreign Policy Formation of the Soviet Union: Two Perspectives." Mimeo. Paper presented to Western Political Science Assn. meeting, Portland, March 1972.

Chang, Parris H. "Research Notes on the Changing Loci of Decision in the Chinese Communist Party." *China Quarterly* 44 (October–December 1970): 169–94.

Charles, David A. "The Dismissal of Marshal Peng Teh-huai." *China Quarterly* (October–December 1961): 63–76.

Chopra, Maharaj K. "Democracy and Defense in India." *Military Review* 47 (August 1967): 9–15.

Cooper, F. "Long-Range Defence Planning in the UK." *Long Range Planning* 3 (December 1970): 18–22.

*Crozier, Michel. "The French Bureaucratic System of Organization." *The Bureaucratic Phenomenon*, Chicago, Ill.: The University of Chicago Press, 1967, pp. 213–36.

Dean, Sir Maurice. "Central Organization for Defence." *RUSI Journal* 114 (June 1969): 53–59.

Erikson, Bjarne. *The Committee System of the NATO Council*. Boston: Universitetsförlaget, 1967.

Farrell, R. Barry, ed. *Approaches to Comparative and International Politics*. Evanston, Ill.: Northwestern University Press, 1966.

Foltz, William J. "Military Influences." Vernon McKay (ed.) *African Diplomacy*. New York: Frederick A. Praeger, 1966, pp. 69–90.

*Frankel, Joseph. *The Making of Foreign Policy*. New York: Oxford University Press, 1967.

Garris, Jerome. *Sweden's Debate on the Proliferation of Nuclear Weapons*. Los Angeles: Southern California Arms Control and Foreign Policy Seminar, June 1972.

*George, Alexander. *The Operational Code: A Neglected Approach to the Study of Decisionmaking*. Santa Monica, Calif.: The RAND Corp., 1970.

German Federal Government. "Control and Planning," *White Paper 1971/72*. Bonn: Press and Information Office, 1972, pp. 114–38.

Gittings, John. "Military Control and Leadership, 1949–1964." *China Quarterly* (April–June 1966): 82–101.

Gurtov, Melvin. "The Foreign Ministry and Foreign Affairs during the Cultural Revolution." *The China Quarterly* 40 (October–December 1969): 65–102.

Hakovirta, Harto. "The Finnish Security Problem." Cooperation and Conflict 4 (1969), 20 pp.

*Halperin, Morton. *Bureaucratic Politics and Foreign Policy*. Washington, D.C.: The Brookings Institution, forthcoming.

Halperin, Morton H., and Kanter, Arnold (eds.). "Interaction between Nations (Part V)." *Readings in American Foreign Policy*. Boston: Little, Brown, 1973, pp. 387–430.

*Harding, Harry, and Gurtov, Melvin. *The Purge of Lo Jui-Ching: The Politics of Chinese Strategic Planning*, R-548-PR. Santa Monica, Calif.: The RAND Corp., February 1971.

Harris, Harry G. *The Special Committee of NATO Defense Ministers—A Study of Political Consultation in the Atlantic Alliance*. Mimeo. Ph.D. dissertation, Harvard University, January 1970.

Henriksson, Arne. "A New Economic System for Defence (Sweden)." *Skandinaviska Banken Quarterly Review* 1 (1968): 6–10.

Heymann, H. (ed.) *Bureaucracy*. Santa Monica, Calif.: The RAND Corp., 1970.

*Howard, Michael. *The Central Organization for Defence*. London: Royal United Services Institute, 1970.

*Huntington, Samuel P. *The Common Defense: Strategic Programs in National Politics*. New York: Columbia University Press, 1961.

Kanter, Arnold. "The European Defense Community in the French National Assembly: A Roll Call Analysis." *Comparative Politics* 2 (January 1970): 203–28.

*Kissinger, Henry. "Domestic Structure and Foreign Policy." James Rosenau, *International Politics and Foreign Policy*, 2d ed., New York: The Free Press, 1969, pp. 261–75.

Klein, Rudolph. "The Politics of PPB." *Political Quarterly* 43 (September 1972): 270–81.

Kolkowitz, Roman. "Interest Groups in Soviet Politics: The Case of the Military." *Comparative Politics* 2 (April 1970): 445–72.

* = particularly recommended.

Kronenberg, Vernon J. *All Together Now: Canadian Defence Organization 1964-1971.* Mimeo. master's thesis, Carleton University, Ottawa, Canada, July 1971.

*Langer, Paul F. *Japanese National Security Policy— Domestic Determinants.* Santa Monica, Calif.: The RAND Corp., 1972, pp. 5–40.

Lee, William. "The Politico-Military-Industrial Complex of the USSR." *Journal of International Affairs* 26, no. 1 (1972): 73–86.

*Leites, Nathan. *A Study of Bolshevism.* New York: The Free Press, 1953.

Lerner, Daniel, and Aron, Raymond (eds.), *France Defeats EDC.* New York: Frederick A. Praeger, 1957.

*Levine, Robert. *The Arms Debate.* Cambridge, Mass.: Harvard University Press, 1963.

Lindsey, George R. "Operational Research and Systems Analysis in the Department of (Canadian) National Defence." *Optimum* 3, no. 2 (1972): 44–53.

London, Kurt. *The Making of Foreign Policy.* New York: Lippincott, 1965.

Ministry of Defence, Sweden. *Summary of the New Planning, Programming and Budgeting System,* Pub. No. 1/1970. Stockholm: Ministry of Defence, 1970.

Moulton, J. L. "Defence Planning: The Uncertainty Factor." *Long Range Planning* (June 1971): 50–53.

Neustadt, Richard E. "White House and Whitehall." *The Public Interest* 2 (1966): 50–69.

———. *Alliance Politics.* New York: Columbia University Press, 1970.

*North, Robert C. *The Chinese Communist Politburo and Its Operational Code.* Stanford, Calif.: Stanford Research Institute, 1965.

Novick, David, and Alesch, Daniel J. *Program Budgeting: Its Underlying Systems Concepts and International Dissemination,* P-4462. Santa Monica, Calif., The RAND Corp., September 1970.

Penkovskiy, Oleg. *The Penkovskiy Papers.* New York: Avon Books, 1966.

Pike, Douglas. *Viet Cong: The Organization and Techniques of the National Liberation Front of South Vietnam.* Cambridge, Mass.: MIT Press, 1966.

Pye, Lucian W. *Warlord Politics.* New York: Frederick A. Praeger, 1971.

Rao, P. V. B. "Government Machinery for the Evolution of National Defence Policy and the Higher Direction of War." *Institute for Defense Studies and Analysis Journal* (India) 1 (July 1968): 1–11.

* = particularly recommended.

Robinson, Thomas W. *Alternative Regime Typology: The Case of Future Domestic and Foreign Policy Choices for Mainland China,* P-4531. Santa Monica, Calif.: The RAND Corp., May 1971.

Rosenau, James N. (ed.) *Domestic Sources of Foreign Policy.* New York: The Free Press, 1967.

*———. *The Scientific Study of Foreign Policy.* New York: The Free Press, 1972.

*Skilling, H. Gordon, and Griffiths, Franklyn (eds.) *Interest Groups in Soviet Politics.* Princeton, N.J.: Princeton University Press, 1971.

*Smith, T. Alexander. "Toward a Comparative Theory of the Policy Process." *Comparative Politics* 1 (1968–69): 498–515.

*Snyder, Richard C.; Bruck, H. W.; and Sapin, Burton. *Foreign Policy Decision Making.* New York: The Free Press, 1962.

*Snyder, William P. *The Politics of British Defense Policy, 1945–1962.* Columbus, Ohio: The Ohio State University Press, 1964.

Thompson, George M. "The Official Opposition Point of View of British Defence Policy." *RUSI Journal* 116 (June 1971): 16–21.

*Triska, Jan, and Finley, David. *Soviet Foreign Policy.* New York: Macmillan, 1968.

Vandevater, E. *Some Fundamentals of NATO Organization,* RM-3559-PR. Santa Monica, Calif.: The RAND Corp., April 1963.

VanGelder, M. M. "An Integrated Department of Defence." *Army Journal* 276 (May 1972): 3–20.

*Waltz, Kenneth N. "The Politics of British Military Policy." *Foreign Policy and Democratic Politics.* Boston: Little, Brown, 1967, pp. 141–80.

Warner, Edward L. III. "Bureaucratic Politics: A Schematic Outline." Mimeo. unpublished manuscript, USAF Academy, Colo., January 1972.

*———. *Bureaucratic Politics and Soviet Defense Policy.* Mimeo. dissertation, Princeton University, 1973.

"Whitehall, Better than Pentagon?" *Armed Forces Journal International* 110, no. 9 (May 1973): 54.

Whitson, William W. "Domestic Constraints on Alternative Chinese Military Policies and Strategies in the 1970s." *The Annals* 402 (July 1972): 55–66.

Wilkinson, David O. "Political Processes." *Comparative Foreign Relations: Framework and Methods.* Belmont, Calif.: Dickenson Publishing Co., 1969, 115–34.

Wise, David, and Ross, Thomas B. *The Espionage Establishment.* New York: Bantam Books, 1967.

*Wolfe, Thomas W. *Policymaking in the Soviet Union: A Statement with Supplementary Comments,* P-4131. Santa Monica, Calif.: The RAND Corp., June 1969.

PART THREE

MILITARY DOCTRINE

INTRODUCTION

PAUL R. VIOTTI

The preceding section treated security policy decisionmaking structures and processes in several countries. Military doctrine and force posture (treated in the next section) are closely related outputs shaped by political interactions within and between members of the leadership or decisionmaking elite, various bureaucratic elements including the armed services themselves, interest groups, and other political factions.

DOCTRINE DEFINED

Military doctrine can be defined as a body of theory which *describes* the environment within which the armed forces must operate and *prescribes* the methods and circumstances of their employment. The primary function of such doctrine is to maximize the effectiveness of a state's military capabilities in support of national objectives. As such, military doctrine has at least two levels of definition.[1] At the national or grand strategy level, military doctrine is concerned with coordinating the separate contributions of the armed services with the diplomatic, economic, and other nonmilitary instruments of policy. At a lower level, each armed service also has its own military doctrine governing the employment of the forces under its command.

What relationship does the military doctrine of a particular service have with military strategy and tactics? In a sense, the latter involve doctrine applied to specific situations. Military strategy is concerned with overall planning for employment of forces to achieve victory or other objectives. Military tactics, by contrast, is more concerned with the details of battlefield employment of troops, aircraft, and other weapons systems. When strategies and tactics are subjected to test either in exercises or actual combat, revision of doctrine may well be the result. For example, as Handel argues, the Israelis have a very flexible and dynamic doctrine which has been subjected to continuing reevaluation and revision in light of changing situations and actual combat tests.[2]

DOCTRINE AND FORCE POSTURE

A perennial question is whether doctrine guides the evolution of force posture or whether the converse is true. In France under de Gaulle, doctrinal advocacy led to procurement of weapons systems designed to provide a nuclear deterrent.[3] But in the Fourth Republic, nuclear weapons development proceeded without benefit of doctrinal justification.[4] In general, for doctrine to be a dynamic force, favorable attitudes toward change must be present within the leadership elite of the state. Moreover, bureaucracies with vested interests in particular weapons systems adversely affected by doctrinal changes must either be coopted or their negative influence must somehow be nullified.

Given that the leadership elite and bureaucratic interests are oftentimes hostile toward innovation in general and doctrinal changes in particular, doctrine is frequently directed toward

---

[1]A lower-level definition used within the American military establishment holds that "basic doctrine" is composed of fundamental principles and concepts for employing military forces in support of national objectives. Henry Kissinger has used a higher-level definition: ". . . strategic doctrine must not be thought of as something theoretical or dogmatic. Its role is to define the likely dangers and how to deal with them, to project feasible goals and how to attain them. It must furnish a mode of action for the circumstances it defines as 'ordinary'. Its adequacy will be tested according to whether the forces developed in their anticipation are adequate to deal with the real challenges." Henry A. Kissinger, "Strategic Doctrine and American Defense Policy," in Kissinger (ed.), *Problems of National Strategy* (New York: Frederick A. Praeger, 1965), p. 9.

[2]See Handel's article below, pp. 279–89.
[3]See Kolodziej's article below, pp. 245–57.
[4]See Scheinman's article above, pp. 140–45.

Captain Paul R. Viotti (USAF) (M.A., Georgetown University, and M.S., George Washington University) teaches political science at the USAF Academy. Areas of speciality include international politics, Middle East studies, and defense policy.

The views expressed herein are those of the author and do not necessarily reflect the views of the United States Air Force or the Department of Defense.

rationalizing the existing force posture rather than providing a rational basis for future force planning. In such situations doctrinal modifications, if they occur at all, are usually made incrementally in response to force posture changes. The development of nuclear weapons or acquisition of other new weapons systems normally results in doctrinal changes to account for the new military capabilities. Indeed, the technology of weapons development has been a major driving force behind doctrinal changes in both the Soviet Union and China.[5] Force posture reductions caused by economic and political constraints have also affected the doctrines of Scandinavian countries and the United Kingdom.[6]

THE FUNCTIONS OF DOCTRINE

Aside from the rational concern of providing the decisionmakers of a state with a logical theory for the employment of its armed forces, military doctrine may also be made to serve several functions.[7] For example, doctrine may be designed to boost morale in the armed forces, balance domestic political factions, demonstrate adherence by the leadership to the tenets of a particular ideology, develop a popular consensus in support of the state's defense policies, contribute to alliance cohesion, and mislead or threaten adversaries. As a result of these often contending functional objectives, formally stated military doctrine may not be a true reflection of de facto or informal military doctrine operative in a particular state. The analyst must, therefore, delve into the actual military practices of the country being examined. Indeed, some countries do not even have a formally and publicly articulated doctrine and one must, instead, turn to the body of informal doctrine established in large part by actual practice.[8]

A distinction can also be made between the military doctrine of a particular state and military doctrine which claims universal applicability. The former is a body of theory concerning mili-

tary employment which is accepted by the decisionmakers of a given state. As such, military doctrine exists to maximize the military power that a state possesses—accentuating its strengths and minimizing its weaknesses. By contrast, military doctrine can also be viewed in the Clausewitzian sense as a body of universally applicable principles of war.[9] In a way, Chinese military doctrine concerning guerrilla warfare typifies both doctrinal types. It seeks to maximize Chinese military capabilities and, at the same time, claims relevance as a theory or set of warfare principles applicable in other countries.[10]

Military doctrines have traditionally been concerned with the employment of military forces to maximize war fighting capabilities. In the post World War II era, however, the development of nuclear and other weapons of mass destruction has resulted in a considerable shift in doctrinal emphasis from war fighting to deterrence capabilities. The results of the first round of strategic arms limitation talks (SALT I) are a clear example of this shift in emphasis. Acknowledgment of the futility of war fighting at the strategic or nuclear end of the conflict spectrum has led the United States and the Soviet Union to agree on freezing the status quo, that is, maintaining mutual assured destruction capabilities as a means of deterring or preventing nuclear warfare.[11]

Arnold Horelick addresses this war fighting and deterrence dichotomy, observing that the shift toward deterrence (or, at least, toward war avoidance) is evident in all the countries examined with the notable exception of Israel. The Israelis see themselves as faced with the real and present danger of attack by a conventional, nonnuclear Arab force. Faced with this "reality," Israel has focussed her attention on maintaining both active and ready reserve war fighting forces.[12]

---

[5]See Lambeth's and Harding's articles below, pp. 200–15, and 216–32 respectively. Cf. George H. Quester, "On the Identification of Real and Pretended Communist Military Doctrine," *Journal of Conflict Resolution* X, no. 2 (June 1966): 172–79. Quester deals with the evolution of Soviet and Chinese doctrine as it is affected by nuclear weapons developments.

[6]See Ørvik's and Brown's articles below, pp. 258–71 and 233–44 respectively.

[7]See Horelick's and Lambeth's articles below, pp. 192–99 and 200–15 respectively.

[8]In Scandinavian countries, for example, the idea of formal military doctrine is said to be a strange and rather foreign concept. See Ørvik's article below, pp. 258–71.

[9]This distinction was made by Professor Ian Bellany, University of Lancaster, England, in remarks to the Conference on Comparative Defense Policy held at the United States Air Force Academy, Colorado, February 7–9, 1973.

[10]Referring to a paper by Dr. Ralph L. Powell of the American University, Dr. Arnold Horelick of the RAND Corporation made this observation at the same Comparative Defense Policy Conference noted above.

[11]See Lambeth's discussion below, pp. 200–15. The *sine qua non* in this balance of terror or, for that matter, in any deterrence equation, is the assumption that the parties will continue to be blessed with essentially rational decisionmakers. For an excellent critique of the mutual assured destruction (MAD) doctrine, see Fred C. Iklé, "Can Nuclear Deterrence Last Out the Century?" *Foreign Affairs* 51, no. 2 (January 1973): 267–85.

[12]See Horelick's article below, pp. 192–99.

AN APPROACH TO THE ARTICLES

One approach to the comparative analysis of military doctrines is to divide the task into three main areas of inquiry—the sources of the doctrine, the description of the doctrine itself, and an evaluation of the doctrine in terms of such criteria as flexibility, adaptability, coherence, and structure. Such an approach may prove useful to the reader as an organizing framework for interpreting the following articles on Soviet, Chinese, British, French, Scandinavian, Indian, and Israeli military doctrines.[13]

[13]A more detailed framework for comparing military doctrines along these lines is developed by Michael I. Handel, a teaching fellow and Ph.D. candidate at Harvard University, in his paper presented to the Conference on Comparative Defense Policy noted above, entitled "The Development of Israeli Political-Military Doctrine." An excerpt from that article is found in this section, below, pp. 000–00.

PERSPECTIVES ON THE STUDY OF COMPARATIVE MILITARY DOCTRINE

ARNOLD L. HORELICK

The author rejects nineteenth-century "classical military doctrine" as a specious set of "principles of war" which are irrelevant in the contemporary era. Instead he prefers to deal with what he calls modern political-military or strategic doctrines—a diverse body of more or less official beliefs which serves a multiciplicity of internal and external functions for individual countries. In general, a country tends to deal in its doctrine only with "manageable" threats, ignoring those which are beyond its capacity "to control or influence substantially." With the development of nuclear weapons since World War II, doctrinal concern has, for the most part, shifted from warfighting to deterrence strategies.

Arnold Horelick is Senior Staff Member in the Social Science Department of the RAND Corporation. A graduate of Rutgers and Harvard, he has written numerous articles and is coauthor of a book, Strategic Power and Soviet Foreign Policy *(1966).*

"CLASSICAL" MILITARY DOCTRINE

The "classical" nineteenth-century military doctrines of Europe's great powers were expressions of a highly specialized art form that caused a great deal of mischief in the real world and had precious little redeeming artistic value. Their foundation was laid by a small group of peripheral military figures of the post-Napoleonic era, including men of great brilliance, like Clausewitz, who sought to bring intellectual order to and extract some broader meaning from the great wars of their formative years. Like most profound thinkers, they were often misquoted and seldom read. The official military doctrines of the late nineteenth and early twentieth centuries were highly stylized, simplistically condensed glosses on the patristic writings, prepared by professional military men, often of considerably higher rank and invariably of lower intellectual stature, who combed the classics for maxims and "principles of war," losing in translation the deeper understanding of war that was their essence. The more or less explicit canons or "principles of war"

This is an original article written for this volume and the Conference on Comparative Defense Policy held at the Air Force Academy, February 7–9, 1973. Copyright © 1973 by the RAND Corporation.

formulated in this manner by the General Staffs of the European powers became the conventional wisdom of the professionals, were taught religiously in the military academies, and, being pitched at a lofty level of abstraction and generality, provided military planners of the time with a rich mine of rationalizations for strategies that suited their temperaments and ambitions, but rarely served any enlightened national strategic purpose.[1]

The popularity of formal military doctrines of the nineteenth-century type entered into a well-earned decline after their catastrophic applications in World War I. While doctrinal writings of the "principles of war" type are still to be found in the field manuals of the armies of the world, they are little read outside of service academies, where, one would hope, they receive the attention they deserve. In any event, the real world influence of "classical" military doctrine is now negligible, and except perhaps for antiquarians and those interested in it as an art form, systematic comparison can serve no useful purpose.

It is probably a misnomer to refer to the systems of ideas treated in the articles prepared for this section as "military doctrines." They are incomparably broader in scope and range, and richer in content, reflecting inputs from an extensive and highly diversified set of intellectual sources, and they perform functions that extend far beyond the confines of professional military edification and indoctrination. In an era when deep concern over the actual or possible use of force has become the constant companion of statesmen and ordinary citizens alike, as well as of the military for whom such preoccupation was in times past a professional monopoly, the formulation and promulgation of military doctrine has, like war itself, become too important to leave to the generals.

The perspectives on military doctrine brought to bear in these articles are quite diverse and there are fewer common analytical categories than a comparativist would like to see. This variety and unevenness are partly reflections of inevitable differences in the interests, preferences, and styles of the individual authors; but more critical is the extraordinary diversity inherent in their material. The states whose doctrines are the subject of our inquiry include, at

one extreme, the USSR, a superpower, armed with the full panoply of nuclear weapons and modern delivery systems, with military and foreign policy interests engaged on a truly global scale, but whose forces have not fired a shot in anger since the close of World War II except against their allies; and at the other end of the spectrum, Israel, a small regional power, with military forces that are inconsequential by great power standards, but which has fought and won three conventional wars in as many decades, the last one against a combination of opponents that included clients of both superpowers.

There is no convenient term that adequately describes the range of concepts that are the subject of this section, but "military doctrine" seems too obviously restrictive and circumscribed to be employed comfortably even for shorthand purposes. Several of our authors appear deliberately to have avoided use of that term, presumably on those grounds, and in this paper I shall follow their example and employ either the term "political-military doctrine" or "strategic doctrine" as a matter of convenience.

CHARACTERISTICS OF MODERN POLITICAL-MILITARY DOCTRINES

Unfortunately for the comparativist, the great diversity of contemporary political-military doctrines applies not only to their content but extends also to their form. In few states is strategic doctrine systematically articulated or formally codified. Ideological regimes, for which the production of doctrines of all sorts is usually a minor national industry, provide us with the neatest sets of materials, but as the Lambeth paper indicates,[2] they tend to obscure precisely those sensitive doctrinal issues that are of the greatest operative military and political significance.

Several West European states issue periodic White Papers on defense policy, but rarely do they even approximate comprehensive statements of doctrine. As Kolodziej indicates with respect to the 1972 French White Paper,[3] they tend rather to focus on budgetary, weapons acquisition and force level issues. The study of U.S. strategic doctrine is complicated by an incredible richness of diverse source material, the most important of which are Presidential State of the World Messages, Defense Secretary Posture Statements, and background briefings by the President's Assistant for National Security. On the whole, the student of comparative military

---

[1]For a trenchant critique of the vulgarization of classical strategic thought at the hands of the general staffs of the major European powers in the late nineteenth and early twentieth centuries, see Bernard Brodie, *Strategy in the Missile Age* (Princeton, N.J.: Princeton University Press, 1959), pp. 21–70. The "principles" so derived have usually included the objective, offensive, mass, economy of force, maneuver, surprise, security, simplicity, and unity of command.

[2]See below, pp. 200–16.
[3]See below, pp. 245–58.

doctrine will have to extrapolate from a large variety of uneven sources, both verbal and behavioral, military and non-military, and cut his way through the heavy fog of ambiguity that covers precisely the most vital issues.

Contemporary political-military doctrines owe their extraordinary complexity and comprehensive character to the post-World War II revolution in the environment of international relations. "Strategic" concerns and conceptual thinking about the role and use of force in interstate relations before the Second World War had been confined essentially to the exclusive circle of major European powers, which alone fielded peacetime military establishments of any consequence. While these states, particularly after the rise of ideological movement-regimes, differed significantly with respect to their military goals, capabilities, national military styles and traditions, they were confronted by a more or less common set of military problems (how to fight yet another massive continental land war) that had not changed radically since the first round in 1914–18. The "principles of war" endured, the cast of main characters remained remarkably stable, the instruments of war changed little and slowly from war to war, and military adaptation to technological change was even slower. The most decisive modern weapons available when World War II was launched—airplanes, tanks, and submarines—had all previously made their appearance as combat arms a quarter century before.

The fundamental reordering of the international system brought about by the Second World War and its aftermath and the revolution in military technology introduced by the use of atomic weapons in its final stage altered this perspective entirely. The cast of characters in international politics changed radically. Out of the ruins of the old European-centered international system, two new superpowers rose to commanding political-military positions, with ideologies, traditions, and national styles radically different from those of the European states that had set the military tone for centuries before. There was an explosive proliferation of new independent states for which modern military establishments appeared either as vital instruments for achieving and maintaining independence and political control or as indispensable symbols of their new sovereignty. The qualitatively new military technologies developed at dizzying speed by the super-states transformed the nature of war and strategy more comprehensively at one stroke than all of the weapons

introduced since the invention of gunpowder, taken together. City-busting weapons and vehicles for delivering them almost instantaneously to targets over intercontinental ranges made available to political leaders the capacity to achieve directly and immediately strategic objectives that were only a few years earlier beyond the reach even of vast armies fighting protracted wars.

Although the weapons systems associated with the new military technologies have been developed and deployed in decisive quantities only by the superpowers, and on a modest or token scale by only three other states, their existence has had a profound effect on the way in which statesmen and soldiers the world over must now think about the role and use of force in international relations. Fear of escalation to general nuclear war, or manipulation of that fear, is a pervasive fact of international conflict and in one way or another influences the political-military doctrines of all states.

Before these revolutionary new facts of military technology and international relations, the irrelevance of classical military doctrine of the nineteenth-century European type stood starkly exposed. Future wars of concern in the nuclear age covered almost all points on the broad spectrum from great power general nuclear war down to insurgency wars in remote corners of Asia, Africa and Latin-America; but the classical, now termed "conventional," world wars on the scale 1914–18 and 1939–45 which prenuclear military doctrines addressed almost exclusively were relegated to the dustbin of military history.

DETERRENCE AND DOCTRINE

Even more profoundly important for the evolution of strategic doctrine than the new image of war associated with nuclear weapons was the change the new weapons induced in conceptions of the central purpose of military force. Before nuclear weapons, no significant distinction could be drawn between the deterrent and warfighting values of military forces. Forces were built to win wars; if their superiority was apparent to a putative opponent, he might be deterred. Deterrence, of course, is not a new strategic purpose discovered by modern nuclear war strategists. But the destructiveness of nuclear weapons shifted the prime focus of military doctrine from defense, or warfighting, to deterrence, and the new technologies imparted to this distinction a significance that was no longer merely theoretical.[4] Different types of military force contribute in different degrees to the objectives of deterrence and warfighting. Forces that contribute substantially to one objective may be only marginally useful for the other, or even counterproductive. Multiple independently maneuverable reentry vehicles for intercontinental ballistic missiles (ICBMs) with zero CEPs[5] would significantly enhance the warfighting capabilities of the force that possessed them, but could be highly destabilizing with respect to deterrence. Submarine-launched ballistic missiles (SLBMs) with comparatively small warheads and modest accuracies make excellent instruments of deterrence but are poor bets for attacking military targets such as silo-hardened ICBMs.

Deterrence, by its very nature is a peacetime objective; defense a wartime goal. So as the focus of strategic thought shifted from defense and warfighting to deterrence, the peacetime deployment and political use of military force became the central doctrinal issues for most advanced states, and warfighting doctrine generally took a back seat.

Everywhere the primacy of deterrence confounds the articulation of coherent doctrine. What one wishes, in peacetime, for the opponent to believe one would do in war may be the least desirable among the remaining alternative wartime courses of action if deterrence should actually fail. Assured destruction is a perfectly logical, if unpalatable, doctrine of nuclear deterrence; it is, in the presence of bilateral capabilities for implementing it, a suicidal doctrine for waging war. Because it inherently strains credibility, the logic of deterrence argues for conspicuously depriving oneself of alternatives (e.g., self-denying ordinances against "damage-limiting" capabilities such as civil defense, ABM, and counterforce capabilities.) But policies to bolster the credibility of an "assured destruction" strategic doctrine inevitably weaken the credibility of the deterring power's commitment to deter attacks against allies, a central commitment in the strategic doctrines of both superpowers. The logic of this argument is, regrettably, indefinitely circular.

---

[4]For a perceptive discussion of this distinction see Glenn H. Snyder, *Deterrence and Defense* (Princeton, N.J.: Princeton University Press, 1961), pp. 3–51.

[5]That is, extremely accurate ICBMs. By convention, CEP (Circular Error Probable) refers to the radius within which 50 percent of the warheads will fall. Thus "Zero CEP" implies that at least half of the warheads delivered will be right on target.

FUNCTIONS OF POLITICAL-MILITARY DOCTRINES

The political-military doctrine of a state must serve a multiplicity of functions, both internal and external. Internally, its prime functions are strategic orientation, policy guidance, and political mobilization. Through the formulation and dissemination of doctrine, the political and military leadership of a state hammers out an agreed set of broad views about the role of force in the international life of the country and communicates them throughout the national security community of the government, to the legislature, and to the public at large. The doctrine is supposed to provide guidance to the armed forces so that they may be organized, postured, and deployed in an appropriate manner; to inform the deliberations of the legislators responsible for committing the resources and raising the military forces required; and to mobilize a broad domestic consensus in support of the foreign and military policies of the government.

There is an inherent strain among these functions, the intensity of which varies in accordance with the domestic political system of the given state and the external political-military circumstances in which it finds itself. The doctrine must rationalize the existing policies, capabilities, and posture of the state in the light of authoritatively perceived threats to its security, interests, and values. How can threats be averted without sacrificing interests and values? Should a particular security threat materialize, how can it be confronted and dealt with successfully given the military capabilities available? No state in today's world can insure itself equally against all conceivable or plausible threats to its security interests. A major function of doctrine is to devise some measure of priority, usually through some weighted combination of probability and consequences, that can be applied to the multiplicity of threats confronting the state. In its orienting function, the doctrine must answer the question: what is the best we can do with what is available to us? But in its role as guide to future policy, the doctrine must also address the question: how can we do better, given our potential, in confronting threats, preserving values, and advancing state interests? The tension arises from the gap that is almost certain to exist between the "what is" and the "what ought to be." If the doctrine exposes urgent threats that overwhelm existing capabilities for dealing with them, it risks internal demoralization. But if it adjusts the rank ordering of threats, interests, and values to accord with capacity, it risks complacency and weakens the utility of doctrine as a guide to future policy.

These internally derived tensions may be further accentuated by conflict with some of the externally oriented functions of the doctrine. For the same set of political-military beliefs is also communicated to opponents, allies, and to the entire international community. Indeed, for the major powers with important interests abroad, the communication of doctrine to the external world has become a major instrument of foreign and defense policy. Ideally, the doctrine should dissuade opponents, reassure and encourage allies, and exert positive influence on other third parties. These functions may be difficult to reconcile. The doctrine is supposed to affect the perceptions of opponents, but if the gap between the image of reality projected in the doctrine and the opponent's perception of it is too great, the doctrine will lack credibility. In the international arena, the credibility problem is similar to the one that confronts governments internally in societies where acts of governments are subject to intense public scrutiny. With respect to allies, and depending on their relative degree of political autonomy, the doctrine must strike a balance between reassurance about existing arrangements and pressure to maintain or increase the ally's contribution to the common cause. The dominance of deterrence strategies has made the maintenance of such a balance particularly difficult, as the Brown, Ørvik, and Kolodziej articles emphasize.[6]

States are unequally constrained by the competing and partly contradictory demands placed upon their strategic doctrines. The strong are less constrained than the weak. But those with far-flung interests and multiple alliances are likely to be harder pressed than those without broad external responsibilities and alliance assets that require cultivation. Governments in comparatively "open" societies will operate with far narrower margins of credibility internally than authoritarian regimes; but in the international arena the asymmetries are less striking. Alternative civil-military relations in states will also exercise differential constraints on the formulation and promulgation of doctrine, for strategic doctrines invariably serve as arenas in the internal struggle to determine the allocation of resources within a society to the military sector, and within that sector, among the various branches.

THREAT PERCEPTION AND DOCTRINE

At the root of a state's strategic doctrine is its orientation toward those challenges confronting the state that involve the use of or threat to use force. In human behavior, the only reality is subjective. Whether an objective reality independent of men's perceptions exists is a question central to philosophy but largely irrelevant to politics. Threats to the security of a state make their impact on doctrine in the form that they are perceived by the leaders who control the state's destiny. Threat perceptions will vary from group to group and from individual to individual, but a viable state presupposes a consensus, or at least an effective accommodation of individual and group perceptions of national threat. This consensus arises from the identity of historical experience, political creed, and from the other common attributes that are the essence of statehood. Dissimilar political units are likely to generate dissimilar perceptions of similar threats. Of course, no two states will in fact be confronted by identical situations susceptible of interpretation as threats. But the variance in perception may be no less important than the variance in circumstances. Here we are dealing with the differential impact on doctrine of predispositions affecting threat perception that characterize the political and military elites of the different states. The articles in this section provide some instructive examples.

Brown points out that the low incidence of armed violence in the domestic historical experience of Britain has encouraged British opinion, and particularly its more liberal wing, "usually to take a more benign view of the outside world than the facts tend to warrant." Similarly, he calls attention to the "quiet but profound confidence of Englishmen that there will always be time to recoup initial set-backs," a national belief that engenders a toleration of under-insurance. By contrast, Bolshevik ideology, Soviet historical experience, and Russian political culture combine, Lambeth shows,[7] to incline Soviet leaders toward an extremely wary global outlook that is frequently manifested in vastly overinflated "worst case" threat assessments.

THREAT MANAGEABILITY AND STRATEGIC DOCTRINE

A state's political-military doctrine also reflects its leadership's assessments of the manageability of the diverse strategic challenges facing

---

[6]See below, pp. 233–44, 258–72, and 245–58 respectively.   [7]See below, pp. 200–16.

the country. Ideology, historical experience, national "style" and character, and the idiosyncrasies of powerful leaders weigh heavily in these assessments, biasing them in different directions, but there appears to be a universal tendency among statesmen and generals to attend more closely in formulating doctrine to challenges that seem manageable or manipulable at the expense of serious attention to others that may be graver, but appear clearly to be beyond the capacity of the state in question to control or influence substantially by its own means. If the potential for developing means to deal effectively with currently "unmanageable" threats is believed to exist, doctrinal neglect, avoidance or downgrading of such threats may merely be transitional, while policy addresses the question of providing an appropriate countering capacity. This option is most congenial to authoritarian regimes that can maintain the necessary separation of doctrine and operational policy free of public scrutiny at home and under a protective cloak of secrecy abroad. Thus, disparagement of nuclear weapons in Soviet doctrine persisted until the USSR acquired respectable capabilities and continues today in Chinese doctrine even as Peking builds its nuclear force.

The impact of perceptions of threat manageability on political-military doctrines perhaps can be illustrated by comparing treatment of the threat of direct nuclear attack in the doctrines of a variety of states possessing unequal capacities for dealing with it by their own means and varying degrees of access to support from more powerful protectors.

1. Defense against all-out nuclear attack by a superpower. Defense as opposed to deterrence, appears now to be an unmanageable problem even for the superpowers, and certainly for all other states. That the state cannot provide its people with a defense against nuclear attack has been an explicit part of West European political-military doctrines since the mid 1950s. The United States, after the loss of its nuclear monopoly and the gradual erosion of its "splendid" first-strike capability, flirted briefly with a comprehensive "damage-limiting" doctrine in the early 1960s but soon abandoned it as unfeasible, opting instead for a more or less ambiguous doctrine of deterrence only, based on maintenance of an "assured destruction" capability against the USSR. While Soviet doctrine persists in asserting that it aims at ensuring the USSR's survival in a general nuclear war, the force of this assertion has been progressively attenuated in the past decade by acknowledgments of the catastrophic destruction that would be inflicted on all

belligerents. The extent to which a Soviet "victory" in nuclear war could under any plausible circumstances be anything but pyrrhic is evidently still a contentious issue, but the supreme priority of deterrence in Soviet doctrine is now unmistakable. Whether the Soviet Union's joint undertaking with the United States not to develop or deploy nationwide ABM defense systems foreshadows an explicit doctrinal acknowledgment that prevalence in nuclear war is no longer a viable concept remains to be seen.

2. Self-reliant deterrence of such an attack. At present this can appear to be a clearly manageable problem only to the superpowers and is the central preoccupation of their military doctrines. China, which perhaps has the potential ultimately to build a nuclear capability of superpower proportions, appears to be implementing a policy that aims at achieving self-reliant strategic deterrence, but has yet to develop or at least to surface a corresponding doctrine. For the time being the issue is dispensed with doctrinally by a cavalier assertion (a form of denial?) and a process of threat transformation in which the unmanageable is converted into the congenial. By adopting a survival criterion compatible with the extermination of up to half the population of the country, Chinese doctrine confidently asserts that the country, even without a nuclear capability of its own, could "survive" a full-scale nuclear attack. The nuclear armed opponent, having exhausted the possibilities of victory through employment of air-deliverable nuclear weapons, would then have no alternative but to launch the massive land invasion of China which Maoist "people's war" doctrine is so conveniently tailored to defeat in a protracted war of attrition and annihilation.

Among the remaining states, France, which lacks both a present capacity and the potential for acquiring nuclear capabilities approaching superpower levels, maintains a doctrine of ostensible strategic self-reliance based on the concept of "proportionate deterrence": Paris was well worth a mass to Henry IV, but she will not be worth the loss of Kiev to the Kremlin. The French rationale is analyzed in detail in Kolodziej's article,[8] but for purposes of the present discussion it should be noted that French belief in the efficacy of their deterrence doctrine is integrally linked to the existence of a strategic nuclear standoff between the superpowers. In this respect ambitious French claims for the *force de dissuasion* are just as dependent upon U.S. strategic nuclear power as the far more modest

[8]See below, pp. 245–58.

British claim that the UK's small nuclear capability makes an independent contribution to American strategic deterrence of a Soviet attack on Europe.

3. Reliance on a superpower ally possessing an independent deterrent force. This is a more or less explicit doctrinal tenet of all the European states, France excepted, that are formally allied to one of the two superpowers. While leaders of such states often acknowledge quite bluntly that deterrence of nuclear attack cannot be ensured by the forces under their direct command, they may achieve some sense of indirect control of the nuclear attack problem through their participation in the affairs of the alliance providing the instruments of deterrence. Characteristically, at least for junior alliance members enjoying a relatively high degree of political autonomy, the strategic doctrines of states in this category are oriented more toward problems of alliance management than toward dealing militarily with the threat posed by the superpower opponent. Thus, the March 1972 majority report of the Commission of Civilian and Military Experts, appointed by the Netherlands Government to assess problems of Dutch defense in the 1970s, states: "The Netherlands' defense effort must be seen as a contribution to the creation of a political climate in which the American President is enabled to maintain both United States nuclear and conventional contributions to NATO."[9]

While the political-military doctrines of these countries all reflect a common dependence for nuclear war deterrence on the alliance of which they are members, small states comparatively removed from the main line of East-West demarcation in Central Europe are likely to manifest a stronger inclination to hedge their bets than, say, the Federal Republic of Germany (FRG). The FRG's doctrine stresses the crucial importance of multi-national, particularly U.S. military presence on its territory, stockpiled American nuclear weapons and forward defense to ensure the earliest possible coupling of alliance and American deterrence capabilities to the contingency of an attack upon itself; however, the Scandinavian NATO allies, as Ørvik shows,[10] seeking to avert automatic linkage with the high levels of destruction that would be associated with any major war in Central Europe, permit neither the stationing of allied forces or of American nuclear weapons on their territories. Iceland provides a particularly striking example of the propensity

of states to concentrate national energies on manageable problems rather than squandering them on challenges, no matter how grave, which they cannot hope to control. Utterly helpless against any direct attack by the Soviet Union, Iceland spends nothing on military forces and in its day-to-day external conduct is largely preoccupied with fending off, sometimes quite aggressively, what it regards as the commercial incursions of competing fishing nations, which include quite prominently its NATO allies, Britain and West Germany.

In a typology that lumped together indiscriminately the junior partners of the two major alliance systems, the Warsaw Pact countries of Eastern Europe would have to be placed side-by-side with the European NATO allies of the United States. The utility of such a typology for generalizing about the salient strategic doctrinal preoccupation of its members is, however, limited. Among the Pact allies, only the leaders of the German Democratic Republic (GDR) can regard the sovereignty and territorial integrity of their country to be dependent on the alliance leader's protection to a degree comparable to the European NATO allies (indeed, the GDR is more acutely dependent, since without the Soviet guarantee the internal threat to the viability of the East German state would almost surely be unmanageable). Polish and Czechoslovak fears of West German irredentism, fears that provided some genuine national interest justification for their alliance with the Soviet Union, have been substantially appeased in recent years, while for at least one Warsaw Pact ally, Rumania, the only serious threat to its independence *is* the alliance leader. While the main thrust of the military-political doctrines of the European NATO allies is aimed at maintaining a close coupling with U.S. military power, Rumania's necessarily implicit strategic doctrine enjoins Bucharest to promote the creation of a European political-military climate in which its superpower ally will lack both incentive and pretext for rendering "military assistance" of any kind.

4. Reliance on irrelevance, neutrality, and the indivisibility of peace. For states lacking both independent means of nuclear retaliation and alliance ties with powers possessing them, strategic deterrence is not a viable doctrine. For most states in the world, security against nuclear attack must be derived from its sheer irrelevance to any contingency in which they and a potential attacker might plausibly be involved. The leaders of small neutral and nonaligned states may not unreasonably believe, and elevate their belief to the level of doctrine, that their country's aloof-

9"The Future of Dutch Defense," *Survival* (Nov.-Dec. 1972): 294.
10See below, pp. 258-72.

ness from both blocs offers no provocation to either; that its strategic insignificance removes the temptation to wage acquisitive war; that its security is safeguarded by spillover from the pervasive fear of escalation that is attached to military employment of nuclear weapons anywhere against anyone; or, that in the final analysis, it will accommodate or yield rather than accept the risk of nuclear destruction entailed by forcible resistance.

Larger states in this category that do have evident global or regional strategic value may also rely on a potential attacker's perception that its superpower opponent attaches such a high value to denying the assets of the threatened nonaligned state to its competitor that it will assume a protective stance toward it even in the absence of alliance obligation. India is the prime example of such a state.

Because of Europe's neurological role in the conflict of great bloc interests, the neutral and nonaligned states of that continent must be regarded as a special subset. The East Scandinavian states of Sweden and Finland belong to this subset, along with Switzerland, Austria and Yugoslavia. But even among this narrower and select group of states major differences in their circumstances, location, size, historical experience with potential enemies, and military capabilities make for considerable diversity in their political-military doctrines.

Yugoslavia has developed a vigorous and innovative doctrine of "total national defense" unmistakably directed against the threat of invasion from the East. For Finland, on the other hand, the restraints imposed by her peace treaties with the Soviet Union, as Ørvik indicates, make any realistic military doctrine a dubious proposition. Finland's limited permitted military capabilities are clearly inadequate to cope with any aggression which her only putative opponent, the Soviet Union, might be determined to launch. But they probably are adequate for dealing with border control problems against any opponent except the Soviet Union and hence might in the event of war fulfill the function of denying the USSR a pretext to occupy the country to secure the northeast approaches. This is a thin reed upon which to rest the security of the country. Hence, the burden of Finnish doctrine is on maintenance of good relations with the Soviet Union, coupled with efforts to promote a broader European policy aimed at crisis avoidance (neutralization of the Nordic area and promotion of various forums to deal with European security).

Sweden, on the other hand, larger than Finland and unconstrained by treaties with either of the superpowers, can hope to mount forces large enough to persuade a potential aggressor that the costs of aggression might outweigh the gains. Of course, since the costs that Sweden could impose upon an attacker like the Soviet Union would in no case be substantial, this presupposes that the expected gains would only be regarded as marginal. To encourage such a cost-benefit calculation in Moscow, Sweden has developed a doctrine designed to impress, particularly upon the Soviet Union, Sweden's determination to preserve its neutrality under all circumstances, including the invasion of Norway and Denmark. The point is to discourage a preemptive Soviet attack in the event of a decision to invade the West Scandinavian NATO states.

AN OPERATIVE WARFIGHTING DOCTRINE

The fundamental security problems of one state in the sample selected for this section have escaped the nuclear threat compass that has directed the course of this inquiry. The state is Israel, and its strategic doctrine merits attention if only because of its demonstrated power and efficacy. Israel's is a warfighting doctrine *par excellence*, but in almost all other respects it is the antithesis of the old "classical" military doctrines. For while classical doctrine was dogmatic and canonical, very slow to change fundamentally or to adapt to technological innovation, the strength of Israel's doctrine, Handel argues, rests precisely in its flexibility, dynamism, adaptability and open-endedness.[11]

What distinguishes Israeli political-military doctrine from those of other states is the perception of threat that drives it and its unwillingness to tolerate "unmanageable" security challenges. In the Israeli perception, the Jewish state is confronted by a mortal threat that is unremitting and essentially undeterrable. Deterrence is a desirable objective, but it must not be pursued at any significant cost to warfighting capacity. Israel's "first strike" capability against its Arab neighbors offers a continuing provocation to them, but it is not negotiable in the currency of deterrence. The difference between this threat perception and the perceptions of other states with which we have dealt is critical. For Israel, a doctrine of deterrence-only or even deterrence-mostly is unacceptable because the consequences of defeat in the event of failure of deterrence are so asymmetrical; for Israel, national if not physical extinction; for its Arab enemies, another

[11]See below, pp. 279–89.

humiliation and another enforced pause before yet another round.

But while Israeli victories in war are a measure of the success of its military doctrine, the nonoccurrence of general nuclear war offers no reliable assurance that the strategic doctrines employed by the nuclear powers to deter it are sound and effective. We can assess doctrines of strategic nuclear deterrence with confidence only in the event of their failure. So long as the survival of mankind depends on nuclear deterrence, we can only pray that the doctrines we have created to ensure deterrence are never put to the test.

THE SOURCES OF SOVIET MILITARY DOCTRINE

BENJAMIN S. LAMBETH

Soviet military doctrine is a "complex and shifting amalgam of thought partly structured by the leadership's Marxist-Leninist belief system, yet in the main determined by essentially the same secular opportunities and constraints that affect all politicians practicing the art of the possible." Factors directly affecting the formulation and implementation of Soviet doctrine include the strategic balance vis-à-vis the United States, the stability of mutual deterrence, the degree of East-West tension, ideological "truths," historical experiences, the need to maintain morale in the armed forces, personal leadership predispositions, and other domestic political considerations. In recent years, an improved strategic force posture and a concomitant rise in Soviet self-confidence and composure have resulted in considerable moderation and refinement of the frequently hard and simplistic doctrinal line of the Khrushchev era.

Benjamin S. Lambeth is a strategic analyst in the Office of National Estimates, Central Intelligence Agency. At the time this article was written, he was a graduate research associate at the Center for International Affairs, Harvard University. Lambeth has previously worked for the Institute for Defense Analyses and the Center for Strategic and International Studies of Georgetown University. He is co-author of The Soviet Union and Arms Control *(1970) and* A Guide to Strategic Concepts *(forthcoming).*

INTRODUCTION

When Western commentators employ the term "military doctrine," it is rarely clear at the outset precisely what they have in mind. Some analysts use it primarily in reference to a specific strategic maxim or operating principle, such as "assured destruction," "damage limitation," "counter-force," and so on. Others invoke it more broadly to denote the dominant theme of a state's overall defense policy at any given moment, such as "massive retaliation" and "flexible response," the two major American strategic "doctrines" of the post-World War II era. Still others, perhaps the vast majority, use it interchangeably to mean both of these things and more. There is nothing intrinsically wrong with this rather indiscriminate and haphazard practice, but one of its consequences is that the term has no commonly accepted meaning in Western strategic discourse

This is an original article written for this volume and the Conference on Comparative Defense Policy held at the Air Force Academy, February 7-9, 1973. Copyright reserved by the author.

and thus stands as little more than a lofty synonym for such commonplace notions as "policy," "principle," and the like.

In the Soviet Union, on the other hand, "military doctrine" is a more or less rigorously defined major component of a systematic and highly structured formal taxonomy of strategic thought. In the somewhat inelegant but typical formulation of an authoritative Soviet spokesman on the subject, the Soviet conception of military doctrine embraces "the sum total of scientifically based views accepted by the country and by its armed forces on the nature of contemporary wars which might be unleashed by the imperialists against the Soviet Union, on the goals and missions of the armed forces in such a war, on the methods of its waging, and also on the demands, which flow from such views, for the preparation of the country and the armed forces for war."[1] How this conception of doctrine fits into and informs the larger Soviet taxonomy of military theory and practice is explained throughout the Soviet literature somewhat along the order of the following:

1. *Military doctrine*, a coherent and internally consistent body of observations on deterrence, war preparation, and war waging, is harmoniously worked out through the joint efforts of the political and military leadership and bears the official imprimatur of the Communist Party.

2. Energizing and reinforcing doctrine are the contributions of *military science*, which include such diverse inputs as lessons derived from historical reflection on the successes and errors of past wars, policy imperatives deduced from the theoretical analysis of present and likely future strategic environmental conditions, and weapons deployment opportunities afforded by developments and breakthroughs in modern military technology.

3. Flowing from doctrine, in turn, are the principles of *military art* that govern the way the armed forces will actually bring their capabilities to bear in combat, ranging from tactics and what the Soviets call "the operational art" to the strategy of intercontinental nuclear missile warfare.

4. Feeding back to doctrine (and, over time, gradually modifying it), finally, are the experiences gained through day-to-day developments and refinements in military art which periodically bring about new possibilities for the application of military power and ultimately necessitate

changes in doctrine in order to bring it up to date.[2]

The conceptual orderliness and pristine simplicity of this officially sanctioned image of how military theorizing goes on in Moscow leaves the uncritical observer with a distinct (and quite intended) impression that the Soviet defense community is endowed with the best of all worlds: a frictionless division of labor, a computer-like efficiency, and an ideologically inspired scientific methodology that is virtually incapable of error. Needless to say, the situation is vastly more complex in reality. To be sure, there unquestionably exists in the Soviet Union a highly integrated and widely accepted notion of what constitutes military doctrine, and the taxonomy of Soviet military theory is probably more elaborate and institutionalized than that of any other country. Yet it hardly follows from this, as some Western analysts have suggested, that the formulation of Soviet strategic policy is a sort of conspiratorial palace intrigue in which the Party elite, with the sublime cooperation of their pliant military leaders, simply survey the international and technological horizon with cool detachment and foresight, reflect calculatingly on what military goals they would like and on what measures they would require to attain them, and then proceed to issue strategic proclamations and weapons deployment decisions with the relentless rationality of a Bolshevik Leviathan.[3] Notwithstanding its authoritarian political system and its ideological compulsion to rock the international status quo wherever possible, the Soviet Union is beset by the same external vagaries, technological trends, and internal bureaucratic pressures that bear upon any modern industrial state. As a result, its military doctrine is neither a rigid and ideologically inspired "master plan" predetermining the Soviet leadership toward certain inexorably policy choices nor an entirely coherent set of dogmatic operating principles worked out *a priori* by the ruling elite. Rather, it is a complex and shifting amalgam of thought partly structured by the leadership's Marxist-Leninist belief system, yet in the main determined by essentially the same secular opportunities and constraints that

---

[1]Lieutenant General I. Zav'ialov, "On Soviet Military Doctrine," *Krasnaia Zvezda*, March 30, 1967.

[2]Among the more prominent of the many detailed Soviet discussions of this taxonomy include Colonel General N. Lomov, *Soviet Military Doctrine* (Moscow: Izdatel'stvo "Znanie," 1963); and Major General S. Kozlov and others, *On Soviet Military Science* (Moscow: Voenizdat, 1964).

[3]See, for example, William R. Kintner and Harriet Fast Scott (eds.), *The Nuclear Revolution in Soviet Military Affairs* (Norman: University of Oklahoma Press, 1968). For a more extreme variant of the same point of view, see also Stefan Possony, "U.S. Intelligence at the Crossroads," *Orbis*, 9, no. 3 (Fall, 1965): 587–612.

affect all politicians practicing the art of the possible.

In the discussion that follows, we shall examine Soviet military doctrine with a view toward identifying these opportunities and constraints (or "causal factors," if one prefers) and attempt to cast some light on how they interact in shaping the content of Soviet military theory and policy. Since the actual substance of Soviet military doctrine has already been superbly and abundantly dealt with elsewhere,[4] we can forgo enumerating its key principles here and proceed directly to a survey of their diverse causal origins. Hopefully in the process, a reconstruction of that doctrine will emerge which shows (if somewhat impressionistically and anecdotally) not only its primary themes but also the alternative wellsprings from which they derive.

OBJECTIVE SECURITY REQUIREMENTS AND THE CHANGING EXTERNAL THREAT

Perhaps the first thing to be said about Soviet military doctrine is that however idiosyncratic it may be, it is anything but unresponsive to the strategic realities of the international landscape. Like any other large power with major stakes and interests beyond its own borders, the Soviet Union must constantly assure that its security preparations adequately accommodate the challenges and threats posed by its perceived adversaries. It is only natural, therefore, that Soviet strategic thinking and policymaking should be conducted with a careful view toward the changing nature of the external environment.

To say this, of course, is hardly to suggest that Soviet military doctrine invariably reflects distortion-free threat perceptions. On the contrary, both their ingrained Bolshevik "operational code" which, since Lenin's day, has admonished them to beware of enemies everywhere and their sobering historical experience which has given them a real sense of beleaguerement by the outside world have, over time, inclined the Soviet leaders to adhere to an extremely wary global outlook which has frequently manifested itself in what, by any objective standards, would have to be regarded as vastly overinflated threat as-

sessments.[5] Notwithstanding this ideologically inspired bias, however, Soviet military doctrine has shown such a keen sensitivity to shifts in the global strategic environment that one is tempted to cite "objective necessity" as its single most important determinant.

To be specific, virtually the entire Soviet image of what a future war between the two superpowers would be like—without question the central component of Soviet military doctrine—stems directly from a Soviet weighing of such shifting external considerations as the relative distribution of military forces between the two opposing blocs, the types of weaponry that would most likely be used in a war, the relative degree of tension or relaxation in superpower relations, and the ability of the nuclear balance to remain stable under duress. Let us examine each of these considerations briefly and observe how they tend to affect the content of Soviet military doctrine.

A. *The strategic balance.* Before commenting on the positive impact of this determinant, we should perhaps first say a few words about what is most probably its negative (or null) role, namely, in governing the physical complexion of the Soviet strategic posture. There has been a good deal of recent commentary in Western writings, most of it more impressionistic than empirically grounded, on the "action-reaction" phenomenon that supposedly fuels the East-West nuclear arms race. Without dwelling on the specific content and problems of this notion[6] (and conceding the obvious basic fact that neither superpower can go entirely unaffected by what its adversary does in the realm of weapons procurement), we may point out that there is little evidence to suggest that Soviet force deployments have in fact been reflex responses to American strategic weapons decisions. This is

---

[4]By far the most notable works in this regard are Thomas W. Wolfe, *Soviet Strategy at the Crossroads* (Cambridge: Harvard University Press, 1964) and, by the same author, *Soviet Power and Europe, 1945-1970* (Baltimore: The Johns Hopkins Press, 1970). Marshal V. D. Sokolovskii, *Soviet Military Strategy* (Englewood Cliffs, N.J.: Prentice-Hall, 1963) is an indispensable source of official Soviet commentary on the same subject and touches in considerable detail on most of the doctrinal issues discussed in the present essay.

[5]To point this out, one should hasten to add, is not at all to assert the "revisionist" thesis that the Soviet Union has essentially been a hapless victim of aggressive Western policies. On the contrary, leaving aside the thorny question of which superpower bears the greater responsibility for the Cold War, it seems reasonable to suggest that, if not because of their revolutionary ideology then because of their repeated efforts to disrupt the global equilibrium, the Soviets have had largely themselves to blame for most of their perceived security problems. At the same time, however, one should not overlook the crucial influence that such sobering experiences as the allied intervention during the Soviet civil war, the Western *cordon sanitaire* of the interwar period, the Nazi invasion of 1941, the postwar period of "capitalist encirclement," and the recent emergence of a new threat from the East in the form of incipient Chinese nuclear power and irredentism must have cumulatively had over the years in aggravating the already hyper-suspicious political psychology of the Soviet leadership. Even certifiable paranoids, after all, occasionally have real enemies.

[6]See, however, Colin S. Gray, "The Arms Race Phenomenon," *World Politics* 24, no. 1 (October 1971): 39-79.

not the place for a discussion of the motive forces governing Soviet-American strategic relations, but it ought to be noted in passing that Moscow's force deployment choices have been outgrowths far more of internal bureaucratic politics, leadership perceptions of "objective necessity," and technological considerations of strategic utility than simply knee-jerk emulations of United States decisions. As early as 1963, for example, Soviet military writers were openly talking of the potential value of "maneuvering warheads,"[7] a fact which suggests that the current Soviet MIRV research and development program has antecedents far pre-dating actual American deployment efforts in this field. In the realm of ICBM deployment, similarly, the long lead-time which necessarily must have preceded the Soviet offensive force buildup which became apparent during the second half of the 1960s indicates that the initial deployment decision was probably made at around the time of the Cuban missile crisis in 1962, two years before the American ICBM force-posture goal of 1054 launchers was announced.

Having noted this important qualification, however, we may safely suggest that shifts in Soviet military doctrine—if not in the hardware base that supports it—often display notable consistency with changes in the external strategic milieu. One illustration of this may be found in the changing emphasis given over time by the Soviets to the relative importance of "quantitative" as opposed to "qualitative" aspects of strategic weapons and postures. As long as the United States held an incontrovertible numerical ICBM superiority over the Soviet Union, Moscow's declaratory pronouncements tended to dismiss the significance of that lead and to stress instead the importance of non-numerical considerations such as overall deliverable megatonnage, in which it was asserted—probably correctly—that the Soviets enjoyed a comparative advantage.[8] Once this missile gap began to narrow and to bring the size of the Soviet ICBM force more into numerical line with that of the United States, however, Soviet statements increasingly began to show a tendency to depart from the qualitative-emphasis theme and to stress instead that Soviet security now rested on

the fact that Moscow possessed a missile arsenal that was "in no way inferior" to that of its American adversary.[9]

Another example of how the strategic balance directly bears on Soviet military doctrine may be seen in the way Soviet perspectives on the rate at which a superpower conflict in Europe would assume nuclear proportions have shifted in the past decade. During the late 1950s and early 1960s, when American strategic policy was still largely dominated by the "massive retaliation" option and when the U.S. commitment to European security rested on a forward defense concept that stipulated an early introduction of tactical nuclear weapons into any conflict, Soviet pronouncements uniformly espoused the doctrinal conviction that any limitation of a war in Europe was simply out of the question. Even when the Kennedy-McNamara team first began to articulate its "flexible response" policy, Soviet declarations tended to remain highly skeptical and to insist that any East-West clash in Europe would nonetheless escalate rapidly to the nuclear level. When the American conventional force buildup on the continent gradually came to give real teeth to Washington's "flexible response" proclamations and to offer a tangible prospect for

---

[7]See Major General I. Baryshev, "Nuclear Weapons and the PVO," *Krasnaia Zvezda*, November 13, 1963.

[8]A representative example of this tendency may be found in the statement contained in the Sokolovskii volume (circa 1963) that "at the present time, in gaining superiority in nuclear weapons, their quality and the technique of their employment are more important than their number." *Soviet Military Strategy*, p. 355.

[9]One could, of course, object to the correlation drawn here by arguing that the early Soviet stress on the "qualitative" factor was merely an ego-reinforcing device aimed at compensating for the hard fact of Moscow's second-best numerical position in the strategic balance, and that in point of fact, the Soviet leadership was, at least in its private calculations, under no illusions at any time about the importance of quantitative considerations in the strategic equation. In bolstering such an argument, one could point, for example, to the frantic Soviet effort to emplace medium-range missiles in Cuba in 1962 as a clear testament to Moscow's conviction that whatever might be said for such qualitative considerations as superiority in megatonnage, relative numbers of offensive missiles also mattered a great deal in determining one's overall strategic standing. To the extent that Soviet doctrine has long paid at least forceful lip service to the importance of achieving strategic supremacy over the United States, this perspective has to be recognized as having considerable merit. But it must be remembered at the same time that even a successful deployment of the missiles in Cuba would not have provided Moscow with numerical superiority; that the Soviet Union's most adventurous international provocations occurred at a time when it was strategically inferior to the United States; and that Khrushchev may well have felt that he had more than sufficient strength in his marginal but not insignificant nuclear capability to "counter-deter" Washington from attempting to thwart his moves by threatening the physical survival of the Soviet Union. After all, in the aftermath of the Cuban missile failure, the Soviet Union did not rush headlong into a numbers race with the United States by increasing the deployment rate of its relatively primitive SS-7 and SS-8 ICBMs, but chose instead to wait calmly for its third-generation SS-9 and SS-11 missiles to come into fruition before moving to repair its image of strategic power which received such heavy battering during the Cuban debacle. For all we know, the Soviets really believed that qualitative considerations were of prime importance during the early 1960s and only began to appreciate the relative advantages of quantitative factors once they had some real numbers in hand whose potentialities they could ponder.

stretching out the likely rate of a European crisis escalation, however, Soviet commentary began to waver somewhat and to concede that a central conflict between the superpowers no longer need "inevitably" escalate into nuclear exchanges. Although this shift fell perceptibly short of asserting that a European war could now be guaranteed to remain restricted to the conventional level, it seemed all the same to reflect a new Soviet belief (and possibly hope) that such a war could lend itself to some restraints, at least during its initial phases. This new perspective first received authoritative weight in a statement by the commander-in-chief of the Warsaw Pact forces, Marshal Yakubovskii, to the effect that Soviet doctrine should increasingly direct its attention to the hitherto largely ignored requirements of waging not only nuclear war in the European theater but also war using conventional weapons only.[10] Apparently taking their cue from this new doctrinal orientation, Warsaw Pact field maneuvers subsequently began for the first time to simulate conflict scenarios whose initiation and early prosecution remained confined to the level of non-nuclear exchanges.[11]

B. *Types of available weapons.* An even more crucial determinant of Soviet doctrine than the relative distribution of military forces is the overall nature of the hardware that would most likely be employed in a future war. The most obvious case in point here, and the one to which we shall restrict the present discussion, is the existence of vast quantities of air and missile deliverable nuclear weapons in the strategic arsenals of the two superpowers. Although it would oversimplify matters a great deal merely to assert the reductionist thesis that "the Soviet Union is unswervingly committed to a nuclear strategy,"[12] there is no question that Soviet declaratory policy reflects a prepossessing concern with the specter of a general nuclear war. If for no other reason than the fact that both superpowers' security ultimately rests on offensive nuclear weapons, the

Soviet political and military leaders seem to be convinced beyond doubt that such weapons would be brought to bear massively and *à l'outrance* in any escalating conflict that endangered the core values of either side. Whether one regards this assumption merely as a crude Soviet variant of "worst-case" analysis or as a truly prescient grasp of what a general war would most probably be like, the deep imprint of its effect may clearly be found across the entire spectrum of Soviet doctrine.

The notion that any global strategic war would necessarily see a widespread use of nuclear weaponry, for example, has led Soviet military doctrine to place considerable emphasis on the role of strategic preparedness and preemption. In part, this emphasis may be derivative simply of the natural desire of military men everywhere to control the initiative and not let themselves get caught with their guard down. For the most part, however, it seems to reflect a genuine Soviet respect for American counterforce potential and a consequent reluctance to stake the future survival of the Soviet state on the questionable war-waging capacity of a post-attack ICBM inventory. Although Soviet statements on this theme have generally tended to exercise great care to avoid suggesting that a standing Soviet launch-on-warning policy exists, their constant assertions since the mid-1950s that the Soviet armed forces would take every measure necessary to "break up" or "frustrate" an American attack add up to a doctrinal position that has every resemblance to serious contemplation of the preemptive first-strike option in a crisis.[13]

To cite another example, the Soviet declaratory expectation that the wrenching dislocations imposed by nuclear war would effectively destroy the adversary's capacity for organized strategic action following his absorption of the initial blows leads to a Soviet doctrinal belief (or at least article of faith) that a general nuclear war could be terminated on terms politically favorable to the Soviet Union without the requirement of Soviet forces physically occupying the homeland of the enemy. In part, this doctrinal precept no doubt reflects both a measure of wishful thinking on the part of the Soviet leadership and an implicit declaratory concession to the

---

[10] Marshal I. Yakubovskii, "Ground Forces," *Krasnaia Zvezda*, July 21, 1967.

[11] As if to underscore the lingering Soviet skepticism regarding the possibility of keeping a theater war in Europe permanently confined to the conventional level, however, these maneuvers eventually devolved into simulated nuclear exchanges. For a detailed listing and description of the major Warsaw Pact maneuvers during this period, see Wolfe, *Soviet Power and Europe*, pp. 478–80. For a well-informed discussion of the impact which the American "flexible response" strategy has had on the evolving Soviet image of theater warfare, see also the Appendix on "Soviet Military Strategy" in Trevor Cliffe, *Military Technology and the European Balance*, Adelphi Paper No. 89 (London: International Institute for Strategic Studies, 1972), pp. 29–35.

[12] Kintner and Scott, *The Nuclear Revolution in Soviet Military Affairs*, p. 390.

[13] Some such statements, moreover, have been far less unrestrained than others, as exemplified by the assertion of I. Glagolev and V. Larionov that in the event of a nuclear war, the Soviet Union's missiles and bombers "would take off *even before the aggressor's first rockets, to say nothing of his bombers, reached their targets*." "Soviet Defense Might and Peaceful Co-Existence," *International Affairs* (Moscow) 11 (December 1963): 32 (emphasis in the original).

practical impossibility of the Soviet Union's actually carrying off a successful invasion of a powerful transoceanic enemy like the United States. Nonetheless, it may additionally be read as indicating a not altogether unreasonable Soviet presumption that if the initial phase of hostilities goes off well, leaving the United States in a state of profound shock and the Soviet Union in possession of a residual strategic force for diplomatic bargaining, the problem of successful war termination may well take care of itself.[14]

C. *Degree of East-West tension.* The principal impact of this factor, which can be dispensed with in brief, is not so much on the actual Soviet image of nuclear war as it is on the Soviet leadership's estimate of the likelihood that such a war might occur. To the extent that their assessments of the probability of war have a substantial bearing on the leadership's overall view of such important matters as resource allocation priorities and combat readiness requirements, however, the relative degree of amity (or at least mutual tolerance) in the superpower relationship is a significant determinant of Soviet attitudes. One rarely finds, of course, a direct linkage between fluctuations in global tension and shifts in the content of Soviet professional military writings, if only because institutional and ideological considerations have long since made it all but ritualistic for Soviet doctrinal essays to begin with the *pro forma* injunction that Soviet military vigilance is necessitated by the supposed "new world war" which imperialist schemers are constantly plotting. The effect of such fluctuations on actual Soviet strategic planning, however, can frequently be clearly discerned in the pronouncements and observable behavior of the Soviet political leadership. To cite only three of the many examples that could be noted in this regard, the successful conclusion of the SALT I agreements between Washington and Moscow,

the on-going East-West discussions on mutual and balanced force reductions (MBFR) in Europe, and the increasing orientation of Soviet verbal statements and force deployments toward the growing Chinese threat may all be traced to authoritative Soviet convictions that the global relationships of major tension have now changed and that former doctrinal articles of faith can safely undergo some reassessment and overhauling.

In particular, the emerging Chinese nuclear threat to Soviet security interests represents an ironic empirical confirmation of the 1963 Soviet propaganda pronouncement that "the atomic bomb does not adhere to the class principle."[15] By revealing the hard truth that strategic rivalry is ultimately a transideological phenomenon, it also makes a hollow fiction of the traditional Soviet doctrinal refrain that any major war would inevitably be a "class war" of opposing social systems. Though Soviet writings continue to pay lip service to that refrain, Soviet force deployments along the Chinese border and Moscow's eagerness to stabilize its European flank offer little room for doubt as to where the real concerns increasingly lie.

D. *Deterrence stability.* Closely related to the role of relative East-West tension in shaping Soviet military doctrine is the relative degree to which the Soviets believe their deterrence relationship with the United States can sustain the combined "system shocks" of intense superpower crises and technological improvements in American weaponry. In effect, this consideration boils down to the extent to which the Soviet leadership can feel confidence in the capacity of its strategic forces to threaten a credible second strike.

For the most part, Moscow's attitudes on this subject must be gleaned by inference and deduction since Soviet military pronouncements do not typically contain the terms of reference and categories of analysis common to Western strategic discussions. In particular, Soviet military writings assiduously avoid embracing deterrence "stability" as the end-all of military planning and emphasize instead the less sophisticated and more ambiguous objective of simply being able to deal a "crushing rebuff" to any nuclear attacker. To some degree, this idiosyncrasy may have ideological underpinnings insofar as the concept of "stability" connotes a preservation of the international status quo, something clearly anathema to Marxist-Leninist theology. In part also, it may stem from a conscious Soviet

---

[14]In this regard, an authoritative senior Soviet military commentator, Colonel General N. Lomov, has suggested that with massive nuclear missile strikes, "the possibility becomes real for the quick removal of a whole series of countries of one or another coalition from the war even without the simultaneous seizing of those countries' territory by land forces and airborne troops," and that such strikes can "at once, from the very beginning of the war, achieve results of great significance, . . . avoiding the methodical, step-by-step development of tactical successes into operational, then strategic, and finally political results." "The Influence of Soviet Military Doctrine on the Development of Military Art," *Kommunist Vooruzhenykh Sil* 21 (November 1965): 21. See also the observation of Colonel S. Tiushkevich that the successful exploitation of a preemptive nuclear strike can, "in almost an instant, disorganize and demoralize the enemy forces, obliging them to operate in uncoordinated and chaotic fashion, and even to cease resistance." "Necessity and Chance in Modern Warfare," *Kommunist Vooruzhenykh Sil* 10 (May 1964): 40.

[15]"Open Letter of the Central Committee of the Communist Party of the Soviet Union," *Pravda* (July 14, 1963).

doctrinal preference for grounding Soviet security on the voluntaristic choices of the Soviet leadership rather than on the blind mechanism of some autonomous "system" of mutual deterrence.[16] It is quite clear, however, that whatever terms of reference they may prefer, the Soviets are strongly committed to the principle—if not the slogan—of nuclear deterrence and plainly favor a strategic balance that is more rather than less stable.

No better testament to this fact may be found than the steady rise in the composure and self-assurance of Soviet strategic statements that has accompanied the Soviet Union's gradual attainment of a secure retaliatory force during the past decade. Throughout most of the Khrushchev incumbency, when the Soviet strategic posture was still largely embryonic, it was characteristic of Soviet doctrinal pronouncements simply to assert unrestrained threats that any serious Western encroachment on Soviet interests would trigger a reflexive and indiscriminate Soviet nuclear response.[17] Whether this Soviet-style "massive retaliation" refrain represented real concern over the survivability of the Soviet deterrent or merely another verbal handmaiden of Khrushchev's blunderbuss approach toward international relations generally, it was hardly calculated to convey a persuasive impression to the West that the Soviet Union could remain composed under situations of stress. Once the Soviet force-posture began to acquire sizable numbers of hardened ICBMs and submarine-launched missiles under the tutelage of the Brezhnev-Kosygin regime, however, this Khrushchevian practice of hurling rhetorical lightning bolts in the direction of every perceived threat became steadily supplanted by a new emphasis on quiet self-confidence and circumspection. Among the doctrinal adjustments stimulated by this new Soviet sense of adequate security were included a substantial downplaying (though not total abandonment) of the former urgency assigned to preemption, a sharply reduced estimate of the probability of American attack against the

Soviet homeland, and a growing willingness to hedge assertions that a central war in Europe would "inevitably" erupt to the strategic nuclear level with qualified pronouncements that such a war might stand a chance of remaining limited. While these adjustments fell considerably short of embracing such controversial American strategic notions as the desirability of restrained targeting and the feasibility of slow-motion counterforce duels, they represented a signal departure from the hair-trigger quality of the previous doctrinal orientation.

THE ROLE OF MILITARY-TECHNOLOGICAL INNOVATION

If the "objective necessities" of Soviet doctrine are largely imposed by the relative challenges of the external environment, the possibilities which it can effectively exploit are predominantly determined (and circumscribed) by the relative state of the art in Soviet weapons technology. Ever since the earliest days of organized warfare among states, it has been characteristic for military doctrine to lag substantially behind military technology. And notwithstanding its asserted claim to "scientific mastery" over the vagaries of history and nature, the Soviet Union has been no more exempt from this feature of military affairs than any other nation. Indeed, the "military-technological revolution" which has received such prominent discussion in Soviet military writing throughout the past decade has been both an exclusive offspring of advancements in weapons development and a sustaining testament to the subordination of Soviet military doctrine to the hard facts of technological life.[18]

One obvious example of this commanding lead which weapons technology has exercised over Soviet military doctrine may be found in the thoroughly uninspired way the Soviet Union first entered (or, more correctly, stumbled into) the nuclear age. Not only was there no *a priori* requirement for nuclear weapons evident in Soviet military doctrine during the 1940s, there was also little apparent effort by the Soviets even in the initial years *after* their acquisition of the atomic bomb to comprehend the potentially far-

---

[16]See, for example, the explicit statement to this effect by Major General N. Talenskii in justifying the Soviet Union's involvement in ABM research and development, in his "Anti-Missile Systems and Disarmament," *International Affairs* (Moscow) 10 (October 1964): 15–19.

[17]Typical of this tendency was the following statement made by Khrushchev in a 1959 interview with Averill Harriman: "Your generals talk of maintaining your position in Berlin with force. That is bluff. If you send in tanks, they will burn and make no mistake about it. If you want war, then you can have it, but remember, it will be your war. Our rockets will fly automatically." Quoted in Daniel Ellsberg, *The Theory and Practice of Blackmail*, (Santa Monica, Calif.: The RAND Corporation, July 1968), p. 1.

[18]In the Soviet lexicon, this "military-technological revolution" has thus far featured three main stages: the advent of nuclear weapons, the emergence of missile delivery systems, and the development of cybernetic systems for military command and control. The Soviets now regard themselves as well into the third stage. See Lieutenant Colonel V. Bondarenko and Colonel S. Tiushkevich, "The Contemporary Stage of the Revolution in Military Affairs and Its Demands on Military Cadres," *Kommunist Vooruzhenykh Sil* 6 (March 1968): 18–25.

reaching consequences of this revolutionary new weapon and to incorporate them into the body of existing Soviet military thought. All the evidence that exists on this subject, in fact, suggests that the Soviets went after the A-bomb not because they had a firm doctrinal need for it, but simply because the theoretical possibility for developing and producing it provided an irresistible target of opportunity for technological exploitation.[19] Indeed, as long as Stalin lived, Soviet military doctrine remained captivated by his dogmatic military traditionalism which refused to admit that nuclear weapons might constitute anything more than another—if more powerful—form of battlefield ordnance. Only during the mid-1950s, after Stalin's departure from the scene had finally released Soviet military thought from the oppressive stranglehold of his self-proclaimed "military genius," did Soviet strategy finally begin to assimilate the truly novel implications of the new weaponry and direct its attention to such important nuclear age concepts as deterrence, preemption, and surprise.

A more recent illustration of this tendency for military-technological innovation to pull Soviet doctrine along in its wake may be found in the "New Look" strategic policy which Khrushchev articulated in 1960. This policy, which sweepingly relegated the once-paramount Soviet ground forces to a subordinate role and simultaneously elevated the strategic missile forces to a place of unprecedented primacy in Soviet military planning, was less a product of any particular doctrinal foresight on Khrushchev's part than simply a natural response to what the Soviet military literature commonly refers to as the "second stage" of the military-technological revolution, namely, the advent of intercontinental missile delivery systems. By wrenching Soviet military policy away from its previous continental focus and explicitly imparting to it a new all-or-nothing focus on nuclear deterrence, Khrushchev did little more than render *ex post facto* doctrinal obeisance to the Soviet Union's final achievement of the technical means to deliver a credible nuclear strike directly on the heartland of the United States.

To say that Soviet military doctrine tends to follow rather than run ahead of military technology, of course, is hardly to suggest that weapons research and development in the Soviet Union has an autonomous life of its own. On the contrary, Soviet planners are acutely sensitive to the importance of harnessing weapons developments to the perceived requirements of military doctrine rather than simply letting them follow a directionless course.[20] Soviet military doctrine does not, however, systematically commission (and indeed can have no way of anticipating) specific military-technological innovations but rather does little more than endow the research and development process with an authoritative hunting license. What military development produces, in turn, is simply what is technically attractive and feasible, leaving it to doctrine to figure out later, at its own pace, how the product should be employed.

THE IMPACT OF AMERICAN STRATEGIC THINKING

One of the most interesting practical questions for Western security planners is the extent to which Soviet military doctrine is affected by (and hence subject to manipulation by) developments in American strategic theory and policy. From the little evidence that can be gathered from observable Soviet doctrine and behavior, it seems that this question does not readily submit to a simple and categorical answer. In principle, Soviet doctrine is no less receptive to the consideration of alien strategic ideas than any other body of military thought which claims to be willing to build upon the strategic ideas and experiences of others. It is common knowledge, for example, that much of Soviet military doctrine derives directly from the classical military-theoretical writings of Clausewitz, and Soviet commentators have frequently been quite unabashed in asserting that Soviet military theory must carefully exploit, among other things, "all the finest achievements of bourgeois military

---

[19] The Soviets were considerably spurred on in their efforts, however, by their knowledge that the United States was busily at work on a nuclear program of its own. Needless to say, while Stalin was resistive to certain major doctrinal implications of nuclear weapons, he was scarcely unmindful of the basic desirability of such weapons, as attested to by his eager efforts to achieve an operational nuclear delivery capability as early as possible. For background discussion on the origins of the Soviet nuclear program, see Arnold Kramish, *Atomic Energy in the Soviet Union* (Stanford: Stanford University Press, 1959). On Stalin's strategic policies, see also the brief but balanced account in Wolfe, *Soviet Power and Europe*, pp. 32–49.

[20] One Soviet commentator, for example, has explicitly argued in this connection that technology can sharply enhance the possibilities of military strategy by offering surprise breakthroughs in weaponry that can abruptly change the strategic balance and deprive one's enemy for a long time of the possibility to develop effective countermeasures against such weaponry. (Lieutenant Colonel V. Bondarenko, "Military-Technological Superiority—A Most Important Factor for the Reliable Defense of the Country," *Kommunist Vooruzhenykh Sil* 17 (September 1966). For a detailed analysis of the Bondarenko article, see Benjamin S. Lambeth, *The Argument for Superiority: A New Voice in the Soviet Strategic Debate*, Institute for Defense Analyses, N-419R (January 1967).

science."[21] As soon as one departs from this level of vague generality and seeks to pinpoint specific instances where Soviet doctrine has assimilated the teachings of its major adversary, however, one quickly discovers that the Soviet learning curve follows anything but a smooth and steadily rising path.

Where Soviet doctrine is perhaps most prone to emulate the strategic thinking of the United States is in the realm of weapons deployment practices whose duplication by the Soviets would materially enhance the security of the Soviet Union. It is quite reasonable to suspect, for example, that the widespread American public discussions during the early 1960s regarding the need for a secure second-strike capability and the consequent move by the United States to emplace its Minuteman ICBM force in underground silos had a considerable influence in calling official Soviet attention to the strategic vulnerability issue, for in the aftermath of its disastrous failure in the Cuban missile crisis, the Soviet Union lost little time both in coming to quick doctrinal terms with the necessity of a survivable retaliatory force and in undertaking the necessary collateral efforts to harden its own ICBMs. In a similar vein, it is also plausible that American calculations that the threat of an ICBM counterforce duel required a back-up strategic bargaining capability in the form of submarine-based Polaris missiles sufficiently impressed the Soviet leaders to induce them to develop their own Polaris-type fleet, something they most likely would not have done merely out of considerations of technical feasibility alone.[22]

In addition to adopting for their own use certain American strategic ideas which, *mutatis mutandis*, have seemed appropriate to the parochial security needs of the Soviet state, the Soviet leaders have also shown an occasional willingness to assimilate explicit American strategic "teachings" in instances where they have been genuinely aimed at reducing the likelihood of inadvertent war. One example of such Soviet responsiveness, as illustrated by the "hot-line"

accord of 1963 and by the more recent Soviet-American agreement on managing the risks of nuclear war, may be seen in the growing Soviet recognition over the past decade that superpower rivalry cannot be safely waged as an exclusively zero-sum game and that certain kinds of tacit cooperation with the United States are required if the East-West conflict is to remain a manageable adversary relationship rather than a volatile standoff beyond either side's control. A much more interesting example is the way the Soviet Union apparently responded to American efforts during the early 1960s to point out to Moscow the supreme importance of effective nuclear command and control mechanisms. Although we know extremely little about Soviet nuclear control arrangements and weapons release procedures, the fact that the Soviets never called full-scale nuclear alerts during their mock combat-readiness exercises of the early 1960s (and indeed never brought their ICBM force to full combat-ready status even during the height of the 1962 Cuban missile crisis) lends considerable support to the hypothesis that the Soviet nuclear control system during that period was sufficiently primitive to leave the leadership with grave doubts about its ability to prevent a possible accident once the mobilization order was given. In the aftermath of the Cuban crisis, U.S. defense officials (nervously mindful of this possibility) went to great lengths toward tacitly trying to "educate" the Soviets in matters of nuclear control by studiously releasing in prominent public speeches formerly highly classified information about such American nuclear safeguards as electronic locks, positive control procedures, and the like. Whether or not the Soviets got the message exclusively through this medium rather than through independent deduction is a matter that we can only speculate about, given the paucity of evidence available in the public domain. It is noteworthy, however, that not long after this American effort, the Soviets began stressing the adequacy of their nuclear safeguard arrangements in their doctrinal statements and holding full-scale nuclear alerts as a normal order of business in their strategic operational readiness exercises.[23]

Any state's willingness to be an active pupil of its adversary's teachings has ultimate limits,

---

[21]Major General Ye. Nikitin, "Lenin and Soviet Military Science," *Soviet Military Review* 4 (April 1972): 51.

[22]One should bear in mind, in this regard, that throughout most of the 1950s even American planners were largely unaware of the importance of the first-strike/second-strike distinction and only came to perceive the need for a protected retaliatory capability after a detailed RAND Corporation study discovered, almost by happenstance, the potential vulnerability of the American bomber and missile force to a surprise Soviet attack. It is hard to believe, therefore, that the Soviets would have done solely through the natural momentum of technological development what it took an intensive systems analysis and considerable bureaucratic arm-twisting to convince the United States to do.

[23]For details of this interesting episode in Soviet-American strategic relations, see Edward Klein and Robert Littell, "Shh! Let's Tell the Russians!" *Newsweek* (May 5, 1969): 47. See also the informative discussion in Johan Jörgen Holst, "Missile Defense, the Soviet Union, and the Arms Race," in Johan Jörgen Holst and William Schneider (eds.), *Why ABM? Policy Issues in the Missile Defense Controversy* (New York: Pergamon Press, 1969), pp. 168–69.

however, and there is a wealth of evidence to suggest that the Soviets draw their line of tolerance sharply at the point where American strategic "instruction" departs from genuinely magnanimous concern over international stability and seeks consciously to persuade Moscow to play the strategic game according to Washington's self-serving rules. To note only the most immediately obvious case in point, Defense Secretary McNamara's fervent efforts during the early part of his tenure to sell the Soviets his "city-avoidance" strategy—during a time, not insignificantly, when U.S. strategic superiority made a counterforce war a much more attractive option for the Americans than for the Soviets—were roundly dismissed by the Soviets as little more than a cynical effort to "legitimize" nuclear war on American terms. To this day (despite their impressive force-level buildup of the past five years), Soviet military doctrine continues to reject out of hand all notions of restrained targeting and limited strategic war that figure so prominently in much of American strategic thinking.[24]

LEADERSHIP PRECONCEPTIONS AND PREFERENCES

Up to now, we have been discussing only the "objective" determinants of Soviet military doctrine, namely, those external challenges, opportunities, and constraints that impose certain minimum security requirements on the Soviet state regardless of its national objectives, ideological commitment, or leadership style of the moment. Were those determinants the only ones affecting Soviet doctrine (or, to put it more correctly, were the Soviet leaders purely "rational strategic men"), we could simply conclude our analysis at this point by observing that the exist-

ence of perceived external threats forces the Soviets to maintain a "sufficient" military posture in order to cope with them; that the availability of nuclear weaponry in the arsenals of the two superpowers constrains Soviet doctrine to adopt a predominantly nuclear orientation; and that the dictates of common sense oblige Soviet military planners to draw upon whatever precepts of American strategic practice that might conceivably enhance the security of the Soviet Union. The fact is, however, that "objective" determinants explain only a part of Soviet military doctrine, namely, that part which would most likely be common to any superpower that found itself in the sort of strategic milieu in which the Soviet Union has to operate. In this section and in the remaining ones that follow, therefore, we must turn our attention to those "subjective" factors that make Soviet military doctrine idiosyncratic and uniquely "Soviet" in complexion and content.

In a strict sense, of course, every principle of Soviet military doctrine is ultimately a reflection of leadership preference, for the simple reason that each emanates from a more or less conscious political or military decision. Yet as much as "objective necessity" imposes inescapable demands and constraints on the Soviet leadership, it also leaves considerable room for choice among multiple options. The destructiveness of modern weaponry, for example, may force the Soviets to adhere to a policy of nuclear deterrence, but it does not necessarily oblige them to base their deterrence concept on the principle of "mutual assured vulnerability" (and they clearly do not). Similarly, while the exigencies of the external environment may dictate certain obvious weapons procurement policies to the Soviets, they do not necessarily assure that the accompanying doctrine will always reflect total value-maximizing "rationality." Domestic political considerations or personal leadership predispositions may, on occasion, enter midway into the decision-making loop and produce doctrinal precepts that either exceed the capabilities of the Soviet strategic force-posture or else fail to exploit existing capabilities to their fullest potential.

An example of the first anomaly (that of doctrinal overextension) may be found in Khrushchev's enunciation in 1960 of what amounted to an almost exclusively nuclear "massive retaliation" doctrine at a time when the Soviet missile force was minuscule and barely beyond the stage of initial deployment. Motivated in part by a desire to assert his authority over the Soviet military establishment and in part by a belief that he could bluff the United States into accepting

---

[24] There is, incidentally, a useful lesson to be learned from this example whose acceptance by U.S. strategic planners could go a long way toward eliminating two occasionally counterproductive propensities of American strategic thinking: (a) the tendency to assume that whatever is strategically rational and desirable for the United States must *ipso facto* also be acceptable for the Soviet Union, and (b) the compulsion to develop highly sophisticated—and often over-intellectualized—strategic theories and scenarios for variants of wars which, if only because the Soviets see things quite differently, will probably never occur. There is nothing, of course, intrinsically wrong with American efforts to manipulate Soviet military doctrine in ways that could eventually redound to the security interests of the United States. What could profitably be avoided, however, is the lapsing from this sensible (if often less than fruitful) posture into the self-satisfied *hubris* of wrongly assuming that the world is, in Stanley Hoffmann's trenchant phrase, merely a projection of American rationality in which "opponents are supposed either to reason like Americans or to be in need of education bringing them to this level." *Gulliver's Troubles, or the Setting of American Foreign Policy* (New York: McGraw-Hill, 1968), p. 160.

his pronouncements at face value, Khrushchev embarked on a daring effort to restructure formal Soviet military doctrine which could scarcely be sustained by the actual weaponry at his disposal and whose prematurity was ultimately confirmed by the Cuban missile setback in 1962 and the rapid retrenchment of Soviet doctrine which ensued.

The opposite anomaly (that of doctrinal lag) is exemplified by Stalin's insistence up to his death in 1953 on keeping Soviet military policy firmly wedded to his outmoded theory of the "permanently-operating factors" long after the Soviet Union had crossed the nuclear threshold.[25] Although nuclear weapons during that period were being introduced into the Soviet force structure as fast as available technology and production capacity could turn them out, Stalin refused to accept that their vast destructive potential warranted any fundamental departure from the traditional Soviet wartime strategy of wearing the enemy down through gradual attrition. As in the case of Khrushchev's premature stress on "massive retaliation," the explanation is essentially non-rational and tied to "subjective" domestic considerations: Stalin was either politically unwilling or psychologically unable to admit that modern technology had seriously compromised the foundations of his long sacrosanct military thought, and he accordingly chose to hold the Soviet Union to his increasingly anachronistic doctrinal preconceptions rather than allow his authority to be eroded by conceding that he could possibly be wrong.

As a general rule, it is probably safe to say that in almost every case where Soviet military doctrine diverges significantly from American thinking (or from the premises that a "rational strategic man" with American values would consider optimal), it is due precisely to the influence of subjective leadership preference or some other domestic determinant insensitive to the "objective" causal imperatives discussed above. Perhaps the most prominent leadership-inspired idiosyncrasy of Soviet military doctrine as contrasted to that of the United States may be seen in the careful attention and consideration the Soviets have given to the problem of coping with a deterrence failure. While the content of actual American nuclear contingency plans could well

suggest something quite different, the publicly available information regarding American strategic policy strongly implies that the United States has placed the overwhelming burden of its national security investment in the deterrence of nuclear war and has paid little heed, by comparison, to what might have to be done if deterrence were to break down. The emphasis on "mutual assured destruction" rather than "improved war outcome" capabilities in U.S. force planning provides a standing confirmation of this American strategic orientation, as does the virtual absence of discussion in American strategic writings of how one might effectively cope with (and terminate) a crisis which devolved into strategic nuclear exchanges. Whether out of a genuine belief in the efficacy of mutual deterrence or out of a reluctance to "think about the unthinkable," American strategic thinking by and large seems to grind to a screeching halt at the point where deterrence gets bowled over by war.[26]

Soviet doctrine, on the other hand, dwells little on such matters as deterrence-maintenance and pre-war crisis diplomacy and devotes by far the greatest amount of its attention to precisely that subject on which American doctrine is most silent: the prosecution and successful termination of nuclear war in the event deterrence fails. Up to a point, perhaps, this may be simply regarded as an altogether natural form of nervous whistling in the dark aimed at reducing Soviet unease over the uncertainties of what Clausewitz called "the fog of war." For the most part, however, it must clearly be laid to a conscious belief on the part of the Soviet leaders—civilian and military alike—that the survival of the Soviet state must be based on far more than blind faith in the stability of mutual deterrence. To note this point is not to assert that the Soviet crystal ball is any clearer than that of American planners or that in the event of a nuclear war, the Soviets would necessarily act in accordance with their preestablished doctrinal precepts. It is, however, to suggest that the Soviet leaders have purposefully taken it upon themselves to devote considerably more rigorous effort than their American opposites toward coping with the imponderables of the nuclear age and that they may, as a result of that effort, be somewhat better prepared organ-

---

[25] Stalin's "permanently-operating factors," which included the stability of the rear, the morale of the army, the quality and quantity of divisions, the armament of the army, and the organizational abilities of the commanders, were put forward in explicit contrast to such "transitory" factors as surprise, which, in Stalin's belief, could not be made to determine the ultimate outcome of a war.

[26] The few exceptions to this general tendency may be found in the collected writings of Thomas Schelling and Herman Kahn. See, for example, Schelling's *Arms and Influence* (New Haven: Yale University Press, 1966), and Kahn's *On Escalation* (New York: Frederick A. Praeger, 1965). See also Klaus Knorr and Thorton Read (eds.), *Limited Strategic War* (New York: Frederick A. Praeger, 1962).

izationally and psychologically to sustain the severe stresses and strains that a nuclear war would undoubtedly generate.[27]

IDEOLOGY, HISTORICAL TRADITION, AND STANDARD OPERATING PROCEDURE

A second "subjective" determinant of Soviet military doctrine, beyond the principal one of conscious leadership preference, stems from those philosophical beliefs, historical experiences, and ritualized ways of doing business that may be regarded as collectively constituting the Soviet Union's strategic "style." All political systems, regardless of their professions of decisionmaking voluntarism or enlightened rationality, are constrained by certain built-in idiosyncrasies which affect and, to a greater or lesser extent, predetermine their policy choices. Notwithstanding its exclusive claim to a "scientific" methodology for dealing with military-strategic affairs, the Soviet Union is no more unbound by this systemic constraint than any other country. Ideological professions, historical burdens, and standardized patterns of behavior may have little intrinsically in common, but they can be fairly treated together for the purpose of the present analysis because, in combination, they make up that unique characterological baggage which Soviet planners must carry as they go about the formulation of their policies.

Ideology is an important stylistic determinant of Soviet doctrine not so much because it prescribes *a priori* imperatives for Soviet policymakers (which, in practice, it does only tenuously) but because it is primarily responsible for generating and authorizing the ground rules and terms of reference that Soviet doctrine must observe. By defining the international system as an intractable confrontation of opposing social

classes, for example, ideology assures the continued maintenance of a basic adversary relationship between the United States and the Soviet Union and stipulates that Soviet doctrine be based on a presumption of ceaseless Soviet competition with the West. In addition to inspiring this Manichaean image of Soviet-American relations, ideology also dictates that Soviet doctrine follow Lenin's classic thesis on imperialism which maintains that war is solely derivative of economic causes. Furthermore, because of its axiomatic assumption of the moral superiority of socialism, Marxist-Leninist theology contributes to the prominent refrain in Soviet doctrine that regardless of the vast destructiveness of modern nuclear weaponry, the Soviet bloc would emerge relatively triumphant in any global war against the capitalists. Finally, as a result of its stress on the necessity for constant struggle and ultimate transcendence, ideology insists that the Soviet Union pay unswerving obeisance (at least in principle) to the goal of achieving strategic superiority over the United States.

Another important characterological determinant of Soviet doctrine, though less explicit than ideology and more subtle in its effect, is the cumulative historical experience of the Soviet Union and the resultant national psychology engendered by it. One manifestation of this determinant may be found in the considerable importance the Soviets assign to strategic defense in their overall hierarchy of national security priorities, an emphasis which may be explained in considerable measure by the bitter Soviet memories of the rapacious Nazi invasion of 1941 and the determination of the Soviet leadership to take every step to prevent a replay of that disaster in the future.[28] (In this same vein, one may further speculate that the Soviet Union's apparent decision to concentrate its initial ABM deployment effort solely on Moscow rather than on its ICBM sites may be explainable in part by the Party elite's abiding historical concern for assuring its own political survival, come what

[27]This fact also points up the erroneousness of the argument advanced by Roman Kolkowicz ("Strategic Parity and Beyond: Soviet Perspectives," *World Politics* 23, no. 3 [April 1971]: 451) that military technology has exerted "a levelling effect on diverse political, military, and ideological doctrines, creating a gradual convergence of strategic concepts and policies derivative from this new iron law of nuclear technology." Although Soviet and American force postures have indeed come, as Kolkowicz puts it, more or less "into phase" with one another in recent years, this scarcely implies that a "progressive symmetry between United States and Soviet doctrines" has also come about. However much the Soviet force posture today may superficially mirror that of the United States, there can be no mistaking the continued uniqueness of the doctrine that underlies it. For a useful overview of the key differences between American and Soviet doctrinal principles, see Thomas W. Wolfe, *The Global Strategic Perspective From Moscow*, P-4978 (Santa Monica, Calif.: The RAND Corporation, March 1973), pp. 9–12.

[28]One should exercise caution, however, against falling prey to the belief currently popular in the United States that this stress on defensive weapons indicated by Soviet declaratory statements and by Moscow's heavy investment in air defense and ABM forces *ipso facto* implies that Soviet military doctrine is somehow hung up on a predominantly "defensive orientation." Although Soviet doctrine indeed ascribes considerable importance to the role of strategic defense, its primary thrust is unquestionably offensive in nature. For a strong Soviet argument to the effect that defense is not an end in itself but rather is integrally tied (through its damage-limiting function) to the overall offensive mission, see Major General I. Zav'ialov, "On Soviet Military Doctrine," *Krasnaia Zvezda* (March 30, 1967).

may to the rest of the country.[29]) Insofar as the Soviet Union can be said to have been laboring under a national "inferiority complex" throughout its half-century of competition with its more economically and technologically endowed American adversary, one may also perhaps attribute to historical-psychological determinants the pervasive stress given over by contemporary Soviet military doctrine and practice to the importance of "bigness" (as in warhead megatonnage and launch vehicle size), "quantity" (as in overall numbers of nuclear-missile weapons), and "precedence" (first earth satellite, first ICBM, first man in space, and so on).[30]

A final influence in this "characterological" category that bears on Soviet strategic doctrine is the momentum of traditional practice, organization process, and standard operating procedure. At the risk of being somewhat reductionist and glib, one may observe that a good deal of what goes on in the realm of Soviet military affairs is frequently due not to any hidden motive or supersophisticated rationale, but rather to little more than the prosaic fact that the Soviets simply do things that way. Two mundane but representative examples of this phenomenon may be inferred from some of the evidence we have about Soviet missile installation practices. The first relates to the Soviet deployment of a number of SS-11 ICBMs in old medium-range missile sites in 1969, at a time when the SALT negotiations were still in the early stages of trying to work out a tentative agreement on the limitation of offensive weapons. Some observers in the West speculated that this dual deployment of the SS-11 represented a clever Machiavellian ploy on the part of the Soviets to gain a free bonus in SALT by shrewdly placing these missiles in MRBM launch complexes so that they could later be claimed to be functionally removed from the category of negotiable "intercontinental" weapons. It seems far more plausible, however (especially in view of the twin facts that many Soviet ICBM sites are collocated with MRBMs and that Moscow evidently made no issue out of the missiles in SALT) that this move was merely a natural and purely organizationally motivated example of Soviet force-structure refinement whereby a number of available SS-11s were deployed in a number of conveniently adaptable MRBM fields.

The second example harks back to the Soviet deployment of medium-range missiles in Cuba in 1962 and relates to an apparent anomaly in the way the Soviets implemented their concealment measures for those missiles. During the initial U-2 reconnaissance overflights which first disclosed the existence of the missiles in Cuba, the weapons were found to have been deployed with no sound attempts at concealment whatever. Once the crisis broke following President Kennedy's October 22 television address, however, subsequent low-level verification overflights revealed that the Soviets were frantically camouflaging their missiles—yet, strangely enough, *after* their nature and location had already been ascertained. The only plausible explanation for this bizarre Soviet performance is that the Soviet technicians in Cuba simply followed by rote the same deployment doctrine as the one used for emplacing similar missiles in the Soviet Union (where presumably camouflaging was scarcely necessary) and lit upon the bright idea of trying to hide their activities only after the overflights had already let the cat out of the bag.

STRUCTURAL CONSTRAINTS OF THE SOVIET POLITICAL SYSTEM

The nature of the decisionmaking process in the Soviet Union imposes both a blessing and a curse on the development of Soviet military doctrine. On the one hand, the authoritarian character of the Soviet political system permits Soviet planners to work in relative freedom from such domestic constraints as the pressures of public opinion and the requirements for legislative approval which frequently complicate strategic policymaking in democratic societies. While this relative absence of public accountability enjoyed by the Soviet leadership does not mean that it can deal with problems with the full consistency and purposefulness of a unitary rational actor, it does provide for a situation in which Soviet military doctrine can be shaped in reasonable accordance with the parochial preferences of the ruling oligarchy. As a result, Soviet doctrine can

[29]For a searching analysis of Soviet foreign policy which attributes considerable significance to this leadership "survival ethic" as a mainspring of Soviet behavior, see Adam B. Ulam, *Expansion and Coexistence: The History of Soviet Foreign Policy, 1917–1967* (New York: Frederick A. Praeger, 1968), particularly pp. 314–15.

[30]One may venture to suggest, however, that on this matter of missile "numbers," it is probably assuming too much consistency and singularity of purpose on the part of the Soviet leadership to argue that the post-Khrushchev Soviet ICBM buildup was directly tied to an *a priori* doctrinal requirement for a preemptive capability, as William T. Lee maintains in "The Rationale Underlying Soviet Strategic Forces," in William R. Kintner (ed.), *Safeguard: Why the ABM Makes Sense* (New York: Hawthorn Books, 1969), pp. 142–78. A far more plausible explanation seems to be the one advanced by John Erickson to the effect that "the phasing of the Soviet weapons buildup makes it clear that no single simplistic 'solution' or 'decision' was behind it," and that the Soviets sought to overinsure themselves against a whole range of possible contingencies rather than merely to seek a calculated preemptive first-strike option. *Soviet Military Power* (London: Royal United Services Institute, 1971), p. 51.

at least endeavor to approach, if not actually attain, the systematic character postulated by the formal taxonomy of Soviet military theory and can also safely embrace certain operating premises (such as the preemptive attack option and the belief in the "winnability" of nuclear war) that might well not be readily acceptable in a democratic state. Moreover, because of the highly centralized nature of the Soviet decision-making structure, Soviet doctrine is largely developed at the General Staff level with the active involvement of the Party leadership. As a consequence, it tends to reflect somewhat more integration and internal consistency than the military policies of countries where interservice rivalries are allowed to go on relatively unrestrained.

On the other hand, however, Soviet military doctrine is hardly immune to the bureaucratic tugging and hauling that occurs in any large and highly institutionalized state, irrespective of its particular form of government. Although spared substantial disruptive pressures by nongovernmental domestic constraints, Soviet doctrine is constantly buffeted within the contained universe of Soviet policymaking by countervailing institutional claims over such issues as how functional roles and missions should be distributed and how the limited Soviet resource allocation pie should be divided.[31] Consequently, it tends to constitute something of a "committee compromise" among the often divergent interests of the military, political, and defense industry elites, and also to mirror, through its occasional internal contradictions, those conflicts which remain unresolved or which seem endemic to the Soviet system. The perennial tension between the Party and the military professionals over the question of how defense decisionmaking authority should be divided, for example, is clearly reflected in the marked ambivalence which Soviet doctrinal statements exhibit toward this highly sensitive issue. Partly loyalists within the Main Political Administration of the Soviet military establishment, on the one hand, frequently downgrade the military's policymaking role and maintain that the complexities and demands of modern warfare require firm political direction and control over all contemporary strategic affairs.[32] Spokes-

men for the military professionals, on the other hand, while not denying the principle of Party supremacy, counter such assertions by pointing to the indispensability of military expertise in the policy process and by insisting that "politics is often forced to reckon with the demands of military strategy,"[33] an area of activity in which the military leaders presumably have a good deal to say. While these two differing perspectives are by no means wholly incompatible, they do point to a measure of Party-military contentiousness over the question of institutional roles and help to explain why Soviet doctrinal pronouncements generally tend to be less than explicit in their treatment of such matters as nuclear command and control arrangements, force-structure planning responsibilities, and the relative importance of the military voice in the overall policy process.

IMPERATIVES OF DOMESTIC AND FOREIGN AUDIENCE MANIPULATION

The question is often asked by Western analysts and commentators whether Soviet military doctrinal writings and policy statements are anything more than elaborate propaganda vehicles aimed at misleading the West about Soviet military capabilities and intentions. The question is by no means an unreasonable one, for the Soviet leadership explicitly regards its public pronouncements, among other things, as instruments for external communication and has not been deterred, on occasion, from consciously using those pronouncements to enhance the credibility of Soviet power in Western eyes by denying or covering up the existence of Soviet weaknesses. During the period of the American atomic monopoly from 1945 to 1949, for example, Soviet doctrinal pronouncements deprecating the strategic significance of nuclear weaponry were almost certainly inspired, at least in part, by the hard fact that the Soviets lacked such weaponry and had to compensate for their deficiency by assuming a public pose that it really made little difference to them.[34] Similarly, until

---

[31]For a careful examination of the institutional dynamics of this process, as well as for one of the best recent analyses of Soviet military policymaking generally, see Matthew P. Gallagher and Karl F. Spielmann, *Soviet Decisionmaking for Defense* (New York: Frederick A. Praeger, 1972).

[32]See, for example, the sharp assertions of Party primacy in military affairs contained in Major General V. Zemskov, "For the Theoretical Seminar: An Important Factor for Victory

in War," *Krasnaia Zvezda* (January 5, 1967), and Colonel A. Babin, "The Party—Leader of the USSR Armed Forces," *Krasnaia Zvezda* (April 6. 1967).

[33]Marshal V. D. Sokolovskii and Major General M. Cherednichenko, "On Contemporary Military Strategy," *Kommunist Vooruzhenykh Sil* 7 (April 1966).

[34]Interestingly, the Chinese followed the same basic pattern of deprecating the significance of nuclear weapons up to the time of their first nuclear test in October 1964, after which they progressively abandoned that line in favor of a considerably more sober and sophisticated attitude. For further discussion on this point, see George H. Quester, "On the Identification of Real and Pretended Communist Military Doctrine," *Journal of Conflict Resolution* (June 1966): 172–78.

U-2 reconnaissance and other sources of intelligence finally exposed his claims as a hollow
bluff, Khrushchev engaged in a systematic and
calculated campaign from 1957 to 1961 to exaggerate in his public statements the number
of ICBMs possessed by the Soviet Union and
thereby deceive the United States into believing
that the Soviets were far stronger than they
actually were.[35] As a general rule, however, this
sort of doctrinal manipulation for deceptive purposes has varied more or less inversely over time
both in feasibility and frequency of occurrence
with the ability of American intelligence capabilities to penetrate it. As long as the Soviet Union
was inaccessible to Western inspection, Soviet
leaders could successfully overstate the number
of military forces at their disposal almost at will.
Since the advent of sustained and highly reliable
American satellite surveillance of Soviet strategic developments, however, such deceptive efforts have lost most of their former ability to
persuade and thus have largely disappeared from
the Soviet propaganda arsenal.

Another way the Soviets seek to influence the
West through doctrinal manipulation is by adopting certain public declaratory stances that have
the effect of preempting or undermining the
strategies of their adversaries. The Soviet
rejection of McNamara's "city-avoidance" notions during the early 1960s, for example, put
the United States on clear notice that it could not
count on fighting a "clean" counterforce war
and thereby deprived it of the ability to seek any
significant self-reassurance from its numerically
superior ICBM capability. Similarly, the long-
standing Soviet insistence that any theater war in
Europe would quickly assume nuclear proportions had the effect of maximizing the deterrent
utility of the Soviet Union's inferior nuclear
forces by throwing a monkey wrench into many
of McNamara's more subtle calculations regarding the possibility of carefully controlled escalation below the nuclear firebreak. In both instances, of course, the United States could continue
to hope that in any real crisis in which the opposing strategic perspectives would be put to the
test, common sense would ultimately prevail over
doctrinal rigidity in Moscow and induce the
Soviets to see the wisdom of American strategic
thinking. Yet in the absence of such a crisis, those
Soviet doctrinal assertions managed to play skill-
fully on American uncertainties by forcing the

United States to base its "worst-case" contingency plans not on its own highly sophisticated concepts but rather on the lowest common
denominator dictated by declared Soviet intentions.

Notwithstanding these examples, however,
there are sharp limits beyond which the Soviets
cannot go in their efforts to structure foreign
audience perceptions simply through rhetorical
fiat. It is important to bear in mind in this regard
that Soviet military doctrine is not primarily a
set of carefully contrived external propaganda
poses but an important body of functional operating principles for internal consumption by the
Soviet military. Since the Soviet leadership can
scarcely afford to lie to its own officer corps about
its strategic intentions and objectives merely to
deceive the West, and since the size and complexity of the Soviet political-military infrastructure
preclude the communication of policy guidelines
solely through secret channels, it should only
stand to reason that the bulk of declared Soviet
military doctrine should reflect a reasonably
faithful image of actual Soviet strategic thinking.
Where the precise line separating propaganda
and reality should be drawn, of course, varies
from case to case and can be legitimately debated
by Western analysts. It is interesting to note,
however, that the contents of the restricted-
circulation Soviet General Staff journal *Voennaia Mysl'* (Military Thought) generally tend to
show a close correlation with the contents of the
unclassified Soviet military literature, suggesting
that the overwhelming majority of Soviet doctrinal pronouncements can be fairly accepted at
face value by the West.[36]

There is, on the other hand, one significant
area in which Soviet military doctrine does tend
to get "bent" by domestic manipulative considerations, and that area centers on the imperative
of maintaining a high degree of ideological *élan*
and fighting spirit among the armed forces. In
addition to its primary function of positing official military policy guidelines, Soviet doctrine
also has an important educational and exhorta-
tive role which manifests itself in occasional
drum-beating exercises aimed more at keeping
the troops motivated than at expressing the real
convictions of the political-military leadership.
The emphasis on the "morale factor" in modern
warfare which pervades Soviet doctrinal writings, for example, and the associated stress on

---

[35]A detailed analysis of this missile deception campaign
by Khrushchev may be found in Arnold L. Horelick and Myron
Rush, *Strategic Power and Soviet Foreign Policy* (Chicago:
University of Chicago Press, 1966).

[36]For an authoritative analysis of selected articles from
Voennaia Mysl' which tends to confirm this proposition, see
Raymond L. Garthoff, *Soviet Strategy in the Nuclear Age*
(New York: Frederick A. Praeger, 1961).

the primacy of men over machines which usually accompanies it, may be read in large part as an effort by the leadership to galvanize the Soviet forces *a priori* against what would undeniably be a severely dehumanizing and emotionally demanding experience for them if a nuclear war were indeed to occur. Similarly, the hard-line assertions in many Soviet military writings which reject as "fatalistic" the notion that a nuclear war cannot be meaningfully won probably reflect far less a genuine Soviet belief that nuclear war really constitutes a viable policy alternative than a desire to assure that the Soviet armed forces avoid embracing the defeatist conclusion that nuclear deterrence has invalidated their traditional *raison d'être*.[37]

SOME CONCLUDING CAVEATS

Having surveyed the various inputs and influences that interact in producing Soviet military doctrine, it remains to be asked how much the emergent picture helps to enhance our overall understanding of the Soviet strategic challenge. Without getting diverted into a detailed discussion of the methodology and problems of strategic threat analysis, we may fairly suggest that one ought to exercise considerable caution against assuming that Soviet doctrine can, by itself, tell us all we need to know. Up to a point, of course, doctrinal analysis is indispensable for providing insights into the nature of Soviet strategic thinking. For one thing, it reveals many of the basic assumptions that inform Soviet perceptions of such aspects of external reality as the nature of international relations, the character of the external threat, the security imperatives posed by that threat, and so on. For another thing, it provides some indication of the dominant image of a future war held by the Soviet leadership, including the way such a war would most likely be initiated, the role which would be played by various weapons and forces in waging it, and the basic hardware and policies necessary for deterring its occurrence, if possible, and for successfully fighting it if deterrence should fail. Finally, it casts useful light on what Soviet planners see as ideal or optimum in the realm of strategic affairs, such as the maintenance of an arsenal superior to that of the United States, the seizure of the initiative during the outset of any war, and the prosecution of war to a meaningful military victory. On all these counts, Soviet doctrine has

a great deal to say and deserves the most careful attention and scrutiny by Western defense analysts.

There are limits, however, beyond which exclusive reliance on doctrinal analysis can be not only unhelpful but downright misleading. To begin with, the mere fact that Soviet doctrine posits a certain imperative or goal is no assurance that Soviet behavior will always abide by it. The avowed Soviet doctrinal commitment to come to the direct aid of any of its socialist allies who might be attacked by the "imperialists," for example, provided little comfort to the North Vietnamese who had to bear the brunt of American bombing throughout the past half decade. Similarly, the strong emphasis assigned by formal Soviet military doctrine to the importance of achieving strategic superiority over the United States has been explicitly contradicted in practice by the Soviet Union's accession during the SALT negotiations to the principle of "equal security" for each superpower and by its consequent disavowal (along with the United States) of any intention to seek a unilateral advantage in the strategic nuclear balance.[38]

Second, the fact that Soviet doctrine prescribes certain textbook-like rules for fighting a nuclear war (such as preempting upon receipt of unambiguous warning of an imminent attack and targeting Soviet forces against enemy cities as well as military installations) in no way guarantees that those rules would necessarily be followed if a confrontation were indeed to get out of hand and come to blows. It has not been uncommon in crises of the past for both superpowers as a first order of business to cast aside their prearranged game plans and fall back on day-to-day improvisation to carry themselves away from the brink of war. Thus while Soviet doctrine formally insists that the administrative and command centers of the enemy would be among the first targets to be attacked in any strategic war, it is not unreasonable to suppose that in a gradually intensifying crisis, the Soviets might well discover a compelling eleventh-hour interest in keeping the American decisionmaking authority in Washington intact for intrawar bargaining purposes.[39]

---

[37] See, for example, Lieutenant Colonel Ye. Rybkin, "On the Essence of World Nuclear-Missile War," *Kommunist Vooruzhenykh Sil* 17 (September 1965): 50–56.

[38] An excellent discussion of this growing dichotomy between actual Soviet strategic policies and many of the formal precepts of Soviet military doctrine is presented in David Holloway, "Strategic Concepts and Soviet Policy," *Survival* (November 1971): 364–69.

[39] The point here is not that we can *count* on the possibility that the Soviets will abandon their doctrinal principles during a nuclear crisis in favor of enlightened self-interest. It is, rather, that we should not automatically dismiss that possibility merely because peacetime Soviet doctrinal pronouncements rule it out.

Last, and most important, Soviet military doctrine has little to contribute toward the prediction of such imponderables as future Soviet strategic intentions and force-posture levels, for the simple reason that these matters are not decided *a priori* by the political-military elite but rather are worked out only after intense internal struggling throughout the entire upper echelons of the Soviet decisionmaking hierarchy.[40] A full understanding of Soviet military policy, therefore, requires far more than simple content analysis of formal Soviet doctrine. It requires an analytical approach which regards Soviet policy not as a neatly structured offspring of leadership fiat, but as a complex and often jury-rigged outgrowth of a dynamic political process that pits such relative constants as ideological imperatives and doctrinal precepts against the vagaries of personal power struggles, bureaucratic rivalries, and related procedural idiosyncrasies of the Soviet political system.

---

[40]Assumptions to the contrary, in fact, have been among the principal causes of past American over-estimations of the Soviet strategic threat. For some valuable and well-informed comments on this point, see A. W. Marshall, *Problems of Estimating Military Power*, P-3417 (Santa Monica, Calif.: The RAND Corporation, August 1966).

THE EVOLUTION OF CHINESE MILITARY POLICY

HARRY HARDING

Disputes in China over military policy involve struggles among complex coalitions containing both military and civilian elements. Since 1949 there have been doctrinal shifts between advocacy of an "army organized to fight a People's War" on the one hand and support for a professional "military establishment designed to engage in modern conventional and nuclear warfare" on the other. Such doctrinal conflicts have been resolved through compromises designed to "satisfy most of the competing interests."

Harry Harding is an Assistant Professor of Political Science at Stanford University who has written a number of articles on Chinese politics. A consultant to the RAND Corporation since 1969, he was graduated from Princeton in 1967 and received his Ph.D. from Stanford in 1973.

Military policy has been one of the most controversial issues in contemporary Chinese politics. On at least four occasions since 1949, military questions, usually in conjunction with other political, economic, or international issues, have become the center of serious conflict at the highest levels of Chinese leadership. Both Chinese defense ministers—P'eng Teh-huai (1954–59) and Lin Piao (1959–71)—were removed from office after dramatic confrontations over military matters.

Why have military issues been so controversial in China? One basic reason is that Chinese Communist leaders have had to cope

---

An earlier version of this chapter appeared as "The Making of Chinese Military Policy," in William W. Whitson (ed.), The Military and Political Power in China in the 1970s *(New York: Frederick A. Praeger, 1972), pp. 361–85.*

For their helpful comments on various drafts of this essay, the author is indebted to William Whitson, Alexander George, John W. Lewis, John W. Woodmansee, and members of the Department of Political Science of the United States Air Force Academy.

with several competing models of military strategy, organization, and weaponry.[1] One has been the tradition of Chinese Communist guerrilla warfare, itself drawn from the rich heritage of local banditry and peasant rebellion in China. Another has been the model of conventional land war, first introduced to China by the West in the nineteenth century, and then, in a more modern and politicized form, taught to young Communist officers by Russian advisers in the 1920s and 30s. Yet another has been the model of strategic nuclear warfare developed in the Soviet Union and the United States since World War II. And still another is the contemporary model of limited war—of "coercive diplomacy"—in which highly sophisticated land, sea, and air forces are employed to support limited diplomatic objectives. Faced with these competing models, Chinese leaders have not always been able to agree which one is best suited to China's strategic needs. What is more, they have not always been able to agree what China's strategic needs actually are. Trained in the pre-nuclear era, and heirs to the Chinese traditions of peasant warfare, senior Chinese leaders have not found it easy to devise a strategic posture for the nuclear age.

A second fundamental source of controversy lies in the Janus-faced nature of the Chinese People's Liberation Army (PLA). Ever since its founding, the PLA has been assigned domestic as well as strategic responsibilities. It has been required, as Mao has said, to be not only a fighting force, but also a political force and a production force. The determination of Chinese military policy, therefore, has involved the search for the best balance among these domestic and strategic roles. This, in turn, has required that Chinese policymakers clearly assign relative priorities to economic considerations, domestic political goals, and external security requirements. In a very important sense, therefore, military policy lies near the heart of the Chinese political process. In it are reflected the most basic decisions concerning China's national priorities.

This essay attempts to summarize the evolution of Chinese military policy since the end of the Korean War, and to analyze the process by which military policy is made. It is divided into three parts. The first section presents a framework for the analysis of military policy in China. It introduces the competing strategic options, defines the terms in which they are discussed by

Chinese leaders, and identifies the major participants in the military policymaking process. In the second section, this framework is used to provide a brief history of the development of Chinese military policy since 1953. The third section, drawing on the chronology, attempts to identify the major trends in Chinese military policy, and to discover the circumstances which have produced serious controversy over strategic issues. It concludes with some speculation concerning the prospects for China's military posture.

Much of the analysis, and even much of the historical narrative, that will be presented below is highly speculative. Although the Cultural Revolution has provided Western scholars with invaluable information about the policymaking process in China, our understanding of the formulation of policy—and particularly the formulation of military policy—is still far from complete.[2] The evidence contained in the public statements of Chinese military planners, the Red Guard materials published during the Cultural Revolution, and the internal Communist Party documents occasionally released by the Chinese Nationalists on Taiwan unfortunately remains highly fragmentary. It must be combined, often in frustrating proportions, with assumptions about bureaucratic politics and the intuition of the "Pekingologist." The resulting analysis is necessarily highly tentative, but the importance of the subject may justify the effort.

A FRAMEWORK FOR ANALYSIS

Alternative Military Options

Ever since 1949, the makers of Chinese Communist military policy have confronted a very fundamental issue: what kind of army should they build? As already indicated, Chinese military planners have had a wide range of alternative models available to them. In their own writings on military policy, however, the Chinese have tended to reduce the issue to a single, stark choice: between the "proletarian" line on military policy and the "bourgeois" line.[3] Accordingly, Western analysts have also discussed Chinese military policy in terms of dichotomies. Some have written of the tension between the

[1]For an elaboration of this point, using a different set of models than those presented here, see William W. Whitson, *The Chinese High Command: A History of Communist Military Politics, 1927-71* (New York: Praeger, 1973), Introduction.

[2]For a summary of the Chinese policymaking process, based largely on information published during the Cultural Revolution, see Michel Oksenberg, "Policy-Making Under Mao, 1949-68: An Overview," in John M. H. Lindbeck (ed.), *China: Management of a Revolutionary Society* (Seattle: University of Washington Press, 1971), pp. 79-115.

[3]See, for example, "Basic Differences Between the Proletarian and Bourgeois Military Lines," *Peking Review*, November 24, 1967, pp. 11-16.

"political" and "professional" orientations toward military problems;[4] others, of the struggle between "reds" and "experts" among Chinese military leaders;[5] and still others, of the conflict between the "old" and the "new" in the Chinese army.[6] Although using different terms, these formulations all imply that the basic decision facing Chinese leaders is whether to maintain an army organized and equipped to fight a people's war, or to develop a military establishment designed to engage in modern conventional and nuclear warfare.

The essential characteristics of these two competing options can be sketched quite quickly. An army designed to engage in people's war would consist of regular infantry forces, guerrilla units, and a large popular militia, each armed with simple weapons and skilled in close combat and night fighting. There would be virtually no air force, no navy, no complex equipment. In defending China against invasion, such an army would employ the strategy known as "luring deep": retreating before an enemy advance, falling back to prepared defense positions deep inside China, encouraging the invaders to disperse their forces and overextend their supply lines, seizing every opportunity to surround and annihilate isolated enemy units, and then launching a general counterattack once the enemy's initial momentum had been spent. To maximize the flexibility and initiative of Chinese forces, and to increase the probability of surviving the initial enemy blow, China would be divided into several regional theaters, with regional and unit commanders assigned a large measure of operational autonomy.

Success in people's war depends not only on the military training of the troops, but also on their morale, and on their ability to rely on the civilian population for supplies, recruits, and intelligence. As a result, people's war strategies assign extensive responsibilities to the political commissar and Party committee of each unit. These political cadres must ensure the political indoctrination of the soldiers, the maintenance of troop morale, and the effective co-ordination of military operations with the activities of local civilian governments.

If a professional army were developed, on the other hand, modern air, ground, and naval forces, co-ordinated at the national level and equipped with highly sophisticated weapons, would largely supplant the lightly armed guerrilla forces and popular militia of people's war. Rather than lure the enemy deep, and thereby permit him to occupy China's coastal cities and destroy much of her industry, the Chinese army would be prepared to conduct a linear defense of China's borders, open a second front against enemy installations outside China, or even preempt an anticipated enemy attack. Compared to the lightly armed infantry forces of people's war, the professional army requires much less logistical support from the civilian population, but much greater technical proficiency from its own soldiers. For both these reasons, the roles of the political commissar and the Party committee—so vital to the success of people's war—would be substantially reduced in a fully professional army. The amount of time devoted to political education would be restricted, so as to permit greater attention to technical training.

An analysis which interprets the evolution of Chinese military policy as a continuing dialogue between proponents of people's war and advocates of military modernization can provide important insights into the military policymaking process, as a glance through the literature on the subject will show. But it can also be misleading in two significant respects. First of all, these two "basic options"—people's war and professionalization—are not as mutually exclusive as they might seem. As we will see, the Chinese have found it entirely possible to strike a balance between the two, and to devise a military posture which combines important elements of both people's war and professionalization. To strike such a balance can have both military and political advantages. Militarily, it provides a way to enjoy some of the strategic advantages of both options; politically, it offers an attractive compromise to all the participants in the policymaking process. The problem facing Chinese military planners, therefore, has generally not been to choose between guerrilla forces and a modern military. Instead, it has been to find the best balance, or combination, of people's war and professionalization.

Second, "professionalization" is not itself a single, well-defined option. In the Chinese context a "professional" army might take one of several forms. Chinese planners, for example, have tended to see a distinction between a modern army designed for purely defensive or deterrent purposes and a modern army capable of

[4]William Whitson, "The Concept of Military Generation: The Chinese Communist Case," *Asian Survey* 8, no. 11 (November 1968): 921–47.
[5]Alexander L. George, *The Chinese Communist Army in Action: The Korean War and Its Aftermath* (New York: Columbia University Press, 1967), Chap. 11.
[6]Ellis Joffe, "The Conflict Between Old and New in the Chinese Army," *China Quarterly* 18 (April–June 1964): 118–40.

projecting military force well beyond China's borders. Perhaps related to this, they have also seen a choice between the modernization of the ground forces and the development of nuclear weapons, nuclear delivery systems, and air defense capabilities. All of these, when compared to the ideal model of people's war, are "professional" options, but they differ significantly one from another. An analysis which focusses exclusively on the conflict between the proponents of people's war and the advocates of military modernization may very well ignore the fact that there are several competing approaches to professionalization. On many occasions, in fact, it would be more accurate to speak of the competition in China among people's war, modern ground forces, and strategic forces than of a choice between people's war and professionalization alone.

The Evaluation of Alternative Policies

The discussion of military policy in China over the last twenty years has reflected three sets of continuing concerns. The first, of course, has been the development of the capability to meet, or deter, expected threats to Chinese security. Beyond this, Chinese leaders have also sought to develop an effective strategic posture at the lowest possible cost, and in a way that would be compatible with their view of the domestic responsibilities of the PLA. Obviously, each of these three concerns has been more salient to some Chinese leaders than to others. But, taken together, they have provided the criteria by which participants in the military policymaking process have evaluated alternative strategic options, promoted the option they favored, and criticized the competing options proposed by others. These three criteria, in other words, have provided the terms of debate for military policymaking in China.

Of the three, the criterion most frequently invoked in public discussions of military problems has been the effectiveness of alternative strategic options in meeting expected threats to China's security. These threats have most certainly changed over time; the fear of a Nationalist invasion supported by American air and naval power has been almost totally replaced by a fear of a Russian preemptive strike against Chinese nuclear installations, for example. But even more important, Chinese leaders have frequently differed in their estimate of the type of threat that China has faced at any given moment, and thus in the strategic posture they believe China should adopt. The relationship between threat perception and policy advocacy is almost certainly a complex one. Some Chinese military planners have undoubtedly attempted to proceed as disinterestedly and objectively as possible to identify the threats facing their country, and then to develop the most effective strategy for coping with them. Others, like their counterparts in other countries, appear to have advocated a military force posture because of its economic or political advantages, and then sought to justify their choice by inventing an appropriate "threat" and by discounting other threatening situations which might support competing options. One can therefore never be sure how seriously a statement of perceived threat should be taken.

In general, public discussions of Chinese strategic policy have referred to three categories of military threats to China. Those who advocate the development of strategic nuclear forces and sophisticated air defense capabilities have warned of the threat of conventional and nuclear air strikes against China, and of the need to develop the capability to defend against them or to launch retaliatory attacks. The proponents of people's war, on the other hand, have argued that China could survive even a full-scale nuclear attack, and that the enemy would be forced to mount a massive invasion of China, comparable to the Japanese invasion of China in the 1930s, in an attempt to bring the war to an end. In such a case, they have argued, China's most effective strategy would be to decline to meet the technologically superior enemy on its own terms, but to utilize her own vast territory and her superiority in manpower, engage in strategic retreat, and "drown the enemy" in people's war. In responding to these arguments, the advocates of more modern, specialized ground forces have usually referred to the possibility that China would have to fight beyond her borders, as in Korea, which would require a projective military capability beyond that provided by people's war. In addition, they have pointed out that a people's war strategy would require the surrender of much Chinese territory, including in all probability China's major cities and her most important industrial areas, and have called for the development of armed forces which could conduct a more linear defense of China's borders.

When viewed in terms of strategic effectiveness alone, the proponents of people's war are at a considerable disadvantage. People's war might well be highly effective against a massive ground invasion, but could hardly deal with air strikes against selected Chinese targets. There is little doubt that some sort of modern army could cope more effectively with a broader range of military threats than could a people's war force.

But strategic effectiveness is not the only criterion used to evaluate military options in China. In her study of Chinese military policy in the 1950s, still the best single study of the period, Alice Langley Hsieh developed the proposition that economic factors play a crucial role in the formulation of Chinese military policy.[7] Chinese leaders concerned with economic development, Hsieh concluded, will attempt to hold the military budget to a minimum.

On this level of debate, it is the proponents of military modernization who are at the disadvantage. The development of specialized ground forces, air defense capabilities, nuclear weaponry, and the rest of the panoply of modern warfare would obviously require a substantial diversion of resources from the civilian economy, with no assured ability to compete effectively with the more advanced economies of the Soviet Union and the United States. The proponents of people's war, on the other hand, are able to point to the relatively low cost of maintaining lightly armed infantry forces, and the ability of a popular militia to contribute actively to economic construction in rural areas. As a result, the proponents of professionalization have frequently tended to exaggerate—or at least to describe very graphically—the threats to Chinese security, in an attempt to justify the economic sacrifices that rapid modernization would entail. In response, their opponents have tended to discount the severity of the external threat, or else to argue that it could be managed successfully by diplomatic means.

Finally, a third element in Chinese military planning, and one that has received insufficient attention in Western analyses, is the fact that the PLA is not confined to strategic roles, but, in accordance with its revolutionary traditions, has been assigned a variety of domestic tasks as well. Ever since 1949, the PLA has routinely provided internal security, manpower for civilian economic projects, support for agricultural activities during peak farming periods, training for government and Party cadres, and, particularly during the 1960s, leadership for ideological reform campaigns. At the same time, as part of a nation undergoing intensive efforts to remold its political culture, the PLA, like all other sectors of society, has been expected to devote time to political indoctrination and ideological education as well as military training.

To a very large degree, all Chinese military leaders appear to accept the necessity and desirability of performing these domestic roles. Nonetheless, beyond a certain point, the performance of domestic roles becomes increasingly incompatible with the creation of a professional army. An air force interceptor unit, for example, must devote so much time to training and maintenance that it cannot readily engage in civilian work. Moreover, its location in relatively remote, high security bases prevents it from having regular contact with civilians.[8] To build a professional army, in short, requires a concomitant restriction of the soldier's sideline occupations as policeman, cadre teacher, ideologue, and laborer.

This has provided the proponents of people's war with perhaps their most persuasive case. Unlike a professional army, an army designed to wage people's war can readily perform domestic economic and political roles. Its simple weaponry requires less time be spent in technical training; its nonspecialized organization can easily be turned to civilian tasks; indeed, its very strategy requires close and continuing ties with the local population. A professional army, on the other hand, runs the risk of becoming "divorced from the masses"—a very serious violation of Maoist political and social values.

All of this suggests an important conclusion: the three criteria—strategic effectiveness, cost and compatibility with the PLA's domestic roles—support somewhat different military postures. The more "professional" options provide the capability to meet a broader range of military threats, but they require a willingness to accept substantial economic burdens and to sacrifice some of the PLA's domestic roles. People's war, on the other hand, may have questionable strategic effectiveness, but remains attractive because of its low cost and its compatibility with the domestic roles of the Chinese military. For this reason, the assignment of priorities to these three criteria is a major factor in the determination of China's strategic posture. And Chinese leaders may find it tempting to try to strike a balance between people's war and modernization, rather than to make a clear choice between them.

Major Participants and Their Preferences

All the available evidence indicates that the policymaking process in China is characterized by conflict, coalition, and compromise among competing bureaucratic interest groups. Unfortu-

[7]Alice Langley Hsieh, *Communist China's Strategy in the Nuclear Era* (Englewood Cliffs, N.J.: Prentice-Hall, 1962).

[8]For a development of this point, see Allen S. Whiting, "China: The Struggle for Power," *The New Republic* (December 4, 1971): 19–21.

nately, however, the evidence is not detailed enough to indicate clearly which policies each group prefers. In the absence of conclusive data, the analyst must rely on theories of bureaucratic politics to advance some speculations about the preferences of different civilian and military agencies concerning military policy.

Basically, models of bureaucratic politics suggest that organizations seek to increase or preserve their prestige and resources, and to prevent encroachment by other organizations on their roles and missions.[9] They do so for two somewhat different, but reinforcing, reasons. First, the members of an organization may selfishly seek the increased prestige, power, income, or self-satisfaction which accompany an extension of their organization's responsibilities or an expansion of its budget. But, second, they may also genuinely believe that their organization is better suited than any other to meet the task at hand. For whichever reason, organization theory predicts that, when problems, challenges, or new opportunities arise, each organization involved with the issue will tend to advocate solutions in which it would play a major role, and will oppose proposals by other organizations that would encroach on its missions or reduce its resources.

These assumptions, it should be emphasized, do not permit infallible predictions of the policy preferences of the participants in the Chinese policymaking process. In China, organizational spokesmen are expected to rise above the advocacy of narrow bureaucratic interests, and seek the best solutions to problems, regardless of their impact on the roles or budgets of the organizations concerned. Blatant organizational opportunism is frowned upon, and those who engage in it are often seriously punished for doing so. Perhaps for this reason, there have been several instances when participants in the military policymaking process appear to have espoused positions that ran counter to a strict definition of their organizational interests, or refused to support proposals that would have benefited their organizations. Bureaucratic interest, in short, represents but one factor in deciding an individual's policy preferences, and is not always the determining one.

Nevertheless, models of bureaucratic politics can help us identify the major participants in the policymaking process, and make preliminary estimates of their policy preferences. For the sake of argument, therefore, let us set the problems with these models aside, and assume that Chinese organizations will support those strategic options that will maximize their own political and economic resources, and will enhance or protect their roles in Chinese society. If we do so, we can identify several civilian and military agencies as having an important interest in the formulation of strategic policy.[10]

In the first place, there are several competing interest groups within the PLA itself. The General Political Department, which is charged with supervising the implementation of the army's domestic roles, and with conducting political training within the PLA, could be expected to support a people's war strategy.[11] Similarly, those units which would play a major role in people's war (particularly the local forces and the militia) could also be expected to oppose the development of a professional, modern army.[12] At the other extreme are the General Staff Department, the navy, the air force, the "Second Artillery Corps," which is the strategic missile arm, and the General Rear Services Department, which is responsible for logistics and weapons production.[13] All these departments and service arms probably advocate the rapid development of a technically sophisticated, highly professionalized army, with minimal political and economic responsibilities. Somewhere between these two rather extreme positions lie the commanders of China's eleven military regions and the commanders of the approximately thirty-five main force army corps. These ground force commanders probably reject traditional forms of people's war (particularly reliance on the militia) as an ineffectual strategic posture, and oppose a level of domestic activity so high that it threatened the military effectiveness of the PLA. On the other hand, they probably also seek to maintain the relative autonomy of the military regions from central command, and defend the budgets of the ground forces from encroachment by the

[9]For a pioneering discussion of the "organizational process" and "bureaucratic politics" models, see Graham T. Allison, *Conceptual Models and the Cuban Missile Crisis: Rational Policy, Organization Process, and Bureaucratic Politics*, P-3919 (Santa Monica, Calif.: The RAND Corporation, August, 1968). See also Anthony Downs, *Inside Bureaucracy* (Boston: Little, Brown, 1967).

[10]For another attempt to identify the interests of various groups in the military decisionmaking process, see William Whitson, "Organizational Perspectives and Decision-Making in the Chinese Communist High Command," in Robert Scalapino (ed.), *Elites in the People's Republic of China* (Seattle: University of Washington Press, 1972), pp. 381–415. Reprinted in this volume, pp. 24–38.

[11]Glenn G. Dick, "The General Political Department," in William W. Whitson (ed.), *The Military and Political Power in China in the 1970s* (New York: Praeger, 1972), pp. 171–84.

[12]Harvey Nelsen, "Regional and Paramilitary Ground Forces," in *ibid.*, pp. 135–52.

[13]Richard E. Gillespie and John C. Sims, Jr., "The General Rear Services Department," in *ibid.*, pp. 185–214.

nuclear weapons program, the air force, and the navy. In addition, because of their close ties with provincial officials, and their membership on provincial Party committees, they are also aware of the desirability of some military participation in public security work, agriculture, and water conservation. On balance, these regional and corps commanders may well desire a more modern variant of people's war: a strategic posture which maintains emphasis on relatively lightly armed ground forces, and which permits a balance between the strategic and domestic roles of the PLA, but which involves more modern equipment—advanced infantry weapons, trucks and personnel carriers, some light armor and artillery—than was available during the Revolution.

In addition, there are several civilian interest groups which have an interest in military policy. Party leaders who are concerned with maintaining the ideological purity of Chinese society may well believe that a professionalized, specialized army is incompatible with revolutionary values. Instead, they favor the concept of "every man a soldier," the organization of a large militia, and the maintenance of a small standing army which could serve as a political work team when required. In short, these leaders would support the strategic posture associated with people's war. Cadres responsible for agriculture, even though less concerned with ideological questions, may also support people's war because it permits the Army to assign substantial amounts of manpower to agriculture during peak farming periods. In contrast, many cadres in heavy industry—particularly in electronics—would benefit from the development and production of the advanced weapons systems associated with military modernization.

Finally, there are probably civilian agencies which favor the modernization and professionalization of the PLA, but at a gradual pace. The economic managers in both the Party and state bureaucracies can be expected to support the concept of a professional army, disengaged from political and managerial activities in the civilian sectors of the economy. In addition, they would also favor the development of the capability to defend the vital economic regions of Manchuria and coastal China, rather than abandon them under a strategy of "luring deep."[14] At the same time, however, these agencies may also fear that their own budgets would be cut to finance the

rapid modernization of the army, and therefore may seek to moderate the pace of military professionalization.

This tentative prediction of the policy preferences of civilian and military interest groups should illustrate a crucial point: the formation of military policy in China is not characterized by a sharp division between military and civilian leaders. Disputes over military policy are not "Party-Army" debates. Rather, there is a wide spectrum of opinion on military affairs both within the Army, and within the civilian bureaucracy. Thus, the participants in military policymaking tend to be complex coalitions, each of which contains both civilian and military elements.

CHANGES IN CHINA'S STRATEGIC POSTURE

The preceding analysis of the major issues and participants in the military policymaking process provides a useful framework for a discussion of the evolution of Chinese military policy since 1953. Of particular interest are the four instances of serious controversy and debate that occurred in 1955–56, 1959, 1965, and 1971. It is important to recognize that none of these four episodes dealt exclusively with military policy; each also involved other issues that, in some instances, were even more significant than military matters. The debate of 1955–56, for example, accompanied a broader discussion of the allocation of resources among various sectors of the economy so as to achieve the most rapid rate of economic growth. The purge of Minister of Defense P'eng Teh-huai in 1959 was part of a bitter controversy over the wisdom of the Great Leap Forward. The so-called "Vietnam debate" of 1965 was not only a response to American escalation in Southeast Asia, but also the opening round of the Cultural Revolution, and reflected the increasing opposition in the Party to Mao's positions on economic, educational, and organizational issues. Finally, the purge of Lin Piao can be attributed not only to his views on foreign relations and military policy, but also to his attempts to strengthen his own position as Mao's successor. As the purpose of this essay is to describe military policy, however, the other issues involved in these four episodes will be described only in passing.

After the signing of the Korean armistice, Chinese leaders intensified a program of military modernization that had been initiated dur-

---

[14]This is suggested in Whitson, *The Chinese High Command*, pp. 455–56.

ing the Korean War.[15] In part, this program was a response to the serious difficulties experienced by the Chinese armies in Korea; but beyond this, it was also part of a broader effort to learn from Soviet experience in all sectors of society. In the PLA, the greatest emphasis was placed on the standardization and modernization of ground force equipment, through both the import of weapons from the Soviet Union, and the establishment of weapons production facilities in China. Substantial attention was also paid to the strengthening of the Chinese air force, again through the purchase of fighter aircraft from the Soviet Union and through the resumption of domestic aircraft production. China did not attempt to develop her own nuclear capability, however, but relied instead on her military alliance with the Soviet Union, signed in 1950, to deter a nuclear attack by the United States.

During this period, the Soviet Union provided China not only with more modern weapons, but also with professional organizational principles and strategic doctrine. Soviet military manuals were translated into Chinese; Soviet military advisers dispatched to China; and Chinese officers sent to the Soviet Union for training. A system of military discipline was established, military ranks and honors created, specialized service branches formed, and formal military training emphasized, all along Soviet lines.

By 1955, however, consensus over the pace at which this modernization should occur began to break down. Some of China's most senior professional officers—most notably Chief of Staff Su Yü, Director of Military Training Liu Po-ch'eng, and Inspector-General Yeh Chien-ying—argued that the Eisenhower-Dulles policies of "containment" and "liberation," the signing of the Mutual Defense Treaty between Washington and Taipei, the establishment of a network of military alliances in Asia, and the American threats to use nuclear weapons against China during the Quemoy crisis of 1954–55, all indicated a significant probability that the United States might launch a nuclear attack against China. In response, they proposed that the modernization of the PLA be substantially accelerated, through the expansion of domestic weapons production, increased purchase of weapons from the Soviet Union, and expanded expenditures for research and development.[16] It is also likely that Su, Liu, and Yeh suggested that China begin developing its own nuclear weapons.

This proposal was made at a time when Chinese leaders had hoped to be able to reduce the military budget and channel all available resources into economic development under the First Five-Year Plan. The arguments of the military professionals that these priorities be reversed were not convincing to a coalition of military and civilian interests desiring an acceleration of economic growth. Led by Defense Minister P'eng Teh-huai, and probably including Liu Shao-ch'i and Finance Minister Li Hsien-nien, this second group reasoned that an American attack on China could be deterred both by a cautious Chinese foreign policy and through the invocation of the Soviet nuclear umbrella. In the unlikely event that deterrence failed, China could ride out an American nuclear attack, and then defeat the inevitable American invasion through reliance on people's war. It was neither necessary nor desirable, they argued, to divert funds from civilian projects to military preparations; balanced military modernization could best be achieved as a part of the long-term development of the economy, not through costly and inefficient "quick fixes."

The debate was resolved in April 1956 by Mao Tse-tung's speech "The Ten Great Relationships."[17] It is extremely significant that, in this speech, Mao accepted the necessity for military modernization. Moreover, despite his earlier claims that atomic weapons were a "paper tiger," and not as "terrible" as they seemed, Mao also endorsed the idea that China should begin the development of its own nuclear arsenal. But Mao also declared that the modernization of the PLA should not be permitted to restrict economic development, and that the military's share should be reduced to 30% of the state budget. Accepting the argument that only a program of sustained economic development could support military modernization, Mao asked, "Do you want atom bombs? Then you ought to reduce defense expenses proportionately and spend more on economic construction. If you only pretend to want atom bombs, you will not reduce defense expenditures proportionately and will spend less on economic construction."

---

[15]For details, see John Gittings, *The Role of the Chinese Army*, (New York: Oxford University Press, 1967), Chaps. 6, 7.

[16]Hsieh, *Nuclear Era.*

[17]Mao's speech is available in Jerome Ch'en (ed.), *Mao* (Englewood Cliffs, N.J.: Prentice-Hall, 1969), p. 71.

Mao's speech set the stage for a compromise between the two competing groups. While Mao indicated that economic development should have priority over the modernization of the PLA, he also made it clear that military modernization should not be sacrificed for the sake of economic development. According to Alice Hsieh, the outcome of the 1955–56 debate was that the military professionals were permitted to begin research on nuclear weapons, and increase the production of conventional weapons, but were required to do so at a slower pace than they had originally proposed.

The domestic responsibilities of the PLA do not appear to have been an issue in the debate of 1955–56. Indeed, both sides in the controversy appear to have assumed that the army's domestic roles were a less important consideration than either the military budget or China's national security. Later in 1956, however, increasing attention was paid to the question of the PLA's role in Chinese society.

At first, the issue was how to reconcile the modernization and professionalization of the PLA with its revolutionary traditions.[18] By the end of 1956, there seems to have been a widespread consensus, both inside and outside the army, that singleminded modernization along Soviet lines had had serious effects on the comradely relations between officers and men, the close relationship between PLA units and the local communities in which they were stationed, and the commitment to ideological principles which had characterized the Red Army before 1949. This concern with preserving the revolutionary heritage of the PLA was related to a growing tendency in all areas to question the applicability of Soviet models to China. At this point, the solution was to strengthen the political education of the troops, but to continue the modernization of the PLA's weaponry and strategy. As in other sectors of Chinese society, the goal was to preserve "redness" while building "expertise."

When the Great Leap Forward was launched in 1958, however, even greater changes were made in Chinese military policy. The amount of uncompensated time the PLA contributed to agricultural production increased fifteen-fold between 1956 and 1958. The average soldier, who had spent 1.5 days in "free labor" in 1956 and 8 days in 1957, now spent 24 days in non-

military activities in 1958.[19] Moreover, the Great Leap seemed to promise a major transformation of both strategic principles and force posture. The validity of people's war as a defense strategy was vigorously reasserted, and the militia, to which little attention had been paid during the early 1950s, was greatly expanded. Indeed, if Chinese statements at the time are to be believed, the militia was considered to be as important to Chinese security as the regular forces, if not more so. The commitment to military modernization appeared to have been suspended, if not revoked.

It is quite probable that the Great Leap Forward initially received broad support within the PLA, among professionals as well as more politically oriented officers. Even the proponents of military modernization may have hoped that the Leap would produce rapid economic expansion, part of which could later be channeled into military development.[20] By mid-1959, however, serious opposition to the Leap had emerged among professional military men. This opposition stemmed, in essence, from three sources. First, the country faced an extremely serious agricultural crisis, both because of the flaws in the very conception of a Great Leap Forward, and because of the exaggerated manner in which it had been implemented. The agricultural crisis, in turn, greatly weakened the morale of Chinese soldiers, most of whom were of peasant origins, and many of whom were receiving word of serious food shortages in their native villages. Second, the emphasis on political training in the PLA, its deep involvement in domestic economic activities, and the disparagement of the regular forces in favor of the militia all contributed to an increasing conviction among China's professional officers that the military effectiveness of the PLA was threatened. And finally, as in 1955, an important role was played by an international factor: the deterioration of Sino-Soviet relations. The 1958 Quemoy crisis had once again underlined America's apparent willingness to go to the brink of war over the offshore islands, and had also brought into question the reliability of the Soviet nuclear umbrella. From the Chinese point of view, Soviet support in the crisis came only after the Chinese had borne the greatest risks, and even then seemed somewhat grudging. Less than a year later, perhaps out of disdain for the Great Leap

[18]For discussion, see Ellis Joffe, *Party and Army: Professionalism and Political Control in the Chinese Officer Corps, 1949–1964*, Harvard East Asian Monograph No. 19 (Cambridge: Harvard University Press, 1967).

[19]For details, see Gittings, *Chinese Army*, Chaps. 8, 9. These figures are calculated from data presented on pp. 181–82 and 305.

[20]Whitson, *The Chinese High Command*, p. 526.

Forward, perhaps out of fear of Chinese "recklessness" in international affairs, Khrushchev cancelled an agreement to assist the Chinese in the development of nuclear weapons.

When viewed from this perspective, the purge of Defense Minister P'eng Teh-huai, Chief of Staff Huang K'o-ch'eng, and other military officers in August 1959 can be traced, at least in part, to their objections to the impact of the Great Leap Forward on China's strategic posture.[21] At the 8th Plenum of the Central Committee, which met at Lushan in August 1959, P'eng submitted a "letter of opinion" to Mao, in which he presented a highly critical assessment of the Leap. Moreover, there is reason to believe that P'eng had discussed this letter, in which he called the Leap an example of "petty-bourgeois fanaticism," with Nikita Khrushchev before presenting it to Mao. P'eng's recommendation, we can surmise, was that China should abandon many of the Great Leap policies, return to a program of military modernization, pay much less attention to developing the militia, and attempt to repair China's deteriorating relations with the Soviet Union. All these steps would be necessary to ensure China's national security.

Although P'eng was dismissed from office, not all of the views he expressed at Lushan were repudiated. Instead, the outcome of the 1959 debate—like that of the 1955–56 controversy—was a compromise, with Lin Piao, P'eng's successor as Defense Minister, redressing the balance between the army's domestic and strategic functions.[22] Lin is most frequently associated with the intensification of political training in the PLA, the rejuvenation of Party branches throughout the army, the reinforcement of the authority of the political commissars, the introduction of the study of the works of Mao Tse-tung, and the abolition of military ranks. But he resumed the commitment to the modernization of the PLA in several significant ways. The amount of time which the PLA was required to devote to nonmilitary activities was reduced. The militia was gradually relegated to

economic, rather than military, duties. And substantial resources were devoted to the nuclear program, the air force, and the navy. Lin's success as defense minister was demonstrated as much by the easy Chinese victory in the Sino-Indian border war of 1962, and the explosion of China's first nuclear device in 1964, as it was by Mao's increasing reliance on the PLA domestically in the years just preceding the Cultural Revolution.

In strategic terms, Lin's program was an intriguing balance of people's war and modernization. The ground forces remained essentially a regionally organized, light infantry force, designed to engage in domestic activities in peacetime, and to wage a protracted people's war in the event of conflict. In contrast, the air force, the navy, and the nuclear weapons program developed along much more professional lines. A five-year program for the modernization of the air force was launched in the early 1960s. As a result of this program, China was able to produce its own MiG-21s by 1965, and its own TU-16 medium bombers and F-9 fighter bombers by the end of the decade. The air defense network was extended to protect the interior of China, as well as the coastal regions.[23] A program of naval construction was also begun, with emphasis placed on the production of missile-carrying patrol boats and submarines.[24] On balance, this program was a well-conceived attempt to meet the conflicting demands placed on the PLA. Although there was some opposition, perhaps on the part of civilian economic planners, to Lin's insistence that China develop and produce her own advanced weapons, rather than buy them from the West, Lin was generally able, as William Whitson has put it, to "satisfy everyone."[25]

In 1964, Mao Tse-tung apparently concluded, perhaps with Lin Piao's encouragement, that deeper involvement of the PLA in domestic affairs might bolster his campaign to stop the spread of "revisionism" in Chinese society. More than any other institution, the PLA had shown itself able to combine a commitment to Maoist values with effective performance of its assignments. In February 1964, therefore, a campaign was launched to "Learn from the PLA." Under this rubric, the army was used as an organizational model for various Party and state bureaucracies, the General Political De-

---

[21]For analyses of P'eng's purge, see Philip Bridgham, "Factionalism in the Central Committee," in John Wilson Lewis (ed.), *Party Leadership and Revolutionary Power in China* (Cambridge, G.B.: Cambridge University Press, 1970), pp. 203–35; David A. Charles, "The Dismissal of Marshal P'eng Teh-huai," *China Quarterly* 8 (October–December 1961): 63–76; Gittings, *Chinese Army*, Chap. 11; and *The Case of P'eng Teh-huai, 1956–1968* (Hong Kong: Union Research Institute, 1968).

[22]See Ellis Joffe, "The Chinese Army Under Lin Piao: Prelude to Political Intervention," in Lindbeck, *China*, esp. pp. 368–69.

[23]Richard M. Bueschel, *Communist Chinese Air Power* (New York: Praeger, 1968), Chaps. II, III.

[24]John R. Dewenter, "China Afloat," *Foreign Affairs* 50, no. 4 (July 1972): 738–51.

[25]Whitson, *The Chinese High Command*, p. 429.

partment became closely involved in the intensifying controversy over art and literature, and PLA cadres were dispatched from the army to establish "political departments" in a wide range of government ministries. Thereafter, any proposal that the PLA withdraw from its domestic roles would, predictably, have aroused Mao's strong opposition.

In March 1965, however, when the United States launched a program of sustained air strikes against North Vietnam, and began to introduce large numbers of combat troops into the South, Chief of Staff Lo Jui-ch'ing made just such a proposal.[26] Lo began to call for a reorientation of China's military posture, so as to assign the highest priority to the PLA's strategic roles. Even with China's relatively cautious policy toward Vietnam, Lo argued, the Americans might "lose all sense of reality" and carry the war to China. If China were to increase its aid to Vietnam, as Lo may well have thought it should, then the risks of confrontation with the United States would be even greater. In speeches and written statements throughout the summer of 1965, Lo warned that China was simply not prepared to meet the threats to Chinese security posed by the United States. To Lo, there were "a thousand and one things to do" before China would be ready for war.

In veiled language, Lo seems to have rejected the strategy of "luring deep" advocated by Lin Piao. Lo implied that a massive American invasion of China, against which a "luring deep" strategy would admittedly be effective, was not the threat China should be most concerned about. Instead, Lo indicated that the PLA should be prepared to conduct a linear defense of China's borders against a much smaller scale American ground strike; to intervene, as in Korea, to help protect North Vietnam against American invasion; to strike preemptively against American installations in Asia to forestall an American attack against China; or to open a second front elsewhere in Asia if the United States escalated the conflict in Vietnam beyond acceptable limits.

If the PLA were to be ready to do all this, Lo apparently argued, an extensive program of defense preparations would be necessary. It is possible, for instance, that Lo proposed a redeployment of air defenses to south China, to strengthen China's border with Vietnam. It is

also likely, as Red Guard criticisms of Lo have indicated, that he proposed that the ground forces be strengthened by intensifying their military training, increasing their numbers, and bringing them under tighter central control. Finally, several new weapons systems—the MiG-21, SAM-2 anti-aircraft missiles, light tanks, and self-propelled artillery—had either entered production early in 1965 or were in the last stages of design. Lo may have proposed that the production of these weapons be accelerated, an effort to produce these weapons in sufficient numbers to reinforce China's defenses against an American attack. To do so, Lo apparently demanded that further research and development—even of nuclear weapons—be suspended or cut back, so as to channel all available resources into weapons production.

The defense preparations proposed by Lo probably aroused the opposition of several interest groups on economic and political grounds. Within the defense establishment, organizations engaged in research and development and regional military commanders whose equipment and personnel would have been deployed to the south both would have suffered under Lo's plans. If Lo's proposals required a diversion of resources from the civilian economy to the military sector, he would have faced resistance from economic planners as well. Perhaps most important, Lo's proposals would have had a crippling effect on the domestic political activities of the PLA and on the roles Mao planned for the army in the future. If security affairs came to demand more of the army's time, then its involvement in domestic political activities would necessarily be reduced.

What is more, Lo's proposals could also be criticized on strategic grounds. It is doubtful, for example, that Lo's defense preparations would have significantly improved China's defense and deterrence postures toward the United States. In fact, such defense preparations might well have been seen by the United States as provocative, and might therefore have increased, rather than reduced, the possibility of Sino-American conflict. Instead, Lin Piao implied in his famous essay "Long Live the Victory of People's War," published in September 1965, China's most effective policy would be to avoid any action that would provoke the United States. The Vietnamese, Lin declared, should be prepared to carry on their struggle against the Americans in a "self-reliant" manner, without any substantial increase in Chinese assistance. The Chinese, Lin implied, should be prepared to defend their country through people's war, without any

---

[26]For further details, see Harry Harding and Melvin Gurtov, *The Purge of Lo Jui-ch'ing: The Politics of Chinese Strategic Planning*, R-548-PR (Santa Monica, Calif.: The RAND Corporation, February, 1971).

dramatic efforts to improve their strategic posture. Lin's conclusion, therefore, was that Lo's proposed defense preparations were, on military grounds, both unnecessary and undesirable.

That Lin (and, most likely, Mao as well) saw Lo's proposals as militarily unnecessary as well as politically undesirable added a significant element to the debate. Since the Maoists could not accept the strategic logic of Lo's plans, they accused him of concocting an elaborate rationalization for proposals whose real purpose was to force the disengagement of the PLA from domestic activities, reduce its political reliability, and thus sabotage Mao's campaign against revisionism in China. As one Red Guard document published during the Cultural Revolution charged:

Lo Jui-ch'ing dwelt considerably on "war preparations," and it seemed as if he was concerned over our country's security. This is not true. What he called "war preparations" were in fact preparations for usurping the army leadership and opposing the Party.[27]

The accuracy of these charges is questionable. It seems more likely that Lo was acting in part out of a genuine conviction that Chinese security was threatened, in part out of the hope that he could use a campaign of war preparations to advance his own career. But it also appears that the Maoists came sincerely to believe that Lo was engaged in a treacherous effort to support Mao's opponents in the Party by distracting the PLA from its domestic roles.

Although Lo was purged in December, the resolution of the strategic debate of 1965 was, in some ways, a compromise. The elements of Lo's program that were especially objectionable to major interest groups were rejected, including his proposals to cut back on research and development in order to permit a crash program of defense preparations. On the other hand, some of Lo's proposals for the strengthening of China's defenses were ultimately accepted. Over-all troop strength was enlarged, defenses in the south reinforced, and aircraft production increased. But these measures were implemented more slowly and geographically more widely than Lo had originally proposed, in accordance both with Mao's preference for long-term defense planning and with the reluctance of China's regional commanders to disrupt the established "balance" among China's military regions.

This compromise permitted the PLA gradually to expand its participation in domestic politics during the first year of the Cultural Revolution. At first, the PLA was restricted to providing logistical support to Red Guards traveling throughout the country. Somewhat later, in the face of increasing disorder, the army was ordered to secure such vital installations as broadcasting stations, granaries, and airports. Finally, in mid-January 1967, when the "proletarian revolutionaries" were authorized to "seize power" from provincial and municipal Party committees, the PLA was instructed to support them. From that point on, the army was deeply involved in the Cultural Revolution. Its somewhat incompatible tasks in 1967 and 1968 were to "support the left," protect state property, supervise governmental operations, participate in the formation of revolutionary committees, guide the rebuilding of the Party, and mediate disputes among rival Red Guard factions.[28] To do so, it is estimated that the PLA assigned some one million men to political and economic activities.[29]

The PLA's ability to meet these domestic responsibilities clearly reflected the two-sided strategic posture developed after 1960 by Lin Piao. The expansion of the domestic functions of the PLA was made possible by increasing the strength of the ground forces; the air force, the navy, and units concerned with nuclear testing and missile development were largely insulated from the Cultural Revolution. People's war was touted as the correct "proletarian military line" for the ground forces, in part because it justified their diversion to domestic tasks, but aircraft production, nuclear testing, and shipbuilding continued with little interruption throughout the Cultural Revolution. On no occasion was the nuclear program or the modernization of the air force described as incompatible with people's war.[30]

---

[27]"Big Military Competition is Big Exposure of Lo Jui-ch'ing's Plot," *Jen-min Jih-pao* (August 28, 1967); in *Survey of the China Mainland Press*, No. 4022 (September 5, 1967): 9–10.

[28]On the role of the PLA during the Cultural Revolution, see John Gittings, "The Chinese Army's Role in the Cultural Revolution," *Pacific Affairs* 39, nos. 3–4 (Fall-Winter 1966–67): 269–89; Jürgen Domes, "The Cultural Revolution and the Army," *Asian Survey* 8, no. 5 (May 1968): 349–63; Jürgen Domes, "The Role of the Military in the Formation of Revolutionary Committees, 1967–68," *China Quarterly*, 44 (October-December 1970): 112–45; Harvey Nelsen, "Military Forces in the Cultural Revolution," *China Quarterly* 51 (July-September 1972): 444–74; Chien Yu-shen, *China's Fading Revolution: Army Dissent and Military Divisions, 1967–68* (Hong Kong: Centre of Contemporary Studies, 1969); and Whitson, *The Chinese High Command*, Chaps. 7, 8.

[29]William Dorrill et al., *China in the Wake of the Cultural Revolution*, RAC-R-81 (McLean, Va.: Research Analysis Corporation, September 1969), p. 23.

[30]Jonathan D. Pollack, "Chinese Attitudes Towards Nuclear Weapons, 1964–69," *China Quarterly* 50 (April-June 1972): 252.

When the Ninth Party Congress opened in April 1969, marking the end of the Cultural Revolution, Lin Piao was at the height of his influence. With the state and Party bureaucracies still in disarray, and the mass organizations dismembered, the PLA was the only organization in the country capable of implementing policy on a national scale. As minister of defense, therefore, Lin headed an organization which was indispensable to the implementation of policy and the maintenance of social order. At the same time, China had just experienced her first serious border clashes with the Soviet Union, along the Ussuri River. The prospect of a Sino-Soviet war could be used to support calls for national unity behind military leadership. Together, these two factors greatly strengthened the political positions of both Lin Piao and the PLA. The Ninth Congress proclaimed Lin to be Mao's "close comrade-in-arms and successor," and elected him sole vice-chairman of the Party. It also appointed central and provincial military men to the Central Committee in unprecedented numbers.

Ironically, these same two factors that strengthened Lin's position in 1969—the influence of the PLA in domestic politics, and the Sino-Soviet conflict—later turned to his disadvantage.[31] The reconstruction of the Party in 1970 and 1971 raised a fundamental and controversial issue: the distribution of political power in post-Cultural Revolutionary China. Throughout the period, it appears that Lin sought to ensure continued military participation in civilian decisionmaking, and perhaps even military domination of the new Party committees. To do so, it was charged after his purge, he opposed the reinstatement of civilian cadres dismissed during the Cultural Revolution, in order to increase the number of military cadres appointed to civilian positions. The contest between military and civilian cadres for positions on the new Party committees became increasingly intense, and apparently significantly delayed the selection of the last few provincial committees. The outcome, however, strongly favored the military: of the 158 secretaries on the 29 provincial Party committees, 59% were military representatives, and 35% were civilian cadres. (The remaining 6% were mass representatives.) Twenty of the 29 first secretaries were military commanders or commissars. Once

appointed, furthermore, these military cadres were encouraged to act as a distinct voting bloc within the Party committees, discussing important matters among themselves before referring their conclusions to the full committee.

These attempts to entrench his own position created conflict between military and civilian cadres and opposition among those who believed that military intervention in civilian affairs had gone too far. They also exacerbated tensions within the PLA itself. Lin's aim, apparently, was not simply to increase the number of military representatives on Party committees, but also to draw as many as possible from his own faction within the PLA, the so-called Fourth Field Army faction. Since his purge, Lin has been accused of having tried to appoint as civilian Party secretaries military men who were personally loyal to himself, then co-ordinating and guiding their activities in the provinces through the military chain-of-command. This tactic probably won Lin the opposition of competing factions, particularly members of the Second and Third Field Armies, whose political influence Lin was trying to restrict.[32]

International relations, and their implications for military policy, were another issue in Lin's purge. Despite the increasing tensions along the Sino-Soviet border, and the possibility for rapprochement with the United States, Lin chose to maintain a dual adversary policy, a policy of rigid hostility toward both nations, similar to that of the early 1960s. To meet the military challenge posed by the Soviet Union, Lin conducted a series of defense preparations highly compatible with a people's war strategy. Grain and other vital supplies were stockpiled, air raid shelters constructed, industries dispersed to rural areas, and lightly armed paramilitary forces established in areas close to the border. Characteristically, the main force units were held in reserve well behind the border; Lin's strategy was to let the paramilitary units draw the Soviet invaders deep inside Chinese territory before counterattacking with regular troops in the front and guerrillas in the rear.[33]

Lin's diplomatic and military policies probably aroused opposition from two relatively distinct sources. To Chou En-lai, and the civilian officials associated with him, China could not afford the risks inherent in a dual adversary policy. China's security should be ensured not only by independent military preparations, but

---

[31]For details, and a discussion of the other issues in Lin's purge, see Harry Harding, "Political Trends in China Since the Cultural Revolution," *The Annals of the American Academy of Political and Social Science* 402 (July 1972): 67–82.

[32]On the role of the field army factions in Chinese military politics, see Whitson, *The Chinese High Command, passim.*
[33]*New York Times*, July 25, 1972, pp. 1, 14.

close to twenty-five years.[10] If the threat had been the most decisive variable in formulating their military doctrines, one would have thought that their military postures would have varied with changes in the threat from the Soviet Union. This is a perceptual question, however, and there is no generally accepted interpretation of the varying levels of the Soviet threat. By and large there are two major views: some feel that during the first two decades the Soviet Union was expansive, aggressive, and therefore dangerous to such border lands as Norway and Denmark. The 1962 Cuban missile crisis taught the Russians a lesson, made them shelve their aggressive designs, and settle for peace and cooperation. The other major view is that during the two first decades, the Soviet Union was much too weak to risk any military confrontation involving the United States. It was only after the 1962 Cuban crisis that it reached a level of military performance which now poses a real threat to the West.

Whether the West Scandinavians subscribed to one or the other of these extreme views, it can hardly have affected their military doctrines. With the exception of a modest peak in the middle 1950s their defense expenses have remained on the same level with a definite declining trend in the last few years. A further indication of both being relatively unperturbed about an imminent Soviet threat is the so-called bases policies which the two West Scandinavian countries have practiced ever since the alliance was initiated. Neither of them allows the stationing of any foreign, allied troops on their territory unless they are attacked or directly threatened.[11] Nor do they allow any deployment or stockpiling of tactical nuclear weapons. NATO made such an offer in the late 1950s but was turned down. As an extra precaution, Norway has added restrictions on allied maneuvers, use of air space and airports north of the 24th meridian.

In view of the special conditions on NATO's northern flank (the many obstacles to be overcome for providing timely assistance from any of the allied countries), one would have thought that if the West Scandinavians felt the threat to be anywhere near imminent they would have urged their allies to put forces and make prepara-

tions in most strategic areas where a conflict might be expected to erupt. Instead, they have laid down these prohibitions and bans which prevent the alliance from an effectively prepared local assistance by allied forces and tactical deterrents.[12] There are no indications of a direct correlation between changes in Soviet military postures and the bans. Since 1949 the trend has been toward a further tightening of the restrictions on allied activities, rather than modifying or abandoning them.

Nor is there any noticeable connection between the changes that have taken place on the allied side, within NATO, over the past few years. It is beyond doubt and discussion that the Soviet forces have been greatly increased in the northern flank areas, which are of most direct concern to the Scandinavian countries. Not only have the forces grown in numbers and in quality of equipment, they have also been deployed and exercised in ways that most military observers find disturbing.[13] The two major events were the *Sever* and *Okean* exercises in 1968 and 1970 respectively. On both occasions Soviet naval forces, combined with troops and gear for amphibious landings, repeated the German invasion pattern of April 1940 by sailing these units along the Danish and Norwegian coasts from the Baltic Sea way up into the North Atlantic.[14]

While thus the Russians have increased their military potential, the trend within the Western alliance, on which Scandinavian hopes for support and assistance depend, seems to point in the opposite direction.[15] Apart from the political difficulties, those related to France as well as to other alliance members, there has been a steady decline in military postures in all parts of the Western world.[16]

The Scandinavians are not unaware of this trend. Situated in one of the most exposed areas on the Western perimeter, one might think that

---

[10]For a historical account of major developments, see Johan J. Holst, *Norsk Sikkerhetspolitik* (Oslo: NUPI, 1962).

[11]Cf. Nils Ørvik, "Base Policy—Theory and Practice," *Cooperation and Conflict* 3, IV (1967): 188–203. See also the present writer and Niels J. Haagerup, *The Scandinavian Members of NATO*, Adelphi Paper No. 23 (London: IISS, 1965).

[12]For Danish nuclear policies, see *Problemer omkring dansk Sikkerhedspolitik*. (Copenhagen: Seidenfaden-rapporten, 1970), and *Dansk Sikkerhedspolitik* (Copenhagen: Danish Foreign Ministry, 1968). For Norwegian nuclear policies, see Nils Ørvik, *Alternativer for Sikkerhet* (Oslo: E. G. Mortensen, 1970).

[13]*Military Balance (1971–72 and 1972–73)* (London: IISS, 1971 and 1972), *NATO Letter*, September issue (1970), and news reports.

[14]Discussed in the present writer's "Scandinavian Security in Transition. The Two-Dimensional Threat," *Orbis* (Fall 1972), pp. 720–42.

[15]Cf. the voluminous literature on recent developments within the Western alliance.

[16]The period of obligatory military service is shortened, equipment is rapidly becoming obsolete, and appropriations barely compensate for the spirals of inflation. The overall performance rate of NATO's military establishment is lower than earlier, in relative terms much lower.

they would try to compensate for the weakened support potential of the alliance by a greatly increased effort of their own. Quite obviously, by tightening their belts and trimming some of their more affluent domestic programs, the Danes and Norwegians should be able to increase, perhaps even double, their defense efforts. They would still keep their GNP percentage below 6%, a proportional figure which many countries of approximately their size have maintained for decades without any damage to their social, economic, or political structure.

Instead, neither of them has moved in this direction. Norway, though clearly shaken by the Soviet naval expansion as well as by recent deployments,[17] has kept the defense appropriations on roughly the same levels as in earlier years. During the debate on Norway's national budget for 1973, it was pointed out that of all the departmental budgets, defense showed the smallest growth.[18] The Danish government, however, decided in 1971 to stop hedging about the issue and proposed to the national assembly a program for reduction of Danish military forces and equipment that would give Danish defense little more than symbolic value. The draft will be maintained but the period of military training is to be only half of what it used to be, that is, reduced to six months, from the present twelve. The army which is now listed at a strength of 27,000 men would be cut down to 7,000. Corresponding reductions are suggested for navy and air force. The proposal envisages certain compensations in terms of an improved homeguard or militia arrangement. However, in view of the most likely defense tasks and the assumed opponents this seems only of marginal relevance.[19]

The proposal has drawn heavy flak in NATO meetings and through direct communication, but there are few signs to indicate that the Danes will budge.[20] Some adjustments seem likely (perhaps nine instead of six months of military service), but there are strong reasons to believe that the reductions will be maintained in principle.

THE EAST SCANDINAVIANS

Finland

Of all the Scandinavian countries, Finland has probably given the most convincing proof of its devotion to the principles of national independence and to the freedoms listed as vital and essential in the Western world. The lonely struggle of the Finns against the towering preponderance of the Soviet Union during the 1939–40 Winter War is now legendary. Less known, but no less impressive in military terms, was the so-called Continuation War of 1941–44 where the Finns fought side by side with the Germans, for a while even closing in on Leningrad.[21] In spite of exceptional bravery and endurance, both wars ended with defeat and the forced acceptance of two major treaties, the peace treaty of 1947 with the Soviet Union and Great Britain and the 1948 Russo-Finnish agreement of Friendship and Mutual Assistance.[22]

These formal restraints have made it very hard for the Finns to apply or even to design in realistic terms any military doctrine. Of the three major variables, their objectives are no different from those of their Scandinavian neighbors. The threat to Finland is also defined in the same Soviet terms. But with the 1948 Treaty of Friendship and Mutual Assistance as the basic guideline for their policies of national security they are bound to suffer from inconsistencies in their military posture and face a number of serious obstacles to countering the threat through a buildup of armed forces. The 1947 peace treaty restricts the Finnish army to a maximum of 34,000 men, the navy to 4,500, and the air force to 3,000. Considering that Finland during World War II had more than half a million men in active service and yet suffered defeat, the forces it is allowed to deploy are much too small for a credible defense. The peace treaty also imposes additional restrictions, such as prohibitions against weapons with primarily offensive uses such as submarines, special categories of surface warships (total allowed tonnage: 10,000), and bombers. Some of these restrictions have been modified over the years as the Russians have grown confident that a Finnish government is unlikely to turn the weapons against the Soviet Union. Thus, over the past decade the Finns have received short range missile weapons, more

---

[17]The celebrated incident of an allegedly Soviet or East European submarine which for nearly two weeks played games with Norwegian search vessels, has caused concern within as well as outside the country.

[18]*Aftenposten* (Oslo) (18 Nov 72).

[19]*Beretning fra Forvarskommissionen af 1969* (Copenhagen: Forsvarsministeriet, 1972), pp. 385 ff.

[20]With some modification the reduction bill was passed in 1973. See Niels T. Haagerup, "Denmark's Defence Reform," *Survival* 4 (1973): 171–77.

[21]It should be noted that the Finns only advanced as far into the Soviet Union as East Karelia, which they regarded as a *terra irredentia*. They refused to join in any attack on Leningrad.

[22]The latter is printed in Urho Toivala, *Introduction to Finland* (Helsinki: Werner Soderstrom, 1960), pp. 109–10. For the peace treaty, see Erik Castrén, "Peace Treaties and Other Agreements Made by Finland," in *Finnish Foreign Policy* (Helsinki: The Finnish Political Science Association, 1963), pp. 50–65.

sophisticated ground combat equipment and a relatively large number of MIG-21 fighters. The fighting value of the latter is, however, somewhat reduced by the fact that the Russians did not include the basic service gears in the delivery. Consequently, after a certain number of air hours, the Finnish MIGs must be flown back to Russia for overhaul and service. On the other hand, Finland has recently bought twelve Swedish *Draken* fighters, which can be serviced and also partly produced in Finland. Some Finnish metal factories as Valmet and Tampella have a very advanced technology and could, if need be, turn out sizeable amounts of lighter types of weapons.

Given these limitations, which may be further modified but are unlikely to be removed, can Finland have a military doctrine in a sense that is comparable to her Scandinavian neighbors who are not subjected to such restrictions on national defense? Is it possible for Finland to use this rudimentary military force as an instrument of national policy?

Finland's declaratory military doctrine is closely linked to its policy of neutrality, which the Finnish government felt free to proclaim after the Soviet Union during the 1955 thaw period had withdrawn its military base in Porkkala, a peninsula near Helsinki, which the Russians had occupied since the end of the war.[23] The idea is apparently to create some notion that corresponds to the Swedish definition: "nonalignment in peace, aiming for neutrality in war."[24] This version of neutrality is based, however, on the assumption that the country commands enough military force to prevent any potential belligerents including Russia from using the neutral's sea or land territory or from violating other sovereign rights. The Finnish government, supported by specialists on foreign and defense matters, maintains that its small but well-trained military forces are able to perform such functions.[25] If need be, the government will order full mobilization calling the whole nation in arms to fight any invader.

We are again faced with the dichotomy between declaratory and action policies. This Finnish claim to a Swedish-modeled neutrality seems questionable for two major reasons: first, a glance at the map of Finland would be enough

to show that if the Soviet Union really wanted to proceed to military occupation of Finland, there would be very little the Finns could do to prevent it from doing so. If a heavily armed, fully mobilized Finland proved unable to keep the Russians out during the World War II, even when allied with Germany,[26] there could not be the faintest chance of success under present conditions. Second, with the Russo-Finnish Treaty of Friendship and Mutual Assistance, which was renewed in 1955 and again in 1970, there is no need for the Soviet Union to resort to military force in order to obtain a more direct control of Finnish affairs. Articles 1 and 2 in the agreement state explicitly that if either of the two countries are threatened by Germany or states allied with Germany, they shall engage in consultations to discuss what steps might be necessary for maintaining the security of the two countries. Such a move was initiated in 1961 during the so-called "note crisis," when Khrushchev asked for such consultations and for a brief period created an atmosphere of deadly crisis until the demand was dropped.[27]

The Soviet influence in Finnish affairs is very substantial as it is. If they for some or other reasons should want a firmer grip, a most likely scenario would be a three-step progression along these lines.[28] First, the Soviet government would tell the Finns that the international situation had deteriorated to a point where consultations for mutual security and assistance had become necessary (Article 2). There is no agreed definition for international crises. Such claim might virtually be made at any time the Russian leaders choose to do so. Given such Soviet initiative, it would seem very unlikely that the Finns could prove or persuade them that they were all wrong—that there was no danger from Germany or its allies.

Having established that a crisis situation applicable to the treaty did indeed exist, the next question would be what were the practical steps of mutual assistance, which in fact would mean "who of us should do what?" The Soviet High Command would turn to the Finnish Commander in Chief, point at the assumed military needs and ask him where he would suggest that the Finnish

---

[23]L. A. Puntila, "Finland's Neutrality," in *Finnish Foreign Policy*, p. 221.

[24]Nils Andrén and Aake Landquist, *Svensk Utrikespolitik efter 1945* (Stockholm: Almquist och Wiksell, 1965), p. 84.

[25]Aimo Pajunen, "Finland's Security Policy," *Cooperation and Conflict* 1 (1968): 75–92; Harto Hakovirta, "The Finnish Security Problem," *Cooperation and Conflict* 4 (1969): 247–66.

[26]The Finns stubbornly insist that "Finland was not an ally of Germany: she was a co-belligerent." Max Jakobson, "The Foreign Policy of Independent Finland," in *Finnish Foreign Policy*, p. 46. There may be legal grounds for this distinction. In its practical consequences of jointly taking on the Russian forces, the matter seems indisputable.

[27]Max Jakobson, *Finnish Neutrality* (London: 1968), pp. 69–87.

[28]N. Ørvik, *Sicherheit auf Finnisch. Finnland und die Sowjetunion.* (Stuttgart: Seewald Verlag, 1972), pp. 56–67.

forces be placed, implicit: what tasks they could or could not perform which otherwise would have to be done by Russian forces.

The third phase would emerge when the Finnish government responded to these demands. If it found them acceptable, the present implied assumption is that the government might order full mobilization with whatever means were available. It is an improbable decision, but let us discuss it. This might trigger the Soviet government into an instant, forced occupation of all major points in Finland, invoking to the world the clauses of mutual assistance and security in the friendship treaty and stressing Finland's legal obligations. Or more effectively, the Russians might do nothing, just sit put and let the Finns mobilize and arm some hundred thousand men.[29] Such a passive response would involve very few risks. There would be virtually no chance of outside assistance to Finland from any NATO country, most likely not even offers of sanctuaries and clandestine assistance from the Scandinavian neighbors. As there are no Soviet forces in Finland, the Finnish mobilized army would have no hostile forces to attack—unless Finnish forces would stage an invasion of Soviet territory—which would hardly be conceivable. Thus, if the Soviet forces did not move and nothing more happened, the chances are that the Finnish government would come under hard, probably irresistible domestic pressure to call it all off.

A second alternative would be for the Finns to do nothing, which would mean an indirect consent to having Soviet forces take up defense positions in Finland for "the mutual protection of the two countries." A third alternative, which seems the most likely one for the scenario designed here, would be Finnish compliance with the Soviet demands with the government trying to have the Finnish forces cover most of the areas that were thought to be of vital importance to Finland's national policy.

If we can conclude from this discussion that there is no credible scenario that provides for a successful use of Finnish forces against the Soviet Union, are there other military tasks which these forces might effectively perform in support of national policy?

The provisions in the peace treaty say that Finnish forces should be limited to a size that would permit local border control and tasks of an internal nature. This could mean that the 40,000 man force should be prepared to act as an extended state police force, ready and able to

put out any attempt at insurrection, revolutionary activities or coups supported by armed force. For such truly internal tasks the Finnish military forces seem indeed credible.

The second stated mission is the border control, which since 1956 has been linked to the policy of neutrality. Despite the brief period of training,[30] the Finnish military forces hold very high standards. Their officers in general and the reserve officers in particular, are highly motivated and very able. Their limitation is number, not quality. Consequently, their task of border protection would become credible—if the Soviet Union is *not* counted among the possible intruders and violators of Finnish neutrality. This is the crux of the matter. Only under this assumption would a Finnish military doctrine be compatible with existing capabilities. In a crisis situation, the Soviet Union would become Finland's closest and most important ally, and as such be expected to take care of any enemies in the external environment. If the Finns had no armed forces of their own, the Soviet army, navy and air force would have to take up positions in Finland as well as in other areas that might be threatened. This would have an adverse effect on Finnish-Soviet relations and make Finland more dependent on her great neighbor than she already is. Consequently, the more and the better trained Finnish forces, the less they would need direct help and assistance from Soviet troops.

Under these assumptions, the Finnish military forces would play a useful role in forming and supporting national policies and thus fulfill the requirements of a workable military doctrine. But such contingencies would have the political disadvantage of bringing Finland even more firmly in on the Soviet side. Any conflict, raising even the faintest possibility of a mutual danger and mutual Russo-Finnish response would display the built-in inconsistencies in the Finnish position and tear off the thin veil of neutrality which is now meant to cover them up. A rational Finnish approach would be to do whatever they could to avoid such situations.

This explains the energetic Finnish attempts, partly as personal initiatives by President Urho Kekkonen, to neutralize the Nordic area and thereby reduce the possibilities of conflicts that might involve Finnish security. The most notorious of these attempts is Kekkonen's May 1963 proposal for a Nordic nuclear-free zone and his "peace-zone" proposal of November 1965. In

[29]*Ibid.*, pp. 67–71.

[30]The compulsory training period for enlisted men is for 8 months, specialists 11–15 months.

the former, which has been bypassed by the nonproliferation treaty of 1968, he asked for formal declaration making all of Scandinavia a nuclear-free zone. In the latter proposal, he suggested a bilateral arrangement between Finland and Norway, where Norway would ban any allied forces approaching from the West to anywhere near Finnish-Norwegian borders, while Finland issued a corresponding guarantee for holding off Soviet forces approaching from the East. As this would have put a virtual ban on meaningful NATO maneuvers on the northern flank, the Norwegians naturally rejected the proposal.[31]

Sweden

With her size and wealth, one would think that of all the Scandinavian countries, Sweden is the one whose military doctrine comes closest to those of the major powers. Her armed neutrality is clear, simple, and under certain circumstances fully credible. Sweden's security objectives are to maintain the nation's independence, its freedom of action while safeguarding her internal development as she defines it, and at the same time also work for international peace and conciliation.[32]

As a means for achieving these goals Sweden continues to practice a policy of "nonalignment aiming for neutrality in a future war." The Swedes maintain that this policy contributes to international peace and stability as well as to their own national security. Sweden sees herself as a most useful buffer between the two contending power blocs. However, in order to play this role as an intermediary peacemaker successfully, her military forces must be strong enough to convince either of the two blocs "that an attack on Sweden is unlikely to pay off."[33]

As far as military doctrines go, this is fair enough. By making the costs of aggression outweigh any possible gains, the two power blocs will be deterred. If we want to test the saliency of Sweden's military doctrine, we will therefore have to estimate the gains that an invader could reasonably hope for and the costs, that is, the kind of damage which Swedish defense forces could be expected to do to any power that should want to try. As is the case with the other Scandinavian states, so far the Soviet Union is seen as the major danger to national security.

In spite of the proclaimed policy of neutrality,

which presupposes a "tous azimut" strategy, all preparations have been geared to meet an attack or incursion by Russian forces. So what we are really talking about are the Soviet gains or incentives for staging military operations against Sweden. In what way would physical control of Sweden improve the overall strategic position of the Soviet Union?

The question of Soviet gains from a militarily controlled Sweden should be seen in two perspectives, strategic and political. In both cases useful references could be made to German policies toward Sweden during World War II. One should, however, keep in mind that due to Russia's abundant natural resources, notably iron ore, these incentives are less important, while the geographical ones seem greater. As the Swedes themselves indicate, compared to Norway and the Danish Straits, Sweden has only marginal military value to the Soviet Union. This has become more evident in recent years with the increased importance of the Baltic entrances and the Northern Cap area.[34] With the Russian naval expansion, the deployment of nuclear missile-carrying submarines, the fishing and merchant fleets and many major industries, the Kola Peninsula with its main port, Murmansk, has become a core area in Soviet strategy.[35] These activities have upgraded greatly the strategic value of north Norway, partly also of Finnish Lapland, but it has few direct implications for Sweden. If the Soviet leaders should see a need or an opportunity to extend their military control to north Norway, the success of such operations could hardly depend on simultaneous control of Swedish territory. The same considerations pertain to operations against positions in the Danish straits.

The one contingency where Sweden would become strategically significant is a situation where the Soviet Union initiated large scale military operations against Norway, to a lesser extent also against Denmark. In that case, Sweden would emerge as an important transit area for getting military logistics and other supplies from the Soviet Union to Norway. By transporting them by rail or road across Sweden, they would reach Russian operational bases in Norway more safely and quickly than by a northern or southern sea route. The Swedes are aware of such possibilities and point in their public writings also at the additional value of

[31] *Morgenbladet* (Oslo) (Dec. 1, 1965).
[32] *Kungliga Majestaatets Proposition No. 75, 1972* (Stockholm: 1972), p. 62.
[33] *Ibid.*, p. 63.

[34] Nils Ørvik, *Europe's Northern Cap and the Soviet Union.* Occasional Paper No. 6 (Cambridge, Mass.: Center for International Affairs, Harvard University, 1963).
[35] *Kungl. Maj. Prop. 75.*, pp. 50-52.

the Soviet Union for NATO having transit rights across Swedish territory.[36]

Logistics is an important part of any military operation, but the Swedes are probably right in their estimates that the Russians are unlikely to stage an isolated attack against Sweden just to secure transit facilities for a subsequent move against Norway. Sweden's problems would emerge in the later stages of an armed conflict after the initiation or completion of military operations as they did during the German invasion of Norway and Denmark in 1940. There are, however, interesting aspects in comparing the German moves in 1940–43 with a possible future situation. The Swedes are unlikely to ignore them.[37]

While observing that most military planners tend to prepare for the last, rather than the next war, the 1940–45 scenario is not irrelevant to a future situation with Russia playing Germany's role. It seems beyond dispute that the most important objectives for a Soviet military move would be the air and seaport facilities in Norway and, at a later stage, possibly also in Denmark. In strictly military terms, the Russians have a good many more reasons for considering such acquisitions in the 1970s than they had in the 1950s and 1960s.[38] One could also see how Norway, at the moment drifting away from the European Common Market, with its severe self-imposed restrictions impeding a timely NATO assistance, could one day present a tempting target for a low-risk demonstration of Russia's power and determination. A major concern would naturally be to keep the conflict area as limited as possible. With the distribution of forces in the area, it would seem feasible for the Soviet Union to stage such a *blitz* operation without involving either Finland or Sweden directly. If operations along these lines should prove

successful, the gains by simultaneously extending Soviet military control to Sweden would not seem very great.

Looking at this costs-benefits analysis from the Swedish point of view, it might at first sight seem quite plausible. Sweden's small but well-trained and equipped military force might prove as effective a deterrent to the Soviet Union as it did to the Germans more than thirty years ago.

However, a harder look raises some additional questions. If we suppose that the *blitz*-operations against Norway had been completed, the *political* aspects of Soviet costs-benefits analyses would become predominant. As political means would seem clearly preferable to military ones, the Soviet leaders would have to estimate how much they could get by threatening invasion, and the Swedes, how to make effective resistance credible—without having to prove it. During World War II, Sweden had avoided a military confrontation by adjusting her political concessions to the shifting degrees of German needs and their propensity for using force. Deterred by the probable costs of military reprisals, the Germans refrained from extreme demands, while on the other side, the Swedes, with a keen and wary eye on Germany's "aggression barometer" always could produce some further concessions when a breaking point seemed near.

The success or failure of such a game or contest would depend greatly on the effectiveness of Swedish military forces, their stamina, and her political will. It would, therefore, seem very strange indeed, if such scenarios were not eagerly studied by those who now formulate Sweden's military doctrine for the 1970s. The curse of such games is the constant risk of misinterpretation, misreading of signs and signals in the formation of perceptions. A precondition for such a military doctrine would be to prevent the Soviet Union from including Sweden in its initial move toward the crucial strategic positions in Norway. Therefore, a first and most important step would be to communicate to the Soviet Union what neutral Sweden sees as the rules of the game. The most vital point would be to convince the Soviet leaders that Sweden would not under any foreseeable circumstances become engaged in an armed conflict unless openly and deliberately attacked or provoked.

This message is in fact already conveyed through Sweden's often repeated assurances that even if the countries in her neighborhood should become involved in armed conflicts Sweden would not necessarily be engaged. This means that if Norway, Denmark, or even Finland get embroiled in a struggle, Sweden would stead-

[36]*Ibid.*, pp. 51–52. As a "true-blue neutral" the Swedish government takes great pains to point out that *either* of the two power blocs have such transport and other belligerent needs that Sweden could fill. References to the Soviet Union are often stated as "the two great power blocs."

[37]Given the duality of their neutral predisposition, they may also have paid some attention to the ill-fated Franco-British enterprise toward Scandinavia in 1939–40, when Churchill set out "to kill two birds with one stone" by staging a military expedition, to land in west Norway, occupy some Norwegian ports, and on its way to aid the hard-pressed Finns also take into custody the Gallivare-Kiruna iron ore mines in north Sweden, which Hitler had deemed vital for his conduct of the war. This attempt by the British and the French to gain an initiative in the "phony war" and divert the interests of the Germans from France and Belgium is well described in a number of books and articles on the German invasion of Norway in 1940.

[38]Jan Klenberg, *The Cap and the Straits. Problems of Nordic Security*, Occasional Paper, (Cambridge, Mass.: Center for International Affairs, Harvard University, 1968).

fastly maintain her neutral position as she did in 1940 when her two Scandinavian neighbors were attacked by Germany; implicit here, Sweden would not join them or their allies, but await Russia's next move. If the Russian leaders got this message straight and believed it, there would be no need for Soviet military planners to include a preemptive strike against Sweden as a necessary corollary to a westward military move. Thus, Sweden's major concern is to avoid what we may call a "conventional first strike."

The most cited public assurance of Sweden's determination not to become engaged, even if her two next-door neighbors, Norway and Denmark, were involved in a great power conflict in northern Europe, appeared in 1965 in a small book written by the then Deputy Minister of Defense, Karl Frithiofson.[39] It has been repeated frequently ever since, most recently in the Swedish government's proposition to the national assembly in 1972.[40] It serves as an effective reassurance to the Soviet Union that Nordic cooperative arrangements will not be carried to a point where Sweden is pledged to come to the assistance of either Norway or Denmark.[41]

Thus, Sweden's message is clear and unambiguous. The Soviet Union can rest assured that unless she deliberately attacks or provokes Swedish territory, Swedish forces will not become engaged. They are there for the sole purpose of protecting Sweden. If Norway and Denmark, either through their own actions or indirectly through their own membership in NATO, should become involved, they will get no military support from Sweden. Swedish forces will not interfere with the ways that the Soviet Union may choose to deal with such problems. For obvious reasons, the Soviet leaders maintain a healthy skepticism of public declarations. In this case particularly, they would like to see them backed up by harder facts. If, as is suggested here, Swedish military doctrine provides for a bargaining process based on the German 1940–43 transit model, one would look

for actions rather than words as indications of intent. This makes it necessary to take a closer look at Sweden's military capabilities and the trends of recent development.

The scenario of neutral Sweden maneuvering between contending power blocs is primarily a political exercise. Sweden cannot take for granted that her neutrality will prevail. Persuasion and deterrence may fail. If the Soviet Union decides that gains outweigh costs, as it did in the Finnish case of 1939–40, how will Sweden respond? If capitulation is unacceptable, what are the alternatives when the military instrument is actually being used—what tasks is it expected to perform and under what circumstances?

In principle there are just two basic alternatives: an isolated defense effort, relying only on national capabilities and resources, or joint defense in cooperation or coalition with other states fighting the same enemy. In more concrete terms, how do the Swedish planners visualize an isolated, national defense effort when the opponent is the Soviet Union? Is this a real alternative? If it is not, does Norway or Denmark provide an alternative model for Sweden with military resistance by national forces during the initial phase, then supplemented by massive support from USA and NATO? One can understand how a neutral government may find it difficult to discuss openly such crudely cut options as these.

When World War II ended, Sweden ranked next to Britain as the strongest military power in Western Europe. Since then it has fallen back in a relative sense, but all through the 1950s and way into the 1960s, Sweden kept abreast with the major powers in military organization and advanced military technology. Her impressive array of military aircraft, from the early "Tunnan," to "Lansen," "Draken" and now "Viggen" were all designed and produced in Sweden in respectable numbers. As late as 1969, the Swedish air force had as many combat aircraft as Britain's Royal Air Force.[42] This also holds for most of her other military equipment, tanks, and electronic guidance systems, all very sophisticated and of first rate quality. The last couple of decades have, however, brought some important choices that seem bound to affect the whole scope of national security and her military doctrine.

The first to be met was the nuclear one. As most highly industrialized countries, Sweden sooner or later had to make a basic decision as

---

[39]Karl Frithiofson, *Sveriges Saekerhetspolitik* (in the series: *Forsvar i Nutid*, Stockholm 1965), p. 12.

[40]"Aeven om stater i vaar naerhet skulle dras in i en konflikt i Europa mellan stormaktsblokker behoever detta enligt utredningen inte noedvendigvis medfoera att Sverige engageras i konflikten," *op. cit.*, p. 66.

[41]In fact, Mr. Frithiofson's statement in 1965 came after a sudden resurgence of public discussion of a Scandinavian defense union, which had been a dead issue since the abortive attempt in 1948–49 to present such a joint arrangement as an alternative to the North Atlantic alliance. It was a mirage that quickly evaporated after the concerned governments had denied any connection with such plans. Kjell Goldmann and Christian Lange, "Nordisk saekerhetspolitik 1949–1965–197?" *Strategisk Bulletin* 2–3 (1966).

[42]Egil Ulstein, *Nordic Security*, Adelphi Paper No. 81 (London: 1971), pp. 22–25.

to whether or not she should develop nuclear weapons for her national defense. She has great resources in natural uranium and carried on an intensive nuclear research throughout the 1950s.[43] In 1958, the Chief of Defense recommended that Sweden should opt for a tactical nuclear weapons program. The military establishment was solidly for it, but most politicians had great doubts.[44] After a nationwide debate, the government, supported by the national assembly, first agreed on a compromise solution. The nuclear energy and the weapons program should be carried on simultaneously to a point where a definite choice for one or the other had to be made. This took about four years. In the meantime, the antinuclear campaigns had gathered momentum and non-nuclear pressures were mounting. In 1957 Norway and Denmark rejected them and in 1961 denied their allies the right to store nuclear charges on their territories. Simultaneously, the Swedish foreign minister launched his "Undén plan" for a worldwide non-nuclear club.[45] In May 1963, President Kekkonen came out with his plan for a nuclear-free zone in Scandinavia and in July, the United States and the Soviet Union signed the Test Ban Treaty. When the issue of a nuclear weapons program came up in Sweden, the political climate was even more unfavorable. The issue was closed in 1965 with a de facto decision not to produce nuclear weapons.[46] The legal responsibility not to develop nuclear weapons was reaffirmed when Sweden signed the Non-Proliferation Treaty, although the Treaty pledges are not irrevocable.[47]

How did the renunciation of a nuclear option affect Sweden's military doctrine? Following our assumption that it is vitally important for Sweden to convince the Soviet Union that she will not become engaged in armed conflicts in the area, not even those involving her northern neighbors, and thus ought not to be subjected to a preemptive strike, manifest non-nuclearity may serve a useful purpose. On the other hand, if we try to visualize a bargaining situation, roughly corresponding to the German 1940–43 scenario, this same decision has made her more vulnerable to nuclear blackmail. In the 1940–43 case, Germany had no means for deterrence or offense to which Sweden did not have an equivalent in kind. In a future situation, with Russia playing Germany's role, Sweden has no answer to a nuclear threat other than complying or gambling on the Soviet Union bluffing—or resorting to conventional means to make her points clear.

According to government sources, "a war in the external environment will primarily be conducted with conventional weapons."[48] If this basic assumption holds good, the Swedish military doctrine would seem very relevant since these are the only kinds of weapons she can have anyway. But even within this conventional framework, recent decisions require further explanation.

Through the 1940s and 1950s, the Swedish forces were charged with the task of defending their country against aggression *both* from across the Baltic and over the Finnish border in the north. In 1963 these tasks were redefined. Instead of the "both-and" came an "either-or." Thus indirectly admitting that taking on invaders from across the Baltic Sea and from the north simultaneously was too much, the task was from then on to prepare for one contingency or the other. Five years later the Swedish government made another decision along the same lines. In order to evaluate the real costs and needs of defense, it introduced in 1958 an arrangement where the national defense budget got an automatic annual increase of 2½ percent before discussing further priorities. However, the Swedish national assembly in 1968 voted for abolishing the automatic 2½ percent increase, allowing each new budget to be judged on the merits of the situation and on current needs.

As seemed predictable, this meant in real terms a lower growth rate and a gradually lowered state of military preparedness. Some acquisitions and building programs would have to be postponed, others cancelled. Existing equipment must be used longer than originally planned. Worst hit was the air force. In 1961 it

[43]Leonard Beaton, *Must the Bomb Spread*? (Baltimore: Penguin Books, 1966.)

[44]Karl Birnbaum, "Sverige och Kaernvapenfraagen," *Strategisk Bulletin* 6 (1965). See also his, "Sweden's Nuclear Policy," *International Journal* 3 (Summer 1965): 279–311; and Jan Prawitz, "A Nuclear Doctrine for Sweden," in *Cooperation and Conflict* 3 (1968): 184–93.

[45]In 1961, Mr. Undén had U.N. Secretary General U Thant send a circular letter to most non-nuclear nations, urging them to form a non-nuclear league. Ironically, the Swedish government was among those who turned it down. Bertil Heurlin, "Nuclear-free Zones . . . ," *Cooperation and Conflict* 1 (1966): 31–45.

[46]"Our (Sweden's) defense is based on the assumption that in case of war it will be conducted with no resort to nuclear weapons. . . . It is not in the interests of the national security of our country to acquire nuclear weapons." Statements in *Forsvarsfraagan, Fakta, underlag och siffror* (Stockholm: 1968), p. 28.

[47]George Quester, "Sweden and the Nuclear Non-Proliferation Treaty," *Cooperation and Conflict* 1 (1970): 52–54. See also Nils Andrén, *Den totala saekerhetspolitiken* (Stockholm: Roben och Sjogren, 1972), pp. 94–99.

[48]*Kungl. Maj: ts. Prop. 72:75*, p. 68.

was decided that the "Viggen" airplane should be developed and produced in: (1) strike, (2) reconnaissance, (3) interceptor versions. Due to budgetary restraints, which still exist, this sequence has been postponed and delayed. The program now runs two years behind schedule, but is not substantially changed.[49] Whether or not it will be implemented depends on budgetary considerations, and in Sweden, as in most other West European countries, recent developments have not raised the prospect for higher appropriations for defense purposes. The "Draken" fighter force is still expected to be in service through the seventies. It is hoped that it will be replaced in the 1980s by a Bofors Rb. 70 defense missile system and by the interceptor version of Viggen JA 37. It should, however, be noted that much of the projected air defense system still is not there, and that it will depend on the willingness of the politicians in the next few years to give continually high priority to arms development, whether it ever will get there, in the quality and the quantity assumed in the plans. The 1968 defense arrangement was termed intermediary, to be reviewed after four years, but there is no indication that the defense establishment will be given the funds it needs to catch up from where it left off in 1968.[50] The reduced priorities for defense are also expressed in a lower percentage of the GNP, which has sunk from its maximal 6% to its present 3.7%.[51] Few deny that the 1968 arrangement has weakened, some say even seriously, the defense value of Sweden's military forces.[52]

If we return to our questions as to the potential use of Swedish military forces—what tasks they are being prepared to perform—the de facto reductions of goals as well as capabilities seem to rule out any scenario of an isolated Soviet attack on Sweden. If this was seen as a real contingency, national defense would rather have gotten a larger share of the growing Swedish GNP. If an isolated national defense effort is out as a viable alternative, this would, in rational terms, seem to be due to either of two major considerations: either Sweden counts on Western

assistance to meet a possible Soviet threat or she does not seriously consider any Soviet threat to Sweden, at least not in a foreseeable future. The first case would mean that Sweden has based her military organization on the assumption that if the Soviet Union should initiate hostilities, Sweden would meet the first assault with her own indigenous forces. They would have a totally mobilized population behind them and would give up no part of Swedish territory without maximal resistance. This is what all the official declarations say over and over again. But given the difference in Russo-Swedish military potential, no rational person would assume that the Swedish forces, even when displaying such outstanding fighting qualities as the Finns in 1939–40, could hold their ground for more than some weeks, at the very best. If no one comes to her aid, the struggle would almost certainly end as the Finnish winter war had done, with massive destruction and a shattering defeat with far-reaching concessions. In rational terms, this would not make sense.

If, however, there were a reasonable chance of getting timely assistance from USA and NATO, Sweden's position would be no worse than that of Norway and Denmark. In fact, with her higher level of military preparedness, Sweden might even be better off than they. Thus, in terms of facts, if not in form, Sweden would have basically the same military doctrine as her two Scandinavian neighbors, whose defense establishments are built on the same basic assumption: meet the first attack with indigenous forces, do what is possible within this national framework, and then hope that allied assistance will arrive before too much territory is lost or destroyed.

As even the slightest indication along such lines might weaken the credibility of Sweden's nonalignment policy, Swedish spokesmen have always denied it vehemently. Some may go as far as to admit that Norway's and Denmark's membership in NATO indirectly contributes to Swedish security by sheltering most of Sweden's land borders, thereby saving her from the tremendous expense of keeping up a neutrality guard to the west as they do in the east.[53] But they will stubbornly deny that Sweden would ultimately count on western military assistance.

However, the decisions on defense, referred to above, might well support the scenario of parallel Dano-Norwegian and Swedish military doctrines. The denunciation of nuclear weapons could mean that Sweden as well as Norway,

---

[49]The 1972 proposal now considers some modifications on the "Viggen" issue, Kungl. Maj:s IS, 1972. (A forthcoming book by Dr. Ingemar Dörfer is expected to deal extensively with the "Viggen" project.)

[50]In fact, the 1972 proposal envisages some further reductions, as two weeks less compulsory training for recruits, motivated by economic difficulties, *Kungl. Maj. 170.*

[51]*Military Balance* 1972–1973, p. 70.

[52]For a further discussion of the 1968 defense arrangement, see the present author's "Maalsetting och Militaermakt," in N.Ø. och Nils Andrén, *Dialog om svensk saekerhet, Strategisk Bulletin* 2–3 (1970). See also Nils Andrén, *Den totala saekerhetspolitiken*, pp. 100–3.

[53]Andrén, *Der totala saekerhetspolitiken*, pp. 61–64.

Denmark, and other NATO countries have found the American nuclear umbrella satisfactory as well as necessary.

The change in 1963 from a "both-and" to "either-or" guideline in repelling attacks over the Baltic and through Finland could indicate that if both should occur at the same time, which would not seem unlikely, someone else would have to deal with the other contingency which the Swedish forces could not realistically hope to manage. The reductions in 1968 seem also compatible with this doctrinal line. The most essential part of the new arrangement is the reduced possibilities of air cover for ground operations. If one counted on Western assistance at all, it would seem that the first, most likely, and most credible contribution would be air support, which could be dispatched quickly.

While Swedish spokesmen will continue to deny that Western assistance forms any part of their strategic planning, outsiders may conclude that without such basic assumptions the military organization that emerged after 1968 as defense for the 1970s seems unable to fulfill the national security objectives which it is expected to meet. The contingency which the Swedish government apparently sees as most probable is the one discussed earlier, where Sweden, because of her marginal strategic objectives and her traditional pragmatic flexibility of neutral policies, is not attacked even if close neighbors are embroiled in armed conflicts. The recent defense reductions might, therefore, be seen as expressing a growing belief in a stabilized Europe where the use of military forces is becoming less and less likely.

This basic assumption was spelled out by the Swedish government as a guideline for the 1968 arrangement:

Sweden's defense policy is based on [the assumption] that the political and military situation in Europe in the foreseeable future will be determined by the existence of two power blocs with at least partially conflicting goals. One can expect that even in the future such a power balance between the great powers will continue to exist, with a high degree of equality between their military resources. Because of this balance, the forces of the great powers will essentially tie each other up and only limited forces can be deployed against us [Sweden].[54]

CONCLUSION

The Scandinavian countries offer a broad spectrum of military capabilities: Iceland with none, Finland with very little, Sweden with very

much. With all the individual differences which we have discussed above, they have one important trait in common: their military doctrines were all formed and developed in the late 1940s and early 1950s. This means that they were based on variables which by now are more than twenty years old. This does not necessarily mean that they no longer are applicable. But with the fast pace of present politics, two decades is a long span of time. One would, therefore, expect that some of the changes that have taken place in this period may have affected the components on which these doctrines rest.

There is hardly a sector within the range of military capabilities that has not changed over the past twenty years. Technological innovations have created new demands for weapons and weapons systems. The costs have gone up. Some items, as combat airplanes and guided missile systems, are moving out of range for small or even middle-size countries. In some cases these countries may still afford to buy the finished products, but the research and development sectors are mostly getting beyond their reach. If they still want them, they will have to accept corresponding ties of interdependence or dependence.

The same is true on the economic and partly also on the political levels. The European Community, which affects all the Scandinavian states in one way or other, is no longer confined to problems of trade and tariffs, but is moving into the political and security fields as well. It has become increasingly difficult to talk about defense only in terms of military hardware. Political moves in the economic field, such as Norway's decision to stay out of the Common Market, are bound to have implications for her national security. The same holds for Sweden's persistent economic nonalignment policies and for Iceland's insistence on extending her fishing limits. While it is still possible to use the term military doctrine, meaning potential uses of military forces, the nonmilitary components require more attention than earlier.

Perhaps the most important variable, pertinent to the Scandinavian states, is the change in the East-West power relations which took place during the decade between the Cuban missile crisis and manifestations of the Nixon doctrine in 1972. Without going into the details of the SALT agreement, the proposed European Conference for Security and Cooperation (ECSC), the mutual and balanced force reductions (MBFR) talks, and other East-West arrangements in Europe, there can be little doubt that the Soviet Union so far has come out on top. Whether or

[54]Andrén, *Den totala saekerhetspolitiken*, p. 92.

not the hardware which it now parades on sea
and land really outmatches that of the United
States and her allies is not of primary political
importance. What counts far more are the *perceptions of power.* The north Europeans can
hardly avoid the impression that the United
States tried to do more than she could manage.
She was over-extended and is being forced to
retreat from the positions she held two decades
ago. While this is readily acknowledged by
President Nixon's "low profile" policy, there
have been no indications as to where the new
outer limits of US influence are supposed to go
in the future. "If what was is too much, how
little is enough?"

.   As we have seen from our discussion of the
Scandinavian defense policies, their military doctrines are, with the exception of Finland, increasingly dependent on contributions and
physical assistance from the United States and
its West European allies. A logical Scandinavian
reaction would be to make an extra effort of their
own to make up for the difference or at least
demonstrate that they are prepared to make a
maximal national effort. But instead of such adjustments to changes in the European power
balance, they seem to take for granted that it
will continue as it has existed in the past. In
fact, they are decreasing their national contributions to defense. The Danes took the most
demonstrative step with their deep-cutting defense proposal, while the Norwegians were
praised in NATO meetings in 1972 for not having followed the Danish example.[55] But as
critics pointed out during the defense debate in
the Storting, the trend in Norway is toward a
"lower defense profile." So is the case in
Sweden. As illustrated by the GNP percentages,
it is not a question of costs, but of national priorities. All the Scandinavian countries could easily
allocate higher portions of their rising GNPs for
defense without essential harm to the domestic
programs they now are pushing. The decisions
on defense reductions are their own free national choices.

Going back to the three major variables which
seem central in formulating military doctrines,
objectives, threats and capabilities, we would
assume that their objectives remain the same.
They aim for as many freedoms, as much national independence as earlier. Capabilities is
not an immediate problem. Their present efforts
are minimal rather than maximal. This leaves
the perceived threat as the most crucial variable.

One gets the impression that the Scandinavian
governments and national majorities either do
not recognize a viable threat to the security of
their countries, or they no longer feel that they
could do much about it—if one should appear.

This may be less true for the East Scandinavians than for their colleagues in West Scandinavia. In terms of military doctrine, the Finns
may be well-placed, as the tasks which their
armed forces are trained to solve are sufficiently limited to give credibility to their performance. While they cannot fight the Soviet
Union, they can credibly take on other states
that might try to get at the Soviet Union through
Finnish territory. The probability of any of the
Western states making such probes is low
enough to give the Finnish forces, small and
restrained as they are, functions which they, at
least at the moment, are able to fulfill.

To some extent this may also be true for the
Swedish forces. With all their impressive gear,
gadgets, and organization, they are no match
for nuclear-armed, overwhelmingly numerous
Soviet forces. They never were. So they lean
ever heavier on their No. 1 scenario with the
marginal attraction and their more-costs-than-
gains deterrence. The second stage, involving
such alternatives as ultimate Western assistance,
is fading along with the American overall superiority on which it was based. With the alternatives of isolated national defense out, and the
prospects of effective Western support actions
becoming ever dimmer, the Swedish position
seems essentially similar to that of Finland,
although with due respect to the differences in
level. While being clearly incapable of holding
back a deliberate Soviet move, the Swedish
forces would seem fully credible for the limited
task of defending Swedish territory against any
power other than the Soviet Union.[56]

The West Scandinavian countries are better
off in the sense that their membership in NATO
provides them with pledges of military assistance. There is no indication at the moment that
the United States and the major allies will refrain from helping one of the smaller members.
But one ought not ignore the fact that NATO is
a *mutual* arrangement. This means that some
degree of reciprocity is required in order to make
the system work. The major members of the
alliance have accepted the numerous reserva-

---

[55] *Nytt fra Norge* 13/12-1972.

[56] This alternative is dealt with in more detail in this
writer's "Maalsetting och Militaerimakt," *Strategisk Bulletin*
2-3 (1970) and "Forsvar mot hjelp. En strategisk modell,"
Norsk Militaert Tidskrift (1970): 545-57.

tions and limitations imposed on them by Norway and Denmark. On the other hand, they have also made it clear that the assistance which they are pledged to provide is being further complicated and jeopardized by the Scandinavian prohibitions and bans on advance preparations. If the downward trend of national defense efforts should continue in the direction now indicated by the recent Danish example, one might reach a point where the essence of mutuality could be dangerously diluted.

One should also keep in mind that within NATO the incentives to action depend on national decisions. A continuation of the US-USSR policy of parity might project Soviet influence in Europe to a point where questions about the effectiveness of a NATO response may become irrelevant for lack of members' requests for armed assistance. In that case, the distinctions between East and West Scandinavian military doctrines may become less significant than they have been in the past.

INDIAN MILITARY POLICY AND STRATEGY

ASHOK KAPUR

India's military doctrine is in a state of evolution, subject to continuing modification as circumstances change. The country is part of a South Asian balance which also includes Pakistan, China, the Soviet Union, and the United States. India is not a signatory of the nuclear nonproliferation treaty, a fact which has not been overlooked by other major powers. Although she may not choose to develop nuclear weapons per se, India is likely "to keep abreast of modern technology," thus keeping her options open.

Ashok Kapur is a lecturer in the Department of Political Science at the University of Waterloo, Ontario, Canada. He has written a number of articles on Indian and South Asian military affairs for various professional journals.

Military strategy and foreign policy are correlated aspects of national policy. In formulating military strategy, the strategic planner must investigate the assumptions underlying foreign policy and military strategy, test the various policies in action, and discover future contingencies and alternative means of action for achieving relevant national objectives. The final task of the military strategist is to develop a preferred policy and strategy in the light of the best means available. British Indian defense policy was based on the idea of a forward posture focused on Afganistan and Tibet—with the USSR as the greater threat to peace in both Afganistan and Tibet and with a weak Chinese Manchu power providing a presence in Tibet.

GEOSTRATEGIC SITUATION

After the withdrawal of British power from the Indian subcontinent in 1947, the geostrategic situation changed. A weak Chinese presence in Tibet was replaced by military rule in Tibet; the forward posture which had been advocated to protect the Indian "ramparts" was no longer available to Indian defense planners; and, although the Soviet threat and ambitions toward south Asia were to be replaced by an immediate Chinese military threat on India's northern borders, the proximity of the Soviet Union to the Indian subcontinent required constant attention.

The changes in the Indian military environment following World War II make close applica-

Reprinted with permission and with a new section by the author from Military Review, 49 (July 1969): 67–74. Copyright © 1969 and © 1973 by the author.

tion of conventional European military practices to Indian conditions difficult. Unlike during the 19th century, India no longer has safe borders which are secure against great power intervention. In fact, India has a hostile frontier of 2,500 miles with China and about 1,500 miles with Pakistan which she must actively defend. Also, until recently, the Indian Ocean and the sealanes extending from the Mediterranean and the Middle East enjoyed the protection of the British and United States navies.

With the British withdrawal east of Suez and the Soviet naval presence in the Indian Ocean, Persian Gulf, and eastern Mediterranean, the security of the sealanes no longer can be taken for granted. A Red Chinese naval buildup could also threaten the Strait of Malacca and the South China Sea.

FACTORS TO CONSIDER

An evaluation of Indian military strategy must take these factors into consideration:

• The Indian perception of the threat from Pakistan and China, including China's possession of nuclear weapons.

• The impact of United States-USSR policies upon the Indian subcontinent in view of their considerable economic and military investment and the political stakes involved.

The post-1947 Indian military theater, like the European theater, lacks depth. Any offensive into Indian territory would require a highly mobile Indian defense in a theater which does not permit a long, attritional defensive campaign. Consequently, the maintenance of an effective deterrent and mobile defense capability becomes a military necessity.

In light of the 1962 Chinese attack upon India, the 1965 Indo-Pakistan war, and India's security dilemma, highlighted by the nonproliferation treaty issue, what is India's own assessment of the strategic threat? What are the military requirements for meeting the threat potential?

Present Indian military capabilities are applicable only to the concept of a limited war. This is due to both internal and external factors. The internal factors concern the political inhibitions within India, the economic-technological-industrial restraints, and the problems of military geography which make general war problematic.

The external factors include the role of great powers, particularly the United States and the Soviet Union. Neither of these powers desires an uncontrollable or unpremeditated conflict in the subcontinent. Thus, the question of Indian deterrence and defense system at the present stage can

be considered only in the context of limited war.

To evaluate Indian defense policy in its proper perspective, it is important to recognize that India is part of the Asian balance. As long as China and India remain antagonistic, India will need to gear her strategic posture to the Sino-Indian strategic model. As long as China remains a political and military problem, the interaction between the United States and China and the USSR and China will constitute important factors in the current military situation in Asia.

Since the question of United States-USSR security assurances to India has been raised at various stages from 1962 onward, the interaction of the strategic models provides a picture of the multiplicity of factors involved. Such factors include different, and often varying, national perceptions of the threat potential, the doctrine or strategy which guide a particular national response, the military systems which are in use or are likely to be used, the precise military environment at a given time, and the ratio of offensive-defensive forces. These foregoing themes are elaborated upon in Models I through IV.

CONVENTIONAL POSTURE

From these models, it may be reasonably assumed that India's conventional military defense posture at present appears to be adequate to meet the limited conventional military threat which China or Pakistan pose to India. However, the emergence of China as a nuclear power, and the maintenance of a massive Chinese military posture in Asia are elements in the military environment which reflect the uncertainty in the strategic balance in Asia.

By 1975, China could have between 400 and 575 nuclear and thermonuclear warheads available for delivery by a combination of manned bombers, submarines, and midrange ballistic missile (MRBM) delivery systems.

India does not have a solid defense against China's strategic threat. As of now, Indian air defense capability consists of a primitive radar system with fighter-interceptor jet aircraft as the mainstay of the air defense system. Three options are open to India for improving her air defense capabilities:

• The establishment of an early warning barrier consisting of a ground-based and airborne radar system in the Himalayan region, with the objective of overseeing about 150 miles across the Himalayas.

• The establishment of a forward-based air defense system with the use of fighter-interceptors armed with air-to-air missiles for inter-

Model I: United States versus China

Doctrine and Strategy	Military System	Military Environment Contingencies	Remarks
Policy of flexible response	Strategic offensive missiles; bombers; limited antiballistic missile system; and limited ground forces	Fluid power situation in China and Asia	Chinese fear of US military threat to China mainland has progressively weakened over the years
Politically build bridges with China		Problem of Chinese nuclear blackmail	
		United States unable or unwilling to commit ground forces in mainland China	
		Strategically, both the United States and China respect each other	Future pattern of China's military threat uncertain because of her internal problems
		China seeks development of intercontinental ballistic missiles and submarines which could conceivably threaten other Asian countries and the United States	

cepting the intruder in the forward, sparsely populated areas.

• A short-range air defense system to defend key areas, military bases, and installations within Indian territory.

THREAT PATTERNS

The problem of an effective air defense system for India's northern borders is only one side of the picture. India's posture is the concern of the strategic aspect of Indian policy. It is impossible to isolate the many variables which will eventually shape India's strategic posture, but it is possible to identify some threat patterns based upon projected Chinese capabilities. It is then possible to project desired Indian strategic options.

In the early time frame, the Chinese threat can be countered by a strong conventional military posture and a strong political and diplomatic posture against China. India's strategic response options during this period include: reliance upon deterrence rather than a nuclear weapons system; achieving deterrence, keeping the nuclear option open, and continuing research and development in missile systems; conditioning the development of nuclear capability upon the

Chinese strategic nuclear force and its threat posture; dependence upon fighter-interceptor aircraft with a fully integrated air defense system which includes surface-to-air, air-to-surface, and air-to-air missiles.

In the longer run, it should be assumed that Chinese MRBM's and intercontinental ballistic missiles (ICBM's) will pose a real threat to India. Chinese ICBM's also will be in a position to threaten US cities against which a thin ABM system will not provide a foolproof guarantee. Consequently, US assurances to India become less valid. Since India cannot field an ABM system because of political or technological reasons, she should develop an indigenous nuclear capability of a counter-city type. Nuclear mines could be used also to seal off Himalayan passes.

Present Indian defense capability allows India to conduct a conventional holding operation against China and Pakistan. Although the use of armor in the central and eastern Indo-Tibetan sectors is out of the question due to geography, there may be areas where it might be feasible to achieve a decisive military breakthrough.

Considerable scope also exists in improving the performance of the Indian Air Force. In the 1965 and 1971 wars, according to official Indian

Model II: United States versus China over India

Doctrine and Strategy	Military System	Military Environment Contingencies	Credibility	Remarks
US military assistance and sales to help India's defense effort against China	Strategic bombers; US 7th Fleet and European Command	2,500 miles of hostile Sino-Indian frontier in inhospitable terrain	US assurance questionable because it is highly conditional	India has capability to conduct holding operations in the Himalayan regions for a limited period
		Possibility of Sino-Pakistan collusion against India		
Highly conditional "assurance" to India against Chinese nuclear blackmail		Long lines of communications		
		Inadequate radar complex in the Himalayan region		
		Problem of night deployments by Chinese forces in Tibet		
		Problem of airborne attacks by Chinese forces		
		Problem of Chinese submarine threats to India		

estimates, the Indian Air Force achieved a favorable situation. This, however, is not the same as air superiority. The Indian Defense Ministry has stated that the lessons from 1965 and 1971 and conclusions from the conflict in western Asia have been, and are being, studied for use in training concepts. If this applies also to the Indian Air Force—and the lesson of Israel's use of air power is quite evident—then one can visualize the possibily of creating a better deterrent or having a military campaign of even shorter duration in the future.

INDIA'S EVOLVING MILITARY DOCTRINE

In a formalistic sense India to date does not have a military doctrine, that is, if a military doctrine is defined as a set of explicitly stated ideas about the conditions, constraints and incentives for the use or threatened use of force in support of national objectives. While military and scholarly analysts in India discuss military problems in the public media, and the Indian General Staff obviously has detailed contingency plans, the fluidity of India's regional and international environment has precluded a firm definition of the external threat. Consequently one needs to speak in terms of India's evolving military doctrine rather than something which is already "in-being."

In the 1950s, as a result of India's relative isolation in the world community on the Kashmir issue and as a result of America's policy in favor of an India-Pakistan military balance (1954–71), India's main military focus was on Pakistan. Its strategic aim was to alter irredentist attitudes in Pakistan toward Kashmir. Two methods were adopted to achieve this objective. First, to change the dynamics of its politics, Kashmir's integration into the Indian body politic was emphasized. The second method was creation of a credible threat of physical coercion if the irredentist attitudes prevailed. The strategic targets were the policies of Pakistan and the United States. India's aim on balance was not necessarily to utilize India's latent military advantage against Pakistan but rather to seek, as far as possible, a bilateral negotiated solution without foreign interference.

Model III: India versus China

Doctrine and Strategy	Military System	Military Environment Contingencies	Credibility
Conduct conventional military holding operations on the Indo-Tibetan border Develop a counter-offensive strike force	Conventional armament Offensive bomber capability limited to old *Canberra* bombers	Same as in Model II. Presently, the threat is essentially conventional	Indian credibility good for conducting conventional holding operations on the Indo-Tibetan border

Model IV: India versus Pakistan

Doctrine and Strategy	Military System	Military Environment Contingencies	Credibility	Remarks
Conduct holding operations Conduct counter-offensive strike aimed at Pakistan's capital and heartland Modernized mobile warfare techniques required Duration of war cannot exceed three weeks because of limited industrial base and possibility of great power intervention Achieve air superiority over the subcontinent	Conventional military forces with strong air support Give attention to Pakistan's superior radar and communication facilities and air facilities India's armor strength is smaller compared to Pakistan's armored forces in division strength	1,500 miles of hostile frontier including the cease-fire in Kashmir	Good at present	Long lines of communications—particularly in the Punjab-Kashmir-Ladakh sector which must be protected Possibility of Sino-Pakistan cooperation

India's 1971 decision to use force was a departure from the conventional approach to India-Pakistan conflict resolution. The 1971 strategy revealed a reorientation in India's definition of a stable balance of power in the subcontinent. Indeed, America's idea of an Indo-Pakistan military balance has been replaced with the Indian idea of a *stable military imbalance* with India as a dominant military power and as a factor for stability in the region.

By contrast, during the early 1960s the military situation was not so favorable for India. At this time the China threat became linked with the danger of 'collusion' or 'parallelism' between China and Pakistan. The emerging three front confrontation (East Pakistan seen as the potential third front) required a search for allies to create a balance of power. In addition it required the growth of two separate military strategies because the political context and tactical military requirements varied between the China and Pakistan fronts. Consequently there emerged the concept of two armies pursuing two different but coordinated military strategies under a single political command.

The Johnson Administration ushered in a period of great change in the premises of Indian strategy. While Moscow continued to support India on Kashmir, Khrushchev's neutrality during the 1962 crisis created an uncertainty about the nature and scope of Soviet commitment on India's behalf against China. The death of President Kennedy robbed India of an opportunity to secure American military aircraft. Moreover, as America became less concerned about the danger of Chinese military aggression in Asia, the rationale of American military assistance began to slip and this was reflected in a slowing down of American military and technological assistance to India. The American choices came to be made in terms of China *or* India—with China as a favored party—and this discrimination naturally did not help India's military position or the strategic context of Indian policy. Consequently, a task of Indian diplomacy and military strategy was to induce an American response on India's behalf and to accelerate military and technological transfers to India. The aim was to establish a well-functioning pipeline between India and the United States as a hedge against the possibility of a peaking in the Indo-Soviet military relationship during the late 1970s.

Overall then, three interests guided Indian military behavior during 1965–71. The first was to prevent the establishment of an India-Pakistan balance; this has been achieved. The second was to prevent the USA from discriminating between India and China in the evolving Asian balance of power; the on-going Indo-US dialogue (1971–73) is geared in part to satisfy this objective. The third interest was to guarantee against the possibility of superpower-directed conflict management à la Tashkent; the 1971 intervention against Pakistan and its outcome secures this aim.

To speculate about the future direction of Indian strategies one needs to keep two factors in mind, one of which has emerged and the other is still emerging. The element which has emerged is that in the 1960s and 1970s (unlike the 1950s) Indian diplomatic and military strategies have become mutually supportive with regard to security planning, targeting doctrines, and the growth of a national defense infrastructure to support national goals. In other words, the uncertainties which bedeviled civil-military relations during the 1950s have been partially removed. India's defense machinery is now more coherent and systematic. Moreover, there is a greater control over the security management process. Another related apect which has emerged from the coordination of national goals, intelligence resources, and military capabilities is that India's conventional military strategy, while it remains at present essentially land-based, nevertheless has an emerging seaward emphasis reflected in the navy's increased share of the defense budget.

Concerning nuclear projects, the foundation of India's program was laid in the mid-1940s. The country now boasts a modest but sophisticated program geared to fusion and fast-breeder research. India has not signed the nuclear nonproliferation treaty (NPT) and has refused to accept international safeguards on its nuclear reactors, except the weak safeguards on Canadian and American supplied reactors. In recent years India has declared that it does not recognise the NPT theory that a peaceful atomic underground explosion is necessarily a military explosion. In addition India has declared its intent to undertake "peaceful" underground nuclear explosions and it has the facilities for that purpose. The emerging link between conventional power and nuclear power lies in the fact that even though sophisticated Indian strategic thinkers recognize that nuclear weapons are not militarily usable, nonetheless there is a clear recognition—and this goes back to Nehru's thinking—that nuclear power has political value. Consequently, unless nuclear weapons actually become frozen assets in the international system and the major powers stop playing the nuclear game, it is likely that to keep abreast of modern technology and to "stay in the game" India will continue to make the link between its conventional and nuclear power more visible in its external behavior.

Overall, one can be certain only about one thing with respect to the doctrinal basis of Indian military and nuclear policy. Unless China deploys missiles against India or provokes it by firing an ICBM test over Indian territory, the China threat is unlikely to be the sole rationale of Indian military strategy during the 1970s. Indian policy is also likely to remain concerned with maintaining a balance between Indo-US and Indo-Soviet relations. Of course, this assumes that the military situation within the subcontinent will remain stable and that there will be no rapprochement between the Soviet Union and China.

CONCLUSION

The traditional role of military power in foreign affairs is no less important today than it has been in past centuries. In fact, the enlarged role of military power in Asian politics has particular relevance for India. Total security at the optimum level is rarely possible. Military strategy is the achievement of security with the best available means and to the maximum extent possible. In the Indian context, the "means" are India's growing, although limited, base of defense production and military imports from friendly powers. Several factors impel India to a policy to prevent war:

- Because of political, military, and geographical conditions, the enemy probably would have the initiative in originating hostilities.
- Prolonged defense is not feasible because the Indian theater lacks depth.
- The possibility of a two-front confrontation with Pakistan and China must be taken into account by Indian planners, even though the danger of joint military action by these countries is not a realistic probability in the foreseeable future.
- Because of restricted resources and difficult lines of communications, particularly in the Kashmir and Indo-Tibetan sectors, a military campaign would be limited.

Consequently, greater attention needs to be paid to deterrence planning.

THE DEVELOPMENT OF THE ISRAELI
POLITICAL-MILITARY DOCTRINE

MICHAEL I. HANDEL

Before the June 1967 "Six Day War" Israel's borders afforded the Arabs considerable military advantage. Territory taken in the war from Syria, Jordan, and Egypt resulted, however, in the establishment of geographically "natural, defensible borders." The basic premise underlying Israeli doctrine is the perception that "the central aim of the Arab countries is to destroy the State of Israel whenever they feel able to do so." The success of the Israeli doctrine in coping with this perceived Arab "threat" can be attributed to the doctrine's logical coherence and its flexibility or adaptability to changing circumstances.

Michael I. Handel, a teaching fellow at the Harvard Center for International Affairs, was born in Israel. A graduate of Hebrew University in Jerusalem, he is currently working toward completion of his Ph.D. at Harvard.

Israel's military and national security problems are unique in many ways. Yet they belong to the group of smaller states, to those who must—rather than those who can. In this respect, there are many valid lessons that other small states can learn from the Israeli experience. Israel has realized that it cannot adopt foreign doctrines of the bigger powers which are irrelevant to its material capabilities, political situation, and cultural milieu. It has had to find its own solutions for its problems. The reserve system, the weapon acquisition and procurement processes, the logistical structure, and all other elements of the doctrine have had to be tailored to Israeli needs, and on occasions developed from scratch. Many of these experiences can be relevant to other small states.

GENERAL BACKGROUND

The Geographic Setting

The evolution of the Israeli military doctrine and the changes that have taken place in it since June 1967 can be properly understood only against the background of its geographic position. "Israel's geographic position until June 1967 was a strategist's nightmare."[1] Israel was sur-

rounded on land by four hostile Arab states, with the additional threat of a blockade from the sea in time of war. From a military point of view it was a state under siege.

The total area of the state until June 1967 was 7,992 square miles, and the total length of the borders was 774 miles (615 miles on land and 159 miles on sea),[2] which created a "vast disproportion between the length of the borders and the depth of the country, turning Israel into a frontier state and making its people frontier conscious."[3] No part of the land borders was defined by natural obstacles. The Syrians enjoyed a considerable advantage sitting on the Golan Heights overlooking Israeli positions and settlements below. The border with Jordan was the longest and most difficult to defend; the West Bank created a large double-edged wedge pointed toward the center of Israel reaching as close as nine miles from the coast, threatening to cut communication between north and south. In the "narrow waist" created by the Jordanian wedge some three quarters of the population as well as the larger part of its industry were concentrated. Jerusalem itself was surrounded from three directions enabling hostile forces to cut it off by a

[1]Michael Brecher, *The Foreign Policy System of Israel* (New Haven: Yale University Press, 1972), p. 65.

[2]Y. Karmon, *Israel's Ceasefire Lines* (Tel Aviv, IDF Chief Education Officer, 1967), pp. 9–10 (Hebrew).

[3]Yigal Allon, *A Curtain of Sand*, rev. ed. (Ha'kibutz Ha' meuchad, 1969), p. 58.

This is an extract of a longer original article, written for this volume and the Conference on Comparative Defense Policy held at the Air Force Academy, February 7–9, 1973. Copyright reserved by the author. An expanded version of this article has appeared as "Israel's Political-Military Doctrine' (Harvard Center for International Affairs Occasional Paper, No. 30, July 1973).

pincer movement from the rest of the country. The border with Egypt was not natural either, while the northern section—the Gaza Strip—constituted a deep wedge reaching as close as thirty miles from Tel Aviv, creating a potential bridgehead for operation against Israeli settlements and lines of communication. This situation forced Israeli strategic planners to allocate adequate forces for containment, the organization of areas in such a way as to enable the continuation of the war effort even if such areas would be cut off, and the organization of peripheral defense systems.[4] Almost all civilian population centers, industrial complexes, and military installations, including first-line combat airfields, were well within the enemy's artillery range on the border as shown on the map.

The implications of this geostrategic situation were no less severe regarding Israel's air defense—it meant a dangerously short warning time for the interception of penetrating enemy aircraft. While most of Israel's territory was covered by its neighbors' radar system, the reverse was not the case. Similarly, most of Israel's population and industrial centers were vulnerable to shelling attacks from the sea. The country lacked any strategic depth and therefore could not, in the event of a surprise attack, try to trade "space" for "time" in order to regroup and organize its defense and counteroffensive. Israel's geostrategic vulnerability was regarded by all its strategists as inviting a surprise attack. The implication for the defensive part of the Israeli military doctrine was the apparent necessity to maintain a constant state of alert, develop its warning systems, stress the role of intelligence, and develop its conventional second strike capability. Its reserve system had to be organized to respond in maximum speed (the complete reserve system can be mobilized within seventy-two hours, while some of the more important units can be activated in a considerably shorter time). In addition, a peripheral defense system of border settlements was organized to hold the first line of defense by its own efforts. The implication of this geostrategic condition on the offensive parts of the doctrine resulted in the development of the doctrine of preemptive first strike (sometimes called interceptive attack)[5] and the capability for the quickest possible transfer of the war to the enemy's territory. In

Dayan's words: "The term 'frontier security' has little meaning in the context of Israel's geography. The entire country is a border and the whole rhythm of national life is affected by any hostile activity from the territory of neighboring states."[6]

It must be added that this predicament was not without some advantages. The first and most salient one was that the Israeli Defense Force (IDF) enjoyed the advantages of interior communication lines, making it easier to shift its forces from one front to another[7] as well as simplifying its logistical problems. Second, the large Arab wedges were subject to envelopment by Israel's forces, turning them from bridgeheads into traps.[8] Third, Israel's central location between Arab states was able to serve as a buffer and block communication and coordination between Arab armies.[9]

Israel's victory in the June 1967 "Six Day War" revolutionized its geostrategic situation. The area delimited by the new ceasefire lines is four times larger than before. The ratio of its land to sea borders was reduced from 4:1 to 2:1.[10]

For the first time Israel has acquired natural, defensible borders. Syria's threatening topographical superiority has been eliminated, and Israeli troops are positioned less than 30 miles from Damascus, creating a potential threat to the Syrian capital. Syria's capacity to cover Israeli air space by radar was reduced, while Israeli capacity to cover Syria was increased and Israeli settlements were removed from Syrian artillery range. The most important changes have, however, occurred along the Jordanian border—the double-edged Jordanian wedge pointing to the sea was eliminated and with it the threat to Israel's "soft underbelly" along the coast. Israel has now obtained a double natural defense line (the first along the river Jordan and the Dead Sea and the second along the central mountain ridge cutting across the "Western Bank") which puts a formidable obstacle in the way of any advancing army. The Jordanian capital is now located less than twenty-five miles from the border. The border with Egypt was pushed way back, eliminating the Egyptian threat to cut the Negev in half and joining forces with Jordan. The new border along the Suez Canal established an excellent "anti-tank ditch," especially when fortified

[4]Y. Raviv, "Israel's Security in the Third Year after the Six Days War," *Maarachot* 45, no. 204 (January 1970): 4 (Hebrew).
[5]The term was suggested by Yigal Allon. See *A Curtain of Sand* and "Active Defense—A Guarantee for Our Security," *Molad* 1 (24), no. 2 (July/August 1967): 137–43, especially p. 142.

[6]Moshe Dayan, "Israel's Border and Security Problems," *Foreign Affairs* 33, no. 2 (1955): 250–67.
[7]Allon, *Curtain of Sand*, p. 59.
[8]*Ibid.*, p. 59.
[9]*Ibid.*, pp. 54–55.
[10]Data Karmon, *Israel's Ceasefire Lines* (Tel Aviv, IDF Education Officer, 1967), pp. 9–10.

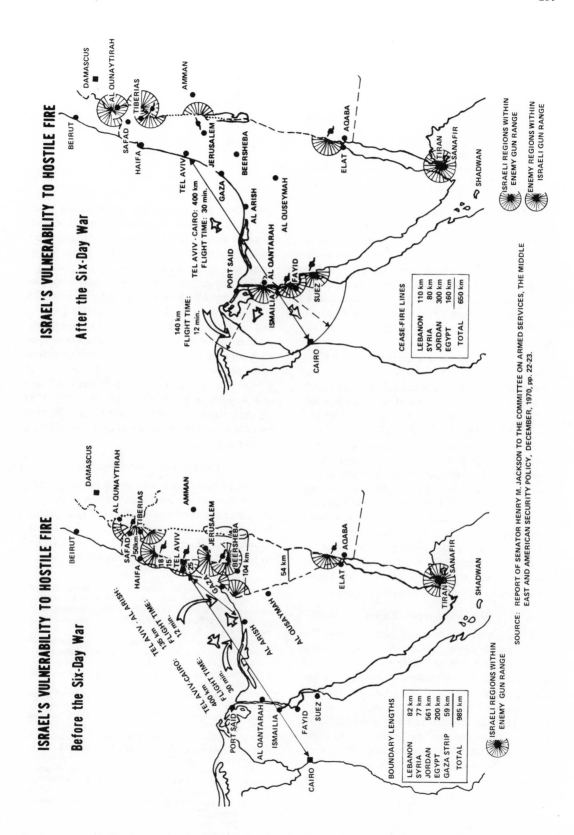

ISRAEL'S VULNERABILITY TO HOSTILE FIRE

After the Six-Day War

ISRAEL'S VULNERABILITY TO HOSTILE FIRE

Before the Six-Day War

CEASE-FIRE LINES	
LEBANON	110 km
SYRIA	80 km
JORDAN	300 km
EGYPT	160 km
TOTAL	650 km

BOUNDARY LENGTHS	
LEBANON	82 km
SYRIA	77 km
JORDAN	561 km
EGYPT	200 km
GAZA STRIP	59 km
TOTAL	985 km

SOURCE: REPORT OF SENATOR HENRY M. JACKSON TO THE COMMITTEE ON ARMED SERVICES, THE MIDDLE EAST AND AMERICAN SECURITY POLICY, DECEMBER, 1970, pp. 22-23.

Table 1. Population: Arab States and Israel (in millions)

	1948	1958	1967
Egypt	19	22	31
Iraq	4.8	5.0	8.3
Syria	2.9	4.0	5.6
Lebanon	1.1	1.5	2.0
Jordon	1.0	1.5	2.2
Saudi Arabia	3.5	4.0	6.0
ARAB TOTAL	32.3	38.0	53.1
ISRAEL	0.65	1.78	2.60
Ratio of Arabs to Israelis	50 to 1	21.3 to 1	20.4 to 1

on the east bank. The Egyptian air threat to Israel from forward airfields in the Sinai has disappeared, while the warning time to Israel has been extended from twelve to thirty minutes, reversing the situation by reducing the warning time for Egypt. Israeli air bases in southern Sinai pose a threat to upper Egypt and can be used to outflank the defenses of lower Egypt, forcing the Egyptians to extend their air defense systems to cover much larger areas than before.

Israel has acquired a greater measure of security by adding strategic depth and better lines of defense giving her more operational maneuverability in terms of time and space. This has led to some important changes in its military doctrine after the "Six Day War"; however, this new geostrategic situation is not without some minor disadvantages. The first is the relatively large Arab population now included in the occupied areas, numbering about one million inhabitants. If we add to them the 350,000 Arabs living in Israel itself then almost a third of the total population under Israeli control could not be relied upon for loyalty to the Israeli government in times of crisis. The second minor disadvantage lies in the extended lines of communication which somewhat complicate Israel's logistical problems.

The Demographic Factor

Israel's small population compared to the Arab states (Table 1) must be accepted as a permanent factor in the Middle Eastern balance of power.[11] Israel has tried to compensate for her small population by total mobilization in times of war, based on a compulsory regular service (three years for all men and two years for women), and on a reserve duty required from every citizen until age 55—a truly remarkable *levée en masse*. It could therefore be said that Israel has

one of the highest military participation ratios (MPR) in the world.[12] The great disparity in manpower is also compensated for by trying to maximize the capabilities inherent in a highly developed society stressing quality over quantity.[13] In this respect, Israel's position has been continually improving with the growing complexities of modern warfare which requires highly qualified and well-trained manpower. One interesting indicator is the large discrepancy between Israel and 15 Arab States in the output of scientific publications per year. Israel publishes 2.4 more such works in a year than all Arab States combined and 4 times as much as Egypt. (In 1971, 1739 scientific works were published in Israel; 750 were published in all the Arab world of which 443 were published in Egypt.)[14]

The Economic Infrastructure

Israel's economy is one of the fastest growing in the world.[15] Its economic position was, however, heavily burdened during the first twenty-five years of its independence by complex security problems. An ever increasing part of its GNP had to be allocated to matters of security.[16]

[11]Brecher, *op. cit.*, p. 68. It must be remembered that these numbers are partially misleading as the "effective population" available for modern military service is much lower than these numbers would indicate. See Nadav Safran, *From War to War* (New York: Pegasus, 1969), pp. 256–65.

[12]This concept was suggested by Stanislav Andreski, *Military Organization and Society* (Berkeley: University of California Press, 1967), pp. 33–39. MPR is defined as "the proportion of militarily utilized individuals in the total population" (p. 33).

[13]For an analysis of the "potential military advantage of a relatively modernized society over a less modernized rival" in the Middle East context, see Dan Horowitz, "Flexible Responsiveness and Military Strategy: The Case of the Israeli Army," *Policy Sciences* 1 (April 1970): 191–205.

[14]Zeev Shiff, "The Scientific Gap between Israel and the Arab States", *Haaretz* (January 19, 1973): 15. A book review on a book by Antoine B. Zahlan from which the data were taken.

[15]U.S. Arms Control and Disarmament Agency, *World Military Expenditures 1971* (Washington, D.C., U.S. Government Printing Office, 1972), p. 12.

[16]Dan Patenkin, "Economy Security and the Balance of Payments," *Maariv* (January 31, 1971): 15. In other words, in the last four years at least 40% of the Israeli government regular budget has been devoted to defense. It must, however, be remembered that since 1967 a large percent of the defense expenditures has actually been *invested* in the military and related industries, thus contributing to the expansion of the economy in the future (p. 17).

The reasons for an ever increasing economic strain lie in the Arab-Israeli arms race, which started to accelerate both quantitatively and qualitatively with the Russian-Egyptian arms deal of 1955. Prior to this deal the Western Powers had had some success in containing the regional arms race under the 1950 Tripartite Agreement.[17] Since then, not only did the quantities of arms in the area increase, but so did the price of modern weapon systems. It must also be remembered that Israel has had to take into account not only Egypt's level of armaments, but also that of other Arab countries, a factor which further complicates Israel's position.

Since Israel almost completely lacks in natural resources and a heavy industrial infrastructure, most of the heavier weapons have to be imported from abroad. This makes the country more vulnerable and dependent, both financially and materially, on foreign countries. The support of the world Jewish community, German reparations in the past, and loans from the United States make up the difference between its own economic capacity and its defense needs. Today Israeli citizens carry on their shoulders the heaviest debt to foreign countries per capita in the world. In this sense Israel is living on credit which future generations will have to pay.

Despite all efforts, economic and military autarky cannot be considered as an attainable goal. At best, dependence on foreign support could be minimized or reduced but not eliminated altogether. Israel can match Egypt but not the USSR. No small state in today's world can compete in an arms race *solely by its own efforts* when its adversary is supported by a super-power.[18]

Political Background

The margins of debate among most Israeli parties over security matters are fairly narrow, and it could be said that for all intents and purposes most of the political parties have tended until recently to support the government on most important security issues, thus reflecting Israeli public opinion on the matter. The government

has, therefore, never had serious opposition to its security policies. This is only natural for a nation under a constant state of siege in which all citizens serve in the army and have a first-hand knowledge of military affairs and matters of security. This must be especially appreciated in view of the otherwise highly fragmented and divided Israeli political system. (There were thirteen parties and splinter parties in the Israeli parliament in 1971.) Generally, matters of security are above party politics.

Regarding civil military relations,[19] Israel can be seen as a modernized state where control over affairs of war and peace is in the hands of the civilian authorities who consult the military professionals whenever it is necessary. This does not mean that the army does not have an exceptionally important role to play within legitimately accepted channels in all matters relating to national security. The government has inevitably to rely on the professional advice of the army in all questions where use of force might be employed and in all matters influencing defense policies. This obviously gives the army an exceptional amount of influence, which so far has not been misused. The army's participation in the governmental decisionmaking process is made through the advice and participation of the chief of staff in the government meetings. Other professional advisors of the general staff include such figures as the head of intelligence, the head of the air force, and the chief of the operations branch. The advice of the chief of staff is usually given directly to the prime minister, who was traditionally the minister of defense as well (an indicator of the central importance attributed to defense issues). This tradition has been changed since the 1967 war when General Dayan became the head of the defense ministry. This change, of course, could potentially lengthen the chain of communication between the army and the government. In case of disagreements between the chief of staff and the prime minister, the latter's opinion always takes precedence and the chief of staff complies with the decision (his most extreme threat is resignation).

External Political Conditions

It is only necessary to mention in this context that Israel, despite earlier efforts by Prime

---

[17]For an interesting analysis of the Middle Eastern arms race, see Safran, *op. cit.*, pp. 143–265.

[18]The economic sphere is considered to be the one in which small states suffer from formidable disadvantage when compared with the great powers. See David Vital, *The Inequality of States* (London: Oxford University Press, 1967); Marshall R. Singer, *Weak States in a World of Powers* (New York: The Free Press, 1972); E. A. G. Robinson (ed.), *Economic Consequences of the Size of Nations* (New York: St. Martin's Press, 1960); and International Peace Research Institute (IPRI). *The Arms Trade with the Third World* (Stockholm: Almquist and Wiksell, 1971), especially part I.

[19]For the best study of civil military relations in Israel, see Amos Perlmutter, *Military and Politics in Israel* (London: Frank Cass, 1969), especially pp. 49–136, excerpts of which appear in this volume, pp. 88–97. See also Ben Halpern, "The Role of the Military in Israel," in John J. Johnson (ed.), *The Role of the Military in Underdeveloped Countries* (Princeton, N.J.: Princeton University Press, 1962), pp. 317–58.

Minister David Ben Gurion in the early 1950s, has not succeeded in establishing a formal military or mutual defense pact with any other state.[20] This is not surprising, as such an agreement would 'automatically' alienate the Arab countries from the country that would sign such a treaty. This situation has made it clear to all involved in the formulation of the Israeli political-military doctrine that ultimately the country has to rely on its own power in times of crisis. Indeed, Israel was unable to secure the support of one power as a permanent source for weapons acquisition. In this respect Israel is probably in a unique position among the free states of the world. It is a traumatic experience that underlies all Israeli strategic thinking; its military doctrine cannot be properly understood without a full understanding of this situation.

This does not mean, however, that Israel completely lacks "alliance value." Being the only militarily powerful and politically stable country in the area, it has reached on more than one occasion, for shorter or longer periods, a de facto alliance with some of the great powers when their interests have coincided (with France in 1955–56, an agreement which lasted almost a decade, and with the United States in the summer of 1970). However, the powers were reluctant on all occasions to formalize this ad hoc cooperation by a formal agreement. Otherwise Israel has had excellent economic and cultural relations with most states in the world, including some of the most important peripheral states in the area—like Turkey, Iran, and Ethiopia—with which it has many common political and strategic interests.

The Evolution of the Israeli Political-Military Doctrine

The best way to understand the current Israeli political-military doctrine is by following its historical evolution.[21] A period of war is followed by a relatively calm period utilized for reorganization, the assimilation of lessons, revision of the doctrine and recuperation, followed again by a period of growing strength combined with intensified military activity culminating in a new war and a repetition of the cycle.[22]

---

[20]The best and only good study available of Israeli foreign policy is Brecher, *op. cit.*, chaps. 2–3.

[21]See my more extensive piece, from which this article is taken, *Israel's Political-Military Doctrine*, unpublished revision of a paper presented to the Conference on Comparative Defense Policy held at the Air Force Academy, February 7–9, 1973, dated May 4, 1973.

[22]Colonel Yuval Neeman while serving as head of the Planning Division of the General Staff in the early 1950s, did a research in which he concluded that intensification of the Arab-Israeli conflict is to be expected every ten years. He deter-

THE ISRAELI POLITICAL-MILITARY DOCTRINE— A SUMMARY[23]

A. The Political Level

1. The basic assumption underlying the Israeli political-military doctrine is the understanding that the *central aim of Arab countries is to destroy the State of Israel whenever they feel able to do so*, while doing everything to harass and disturb its peaceful life.[24]

2. Peace is greatly desired, but security is more important (i.e., any peace settlement that would compromise or undermine Israel's security is not acceptable).

3. Israel is militarily, and to a lesser extent, politically isolated from the rest of the world; it is not a member of any political or military alliance and *must* ultimately *rely completely on its own power in case of emergency.*

4. In case of an imminent war Israel should try to *gain the support of at least one of the big powers*, or at worst, *the understanding* and sympathy of one (or more) of the great powers in order to *neutralize* any potential threat from another great power intervening on behalf of its enemies.[25] The friendship of at least one power is also highly desirable in peacetime in order to secure the procurement of weapons that cannot be manufactured in Israel.

5. Israel has included in its declared *casi belli* the following potential developments in or by its neighboring states:[26]

---

mined on the basis of historical evidence that the Jewish population in Palestine faced an intensified Arab attack every ten years: 1920–21, 1929, 1936–39, 1947–49, 1956, 1967. On the basis of this analysis he predicts an intensification of the conflict around 1977. See Yuval Neeman, "How Shall We Preserve the Achievements of the 1967 War?," *Maariv* (July 18, 1967):3.

[23]Only those elements which are unique or typical of the Israeli political-military doctrine have been included; universal principles (e.g., concentration of power, economy of force, etc.) have not been included in this summary.

[24]This must be understood on the basis of Israel's historical experience in its relation with its neighbors since its independence, in Jewish history in general, and with Arab declarations and attitudes toward it. See Y. Harkabi, *Arab Attitudes to Israel* (Jerusalem: Israel University Press, 1971). This is an excellent content analysis of Arab attitudes toward Israel as reflected in Arab newspapers, radio and literature, studied from a social-psychological approach. Also, see Brecher, *op. cit.*, pp. 280–90.

[25]This principle was formulated by Prime Minister D. Ben Gurion who was always against taking the risk of war without the support of at least one great power. He objected to the opening of the 1967 War without the clear support of a great power. Until now Israel has succeeded in adhering to this principle. It gained Russian help and support during the War of Independence, 1947–49; French active help and support during the Sinai Campaign (and almost a de facto alliance with France for almost a decade afterward); and American sympathy during the 1967 War and during the war of attrition, thus neutralizing a potential Russian threat.

[26]Brecher, *op. cit.*, p. 67; Allon, "Active Defense, the Guarantee for Our Survival," p. 141; Saul Friedlander,

a. *A threatening concentration of Arab military forces on one or more of its borders* (especially when combined with new military treaties among Arab neighboring states directed against Israel).[27]

b. The closing of the Straits of Tiran or *any* other *direct air and sea routes to Israel.*

c. If Arab guerrilla or any other intensified military semi-warfare reaches an intolerable level, and reprisal or retaliation policies prove to be inadequate to cope with the situation.[28]

d. If an Arab state, more powerful than Jordan, attempts to take control over Jordan and change the balance of power on Israel's eastern border.[29]

e. A situation in which Israel's security is seriously undermined by *unbalanced arms supplies* to Arab countries not matched by similar supplies to Israel.[30]

None of these *casi belli*, if provoked, would lead to an automatic or reflexive type of reaction, but rather in each case, an ad hoc decision would be reached, based on general developments and according to other elements of the doctrine.

6. Israel has made it clear that every Arab state bears the responsibility for acts of aggression ensuing from its territory against Israel.

7. Israel will continue efforts to reach the maximum level of military self-sufficiency by domestic production, generally within the limits of cost/benefit considerations, but in exceptionally important weapon systems even in disregard of economic considerations.

8. Israel has made it clear that it desires no confrontation with any of the superpowers, but

that it would fight back if directly threatened or attacked by one.

9. Israel would not be the first state to introduce nuclear weapons into the region, but would keep a nuclear option just in case some other state in the region acquires one. In order to improve its bargaining position vis-à-vis the great powers, it maintains a deliberately ambiguous policy on this issue.

10. Israel is a Jewish state desiring to maintain its national character.[31] It sees as one of its major duties and part of its ideology the protection of the welfare and well-being of Jews all over the world, and speaking on their behalf if necessary. It desires to improve its relations with Jewish communities in the world. The support of Israel by Jewish communities is viewed as the only permanent and reliable source of support for the state.

B. The Strategic Military Level of the Doctrine

1. The IDF would *undertake a preemptive (interceptive) attack if the security of the state is ever endangered.* The political and military intention is defensive, but the strategy is offensive.[32]

2. It is an *iron law* of the Israeli strategic military doctrine that if a war breaks out, it must be *transferred and fought on the opponent's territory as soon as possible.*

3. The IDF should do the best it can to maintain the initiative and dictate the terms of battle.

4. The time available for the conduct of military operations once war has started is extremely short due to the international environment (e.g., the great powers and the UN). Decision and victory must therefore be achieved in the shortest possible time. The strategic doctrine of the IDF stresses the element of speed.[33]

5. As the threat to the security of the state is perceived as a continuous one, a constant state of

---

"Policy Choices before Israel," in Paul Y. Hammond and Sidney S. Alexander (eds.), *Political Dynamics in the Middle East*, pp. 148–49.

[27] This was the *casus belli* leading to the 1967 War, combined with the closure of the Tiran Straits and the signing of the Egyptian-Syrian and Egyptian-Jordanian military agreements. Under different political circumstances ("Operation Rotem") this *casus belli* was not provoked.

[28] This was the major *casus belli* leading to the Sinai Campaign.

[29] Numerous statements to this effect have been made by Israeli politicans and senior military officers. It was close a few times during the 1950s—a possible Iraqi intervention in 1955-56; in 1958 Israel enabled British troops to fly over Israel to prevent a pro-Nasserite coup d'état, and in the summer of 1970, Israel indicated its support for Jordan against a Syrian invasion. Otherwise one of Israel's important principles is *not to intervene* in internal Arab politics.

[30] For such considerations, a year before the Sinai Campaign, after the so-called "Czech-Arms Deal" and before the situation was balanced by arms shipments from France, see David Ben Gurion, *Uniqueness and Mission* (Jerusalem: Maarachot IDF Publishing House, 1971). This was discussed in a meeting with senior officers on December 16, 1955; see "Is There a Need for a Preemptive War Against Egypt?" pp. 218–25. Also, see Friedlander, "Policy Choices Before Israel," p. 149.

[31] This is a central element in the Israeli political doctrine. It indicates, among other things, that it would not accept any settlement of the conflict which might undermine its national character (e.g., a mass return of Arab refugees is unacceptable after a de facto exchange of population has been made with Arab countries.) It does not try permanently to control areas of which the majority population is Arabic in character (the West Bank and the Gaza Strip), but would maintain control over them as long as no solid peace agreement has been reached.

[32] The new borders acquired after the 1967 War considerably reduce the pressures to resort to a preemptive attack.

[33] One other important reason why the element of speed is so important is Israel's inability to carry for an extended period the economic burdens of war or even of a prolonged full reserve mobilization. In accordance the IDF stressed the development of those forces capable of high speed and of moving the war into the enemy's territory. Other forces suitable for more extended types of warfare have received only relatively low priority.

alert must be kept by the IDF, especially by intelligence elements and the air force.

6. Due to economic and demographic constraints, the IDF must base its major forces on a reserve system. Ample warning time is necessary in order to mobilize the reserves under the protection of the regular armed forces. The reserve system must be capable of mobilizing within the shortest possible time.

7. The IDF has to build up and develop its forces, and design its strategic plans according to the assumption that it would have to face *a combination of a coordinated military effort by all neighboring Arab armies* at the same time.

8. In case of war on more than one front the strongest opponent must "be taken care of first."[34]

9. Strategic planning and military thinking are based on the philosophy of indirect approach: the line of least expectation, careful adjustment of means to ends, flexible planning, dislocation of enemy forces, etc.[35] By the strategy of indirect approach, a frame of mind, more than a fixed set of rules or principles is what characterizes the IDF's planning. Considerable attention is given to the study of the enemy's character.

10. The IDF's central peacetime goal is to establish a strong posture of credible deterrence in order to prevent Arab miscalculation regarding the IDF's real power.[36]

C. The Tactical Level of the Doctrine

1. Strategic planning leaves the greatest possible freedom for the commanders in the field—the doctrine stresses initiative, flexibility, improvisation, and the ability of the local commander to exploit unexpected developments and change the original operational plans—as long as they maintain and achieve the objectives assigned to them.

2. One of the most important elements on the "tactical level" is the central attention paid to the quality of middle and lower echelons of command. (This is also the reason why so much freedom for maneuvering and decision can be left to the tactical level.)[37]

3. The IDF stresses quality over quantity trying to maximize the use of highly trained and motivated personnel in relation to the best available weapon systems. Related to this are the high standards for maintenance of equipment.

4. A principle guiding all tactical and strategic planning is the desire to minimize losses and casualties in any possible way.

A BRIEF EVALUATION OF THE DOCTRINE

Small states trying to develop their own political-military doctrines have fewer options and less freedom to formulate their own doctrines. A great power can *first* design its desired doctrine and then build and acquire the weapons best suited for the implementation of the doctrine it chooses. A small and relatively weak state has to find what weapons are available. Only then can the country formulate its doctrine. In other words, its options are considerably more limited. This can be clearly seen by the evolution of Israeli military doctrine, which to a large extent was a function of the weapons that were available. Israel has entered the ranks of those few small states which have succeeded in developing their own original doctrines (others, for example, are Sweden and Switzerland). Israel has developed an original doctrine after realizing that the doctrines of the bigger powers have only limited applicability to the problems of a small state. It has tried to do its best to learn from the lessons and doctrines of other states, and has successfully adapted many of the lessons learned by other states to its own unique needs. Most of the Israeli doctrine is the product of lessons learned through a process of trial and error. Israel has had no other choice; its survival has depended on its military ingenuity and, in this respect, it has found no other states to rely on. Mirabeau once said that "war is the national industry of Prussia." Despite the great difference between the two, this aphorism aptly describes Israel's situation too; the questions of war and survival are the main preoccupations of the community.

There are two criteria according to which we can evaluate the success of a given doctrine—flexibility or adaptability, and coherence.

---

[34]This stands in contradiction to B. H. Liddell-Hart's opinion: "A further deduction, perhaps not positive, but at least suggestive from our survey, is that in a campaign against more than one state or army it is more fruitful to concentrate first against the weaker partner, than to attempt the overthrow of the stronger in the belief that the latter's defeat will automatically involve the collapse of the others." *Strategy of the Indirect Approach* (London: Faber and Faber, 1967), p. 164. This is like the German position on the eve of World War I and Schlieffen's decision to attack first on the French front. See Ritter Gerhard, *The Schlieffen Plan* (London: Oswald Wolff, 1958).

[35]Liddell-Hart, *Strategy of the Indirect Approach*, pp. 333–72.

[36]Israel's policy of reprisals must be understood as part of its deterrence policy.

[37]It may be interesting to note in this context that the longest *basic* officer training course of the IDF (excluding the navy and air force) is between three to six months. Israel does not have any equivalent institute to St. Cyr, West Point, Sandhurst, etc.

Flexibility or Adaptability

The Israeli doctrine could be judged as a clear success according to these criteria. If we usually understand a doctrine as more or less a rigid set of rules serving as a basis for action, this holds true only to a very limited extent for Israel. Its approach to its doctrine is nondoctrinaire and undogmatic. The doctrine is constantly and continuously changed, revised and updated; it is open-ended and one can probably add to its principles—the principle that the doctrine itself, through a continuous feedback process, must never remain static. Everything is done to encourage innovation and change. There is little doctrinal commitment built into the doctrine.

Despite the ever present security problems posing serious pressures, forcing the IDF's senior decisionmakers to direct most of their attention to *current security problems*, they have succeeded remarkably well in focusing their attention on long-range planning and future-oriented problems. They have realized that in order to maintain their success, they must always look forward. Despite successes and victories they are always quick to find weaknesses, mistakes and ample room for improvement. Since the very beginning of the IDF it became clear that the next war will and must be fought very differently from the last one. This was also the reason why the doctrine and its designers paid considerable attention, not only to the *positive* lessons of their war experience, but also to the *negative* lessons, i.e., *what should not be considered relevant in the next war.* They studied the lessons of each war as if they had lost, not won it. In this respect the doctrine can be characterized as being flexible and open-ended. Perhaps it is in this respect that a small state does have a relative advantage over a bigger one. It is more difficult to change a doctrine of a great power. The sheer size of a large army makes centralization into a considerably more difficult problem and, as a result, there is a need for a more rigid set of guiding principles. Frequent changes in the military doctrine of a great power might end in chaos. Also, the bigger the state, the larger the military bureaucracy and the more difficult it becomes to introduce reforms and changes. The process may turn out to be too slow and too many groups with vested interests may attempt to block such changes. A small state operating in one relatively narrow subsystem has usually to develop one major strategy relevant to regional conditions. A great power having worldwide interests cannot enjoy the benefits of "regional specialization." It has to develop a complicated nuclear strategy on various levels; it has to develop a military doctrine for waging a limited war in different areas of the world; it has to develop separate counterguerrilla doctrines, etc. All these are problems spared the policymakers in small states.

The IDF's simple and highly centralized military organization and unified command are one of the explanations for its greater flexibility and receptiveness to change. In terms of adaptability the IDF was always aware of the fact that it cannot simply adapt the doctrines of other states. By contrast, the Egyptian armed forces have been heavily dependent on foreign advice and have mechanically adopted British, German, and Russian doctrines which have, to a large extent, been irrelevant to the area and to the qualities of the Egyptian soldier. Israel tried to develop its own original concepts and weapon systems, an approach which it has found to be very successful. During the years, as the IDF gained in confidence, the trend was to search more and more for such original solutions. A large part of its success lies also in its realistic understanding of its enemy's character capabilities and weaknesses.

Coherence

The principles of the Israeli doctrine were well coordinated between the political and military (strategic and tactical) levels. There is a clear hierarchy and order among those principles summarized above. The military and civilian decisionmakers have successfully cooperated in the formulation of these principles. The politicians, for example, have stressed the international constraints limiting the time available for any military operation and the military has succeeded in translating these limitations imposed on them into a set of military principles—such as in strategic planning, choice of weapons, and tactics—so as to design a suitable military doctrine. In the same way we can see the correlation between the tactical and the strategic levels. For example, strategic planning relies heavily on the improvisation and freedom of action of the tactical commands as the basis of success more than is the case in other armies where the operational plans are designed in detail by the higher echelons. The principles of the doctrine are clearly formulated and synchronized with few, if any, internal contradictions. This is why the doctrine has proven to be a successful guide to action and has led in its application to such positive results.

Israel's success in formulating its doctrine, however, was not as easy and smooth as the results may indicate. The future would pose new problems for those involved in the shaping and continuous process of updating the doctrine. In the last few years the IDF has moved at an accelerated pace into the supersophisticated and highly technical age of military equipment: electronic and counter-electronic warfare, computerized radar control and logistics, helicopter borne infantry, a guided missile navy, and the latest tank and aircraft equipment. The gradual disappearance of the old fashioned infantry and armor and the movement into a highly skilled men/machine type of army is bound to change the character of the IDF. Will it be able to maintain its traditional high moral, ideological and spiritual values? Will it be able to maintain its sense of a mission and dedication and not just become another part of a highly industrialized society? Only time will tell. Other problems will be to attract young and bright people to a growing, bureaucratized, and routinized army, enabling them to develop their individuality and to advance rapidly in the ranks on the basis of their merit. It will become considerably more difficult to recruit such brighter young officers in an industrial society where the military vocation is usually on the lower rungs of the status ladder. On the other hand, the IDF will face the task of rejuvenating the higher command which has reached middle age in the last few years. For an army which has consciously tried to maintain an open-minded attitude to military problems and develop an open-ended doctrine, it will be a task of the first importance to infuse new blood into the high command and prevent sclerosis and decay.

On a different level it seems possible that security problems of a new nature, like terrorism, will shift the focus from conventional military strategy and doctrines more to the direction of cloak and dagger type counter-terror activities. The Israeli doctrine will have to adapt itself to new types of war, which the IDF has not trained to do before. With a possibility of a gradual decline in conventional and counter-guerrilla operations the IDF might develop a growing interest in counter-terror operations of various sorts. No doubt that the IDF experience could prove to be very helpful in many such activities, but on the other hand, an exaggerated amount of attention on part of the IDF's high command to counter-terror operations could lead to some neglect of its more important duties.

As for how the Israeli doctrine will respond in detail to Arab terrorism, it is too early to know in detail, but on a more general level the existing doctrine as outlined above can give us a general idea of the direction it will take. For example, it will try to maintain the initiative wherever possible, transfer the war against terror to the enemy's territory, dictate the terms of the battle

by choosing the place and the means, and above everything, provide a central role for intelligence. Israeli counter-terror operations at this stage already indicate that a combination of conventional and nonconventional means, including the possible use of terror, will be applied.

The Sources of the Flexibility and Coherence of Israeli Doctrine

Israel's success in maintaining a flexible and open-minded attitude towards problems of national security and military affairs is of course of great interest. *On the historical level* earlier pre-statehood experiences were crucial in the formation of a psychological environment conducive to change. The very first paramilitary organization established was the "hashomer" which was at least partly revolutionary in character and, *in contradiction* to Jewish tradition, stressed the need to *break up* with the past and fight back.[38] In the 1930s the 'Yishuv's' main military "indoctrination" was closely tied to Orde Wingate, an unconventional British soldier, who stressed on all levels the need for innovation, daring, and an open-minded approach to military problems; Dayan and Allon were his disciples.[39] In the early 1940s the local Jewish population trained and prepared itself in cooperation with the British army for unconventional *partisan warfare*, a type of warfare stressing individualism, self-reliance, and resourcefulness, against the advancing German Afrika Corps. This period of cooperation with the British army led also to better understanding for the first time of how conventional armies fight and work. Yet, the attitude was not one of uncritical imitation of British military organization, strategic thinking and military operations and conduct.[40] The later underground organizations were also forced to think unconventionally, be capable of adapting themselves to rapidly changing situations, and learn to do the best with the little that was available. In other words, these historical experiences, combined with the pioneering spirit of a young and dynamic society, created a milieu that was conducive to the acceptance of change and nondogmatic attitude toward problems of security. It must be remembered that the whole Zionist experience was a conscious attempt to create a new Jewish identity and break away from centuries-old traditions.

---

[38]See Amos Perlmutter, *Military and Politics in Israel*, pp. 3–48.

[39]See Yigal Allon, *The Making of Israel's Army*; Shabta Tereth, *Moshe Dayan*; and Christopher Sykes, *Orde Wingate* (Cleveland, Ohio: World Publishers, 1959).

[40]See, for example, Yigal Allon, *The Palmach*, pp. 17–18.

On yet another level, Ben Gurion as well as the Israeli military elite encouraged the advancement of young and dynamic officers who dared to put forward new ideas. The capability to innovate as well as fight for one's ideas was made an essential requirement for ambitious officers who wanted to advance. In other words, the career-advancement pattern encouraged nonconformity rather than the conformity in regard to the intellectual requirements demanded of officers.

The Israeli army does not have any military academies for officers. As a result, the body of officers has much less of the corporate character of other armies. And the lack of such common education and indoctrination, therefore, also means that there is less of a common, narrowly limited *weltanschauung*, little group consciousness or uniformity of attitudes. Consequently, there is more room for diversity, checks and balances, and readiness for change.

BIBLIOGRAPHY: MILITARY DOCTRINE

*Aron, Raymond. *The Great Debate*. Garden City, New York: Doubleday, 1965.

Augenstein, B. W. "The Chinese and French Programs for the Development of National Nuclear Forces." *Orbis* 2, (Fall 1969): 846–63.

Baritz, Joseph J. "The Soviet Strategy of Flexible Response." *Institute for the Study of the USSR Bulletin* 16 (April 1969): 25–35.

————. "The Warsaw Pact and the Kremlin's European Strategy." *Institute for the Study of the USSR Bulletin* 17 (May 1970): 15–28.

Bartlett, C. J. *The Long Retreat: A Short History of British Defence Policy 1945–1970*. London: Macmillan, 1972.

Beaton, Leonard. *The Strategic and Political Issues Facing America, Britain and Canada*. London: British-North American Committee, 1971.

————. *The Strategy of Action*. New York: Frederick A. Praeger, 1968.

*Beaufre, Andre. "French Defense Policy." *RUSI Journal* 115 (March 1970): 3.

Bell, Coral. "Australian Defence in the Asian Context." *Royal Central Asian Sociological Journal* 55 (October 1969): 276–87.

Bellany, Ian. *Australia in the Nuclear Age*. Sydney, Australia: Sydney University Press, 1972.

*Bobrow, Davis B. "Peking's Military Calculus." *World Politics* (January 1960): 287–301.

*Boorman, Scott A. *The Protracted Game: A Wei-chi Revolutionary Strategy*. New York: Oxford University Press, 1969.

Boyce, P. J. "Australian Attitudes to Security." Millar, T. B. (ed.) *Australian-New Zealand Defence Cooperation*. Canberra: Australian National University Press, 1968, pp. 16–34.

Brodie, Bernard. *Strategy in the Missile Age*, R-335. Santa Monica, Calif.: The RAND Corp., January 1959.

————. *A Guide to Naval Strategy*. New York: Frederick A. Praeger, 1965.

Brooks, Philip C. "Some Antecedents of British Defence Policy." *Army Quarterly* 102 (October 1971): 70–80.

Brown, Neville. *Arms without Empire: British Defence in the Modern World*. Baltimore: Penguin Books, 1967.

*————. *British Arms and Strategy, 1970–1980*. London: RUSI, May 1969.

Buchan, Alastair. *Europe's Futures, Europe's Choices*. New York: Columbia University Press, 1969.

*————. (ed.). *Problems of Modern Strategy*. New York: Frederick A. Praeger, 1970.

Caldwell, Lawrence T. *Soviet Attitudes to SALT*, Adelphi Paper No. 75. London: IISS, February 1971.

"The Canadian Defence White Paper." *Survival* 13, no. 11 (November 1971): 379–82.

*Debre, Michel. "France's Global Strategy." *Foreign Affairs* 49 (April 1971): 395–406.

DeWeerd, H. A. *The British Effort to Secure An Independent Deterrent 1952–1962*, P-2692. Santa Monica, Calif.: The RAND Corp., January 1963.

Drummond, Stuart. "The West German White Paper of 1970." *Army Quarterly* 101 (January 1971): 158–62.

Dutt, D. Som. *India and the Bomb*, Adelphi Paper, No. 30. London: IISS, November 1966.

*Earle, Edward Mead (ed.). *The Makers of Modern Strategy*. New York: Atheneum, 1966.

*Erickson, John (ed.). *The Military-Technical Revolution: Its Impact on Strategy and Foreign Policy*. New York: Frederick A. Praeger, 1966.

Fontaine, Andre. "What is French Policy?" *Foreign Affairs* 45, no. 1 (October 1966): 56–76.

"For the First Time—A Distinctly Canadian Approach." *Armed Forces Journal International* 110, no. 8 (April 1973): 28–32.

Galloway, Strome. "The Search For a Defence Policy in Canada." *Army Quarterly* 101 (April 1971): 287–94.

Garthoff, Raymond L. *Soviet Strategy in the Nuclear Age*. New York: Frederick A. Praeger, 1958.

———— (ed.). *Sino-Soviet Military Relations*. New York: Frederick A. Praeger, 1966.

*————. *Soviet Military Policy*. New York: Frederick A. Praeger, 1966.

Gelber, Harry G. "Nuclear Weapons in Chinese Strategy." *Problems of Communism* 20 (November-December 1971): 33–64.

*Gelber, H. G. (ed.). *Problems of Australian Defence*. New York: Oxford University Press, 1970.

Giap, Vo Nguyen. *People's War, People's Army*. New York: Frederick A. Praeger, 1962.

Goodman, Elliot R. "DeGaulle's NATO Policy in Perspective." *Orbis* 10 (Fall 1966): 690–723.

Goure, Leon. *The Role of Civil Defense in Soviet Strategy*, RM-3703-PR. Santa Monica, Calif.: The RAND Corp., June 1963.

————. *Notes on the Second Edition of Marshal V. D. Sokolovskii's "Military Strategy,"* RM-3972-PR. Santa Monica, Calif., The RAND Corp., Feb. 1964.

*Gray, Colin S. *Canadian Defence Priorities: A Question of Relevance*. Toronto: Clarke, Irwin, 1972.

Gröndal, Benedikt. *Iceland: From Neutrality to NATO Membership*. Oslo: Universitetsforlaget, 1971.

Grosser, Alfred. *French Foreign Policy Under DeGaulle*. Boston: Little, Brown, 1965.

Gurtov, Melvin. *Indochina in North Vietnamese Strategy*, P-4605. Santa Monica, Calif.: The RAND Corp., March 1971.

Gyani, P. S. "India's Military Strategy." *India Quarterly* 23, no. 1 (Jan.-Mar. 1967): 21–27.

*Halloran, Richard. "Japan's First Defense Plan Since the War Is Disclosed." *New York Times* (March 4, 1973), p. 1.

* = particularly recommended.

Halperin, Morton H. "Chinese Attitudes toward the Use and Control of Nuclear Weapons." Tang Tsou (ed.) *China in Crisis*, vol. II. Chicago: University of Chicago Press, 1968, pp. 135–60.

*Handel, Michael I. "Israel's Political-Military Doctrine." Mimeo. unpublished paper, Harvard University Center for International Affairs, May 1973.

Hanreider, Wolfram F. *The Stable Crisis*. New York: Harper & Row, 1970.

———. *Foreign Policies and the International System: A Theoretical Introduction*. New York: General Learning Press, 1971.

Hawkins, David. *The Defence of Malaysia and Singapore—From AMDA to ANZUK*. London: *RUSI*, Aug. 1972.

*Herrick, Robert W. *Soviet Naval Strategy*. Annapolis, Maryland: U.S. Naval Institute, 1968.

Hinton, Harold C. *China's Turbulent Quest*. Bloomington, Ind.: Indiana University Press, 1972.

Hoag, Malcolm W. "Nuclear Policy and French Intransigence." *Foreign Affairs* 41 (Jan. 1963): 286–98.

Hoeffding, Oleg. *Troop Movements in Soviet Tactical Doctrine: An Annotated Translation*, R-878-PR. Santa Monica, Calif.: The RAND Corp., Nov. 1971.

Hsieh, Alice Langley. *Communist China's Strategy in the Nuclear Era*. Englewood Cliffs, N.J.: Prentice-Hall, 1962.

———. *Communist China's Evolving Military Strategy and Doctrine*, P-646. Arlington, Va.: Institute for Defense Analyses, June 1970.

*Huck, Arthur. *The Security of China*. New York: Columbia University Press, 1970.

Huff, Curtis E. "Foreign Relations of 35 African States: Regional Patterns and Changes After Military Coups d'Etat." Mimeo. paper presented to American Political Science Association Meeting, Chicago, September 1971.

Hunt, Kenneth. "Japan's Military Policy: A New Era Begins?" *Interplay* 4 (Mar. 1971): 44–48.

International Institute for Strategic Studies. *Survey of Strategic Studies*, Adelphi Paper No. 64. London: IISS, Jan. 1970.

———. *Strategic Survey 1972*. London: IISS, 1973.

Iwashima, Hisao. "Japan's Defense Dilemma, Principles and Realities." Mimeo. paper presented to convention of the International Studies Assn., New York, March 1973.

Jabber, Fuad. *Israel's Nuclear Option and U.S. Arms Control Policies*. Los Angeles: Southern California Arms Control and Foreign Policy Seminar, 1972.

*Johnson, A. Ross. *Total National Defense in Yugoslavia*, P-4746. Santa Monica: The RAND Corp., Dec. 1971.

Jukes, Geoffrey. *The Indian Ocean in Soviet Naval Policy*, Adelphi Paper No. 87. London: IISS, May 1972.

Kapur, Ashok. "Peace and Power, India's Nuclear Policy." *Asian Survey* (1970): 779–88.

———. "Nuclear Weapons and Indian Foreign Policy: A Perspective." *World Today* 27 (Sept. 1971): 379–89.

Kekkonen, Urho. *Neutrality: The Finnish Position*. London: Wm. Heinemann, 1970.

*Kissinger, Henry A. (ed.). *Problems of National Strategy*. New York: Frederick A. Praeger, 1965.

———. *The Troubled Partnership*. Garden City, N.Y.: Doubleday, 1966.

Klenberg, Jan. *The Cap and the Straits: Problems of Nordic Security*, Occ. Paper No. 18. Cambridge, Mass.: Harvard University Center for International Affairs, Feb. 1968.

Knorr, Klaus (ed.). *NATO and American Security*. Princeton, N.J.: Princeton University Press, 1969.

*Kohl, Wilfred. *French Nuclear Diplomacy*. Princeton, N.J.: Princeton University Press, 1971.

Kolkowicz, Roman. *The Dilemma of Superpower: Soviet Policy and Strategy in Transition*, P-383. Washington, D.C.: Institute for Defense Analyses, Oct. 1967.

———. "The Warsaw Pact: Entangling Alliance." *Survey*, no. 70/71 (Winter/Spring 1969): 86–101.

———. *Soviet Strategy in the Nuclear Era: Deterrence, Parity and Beyond*, N-789. Washington, D.C.: Institute for Defense Analyses, Sept. 1970.

———. "Strategic Parity and Beyond, Soviet Perspectives." *World Politics* 23, no. 3 (April 1971): 431–52.

Kolodziej, Edward A. "Revolt and Revisionism in the Gaullist Global Vision: An Analysis of French Strategic Policy." *Journal of Politics* 33 (May 1971): 448–77.

*———. "France Ensnared: French Strategic Policy and Bloc Politics After 1968." *Orbis* 15 (Winter 1972): 1085–1108.

Langdon, Frank. "Strains in Current Japanese-American Defense Cooperation." *Asian Survey*, 1969, pp. 703–21.

Lindsey, G. R. *Canadian Maritime Strategy: Should the Emphasis Be Changed?* Ottawa: Department of National Defence, Defence Research Analysis Establishment, July 1969.

*von Loringhaven, Gen. Maj. Bernd Freytag. "Conventional Defence and Nuclear Deterrence—A German View." *Brassey's Annual 1970*. New York: Frederick A. Praeger, 1971. pp. 12–27.

McLin, Jon B. *Canada's Changing Defense Policy, 1957–1963*. Baltimore, Md.: The Johns Hopkins Press, 1967.

MacIntosh, Malcolm. "Soviet Strategic Policy." *World Today* 28 (July 1970): 269–76.

Macridis, Roy C. (ed.). *Foreign Policy in World Politics*, 4th ed. Englewood Cliffs, N.J.: Prentice-Hall, 1972.

Martin, L. W. *British Defence Policy: The Long Recessional*. London: IISS, Adelphi Paper No. 61 (Nov. 1969).

Marzari, Frank. "Deterrence, NATO's Military Strategy and the European Allies." *Queen's Quarterly* 75 (Oct. 1968): 410–71.

Mendl, Wolf. "Perspectives of Contemporary French Defense Policy." *World Today* 24 (Feb. 1968): 50–58.

* = particularly recommended.

*———. *Deterrence and Persuasion: French Nuclear Armament in the Context of National Policy, 1945-1969*. New York: Frederick A. Praeger, 1970.

Michaud, Michael A. G. "India as a Nuclear Power?" Mimeo. a paper written at UCLA under the auspices of the National Security Studies Program, June 1963.

Ministry of Defense, Sweden. *Swedish National Security Policy*, Pub. No. 5/1970. Stockholm: Ministry of Defence, 1970.

Mirchandani, G. G. *India's Nuclear Dilemma*. New Delhi: Popular Book Services, 1968.

Moorsteen, Richard, and Abramowitz, Morton. *Problems of U.S.-China Relations and Governmental Decision-Making*, R-659-DOS/ARPA. Santa Monica, Calif.: The RAND Corp., April 1971.

Morse, Edward L. *A Comparative Approach to the Study of Foreign Policy: Notes on Theorizing*, RM No. 36. Princeton University: Center of International Studies, Nov. 1971.

Moulton, J. L. "The British Role in the Defense of Western Europe: Stopgap or Strategy," Moulton (ed.) *Brassey's Annual 1969*. New York: Frederick A. Praeger, 1969. pp. 142–54.

Mueller, John E. "Canada as a Non-Nuclear Power," Mimeo. a paper written at UCLA under the auspices of the National Security Studies Program, June 1963.

Mukerjee, Dilip. "India's Defence Perspectives," *International Affairs (London)* 44 (Oct. 1968): 666–76.

Muraoka, Kunio. *Japanese Security and the United States*, Adelphi Paper No. 99. London: IISS, Feb. 1973.

Nihart, Brooke. "United Kingdom's Defense Philosophies and Policies," *Armed Forces Journal International* 110, no. 9 (May 1973): 24–26.

Osgood, Robert E. *NATO: The Entangling Alliance*. Chicago: University of Chicago Press, 1962.

*Paret, Peter. *French Revolutionary Warfare From Indochina to Algeria: The Analysis of Political and Military Doctrine*. New York: Frederick A. Praeger, 1964.

*Pierre, Andrew J. *Nuclear Politics: The British Experience with an Independent Strategic Force, 1939-1970*. New York: Oxford University Press, 1972.

Pike, Douglas. *The Viet-Cong Strategy of Terror*. Saigon: U.S. Mission, Feb. 1970.

Plischke, Elmer. "West German Foreign and Defense Policy." *Orbis* 12 (Winter 1969): 1098–1136.

Poirier, Lucien. "Deterrence and the Medium-Sized Powers." *Military Review* 52, no. 11 (Nov. 1972): 22–34.

Pollack, Jonathan D. "Chinese Attitudes towards Nuclear Defense, 1964-9." *China Quarterly* 50 (April-June 1972): 244–72.

Powell, Ralph. "The Military Doctrines of the People's Republic of China." *Proceedings of the Conference on Comparative Defense Policy*, USAF Academy, Colo.: Department of Political Science, 1973.

Quandt, William B. *Palestinian Nationalism: Its Political and Military Dimensions*, R-782-ISA. Santa Monica, Calif.: The RAND Corp., Nov. 1971.

*Quester, George H. "On the Identification of Real and Pretended Communist Military Doctrine." *Journal of Conflict Resolution* 10, no. 2 (June 1966): 172–79.

———. "Japan and the Nuclear Non-Proliferation Treaty." *Asian Survey* (1970): 765–78.

*Richardson, J. L. *Germany and the Atlantic Alliance: The Interaction of Strategy and Politics*. Cambridge, Mass.: Harvard University Press, 1966.

———. *Australia and the Non-Proliferation Treaty*, Canberra Paper #3. Canberra, Australia: Australian National University Press, 1968.

———. "Australian Strategic Perspectives." *International Journal* 26, no. 4 (Autumn 1971): 725–34.

Robinson, Thomas W. *Peking's Revolutionary Strategy in the Developing World: The Failures of Success*, P-4169. Santa Monica, Calif.: The RAND Corp., Aug. 1969.

Rolph, Hammond. "'People's War': Vision Vs. Reality." *Orbis* 14 (Fall 1970): 572–87.

*Rosecrance, R. N. *Defense of the Realm: British Strategy in the Nuclear Epoch*. New York: Columbia University Press, 1968.

Rosenbaum, H. Jon. "Brazil's Foreign Policy: Developmentalism and Beyond." *Orbis* 16 (Spring 1972): 58–84.

Rosenbaum, H. Jon, and Cooper, Glenn M. "Brazil and the Nuclear Non-Proliferation Treaty." *International Affairs* 46 (Jan. 1970): 74–90.

Ross, Anthony C., and King, Peter. *Australia and Nuclear Weapons*. Sydney, Australia: Sydney University Press, 1966.

Rusinow, Dennison I. *The Yugoslav Concept of "All-National Defense."* Hanover, N.H.: American Universities Field Staff, Nov. 1971.

Russell, Charles A., and Hildner, Robert E. "Revolutionary War: A Comparison of Chinese Communist and North Vietnamese Strategy and Tactics." *Air University Review* 24, no. 2, (Jan.-Feb. 1973): 2–12.

Russett, Bruce M., and Cooper, Carolyn C. *Arms Control in Europe: Proposals and Political Constraints*, Monograph 2, Vol. 4, 1966–67. Denver, Colo.: Social Science Foundation & GSIS, 1967.

Salpeter, Eliahu. "Egypt's New Strategy." *New Leader* 54 (Mar. 8, 1971): 5–7.

Schmidt, Helmut. "Security and Detente—Cornerstones of Bonn Policy." *German International* 15 (June 1971): 20.

Schütze, Walter. *European Defence Cooperation and NATO*, Atlantic Paper 3, 1969. Paris: The Atlantic Institute, 1969.

Schwab, George. "Switzerland's Tactical Nuclear Weapons Policy." *Orbis* 13 (Fall 1969): 900–14.

Shah, A. B. (ed.). *India's Defence and Foreign Policies*. Bombay, India: Manaktalas, 1966.

Skoglund, Claës. "The Total Defence of Sweden." J. L. Moulton (ed.), *Brassey's Annual 1971*. New York: Frederick A. Praeger, 1971, pp. 158–71.

*Sokolovskii, V. D. *Soviet Military Strategy*, with analysis and annotation by H. Dinerstein, L. Goure, and T. Wolfe, R-416-PR. Santa Monica, Calif.: The RAND Corp., April 1963.

Spence J. E., and Thomas, Elizabeth. *South Africa's Defense*, Security Studies, Paper No. 8, Los Angeles: UCLA, 1966.

Stewart, Michael. "Britain, Europe and the Alliance." *Foreign Affairs* 48 (July 1970): 648–59.

Suryohadiprojo, Sayidiman. "The Territorial Defense Concept." Mimeo. unpublished. Jakarta, Indonesia.

Sutherland, R. J. "Canada's Long Term Strategic Situation." *International Journal* 17, no. 3 (Summer 1962): 199–223.

"Swiss Concept of Defense." *Military Review* 47 (Dec. 1967): 65–71.

Tanham, George K. *Communist Revolutionary Warfare*, rev. ed. New York: Frederick A. Praeger, 1967.

"To Stay Neutral, Be Ready to Fight." *Armed Forces Journal International* 110, no. 6 (Feb. 1973): 28–32.

Tsau, Tang, and Halperin, Morton. "Mao Tse-tung's Revolutionary Strategy and Peking's International Behavior." *American Political Science Review* 59, no. 1 (March 1965): 80–100.

*Ulstein, Egil. *Nordic Security*, Adelphi Paper No. 81. London: IISS, Nov. 1971.

van der Kroef, J. M. "Australian Defence: Uncertain Fortress." *Far Eastern Economic Review* 63 (1969): 15–18.

———. *Australian Security Policies and Problems*. New York: The National Strategy Information Center, May 1970.

Vigor, Peter, and Erickson, John. "The Soviet View of the Theory and Strategy of War." *RUSI Journal* 115 (June 1970): 3–13.

Weinstein, Franklin B. "The Uses of Foreign Policy in Indonesia: An Approach to the Analysis of Foreign Policy in the Less Developed Countries." *World Politics* 24 (Apr. 1972): 356–81.

*Welfield, John. *Japan and Nuclear China*, Canberra Paper No. 9. Canberra, Australia: Australian National University Press, 1970.

Wilcox, Wayne. *Nuclear Weapons Options and the Strategic Environment in South Asia*. Los Angeles: Southern California Arms Control and Foreign Policy Seminar, June 1971.

Wilkinson, David O. *Comparative Foreign Relations: Framework and Methods*. Belmont, Calif.: Dickenson Publishing Co., 1969.

Williams, Shelton L. *The U.S., India, and the Bomb*. Baltimore: The Johns Hopkins Press, 1969.

———. *Nuclear Non-Proliferation in International Politics: The Japanese Case*, Vol. 9, Mono. 3. Denver: Social Science Foundation and GSIS, University of Denver, 1972.

*Wolfe, Thomas W. *Soviet Strategy at the Crossroads*. Cambridge, Mass.: Harvard University Press, 1964.

———. *The Soviet Voice in the East-West Strategic Dialogue*, P-2851. Santa Monica, Calif.: The RAND Corp., Jan. 1964.

Zagoria, Donald. "The Strategic Debate in Peking." Tang Tsou (ed.), *China in Crisis*, Vol. II. Chicago: University of Chicago Press, 1968, pp. 237–68.

Zedler, John N. *The Multilateral Force: A Misreading of German Aspirations*, Security Studies Paper No. 14, Los Angeles: Security Studies Project, UCLA, 1968.

Ziemke, Earl F. "West Germany's Security Policy." *Current History* 62 (May 1972): 239–43.

* = particularly recommended.

PART FOUR

FORCE POSTURE

INTRODUCTION

OWEN W. LENTZ

Of the various elements of defense policy being surveyed in this book, force posture is the only one that has traditionally been approached from a comparative standpoint. When setting out to develop their force plans, national defense decisionmakers have almost always begun by evaluating the "threat." This means that they collect as much information as possible about the forces of potential adversaries, against which they then judge the adequacy of their own forces. Actual force capability in terms of numbers of military personnel under arms and the number and types of weapons in a nation's inventory has long been the focal point for such comparisons. Decisionmakers have tallied the forces that might be arrayed against their nation and then endeavored to match or surpass such forces either quantitatively or qualitatively.

THE DEVELOPMENT OF COMPARATIVE ANALYSIS

In many ways, this interest in the pure "structure" of the forces of potential adversaries paralleled the type of interest displayed in the earliest attempts at comparison in the field of political science generally. Early comparative politics, too, tended to focus almost entirely on "structural" (in this case, legal and governmental) forms within various governments—most often with less effort at comparison than that undertaken by the military planners in the realm of force posture. Early in the field of comparative politics, country-*by*-country studies were more the norm than country-*to*-country comparisons. What has happened in both fields as they have developed has been an increasing concern for delving beneath the surface structures in order to discover the *explanatory Whys*? behind the more readily apparent but simply *descriptive Whats*? and *Hows*?

In the general field of comparative politics, this interest in "sub-surface" variables—in what

actors and actions shape governmental structures and give them "life," and why—led to what has been labeled the "behavioralist revolution." Without unfolding the entire "behavioralist" *vs.* "traditionalist" debate, suffice it to say that those involved in the behavioralist movement see themselves as espousing more closely the "scientific method" as it has been applied in the basic sciences, i.e., they see themselves as endeavoring to develop theoretical explanatory postulates which are capable of being empirically tested, hopefully in an environment consciously controlled for any value biases that may be held by the investigator. The construction and testing of various models or paradigms that logically incorporate their empirical postulates have characterized the efforts of the behavioralists over the past two decades. The approaches one finds being pursued in this field are wide-ranging and include systems theory, functional analysis, game theory, decisionmaking theory, cybernetics, political culture analysis, survey research, political socialization and development studies, and political psychology. Some, if not all, of these approaches for exploring the subsurface explanatory variables are potentially relevant to the study of force posture.

CAPABILITIES, INTENTIONS, AND ARMS RACES

In the area of force posture analysis, the division between those content with describing the surface structure and those interested in exploring the more deeply buried causal variables pre-dates the behavioralist revolution in the general field of political analysis. Within intelligence bureaucracies, where the collection and analysis of data about foreign force postures have traditionally been performed, there has long been a debate over the emphasis to be placed on structural *capabilities* versus the *intentions* of the decisionmakers responsible for acquiring those capabilities. Given the difficulty of evaluating in-

Major Owen W. Lentz (USAF), M.A., Georgetown University, teaches political science at the USAF Academy, and is currently completing his dissertation to fulfill Ph.D. requirements at M.I.T. His special areas of teaching and research are political theory and defense studies.
The views expressed herein are those of the author and do not necessarily reflect the views of the United States Air Force or the Department of Defense.

tentions, those stressing analysis of capabilities have generally won, but the debate has nevertheless endured. Those military decisionmakers holding to the capability side of this debate have often been suspected of being motivated by the narrow bureaucratic interests of justifying larger forces for their particular service. Whether or not this has indeed been a prime motivator, the prevailing emphasis on capabilities over intentions has tended to exacerbate the arms race.

In fact, concern over reactive arms races based on trying to match, surpass, or offset an adversary's capabilities has kindled interest in control through understanding and perhaps influencing the motives of the decisionmakers. The paradox of such races is that the more intensely they are pursued the more expensive and generally unstable they tend to become, thus threatening (instead of contributing to) national security. Although it is difficult to ascertain the precise influence of arms races on the incidence of war,[1] it has nevertheless been discomforting to realize that an opponent weary of the race who has just achieved a temporary element of superiority, either qualitatively or quantitatively, might decide to preempt and thus be done with it. Also, interest in better understanding and hopefully controlling arms races has received added impetus from the dawning realization over the past decade of the folly of such races at the nuclear level and of the rising costs of sophisticated weaponry even at the conventional level. Hence, as a result of concern over the paradoxical threat to security posed by arms races and over the intentions underlying adversary force postures, recent years have seen increased interest among students of defense policy in analyzing the actors and actions behind the simple "capability" structure of adversary forces.

DIGGING BENEATH THE SURFACE

Those chiefly involved in these deeper analyses of force posture have employed some of the same methodologies that have emerged through the behavioralist revolution in political science. Given the as yet embryonic nature of the discipline of behavioralist research in political science, each of the methods employed still has certain shortcomings.[2] Nevertheless, the section on force posture which follows is demonstrative of

the increased depth of understanding that can be gained by employing a variety of these methodologies.

While Paul Hammond's lead article on force posture suggests "functionalism" as an approach, a reading of the other articles makes it apparent that not all scholars necessarily see this as the most promising avenue of research. In fact, most articles in this section tend to employ a "mixed bag" of analytic techniques. All delineate in some fashion—whether by an accounting of actual forces, or an accounting of the costs of those forces—the "structure" of the military forces under consideration, and each employs the additional "traditional" technique of *describing* the strategic and geographic setting of the countries concerned. Significantly, however, they all go beyond these "surface" manifestations of posture to explore the possible *explanatory* variables lying behind them. In pursuing this exploration one finds examples of functional analysis, system analysis, and decisionmaking process analysis (including both bureaucratic and organizational "imperatives" and leadership "styles").

Clearly, the approaches taken in these articles and their general tenor reflect the shift that has been taking place among the more sophisticated students of force posture from asking: "How many will it take to match (or surpass)?," to "How much is *really enough*?" Comparative force posture analysis, by its very nature, appears to hold out the promise of at least helping us get a better grasp on answers to this latter question. Also, because it provides a convenient avenue for linking "structure," "function," and "process," force posture analysis appears to perhaps be the most promising focal point for pursuing further comparative defense policy studies. There are few things which you can observe and verify in the real world. But force posture—wings, divisions, etc.—is just such an observable phenomenon. The question posed for those writing the articles in this section was simply how might we explain that observable phenomenon, and under what circumstances do the explanations differ. All too often, decisionmakers and academics tend to interpret those tangible phenomena as having been built and deployed according to a rational calculation of potential external use—an explanation which can be incomplete, misleading, or even quite wrong.[3]

[1]See Colin S. Gray, "The Arms Race Phenomenon," in Richard G. Head and Ervin J. Rokke (eds.), *American Defense Policy*, third edition (Baltimore: The Johns Hopkins Press, 1973).

[2]For an excellent discussion of both the strengths and the shortcomings of the various methodologies being employed in

behavioralist research, as well as the traditionalist vs. behavioralist debate mentioned earlier, see Lawrence C. Mayer's *Comparative Political Inquiry: A Methodological Survey* (Homewood, Ill.: The Dorsey Press, 1972).

[3]Remarks by Major Frank Horton, Conference Co-director, during discussion at the Conference on Comparative Defense Policy, 7–9 February 1973, USAF Academy, Colorado.

THE CROSS-NATIONAL COMPARISON OF FORCE POSTURES

PAUL Y. HAMMOND

While noting that objective *force description—meaning the current force structure of a nation's military establishment and its planned longer-term* output *capabilities—is the usual way of defining force posture, Hammond departs from this norm to delve into the more* subjective *question of the functional motives underlying the development of forces and the functional perceptions nations develop about these objective capabilities. Through the use of brief case examples, he develops a functional model for looking at the inputs to force postures, emphasizing that "force posture varies not only according to military and economic 'logic,' but also according to how inclusive of nonmilitary functions it is."*

Professor Hammond is Associate Head of the Social Science Department at the RAND Corporation and has served on the faculty of several universities. Additionally, Professor Hammond has consulted for a number of organizations including the Institute for Defense Analysis and the Hudson Institute, and is the author of Organizing for Defense *(1961);* The Cold War Years *(1969); and coauthor of* Strategy, Politics, and Defense Budgets *(1962);* American Civil-Military Decisions *(1963); and* The United States in a Disarmed World *(1966).*

THE CONCEPT: ITS MEANING AND USE

The term *force posture* came into prominence as a concept in the fifties as a way to focus on the output or program capabilities of military forces-in-being, rather than an input description of armed forces after their next preferred increment—which is the usual preoccupation of military spokesmen. Force posture also drew attention because of its key role in any concern about the effect of military policies on opposing forces—the dynamic interaction so crucial to arms control analysis. It is also valuable because of its hard empirical qualities: (1) It deals in capabilities that can be observed from both sides; (2) It is the *actual* "output" of one's own resource inputs and organizational process and, as such, is not always what one anticipated.

Our concern here will be with comparing force posture cross-nationally. We will not treat it to the exclusion of other approaches—doctrine, strategy, ideology, etc. Force posture makes little sense when it is entirely isolated from these other concepts.

I take *objective* force posture to mean the current military force structure of a nation-state's military establishment, stated as immediate, short-term, and planned longer-term *output capabilities*. *Subjective* force posture consists of *perceptions* about these capabilities. While there can be as many subjective force postures as there are observers, two—the force owner's and his opponent's—are particularly relevant.

Force posture, like doctrine and strategy, reflects the stream of past decisions and ongoing practices concerning the military establishment, past views, and to a lesser extent present ones, about the nature of the military threat, the current organizational process and the political process situations, previous and current armed service rivalries, the adaptation of forces-in-being to changing perceptions of the military threat, the risk-bearing propensities of political and military decisionmakers, etc.

The range of tolerable threat perceptions mortgaged to past decisions is limited by bureaucratic, if not cognitive, dissonance. Any American service or service component is reluctant to admit that it is incapable of meeting a recognized military threat, even when it becomes alarmed by its apparent inferiority to an opposing force, for fear of jeopardizing its competitive claim on re-

This is an original article written for this volume and the Conference on Comparative Defense Policy held at the Air Force Academy, February 7–9, 1973. Copyright © 1973, the RAND Corporation.

sources and missions. The fulfillment of its national security function will always be claimed to be within immediate reach.

Force posture deals with present capabilities—with the military status quo. In doing so, it also describes important constraints on government-wide attitudes about national security policy. How the government responds militarily to external developments turns on what it can do, at least to begin with, in the short run.

Force postures can correspond to distinct and familiar political styles. A conservative position on force posture is likely to coincide with a conservative position on the function of the military establishment and of strategy and posture in the internal political system. A particularly strong military capability vis-à-vis one's adversary's makes it easier to pursue foreign policies that bolster the government's authority by strengthening its prestige and public support. De Gaulle's foreign policy was of this nature. His nuclear military policy supported his diplomatic claim for France of a major position as a world power. Consistent with his long-held view about the international system, he played down the ideological verities of the Cold War in favor of the secular verities of nationalism and power conflict. But his position was not incompatible with that of anti-Communist ideologues on the French Right. De Gaulle had come to power through doubtful constitutional means and had immediately faced a threat from rigid and narrow right-wing military ideologues. The broadly nationalist appeal of a distinct set of policies that included ambitious force posture aspirations, helped to eliminate his dependence on the French Right and win wider support for his regime. This striking French example shows that force posture may be used for internal political purposes in addition to its function of dealing with perceived external military threats. As it should also indicate, the varied *functions* that force posture performs in the governing process makes comparisons across states tricky. It will be helpful to look more closely at functional variants in order better to control for them.

A FUNCTIONAL APPROACH TO POSTURE

Military establishments play a variety of roles (sometimes simultaneously) in national states. They may provide the ruling elite or serve as a constitutional arbiter. They are sometimes a privileged interest group and sometimes play more subordinate instrumental roles as implementers of national development projects and guardians against internal and external threats,

as their superiors specify these tasks. Usually they trade on their instrumental roles to get privileges and thereby modify their subordinate status. Of these many functions, the most widely recognized (hence, most legitimate) is providing security against external threats. This is the one that is given emphasis in the concept of force posture.

For schematic convenience, one might order the military institutional roles that are particularly germane to force posture, as follows:

1. National unifier: using military institutions and policies as a source of national political cohesion by setting aside (not solving or accommodating) interest and goal conflicts.
2. National accommodator: using them to achieve more political cohesion by narrowing and eliminating political differences.
3. External buffer and accommodator: using them to narrow and eliminate differences between internal or domestic interests and external or foreign interests.
4. Military defender: meeting perceived foreign military threats.

Many states can reduce internal political conflict in times of crisis. The military, in their role as national unifier, are often vital to that effort. Military establishments also get involved in distributional politics—where to locate a base, where and with what firm to place a contract, what civil services to provide what local political interests. In doing these things, the military act as an accommodator of interests within the state. As elements of alliance mechanisms and as instruments of diplomacy, military institutions and policies buffer and accommodate internal interests with external interests. Finally, the distinctly military function of military institutions is to cope with military threats from other states.

If we now deal with these roles as they apply to force posture, we can put aside certain finer points of comparison across national variants.

Force posture and associated elements (strategy and doctrine, e.g.) have been used as national unifiers. De Gaulle's claim about the *force de frappe* and French force posture was an essential part of his claim to a high status and high prestige position for France in international affairs that helped win his regime legitimacy in France while it allowed him so to undercut the French military establishment as a rival right-wing rallying point. Similarly, the abrupt shift in force posture goals that India made after the Chinese attack in 1962 helped to rally Indian public sentiments in favor of the government and enhance the Indian military's role (until then quite limited) as a symbol of national unity. Evidently the Indian Army's success in Bangladesh added to this rallying point or national unifier role for the Indian Army.

The promotion of national political unity through military posturing is a familiar pattern and supposedly one of the worst features of the state system. The force postures that are compatible with the effort to use foreign successes to unify the country politically are provocative or at least menacing. The UAR's posture towards Israel tends to be openly (and emptily) menacing. Israel's posture certainly menaces in return. Its strategic position permits it no alternatives when its neighbors menace it in response to their own difficult internal political situations. Sukarno made much of expansionist jingoism in his last years of rule in Indonesia, evidently as part of that complex process of symbol manipulation that he used to aggregate power in a state that had very limited political cohesion.

De Gaulle's nuclear posture may appear to have been a compensation for his giving up of French political claims in Algeria, and doubtless India's military policy after 1962—the substantial expansion of her armed forces and her takeover of Goa—should also be viewed in part as compensatory action; but unlike the French case, there is little assurance that India will not take more expansionist military action—if, indeed, it has not already done so.

Military posturing as a *national unifier* can be more parades than combat readiness—more force posturing than force posture. When that happens, the prestige that attaches to the military establishment may not be entirely justified by even the narrow standards that are applied. Nevertheless, the parade capability is not of negligible political value. Few military establishments neglect it, and the powerful as well as the weak exploit it. For the less obvious demonstrations, one can substitute for the spit and polish and the massing of troops and hardware on parade the reputation of technological achievement manipulated by other means—demonstrated so that it will be reported in the mass media or simply conveyed through the elite channels of the military-industrial-technological complex. Some of the appetites for advanced aircraft among less developed countries (LDCs) that puzzle and dismay observers in the industrialized states are quite justifiable for the wide public impact that can be achieved with them in the villages—well beyond the "reach" of parading troops.

It should be evident that where military establishments serve as national unifiers, internal political forces can combine with military aspirations to induce external military assertiveness. Some critics of Gaullist France's force posture and doctrines claimed that they unnecessarily provoked the Soviet Union. (Other criticisms of the *force de frappe* undercut this charge.) The specialized nature of the *force de frappe* may have assured that any French jingoism that resulted from it would not get very far because the *force* could be used for no other purpose than deterring the Russians. General purpose forces that serve as national unifiers—India's, Israel's, Iran's—would have more opportunities for pursuing expansionist inclinations that their existence may serve to generate because they are (or appear to be) capable of the military actions that would be entailed.

A military force that is a *national accommodator* has a weak or nonexistent force posture and plays its role in national political life mainly through civic action activities. When military activities are involved, these other outputs usually suffer. In peacetime, the military establishment is an instrument of national economic and political development. The United States Army from the end of the Civil War and until World War I was mainly a means to civil goals. (The Spanish-American War did not have much impact, even temporarily, on this civil role.) The dispersed Western Indian fort location of the American Army and its involvements with civil functions left little room for a force posture. The Brazilian Army has usually played a comparable role in national development (a role that the military coup of 1964 much complicated, to be sure). In both of these cases, the result of greater national unity does not mean, as it does where the military is a *national unifier*, the centralization of authority. We have termed this role *national accommodator* because the military becomes a means for accommodating conflicting interests through its capacity to distribute goals and services. Specifically, it serves as an instrument of log-rolling and pork-barreling that facilitates the spreading of power to some extent. It is interesting to note that the cohesion in public affairs that it facilitates is structurally "flat"—a legislative-like cohesion rather than the structurally "tall" authoritarian and deferential politics that the appeal to rally round the prestigious leader will induce. The third type of function, the *external buffer* and *accommodator*, is comparable to that of the second, but deals with the state's relationship to other, not unfriendly powers, including allies, clients, donors, and vendors. Force posture in these circumstances is likely to accommodate through ambiguity or obfuscation the differences in military purposes between the two or more military partners.

The function of *military defender* is the most straightforward and narrow of the four. When it is performed well it includes a peculiar forestalling role that protects against the acquisition of broader roles. For example, rather than serving as a rallying point to strengthen the national regime and fire public enthusiasm for national achievements and aspirations as they are being expressed through military means, a successful force posture in this narrow sense would forestall the negative public anxieties that become the stuff that produces authoritarian politics.

In sum, any attempt we make to compare military establishments or their force postures should take into account differences in the function that military force postures play within each state. Military establishments and military force postures play surprisingly similar roles in many states—as symbols of national unity, as instruments of national economic and social development, as distributors of political and economic valuables. Sometimes these role similarities are overdrawn. The literature of the early 1960s on the military as modernizers in the LDCs probably presented an overly uniform picture of the military as modernizers. There is no doubt that one can talk about common roles to some extent. But many of these common functions or purposes were peculiarly nonmilitary. The variations in the mix and strength of such roles has had an important bearing on force posture. In the next section we will describe patterns of variance as they can be associated with general differences in force postures.

THE PRINCIPAL FUNCTIONAL VARIANTS

Geoffrey Kemp accounts for Israel's force posture first on the basis of the extreme time pressure on Israel's military readiness requirements, and then on the basis of three elements: *resources, milieu,* and *capacity for collective action*.[1] Explaining force posture in this way implies or assumes a strongly deterministic military rationalism that responds to identifiable requirements or vectors. Israel may in this respect be a misleading case. Her threat is highly visible and quite immediate; the margins for her survival are narrow, or seemingly so. If Israel has avoided becoming a garrison state, it is not because she lacks the external determinants of one. Her military imperatives are severe and compelling. They require the highest priority.

However, even in the extreme case of Israel, as a nation-state under long-term siege, other factors than military logic help account for force posture. For example, judging by the debate that went on within Israel after the Six Day War concerning the disposition of the newly occupied territories, one is able to conclude that the decision against any significant withdrawal turned on considerations about how to deal with the enemy in political or diplomatic terms, as well as in military logic.

Force postures and threat perceptions will not all be equally determined by nonmilitary factors at any one time, and they may vary over time. Greenwood, in another article on force posture,[2] argues that the three major West European powers, West Germany, France and Great Britain, are converging in their military postures as they cast off the components. This thesis can be readily recast to state it as a convergence on military and economic logic (at least the kind of "logic" that has usually looked so self-evident from Washington). Furthermore, if the Israeli case is an extreme one, then one can imagine that when states are much less tightly constrained by military logic than is Israel, they would be more able and therefore more inclined to use military posture for other purposes. When Elihu Root, in his first army *Annual Report* on the War Department (in 1899) took the extraordinary step of stating that the purpose of the U.S. Army was to fight wars, he must have been reacting to an extreme opposite of the modern Israeli case. In fact, it is quite true that the American Army between the Civil War and World War I tended to lose sight of its warfighting purpose, the Indian wars and the Spanish-American War notwithstanding, as it acquired a variety of peacetime functions. We can take it at the turn of the century as an extreme opposite of the Israeli Army today with respect to a readiness-demanding milieu. Its performance in World War I confirms that the resources available to it when necessary, and the capacity of the state (including the Army) for collective action were amply adjustable constraints.

The post-Civil War U.S. Army has contemporary cognates—in China's PLA, in the Brazilian Army, in Iran's Ground Forces, in Haile Selassie's garrison-ridden army (at least before the reforms of the mid-sixties). It is in fact the rule, rather than the exception, that states without a widely recognized military threat use their armies for other than "military purposes."

---

[1] See his article in this volume, pp. 391–405.

[2] See below, pp. 340–62.

I have stated this point as though armies are passive instruments, and have left in doubt whether by "armies" I mean as well the other services. As for how inclusively I use the term, let me leave that until later. It deserves close attention, but at a more appropriate place. As for the passivity of the army, here it is mainly a convenience that could be misleading. Armies get drawn off into other than military activities mainly when military activities are unappealing to the major elements of the state. Armies prefer to do military things when they have choices. Other tasks mean less autonomy and usually less status for them. (The PLA may be an exception, but is more probably a significant variant of several factors.) Military tasks are normally preferred unless they are sure to be less rewarding. When the demand for military services is very low, armed forces will settle for performing other tasks. A high demand for their services may also draw them into nonmilitary roles as well, in an effort to assure them the resources they need to do their thing. This bivariate distribution in the breadth of military participation in public affairs describes and partially explains military domination in national politics when it occurs. It also suggests that we should expect to find the most assertive behavior of the military at the two extremes and the most passive behavior in the middle. The one extreme is the garrison state, the other extreme is the nonmilitary state. Just as Israel does not fit the garrison state because of factors not included in this model, so in other states—Indonesia, Pakistan, Argentina—the military are prominent for reasons other than what this model includes. Rarely in the contemporary world have military elites come to power strictly on the grounds of the urgency of the external threat. Hence, we leave this variant of military nonpassivity aside here and use the case of weak military justification as the extreme contrast from strict military demands.

But if we broaden the frame of reference to include other vectors when the military requirements are weak, does the condition of weak military requirements as perceived go with military institutions—and hence a force posture—that are broadly inclusive of nonmilitary as well as military functions?

We are now ready to state the main thesis of this chapter. Force posture varies not only according to military and economic "logic," but also according to how inclusive of nonmilitary functions it is. In this section we will examine the differences these nonmilitary elements seem to induce in force posture. We should then be in a position to sort out some of the commonly identified norms that are applied to force posture to determine to what extent they rest on the logic of military operations and economy and the extent to which they reflect other purposes and objectives. In the last section we will attempt to state some general norms by which to judge and appraise force postures.

Weak Force Posture

Weak force posture and low concentration on military functions tend to go with ground forces that are heavily involved in national political and economic development. The post-Civil War U.S. Army is a case in point. Many Latin American armies, certainly including Brazil's, Argentina's, Peru's, and Venezuela's, should also be included.

In the case of Latin American states, the threat has commonly been stated to be on three levels: hemisphere, regional-external, and internal security. If this is true, then we should expect force postures to be complex because it will reflect the complex and contingent character of its threat analysis. But this would be to miss the main point.

The location and activities of the Brazilian Army in Brazil, as an example, includes civil functions that are a distinct diversion from strict military activities. The Brazilian military establishment has traditionally had an important internal security function. But it has, in addition, performed strictly civil activities as well. Internal security functions are viewed in the Brazilian Army as considerably broader than policing activities, and at least to the extent that this broader view draws the army into noncoercive civic programs, this view may be commendable. Nevertheless, a Brazilian force posture statement must be diffuse and weak because it must either exclude the legitimate functions of the Brazilian armed forces or, in order to include them, be a lengthy and complicated report about the local activities of a military establishment that operates normally under considerable regional autonomy.

The Japanese Self-Defense Forces are also concerned mainly with internal security. Unlike the Brazilian military, however, the Japanese force confines itself quite exclusively to policing activities. It is a highly specialized force, as befits a highly differentiated industrial state.

In China, the PLA has a broad set of functions to perform—political, economic, and military. The Chinese government, or PRC, has publicized statements that minimize the vulnerability of China to nuclear weapons, at the same time that it has sacrificed heavily to acquire them. This disparity between declarations and policies, together with the strongly regionalized structure of the PLA, makes it difficult for the outsider to be clear about the coherence of Chinese force posture. Nevertheless, the multiple functions which the PLA (but not the Chinese naval and air forces) play in the governing of China should make it clear that force posture as a statement about instantaneous and short-term Chinese military actions and reactions would have to be heavily cluttered with the varied and ongoing roles of the PLA.

It has been argued that a "civilianized" military establishment—one that is embroiled in internal civil tasks—is desirable because it deflects military energies away from socially less productive activities. A diffuse force posture that is the result of such broad involvement by the military would, then, seem to be a positive indicator where external threats are not important. Even in the case of a negligible threat environment, other factors enter in, however. Military establishments that become involved in national political and economic development sometimes generate from that experience a great deal of impatience about "impediments" to development. As Stepan has shown,[3] the precedent-breaking military coup in Brazil in 1964 was driven by strong collective military ambitions to form and restructure Brazil's political and economic system. Ayub Khan's coup in Pakistan in 1958 evidently represented a comparable personal ambition, combined with an additional factor, a strong malaise in the Pakistan Army about "politicians" because of the way they used the Army to cope with severe law-and-order problems. The Pakistan Army was in a position to choose not to be used in that way. If military rule should be avoided, then military involvement in civil affairs under the direction of civil authorities is not a good thing when it serves to induce military rule.

Militant or Pretentious Force Postures

At the opposite extreme of the weak force posture associated with immersion in domestic tasks is the classical problem type that is provocative and threatening. Nasser's UAR (to a lesser extent, Sadat's), and Sukarno's Indonesia, can be said to have had militant and pretentious force postures because they threatened neighbors with military measures, took some but not enough steps to carry out their threats, and did these things under circumstances that indicated

that an important motivation for their action was its effect on internal mass politics (and for Nasser, on the rest of the Arab world, as well). Such military postures are pretentious in part because they play to the political galleries, but also because more is threatened than the military facts—the objective force posture—will support. Pretentiousness, by the way, in these circumstances, may be a very good thing. On the one hand, if the point of reference is how much trouble is caused by a given amount of military capability, pretentiousness is an extension, an add-on, beyond what one could expect from the prudent use of military force. On the other hand, if pretentiousness reflects how much less actual trouble is caused than passing annoyance from posturing in response to internal political considerations, then it represents a desirable short-fall.

In the Egyptian example, the militant and pretentious force posture patently has an important and, one can argue, a legitimate political role. The appeal of a common outside enemy and of the persistent goal of war against Israel remains a convenient source of short-term political appeal in Egypt, to which in 1967 was added the recovery of substantial lost territories. The objective military situation is surely grounds for a force posture that identifies Israel as the enemy. The militancy and pretentiousness enter when Egyptian rulers turn hostility toward Israel into an instrument of internal political cohesion.

While Egypt is an extreme case, few, if any, force postures are free of this characteristic. For states rarely adopt force postures that cost them heavily in domestic political support; rather, they design force postures to have sufficient domestic appeal to assure the necessary internal support over the required time period. When General Marshall supported universal military training at the end of World War II, evidently a significant quality of the mobilization policy implied by that proposal was that the American public would be able to live with it over the long term. The severely erroneous assumption involved does not invalidate the general objective to square military posture with public moods and sentiments.

One could argue that the trouble with pretentious policies like Nasser's or Hitler's that distinguishes them from Marshall's is that their force posture is part of an effort to arouse public excitement in order to induce greater national cohesion, whereas Marshall's was a more passive, nonmanipulative approach to public opinion. Yet there are other examples of arousal that pass for legitimate and appropriate use of force posture in the political dimension, as well. Suppose Presi-

[3]Alfred C. Stepan, *The Military in Politics: Changing Patterns in Brazil* (Princeton: Princeton University Press, 1971), pp. 178–87.

dent Kennedy had managed the Cuban missile crisis in such a way that the crisis force posture, together with other elements in his handling of the crisis, had lost for him support rather than winning it. Suppose, as a consequence, that when he announced to the American public the presence of Soviet missiles in Cuba, the public reaction had been against rather than supportive of his actions. These can only be matters of speculation, but it seems unlikely that he would have dealt with Moscow with as strong a hand. He in fact carefully orchestrated his public performance in the missile crisis—including the public view of force posture—evidently to achieve just the supportive public response that he got.

Gaullist nuclear strategic force posture is probably justifiable on the same basis, however irritating it has been, especially to U.S. officials. That posture was part of a larger pattern of foreign political and military policy that aimed for high status and prestige for the French nation. We alluded earlier in this article to the fact that De Gaulle came to power with the assistance of the French military, that he rapidly established a regime whose legitimacy was wholly independent of the French military. De Gaulle's foreign and domestic policies were scarcely beyond criticism, but he seems to have accomplished an extraordinary feat in rallying the French public to the authority of his regime: the founding of a French polity of unprecedented stability and prosperity. Surely not an insignificant part of that feat was the French military posture that he adopted, including a nuclear force posture that claimed for France equality with the Soviet Union and the United States, and established or purported to establish France as a major force in world diplomacy; and an independent conventional force posture accomplished by extricating French forces from the NATO command structure and from NATO deployments. Given the function that De Gaulle's force posture performed as an aid to the regime's consolidation, it is not at all surprising (and was perhaps commendable) that he avoided quibbling about the feasibility of its implementation and tolerated a certain lagging in the effecting of his policies of noncooperation with the NATO commands, or that in more recent years some of the weaker features of this militant and pretentious force posture would be quietly abandoned.

France was in fact the second nuclear power to attempt to achieve an entirely independent posture that it could not sustain. In the United Kingdom nuclear prestige had also appeared to be an attractive source of comfort for an incumbent Conservative government suffering from the political symptoms of a shrinking empire that were particularly acute after the debacle that Suez was for it in 1956. It may, however, be easier to dismiss the political functions the British nuclear force posture performed because it appears to have been more partisan in a highly competitive political system.

Dependence and Independence

Another broad function force posture plays is to assist the state in asserting or establishing its independence, or in acknowledging or sometimes exploiting the position of dependence on other states. Again, France is a notable case. During the mid-sixties, along with its nuclear force policies, it extricated its armed forces from the NATO command structure and deployments in an attempt to achieve independence from its NATO allies, and from the United States in particular.

The demand for national independence stands outside any scheme of military logic. The acceptance of a dependent position, such as Finland's with respect to the Soviet Union, or the dependence of LDCs on industrialized powers for modern weapons, seems to be dictated by a kind of plain military or economic necessity. Yet even here the function of force postures may serve to explain the difference between accepting and defying military logic—the difference, for example, between France and Finland or Japan. Finland's strategic position should perhaps be classed with Israel's—so close to the line of military logic, so constrained by circumstances, as to permit little that is not inevitable. Finnish force posture stresses instant and short-term response capabilities that will minimize the dependence on the Soviet Union which they evidently expect in any case. Similarly, underlying Japan's unwillingness to rearm is, among other things, the recognition of her unavoidable dependence on U.S. military power.

Sweden has a different problem—to design a force posture that will maintain the credibility of its assertion that it intends to remain neutral. By designing a force posture the instant response capabilities of which are purely defensive, so that it is incapable of helping its neighbors, Sweden contributes to the credibility of a claim that rests on long historical precedence. One might say that Sweden's force posture is intended to bolster its reputation as a neutral. Beyond the threshold of war, however, while still professing neutrality, Sweden has quietly taken steps that would enable it to cooperate with the Western alliance structures. Sweden's force posture includes a fallback position of interdependence.

If the function of force posture is to assert the independence of the state, it may find that military technology is its major enemy. The PLA's acceptance of poor equipment standards may reflect more the Chinese determination to be independent than any authentic judgment that different equipment standards would be more effective. As in its handling of nuclear military policy, the PLA may have attempted to cope by using bombast with its aspirations for independence at the same time that it has evidently chosen a low standard of equipment for its ground forces.

India and Pakistan offer interesting contrasts and parallels in force posture efforts that seek to weaken the strands of dependency. Until 1962, Indian supply policy reflected a high priority assigned to independence from any military supply sources. This was accomplished by acquiring weapons from a wide variety of sources, and tolerating or ignoring the enormous logistics problems that accompany multiple sources and systems. The Chinese victory in Ladakh in 1962 increased the Indian government's interest in military efficiency. Some consolidation of weapons systems occurred, and the Indian Defence Ministry, still intent upon minimizing its dependence on other governments for military equipment, began an ambitious program to expand its own military production capacity. Domestic sources became more important after 1965, when the United States stopped granting military aid to India and Pakistan when they fought over Kashmir again. After that, the Soviet Union became India's predominant foreign arms supplier.

Pakistan had begun in the early sixties to extricate itself from a severe supply dependency on the United States by looking to Moscow and Peking for arms. The Chinese Communists proved the more helpful of the two rival communist powers. Washington grumbled, but continued its reduced rate of supply until 1965, and later resumed the supply of "non-lethal" items on credit (available to both India and Pakistan). Pakistan, however, did not attempt to develop domestic sources of supply, preferring to use foreign exchange for that purpose.

Force posture can be a statement about illusions as well as realities. Few national regimes find high-prestige military activities of negligible political value to them. It is particularly noteworthy, therefore, when a state makes a clear choice not to seek parity or superiority in force posture with its opponents, and even more, to accept subordination, dependence or inferiority in its military position towards its opponent. If independence is actually within reach, and the costs of dependence are high, a force posture that accepts inferiority or dependence when it need not may be a serious mistake of statecraft. That, of course, was Churchill's judgment about British air power in the late 1930s, and few people any longer disagree with the position he took. At the same time, Finland's handling of her dependent contemporary situation with respect to the Soviet Union, seeking a limited but definite amount of autonomy, seems to be shrewd and prudent.

Forward Strategies

The North Atlantic Alliance is committed to a forward defense strategy on the flanks as well as the central front—in Scandinavia, Greece, and Turkey, as well as Germany. It has gone to a great deal of trouble to gain some credibility for claiming to hold at a forward line that would shield almost all of Western Europe from an attack from the East. In the central front, where what we might call the value-to-space ratio is very high, it is not altogether surprising to find a strong commitment to a forward defense that would assure or promise to avoid the destruction of territory by conventional war. Turkey, however, is another matter. Trading space for time there could be a distinct asset.

Force postures are rarely widely known. Some of their elements are military secrets. NATO force posture, however, has been subjected to considerable public scrutiny by public officials, journalists, and other writers—more scrutiny, at least, than is normal with national force postures. It may be that this exposure, by drawing attention to the values at stake in the early stages of a war in Europe, has led to this extreme attention to a forward strategy, although this explanation is also unsatisfactory for explaining its appearance on the southern flank.

American military planners characteristically design forward defense lines as shielding strategies, and it may be that this fact would explain its presence on the southern flank, and to some degree on the central front. Forward strategy, however, may also be linked into a larger set of issues that persistently underlie force posture. As contingent plans and capabilities for an immediate response to attack, force posture deals in uncertainties and latitudes. It reflects, in how constraining its command guidance and doctrine are, and in the collateral provisions for formal consultation and clearance, the confidence placed in the officers who man the chain of command—or rather, the delicate balance between that confidence and the confidence with which these officials and their superiors peer into the contingent future.

Few of the uncertainties that involve threats to social values can be settled by military planning, even conditionally, in advance. Unpredictable choices have to be made among non-military values during war-fighting. Nowhere is this clearer than with respect to the use of territory to absorb the energy of an attack and gain time to respond. The PLA is perhaps the extreme case in the contemporary world of an armed service that declares its willingness to sacrifice national territory (hence, the valuable things located in it) as a principle of its defense posture. Certainly one asset of Chinese force posture is this claimed willingness to take punishment. (Given the advance declarations involved, we have no reason to doubt that political authorities approve of these pronouncements, whatever we may think about their reliability.) The PLA is an integral part of China's political and economic life. Could it be that these declarations indicate that the Chinese ground forces enjoy more confidence from civil authorities in China, and indeed even from wider elements in Chinese society, about the way they would make decisions where societal values are at stake, than the NATO military commanders deciding which segments of the civil populace will have to bear the greatest burdens of war?

Perhaps NATO's forward strategy reflects the lack of cohesion within the defense community. West Germans must be assured that their territory and their population will not be chewed up according to a military plan that will keep the war off French, Dutch, and British territory.

A striking variation on this problem is the case where military plans write off a major segment of the national territory as indefensible. Such was the case in Pakistan for nearly two decades, beginning in the early 1950s. The Pakistani government kept its shield forces for defending against India in the West Wing, stationing only internal security and law-and-order forces in East Pakistan (now Bangladesh), where more than half the population of Pakistan was located. This extraordinary force posture seems to have contributed to the breakup of Pakistan.

Any military command arrangement is an agreement beforehand to permit military preemption of civil authority in some degree—how much depending on how much more expeditiously the military command can act than can civil authority and how much its future command problems can be anticipated. Accordingly, it is fair to say that force posture reflects how trustful

the relationship between civil and military authorities is. Perhaps it also tests the cohesion of the state.

Internal Disparities in National Force Postures

Military establishments are not unitary structures. They sometimes speak with several voices. The PRC speaks with at least two voices about the efficacy of nuclear warfare. Its forced draft development of nuclear weapons voices a serious concern about them, while its pronouncements have usually minimized the possible effects of nuclear war on China. This disparity is easy to explain yet nonetheless troublesome. There also seem to be considerable disparities between the PLA and the Chinese air and naval forces with respect to the importance of modern weapons. Other governments sometimes also display disparities among their services, although seldom so conspicuously. The U.S. military services carried on quite conspicuous force posture and strategy disputes during the late forties and throughout the fifties, but have kept their competitive behavior less conspicuous since that time.

We should expect national force postures to reflect interservice rivalry and other internal tensions. For outside observers, the resulting confusion can be disconcerting, but at least it should provide some reassurance that the government involved learns what some of its military options are.

FORCE POSTURE NORMS

States have generally used military policy to win popular, or at least elite, support and to gain control over resources. When they do this, force posture reflects an inward-looking preoccupation, or at least a disparity between the state's internal behavioral constraints and the demands or requirements of national security that originate in its external environment. A conspicuous feature of the Cold War has been the propensity of states involved in it—including the United States, most specifically—to overly dramatize external threats in order to win and maintain the necessary internal political support for external efforts. To note incongruities such as these between internal and external behavior constraints is a way to identify problem areas in a state's external relations by the application of a behavioral metaphor. By implication, the norm is the adaptation (hence, the ability to adapt) of national actors to changing external conditions without producing inadvertent, unnecessary, or unanticipated effects, without losing control of the situation, and without inducing catastrophes.

Even where this behavioral criterion is applied to force posture, it is not confined to behavior that performs only a military function. It may apply as well to behavior that has also a political function. De Gaulle's vision of France's position was of a stable role in the international system, even though the role he sought for France required more resources than France could continue to supply. On the other hand, the role assigned French military power by American strategy in the early 1960s was incompatible with France's internal political constraints. A "healthy" internal political situation in France demanded, or seemed to demand, a more prestigious and independent strategic role. Which force posture—Washington's or Paris'—was "right"? Professor Kolodziej, in an article on French military doctrine elsewhere in this volume,[4] has explained French military doctrine in sufficient detail to make it clear that from the standpoint of French doctrine, the American position was wrong, just as, from the standpoint of Secretary of Defense McNamara's Athens and Ann Arbor speeches in 1962, French nuclear posture was wrong.

So long as we look at force posture norms as an extension of national military doctrines, any state with a reasonably consistent doctrine will justify its own program—its own force posture—at the expense of others. We are nevertheless justified in looking for a convergence on common norms because of certain common goals. Military action can be very costly to both sides—a game that no one wins, or in which everyone loses highly valued things. For this reason, we should expect to find a common (though scarcely a universal) preference in favor of states that can adapt their internal and external aspirations to international conditions so as to minimize the prospects of substantial inter-nation violence. Hence, it should be possible to state a limited set of behavioral norms. We will do so according to whether a prospective norm (1) addresses the external world, (2) connects war-fighting capabilities with internal political and economic constraints, and (3) deals with intrinsic or strictly internal factors.

Norms That Take Account of External Conditions

The force posture norms directed to the external milieu have been intensively explored in nuclear strategic theory. In their application to force postures in general (or at least prewar-fighting force postures), they can be clustered in four groups.

Credibility. Whatever the intent of its "owner," a force posture, to be credible, must satisfy the criteria the opponent uses to judge it. The capability of the military force must be impressive *to him.* The intent to use the capability must be demonstrated by factors impressive *in his terms. Stable Effects.* In established nuclear strategic theory, a first-strike capability (one that must go first because it cannot survive to go second) is provocative and unstable, while a second-strike capability is stable and restraining. Two opposing forces are in a stable relationship if neither can be substantially destroyed by surprise. To work, this theory depends upon sufficient information being available to each side about the behavior (at least the force posture) of the opponent to determine that it meets the second-strike criteria and knows it. Beyond that, additional cognitive conditions augment the applicability of the theory. In order for each side to know adequately about the state of mind and the state of the force posture of its opponent, declaratory and actual force postures ought to be in some congruence, unless there are substantial independent sources of information about both.

The simple model of opposing strategic nuclear systems becomes more complicated as its norms are applied to opposing conventional forces. Low thresholds and ambiguous geographic delineations are dangerous for conventional force stability. Toe-to-toe opposing conventional forces need the high thresholds that permit mistakes and misunderstandings to occur safely.

Highly asymmetrical conventional forces that are toe-to-toe, such as the contemporary Israeli confrontation with her Arab neighbors, as Kemp points out in an article on force posture,[5] pose special problems for maintaining or inducing stability. The low threshold against guerrilla action is particularly troublesome to Israel. She has attempted to raise it by a policy of selective retaliation. In addition, Israel is heavily dependent for her military viability on air superiority, and on short, decisive campaigns to avoid wars of attrition. The incentives for the other side—for the UAR and other Arab states—favor low-level military activities (mainly guerrilla warfare) which they could permit to grow into a sustained and slow war-fighting action. Moreover, a decisive surprise effectively executed against Israel would be disastrous to her, while the UAR has survived two such surprises from Israel. Israel has demonstrated that it is possible to develop stabilizers in highly asym-

[4]See Edward A. Kolodziej's article, pp. 245–57.

[5]Geoffrey Kemp, "Israel and Egypt: Military Force Posture 1967–1972," pp. 391–405.

metrical confrontations of conventional forces. The stable, conventional confrontation need not be symmetrical.

Congruence with External Threats. Since force postures are partially derived from powerful internal bureaucratic forces, one cannot take for granted that they will be designed to fit the perceived external threat. Furthermore, threat perceptions are likely to be biased by the same pressures. Given the economy and the convenience of distinct organizational goals, there will be a strong propensity to narrow the threat to a single, clearly defined enemy. Furthermore, in structuring the force posture, military planners are inclined to simplify their operational planning by overvaluing limited options. The identification of these two biases should be helpful in establishing congruencies with external threats. In addition, organizational process and information-handling norms could help establish congruency: genuinely competitive sources of information about the external threat, for example, are imperative.

Are Inter-State Dependencies and Entanglements Preferred? We enter here particularly contingent territory. When Pakistan attacked India in 1966, the Pakistani armed forces were to a considerable extent dependent on American hardware and POL. Pakistan had, it has been reported, three months' supply of POL, stretched beyond American calculations by reduced training routines. Was Pakistan's dependence on the United States an inhibition to her attack on India? Or did American military supplies to Pakistan enable her to make the attack? Similarly, does Israel's supply dependency on the United States or the Arab states' dependency on the Soviet Union encourage or discourage military conflict in that region? Theoretically, if the outside powers want to dampen down a regional conflict, and the regional powers are dependent upon them, then dependency can aid the avoidance of conflict. The evidence suggests, however, that outside powers do not always want to avoid intra-regional conflict, and that sometimes when they do they are unable to. By one account, the Arab-Israeli War of 1967 was begun by a Soviet miscalculation. Moscow, according to this account, did not really want to see Israel engaged in war with the UAR or Jordan. Similarly, during the Taiwan Straits crisis of the mid-1950s, U.S. diplomacy at times dampened and at other times aggravated the conflict.

Where states are entangled with one another in mutual defense arrangements—here NATO is the prime example—the mutuality of the defense arrangements—the multinational commands and consultative procedures—may dampen escalative pressures and moderate fears. The result is a desirable high threshold to war. On the other hand, once military operations commence, the mutual arrangements will generate some escalative pressures. On balance, mutual entanglements probably are preferable force posture norms where stabilizing the military environment is desirable. Client-state dependencies, however, are too varied to permit of generalization, except this general caveat: states that sponsor smaller states as their military clients often overestimate—sometimes dangerously—how much they thereby gain control of the local military milieu.

Norms about Factors Internal to a State

The internal conditions on which force posture rests should permit it to be stable, credible over time, yet adaptable to changing external circumstances. At minimum, force posture must not simply solve internal problems such as national political cohesion where it is unrelated to the external threat to which the force posture would be directed. Further, force posture should be designed so that it will not have to change with every shift in public or political mood that is unrelated to the external threat. This has long been a norm popular with military planners, although it is rarely achieved. Perhaps a more realistic norm is one that acknowledges military policy to be a component of the national political milieu: force posture ought to be politically self-supporting in the sense that it generates enough active approval to offset the political burdens it imposes.

Where force posture is not provocative—where it has little potential for inducing counteractions that are dangerous—the above norms could simply be ignored. In fact, under these circumstances there is no reason that force posture could not be turned to other purposes to achieve other norms.

Under some circumstances, force posture needs to balance its internal political accounts in the very short run. In the Cuban missile crisis, when President Kennedy made his first public moves, he was able to confront the Soviet Union with a public reaction that was solidly supportive of his actions. Had short-run American public reactions been negative, it is possible that they would have complicated Kennedy's handling of the crisis by tempting the Russians to exploit the imbalance in political accounts.

Force posture also should be congruent with internal political values. It ought to offer protection to all or enough components of a state to assure its solidarity. To neglect attempting to defend a major segment of the state, like East

Pakistan, as Pakistan did, or to impose inequitable burdens on distinct classes or segments of society—for example, by drafting mostly blacks or poor people—is to hazard a serious weakening of the national solidarity that effective military establishment should be recruited and trained to assure it shares the values of the larger society, and organized to assure its self-control. The latter norm is directly applicable to force posture.

Integral or Intrinsic Norms

Certain norms that are associated with bureaucratic rationality can also be applied to force posture. The forces involved should be organized so that they are controllable, structured so that they are efficient and nonredundant (except where redundancy is a planned method of coping with uncertainty), arranged so that they are compatible with military doctrine and strategy (providing doctrine and strategy are valid), and designed to provide the political authorities of the state the options they insist upon or believe they have.

CONCLUSION: CAN THERE BE A CONVERGENCE OF NORMS?

Nuclear strategic theory has inspired arms control tenets that develop common standards—norms—by which opposing military forces can pursue their mutual interests, providing both sides accept the status quo and want to avoid war. War has seldom been the preferred option of statesmen and generals, but it has often been the best available option, given the goals and constraints of statecraft. Because states use force posture to cope with political factors as well as military threats, it is probably overly optimistic to expect them to converge toward a common standard for force posture by reducing the political uses to which they put it, stripping away the political barnacles, as it were, so that the rational lines of military logic will become clearer.

In the case of convergence that Greenwood[6] notes among French, British, and West German force postures, it has occurred among friendly states while they have been relatively stable internally and under no severe external security challenges. Their convergence looks as much like a product of other desirable conditions as it does the cause of these conditions. Convergence under less favorable circumstances could just as well be destabilizing and provocative. As troublesome as French nuclear policy seemed to be in the early sixties from Washington, where the concern was with France's spoiling effect on the goals of stabilizing nuclear deterrents and discouraging the proliferation of nuclear weapons, a worse eventuality—one that would have been more destabilizing—was a chaotic France, which was what Gaullists used force posture, along with other elements of governing, to avoid. Whether or not one agrees with the way De Gaulle brought France stability, it is clear that he addressed the structural problems of the French polity, which is to say that at least he did not assume he could stabilize France by governing it forever. Even from the viewpoint of his American critics, it is not clear that his use of force posture and military strategy was unjustified, for his statecraft helped to make possible the political conditions that now permit his successor to abandon (albeit quietly) his grand posturing and converge French force posture toward British and West German force posture.

---

[6]David Greenwood, "The Defense Efforts of France, West Germany, and the United Kingdom," pp. 340–62.

SOVIET STRATEGIC FORCE POSTURE: SOME ALTERNATIVE EXPLANATIONS

EDWARD L. WARNER III

While recognizing that Soviet force posture has resulted from a complex interacting milieu of both external and internal factors, Warner has chosen to focus on what has been the most obscure set of these factors—those surrounding the workings of bureaucracies within the Soviet state. Although the difficulty of obtaining complete data for this area of investigation leaves some of his conclusions in the imaginative, hypothetical state, and space permits him only to survey those Soviet bureaucracies concerned with strategic forces, the approach undertaken by Warner in this article nevertheless shows promise for deepening our understanding of the possible internal motivations generating Soviet forces. His presentation of this internal side of the picture is enhanced throughout by brief looks at the arms race interactions between the USSR and the U.S.

Major Warner, a 1962 graduate of the U.S. Naval Academy, is a member of the United States Air Force and has taught in the Department of Political Science at the U.S. Air Force Academy. He is currently working in the national security community in Washington, D.C. and is completing his doctorate for Princeton University. Co-editor of this book, he has also contributed a chapter, "The Development of Soviet Military Doctrine and Capabilities in the 1960's," in American Defense Policy *(second edition, 1969).*

AN OVERVIEW OF EXPLANATIONS

The development of Soviet military capability since World War II has occurred within the context of an arms race with the United States. That is, Soviet force posture has developed in an environment characterized by: (1) Conscious antagonism between the Soviet Union and the United States; (2) A mutual structuring of forces with attention to their deterrent and combat effectiveness against one another; and, (3) An ongoing competition in terms of both the quantitative size and the qualitative characteristics of their armed forces.[1] While this armaments competition has produced irregular spurts of deployment activity on both sides, it has been marked by mutually sustained efforts in weapons research and development across a wide spectrum of systems.

The Soviet-American arms race has included two basic types of weapons interaction, the emulative and the offsetting patterns.[2] Both countries have displayed an inclination to imitate the weapons development and procurement actions of their adversary. The emulative type of interaction was evident in the much publicized bomber and missile gap deployment reactions of the United States in the mid-fifties and early sixties and appears to have been the case in the Soviet ICBM build-up between 1965 and 1971 and in their deployment of Y-class ballistic missile launching submarines. While in some cases the emergence of highly similar weapons systems in both inventories may reflect conscious imitation, in others it appears to be merely the product

[1]Colin S. Gray, "The Arms Race Phenomenon," *World Politics* (October 1971): 41.

[2]Colin S. Gray, "The Arms Race Phenomenon," *World Politics* (October 1971): 54; Johan J. Holst, "Missile Defense, the Soviet Union and the Arms Race," in J. Holst and W. Schneider, Jr. (eds.), *Why ABM?: Policy Issues in the Missile Defense Controversy* (New York: Pergamon Press, 1969): 161–63.

of parallel development efforts by similarly endowed rivals.[3]

More frequently the Soviet-American force posture interaction has been of an offsetting variety in the manner of the classical offense vs. defense competition. Examples of this action-reaction pattern include mutual Soviet and American activities in the procurement of strategic missile launching submarines and antisubmarine warfare systems to counteract this threat, strategic bomber-bomber defense activities on both sides and somewhat later a similar ballistic missile-missile defense competition. The latter case has included three discrete stages; the development of the basic launch vehicle, the ICBM, the offsetting reaction in the antiballistic missile (ABM) development, and the development of a series of tactical and technological measures including the acquisition of various penetration aids and multiple warheads designed to neutralize and overcome the opponent's missile defenses.

While the emulative/offsetting distinctions are straightforward in theory, the actual pattern of Soviet-American weapons interactions has been highly complex. In light of the lengthy lead times involved in the development of modern weaponry, the efforts to acquire sophisticated offensive and defensive systems are often begun simultaneously. Thus for example Khrushchev noted that the Soviet ICBM and ABM development programs were both initiated at the same time.[4]

With both the Soviet Union and the United States supporting extensive weapons development programs, the military-political leadership on both sides, often relying upon worst possible case analysis, has been prone to attribute maximal weapons development efforts and accomplishments to the adversary. Given the extreme secrecy surrounding modern weapons research, initial development efforts for offsetting systems are often begun based upon the anticipated or vaguely perceived rather than the directly observed activities of the opponent. As a practical matter, the efforts attributed to the enemy are likely to be those which one's own weapons researchers have conceived and proposed. As a result, programs undertaken in response to such anticipated development activities can produce a kind of arms race against oneself in which

one's own offense is pitted against one's defense in a manner which fortifies the claims of each. Uncertainty can easily produce an action-over-reaction pattern, where, although the anticipated threat fails to materialize, the response nevertheless results in the procurement of a major weapons systems.[5]

Another difficulty arises in seeking to identify various arms race interactions. Identical systems often have significant destructive potential vis-à-vis one another. For example, ICBMs, if sufficiently accurate and targeted against the land-based missile force of the enemy, could seriously endanger the survival of his strategic strike force. In this sense, the procurement of a strategic counterforce capability most certainly represents a neutralizing move with relation to the opponent's strategic offensive force. Thus the spurts of ICBM construction on both sides over the past decade have had both emulative and offsetting dimensions.

Arms race competition with the United States has by no means been the sole external factor influencing the evolution of contemporary Soviet force posture. Concern about the projection of Soviet political influence throughout the world, about the political reliability of the Eastern European communist states, and increasingly in recent years concern about the political and military challenge presented by the People's Republic of China are additional considerations which appear to shape the composition and deployment of the Soviet force posture.

All of these foreign policy considerations acquire significance only when perceived and acted upon by influential members of the Soviet defense policymaking community. The perceptions and actions of these participants tend to be importantly influenced by their fundamental political persuasions, and, in many cases, the institutional roles they occupy. Conservative elements, like the members of the Soviet military, are prone to emphasize the threats posed by capitalist imperialism and probably China as well and to counsel the pursuit of strategic superiority over these enemies. In contrast, persons viewing these countries less malevolently will be inclined to endorse small military procurements.

The contours of Soviet force posture are also importantly affected by a number of domestic considerations. The maintenance of comprehensive weapons development and production pro-

[3]Samuel P. Huntington, "Arms Races: Prerequisites and Results," in R. J. Art and K. N. Waltz (eds.), *The Use of Force: International Politics and Foreign Policy* (Boston: Little, Brown, 1971), pp. 391–92.

[4]Arthur Sulzberger, interview with Khrushchev, *New York Times* (September 8, 1961).

[5]George W. Rathjens, "The Dynamics of the Arms Race," in Art and Waltz (eds.), *op. cit.*, pp. 488–91.

grams is strongly promoted by those with a commitment to the continuous modernization of the Soviet force posture. Such a commitment to the "doctrine of quality"[6] is generally prevalent among those weapons designers and defense producers whose institutional and personal prosperity is closely tied to the level of Soviet activity in this area.[7] These constituencies receive additional support from the services and branches of the Soviet armed forces who share their devotion to the acquisition of numerically large and qualitatively advanced weapons inventories. With each service and its attendant designers and producers seeking attention and budgetary support, the distribution of resources among these groups is bound to reflect their relative political power and ability to convince the political leadership of the priority of their demands.

Not only the promotion of institutional interests but also established traditions and standardized organizational practices in the process of weapons development and force deployment have importantly shaped the evolution of Soviet force posture. Traditions, frequently embedded in explicit military doctrine, can provide an important source of advantage for a particular military service and its associated weapons producers. Thus the Soviet doctrinal commitment to the massive, combined arms theater offensive as an integral part of modern war strengthens the claims of the ground forces and tactical aviation for the maintenance and improvement of their extensive and diversified military capabilities. Similarly traditional emphasis upon military operations in Europe may help account for the priority accorded to the procurement of the large numbers of medium and intermediate range ballistic missiles and medium-range bombers during the past two decades.

With regard to organizational process, weapons acquisitions and deployments can be strongly influenced by the normal operation of regularized bureaucratic routines. Thus the apparent practice of allotting sizable budgetary shares to each of the five independent military services appears to stimulate across the board weapons developments and acquisitions.

In the area of force development, the Soviet movements of men and weapons into distant areas such as Cuba and Egypt appear to have been accomplished in accordance with standard operating procedures originally developed for the employment and use of these forces in the USSR and its contiguous areas. Thus the medium and intermediate range missiles and their associated anti-aircraft SAM sites clandestinely moved into Cuba in 1962, were erected in the same basic configuration as similar systems deployed in the Western USSR (a practice which contributed importantly to their identification by U.S. intelligence).[8] In a similar manner, Soviet ground force divisions deployed to Cuba in 1962 and the Soviet equipment provided to the Egyptian Army in the mid-sixties included the complete inventory of weapons: tanks, personnel carriers, forest clearing equipment, etc., carried within a standard Soviet division designed to fight in central Europe, without apparent concern for local theater requirements.[9]

The discussion that follows offers a variety of explanations for the character of contemporary Soviet force posture. In light of the size of the Soviet military arsenal and the space limitations of this article, only their strategic offensive and strategic defensive forces are examined. It is hoped that these examples will adequately demonstrate the importance of supplementing those explanations which rely heavily upon foreign policy motivations attributed to the Soviet leadership with alternative hypotheses that focus upon forces internal to the Soviet policy process.

STRATEGIC OFFENSIVE FORCES

Land-based Missiles

The Soviet inventory of strategic missiles currently includes some 1530 intercontinental ballistic missiles and 600 of an intermediate and medium range.[10] The ICBM force includes a mix

---

[6]For a discussion of this concern and its impact within the American defense community see, Richard G. Head, "Doctrinal Innovation and the A-7 Attack Aircraft Program," in R. G. Head and E. J. Rokke, *American Defense Policy*, 3rd ed. (Baltimore: The Johns Hopkins University Press, 1973).

[7]Examples of designer promotion of their own weapons are often encountered within Soviet memoir literature. Cf., Alexander S. Yakovlev, *Tsel' zhizni: zapiski aviakonstruktora* [The Goal of Life: Notes of an Aviation Designer], 2nd ed. (Moscow: Izdatel'stvo Politicheskoi Literatury, 1968), p. 491. F. Petrov, "Search for Design Perfection," *Teknika i vooruzheniye* [Technology & Armaments] 11 (November 1960): 2; and V. Grabin, "Contribution to Victory," *Teknika i vooruzheniye* 5 (May 1970): 7, for such activity in the artillery field; and A. Nikitin, "History of the Creation of an Anti-tank Aviation Bomb," *Voenno-istoricheshii zhurnal* [Military-History Journal] 9 (September 1969): 72–73.

[8]This point is made by a leading advocate of the organizational process approach, Graham T. Allison, in *Essence of Decision: Explaining the Cuban Missile Crisis* (Boston: Little, Brown, 1971), pp. 102–13.

[9]*Ibid.*, p. 105; Lecture by Colonel Eliyahu Ze'ira, Chief of Operations, Israeli Army General Staff, November 1967, U.S. Air Force Academy, Colorado.

[10]These and all subsequent figures on the current size of Soviet military forces are extracted from *The Military Balance: 1972–1973* (London: International Institute of Strategic Studies, September 1972).

of older systems, 210 SS-7's and 8's which were deployed during the early sixties, and the new, 290 SS-9's, 970 SS-11's, and 60 SS-13's, all third generation weapons developed in the sixties and deployed from 1964 onward. The more modern ICBM's are emplaced in a series of launch complexes spread throughout the Soviet Union in dispersed underground silos,[11] while the second generation systems are deployed in both "soft," aboveground launch position and hardened silos.[12] The Soviet practice of hardening these launch positions followed American efforts of the type by a couple of years, thus representing an interaction with both emulative and offsetting aspects.

The pace of Soviet missile deployment and the characteristics of their different systems have varied considerably. In an attempt to explain these differences the recent history of Soviet missile development and particularly the major decisional points in its evolution are discussed below.

At the conclusion of World War II, the Soviets possessed two separate resource bases to support their initiation of a major missile research and development program. The last days of the war had brought the Soviet capture of a number of scientists, many of the plans and blueprints and most of the production and test facilities associated with the extensive German rocket development program.[13] In addition, a substantial cadre of Soviet scientists with lengthy experience in missile research was available. Led by such figures as S. P. Korolev, V. P. Glushko, and F. A. Tsander, this group of Soviet researchers had worked on basic missile design and research under direct government sponsorship since the 1920s. By April 1932, they were organized into specific design teams working on different aspects of the rocket research effort.[14]

The initiation of the major postwar Soviet missile development program was directly authorized by Stalin and the Party's Politburo

in 1946.[15] While undertaken as a portion of the emerging Cold War competition with the United States, this effort represented an independent Soviet initiative that preceded the beginning of a major American missile development program.

Building upon the closely supervised efforts of the captured German scientists and the parallel work of their own missile design teams,[16] by the mid-fifties the Soviets had produced their first generation of operational ballistic missiles. Their original MRBM, the SS-3, was test fired by 1954 and operationally deployed beginning in 1955, while the first ICBM, the SS-6, was tested in August 1957, and its deployment began in 1958.[17]

The SS-6 was a dual purpose system, employed both as a military weapon and as the primary launch vehicle for early Soviet space efforts. It had a decidedly large booster which may be explained by the fact that the parameter for launch capacity was established for the anticipated use of bulky and low-yield plutonium fission warheads, prior to a Soviet breakthrough in the area of thermonuclear weapons technology that greatly reduced the size and weight of these warheads.[18] The SS-6 program helped establish a Soviet tradition of powerful boosters which appears to have been sustained by the efforts of a specialized "big-missile" design team.

Deployment of the SS-6 was limited to a single-launch complex in the northwestern USSR.[19] This abbreviated deployment appears to have been necessitated by the logistic problems associated with servicing the unstable, nonstorable liquid fuels used in this system.[20] Its cumbersome nature precluded the emplacement of the SS-6 in protected launch sites and apparently produced significant problems with its soft configuration as well.[21]

[11]Press reports indicate that there are 6 major SS-9 complexes, each containing several flights of 6 missiles each, and 10 large SS-11 complexes which have a number of 10 missile clusters within them. W. Beecher, "U.S. Data Indicate Moscow is Slowing ICBM Deployment," *New York Times* (December 17, 1970).

[12]Thomas Wolfe, *Soviet Power and Europe, 1945–1970* (Baltimore: The Johns Hopkins Press, 1970), p. 183.

[13]Asher Lee and Richard E. Stockwell, "Soviet Missiles," in A. Lee (ed.) *The Soviet Air and Rocket Forces* (New York: Praeger, 1959), pp. 147–59.

[14]G. A. Tokaty-Tokaev, "Foundations of Soviet Cosmonautics," *Spaceflight* (October 1968): 335–46; Tokaty-Tokaev, "Soviet Space Technology," *Spaceflight* (Febuary 1963): 58–64; Michael Stoiko, *Soviet Rocketry: Past, Present and Future* (New York: Holt, Rinehart and Winston, 1970), pp. 42–65.

[15]Tokaty-Tokaev, "Foundations of Soviet Cosmonautics," *Spaceflight* (October 1968): 343.

[16]*Ibid.*, pp. 343–45; Lee and Stockwell, in Lee (ed.), *op. cit.*, pp. 149–57. A Soviet defector, Leonid Vladimirov, identifies S. P. Korolev, M. Yangel, and V. Chalomei as leaders of the major Soviet ballistic missile design teams in the fifties and sixties. Leonid Vladimirov, *The Russian Space Bluff* (London: Tom Stacey Ltd., 1971), pp. 53, 82. See also Nicholas Daniloff, *The Kremlin and the Cosmos* (New York: A. A. Knopf, 1972), pp. 57–58.

[17]Johan J. Holst, *Comparative U.S. and Soviet Deployments, Doctrines, and Arms Limitation* (Chicago: University of Chicago Press, 1971), p. 10.

[18]Henry T. Simmons, "The Soviet Space Program," *Space/Aeronautics* (December 1965): 54.

[19]Desmond Ball, "The Strategic Missile Program of the Kennedy Administration, 1961–1963," Ph.D. dissertation (Canberra: Australian National University, June 1972), p. 102.

[20]Charles J. V. Murphy, "Khrushchev's Paper Bear," *Fortune* (December 1964): 228.

[21]Oleg Penkovskiy, *The Penkovskiy Papers* (Garden City, N.J.: Doubleday, 1963), pp. 339–43.

Despite Khrushchev's personal enthusiasm for missiles and frequent claims regarding Soviet ICBM strength,[22] only a few SS-6's were operationally deployed.[23] This fact, coupled with accelerated American ICBM deployments that had been stimulated by fears of an impending missile gap strongly favoring the Soviets, produced a significant strategic missile superiority for the United States in the early sixties.

Two factors may have influenced the Soviet decision to procure such a small ICBM force. It is most likely that the SS-6 deployment was halted as a result of the technical difficulties noted above. Additionally, since strategic missiles had not been assigned to an independent military service during the fifties but instead were apparently controlled by the artillery branch of the Ground Forces, the early stages of the ICBM effort may have suffered from the absence of adequate institutional support within the Soviet defense establishment.[24]

The abbreviated SS-6 procurement was followed by the leisurely acquisition of two second generation systems, the SS-7 and SS-8. Developed in parallel, perhaps by competitive design teams, some 220 of these missiles were deployed between 1962 and 1965. Still operational at this time, these liquid fueled ICBMs reflected the Soviet preference for powerful boosters. More manageable than the SS-6, they were deployed in dispersed and hardened launch sites in the latter phases of their acquisition.

During this same period, the Soviets moved more rapidly toward the acquisition of a substantial medium and intermediate range ballistic missile capability. They began with the SS-3, a 600 mile range missile acquired in the mid-fifties, followed by the 1200 mile range SS-4 whose development began in 1959 and the 2300 mile range SS-5 beginning in 1961.[25] By 1963 they had deployed a force of 750 M/IRBMs in the Western USSR, all apparently targeted against strategic and tactical targets in Western Europe.[26]

Factors explaining the pronounced build-up of the I/MRBM force appear to include the ab-

sence of the technical difficulties which plagued the early ICBM program, the emphasis in Soviet military doctrine upon a massive theater campaign in Europe, and a rational Soviet strategy of deterring hostile American actions by holding Western Europe as a visible "hostage." The doctrinal tradition may have been reinforced by the leading role of artillery officers in the Soviet missile program, noted previously. These men are likely to have been inclined to integrate the newly developed systems in a kind of extended contiguous support mission similar to the role played traditionally by artillery rather than directing their efforts toward the fulfillment of a completely novel intercontinental mission.

Returning to Soviet ICBM efforts, a landmark decision appears to have been taken sometime in 1963 to commence a general expansion of Soviet strategic capability. Factors bearing upon this crucial decision appear to have included a commitment within the political leadership in the wake of the Cuban crisis of 1962 to attain a position of at least strategic parity and perhaps superiority vis-à-vis the United States, pressures from the Soviet military to acquire a viable war-waging capability at the strategic level, and the parochial lobbying of the strategic rocket forces, created in 1959, and their industrial producers who sought to expand the ICBM inventory at a time when the M/IRBM construction program was nearing completion.

This decision has all the earmarks of an emulative reaction triggered by the overreactive build-up of American strategic power that had begun three years earlier. Upheld and perhaps expanded by the collective leadership which succeeded Khrushchev in October, 1964, it produced a steady expansion of the Soviet strategic missile capability throughout the decade. This sustained effort eventually yielded the 3:2 advantage in land-based ICBM's currently held by the Soviet Union over the United States.

Included within the 1963 force expansion decision was the choice to begin deploying two third generation ICBM's, the SS-9 and the SS-11. The SS-9 is an exceptionally large, storable liquid fueled missile. It is currently capable of carrying a single 25 megaton warhead or a three-part multiple warhead, the so-called "MRV triplet," in which each individual warhead has an explosive equivalent of 5 megatons. The SS-11 is also a storable liquid missile, but significantly smaller, being comparable to the American Minuteman in overall size and warhead power, which is approximately one megaton.[27] Develop-

[22]Arnold L. Horelick and Myron Rush, *Strategic Power and Soviet Foreign Policy* (Chicago: University of Chicago Press, 1966), *passim*.

[23]Precise numerical estimates are difficult to locate as authors frequently speak in terms of a "handful" of SS-6's. Cf. "Pentagon Bares Figures Showing Atom Arms Lead," *New York Times* (April 15, 1964); Wolfe, *Soviet Power and Europe*, p. 182.

[24]Allison, *op. cit.*, p. 116.

[25]*The Military Balance, 1972–1973* (London: International Institute of Strategic Studies, 1972), p. 65.

[26]*The Military Balance, 1962–1963* (London: Institute of Strategic Studies, 1962), p. 3.

[27]*The Military Balance, 1972–1973*, p. 65.

ment work on both the SS-9 and 11 was probably begun in the early sixties.

The SS-9 appears to be the product of the heavy missile design tradition noted earlier. Approval for its development may have been facilitated by Khrushchev's interest in large yield "terror weapons,"[28] for whose delivery the SS-9 was ideally suited. Alternatively, it may have been developed as a counterforce weapon for use against American silo-based ICBM's in order to improve Soviet war-waging capabilities. The decision to proceed with the deployment of this system may also have been influenced simply by the availability of the system for prompt deployment without reference to its possible employment. Whatever the original Soviet intentions, by the late sixties it was its potential for carrying hard target killing multiple warheads that became the critical element in Western discussions of the SS-9.

Soviet multiple warhead development efforts appear to postdate the original SS-9 deployment decision, with initial design work probably beginning in the mid-sixties and the first flight tests of their MRV triplet initiated in August 1968.[29] Soviet activity in this area could have been motivated by a variety of considerations. They may have sought a MRV capability in order to attain more efficient city destruction in that the reinforcing character of three separated smaller warheads can produce a cumulative effect that is more powerful than a single warhead.[30] While this may be the reason for the development of the MRV for the SS-11 whose testing began in July 1970,[31] there is disagreement whether the geographic separation of the SS-9's triplet is sufficient to produce greater destruction than the single large warhead.[32] Alternatively, the MRV, still designed for counter-city attacks, may have been developed to multiply the number of incoming Soviet at-

tack vehicles as an offsetting measure in anticipation of an American decision to deploy an ABM system. (The United States did announce its intention to proceed with the deployment of the Sentinel ABM system which provided for a "thin" city defense in September 1967.) Finally, basing their case upon the reported "footprint" or dispersal pattern of the SS-9's powerful triplet, some American defense spokesmen have stated that this system was expressly designed for counterforce strikes against the American Minuteman force. These interactive concerns are likely to have been reinforced by the parochial lobbying of the MRV development design teams and the members of the strategic rocket forces, who press for the acquisition of such a Soviet capability because: (1) it is technologically feasible, and (2) with adequate accuracies it could further improve Soviet ability to wage nuclear war, a firm doctrinal commitment of the Soviet armed forces.

While the counterforce capabilities of the SS-9 MRV triplet have recently been discounted,[33] it will most certainly represent a valid concern when the Soviets achieve a true MIRV (multiple independently targetable reentry vehicle) capability.[34] Nevertheless, one should avoid complete reliance upon this line of argument in accounting for the SS-9. The existence of a well-established large booster tradition in Soviet missile development, the timing of the SS-9 development and deployment decisions and the presence of other plausible explanations for the development of both the large 25 megaton warhead and the MRV triplet all suggest that it is highly questionable to cite the characteristics of the SS-9 as obvious proof of its intended application as a counterforce, first-strike weapon.[35]

---

[28]Khrushchev boasted publicly about the Soviet possession of such weapons and the atmospheric thermonuclear test series conducted in August-September 1961 included the explosion of a super-warhead with a yield of approximately 50 megatons.

[29]Holst, *Comparative U.S. and Soviet Deployments, Doctrines and Arms Limitation*, p. 16.

[30]Peter Ognibene, "ABM Pact is Better Than None," *Washington Post* (July 4, 1971).

[31]Michael Getler, "Soviets Test New Version of Missile," *Washington Post* (August 2, 1970).

[32]Johan Holst asserts that the impact pattern of the SS-9's MRV triplet is too closely clustered to produce the necessary reinforcement effect that improves destructive efficiency, while Ian Smart claims that the triplet's separation is approximately 10 miles, which will produce the desired increase in blast overpressure. See Holst, *Comparative U.S. and Soviet Deployments, Doctrines, and Arms Limitation*, p. 16, and Ian Smart, *Advanced Strategic Missiles: A Short Guide*, Adelphi Papers, No. 63 (London: Institute of Strategic Studies, December 1969), p. 24.

[33]There have been various press reports and statements attributed to Dr. John Foster, the former Director of Defense Research and Engineering of the Department of Defense, that indicate that the MRV for the SS-9 is not sufficiently accurate to threaten the U.S. Minuteman force. See Michael Getler, "Soviet Missile Faulted," *Washington Post* (June 17, 1971), and William Beecher, "Soviet Missile Peril Now Found Unlikely by U.S. Til 1980's," *New York Times* (March 22, 1972). See also Admiral Thomas H. Moorer, *United States Military Posture for FY 1974, Statement before the Senate Armed Services Committee* (Washington, D.C.: G.P.O., March 1973), p. 11.

[34]Secretary of Defense James R. Schlesinger announced successful Soviet flight testing of MIRV's on two of their new generation ICBM's, the SS-X-17 and SS-X-18, which are discussed below. Michael Getler, "Soviet MIRV Test Seen Successful," *Washington Post* (August 18, 1973).

[35]Cf. Senator Henry Jackson's rhetorical question made during Senate debate on the SALT agreements on August 3, 1972: "Mr. President, for what possible purpose would a nation deploy a missile with a 25 megaton payload capability if it was not for some sort of counterforce?" *Congressional Record—Senate* (August 3, 1972), p. 18.

Whatever Soviet intentions regarding the SS-9, their inventory of these weapons expanded steadily between 1965 and 1970, reaching a strength of approximately 290. The SS-9 force has remained basically stable since that time, although an additional thirty large and as yet empty missile silos were constructed during 1971 which may be slated to receive the present or a modified SS-9 or a completely new heavy missile.[36] Sizable new Soviet deployments in this area appear to be effectively constrained at least for the next few years by the Interim Offensive Agreement signed in May, 1972, at the conclusion of the first round of the Strategic Arms Limitation Talks. This agreement includes a provision limiting Soviet "heavy" missile deployment within a ceiling of 313 missiles.

The SS-9 also serves as the launch vehicle for the Soviet depressed trajectory ICBM (DICBM) or fractional orbital bombardment system (FOBS). First flight tested extensively in 1967, the Soviet FOBS has prompted Western speculation that it is intended for South Polar attack[37] against U.S. strategic bomber bases. The system appears capable of carrying a 1-3 megaton warhead but with only moderate accuracy, thus limiting its probable use to attacks upon "soft" targets.[38] The Soviet decision to develop this system despite its obvious capability limitations suggests that a particularly favorable attitude toward strategic weapons development prevailed within the political leadership in the mid to late sixties. Given the fact that the Soviets had already invested in the development and deployment of the SS-9, the FOBS system may have been a relatively inexpensive system.

While deployment information on the FOBS is unavailable, periodic testing of the system suggests its inclusion as an operational system within the Soviet inventory.

The "light" SS-11 was the central element of the sizable Soviet ICBM expansion between 1965 and 1972. Approximately 970 of these missiles were emplaced during this period. Its resemblance to the American Minuteman is marked, although it has a storable liquid booster rather than solid fuel, a difference that may have been caused by a Soviet lag in this technological area. A closer replica of the Minuteman, the solid fueled SS-13, did make its appearance as an operational weapon in 1968. To date, however, its procurement has been quite modest with only 60 deployed by September 1972.[39] This small SS-13 force may reflect the dependability of the SS-11 or merely the tardy arrival of the 13 at a time when the momentum of the SS-11 program made it difficult for the newer system to gain adequate deployment support.

An interesting aspect of the SS-11 deployment has been the emplacement of approximately 100 of them in launch complexes in the Southwestern USSR which had been previously devoted exclusively to M/IRBMs. This practice was initiated in late 1969, at the same time that the Soviets dismantled a force of 70 SS-4's and SS-5's deployed in the Soviet Far Eastern maritime provinces that were presumably targeted against China and U.S. forces in Asia. This move appears to have been a simple replacement maneuver in which specially configured, variable range SS-11's emplaced in hardened silos and far removed from the tense Sino-Soviet border which can cover targets in the Far East were substituted for the older and generally soft-sited SS-4's and SS-5's.[40] Some have suggested that the move was undertaken to complicate American verification efforts, perhaps in anticipation of a possible SALT agreement.[41] In light of their intercontinental capability, Western sources continue to count these SS-11's within the Soviet ICBM inventory.

The size of the Soviet M/IRBM force showed little change between 1964 and the initiation of the variable range SS-11 deployments in late 1969, remaining at roughly 700 missiles throughout the period. The transfer of the 70 SS-4's and 5's noted above from the European USSR to the Soviet Far East apparently took place in 1966 or 1967. This move was probably undertaken to cover Western military targets in East Asia and targets in the People's Republic of China. The deactivation of these soft configuration systems in 1969-70 suggests that this may have been a

[36]See William Beecher, "Soviet Prepares Big New Missiles," *New York Times* (April 23, 1972); Stewart Alsop, "Good News at Last," *Newsweek* (June 14, 1971); Michael Getler, "New Soviet Silo Building Seen As Protection for Two Missiles," *Washington Post* (May 27, 1971). This follow-on to the SS-9 has been designated the SS-X-18, David Binder, "A Soviet Success Reported in Test of New Missiles," *New York Times*, August 20, 1973.

[37]This mode of attack would avoid approach detection by the American ballistic missile early warning system (BMEWS) which monitors the northern attack routes. It has prompted an American offsetting response in the deployment of an over-the-horizon radar system that now covers the South Polar approaches.

[38]Cecil Brownlow, "Soviets Prepare Space Weapon for 1968," *Aviation Week and Space Technology* (November 13, 1967).

[39]*The Military Balance, 1972-1973*, p. 6.

[40]William Beecher, "Soviet Is Said to Dismantle Some of Its Older Missiles," *New York Times* (March 3, 1972); "100 Old Missiles Retired by Russia in Five Years," *Washington Post* (March 4, 1972).

[41]William Beecher, "Soviet ICBM Shift Detected by US," *New York Times* (February 11, 1970).

precautionary move undertaken in response to the pronounced deterioration of Sino-Soviet relations that had included significant border skirmishes in the spring of 1969. Since 1969 the Soviets have retired approximately 100 SS-4's and 5's, although, given the variable range character of a portion of the SS-11's, the overall size of the peripheral range ballistic missile strike force remains at approximately 700.

The Soviets displayed two mobile I/MRBM's in the mid-sixties. The SS-14 system, given the NATO designation "Scamp" and employing a two stage version of the solid-fuel SS-13 with a 2500 mile range[42] was first shown publicly in 1967. The SS-XZ, "Scrooge" system, which has a range of 3500 miles, was similarly paraded in 1967. While these systems may be employed as follow-ons to the SS-4 & 5, to date there have been no reports of their operational deployment. Should they be deployed, their mobility would present considerable difficulties for the verification of any agreement controlling I/MRBM's that might emerge from SALT II or the Mutual Balanced Force Reduction (MBFR) talks.

The tapering off of the Soviet land-based missile expansion in the early seventies followed by Soviet willingness to accept quantitative ceilings in the SALT I Interim Offensive Agreement requires some attempt at explanation. Whatever the Soviet military's desire for the attainment of a war-winning strategic superiority, the political leadership appears to have decided upon at least partial restraint. This is likely to be the result of a collective judgment that continued launch vehicle expansion threatened to elicit major American emulative and offsetting responses in the form of both a substantial ABM defense of the Minuteman force and possibly an unrestrained SLBM expansion. To offset such American reactions would entail a Soviet effort, which although not financially unbearable, would require a substantial additional investment at a time when alternative resource claimants, including agriculture, consumer goods production, and investment for economic growth are in need of major financial inputs.[43] These budgetary competitors are likely to have found representation among the various political leaders, who in turn could find support for their case from the few Soviet advocates of a mutual deterrence stalemate with the United

States[44] and apparent American interests in the negotiation of joint restraint. Whatever their motivations, given the momentum of the Soviet build-up of strategic power, it must have required a specific decision by the Politburo to curb the continuing numerical expansion of the Soviet land-based missile force.

The limited nature of the restraints imposed by the Interim Offensive Agreement are highlighted by current Soviet efforts in development of a fourth generation of ICBM's. They are reported to be developing two new light ICBM's, the SS-X-16 a follow-on to the solid-fueled SS-13 and the SS-X-17 a follow-on to the SS-11, and the heavy SS-X-18 a follow-on to the SS-9 noted earlier.[45] This activity is consistent with General Secretary Brezhnev's reported comment that the Soviets fully intend to press ahead with a vigorous research and development program during the five-year life of the Interim Agreement.[46] This effort, particularly if it should produce major deployment programs to replace significant portions of the current SS-9, 11 and 13 force, augurs well for the fortunes of the strategic rocket forces and their defense industrial suppliers.

Submarine-Launched Ballistic Missiles

One of the most dynamic elements of Soviet strategic missile development in recent years has been the ballistic missile launching submarine force. By September 1972, the Soviets possessed 560 ballistic missiles carried aboard 61 submarines. The backbone of this force is the nuclear powered Y-class submarine carrying sixteen SS-N-6 missiles, which can be fired from a submerged position and have a range of 1500 miles. In the summer of 1972, the Soviets were reported to have 29 Y-class boats completed and another 14 under construction.[47] The latter group includes a modified Y-class submarine which has

---

[42]Holst, *Comparative U.S. and Soviet Deployments . . .*, p. 17.

[43]See Thomas W. Wolfe, *Soviet Interests in SALT: Political, Economic, Bureaucratic and Strategic Contributions and Impediments to Arms Control*, P-4702 (Santa Monica, California: The RAND Corporation, September 1971), *passim*.

[44]For example, G. Gerasimov, who has written about the folly of war in the nuclear age and the meaninglessness of strategic superiority. Cf. Gerasimov's "Pentagon, 1966," *International Affairs* 5 (May 1966): 26, and *Pravda Ukrainy* (March 23, 1969).

[45]*Statement of Defense Secretary Elliot L. Richardson before the House Armed Services Committee* (Washington, D.C.: G.P.O., April 10, 1973), p. 2. A fourth new ICBM, the SS-X-19, a small liquid-fueled missile, was announced as under test in August 1973. David Binder, "A Soviet Success Reported in Test of New Missiles," *New York Times*, August 18, 1973.

[46]President Nixon reported this comment by Brezhnev in his remarks at a Congressional briefing on SALT held at the White House on June 15, 1972. *Strategic Arms Limitation Agreements—Hearings before the Committee on Foreign Relations, United States Senate, 92nd Congress* (Washington, D.C.: G.P.O., 1972), p. 393.

[47]"Second Thoughts on SALT I," *Time Magazine* (July 10, 1972): 6.

bèen designated the D-class.[48] This submarine is apparently designed to carry 12 of the newest Soviet SLBM's, the SS-N-8, "Sawfly," a submerged launch missile with a 4000 mile range and carrying a stellar inertial guidance system.[49]

Soviet interest in the use of the submarine as a launch platform for missiles dates from the immediate post-World War II period when they studied an unsuccessful German program to launch the V-2 rocket from a submarine-towed container.[50] By 1950, the Soviets had begun the development of two separate submarine missile programs.

In the strategic area, the Russians developed the 300 mile range SS-N-4, "Sark," designed for firing from a surfaced submarine. In the fall of 1955, this system was successfully fired from a specially converted Z-class diesel submarine.[51] It was eventually deployed on 10 such Z-V class submarines carrying 2 missiles each as well as the G-class diesel and the H-class nuclear subs.

Tactically, the Soviets fitted their adapted land-based Shaddock missile to a specially configured W-class submarine. This was part of a broader development program which yielded a substantial cruise missile capability for both surface ships and submarines. These weapons appear to have been designed for an anti-ship role with their most likely target the American attack carriers. Soviet cruise missile firing submarines include the J-class diesel and the E-class nuclear boats.

The Soviet deployment and procurement of missile-launching submarines in the fifties appear to reflect a number of factors. At the political level, Nikita Khrushchev, a key figure in defense policy decisions from 1953 onward, was a firm supporter of both missiles and submarines. Khrushchev was also outspoken in his criticism of the utility of large surface vessels. This was important in that it appears to have been an important factor in the post Stalin decision to cancel an ambitious twenty-year naval building program which had included significant expansion in this area.[52] Opposition to this program was apparently shared by number of senior figures in the Ministry of Defense, including the Minister himself, Marshal Zhukov. This may well reflect Ground Force resistance to the budgetary and mission expansion ambitions of a rival service.[53]

Denied the opportunity to expand their heavy surface forces, the Soviet Navy appears to have opted to shift its parochial advocacy into the submarine area where the climate of opinion was more favorable. From a ship construction standpoint, this certainly proved to be the case as some of the ways slated for capital ship construction were transferred instead to the building of submarines.[54]

The development of a submarine strategic strike force found mixed justification in Soviet naval doctrine. Since the thirties, Soviet naval strategy had been dominated by the so-called "Young School" which emphasized a peripheral maritime defense conducted by light naval forces and land-based aviation rather than a doctrine based upon an oceanic fleet and involving far-flung offensive operations.[55] Consequently, the emergence of a naval force for delivering strategic attacks upon the homeland of the enemy faced significant obstacles in that it represented a major doctrinal innovation. However, the Young School's light vessel approach included a strong emphasis upon the construction and use of submarines, thus providing a supportive element for an expanded submarine role in the overall Soviet strategy.

Extensive Soviet submarine construction in the past presumably strengthened the case for the development of an SLBM system from a defense production standpoint. Sizable submarine building facilities were readily available for such a program and well-established submarine design teams, which have remained intact to this day,[56] could be expected to vigorously promote the procurement of new submarine systems.

---

[48]"USA-USSR: New Soviet Missile Submarine," *Interavia Air Letter* (June 9, 1972): 27; *Statement of Defense Secretary Richardson*, April 10, 1973, p. 32.

[49]William Beecher, "Soviet Advance on Missile Seen," *New York Times* (October 1, 1972) and "Russia Tests New Sub Missile," *Baltimore Sun* (November 29, 1972).

[50]Thomas W. Wolfe, *Soviet Naval Interaction With the United States and Its Influence on Soviet Naval Development.* P-4913 (Santa Monica, California: The RAND Corporation, October 1972), p. 16.

[51]*Ibid.*, p. 17.

[52]Michael MccGwire, "Soviet Naval Procurement," in *The Soviet Union in Europe and the Near East: Her Capabilities and Intentions* (London: Royal United Services Institution, August 1970), pp. 76–78.

[53]The Commander-in-Chief of the Soviet Navy, Admiral S. G. Gorshkov, commented on these interservice rivalries which included antipathy toward the submarine as well as surface ships as follows in 1967: "Unfortunately, we had some quite influential 'authorities' who believed that the appearance of nuclear weapons meant that the Navy had completely lost its significance as a branch of the armed forces. In their opinion, all the basic tasks of a future war could be resolved without the participation of the Navy at all.... Not infrequently, it was claimed that landbased missiles alone would suffice for the destruction of surface strike forces and even of submarines." S. G. Gorshkov, "The Development of Soviet Naval Art," *Morskoi Sbornik* [Naval Collection] (February 1967): 19. See Robert Waring Herrick, *Soviet Naval Strategy: Fifty Years of Theory and Practice* (Annapolis, Md.: United States Naval Institute, 1968), pp. 67–71.

[54]MccGwire, *op. cit.* p. 78.

[55]*Ibid.*, p. 82; Herrick, *op. cit.*, pp. 19–27.

[56]*Status of Naval Ships*, Hearings Before the Special Subcommittee on Sea Power of the Committee on Armed Serv-

Finally, American efforts in this area, in particular the Polaris program of the late fifties, could be expected to strengthen the arguments of those pressing for continued investment in the development and acquisition of a Soviet SLBM capability.

The Soviets continued their efforts in the SLBM field throughout the sixties and early seventies. The surface launched SS-N-4 was succeeded by the SS-N-5, "Serb," a 650 mile range, liquid-fueled weapon which could be fired from a submerged position. It was developed in the early sixties and became operational on converted G-II class (diesel) and H-II class (nuclear) submarines in 1964.[57]

The most important activity in this area centered around the third generation system, the SS-N-6, a submerged-launch missile with a 1500 mile range, and its carrier the nuclear-powered Y-class submarine. The development of this system is likely to have been authorized as a part of the general post-Cuba force expansion discussed earlier. The configuration of the Y-class sub with its 16 missile capacity, identical to that of the American Polaris which was operational in 1960, suggests a strong imitative element in its development. Since the first operational Y-class was delivered in late 1967, modern SSBN's have come off the construction ways at Severodvinsk in Northern Russia[58] and at a yard in the Soviet Far East at the rate of 6 to 8 per year, producing the force of 43 in service and under construction by mid-1972. Since mid-1972, these boats have been supplemented by the D-class submarine which is scheduled to carry 12 of the new SS-N-8 "Sawfly" missiles.

Sustained Soviet ballistic missile submarine activity is understandable on a number of grounds. The SLBM submarine with its mobility and concealment appears to be the most secure of contemporary strategic strike systems and thus a very rational choice for continued expansion. Additionally, in a period of a comprehensive and sustained military build-up, when the Soviet leadership appeared to have made a commitment to attaining first numerical parity and then a marginal superiority with respect to the United States, it was only logical that they include a substantial effort in the area where the United States had maintained a distinct qualitative and quantitative advantage. In addition, the general-

ized force expansion of the mid and late sixties is likely to have made additional funds available to all of the major services. With the existence of a submarine force/sub construction lobby, buttressed by a firm role assignment within Soviet military doctrine for submarine launched ballistic missiles as an important element of the strategic exchange[59] and a sizable submarine construction capacity, it is not surprising that the Soviet submarine program has enjoyed such prosperity in recent years.

Strategic Aviation

The Long-Range Aviation Command of the Soviet Air Forces currently controls 140 long-range bombers consisting of 100 TU-95, "Bears," and 40 MYA-4, "Bisons,"[60] and a medium bomber force of 700 aircraft, including 500 TU-16 "Badgers," and 200 TU-22, "Blinders." This force is supplemented by the shore-based bombers of Soviet Naval Aviation. Its inventory included 300 Badgers, armed with air-to-surface missiles apparently slated for an anti-ship role, 50 specially configured reconnaissance and tanker Badgers, 60 reconnaissance Blinders, and 40 long-range reconnaissance Bears.[61]

The overall size of the Soviet strategic bomber force has declined steadily over the past decade. While the long-range bomber strength has remained constant, the medium bomber force has declined by almost one-third. The internal composition of the medium bomber inventory has been altered as well with the gradual replacement of the older TU-16 Badgers procured between 1955 and 1960, by the newer TU-22, Blinder, which first entered service in 1962.

A prototype strategic bomber, the Tupolev designed variable geometry "Backfire," has been sighted frequently since 1969. While a series production decision apparently remains to be made, Western sources are in conflict regarding the Backfire's range capabilities. Some call it a truly long-range system,[62] while others attribute shorter-range characteristics to it, limiting the aircraft to a peripheral attack role and thus dis-

ices, House of Representatives, 90th Congress, 2nd Session; and 91st Congress, 1st Session (Washington, D.C.: U.S. Government Printing Office, 1969), pp. 226, 233.

[57]McGwire, p. 84.

[58]"Soviets Stressing Offensive Mix of Strategic Arms for Which the U.S. Has Little Defense," *Aviation Week and Space Technology* (October 11, 1971): 38.

[59]The Soviet Navy appears to have been forced to lobby strongly to acquire a substantial cut of the strategic exchange in Soviet military doctrine. See Admiral V. A. Alafuzov's review of the first edition of Sokolovskii's *Military Strategy*, which was part of a successful naval effort to gain recognition of the role of SLBM's as important strike weapons. Admiral V. A. Alafuzov, "On the Publication of the Work 'Military Strategy,'" *Morskoi Sbornik* 1 (January 1963): 95.

[60]There are an additional 50 Bisons configured as tankers for in-flight refueling.

[61]*The Military Balance, 1972–1973*, p. 7.

[62]Edgar Ulsamer, "Backfire: Special Report on the New Soviet Strategic Bomber," *Air Force Magazine* (October 1971): 35.

qualifying the Backfire as the possible successor within the Bear-Bison force.[63]

Historically, a critical point in the development of contemporary Soviet strategic aviation was the leadership's decision in the mid-fifties not to deploy a large long-range bomber force. While American officials and commentators were anticipating a major Soviet build-up and speaking of an impending bomber gap (an estimate that the Soviets themselves encouraged by their ploy of creating the impression of a sizable Russian bomber force by a cleverly manipulated fly-by of their limited inventory at the 1955 Air Show[64]), the Soviets chose instead to build up their medium-range bomber force, while never acquiring more than 150 of the long-range Bisons and Bears.

A variety of explanations can be put forward regarding this choice. The small long-range bomber acquisition may have represented a rational choice to concentrate Soviet efforts on the development of their first ICBM, which was at that time approaching operational capability. In addition, Khrushchev's personal predilections may have been an important factor in that he publicly displayed a strong aversion for strategic aircraft while enthusiastically endorsing the ICBM.[65]

The decision to procure a substantial medium-range Badger force while eschewing a substantial long-range capability may be traced to the continental perspective prevailing within the Soviet Armed Forces that was noted in the earlier discussion of the parallel M/IRBM build-up. It also may reflect the limited organizational strength of the air forces in general and long-range aviation in particular within the Soviet military establishment. Despite sporadic attempts to establish a true strategic aviation capability in the past,[66] the Soviet Air Forces had been traditionally assigned an auxiliary role as a kind of flying artillery force in Soviet military planning and operations.

Soviet strategic aviation procurements during the fifties are likely to have been prompted by the design/production ambitions of the major aircraft design bureaus and those in charge of the production facilities of the Ministry of Aviation Industry. The design bureaus are headed by a small number of prominent designers, who often have been educated at the Zhukovsky Air Engineering Academy run by the Soviet Air Forces and in many cases hold honorary general officer rank within the engineering and technical services.[67] Their sizable staffs appear to enjoy considerable autonomy in the creation of new aircraft designs, maintain strong institutional and personal ties with the Soviet Air Forces, and are likely to engage frequently in the type of self-promotional activity evident in the Yakovlev case cited earlier.[68]

During the fifties, the design collectives led by A. N. Tupolev, V. M. Myasishchev, and S. V. Ilyushin were engaged in strategic bomber design competitions. In this period, the Tupolev collective produced the TU-95 Bear and TU-16 Badger while Ilyushin's group failed to gain authorization for the production of a single design in this area[69] and Myasishchev was successful only once, with his MYA-4, Bison.

Despite the Soviet decision to limit the size of their strategic aviation inventory to the modest level attained by the beginning of the sixties, these designers were able to sustain their design organizations in this and other areas. Even in this restricted environment, Tupolev continued to find success in the development of strategic aircraft. His group designed the medium-range TU-22, Blinder, the only strategic bomber produced in the sixties which was procured as a replacement for a portion of the Badger force, as well as the TU-VG Backfire which currently awaits a high level series production decision.

[63] *The Military Balance: 1972–1973*, p. 5.

[64] For an excellent discussion of the American bomber-gap perceptions, the role of intentional Soviet deception in its emergence, and its eventual disappearance, thanks largely to the American U-2 program, see Ervin J. Rokke, "The Politics of Aerial Reconnaissance: The Eisenhower Administration," Ph.D. dissertation (Cambridge, Massachusetts: Harvard University, June 1970), pp. 185–204.

[65] In the late fifties and early sixties Khrushchev frequently spoke of the obsolescence of the manned bomber and its impending replacement by missiles. His attacks included this statement before the Supreme Soviet in January 1960: "Military aviation is being almost entire replaced by missiles. We have now sharply reduced and probably will further reduce and even halt the production of bombers and other obsolete equipment." *Pravda* (January 15, 1960).

[66] During the thirties, a cadre of Soviet Air Forces commanders led by V. V. Khripkin vigorously pushed for the development of a Russian strategic aviation arm capable of long-range independent operations. This effort languished after the military purges of 1936–38, whose victims included Khripkin, see John Erickson, *The Soviet High Command, 1918–1941* (New York: Macmillan, 1962), pp. 382–83.

[67] The prestige of the leading Soviet aviation designers is enhanced by the practice of designating aircraft with letters derived from the chief designers names. Thus the Mikoyan-Gurevich team produced the MIG series, Yakovlev-the YAK's, Antonov-the AN's, Tupolev the TU's, Sukhoi, the SU's, etc.

[68] For a discussion of Soviet aircraft design and production practices see Arthur J. Alexander, *R & D In Soviet Aviation*, R-589-PR (Santa Monica, California: The RAND Corporation, November 1970), and his further comment on this subject in this volume, pp. 426–43.

[69] Ilyushin's IL-46, a scaled-up version of his tactical bomber, the IL-28 Beagle, competed unsuccessfully with the TU-16 Badger in the early fifties. This information and that which follows on specific aircraft designs is extracted from a comprehensive listing of Soviet aircraft provided the author by Arthur J. Alexander.

The Tupolev collective also designed other military aircraft that were authorized for production including the TU-28 Fiddler fighter-bomber and the airborne warning and control system (AWACS), the TU-114B, Moss, as well as a number of civilian transports including the TU-134 and the supersonic transport, the TU-144.

Ilyushin and Myasishchev turned to other design activities. After failing to have his supersonic MYA-Delta, the Bounder, selected for production in the late fifties, Myasishchev's group became a leading force in Soviet spacecraft design.[70] During the same period, Ilyushin as well appears to have abandoned the military field, devoting his efforts instead to the design of civilian transport aviation.[71]

While these design organizations were shifting their attention into related areas, the production facilities of the Ministry of Aviation Industry displayed similar flexibility. Virtually continuous innovation in the development of tactical fighters and civilian and military transport was sufficient to maintain a substantial level of aircraft production. In addition, their manufacturing facilities have been increasingly devoted to the production of a wide variety of consumer goods including refrigerators, vacuum cleaners, and pleasure boats.[72] The availability of these alternative production areas is likely to have been an important factor lessening the pressures from the aviation design-production complex for the procurement of a larger strategic bomber inventory.

Despite its failure to fulfill American expectations in the procurement of a massive strategic bomber force, Soviet long-range aviation has successfully acquired and maintained a modest intercontinental capability and a substantial medium-range inventory. The capability of this force has been augmented considerably by the development of a variety of air-to-surface missiles. These weapons provide the Soviet strategic air arm with a stand-off capability which permits it to attack many targets without encountering their point defenses. The addition of these weapons has been reflected in the Soviet discussion of their strategic bomber capability which rou-

tinely extol the virtues of their "jet-propelled, missile-carrying aircraft."

The relatively low priority accorded to strategic aviation within the family of Soviet strategic offensive systems was evident in its failure to share in the broad expansion of Soviet military capabilities that occurred in the mid-sixties. While missile-carrying strategic aviation successfully resisted Khrushchev's determined attack upon its very existence, its partisans apparently lacked the strength to capitalize upon the disposition of the Soviet political leadership which allowed a major expansion of the land- and sea-based ballistic missile forces described above.

However, the appearance of the Backfire in 1969 after a delay of some ten years since the emergence of the previous new Soviet long-range bomber design provides ample proof of the persistence of those who seek to maintain or expand a substantial Soviet strategic aviation capability. This Soviet effort appears similar to those which have accompanied the development of the B-1 strategic bomber design in the United States. While the parallel developments of the Backfire and the B-1 appear to represent cases of independent but similar activity on both sides, the procurement decisions on both aircraft are likely to be highly interdependent. The series production of either one could importantly influence events within the decisional arena of the other. Such a move would be bound to arouse fears of a new bomber gap, thus strengthening the arguments of those favoring a similar procurement in the second country.

STRATEGIC DEFENSIVE FORCES

The Soviets have expended a great deal in the development and maintenance of a large and diversified national air defense system. This mission is assigned to one of the five independent military services of the Soviet armed forces, the National Air Defense Forces which is frequently identified by its Russian abbreviation *PVO-Strany*.

A variety of weapons systems have been procured to defend the Russian homeland from attack by enemy aircraft and missiles. Their vast anti-aircraft system includes an extensive radar detection and tracking network, a large fighter-interceptor force of approximately 3000 aircraft and some 10,000 surface-to-air missiles (SAM's) of a variety of types located in 1600 different launch sites. The Soviets have also deployed a modest anti-ballistic missile (ABM) system centered around Moscow which currently includes some

[70] William H. Gregory, "Soviet Union Seeks Balance In Technology Growth," *Aviation Week and Space Technology* (March 18, 1968): 87.

[71] These include the IL-18V, Coot, a standard aeroflot passenger aircraft and the IL-62, Classic, a deluxe passenger liner which has partially replaced the TU-114.

[72] This development has been noted publicly by a number of prominent Soviet figures including Premier Kosygin in his major address before the Twenty-Fourth Party Congress, *Pravda* (April 7, 1971). See also the article by P. Dementev, the Minister of Aviation Industry, "More Than Just Airplanes," *Izvestia* (May 22, 1971).

64 launchers housed in four separate complexes.[73] Under the terms of the ABM Treaty negotiated at SALT I, they may expand this system to a maximum of 100 launchers and are additionally authorized to construct a second 100 launcher system deployed to defend one of their ICBM launch complexes, although to date no reports about the initiation of the latter system have been heard.

The large and continuing Soviet investment in strategic defense is frequently attributed to a long-standing Russian tradition of defense-mindedness. In light of their bitter experiences at the hands of the invading armies of Charles XII of Sweden, Napoleon, Kaiser Wilhelm, the Western powers during the Russian Civil War, and Adolf Hitler, such a Russian concern is perfectly understandable.

Substantial strategic defense efforts are also justified within Soviet military doctrine. Although throughout the Soviet period their doctrine has been marked by a preference for seizing the initiative and boldly conducting offensive operations, their simultaneous commitment to the "combined arms concept" provides a firm basis for substantial defensive measures as well. In addition, in the adjustment of their military strategy to the nuclear-missile revolution, the Soviets have flatly refused to adopt an assured destruction approach to the problems of modern war. Led largely by the theorists of the Ministry of Defense, the Soviets have endorsed instead a strategy which calls for comprehensive preparations for the waging of thermonuclear conflict, including serious attention to measures designed to limit possible damage to the Soviet Union itself. Consequently, the fundamental thrust of Soviet military doctrine fails to share the judgment that contemporary strategic defense is basically a futile exercise, a conclusion which has predominated in American strategic thought.[74] With the growth of antagonism between the Soviet Union and the People's Republic of China and in light of the much more modest strategic capabilities possessed by the Chinese, this doctrinal commitment to damage-limiting defense may have received some practical reinforcement.

Whatever the bases of its mandate, in PVO-Strany the Soviet strategic defense mission has found a vigorous institutional advocate that has been demonstrably successful in acquiring and maintaining substantial budgeting support for that purpose. In the late forties and fifties, their efforts to gain support for the development of an antiaircraft defense capability were probably assisted by the fact that the chief antagonist, the United States, made strategic bomber attack on the Soviet homeland the keystone of its military policy. In addition a substantial aviation threat to the Soviet Union has existed in the past and continues to exist which includes American long-range strategic bombers and forward-based fighter bombers as well as the strategic attack aircraft of third countries including France, the United Kingdom, and China. Subsequent Soviet ABM development and procurement activities could be similarly supported in a straightforward offsetting manner due to the growth and importance of American missile capabilities. While such arms race interaction reinforced by the Soviet predisposition to pay close attention to active defense are adequate to substantiate the sizable Soviet air defense effort, there are some anomalies in the composition of this force which merit further discussion.

In the forties and fifties the Soviets procured a truly massive conventional anti-aircraft artillery (AAA) capability. The nationwide emplacement of these weapons ran well beyond that which could be rationally justified in the face of the numbers and characteristics of the increasingly jet-powered American bomber force.[75] During the same period they procured a large inventory of fighter-interceptors centered around the MIG-17 and the early MIG-19 with exclusively daylight capabilities. Given the probabilities of night assault by the enemy, this acquisition also confounds the logic of rational interaction.[76] Instead, these decisions appear to reflect the efforts of PVO-Strany, which had achieved the status of an independent service in 1948, to fully expend its sizable annual budget. Viewed from this organization perspective, these procurements which increase the weapons inventory under PVO's control and apparently increase its ability to fulfill its assigned role make great sense despite the deficiencies of these systems.

Apparently following the same bureaucratic logic, the Soviets followed their oversized AAA procurement with a similar saturation acquisition of surface-to-air missiles (SAMs) as soon as these systems became available. Their SAM acquisitions began in the mid-fifties with the SA-1 system

---

[73]*The Military Balance, 1972–1973*, p. 7.

[74]For the most comprehensive recent exposition on Soviet military doctrine and capabilities see John Erickson, *Soviet Military Power* (London: Royal United Service Institute of Defense Studies, 1971), pp. 7–12, 41–74. See also Thomas W. Wolfe's excellent discussions in *Soviet Power and Europe, 1945–1970*, pp. 195–216, 427–58, 501–10.

[75]Johan J. Holst, "Missile Defense: The Soviet Union and the Arms Race," in J. J. Holst and W. Schneider, Jr. (eds.), *Why ABM? Policy Issues in the Missile Defense Controversy* (New York: Pergamon Press, 1969), p. 147.

[76]*Ibid.*, p. 146.

whose deployment revealed another tendency evident in the development of the Soviet air defense system. This weapons system was apparently prematurely deployed in that its use was restricted to its original Moscow-centered configuration.[77] The practice of moving rapidly from development to an initial operational deployment, which was to appear again in the ABM area in the sixties, may have been prompted by PVO's budget spending imperative as well as a standardized Soviet practice of emplacing systems when additional development and testing remained to be done. A similar practice has frequently been followed in the Soviet Navy, where new ship designs are routinely deployed as "production prototypes" to undergo continuing sea trials during their initial years of operation.[78]

The limited acquisition of the SA-1 was followed by the large-scale procurement of the second generation SA-2. This missile which first appeared in 1958 may have been designed by the design bureau of P. A. Lavochkin, formerly a major aircraft designer who had turned to missile development after failing repeatedly in a number of fighter design competitions in the late forties and early fifties.[79] SA-2 production was voluminous as it became the workhorse of the extensive Soviet SAM network and was regularly included in arms shipments to a variety of nations including Cuba, Egypt, and North Viet Nam. Its apparent deficiencies against low altitude attackers prompted the development and procurement of the complementary SA-3 system beginning in the late fifties and continuing to the present day.

The early sixties saw the appearance of the Griffon missile which was employed in a Leningrad-centered deployment which never became operational and has been generally described as an unsuccessful ABM system.[80] From a characteristics standpoint, the missile was capable of high altitude interception, thus providing it with a marginal capability against the first generation Polaris A-1 missile and the medium-range Thor[81] that was emplaced in Europe in the early sixties.

Following the abortive Leningrad deployment, another high altitude defensive missile, the SA-5, was deployed, particularly in the so-called Tallinn Line, an arc of launch sites extending northeast from the Baltic city of Tallinn and protecting the northwestern approaches to the European USSR.[82] The Tallinn Line appears to represent an offsetting Soviet response to American attack systems that were not in use by the time it became operational. This system may have been directed against the Polaris A-1 missile, a possibility suggested by the fact that the oceanic launch area for this 1300 mile range SLBM was limited to the Barents Sea, thus bringing their flight path to the European USSR directly through the area covered by the Tallinn Line.[83] If this was the case, it has proved to be a costly and futile Soviet effort in that the Polaris A-1 has been replaced by the longer range A-2 and A-3 thus extending its potential launch areas and changing its entering trajectory in a manner making it less likely to be vulnerable to the SA-5. Alternatively, the SA-5 may have been designed as an anticipatory measure to combat the American supersonic bomber, the B-70. If this was the case, Soviet planning was once again rather grieviously in error as this aircraft, although advancing to the prototype stage, was never procured as an operational system.

Whatever their original intentions, the Soviets have deployed some 1000 SA-5's,[84] both in the Tallinn Line and in the southeastern USSR. Its capabilities against high-flying strategic bombers and perhaps their air-to-surface missiles appear formidable. Western concern about a possible ABM role for the SA-5, particularly if it could be successfully integrated with the sophisticated radar network of the Soviets' unambiguous ABM, the Galosh/Moscow system, persisted into the early seventies.[85] This possibility has been explicitly prohibited in the ABM Treaty signed at the conclusion of SALT I.

In the mid-sixties the Soviets began to deploy an ABM system in a series of launch complexes around Moscow. This system utilizes the Galosh missile, an area defense vehicle capable of intercepting incoming vehicles outside the earth's atmosphere where it can utilize its nuclear warhead to produce a lethal electromagnetic pulse (EMP).[86]

[77]Thomas W. Wolfe, *Soviet Power and Europe, 1945–1970,* p. 185.

[78]Michael MccGwire, "Soviet Naval Capabilities and Intentions" in *The Soviet Union In Europe and the Near East: Her Capabilities and Intentions* (London: Royal United Service Institution, August 1970), p. 43.

[79]Robert A. Kilmarx, *The History of Soviet Air Power* (New York: Praeger, 1962), p. 229.

[80]Wolfe, *Soviet Power and Europe,* p. 188.

[81]*The Soviet Military Technological Challenge,* Special Report, Series: No. 6 (Washington, D.C.: The Center for Strategic Studies, September 1967), p. 61.

[82]*Ibid.,* p. 63.

[83]Geoffrey Jukes, *The Indian Ocean in Soviet Naval Policy,* Adelphi Papers, No. 87 (London: International Institute for Strategic Studies, May 1972), p. 5.

[84]Erickson, *Soviet Military Power,* p. 47.

[85]Cf. Joseph Alsop, "Soviet Missile Analysis," *Washington Post* (June 4, 1971).

[86]*The Soviet Military Technological Challenge,* pp. 63–64.

The deployment of the Galosh was probably authorized in the landmark Soviet force expansion decision of 1963. Its construction pattern shows signs of the Soviet premature emplacement syndrome noted earlier in that the construction was temporarily halted in 1968 with only 64 launchers completed. Construction around Moscow was resumed in the spring of 1971, perhaps to accommodate an improved missile,[87] although it will have to be kept within a maximum of 100 launchers as agreed upon in the ABM Treaty of 1972.

The limited Soviet ABM deployment may be traced to second thoughts regarding the probable effectiveness of the system.[88] First their own self-restraint and then their willingness to agree to the explicit numerical limitations embodied in the SALT-negotiated ABM Treaty represent a serious setback to PVO-Strany. Although authorized by the Treaty to construct a second 100 launcher system for the protection of an ICBM launch complex, PVO-Strany has been denied the opportunity to emplace a thick ABM network. As a result they may prove vulnerable to pressures from the other military services for a reduction of PVO's share of the defense budget.

Soviet ABM development which began in the late forties provides an example of self-generated weapons development with obvious arms race impact. As in the entire air defense area there were elements of rational offsetting response to American offensive development mixed with the shaping influences of their active defense tradition and internal bureaucratic factors. The Soviet propensity to deploy air defense missile systems at the first possible opportunity has meant that they have triggered American reactions rather than responding in an emulative manner.[89]

The 3000 aircraft inventory of fighter interceptors assigned to PVO-Strany has gradually been reduced from a strength of 8000 a decade

ago and has undergone continuous modernization.[90] The predominance of day-fighters noted previously began to disappear with acquisition of the all-weather YAK-25 and the MIG-19P in the late fifties. While sizable numbers of the fifties aircraft remain in active service, the capabilities of air defense interceptor aviation have been steadily improved with the addition of a new generation of advanced fighters including the SU-9, YAK-28P, TU-28P, SU-11, and MIG-23, all of which are equipped with modern avionics and air-to-air missiles.[91]

The maintenance of this large interceptor force is supported by the various components of the Soviet commitment to strategic defense discussed above. It probably benefits as well from the existence of two institutional sponsors within the Soviet Armed Forces. The aircraft assigned the air defense role are simultaneously an element of the Soviet Air Forces with regard to training and logistic matters and of PVO-Strany which acts as the operational command. The pressures for continuous fighter development and series production are also likely to emanate from the prestigious Mikoyan, Sukhoi, Tupolev, and Yakovlev design bureaus. The appearance of new fighter prototypes at regular three- to four-year intervals suggests the potency of this group. In addition, the manufacturing plants within the Ministry of Aviation Industry are likely to lobby for additional aircraft acquisitions in accordance with their own "production line imperatives."[92] Blessed with this array of parochial advocates and the continued existence of a plausible aviation threat from the West and now China, the PVO air arm appears to be in a good position to maintain and improve its substantial capabilities.

From an interaction standpoint, the Soviets are known to monitor carefully Western aircraft de-

[87]William Beecher, "Laird Says Soviet Renews ABM Work," *New York Times* (April 29, 1971).

[88]From the scientific community, the voice of the dissident nuclear physicist Andrei Sakharov was raised against the Soviet deployment of an ABM on grounds of its projected ineffectiveness and undesirable political consequences in his underground manifesto, *Progress, Coexistence and Intellectual Freedom* (New York: W. W. Norton, 1968), p. 35. There were also signs of disagreement concerning the effectiveness of their ABM among senior figures within the Ministry of Defense in early 1967. See Wolfe, *Soviet Power and Europe*, p. 439.

[89]Soviet construction of the Moscow/Galosh system proved to be an important precipitating factor that influenced political calculations within the Johnson administration and prompted the imitative initiation of deployment of the American Sentinel ABM system in 1967-68. For an insightful analysis of this decision see Morton H. Halperin, "The Decision to Deploy the ABM: Bureaucratic and Domestic Politics in the Johnson Administration," *World Politics* (October 1972): 62-95.

[90]Cf. Cecil Brownlow, "Soviet Air Force Unveils Advanced Designs for Expanded Limited War Capability," *Aviation Week and Space Technology* (July 17, 1967): 32-35; "Soviets Push Advances in Fighters," *Aviation Week and Space Technology* (October 18, 1971).

[91]"Soviets Closing Gap in Avionics, Computer Science Military Development," *Aviation Week and Space Technology* (October 25, 1971): 28-30.

[92]A provocative discussion of the impact of available production capacity on the awarding of aviation contracts in the United States is found in James Kurth, "Corporate and Bureaucratic Imperatives In American Weapons Procurement," in R. Head and E. J. Rokke (eds.), *American Defense Policy*, 3rd ed. (Baltimore: The Johns Hopkins Press, 1973), pp. 626-40. For a trenchant critique of Kurth's "production line imperative" hypothesis see Arnold Kanter and Stuart J. Thorson, "The Logic of American Weapons Procurement: Problems In the Construction and Evaluation of Policy Theories," paper delivered at the 1972 Midwest Regional Meeting of the International Studies Association and the Peace Research Society, Toronto, Ontario, May 11-13, 1972. We lack sufficient information on Soviet aircraft production to test the validity of this theory on the Soviet scene.

velopment, a practice with obvious emulative and offsetting design implications. Soviet interceptors are most certainly designed with an eye toward their capabilities against probable Western attackers. Thus the supersonic, high altitude characteristics of the MIG-25 Foxbat suggest that it may have been designed as a counter to the anticipated American procurement of the B-70. The convergence of Western and Soviet aircraft design activity in such areas as vertical take-off and landing and variable geometry airframes appears largely attributable to the simultaneous advance of the technological state-of-the-art by similarly proficient aviation design complexes rather than an imitative action-reaction sequence on either side. Yet, when one side develops and acquires a particular capability it is likely to strengthen the demands for the funding of both imitative and offsetting activity within the decisional arena of the other.

CONCLUSION

The examination of the evolution of Soviet strategic force posture presented above indicates that it has been shaped by a variety of factors. While in many respects responsive to American weapons developments, it has also exhibited distinctive characteristics traceable to the influences of Soviet military doctrine, the parochial interests of the various organizations involved in the development of Soviet defense policy, and the routine processes of Soviet weapons design and acquisition. As a result, one must agree with the conclusion of one student of Soviet weapons development, A. W. Marshall, that "the interaction between American and Soviet force postures is muffled, lagged and very complex.[93] While evidence to test hypotheses concerning the impact of internal organizational factors is difficult to obtain, imaginative and empirical work along these lines nevertheless holds great promise for improving our understanding of the development of Soviet force posture.

[93]Quoted in Allison, *op. cit.*, p. 98.

CHINA'S FORCE POSTURE:
FACTORS IN THE POLICY PROCESS

JOSEPH J. HEINLEIN, JR.

By carefully analyzing both the internal and external roles that the various elements of China's force structure might be seen to support, Heinlein has provided a meaningful perspective from which to view contemporary pronouncements of Maoist doctrine. His account reveals the difficulties faced by the Peking government (1) in balancing advanced weaponry R & D taking place primarily in the air and naval forces with economic development in other domestic areas, and (2) in endeavoring to keep the ground forces satisfied with their minimal economic allocations by utilizing them in civil roles offering certain intrinsic rewards. His discussion of these issues is deepened by the inclusion throughout of the impact of the traditional tension between the central and regional governments and of the relationship of China with other countries in the realms of international politics and economics. His analysis allows one to see present enunciations of Maoist doctrine as not so much determining the Chinese force posture as simply providing rationalizations for an almost inevitable turning of events shaped, for the most part, by the "micro" regional and bureaucratic imperatives within China and by the "macro" economic and political imperatives of China's relations internationally.

Lt. Colonel Heinlein is an Assistant Professor, Department of Social Sciences, U.S. Military Academy. He completed his M.A. in Far Eastern Area Studies at American University in 1965. He is the author of North Korea's Doctrine and Strategy *(1969) and "The Ground Forces," in Whitson,* The Military and Political Power in China in the 70's *(1972).*

It is fairly difficult to describe the numbers and composition of China's military forces with any great assurance in the correctness of the description (see Table 1). However the description of the forces is far more easily accomplished than an explanation of the causal factors at work in the policy process of the Chinese political system which have served to shape China's military force posture. This paper attempts such an explanation by initially scanning China's environment, both internal and external, in order to discern the threat with which the Chinese military could be required to contend, the economic parameters of the problem, and some of the demands the environment might place upon the Chinese leadership. However, instead of treating China and its leaders as a unitary "rational actor"[1] selecting what are perceived to be the most effective alternatives in pursuit of well-defined objectives, we will attempt to show that Chinese perceptions of the environment and the demands emanating from it are not necessarily uniform and that the policy process in China manifests considerable diversity of interest. An effort is also made herein to describe the direction and control of programs related to force posture, the arena in which related decisions are formulated and relevant interests articulated, and what programs are currently on going which contribute to incremental change in force posture.

---

[1] The term "rational actor" refers to the characterization of a nation and/or its leadership as the personification of rational behavior reflecting unified purpose, goal, and calculated solutions to problems. This concept and those used below which employ organizational outputs as influences in the policymaking process are drawn from Graham T. Allison, *Essence of Decision* (Boston: Little, Brown, 1971), *passim*.

This is an original article written for this volume and for the Conference on Comparative Defense Policy held at the Air Force Academy, February 7–9, 1973. Copyright reserved by the author. The views expressed herein are those of the author and do not necessarily reflect the views of the United States Army or the Department of Defense.

Table 1. Force Posture

GROUND FORCES

Strength: Approximately 2.5 million.

Combat Divisions: About 150, of which 110 are infantry, 6 armored, and a few horse cavalry; in addition there are border defense and public security forces that could be used for combat; separate gun and howitzer artillery divisions provide support.

Firepower: Most units short of heavy artillery; small arms probably adequate; ammunition dispersed and stockpiled; armored units deficient in tanks, especially more modern types.

Disposition: Generally along lines of population and industrial pattern; heavy concentrations in northeast and along the coast.

Mobility: Generally poor; some motorized infantry have full complement of vehicles; no more than half of armored divisions fully equipped; some armored personnel carriers in use; rail-bound for strategic moves; tactical foot mobility excellent.

Training/Readiness: Uneven throughout; certain elite units (perhaps a strategic reserve) may maintain higher standards; combined arms exercises not as frequent or as effective as needed.

Logistics: Handled by General Rear Services Department (procurement and distribution agency for all services); resupply tied to road and rail nets; no organic capability to satisfy large-scale manuever; heavy reliance on stockpiling and local acquisition.

Tactical Organization: Triangular concept of 3 regiments/division; number of divisions per region (U.S. corps equivalent) varies widely; long-fixed ties of divisions to geographic regions, of which there are 11, inhibit strategic employment; about 14,000 men in an infantry division and 10,000 in an armored division.

AIR FORCES

Strength: Approximately 250,000 (as many as 50% of personnel are assigned to AAA, radar, and SAM-2 air defense units).

Aircraft: About 3100 jet fighters (majority are MIG-15, 17; a few MIG-21; Chinese version of MIG-19 being serially produced); some 150 IL-28 jet light bombers; about 50 TU-16 medium bombers (also in series production).

Missiles: It has been estimated that MR/IRBM's are now deployed at 3 to 5 sites. Reduced range firing of ICBM may already have occurred, however first deployment would not likely begin prior to 1975 with some 10–20 missiles being operational by mid-1976 (the missiles are included here even though the subordination of the 2d Artillery is not certain). There are about 50 SAM sites and 1500 air defense radars under the operational control of the air forces, plus some 4500 AAA guns.

Training/Readiness: Much improved over mid-60's when fuel and spare parts limited training; well coordinated and exercised air defense capability; much less effective in ground support role; regional manned-bomber capability includes nuclear weapons.

Logistics: Adequate to maintain training; would probably be strained in actual combat of any duration; stockpiles heavy at older bases, continuing at newer fields; use same logistics net as ground forces (GRSD).

Command/Control: Air forces are theoretically subordinate to the military region command in which they are based. In practice, however, strategic mission and mobility make them operationally amenable to centralized control; inter-regional re-disposition of aircraft and air defense missiles is not unusual, indicating cross-region authority exists; air defense system is also supra-regionally coordinated.

NAVAL FORCES

Strength: Approximately 150,000 (including 16,000 naval air force and 28,000 marines).

Vessels: 35 submarines (including one Chinese-built G-class; no missiles believed to be available).

   4 destroyers
   9 destroyer escorts
   11 escorts
   10 Osa-Komar missile boats (with Styx missiles)
   31 sub-chasers
   160 fast gunboats
   240 fast torpedo boats
   22 coastal and river defense craft
   54 amphibious ships and landing craft
   33 auxiliaries and support ships
   375 miscellaneous and service craft
(except for the submarines and patrol craft, the majority of the above vessels are aged and obsolete by U.S. standards).

Training/Readiness: Despite the age and obsolescence of the majority of the craft, training has nonetheless been persistent and performance in skirmishes with the Chinese Nationalist navy has been credible. Submarine training extremely limited and readiness poor; no match for a modern force.

Command/Control: Organized into 3 coastal fleets; theoretically subordinate to military region in which based; probably responsive operationally to supra-regional authority; naval air consists of allocations from aircraft listed above under air forces; aircraft are integrated for operations with naval forces but are also responsive to air defense network; marines appear to be ground troops trained in amphibious operations and associated with naval installations.

Logistics: Procurement and support through GRSD; difficulties evident in spare parts for aged craft and associated weapons systems; Chinese built fast boats and Styx missile craft less a problem.

Sources: Franz J. Mogdis, "The Role of the Chinese Communist Air Force in the 1970's," and J. Heinlein, "The Ground Forces," in W. W. Whitson (ed.), *The Military and Political Power in China in the 1970's* (New York: Praeger, 1972); *Annual Defense Department Report, FY 1973*; *Jane's Fighting Ships and Jane's Weapon Systems* (New York: McGraw-Hill, 1972); Gerald Ellis, "China's Military Strength," *Military Review* (April 1971).

EXTERNAL THREAT AND
ALLIANCE ENVIRONMENT

The evidence is quite clear that the threat to China and the appropriate response to that threat, to include the role of alliances, have been central issues in debates over military policy. Furthermore, the parameters of the threat and the complexion of the alliance structure in Asia have both undergone considerable alteration during the past two decades and these changes have had impact upon the current and future composition of Chinese military forces.

It was the Korean War, at a time of Sino-Soviet amity, which caused the Chinese to react forcefully, to taste modern, large-unit type warfare and to welcome Moscow's military aid and doctrinal influence. This was the stimulus for modernizing the PLA* along Soviet lines and with Soviet assistance. More importantly it served to breed professional attitudes within the military leadership which were to surface in recurring struggles among the ruling elite in Peking. While these debates have invariably expanded to include ideological and economic issues, the core of the argument over military policy has remained the question of strategy and tactics for the defense of the mainland: was China to develop military forces appropriately equipped and trained to contend with an adversary in terms of modern warfare, denying an invader access to Chinese territory, or was reliance to be placed on the Maoist techniques of guerrilla warfare by luring the enemy to destruction within Chinese territory?

As de facto changes in the alliance pattern were evolving in Sino-Soviet relations, the "people's war" concept of guerrilla-type operations was invoked as the rationale for defense despite the qualitative increase in the threat. Even before the Moscow-Peking split many of those within the upper echelons of military leadership who favored modernization of the armed forces were purged. Similar debates attended the U.S. escalation in Vietnam: a similar dichotomy was evident and another purge ultimately ensued.[2]

Perhaps the most significant impact on Chinese calculations of the threat they faced came in the Soviet turnabout from ally to adversary. It was quite obvious that Peking lacked the wherewithal to match either Soviet or U.S. military capabilities and according to Chou En-lai the decision to improve relations with the United States was made at a time when the Soviet force build-up was reaching its peak in the Far East.[3] Recent shifts in policy have included a cutback in military spending and a reordering of economic priorities. True to earlier patterns of purge, Lin Piao, Wu Fa-hsien, and Huang Yung-sheng fell from positions of power.[4]

Peking could not help but appreciate the opportunities available in the Asian alliance environment. The formal alliances are a product of the cold war era and the alliance structure belies the qualitative changes which have taken place. But such vague meanderings on a strategic plane did not have as immediate an influence on Chinese military policy as do the hard facts related to the presence of 47 Soviet divisions across the border, the experience of the Korean war, the potential threat embodied in the U.S. buildup in Asia in the late 1960s, and superpower aid to such clients as India, South Korea, and Taiwan. There is reason to believe that the consensus in Peking discarded any thought of attempting to compete head on with the U.S. or the USSR in an arms race, but any realistic evaluation of past experience and current developments must have also indicated that the more likely threat to China was from conventional forces, or perhaps a limited nuclear attack confined to a low level. The gradual modernization of the PLA may indicate that Peking had not ignored such an eventuality.[5]

---

*People's Liberation Army (PLA) is the generic term applied to China's armed forces which embodies ground, air, and naval forces.

[2]For a concise chronology of Chinese military policy since 1953 rendered in the context of force development, with a definition of major participants (four are used: "people's war" advocates, balancers of the strategic and domestic roles of the PLA, civilian agencies who guard their own budgets, and the "professionals" who advocate modernized forces) and their preferences see: Harry Harding, Jr., "The Making of Chinese Military Policy," in W. W. Whitson (ed.), *The Military and Political Power in China in the 1970's* (New York: Praeger, 1972), pp. 361–88, and reprinted in this volume, pp. 24–38.

[3]Warren H. Phillips, "Chou's Tale of Lin Piao Rivals Fiction—Which It Might Be," *Wall Street Journal* (Oct. 12, 1972): 1.

[4]For an analysis which uses the air forces as a case study and sees Lin, Wu, and Huang as part of a faction which argued for retention of the priorities on military development see Franz J. Mogdis, "The Role of the Chinese Communist Air Force in the 1970's," in Whitson (ed.), *op. cit.*, pp. 253–66. Mogdis also presents an analysis of threat perception which has the Chinese viewing the Soviet Union as their "number 1 enemy." For interpretations which find Lin caught in a struggle between Mao and his generals in which Lin remained loyal to Mao see Derek Davies, "China: After 25 Years, the Death of a Revolution," *Far Eastern Economic Review* (hereinafter cited as *FEER*) (Mar. 11, 1972): 7–14; and Simon Leys, "Downfall of a Trusting Zealot," *FEER* (Feb. 26, 1972): 20–22.

[5]Jonathan D. Pollack, "Chinese Attitudes towards Nuclear Weapons, 1964–69," *The China Quarterly* (April/June 1972): 244–71, demonstrates that Chinese perceptions are expressed from a perspective of distinct inferiority; that a nuclear Japan rates high in perceptions of danger. The Chinese recognition of constraints auguring against arms-racing is treated in Alice Langley Hsieh, "China's Nuclear-Missile Programme: Regional or Intercontinental?" *China Quarterly* (January/March 1971): 85–99.

And we could as well be witnessing a "double-think" of sorts which led the Chinese to program against a threat which their resources could reasonably contend with, ignoring the larger threat of nuclear weapons and sophisticated systems as being beyond their means to cope with and therefore not worthy of serious consideration.[6]

INTERNATIONAL TECHNOLOGICAL AND ECONOMIC ENVIRONMENT

The capabilities one might attribute to China's military force posture, and the contribution made by this posture to China's stance on foreign and domestic issues must be examined in a relative sense, i.e., vis-à-vis other actors on the international stage. China's present capabilities must be assessed as inferior to both the U.S. and USSR and even the potential for improvement and expansion in modern terms is likely to be inferior to Japan's potential. Relatively low levels of economic development and technology can be isolated as basic constraints impacting upon any Chinese attempt to achieve a more competitive military force posture. In general, the gap between the level of China's economic development and that of the advanced economies is not likely to narrow in the near future. The exponential rate of technological invention and growth in these countries will cause Peking to be forever playing catch-up.

Investment capital and advanced technology are primary requirements for a rapid and steady development of China's economy. From its own resources Peking can generate neither of these in any great amount but has nonetheless for many years remained chary of foreign sources of technology and foreign investment, development loans or regularized arrangements which hold commitments. However, Peking's emergence from the Cultural Revolution and the new-found rapport with Tokyo and Washington in the seventies indicate a realization that China cannot hope to develop its economy without access to the international market-place.

With regard to internal Chinese affairs and more specifically with regard to military force posturing, it is apparent that the initiative to seek scientific and technological innovations that may develop on the world market must come from China. Furthermore, when Chinese initiatives are forthcoming they will be channeled through a centrally controlled procurement process, implying a decision by the central leadership. Ad hoc access to the transnational environment by, for example, a sort of military-industrial complex is not likely. This situation would of course impede the independent satisfaction of self-generated demands by such a hypothetical interest group within China insofar as such satisfaction would depend upon input from abroad. Independent pursuit of such inputs by sub-national interests is virtually impossible without at least the tacit consent of central authorities. When the Chinese do in fact solicit such inputs it very likely reflects the culmination of an internal political process of decision to do so. It would follow that the character of the inputs sought would therefore be a fairly reliable indicator of the character of the program or programs the inputs are intended to service. In addition these programs would themselves most likely be centrally directed.

THE INTERNAL POLITICAL AND MACRO-ECONOMIC ENVIRONMENT

The questions to be asked in examining China's force posture are somewhat different from those which are pertinent to the policy process in most other countries. Factional and bureaucratic interests are not easily discernible nor readily defined. And the generally accepted conventional wisdom that China's military forces are a product of a unified, centralized decision-making process makes for ease of analysis but deserves challenge. The internal political and macro-economic environment therefore demands examination for what it may reveal with regard to a plurality of interests and to some extent a description of the means by which these interests are accommodated. These considerations are especially pertinent to China's force posture since the generation and maintenance of military programs is more often than not in competition with general economic development and the high profile of the military on the Chinese political scene has been a persistent factor when hard choices have been demanded.

A number of patented models may be instructively applied to China's internal environment, but none alone is wholly adequate. Peking's attempts at rationalization and legitimacy though ideology, ambitious undertakings, monopoly of communications, an internal security apparatus and the generation of tension keyed to adversary relationships, would tend to characterize the Chinese domestic scene as totalitarian. But while there are mass movements galore, the supremacy of the Party has in a practical sense been chal-

---

[6]According to James Blaker "there is a hint that the production of infantry weapons and perhaps tanks was considered by some Chinese leaders to be more than sufficient for their own needs as early as 1966"; "Conventional Weapons" in Whitson (ed.), *op. cit.*, p. 219.

lenged by the PLA, its control of non-party organization especially in the provinces can be severely questioned, central control of the economy is far from complete and factionalism is quite evident. However, the degree of denigration of central authority is far from being sufficient to totally abrogate Peking's overriding control.

Certain aspects of an oligarchic model are apparent in the makeup and functioning of the central leadership which appears to be a collegial dictatorship even though Mao emerges *primus inter pares*. It is clear that this central oligarchy is not monolithic and that its members often jockey for relative preeminence over their colleagues, that open conflict often flares over policy issues, and that particular group interests are often manifested in debate.

In some cases both the economic and political arrangement tiered below the central leadership can be modeled along bureaucratic or organizational lines (e.g., the technocratic elements in the government administration, and the air force in the PLA each evidence a degree of organizational conformity). However the Party and the PLA both reflect horizontal cleavages which are mostly coincident with a degree of regional or provincial autonomy and are aligned with parochial preferences. The central oligarchy appears to reflect both organizational and regional cleavages and its members undoubtedly carry more or less influence in councils, depending upon the degree of power these interests represent. However, it also seems that personages such as Mao and Chou are in many ways "above the fray" and that at least some of the governing apparatus is consistently at their bidding in putting national goals above local or organizational interests.[7] Military programs in many cases require that local interests be subordinated.

Chou En-lai's recent discussion of the succession problem went far to reinforce analyses which relate individual members of the Central Committee to regional, military or bureaucratic interests when he maintained that a single successor to Mao was out of the question because of China's domestic diversities and problems. He further hinted at the functioning of the committee in describing its rejection of the report Lin Piao proposed to deliver to the Ninth National Party Congress in 1969, and the subsequent re-draft by the committee which Lin "only read . . . but his thinking ran counter to the report." In addi-

tion Chou's reference to a "handful of sworn conspirators" could give credence to the formulation that Air Force commander Wu Fa-hsien, Chen Po-ta, and Army Chief of Staff Huang Yung-sheng were in league with Lin and their disappearance is indicative of the manner in which intra-party disputes of singular bitterness are solved.[8] These and earlier purges of high ranking military men (P'eng Te-huai in 1959 and Lo Jui-ching in 1966) very definitely place military interests in the policy process at the highest levels. The suggestion of course is that these prominent military leaders were a reflection of organizational interests, that they had a following from among the forces they commanded.

Regional interests are articulated in the Central Committee by the 202 members from the provinces (70% of the full and alternate membership): figures which imply constraints upon arbitrary policy formulation by the central elite. These figures include some 76 PLA men from the provinces whose sympathies most likely are with the local authorities given heavy PLA involvement in local administration.[9] This PLA fixation on local economic and administrative chores demonstrates how horizontal cleavages would disrupt vertical organizational disaggregation and is especially pertinent to the ground forces.

Conversely the air and naval forces are less involved in nonmilitary tasks, are oriented toward mobility and outward looking military missions, and are organizationally tied to nationally administered equipment programs; as organizational monoliths (relative to the ground forces) these elements are suited to the organizational model which would suggest a specific orientation of interests toward organizational mission and goals. Much the same could be said for the orientation of national level economic planners and foreign ministry bureaucrats; their bias would probably be toward national level goals and, like the naval and air forces, would most likely demonstrate a greater degree of responsiveness to central direction than would regional factions.

The most prominent feature of the post-cultural revolution political environment was the PLA's preeminence over Party and bureaucracy in the administration of the government and economy at all echelons. Insofar as the PLA's involvement extended well below regional and provincial levels, and assuming a conscientious

---

[7]Victor C. Falkenheim, "Continuing Central Predominance," *Problems of Communism* (July/August 1972), especially the discussion of "pattern of controls," pp. 79–80.

[8]Reportage on Chou's comments is found in *Wall Street Journal* (Oct. 12, 1972): 1 and 35; and in *The Christian Science Monitor* (Oct. 12, 1972): 1 and 6.

[9]Parris Chang, "Decentralization of Power," *Problems of Communism* (July/August 1972): 67–75.

attitude on the part of these uniformed administrators, it would follow that their orientations would coincide more with local than with national interests. However this inordinate power in the hands of the PLA is likely to create an abrasive relationship with the Party and administrative cadres whose authority has been coopted. Writ large this would imply that current efforts at rehabilitation of the Party apparatus are an attempt to restore the balance among Party, PLA and technocrat (although a case can be made that this was never a very stable balance).[10]

This analysis suggests that the generally accepted interest categories of Party, PLA, administrative (technocratic) bureaucracy, and regions (or provinces) are inadequate for conducting an examination of defense policy formulation in China. It suggests that at a minimum there is reason to expect cleavages within the PLA, the Party apparatus, and the central leadership.

The macro-economic environment serves to fortify the authority of Peking in defining military and economic policy but simultaneously delimits central authority and engenders considerable political and economic autonomy. Over time only the requirement to provide security has been able to compete with economic development for resource allocation. The macro-economic pattern which has evolved is necessarily at the core of this recurring debate.

The autonomy in the economic system is clearly evident not only in the decentralization of management and investment in small industry and agriculture of recent years, but in the recognition quite early on that centralized planning of such a wide-ranging economy could only be effective if the scope was kept narrow.

Current trends toward localized economic development, freedom to plan and invest locally, to manufacture capital equipment and goods locally, and to achieve a degree of local self-sufficiency can only enhance the position of a given province in negotiations with Peking over material and financial surpluses which central planners would attempt to redistribute. This is especially relevant to the more sophisticated military production programs, a full range of which no single province or military region can undertake on its own. And Peking can only implement programs by financing them through extractions from the provinces.

The central authorities can pursue national goals which require economic support, to include those related to military force posture, only

with the cooperation of the quasi-autarkic provincial economies. The five year economic plans still attempt to direct the economy but a combination of the overwhelming magnitude of the task and the de facto limits upon how much arbitrary extraction the provinces will tolerate has gradually led to an economic structure which in large measure prohibits the central leadership from defining goals by fiat.[11]

LEADERSHIP PERCEPTION OF POLICY REQUIREMENTS

The environment thus far described is the source of demands placed upon the Chinese political leadership to formulate defense, economic and foreign policies. Combining internal factors with the external environment complicated our discussion and refuted the rational actor model of China's leadership. But insofar as we can perceive of an oligarchic model of the Chinese elite we can attribute to it national-level orientations. That is to say that despite the pluralism inherent in the Chinese political system, there remains a preeminent central authority whose perceptions include a commitment to national cohesion. This central authority has defined goals to maintain this cohesion and perceives that certain policies are required to achieve these goals.[12]

There is considerable evidence that the leadership perceptions of policy requirements related to the security of China have not been candidly articulated in the highly publicized strategic doctrine of "people's war." That this has essentially been a rationalization is evident when one goes beyond the statements of policy to the programs which have been implemented.[13] Without Soviet aid this leadership was for the first time struck by the magnitude of the economic problem, made worse by the failure of the Great Leap and the agricultural disasters in the early 1960's. By this time a commitment had been made to modernize the armed forces, but it now had to compete with overriding economic issues.

It was a natural tendency for Peking to find solace in the earlier routines of military opera-

---

[10] Leo Goodstadt, "Rice vs. Rockets," *FEER* (Oct. 2, 1971): 5–7.

[11] For example, the March 5, 1972, *Nan-fang Jih-pao* article "The Policy of the Party May Not Be Forgotten at Any Time" argues that material incentives are virtually a right of the farmer and cites the Party line to justify this contention. *Survey of China Mainland Press* 304 (1972): 20–28 (hereafter referred to as *SCMP*).

[12] The five-year economic plans are specific examples. See *Hung Ch'i* (Oct. 1969).

[13] This is strongly implied by Pollack, *op. cit.*, in his analysis of threat perception; it is argued below in terms of military-related production programs.

tions and to attempt to voice a confidence in the guerrilla war option for defense. But this was never the preferred military solution. It was forced upon the leadership. The return to economic development along the lines of heavy industry and machine manufacturing—the base for a defense industry—was forthcoming each time the agricultural sector began to display enough health to warrant it.[14] And even through the periods of emphasis to agriculture and broad guage economic development, specific military production programs continued: aircraft, missiles, nuclear weapons, tanks, naval craft, radar, artillery, and small arms. These programs have been consistently at a deliberate pace and most at low profile, but they have continued. Peking's statements of a people's war strategy belie the modern caliber of China's emerging air, naval, and air defense capability. These developments could lead one to surmise that the purges of P'eng and Lo need not have been due to their advocacy of a modern force, but rather to their insistence on quickening the pace to that end and their willingness to accommodate to Soviet terms in order to elicit Moscow's assistance.[15]

China's present force posture, albeit hampered by the PLA's involvement in politics, is considerably improved over what it was fifteen years ago and many weapons production programs have yet to peak (e.g., medium bombers, fighter aircraft, tanks, and vehicles). This would seem to suggest that at least at the time the programs were initiated the leadership considered the people's war strategy a stop-gap, self-assuring military stance.

Leadership perceptions of the economic imperative have probably been the greatest factor in the gradualism characteristic of China's military modernization (save perhaps the adamant anti-Soviet policies which have foreclosed the possibility of aid). The decisions related to allocating economic and defense priorities have been the root of the political turmoil which has racked China on a recurring basis. Leadership perceptions have been divergent enough to give

substance to the superficial "power struggles." The catharses of continuing revolution that have set faction against faction have invariably included disputes over both economic and defense policy.

It appears that the leadership fully appreciates that it must deftly balance economic and military demands in order to retain its hold on the reins of power. This becomes a complex problem if one accepts the pluralism implied in the descriptive model of the Chinese internal political and economic environment set forth above.

ECONOMIC INTERESTS

Insofar as interprovincial trade is directed by an administrative apparatus of the central government, transfers from surplus to deficit geographic localities, and demands for complementary inputs of commodities flow through formal channels. But the entrepreneurs in China, who appear as collectives rather than as individuals, can voice demands as well by shading reports, altering centrally established goals, footdragging, investment according to local rather than national preferences and resisting attempts by Peking to extract funds or commodities to finance nationally directed programs.[16] The trend toward decentralization in economic planning has eased Peking's planning problems but has also compounded the "mountain stronghold" attitude of giving regional needs priority over national goals. As a result there is a constant pressure applied by Peking upon the provinces to maintain conformity with the national plan. Orientations on these economic issues often cross organizational lines and challenge the concept of total direction by Peking of even the relatively narrow scope of central planning.

An example of how policies are reacted to across organizational lines was the concern expressed by the PLA that attempts to reduce material incentives in local agriculture and industry would be difficult to implement. An essentially economic issue, it elicited a reaction from the military for a number of probable reasons: the PLA proximity to and involvement with local administration in the aftermath of the Cultural Revolution may have induced a sympathy with local interests; the local PLA may be concerned that it will again be called upon to assist in implementing an unpopular policy; or certain mili-

[14]The current economic line, for example, still quotes Mao in pointing out the "correct relationships" in the economic sector: "The economic construction of our country is centered on heavy industry: this point must be affirmed. But at the same time it is imperative to pay full attention to the development of agriculture and light industry." *SCMP* 304 (1972): 1.

[15]Harding implies that the dichotomy between those who favored a "politicized" army and those like P'eng whose concern was with improved combat effectiveness should be the crux of any analytical disaggregation of the PLA ranks. He views Mao's "Ten Great Relationships," in April 1956, as the basis for the compromise which permitted modernization to continue. Harding, *op. cit.*, pp. 374–75.

[16]Jack Gray, "The Economics of Maoism," *Bulletin of the Atomic Scientists* (Feb. 1969): 42–51.

tary men may be astute enough to appreciate that material incentives can contribute to economic health.[17]

On the issue of economic incentives the PLA found itself in tune with local attitudes which have steadfastly resisted innuendo by Peking that ultimately private holdings would revert to collective ownership. Local preferences in this regard are unambiguously stated with surprising clarity indicating that not only do local interests at times differ with central policy but also that the provincial authorities feel sufficient strength in their position to voice their views.[18]

This local economic independence seems to be an area where compromise and balance are sought. Peking is constantly urging local officials to give the needs of the state first priority, yet even Mao has repeatedly admonished the Party to respect local initiative. National goals may ultimately ride on how well disparate interests in the provinces can be cajoled into accepting the challenge to build a strong China.[19]

Defense production interests revolve in large measure around the central elite. However, the armed services are keyed to program outputs in terms of military capabilities or to the power and prestige attendant to enhanced military capabilities. The production facilities related to programs are ultimately tied to specific localities and these localities can generate a vested interest in specific programs. This sort of interest would very likely apply only to factories and plants producing military-peculiar items which find no diverse application elsewhere. Hence machine-tools and steel, while essential to military programs, are just as important to a wide range of nonmilitary production for which a demand exists in China's nascent economy. Even so, the aircraft, motor vehicle, missile, radar, and weapons producers in Chinese industry together with their ancillary fabrication network represent important interests which augur for implementation and continuation of a variety of military production programs. Their importance is increased because they are technology-heavy and absorb considerable sci-

entific and skilled talent—all scarce commodities in China. Because of the geographic distribution of these production facilities the demands they generate have impact in regions as well as within the central councils in Peking which have created and sustained them.[20]

At times these interests may be in tandem with factions within the military forming a coalition not unlike the capitalist "military-industrial complex" to lobby for increased spending in certain economic sectors.[21] In 1970 for example the announced emphasis on shipbuilding for the dual purpose of alleviating China's reliance on chartering and increasing naval capabilities to compete with U.S. and Soviet naval forces certainly indicated a shared interest between the industry and the navy; and in 1971 Peking elicited a sharp reaction from the industry which argued for continued importation of foreign design and technique while official policy stressed indigenous innovation.[22] The purge of air force commander Wu Fa-hsien in 1971 is similarly seen by many to be related to the drastic downgrading of the electronics industry in which the air force has a vested interest. This same economic policy called for the air force to bear the brunt of reductions in military spending. Examples such as these indicate that economic interests are not solely defined by the "central vs. provincial" dichotomy but may appear as organizational interests associated with a particular industry and in some cases shared by one of the military services.[23]

In sum, there is sufficient evidence to indicate that economic interests have a voice in the policymaking process in China and that while these interests may not have the same complex-

---

[17]The PLA, in the May 1971 issue of *Hung Ch'i*, emphasized the difficulties involved in "eradicating private ownership" and suggested "a hundred and even a thousand years" was required to do so. *FEER* (Nov. 21, 1971): 23.

[18]*FEER, ibid.*, p. 20.

[19]Constant references to the problem of autonomy appear in Peking's propaganda, e.g., "The characteristics of a departmentalist are: disregard the needs of the whole nation and ignore other departments, other places, other people. . . . The correct policy is: unified planning, all-round consideration, and proper arrangements." *Hung Ch'i* (April 1972), *Survey of China Mainland Magazines* (SCMM): 727–28.

[20]The General Rear Services Department, which is the logistic and procurement agency for all PLA services is an organization which needs further study in this context (for background on the GRSD see Richard E. Gillespie and John C. Sims, Jr., "The General Rear Services Department," in Whitson [ed.], *op. cit.*, pp. 185–213). That there is a direct relationship between the services and the ministries which oversee production can be seen in such assignments as those of Fang Chiang, former commander of the navy, to head the Sixth Ministry of Machine Building responsible for naval armaments in 1963, and the one-time director of equipment planning for the PLA general staff, Wan I, to head the Second Ministry (munitions); Anne B. Clark, "Selected Biographies of Chinese Communist Leaders" (mimeographed) (Harvard East Asia Reseach Center, July 1964), Simon Leys places interests such as those of a military/regional clique in the context of recent purges. Leys, *op. cit.*

[21]"Some comrades often view the development of heavy industry and that of agriculture and light industry separately. They see only the contradictions among the three in the distribution of manpower, funds, equipment, and materials." *Hung Ch'i* (June 1, 1971), in *SCMM*, no. 731–32.

[22]*FEER 1971 Yearbook*, p. 144d.

[23]*FEER* (Nov. 27, 1971): 20–24; also Mogdis' analysis in Whitson (ed.), *op. cit.*

ion as their capitalist counterparts, at times they do find sympathy in the government, Party, and military bureaucracies which can aid them in having greater impact at national level.

MILITARY PERCEPTIONS [24]

The historic roles and missions of the PLA's ground, naval and air forces have been sufficiently dissimilar to enable one to analyze each as a distinct organization with its own perceptions of organizational goals and special programs suited to achieving those goals. The ground forces stand out as being especially significant since their organizational routines manifest as much of a political/economic function as they do a military orientation.

It could be argued that this multifunctional ground force mission and the acknowledgment of it by ground force commanders has assisted the central leadership in Peking in achieving the balance between defense and economic priorities. However, this assistance has been gained at the cost of considerable political influence garnered by the PLA in the process.

Ground Forces [25]

The ground forces have the longest and most respected tradition in the PLA. They are the most versatile of the forces and in general the most conservative as regards doctrine, strategy and policy. The most striking feature of the ground force tradition is its routine involvement in non-military activities. Senior officers have come to accept that political, social and economic involvement is not an unusual role for the military. The Communist military tradition very early on incorporated notions of social revolution and Leninist organizational technique which emphasized "Party control of the gun." These notions were reinforced by a fusion of Party, military and government roles which persisted until the 1950's and finds the elite leadership in Peking even now made up in large measure of former military men.

With the possible exception of the venture into Korea, the ground forces have been rather consistently attuned to waging war on Chinese territory or to safeguarding China from intrusion.

There has been little occasion to consider far-reaching, sustained military operations beyond China's borders or to develop forces for such a mission (even the Korean War involvement can be said to have been waged with substantial Soviet expertise in logistics and planning, and was not the fruition of military force planning by the Chinese). Tactics have been traditionally characterized by quasi-guerrilla, hit-and-run operations—and these tactical concepts have notably prevailed in the formulation of the "people's war" strategy for the defense of China.

However, the Korean War and the close association with Soviet military doctrine, training, tactics, and weaponry, did give cause for the PLA to question these traditional orientations. The trend toward modernization through the 1950's gave rise to a new professionalism based upon conventional military force structure and was to lead to the bitter disputes over the "bourgeois military line" in the context of the Sino-Soviet dispute. The "red vs. expert" dichotomy was seemingly bridged with the re-politicization of the PLA under Lin Piao, but its significance runs deep. It relates to a generation gap in the armed forces as much as it does to purely political orientations. The military "elders" are naturally more prone to persist in traditional notions of quasi-guerrilla operations while innovation, if it is to come at all, will probably be a product of a rising young leadership. But this sort of leadership is not being developed. On the contrary it is being stifled by outmoded doctrine and continuous involvement in nonmilitary functions.

The Cultural Revolution had the general effect of entrenching traditional ground force attitudes. It was largely the ground forces that were used to maintain order; their typical association with economic enterprise was reinforced; they were called upon to fill the void left by the assaults upon Party and bureaucracy. They may well have learned to savor their new-found influence.

All of this has served to distract the ground forces from their military mission of defense. In addition it has probably caused them to more fully share local attitudes on economic and political issues. One might conclude that, despite some evidence of professional attitudes among the ground forces, based on traditional and recent experience the weight of orientations is away from a modernized, well trained military force. Evidence of professionalism is nonetheless readily available in ongoing weapons programs to include tanks, artillery and means of mobility. Both a "strategic" and "local" force syndrome

---

[24] There are a variety of perspectives on military perceptions in Whitson (ed.), *op. cit.*, on which much of this section is based, especially the articles by Harding, Elmquist, and Simmonds.

[25] Joseph J. Heinlein, "The Ground Forces," in Whitson (ed.), *op. cit.*, pp. 153–70.

seem to persist but the ground forces display a "political" complexion that their sister services share only slightly.

Included here under the rubric of ground forces would of course be the militia, the public security forces, and the labor and construction corps insofar as these organizations have a quasi-military structure and since the Cultural Revolution have been operationally controlled by the PLA (even before the Cultural Revolution the Military Affairs Commission of the Party provided "direct guidance" of these organizations). Estimates of militia strength are wide-ranging but generally are upwards of five million; the militia has served as a basis for mobilization and recruitment with the "basic" militia being better trained and equipped than the "ordinary" militia which is largely used as a labor force (e.g., at harvest time). The public security force, although some are trained and equipped well enough for combat operations, is mainly a police organization of some half million men (augmented somewhat during the Cultural Revolution) which is subordinate to local/provincial party or revolutionary committees and under this aegis closely associated with the local PLA (de facto PLA control has resulted from military domination of these committees). The construction forces are similarly tied closely to the PLA, developing for example the virgin northeastern forest lands.

Insofar as these organizations are highly parochial in membership and function, i.e., mission-oriented toward province and locality, the attitudes they evidence are likely to be coincidental with the regional or local force PLA organizational orientations.

Naval Forces[26]

While some of the traditional political orientation noted within the ground forces is also apparent in the PLA's naval arm, the very nature of the naval mission, its view beyond land bases, and necessary interest in signature equipment have made this orientation less fixed and its exposure to political missions less intense. Naval forces must have vessels and associated weapons systems. Organizational goals necessarily include procurement of these items. In addition, the navy has had a more or less constant mission of protecting coastal waters and patrolling inland water boundaries. They have not had the dubious luxury of being able to rationalize a

paucity of equipment in terms of "people's war" strategy. The on-going mission will not permit it.

Organizational routines of the naval forces have long been predicated upon the presence of the U.S. and Chinese Nationalist flotilla in the Taiwan straits. This situation has demanded that readiness and training be given higher priority than that necessary in the ground forces. And while construction programs related to naval equipment have not been overwhelming, they have been persistent, indicating that as a minimum a coastal patrol capability is a well-defined goal. In addition there seems to be an aircraft allocation to the navy which may embody the organizational structure of a naval air arm.

The naval forces would therefore represent an interest in specialized production programs which would support modernization and a general orientation toward expertise which is imperative in the context of the active nature of the primary naval mission. While the evidence is spurious, it would follow that the naval forces share the interest of the ship building industry in procuring the most advanced technology available to service their construction programs.

Air Forces[27]

Aside from its earliest days in which the air forces leadership was drawn from the ground forces, the air arm of the military developed in a direction which was largely away from tradition and the mainstream of the majority of the PLA. As it began to generate its own leaders they were invariably younger than the PLA's elite generation simply because they were aviators whose selection was initially based in part on youth. And like the naval forces, the air forces have consistently had a mission which demanded modern technology, equipment, readiness, and training expertise in every sense. Much more than the other services the air forces became heavily reliant upon Soviet aid, and upon the development of an advanced industrial base thereafter. Throughout their history of thirty-odd years the air forces have had to contend with a more or less constant threat (even more so than did the naval forces) from Taiwan, the United States, first in Korea and then in Southeast Asia, and, more recently from the Soviet Union.

The on-going production programs for air and air-defense-related weaponry represent the major slice of resources that has been regularly

[26]John R. Dewenter, "China Afloat," *Foreign Affairs* (July 1972): 738–51.

[27]Franz J. Mogdis, "The Role of the Chinese Communist Air Force in the 1970's," in Whitson (ed.), *op. cit.*, pp. 253–68.

dedicated to maintaining and improving air force posture. Their high profile, modern orientation, and dynamic character had very likely engendered elitist attitudes in the air forces even before China's acquisition of a nuclear capability. The training and readiness of these forces is apparent in the downing of a number of U.S., Chinese Nationalist, and Soviet aircraft which have intruded upon mainland airspace over the years.

More than either the naval or ground forces, the air forces have placed heavy demands upon China's nascent industries and technological base. While certain elements in the economic sector have shared the benefit of such an application of resources, the wider sector of the economy has had to relinquish considerable potential for diversification and expansion to air force-related programs. In this respect both ground and naval forces have also paid a price.

It is far from certain at present if China's nuclear forces will emerge as a separate organizational entity or if they will be subsumed under the aegis of the air forces. In any event the production of nuclear-delivery-capable TU-16 medium range bombers enables the air forces to share the nuclear prestige.

Insofar as the PLA harbors a cleavage of interests along strategic-local force lines, the air force in toto would fall into the strategic category along with the 2nd Artillery, China's nuclear missile unit, the air defense artillery forces (already organizationally related to the air force and "strategically" employed in North Vietnam for a time), and probably the majority of the naval forces by virtue of their outward orientation and mission. The ground forces might contribute the elite and mobile armored divisions to this strategic category—it appears that certain of these forces are better equipped and trained than most of the ground forces, and that they are more directly responsive to control from Peking.

In terms of improved defense posture, certain types of programs would constitute a contribution to force development: programs which generate firepower, mobility and sophisticated weapons systems which would befit a force capable of defending China against modern opposition. One might add manpower, both in numbers and expertise, and readiness to a force posture equation. Lastly, a modern organization, both flexible and dynamic, is a requirement for any military force of stature.

On all of these counts save manpower the ground forces appear to be lacking. The only weapons systems in production which suit the ground forces are small arms, artillery and tanks;

vehicles can of course provide mobility but what little is known about the levels on hand in units indicate shortages, and these have the added purpose of supporting the civilian economy. The ground forces are in large measure rail-bound, unable to maneuver except as foot soldiers. Tanks and artillery are also below par in numbers and sophistication. And the strategic organization of the military forces is tied to geographic regions.

While both naval and air forces are theoretically included in this terrain-bound organizational structure, by their nature they retain an inherent mobility. Even so their bases are fixed. And like the ground forces they have no apparent alternative organizational mode for deployment beyond China's borders on any large scale. But in a relative sense, both the naval and air forces are better off in terms of modern weapons and equipment as well as level of training and readiness.

THE PROCESS OF DETERMINING CHANGE IN FORCE POSTURE AND PATTERNS AFFECTING THE PROCESS

The types of programs noted above which contribute to a modern force posture are necessarily coordinated if not controlled by Peking, implying that the decisionmaking process related to force posturing is conducted in the central councils of leadership even though the impact may also be felt in the regions.

This centralized coordination and control of weapons programs is indicated in a number of ways. To begin with, the distribution of industry throughout China is such that no single military region—except perhaps Nanking, Shenyang, and Wuhan—seems to possess the capacity to produce all the conventional weaponry required for troops within their borders.[28] Such a capacity is even less likely to accrue in the case of more sophisticated weapons systems. A weapons mix of the sort now being produced in China therefore requires overall coordination if it is to achieve widespread distribution among the forces.

Secondly, the raw material and fabricated component inputs for the more elaborate weapons systems such as radar, aircraft, missiles and especially nuclear weapons must come from a variety of domestic and even foreign sources. This is as much or more the case with technology as it is with hardware, especially insofar as the most advanced technology is only available on foreign markets. Likewise one finds that the ex-

[28]James R. Blaker, "The Production of Conventional Weapons," in Whitson (ed.), *op. cit.*, pp. 215–27.

pert knowledge of managers and high-level technicians is one of China's scarcest resources and has been pooled in order to satisfy the requirements of modern weapons production.

A third indicator of centralization which is directly related to technology and refined hardware inputs is the established system for control of access to foreign sources and the management of interprovincial trade by the bureaucracy. Transfers from one province to another are effected by Peking. More importantly, the channels of foreign trade are even more restrictive and funnel all negotiations through Peking, giving the central leadership both a monitoring capacity and an opportunity for initiative to seek specific technological and hardware inputs abroad.

As a fourth indication one might add the evidence of debates over policy in the past. The contending personalities have invariably included central figures. While they may have had regional or provincial ties, for the most part it was in their capacity as members of the central leadership that they have been criticized for advancing deviant policies.

While Peking is the arena in which policies are hammered out both the regions and the wider bureaucracy play a large role. Resources and finances must be provided by the provinces through surpluses. In addition they must cooperate with national economic objectives in order to facilitate program implementation. On both counts the provincial economic authorities can wield considerable weight, either actively or passively. They may be strongly behind a particular program and be prone to support it, or conversely, they may see centrally defined goals and programs as detrimental to local interests. As noted above, the provinces can react negatively in a number of ways while paying lip service to Peking.

The bureaucracy can contribute to the equation in its capacity as economic manager and administrator. Insofar as military programs depreciate general economic development one might find a large segment of the economic planners adverse to such programs. The primary orientation of the economic bureaucracy would naturally be toward broad gauge economic progress and one might expect to occasionally find a coincidence of interest between localities and technocrats in this area.

Of real significance here is the trend toward decentralization of the economy and the attempt to make regions more self-sufficient. This policy necessarily gives local authorities much more leverage vis-à-vis Peking. While purely speculative, it is nonetheless feasible that one of the

peripheral advantages in allowing greater autonomy was the notion that provincial preferences might assist in braking the momentum of military programs by expressing a reluctance to finance them. This assumes that the leadership saw a need to curtail military expenditures or that the provinces voiced a concern independently, not unreasonable assumptions in view of the 1970–71 economic policies which gave emphasis to economic development.

A primary tactic of the strategic-minded military factions is to cite the threat to China and to persuade the decisionmakers to arm against it. More subtle is their ability to withdraw support from the central elite, or to threaten such an action.

The central elite must retain the support of the military but it is not without resources and methods to do so. They can always point to the reality of a developing economy with its inherent limitations. Nonetheless ongoing weapons programs indicate that modernization of the armed forces is being gradually undertaken and something of an accommodation has been reached with strategic force interests. But none of these programs has been so aggressive and intense to indicate that military interests have been able to run rampant in the central councils of leadership. On the contrary the concept of a rational actor, powerfully endowed, does seem credible when one views the balance between military and economic goals and resources applied toward each.

In a relative sense, the professionals within the military, i.e., strategic, air, and naval forces, have received the greater share of what allocations have been made to the military sector. That there have been bitter disputes is evident from the purges and recurring "redness" campaigns. But that the ground forces have received short shrift in allocations is not necessarily due to their voice being weakest. They have after all emerged with inordinate influence vis-à-vis the party and bureaucracy in nonmilitary matters. It could be argued that the traditional orientations of the ground forces have prepared them to accept this nonmilitary mission and that they may even cherish it.

The political orientation of the PLA, especially of the ground forces, has been a major contribution to policies which attempt an equitable distribution of resources and effort between economic development and defense programs. The traditional ethic of the PLA which dictates the involvement of the organization in a wide range of nonmilitary activities, which holds the military subservient to the party by its ideological premises, and which has in practice placed military men in prominent positions among the governing elite, has served to elicit military support for the national goals of development and socialization and simultaneously tempered demands for modernization and resource allocation to military programs.

Intra-military preferences are, however, far from homogeneous. Both the air and naval forces must necessarily strive for a heavier share of allocations reserved for military programs because of their organizational goals which must have modernity and equipment inputs. These organizational orientations lack in large measure the ingredient of non-military purpose the ground forces mission embodies. Thus interservice competition for resources is less intense. The support of the naval and air forces can be elicited by allowing them the satisfaction of modernity and even expertise. Much of the satisfaction given to the ground forces, however, can come from a different source: prominence in politics, emulation and a degree of autonomy in their regional activities.

While this pattern may go far to alleviate inter-service competition, it does thrust the PLA into a competitive stance vis-à-vis the party and the bureaucracy. But even this posture does not necessarily fuel the debate over military programs since in their political/bureaucratic role the ground forces are likely to sound a sympathetic note with nonmilitary rather than armed service interests.

These are, of course, generalizations and should not imply that ground force attitudes are devoid of "expert" and professional motivations which would augur for a more modern, better equipped, trained and ready army. But the net weight of ground force orientation seems to be away from these attitudes. Nonetheless programs are in fact being undertaken, albeit gradual, to improve the ground force posture. In context, however, these are relatively low profile and inexpensive even though they may salve the professional ego.

The on-going military production programs certainly bear witness to the imbalance of resources allocated in favor of the naval and air forces. In addition they serve as a fair indicator of the direction, be it planned or random, of Chinese force development.

In the nuclear field the dozen or so tests since 1964 indicate considerable sophistication in warhead development. The most recent tests have been low yield (less than 20 KT) and could indicate that some thought is being given to tactical systems. Considerable investment in the program has already been made (e.g., the Lan-chou gaseous diffusion plant, a complex and costly enterprise) which indicates a built-in momentum even though continued progress will demand a constant input of resources.[29]

Missile development has been equally impressive. The two space satellites probably were orbited by an IRBM-type vehicle and have been considered a progression toward ICBM development. Focus has been on liquid-fueled systems, however, an established solid propellant manufacturing facility is thought by some to be part of a second generation ICBM program.[30]

The Chinese appear to have their own design teams and research establishments at work in the aircraft industry. Plants near Mukden are now producing in series Chinese versions of both the TU-16 (at about 25–30 per year) and the MIG-19 (rate: 200–300 per year). Radars and air defense missiles are also produced in significant quantities.[31]

Naval programs are under way to produce guided missile destroyers and missile equipped patrol boats. Interest in nuclear powered submarine technology is high. Some estimates hold that three nuclear powered submarines have been under construction since 1969. The single G-class sub was built by the Chinese at Dairen in 1964; the 20 or so W-class boats were assembled in Chinese yards. Destroyer escorts and sub-chasers have been constructed at Canton and Shanghai. The fast boats in the fleet were specifically designed for series production in China.[32]

By comparison with these naval and air force programs the production and development of ground force weaponry and equipment seem meager. A Chinese copy of the Soviet T-54 tank has been in production since 1964 and an improved version is reported to be rolling out. Armored personnel carriers and a wide range of light and heavy artillery are produced in significant numbers as are small arms, ordnance, and vehicles.[33] Few items incorporate advanced design, however. But all told, these programs represent a well-rounded development pattern and are considerably less expensive than missiles, aircraft, and nuclear submarines. Nonetheless the production mix reflects an emphasis on naval and

[29] Jane's Weapon Systems (New York: McGraw-Hill, 1972), p. 2.
[30] Ibid., p. 526.
[31] Secretary of Defense Annual Report (Washington: G.P.O., 1972), pp. 44–46.
[32] Jane's Fighting Ships (New York: McGraw Hill, 1972), pp. 62–67.
[33] Jane's Weapon Systems, op. cit., p. 211; Gerald Ellis, "China's Military Strength," Military Review (April 1971): 71–76.

air force missions over that of the ground forces and perhaps an attendant perception of the sort of threat these forces would engage.

In this regard the deployment of an MR/IRBM, a more costly option than proceeding directly to an ICBM, could be based on the perception of the threat from the Soviet Far East which happens to reinforce organizational pressures from the military to add an immediate nuclear capability to the arsenal. The persistence of the Soviet threat may augur for little change in current programs.

Where weapons production programs are used as clues to the decisionmaking process, as has been done here, it should be remembered that current programs are the result of decisions a decade past. Current decisions will reflect threat perceptions, economic imperatives, and bureaucratic/organizational proclivities in a changed international and domestic environment. But the inherent momentum of on-going programs will be a prime factor. And unless the Chinese radically alter their secretive style we will only begin to see evidence of changes over time.

Some guesses are nonetheless possible. Accepting that the many factors considered here all in some measure bear on the formulation of military policy, one might speculate that the current emphasis on economic development is only the beginning of an alteration in Peking's priorities. The threat and alliance environment has seen a net decrement in the adversary relationships involving China, the PLA ground forces have accrued unprecedented political power, and there is reason to describe the ground force orientations as being in some ways congruent with regional and local interests. Out of this symbiosis at least three outcomes related to incremental change in force posture are possible: first, as now seems the case, strategic programs coincident with air and naval force organizational missions and goals could be deemphasized along with military spending as a whole, but by their very momentum continue to ramble on; second, ground force commanders could increase their bid hoping to displace the more sophisticated programs with the hardware they have received

only sparingly in the past; a dialogue could develop with Peking over distribution of end items with regions using locally held scarce resources as bargaining chips; and third, the services could rally around their common military interests to resist the reassertion of civilian authority through a rehabilitated Party—such an affront to Peking by the PLA could also conceivably lead to regional interest in general being more aggressively advanced, especially if the regional ties of military commanders cannot be reconciled with national interests. And of course there are many possible variations on the above themes.

Debates over military policy in China are invariably intertwined with economic issues. The fragility of the developing economy is at times demonstrated by the way the whims of nature disturb its agricultural base and compound the problems of planning and distribution. As a result economic demands compete regularly with military spending. Investment and expertise are required in both sectors, and these sectors are natural contestants for China's scarcest resources. The macroeconomic environment tends to make Peking the arbiter in the contest and this position is one of the primary assets of the central leadership in maintaining its power.

Since the alternatives available to the Chinese leadership with regard to force posture invariably hinge on economic inputs and simultaneously compete with economic development, these alternatives are as much described by the degree of impact each might have upon the economy as they are in terms of objective assessment of the threat they seek to counter. As seen at the outset of this writing, there is little reason for Peking to attempt to match the superpowers in military capability simply because of the magnitude of the chore. Yet there is some logic to maintaining a modicum of defensibility in order to deter lesser adversaries or even the U.S. or USSR below the nuclear threshold. In the realm of weaponry then, there appears to have been a deliberate attempt to satisfy those who would highlight the threat to Chinese territory, but just as deliberate an effort has been made to develop a force posture which demands less of the scarce commodities needed by the economic sector.

THE DEFENSE EFFORTS OF FRANCE, WEST GERMANY, AND THE UNITED KINGDOM

DAVID GREENWOOD

Professor Greenwood's analysis of the defense postures of France, West Germany, and the United Kingdom does not address the "functional" question per se. Rather, he has chosen to focus upon the "objective" force postures of the three, defined, for the purposes of his analysis, more in terms of military budget *outputs than actual military forces. The major thesis of his study is aimed at determining whether or not the force postures of the three are converging or diverging. He accomplishes this by first exploring commonalities among them in terms of "the interplay of shared strategic objectives and aspirations on the one hand, and commonly felt resource constraints on the other." Second, he examines the differences among them as reflected in "the uniquely national aspects of both perception of the international environment and experience of domestic pressures." Given the successive levels of analysis on which the force posture question can be tackled, Greenwood's approach is clearly aimed at the "macro" level with the focus being on describing "posture" or "stand" as the "quantitative output" of governmental processes reacting to both domestic and foreign constraints and imperatives. Greenwood's study superbly demonstrates the richness of insight still to be gained by comparative studies aimed at the "macro" level in a time when the major thrust of many defense-related studies has been to delve almost exclusively into the "micro" "input" levels of internal bureaucracies.*

Professor Greenwood is Senior Lecturer in Political Economy (Higher Defense Studies), University of Aberdeen, Scotland. After receiving his M.A. in Economics at Liverpool University in 1959, he became an officer in the RAF and served as a lecturer in Economics at the RAF College, Cranwell. In 1966–67 he was Economic Advisor at the Ministry of Defense. He has written Budgeting for Defence *(1972).*

From time to time students of contemporary affairs must take stock, survey the actors on the international scene, and note where and how particular nations stand in relation to the main issues and developments upon which peace and security depend; and where and how the nations stand in terms of military and political power and influence. The concept of *posture* has been developed in this connection. Yet there is no self-evidently correct way of describing and elucidating so complex and comprehensive a thing as a state's overall stance in world, or regional, affairs. Nor is the problem any simpler if atten-

tion is confined to the military dimension, to discussion of what is conveniently termed defense (or force) posture. Examination of alliance obligations, treaty commitments and general policy declarations, together with analysis of orders of battle, deployments and inventories of military matériel can yield a broad picture. But it is hard to impart coherence to such an account. The economist who turns his attention to defense matters is attracted by a different technique, by an approach based on the fact that defense is an economic activity. His inclination is, first, to ask such questions as: what resources are committed

This is an original article written for this volume. An earlier and much longer version of this paper was presented at the Conference on Comparative Defense Policy, held at the Air Force Academy, February 7–9, 1973. I wish to thank Paul Y. Hammond for comments on the earlier paper; Anthony C. Rogerson for guidance on compression; and Helen Perren for typing successive drafts. Copyright reserved by the author.

to military purposes, and to what military purposes? His disposition is to review national *defense efforts*, which has the notable advantage of exposing both the pattern of defense priorities, via examination of how resources are distributed among military capabilities, and the place of defense or security objectives in the structure of national priorities, via examination of the share of total national resources assigned to the military rather than to civil purposes.

Such an approach is taken here in looking at the defense efforts of the three major European members of the North Atlantic alliance—France, West Germany, and the United Kingdom. To some extent it is simply an exercise in comparative, or transnational defense analysis. But there is a certain utility in taking stock of the situation of these three powers in the early 1970s. For it is to these three countries that the smaller nations of Western Europe will look for leadership should the United States persist, as seems likely, with the reappraisal of her role in relation to European security which has already begun. Furthermore, as the three core powers of the enlarged European Community of Nine, any momentum for greater political, and later defense, co-operation in the Community must be both created and sustained by them.

DEFENSE AS AN ECONOMIC ACTIVITY

It is legitimate to regard defense as an economic activity because establishing, equipping and maintaining armed forces entails the commitment of scarce resource *inputs*, of manpower and matériel, technical ingenuity and organizational skill, to the production of an *output*. A defense effort 'produces' some contribution to safeguarding national security; and security is an objective or value to which governments attach importance and which, in the present state of the world, is not available as a 'free good'. But it is only one objective among many. States and peoples are also concerned about other things—education, health, the quality of life in cities and countryside, and the material well-being of their society. Moreover resources allotted to security have alternative uses in satisfying these other aspirations. Defense is bought at a price in forgone opportunities to enjoy other benefits, and people know it.

Every country faces this dilemma and resolves it by *budgeting*—by deciding how much for private as opposed to public purposes when setting the size of the government budget, and by deciding how much for military as opposed

to civil purposes when planning the pattern of public spending. What determines the weight given to any specific element, like defense, in the structure of national priorities? Formally, the problem is one of maximizing some concept of social welfare. But this is not an operational prescription. In practice, governments "muddle through"; that is, they proceed incrementally, responding to change. At any point in time there is a social value ordering enshrined in the balance among on-going programs, but it is not fixed, permanent, immutable.

Two kinds of development may prompt change. First, there are pressures which are, in a sense, endogenous or 'internal' to the allocative exercise. Even though there has been no change in the objective realities of, say, a poverty problem, a government may decide to give more weight to an income maintenance program and *ipso facto* less to, say, arms programs. This may reflect either a straightforward rethinking of domestic priorities or, more plausibly, a response to pressure—from interest groups or, indeed, from the internal economics of particular programs. Second, there are exogenous considerations: circumstances may change. The threat to national security, or that to the environment or customary living standards, may assume a fresh form or new proportions which seem to invalidate existing appropriations based on an earlier pattern of priorities.

This last distinction is important, for it provides a basis for examining national defense efforts. If this is the manner in which the allocation of resources to and within defense is settled, what provision for defense a country makes, and what particular military capabilities it chooses to have, is determined by the interplay of two sets of influences; namely, the structure of domestic priorities on the one hand, and the politico-strategic environment on the other. (The latter, we should note, is not simply a matter of 'threats' in the conventional military sense. Change in the politico-strategic environment may be brought about by the behavior of allies as well as by that of candidate opponents. Moreover, it is obviously the *perception* of threats, or pledges of support, that matters.)

Comparative or transnational studies invite the investigation of similarities and differences of convergence and divergence. In examining the defense efforts of France, West Germany, and the United Kingdom interest must focus, therefore, on what is like and what is unlike in the roles and structures of their respective armed forces and on whether they are getting more or less alike. Because two sets of influences contribute to shaping individual national defense efforts, and because interest centers in this way on like and unlike, it is clear that four themes call for consideration in the present exercise. They can be expressed in the form of questions. We must ask:

1(a) To what extent do the three states share a common perception of the politico-strategic environment, and especially of the scale and nature of the threat(s) to their national security (or stature): and are they agreed about what responses are appropriate, feasible and effective?

(b) In what respects do they have a unique national viewpoint, either because they view the same things differently or because they pay attention to different things?

2(a) How far do the three countries share a common view on domestic priorities, in particular about the balance to be struck between military and nonmilitary claims on resources, and about the pattern of intra-defense priorities?

(b) Do individual countries experience exceptionally strong internal pressures for particular resource allocations?

DEFENSE BUDGETING AND RESOURCE CONSTRAINTS

Superficial scrutiny of the situations of the states confirms that these four questions are pertinent ones and offer worthwhile perspectives from which to consider their defense efforts. In their external circumstances France, West Germany, and the United Kingdom have a great deal in common. Yet each has independent national commitments, obligations and aspirations which set it apart from the others. The existence of common ground does not connote an identity of interests. Likewise much the same internal pressures affect defense policymaking and planning in the three countries. But each has particular concerns, while even where they are grappling with similar problems this does not mean that the same solutions commend themselves.

Because of this there are numerous similarities in the scale and content of the defense efforts of France, West Germany, and the United Kingdom, but also several marked differences. The particular thesis to be examined here is that the general configuration of the national provision for defense has been shaped, in each country, by the interplay of the *shared* strategic objectives and aspirations and the *commonly felt* resource constraints; and that the differences among them—in terms of force structures, levels, deployments, and doctrine—reflect the uniquely national aspects of both perception of the international environment and experience of domestic pressures. Further, in considering how the defense policies and programs of the three powers have developed in the past five to ten years, it can be shown that uniquely national concerns are becoming less and less important.

France has a population of around 52 millions, the Federal Republic one of about 60 millions: the population of the United Kingdom is just over 56 millions. The Three are thus of comparable demographic size.[1] They are also similar in their economic structures, as is brought out clearly by data on the industrial (or sectoral) origin of gross domestic product such as those in Table 1 below.

[1] We have had the Six, the Seven and we now talk of the Nine. One hesitates to add to the list. But occasionally I shall refer to France, West Germany and the UK as the Three, mainly because constant repetition of phases like "the three countries in question" and "the three leading European powers" would soon become tiresome.

Table 1. Industrial Origin of Gross Domestic Product at factor cost 1967–68, France, West Germany and the United Kingdom (Percentages)

Industry/Sector	France	FRG	UK
Agriculture	7	4	3
Industrial activity			
manufacturing	35	39	34
other	3	4	5
Construction	9	7	7
Transport and communications	5	6	8
Trade and Commerce	14	14	11
Others	29	27	32
	100	100	100

Source: *UN Statistical Yearbook*, Table 186.

In terms of their commitment of resources to defense the Three also stand together, as the major spenders among the European members of NATO. In 1972 their aggregated defense spending represented approximately 72% of the total military outlays of the thirteen members of the Alliance outside North America (France 22%; West Germany 26%; United Kingdom 24%). Estimated defense expenditure (or defense budget) figures of NATO Europe for 1971 and 1972 are given in Table 2. That the Three do stand together, and apart, is readily apparent.

The most widely used basis for transnational comparisons of defense efforts, however, is the relationship between defense spending and Gross National Product (GNP). The latter concept is the most serviceable general measure of the resources available to a country for all purposes, private and public, military and civil. But there are different ways of defining GNP and alternative ways of estimating its value. Nor is 'defense spending' an unambiguous concept. There are alternative ways of defining it—creating coverage problems; and difficulties over the costing of defense programs—and hence valuation problems. Some international organizations (e.g., NATO) do prepare defense expenditure data on a standardized definition. There are, however, no regularly published series based on a valuation technique which completely eliminate the danger of erroneous inference when interstate comparisons are made.

Because defense expenditure can be defined in several ways, and because GNP can be calcu-lated by more than one method, one finds a nation's defense expenditure/GNP proportion quoted by different authorities at wildly different values. Much misunderstanding and sterile dispute arises because of this. Thus one is reluctant to state how the Three compare on this measure, and to draw inferences from any single estimate of the proportion. Values for defense expenditure as a percentage of GNP, according to two definitions of defense expenditure and two GNP computations, are set out in Table 3. The proportions in part (B) have the merit of being based on NATO's standard definition of defense spending. They lie within a fairly narrow range. When one recognizes that the UK has no conscripts, whereas France and Germany each have over 200,000, the percentage point difference shown here is not surprising. The conclusion is that this evidence does not establish with any certainty whether the 'burden' of defense on one economy is greater or less than that on the others. In view of this the readiness of participants in burden-sharing disputes to base their arguments on two- or three-*tenths* of a percentage point difference in GNP proportions is really quite remarkable.

To complete this initial appreciation of the scale of the French, West German, and British defense efforts we may consider manpower. Statistics of the strengths of the armed forces of the Three provide a basis for comparison which is not bedeviled by the problems that arise with expenditure data. But there are difficulties here too, particularly over the treatment of para-

Table 2. Defense Expenditure or Budget and Defense Expenditure per Capita,
NATO Europe 1971 and 1972

Country [a]	Defense expenditure or budget ($US million)		Defense exp. per capita ($US)
	1971	1972	1971
France	5,202	6,241	101
Germany	5,961	7,568	100
United Kingdom	6,108	6,900	109
Italy	2,651	3,244	49
Netherlands	1,161	1,562	87
Belgium	594	724	61
Turkey	446	573	12
Greece	338	495	37
Norway	411	491	105
Portugal	398	459	41
Denmark	410	438	82
Luxembourg	9	6	26
TOTAL	23,689	28,701	

Source: The Military Balance 1972–73 (London: IISS, 1972), Table 2.

[a] Iceland is not included in this table since she maintains no armed forces.

Table 3. Defense Expenditure as Percentage of Gross National Product

(A) Defense expenditure, national definition, as % of gross national product at current market prices. IISS calculation.

	1967	1968	1969	1970	1971
France	5.0	4.8	4.4	4.0	3.1
West Germany	4.3	3.6	3.6	3.3	2.8
United Kingdom	5.7	5.4	5.0	4.9	4.7

Source: The Military Balance 1971–72 and *1972–73* (London: IISS, 1971, 1972).

(B) Defense expenditure, NATO definition, as % of gross national product at factor cost (current prices). NATO calculation.

	1967	1968	1969	1970	1971
France	5.9	5.5	5.1	4.7	4.5
West Germany	5.6	4.7	4.7	4.3	4.4
United Kingdom	6.5	6.3	5.9	5.7	5.3

Source: NATO Document ISM (71)60.

military forces and reserves—especially reserves who train frequently and can take places in front-line units at very short notice. And ideally one should not neglect the contribution of armed forces' civilian employees, especially when in one country they do jobs which in another are performed by uniformed servicemen. It must suffice to note that there are these problems: finding the 'proper' basis for manpower comparisons is a task for another occasion. Table 4 gives the bare facts for military, para-military and reserve forces as assembled by the International Institute for Strategic Studies (IISS). It shows the position at mid-1972. The forces recorded here represent 3.4% of the male population of military age in the United Kingdom, while the percentages for France and the Federal Republic are 5.1% and 4.2% respectively. On this measure, therefore, the UK is bottom of the league, whereas she stands at the top on the basis of the GNP proportion (cf. Table 3)—a further reason for believing that the countries bear broadly similar defense 'burdens'—albeit in different ways.

France, West Germany, and the United Kingdom are demographically and economically of the same stature and they allot resources of money and manpower to defense to much the same extent. We must now consider the military capabilities that these resources are used to provide. It is not intended to offer a detailed order of battle of the Three or a complete inventory of the weapons systems with which their forces are equipped. Statements of their force postures in such terms can be found elsewhere.

It suits our purpose better to approach things differently.

DEFENSE BUDGETING RELATED TO "OUTPUT" CAPABILITIES

Functional costing involves calculating the costs associated with achieving a given objective, or fulfilling a specified purpose (or mission), by grouping the outlays required to pursue the activities which contribute to the mission. Where all the functions or missions under the aegis of a particular government spending department are costed in this fashion, that department (e.g., a Defense Ministry) has an output budget. If expenditure plans are formulated for a sequence of future years, with all expenditure attributed to functions or outputs in this way, there exists a *program budget*.

Output budgeting (or program budgeting) imposes on governments an obligation to identify what their major purposes actually are—in defense and elsewhere. Thus any country which uses output budgeting, and publishes in this format data on the resources committed to defense, necessarily gives an explicit indication of the purposes which it sees its defense effort serving. Moreover the resources assigned to particular outputs or programs (in defense terms, to the provision of different military capabilities) provide a measure of the relative importance which the country ascribes to these several purposes. A defense budget, when cast in the output format, thus exposes the anatomy of a national defense effort more informatively than a count of major units or an inventory of weapons.

Table 4. Military Manpower of France, West Germany and the
United Kingdom (Estimated Strengths mid-1972)

	France		FRG		UK[b]
	No.	% con-script	No.	% con-script	No.
Army	328,000	64	327,000	57	180,000
Navy[a]	68,000	23	36,000	25	82,000
Air Force	105,000	36	104,000	37	110,000
Total	501,000	52	467,000	50	372,000
Para-military forces	73,000[c]		18,500[d]		—
Trained reservists	450,000		645,000[e]		429,400[f]

Source: The Military Balance 1972-73 (London: IISS, 1972), Table 3.

[a] Including naval air arms.
[b] Including forces enlisted outside the UK.
[c] Gendarmerie, 58,000: Compagnies Republicaines de Securité 15,000.
[d] Border Police, whose equipment includes armored cars and coastal patrol boats.
[e] Of whom over 80% are stated as 'on immediate recall'.
[f] Regular Reserves 356,100: Volunteer Reserves 64,800: Ulster Defense Regiment 8,500.

France

The French defense budget for 1972, analyzed by major programs, is shown in Table 5. That tabulation is a succinct statement of the military priorities of contemporary France. The French defense effort is founded on a nuclear retaliatory capability, a capability for theater operations in and around Europe, a territorial defense capability, a modest capacity for operations outside Europe and the provision of 'Utility' forces. In theory the whole of the French defense budget could be assigned to these five major programs, for all her expenditure is directed ultimately to the fulfilment of these missions. But, like others who use output budgets, the French planners have recognized that, beyond a certain point, the attribution of costs to front-line functions becomes increasingly arbitrary. Their output budget accordingly includes four 'support' programs covering those activities which help sustain the combat forces as a whole rather than particular parts of them. But the five 'mission' programs are what French defense is actually for.

In 1972 the French are spending 15% of their defense budget on the *forces de riposte nucléaire*, although in these forces one finds only 4% of her total armed forces. The disparity is easily explained. Capital expenditure still looms large in the provision on this program as France struggles to establish her land- and sea-based missile capabilities, though even when they are established these will be 'capital-intensive' forces. At present these forces comprise:

—58 Mirage IVA bombers.
—Two units of 9 strategic ballistic ground-to-ground missiles (SSBS).
—The first of five ballistic missile launching submarines (SNLE) which France is to deploy, each with 16 of the M-1 sea-to-ground missiles (MSBS).

The largest of the French 'mission' programs, absorbing between a quarter and a third of the 1972 budget and almost two-fifths of Servicemen, is that of the *forces de manoeuvre*. These are the units whose task is "to fight and check an enemy attacking France or her allies in a nuclear or conventional war in Europe."[2] Some Army

[2] *Le Plan Militaire 1971-75* (Paris: Armed Forces Public Relations and Information Department, 1970). The quoted phrase is from an English summary of this document published as a *Note d'Information* in January 1972. For fuller comment on the French defense effort see the *Exposé des Motifs* of the Third Programme Law: *Project de Loi de Programme (equipements militaires).* Assemblée Nationale, Doc. No. 1361 (rectifié), 31 August 1970; D. Lewandowski, "Le Budget de la Défense Nationale pour 1972," *Revue de la Défense Nationale* (28 January 1972): 22-38, and *The Military Balance 1972-73* (London: IISS, 1972).

Table 5. The French Defense Program and Budget

Major program[a]	Expenditure francs (millions)	% of total	Military manpower
1. Forces de riposte nucléaire	4,746	15	19,064
2. Forces de manoeuvre	9,181	29	191,444
3. Forces de securité générale	2,966	10	100,519
4. Forces d'action exterieure	1,208	4	44,529
5. Forces d'usage général	2,419	8	79,901
(mission programs)[b]	20,520	66	435,457
6. Research, development and testing	(2,200)	7	
7. Training and personnel services			
8. Matériel support, infrastructure	(8,485)	27	
9. Administration and other			
(support programs)[b]	10,685	34	(65,500)
GRAND TOTAL	31,205	100	(501,000)
Capital expenditure (Titre V)	14,552	47	
Operating expenditure (Titre III)	16,653	53	

( ) denotes imputed figure.

Source: Lewandowski, D., "Le Budget de la Défense Nationale pour 1972," *Revue de la Défense Nationale* 28 (January 1972): 22–38.

[a] The French nomenclature has been retained for major programs 1–5 to conform to the usage in the text.

[b] The attribution of expenditure on R & D training, support and suchlike to 'mission' programs is almost certainly greater than in UK output budgeting practice.

units equipped with France's own short-range PLUTON missile will furnish a nuclear capability, when PLUTON eventually enters service: the conventional capability resides in five mechanized divisions (2 in Germany, 3 in France). These ground forces are supported by a tactical air force. In addition most of the French Navy is regarded as part of these *forces de manoeuvre*. The *forces de securité generale*, 100,000 strong and accounting for 10% of the 1972 budget, must be regarded as complementary to the *forces de manoeuvre*. Their job is to protect vital military (and other) installations in France and generally to oppose any attempt at penetration by an enemy. They include elements of all three services.

The *forces d'action extérieure* and the *forces d'usage generale* include:

—A strategic reserve/mobile force of two parachute brigades, one airborne brigade and supporting elements.
—The air movement capability represented by the French Air Force's Nord 2501 and

Transall transport aircraft.
—Units permanently stationed at overseas bases.

Since the nuclear retaliatory capability is really an element in the order of battle for European operations, these forces constitute the whole of France's specific provision for possible action elsewhere. If one ascribes to them a realistic share of the costs of the general 'support' programs of the output budget, it appears that at most only one-sixth of the French defense effort can be construed as provision for extra-European commitments and concerns. In other words, for all that she has withdrawn her forces from NATO's integrated military command arrangements, *European* security is what the French defense effort is (almost) all about.

West Germany[3]

There is not even such a token acknowledgment of a world beyond Europe in West Ger-

[3] Based on White Paper 1970 (*On the Security of the Federal Republic of Germany and the State of the German Fed-*

many's provision for defense. The entire effort of the Federal Republic is conceived as a contribution to collective security in Europe. German rearmament was acceptable to other Europeans, and to the people of West Germany themselves, only on condition that the military capabilities created were limited, predominantly defensive in character, and wholly assigned to the integrated military command of the Atlantic Alliance. Thus the role and missions of the Federal Armed Forces have been defined from the outset in terms of the defense of northwest Europe. West Germany does not appear to prepare, and certainly does not publish, a full output or program budget like that which has been available for the UK since the mid-1960s and for France since 1971. Fortunately, this exclusive commitment to the European theater means that analysis of expenditure and manpower by service is an adequate proxy for an output budget. Thus an elucidation of West Germany's force posture can be based on the data in Table 6.

eral Armed Forces), English edition, pp. 174–78, and the following years publication Weissbuch 1971/72 (*Zur Sicherheit der Bundesrepublik Deutschland und zur Entwicklung der Bundeswehr*), pp. 129–37. (An English edition of this is also available now.)

Ground forces absorb three-quarters of the men in the Federal Armed Forces and between a third and two-fifths of the West German defense budget. Apart from some territorial defense units (35,000 men) these troops are wholly assigned to NATO. They are organized in three corps containing a total of 12 divisions: four armored, four armored infantry, two rifle divisions (for the Hessian hills and the Bavarian forest), one mountain, and one airborne division.

The small West German *naval forces* are assigned to roles in the Baltic (coastal protection and the surveillance of the approaches) and in the North Sea (maritime reconnaissance and surveillance) with the emphasis on anti-submarine warfare capabilities. The Federal Republic's air force is essentially a tactical air force. For a number of years the main combat aircraft have been the F104G Starfighter (in a variety of strike, reconnaissance and interceptor roles) and the Fiat G-91 (in the ground attack/battlefield reconnaissance role). But the *Luftwaffe* has begun to replace the reconnaissance F104s with RF-4E Phantoms and over the next few years F-4F Phantoms will take over the air superiority roles. The multi-role combat aircraft (MRCA), which is under joint development with the UK

Table 6. The West German Defense Program and Budget

	1969 Expenditure DM millions[a]	% of total		1971 Manpower 000s[b]
Army	7,051	37		325
Navy	1,663	9		35
Air Force	4,820	26		107
Unallocable	5,265	28		—
Total programmed funds	18,800	100	Total strength	467
Actual expenditure in 1969	19,486			
of which				
Capital expenditure	7,696	40		
Operating expenditure	11,790	60		

Source: White Paper 1970 on the Security of the Federal Republic of Germany and the State of the German Federal Armed Forces (English edition) (Bonn: Press and Information Office of the German Federal Government, 1970).

[a] Estimated expenditure based on the pattern used by all nations for purposes of the NATO annual review, which does not fully coincide with the German Budget classification system. 1969 figures are given because this particular analysis was not published in the 1971–72 White Paper.

[b] From the 1971–72 White Paper (Weissbuch). The tabulation on p. 55 of this book gives a comprehensive picture of West German military manpower by service, rank and terms of service.

and Italy, will fill the Starfighter's other missions: the Franco-German Alpha-Jet is Scheduled to replace the G-91. The air force also mans Nike-Hercules and Hawk batteries (surface-to-air missiles), and 2 wings with Pershing (surface-to-surface missiles). The Luftwaffe's tactical transport capability is provided by C-160 Transall aircraft and helicopters. This comprehensive array of tactical air power, geared exclusively to operations in Europe, employs just under 25% of the manpower of the Federal Armed Forces and absorbs just over 25% of the expenditure which is clearly allocable to individual services.

United Kingdom[4]

The United Kingdom has published a functional analysis of defense expenditure, in terms of 14 major programs, each year since 1965.

[4]The commentary on the UK 'output budget' in the following paragraphs is based on the official Statement on the Defence Estimates 1972-73, Cmnd. 4891, and (inevitably) The Military Balance 1972-73. I have also drawn on some material recently submitted as evidence to a Sub-Committee of the House of Commons Expenditure Committee and published in Second Report from the Expenditure Committee (Defence and External Affairs Sub-Committee) 1971-72, House of Commons Paper 141 of 1971-72 (London: Her Majesty's Stationery Office, 1972).

The analysis for estimated defense expenditure in the financial year 1972-73 (ending 31 March 1973) is shown as Table 7. The output budget comprises six 'mission' programs—to which in theory the whole of UK defense expenditure might be attributed. But the functional analysis is designed as a planning aid so that the costs apportioned to any activity need to be those (and only those) which are assuredly and inescapably bound up with having that activity in the overall program and budget. Certain tasks, however, like the running of reserves and auxiliaries, R & D, training, the provision of a range of family and personnel services, and also the higher management of defense, though ultimately subordinate to and undertaken only to support, sustain, and direct the forces assigned to 'prime missions', stand in no precise relationship to these forces. Hence the UK regards them as functions or activities in their own right. Radical change in the composition of the combat forces would entail modification in the support functions. But it is more illuminating to trace out such effects, by investigating the implications of change in one program for others, than to indulge in arbitrary and meaningless attributions. Thus just over half of total expenditure is shown on eight 'support' programs.

Table 7. The UK Defense Program and Budget

	Major program	Expenditure £m	% of total	Military manpower
I	Nuclear Strategic Force	38	1.3	2,200
II	Navy GP Combat Forces	330	11.6	36,200
III	European Theater Ground Forces	412	14.4	98,000
IV	Other Army Combat Forces	52	1.8	17,900
V	Air Force GP Combat Forces	410	14.3	50,000
VI	Air Mobility	114	4.0	17,400
	Mission programs	1,356	47.5	221,700
VII	Reserves & Auxiliaries	47	1.6	2,400
VIII	Research & Development	330	11.6	1,200
IX	Training	308	10.8	88,700
X	Production, Repair & Associated Facilities in the UK	253	8.9	10,000
XII	Other Support Functions	536	18.8	52,500
XI, XIII & XIV (net)		24	0.8	—
	Support programs	1,498	52.5	376,500
	Grand Total	2,854	100.0	

Source: Statement on the Defense Estimates 1972. Command Paper 4891, Annex D.

For our purpose attention can be confined to the six 'mission' programs. One fact is particularly arresting. Major programs II, III, & V—Navy General Purpose Combat Forces, European Theater Ground Forces, and Air Force General Purpose Combat Forces—account for almost 85% of all expenditure on main missions. The UK no longer has a Far East Fleet; naval forces deployed East of Suez are (in theory anyway) found from units whose primary role is a NATO one. Similarly, few Royal Air Force combat aircraft are stationed outside Europe (including the UK) and the Mediterranean. Thus all but a small fraction of these forces are in the budget with the requirements of deterrence and defense in and around Europe in mind. For the UK, as for France, five-sixths of her defense effort is directed to European roles and missions.

The UK's Nuclear Strategic Force currently absorbs 1.3% of the total budget (just under 3% of expenditure on combat forces). This is the price the country is paying now to maintain the strategic retaliatory capability provided by her four ballistic missile submarines equipped with Polaris. It is deceptively low, for it represents only the running costs of the 'R' boats, and of the facilities at the Clyde Submarine Base which are part and parcel of the 'force'. The capital costs of the submarines, missiles, warheads, and of the extensive shore facilities associated with them, fell on earlier budgets.

Navy General Purpose Combat Forces—the Fleet—provide the UK with the capacity to coduct a varied range of operations at or from the sea—amphibious and helicopter landings, the protection of shipping, defensive and offensive anti-submarine warfare, the provision of naval 'presence', fishery protection, and mine hunting. The major units of the surface fleet are the one remaining attack carrier (ARK ROYAL), 2 commando carriers, 2 assault ships, 2 helicopter/cruisers, and 9 guided missile destroyers; in addition there are 60-odd escorts (frigates) and 40-odd mine countermeasures vessels. The Royal Navy is building up a nuclear-powered Fleet submarine force: it will shortly be 8 strong and 2 further boats are under construction. But most of its submarines are of the diesel-powered patrol variety.

The British Army is now almost like the West German, committed exclusively to European tasks. *European Theater Ground Forces*—the third major program of the UK output budget—is where 85% of all troops in, or directly supporting, field force units are to be found (Table 7 final column). This capability has three components:

—the British Army of the Rhine, organized as a corps of 3 divisions each of 2 brigades (5 armored, 1 mechanized), with 2 armored car regiments, 2 artillery brigades, and an air defense regiment equipped with the Thunderbird (surface-to-air missile).
—the Berlin garrison consisting of a 3,000-strong infantry brigade.
—UK Forces (meaning actual combat units stationed in Britain and not troops at training units, regional headquarters). The main force component here is the land element of the UK mobile force—including 3 divisions (3 airportable brigades) and a parachute brigade.

The 'major program' *Other Army Combat Forces* is not really a major program at all nowadays. Only a handful of fighting units of the British Army are now deployed outside Europe.

The RAF's combat aircraft are also concentrated in the single operational home command—Strike Command—and RAF Germany. Five squadrons of various types are deployed in the Mediterranean, and there are detachments of Nimrod maritime reconnaissance aircraft and Wessex helicopters in Singapore—but that is all. In Germany there are squadrons of F-4 Phantom, Buccaneer, Lightning, and Harrier aircraft. Additional squadrons of these types are operated by Strike Command from UK bases. Vulcan medium bombers, Victors, and Canberras in the reconnaissance role, and Nimrods are also based in the UK. These are the UK's Air Force General Purpose Combat Forces. The British Air Mobility capability—the last of the major programs we have to consider—is provided by 5 strategic transport squadrons, 7 tactical transport squadrons equipped with C-130 Hercules, and several helicopter squadrons.

SHARED STRATEGIC PERCEPTIONS

The foregoing descriptions of three national defense efforts have been presented as an elucidation of the 'output budgets' of the countries concerned. Those budgets are not fully and precisely comparable. The Three do not plan on the basis of a common mission programs/support programs format. Nevertheless, the rough comparison which our data permit is sufficient to verify the first of the two hypotheses formulated earlier. The Three are currently committing resources to broadly similar purposes and on a similar scale: and the similarities reflect common ground in perception of the strategic environment and common experience of domestic constraints.

In highlighting the main similarities in force structures we may note, first, that the defense efforts of the Three yield balanced forces—each has something of almost everything. Second, although each country, and in each country each arm, has its share of equipment which is obsolescent (if not obsolete) the aspiration is to be able to compete with any opposition. Paucity of numbers is acceptable, inferiority in quality of equipment is not, except as a price grudgingly paid in one quarter to allow resources to be used to hold the country in the front rank elsewhere. There is more than a token R & D effort in each country too, indicating that complete technological dependence, on a super power or on other medium powers, is equally unacceptable. Finally, deployment as well as equipment reveals, for all three, a preoccupation with security in Europe. If defense is a kind of active insurance these are 'all risks' policies so far as European contingencies are concerned.

That it is a shared perception of the contemporary politico-strategic environment which determines these quantitatively and qualitatively similar dispositions is not really in dispute. The national orders of battle follow naturally from the fact that the Three are all signatories of the North Atlantic Treaty and, what may be more important, of the Brussels Treaty. It is the obligation clause of the latter which is the more demanding: "If any of the High Contracting Parties should be the object of an armed attack in Europe, the other High Contracting Parties will . . . afford the Party so attacked *all the military and other aid and assistance in their power*."[5] The Soviet Union and Warsaw Pact are the only powers judged capable of producing a situation in which that commitment might have to be honored. Their capability is so potent that, for so long as there remains uncertainty about the intention to use it, prudence dictates the assumption of a credible deterrence posture based on a capacity for prompt reaction to any hostile move and successful defense against it—by conventional means so far as possible, by controlled escalation thereafter. None of the Three regards a major Soviet thrust into Western Europe as a

likely contingency.[6] Nor are most of the scenarios of limited aggression by Eastern Europe particularly plausible. What prevents the dismantling of the security apparatus of the West Europeans is uncertainty about—in fact the logical impossibility of knowing—just how far this situation is itself attributable to the capability for defense and riposte which the NATO countries present. There is also a real fear of "political pressure overtly or covertly supported by military means."[7]

Whether there is consensus about what flexibility in response the European situation requires might be disputed. France is not committed to the flexible response strategy formally adopted at Brussels in 1967. Moreover, Bonn cannot view with the same equanimity as Paris (or London) the implications of even a few days conventional fighting while political bargaining takes place—negotiation in which the use of nuclear weapons in a battlefield context would probably be threatened in the name of 'risk manipulation'. Yet recent formulations of the French concept of operations in Europe indicate that France has at last broken with the principle of 'all or nothing' in nuclear affairs. Her strategy now rests on a notion of "forward deterrence" which, incidentally, is only workable with the close cooperation of allies. Moreover such cooperation does take place. French forces have collaborated in land exercises in Germany, maritime exercises in the Atlantic, and surveillance operations in the Mediterranean; French commanders are in contact with NATO commanders and there are agreed contingency plans for the use of French forces in conjunction with NATO forces in case of attack.[8] France does not, it is true, show any inclination to 're-integrate' her defense effort in NATO's military command structure. But she evidently views the European security scene much as other Europeans do.

"Forward deterrence" also appeals to the West Germans. Unfortunately, because of the Federal Republic's geographical characteristics

---

[5]The Brussels Treaty was signed in March 1948 by Belgium, France, Luxembourg, the Netherlands, and the United Kingdom. The obligation clause quoted was Article IV of the original treaty. The Paris agreements of October 1954 covered accession to the treaty of the Federal Republic of Germany and Italy. (The text of the amended treaty has been reproduced in several books on European affairs, for example B. Burrows, B. and C. Irwin, *The Security of Western Europe* (London: Charles Knight, 1972), Annex III. The original treaty and full details of the Paris agreements can be found in *NATO Facts and Figures* (Brussels: NATO Information Service, 1970), Appendices 2 & 10.

[6]See, for example, the West German White Paper, 1970 *op. cit.*, p. 20.

[7]*Ibid.*

[8]See Neville Brown, *European Security 1972–1980* (London: Royal United Services Institute), p. 41; and B. Burrows and C. Irwin, *op. cit.*, p. 7. Even after her withdrawal from the military organization in 1966 France continued to participate in the NATO early warning system (and other agencies) and maintained liaison at most of the major NATO headquarters. Furthermore, as we have noted, she keeps her 2nd Corps, of two mechanized divisions, in southern Germany where they join in various international exercises; and her garrison remains in Berlin (under Four Power arrangements). See also Andre Beaufre, "French Defence Policy," *RUSI Journal* 115, 657 (March 1970): 3–9.

and position it cannot be had on quite the same terms. But the Germans have squared their circle too in the last decade. Under Schroeder, and particularly under Helmut Schmidt, realistic policies were evolved for the defense of the Federal Republic should deterrence fail; indeed the European version of 'flexible or graduated response' as accepted at Brussels in 1967, was based on them. There have been further developments since, in the guise of a fashioning of tactical doctrine for the implementation of the strategy by the *Bundeswehr*. The structure and deployment of the Federal Armed Forces were adapted in 1970 and 1971 to suit the conditions of conventional land defense. The basis of current West German thinking is defense close to the border, executed primarily by armored infantry and motorized infantry divisions whose structure and equipment are tailored to the area in which they are most likely to be employed. These are backed by a main body of mobile forces comprising armored divisions which can move quickly to focal points, and the airborne brigades which can be deployed rapidly over long distances. The task of territorial units is to ensure freedom of maneuver for the field army and provide rear area security against enemy forces which may have infiltrated, penetrated or been air-landed behind friendly forces. This is warfighting on German soil—something it was for long thought the Federal Republic would not countenance. But it is also *Vorneverteidigung*—the forward defense which the West Germans have consistently advocated. The trick is that 'forward defense' used to connote 'forward deterrence—all or nothing'. It now means exactly what it says, and carries with it the threat of "controlled intensification of combat, geographical expansion of the conflict or controlled selective use of nuclear weapons . . . to demonstrate to the aggressor that the risks he runs are utterly disproportionate to the objective he is seeking to achieve"[9]—the whole adding up, hopefully, to a credible deterrent.

The development of the United Kingdom approach to the European security problem can be traced in the brief essays on the topic which appeared in the Defense White Papers of 1965–70. This was Denis Healey's term as Secretary of State for Defence, and the 'essays' bear the signs of having been written by the Minister himself. The UK position is very close to the West German, largely because Healey and Schmidt established an important rapport. Carl Amme has observed that the British strategic concept is also "little different from the latest French formulation of testing the enemy's intentions." According to Amme, "the only difference is that Britain visualizes its actions as part of NATO strategy, whereas France sees its actions as independent—although profiting by the action of allies."[10] That may be going too far. But the fact that the argument comes full circle, back to the French, is significant in itself.

This argument is plausible so far as it goes. France, West Germany, and the United Kingdom mount comparable defense efforts, to produce military capabilities which have much in common, because they interpret the requirements of their security situation in Europe in similar ways. Those requirements are of two kinds: for a broad range of capabilities of high quality, and for a strategic and tactical doctrine which furnishes deterrence and defense.

But the argument does not go far enough. In the first place none of this hangs together without the backing of the US intercontinental nuclear strike capability and the availability of US-held nuclear warheads for allied divisions in Germany. The essence of 'flexible response'— or the French 'test'—is controlled escalation. Its effectiveness depends crucially on presentation of the risk that such escalation could go all the way to the use of tactical nuclear weapons, and ultimately to massive retaliation—for that is what it would be—by the United States' strategic nuclear forces. Thus whatever security benefits NATO European powers may feel their own forces afford directly, these pale into insignificance by comparison with the part those forces play in sustaining the collective security arrangement which entangles the US in Europe. European security and the Europeans' sense of security hinge on that.

Second, it is necessary to stress that the force postures of the Three today have been shaped in a period during which *détente* has not only been 'in the air' but part of official NATO policy (and an objective of French policy too). More-

---

[9]White Paper 1970 (English edition), p. 20. There is however a growing amount of criticism in West Germany that this formula offers no escape from the Federal Republic's strategic dilemma and entails "destruction by defense." The debate received fresh impetus in 1970–71 with the appearance of a monumental study on the consequences of nuclear war in West Germany. See Carl von Weizsacker (ed.), *Kriegsfolgen und Kriegsverhütung* (Munich: Carl Hanser Verlag, 1970), 699 pp.

[10]C. H. Amme, "National Strategies within the Alliance: Great Britain", *NATO's Fifteen Nations* 17, 5 (Oct.–Nov. 1972): 18–22. The present (Conservative) administration in the UK appears to have accepted the policy formulation vis-à-vis Europe which it inherited in 1970. No further intellectual refinement seems to have taken place, and the White Papers no longer contain discursive essays.

over, there is the clear feeling that this is not just a momentary relaxation of tensions which is vulnerable and fragile.

Finally, there is the sense of keener threat that has been borne in on the governments of the Three where other public policy objectives are concerned. As the threat to security has seemed to wane, others have come to the fore. The threat to the environment from pollution by noise, fumes and effluent has become a major preoccupation of governments, for example. It is accepted that solving this, and other problems of cities and countryside, and providing better opportunities for the young, the poor, the sick and the unemployed, require greater allocations of resources to social and economic purposes than in the past. The opportunity costs of provision for defense have risen; and, since there have also been increases in the money cost of both military manpower and matériel, defense efforts are under pressure from two directions.

These three apparently disparate things—concern to maintain a US presence in Europe, the developing détente, and the costs of defense—interact significantly in the current defense policymaking and planning of France, West Germany, and the UK. The three powers share in the enthusiasm over détente, although some are more enthusiastic than others. West Germany has made the recent running, for motives which are open to various interpretations.[11] France applauds the developments, for they can be construed as movements in the direction of a European security arrangement without super-power dominated pacts. The UK welcomes them because of the possibility of eventually attaining greater security at substantially lower cost. Yet there is no immediate "détente dividend" for the European powers, no real likelihood that it will be possible to move to lower defense budget levels soon. Indeed, the contrary is true. Leaders of the Three insist that the West must be sure to negotiate from strength, not so much an impressive conglomeration of individual 'strengths', but that which flows from a lack of doubt about a US presence in Europe of about the present size. However, there are fears that the US may have a unilateral withdrawal of troops in mind again; and the possibility of the strength of the Seventh Army falling anyway, through reorganization to cope with manpower shortage or under-manning following the ending of the draft, has also been

discussed.[12] Hence the eagerness with which members of NATO Europe—including the UK and FRG—have committed themselves to the European Defense Improvement Program (EDIP), and to higher contributions outside it. The Europeans have been prepared to give marginally more to defense purposes—for fear of what the US might do. At a time when defense budgets are under tight ceilings because of the strength of civil claims, Defense Ministries stand in the paradoxical position of clamoring for more funds while welcoming the era of negotiation.

A felt need to help the US President stave off Congressional pressure for disengagement from Europe is not the only reason why the French, West German, and United Kingdom Defense Ministries want to assign more resources to defense despite détente. Another factor pressing them in this direction, one by which France sets greatest store, is a desire to be less dependent on US power (where possible) whether the Americans are pressing for more effort from Europe or not. The motivation for this springs from three sources: first, an aspiration for some European defense identity to emerge *pari passu* with the movement towards political union recently set in train among the Nine; second, reflection on the implications of SALT, where super-power talked to super-power without allied participation, creating anxiety that new areas may be defined where the interests of super-powers will take precedence over the interests of allies; and third, a desire to keep advanced defense technologies alive. And there is a further basic reason why the pressure on defense budgets is not relieved by détente. Because of the operation of resource constraints arising from higher allocations to nonmilitary programs in the past each of the Three regards itself as having a backlog to make up. To quote British examples, it gives the Royal Navy no satisfaction to see how the ages of its major units compare with those of, for instance, the Soviet Navy; nor is the Royal Air Force enamoured of a situation in which, because of 'adjustments' of several kinds in its equipment programs, the Canberra—first deployed in 1955—continues to have a key front-line role.

DOMINANT ISSUES IN RESOURCE ALLOCATION PROCESSES

The defense budgets of the Three are subject to these pressures from the demand side, so to speak. More output in the form of military capa-

[11]Compare, for example Theo Sommer's views on the appropriate ambition for an Ostpolitik in *Die Zeit*, 28 March 1969 (reprinted in *Survival* [June 1969]: 194, 196) and A. Watson, *Europe At Risk* (London: Harrap, 1972), chap. 3, for a view on what Willy Brandt has really been doing.

[12]Trevor Cliffe, *Military Technology and the European Balance*, Adelphi Paper No. 89 (London: IISS, 1972), p. 2.

bilities, and output of a higher quality, are being sought. But the claims of defense must be set against those of other uses of resources in the national allocative competition which the governments of each of the Three adjudicate. To shed light on why the budgetary outcomes for defense have been as they have for the Three, and in particular why pressures for higher appropriations have not produced larger defense budgets, it will be sufficient to identify the issues that have been dominant in the allocation exercises of the countries in recent years. By and large, as was suggested earlier, they have been similar issues.[13]

In public expenditure planning resources are assigned to purposes according to the social valuation of those purposes. That is the nature and purpose of the exercise. Three sets of circumstances can be distinguished in which the allotment to defense will be under pressure in such a context:

First when the 'internal economics' of particular defense programs, or defense programs generally, go awry; that is, when the resource inputs required to achieve a given level of military capability (effectiveness) rise, raising its *opportunity cost*, and making the satisfaction of other values more 'cost-effective'.[14]

Second when the claims of civil uses of resources become greater, e.g., for road maintenance because of increased traffic levels, or for drugs (say, tranquilizers) because of growth in population and the incidence of particular ailments (say, stress conditions).

Third an autonomous shift in the decision-takers' value ordering or one arising from public pressure for change in social priorities.

Each of these has affected the annual allocation of resources to and within defense in France,

West Germany, and the United Kingdom more or less continuously in recent years. There is no precise way of testing this proposition, but the circumstantial evidence is plentiful.

Before considering the rising cost of military inputs we must glance briefly at the 'input budgets' of the three countries. France and West Germany both publish expenditure data with a distinction drawn between capital spending and operating costs. In 1972 the French budget of 31,205 million francs was split 47%: 53% between the two. Analyses of budgeted capital and operating costs for West Germany show in 1972 a capital:operating cost ratio of 30%: 70% compared to 40%:60% only three years earlier. No distinction between capital and running costs is made in the United Kingdom's published 'input budget'; my own estimate of the ratio is 37%:63%. Table 8 gives a summary of the pattern of input costs by four categories for the three countries based on the latest budgets. These are very different patterns, but the differences are not crucial for the present argument. Both manpower costs and the costs of military equipment have been rising rapidly. Each of the Three has thus found that the resource costs of all capabilities have risen; and to such an extent that many provisions have had to be abandoned or curtailed because, at the higher price, the security benefits have not been thought worth the sacrifices necessary elsewhere. Rising personnel expenditures reflect two developments. First, pay and allowances have risen to keep pace with rising incomes in civil occupations. Thus in the UK in 1966-67 the pay and allowances of the armed forces, of whom there were c.450,000, totaled £480 millions: currently the c.375,000 forces receive £748 millions. This near-doubling of per capita manpower costs compares with a 65-70% national average increase in income from employment per head. Labor for defense has become more expensive than labor for other

---

[13]For an account of public expenditure planning procedures and issues in the UK in the 1960s, see David Greenwood, *Budgeting for Defence* (London: Royal United Services Institute, 1972), especially chaps. 3, 4, & 5. I have reviewed the French and German systems briefly in "Economic Constraints and National Defence Efforts," chap. III of *European Military Institutions: A Reconnaissance*. Third Report (1970–71) of the Universities-Services Study Group (Scotland), esp. pages 73–81.

[14]In simplified terms if the cost of converting a Polaris submarine to Poseidon is 50 million I may judge (value) that the enhancement of the security argument in the social welfare function (and hence social welfare) through authorizing that conversion just exceeds the increment to social welfare that would accrue (by way of 'urban renewal' benefits) from building the 10,000 municipal dwellings that are the real opportunity cost of the conversion. If it transpires that the cost of a second conversion a year later is 60 million (opportunity cost, say, 11,500 dwellings) I may judge the additional retaliatory capability not worth the 'sacrifice' of 11,500 homes.

Table 8. Defense Costs
France, West Germany and United Kingdom
by main input categories

Category	France	FRG	UK
Capital			
Equipment	35	16	27
Works	12	13	10
Operating			
Personnel	40	46	50
Other	13	25	13
	100	100	100

Source: Appendix tables and author's estimates.

things.[15] Similar developments have been in train in France and West Germany. Manpower problems in all three countries have also prompted much additional expenditure recently on improving the living and working conditions of the armed forces and the range and quality of personnel services available to them. This represents a second factor which has raised the cost of furnishing given military capabilities—'given', that is, in operational terms.

The rising cost of military equipment simply exacerbates this tendency. There are numerous examples, from each of our three countries, of systems dropped from defense programs (or numbers cut) through having ceased to be 'cost-effective'. During the course of her second military plan (1965–70) France abandoned plans for a VTOL Mirage, an area surface-to-air missile, heavy-lift helicopters and a nuclear-powered Fleet submarine. The Jaguar program was reduced, and virtually all Army re-equipment plans were cut but those for the AMX-30 tank and the PLUTON missile. The Critical Review of the *Bundeswehr* led to abandonment of plans for a joint US/German main battle tank and of the Frigate 70 development, while the planned purchase of 800 Multi-Role Combat Aircraft (MRCA) was reduced to just over 400. In the UK a new generation of attack carriers and the TSR2 aircraft are the more conspicuous among several items which priced themselves out of the program in the later 1960s.

Meanwhile the cost of meeting social policy objectives has been rising too, because of population growth, insistence on higher levels of service in existing areas of activity, and pressure for action in new areas. Bids for funds for these purposes have mounted steadily in the Three—nowhere more so than in France since the events of May 1968. Moreover, in all three countries the social valuation of civil goals has risen vis-à-vis the value assigned to meeting security objectives. Popular (and Parliamentary) perceptions of the 'threats' in social policy areas have been heightened at a time when perceptions of the security 'threat' have subsided—thanks to détente. Assertions by Defense Departments that there is no 'détente dividend' make no impression, especially on those skeptical about the rationale of earlier levels of expenditure anyway. John Tuthill has summarized the position admirably:

There is a general conviction in the Atlantic area that a number of internal needs have not in the past, received the means to which they have been entitled. Such internal needs would include urban development, improved educational facilities, expenditures designed to improve the lot of racial minorities, public health and environment; and all demand vast increased funds and, therefore, resources. Not only does public opinion insist on increased expenditures in the non-defence field; there is also considerable public apathy or outright opposition to the current level of defence expenditure. A new generation, which cannot conceive of a Security crisis, opposes defence expenditures in themselves.[16]

This is why the French, though anxious to build the apparatus for an 'independent' posture, accepted a more modest nuclear forces program and virtually put their conventional forces on a 'care and maintenance' basis after 1968. It is a state of affairs which West German defense planners recognize. It is what induced the Labor government which held office in the UK from 1964–70 to reshape the national defense effort, holding it constant (in real terms) so that the benefits of what growth the UK achieved in those years might be enjoyed in the civil sector.

The share of defense expenditure in central government budgets is a rough indicator of the effect of such developments as these. International differences in this indicator need to be interpreted with caution, because of differences in the scope of public provision among nations. But a consistent trend in the value of the proportion for a single state does register a shift in social priorities. The data in Table 9 confirm clearly that in the public expenditure resource allocation exercises in the Three in the last decade there has been such a shift.

[16] J. W. Tuthill, "Economic Slowdown and NATO," *Survival* (March/April 1972): 60.

Table 9. Defense Expenditure as % of Total Government Expenditure, 1961–71 (alternate years)

	France	FRG	UK
1961	27.2	32.6	27.8
1963	23.6	39.5	27.8
1965	24.0	33.5	25.2
1967	22.7	32.2	21.3
1969	21.1	29.4	18.0
1971	20.0	28.8	19.5

Source: NATO Document ISM(71)6.

[15] David Greenwood *Budgeting* . . . op. cit., p. 47 and Table 4; and *National Institute Economic Review* 60 (May 1972): 77 (Table 8). Civilian strengths fell more rapidly than service strengths over 1966–72, but the civilian wage and salary bill rose by 80%.

ASYMMETRIES AMONG DEFENSE PROGRAMS OF THE THREE

The argument thus far has been directed to elucidating the central thesis of the paper. The defense efforts of the Three are broadly similar, in terms of how much and what kind of provision for defense they make, and the purposes for which they make it. This is because they share a common perception of the politico-strategic environment—in essentials at least. They have the same 'enemies' and the same allies, so far as Europe is concerned. There is a central body of agreement on what to do to ensure the continuing good behavior of both, and on what would have to be done if this state of affairs were to end. But the Three do not make the provision which their own military would like, nor that which the United States would like. This is because they share a common appreciation of the claims of other public policy purposes. They have most of the same internal needs, and agree that these "have not in the past received the means to which they have been entitled." But what of the corollary to this main thesis—that where there are differences among the Three in the size, shape, equipment, and deployment of their armed forces these can be traced to certain marginal differences in the interplay of external and internal factors on their decisionmaking for defense. This theme is overdue for discussion.

There are in fact several notable triangular asymmetries. France and the United Kingdom (but not Germany) maintain semi-independent nuclear retaliatory forces and have overseas defense commitments which oblige them to maintain intervention forces as well as garrisons outside Europe. The Federal Republic and the United Kingdom (but not France) have all but a small fraction of their forces earmarked for, or assigned to, NATO command, accept US tactical nuclear weapons under the two-key system, and are prepared to buy even their most advanced weaponry from the Americans. Both France and West Germany (but not Britain) maintain conscription systems and assign substantial forces to territorial defense. West Germany alone takes 'forward defense' really seriously. Only France has the prospect of a tactical nuclear capability which does not depend on the United States. Only the United Kingdom possesses a really substantial and comprehensive capability for operations at sea. One could cite other differences—but these are the main ones.[17]

Important though they are it is necessary to hold these differences in perspective. It is a precarious nuclear status that France and the UK enjoy and their world roles are just about played out. Inferences from the fact of West German and British 'integration' in NATO must be tempered by the knowledge that although the three NATO Supreme Commanders have 'integrated' headquarters and planning staffs they do not in normal times have ships, troops, or aircraft actually under command. There are plans for 'integrated' operations, and forces committed to be put under joint command in specified circumstances; but the various stages of Alert procedure have to be agreed "and this agreement includes confirmation that, at the appropriate stage, the country's forces or that part of them committed to NATO *will* be put under integrated command."[18] Nor is it likely that the French and German conscription systems will last much longer.

The nuclear forces asymmetry is normally 'explained' in terms of French and British delusions of grandeur. If one were addressing the question: "why have France and the UK chosen to create and maintain these small 'independent' deterrents?"—such an argument might be appropriate. But for our purposes it is beside the point. For the question here is "why do the French and British have such a capability and the West Germans not?" And the answer to this lies squarely in West Germany's circumstances, since in a different context it seems most unlikely that the Federal Republic would not have delusions too. What, then, are these circumstances? First, and formally, at Paris in 1954 the Federal Republic undertook not to produce nuclear, chemical or biological weapons on her territory and to accept international verification to that effect; later, in 1963, by signing the Non-Proliferation Treaty, she renounced the options to purchase or produce abroad. Second, and equally important, the West German people have shown over the years a violent opposition to the possession of nuclear weapons. The decision to equip the *Bundeswehr* with delivery vehicles with a nuclear capability—but with US custody of warheads—was surrounded by a debate in Parliament and elsewhere which has not wholly subsided. In March 1958, the month of the crucial 'atomic debate' in the *Bundestag*, opinion

---

[17] Each is discussed in the following paragraphs. I owe the felicitous phrase 'triangular asymmetries' to Major-General W. G. H. Beach of the British Army.

[18] B. Burrows and C. Irwin, *op. cit.*, pp. 49–50 (emphasis added). Thus the UK and FRG can 'opt out', just as France can 'opt in'—so that in the event the Three are not on totally different footings.

polls showed 68% against and only 15% positively for giving the *Bundeswehr* the means to deliver nuclear weapons. The Parliamentary vote went in favor even so. But, though opposition tailed off after this, even in 1966 poll data suggested that nearly 50% of West Germans were still opposed to the idea.[19] In short, it is the unique position of West Germany, and her nuclear self-denial, which is the important explanation for the 'nuclear' asymmetry.

Forces for operations outside Europe are the second capability for which France and the United Kingdom, but not West Germany, make provision. The UK retains an extra-European capability because she has not yet completed the 'long retreat'. It seems unlikely that she will abrogate all strategic interest in the East of Suez area, for so long as there are remaining dependencies (like Hong Kong), multilateral security arrangements (as for Singapore and Malaysia) and pressures to show concern for the old Commonwealth (especially Australia and New Zealand). But ANZUS—the Pacific Security Treaty concluded in 1951—is now more important to Australia and New Zealand than their link with the UK. The Five Power Agreement over Singapore and Malaysian defense may eventually reduce to a local Four Power arrangement—and the incorporation of Hong Kong under such a regional organization is not out of the question. Thus in strategic terms the case for even the present minimal provision in the UK defense budget seems unlikely to hold much longer. The insistent pressures for the retention of overseas bases arise internally rather than externally, and notably in the UK services themselves. For instance, old (and not so old) soldiers continue to insist that East of Suez soldiering is "real" soldiering and that recent withdrawals are to be regretted mainly because they mean fewer opportunities for the Army to 'justify itself' by the conduct of the kind of operation in which it has considerable expertise and experience. In naval circles also there is a sense of regret that opportunities for 'showing the flag' are becoming fewer. Naval and military tails wag strategic dogs a little, or the UK provision for operations outside Europe would be even less than it is. Adjustment to the over-riding priority of the 'Continental commitment' has not gone as far as one might have expected.[20]

A comparable mixture of military vested interest and political nostalgia lies behind the continuing French provision for *forces d'action extérieure*. The reservations felt in the UK armed forces about the attenuated role which a Eurocentric posture entails are shared by their French counterparts. This is obvious from the campaigning in the pages of the *Revue de Défense Nationale* for retention of those elements of French military power which furnish the capacity for operations outside Europe. But the French government itself has not turned away from the world outside Europe to quite the same extent as the British. Indeed, French concern for her cultural and big-power status has shown itself in the past few years in renewed interest in the remnants of her overseas empire, and in an urge to extend French influence in new directions. Having shed the burdens of Indo-China and Algeria, considerable importance now attaches to Francophone Africa. This is partly a matter of economics: it is also a matter of prestige—and here the African states are important as existing members of the family of French-speaking peoples which President Pompidou is so keen to develop. The French approach to the world outside Europe is thus not quite the same as the British. Whereas the UK, having lost her empire, is looking to Europe as the stage on which to play a new-found role, France appears keen to show that the old European actress has a wider repertoire.

The French withdrawal from the 'integrated' command structure of the Atlantic Alliance—which is one aspect of the second of the major asymmetries identified earlier—has been widely discussed in the literature and does not, therefore, call for much attention here. But unwillingness to rely on outside sources of military matériel, and unwillingness to countenance the notion of a second party veto on the use of her own forces—these are other distinguishing features of the independent French position. What is it about either the French view of the strategic environment, or the French domestic pressures, which makes her insist on this costly independ-

[19]See E. Noelle and E. P. Neumann, *Jahrbuch der öffentlichen Meinung*, 1956, 1958–64 & 1965. (Allensbach 1956, etc.) I am indebted to Dr. W. R. Vogt of the University of Hamburg for this reference. See also Haus Speier, *German Rearmament and Atomic War* (Evanston, Illinois: Row, Peterson, 1957) and U. Nerlich, "The Nuclear Dilemmas of the Federal Republic of Germany," *Europa-Archiv* 10 (Sept. 1965).

[20]Directors of Music may have something to answer for here. At recruit center and academy passing-out parades a favorite march is the stirring "Imperial Echoes." More seriously, for a good account of the UK withdrawal from overseas since 1945, see C. J. Bartlett, *The Long Retreat* (London: Macmillan, 1972), and on the gradual acceptance by political and military leaders of the priority of European security over imperial defense see Michael Howard, *The Continental Commitment* (London: Temple Smith, 1972).

ence? It is not a question to which one can do justice in a short paragraph or two. But the main lines of the answer are straightforward. First, on the strategic perception, Michel Debré's speech to the Institut des Hautes Etudes de Defense Nationale, in June 1971, contained a stark presentation of the essential point:

Pour faire abandon à une organisation internationale de sa capacité de défense, pour aligner son effort national sur un ensemble qu'on ne commande pas entièrement, il faut être assuré à la fois de l'identité de politique face à la menace et de la solidarité profonde de tous les Etats associés, chacun mettant sa puissance, son existence à service de tous. *La défense, c'est la mise en cause de la nation, de la liberté, de l'honneur, de la vie des hommes et des femmes.*[21]

This is the nub of the French position. It allows scope for some cooperation with 'integrated' elements of others' forces, for receiving military support provided there are no strings, and for participation in collaborative weapons development. Nor is it at odds with the view that "les armaments nucléaires americains qui sont les plus puissants de tous demeurent la garantie essentielle de la paix mondiale."[22] But it cannot accommodate the relinquishing of French control over the defense of France, and over whether France would be defended or not.

There are domestic pressures ranged in support of, and in opposition to, this posture. The *capacité de défense* embraces defense-related industry. Self-sufficiency is a desideratum here as for the forces themselves. Thus the policy enjoys the support of large sectors of French industry which benefit from domestic procurement spending and also from the government's pragmatic arms sales policy. There is also a deeper and more general strand of support for an independent posture, at least among the *milieux*

dirigeants of French society, one which predates de Gaulle's assumption of power in 1958. In August 1954 the French National Assembly declined to ratify the European Defense Community (EDC) Treaty following months of vigorous debate in which France was deeply divided. Daniel Lerner has argued that both sides in this debate drew their conclusions "from profound preferences that are often refractory to the demonstrations of logic." He suggests that: "the defeat of EDC reflected an extra-rational act of *will* . . . To the familiar sense of France as a great autonomous *presence* in the world, EDC opposed the strange new vision of France as a cog in the wheel of Europe. It was this vision that was being rejected by many of those who opted against EDC."[23] Much the same sort of feeling—'extra-rational' perhaps, no more than 'profound preference'—probably remains in influential circles in France today, underpinning the present posture. Popular opinion, however, has shifted. The independent posture does not commend itself to a majority of Frenchmen nowadays, according to a survey of public attitudes to the state conducted in 1971.[24] Only 43% of respondents to this survey felt that the French state was "destined to survive for a long time yet": 32% thought it "destined to merge itself (*se fondre*) in a larger political grouping." More significantly for the defense policymaker, 40% of those questioned doubted the effectiveness of a purely national military effort: 53% doubted the effectiveness of the deterrent force: and a surprising 75% declared themselves in favor of "une défense intégrée à un système plus vaste que la cadre nationale" ["defense integrated in some larger system than the nation state"].

Official policy, however, does not envisage integration, even in an exclusively European setting, for many years yet—if at all. In a recent interview President Pompidou was asked whether a remark that "a strong Europe is a good thing for the whole world" referred to defense. His answer was short and to the point: "I have already said a great deal on this subject. My answer is the same as ever. Defense will come last, because it is what raises the most problems

---

[21]"Before you entrust your ability to defend yourself to an international organization, before you assign your resources to a collective arrangement over which you do not have complete control, you have to be certain that all your partners have identical policies regarding the threat and that there is complete solidarity, with each putting his capabilities, his very existence, to the service of all. Defense is what the nation, liberty, honour, people's lives are all about." Text in Revue de défense Nationale, 27 October 1971, under the title "Europe 1971: deux échecs, deux succès, deux épreuves, deux certitudes." (Emphasis in the original.) See also Wolf Mendl, *Deterrence and Persuasion: French Nuclear Armament in the Context of National Policy 1945-69* (London: Faber & Faber, 1970), for the evolution of policy. Quite apart from its sound analysis this book contains an excellent guide to further reading.

[22]"America's nuclear forces, which are the most powerful of all, continue to be the essential guarantee of world peace." Assemblée Nationale, Doc. No. 1376, 6 October 1970, p. 7. (Report of the Commission on National Defence) quoted in Maj.-Gen. W. G. H. Beach, "The Springs of Policy," in *European Military Institutions—A Reconnaissance, op. cit.,* p. 18.

[23]D. Lerner and R. Aron (eds.), *France Defeats EDC* (New York: Praeger, 1957), chap. 9 (by Lerner), p. 208. It might be objected that France was later to participate in the European Economic Community—as a cog in the wheel. But the diminution of sovereignty entailed by membership of the Communities is not of the same order as that which EDC would have involved. In particular it does not, for any country, "obscure the national identity represented in its national army" (*ibid.*, p. 216).

[24]Actualités—Documents: études d'opinion *Les Français et L'Etat* (Comité Interministérice pour l'Information, *Actualités-Service*, No. 111 Supplement, April 1971).

and difficulties. Let us begin with the rest."[25] Whether a conflict between popular sentiment and the views of the leadership will arise in the later 1970s is an open question. One suspects that forging the economic and monetary union, and harmonizing foreign policy positions on the Davignon formula, will be quite enough for France and the rest of Europe for some time yet.

The contrast between the official French and West German attitudes to 'integration' could hardly be more stark. Statements in the Federal Republic's White Papers read like French policy pronouncements stood on their heads. "The Federal Republic pursues no world power policy," "Security can only be based on a firm foundation of Western partnership"—these sentences appeared in both the 1970 and 1971–72 *Weissbücher*. The former also contains the categorical statement that "the Paris Agreements of 1954 and our commitments within NATO are beyond discussion." It is the unique character of the interplay between politico-strategic influences and domestic factors in the Federal Republic which accounts for this situation. The rearmament of West Germany would not have been acceptable to the Western powers, to the Soviet Union, or to the West German people themselves, on any terms other than 'integration'. The powers made this clear in the international debate over rearmament and framed the Paris agreements accordingly. But interest groups in the Federal Republic campaigned for precisely the same restraints—among them the German Trade Union Federation (DGB). The adoption of Germany into the Western European community was seen as a means of expiating the past. 'European' lyricism and 'European' metaphysics were developed in Germany, it has been suggested, "for the simple reason that it is pleasant to wish for such a thing having lost a war." Similarly, many felt that "if we became European we could rid ourselves of the whole mortgage we acquired as Germans."[26] The contrast with the French is complete: for their posture is founded on the retention of 'French-ness' within the European setting. The question is whether in the mid- or late-1970s a 'cross-over' point occurs. The price of independence for France is high, and public opinion appears to be balking at it. At the same time West German

national self-awareness is developing rapidly. Lodged among the sentences in the White Papers stressing integration is one which declares that "the Federal Republic cannot afford to renounce a policy of self-assertion."[27] Does the formal difference in their positions vis-à-vis the Alliance then count for much?

At the purely military level it obviously does. But that is about as far as it goes: indeed we seem to be near the 'cross-over' point already. Chancellor Brandt's *Ostpolitik*, for example, is a West German not a European one. Insistence in official statements that it is "no solitary venture" and that the *Ostpolitik* "presupposes—if it is to succeed—a strong Western Alliance and its unity of purpose"[28] can be taken more than one way. One commentator has noted that in relations with the East "Brandt was right in his perception that Germany's negotiating position was strongest while NATO and EEC *were cohesive enough to offer him concerted political support and yet remained loosely-knit organizations."*[29] A further gloss on this is provided by Brandt's remarks in a recent television interview:

" . . . in addition to economic integration we now may be able to bring about what I would call a qualified political cooperation—in other words not to introduce supra-national elements at this stage into the area of foreign political and security operations . . . we will have to depend more upon inter-governmental operations than upon, as I said, supra-national methods."[30]

It was Brandt, not Pompidou. So much for 'integration': the mortgage has been paid off.

Brandt's remarks might equally well have been made by Edward Heath or even Harold Wilson. The United Kingdom, like France and West Germany, treads warily in the new political climate in Europe. However, it would be wrong to press the parallels too far, since the paths of the Three are not running in the same direction at present. Nor are all Three dressed for the same occasion: Britain struggles to don the 'European' cloak at a time when France wears it loosely round her shoulders and West Germany indulges in a kind of political strip-tease to hold Soviet interest. Given this political setting the second of our major asymmetries—the West German and United Kingdom commitment to NATO, the French rejection of this status—is not one of which too much can be made.

[25]Interview on Dutch television, 18 June 1972. (Excerpts in French Embassy, London: *Monthly Information Bulletin*, series 14, no. 7 [July 1972].)

[26]Professor Carlo Schmid at the SPD Party Congress in 1965 quoted by G. Bailey, *The Reporter* (6 October 1966) (in *Survival* [Dec. 1966], pp. 388–89). I owe this reference to Maj.-Gen. W. G. H. Beach, *op. cit.*, p. 25.

[27]White Paper 1970, *op. cit.*, p. 3, and Weissbuch 1971/72, *op. cit.*, p. 3.

[28]White Paper 1970, *op. cit.*, p. 11.

[29]Nina Heathcote, "Brandt's Ostpolitik and Western Institutions," *The World Today* (August 1970) (emphasis added).

[30]Interview on BBC television, March 2, 1970, quoted in A. Watson, *op. cit.*, p. 75.

The aspect of force posture in which France and West Germany are alike and the UK exceptional is the reliance on conscription for around half the military manpower requirement and the assignment of substantial forces to territorial defense. The two are related, since the 'operational requirement' for territorial defense swells the numbers needed in the forces as a whole, notably in the land forces. But it is convenient to consider conscription separately.

There are powerful arguments for all-regular, volunteer forces given the technological complexity of late twentieth century warfare. As soon as these became compelling, and there seemed to be ways of maintaining key military capabilities more capital intensively, the United Kingdom abandoned conscription. Why did France not follow suit? Why did West Germany not create a professional military force from the outset?

For West Germany it is only necessary to pose the question in that form for the answer to be clear. When enlistment into the *Bundeswehr* began in 1956 it was intended to recruit as many men as possible on a voluntary basis, either for a full career or for a limited period. The balance was to be found by conscription. Given the extent of popular hostility to the whole idea of rearmament (or remilitarization), it was inevitable that a large part of the requirement would have to be met this way. Indeed, since the West Germans were anxious to avoid creating a military state within the state, and were determined from the outset to establish a New Model army based on the conception of the soldier as "citizen in uniform," motivated by *Innere Führung*, it is interesting to speculate what the reaction would have been had volunteers come forward in vast numbers. But the position today is different. The West Germans have learned to live with their new military—though they do not yet take it for granted as the British do. It is also apparent that the apparatus of civilian control, parliamentary supervision and *Innere Führung* training is sufficiently well-established that the Federal Republic could now contemplate moving to an all-regular basis. Whether the tactical doctrine now evolving in the *Bundeswehr* could accommodate such an arrangement is another matter. The requirement for substantial territorial defense forces suggests that some form of conscription will persist for several years.

Why do the French still draft? There is, in the first place, the tradition of the *levée en masse*, founded on the principle of *l'égalité de tout devant l'impôt de sang* ["the equality of all men facing the tax on blood"]. But contemporary French thinking goes beyond this. In strategic terms the system of universal service is justified as a means of preparing the whole nation for combat, and there is an important place for former conscripts in the overall deterrence posture. Should the 'test' fail there might be invasion—a contingency which a nation invaded three times within a century does not discount lightly even in the nuclear age. The regular *forces de sécurité générale* would then need all the help they could get. What better than a nation-in-arms? Michel Debré has also emphasized conscription as a training ground for character and national solidarity: "the universality of military service . . . and the degree of social mixing (*brassage social*) that is involved make conscription an ideal ground for character-building (*la formation des hommes*) and the apprenticeship of solidarity."[31] Tradition and rationale thus mesh. But the pattern may change, especially when Debré steps down, for several reasons. The mixture of regulars and conscripts in the army is not a happy one. The training of conscripts is costly and the uses to which they can be put, in what remains of their twelve months service, are limited. The territorial defense forces organization, though impressive on paper, has low prestige; the regular units are scornful of the reserve formations, while they themselves are heavily committed to ceremonial duties and peace-time routines. These factors together explain why the notion of a two-tier army—all regular mechanized divisions and a conscribed militia—has been raised in France as it has in Germany.

Conscription of some sort seems likely to be retained, therefore, by both France and West Germany, to meet the requirement for general territorial defense. That requirement is not shared by the United Kingdom for the simplest of reasons: in the British concept of operations the Channel still counts. The British Army can be smaller than those of the two Continental powers, and it was able to dispense with conscription ten years ago.

CONVERGENCE OR DIVERGENCE?

A few final questions remain. The general configuration of the defense efforts of France, West Germany, and the United Kingdom has been shaped, in each country, by the interplay of shared strategic objectives and aspirations on the one hand, and commonly felt resource con-

---

[31]Quoted in Maj.-Gen. W. G. H. Beach, *op. cit.*, p. 57, on whose account of the French system this paragraph is based.

straints on the other. The differences among them, in terms of force structures, levels, deployments and doctrine, reflect the uniquely national aspects of both perception of the international environment and experience of domestic pressures. Such at least has been our thesis. But is there now more or less common ground than two, five, or ten years ago? Are the uniquely national concerns or inhibitions more or less important? Do we have convergence as well as similarity, and divergence as well as difference?

The outlines of answers to these questions have been discernible at several stages of the argument. Some firm and definite instances of convergence and divergence have been noted here and there. But what if we bring back into focus the actual size, shape, equipment, and deployment of the three countries' armed forces and compare these facts with the position, say, a decade ago? In 1963 the defense expenditures of the Three, on a standardized basis, in US dollars at 1960 prices, and exchange rates, were as follows:[32]

	France	FRG	UK
$ mill.	4,110	4,371	4,768

Since then all three defense budgets have risen markedly in terms of *current* prices. Table 10 shows that the French budget almost doubled over 1960–72; the West German more than doubled in this period; and the British rose by 75%. But at *constant* prices the picture is very different. Estimated expenditures for 1972, on the same basis as those for 1963 above, are:

	France	FRG	UK
$ mill.	4,725	4,643	4,707

Remarkably, these figures lie within a range of $82 million; the lowest on this measure (FRG) is less than 2% below the highest (France). There has been convergence in statistical terms if nothing else (Table 11). To ascertain whether there is more to it than this we may ask the following questions: When there was a change of government in one of our countries, and adjustment of the defense effort as a result, which military capabilities were eliminated, and which suffered disproportionate cuts (or vice versa, of course)? When there was pressure to reduce all public demands because of unfulfilled growth expectations and/or more pressing civil claims—which defense programs were affected? If the supplementary thesis to our main theme is valid we would expect those programs geared to uniquely national concerns or aspirations to be the ones which were curtailed or dropped.

We may test the proposition in three settings:
—*the United Kingdom, 1964–early 66*: this was the period when a Labour government, having entered office with a commitment to allot more to social programs without diverting more resources from the private sector, sought to hold defense budgets in check.
—*the United Kingdom, late 1966–68*: a period when the same administration sought to reduce defense spending because of slow growth of GNP (to mid-1967), as part of a general restraint on domestic demand (after devaluation in November 1967).
—*France, 1967–69*: a period when an administration first cut defense spending because of insufficient growth (in 1967, affecting the 1968 budget): and later repeated the process to moderate defense's claims on total resources so that more might be spent on civil programs—this following the 'events' of the spring and early summer of 1968 and the monetary débacle of November (affecting the 1969 budget).

The test itself is simple enough. Where did the crunches come? Did they affect the 'independent' nuclear forces and the extra-European presences and capabilities of France and the United Kingdom rather than their European theater forces? In the United Kingdom in 1964–66 the

Table 10. Defense Expenditure
France, Germany (FRG), United Kingdom
Current prices and exchange rates: Index Numbers

Year	France	FRG	UK
	Index 1960=100	*Index 1960=100*	*Index 1960=100*
1961	106	109	103
1962	116	142	110
1963	119	164	113
1964	127	161	121
1965	132	164	126
1966	140	167	130
1967	151	177	138
1968	158	159	141
1969	165	178	139
1970	173	186	148
1971	183	212	163
1972	197	232	175

Source: SIPRI (1972), Table 4A.3.

[32] The data here are from SIPRI (1972) *op. cit.*, where there is full explanation of the conventions used in compiling them. (pp. 74–81).

Table 11. Defense Expenditures: France, Germany (FRG), United Kingdom
(US dollars [millions], at 1960 prices and exchange rates)

Year	France $	France Index 1960=100	FRG $	FRG Index 1960=100	UK $	UK Index 1960=100	Total NATO Europe	Index 1960=100
1961	3876	99	3082	106	4628	100	14646	101
1962	4182	107	3894	134	4712	101	16120	111
1963	4110	105	4371	150	4768	103	16755	116
1964	4225	108	4193	144	4935	106	17037	119
1965	4293	109	4131	142	4925	106	17159	120
1966	4415	113	4057	140	4875	105	17255	121
1967	4651	119	4227	146	5023	108	17977	126
1968	4645	118	3746	129	4923	106	17544	123
1969	4582	117	4080	140	4614	99	17527	123
1970	4560	117	4112	142	4604	99	17742	124
1971e	4591	117	4451	153	4610	99	18270	128
1972e	4725	121	4643	160	4707	101	n.a.	n.a.

Source: SIPRI (1972), Table 4A.2.
e = estimate
n.a. = not available

first crunch certainly came on the nuclear force. The new government cancelled a fifth Polaris submarine within weeks of taking office. There followed another dramatic cancellation—of the TSR-2 aircraft. But a 'compensating' decision, to buy the F-111K, was made and other adjustments to the RAF re-equipment program in 1965–66 were shifts to 'better buys'. The major program change of this first defense review was the decision not to provide for an attack carrier force in the 1970s, and hence not to begin building the first of a new class of carriers—CVA-01. This decision entailed limitations on the UK's capability for operations outside Europe—viz., in possible intervention operations without allied support and without the benefit of a 'red carpet' provided by the host state. The European capability was virtually unaffected; most European maritime air tasks were thought to be within the capacity of land-based aircraft.

In the second of Britain's "defense reviews" of the 1960s the emphasis was squarely on reducing force levels outside Europe. The first phase—to July 1967—was prompted by unfulfilled growth expectations which led the government to look for economies in public spending generally. But the defense program was cut more than most. At the end of this phase a major rundown of force levels in the Far East was announced, to lead to eventual withdrawal from Singapore and Malaysia by the mid-1970s. One brigade was 'redeployed' from West Germany, to produce a marginal saving in foreign exchange costs. However, the unit stayed in the order of battle of Rhine Army and its heaviest equipment stayed in Germany. There was a

second phase to this defense review following the devaluation of the £ in November 1967, which led to an announcement that the Far East rundown was to be accelerated—to complete withdrawal by end-1971. A decision to pull out of the Persian Gulf was made at the same time, and an earlier phasing-out of the existing carrier force was programmed. Of these changes only the 'redeployment' of the BAOR brigade directly impaired the European capability. The others actually led to a strengthening of the UK's capacity for operations in the NATO area. Freed of extra-European tasks—other than to afford a 'general capability' for use world-wide in extremis—the strategic reserve was reconstituted (in fact, renamed) as a UK mobile force at SACEUR's disposal, and the amphibious forces were assigned a role in the defense of NATO's northern flank.

In France in 1967 growth of total output was slower than had been anticipated, which compelled reappraisal of the Second Military Plan. In drawing-up the 1968 defense budget the ax was brought down first and foremost on the Army re-equipment program. However, AMX-30 tank procurement and the PLUTON missile development were not affected. The non-nuclear force elements of the French Navy were also cut and the AFVG aircraft project was cancelled. The priority program—the strategic nuclear force—was least affected. Moreover the momentum of the Jaguar, Mirage F1, and tactical helicopter development and production programs was maintained. Setting aside the nuclear force and considering only the impact of these changes on the *forces classiques*, it is apparent that those with a European rationale suffered least.

The events of May 1968 impelled the French government to stabilize real defense expenditure for the remainder of the duration of the Second Plan so as to free resources for civil programs. Economies in operating costs were effected across-the-board. It was announced that there would be cuts in the strength of the services, the amphibious warfare and air mobility capabilities being the main victims. As for equipment expenditure, the Mirage F1 program was cut. But, most important, the time-scale for the introduction of both the SSBS and SNLE/MSBS deterrent systems was stretched—and the later reduction of the SSBS force from the originally planned 27 to 18 was effectively foreshadowed by this. Again the burden of adjustment fell not on the *forces de manoeuvre* but on France's other military capabilities, including in this instance the nuclear force.

The supplementary hypothesis is not fully borne out by these tests. In the United Kingdom experience, however, disengagement outside Europe was a clear priority. When pressure from economic policy and from a desire to shift the balance of public spending towards internal needs prompted a reshaping of the UK defense effort the interests of European security were held paramount. The French too, when their crunch really came in 1968, accepted a marked degradation in their capacity for overseas operations, and did not shrink from reducing the allocation of resources to the nuclear forces, letting the tactical forces for European operations off very lightly.

The conclusion to be drawn is obvious. The three major powers of NATO Europe—clearly comparable in economic and military stature—mount similar defense efforts which reflect for each the reconciliation of the competing claims of security on the one hand and social and economic satisfactions on the other. There are differences among them, however, for their images of the strategic environment are not identical nor are their internal needs.

But French and British defense policies and programs have developed over the past decade in such a way that these differences are less pronounced than once they were. In defense terms, therefore, where France, West Germany, and the United Kingdom now stand is readily apparent. They stand apart, prepared to collaborate but attentive to self-interest. They also stand together, in the shade of one superpower and the shadow of another, subject to similar social claims and economic pressures, with their central security priorities in broad harmony—to this extent, on common ground.

JAPAN'S DEFENSE POLICY AND THE SELF-DEFENSE FORCES

MARTIN E. WEINSTEIN

Of all the studies in this section, Professor Weinstein's fits most closely the functional approach suggested by Paul Hammond. He traces Japan's defense policy and resulting force postures from the initial postwar proposals of Yoshida, Katayama and Ashida in 1947 to the present time, describing throughout the functions for which Japanese leaders have sought to procure both their own forces and the guarantee of the forces of the United States. In his analysis, Weinstein describes (à la Huntington) how the strategic outlook of Japan's leaders and the resulting functions required of its defense posture have continued to remain in harmony with the defense posture made imperative by the internal domestic structure of Japanese politics. In concluding his analysis, Weinstein describes very cogently why it has been quite rational for Japan's leadership to remain content with a very stable force posture (both quantitatively and qualitatively) despite the vast differences in Japan's economic stature over the past two decades.

Professor Weinstein is Associate Professor at the University of Illinois. He has served as an officer in the Air Force, and as Executive Editor and Research Associate in the East Asian Institute, Columbia University, after completing his doctorate there in 1969. He is author of Japan's Postwar Defense Policy, 1947–68 *(1971) and numerous articles on Japan's foreign and defense policies.*

The Japanese Self-Defense Forces have been at the center of a bitter political controversy since their inception in 1950. For two decades the Socialists, the principal opposition party, have been insisting that these forces are unconstitutional. They have characterized them as a tool of American imperialism and as part of a reactionary plot to restore military rule. Other critics of the government, ranging from thoughtful journalists to ultra-rightists, have charged that the Self-Defense Forces are a militarily inadequate concession to American pressure for rearmament. Government officials and conservative politicians have responded to the socialists by arguing, with apparent success judging by their election victories, that the Self-Defense Forces are a legitimate expression of Japan's right of national self-defense. To the second set of critics, they have hardly attempted to respond at all. Many words have gone into the debate over the Self-Defense Forces, but little has been said to clarify their actual function. In short, apart from the small group of officials particularly in the Defense Agency, and the Finance and Foreign Ministries who have drawn up

defense budgets and plans, few people in or outside Japan have had any concrete notion of how the Self-Defense Forces serve to defend their country.

The purpose of this article is to clarify the function of the Self-Defense Forces by examining their role in the Japanese government's defense policy—conceived early in the Occupation, and developed and modified through the 1951 and 1960 security treaties with the United States.[1]

HISTORICAL DEVELOPMENT TO 1954

Japan's defense policy has not, contrary to common belief, been a derivative of United States Far Eastern security policy. Its origins predate the 1949 Communist victory in China and outbreak of the Korean War in 1950, the two events which led the United States to define its military responsibilities in East Asia. The spe-

[1] The following outline of the evolution of Japan's defense policy is a summary of the more detailed treatment I gave to this subject in, *Japan's Postwar Defense Policy, 1947–1968* (New York: Columbia University Press, 1971).

This is an original article written for this volume and the Conference on Comparative Defense Policy held at the Air Force Academy, February 7–9, 1973. Copyright reserved by the author.

cific objectives of Japan's defense policy, further-more, have always been distinct from those sought by Washington. As far back as 1947, the Japanese government, first under Prime Minister Yoshida and then under Prime Minister Kata-yama and Foreign Minister Ashida, decided that a United States-Soviet conflict was inevitable; that neutrality or reliance on the United Nations for military security was impractical; and that Japan, already under an American controlled oc-cupation, should cast its lot with the United States after regaining its sovereignty. They an-ticipated that the Soviets would attempt to draw Japan away from association with the United States and into the Socialist camp by instigating and supporting communist-led insurrections and by threatening or actually launching a direct at-tack from the north, through Hokkaido.

Prime Minister Yoshida and Foreign Minister Ashida believed that if permitted to build para-military, centralized police forces, they would be able to handle the internal threat themselves. Given the superiority of United States naval and air power, they believed that a direct Soviet at-tack could be deterred by an American guarantee of Japan's external security. That included maintaining bases in Japan for emergency use by the United States and stationing American forces in the areas adjacent to Japan, which at that time probably meant the Ryukyu and Bonin Islands. In a memorandum prepared by Foreign Minister Ashida in 1947, and transmitted to the U.S. government, the Japanese government pro-posed to implement this defense policy through a mutual defense agreement with the United States, under which the two governments would consult and cooperate in the defense of Japan.

The Japanese government believed then that their country's strategic value, their willingness to assume complete responsiblity for the internal communist threat, to cooperate in external de-fense, and to maintain close political-economic association with the United States constituted a realistic and reasonable basis for a mutual de-fense arrangement.

Thus, the original role planned for the Japa-nese armed forces was both military and diplo-matic. These forces were to maintain internal security. By so doing, they would contribute to the creation of a mutual defense relationship with the United States including a guarantee of Japan's external security. Mr. Yoshida and Mr. Ashida did not want simply to hand Japan's security problems over to the United States, which would have meant making Japan into an American military dependency. They anticipated that it would be a matter of vital interest to the

United States to prevent a Communist take-over in Japan. They thought that such a take-over was as likely to result from subversion and insur-rection as from direct attack. By undertaking to build adequate internal security forces, and to make available in Japan emergency-use bases, they were, from their point of view, offering to share with the United States in the task of de-fending Japan.

From 1947 to 1951 neither SCAP nor the United States government seems to have paid much attention to the Japanese government's proposals for post-peace treaty security arrange-ments. Despite the abortive general strike of February 1, 1947, and continuing labor disorders and violence, it was not until July 1950, when the bulk of American units based in Japan were sent to Korea, that General MacArthur finally au-thorized Prime Minister Yoshida to establish the 75,000 man National Police Reserve.

When Prime Minister Yoshida met Special Ambassador Dulles in January 1951 for the security treaty negotiations, he proposed a mu-tual defense agreement along lines set down in the Ashida Memorandum. Instead of emergency-use bases, however, he offered the United States use of whatever installations were necessary for the conduct of the United Nations operation in Korea. Thus, *despite the Korean War, the role which Prime Minister Yoshida envisaged for the Japanese forces was still limited to the mainte-nance of internal security.* Mr. Dulles, however, insisted that a mutual defense agreement would be possible only if Japan rearmed to the level where it could assume primary responsibility for defending itself against a direct Soviet attack, and could assist militarily in protecting regional security. He urged rapid expansion of the Na-tional Police Reserve into a 350,000-man army.

Prime Minister Yoshida refused to rearm on the scale urged by Mr. Dulles. The upshot of their disagreement was the provisional 1951 Security Treaty, which was not a mutual agreement and which satisfied neither side. The Treaty did, how-ever, provide for the stationing of United States forces in Japan, forces which were a *de facto* guarantee of Japan's external security.

Disagreement on rearmament between Prime Minister Yoshida and Ambassador Dulles de-rived essentially from different estimates of the Soviet threat. Ambassador Dulles seems to have believed that a Soviet invasion of Japan was a distinct possibility, and that it would take all the naval and air forces the United States could spare, since they might also be occupied else-where, plus a 350,000-man Japanese army to defend Japan against such an invasion. Prime

Minister Yoshida, on the other hand, did not think an amphibious attack against Japan was likely so long as the Americans remained committed to the defense of South Korea, held naval and air superiority around Japan, and were willing to guarantee Japan's security. As he saw it, an American guarantee would *deter* a Soviet attack. It was the key to Japan's external defense. He believed that without such a guarantee, Japan in 1951 was too weak economically and spiritually to cope with Soviet Russia or to build the army Mr. Dulles wanted—an army which he considered unnecessary if the American guarantee was forthcoming.

Although unwilling to accept Mr. Dulles' arguments, Prime Minister Yoshida saw that he would have to compromise on the rearmament issue in order to build the mutual relationship he wanted with the United States. He had no intention of building forces capable of participating in regional defense, or even capable of assuming primary responsibility for external security. He did, however, decide to expand the National Police Reserve from an internal security force into armed forces capable of participating in Japan's external defense.

Thus, in the spring of 1952 when the Peace Treaty and Security Treaty came into effect, Prime Minister Yoshida reorganized the National Police Reserve. Renamed the National Safety Agency, it was expanded to include the 110,000-man National Safety Force and the 8,900-man Maritime Safety Force. While not explicitly authorized to combat foreign invaders, elements of the National Safety Force were deployed to Hokkaido, where they replaced American units responsible for defending the island against a Soviet attack. In July 1954, Prime Minister Yoshida pushed the Defense Agency Establishment Law and the Self-Defense Forces Law through the Diet. These laws again reorganized and expanded the armed forces, and explicitly authorized them "to defend Japan against *direct and indirect aggression*, and when necessary, to maintain public order."[2]

In 1954, the actual strength of the combined Ground, Maritime and Air Self-Defense Forces was 146,285 men. They were equipped with United States World War II vintage machine guns, mortars, recoilless rifles, armored personnel carriers, trucks, and a small number of propeller driven aircraft, destroyer-escorts and patrol boats.[3] These forces had adequate equipment to carry out their internal security mission.

They were, however, prepared to play only a minor role in Japan's external defense, which was being taken care of by the United States forces in South Korea, in the Western Pacific and in Japan itself. Close to 200,000 American servicemen, including combat infantry units, were still stationed in the country.[4] This is not to say that the Self-Defense Forces were merely an instrument of the government's Security Treaty diplomacy. They did reflect Japan's determination to fight in its own defense, and if the Soviets had attempted a landing on Hokkaido in 1954, they would have been met by Japanese as well as by American forces. But the role of the Self-Defense Forces (SDF) in defense policy, although widened by law to include external defense, was still in practice very similar to that projected in the Ashida Memorandum. Militarily, their primary function was internal security. Diplomatically, they were a compromise intended to gain for Japan the mutual security arrangements and the explicit guarantee which the government wanted from the United States.

THE STATIC ROLE OF THE SDF
SINCE 1954

The argument of this article is that the role of the Defense Agency and the Self-Defense Forces in Japan's defense policy in the early 1970s remains essentially what it was in 1954; and that this limited role continues to reflect the government's estimate of both external and internal threats and forces required to counter these. Diplomatically, the role of the armed forces has shown no significant change. Prime Ministers Hatoyama and Kishi gradually built up the Self-Defense Forces in order to replace the 1951 Security Treaty with the 1960 Treaty of Mutual Cooperation and Security. Prime Ministers Ikeda, Sato and Tanaka have continued that gradual build-up to maintain the mutuality and explicit guarantee gained in the new treaty. But the Self-Defense Forces are obviously more powerful than they were in 1954, and the argument that their military role in defense policy remains essentially unchanged required a more detailed exposition.

As a result of almost twenty years of gradual growth the Self-Defense Forces are clearly larger and better equipped than they were in 1954 (see Table I). Their total strength is approximately 235,881 men—157,571 Ground Self-Defense Forces, 36,869 Maritime Self-Defense Forces, 41,363 Air Self-Defense Forces, and 78 Joint

[2] *Bōei jitsumu shoroppō* (Tokyo, 1968), p. 66.
[3] *Bōei nenkan* (Tokyo, 1955), pp. 227–47.

[4] *Ibid.*, p. 249.

Table 1. Personnel Strength of the Self-Defense Forces (SDF) and of
United States Forces in Japan (USFJ)

	Authorized Strength of SDF	Actual Strength of SDF	United States Forces in Japan
1954	152,110	146,285	210,000
1955	179,769	178,290	150,000
1956	197,182	188,030	117,000
1957	214,182	210,603	87,000
1958	222,102	213,830	77,000
1959	230,935	214,682	65,000
1960	230,935	206,001	58,000
1961	242,009	209,015	48,000
1962	243,923	215,649	46,000
1963	243,923	212,904	45,000
1964	246,094	216,218	46,000
1965	246,094	225,450	40,000
1966	246,094	226,640	34,700
1967	250,372	231,438	36,400
1968	250,372	234,849	
1969	258,074	235,564	
1970	259,059	235,881	39,500
1971	260,688		28,000

Note: Figures for authorized and actual strength of the SDF for 1954–59 are from *Jieitai jyūnen shi* [Ten Year History of the SDF] (Tokyo, 1961) p. 271; for 1960–67, from *Nihon no anzen hoshō* (1968), pp. 366, 367; for 1968–71, from *Jieitai nenkan* (1971), p. 206. These are official Defense Agency figures.

Strength of United States Forces in Japan is from *Jieitai* (SDF) (Tokyo, 1968), p. 266, and from *Bōei Nenkan* (1972), p. 367.

The discrepancy between authorized and actual strength of the SDF is accounted for almost entirely by deficiencies in the Ground SDF. Because of Article IX of the Constitution, there is no compulsory military service, and all SDF members are volunteers.

Staff Council. Their inventories include the latest model Type 61 tanks, heavy artillery, transport helicopters, F-104 supersonic jet fighters, Nike-Hercules antiaircraft missiles, plus forty destroyers and destroyer-escorts especially equipped for antisubmarine warfare.[5] Since the American military presence in Japan has been drastically reduced from close to 200,000 to approximately 28,000, it is tempting to conclude that the Japanese armed forces have assumed primary responsibility for external defense.

In public statements, the government and the Defense Agency make a practice of dodging this question by saying that defense of Japan is a joint Japanese-American responsibility under the Treaty of Mutual Cooperation and Security.[6] However, a National Defense Council staff paper prepared in 1966 for limited circulation within the government, sets forth in greater detail the

military role of the Self-Defense Forces.[7] According to this staff paper, which appears to be still valid, Japan's security in the late 1960s and the 1970s is endangered by three kinds of threats.[8]

First, Japan is presently threatened by Soviet nuclear missiles, and in the 1970s, it may also face a nuclear missile threat from Communist China.[9] Second, there is the threat of conven-

[5] *Bōei nenkan* (1972). Also *The Military Balance 1972–1973* (London: IISS, 1972).

[6] For instance, see *Nihon no anzen hoshō* (1967), pp. 73–78; and *Jimintō anzen hoshō chōsakai* [LDP Security Research Committee], *Nihon no anzen to bōei* [Japan's Security and Defense] (Tokyo, 1966), Part II, chapter IV, pp. 266–79.

[7] "Waga kuni bōei ryoku no honshitsu to bōei ryoku seibi no arikata [The Essence of Japan's Defense Power and a Program for Defense Equipment]" (October 1966).

[8] Interviews with Mr. Kaihara Osamu, Secretary-General of the National Defense Council on April 2, and June 5, 1968 and with General Takenaka Yoshio, Military Attache, Embassy of Japan, October 5, 1972.

[9] It should be noted that defense policy planners in Japan have viewed the Soviet and Chinese threats in terms of capability rather than intention. As a consequence, although defense policy vis-à-vis mainland China has been given considerable attention, the Chinese threat has been rated as distinctly smaller than the Soviet. The two aspects of Chinese capability that have received the most attention are: (1) the progress of China's nuclear weapons program; and (2) the possibility that Mao's brand of Communism and his insurrectionary tactics would be adopted and applied by the Communists and left Socialists in Japan. Defense planners have, of course, taken cognizance of the Sino-Soviet rift. Their reaction, however, has been skeptical and cautious. They generally agree that so long as the dispute continues it reduces the chances of a Soviet attack on Japan. They also feel, especially since 1966, that

tional, local war, which is most likely to take the form of attacks by the Soviet Union. Third, there is the threat of large-scale internal disorders, which can develop into a war of national liberation, led by Japanese Communists and supported by Communist China and perhaps the Soviet Union. This last threat is seen as most likely to materialize if war were to break out again in Korea.[10]

For countering the nuclear missile threat, Japanese policy is to rely entirely on the United States strategic deterrent; for internal security, on the police and Ground Self-Defense Forces. Against conventional attacks, government policy is to cooperate with the United States within the framework of the Security Treaty. Defense planners recognize that the conventional external threat ranges from infiltration of guerrillas, weapons and supplies for insurrectionary elements in Japan, amphibious probing attacks, air attacks on Japanese cities and interdiction of Japanese shipping, all the way to a full-scale invasion from the north.

The Ground, Maritime and Air Self-Defense Forces acting together are believed strong enough to prevent infiltration and to repel probing attacks. The air defense network is built around the electronic Base Air Defense Ground Environment (BADGE) system, the F-104 jet fighter-interceptors, Nike-Hercules missiles, and antiaircraft artillery. It can play an important role in conventional air defense, but only so long as the Self-Defense Forces have adequate fuel and ammunition, which depend on imports by sea.[11] Defense planners anticipate, however, that the Maritime aided by the Air SDF could only protect Japanese shipping against submarine, surface and air attacks in territorial and coastal waters, and to a very limited degree in the peripheral seas. This means that if air attacks were combined with interdiction of shipping, Japan could not be defended unless the United

States employed its naval and air forces in the Pacific and Indian Oceans to keep open shipping lanes to Japan.[12]

As for a large-scale invasion from the north, the National Defense Council and the Defense Agency recognize that the Self-Defense Forces are not prepared to cope with it. Officially, the Self-Defense Forces are supposed to have two months reserve ammunition. According to informed officials, however, reserve ammunition figures are computed on an unrealistically low rate of consumption. They estimate that in actual combat the reserves would probably be used-up in a week or less.[13] In effect, the government still relies on the American guarantee to deter a large-scale conventional attack. Such an attack, they believe, could only be repulsed by a rapid and equally large-scale American intervention. If this response were not forthcoming or were to prove ineffective, the last line of defense would be a protracted guerrilla war against the invader—a war of national liberation led by the government.[14]

To sum up, Japanese defense planners believe that the Self-Defense Forces are capable of handling internal security, preventing infiltration and repelling probing attacks. They can play an important role in Japan's air defense, and a minor role in protecting Japan's essential shipping. But despite their growth since 1954 and the reduced American military presence in Northeast Asia, they have not assumed primary responsibility for external defense. They have rather developed a capability to repel the lesser forms of external attack. This capability is intended to reduce the likelihood of small-scale attacks and thus increase the probability that a Soviet or Communist Chinese thrust against Japan would be on a scale large enough to activate the Security Treaty and provoke an American response.

In the jargon of the strategists, the function of the Self-Defense Forces is to raise the threshold of attack. In simpler language, their role in external defense is to strengthen the American guarantee. It should be noted that as in 1947 and 1951 the Japanese government still apparently views that guarantee primarily as a deterrent, and only remotely as a fighting defense. The dominant view among officials concerned with defense policy is that neither the Soviets nor Communist Chinese are likely to attack Japan so long as the

conditions in China are highly unstable, and that the rift could be quickly closed by a sudden, unpredictable change in Peking's policy.

See Kotani Hidejirō and Tanaka Naokichi, "Nihon no anzen hoshō no tembō [The Prospects for Japan's Security]," in *Nihon no anzen hoshō* (Tokyo, 1964), pp. 753–87 and 908–17. *Nihon no anzen hoshō* (Tokyo 1966), pp. 60–64. Tanaka Naokichi, *Kaku jidai no Nihon no anzen hoshō* [Japan's Defense Policy in the Nuclear Age] (Tokyo, 1967), pp. 118–27. Kishida Junnosuke, *Chūgoku no kaku senryoku* [Communist China's Nuclear War Power] (Tokyo, 1967). Doi Akio, *Shin Senryaku to Nihon* [The New Strategy and Japan] (Tokyo, 1968), pp. 155–76.

[10]"Waga kuni bōei," pp. 1–4, treats this and the following points.

[11]Sakanaka Tomohisa, *Nihon no jieriryoku* (Tokyo, 1967), pp. 52–53. *Nihon no anzen hoshō* (1967), pp. 193–202.

[12]Sakanaka, p. 59. "Waga kuni bōei," p. 6.

[13]This point is also made, somewhat less strongly in Sakanaka, p. 52, where the estimate is that, "the ammunition reserves would last no more than two weeks."

[14]"Waga kuni bōei," pp. 4, 5.

United States holds up its end of the nuclear balance, remains committed to the defense of South Korea and maintains the naval and air superiority in the Western Pacific necessary to sustain that defense. Given this favorable disposition of American forces, they believe that Japan can be secured from external attack by an explicit American guarantee reinforced by the threshold-raising Self-Defense Forces.

Several thoughtful critics of government policy have argued that with American military superiority in the Far East, Japan would be as safe from attack without American bases in the country and the Security Treaty guarantee.[15] The government's position is seldom presented in public,[16] but what it amounts to is a belief that United States forces in Japan are an essential element in the American military position in the Far East, and that their deterrent value is much greater with an explicit guarantee than without. The government does not directly challenge the argument that the United States would come to Japan's defense even without a security treaty. Their view, rather, is that the treaty and the bases make explicit the American intent to defend Japan, and serve to prevent an attack. In short, policy on external defense rests on the conviction that an ounce of deterrence is better than a pound of intervention.

THE INTERNAL THREAT

One might suppose that Japan's phenomenal economic growth in the 1950s and '60s, and its apparent political stability, signified disappearance of the internal security threat which so exercised the government in the poverty-stricken, chaotic period from the surrender until after the Korean War. There is no doubt that the present government of Prime Minister Tanaka appears less likely to be overthrown by labor disorders or by a Communist-led coup than did Yoshida's government of 1947. The mood of the labor movement, mellowed by Japan's prosperity, is less revolutionary. Communists and radical Socialists are divided and weakened by internal

disputes which have been aggravated by the Sino-Soviet split. Furthermore, the police and Self-Defense Forces are much better prepared to maintain internal security than they were during the occupation and immediate post-occupation years.

Nevertheless, the Hatoyama, Kishi, Ikeda, Sato, and Tanaka governments have continued to take the internal threat seriously; throughout the last two decades the SDF, in particular the Ground Self-Defense Forces, have been equipped, deployed and trained to maintain internal security.[17] It is true that in the late 1950s, when the first Defense Build-up Plan (1958–61) was being implemented, the Defense Agency de-emphasized the internal security mission as a consequence of their push to rapidly develop an external defense capability. Prime Minister Kishi remained concerned over the internal threat, however, and was anxious to counter it by amending the Police Duties Execution Law to widen police powers to deal with civil disorders. Whatever apathy may have developed in the Defense Agency toward internal security issues in the late 1950s was abruptly dispelled by massive demonstrations and riots in 1960 which led to Prime Minister Kishi's resignation.

Since 1960, the Defense Agency and the Self-Defense Forces have shown renewed awareness of the internal threat, and have been preparing to deal with it.[18] During the late 1960s they were spurred on by the well publicized intent of Communists, revolutionary student groups and radical Socialists to succeed in 1970 where they failed in 1960, to "overthrow" the government on the issue of continuing the Security Treaty. The war in Vietnam has turned the attention of defense planners from 1960-style disorders, which they feel confident of being able to prevent, to dealing with insurrections in the form of a protracted guerrilla war probably supported, and to some extent directed, by Peking and/or Moscow.[19] As already noted, it is anticipated that such a war of national liberation would be likely to accompany the renewal of war in Korea. This was the hypothetical threat being countered in the secret "Three Arrows Plan," leaked in 1965,[20]

[15]For example, see Rōyama Michio, "Kaku senryaku no igi to Nihon no shōrai [The Meaning of Nuclear Strategy for Japan's Future]," Chūō kōron 966 (March 1968): 50–67. Also, the record of a colloquium by Etō Shinkichi, Hoshino Yasusaburō, Kishida Junnosuke, and Murakami Kaoru, "Sekai senryaku to Nihon no anzen kōsō [World Strategy and Japan's Security]," Gendai no me 8, no. 8 (August 1967): 89–101.

[16]For example, see Saeki Kiichi, "Ajia no anzen to Nihon [Japan and the Security of Asia]," Kyokutō no anzen hoshō [The Security of the Far East] (Tokyo, 1968), pp. 9–36. Nagai Yonosuke, "Japanese Foreign Policy Objectives in a Nuclear Milieu," Journal of Social and Political Ideas in Japan 5 no. 1 (April 1967): 27–42.

[17]The socialists and communists have viewed the Self-Defense Forces since their inception as a militarist-capitalist tool, armed specifically at them. But their writings on this point, while not entirely devoid of truth, have been marred by ideological stereotypes and exaggeration. A well-informed, relatively detached and yet critical study of this question appears in Sakanaka, pp. 42–51, 72–86.

[18]Sakanaka, pp. 42–51. Nihon no anzen hoshō (1967), p. 137. Jieitai (Tokyo, 1968), pp. 56, 63.

[19]"Waga kuni bōei," pp. 35–39.

[20]Sakanaka, pp. 72–86.

which caused such an uproar in the Diet and press. It continues to be the major internal threat envisaged by the National Defense Council.

The defense planners do not see this threat materializing so long as Japan is prosperous. As the National Defense Council staff paper implies, however, and as numerous discussions with Japanese of various political persuasions confirmed, it is widely believed by Japanese that prosperity and stability are extremely fragile. The general strike attempt of 1947 has not been forgotten, and memory of it was freshened by the French general strike in May 1968. Defense planners as well as most economists and businessmen are convinced that a general strike would cripple the economy in a matter of weeks, and would be likely to undermine government authority and the parliamentary democracy which it represents. In a somewhat less dramatic but equally disastrous scenario, officials anticipate that the economy would be seriously disrupted either by a prolonged dock workers' strike or a communication workers' strike, either of which would be as effective as interdiction at sea in cutting off the flow of imported fuels and raw materials essential to Japanese industry.

One might suppose that to protect the nation from economic collapse, the government could be expected to promptly order the Defense Agency to operate the ports and railroads. This supposition, however, rests on the further assumption that the public, in particular urban industrial and white collar workers, are basically loyal to the existing parliamentary institutions, and would in a crisis uphold the legitimacy and authority of the elected government. It is exactly this assumption, however, which defense planners and many other conservatives are not willing to make. They argue that close to one-third of the voters support the Japan Socialist Party and that the Socialists, although not as unabashedly revolutionary as the Communists, are aiming at a peaceful revolution and therefore refuse to accept the legitimacy of the government.

There is, then, an ambiguity in this approach to the internal threat which reflects the government's and Defense Agency's appreciation of the delicately balanced and contradictory elements which hold a political community together, and which make government possible. Defense planners seem to believe that use of military force to protect parliamentary government may become unavoidable, and that they must be prepared for this contingency. But they do not think that Japan's internal security can be maintained simply by equipping the Ground Self-Defense Forces with helicopters and drilling them in riot control

and counter-insurrectionary tactics.[21] On the contrary, they seem painfully aware that employment of Self-Defense Forces to settle an economic-political crisis would be extremely risky, as likely to trigger an insurrection as to prevent one, and as likely to wreck Japan's political institutions as to preserve them. The defense planners fear that many Japanese would interpret use of Self-Defense Forces as an open admission by the government that their authority is not respected, that they can rule only by force. Moreover, even if the Self-Defense Forces were successful in quickly suppressing an internal disturbance, officials expect that many Japanese would interpret that success as a return to militaristic, authoritarian, prewar government. They recognize a kernel of truth in this interpretation. For if the government became dependent upon them for survival, what would prevent the Self-Defense Forces from dominating the government? Legally and organizationally the Defense Agency and SDF are under firm civilian control.[22] Most conservative politicians, businessmen and bureaucrats, including those in the Defense Agency, seem strongly opposed to revival of strong military power. But would the government be able to order the Self-Defense Forces out of politics once they had been called in? Would twenty years of civilian control offset a thousand-year tradition of military rule?[23]

No one, of course, can answer these questions with certainty, and as the following incident suggests, civilian leaders of the Defense Agency have been reluctant to experiment. In June 1960, at the height of the Security Treaty crisis, a group of Liberal-Democratic leaders are reported to have asked Defense Agency Director-General

[21]"Waga kuni bōei," p. 75. This point has also been made in a vague way in *Nihon no anzen hoshō* (1967), pp. 47–58; and (1968), p. 111.

[22]Article 66 of the Constitution states, "The Prime Minister and other Ministers of State must be civilians." Under the Defense Laws, the Defense Agency is an external organ of the Prime Minister's Office, and is subordinate to the Prime Minister. Moreover, the laws require that the Defense Agency Director-General be a civilian, and the Defense Agency, with only few exceptions, be staffed by civilian officials. The three Self-Defense Forces are headed not by commanders, but rather by staffs, each of which is subordinate to the Prime Minister and the Director-General. The Joint Staff Council, composed of the Chiefs of Staff, is the highest body of uniformed officers. It functions as an advisory body to the Director-General.

Before 1945, the War and Navy Ministers were officers on active duty and were constitutionally the equals of the Prime Minister. See Yale C. Maxon, *Control of Japanese Foreign Policy* (Berkeley: University of California Press, 1957).

[23]Fujiwara Hirotatsu and Tomita Nobuo, *Hoshu dokusai no teihen* [The Foundations of Conservative Despotism] (Tokyo, 1968), pp. 460–68. Fujiwara and Tomita have analyzed this uncertainty and lack of confidence on the basis of opinion poll data, on pp. 193–98, 273–76.

Akagi Munenori if he would use the Ground Self-Defense Force to protect the Diet and executive buildings from invasion by demonstrators and rioters. The Party leaders were surprised by Director-General Akagi Munenori's response. He was not eager to take action. On the contrary, he replied that while the Self-Defense Forces had been alerted, he was loath to commit them to action unless the police proved completely incapable of controlling the riots, or the confrontation developed into an armed insurrection.[24]

Critics of the government have explained Mr. Akagi's reaction in terms of the Defense Agency's determination to build popular support for the armed forces. The left opposition argued that Mr. Akagi wanted to suppress the disorders, but hesitated because he was afraid to damage the image of "the people's Self-Defense Forces"—an image necessary to rebuild the nationalist, militarist spirit upon which a future military takeover must be based.[25] Rightist critics accused Defense Agency bureaucrats of using the armed forces as a "toy," placing their own ambitions above the safety and order of the country.[26] Most illuminating is the general agreement that Mr. Akagi's determination to avoid intervention was based on his concern over the popular response to use of the SDF for suppressing internal disorders.

Judging from the perilous situation in which the government found itself in 1960, it is not surprising that twelve years later in 1972, only four of the thirteen GSDF divisions are stationed on Hokkaido against external attack, while the remaining nine divisions are deployed in heavily populated areas close to major cities and industrial complexes where they can better counter any internal threat.[27] Nor is it surprising that defense planners take the position that ultimately Japan's security depends on its political stability, which in turn, must derive from a sense of national loyalty of the people.[28]

The SDF is the government's last resort in a showdown with the antiparliamentary and radical opposition. For the Ground Self-Defense Forces, in particular, the maintenance of internal security remains the basic mission. Official policy seems to assume that by being well equipped,

carefully trained and properly deployed, the GSDF can prevent the very insurrection they are preparing to crush.

THE LEVEL OF DEFENSE EXPENDITURES

The contention that the government has continued to view the Self-Defense Forces as a necessary but subordinate element in its defense policy is supported not only by its strategic estimates and plans but also and perhaps more decisively by its defense budget. Examination of Japanese defense budgets as compared to GNP and total government budgets shows that while defense budgets have more than quadrupled ($372 million in 1954 to $1.86 billion in 1972), the defense budget has shown a steady decline as a percentage of GNP and total government spending (1.72% and 12.87% in 1954; .80% and 7.13% in 1971). (See Table 2.) The absolute increase reflects the building of the SDF, from an internal security force into one capable of participating in external defense, and also rising prices of modern weapons. On the other hand, the decreasing proportion of both GNP and the government budget devoted to defense, as well as extremely low level of defense expenditures, indicates that expansion of the Self-Defense Forces has not been pushed to the limits permitted by economic and domestic political considerations.

There is no doubt that public opposition to rearmament and the high priority assigned to economic growth have set limits to the level of defense spending. However, these decreasing percentages indicate that defense spending has not approached these limits. The war-weary, demoralized, economically insecure Japanese of 1954, could devote 1.72% of their Gross National Product and 12.87% of their taxes to defense; revitalized, confident and increasingly affluent Japanese of the 1970s could do at least as much, if the government were asking them to.

This does not suggest that the voters have been willing to amend Article IX, build nuclear weapons, raise the Defense Agency to a ministry or to dispatch Japanese forces overseas. All these imply huge defense outlays not to speak of a restoration of the military establishment, authoritarian government and a disastrously aggressive foreign policy. Public opinion polls show that such measures have been highly unpopular.[29]

---

[24]Sakanaka, p. 44. Also see Shinobu Seizaburō, *Ampo tōsō shi* [History of the Treaty Struggle] (Tokyo, 1962), pp. 418, 465.

[25]*Ibid.*, pp. 418, 465.

[26]Hokugo Gentaro (pseudonym), "Kaihara kanbōchō nō seppuku [Secretary-General Kaihara's Suicide]," *Gunji kenkyū* (November 1966): 132–37.

[27]*Bōei nenkan* (1972). Map inside front cover shows disposition of all thirteen divisions. Sakanaka, pp. 44–50, 51, discusses troop strength, weapons, training, etc.

[28]*Ibid.*, Table I-6. "Waga kuni bōei," p. 74.

[29]For public opinion poll data on these issues up to 1960, see Douglas H. Mendel, *The Japanese People and Foreign Policy* (Berkeley: Univerity of California Press, 1961), pp. 68–101. For results of more recent polls see Fujiwara and Tomita, pp. 460–68. This book is an analysis of opinion polls

Table 2. Comparison of Japanese Defense Budgets, Government Budgets and Gross National Product (billions of U.S. dollars)

	Defense Budgets (A)	Government Budgets (B)	Gross National Product (C)	A/B%	A/C%
1954	.372	2.89	21.65	12.87	1.72
1955	.356	2.83	24.40	12.58	1.46
1956	.367	2.97	27.48	12.36	1.33
1957	.417	3.30	31.13	12.64	1.33
1958	.410	3.70	31.99	11.08	1.28
1959	.427	4.15	37.16	10.29	1.15
1960	.438	4.90	44.55	8.94	0.98
1961	.503	6.01	53.63	8.37	0.94
1962	.594	7.12	58.86	8.34	1.01
1963	.688	8.49	68.71	8.10	1.00
1964	.780	9.28	79.40	8.41	.98
1965	.848	10.40	87.08	8.16	.97
1966	.959	12.43	101.87	7.71	.94
1967	1.075	14.45	118.56	7.44	.91
1968	1.173	16.16	132.89	7.25	.88
1969	1.375	19.25	173.43	7.14	.79
1970	1.640	22.82	201.93	7.19	.81
1971	1.864	26.15	234.22	7.13	.80

Note: Currency conversions have been computed at 360 Yen equals one dollar. The Yen was revalued at 308 Yen to a dollar in 1972.

Defense, budgets and government budgets are Defense Agency statistics. The data for 1954–61 were taken from Kajima kenkyu jo, *Nihon no anzen hoshō* [Japan's Security Policy] (Tokyo, 1964), p. 941; for 1962–68, from *Bōei nenkan* (1968), p. 350; for 1969–71 from *Jietai nenkan* (1972), pp. 590–91.

Gross National Product figures are Economic Planning Agency (EPA) statistics, extracted from *Asahi nenkan*, Economic Sections, volumes for 1964 through 1968. *Bōei nenkan* (1968), p. 350, uses identical Gross National Product figures for 1961–68.

It should be noted that since 1965, the EPA has been using revised methods for computing Gross National Product, which result in higher figures than the pre-1965 methods. For example the pre-1965 statistics show Gross National Product for 1962 as 39.74 billion dollars as compared to 58.86 billion dollars above. The result of these statistical revisions, of course, is that the percentage of Gross National Product devoted to defense is even less than previously believed. Thus, *Nihon no anzen hoshō*, p. 941, shows A/C for 1962 to be 1.4%, while *Bōei nenkan* (1968), p. 350, using the revised Gross National Product shows A/C for 1962 to be 1.01%, as does the above table.

These same polls also show that a majority believe that conventional, strictly defensive forces are necessary, and that they neither violate the Consitution nor create an intolerable tax burden. This suggests that if the government had wanted to buy more jet fighters, helicopters, destroyers, tanks or ammunition for the Self-Defense Forces, it could have done so without great political risk.

Moreover, it is hard to believe that Japan's phenomenal rate of economic growth would have been noticeably slowed if defense spending had been held at the 1954 or 1958 level. Prime Ministers Hatoyama, Kishi, Ikeda, Sato, and Tanaka, nevertheless, have permitted defense spending levels to slip lower and lower, apparently being satisfied that their defense budgets have met

Japan's military needs, especially as these needs have been conceived within their overall defense policy.

There has, naturally, been disagreement within the government over the level of defense spending. As one might expect, the Defense Agency has tried to increase its budgets, annually wrangling with the Finance Ministry over the exact amount. More importantly, long-range levels of defense spending have been set in the Defense Build-up Plans. Available evidence shows that in 1961, when the Second Plan (1962–66) was adopted, and again in 1966–67 when the Third Plan (1967–72) was settled on, Defense Agency Director-Generals argued in the National Defense Council and in the Cabinet for an increase of defense expenditures up to 2% of the GNP.[30] This amounted to a request for a 100% in-

including the raw data. Doi, pp. 73–83. Also "Nihon no bōei— Anata wa dore o erabu (Japan's Defense—What Do You Choose?)," *Shukan Asahi* (April 5, 1968): 22–37. (This account also includes a well written note on methods and samplings.)

[30]For an account of the debate in 1961, see Weinstein, Master's thesis, Columbia University, 1965, "Rebuilding Japan's Armed Forces," pp. 36–39. The 1966-67 controversy is

Table 3. International Comparison of Levels of Defense Expenditures, 1965

Country	Gross National Product (GNP) ($ Billions)	Defense Expenditures as Percentage of Gross National Product
United States	1,073	7.3
Soviet Union	536	11.0
Japan	234	.8
West Germany	210	2.8
France	170	3.1
United Kingdom	130	4.7
Italy	104	2.6
China (Mainland)	90	10.0
India	49	3.4
Poland	45	5.2

Note: This table is compiled from data in *The Military Balance, 1972-1973* (London, International Institute for Strategic Studies (IISS), 1972. Because of the lack of dependable governmental statistics on Soviet and Mainland Chinese defense budgets, the figures for these two countries are necessarily uncertain approximations. The figures for Japan are from Table 2 above, and are slightly different than the IISS data, which gives Japan's GNP as $255 Billion, defense expenditures at $1.86 Billion, for a percentage figure of 0.7.

crease in the defense budget. To support their request for a larger cut of the GNP, Defense Agency spokesmen pointed to Japan's economic growth, extremely low levels of defense spending and to reductions in the United States forces in and around Japan. On both occasions, the Defense Agency was opposed by the Finance Ministry, Ministry of International Trade and Industry, and Economic Planning Agency. They argued that the present rate of SDF expansion satisfied Japan's needs within the Security Treaty framework, and fulfilled Japan's obligations under the 1954 Mutual Defense Assistance Agreement. A higher rate of defense spending was, they claimed, unnecessary, and might interfere with their plans for economic growth.

In 1961, 1967, and 1972, the economic planners prevailed, but not simply because economic growth had played a key role in shaping Japanese policy. Just as importantly, the Defense-Agency Director-Generals were unable to convince the Prime Ministers and their Cabinet colleagues that 2% rather than 1% of the GNP was necessary to build and maintain the threshold-raising internal security forces called for in Japan's defense policy. In brief, economic planners and Defense Agency spokesmen seem to have been in general agreement on defense policy and strategy, differing only on how much money has been necessary to build forces capable of im-

plementing this strategy. Thus, given the success of the government's security treaty diplomacy and apparent effectiveness of the Self-Defense Forces in carrying out their limited mission, it has been difficult for the Defense Agency to make a strong case for a larger share of the budget.

It seems fair to say that the limited role and small budget of both Defense Agency and SDF cannot simply be accounted for by the Japanese Government's preoccupation with economic growth, and the public's pacifism and opposition to rearmament. Of at least equal importance, the size, equipment, organization, training and deployment of the Self-Defense Forces have been consistent with overall defense policy. The defense establishment has reflected the government estimates of external and internal threats to Japan's security, and its strategic judgment on the forces necessary to counter these threats.

STRATEGY VS. STRUCTURE

The defense policy described in this study is also meaningful in terms of the theory of defense policy and its formulation. According to Huntington:

The most distinctive, the most fascinating, and the most troublesome aspect of military policy is its Janus-like quality. Indeed, military (defense) policy not only faces in two directions, it exists in two worlds. One is international politics, the world of the balance of power, wars, and alliances, the subtle and the brutal uses of force and diplomacy to influence the behavior of other states. The principal currency of this world is actual or potential military strength; battalions, weap-

covered in Maeda Hisashi, "Nihon no bōei seisaku [Japan's Defense Policy]," Asahi Newspaper Security Policy Research Council Report No. 20 (July 1, 1967). A less detailed version of this study appears in Sakanaka, pp. 225–62. It should be noted on the Fourth Plan that the Defense Agency scaled its budget projections down to 1% of GNP by spring of 1970.

ons and warships. The other world is domestic politics, the world of interest groups, political parties and social classes, with their conflicting interests and goals. The currency here is the resources of society: men, money, material.[31]

Military policy can be roughly divided into strategy and structure. Decisions made in the categories or currency of international politics may be described as *strategic* in character. Strategy concerns the units and uses of force. More precisely, strategic decisions may be subdivided into two broad divisions: 1) program decisions concerning the strength of military forces, their composition and readiness, and the number, type and rate of development, commitment, and deployment of their weapons; and 2) use decisions concerning the deployment, commitment, and employment of military force, and manifested in military alliances, war plans, force movements, and the like. A strategic concept identifies a particular need and implicitly or explicitly prescribes decisions on the uses, strengths, and weapons of the armed services. *Structural* decisions, on the other hand, are made in the currency of domestic politics. They deal with procurement, allocation, and organization of men, money, and material which go into the strategic units and uses of force. Among the more important types of structural decisions are: 1) budget decisions concerning the size and distribution of funds made available to the armed forces; 2) personnel decisions concerning the number, procurement, retention, pay, and working conditions of members of the military services; 3) material decisions concerning the amount, procurement and distribution of supplies to the armed forces; and 4) organizational decisions concerning the methods and forms by which the military services are organized and administered.[32]

The history of military (defense) policy, like that of other areas of public policy, can be divided into phases of controversy and change (or disequilibrium) and phases of harmony and stability (or equilibrium). Military policy is in equilibrium when: 1) no sharp conflicts exist among the dominant goals of domestic policy, military policy, and foreign policy; and 2) no major changes in policy are taking place.[33]

In his study of American defense policy in the 1950s, Huntington found that the strategic-structural relationship in this country was marked by conflict and instability—that our policy was an uneasy compromise between what our strategists believed were the forces and weapons necessary to protect us against the Soviets and Communist Chinese, and the determination of our economic planners to curb inflation and reduce taxes.

Placed against Huntington's model, Japanese policy has been characterized by extraordinary harmony and stability. When formulated in 1947 and first implemented in the early 1950s, it appears to have been shaped primarily by strategic considerations. This is not surprising. Mr. Yoshida and Mr. Ashida had served most of their lives in the Imperial Japanese Foreign Ministry. The world of international politics was more familiar and congenial to them, especially to Mr. Yoshida, than that of domestic politics. Moreover, the evidence of this study suggests that for these men, Japan's fate in the postwar world depended first and foremost upon the proper course being set in foreign and defense policy. They seem to have believed that economic recovery, and social and political stability depended above all on forming the right relationship with the United States, and on rebuilding Japan's foreign trade. During the late 1950s and through the 1960s, the high priority assigned by the government to rapid economic growth no doubt reinforced the existing strategy and produced the seemingly unshakeable harmony between strategy and structure that still prevails today.

The obvious key to this harmony has been the exceedingly small demands made on the economy by the Yoshida-Ashida strategy. It is clear from the Huntington book, that when strategy translates into huge budget requests and expensive, lucrative procurement contracts, it will unavoidably become the object of domestic political and economic concern. In a nutshell, so long as the government's strategy costs less than one percent of the Gross National Product, and less than 10% of the taxpayers' yen, there is not likely to be a strategic-structural conflict in Japan.

Useful as Huntington's model is, however, it is not entirely adequate to describe Japan's defense policy, or the policy of most states. For in the Huntington model, a state's armed forces are conceived as defense solely against external attack. In this study, however, it is apparent that the Japanese government has seen its defense policy and its armed forces as a means of countering both internal and external threats to national security. Indeed, when their policy was first made in 1947, it seems to have been based on the belief that the internal threat was greater than the external threat. As a consequence, it seemed perfectly reasonable to Prime Minister Yoshida and Foreign Minister Ashida to propose a "mutual" defense agreement with the United

---

[31]Samuel P. Huntington, *The Common Defense* (New York: Columbia University Press, 1961), p. 1. See also the excerpt in this volume pp. 107–12. In his first note on Chapter I, Huntington writes that his *strategy-structure* model parallels that drawn by Charles H. Donnelly in his annual surveys of *United States Defense Policies*, and also is derived from Paul H. Nitze, "Atoms, Strategy and Policy," *Foreign Affairs* (January 1956): 187–88; and Roger Hilsman, "The Foreign Policy Consensus: An Interim Research Report," *Journal of Conflict Resolution* (December 1959): 376–77.

[32]*Ibid.*, pp. 3, 4.

[33]*Ibid.*, p. 7.

States, while asking our government to assume virtually the entire burden of Japan's external defense. For in undertaking to maintain internal security and to prevent a Soviet-Communist take-over of Japan from within, they believed themselves to be shouldering a comparable burden, and to be performing a vital service for the United States.

Since the Huntington model grew out of a study of American defense policy in the 1950s, this limitation is understandable. During the 1950s there was no serious internal threat to American national security—certainly none that was likely to require the use within the country of the armed forces. It would appear, however, that most governments in the world are as concerned over internal as external security; that the two are in many cases closely related; and that the armed forces play an important role in both. This is true in China, on Taiwan, in Korea, Latin America, Africa, Southeast Asia, in the Soviet Union and throughout Eastern Europe. It also seems to be the case in Greece, Spain, and perhaps France as well. One has only to recall President de Gaulle's conference with his military commanders in West Germany during the general strike in 1968. And one wonders in this regard, whether racial and student violence in this country may not be changing the Huntington definition of defense for us.

THE ALLOCATION OF NOT-SO-SCARCE RESOURCES

Lastly, the conception and implementation of Japan's defense policy suggest that the government, throughout the postwar period, has approached the problem of national security very much in accordance with the general prescriptions set down by Hitch and McKean in *The Economics of Defense in the Nuclear Age*.[34] Although this may seem paradoxical after giving so much emphasis to strategy, it is not, for:

Economics is not exclusively concerned . . . with certain types of activities (industrial) rather than others (military), or with traditional points of view of budgeteers and comptrollers. Being truly economical does not mean scrimping—reducing expenditures no matter how important the things to be bought. Nor does it mean implementing some stated doctrine regardless of cost. Rather economics is concerned with allocating resources—choosing doctrines and techniques—so as to get the most out of available resources. To economize

in this sense may imply spending less on some things and more on others. But always economics or economizing means trying to make the most efficient use of the resources available in all activities and in any circumstances.[35]

Using this definition, there is no conflict between strategy and economics. On the contrary, defense policy becomes the application of economics to the problem of national security— choosing among alternative strategies and forces the ones that make the most efficient use of available resources. Hitch and McKean hoped to convert our Congresssmen, generals and comptrollers to this approach, and by so doing to end our strategic-structural conflict, our squabbling over absolute budget ceilings and indispensable weapon systems.

In Japan, no such injunction has been necessary. Throughout the postwar period, the Prime Ministers, Foreign Ministers and the small group of advisers who have helped them to make defense policy, seem to have understood that: "National security . . . depends on three things: (1) the quantity of national resources available, *now and in the future*; (2) the proportion of these resources allocated to national security purposes; and (3) the efficiency with which the resources so allocated are used."[36]

The evidence presented suggests that in addition to taking steps to deal with the immediate problem of how to defend Japan, the government has also made a conscious effort to minimize the proportion of resources allocated to national security, in order to maximize total resources available *in the future*. In 1947, in 1951, and again in 1954, when the Mutual Defense Assistance Agreement was concluded, the government explicitly argued that Japan's security depended first and foremost on economic recovery. They were saying to the United States, in effect, that the resources then available were not adequate to permit a meaningful military effort, and that therefore, the most satisfactory strategy they could afford was one which placed the primary responsibility for Japan's external defense upon the United States, while they devoted themselves to developing the economic resources necessary to take on this task in the future.

Judging from the success of Japan's economic recovery, and its rapid rate of economic growth, it is tempting to conclude that during the last decade Japan has developed a large enough economic base to enable the government to build much more powerful forces than it has, and to

---

[34]Charles J. Hitch and Roland M. McKean, *The Economics of Defense in the Nuclear Age* (New York: Atheneum Press, 1965).

[35]*Ibid.*, p. 1.
[36]*Ibid.*, p. 4. (Italics added.)

take over the burden of its external defense from the United States. Quite apart from the question of public opposition to large-scale rearmament, however, the Japanese government seems to have taken the view that there is no strategy in sight equal or superior to the present one, which the bigger forces they might build could serve.

As the strategic discussions in the previous sections indicate, the defense planners still see Japan as caught between the super-powers, almost as vulnerable militarily and economically as in 1947. Despite Peking's nuclear missile program, the government does not seem to think that Communist China will pose a serious external threat to Japan during the 1970s, unless the Sino-Soviet rift were suddenly to close. For China still does not have the naval and air forces to threaten Japan, and their missile forces are very small compared to the Soviet arsenal, which is offset by the American deterrent. Although Japan now ranks third in Gross National Product in the world, the United States and the Soviet Union are still far out in the lead economically. The Japanese defense planners know that Japan has the necessary economic and technological base to build a *force de frappe*. But most of them do not agree with General Gallois' strategy,[37] and none of them believes that Japan can afford to build a force of offensive missiles, or an ABM system powerful enough to protect Japan against the Soviet or American nuclear arsenals.

They could probably buy conventional naval, air and land forces strong enough to enable Japan to single-handedly repulse a Soviet conventional attack. But so long as the United States is committed to the defense of South Korea, and

seems likely to retain its naval and air superiority in the Western Pacific, such forces seem to them to be an unnecessary duplication of effort. Finally, the concern of the defense planners over the possibility of interdiction of Japan's maritime shipping indicates that the government today is as keenly aware as Mr. Yoshida and Mr. Ashida were in the 1930s, that: (1) Japan's economic survival depends on access to distant resources and markets (oil from the Persian Gulf, iron ore from Australia and India, timber from Canada, just to mention a few); and (2) that Japan is still far from having the resources to build the naval and air forces required to protect this essential shipping in the event of a protracted war. Only American naval and air power seem capable of performing this mission.

As in 1947, Japan cannot defend herself against either of the super-powers. The United States can still defend Japan against the Soviet Union (and Communist China). No one can defend Japan against the United States. In short, despite their greatly increased resources, it is still difficult for the Japanese government to see a reasonable alternative to their present strategy and defense arrangements. The defense budget may, on occasion, appear embarrassingly tiny, but it buys the forces necessary to implement the present policy. Just as importantly, the government believes that this tiny defense budget, by being tiny, contributes to the economic growth rate. They have been and they continue to minimize the proportion of resources allocated to national defense, in order to maximize the quantity of resources available in the future.

Why choose a new strategy and buy bigger forces now, when the old, inexpensive strategy remains the best available? Better instead to hang on to the old strategy, use the savings to build the Gross National Product as rapidly as possible, so that if and when in the future it becomes necessary to buy a replacement, there may be enough resources to buy one as least as good.

---

[37]The views prevailing in the government on an independent nuclear force and the awareness of and reaction to General Gallois' ideas are presented in *Nihon no Anzen Hoshō* (1967), pp. 13–18, and also in Saeki's "Ajia no Anzen Hoshō to Nihon." A thoughtful Japanese proponent of a *force de frappe* is former General Doi Akio, who recently published his strategic views in *Shin Senryaku to Nihon* [The New Strategy and Japan].

FORCE POSTURE: INDIA AND PAKISTAN

LORNE J. KAVIC

Professor Kavic has provided a tightly reasoned, well-organized study of the determinants of force posture in India and Pakistan from the time of partition to the present. His analysis provides insight into the strategic context, the external dependency relationships, the internal situational environments, the economic context, and the policymaking impact of various individuals and groups on the determination of force structure in both countries. Like the articles by both Greenwood and Kemp in this section, Kavic's is comparative within itself and provides another example of how the force postures of different countries—in this case, geographically proximate rivals—can be more comprehensively understood in a comparative perspective.

Professor Kavic is Sessional Lecturer in Political Science, University of British Columbia. Since completing his baccalaureate in 1959, he has served as a Foreign Service Officer in Canada's Department of External Affairs and completed a Ph.D. in International Relations at the Australian National University. He is author of India's Quest for Security: Defence Policies 1947-65 *(1967) and many articles.*

During the period of Crown rule (1858–1947), the Indian peoples lived united under one paramount rule and in unexampled security from internal disorder and external aggression. Great power rivalries, skillful British manipulation of the balance of power, and British naval domination of the Indian Ocean minimized the possibility of a serious threat to India, and the only continuing threat perceived involved militant tribes in the northwest, Afghanistan and Russia. In accordance with India's meager financial resources, its military liabilities were generally limited to internal security, tribal control on the frontiers, and defense against a minor power like Afghanistan and against a major power like Russia, pending the arrival of imperial aid. Decisions regarding force posture were heavily influenced by budgetary constraints.[1]

FORCE STRUCTURE PRIOR TO PARTITION

Indian nationalists developed a general disbelief in the possibility of any Russian invasion and a marked tendency to minimize the threats posed by Afghanistan and the tribals on the North-West Frontier, and to attribute much of the problem to the imperialist urges of British authorities. But the need for armed forces was readily acknowledged, and tentative conclusions of the interim government, which took office in September 1946, envisaged an annual outlay on defense of about Rs 110 crores for a military program involving a well-equipped and mobile army of about 200,000 men backed by a reserve and a large territorial army, a balanced air force of 20 squadrons, and a small naval task force built around 3 light cruisers and including 2 aircraft carriers. In accordance with India's weak finances and her pressing problems of internal development, her military liability was restricted to the roles discharged under the Raj, the intervention of friendly powers in the event of an attack by a major country like the Soviet Union or China being regarded as well-nigh axiomatic.[2] The defense planning of the interim government was undercut, however, by partition simultaneous with the formal withdrawal of British power from the subcontinent. The events surrounding partition created grave suspicions and intense animosities between the 2 states, aborting con-

[1]For further details, see Lorne J. Kavic, *India's Quest for Security: Defence Policies, 1947–1965* (Berkeley and Los Angeles: University of California Press, 1967), pp. 8–20.

[2]*Ibid.*, pp. 21–31.

This is an original article written for this volume and the Conference on Comparative Defense Policy held at the Air Force Academy, February 7–9, 1973. Copyright reserved by the author.

sideration of joint defense arrangements and causing both governments to prepare for possible renewed hostilities.

THE STRATEGIC CONTEXT OF INDIAN FORCE PLANNING

In the prevailing geopolitical context down to the traumatic events of October-November 1962, Pakistan constituted the only direct threat that the Indian people and their elected representatives were prepared to acknowledge. Its Islamic character was regarded as constituting a challenge to the secular basis of the Union, while its bitter sense of grievance over Kashmir confronted India with a range of possible contingencies, of which the most likely was believed to be another effort to wrest Kashmir from Indian control. The situation provoked some alarmism in sections of Indian opinion, especially after Pakistan began receiving United States military aid and acquired membership in the Central Treaty Organization and the Southeast Asia Treaty Organization. Most Indians, however, continued to manifest a general smugness regarding their national security, given the perceived weaknesses and vulnerabilities of the smaller Pakistani state and the assumption that Pakistan's Western allies would not support an 'aggressive' policy toward India but would act to effect an early cessation of any renewed hostilities.

The Himalayan conflict in 1962 jolted Indians out of their relative complacency about the nation's security. It brought into focus a grave threat in a quarter where geography had been regarded as an almost insurmountable barrier to serious attack by land, and from a country on which Indian official and popular views had been more wishful than reasoned. It evidenced that neither India's size and supposed importance, nor the balance of power thesis precluded a limited conflict in which an aggressor could initiate hostilities and terminate action at will, and without interference by the great powers. It exposed an unreal preoccupation with the 'historical ghost' of Muslim Pakistan to the detriment of suitable adjustments to accord with the changing geopolitics in the Himalayan region. It created momentous new problems involving a major power along a 2800-mile border broken only by several powerless kingdoms, while aggravating rather than alleviating existing ones with a minor power, Pakistan. It appeared to force India to contemplate a spectrum of threats embracing insurgency, limited conventional war with Pakistan, limited conventional war with China, collaborative conventional attack by

Pakistan and China, and nuclear blackmail-cum-coercion from China.

During the decade which has elapsed since India's Himalayan debacle, official and public perceptions of threats to the national security have been characterized by reduced concern for several contingencies involving Pakistan, adjustments as regards the nature of the Chinese threat, and an increasing tendency to suspect possible collusion among the United States, China, and the Soviet Union aimed at denying India her 'rightful' role in regional and world affairs. Concern regarding contingencies involving the 'historical ghost' gradually eased as India's military build-up proceeded after 1962, the conflict in 1965 demonstrating India's ability to contain Pakistan's offensive capability, with 1971 witnessing Pakistan's decisive military defeat and reduction to its western wing. The specter of a joint onslaught by Pakistan and China failed to materialize in either 1965 or 1971 and, while it continues to hold a certain fascination for some Indians, it is widely regarded as being a remote prospect given Pakistan's weakened state and the existence of the twenty-year Indo-Soviet treaty of peace, friendship and cooperation. The dreaded image of an endless sea of Chinese soldiers flooding over the Himalayas bent on destruction of the Indian Union remains deeply imbedded among the unsophisticated majority of Indians, but more knowledgeable circles are inclined to regard such a contingency as beyond China's capabilities and interests; more seriously viewed is the possibility of China acting on the strategic options available to her in the Himalayan kingdoms, and among the restless tribals of the northeast—Indian officials being haunted by the specter of a major and coordinated insurgency by well-armed and -trained tribals, with considerable opinion viewing this as China's most attractive option in the intermediate term. Even more alarming is the prospect of a pro-Chinese 'satellite' in Bangladesh should the new nation fail to manage its severe problems.

Indian views about Chinese nuclear options being exercised against their country range from disbelief through qualified concern to presumptions of inevitability. The contingency has been dismissed on the grounds that China's conventional superiority over India is so marked as to rule out the necessity of nuclear weaponry,[3] that China could not usefully employ tactical

---

[3]D. R. Manekar, "Avoid Nuclear Folly," *Swarajya* (Annual Number 1965): 806-d. For similar views see Major-General P. S. Bhagat, *Forging the Shield* (New Delhi, The Statesman): 3, 8; P. N. Dhar, director of the Institute of Economic Growth (Delhi), cited in *Statesman* (May 29, 1969).

nuclear weapons in the Himalayan region,[4] and that a Chinese nuclear attack on India would mean world war.[5] Majority sentiment, however, has challenged the credibility of all these assumptions. There is a fairly widespread belief that neither of the two superpowers would risk a nuclear confrontation with China solely on India's behalf once China acquires the means to strike at their homelands.[6] Doubts have also been expressed regarding Moscow's willingness to employ nuclear weapons against a fellow communist power on behalf of a non-communist India,[7] the value of implicit guarantees from a Britain withdrawing militarily from Asia and a United States manifesting disenchantment with military commitments in the region,[8] and the relevance of an external deterrent to Chinese use of tactical nuclear weapons in a restricted sense.[9] Perceived trends in the policies of the nuclear powers over the past several years have tended to strengthen rather than to alleviate these fears, resulting in the considerable disquiet and no little alarm with which most Indians view a disciplined, powerful and nuclear China.

Indians have never been unmindful of the regional and global incidence of their security, and nationalists have long attributed many of South Asia's problems to what has been described as "manipulation of historical hangovers or differences inherent in traditional societies by outside powers."[10] Long a factor in Indian responses to Western alignment with, and provision of large-scale military aid to, Pakistan, this sentiment has been strongly manifested towards Chinese and Soviet policies in the subcontinent during the past decade. In a larger sense, Indians have displayed a strong belief that the Non-Proliferation Treaty is but a device by which the nuclear powers are seeking to maintain their nuclear hegemony and deny India its rightful major power status in world affairs. Girilal Jain, a publicist, suspects that "something in the nature of 'Pax Sovietica Americana' is sought to be established."[11] M. S. Venkataramani, a professor of American Studies at the Indian School of International Affairs, has written that "the United States and the Soviet Union are jointly and separately striving to keep India frozen in its present power posture vis-à-vis themselves and other Asian countries . . . ,"[12] while economist Subramaniam Swamy has charged that the great powers recognize that India is the only power capable of challenging their hegemony, and that the Non-Proliferation Treaty is one instrument by which they seek to reduce India's potentiality.[13]

THE STRATEGIC CONTEXT OF PAKISTANI FORCE PLANNING

Pakistan's defense problems, by comparison, have been massive from the outset. Its government has had the onerous task of securing against external aggression two utterly dissimilar wings 1,000 miles apart, the historic North-West Frontier, 'exterior' boundaries with Iran, Burma, and China, and 'interior' borders with India extending for over 3,000 miles. The security of the 'exterior' frontiers has generally proven unproblematical as the tribals have remained quiescent and seemingly loyal to their citizenship in a Muslim Pakistan, relations with Burma, China, and Iran have remained correct to excellent, and Afghanistan's fluctuating campaign for a 'Pakhtoonistan' has not been viewed as representing a serious or immediate threat to the integrity of the state. The threat from India, however, has been consistently viewed with alarm since partition, given its perceived perfidy in Kashmir and long-term intent to establish hegemony within the subcontinent preparatory to eventual reabsorption of Pakistan into a larger Hindustan. The magnitude of the threat has caused Pakistani leaders to be particularly receptive to exploiting opportunities for alignment with other powers which directly or indirectly strengthen their countries diplomatic and military position vis-à-vis her more powerful

[4]Major-General D. Som Dutt (retd.), *The Defense of India's Northern Borders*, Adelphi Papers No. 25 (London: International Institute for Strategic Studies, 1966), p. 9. See also, J. N. Chaudhuri, who served as Chief of Army Staff from 1962 to 1966, *Arms, Aims and Aspects* (Bombay: Manektala, 1966), p. 115.

[5]See the statement by Prime Minister Lal B. Shastri at the Durgapur session of the All-India Congress Committee in January 1965, cited in Congress Bulletin, January–March 1965, p. 49.

[6]See J. K. Ray, *Security in the Missile Age* (Bombay: Allied Publishers, 1967); H. M. Patel, "Deterrence," *Seminar* 83 (July 1966): 28–9; Major-General D. K. Palit (retd.), *War in the Deterrent Age* (London: MacDonald & Co., 1966), pp. 176–85.

[7]See J. Kripilani, "Need for a Foreign Policy of National Self-Interest," *Swarajya* (Annual Number 1965): 81–83; John Grigg, "India Must Turn Nuclear," *Hindustan Times* (April 19, 1968); Major-General D. K. Palit, *loc. cit.*

[8]See John Grigg, *loc. cit.*; and C. Rajagopalachari, "Shall India Make Her Own H-Bomb?," *Swarajya* 13, no. 17 (October 26, 1968): 1–2.

[9]Bishwaneth Singh, "National Defense in the Nuclear Age: Dilemma of India," *Political Scientist* II, no. 2 (January–June 1966): 1–17.

[10]M. J. Desai in Tang Tsou (ed.), *China in Crisis*, vol. II (Chicago: Chicago University Press, 1968), p. 439.

[11]"Russo-American Duopoly," *Times of India* (May 5, 1968): 6.

[12]"Converging Interests," *Seminar* 96 (August 1967): 31–35.

[13]"System Analysis of Strategic Defense Needs," *Economic and Political Weekly* (February 22, 1969): 402.

neighbor. Circumstances have also dictated a willingness to adjust external relationships to accord with shifts in the policies of the major powers towards Indo-Pakistan relations. In the mid-'fifties, Pakistan capitalized upon Western desires to contain Soviet and Chinese communism to secure membership in CENTO and SEATO and large-scale United States military aid. In response to India's major military build-up after 1962 and a perceived weakening of United States partisanship, President Ayub Khan sought compensatory advantage through normalization of relations with China and Moscow, a shift which was strengthened by Washington's 'neutral' stance during the 1965 Indo-Pakistan conflict and subsequent reluctance to resume grant arms aid. The resultant 'triangular tightrope' based on Soviet arms aid, Chinese diplomatic support and United States economic assistance failed, however, to prevent Pakistan's crushing defeat and bifurcation in 1971. This second partition has tended to confirm, in Pakistani minds, their long-standing fears of Indian intent. The Indian threat has assumed almost overwhelming dimensions while credible counterweights have become more speculative then ever before.

EXTERNAL DEPENDENCY
RELATIONSHIPS

The dependence of India and Pakistan upon the developed countries for concessional assistance and debt relief, advanced technology and military arms and equipment has always been marked.

Foreign economic aid, while modest in terms of the total incomes of India and Pakistan, has been crucial to their economic growth, given their acute development needs and chronic foreign exchange problems.[14] It has constituted a vital element in the total investments made in the five-year economic plans undertaken by both countries, consequently increasing the amount available for consumption and for investment.[15] It has financed a considerable proportion of their imports of essential capital goods, fertilizers and food, accounting for 35 percent and 30 percent of the imports of India and Pakistan, respectively, in 1967, and for an annual average of 33 percent

and 37.5 percent, respectively, in 1968–70. India has benefited modestly, and Pakistan in a major way, from Western military aid, India obtaining about $100 million worth from the United States, Britain, and the 'old Commonwealth' following the conflict with China in 1962, and Pakistan receiving over $1,500 million worth of United States military assistance in 1954–65. Foreign-controlled firms are prominent in both countries in technologically sophisticated fields of direct relevance to defense such as petrochemicals, pharmaceuticals, data processing, and communications.

Both countries have remained heavily dependent upon military equipment of foreign manufacture or design. Due to her weak industrial base, Pakistan has had little choice but to accept an almost total foreign dependency primarily upon arms and equipment of United States origin, although circumstance has required the acquisition of Soviet, French and Chinese equipment since 1965. India has been consciously and progressively reducing its external dependency since independence, at which time about 90 percent of her military equipment and stores was imported, largely from Britain. But India still remains heavily dependent upon external sources for much sophisticated equipment, for designs, vital armaments components, and many of the vital chemicals and intermediates required for the manufacture of ammunition and explosives. Soviet, British, American, and French assistance has figured prominently in defense electronics; India's missile program is proceeding with French collaboration; India's nuclear reactors and much of her nuclear information comes from Canada and the United States; the navy and air force remain acutely dependent upon foreign procurement; and the army's primary tank, the 'Vijayanta', is of British design and some of its vital components are imported.

The impact of this foreign dependence on Pakistani force posture has been clearly of major significance, and of lesser but still substantial importance to the force levels developed by the Indian Union. External economic assistance has both stimulated economic growth and released local resources for disbursement on the armed forces with a consequent easing of the defense burden on the struggling economies of India and Pakistan. United States military aid enabled Pakistan to develop a military establishment considerably in excess of local economic capability, while Western 'emergency' military aid to India following her conflict with China in 1962 had a value considerably in excess of its assessed 'book

[14]For some brief but pertinent observations, see *Partners in Development: Report of the Commission on International Development* (London: Praeger, 1969), pp. 282–317.

[15]Foreign aid, for example, represented 5.9 percent of total investment in India's First Five-Year Plan, 13.2 percent in the Second Plan, 16.9 percent in the Third Plan, and an estimated 10 percent in the Fourth Plan, and has averaged $1,500 million per annum during the past decade.

price'. The policies of foreign governments and firms have collectively determined the manner of development, the composition and the operational effectiveness of the armed forces of both countries, complicating their ability to manage their own security postures, including their ability to wage sustained conflict against each other. Both countries have acted upon the perceived wisdom of diversifying their external dependency in the defense sphere, especially India, which has been particularly careful to spread its procurement of end-items and technology quite widely between the West and Soviet Union, and between the super-powers and the middle powers, but the military policies of both countries continue to remain highly vulnerable to foreign decisionmakers. The truncated Pakistani state will be unable to maintain her current force posture without direct and indirect foreign subsidies on a scale considerably higher than what West Pakistan's equitable share of the aid receipts of an undivided country would have been, and the prospects for even a continuation of former aid levels must be considered poor.[16] India will remain less dependent than her neighbor on foreign aid and, given the nature of her external procurement of military weapons and equipment, and her expanding indigenous defense production base, will be much less vulnerable to foreign pressures with regard to her conventional military posture. But her future force posture will be influenced to a still significant degree by the availability of external assistance and advanced weaponry, due to the requirements of her expanding economy and population, the continuing revolution in weapons technology, and the probability that a nuclear weapons program would not only constitute a serious burden upon the national economy but would also threaten the continuance of existing foreign development assistance upon which India will continue to rely in order to satisfy the rising expectancy of her rapidly growing population.

INTERNAL POLITICAL-MILITARY ENVIRONMENTS

The internal political environments of India and Pakistan have been characterized by certain similarities and some marked contrasts.[17] Both

societies have manifested strident nationalism sensitive to perceived threats to the territorial integrity and political viability of the nation-state, and unalterably opposed to alienation of any portion of the national domain. Both have experienced the fissiparous forces of regionalism and provincialism. Both have contained insecure elites concerned for their power, status and wealth and especially prone to making major investments in police and military forces as a prop to national unity and civil order in periods when they are undergoing great challenge. In marked contrast, however, has been the functioning of the two political systems. India has been continuously governed by the Congress party, which has successfully overcome internal cleavages and occasional pronounced public dissatisfaction with some of its policies, and the passing of Jawaharlal Nehru. Pakistan's 'freedom party', the Muslim League, proved unequal to the twin tasks of political mobilization and interest aggregation, and the country's quest for political stability has involved no less than ten ministries of varying complexion, two major interventions by the Army, and ultimate bifurcation into two sovereign entities. Political power in India has been continuously held by elements occupying the central sector of the political spectrum, minimizing the influence on defense policy of extreme groups such as Gandhians, Hindu communalists, and communists. Pakistan has been dominated, until recently, by a Punjabi gentry and a refugee upper-middle class elite centered in Karachi and Islamabad and possessed of intense feelings towards India, the potentially moderating influence of Bengali political leadership being virtually excluded from national politics through manipulation since the early 'fifties and, since the December 1970 elections, by suppression culminating in secession of the eastern wing.

The political histories of the two countries have been reflected in their respective approaches to national security. The problem of national survival has always bulked prominently in Pakistani national life, and differences of opinion over priorities (defense or development, foreign or domestic) have consistently been resolved in favor of military and foreign policies, with the Army exercising its considerable leverage whenever its conception of national

---

[16]Unless Bangladesh can be persuaded to pick up a proportionate share of debt repayment on Pakistan's external liabilities of over $3,000 million, debt servicing could account for over 30 percent of Pakistan's projected foreign exchange earnings, as against only 17 percent in 1968.

[17]For some useful insight into the politics of the two countries, see Hugh Tinker, *India and Pakistan* (New York: Prae-

ger, 1962); Pran Chopra, "Political Re-alignment in India," *Pacific Affairs* (Winter 1971–72): 511–26: Mohammed Ayoob, "The Military in Pakistan's Political Development," *South Asian Studies* (January 1972): 14–29; and William J. Barnds, "Pakistan's Disintegration," *The World Today* (August 1971): 319–29.

security needs appeared to be threatened—notably by coup d'états in 1958 and 1969, and the abortive effort to suppress Bengali separatism in 1971. In India, relative unconcern about the nation's security during the first fifteen years of independence caused defense and foreign policies to be given a decidedly lower priority than domestic policy, while increased sensitivity since 1962 has resulted in all Indian political parties becoming much more interested in defense issues in accordance with heightened public sensitivity toward the nation's security. Resource allocation between defense and development has never been a politically divisive issue in India, but it aggravated relations between Pakistan's two wings and contributed toward eventual secession of East Pakistan. The dominance of the national politics of both countries by elites resident in those parts of the country most exposed to operational contingencies has reinforced the primacy of the armies and air forces of India and Pakistan in claims upon the defense budget, and has relegated the navies to a 'Cinderella' category. The 'neglect' of the Navy has long been a source of grievance to those areas of India conscious of their past maritime traditions, prone to alarmist perceptions of the country's maritime security, and sensitive to the largely north Indian composition of the Army. In Pakistan, the overwhelming domination of the three armed services by West Pakistanis, the symbolism of the naval branch, and the absence of other than token provision for the defense of East Pakistan reinforced latent Bengali feelings of alienation from the national government and western wing, and strengthened a perspective on national security that posed a fundamental threat to policy requirements as defined by the Army and West Pakistani elite. The expectation that a Bengali prime minister would adjust resource allocations in favor of the eastern wing and economic development at the expense of the western wing and military defense, and would effect a major increase in Bengali representation in the armed forces, was a major factor in Yayha Khan's decision to deny the Bengali-based Awami League the fruits of the national plurality it won in the December 1970 election. The dramatic events of 1971 have served to greatly ease the politically sensitive issue of the 'historical ghost' in Indian national politics, for which China provides no comparable substitute. For the truncated remains of Pakistan, however, they have caused defense to assume a more acute form than at any time since partition, although the problem will lack the previous divisiveness due to the creation of Bangladesh.

THE GENERAL ECONOMIC CONTEXT

Acute economic weakness has characterized India and Pakistan since the withdrawal of British power and, despite important achievements in comparative terms with the situation prevailing in 1947, rapid population growth has served to limit the scope of real gains for the average citizen of the two South Asian states. India's cumulative economic growth rate averaged only about 3.5 percent of Gross National Product (GNP) per annum in 1950–65, and the attainment of a growth rate of slightly over 5.0 percent per annum in 1966–70 was unfortunately followed by the influx of Bengali refugees in 1971 which forced major outlays on relief, necessitating increased taxation and deficit spending and the deferment of implementation of the current economic plan for a year. Pakistan's economic performance compared very favorably with that of India through the 'fifties and 'sixties, with a 5.3 percent increase in the GNP being recorded on an annual average in 1961–66, 7.5 percent in 1967, 5.7 percent in 1968, and 6.3 percent in 1969. Growth declined sharply to only 1.4 percent in 1970, however, and the country faces serious economic problems, at least in the short-term, consequent on the secession of East Pakistan.[18]

In light of these severe economic problems, the basic dilemma of defense—how to achieve maximum security with minimum expenditure on the armed forces—has proven particularly difficult of solution for the governments of India and Pakistan. The quest for security has required acute sensitivity to the competitive claims that exist on scarce resources, and to the adverse effects of even minimal defense outlays on economic and social programs.

THE ECONOMICS OF
DEFENSE IN PAKISTAN

Pakistani outlays on defense remained relatively stable during the 'fifties, rising only 25 percent in 1953–60, and inflation accounted for much of the increased expenditures in the 1960–69 period as defense outlays, adjusted to the wholesale price index using 1960 as the base year, rose only 88 percent, as compared to a 225 percent rise in actual expenditures. However, while the burden of defense in terms of GNP actually

[18]For some comments, see Boudhayan Chattopadkyay, "Economic Dimensions," *Seminar* (February 1972): 24; W. Klatt, "The Indian Subcontinent After the War," *The World Today* (March 1972): 108–16.

eased slightly in 1965–71, representing 5.3 percent in 1965, 4.5 percent (1966), 3.4 percent (1969), 3.8 percent (1970) and 4.2 percent (1971), it nonetheless required a reallocation of resources away from social overhead and increases in taxation leading to strong political discontents which led to the deposition of Ayub Khan by the Army in 1969, and the elections of December 1970 which released forces ultimately destructive of national unity. The loss of revenues from its former east wing has virtually doubled Pakistan's defense burden, and the ability of the economy of the truncated state to support current force levels is extremely doubtful without massive external subsidization, which must be deemed unlikely. A drastic reduction in defense expenditure may be mandatory if the new Pakistani government is to satisfy the social and economic needs and aspirations of its restless people, although the return through demobilization of large numbers of young men to an economy suffering from large-scale unemployment is itself fraught with serious problems.

THE ECONOMICS OF DEFENSE IN INDIA

Amidst the general apathy toward national security prevailing prior to 1962, Indian defense planners were faced with strong budgetary constraints from a government determined to achieve rapid economic growth and headed by a charismatic figure with a pronounced distaste for the 'military approach' to resolution of problems. Thus, while actual outlays on defense rose from Rs 188 crores to Rs 331 crores in 1950–62, accounting for about 55 percent of the central budget deficit, they fluctuated downward in terms of current expenditure from 29.0 percent (1950) to 21.1 percent (1961), while remaining relatively stable in terms of the GNP—averaging just under 2.0 percent per annum. The sense of crisis ushered in by the Himalayan conflict in 1962 and somewhat aggravated by the Indo-Pakistan war in 1965 was widely accepted as requiring sharply increased allocations for defense in absolute terms, and the tripling of the defense budget within three years of the Himalayan debacle pushed the defense share of the central budget deficit to 78 percent, and of the GNP to over 4.0 percent. But the responsible politician and bureaucrat by no means lost sight of the imperatives of economy, attested by the continuing low priority attached to the naval branch, and the economic burden of the substantially larger disbursements on defense was fortunately held down by a major increase in foreign aid receipts and an improved economic growth rate. The defense budget has continued to rise, but at a declining rate, and the defense burden has dropped from 3.8 percent of GNP in 1965 to 3.4 percent in 1971. While some elements of Indian opinion argue that the country can afford, and must absorb at whatever cost, substantially larger defense burdens in future years,[19] there has been a noticeable subsidence of public concern with defense in an immediate sense since the mid-'sixties and renewed awareness of the country's pressing economic and social problems and a mounting sense of urgency that they must be much more aggressively tackled if mounting public discontents are to be alleviated. There are rising criticisms of the nature and scope of Indian defense expenditures from a varied spectrum of opinion which perceives current force levels as adequate to meet practical contingencies within the limits of India's economic weakness, or even excessive to likely needs. While the central government is unlikely to feel that the situation requires any overall reduction in defense spending, the increasing demands for greater outlays on economic development from the states and the Planning Commission, and political prudence, have prompted the Union government to commit itself to a direct and major attack on poverty in the Fifth Plan (1974–79). While the impact of a sluggish economy and mounting popular discontents on the defense budget cannot be forecast with any accuracy due to the numerous imponderables involved, the implications are more obvious—the unlikelihood of continuing large annual increases in defense allocations, aside from accommodating inflation. India's continuing financial and economic weakness would seem to constitute major obstacles to the realization of the hopes of the 'big navy' school, who perceive the lessons of the country's past and her future needs largely in maritime terms, and to those advocates of strategic autonomy who view development of a credible nuclear capability as a sine qua non of national security, national self-respect, and regional and international status and role.

LEADERSHIP PERCEPTIONS AND STYLES

The political leadership of India and Pakistan have had to cope with many problems in their

[19]Such opinion has strongly manifested itself with regards to nuclear and naval policy. For a favorable analysis of India's ability to support an optimal nuclear strategy, see Subramanian Swamy, "Systems Analysis of Strategic Defence Needs," *Economic and Political Weekly* (February 22, 1969): 401–09; *ibid.*, "A Sequel," (May 3, 1969): 772–77.

search for appropriate national security policies, but their perceptions of the policy requirements have reflected differences in approach and in the circumstances with which they have been confronted.

During the first fifteen years of independence, India's political elite perceived no immediate and serious threats to the country's security, even Pakistan being regarded more as a nuisance than a direct military threat. The strained state of Indo-Pakistan relations and the unresolved matter of Kashmir dictated preparedness against the contingency of another 'tribal' invasion of the Indian-occupied portion of the state, as did the mood of the Indian people, but the situation was not deemed such as to require other than an economical level of defense spending. Quantitative and qualitative improvements of the Pakistani armed forces had to be countered to ensure an adequate margin of superior military strength, especially in tanks and aircraft, but all 'nonessential' expenditure was deferred to permit maximum attention to the pressing problems of economic development. In retrospect, Prime Minister Nehru was to contend that the absence of public concern with defense precluded outlays on equipment and higher force levels, that "It is only when danger comes and shakes you up that you can get more money by taxation, loans, credits and gifts from outside."[20] For various practical and emotional reasons, Nehru and his associates in the Congress party hierarchy were strongly disinclined to regard China as either an immediate or potential threat, and mounting signs of Peking's toughening attitude in the Himalayan region were not considered to presage any deterioration of relations to the point of conflict. Thus, while strong public feelings about Chinese policy required that New Delhi provide evidence of its intention to defend the country's territorial integrity, honor, and self-respect, Nehru deliberately avoided measures that might be too provocative to China and treated the matter as little more than a policing problem. No need to reorient defense strategy away from primary focus on Pakistan was acknowledged, Nehru coldly rejecting Ayub's proposal of joint defense, and even the declared intent to eject Chinese troops from India's territory in 1962 was not regarded as requiring redeployment of Indian forces on any sizable scale.

The Himalayan conflict of October-November 1962, however, had a traumatic impact upon the Indian scene, and upon the political elite. A new threat of major proportions had appeared and had to be dealt with; the old minor security problem, Pakistan, remained and could not be ignored. The country had been humiliated, and was aroused. The government had mismanaged the country's security and could ill afford to risk a recurrence. A new range of operational contingencies had to be envisaged ranging from insurgency to limited conflict against a major power (China) and a minor power (Pakistan), possibly acting in collusion. In the view of government leaders, the altered strategic situation required the development of a military capability adequate to contain simultaneous limited attacks from both China and Pakistan pending external intervention. The nationalism of the Indian people remained a strong barrier to foreign alignment, and was deemed to require a more concerted drive toward the long-standing goal of maximum self-reliance in defense, with defense to be regarded as an integral part of the national economic plan.

The sense of urgency which typified the perceptions of India's political leadership of national security in the several years following the Himalayan debacle has eased greatly in recent years as a result of India's defense build-up and various extraneous developments. The spectre of the 'historical ghost' eased as a result of the 1965 war and has dissipated to a considerable extent consequent upon Pakistan's crushing military defeat and bifurcation in 1971. Alarmist assumptions about China have gradually given way to a more considered assessment of the Chinese threat as being more diffuse, low-cost, localized and long-term, and China's nuclear missile capability is not regarded in responsible circles as posing a serious military problem for India in the foreseeable future. But there is unease regarding Pakistan's future postures, and an appreciation that Bangladesh may present security problems far more momentous than East Pakistan ever did. There is an acute sensitivity over China's lead in nuclear weaponry, and some strong doubts regarding the credibility of external guarantees in all circumstances. There is a growing awareness that India's national interest may not always coincide with that of the super-powers, and apparently genuine suspicions that Peking, Washington and Moscow harbor desires to deny India her rightful role in regional and international affairs. There has been growing interest in maritime security issues, prompted by Pakistan's acquisition of submarines, the domestic political repercussions of any intrusion by Chinese submarines into the Indian Ocean, and increasing Soviet and American naval activity in the oceanic

[20]Statement in the Rajya Sabha, cited in *Hindu Weekly Review* (September 9, 1963).

core of India's cherished 'peace area'. There is a consensus that, while an Indian nuclear weapons capability is not an immediate necessity, prudence and the mood of the Indian people dictates that the option be kept open and in fact be widened through stepped-up research and development on weapons and delivery vehicles. But there is also a recognition among India's ruling elite that every contingency cannot be provided for, that the country's search for security cannot be conducted heedless of the antagonisms which that quest may provoke among other powers or among its own people, and that there must be a considered relationship between military commitments and power and between power and resources. Like many nations before her, India must accept that security can never be absolute and that insecurity must be lived with. While it is by no means clear that India's political hierarchy has yet accommodated itself to this state of affairs, the government has demonstrated an ability to take minor trouble in its political stride, to handle crisis situations in a fairly rational manner, and to maintain a far more realistic perspective on defense needs than has been true of many elements of the Indian population and articulate elite.

The perceptions of the requirements of national security by Pakistan's principal political leadership are extremely difficult to summarize, given the fluidity of the politics of the country since its birth, but certain generalizations are permissible. External threat has been equated with India by the entire spectrum of 'national' political parties as they have emerged and disappeared, the basic aim of Indian policies being widely regarded as involving the eventual absorption of Pakistan into a larger Hindustan. The legacy of history, and the communal slaughter and population shifts surrounding partition precluded any easy accommodation with India following the cease-fire in Kashmir in 1949, and the subsequent postures of New Delhi on this and other issues of deep concern to Pakistanis served to sustain the fear, suspicion, distrust and bitterness with which Pakistan's political elite viewed their more powerful neighbor. The need for external supports has been accepted as a virtual sine qua non of national security, and pragmatism has prevailed over ideology as regards the choice of such supports. The defense posture and military policies adopted and pursued by successive national governments, however, have reflected the perceptions of the West Pakistani political leadership rather than a genuine national consensus or compromise acceptable to both wings. Kashmir was a far more meaningful issue to a Punjabi or Sindi than it appeared to the distant resident of East Bengal.

Realistic as the deployment of the country's defense forces in the west may have been on narrow military grounds, it was acutely discomforting to the native leadership of the exposed eastern wing which provided a disproportionate share of the country's revenues allocated toward defense. The restriction of Bengali representation in the armed forces to token symbolism further limited the ability of East Pakistan's popular leaders to identify closely with defense policies over which they exercised virtually no constructive influence. Under the circumstances, Bengali political leaders were more strongly disposed to policies which provided increased local comfort and benefits, and which contrasted rather sharply with views prevailing in West Pakistan and mirrored directly in national policy. Acknowledgment by the western elite of the divergent outlook of the native leadership of East Bengal was reflected in the determined exclusion of this leadership from the national policymaking process. Differences of perspective existed, of course, within the political hierarchy of West Pakistan, but they involved emphasis rather than substance and were constrained by the risks attendant with views that failed to reflect the popular bitterness toward India and challenged the Army's definition of needs. While the government of a truncated Pakistan can be expected to reassess policy requirements in light of the altered situation consequent on the secession of the east wing and India's increasing margin of military superiority, the nature of its leadership and electoral support, the heightened threat perception of India, and its ultimate dependence upon the support of an embittered Army constitute strong constraints upon any early or fundamental changes in the approach to the problems of defense. The maintenance of the pre-1971 defense posture may be impractical, but the alternatives are likely to appear even more unattractive.

INTEREST GROUP AND BUREAUCRATIC STAKES, CIVIL & MILITARY

Both India and Pakistan contain economic interests possessed of substantial stakes in defense posture. The armed forces of both countries, especially the armies, provide valued employment for certain castes, classes, and regions in national economies afflicted with high unemployment. Military bases, cantonments and ordnance factories are important employers and consumers of local services in areas in which they are sited, and their placement and retention are a matter of no small consequence in national politics. The scientific communities of the two neighboring states, notably those associated with atomic energy, defense research and development welcome and assert pressure in favor of expanded efforts in these fields. Private industry profits from defense procurement, especially in India, but the nature of the two economies and their manner of development has not facilitated the development of any major interest by the private industrial sector in defense production.[21] Pakistan's weak industrial base has virtually precluded the development of private capacity relevant to defense requirements, while the interest of Indian industrialists in the equipment needs of the armed forces has been strongly inhibited by the vast civilian market, the official policy of concentrating defense production in the public sector and the comparative modest size of orders placed for private tender, and the close tolerances and strict quality control demanded by the Ministry of Defense as compared to the civilian consumer. New Delhi has attempted to stimulate private sector interest in defense, but its efforts and the response have failed to bear major fruit to date. There is nothing remotely analogous to the lobbying of private industry for defense contracts in Western countries. The private sector in India and Pakistan are rather inclined to view defense spending as restrictive of their activities, due to the fiscal and economic consequences of rising defense expenditures, with such influence as they have been able to project exerting a constraint upon allocations for defense, rather than a stimulus.

The historic roles and missions of the military services of India and Pakistan involved support to the civil power, and local defense against a 'minor' power with reliance upon external assistance in the event of attack by a major power. No specific provision was made for deployment of forces beyond the confines of the subcontinent, although an expeditionary role was allowed for and periodically assumed without prejudice to local security. Partition and strained relations between the two new countries created new strategic problems for the defense planners, although circumstances largely dictated the continuation of a limited conception of military liabilities by both governments. Operational contingencies involved defense of a common border in a narrow sector of the northwest. Strategy emphasized defense and deterrence. The army was seen to constitute the primary sanction of in-

ternal order, national unity and independence, and the main sword and shield of the country, and armor was regarded as the decisive weapons system. The air forces were conceived essentially as affording tactical support to the land operations in battle zones, while successive governments of India and Pakistan have treated the naval branch as incidental to basic strategy.

Pakistani military officers have shown a considerable reticence to articulate views on force posture for public perusal,[22] but the leverage which the armed forces have exerted in the determination of Pakistan's defense policy since at least 1951 permits interpretation of actual force posture as representing the minimal demands of the military services, and the general conclusions of the dominant army. The low priority attached to naval defense, and the only token provision made for the direct defense of East Pakistan prior to the tragic events of 1971, was defensible on strictly military grounds given Pakistan's strategic predicament and limited resources, but it also reflected the overwhelming Punjabi-Pathan nature of the officer corps,[23] and the Army's preeminent position within the defense service establishment. The secession of East Pakistan in 1971 will probably reinforce the long-standing perspectives of the military services, and could further weaken the budgetary position of the Pakistan Navy, although increased emphasis upon relations with the Muslim countries would possibly lead to increased, rather than decreased, emphasis upon this service.

Prior to 1962, no noticeable alarm was manifested by the Indian military services over the force levels sanctioned to cope with the roles and missions assigned by the government.[24] There was the normal desire by all three services for greater margins of superiority over the forces maintained by Pakistan, and some envy at the qualitative superiority of certain Pakistani weapons systems such as tanks, fighter and fighter-bomber aircraft but qualified confidence

---

[21]For one of the few direct treatments of the relationship between the private sector and defense in India, see S. D. Verma, "Role of Private Enterprise in Defence Production," *The Institute for Defence Studies and Analyses Journal* (July 1968): 53–59.

[22]The *Pakistan Army Journal* is the primary vehicle for recorded military views on various issues relevant to defense, but it is not publicly circulated. Of some value regarding military opinion are Major-General Fazal Muqeem Khan's *The Story of the Pakistan Army* (Karachi: Oxford University Press, 1963); and Field Marshal Ayub Khan's autobiography *Friends Not Masters* (New York: Oxford University Press, 1967).

[23]For some details on the regional composition of the Pakistani armed services, including the officer corps, see Mohammed Ayoob, "The Military in Pakistan's Political Development," *South Asian Studies* (January 1972): 28.

[24]See the quarterly *Journal of the United Services Institution of India*, which contains many quality articles on various general and specific aspects of Indian defense and military policy. See also Lorne J. Kavic, *India's Quest for Security*, chapters 3–7 and 9.

in India's ability to cope with any military threat posed by the neighboring Muslim state. The assignment of Himalayan responsibilities to the army in 1959 prompted the Chief of Army Staff, General K. S. Thimayya, to propose the development of a defense scheme consisting of special mountain divisions deployed forward and backed by a strong and highly mobile mechanized force based in the plains. The failure of the government to sanction such a scheme did not cause any serious alarm in service circles, however, as the contingency was perceived to be remote. In the event of limited Chinese attacks, contingency planning assumed that the requisite forces could be redeployed from the Pakistani threat without prejudice to Indian security in that quarter.

Since the traumatic developments of 1962, Indian military opinion has become more sensitive to the nation's military security with opinions ranging from anxiety to a qualified belief in India's ability to meet likely military contingencies. The expansion of the army appears to satisfy the hierarchy of the service, its ability to cope effectively with its Pakistani opponent amply demonstrated in 1965 and, particularly in 1971, and its Himalayan posture viewed as capable of containing any renewed attacks likely to be considered by Peking. No sympathy has been manifested for proposals periodically advanced by various civilian commentators involving creation of an army of between one and two million men backed by large reserves, but a section of service opinion feels that greater emphasis should be placed upon counterinsurgency. The doubling of the Indian Air Force to 45 squadrons has seemingly pacified even the more expansive minds in the service, the most noticeable complaint being the lack of a strategic capability against China— although this view is advanced without strong conviction, given doubts as to the need for such a capability in a practical sense, and the future of manned bombers in a missile age. The low priority accorded to the navy in the first five-year defense plan sparked general concern among the Indian military, and strong resentment in the Indian Navy,[25] the need for a stronger and two-ocean maritime capability being stressed, and one anonymous commentator suggesting the need for two fleets each consisting of 3 aircraft carriers, 9 cruisers, 36 destroyers, 27 antisubmarine and antiaircraft frigates, 36 minesweepers, 20

submarines, and 58 other ships of various types.[26] The decision by the government to view India's maritime requirements more sympathetically in very recent years has only partially appeased the naval service, whose aspirations for much higher force levels remain strong despite the decisive verdict over Pakistan in 1971. Opinion within the armed forces remains divided on the need for nuclear weapons, but support for such a capability is growing, and the military establishment, which regards the immediate threat from China as a conventional one, accepts that India will one day have to stand on its own to take its rightful place in the world.[27]

THE POLICYMAKING NON-ROLES OF THE PUBLIC AND THE LEGISLATIVE BRANCHES

The determination of incremental change in force posture in India and Pakistan has always been essentially elitist and highly institutionalized. Considerable public interest has been manifested in both countries on defense issues, although it has fluctuated sharply in time and place, and has been much more marked in West than East Pakistan, and in northern than southern India. Articulation and debate in the public sphere has been greater in India than in Pakistan, despite the greater sense of urgency with which citizens of the latter have perceived defense requirements, but has been strongly inhibited in both states by lack of information regarding actual policy, and a general acceptance of the oft-reiterated official view that the national interest required secretiveness, and that a subject of such a highly technical and complex nature is best left to those possessed of the requisite knowledge and experience. The role of the legislative branch was severely circumscribed in Pakistan by chronic instability of factional politics leading to severe restrictions upon political activity. In India, parliamentarians consistently passed by unanimous vote whatever defense estimates were placed before it, the annual debate on the defense grants being described as the "duet of the deaf"[28] and as "an elegant or inelegant repetition . . . spiced with Opposition criticisms, interspersed with sallies and enlivened occasionally by an odd fresh incident, such as the buying of MIGs or

[25]See, for example, "A Contemporary Pattern for the Indian Navy," by the military correspondent of the *Statesman* (February 4, 1965); "Editorial: A Stronger Navy," *Journal of the United Service Institution of India* (January–March 1965): 1–2; Anthony Harrigan, "India's Maritime Posture," *Military Review* (April 1969): 24–30.

[26]"Fremen', "India Can Ignore Her Navy Only at Her Peril," *Journal of the United Service Institution of India* (October–December 1963): 321–28.

[27]Dilip Mukerjee, "Big Power Guarantee Sharpens India's Nuclear Dilemma," *Statesman* (15 March, 1969).

[28]*Hindu Weekly Review* (23 March, 1959).

appointment of the chief of staff."[29] Successive governments in both countries have professed a sensitivity to the public mood, but there is no evidence that any adjustments in force posture were attributable to public demands not in accordance with considered opinion originating within the governing political hierarchy and bureaucratic establishments. This pattern seems unlikely to change significantly in the immediate future, notwithstanding the surge of Indian public interest in defense since the traumatic events of 1962 and the altered political scene in Pakistan since December 1970.

THE POLICYMAKING ROLES OF THE EXECUTIVE AND THE MILITARY

Under the Constitution of India, the President is the Supreme Commander of the armed forces, and is required to act in accordance with the advice of the Prime Minister and the Council of Ministers. The executive management of defense, however, is characterized by a hierarchical structure of committees arranged in the classic pyramid based on the three services, with the Cabinet at the apex. A superimposed conciliar structure provides a formal means for lateral communication among officials at similar levels in different hierarchies, but the vertical 'superior-subordinate' relationship constitutes the 'skeleton'. It is within this system that the three services struggle concurrently against each other and against budgetary pressures from Finance and an economy-minded administration.

This committee system of policy management evolved largely ad hoc after independence, but the system has afforded, in theory, a coordinated approach with a measure of consistency being ensured by all branches being served by the military wing of the Cabinet Secretariat. Proposals relating to the annual defense grants are initiated by the respective services, and the estimates are studied by the appropriate division of the individual service branch under the scrutiny of Deputy Financial Advisers. The revised estimates are then discussed in the Defence Minister's Army, Navy, and Air Force Committees, after which they are examined by the Defence Ministry. The resulting estimates are then sent to the Defence Committee of the Cabinet for

consideration, and the conclusions of this body are forwarded to the full Cabinet for approval. The assessment of military needs that emerges from this process has to date constituted policy, given the ability of the government to presume parliamentary approval of its proposals.[30]

In the opinion of a former Defence Secretary writing in 1963, the policymaking organization of the Defence Ministry was "sufficiently flexible to ensure that every relevant point of view has a chance of being presented at the appropriate level and to have it considered at the highest level if necessary."[31] To whatever extent this may accurately describe policymaking, the results were highly discomforting to India in 1962, given the manifest inadequacies of the prevailing force structure to cope with the contingency which erupted so dramatically.

The military contribution to policy has been variously vitiated. Between the ceasefire in Kashmir and the eruption of conflict in the Himalayas, the attachment of undue importance or glamour to the military was well-nigh precluded by the absence of any apparent real threat to Indian security, reinforced by the government's moralistic postures, antimilitarist attitudes, nonaligned stance, and stress on economic development as the ultimate source of a nation's strength. India's inheritance of able political leadership, a trained bureaucracy, and a capable middle class served to lessen the value of the military as a vehicle of modernity and progress. From a position of having direct access to the highest level of government, the armed forces was reduced to the base of a hierarchical structure of committees. Financial officials possessed of a single-minded devotion to economy applied a pervasive system of budgetary controls, service proposals were subjected to veto and modification by civilian officials of the Defence Ministry lacking the requisite expertise to properly judge such matters, and manifesting strongly civilian perspectives. The absence of a unified command posed a serious obstacle to the development of a consensus permitting forceful professional arguments on budgetary allocations. Instead of a single Commander-in-Chief as in the British period, there were three autonomous services competing with each other for budgetary allocations from an economy-minded and markedly apathetic political executive. Such a system placed a heavy responsibility upon the Defence Minister to

[29]Military correspondent in the *Indian Express* (9 June 1962). An opposition censure motion against the government's Himalayan posture against China in early 1962, for example, was defeated by 185 votes to 35, less than one-third of the members of the House appearing to record their judgment on matters pertaining to the disposition of one-quarter of the budget.

[30]A number of new committees came into existence following the Chinese attack in 1962, but ultimately disappeared.
[31]H. M. Patel, *The Defence of India* (Bombay: Asia Publishing House, 1963), p. 3.

effect compromises within the budgetary ceilings laid down by the Cabinet, yet all Ministers before the appointment of V. K. Krishna Menon to the post in 1957 were political light-weights, and only one had any real interest in security issues. Menon's appointment should have augured well for defense given his intelligence and energy, his administrative drive, and his intimate relationship with Nehru. Unfortunately, his strong predilections in foreign policy, his political ambitions and his universally acknowledged arrogance were to exert a negative influence on defense policy during the very period when clear thinking and close cooperation between the political, military, and civil arms of government were required as never before.[32] Since the Himalayan debacle in 1962, the influence of the armed forces in state and society has resurged strongly, especially that of the Army which has reestablished its former image as a highly efficient military force, the symbol of national purpose and a source of genuine national pride. Whether the policymaking machinery has over-adjusted is the subject of some discussion in India, although the problems being experienced by the Indian Navy in satisfying its perceived needs suggest that the leverage currently available to the military is not unlimited.

The executive management of defense in Pakistan has borne some structural similarities to the Indian pattern, but the dominant characteristic has been in dramatic contrast—the powerful and central role occupied by the military, notably by the Army, which has vitiated the input into the decisionmaking process of the civilian politician and bureaucrat.[33] Military policy has accordingly reflected decisions reached within the military establishment in accordance with Army definitions of needs and priorities. The influence over policy of the civil bureaucracies and political elite has been effectively neutralized by infiltration, accommodation and, when necessary, by force. The nature of Pakistan's defense problems, as perceived by the leaders of the Army, propelled them into the center of the decisionmaking process, first as its arbiter and then its monopolist. The GHQ (General Headquarters),

especially following the appointment of Ayub Khan as first Pakistani Commander-in-Chief of the Army in 1951, has been able to project its influence into the inner councils of the decisionmakers even on matters remotely related to defense, and has always played a crucial role in the determination of defense and foreign policies. So long as the Army's financial autonomy was maintained and its definition of security needs was basic to national policy, it remained formally aloof from politics, while seeking to stabilize its role within the system through securing foreign arms aid and consolidation of ties with the bureaucratic establishment. When threats were perceived to its position and definition of defense needs, it acted—against discredited politicians in 1958, against incompetent and corrupt bureaucrats in 1969, and against Bengali separatism in 1971, this final act of politicization borne of desperation and divisive of the unity of the officer corps. At the moment, the prestige of the Army has yet to recover from its humiliation at India's hands in 1971 and senior officers associated with that debacle have been purged by President Z. A. Bhutto. But its ultimate position in the society and state seem assured, given the absence of credible alternatives and, as Wayne Wilcox has commented: "whatever the evolving state structure, military officers will walk the corridors of power."[34]

CONCLUSION: THE FORCE POLICY RESULTANTS

Indian military policy down to 1962 was one of continual compromises between what was politically desirable, militarily prudent, and financially feasible.

The government's declared preference for a small, mobile, and well-equipped army of about 150,000 men did not eventuate, the 280,000-man force inherited at partition growing to 325–350,000 by 1953, and some 550,000 including civilian employees and enrolled noncombatants by 1962. The composition of the service changed only moderately between 1953 and 1962, only two infantry divisions and several unattached formations being added to the 1953 establishment of six infantry divisions, one armored division, one independent armored brigade, one paratroop brigade, and miscellaneous units. The additions resulted from commitments to United Nations peace-keeping (one battalion in UNEF, and an infantry brigade in the Congo), deployment of

[32]For a discussion of civil-military relations in India during the 1947–62 period, see Lorne J. Kavic, *India's Quest for Security*, chapter 9.

[33]For analyses of the political role of the Army in Pakistan, see Wayne A. Wilcox, "Political Role of Army in Pakistan," *South Asian Studies* (January 1972): 31–44; *ibid.*, "The Pakistan Coup d'Etat of 1958," *Pacific Affairs* (Summer 1965); Mohammed Ayoob, "The Military in Pakistan's Political Development," *South Asian Studies* (January 1972): 14–29; and Stephen P. Cohen, "Arms and Politics in Pakistan," *India Quarterly* (October–December 1964).

[34]Wayne A. Wilcox, "Political Role of Army in Pakistan," *op. cit.*, p. 44.

an eventual 14 battalions to counterinsurgency operations against Naga tribals, and allocation of an infantry division and four brigades in the Himalayan region. This expansion was partly offset by deferment of re-equipment, except for tanks, which were readily acknowledged as the decisive weapons system in any renewed conflict with Pakistan. The service was fairly well-prepared for conventional operations against a familiar Pakistani opponent, but contingency preparations against China were based upon an assumption that serious conflict was highly improbable.

The 25-squadron air force was somewhat larger on the eve of the border war than envisaged in early planning revealed in 1949, which aimed at development of a balanced service of 20 operational squadrons by 1960, representing unplanned increases of fighter-bomber and light bomber strength motivated by additions to the Pakistan Air Force, and of transport units required to provide logistic support to the Army in the Himalayas, primarily in Ladakh. The service was trained, equipped and deployed for operations against Pakistan in an essentially tactical role, the air defense system being rudimentary, and the contingency of combatant activity against China being virtually ignored.

The development of the navy into a small carrier task force of 1 aircraft carrier, 2 light cruisers, 3 destroyers, 17 frigates and miscellaneous draft represented a reduction from the initially sanctioned force of 2 aircraft carriers, 3 light cruisers, 8–9 destroyers and other craft, and was attributable to financial stringency rather than changing perceptions of naval requirements. Operational planning contemplated operations, if at all, only against Pakistan.

The inadequacy of the Army's force levels for Himalayan contingencies dramatically exposed by the brief border conflict with China in October-November 1962, and perceived threats from this quarter involving air power aroused the nation, severely embarrassed its government and divested the services of their all-too complacent attitudes regarding a Chinese military threat. The immediate result was a crash program involving expansion of the army to 825,000 men organized into 21 divisions, including 10 mountain divisions; expansion of the air force to 45 squadrons; modernization of the navy; expansion of the defense production base to materially reduce external dependency; and improvements to the operational infra-structure in the Himalayan region. A reassessment of naval policy in 1964 resulted in a decision to expand the navy, initial efforts in this direction involving

creation of a submarine service comprised of 4 units acquired from the Soviet Union, and of destroyer escorts and patrol boats purchased from the same source. No firm decisions appear to have been taken, however, regarding the scope of the navy's role.[35] The government has reiterated its non-nuclear stance, but has declared its intention to keep the option open. The adequacy of the new force levels with regard to operational contingencies involving Pakistan has been demonstrated on two occasions (1965 and 1971), but there continues to be varying degrees of unease manifested regarding India's ability to cope with Chinese options, and with the more general security of Indian interests, and moderate-to-strong pressure upon government to develop a more powerful navy and to exercise its nuclear option at an early date.

Pakistani military policy has been dictated by the perceived need to maintain a credible counter to India's military capability deployable against Azad Kashmir and the west wing, and the attraction of securing an operational advantage sufficient to threaten the Indian position in Kashmir. The flow of United States military aid after 1954 enabled Pakistan to acquire the force posture evidently considered to provide an acceptable measure of security against perceived contingencies involving India. By 1962, Pakistan maintained a field force and a combatant air arm approximately comparable in size and composition to the Indian forces deployed against them, and so deployed and equipped as to warrant more than passing confidence in the event of renewed hostilities. The navy was so composed, however, as to have only marginal relevance to operational contingencies involving India.[36] India's defense build-up begun in late 1962 stimulated deep concern, confirmed by the 22-day conflict in 1965, and provoked a substantial strengthening of the army and air force, and moderate increases to the navy aimed at maintaining a credible defensive posture. The higher force levels,[37] which

[35] For a breakdown of the current force levels, see *The Military Balance 1971–72* (London: International Institute for Strategic Studies, 1971), pp. 62–63.

[36] The army comprised about 225,000 men organized in 6 infantry divisions, 2 independent infantry brigades, 1 paratroop brigade, 1 armored division, and 1 independent armored brigade deployed principally in the Lahore-Sialkot-Rawalpindi-Peshwar, only 1 infantry division being in East Pakistan. The air force deployed 8 squadrons of subsonic fighter-bombers, 1 squadron of supersonic fighter-interceptors, 1-to-2 squadrons of tactical light bombers, and reconnaissance, transport, and coastal search units. The navy was an antisubmarine force comprising 1 light training cruiser, 7 escorts, 6 minesweepers, and miscellaneous minor craft.

[37] According to the most recent edition of *The Military Balance*, the Pakistani armed forces comprised, on the eve of the Bangladesh affair, 2 armored and 10 infantry divisions,

necessitated resource allocations severely bur-
densome to the economy and aggravated political
discontents, failed to forestall defeat in 1971, and
has placed in question the country's fundamental
defense posture. The Indian threat is growing
steadily, virtually precluding the continuation of
a policy of approximate parity on the 'western
front', and the loss of East Pakistan and its
revenues has doubled the burden of defense and

rendered even retention of the existing military
establishment impossible without major external
subsidization. The traumatic events of 1971,
while improving the strategic position of West
Pakistan, have been psychologically damaging to
public opinion in the truncated remains, and have
disrupted the long-standing power structure in
the state, although the central importance of
the Army in the politics of the country is likely
to continue, given the momentous nature of
Pakistan's problems and the absence of any credible alternative to the force as a stabilizing factor
internally and a symbol of national purpose.

---

1 independent armored brigade, and 1 air defense brigade;
3 submarines, 1 cruiser, 4 destroyer escorts and support craft;
2 light bombers, 13 fighter-bomber/interceptors and 1 reconnaissance squadron plus transport unit.

ISRAEL AND EGYPT: MILITARY FORCE POSTURE 1967–1972

GEOFFREY KEMP

*In contrast to most of the articles in this section—David Greenwood's
excepted—Kemp's study focuses directly on objective military force posture
instead of the functional political-bureaucratic inputs and resultant perceptions
suggested by Hammond and appearing either implicitly or explicitly in the
remainder of the articles. In focusing on objective military capabilities, Kemp
notes that one should consider certain fundamental elements—time, resources,
milieu, and capacity for collective action. With these elements in mind, he then
compares the force postures of Israel and Egypt, providing for us an analysis of
neighboring protagonists in the same comparative vein as Kavic's on the Indian
subcontinent, but with the focus shifting in Kemp's study to objective force
analysis instead of the more subjective functional and policy process analysis
characterizing Kavic's study. The emphasis on Israeli doctrinal flexibility
pointed out in Michael Handel's article in an earlier section of this book finds its
companion in the Israeli force posture flexibility identified by Kemp. After
studying Kemp's excellent comparative essay, the reader should gain an
appreciation for the fact that in areas of direct military confrontation like that
existing between Israel and Egypt where forces have such a real and immediate
impact on national survival, the functional and bureaucratic variables that
loom so large elsewhere tend to pale in significance. Simple models do tend to
apply in the case of Israel and Egypt, and one can define simple rational
objective force options.*

*Professor Kemp is Associate Professor of International Politics, The
Fletcher School of Law and Diplomacy, Tufts University. He received his B.A.
and M.A. from Oxford University and his Ph.D. from M.I.T. and has served as
Research Associate at the Institute for Strategic Studies and at the M.I.T.
Center for International Studies. He is the author of* Arms and Security: The
Egypt-Israel Case *(1968);* Classification of Weapons Systems and Force Designs
in Less Developed Country Environments *(1970); plus many other contributions
to books and articles.*

INTRODUCTION

This paper discusses changes in Israeli and
Egyptian military force postures since the Six
Day War of 1967. To understand fully the overall
military balance between Israel and Egypt we
would need to discuss in some detail the military
postures of other key actors in the Arab-Israel
conflict, in particular, the United States, the
Soviet Union, Jordan, Syria, Lebanon, Iraq,
and Libya. This will not be attempted here.

Nevertheless, in spite of these constraints a
narrow focus upon Israeli and Egyptian force
postures has a certain analytical utility. The
withdrawal in July and August 1972 of large
numbers of Soviet military personnel from Egypt
once again enables us to examine the Egypt-
Israel balance in isolation from other military
forces. Within the Arab-Israeli context the
Egyptian-Israeli balance is by far the most important political and military factor.

THE STRATEGIC ENVIRONMENT

The ability of either Egypt or Israel to operate modern military forces in the pursuit of military power objectives is limited by certain en-

*This is an original article written for this volume and the Conference on Comparative Defense Policy
held at the Air Force Academy, February 7–9, 1973. Copyright reserved by the author.*

demic features of the Middle East strategic environment. To the extent that objectives vary, so will the preferred strategies and force structures required to achieve those objectives. Preferred strategies and force structures are also dependent upon the particular resources available to the two countries over any given time.

The milieu in which the Arab-Israel conflict has taken place poses particular problems for the operation of various types of military forces. More will be said of the unique geography of the Middle East in the section on air power. In both Egypt and Israel the human and physical resources required to maintain and operate military forces are either in short supply or subject to the control of external countries.

It is not only important to identify the major elements of military power in a particular environment, it is also essential to specify the *time frame* in which the examination is to focus. In his study of the theory of the firm the famous economist Alfred Marshall distinguished three time periods depending upon whether supply elements (in this analogy supply elements in question would be "available military force") have time to make (1) no adjustments, (2) some adjustments, or (3) full adjustments. Marshall's three time periods are momentary, short-run, and long-run. Applying this very important concept to the discussion of military forces, three types of military capabilities can be distinguished.

1) *Momentary Military Force.* This refers to "force in being" or actual force available before mobilization and before full utilization of existing operational inventories. To be more specific, it refers to the number of trained men and women and serviceable material that can be placed on combat alert at a moment's notice. In terms of the supply and demand analogy, the supply curve of military force in this case is a vertical straight line. For example, the number of combat aircraft ready for use *at any given moment* in a particular theater or the number of artillery pieces ready to fire *at any given moment* would be examples of momentary military force.

2) *Short-Run Military Force.* This also refers to trained men and serviceable materiel that comprise a "force in being" but there is assumed to be a sufficient warning time to allow for partial or complete mobilization of trained front-line reserves and time to allow front-line combat inventories to become fully operational. It refers to the amount of military force a political unit can put into the field from *existing* rather than *potential* military resources. In the Arab-Israel analogy, it clearly has great importance for

Israel since Israel is able to mobilize upwards of 300,000 men and women within a 72-hour period but during normal "peace time" conditions the total armed forces number no more than 77,000 (25,000 regular; 52,000 conscripts).

3) *Long-Run Military Force.* This is truly potential force. It refers to the total resources a country can mobilize over a long time. Though it does not concern us in this analysis, it would have to take into account factors such as future indigenous arms production in Egypt and Israel, economic growth and industrialization, and demographic factors such as changes in population size, distribution, and composition.

Having discussed the problem of time constraints, it is now possible to list some of the elements *required in any time frame* for the use of military forces in certain environments in pursuit of certain political goals. Raymond Aron has suggested three fundamental elements of military forces that subsume the requirements for raising and operating either a modern ten-million-man army or a small guerrilla group operating in the jungle. The three elements are *resources, milieu,* and *capacity for collective action.*[1]

Two types of resources are in particular demand in both countries. The first is human resources in the form of trained, skilled military personnel. In this category it has generally been assumed that Israel, despite its very small Jewish population (about 2,700,000) has a much higher potential for mobilizing skilled human resources than Egypt. However, in the long-run, the trend could change dependent upon the success or failure of Egypt's attempts to modernize its society. The second resource constraint would be advanced arms. Since neither Egypt nor Israel produces advanced arms their dependence upon external suppliers has increased rather than diminished since the Six Day War. While it is true that Israel has made great progress in developing certain categories of independent armaments production and maintenance—especially in the fields of small arms and artillery—its reliance upon sophisticated technology in the form of jet aircraft, tanks, and heavy guns has made it extremely dependent upon the United States to supply its modern inventories.[2] Egypt is even more dependent upon the Soviet Union for its arsenal.

---

[1]Raymond Aron, *Peace and War: A Theory of International Relations* (New York: Praeger, 1968), pp. 48-50.

[2]However, Israel has improved its capacity to maintain and service sophisticated weapons such as the F-4 Phantom.

In terms of the milieu found in the Egyptian-Israeli strategic environment, three points are worth noting. First, since the 1967 war, Israel has a clear geostrategic advantage over Egypt. The occupation of the Sinai Desert means that Israel now has shorter and more easily defended borders with Egypt than it had in 1967. Furthermore, the Sinai allows Israel to disperse its forces more in depth and thereby avoid the dangers of concentration that were so apparent before 1967. Alternatively, Egypt has had to withdraw all its major forces from the Suez Canal zone and, given the physical constraints of the Suez Canal (perhaps the world's largest antitank ditch) and the range limitations of its current inventory of combat aircraft, it is in a much more difficult position to threaten the main concentration of Israeli targets.

The second geographical observation to make concerns climatic conditions. Weather conditions in the Middle East are stable and predictable. The skies over the Sinai, Suez, and the Nile valley are much clearer than those found in many other strategic areas, (e.g., Central Europe and South-East Asia). This means that airpower can be relied upon to undertake a great many military operations. The absence of a permanent cloud base and the absence of jungle terrain on the ground (as in South-East Asia) means that many of the elaborate navigation techniques required for target identification and destruction in other milieus are not presently required in the Egypt-Israel context.

A third important geographical variable concerns the Israeli occupation of Sharm-el-Shaykh and the control this gives Israel over the passage of military vessels into the Gulf of Eilat.

The third component of military force is capacity for collective action. A measure of the capacity for collective action in the military arena involves far more than an aggregation of the administrative, technical, and fighting skills of a country. It refers to certain incommensurable qualities such as morale, leadership, and the ability of the country as a whole to involve itself in the process of political mobilization for conflict and war.

It is generally accepted by most objective observers, including, incidentally, many Egyptians, that at the present time (February 1973) there is no doubt that Israel's overall political will to fight and to fight determinedly against Egypt is

greater than Egypt's capacity to do likewise. Whether this state of events will continue indefinitely is a subject that needs careful discussion. Perhaps it should be added here that while it may well be true that Israel is in a more superior military position vis-à-vis Egypt than at any time in its short history, the growing domestic situation in Israel gives pause for thought about the long-run political future of the country. One of the ironies of the success on the battlefield has been the relaxation of domestic unity and the emergence of many squabbles that had been brushed under the carpet during the traumatic twenty-five years between 1948 and 1973. It would not be too trite to say that the future domestic issues (the distribution of income between the various classes within Israel, the debate over the future concept of the Jewish role in Israel, etc.) mean that internal political dissension may be a vulnerable component of future Israeli grand strategy vis-à-vis the Arab countries.

THE EGYPT-ISRAEL MILITARY ENVIRONMENT, 1967–1972

Although Israel won the Six Day War with astonishing speed and skill, the period 1967–70 was very active militarily for Israel and its neighbors. A brief reminder of the military events of those years is in order:

1967	July–Sept.	Israeli and Egyptian artillery duels across Suez Canal.
	Oct. 24th	Egyptians sink *Eilat* destroyer; Israelis shell Suez oil refineries.
	Nov.	Israelis shell PLO bases in Jordan.
1968	Jan.–Dec.	Major Israeli, PLO and Jordanian clashes in Jordan valley.
	Oct.	Egyptian artillery barrage across Suez Canal.
	Nov.	Israelis raid across Canal to Nile River.
1969	Jan.–Dec.	Major clashes in Jordan valley continue.
	Jan.–Mar.	Artillery duels across Canal increase.
	April 1st	Nasser announces "War of Attrition."
	April–Dec.	War of Attrition continues.
	July 20th	Israel begins massive air attack on Egyptian Canal zone.
1970	Jan. 2nd & 3rd	Israeli deep penetration raids of Egypt begin.
	Feb. 12th	Israeli F-4's hit El-Khanka factory near Cairo.
	April	Soviet Union assumes responsibility for air defense of Nile valley.

Indeed, Israeli engineers have shown great imagination in *improving* certain features of modern French and American aircraft.

April 13th	Deep penetration raids suspended.
May	Egyptian commando raid across Canal.
	Massive Israeli air attacks against Egyptian artillery on Canal.
	Egyptians begin to rebuild SAM sites in Canal zone.
June	Soviets move SAM-2 and SAM-3s into Canal zone.
July	5 Israeli F-4s downed by SAMs.
Aug. 7th	Suez Cease-Fire.[3]

THE IMPORTANCE OF CASUALTY LEVELS AND AIR SUPERIORITY

During the height of the War of Attrition enunciated by President Nasser in April of 1969 and terminated with the cease-fire in August 1970, Israeli military casualties were averaging about 50 per week throughout that seventeen-month period (see Figure 1). This would have been equivalent to approximately 4,000 U.S. casualties per week at the height of the Vietnam War based upon per capita comparisons. Egyptian casualties during this war were much higher in absolute terms though in per capita terms probably lower. Unfortunately, data on Israeli casualties are very much better and more reliable than the data on Egyptian casualties. There have been reports that the high attrition caused by Israeli air strikes along the Suez Canal in the closing days of the War of Attrition was a determining factor in persuading President Nasser to agree to the cease-fire. Furthermore, we can speculate that the casualties Israel was inflicting upon Egypt were very high in terms of the skilled, trained personnel which are in such short supply in Egypt. Thus, although Israel's sensitivity to casualties is correctly regarded as a barometer in determining Israeli military behavior, it should not be thought that Egypt has an infinite capacity to absorb casualties, especially those of the military variety.[4]

During the period April 1969–August 1970, Israel suffered approximately 1,000 military combat casualties in the Suez-Sinai theater, including 274 killed in action. Of these, nearly 800 or 80% were caused by Egyptian small arms, artillery, and mortar fire.[5] Reliable data on Egyptian military casualties are not available, but some sources have estimated that during this same period Egypt lost over 10,000 military casualties. By far the greatest percent of these were caused by Israeli air attacks.[6]

An examination of the data shows that the casualties began to rise very dramatically on a monthly basis when the War of Attrition began. The casualties suffered in 1967 after the June War and in 1968 were, by Israeli standards, high, but they were primarily related to other theaters of operation, especially the Jordan front where the terrorist campaign was at its height. By far the largest proportion of Israeli casualties in 1969 and 1970 came from the Suez-Sinai front.

It has been pointed out that the largest number of Israelis along the Suez Canal were killed by Egyptian artillery, mortar, and small arms fire. On very few occasions did Egyptian air power contribute to Israeli casualties.

Three very important lessons can be drawn from this particular experience. First, Israel realizes that a war of attrition with Egypt, however painful to Egypt, will also result in major Israeli casualties from traditional weapons such as artillery, small arms, and mortars. Second, that air power, used systematically and over a period of time, inflicts high casualty levels on ground forces.[7] Third, that so long as Israel retains air superiority the ability of Egypt to inflict very high casualties by use of air power against Israel will be minimized.

Thus any redress in the balance of air power between Egypt and Israel would have the most severe consequences for Israel. So long as Israel retains air superiority it requires proportionately fewer military personnel to hold the Suez front along the Bar Lev Line. Of course other methods can be adopted to offset the Egyptian artillery and the purchase of the huge M-107 170mm self-propelled gun from the United States will make a major difference in Israel's ground force capability. But in the absence of Israeli air superiority,

---

[3] For an excellent and detailed treatment of this period see Lawrence L. Whetten, "June 1967 to June 1971: Four Years of Canal War Reconsidered," *New Middle East* 33 (June 1971): 15–25.

[4] More elaboration and data on the relationship between strategy, casualties, demography, and military power can be found in a forthcoming paper, *Population and War: Strategy, Demography, and Military Power*, by the author, which is part of an on-going project funded by the Population Council on "Population Dynamics and Organized Armed Conflict." This paper attempts to relate the three population variables, size, composition, and distribution, and changes in these variables to considerations of strategy and how strategy, in turn, affects the military force postures of various nations in various types of military conflicts.

[5] *Ibid.*

[6] Whetten, *op. cit.*

[7] This is not meant to imply that the Israeli air war over Egypt during this period was a "success" from the political perspective. This requires a detailed cost-benefit analysis of the deep penetration raids and the subsequent Soviet build-up which cannot be attempted here.

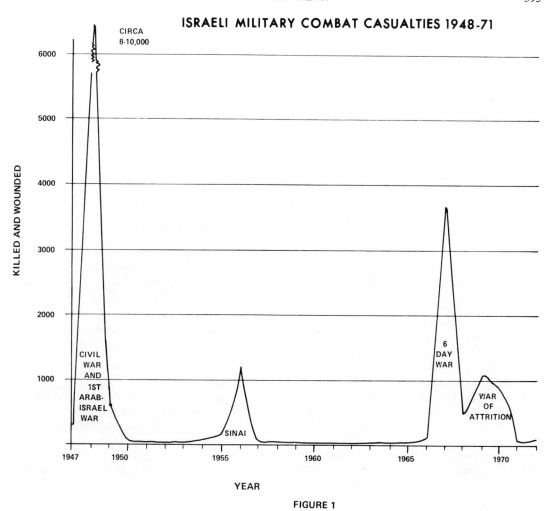

ISRAELI MILITARY COMBAT CASUALTIES 1948-71

FIGURE 1

no matter what Israel's qualitative advantages on the ground, the expected casualty levels might change dramatically in the event of the resumption of a war of attrition by Egypt.

It is this fact, probably more than any other that has influenced Israel's decision to emphasize air power as the most important component of its current and planned force posture. Furthermore, as we will see in the discussion on air power, it puts a high premium upon interdiction and close support missions for aircraft as distinct from point air defense.

It is in the context of comparative air strength that the role of the Soviet Union during this period was of most concern to Israel. The most important effect of the introduction of Soviet combat air teams into Egypt was the fear that at some time in the future they might challenge Israeli air superiority. Their ouster earlier this year was a godsend for all Israel military planners no matter what caution they may have expressed in public.

So long as the Soviet Union does not maintain its own air capability in Egypt, the relative amounts of equipment it gives Egypt are not so important. Some Israelis would prefer the Russians to abandon Egypt altogether. Others argue that some Soviet presence there acts as a deterrent against irrational Egyptian behavior. So long as the Soviet Union does not have the capacity to challenge Israel's air power, the presence of Soviet technicians manning SAM sites is a situation Israel can live with, though of course the SAM build-up in the Canal zone since the ceasefire would undoubtedly cause higher Israeli aircraft attrition rates if full scale fighting were to resume. Thus Egypt's potential ability to challenge Israeli air power over the Suez Canal zone with its SAM missiles is one of the more important elements in the relative balance of power.

THE BALANCE OF MILITARY POWER, 1972/73

In assessing the relative balance of military power between Israel and Egypt in 1973, one overriding factor needs to be stressed, namely that the defense budgets in both countries are extremely high. Despite its ten-fold advantage in terms of total population, Egypt's GNP approximates that of Israel (both are estimated in 1972 to be approximately $7.0 billion). As Table 1 points out, one dramatic and ironic effect of the June War was the quadrupling of both the Egyptian and Israeli defense budgets. Although the Israeli budget estimates for 1973 have not yet been agreed upon (December 1972), the final figure will no doubt be well in excess of one billion dollars. In the case of Egypt, the figures are equally high although their reliability is more in question. Both countries are spending in excess of 20% of their GNP's on defense. These are possibly the highest levels in the world.

Unfortunately, it is not possible to give a detailed, functional breakdown of these budgets. Egypt does not publish the figures. Israel does use very carefully prepared functional cost breakdowns since the formulation of the Israeli budget is a sophisticated and rational process which is based upon many of the techniques developed in the United States over the past ten years. However, Israel does not publish a functional breakdown of its budget. What we can glean from the open sources has to derive from statements by government spokesmen and odd items appearing in the foreign press.

In a speech on Thursday, August 17, 1972, Defense Minister Moshe Dayan discussed the relative progress of Israel's forces in comparison with the Arabs. He pointed out that over 50% of the present security budget has been invested in the air force and that this percentage will grow. In his speech he identified five important components of the defense budget and discussed the relative funds that had been allocated to them over the past five years. They were fortifications and infrastructure, security production, electronics, the armored corps, and the air force. Since this is an important statement and one that gives us information usually fairly difficult to come by, the key features of the speech are summarized here.

A. *Fortifications and Infra-Structure*
   1. Investments from 1967 through April 1973 will be about I.L. 1,364,000 m. ($320 m.[8]).
   2. Over half this sum ($160 m.) has been invested in Sinai. 40% of this sum was spent 1967—August 1970. 60% has been spent since the 1970 cease fire.
   3. The main investments have been in roads, fortifications, wire communications, control installations, camps, and airfields.

B. *Security Production, 1966–72*
   1. Since the Six Day War production has grown five-fold from approximately $81 million in 1966 to $450 million in 1972.
   2. The munitions industry has reached "full capacity" in most types of ammunition, light and medium weapons, and artillery.
   3. Continued growth at the rate of approximately $50–60 million/year is estimated.

C. *Electronics*
   Because electronics are a crucial input in modern sophisticated warfare, investments

[8]4.25 Israeli pounds = $1.00, 1 July 1972.

Table 1. Israeli and Egyptian Defense Expenditures, 1965–72*

	Israel		UAR	
	$ million	% GNP	$ million	% GNP
1965	382	11.7	437	8.6
1966	447	12.2	494	11.1
1967	498	11.5	645	12.7
1968	628	15.4	690	12.5
1969	1130	24.1	805	13.0
1970	1429	26.5	1262	19.6
1971	1484	23.9	1495	21.7
1972	Est. 1247	n/a	Est. 1510	n/a

Source: The Military Balance, 1966/7; 1967/8; 1968/9; 1969/70; 1970/71; 1971/72. (London: The International Institute for Strategic Studies, 1966, 1967, 1968, 1969, 1970, and 1971).

*Based on IISS estimates. Figures are expressed in current dollars.

have risen from about $14 million in 1967 to about $300 million over the period 1967–72.

D. *The Armored Corps*

1. The strength of the Israeli armored corps has doubled since 1967.
2. The average price of a tank that fought in 1967 was about $82,000 (1972 prices). The price of an improved tank in 1972 is about $170,000.
3. The price of the new tanks the armored corps will receive at the end of the 1970s will come to $400,000 each.

E. *The Air Force*

1. The strength of the air force has doubled since 1967.
2. Over 50% of the defense budget now goes to the Israeli air force. This percentage will grow in future.
3. The cost of modern aircraft is rising very sharply. A Mirage III in 1967 cost $1.4 million (1972 prices). The F-4 Phantom in 1972 costs between $4.8–7.8 million depending upon the model. The latest U.S. fighters, F-14 and F-15, cost over $14 million.

4. However, "our forecast of an expansion of the air force during this decade is not built on these planes" [the F-14 and F-15].

In conclusion Dayan said, "In the expansion of the IDF for the coming years, the emphasis is being placed upon the two decisive corps: the air force and the armor. In the expected budgets for the next five years, these two corps will take about 80% of the expansion budget and about 70% of the current budget while the rest of the corps of the IDS and the Security Establishment will have to divide only 20% among them."[9]

Israeli and Egyptian Air Power, 1972

Simple aggregate comparisons of Israeli and Egyptian air power based upon respective numbers of combat aircraft are a very poor guide for discussing the relative balance of air power. Table 2 suggests a mission-oriented comparison of Israeli and Egyptian air strengths based upon the latest IISS figures.

The four missions considered are:

1. *Air Superiority and Air Defense.* Air superiority missions are flown to protect friendly

[9] *The Jerusalem Post* (Weekly Overseas Edition) (August 22, 1972): 9.

Table 2. Comparison of Primary Missions of Israeli-Egyptian Air Power, 1967 & 1972

	1967 (June 4)		1972 (July)	
	Israel	UAR	Israel	UAR
Air Defense and Air Superiority	20 Super-Mystere 24 Hawk SAMs	163 Mig-21 40 Mig-19	9 Super-Mystere 48 Hawk SAMs	220 Mig-21 600 SA-2, SA-3**
	92 Mirage IIIc* 50 Mystere IV*		90 F-4E* 50 Mirage IIIc*	
Deep Interdiction and Reconnaissance	40 Ouragon 24 Vautour	30 TU-16 43 IL-28	10 Vautour 125 A-4EH 6 RF-4E	18 TU-16
Close Air Support	60 Jet Trainers	100 Mig 15/17 55 SU-7 Some Jet Trainers	132 Jet Trainers and reserve aircraft	200 Mig-17 120 SU-7 200 Jet Trainers
Tactical Air Lift	32 Stratocruisers & Noratlas 30 Helicopters	70 IL-14, AN-12 48 Helicopters	10 Stratocruisers 20 Noratlas 10 C-47 2 C-130E 72 Helicopters	40 IL-14 20 AN-12 180 Helicopters

Sources: Derived from *The Military Balance, 1966/67, 1972/73*; Geoffrey Kemp, *Arms and Security: The Egypt-Israel Case*, Adelphi Paper No. 52 (London: Institute for Strategic Studies, September 1969); Nadav Safran, *From War to War* (New York: Pegasus, 1969).

*These aircraft can be used for both air superiority and deep interdiction.

**There remains some doubt as to whether the USSR left behind the more advanced SA-4 (Ganet) and SA-6 (Gainful) after its withdrawal. If a number of these very advanced missiles remain, they further increase Egypt's point defense capability, assuming they can be operated effectively.

air, sea, and ground forces from enemy air attack. This overall mission can include specialist roles such as air-to-air escort capabilities, and long-range point interception. Air defense also refers to the ability to protect ground forces and installations from attack by air, but includes missions assigned to weapons systems other than aircraft, e.g., surface-to-air missiles (SAMs) and anti-aircraft artillery (AAA).

2. *Deep Interdiction and Reconnaissance.* Deep interdiction missions include medium range bombing of fixed or mobile enemy military or logistic installations with a variety of different ordnance, including cannon, machine guns, rockets, napalm, HE, delayed-fuse mines, anti-personnel weapons, and air-to-surface missiles. Reconnaissance missions are designed to provide information of all branches of enemy activity.

3. *Close Air Support.* These missions are flown for ground attack roles against enemy forces operating in close proximity to friendly forces.

4. *Tactical Air Lift.* This provides the theater commander with logistics support for ground forces both within the theater of operations and from air and sea points to the theater.[10]

With reference to Table 2, two things should be initially pointed out. First, the breakdown of the inventories into primary missions is somewhat arbitrary since many of the aircraft, especially those in the Israeli inventory, can perform more than one mission. This is particularly true of multi-purpose systems such as the Mirage and the Phantom. However, what I have tried to do in Table 2 is to suggest that certain aircraft are better suited for certain missions than others and that in any overall comparison Israel presently has more mission flexibility than Egypt, whose systems tend to be tied much more to the single purpose mission.

Another simple point to make—which relates back to the high levels of defense expenditure discussed earlier—would be the impressive growth of both air forces since the June War in 1967. In weighing the respective growth rates it should be recalled that Egypt suffered very high losses during the Six Day War and therefore the comparison of the two inventories should also take into account aircraft destroyed and aircraft replaced. This would suggest that the total turnover of new aircraft in Egypt has been much

higher than is reflected in this Table. Both air forces are now very dependent upon single suppliers: Egypt and the Soviet Union; Israel and the United States. In the case of Israel, the United States has replaced France as the major supplier and in particular, as the supplier of the two aircraft that are now very visible in the 1972 inventory (the F-4 Phantom and the A-4 Skyhawk).

Air Superiority and Air Defense

A more detailed comparison of the various missions will now be made. Egypt, rather than Israel, has developed by far the most impressive point air defense capability with the introduction of large numbers of sophisticated SAM missiles and their associated radars. These, in conjunction with the Mig-21 force, provide Egypt with probably one of the most sophisticated air defense environments in the world. However, whereas this capability—assuming it can be operated effectively—has undoubted advantages in terms of protecting fixed facilities against Israeli air attack, it is not a very flexible investment in military force structure. The restricted combat radius of the Mig-21 and its reliance upon the ground environment suggest that its primary function is to protect Egyptian military installations along the Suez Canal and along the Nile valley.[11]

Although Israel has an impressive air defense capability in the form of aircraft that can be used for the interception and air-to-air role (the F-4's and the Mirage 3's), it has invested trivial amounts of money in surface-to-air missiles (only 48 Hawks) suggesting that Israeli planners are presently less concerned about point air defense and more interested in maintaining air superiority through the flexible use of both interdiction and air-to-air capabilities that can be conducted by the F-4 and the Mirage 3. However, if the Soviet Union were to reintroduce a major air component into Egypt again or if it were to hand over large numbers of Mach 3.0 Mig-23's, Israel will need to upgrade further its air-to-air capabilities. Although this could, in theory, include a request for the U.S. F-15 aircraft, the costs of such an option would be extremely high. Instead, continued efforts will probably be made to increase the capabilities of the F-4 by introducing longer range air-to-air missiles.

[10]There are other more esoteric support missions not listed here which certainly Israel and possibly Egypt have some capabilities for, e.g., electronic countermeasures (ECM), tactical air control, airborne warning and control, and inflight refueling.

[11]As pointed out earlier, this capability enhances Egypt's ability to conduct some offensive military operations across the canal, especially the protracted use of artillery against Israeli ground positions.

The Mig-23, by itself, would not pose a major military threat to Israel since it is essentially a high flying interceptor and reconnaissance aircraft. However, the possible political and psychological effects of immune Egyptian overflights of Israeli-held territory are themselves important.[12]

Deep Interdiction and Reconnaissance

This mission refers to the ability to hit targets deep in enemy territory. Some of the most sensitive arguments between the Soviet Union and Egypt have concerned the poor capabilities Egypt has for this mission. The small numbers of TU-16's and IL-28's in the Egyptian inventory reflect Soviet unwillingness to build up Egyptian offensive capabilities, in comparison to their investment in Egyptian air defense. The TU-16, because of its high payload, has a great deal of military utility, but the few numbers owned by Egypt and its subsonic speed mean that in comparison with the F-4 Phantom it is a very second-rate substitute.

Israel, on the other hand, has developed what can only be described as one of the most sophisticated interdiction capabilities for any small air force in the world. The Phantom/Skyhawk com-

bination and their associated weapons are very impressive and are built around two of the most tested combat aircraft in the world. Not only have both aircraft been tested in battle, but they also have good performance characteristics. In particular, both have a high combat radius. This has two primary advantages. First, it enables Israel theoretically to reach most targets in Egypt, Syria, Jordan, Iraq, and Lebanon with these aircraft. In the case of the F-4 it also means that for the air interception and air superiority missions, Israel can trade off its bomb load capacity for extra fuel so that the combat air patrol capability of the F-4 Phantom is such that it can remain airborne for a much longer time than the Mig-21, which in this mission would be its most severe challenger.

Table 3 makes some simple aggregate comparisons between three primary Israeli and three Egyptian combat aircraft. Table 3 includes some rough cost estimates that are so important when considering future planning options. It can be seen that if one uses *total pay load* as an index of capability then Israel has a three-to-one superiority over the current Egyptian Air Force.

The introduction of the F-4 and the Skyhawk since 1967 represents the most dramatic change in the balance of air power for the interdiction mission between Egypt and Israel. If the performance characteristics of these two aircraft are related to the new geography which has been mentioned earlier, it can be seen why the Egyptians who are knowledgeable about the impor-

---

[12]For a more detailed discussion of some general aspects of the balance between point air defense systems and interdiction aircraft see E. Luttwak, "(Mig-21 + Mig-23 + SAM-3) − (F.4 + A.4 + AGM) = ?" *New Middle East* 39 (December 1971).

Table 3. Selected Performance Characteristics of Egyptian and Israeli Combat Aircraft, 1972

Aircraft	Number	Maximum Payload (lbs.)	Maximum Speed (mach. no.)	Maximum Radius with 3,000 lbs.* Payload	Approx. Unit Cost ($ million, 1972 prices)
Egypt					
Mig-21D	220	2,000	2.0	150–200	1.00
SU-7	120	4,500	1.6	150–200	1.00 Est.
TU-16	18	20,000	0.85	1,500	.70
Israel					
Mirage III	50	6,000	2.0	460	1.4
Phantom F-4E	90	16,000	2.0	700	5.0
Skyhawk A-4E	125	11,000	0.9	750	1.5

Sources: Janes, *All the World Aircraft, 1968–69* (New York: McGraw-Hill, 1967); John H. Hoagland, *World Combat Aircraft Inventories and Production, 1970–75, Implications for Arms Transfer Policies* (MIT Center for International Studies, Publication No. C/70-6, February 1970). *The Military Balance 1971–72, op. cit.*

*The combat radius figures have been calculated on the basis of a "hi-lo-hi" mission. This means that the aircraft flies to target at a high altitude (35,000 ft.) where fuel consumption

is at a minimum, descends to target to offload ordnance (0–1000 ft.) and then returns to base at original height. If the mission were "lo-lo-lo," that is to say, the entire mission were flown at low altitudes, the figures for combat radius with 3000 lb. payload would drop dramatically. However, the great advantage of flying "lo-lo-lo" is that at low altitudes the probability of being detected on enemy radar screens is at a minimum. The Israeli air strikes against Egyptian air bases on the morning of June 5, 1967, were flown at low level.

tance of the interdiction mission are so frustrated over the lack of cooperation they have received from the Soviet Union in supplying them with comparable weapon systems.[13] This is not to say that if they were supplied with the equivalents of the Phantom and the Skyhawk they would be able to use them effectively. To do that requires very careful training and it is believed that Egypt is still very deficient in this arena. Furthermore, there are other quantitative methodologies that should be discussed if a very detailed comparison needs to be made. For example, perhaps as important as the range-pay load index would be the number of sorties that each air force could generate in a particular time frame. This is a function of crew training, the relative ease of maintenance for the particular aircraft, the ordnance requirements for the mission, and the number of pilots. If crews are well trained, then turn-round times can be reduced to a very short period if the aircraft are easy to maintain. It is possible to keep one aircraft operational for many hours a day provided back-up air crews are available. Thus Egypt's shortage of trained pilots is a very serious constraint.

Close Air Support

Since the close air support mission could be termed as an "interdiction" mission, many of the aircraft that are suitable for deep interdiction can also be used for close air support. However, certain aircraft, such as jet trainers, that are suitable for close air support, cannot be used for deep interdiction. Hence one can argue that in order to compare the close air support capabilities one really needs to take into account both deep interdiction aircraft and close air support aircraft. In Table 2 it can be seen that Israel again has a qualitative and quantitative advantage in this arena. Particularly important are the Magister trainers which have a very effective antitank capability and cost much less than the A-4 Skyhawk or F-4 Phantom.

Tactical Air Lift

This is an important mission, especially for Israel who has to plan to fight a war on three fronts. It can be seen that since 1967, both Egypt and Israel have increased their tactical air lift capabilities, especially in the field of helicopters. Helicopters can be used for many purposes and

the various commando raids that Israel has conducted since 1967 against both Egyptian and other Arab targets are perhaps the single most impressive demonstration of their effectiveness in the Israeli inventory.

For the more day-to-day, mundane work-horse roles of supplying the Bar Lev Line and quickly moving reinforcements from one front to another, both the helicopters and the new C-130 Hercules aircraft add to a capability that was somewhat deficient in 1967. Similarly, if Egypt were to wish ever to cross the Suez Canal in strength, an ability to air lift personnel in an initial assault on Israeli positions would probably require the use of helicopter forces. In this sense the addition of the Soviet helicopters is one of the more important capabilities that the Egyptians have built up since 1967.

To sum up, this cursory comparison of air strength on a mission specific basis between Egypt and Israel suggests that Israel presently has some important advantages in all mission capabilities apart from point air defense. With regard to the future direction of air power between these two countries, we would need to take into account the future supply policies of the United States and the Soviet Union which, in turn, cannot be dissociated from their overall political and strategic goals. Perhaps a more useful exercise at this stage, especially for those interested in defense planning, would be to focus upon the extraordinarily high costs of modernization in both countries. If the current unit costs of an F-4 Phantom is between $5.0–8.5 million, then for this amount of money Israel could purchase at least two new Skyhawks (A-4 M), four or five Magister trainers, or one C-130 Hercules.

It might be useful to speculate about what types of trade-offs are made in Israel in deciding whether to invest in Phantoms or any of the other alternative packages that could be derived. Furthermore, it is not only in the arena of alternative combat aircraft that trade-offs can be made. A large number of M-107 guns or even M-60 tanks can be procured for the price of one F-4. More will be said of the importance of armor in the following section and there is no doubt as air power and armor compete, however subtly, for the defense budget there must be some discussion in Israel as to the wisdom of putting so much emphasis upon very advanced aircraft.

However, it would seem that Israel's overriding need to hold down casualties in any military situation will be the determining procurement factor rather than esoteric budgetary tradeoffs. Both the empirical evidence and Israeli perceptions of the evidence suggest that air supe-

---

[13]According to one report, the Egyptians wanted the Soviet Union to supply them with TU-22 medium-range bombers armed with Kitchen air-to-surface missiles and 720 km range Scud surface-to-surface missiles. *The Jerusalem Post* (August 1, 1972): 6.

riority is indeed a key for holding down Israeli casualties in combat situations. Thus a criterion for determining weapons "effectiveness" in this situation would be "effect upon Israeli casualty levels." The priority must be to win war as quickly as possible since it is the duration of conflict that is closely related to casualty levels. In this case, one can expect Israel to continue to invest in many of the most sophisticated weapons systems that are available in the American market and this would include investment in the vital subsystems (ECM, advanced avionics, and SMART bombs) which have been developed in Vietnam.

Israeli-Egyptian Armor and Ground Weapons Comparisons, 1967 and 1972

A comparison of Israeli and Egyptian armor and major ground weapons in 1967 and 1972 is given in Table 4. As mentioned earlier, the emphasis upon armor in the Israeli defense

forces is almost as important as the emphasis upon combat air power. Thus while the overall modernization of the Israeli ground forces has proceeded at a substantial rate since 1967, the modernization of the armored component represents the most significant change.

This is not to say that improvements in other sectors of the ground forces are to be discounted. Far from it. In fact, it is sometimes not appreciated that when the Israeli army went to war in 1967 it was equipped with a very motley selection of small arms and the support systems that are required for basic infantry operations. Rifles were not standardized throughout the army and many of the mortars and machine guns were antiquated. There has been a major emphasis upon standardization and modernization of the infantry since 1967.[14]

[14]It has recently been reported that the Israeli Military Industries has produced "the most advanced assault rifle in

Table 4. Israeli-Egyptian Armor and Major Ground Weapons, 1967 and 1972

	1967		1972	
	Israel	UAR	Israel	UAR
Tanks	200 M-48 250 Centurion 150 AMX-13 200 Sherman	350 T-34 450 T-54 Some T-55 60 JS-3 30 Centurion 20 AMX-13	450 M-48 250 Ben Gurion 700 Centurion 200 Isherman and Super Sherman 100 T1-67 Some M-60	50 JS-3 1500 T54/55 10 T-62 400 T-34 100 PT-76
	800	At least 1000	At least 1700	2600
Armored cars and APCs	n/a	n/a	AML-60 AML-90 Staghound 1000 M-2, M-3 M-113 APCs	2000 APCs
	n/a	n/a	At least 1300	2000

Howitzers and
self-propelled guns
	c. 250 105 mm
	  and 155 mm
		150 SU-100 HOW	352 105 mm and
			  155 mm
			Some M-107
			  175 mm
			Some 155 mm on
			  Sherman
				150 SU-100 and
				  ISU-152 HOW
				1500 122 mm,
				  130 mm, 152 mm
				40 203 mm

	At least 250	150	At least 400	1690
SSMs	none	none	(Jericho)*	24 FROG-3 Some FROG-7 25 Samlet
				c. 50

Sources: See Table 2.

*Not yet in service.

Egypt, too, has received large quantities of Soviet armor since 1967 and has also up-graded its general ground-force capabilities including the addition of thousands of pieces of small arms and artillery which were used in the War of Attrition and still remain along the Suez Canal.

Table 4 breaks down the weapons into four categories: tanks, armored cars and armored personnel carriers, howitzers, and self-propelled guns, and surface-to-surface missiles. Israel has doubled its tank strength since 1967. Aside from the hundred converted Soviet tanks it now has in its inventory (T1-67; they are Soviet T54/55s with 105 mm gun), more Centurions have been added and more of the older British Centurions have been up-graded with 105 millimeter guns. Over 250 M-48 Patton tanks have been added to the inventory and now Israel is beginning to receive the much more sophisticated version of the M-48, the M-60. Despite the fact that these tanks have come from Soviet, British and American inventories, the Israelis themselves have proven to be very adept at converting them for the particular conditions they find in the Sinai and elsewhere.[15]

Although precise figures are not available as to the number of armored cars and APCs that Israel had in 1967, it is believed that many of those now in the inventory have been added since that period. These complement the build-up in the tank category since the overall armored capability of Israel would integrate both tanks, armored cars, and armored personnel carriers in combat conditions. Taken together these two categories of equipment provide Israel with much more mobile ground fire power than it possessed in 1967 and given the relatively small deployment of forward forces along the Bar Lev Line the ability to reinforce rapidly should the Egyptians attempt a Canal crossing is a key goal of Israeli planners.

For this reason one would need to look not only at the ground forces but the theater air lift capabilities mentioned in the previous section. These, together with the tanks, armored cars, and APCs, should be seen as giving Israel an impressive reinforcement capability should combat conditions deteriorate along the Suez Canal and in the Sinai Desert.

All these weapons have utility in other theaters of operation though less so. Consequently, it can be argued that the massive build-up of armor and ground forces is again, as in the case of the air force, very closely linked to the Egyptian contingency and the possibility of having to fight another Sinai war or even a war across the Canal.

In a discussion with military correspondents on Sunday, October 22, 1972, Aluf Adan, O.C. Armored Corps, said that his planners have concentrated on giving the tanks greater logistical independence and longer range. He believed that new basic strategy and new doctrines were required to prepare for the possibility of much longer armored confrontations with Arab forces. In particular, emphasis has been given to training for crossing water hazards and combating minefields. He pointed out that Egypt was engaging in similar training maneuvers.[16]

It can be inferred from this statement that both Israel and Egypt have made careful contingency plans for crossing the Suez Canal with major armored units. Although Israel has used tanks on the other fronts, the importance of the new equipment, strategy, and doctrines relates primarily to the Suez-Sinai front.

Although Israel would probably be extremely reluctant to engage in a major canal crossing for both political reasons and because of high expected casualties, the strategic environment could change to the point when a massive Israeli air and armored assault across the Canal would be a serious military option.

This contingency is also reflected in the increasing emphasis Israel has placed upon howitzers, self-propelled guns, and surface-to-surface missiles. Throughout the War of Attrition, Israel was consistently outgunned by the big guns that the Soviets had provided the Egyptians, especially the 130 mm with its 27 km range. It was for this reason that Israel decided to purchase the M-107 175 mm self-propelled gun from the United States which has a range of 32.7 km. Although not many of these have so far entered the inventory, their potential for shifting the balance of artillery power along the Suez Canal is an important one. These guns are highly accurate (with CEPs of only a few meters over 32 kms) and highly mobile. These two characteristics alone can more than compensate for the few numbers that Israel will probably end up with. The M-107 will be able to target SAMs and their radars as well as more traditional ground targets. It should be noted that Egypt has no

---

the world" (according to *Infantry*, the journal of the Infantry School of the United States Army). The rifle is called Galil and will eventually replace all company weapons. *The Jerusalem Post* (October 24, 1972): 3.

[15]Evidently one major problem Israel had in converting the Soviet tanks was that they were so uncomfortable and difficult to operate. Furthermore, they had been designed for cold climates, not the desert. *The Jerusalem Post* (October 24, 1972): 1.

[16]*Ibid.*

equivalent gun in its own inventory since the Soviet Union has not emphasized self-propelled guns. Soviet guns, although very good for most purposes, have to be hitched to tractors and towed, thus making them much more vulnerable than the M-107.

The Jericho surface-to-surface missile Israel has been developing is not yet believed to be in service. A great deal of speculation exists concerning the role that this missile would play in any conventional military scenario with Egypt. It does not seem a very useful system, given its inevitable high costs, if it is to be used solely in a conventional mode. There has been speculation that it could provide the delivery capability for a tactical or low-yield strategic nuclear missile system should Israel ever decide that it needed to deploy such a capability.

Without devoting too much time to speculation, it has always been the opinion of this author that Israel has, indeed, taken a great many steps towards the option of building nuclear weapons and clearly an ability to operate and maintain sophisticated missiles systems could be seen as part of this long-run insurance policy.

Nevertheless, if one discounts the nuclear role that the Jericho might play, its conventional utility would depend upon its accuracy, its mobility, its range, and its cost if it were to be integrated into the conventional armed forces. Surface-to-surface missiles with a range in excess of 200 miles could be used by Israel against Cairo and other large, soft Egyptian targets. Whether the terror effects of a conventional missile bombardment of Cairo would have any psychological pay-off is a matter for debate. The Egyptian surface-to-surface missiles (Frog 3 and 7) are not believed to be related at all to any nuclear option. It has always been suggested that they are primarily there for terror purposes. That is to say, the ability to threaten Tel Aviv or Jerusalem.

The Egyptians, too, have built up their tank strength. Not only have they increased the inventory they possessed in 1967 by a factor of 2.5, but because of the losses they suffered during that war, the absolute additions of their inventory have been much higher, in excess of 400%. Although the numbers of tanks and armored cars and armored personnel carriers in the Egyptian inventory are numerous, there is some doubt whether they have yet mastered the ability to maximize the effectiveness of these systems in combat profiles. Egypt does not have the indigenous capacity that Israel possesses for innovating and modifying basic Soviet equipment which reflect Soviet doctrines and tactics.

Egypt's capability in howitzers and artillery is impressive and very relevant to the current military balance. It should be repeated that the effectiveness of these weapons is compounded many times when they are used in conjunction with the point air defense systems.

Israeli-Egyptian Naval Forces, 1967 and 1972

The navy remains the Cinderella service in both Egypt and Israel. It is not possible to specify exactly how much money is spent on both navies, but a glance at the inventories points to the fact that both are, by comparison with land and air forces, very small.

Nevertheless, there are some events and changes that have occurred since 1967 that are worth stressing. The first event was the sinking of the Israeli destroyer, Eilat on October 24, 1967 by Egyptian Styx missiles fired from Komar patrol boats. This incident has had worldwide repercussions. It has persuaded the United States Navy that surface-to-surface antishipping missiles are an important adjunct to any modern naval force and since 1967 more emphasis has been placed upon attaining this capacity in the Western navies.

Israel, too, would seem to have learned from the bitter experience. As can be seen in Table 5, Israel has developed a sea missile system called the *Gabriel*. This is believed to be very efficient and very cheap and has already been ear-marked as a possible export-earner for the hard-pressed Israeli economy. It has been fitted to the twelve fast patrol boats (FPB) which Israel surreptitiously removed from France in 1969. Thus Israel, and to a lesser extent Egypt, would seem to be emphasizing small, fast naval capabilities rather than the more traditional trappings of naval power built around cruisers, destroyers, and submarines.

The reason why both countries should attach fairly low priorities to attaining multi-purpose naval capabilities is fairly obvious. Naval forces play a very important role in any conventional military operation provided that either the ocean or seas themselves are an important milieu in determining the strategic outcomes, or provided that the war be protracted and reinforcements be dependent upon sea logistics. (For instance, during the Egyptian intervention in Yemen between 1962 and 1967, most of Egypt's supply came by sea.) However in the current strategic context of the Egyptian-Israeli confrontation it is difficult to imagine that sea-borne operations would have a decisive effect upon overall military outcome. This is not to discount the utility of either navy for limited support missions. How-

Table 5. Israeli–Egyptian Naval Forces, 1967 and 1972

1967		1972	
Israel	Egypt	Israel	Egypt
2 destroyers	4 destroyers (Skory Class)	1 destroyer	5 destroyers
1 anti-aircraft Frigate	2 destroyers (Z Class)	2 submarines	2 Corvettes
4 submarines	6 escorts	12 FPB (with Gabriel SSM)	12 SO-1 submarine-chasers
1 patrol vehicle	9 submarines	4 motor boats	12 submarines
3 landing craft	6 submarine-chasers	12 patrol craft less than 100 tons	9 fleet minesweepers
14 patrol craft less than 100 tons	14 minesweepers	10 landing craft	2 inshore minesweepers
	10 missile patrol boats (Komar)		12 Osa FPBs
	44 MTBs		6 Komar FPBs (with Styx SSM)
	10 landing craft		20 MTBs (less than 100 tons)
			12 landing craft

Source: The Military Balance, 1966/67; 1971/72.

CONCLUSIONS

A comprehensive analysis and comparison of Egyptian and Israeli force postures would need to take into account other military factors in the Middle East conflict including the major external powers. Furthermore, the basic asymmetries in the political strategies and military doctrines of both countries would need to be discussed in some detail. Nevertheless, a simple comparison of Egyptian and Israeli military force postures in isolation from these other variables allows us to make some interesting, if somewhat restrictive, observations. The most important are:

1. Since the end of the June War both Israel and Egypt have invested much higher proportions of their total GNPs in defense budgets than they did before the war. Virtually all the Egyptian investment has been directed towards three goals: rebuilding the forces destroyed or captured in the 1967 war; providing men and material for conflict with Israel during the War of Attrition,

ever, it is not to be expected that the priorities will change over the next few years.

1969–70; and restructuring and retraining its forces in preparation for another possible major confrontation with Israel. Although Israel's defense effort has had to cover more contingencies than the threat posed by Egypt, and, for a period, the Soviet Union, the Suez-Sinai contingency has absorbed the highest proportion of the Israeli defense budget. It is not likely that these budgetary trends will change very much unless a major political settlement between the two countries is reached.

2. The War of Attrition convinced Israel that its overall emphasis upon attaining air superiority had been basically correct when viewed from its special perspective which places such a premium upon minimizing its own casualties. However the War of Attrition also showed that Israel could still be severely hurt by Egypt's protracted use of artillery and other ground weapons. Alternatively, Egypt should have learned that so long as Israel retains air superiority, Egyptian military casualties will invariably be much higher than Israel's in any new conflict. Although in absolute terms of comparative population size, Egypt can afford to absorb

higher casualties, in terms of expected losses of trained military personnel, the effect would be very great.

3. The withdrawal of Soviet personnel and air combat units from Egypt in 1972 has radically shifted the overall balance of military power in Israel's favor, at least for the present. The most serious direct military threat posed by the Soviet presence was an ability to challenge Israel's air superiority. With that threat removed for the time being, Israel can probably cope with a further increase in Egyptian air strength, even if it were to include substantial numbers of Mig-23s.

4. A mission-specific comparison of Egyptian and Israeli airpower suggests that whereas Egypt has deployed one of the most sophisticated point air defense systems in the world, in all other mission categories, including at the time of writing the air-to-air combat mission, Israel has an overwhelming advantage. The addition of the U.S. F-4 and A-4 aircraft to the Israeli inventory since 1967 reflects this superiority. However it also reflects Israel's present dependence upon the United States for advanced weapons. Israel is also believed to have deployed very sophisticated U.S. support systems for its aircraft including some of the latest ECM techniques and air-to-ground (AGM) missiles.

5. Armor is the next most important category in the two force structures. A strong armored capability would be essential to either side if a major confrontation were to recur in the Sinai or even across the Suez Canal. Both countries have invested heavily in modern tanks, APC's and howitzers, although only Israel has been able to procure a long-range, accurate self-propelled gun, the U.S. M-107. The M-107 should provide Israel with an extremely effective weapon to challenge not only the big Egyptian guns across the canal but also the Egyptian SAMs and their radar components which protect the guns.

6. In sum it can be argued that so long as the Soviet Union does not reestablish a major military presence in Egypt, Israel's military power is probably sufficient to ensure an eventual Israeli victory in event of a resumption of hostilities between the two countries. However whether this "superiority" is sufficient to deter an Egyptian leader from engaging in future hostilities remains an open question. Although Israel may well be able to "win" a new war with Egypt, it would do so at a price that might be very high in terms of expected Israeli casualties. For this reason Israeli defense policy will continue to reflect a military doctrine that is designed to exploit Israel's technical superiority by emphasizing modern, mobile force structures that have been adapted for the unique environment of the Middle East. Israel's primary goal will continue to be to "deter" full scale war but if "deterrence" fails, to defeat the enemy main force units in as short a period of time as possible.

American Assembly. *A World of Nuclear Powers?* Englewood Cliffs, N.J.: Prentice-Hall, 1966.

Armbruster, Frank E. "China's Conventional Military Capability." Tang Tsou (ed.), *China In Crisis*, Vol. II. Chicago: University of Chicago Press, 1968. pp. 161–200.

Ashcroft, Geoffrey. *Military Logistic Systems In NATO: The Goal of Integration; Parts I & II* Adelphi Papers Nos. 62 & 63. London: IISS, Nov. 1969 & June 1970.

Baldwin, Hanson; Martin, Laurence W., et al. *Soviet Sea Power*, Special Report Series No. 10. Washington, D.C.: The Center for Strategic and International Studies, Georgetown University, July 1969.

*Beaton, Leonard. *Must the Bomb Spread?* Baltimore: Penguin Books, 1966.

Beaton, Leonard, and Maddox, John. *The Spread of Nuclear Weapons.* New York: Frederick A. Praeger, 1962.

Bellany, Ian. *An Australian Nuclear Force*, Canberra Paper No. 4. Canberra, Aus.: Australian Nat'l. University Press, 1969.

*Blackman, Raymond V. B. (ed.). *Jane's Fighting Ships 1972–73.* New York: McGraw-Hill, 1973.

Blechman, Barry M. *The Changing Soviety Navy.* Washington, D.C.: The Brookings Institution, 1973.

Booth, K. "NATO Ground Forces and the Soviet Threat." *Army Quarterly* 101 (July 1971): 426–36.

Booth, Richard. *The Armed Forces of the African States*, 1970, Adelphi Paper No. 67. London: IISS, May 1970.

*Boulding, Kenneth. *Conflict and Defense.* New York: Harper & Row, 1962.

Breyer, Siegfried. *Guide to the Soviet Navy.* Annapolis, Md.: U.S. Naval Institute, 1970.

*The Brookings Institution. "The Soviet Defense Budget." *Selling National Priorities: The 1973 Budget.* Washington, D.C.: The Brookings Institution, 1972.

Buchan, Alastair, and Windsor, Philip. *Arms and Stability in Europe.* New York: Frederick A. Praeger, 1963.

Buck, James H. "Japan's Defense Options for the 1970's." *Asian Survey*: 10, no. 10 (October 1970): 890–99.

*Bull, Hedley. *The Control of the Arms Race*, Second ed. New York: Frederick A. Praeger, 1965.

"Canada's Budget Crunches Are Behind It." *Armed Forces Journal International* 110, no. 8 (April 1973).

*Chayes, Abram. "An Inquiry Into the Workings of Arms Control Agreements." *Harvard Law Review* 85 (March 1972).

Chiu, S. M. "China's Military Posture." *Current History* 53 (September 1967): 155–60.

Clemens, Walter C. *The Arms Race and Sino-Soviet Relations.* Stanford, Calif.: The Hoover Institution on War, Revolution and Peace, 1968.

Cordier, Sherwood S. "Japan: Present and Potential Military Power." *U.S. Naval Institute Proceedings* 93 (Nov. 1967): 68–78.

De Strihou, Jacques van Ypersole. "Sharing the Defense Burden Among Western Allies." *Review of Economics & Statistics* 49 (Nov. 1967): 527–36.

*Dolian, James P. "The Military and the Allocation of National Resources: An Examination of Thirty-Four Sub-Sahara African Nations." Paper presented to the International Studies Association meeting, New York, March 14–17, 1973.

*Dupuy, T. N., and Blanchard, Wendell. *The Almanac of World Military Power*, second edition. New York: R. R. Bowker Co., 1972.

Ellis, Gerald. "China's Military Strength." *Military Review* 51 (April 1971): 71–76.

*Emmerson, John K. *Arms, Yen and Power: The Japanese Dilemma.* New York: Dunellen Publishing Co., 1971.

*Enthoven, Alain. "Arms and Men: The Military Balance in Europe." *Interplay* 2 (May 1969): 11–14.

Enthoven, Alain, and Smith, K. Wayne. "What Forces For NATO? And From Whom?." *Foreign Affairs* 48 (Oct. 1969): 80–96.

*Erickson, John. *Soviet Military Power.* London: RUSI, 1971.

Fabian, Larry L. *Soldiers without Enemies: Preparing the United Nations for Peacekeeping.* Washington, D.C.: The Brookings Institution, 1971.

Fraser, Angus. "Some Thoughts on the Resurgence of Militarism in Japan." Mimeo. unpublished manuscript, Washington, D.C., 1972.

French White Paper on National Defense. New York: French Embassy, 1972.

Gallagher, Matthew P. "Military Manpower: A Case Study." *Problems of Communism* 13, no. 3 (May-June 1964): 53–62.

*German Federal Government. *White Paper 1971/1972: The Security of the Federal Republic of Germany and the Development of the Federal Armed Forces.* Bonn: Federal Ministry of Defence, 1971.

Goldstein, Walter. *The Dilemma of British Defense: The Imbalance Between Commitments and Resources.* Columbus, Ohio: Ohio State Univ. Press, 1966.

Goure, Leon. *Civil Defense in the Soviet Union.* Berkeley, Calif.: Univ. of California Press, 1962.

———. *Recent Developments in the Soviet Civil Defense Program*, June 1963. Santa Monica, Calif.: The RAND Corporation, June 1973.

*Greenwood, David. *Budgeting For Defence.* London: RUSI, December 1972.

*———. *The Economics of the East of Suez Decision.* Mimeo. unpublished, King's College, Scotland, 1973.

Griffith, Samuel. "Chinese Defence Capabilities." *USI Journal* 100 (Oct./Dec. 1970): 457–74.

*Particularly recommended.

Häckel, Erwin. *Military Manpower and Political Purpose*, Adelphi Paper No. 72. London: IISS, December 1970.

Halperin, Morton H. *China and the Bomb*. New York: Frederick A. Praeger, 1965.

—— (ed.). *Sino-Soviet Relations and Arms Control*. Cambridge, Mass.: MIT Press, 1967.

*Halperin, Morton, H., and Perkins, Dwight H. *Communist China and Arms Control*. New York: Frederick A. Praeger, 1965.

*Huntington, Samuel P. "Arms Races: Prerequisites and Results." Carl J. Friedrich and Seynow E. Harris (eds.), *Public Policy*. Cambridge, Mass.: Harvard Graduate School of Public Administration, 1958.

*Hurewitz, J. C. *Middle East Politics: The Military Dimension*. New York: Frederick A. Praeger, 1969.

Hutchings, Raymond. "Soviet Defense Spending and Soviet External Relations." *International Relations* (London) 47 (July 1971): 518–31.

Hutzel, John M., and Edwards, M. O. *Japanese Security Posture and Policy, 1970–1980*. Menlo Park, Calif.: Stanford Research Institute, 1971.

*International Institute for Strategic Studies. *The Military Balance 1972–1973*. London: IISS, 1972.

Kaul, Ravi. "India's Mammoth Army." *Army Quarterly* 101 (April 1971): 314–22.

*Kavic, Lorne J. *India's Quest for Security: Defence Policies, 1941–1965*. Berkeley: University of California Press, 1967.

Kim, Samuel. "Communist China's Nuclear Capability." *Military Review* 50 (Oct. 1970): 35–46.

*Knorr, Klaus. *The War Potential of Nations*. Princeton, N.J.: Princeton University Press, 1956.

*——. *Military Power and Potential*. Lexington, Mass.: D. C. Heath & Co., 1970.

Lambeth, Benjamin S. "Moscow and the Arms Race." *Current History* 61 (Oct. 1971): 215–21.

Lang, William W. "Can Sweden Defend Herself?" *U.S. Naval Institute Proceedings* 93 (September 1967): 47–57.

"Less Pounds, More Muscle." *Armed Forces Journal International* 110, no. 9 (May 1973): 33–34.

Llahn, Walter F. "Nuclear Balance in Europe." *Foreign Affairs* 50 (April 1972): 501–16.

*Loftus, Joseph E. *Latin American Defense Expenditures, 1938–1965*, RM-5310-PR/ISA. Santa Monica, Calif.: The RAND Corporation, January 1968.

*McGuire, Martin. *Secrecy and the Arms Race*. Cambridge, Mass.: Harvard University Press, 1965.

Mackintosh, Malcolm. *The Evolution of the Warsaw Pact*, Adelphi Paper No. 58. London: IISS, June 1969.

Marshall, S. L. A. "The Army of Israel." *Military Review* 48 (April 1968): 3–9.

Matsuura, Noboru. "Japan's Defense Forces." *Military Review* 51 (February 1971): 48–55.

*Mendershausen, Horst. *Defense Policies and Developments in the Federal Republic of Germany*, P-3792. Santa Monica, Calif.: The RAND Corporation, February 1968.

——. *Will West Germany Try To Get Nuclear Arms—Somehow?*, P-4649. Santa Monica, Calif.: The RAND Corporation, May, 1971.

*Millar, T. B. *Australia's Defence*, 2nd edition. Carlton, Vic., Aus.: Melbourne University Press, 1969.

*Morley, James W. (ed.). *Forecast for Japan: Security in the 1970's*. Princeton, N.J.: Princeton University Press, 1972.

*Morse, Howard L. *Defense Autonomy In Gaullist France: Welfare vs. Warfare and the Dilemma of Insufficient Reserve*. Morristown, N.J.: General Learning Corp., 1972.

Murthy, Narasimha P. A. "The Self-Defence Forces of Japan." *Institute for Defense Studies and Analyses Journal* 4, no. 2 (October 1971): 223–40.

Narkiss, Uzi. "The Israel Defence Forces in the 1970's." *Brassey's Annual 1972*. New York: Praeger, 1973, pp. 90–102.

"The Next Seven Years: More Than $2 Billion for Arms." *Armed Forces Journal International* 110, no. 8 (April 1973): 52–55.

*Pretty, R. T., and Archer, D. H. R. (eds.). *Jane's Weapon Systems 1972–73*. New York: McGraw-Hill, 1973.

Rawlings, John. "World's Air Forces." *Flight International* (June 1971): 922–41.

*Richardson, Lewis. *Arms and Insecurity*. Isle of Palms, Calif.: The Boxwood Press, 1960.

*Rosecrance, R. N. (ed.). *The Dispersion of Nuclear Weapons*. New York: Columbia University Press, 1964.

*Safran, Nadav. *From War to War: The Arab-Israeli Confrontation, 1948–1967*. New York: Pegasus, 1969.

*Schelling, Thomas C., and Halperin, Morton H. *Strategy and Arms Control*. New York: The Twentieth Century Fund, 1961.

Sellers, Robert C. *Armed Forces of the World*, 3rd edition. New York: Frederick A. Praeger, 1971.

Speed, F. W. "Australia's Armed Forces." *Army Quarterly* 47 (October 1968): 30–37.

——. "Japan's Self-Defense Forces." *Army Quarterly* 48 (April, 1969): 28–37.

*Stockholm International Peace Research Institute. *World Armaments and Disarmament: SIPRI Yearbook 1972*. New York: Humanities Press, 1972.

*Subramanyam, K. "Five Years of Indian Defence Effort In Prospective." *International Studies Quarterly* 13, no. 2 (June 1969): 159–89.

"Sweden Has A Budget Crunch, Too." *Armed Forces Journal International* 110, no. 6 (February 1973): 34–35.

"The Swedish Air Force." *Armed Forces Journal International* 110, no. 6 (February 1973): 46–48.

"The Swedish Navy." *Armed Forces Journal International* 110, no. 6 (April 1973): 40–42.

Taylor, John W. R. "Soviet Airpower." *Military Review* 49 (November 1969): 89–96.

—— (ed.). *Jane's All the World's Aircraft 1972–73*. New York: McGraw-Hill, 1973.

*U.S. Arms Control and Disarmament Agency. *World Military Expenditures 1970*. Washington, D.C.: U.S. Government Printing Office, December 1970.

*Particularly recommended.

Varma, Paul. "The Defense of India: The Economic Base to Military Security." *USI Journal* 96 (Oct./ Dec. 1966): 282–99 and vol. 97 (Jan./Mar.): 13–29.

*Weinstein, Martin E. *Japan's Postwar Defense Policy, 1947–1968*. New York: Columbia University Press, 1971.

*Whitson, William (ed.). *The Military and Political Power in China in the 1970's*. New York: Frederick A. Praeger, 1972.

Wolfe, Thomas W. *The Soviet Quest for More Globally Mobile Military Power*, RM-5554-PR. Santa Monica, Calif.: The RAND Corporation, December 1967.

*———. *Soviet Power and Europe, 1945–1970*. Baltimore, Md.: The Johns Hopkins Press, 1970.

Wood, David. *The Armed Forces of African States*, Adelphi Paper No. 27. London: IISS, April 1966.

Yahuda, Michael B. "China's Military Capabilities." *Current History* 57 (September 1969): 142–94.

Yiu, Myung-Kun. "The Prospect of Japanese Rearmament." *Current History* 60, no. 356 (April 1971): 231–36, 245.

* = particularly recommended.

PART FIVE

WEAPONS ACQUISITION

INTRODUCTION

RICHARD G. HEAD

THE NATURE OF WEAPONS ACQUISITION

Weapons acquisition is essentially a process of research and development or importation that converts national resources into usable military hardware. Weapons acquisition can be further defined to mean the research, development, production, and purchase of technically advanced equipment to accomplish specific military missions. The concept of weapons acquisition as a process is central to the following discussion, for it emphasizes the continuous stream of decisions and activities during weapons programs. There are three main sets of actors in this process: the suppliers (defense contractors in the home country or abroad); the buyers (national governments); and other interested parties (allies, neutrals, and opponents). The word "comparative" in the title means that we will be looking at several national systems of procurement, selected for their significance, and representative of the diverse approaches to weapons acquisition.

Thus far this volume has discussed comparative defense policy from the perspective of the military profession, structure and process, military doctrine, and force posture. Weapons acquisition is affected by all of these areas, but two—structure and process and force posture—are of special significance. A state's defense policy-making structure determines the action channels for the weapons acquisition process. A state's force posture, once it is established through bureaucratic and political channels, often provides a self-legitimizing goal—a military requirement—for the development of new weapons. The weapons acquisition process produces an output—military hardware—which becomes, in turn, an input to the state's force posture.

But the purpose of supplying a nation's force posture is only one of several reasons for having a weapons acquisition process. A second, and often influential, purpose is the use of weapons acquisition to create and maintain a domestic industrial base. A third purpose may be to assist and promote national economic growth. A fourth may be to use weapons acquisition as a tool of diplomacy, to create or reinforce alliances, communities of interest, etc. These purposes do not all stem from direct security requirements in the international arena; several of them relate more to domestic political issues. This is part of the complexity of comparative weapons acquisition, because the process serves different purposes in individual states. Indeed, one school of thought argues that there can be no comparison of weapons acquisition processes without a complete study of each state's political, economic, and cultural systems. There is a great deal of truth in this argument, for each weapons development program is the product of a unique set of external and internal factors that relate directly to the concept of political culture. This argument is compelling for those who have the time and inclination to immerse themselves in both the study of a national political culture and weapons acquisition, but the alternative approach has advantages too.

This chapter focuses on comparative weapons acquisition as a series of processes, each with unique characteristics, but possessing a core of similar actors, problems, issues, and events. The subdivisions of the process vary according to the purposes of the analyst. Gregory and Simpson in this chapter outline an eleven-step process, but for our purposes there are five main phases, graphically presented below. They are defined in the article which follows.

A COMPARATIVE PERSPECTIVE

The articles selected for this section reflect a spectrum of acquisition strategies. Alexander examines the United States, France, and the Soviet Union and concentrates on the dominant actors in each state's acquisition process. He

Lt. Colonel Richard G. Head (USAF) is an Air Force Academy graduate with an M.P.A. and D.P.A. from Syracuse University. At the time of this writing he was Assistant Professor of Political Science at the USAF Academy. His doctoral dissertation is on the U.S. weapons acquisition process and he is co-editor of American Defense Policy, *third edition (1973).*

The views expressed herein are those of the author and do not necessarily reflect the views of the United States Air Force or the Department of Defense.

Table 1. The Weapons Acquisition Process

Conceptual	Validation	Full-Scale Development	Production	Operation
	Prototype	Hardware	System	
Economic	Definition	Develop-ment and Testing	Production Logistics Develop-ment	Deployment
Military Technical Bases	Tech, Cost & Schedule			

spotlights a critical issue that is being debated in many countries today—should hardware be primarily developed as integrated weapons systems or should R & D proceed in an essentially incremental manner? The United States pioneered the weapons system concept, and Gregory and Simpson document the current trend for Great Britain and West Germany to move in that direction. As Dorfer points out, Sweden has organized its process around specific weapons systems, but here the small number of systems and the pace of development place it in a different class from the superpowers and the major nations of Western Europe.

The size and economic capacity of the state in question have a great effect on weapons acquisition, such that some acquisition strategies are simply not available to smaller nations. The United States, the Soviet Union, France, and Great Britain have generally developed their weapons under a national policy of self-sufficiency. Other nations have had the greatest difficulty in striving for weapons autarky, although it is the established goal in many medium and small powers. These difficulties exist because modern weapons are very expensive in an absolute sense and are relatively expensive compared to the size of national defense and service budgets. In Western Europe these high costs have reversed national tendencies toward autarky and have generated new interest and political support for cooperative projects like the Multi-Role Combat Aircraft (MRCA). Still, self-sufficiency (or the progress toward it) is a major theme in the articles on China, Sweden, India, Israel, and Egypt.

Having identified several themes of the articles in this section, it remains to discuss briefly

their limitations. The major constraint is caused by the lack of basic information; our ability to conceptualize a weapons acquisition process has outpaced our ability to collect data for comparative purposes. This gap between model-building and data collection in foreign political cultures is partially an ethnocentric characteristic of U.S. analysts. This is due to the unusual variety and depth of data available in the United States on virtually all public policy issues, even ones where national security is involved. For good or ill, the United States is an open society and American analysts tend to design models assuming this availability of data. The Official Secrets Act in the United Kingdom, the intense concern with secrecy in the Soviet Union, the British-style tradition of aloofness in the Indian Civil Service, and the politics of emergency in Israel all combine to limit severely the amount and kind of data available on international weapons acquisition.

Another limitation inheres in the interdisciplinary nature of weapons acquisition, falling as it does into an ill-defined area where the academic disciplines of economics and political science overlap. The problem is exemplified by some of the articles in this volume; economists tend to stress the domestic imperatives of the industrial process while political scientists tend to stress the role of international arms races and external threats. What is needed is more cross-fertilization of the disciplines and more case studies to analyze the relative effects of internal and external determinants. Despite the limitations, the present effort attempts to bring together various inputs and synthesize them into a format for the comparative study of weapons acquisition.

THE WEAPONS ACQUISITION PROCESS: ALTERNATIVE NATIONAL STRATEGIES

RICHARD G. HEAD

The weapons acquisition problem is different for every nation. Various strategic environments and diverse domestic imperatives combine to create uniqueness. Despite their differences, states tend to acquire weapons in only a few ways. This article describes the four prominent strategies—national self-sufficiency, cooperative projects with other states, license production of an established model from a major power, and off-the-shelf acquisitions through either grant aid or direct purchase.

Lt. Colonel Richard G. Head (USAF) is an Air Force Academy graduate with an M.P.A. and D.P.A. from Syracuse University. At the time of this writing he was Assistant Professor of Political Science at the U.S. Air Force Academy. His doctoral dissertation is on the U.S. weapons acquisition process and he is co-editor of American Defense Policy, *third edition (1973).*

Weapons acquisition is the process of designing, developing, producing, and buying military hardware for use in a state's force posture. Here we will define and describe this process, relate it to the process of national research and development, examine the alternative methods nations use to acquire weapons, and discuss the foreign policy implications of various acquisition strategies. Among the substantive questions examined will be the nature of weapons acquisition in the United States, the effect of large-scale U.S. and Soviet production on the acquisition strategies of less developed countries, the European trends toward cooperative development, and the growing movement of smaller states to produce their own weapons under license.

RESEARCH, DEVELOPMENT AND WEAPONS ACQUISITION

The procurement of weapons is affected by multiple factors, including technological, economic, geographic, strategic, tactical and political inputs. In the idealized case there are two classic justifications for new weapons programs—the external threat and technological opportunity. New external threats tend to lead to a situation of strategic disequilibrium and new

technology tends to produce technological disequilibrium. In both cases there are persuasive arguments to move the situation back in balance, to a condition of equilibrium. This dynamic tension is an inherent characteristic of any research and development (R&D) process, but it is especially acute in weapons acquisition.

Another way of discussing the tension between stability and change in R&D is to identify two central concepts—innovation and obsolescence. Innovation represents the new, the novel, the proposal for an advanced weapon and ideas about how to use it; obsolescence is the opposite side of the same coin, how to decide when an old weapon has lost its utility. All states are affected by innovation and obsolescence, and the replacement of the old with the new is the essence of the weapons acquisition process.

A major factor stimulating new weapons development is the increasing rate of technological change. For example, the "Brown Bess" rifle was the standard British infantry weapon from 1690 to 1807. But with the advance of science and technology, weapons in modern times have had much shorter operational lives. The U.S. model 1903 Springfield rifle was standard equipment for only thirty-three years; its replacement, the M-1 Garand, for only twenty-one. Recently, the U.S. Army has had two new rifles—the M-14 and

This is an original article written for this volume. I would like to thank Arthur Alexander, Barry Horton, and Ian Bellany for their stimulation, advice, and assistance in the preparation of this paper. The views expressed herein are mine alone and do not represent the views of the U.S. Air Force or the Department of Defense.

M-16—since 1957, or one every eight years.[1] This reduction in the operational life of weapons has led to the notion that by the time a weapon achieves an initial operational capability, it is obsolescent compared to weapons still on the drawing board. Of course, the implicit assumption behind this notion is that each succeeding weapon is qualitatively superior to the previous model, an assumption that is currently being challenged by some skeptics.

The fear of obsolescence has operated to place great pressure on two weapons development parameters—performance and schedule—in order to provide security and to remain competitive in bilateral or multilateral arms races. In a very general sense, the purpose of R&D is to advance scientific knowledge and to develop new products. Thus, military R&D also has the effect of making one's own weapons obsolete—a kind of unilateral arms race. A further factor complicating the weapons process is the differential nature of technological change. Not only is the general rate of change increasing, but it changes faster for aerospace technology and computers than for rifles and tanks.

An indication of the importance of technological change and innovation in weapons programs is the steady rise in R&D funds as a percentage of total acquisition costs. In the late 1940s North American Aviation spent less than 1% of the total cost of the F-86 Sabrejet program on R&D, while R&D dollars accounted for 24% of the total (R&D, investment, and operation) costs of the Polaris Fleet Ballistic Missile Program.[2] This trend toward R&D being an increasing proportion of the total costs of a weapons program is international in scope, and it is reflected in the projected R&D costs of 38% for Sweden's System 37 Viggen.

Increasing R&D percentages are one indication of rapid technological change but others include increased weapon performance, increased unit cost and shorter production runs. All of these characteristics are typical of weapons acquisition in the 1970s.

INTERNATIONAL R&D EXPENDITURES

Since World War II national expenditures on R&D have grown dramatically in all of the industrial nations. For instance, U.S. government ex-

penditures on R&D in 1940 were less than $100,000 but by 1973 had risen to over $16 billion annually. Nonfederal R&D funds have also grown impressively, from $2.4 billion in 1954 to $12.2 billion in 1973. U.S. R&D funds devoted to military development have generally led the U.S. growth pattern, but the percentage of military R&D as a proportion of U.S. (public and private) R&D has declined steadily from 63% in 1956 to 34% in 1971. However, U.S. investment in R&D has almost leveled off, with the 1973 increase being only 3%.

The international R&D picture shows a similar pattern of growth, with the U.S. and USSR dominating. Worldwide expenditures on military R&D by 1970 were averaging $15–16 billion annually, with the United States and the Soviet Union together accounting for 85% of that figure. The United Kingdom, West Germany, France, and China together accounted for another 10%, while the rest of the world contributed only 5%. By contrast the countries with the most rapid growth in military R&D expenditures were Japan, Israel, and India. Thus, there is a very close relationship between expenditures on military R&D and international significance as weapons producers; the world's top nations in weapons production are the United States, the Soviet Union, the United Kingdom, and France with Japan, West Germany, Israel, and India increasing their capabilities rapidly. For a comparison of total R&D expenditures, see Table 1.

A brief conclusion can be drawn—nations with high overall R&D expenditures tend to spend the most for military R&D and tend to be leaders in weapons development. Further, we can predict on the basis of these figures that nations without a well-developed R&D base will have extreme difficulty in building a self-sufficient weapons development capability. As we will discuss shortly, the developed nations also dominate the weapons acquisition situation for less developed countries, since they become the *suppliers* in arms transfers relations. In specific local conflict situations, the existence of an R&D asymmetry can also be an indicator of relative military capabilities. For instance, it is noteworthy that Israeli scientists annually produce two and one-half times the number of scientific publications than do all the scientists in the Arab world.

[1]George Thayer, *The War Business: The International Trade in Armaments* (New York: Simon & Schuster, 1969), p. 24.

[2]The general trend was reported by Merton J. Peck and Frederic M. Scherer, *The Weapons Acquisition Process:*

An Economic Analysis (Boston: Harvard Graduate School of Business Administration, 1962), p. 26. The Polaris figure is from Harvey M. Sapolsky, *The Polaris System Development: Bureaucratic and Programmatic Success in Government* (Cambridge: Harvard University Press, 1972), p. 163.

Table 1. International R&D Expenditures

	R&D Expenditures ($ bil*)			All R&D as % of GNP	
	1960	1970	Growth Rate in 1972	1960	1970
U.S.	$13.7	$26.9	3%	2.7%	2.7%
USSR	7.8	21.3	13%	—	—
U.K.	1.8	3.0	—	2.6	2.7
Germany	1.13†	3.0**	30–40%	1.4†	2.0**
France	1.0*	3.2	13%	1.5*	2.2
Japan	0.5	3.0	25%	1.2	1.5
Sweden	—	.3**	—	—	1.3**

*At exchange rates and prices for years shown.
†Figures for 1962.
**Figures for 1969.

Source: Aerospace Industries Association, *International R&D Trends and Policies,* 1972.

In summary, general economic capacity as represented by the gross national product has long been accepted as a significant measure of a nation's military potential. However, in a technological age the rate of innovation becomes a critical factor, and this capacity is perhaps best approximated by measurements of national investment in research and development. Further, if a nation is to be self-sufficient in weapons acquisition, it is absolutely essential to have a well-developed R&D capability, and for the government to invest in the continued upgrading of that capability.

ALTERNATIVE NATIONAL ACQUISITION STRATEGIES

Weapons acquisition is embedded in the nation's larger R&D process, and Robert Gilpin has noted that there are really only three categories of national strategies for the development of science and technology.[3]

1. Broad front approach—Only the U.S. and the Soviet Union can afford this large-scale, expensive sponsorship of nearly all the sciences and engineering fields considered to be important militarily, economically, or politically. However, Great Britain attempted to follow this strategy until the early 1960s and France attempted it under President Charles de Gaulle.

2. Special focus approach—This involves concentration of research and development in specialized, narrow bands, and the critical choice is

which of the beckoning technologies should be funded. Sweden, the Netherlands, Switzerland, and, increasingly, the United Kingdom are the best examples.

3. Technology import approach—Realizing that both broad front and special focus approaches are expensive, many states like Japan, Australia, and India make extensive use of technology transfer to build their R&D base. Even scientifically advanced West Germany imports U.S. technology in the specialized fields of computers, nuclear energy, and aerospace.

Similarly, in the study of weapons acquisition we can distinguish among four major national acquisition strategies with one having two subcategories:[4]

1. Self-sufficiency
2. Cooperative projects
3. License production
4. Off-the-shelf
   a. Grant aid
   b. Military sales/Direct purchase

The acquisition process described in the introduction to this section assumes national self-sufficiency, that is, the nation that can and does fund and independently develop a weapon through each of the process's five phases will be self-sufficient. All nations can, and probably do in the abstract, strive for national self-sufficiency, but there are two obstacles—scarcity of R&D

[3]Robert Gilpin, "Technological Strategies and National Purpose," *Science* (July 31, 1970): 442.

[4]The most helpful article on this subject is Ian Bellany, "Military Aircraft Procurement and the Small State: The Australian Case," paper presented at the Conference on Comparative Defense Policy, USAF Academy, February 7–9, 1973. The following discussion is an expansion of Bellany's framework.

talent and funds. These obstacles can only be overcome by large and wealthy states, with the vast majority of states having to find lower-cost alternatives. For example, only the United States and the Soviet Union are self-sufficient in weapons. Medium and small states are forced to seek alternatives to self-sufficiency that will reduce the overall high cost of development by sharing or avoiding altogether the R&D phases of the process. The question for these states is at what point they should enter the overall process, as seen in Figure 1.

Self-sufficiency

Self-sufficiency is a strategy we will discuss in detail because it is the theoretical basis of all the alternatives and it is the strategy of the superpowers. We have noted that the acquisition process is very expensive, and that scarce resources are the major drawback of this alternative. The benefits for the powerful states are also high, both in terms of the military balance (U.S.-Soviet or NATO-Warsaw Pact) and in terms of the export potential of weapons to less developed countries. The major benefit of self-sufficiency is strategic autarky—retaining the right of self-determination of postures and policies through complete control over weapons and their replacement parts. The advantages of autarky for the superpowers are obvious, but even neutrals like Sweden are attracted to self-sufficiency. Sweden is a unique example where a foreign policy of neutrality combines with extreme domestic technical competence to provide a "critical mass" of weapons acquisition capability. (The actors, institutions, and factors in the Swedish weapons process are excellently described by Dorfer in the System 37 Viggen case study, later in the section.)[5]

There are three major aspects of self-sufficiency to be discussed below. The study begins

[5]Ingemar Dorfer, "System 37 Viggen: Arms, Technology and the Domestication of Glory," this volume, pp. 465–78.

with a description of the phases of the acquisition process, using primarily the U.S. example. Second, the concept of uncertainty is outlined as it affects program performance, schedules, and cost. Third, a brief mention is made of the relationship of bureaucratic politics to weapons acquisition.

The Life Cycle of a Weapons System

The weapons acquisition process includes three interrelated but conceptually distinct types of activity—R&D, production, and operation. The R&D phases are conceptual, validation, and full-scale development, with the annual costs of the program rising with each succeeding phase. A typical cost profile of a weapons program might look like Figure 2.

The *Conceptual* phase combines knowledge developed in basic and applied research with operational needs, known as "requirements." The purpose of this phase is to provide the technical, economic and military bases for the program and seriously to nominate the program for Validation. The cost of the Conceptual phase is very low compared to the later phases of the cycle, and thus many systems may compete for selection to the next step.

The *Validation* phase is an outgrowth of the Contract Definition phase introduced to U.S. weapons development under the guidance of Defense Secretary Robert S. McNamara in the early 1960s. McNamara's purpose was to further define the cost, schedule and performance estimates of the Conceptual phase before committing the government to the high cost of Full-Scale Development. Contract Definition under McNamara was essentially a competition, usually between two contractors, to present detailed design proposals and cost estimates for the entire weapons program. The intention was to reduce technical uncertainty through the application of engineering resources, with the winning company being awarded a contract for full-scale development. These competitions tended to be in

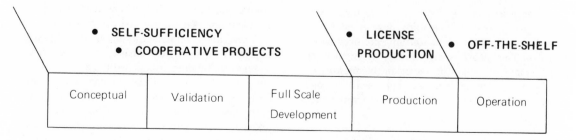

Figure 1. ALTERNATIVE ACQUISITION STRATEGIES

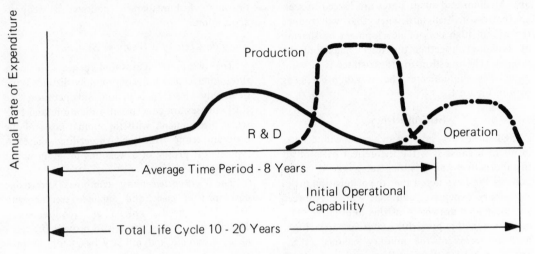

Figure 2. COST PROFILE OF A TYPICAL WEAPONS PROGRAM

the form of paper studies with some testing of components to verify certain aspects of the system. The amount of hardware testing was never very large compared to the whole development to follow, however, and the paper studies in practice tended to underestimate the technical difficulties of development. The name change from Contract Definition to Validation under Deputy Secretary Packard signaled a change in philosophy and was intended to reflect the increased emphasis on hardware development and testing before a decision to begin Full-Scale Development. The popular name for this hardware prototyping and advanced testing is "fly-before-you-buy." There are costs and benefits associated with each method, and the selection of paper versus prototype styles is one of the controversial issues of weapons acquisition in the 1970s.[6]

Full-Scale Development is the most expensive of the R&D phases, since the government must pay for extensive hardware development and testing in addition to certain pre-production costs. This phase is also known as engineering development, since the major problems are not basically scientific in nature, but revolve around design, fabrication and testing of components,

subsystems, and eventually the whole, integrated weapons system.

Production relates less to the research and development nature of the process than to its manufacturing characteristic. However, technologically advanced weapons are historically difficult to mass produce, and many developmental efforts have to be made, both to resolve specific production problems and to handle the many engineering change proposals that affect a system while it is in production and operation.

Operation begins when the weapons system is delivered to the military service and ends only when the last item is retired from the inventory. Although crew training and logistics support begin quite early in the program, they intensify after the first item is delivered. However, the service has no meaningful capability with the new weapon until it has achieved an Initial Operational Capability (IOC), where at least one operational unit is equipped and combat-ready.

There are several factors about the life-cycle cost profile that merit emphasis. First, the largest increase in funding occurs with the decision to enter the Full-Scale Development phase. This decision is probably the most critical in the program, because once development has been undertaken powerful bureaucratic forces are activated to continue the program into production and eventual operation. Alexander notes the importance of this decision to proceed from a "pre-

[6]For a discussion of the conditions under which prototyping has advantages, see Robert Perry, *A Prototype Strategy for Aircraft Development*, RM-5597-1PR (Santa Monica, California: The RAND Corporation, 1972).

project" into full development, and he has gathered valuable data on how such decisions are made in the Soviet Union.[7] Second, we may note that various phases of the weapons acquisition process overlap, with some production activities beginning early in the R&D phases and R&D testing, evaluation, and modification extending almost to the very end of the life of the weapon.

Third, the cost of most advanced technology programs (the area under the various curves in Figure 2), especially in the aerospace sector, is extremely high. Average annual funding during the Full-Scale Development and Production phases may run over $1 billion, with total programs costing between $2 and $10 billion. It is no wonder that many nations look for alternative methods to acquire weapons without going through the whole expensive process. Fourth, there has been a tendency in the past for force development studies to focus on R&D costs and to neglect the costs of operating and maintaining the weapon once it has entered the force structure. Yet these operational costs affect all states, regardless of where they obtain their weapons. It is not uncommon in weapons systems with a 10 to 20 year life expectancy for the cumulative operating costs to equal the sum of the weapon's R&D and production costs (although Figure 2 does not represent this relationship).

Uncertainties in Weapons Development

Research and development is an unusual industrial enterprise because it is future-oriented and attempts to produce something often radically different from past experience. Weapons acquisition reflects this difficulty which is perhaps most concisely represented in the concept of uncertainty. Uncertainty can be defined as incomplete knowledge or the relative unpredictability of the outcome of a contemplated action. The unpredictability associated with weapons programs directly relates to the three major parameters of performance, schedule, and cost. Thus, at the initiation of a program there is high uncertainty with regard to the final performance of the weapon, its development time (schedule), and costs (both total program cost and final unit cost). The uncertainty surrounding each of these weapons parameters is an accumulation of smaller uncertainties in each of four major areas:[8]

Target uncertainties. Target uncertainties reflect the incomplete knowledge of the final physical and performance characteristics that will be required to satisfy a military need. Target uncertainty also encompasses the unpredictability of the final cost and schedule goals of the program. A major source of target uncertainty is the technological change occurring in both the home country (what is available) and in opponent countries (what is required). It also relates to the difficulty in describing the goal. The difficulty associated with target uncertainty was aptly described by an Assistant Secretary of the Navy:

The whole point of the development process is to get something that we haven't got, something that we have never seen, and something that we really don't know can be produced. . . . We simply cannot unambiguously describe before the development begins, or at any point in fact until we have a final object, what it is we are actually buying.[9]

Technical uncertainty. Technical uncertainty surrounds estimates of engineering feasibility and "state of the art" projections. Technical uncertainty begins with the question of whether a weapon can be developed at all, within *any* time and for *any* cost and proceeds to refined estimates of development time and cost. An important point for students of comparative politics is that technical uncertainty is inherently culture-bound. Recent RAND studies using technological trend analysis have confirmed what many engineers felt subjectively—namely, that on the average the U.S. state of the art is more advanced than either European or Soviet technology. Jet engine performance within easy reach of U.S. engineers, and consequently of low technical uncertainty, can be achieved in Europe only with difficulty and high technical uncertainty.[10]

Internal program uncertainty. Uncertainties also originate from the manner in which programs are organized, planned, and managed. This relates to selection of an acquisition strategy (contracting internally, cooperative development, or license-building), the authority of the program manager, and the administrative details of the program. A classic case of internal program uncertainty dominance was the ill-fated British TSR-2 tactical strike/reconnaissance aircraft. The failure to resolve internal program uncertainties in the form of organizational relation-

---

[7]Arthur J. Alexander, "Weapons Acquisition in the Soviet Union, United States and France," pp. 426–43 in this volume.

[8]These categories were developed from Peck and Scherer and other sources and are elaborated on in the *Final Report of the USAF Academy Risk Analysis Study Team*, by Colonel Robert R. Lochry, Major Richard G. Head, et al. (A study sponsored by Aeronautical Systems Division, USAF, August 1, 1971.)

[9]Robert A. Frosch, Address at the Sixteenth Annual Institute on Government Contracts, George Washington University/Federal Bar Association, Washington, D.C., May 8, 1969.

[10]Arthur J. Alexander and J. R. Nelson, *Measuring Technological Change: Aircraft Turbine Engines*, R-1017-ARPA/PR (Santa Monica, California: The RAND Corporation, 1972.)

ships and authority contributed to cost growth, schedule slippages and ultimately to cancellation of the program before a single prototype had flown. Briefly, the problem arose when the British government forced a merger of English Electric and Vickers-Armstrong into the British Aircraft Corporation (BAC), designated BAC the prime contractor for the program, and then failed to give BAC sufficient authority to integrate the various subsystems. The problem was complicated by government bureaucracy as BAC was working for both the Ministry of Aviation and the Air Ministry in a highly uncertain triangular relationship. The difficulties of the prime contractor and the program personnel can be summarized in one statistic; BAC was expected to handle all the systems integration problems of the TSR-2, but it had control over only 30% of the total costs. Internal program uncertainty, coupled with target and technical difficulties, combined to warrant cancellation of the program.[11]

Process uncertainty. Whereas program uncertainties arise from arrangements internal to the development organization, process uncertainty originates in the external environment, primarily in the political process of the country. Examples of process uncertainty are interservice rivalry for missions, *intra*service competition for weapons, the government budget, and legislative actions. These cause two major problems from the point of view of the individual weapons program: first, they produce uncertainty about the criteria for program initiation and approval; and second, they produce uncertainty that appropriate funding will be available when planned to support the program.[12]

Bureaucratic Politics and Weapons Acquisition

The basic objective of the weapons proponents within a government is to get their system into operational service in the shortest possible time, and this objective is often cited as an argument to gain organization autonomy. These advocates often have two specific subobjectives: (1) to attract a broad base of support for their system both inside and outside their government; and (2) to prevent the rest of the government from interfering in the management of "their" program.[13] To accomplish these objectives innovation advocates have used variations on four bureaucratic strategies, drawn here from the U.S. Polaris program:[14]

Differentiation—"the attempts of organizations to establish unchallengeable claims on valued resources by distinguishing their own products or programs from those of their competitors."

Co-optation—"attempts of an organization to absorb . . . new elements into its leadership or policy-determining structure . . . as a means of averting threats to its stability or existence."

Moderation—"attempts of organizations to build long-term support for their programs by sacrificing short-term gains."

Managerial innovation—"the attempt of an organization to achieve autonomy in the direction of a complex and risky program through the introduction of managerial techniques that appear to indicate unique managerial competence."

The advocates of a strategy of differentiation believe in organizing R&D around the individual weapon—the weapons system concept. This method of organization achieved a great deal of publicity through the strategic missile programs of the late 1950s, and it has achieved a level of official acceptance in the United States that approaches orthodoxy. Virtually every major U.S. weapons program since 1960 has been organized around the weapons system concept with a designated program manager in authority. Despite this vast experience it is not at all clear that the weapons system concept should be used in all weapons programs. Sweden and the United Kingdom are redesigning their acquisition processes to use the systems approach more completely, as the following articles describe, but France and the Soviet Union use more incremental approaches. Arthur Alexander, through his study of European and Soviet R&D, has come to believe the weapons system concept leads to inflexibility, excessive reporting systems, inaccurate planning too far into an uncertain future, and a reduction in competition. In the following article he provides a valuable comparative analysis of the U.S., Soviet, and French processes.

---

[11]For the complete story of the program, see *Crisis in Procurement: A Case Study of the TSR-2*, by Geoffrey Williams, Frank Gregory, and John Simpson (London: Royal United Service Institution, 1969).

[12]For a detailed examination of how political events produce process uncertainties see the author's "Decision-Making on the A-7 Attack Aircraft Program" (doctoral dissertation, Syracuse University, 1971).

[13]There are many accounts of the use of bureaucratic politics by weapons proponents. An excellent integration of conceptual material with case studies is the short piece by Vincent Davis, "The Politics of Innovation: Patterns in Navy Cases," in *American Defense Policy*, 3d ed., ed. by Richard G. Head and Ervin J. Rokke (Baltimore: The Johns Hopkins University Press, 1973), pp. 391–406. Perhaps the richest work is Sapolsky, *The Polaris System Development*. The latter provides the basis for much of the following discussion.

[14]Sapolsky, *ibid.*, pp. 43–59.

Co-optation and moderation are discussed by Sapolsky as to their application to the Polaris program, but they will not be elaborated on here. The fourth technique, managerial innovation, merits specific attention, because many experienced managers are skeptical that elaborate reporting systems can, in reality, deliver the benefits their advocates promise.

In the U.S. Polaris program these managerial innovations included the much-advertised Program Evaluation and Review Technique (PERT), the extension of PERT to include financial management (PERT/COST), Reliability Management Index, the concept of project management, the program management center, weekly program review meetings, and managerial graphics. Sapolsky notes that these management techniques did contribute substantively to the Polaris development, but their primary achievement was to gain and protect the autonomy of the program from external comptrollers and auditors.[15]

Cooperative Projects

The rising costs of maintaining self-sufficiency have led many nations to consider cooperative projects where the R&D and production costs are shared. This alternative is still expensive and requires a competent R&D base, which has generally limited cooperative projects to medium-sized states with advanced technological capabilities. Because of the need to agree on common specifications (the military requirement) cooperative projects will probably always be limited to countries which share a relatively common conception of the military threat, such as in the

European security community. In fact, one may surmise that prior economic cooperation was a valuable asset to collaboration on weapons projects.

There are two basic factors which have led to a European predisposition to cooperate in weapons development. First, West European nations are increasingly seeking collective political, economic, and strategic independence. Whereas Europe after World War II was almost completely dependent on the United States for weapons, this dependence is decreasing. The percentage of U.S.-produced military aircraft in Western European forces has dropped from 65% in 1963 to 50% in 1970.[16] European-U.S. economic competition is clearly on the rise. Second, there has been a steady decline in the number of aerospace firms (especially in Great Britain) as the costs of R&D increased and the domestic market decreased. For instance, in 1955 there were 21 British aircraft producers; by 1972 the number had been reduced to 2, British Aircraft Corporation and Hawker-Siddeley.

The initial incentive for cooperative European weapons development came from NATO because of the military and economic advantages of commonality of equipment among allies, but the standardization of defense equipment was never really achieved in any meaningful sense.[17] Bilateral and multilateral arrangements had more success with several aircraft, missiles, army and some naval projects. Probably the most ambitious in R&D terms is the joint British-German-Italian Multi-Role Combat Aircraft (MRCA) which entered a limited production phase in 1973. Less risky and less costly projects include the Anglo-French Jaguar tactical fighter/advanced trainer, the Franco-German Transall military transport, three Anglo-French helicopter projects, the Anglo-French Martel air-launched missile, the Franco-German Hot and Milan antitank missiles and the Roland anti-aircraft missile. Only a few joint naval projects have been attempted, and some of them have not been successful.

The major advantage of cooperative projects, as we have noted, is reduced national expenditure. The MRCA project is a good example. The MRCA program as planned will total nearly $9 billion, with $1.7 billion being R&D costs. If the United Kingdom had built the same aircraft by itself, the R&D costs were estimated to be $1.3

---

[15]On this point about the limited utility of managerial techniques in general and PERT in specific, Sapolsky is quite direct. PERT was resisted both by contractors and by the Polaris technical staff. "Contractor opposition was demonstrated quite early . . . . Eventually, of course, the contractors complied with the PERT directives, but their compliance was unenthusiastic and subversive. The system was designed originally to gather estimates directly from the bench engineers and to process the resulting data centrally in a Navy computer. The contractors, however, had an irresistible urge to process—review and correct—the data at their own sites before releasing them to the Navy. Moreover, practice soon led to the establishment in each plant of specialized PERT staffs which became responsible for the actual generation of time estimates. The PERT staffs tended to be kept carefully isolated from both the bench engineers and the regular management control groups" (Chapter 4). The real lesson was not the magic of PERT, but the independence it provided. "The Polaris Special Projects Office gained an unparalleled independence within the Navy and within the Department of Defense that has only recently been eroded. In drawing general lessons from the experience of the Fleet Ballistic Missile Program, defense officials have tended to emphasize the efficacy of managerial techniques and depreciate the importance of the organizational autonomy of the agency that produced both the techniques and the Polaris" (p. 59).

[16]John Stanley and Maurice Pearton, *The International Trade in Arms* (London: Chatto and Windus, 1972).

[17]John Simpson and Frank Gregory, "West European Collaboration in Weapons Procurement," *Orbis* 16 no. 2 (Summer 1972): 435–61.

billion, or three-quarters of the joint development. As it is the United Kingdom expects to pay only 42.5 percent, or $720 million for the eight-year R&D phase. Further, the three-nation buy of 1,000 aircraft is two and one-half times what Britain could have afforded if she had done it alone. The increased production run is expected to reduce unit costs significantly. However, MRCA is not without problems. In early 1973 some German political voices were advocating withdrawal from the joint project on the ground that the cost growth of the program (up to $6.5 million per copy) was too high and was expected to go higher, making the aircraft much too expensive for its military mission. In addition, the Initial Operational Capability date has steadily slipped from 1975 to late 1970s to the early 1980s, necessitating German plans to order more F-4 Phantoms and Italy to build more F-104S Starfighters than had orginally been planned.[18]

Briefly, there are several major points to be borne in mind when discussing cooperative projects. First, it is extremely difficult to get independent nations to agree on a common military requirement and common mission definition for a weapon. For example, the British and German versions of MRCA will be substantially different, with national avionics and subsystems. As, and if, detente continues, it may be even more difficult in the future to get transnational agreement on military requirements. Second, national industrial firms participating in cooperative projects have not yet moved to the stage of a permanent transnational merger or takeover, a stage that will perhaps be necessary for the creation of permanent, formal, institutions for cooperative programs. Third, nations join cooperative projects for a variety of reasons, not the least of which is to build up their own, national R&D base at the expense of the more experienced partners. Thus, Germany is probably learning more than Great Britain from MRCA, a factor in the network of political and economic incentives that does not necessarily contribute to efficiency of the acquisition process. Fourth, another source of inefficiency is the clamor for national quotas in the distribution of funds—the principle of the "just return." Assuring that each participating national industry gets a fair share of the project funds is much less efficient than allocation by competitive merit. Fifth, with all these inefficien-

cies it is not at all clear that European cooperative projects are inherently preferable to buying or license-producing U.S. equipment. In fact, Belgium, Holland, and Canada all withdrew from MRCA at an early stage to embrace the alternative of license-production. Still, cooperative projects, at least in Western Europe, have an amazing amount of political backing, and experts are predicting that European competition with the United States will continue to grow, spurred by the merger of European aerospace companies into two, large integrated firms within five or six years.

License Production

Building weapons under license from a major power is an attempt to by-pass the R&D phase of weapons development completely by entering the process after R&D has been completed (see Figure 1). This alternative has been used extensively, both by medium and small states and is even on the increase among less developed nations. A few examples among aircraft systems include Japanese production of the U.S. T-33, F-86, and F-4EJ, Chinese production of the MiG-19, Indian production of the MiG-21, German and Italian production of the F-104 and Australian production of the F-86 and Canberra. In addition to the goal of reduced government expenditure for weapons, license-production serves the goal of increasing a nation's industrial capability in what is essentially a technology transfer process.

As with cooperative projects, the advantages of license-production seem more obvious at first sight than the problems. An example of a very successful program was the Japanese production of the Lockheed F-104 Starfighter.[19] In 1959 Mitsubishi was selected as the prime contractor for Japanese production of the F-104, modified to increase its performance in the avionics area. The program was to encompass 200 aircraft, with the early models produced in the United States and the bulk of the program being completed in Japan, after sufficient technological transfer had occurred. The result was substantially as planned, with Japanese industries doing a major share of the fabrication. Japanese production of the airframe became virtually self-sufficient after the first twenty airframes; engine technology took somewhat longer to transfer; and avionics (despite popular notions about Japanese

[18]"MRCA Slippage Sparks Italian F-104 Buy," *Aviation Week and Space Technology*, February 12, 1973, p. 19.

[19]A case study from G. R. Hall and R. E. Johnson, *Transfers of United States Aerospace Technology to Japan*, P-3875 (Santa Monica, Calif.: The RAND Corporation, July 1968).

wizardry with commercial electronics) were never really transferred, but were simply imported from the United States.

The direct costs of a license-production program occur in the areas of license fees, royalties, and technical assistance payments. Royalties on the Japanese F-104 program amounted to about 5% of the invoice price with the total fees averaging about 7.8% of airframe and engine costs. Additionally, indirect costs resulted from dividing the production between two locations, and from "double learning," i.e., the Japanese starting the F-104 learning curve from the bottom. However, a major finding of the RAND study was that Mitsubishi applied Lockheed's experience with the F-104 successfully, and completed the first airframe with 25% fewer man-hours than had Lockheed for its first F-104.[20] If one compared the total Mitsubishi work load with the alternative of buying the 200 F-104s directly from Lockheed, Mitsubishi invested twice as many man-hours, but this difference was more than made up by the large difference in wage scales. Thus, Japan built 200 F-104s for a unit cost of $852,000, compared to a unit cost of $973,000 if she had purchased them directly from the United States.

The Japanese example with the F-104 may be atypical, since many other nations have tried license-production and have found the costs to be much more than the alternative of direct purchase. For instance, Australia produced the British Canberra light bomber and the North American F-86 (in a greatly improved version). The Canberra was produced in Australia from 1950 to 1958, and the 112 F-86s were produced from 1951 to 1961. The costs of producing these aircraft locally instead of importing them has been variously estimated at 40–100% higher than the parent versions.[21] These high costs may be partially due to the technical improvements made in the F-86 aircraft, but they are more likely to relate directly to the small size of the programs and the extremely slow rate of production. Despite the costs, Australia replaced the F-86 with the Mirage III-0 and produced about 100 under license. In an effort to reduce costs, certain parts of the Mirage were imported directly from France, but this led to a reduction in strategic autarky.

Thus, the experience with license-production has been mixed, but several potential advantages can be observed. They include:

(1) lower costs as compared to cooperative projects and in some cases lower than direct purchase; (2) increased strategic independence as compared to grant aid or military sales (assuming that spare parts are locally manufactured); (3) simplified maintenance and operational support; (4) the transfer of technology to domestic industry; and (5) in some cases, balance of payments benefits. The primary disadvantage may be higher cost, but even this is not always the case as seen in the F-104 example. Dominating all these reasons are powerful political factors which in many countries lead to pressure for local weapons production. Domestic production does not have the political implications of dependency that foreign production has. Thus, in China, India, and Japan, to mention just a few examples, license-produced weapons are not thought of as being Russian or American, they are Chinese or Indian or Japanese. With this myriad of factors, it is no wonder that the current trend is for less developed nations to demand consideration of license-production in their contracts to buy U.S., French and British weapons.

The use of license-production has been most pronounced in jet combat aircraft, which corresponds to a general increase in the number of aircraft in production worldwide. The trend is indicated in Table 2.

Table 2. Major Civilian and Military Aircraft in Production

	1950	1960	1970
Programs	63	85	110
Combat Aircraft	30	40	45
Countries	8	17	20

Source: Amelia C. Leiss, *et al., Arms Transfers to Less Developed Countries,* 1970.

Off-the-Shelf

Grant Aid

Grant aid is one of the two subcategories of off-the-shelf acquisition. It is most notably reflected in the U.S. Military Assistance Program which has transferred billions of dollars of equipment to more than 80 nations around the world. The Soviet Union has a similar program although it started later and has reached only 15 or so nations. The advantages of grant aid for the recipient country are that it acquires the weapons virtually free, and in addition usually gets military advisers to train local users. Of course, the

[20]*Ibid.,* p. 69.
[21]Ian Bellany and James Richardson, "Australian Defense Procurement," in *Problems of Australian Defence,* ed. by H. G. Gelber (Melbourne: Oxford University Press, 1970), pp. 255–56.

weapons are not politically free, as the United States usually extracts bilateral assurances, in the form of Mutual Defense Assistance Agreements, and the Soviet Union does likewise.

From the perspective of the recipient country the low costs of acquiring weapons through grant aid may be overshadowed by the high cost of maintaining them. Figuring the true alternative costs of military assistance is one of the most difficult problems for political policymakers. There are two sharply contrasting views with regard to the effects of military assistance on the economic development of recipient countries.[22] One view is known as "resource diversion" which argues that military assistance diverts resources from economic development in order to operate and maintain the "free" equipment. This view stresses that skilled manpower is a critical resource for a less developed country, and by diverting it to work on military projects civilian capital formation suffers, retarding overall economic development. The opposite view, called "resource addition," argues that the equipment provided through military assistance represents a genuine addition to the recipient's economic base. These additions include not only the equipment itself which is supplied free by donor nations, but by training and an increase in manpower skills. Resource addition, then, argues that military assistance accelerates economic development through technological transfer.

Conceptually, these two views are useful in setting the limits of policy debates over military assistance, but in a complex world it is unlikely that one of the views will be completely substantiated by the varieties of development experience. It is more likely that each view has some truth, and policy discussion should be directed toward finding the appropriate conditions where military assistance can be most useful. In Charles Wolf's analysis, resource-diversion probably occurred during the 1960s in India, Pakistan and Castro's Cuba.[23] If these countries had received less military assistance, their defense programs would probably have been smaller, development efforts larger, and the rates of economic growth probably higher. On the other hand, Wolf argues that resource-addition more accurately represents the cases in Korea, Taiwan, and Thailand, where security assistance has had a substantial and beneficial effect on economic development. Whether military assistance in the future will have

the effect of resource-diversion or resource-addition in specific countries is a fertile ground for further research.

The trend in weapons acquisition, however, is definitely away from military assistance/grant aid toward direct military sales. There are many reasons for this change, including the desire to shift defense responsibilities from the United States to allied nations, the continued attacks on military assistance in the U.S. Congress, the perceived dependency relationship between donor and recipient, and the desire of recipient nations to be more independent of their weapons suppliers.

Military Sales/Direct Purchase

In the United States overseas military sales are also handled by the Military Assistance Program, but the requirements of that program state that sales must be substituted for grant aid whenever a country can afford to pay, either by cash or credit. Such a policy in the United States is consistent with both the Nixon Doctrine and sound economic practice. As was noted earlier, there is a trend toward fewer sales to the industrial nations and more sales to the less developed nations of the world. For instance, in 1965 the United States sold $1,146 million worth of equipment to the industrialized nations while selling only $96 million to the less developed countries. In 1969 the United States sold approximately the same amount to industrialized nations, while the less developed countries bought $1,665 million worth of equipment, or seventeen times as much as four years earlier.

Taken together, military sales and grant aid form a system of arms transfers that may be studied as a whole. In a major systematic study from the arms control viewpoint, Amelia Leiss and her colleagues at M.I.T. uncovered some interesting facts and trends.[24] The overall arms transfer system from the developed donor states to a sample of fifty-two less developed recipient states is characterized by four trends. (1) The number of transfers of weapons has grown quantitatively since 1945 and especially since 1955, when the Soviet Union entered the picture as a major donor. (2) The rate of growth has stabilized or even declined since 1964. (The major exceptions are helicopters and tanks which continue to increase in numbers.) (3) The quality of transferred arms has increased with steady modernization, such that the weapons acquired are in-

[22]Charles Wolf, Jr., *Economic Impacts of Military Assistance*, P-4578 (Santa Monica, California: The RAND Corporation, 1971).
   [23]*Ibid.*, p. 3.

[24]Amelia C. Leiss, et al., "Arms Transfers to Less Developed Countries," unpublished study for the U.S. Arms Control and Disarmament Agency, C/70-1 (Cambridge, Mass.: MIT Center for International Studies, 1970.)

creasingly costly to procure, to maintain, and to operate. This trend of high unit cost and low maintainability is likely to continue. (4) There is an increasing number of donors and increasing supplies of advanced weapons available for transfer.

The overall demand for weapons among the less developed countries is at an all-time high; e.g., approximately 400 combat aircraft, 90 transport aircraft, 200 trainer aircraft, 500 tanks, 300 armored personnel carriers, and assorted other weapons are transferred per year. In other words, the market for weapons among the less developed nations alone is high, and this market will probably produce new incentives for suppliers.

Supplier patterns are important because they indicate the relative influence of the great powers on weapons supplies in other nations. Figure 3 shows the early influence of the United States on weapons inventories after World War II, and it demonstrates vividly the dramatic rise in the impact of Soviet weapons after 1955. Thus, the United States has transferred more total combat aircraft (2,523) than the Soviets (2,376), but the Soviet Union has had a more recent impact on the market.

In conceptual terms, we can also view the relationship among suppliers as varying among three alternatives: monopoly (the dominance of a single supplier); duopoly (the dominance of two essential suppliers); and "free market" where a group of suppliers exists with no one or a group able to achieve dominance. Using these terms to describe various categories of weapons, Leiss and her colleagues distinguish periods of changing weapons acquisition patterns.

In combat aircraft prior to 1955 the situation was one of *duopoly* between the *United States and Britain*, with the former supplying quantitatively more systems but the latter supplying qualitatively more advanced systems. . . . *Combat aircraft* transfers *between 1955 and 1965* were also *duopolistic* in nature, with the *United States and the Soviet Union* jointly dominating the quantity transferred. . . . *Since 1965*, transfers of *combat aircraft* have continued to be a *U.S.-Soviet duopoly*, with declining British and increasing French involvement. . . .
Perhaps the most significant development in combat aircraft transfers has been the growth of transfers by donors other than the four major suppliers. These include only small numbers of indigenously produced aircraft. For the largest part, they constitute retransferred aircraft, largely of U.S. origin. The trend in *combat aircraft transfers* is thus toward a "*free market*" situation.[25]

Tank transfers in the 1945–55 period were primarily a U.S.-British duopoly, but since 1955 they have become a U.S.-Soviet duopoly with no change in sight. Transport aircraft were monopolized by the United States in the 1950–55 time period, but since then have moved steadily toward a free market. Trainer aircraft present the same pattern as transports, but the shift is even more markedly toward a free market. The United States is the major single supplier of warships, but the market is basically free with the Soviets, British, and many smaller powers supplying ships.

It is significant to note that where Leiss identified patterns of duopoly, the major rivals tended not to compete with each other. Rather, each superpower transferred arms to its allies and did not disturb the bipolar relationship. However, many less developed countries attempt to exploit the superpower competition for their own purposes. They often seek weapons from both the United States and the Soviet Union to maximize their total resource gain and to avoid being totally dependent on any one supplier. This strategy is especially attractive to states, like India, which value their neutrality highly. The legacy of this bargaining strategy is too often an ill-conceived and unbalanced force structure with a logistics problem that can only be characterized as a nightmare, as some African states have found out.

Two other minor patterns may be noted here. First, the Soviet Union tends to use the "surge" style of transfer, with major donations and sales in a short time-span, while the United States tends to use only the replacement style. Second, until recently, Western European nations tended to supply a higher proportion of modern weapons than either the USSR or the United States. With the U.S. supply of F-4Es to Israel and perhaps Iran and Saudi Arabia this pattern is now being modified slightly. Further, states with large combat aircraft inventories tend to be supplied by the Soviet Union; while states with moderate and small combat aircraft inventories tend to be supplied by the United States.[26]

Another problem in weapons acquisition is the retransfer of weapons from their original user. In such cases it is particularly difficult for the original donor nation to exert its political influence over the projected military use of the weapons it supplied. A case in point was the 1973 Libyan purchase of 100-plus Mirage jet fighters. One of the stipulations of the contract between Libya and France was that the advanced jet

[25]Leiss, *ibid.*, pp. 55–56.   [26]*Ibid.*, p. 136.

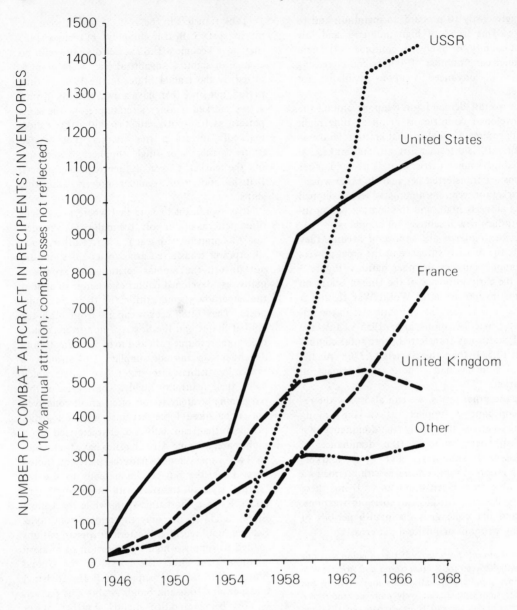

Source: Amelia C. Leiss, et al., Arms Transfers to Less Developed Countries, 1970, p. 45

Figure 3. DONOR IMPACT ON INVENTORIES: COMBAT AIRCRAFT

fighters were not, under any circumstances, to be made available to the Arab countries in conflict with Israel. Shortly after the first delivery of the Mirages, Israel charged the aircraft were being flown to Egypt and had been sighted on airfields there. A political crisis developed in April 1973 with the Mirages being the center of controversy among the governments of France, Libya, and Israel. The net result of the crisis was the withdrawal of the Mirage fighters from Egypt, but not until French embarrassment had been brought to international attention. This brief episode exemplifies just one of the foreign policy implications of weapons acquisition, but it demonstrates the continuing potential for weapons becoming the center of crisis.

CONCLUSION

To summarize, we have discussed four basic types of acquisition strategies: self-sufficiency, cooperative projects, license-production and off-the-shelf deliveries through grant aid or direct military sales. The selection among these alternatives depends on a great many factors, including R&D base, industrial capability, foreign policy inclinations, and domestic political factors. The articles in this chapter elaborate on the specific factors, policies and trends in the countries studied. Their purpose is to illuminate the individual approach that nations take amid this spectrum of international, institutional and domestic factors. In conclusion, it may be useful to attempt to project some future possibilities for international weapons acquisition:

1. All factors point to a continuing high demand for weapons in countries around the world.

2. The global industrial capability for local production of weapons, especially those of low technology, is increasing.

3. The incentives for local production will increase in less developed states, while incentives for cooperative programs in closely allied, industrial nations will increase.

4. Many states will desire local production, but only a few will develop the R&D base to support this strategy. Therefore, for the majority of less developed states, weapons acquisition will continue to consist of arms transfers with increasing provisions for local production through licensing.

5. The number of potential suppliers will increase toward a free market atmosphere, while the supply of weapons available for transfer will increase.

6. Due to technical complexity and increased unit cost of advanced weapons, there will be a further tendency of less developed countries to produce and purchase less modern weapons (except for a few prestige weapons of high quality).

7. Although arms control has had a major effect on strategic weapons through the SALT agreements, the effect on non-nuclear weapons has been only slight. The demand for security through weapons acquisition, especially among the less developed states, appears to be the continued trend.

WEAPONS ACQUISITION IN THE SOVIET UNION, THE UNITED STATES, AND FRANCE

ARTHUR J. ALEXANDER

Conventional wisdom has it that the superpowers of the U.S. and the USSR are driven in the development of weapons by similar strategic and bureaucratic factors. Alexander explodes this ethnocentric fallacy by exploring the unique cultural factors that direct weapons acquisition in the two superpowers and France. In the Soviet Union the most important organization is the semi-autonomous design bureau, while the distinctive features of Soviet aircraft are simplicity, commonality, and incremental change. In the United States the existence of multiple decision centers tends to diffuse program authority, and the resulting high level of government participation has tended to reduce the efficiency and increase the cost of weapons programs. In France the Dassault Company incorporates many features of the Soviet design bureaus and continues to develop incrementally advanced designs at remarkably low costs. The most interesting feature of the weapons acquisition process in these three countries is the long-standing tradition of prototyping in the Soviet Union and France, and the growing acceptance of this technique in the United States.

Arthur J. Alexander is an economist with the RAND Corporation. He holds a M.S. degree from the London School of Economics and a Ph.D. from Johns Hopkins University. He has been a junior staff member of the President's Council of Economic Advisors. His RAND publications include Structure, Income and Race *and* R&D in Soviet Aviation, *and he is co-author of a recent book,* Economics and Public Library Service, *1972.*

INTRODUCTION

The weapons acquisition process of any country is a heterogeneous activity that varies considerably over many dimensions. The specific military service, the class of equipment, and the vagaries of time are but a few of the dimensions over which enormous disparities are observed. In order to reduce to a manageable size the problem associated with a comparative description and analysis of weapons acquisition in three dissimilar countries, some simplifications are necessary. First, I shall focus on aircraft. Aircraft absorb substantial fractions of most military budgets; they are technically advanced; and the acquisition strategies for obtaining similar items of equipment differ considerably in the three coun-

tries to be examined. The second simplifying strategem will be to concentrate on different parts of the acquisition experience in each country. The organizations that dominate the process vary according to national characteristics and other internal forces; equal attention to every actor in the acquisition process is not warranted. In the Soviet Union the design bureau is at the center of the stage; the government dominates the action in the United States; and in France the firm of Dassault is the principal performer.

Despite the use of simplifying stratagems, I shall attempt to draw some general conclusions about the acquisition process in the final section. In particular, I shall focus on the development or R&D phase, as it is there that the systems are generated and there that the success or failure of the process can be discerned.

This is an original article written for this volume and the Conference on Comparative Defense Policy held at the Air Force Academy, February 7–9, 1973. Copyright © 1973, The RAND Corporation, Santa Monica, California.

Any views expressed in this paper are those of the author. They should not be interpreted as reflecting the views of The RAND Corporation or the official opinion or policy of any of its governmental or private research sponsors. The author gratefully acknowledges the always intelligent and often critical advice of Robert L. Perry and Alvin J. Harman.

CENTRALIZED AUTONOMY: THE USSR

Organization of the Aviation Industry

Most of the effort devoted to aviation in the Soviet Union is centralized under the authority of the Ministry of Aviation Industry (MAP).[1] This centralization brings under the roof of one ministry the research, design and development, and manufacturing functions. The Ministry also produces those materials and products that are important to the manufacture of aircraft, such as rolled aluminum and aviation instruments. Despite this concentration within MAP, the various functions are performed by administratively separate organizations. Research is performed in research institutes; design and development is conducted in design bureaus and their prototype construction shops; manufacturing goes on in plants that are not formally linked to the design bureaus. There are approximately six research institutes, eleven aircraft, helicopter, and aerodynamic missile design bureaus, five engine design bureaus, and 30–40 manufacturing plants.

The main outline of the present structure can be traced back to 1939–40. These years followed a period of intense purges. A reorganization of the aviation ministry that began in 1939 raised a number of young individuals to positions of authority. The threat of war provided a strong stimulus to search for new solutions to the problems of the industry. The wartime experience itself served to solidify or sanctify those procedures and solutions that proved to be successful. The personality of Stalin also had a recognizable influence on the pattern of behavior within aviation. Despite organizational changes since then, the principal features of the system that were established or confirmed from 1939 to the end of the war have remained relatively intact.

A feature of the Soviet industry that differs substantially from the American is the highly concentrated nature of production in the aviation ministry. Certain features of the Soviet system contribute to this pattern of industrial concentration. There is a notable lack of control over establishments outside one's own organization (be it ministry or plant). The proven undependability of outside suppliers, together with great pressures to meet planned output targets, have led Soviet industrial ministries, as well as individual plants, to try to keep as much of the manufacturing process as possible within the organization. Of the thousands of components going into aircraft, 90 to 95 percent are produced in the aviation ministry itself. The Ministry of Aviation Industry includes metallurgical plants that roll aluminum and magnesium alloys, stamping and extruding facilities, and plants that manufacture plastic and rubber goods. The prime assembly plant of the 84 passenger, 4 turboprop Il-18 manufactured all components except the engines, radio equipment, accessories, propellers, and wheels. It produced, in-house, the landing gear and shock absorbers, hydraulic system accessories, seats, cast parts, rivets, nuts, and bolts.

Information Flows

With the R&D function separated into autonomous organizations, efficient communications across functional boundaries is necessary for project success. Communications between research institutes and design bureaus perform two main functions. Research results are transmitted down to the design bureau in a usable form, and problems and requests for information are sent to the research institutes. The chief vehicle for the transmission of research results is the handbook for designers published by TsAGI and the other institutes.[2] One of the most important innovations of the early period was the development of this handbook. Sections of the handbook are written by leading research scientists. It is intended to keep the design bureaus abreast of the latest research results, and to constrain the designers to work within a common, proven technical code. The emphasis on the use of handbooks in the design process leads to certain similarities in approach from one design bureau to another. A British observer writes that the wing planforms used on a number of aircraft are so similar "it is difficult to believe that they were arrived at independently."[3] In addition to controlling the approved list of structures and aerodynamic forms, the research institutes publish lists of approved materials and manufacturing techniques. TsAGI also provides specific advice and instructions for every officially approved project. These instructions are project-specific and are growing in importance.

[1] Except where noted, detailed supporting references for the material on the Soviet Union can be found in: Arthur J. Alexander, *R&D in Soviet Aviation*, R-589-PR (Santa Monica, Calif.: The RAND Corporation, 1970). Additional information has come from conversations and interviews with individuals in Soviet aviation, or with outsiders who are familiar with the industry at first or second hand.

[2] The Central Aerohydrodynamics Institute (TsAGI) is the oldest and most important aviation research institute in the Soviet Union.

[3] He goes on to say that "as long as swept wings defy exact theoretical treatment and consequently require prolonged aerodynamic development by trial and error, there is much to be said for such an approach." R. M. Braybrook, "Russian Blinder," *Flying Review International* 19, no. 11 (August 1964): 30.

The need for handbooks and special instructions is partly dictated by the lack of test and research facilities at the design bureaus. The research institutes have a monopoly on the largest wind tunnels, test rigs, and so on, as well as on the most highly qualified scientists. By necessity, then, the design bureaus must rely on the research institutes to supply the day-to-day guidelines on design. The normal problems that occur throughout all phases of design must be given to the research institutes for solution.

The research institutes' relations with the factories are similar to, but probably not so intimate as, those with the design bureaus. Handbooks on approved materials and production techniques are issued by the All Union Institute of Aviation Material (UIAM) and the Scientific Research Institute for Aviation Technology and Production (NIAT). Production problems go to the institutes for solution. New processes are worked out jointly by the plants, research institutes, and design bureaus. Even more than the design bureaus, the factories lack the laboratories and personnel that would be needed if they were to take on the functions now being performed for them by the institutes.

Typically, the culmination of a design project is the construction of a prototype by a special experimental plant associated with, and under the control of, the design bureau.[4] Physically, the experimental plant may be a department of a large production plant or it may be located on the premises of the designer, but regardless of its location, it is administered by the design bureau. Unlike the prototype plants, series production plants are not permanently linked to a specific design bureau, although there are some traditional bonds between a plant and a designer that may extend over several decades. During the period that an aircraft is under production, the designer has a good deal of authority over the plant manager on questions concerning manufacture.

When detailed design begins, production engineers from a series plant are drawn into the design work. They convert the preliminary drawings used for the construction of the prototype into production drawings suitable for plant use. The series plant engineers advise the designers on plant capabilities and the costs of alternative technologies. The production engineers become familiar with the design and prepare the plans to enter the aircraft into production. As the proto-

type is built and flown, changes necessitated by actual flight tests are incorporated into the production drawings. Often in the past, a prototype that incorporated all changes was submitted to the plant, along with the drawings, to serve as a standard. When the aircraft is formally transferred to the series plant, engineers from the design bureau and the plant's manufacturing engineers that had been advising on the design transfer to the plant. So long as the aircraft is in production, a design bureau representative remains at the factory. During the course of production, the series plant sends suggestions for improvements back to the design bureau.

The above description enables us to focus on how information flows influence the output of the system. The research institutes provide proven up to date research results to design bureaus and manufacturing plants through the medium of handbooks and project instructions. The handbooks prevent the design bureaus from incorporating into their designs new technologies that appear promising but that have not yet been tested, proven, and approved. The institutes themselves are kept informed of the problems of the other functional organizations. They get this information from the tests that are run on models and prototypes, from the specific requests for research to solve current problems, and from their membership on various review committees (see below). The design bureaus and plants transmit information to each other through the temporary posting of personnel in each other's establishments and through the dissemination of research results. By the construction of a prototype, the experimental plant of the design bureau proves out the design both in its production and in its performance characteristics. The information thus transmitted to the plant in the form of drawings (and sometimes the prototype itself) is highly reliable.

It is important to note that in other sectors of the Soviet economy, research, design, development, and manufacturing quite often take place in different ministries. The barriers that exist to communications across ministerial boundaries are usually enough to impede effective R&D, but there are other problems as well. Research institutes do not provide usable output to designers and are often not aware of the problems of design. Design bureaus do not turn over producible designs to plants. Often the plants complain that the first year or so of preparation for production is taken up by conversion of the design into a workable product that can be produced. Prototype construction is not universal; where it does exist, the designer must often go hat in hand to a

[4]The Russian term for design bureaus in aviation is *opytno-konstruktorskoe byuro (OKB)*. This is usually translated as "experimental design bureau." However, the word translated as "experimental" has other shades of meaning—"trying out" or "proving" an idea in practice.

plant to have the prototype built, and the plant retains its independence from the design bureau. The authority possessed by an aviation designer over the series production plant appears to be absent elsewhere.

The Process of Development

There is a standard sequence of steps in the design process that takes a concept from initial proposal to operational aircraft. The formal procedures serve as the skeleton that gives shape to the process, and on which the various forces of personality, bureaucracy, and politics act to give a project its detailed appearance. Deviations from the established procedures do seem to be recognized as deviations,[5] and there is enough evidence to support the contention that all of the steps described below are normally encountered.

A proposal for a new aircraft is put forward by either the users or by designers within the aviation ministry, although it has been claimed by one highly knowledgeable observer that the designers are fairly conservative with respect to new approaches. "They would rather improve an old design than try something completely new."[6] If there is no definite customer for a design who is willing to pay for the finished product, the aviation ministry itself can finance development as long as it is considered experimental. Since the aviation ministry has a limited experimental budget, proposals that originate within the industry are ordinarily sold to a customer ministry before design work proceeds very far.

The proposal is submitted for approval to the Council of Ministers. Military leaders sit on the Council and it is here that military demands come into open conflict with alternative resource uses. For example, the heavy forging capacity required for a wing spar might conflict with the demands to produce electricity generating equipment. Some Soviet aviation people have suggested that their military leaders are more likely to see decisions in a national framework than are their American counterparts. Soviet education as well

as the position of military leaders in high decisionmaking councils are said to contribute to this result.

When the proposal is tentatively approved by the Council of Ministers it is sent to the aviation research institutes who study the request and give broad direction to the future project. It then goes before a scientific-technical commission composed of members of the customer and production ministries. This commission works out differences of opinion and develops the detailed specifications and technical parameters of the new design as well as project-specific advice. The pre-project, as the proposal is called at this stage, is usually assigned to more than one design bureau for elaboration. Design bureaus often request to be included at this stage of design, even when they have no real chance of continuing the project to completion. The pre-project does not appear to be a complicated document. It describes the purpose of the aircraft, tasks and conditions of operation, performance characteristics, and the relative importance of the various requirements.

A senior designer works out the general outlines of the aircraft based on the specifications of the pre-project. A small group of highly experienced designers, assisted by aerodynamic, strength, and other specialists, develops a more detailed design over a period of several months. The designers then present the completed pre-projects to the same expert commission that had original responsibility for the project. The commission, after intensive study and evaluation, chooses one or more of the pre-projects for continued development. Typically, a single design is selected at this stage for nonmilitary aircraft. For fighter aircraft, or other advanced technology applications, two or more designs might be retained for detailed elaboration.

As the engineering drawings are produced, they are sent to the prototype shops where the prototype is constructed. In these drawings, only the most critical or complicated components, assemblies, and technological processes are specified in detail. The prototype plant is manned by highly skilled machinists working general purpose machines. Consequently, they are able to work from relatively unfinished drawings, saving the time that would be needed for production drawings and specially designed tools.

The completed prototypes are first flown by the design bureau to establish the gross performance characteristics, and then turned over to the Flight Test Institute (LII) for more detailed testing. The detailed tests are prescribed by the expert commission, and both production and customer

---

[5]Yakovlev writes that in 1951 he decided to skip the usual procedural steps and instead appealed directly to Stalin for a particular decision. Realizing the seriousness of his actions, Yakovlev justified himself by saying that he had no other recourse. "I was afraid that my proposal might get bogged down in going through normal channels." A. S. Yakovlev, *Target of Life*, AD674316 (Washington, D.C.: Clearinghouse, Department of Commerce, NO). Translated from *Tsel'Zhizni*, (Moscow: Isdatel'stvo Politicheskoy Literatury, 1966), pp. 173–76.

[6]This point is supported by a leading test pilot who did not find it strange that a designer turned down a good idea of one of his subordinates "because plane builders rarely accept innovation out of love for progress." M. Gallai, "From the Memoirs of a Test Pilot," *Novyi Mir* 2 (1965): 92–143.

ministry personnel take part. At the completion of state tests, production decisions are usually made. Sometimes, however, the decision to produce a design is made prior to the completion of testing, but actual manufacturing rarely begins until all the changes dictated by test results are incorporated into the production drawings and prototype. After the decision is made to manufacture, the design is formally turned over to the series production plant; however, ultimate control over the design is retained in the hands of the chief designer.

The Role of the Scientific-Technical Commission

The scientific-technical commission plays a critical role at several strategic points in the development process. Members of the commission, drawn from the senior staffs of research and user organizations, are highly experienced in most aspects of aircraft technology and operations. The continuity of membership over the life of a project together with the prestige and competence of the members give the commission's decisions an unusual degree of authority.

At the earliest stage, the commission reviews the technical feasibility and probable cost of a proposal. They later act as a source selection board in choosing the winning designs. During the selection process each of the contending designers may sit with the commission to review and criticize the proposals of their competitors. However, after the selection is made, the authority of the commission appears to preclude extensive complaints by the losers.

At various times during development, the commission reviews the projects and offers advice on proceeding to the next stage. It thus receives information as it becomes available and can make sequential decisions without entering into the day-to-day operation of the design bureaus.

Design Philosophy

The concept of competition has remained as a dominant force in the aviation industry over the years. In military aviation, competition is generally carried through to the prototype stage. In fighter and interceptor aircraft, where prototype competition had been most active in the past, the ratio of prototypes to production articles has fallen somewhat from around 3 to 1 in 1945–49 to approximately 2 to 1 in recent years. Note, however, that there are still two prototypes for every type to enter service. By defining a standard interface, competition is often extended to the subsystem level. Rarely is more than one wholly new subsystem incorporated into a new aircraft. What is lost in global optimization is gained in systems that work.

The design practices of simplicity, commonality, and inheritance, stemming in part from the forces of competition and the importance attached to production, have also been given status in their own right. These terms describe concepts that are interrelated, though basically different from each other. Simplicity here means uncomplicated, unadorned, unburdened, the performing only of what is required and no more. Examples of simplicity are the absence of powered controls on large passenger jets, the use of common materials, and the lack of detailed finishing on parts where it is not required. Commonality means the use of standardized parts, assemblies, and subsystems wherever possible, as well as the sharing of design features among different aircraft. The same guns, radars, and pumps are found on a wide variety of aircraft. The Su-7 (ground attack and tactical air cover) and the Su-9 (all weather interceptor) had common fuselages, tails, and (originally) engines, whereas the wings, armament, and the equipment were chosen for their different roles. Design inheritance is similar to commonality, but it is inter- rather than intragenerational. We find this in the long series of models and modifications of the MiG-21 (first designed in the mid-1950s), which have incorporated new versions of engines, armaments, radars, and aerodynamics as they have become known and available.

These features of Soviet design were strongly influenced by Stalin's often expressed attitudes. His comments concerning the importance of avoiding complicating changes are pertinent. He felt that the designer was the one individual who could be held responsible for the success or failure of a product, and that the designer had the duty of protecting the integrity of his design from the demands of others. The most insidious kind of degradation, Stalin thought, was the "epidemic of improvements." "The designer must not be at everybody's beck and call . . . . He has to protest irresponsible demands . . . . The designer has to be tough and he has to protect his machine from irresponsible advisers. It's hard to make a good machine and very easy to spoil it. And it's the designer who is responsible."[7]

Simplicity has been built into the operating procedures of the industry. Every design team has a standards section. This group examines the design to see whether all state and industry standards are adhered to, whether off-the-shelf

[7]Yakovlev, *op. cit.*, pp. 282–83.

items can be used instead of newly designed equipment, and whether standardized tooling can be used in production. The various handbooks limit the number of structures, materials, and processes that may be used. The unreliability of supply, especially of newly designed equipment from other ministries, induces designers to specify proven materials from traditional sources.

Another factor leading to simplicity is the importance given to the reactions of test pilots and operational pilots of the aircraft. The test pilot, who is usually an engineer, is an integral unit of the design team. A test pilot's critique may affect the course of development.[8] The test pilot has been described as "the designer's best assistant in creating a new aircraft."[9] Pilots are said to take part in all discussions connected with a new design. The opinions of the pilots who fly the aircraft in routine operations are also actively sought.

Design inheritance has the tendency of confining development to proven techniques. Innovation takes place in small increments. The large uncertainties of large jumps in technology are avoided. Design inheritance is prescribed as the desired form of development in a Russian textbook on aviation technology. But, the text warns, "the dogmatic utilization of this method can result in slowing down the rate of technological progress . . . . Upon reaching a certain stage in the development of a given type of aviation design, it is necessary to forego the design inheritance method and to look for new solutions with the purpose of substantial improvements."[10]

The design philosophy of incremental change, marginal advance, and design inheritance, if followed rigidly, would eventually lead to technological stagnation. Since these concepts are an established part of the system, discontinuous change must be sought through temporary deviations from the normal patterns in the form of crash programs, the establishment of problem oriented *ad hoc* organizations and committees, temporary suspensions of the usual procedures, or high level political intervention. When a problem is recognized as such by the Communist Party, the attempted solution will be episodic and *ad hoc*, with close attention paid it by the political leadership.

The Structure of Incentives

Compared to almost all civil R&D and much military R&D in the Soviet Union, the aircraft industry is remarkably efficient and successful. Large numbers of designs that are militarily competitive are developed quickly, at low development and production cost. What is it that drives the system, that produces the observed results? To answer these questions, a sequence of influences can be briefly outlined. Designers are rewarded for aircraft that are produced. State prizes and awards are presented for those designs that successfully enter production and that make a substantial military or economic contribution to the nation. Success leads to follow-on orders, modifications, new assignments, more manpower, and larger and better facilities, as well as to honor and esteem. Substantial monetary state prizes are often distributed among members of the design bureau, providing a boost to morale. Lack of production success is marked by the absence of the above benefits and may, in fact, lead to the dissolution of the design bureau.

In the competitive system of design, the aircraft that flies first historically has had the best chance of winning a competition. Both the design and the experimental prototype can be produced more quickly if the design is uncomplicated and is derived from earlier work. Manpower that is relatively fixed in the short run constrains the designer to solutions that do not require excess design efforts.[11] Also, the plane that is simplest to build and maintain, that has the fewest radical innovations, and that makes use of previous experience appeals to the predispositions of the aviation hierarchy.[12] Since the chief reason for building an aircraft is its military or commercial value, the designer must have a keen appreciation of the characteristics that enhance the value of the aircraft. In the military area especially, aircraft requirements are subject to frequent change

---

[8] During testing of the Yakovlev VTOL, the test pilot brushed off design bureau suggestions for overcoming stability problems; he demanded and received more detailed data analysis of flight parameters and subsequent modifications to the stability systems before he would perform further tests.

[9] V. I. Tikhomirov, *Organization and Planning of an Aircraft Construction Enterprise* (Moscow: State Publishing House for the Defense Industry, 1957). Translated from *Organizatsiya i Planirovaniye Samoletostroitelnogo Predpriyatiya* by Technical Documents Liaison Office, Wright-Patterson Air Force Base as document F-TS-9503/V, p. 434.

[10] D. P. Andrianov, M. Z. Gendel'man, *et al.*, *Management, Planning, and Economics of Aircraft Production*, (Moscow: State Publishing House for Science and Technology, 1963). Translated from *Organizatsya, Planirovaniye i Ekonomika Aviationnogo Proizvodstva* by Foreign Technology Division, Wright-Patterson Air Force Base as document FTD-TT-63/1121/1+2, December 1964, p. 296.

[11] The size of Soviet airframe design bureaus seems to range from about 1000 people to somewhat less than 10,000, including designers, draftsmen, and prototype construction workers.

[12] These predispositions are partly based on cost considerations. In addition, most of the hierarchy, who have had long experience in the industry, seem to have a highly developed penchant for the simple solution since, historically, simple solutions have had a high payoff, especially in wartime.

as a result of shifting strategic factors, new technologies, and specific enemy decisions. Successful design in this kind of situation requires a certain prescience as to what the military requirement will be at the time an aircraft is scheduled to enter into service. Forethought, luck, and perhaps a good deal of salesmanship have characterized those whose designs are produced.

The forces of competition, wartime demand, and Stalin's personal influence also enhanced the importance of speedy design practices. Often, the prototype that first flew was chosen for production, even though a later competitive model had better characteristics. Stalin quite explicitly stated that the winner of a design competition "will be the one who not only gives the best fighter in terms of flight and combat qualities, but who also delivers first."[13] The emphasis on getting a prototype into the air as quickly as possible continues to the present day even though the original motivating forces are no longer present.[14] The goal has been built into the structure and procedures of the aviation industry. The standard procedures by which drawings are made, tooling designed, and prototypes built reflect the original motivation.

The benefits of foresight do not, in general, require much discussion. But the forces that induce people in one organization to be more discerning of possible future events than individuals in another organization require some examination. Part of the importance of foresight in Soviet aviation derives from the manner in which new systems are generated. When a prototype is built and flown, the technical characteristics as proven in flight can be assessed by the potential user. It is at this point that the military value of the aircraft is evaluated.[15] This sequence may be contrasted to recent U.S. practice where the mission or specifications are first decided upon by the military and then the plane is designed to meet the chosen requirements. The Soviet designer thus has a greater amount of responsibility in the total innovation process. He can properly be described as a technological entrepreneur. The tendency in the Soviet Union therefore is to give more weight to the designer, whereas in the United States the balance is shifted toward the military proposer. Consequently, the Soviet design bureau is more closely linked to the success or failure of a project, leading the designer to exercise considerable thought over his conception of the role of the intended aircraft.

The Soviets pay a good deal of attention to predicting costs and trying to attain low costs, but their probable success in achieving these goals depends more on the style of development than on any breakthroughs in cost control.[16] Pushing technology and attempting to manufacture unproven designs have been the most important causes of high production costs in the United States. As shown above, the Soviets avoid both of these pitfalls. Prototype testing, simplicity, commonality, and design inheritance minimize technological advance in each program, shorten the development period, and hold the development program to a relatively small size. All of these features work to control costs. By localizing uncertainties to the organizations best situated to cope with them, the problems associated with uncertainty are not transmitted through the system. The constraints placed upon the R&D system effectively control the costs of development and production.

Soviet aviation R&D operates in a system of constrained autonomy. Design bureaus are autonomous; daily operations are under the organization's own control. The formulation of a design, assignment of manpower, reactions to problems, and detailed management are the organization's own responsibility. However, resource limits and tight development schedules, together with officially approved technologies, processes, and hardware place limits on the freedom of the designer. Feedback from the scientific-technical commission and later from production runs and state prizes provides critical information on organization performance.

The ability to live within very detailed and often arbitrary constraints is a noted characteristic of Soviet man.[17] The unacceptability of these constraints to other nationalities was remarked on by a German aircraft designer who had spent several post–World War II years in Soviet aviation. When he complained to a leading

---

[13]Yakovlev, op. cit., p. 165.

[14]The demand for new military systems has, of course, continued; and the solutions to earlier problems have continued to be effective. The system that was set in motion in World War II has established itself strongly because it has been successful. No crisis born of failure has arisen that would impel a reexamination of how things ought to be done.

[15]An example derived from World War II experience can be cited. Polikarpov had written to Stalin concerning a new design possessing increased speed and range. Stalin replied, "First flight-test its range, *then* we'll decide what to do with it." Yakovlev, op. cit., p. 280.

[16]The head of the aviation ministry has complained that most of the design bureau's cost predictions were grossly optimistic. Nevertheless, it is the actual level rather than the overrun that is ultimately important.

[17]See, for example, Michel Crozier, The Bureaucratic Phenomenon (Chicago: The University of Chicago Press, 1964), p. 228.

Soviet designer about the extraordinary number and detail of design rules they had to follow he was told, "you will never be able to understand the system unless you are born in Russia."

The military customer also is constrained by the approved technology and by broader national or interservice resource limits. But the buyer is able to make critical decisions based on solid information generated by the development process itself. That the customer is not frozen out of the process is attested to by a statement by the head of the Soviet Air Force procurement command. He described himself as being "in charge" of weapons acquisition. As we shall see, this entire process is quite different from that found in the United States.

BUYER PARTICIPATION: THE UNITED STATES

Participation

One of the most important features of U.S. military R&D is the extent of buyer participation in the total acquisition process. By participation I mean the detailed specification and management of research, development, and procurement by the system buyer. Participation is so embedded in American political philosophy and culture that it is undoubtedly an abiding feature of contemporary life.

The abstracted experience of World War II sharply changed the assumptions as to the place of R&D in military affairs. It became the nearly unanimous opinion of military leaders, Congress, and the public that the large and widespread R&D efforts mobilized during the war years should be continued at high levels. The military was expected to lead, rather than follow, in research and technology. This important doctrinal shift (which has been observed after most wars since the mid-nineteenth century) helped set in motion the events of the next twenty-five years.

Participation stems primarily from Congressional and private concern with due process, combined with American cultural patterns of decisionmaking.[18] Due process dictates that fairness be evident in government procurement practices. Competition of private firms for government business is bound in an elaborate web of regulations that attempts to guarantee that the

allocation of business is demonstrably fair and repeatable. Complaints of losers can be dealt with by referral to the regulation; a company's performance can be judged according to the rules of the game. *Equity rather than efficiency is the dominant feature of this game.*[19] But as the total cost of many weapons has come to be measured in the billions of dollars, the acquisition process now encompasses major decisions with political, regional, and industrywide impact. The greater the intrusion of political and bureaucratic forces into the acquisition process, the more complex becomes the structure of regulation. This pernicious circle is closed, as the larger the program and the more complex the system of regulation, the greater is the likelihood of external interference in the formal system.

The role of culture in American bureaucratic processes derives from American individualism and a personal resistance to authority. The organizational counterpart to these personality traits can be found in the existence of multiple decision centers with autonomous legal prerogatives.[20] While this system allows many human resources to be tapped and promotes the flourishing of individual initiative, it also requires an extremely complex array of procedures and regulations that both protects the individual and provides the required coordination of the diffuse decisionmaking power.

The impact of American culture on bureaucracy, as described here, is not of recent origin. Bureaucratic traits that exist today were described and analyzed by De Tocqueville 125 years ago. For the past quarter century, problems associated with the acquisition of weapons have been scrutinized in a series of almost continuous hearings in the Congress and have also been the subject of at least twenty high level reviews, one example of which was the Presidential Blue Ribbon Commission appointed by President Nixon in 1969.[21] Not surprisingly, the same symptoms

---

[18]There are of course other forces leading to participation and excess regulation. The desire of civil servants to be able to justify their decisions if later questioned, the attempt to prevent corruption, the aim to regulate excess profits, and the desire to outlaw waste are all additional elements of the American mind that makes efficiency in acquisition so difficult to attain.

[19]In free, competitive markets efficiency and equity are not incompatible, as was first pointed out by Adam Smith two hundred years ago. However, the pursuit of equity by U.S. governmental bureaucracies leads to controls and regulations that reduce the flexibility and autonomy of the producing organizations with a resulting loss of efficiency. For examples of the principles of equity in contract award, see James R. Kurth, "Aerospace Production Lines and American Defense Spending," in *American Defense Policy III*, ed. by Richard G. Head and Ervin J. Rokke (Baltimore: The Johns Hopkins University Press, 1973) pp. 626–40.

[20]Crozier, *op. cit.*, pp. 231–36.

[21]A continuing theme running through these reviews is well described in the following point taken from a 1957 report: "A growing lack of trust in people at the working level has taken away the authority but not responsibility, diffused this authority throughout higher echelons, increased detailed directions from these echelons, constrained the use of resources at

have been observed over the years—excess regulation, complex lines of authority, difficulty of coordination across organizational boundaries, high cost, inefficiency, waste. Organizational boundaries have shifted frequently and new sets of regulations have attempted to cut through the morass of existing rules, but (with interesting exceptions) the problems remain.[22]

The Organization of Systems Acquisition

All but the smallest of organizations involved in R&D are separated into distinct components. This simple fact means that the flow of the R&D process is broken by organizational boundaries. The location of these boundaries and the means by which they are bridged must be determined by all R&D establishments. American practice has been to place the overall management of acquisition in the hands of the buyer (the Air Force), and the performance in private industry.

A striking feature of the Air Force acquisition bureaucracy has been the periodic changes in organizational responsibility in response to recurring dissatisfaction with existing methods. Boundaries between research, development, and procurement have shifted at least once a decade since the establishment of the Airplane Engineering Division in 1918.[23]

The standard form of organization has been the project office, organized to acquire a new type of equipment (the F-15 is a recent example), or a class of equipment (fighter aircraft). From the mid-1930s to the early 1950s, an experimental engineering project office monitored the weapon through R&D, at which time control passed to a production engineering project office. Subsystem development was the responsibility of the project

offices with integration of subsystems for production being the job of the manufacturer. Development of the B-29 bomber was an exception. A single project office managed development and production, as it was considered too complex to be managed within the standard framework. With the B-47 development in 1951, joint project offices were formed that were physically co-located in order to smooth the transition from engineering to procurement. Project offices at this time were quite small, averaging ten people or less. They had little technical expertise and relied on Air Force laboratories for in-house technical support. The problems of coordination of the joint project offices and the lack of technical personnel were reduced by the assumption of detailed technical management by the airframe manufacturer—the "prime" contractor.

Appearing at the same time as the joint project office was the development strategy enunciated under the name of "weapon system concept." Increasing complexity of new weapons and the interdependency of their components, together with success of the wartime B-29 development, which was conceived of in its later phases as a "system," were contributing factors to the growth of the concept. Other elements also entered into the weapon system concept, as practiced: belief in the efficacy of thoroughly detailed preplanning; the high costs associated with competitive prototype development and testing; the conviction that the problems of a military project office could be contracted out to a prime contractor; and finally the notion that maximum weapon efficiency could be obtained if component design were completely subordinated to the requirements of the total system.[24]

Most of these elements contributed to the increasingly complex burden of control and coordination. Reliance on a prime contractor meant that the problems were not necessarily solved, but duplicated in a civilian organization. Integration of component design required that every component be coordinated with every other. Another outcome of the weapon system philosophy was the generalization of the process. It was thought that a single set of regulations and a common organizational form could be designed to manage a wide variety of acquisitions. "The process of developing weapon systems rather than the development of any single system became the principal concern of development managers. Procedural matters were increasingly emphasized."[25]

---

the working level." Dr. H. Guyford Stever (Chairman), *Report of the Ad Hoc Committee on Research and Development,* Reporting to Chief of Staff, U.S.A.F., 1957.

[22]An example that illustrates the situation is provided in Congressional testimony by nuclear submarine developer Admiral Rickover. The Assistant Secretary of the Navy for R&D and the Director of Defense Research and Engineering had both approved the development of a new item.

But then a man in the lower levels of the Navy Department, a hard worker, called me at 7:30 last night and said 'I am not going to approve the money for this project until you give me a thorough technical explanation!'

So here is an item that has been approved by the top R&D official in the Navy and the top R&D official in the Department of Defense, yet I still have to take time away from running my job to set up meetings and work my way through the organization chart. I now have to convince people who know little about the issue, simply because they have positions of authority.

H. G. Rickover, *Weapon Systems Acquisition Process.* Hearings before the Committee on Armed Services, United States Senate, 92nd Congress, 1st Session, 1972, p. 300.

[23]For a concise organizational history of Air Force acquisition, see: W. D. Putnam, *The Evolution of Air Force System Acquisition Management* R-868-PR (Santa Monica, Calif.: The RAND Corporation, 1972).

[24]Robert L. Perry, *System Development Strategies* RM-4853-PR (Santa Monica: The RAND Corporation, 1966), pp. 18–19.

[25]*Ibid.,* p. 21.

An exception to the standard development strategy was chosen for the high priority ballistic missile program. Since elements of this strategy influenced later events, the program deserves a brief description.[26]

The ballistic missile projects were explicitly planned to be exceptions. Almost from their beginning they existed in a deliberately contrived atmosphere of program uniqueness. In 1954, a special Strategic Missile Evaluation Committee (SMEC) reaffirmed the opinion of a number of scientific groups at the time that a useful intercontinental missile could be developed by 1960, if certain procedural difficulties embedded in the current doctrine and organizations could be overcome. They recommended an "exempt" program commanded by a particularly well-qualified general officer who was to be given full authority over the program. The Air Force assigned highest priority to the Atlas program and established a special field office with complete control. Within weeks, the Air Force Scientific Advisory Committee reviewed the development plans and concluded that no single prime contractor could adequately manage the ICBM program and that neither the civil service nor the military could attract the required engineering talent to provide technical control. It was agreed that the newly created private firm of Ramo-Wooldridge with its elite engineering group should be made responsible for systems engineering and technical direction under contract to the program office. This arrangement effectively bypassed the existing project office organization with its technical support in the Air Force laboratories. Communications between the ballistic missile program office and Ramo-Wooldridge was unimpeded by organizational formalities as they sat side by side in daily contact. According to Perry, the Air Force acquired two valued abilities: "(1) direct control over the actions of the technical program managers without having to invest in ritual correspondence, and (2) rapid and continuous cognizance of the details of program activity which was dependent neither on periodic reporting nor inexpert observation."[27]

Concentration of program authority did not include financial independence of the ballistic missile program from the established organizations in the Air Materiel Command, and by 1955 it had become apparent that the ability to exact prompt technical decisions meant little if their effect depended on financial resources controlled elsewhere. To meet this problem the so-called "Gillette procedures" were enacted that gave to the program office (as reviewed and approved at only one place in the Air Force—the specially created Air Force Ballistic Missiles Committee) exclusive authority to approve and to alter the technical and financial content of the development effort. A development plan for the forthcoming year containing the complete fund requirements—the program package—was prepared by the program office. This package was routinely subject to later amendment as events transpired, but the "package" concept was useful in gaining high level endorsement of plans and expenditure levels as well as in providing stable finances under which necessary reallocation could take place as dictated by the actual course of the program.

The Gillette procedures insured that one portion of the program was not held up in financial channels throwing the whole development program out of alignment. They also reduced substantially the review and approval process through the direct, short, and uncluttered communication links between the program office and the Air Force Ballistic Missile Committee.[28]

An attempt to further insulate the program from expected outside influences involved the creation of heightened security protocols. Many of the documents were classified top-secret and "the atmosphere of a closed society was preserved by vigorous enforcement of 'a need to know' secrecy standard."[29]

In contrast to development strategies that were to come later, the primary organizational characteristic of the ballistic missile development group was its responsiveness to the project orientation of the task. The responsibilities assigned the Ballistic Missiles Division "tended to influence its structure far more than did any preordained concepts of organizational propriety."[30]

In the "non-exempt" part of the world, growth of the systems concept throughout the 1950s made it more difficult to develop subsystems independently of main systems. This trend weakened the links between the laboratories and the systems developers as the project offices added subsystems specialists to their own staffs.

Air Force Systems Command (AFSC) was established in 1961, concentrating in one command all of the R&D, procurement, and production engineering activities, leaving to the new Logistics Command the post-acquisition management of supply and maintenance. Accompanying this reorganization was an attempt to incorporate the

[26]This section draws heavily on Perry, *ibid.*, pp. 60–81.
[27]*Ibid.*, p. 9.
[28]Putnam, *op. cit.*, p. 9.
[29]Perry, *op. cit.*, p. 70.
[30]*Ibid.*, p. 76.

best features (as perceived at the time) of the nonstandard ballistic missile development experience into the existing organizational framework.

The principal element of the ballistic missile program that was adopted was a bastardized form of the Gillette procedures. The new management system was built around the package program concept and a System Program Office was responsible for compiling and executing the package, but without the flexibility or financial authority exercised by the ballistic missile program. The adoption of new techniques (which were altered in the adoption process) by the established bureaucracy was accomplished by a complex series of regulations and procedures.

A new Administration in 1969 was faced with the apparent breakdown of the existing system of weapons acquisition. Cost overruns, while not greater in percentage terms than those of the previous decade, were extraordinarily large in absolute amount with sums running into the billions of dollars.[31] Highlighted by Air Force problems with the C-5A and F-111, the other services had their troubles too with tanks, helicopters, torpedos, and light landing craft. Along with ballooning costs were performance shortfalls and reduced procurement quantities as the excessive costs absorbed limited budgets. In searching for a solution to the crisis, the Department of Defense turned toward an acquisition strategy that had survived as an exception to the established style of the previous decades.

Prototype development of aircraft had been the standard strategy in the United States in the 1930s and 1940s. It is still the preferred strategy in the Soviet Union and France as described elsewhere in this paper. But the growth in the United States of the weapon system concept in the 1950s and the package program of the 1960s displaced the use of prototypes for two decades. A number of nonstandard programs in recent years that used the prototype approach appeared to be efficiently conducted without the hindrances of the normal bureaucratic restraints. The ballistic missile program itself, until the initiation of full-scale production in 1958, was to a large degree managed according to a sequential, prototype strategy despite its reputation for having established the feasibility of "package procurement." The Agena-D rocket, Sidewinder missile, and all of C. L. "Kelly" Johnson's "skunkworks"

projects at Lockheed were examples of nonstandard prototype developments. Many of these programs were also characterized by streamlined management procedures and austere budgets.

The prototype strategy, or "fly before buy" as it is popularly called, together with attempts to cut through the regulatory jungle that has flourished over the years, was the subject of a major policy initiative in 1970. Deputy Secretary of Defense Packard stressed that improved management was dependent on selecting capable people and keeping them in their job long enough to become effective. Tests of hardware and proofing of both systems and components was called on to minimize risk and to avoid the problems of early commitments to immature or infeasible designs. Tradeoffs between costs, performance, and availability date were to be emphasized throughout the development phase. Matters dependent on final design were to be delayed as much as possible until the production phase of the program. Documentation and reports not vital to actual development should be eliminated from the R&D phase. And production resources should be minimized until demonstration that all development problems had been solved.[32] This policy formalized many of the procedures observed in the successful, nonstandard programs of the past.

A new prototype program office was established at AFSC to manage the development of two advanced aircraft types—lightweight fighter and STOL transport. The office is very small with the fighter management group consisting of only a four-man team. Both developments are under fixed maximum obligation contracts. Another innovation is the "design-to-cost" concept where a unit production cost is set in advance and performance is maximized subject to this constraint.

If the program offices can be maintained at low manning levels and if the modest funding levels can be sustained, at least through testing of the prototype, perhaps efficiency in development can be attained. However, the forces leading to growth, regulation, participation, and inefficiency are always present and very strong. Past experience suggests that it has not been possible to standardize the exceptional. Mimicry of misperceived experience has generally resulted in crucial omissions. An important aspect of present innovations is that the new style is being imposed by fiat from higher authority. There is no

[31]For evidence that the acquisition experience of the 1960s was no better than that of the 1950s, see: Alvin J. Harman, *A Methodology for Cost Factor Comparison and Prediction* RM-6269-ARPA (Santa Monica: The RAND Corporation, 1970).

[32]David Packard, Deputy Secretary of Defense, Memorandum, *Policy Guidance on Major Weapon System Acquisition*, May 28, 1970.

strong continuing motivation to make system developers want to behave in an efficient manner, to seek out the best techniques that are applicable to their own development problems. Development and production cost limits may provide some of the required incentives, but it is predictable that the demands of due process will force excess regulatory complications on prototype source selection and competition, and that the prerogatives of diffuse decision authority will destroy the potential simplicity of maximum obligation contracts and design-to-cost. Finally, it is important to remember that military budgets are not controlled by military buyers of equipment nor by the developers, but by Congress and the President. And so we return to a basic theme of American culture, a diffuse decisionmaking power where no single agency has final or dominating authority.

Industry Structure

It is difficult to describe in brief terms the American aircraft and missile industry because of its heterogeneity across firms and even within a firm. Lockheed, for example, includes within its corporate boundaries such diverse divisions as Lockheed Georgia operating in a government owned plant where the C-5A was built; Lockheed California that is developing the L-1011 civil transport (Tristar); and C. L. (Kelly) Johnson's "skunkworks," operated somewhat like a Soviet design bureau and turning out over the years such diverse, technically advanced aircraft as the U-2, F-104, and SR-71.

Despite this diversity, several points do stand out. Buyer and seller concentration is moderately high. The military customer purchases over 50 percent of the output of the aircraft and missile industries, and the largest four firms account for over 60 percent of military sales.[33] Of the 100 largest defense contractors, the top 7 were companies involved in airframes, engines, or missiles with McDonnell-Douglas, General Dynamics, and Lockheed as the top three. For these 3 companies, military prime contracts amounted to over 75 percent of their total corporate sales in 1967.

This high degree of buyer and seller concentration promotes the kind of participation noted above, as the parties find themselves in a position of bilateral bargaining. Since the buyer (the Air Force) is not bound by normal economic con-

straints and the product has no market determined price or standard of quality, the seller finds it to his advantage to use nonstandard selling devices such as political lobbying, and to accept buyer participation in management as a *quid pro quo* for a share of the military business. Despite the fact that most defense contractors complain bitterly about the way the government plays the game, it remains true that for many of the companies this is the only game in town.

The tier of companies below the prime contractors is populated by thousands of participants, and the further one goes from the final weapon system the broader this industrial base becomes. For example, when buying integrated avionics systems, the Space and Missile Systems Organization faces five or six major producers. However, at the component and circuit level, there are hundreds of tiny firms around the country competing for part of the secondary or tertiary business.

The major aerospace companies are vertically integrated over the research, design, and manufacturing functions. Nevertheless, a good deal of their technological input comes to them from outside the firm. Laboratories financed by the National Aeronautics and Space Administration (NASA), Air Force laboratories, and universities provide basic scientific inputs. Firms selling to the prime contractors provide advanced technology embodied in their products.

A major disadvantage of the integrated structure is that research and design resources tend to follow the fortunes of the production side of the business. Merger of firms, or the failure of a company results in the loss of R&D resources, whereas in the Soviet Union production and design are administratively separate and the level of support for one area is not necessarily tied to another. It would be difficult to support a level of design capability in the United States that was independent of production capacity, at least under the present industrial structure. On the other hand, experience has shown that a sudden production-oriented growth in military demand can be met quickly and flexibly by private industry if there is a buck to be made. This must be contrasted to the ponderous Soviet bureaucracy which does what it is designed to do quite well, but which would probably experience great difficulty in doing things differently.

Cost Control

Much research has been performed at RAND on the topic of defense costs; cost estimating, the reasons for and components of cost overruns, and the R&D processes associated with high costs

---

[33]The statistics in this paragraph are taken from 1966 and 1967 data compiled in, James W. McKie, *Concentration in Military Procurement Markets: A Classification and Analysis of Contract Data* RM-6307-PR (Santa Monica, Calif.: The RAND Corporation, 1970).

have all been investigated in detailed studies. Statistical analysis of hundreds of defense contracts over the 1950s and 1960s indicates that total cost growth (after correcting for inflation and changes in the quantity purchased) can be broken down into several components: changes to systems specifications after programs have begun accounted for about 50 percent of cost growth; unforeseen engineering difficulties accounted for another 33 percent; and cost estimating imprecision was responsible for the remaining 15 to 20 percent.[34] A large part of the estimating imprecision and the engineering difficulties appear to be related to the degree of technological advance sought in a program. A major study ranked the amount of technological advance sought in a program on a scale from one to twenty. Examples of the rankings include the KC-135 with a rank of 8.3, the F-111 with 14.8, and the B-58 with 16.[35] On the average, program ranks of 8 to 12 experienced cost overruns of about 25 percent (over a five-year program length) whereas an advanced project of 16 could expect an overrun of 250–300 percent. Furthermore, cost growth increased as the program extended over longer periods of time. Cost growth is only one aspect of a well-publicized problem. More important is the absolute level of costs. Of course, forces that drive up expected costs of a program by a factor of three will also have powerful effects on the absolute cost level. The same elements entering into the cost growth analysis—technological advance, program length, and program changes— also appear to strongly influence cost levels directly.

For military products then we find a vicious circle of circumstances. Demands for technologically advanced weapons require large programs that extend over long periods of time. Participation by the buyer throughout the lengthened development period creates inefficiencies and also countless changes in the program. All of these things drive up the cost. Increasing costs have led to increased regulation and control by outside organizations.

A peculiar feature of the spiralling costs of weapon systems is that regardless of the forces driving costs higher, until recently budgets have expanded to cover the costs. So long as budgets follow costs there is no incentive in the system to control them. It is not accidental then that spirited attempts to invent more effective cost

control techniques arise in a period of budget stringency. Budget constraints, to be most effective, should operate on the periphery of the organization rather than on the details of performance and management. Two simple recent examples will suffice to illustrate the importance of what I earlier called constrained autonomy. The developers of the competitive prototype AX attack aircraft were informed during the development that the Air Force was only prepared to pay a relatively low, fixed price. For the first time in thirty years unshaved rivets were seen on American aircraft. Aerodynamic efficiency suffered by a fraction of a percent and weight increased by about 100 pounds, but cost constraints induced the designers to do without these refinements. The military buyer did not have to specify anything about rivets or enter into detailed participation in the design process—the budget constraint provided the incentive.[36]

Another example is provided by Northrop which helped design and build the fuselage for the Boeing 747. Boeing gave Northrop a price incentive to reduce the weight of the fuselage section but without any other detailed instructions. Northrop succeeded in reducing the weight by a substantial amount using, as they described it, "brains, not beryllium."

PERSONAL AUTHORITY: FRANCE

Industry Structure

During the 1960s, extensive consolidation and merger activity reduced the number of active companies in French aviation until the present time when only two large companies share the bulk of military and civil business. Among the airframe companies, the nationalized firm of Aerospatiale employs about 80 percent of the labor force and the private firm of Dassault accounts for most of the remaining 20 percent. For the aerospace industry as a whole, more than half is nationalized. In addition to the nationalized design and production facilities, most of the large test centers and laboratories are state-owned. Dassault therefore occupies a unique and somewhat sensitive position as the only large, privately owned and managed company in French aviation.[37]

[34]Robert L. Perry, Giles K. Smith, Alvin J. Harman, and Susan Henrichsen, *System Acquisition Strategies*, R-733-PR/ARPA (Santa Monica, Calif.: The RAND Corporation, 1971), pp. 16–19.

[35]Harman, *op. cit.*, p. 62.

[36]Western observers have long noted the rivet-studded surfaces of Soviet aircraft. They generally have smooth skins only in aerodynamically critical areas.

[37]Much of the information on Dassault and its relations with the French military comes from unpublished interviews of colleagues. These interviews with both company and government officials cover a period of years extending back to the mid-1950s. One report which has been invaluable is Robert L.

The influence of the government extends beyond its ownership of Aerospatiale and the leading engine producer (SNECMA). Through its planning activities, the government attempts to guide the overall strategy of the industry. The mergers of the past decade were initiated by the government, and their financing of large projects has provided roughly 200 million dollars of repayable capital for several civil developments. The national budget also includes equally large amounts of credit for capital expenditures and working capital to finance production.

A fundamental aim of the current plan is to emphasize the growth of civil and military exports. This thrust derives from the national objective of "maintaining the capability of French industry to produce—either on its own, or by international cooperation—all the equipment necessary for its own defense."[38] In order to meet this objective, it is thought necessary to strengthen the policy of increasing exports in order to preserve the profitability of existing industrial capacity.[39] In the absence of significant domestic competition, the international export markets are also expected to provide competitive pressures on French management—pressures that the government believes are required to control costs and advance technology.

Unlike American practice, dealings between the French government and industry are on an intimate basis, with a great deal of administrative discretion practiced by executive agencies. It is often said by participants that a sense of partnership pervades the relationship. These features reduce to a minimum the adversary-like, formal structure found in the United States. According to a high government official, source selection, contract preparation, and project management are flexible and pragmatic, and not tied up in regulatory constraints.[40]

Fixed-price contracts are the preferred financial instruments, even for the development phase. A program is divided into small segments which limit the contractor's risk. If cost-reimbursement contracts must be used, contractors are encouraged to believe that costs greatly exceeding the budgeted amount are likely to lead to program cancellation. But since these contracts cover such short periods of time as a single month, the potential of large unanticipated overruns is minimized.

Despite a large degree of government control of the industry, which would be impossible to attain in the United States, Dassault is able to operate with almost complete internal autonomy. This autonomy has largely been earned by Dassault's demonstrated capability. A defense ministry procurement official stated, "I want to keep more control over the other companies because I am not sure they are as sharp as Dassault."

Dassault: Development, Philosophy, and Style

As the firm of Dassault has characterized French aviation, so has the man Marcel Dassault dominated his company. His authority, experience, intuition, and philosophy govern the organization's operations. Dassault feels very strongly that there should be one boss, a "master of the project," in which one company or individual dominates. The president of the company has commented on Dassault's notion of company and individual leadership. "It seems to me indispensable that there should be a project leader. Project leadership is not a function which is taken or given. It is earned by merit relating to the technical, industrial, and commercial experience of an individual or team which will have considerable authority over a project."[41]

Within the company, Dassault has continued to exercise detailed authority into his 80th year (in 1971). His colleagues describe the many times when something has been wrong with a design and Dassault, more or less intuitively, changed several things. It usually works out that these changes do improve the design but many of the engineers do not understand why. "And Dassault does not care why," a project leader has said. "To make science is not his aim." An example of this approach concerned Dassault's personal decision to manufacture the Falcon 20 executive transport against the advice of his principal engineers and market research staff. He also insisted on a longer fuselage, an option that his engineering staff had explicitly rejected earlier.[42]

An element of Dassault's management philosophy is his insistence on limiting the size of

---

Perry, *A Dassault Dossier: Aircraft Acquisition in France* R-1148-PR (Santa Monica, Calif.: The RAND Corporation, 1973).

[38]"The French Aerospace Industry and the State's 6th Plan," *Interavia* 5 (1971): 526.

[39]One must not accept without question the efficacy of French planning. Undoubtedly, the Concorde would not have proceeded without government approval and financing, but Dassault's Mercure program is less clear-cut, and the exportability of the Mirage was demonstrated independently of the official plan.

[40]Crozier claims that there is not so much respect for due process in France as in Anglo-Saxon countries. Crozier, *op. cit.*, p. 222.

[41]"Project Leadership Depends on Merit" (interview with B. D. Vallieres of Dassault-Breguet), *Interavia* 5 (1971): 522.

[42]Perry, *op. cit.*, p. 3.

the company. Until the merger with Breguet Aviation in 1967, the total work force was about 5,000. By 1972, this number had climbed to 14,000, still substantially smaller than its chief French competitor, and minuscule compared to American companies. One reason for Dassault's concern with size may be the threat of nationalization if the firm absorbs too much of the capacity of its competitors and suppliers. However, the advantages attendant upon small size also contribute to its continuance.

Design teams are small and stable. A core of 20–25 engineers may expand to a maximum of around 100 at the peak of a project. The small size and team-like attributes of the project group allow coordination of effort with little formal structure or communications. Stability of employment enables members of the group to become fully familiar with all aspects of the work and with each other, further reducing the necessity for structured coordination.[43]

The small size of the creative sections of the organization appears to have allowed Dassault to reduce or eliminate a potential deleterious effect of French culture as it impacts on bureaucracies. The typical French system of bureaucratic organization resolves a dilemma imposed by two contradictory features of individual Frenchmen—the feeling that omnipotent authority is indispensable if cooperative activity is to succeed and the requirements for individual independence. Dassault has retained the personal authority traditional in French organizations, without the accompanying dysfunctions of apathy, impersonal rules, and rigidity that customarily protect the French individual.[44] French culture, however, is fully manifested in other parts of the organization. A strong caste system prevails with project leaders coming from the list of honor graduates of *les grandes écoles*, and other technical staff from *les petites écoles*.[45] The highly skilled draftsmen and shop workers, like the graduates of the lesser technical schools, are not expected to advance beyond well-established levels within the company. It is both a reflection of French bureaucratic style and a source of design excellence that one engineer has been the principal designer of every wing found on Mirage aircraft.[46] Despite the existence of rigidity, a critical part of the firm has managed to maintain in many of its operations the flexibility and adaptability necessary in a successful development organization. This has been achieved largely through the high quality of the individuals and the small size of project groups.

Dassault has kept the firm small through a policy of substantial subcontracting of production work. More than half the work force is occupied in development. The Mystère IV manned bomber, for example, had over 80 percent of the airframe subcontracted and 75 percent of the finished aircraft. The importance of Dassault to the national economy, however, is evident in the fact that in the mid-1960s about 32,000 people, or one-third of the total manpower of the French aircraft industry, were engaged in the Mirage III project although only 16 percent of this total were from Dassault.[47]

In many ways the Dassault company operates like a Soviet design bureau, but differs substantially in other important matters. First, consider the differences.

Dassault is faced with direct commercial competition. It exports its products in world markets where British, American, and sometimes Soviet equipment is also available. Domestically, it faced the competition of wholly French products in the past, and of cooperative international ventures at the present time.

The French company is not bound to work within prescribed handbooks and other detailed design and technological constraints imposed upon the Soviet designer. Dassault is also free to contract for research with private or government laboratories or develop its own solutions to development problems. In fact, most of the research Dassault requires is of a very applied nature.

The ability to develop experimental prototypes with company financing has proved to be a major advantage to Dassault. Several of its greatest successes (including the Mirage III) have come about from company-sponsored designs which it was then able to demonstrate to the French Air Force.

Finally, Dassault is ultimately dependent on profits. The experience of most other French aircraft companies as well as the fate of several British and American firms demonstrates that there is no substitute for profitability if the firm is to remain viable and in private hands.[48] It is

43Albert Shapero, "Life Styles of Engineering," *Space/Aeronautics* (March 1969): 61.

44This paragraph owes much to Crozier, *op. cit.*, pp. 220–28.

45*Les grandes écoles* are the three best technical universities in France. Perry, *op. cit.*, pp. 3–4.

46Perry, *op. cit.*, p. 36.

47Perry, *op. cit.*, pp. 7–8.

48Discussions with procurement officials in Western Europe yield the unanimous opinion that nationalization is the last alternative to maintaining domestic military production capability. Where it is considered necessary, the preferred approach is to preserve as much of the competitive market attributes as possible, including profitability. Nevertheless, interesting to observe that dependence on profits produces many of the same results at Dassault that an array of direct constraints yields in the USSR.

Turning to the similarities between Dassault and Soviet design practices, one is struck by the number of points that are alike. The similarities include the following:

- Small design teams.
- Prototype development strategy.
- High level technical review committees.
- Austere and rapid design and prototype construction phase.
- Flight test prior to production decision.
- Incremental development strategy.
- Simple designs.
- Briefly stated requirements.
- Concentration on design and development rather than production.

The "incremental development" strategy of Dassault is perhaps its most distinctive feature and the Mirage series of fighter aircraft graphically demonstrates the meaning of this term. From 1955 to 1972, the Mirage I (originally the MD 550) has generated 24 major variants and 41 separately designated models.[49] The aircraft found in this family tree include a strategic bomber (Mirage IV), a cheap, lightweight ground attack aircraft (Mirage 5), several VTOL prototypes (Balzac and Mirage III-V), a series of variable geometry designs (Mirage G, G-4, and G-8), and the newest addition to the French Air Force—the Mirage F-1 with both intercept and ground attack capabilities.

The development history of the F-1 exemplifies the incremental approach and highlights two additional features of Dassault's operations— the ability to absorb failure and an opportunism that converts unanticipated results into successful aircraft.

In order to test the concepts embodied in a vertical lift fighter, Dassault built two test-beds.[50] The Balzac, converted from the Mirage III prototype, tested the lift engine system; a modified Mirage III-T was intended to be the test-bed of the main power source. Early flight testing revealed that the latter was not an appropriate vehicle to test the main engine, so Dassault constructed a new two-place prototype by installing

a new swept wing (the first to be seen on a Mirage) on a slightly enlarged Mirage III fuselage. Subsequently known as the F-2, its excellent performance immediately suggested further development as a close support fighter. This was proposed to the French Air Force. By the date of first flight of the F-2 in June 1966, Dassault was already well into a study of a smaller version (F-3) as a single-place air superiority and close support fighter. With company financing, Dassault initiated another variant, the F-1, to replace the Mirage III-C as an air superiority fighter.

Changes in defense policy led to cancellation of the F-2, and further studies of the F-3 indicated that it would be larger and more expensive than was desired by the Air Force, so it too was canceled. Dassault then financed the construction of an F-1 prototype with an engine that had appeared in earlier models of the Mirage III. The French Air Force decided to support subsequent F-1 development and, after delays caused by budgetary problems, the prototype made its first flight in December 1966. It demonstrated exceptional performance early in its flight test program and was subsequently ordered into production.

This process is not yet over. To create a prototype variable-sweep fighter, a new wing and pivot were mounted on the F-2 prototype. The result— the Mirage G—went from prototype construction approval to first flight in 16 months. The total cost of the Mirage G program, including engines, was about $35 million.

The development history of the Mirage F-1 included a design failure (the modified Mirage III-T), a cancellation due to a requirements change, and another cancellation because the design looked unproductive. The unanticipated good performance of the F-2 led to a later success in the F-1. In the case of Dassault, success has built on success, but failure has not been crippling. Designs are shown to be undesirable before the scale of resource commitment has been allowed to grow very large. Feedback from design and test programs and from the buyer has been available for early decisions.

Costs are an important variable in this process, as was demonstrated with the F-3. Defense budgets have been relatively fixed with a high proportion of the available funds going to the French strategic deterrent forces. The Air Force has operated on a stringent budget over the past decade, with the military demand for aerospace industry resources falling in the last few years.[51] The military simply cannot afford expen-

---

there are often problems with direct government participation in the affairs of the nationalized companies; defense managers in France emphasize that the director must be someone with enough stature to preserve the independence of the company and to operate it as if it were privately owned.

[49]See Perry, *op. cit.*, Section IV for the Mirage genealogy.

[50]This description leans heavily on Perry, *op. cit.*, pp. 27–29.

[51]"The French Aerospace Industry," *Interavia* 5 (1971): 513.

sive equipment. Cost estimation and the achievement of predicted costs become critical features of development strategy. Dassault claims that its cost estimating accuracy is normally no more than 10 percent in error.[52] As noted earlier, the chief causes of cost misestimation are program length and technological advance sought. Dassault, through the incremental approach, avoids large amounts of technical risk; and through speedy design and prototype construction, keeps the uncertain part of the program as short as possible. Design changes are further reduced by transferring design staff from a project as quickly as possible; if an engineer is no longer assigned to a project, he cannot change it. Marcel Dassault believes that cost-plus contracting is dangerous in that cost indifference is likely to be introduced throughout the company through a customer's willingness to pay for high-risk developments of unproven worth.[53]

Dassault represents a peculiar blend of technical audacity and conservativeness. Risk is reduced to a minimum by changing only one aspect of a design at any one time. However, if this is done often enough, substantial technological advance can be wrought over time.

Flexibility in the midst of rigidity, profitability where others have failed, and smallness in a world where growth and size are the usual measures of success are other salient aspects of Dassault. The exceptional qualities of the company must be attributed to a combination of factors. Of principal importance is Marcel Dassault's philosophy that emphasizes risk minimization and small size. A French system of government that permits intimate dealings between the private and public sector reduces the need for official regulation and surveillance. The French habit of employment stability has allowed team behavior to develop. And the French acceptance of concentrated personal authority in organizations has permitted the firm of Dassault to flourish under the genius of its founder.

CHOICE AND STYLE

In order to illuminate several features of the acquisition process I shall draw explicit attention to two separable issues. The first of these is the determination of what to produce. By this I mean the selection of performance characteristics, production costs, and development expenditures. These three factors are interrelated: the specification of any two of them in great measure determines the magnitude of the third.[54] Industry cliché agrees with statistical analyses that the last "small" percentage of performance accounts for some "large" proportion of total costs. Development resources, however, do not have to be devoted solely toward enhancing performance. A given development effort can also be allocated in varying proportions toward cost reduction. Other things constant, however, the higher the performance goals, the greater the required expenditures on development.

The second important issue involves the efficiency or effectiveness of the process. Regardless of the performance sought in a project, the process of achieving it can be austere or lavish and the final product useful or valueless. Efficient R&D—that is, R&D that yields valuable outcomes at relatively low cost—is largely dependent on the manner or style in which development is conducted.

Choice and style, though conceptually separate, are often closely related. The demand for high performance in the United States usually results in a development style that is inimical to efficient R&D as the large programs that are set up to manage these projects invite regulation, undue participation by the client, and inflexibility. By way of contrast, in the Soviet Union it is the development style that to a large degree limits the range of choice. The technology available to design bureaus is dictated by handbooks and instructions produced by the research institutes. Limited manpower is another constraint. The design bureaus are not free to go into the labor market to build up their design staff for a particular project.[55] A third constraint is provided by tight deadlines for important milestones such as first flight. These constraints, operating in a competitive design environment, make it virtually impossible to go very high up on the performance-cost surface. Despite these many constraints, design bureaus have a great deal of internal autonomy and can respond flexibly and

---

[52]Perry, op. cit., p. 14.

[53]This same observation has been made by French government officials who think it essential that defense and commercial work be co-located in order to gain the cost-consciousness of commercial enterprises. Diversification into commercial activities has not drained talent from the defense area, but the reverse is held to be true.

[54]For a given level of efficiency, this expression takes the form: $F(D,T,C) = 0$ where D is the cost of development, T is the level of technology (performance) and C is production unit costs. For a more detailed discussion, see A. J. Alexander, and J. R. Nelson, "Measuring Technological Change," *Technological Forecasting and Social Change* 5, no. 2 (1971).

[55]Nor are the design bureaus likely to dismiss employees during slack periods. Consequently, when there is excess capacity there is an incentive to keep staffs fully employed by either actively seeking new projects or by overmanning ongoing projects.

adaptively to the recurring uncertainties of any development program.[56]

As noted in an earlier section, not all American acquisition programs have followed the same pattern. A key feature of many of the nonstandard post-World War II American programs is that they appear to have been conducted efficiently. Some of these have been expensive, others rather cheap. They are situated at various points on the performance-cost surface. The one unifying feature is the development style, which is not unlike that of the Soviet or French examples.

I suggest that there is a multilayered structure of incentives and techniques in R&D. Of primary importance are three key elements: autonomy, constraints, and feedback. The presence of these elements provides the incentives for development organizations to seek out for themselves the techniques that have been so often observed in successful projects, such as early hardware proofing of concepts, parallel developments of high-risk technology, sequential decisionmaking, etc.[57]

Internal operational autonomy is necessary for the quick response and flexibility required for good R&D. Lack of autonomy requires management by outsiders who do not have detailed information of either the organization or the project. Communications links are lengthened and decisions lag behind events. Multiple participation of outsiders requires even greater efforts of coordination and regulation, often culminating in formalized and generalized command and control structures.

The lack of constraints typically leads to a growth of inputs without a concomitant growth of output. Organizational slack, dulled management incentives, and the loss of inventive imagination are the expected outcomes of permissive budgets and a too beneficent environment. In the case of Dassault, size constraints were part of his personal operating philosophy, abetted by a perceived probability of nationalization should the company grow too large.

Feedback provides the development organization with an appraisal of its performance. If additional resources or other rewards depend on the quality of the appraisal, the feedback mechanism plays a critical role in guiding the organization toward correct solutions. Note that feedback implies a two-way flow. Information must be forthcoming from the development process, then the information must be evaluated and the appropriate message transmitted back to the developers. Failure of any one of these stages destroys the feedback mechanism.[58] When feedback is missing, the outcome is an "arsenal mentality" where there is no need to do anything differently because nothing will happen anyway.

Most successful technological developments are associated with identifiable individuals. Mikoyan, Tupolev, Kelly Johnson, General Schriever, Marcel Dassault are names to which we can attach specific projects. What is the relationship between the individual project leader and the characteristics discussed in the preceding paragraphs? I suggest that it is the individual who generates the privilege of autonomy for his organization. Where autonomy is the exception, exceptional men are required to gain it and to maintain it. And often, special circumstances that give great value to the project's output provide incentives for the exceptions to be tolerated. It is remarkable that organizational autonomy is all but absent in the Soviet Union, except in aviation design bureaus and a few other scientific organizations, especially those with military connections. Kelly Johnson's "skunkworks" is almost unique in the universe of American military system acquisition. The notion that autonomy is a privilege, and a jealously guarded one, is directly acknowledged by these technological entrepreneurs. The first (of 14) operating rule of the "skunkworks" is: "Program manager must be delegated almost complete authority of all aspects of the program."[59] General Schriever in the ballistic missile program sought autonomy through secrecy (on grounds of national security) and through control over funds. In the Polaris missile program, autonomy was generated by a reputation for good management that was astutely cultivated by the project leaders.[60] Autonomy can also be gained by being small and re-

---

[56]These national differences in the weapons acquisition process can be summed up rather baldly. In the United States the general tendency is for choice to dictate style, whereas in the Soviet Union style limits choice.

[57]For a concise description of good R&D technique, see B. H. Klein, W. H. Meckling, and E. G. Mesthene, *Military Research and Development Policies*, R-333 (Santa Monica, Calif.: The RAND Corporation, December 1958).

[58]Feedback can be either short-term or long-term, and can flow from a variety of sources. Recall that during Dassault's development of the Mirage F-1, timely project-specific evaluations come from the French Air Force, whereas a favorable appraisal by the Ministry of Defense of the company's performance over many years was a condition for granting autonomy.

[59]Other rules include: strong but small project offices; severely restricted number of people connected with program; minimum number of reports; monthly cost review—no surprises; control access by outsiders to program by strict security measures; reward good performance.

[60]See Harvey M. Sapolsky, *The Polaris System Development* (Cambridge, Mass.: Harvard University Press, 1972).

maining under cover. The Sidewinder air-to-air missile is an example where the project surfaced only after hardware had been developed to the point where it could be demonstrated. Resources had been bootlegged from other projects and a very small group worked in obscurity until success was at hand.

Constrained autonomy with feedback generated by performance is nothing more than the "invisible hand" of classical economics. That it is so difficult to attain outside of competitive markets is one of the general lessons of this exercise. It is probably impossible to devise a standard organizational structure or strategy for American government that will yield the efficiencies demonstrated by the exceptional weapons acquisition programs in the United States or by the Dassault or Soviet examples. Deeply rooted cultural factors underlie that observation.

The difficulty of transferring a style where the preconditions are missing is emphasized in a statement by Kelly Johnson. A certain military project was canceled because of excess costs and technical shortcomings after a half billion dollars had been spent. "I trained the whole management, including the top engineers. They were in the skunkworks for six months. They were to apply our system to their project. Three months after they got started, under the restraints placed upon them primarily by the military, but also by internal company groups as well, their purchasing department was three times the size of my complete engineering group, which is working on seven projects."

WEAPONS ACQUISITION: CHINA

JAMES R. BLAKER

Chinese weapons acquisition can be conceptually divided into three general post-1950 periods: the postwar restoration period (1949–51); the era of Soviet assistance (1951–60); and the era of self-sufficiency (1961–present). In this article, Blaker covers virtually every major economic and industrial activity affecting weapons acquisition in the Chinese People's Republic. The most significant strategic determinant of the Chinese weapons acquisition process is the continued presence of a Russian military threat, while the most prominent internal characteristic is regionalism.

James R. Blaker is Assistant Director, Defense Program Analysis and Evaluation, Office of the Secretary of Defense. He has a Ph.D. in political science and has served in Intelligence with the Department of the Army. He is the author of many articles on China and a book, Chinese in the Philippines *(1970).*

ECONOMIC AND POLITICAL AUTARKY

China has, over the last two and a half decades, virtually reversed the condition of its non-self-sufficiency in terms of weapons acquisition, moving from almost total dependence on supply from external sources to nearly complete self-sufficiency in all phases of the weapons acquisition process. The shift has not been without economic stress and a high degree of political trauma, but the fact remains that China is one of the handful of nations presently capable of and now producing a broad spectrum of conventional and nuclear weaponry without outside help. Part of the change is due to the fact that China possesses more than enough of the natural resources

This is an original article written for this volume and for the Conference on Comparative Defense Policy held at the Air Force Academy, February 7–9, 1973. Copyright reserved by the author.

necessary to support a broad indigenous weapons industry.[1] But it is also clear that Chinese political leaders have made a conscious and fairly consistent effort since the 1950s to assure autarky.

The movement toward self-sufficiency in weapons production developed gradually over an extended period of time.[2] Chinese Communist military forces initially relied almost entirely on weapons captured from the KMT areas, the Japanese, or to a much lesser extent until the early 1950s at least, received from the Soviet Union. In December 1948, for example, the US military attache at Nanking reported that communist forces had probably captured over 80 percent of all the US equipment supplied to 17 Nationalist Army divisions. And in July 1949, the People's Liberation Army headquarters claimed that it had captured—over the previous four years—about 60,000 artillery weapons, 250,000 machine guns, 2 million small arms, and over 500 tanks.[3]

Until the mid-1950s, however, the conventional military equipment possessed by the Chinese Communists, although extensive enough to give the People's Republic the fourth or fifth largest arsenal in the world, was a mixed bag of US, Japanese, and Russian materiel of widely varying age and effectiveness.

There was some indigenous weapons production capability in China prior to the formation of the People's Republic. During the war against Japan, the Chinese Nationalists developed 15 fairly large small arms and ammunition arsenals —5 smaller arsenals were also developed by 1945—and these production facilities were in fact capable of producing enough small arms ammunition to supply Chiang's forces. There were also some reports of a few arsenals producing both small arms and ammunition in communist-held areas as early as 1942, but the industry as it exists today did not really begin until the end of the civil war in 1949.

For a relatively short period between the end of the civil war and China's entrance into the Korean conflict, Chinese leaders actually sought to avoid or at least delay expansion of the almost negligible armaments production base in favor of the reconstruction effort. Gittings points out that until the Korean war no positive steps were taken toward modernization of the People's Liberation Army and that Chinese leaders sought to ensure that the requirements of the army remained subordinate to domestic economic priorities. The main emphasis was placed on preparation for demobilization.[4] That the Chinese were not particularly interested in the rapid development of an indigenous arms production capability was also hinted by the fact that as late as the autumn of 1951, most of the military materiel used by the Chinese consisted of ex-KMT weapons. In Korea, it was common to find several different kinds of rifles of varying origin and caliber in the same regiment.[5]

Regardless of the extent to which the Chinese played with the idea of avoiding the costs of developing their own arms industry, the debate was probably ended as a result of the Korean conflict. Armament limitations contributed to the kind of man-killing tactics adopted by the Chinese in Korea, as they necessitated the reliance on foot mobility and mass to compensate for the US superiority in firepower. The losses sustained by the use of such tactics underlined the criticality of establishing a self-sufficient arms industry in China. In the interim, the Chinese were initially willing to pay the political and economic price for Soviet assistance.

By October 1951, China was formally committed to the development of an extensive arms industry by Article 22 of the Common Program of the People's Political Consultative Conference. Chou En-lai reportedly insisted at the conference that all production should point toward strengthening the military. A month later, Ch'en Fy, at that time minister of heavy industry, indicated that investment funds were being diverted from nonmilitary industrial goals toward defense industries and Li Fu-ch'un, then vice-chairman of the Finance and Economic Committee, stated that defense industry would receive the highest priority in terms of the allocation of funds. The models and technical expertise for the effort were to be supplied by the USSR.

Soviet industrial aid expanded rapidly after Stalin's death in March 1953. The allocation of the assistance indicated a clear preference for the development of heavy industrial sites, some of which had already been associated with arms production. And assuming that many of the early Soviet aid projects were related to Chinese de-

---

[1]China possesses fully adequate reserves of most industrially significant minerals and metals. The only exceptions appear to be chromite and cobalt, both used primarily in the production of special steels. See K. P. Wong, "The Mineral Resource Base of Communist China," in Joint Economic Profile of Mainland China: An Economic Profile of Mainland China (New York: Praeger, 1968), pp. 169–70.

[2]Most of the discussion in this section is taken from the author's "Production of Conventional Weapons," in Whitson (ed.), The Military and Political Power in China in the 1970's (New York: Praeger, 1972), pp. 215–27.

[3]John Gittings, The Role of the Chinese Army (New York: Oxford University Press, 1967), p. 25.

[4]Ibid., p. 25.

[5]Blaker, "The Production of Conventional Weapons," p. 217.

fence industries, the new industrial centers at Paot'ou and Chengtu, and the expansion of the industrial base at Wukau were probably all highly dependent on Soviet aid and expertise.

Although Mao Tse-tung had alluded to the necessity for self-sufficiency prior to the period of Sino-Soviet cooperation, these expressions were submerged by the rhetoric of alignment until the Great Leap of the late 1950s. When the Soviet Union pulled its technicians out of China in 1960, "self-sufficiency" again emerged and rose to the level of shibboleth. Thus, for over ten years, the Chinese have made a distinctly conscious effort to achieve industrial self-sufficiency.

STATE OF TECHNOLOGY

The Chinese Communists have consistently attached great importance to scientific and technical development, but have generally tended to emphasize applied as opposed to basic scientific research. Thus, although the Chinese Academy of Sciences—the Communist successor to the Nationalists' Peking Academy and the Academia Sinica—was formed with great fanfare the same month the People's Republic was proclaimed, it was soon oriented toward adapting existing scientific and technical attainments to China's needs rather than research for the sole aim of achieving a fuller understanding of a subject. In 1951, for example, the Academy was instructed to make a systematic determination of the requirements of the production sectors of the economy and to gear scientific research toward meeting these demands.

An adjunct of the emphasis on applied research has been the conscious effort to supplement state-sponsored technical research with the quest and demand for "innovation" throughout society. Chinese reports claim that thousands of new products are developed each year, most originating from the pseudoscientist. The "fighter" who has come up with a new feed for pigs, the farmer who has "discovered the law governing the growth of peanuts," the worker who invented a drill "which surpasses the world's advanced level," and the member of the Academy who develops an X-ray spectrophotometer are all "scientific innovators." Their discoveries and developments are well publicized not only as a means of underlining the commitment to self-sufficiency, but because of the value placed on applied sciences. The much publicized practice of "sending down" scientists and other intellectuals to work in factories or rural communes is partially a reflection of the same commitment.

As Leo Orleans points out, the Chinese emphasis on applied as opposed to basic research has not meant an absence of technological achievements.

China has already demonstrated that limiting research to practical requirements need not restrict achievement. By no means has she lost interest in advanced science and technology and despite the Cultural Revolution, Chinese scientists have managed to stay abreast with most of the latest developments.[6]

But if the state of technology in China is far from primitive, neither has it been known for many technological breakthroughs in terms of the levels of technology in modern western nations or Japan. The Chinese have, over the last twenty years, made remarkable technological advances and narrowed the gap between the technology in China and the general level of technology in the United States or Japan. These successes have in large measure been the result of a conscious effort to borrow technology from the more advanced nations, a strategy the Chinese show no intention of abandoning over the next several years.[7] But in adopting the kind of strategy which downgrades basic scientific research, the Chinese may find themselves in a kind of modern-day Aesop's paradox—moving closer and closer to the levels of technology found elsewhere but never surpassing them. And the distance remaining is great in many of the industrial sections associated with military materiel.

Generalizations on where China stands vis-à-vis the United States or Japan in terms of military-related technology are obviously dangerous, but China may be up to ten years behind in electronics and communications, and about five to ten years behind in steel production technology, two sectors of industry which are often taken as indicators of weapon-related technology. Reichers, for example, points out that although the Chinese electronics industry has expanded greatly since the withdrawal of Soviet aid in the 1960s, it is at least five years behind the US and Japan in semiconductor production

---

[6] Leo A. Orleans, "China's Science and Technology: Continuity and Innovation," in U.S. Congress. Joint Economic Committee, *People's Republic of China: An Economic Assessment* (Washington, D.C.: Government Printing Office, 1972), p. 186.

[7] Nearly two years ago the Chinese were publicly arguing that "We do not oppose learning advanced techniques from foreign countries. . . . We must take the initiative in learning and use what they have learned to serve our purpose." (Peking Radio Domestic Service, April 19, 1971.) For more recent indications see N.Y. Times, "China Looking to Japan for Industrial Know-How" (November 13, 1972).

equipment, and that further development of China's semiconductor industry—essential to solid state electronics and communications equipment—depends on China's continued access to non-Communist technology.[8] Advances have also been made in computer technology, but in the development of digital computers, China is still at least five years behind the USSR and ten years behind the United States.[9] In general, it appears that the Chinese lag technologically up to ten years behind the US in military electronics.[10]

China's quest for steel-making technology, highlighted currently by a parade of Chinese technical survey missions to Japan, reflects the growing obsolescence of the Chinese steel industry, most of which was based on Soviet technology of the 1950s. China has and will continue to modernize her steel industry under the fourth five-year plan, but technologically will probably still be about five years behind Japan when the plan ends in 1975.

STRUCTURE OF INDUSTRY

In the broadest sense there are still "two economic systems" in China. On the one hand, small scattered rural communities, in which most of the population lives, maintain much the same economic life and intercourse as they did prior to the formation of the People's Republic. Here, centralization and direct state control are essentially peripheral to economic life. Decisions made in Peking can, of course, have profound impact on the rural, agricultural economy, but as Donnithorn and others argue, the economy of rural China is far from completely centralized, planned, or monolithic.

This is much less the case as far as industry is concerned, and particularly those sectors of the industrial economy which build weapons. Centralized governmental control of industrial enterprises had existed in China before 1949. Indeed, industry under state ownership inherited by the communists accounted for more than one-third of China's industrial output by value in 1949, much of this coming from confiscated Japanese plants in Manchuria, North China and Shanghai.[11] But following a brief interlude (1949–53) in which private industry blossomed, the commu-

nists moved rapidly to expand state ownership. At first the transformation was made enterprise by enterprise, but in 1956 whole trades and branches of industry shifted toward state control and by the end of that year virtually all private industrial enterprises had been nationalized.

A note regarding the structure of industry within China is necessary before we attempt to describe in somewhat greater detail the government-industrial relationship. It is important to comment briefly on the regional distribution of industrial centers, for the regional of distribution of these facilities probably colors the selection of sources for weapons and the manner in which they are acquired.

About 75% of China's total industrial capacity is found in seven provinces—that is, roughly three-fourths of the Chinese industrial capacity is located in about one-fourth of China's provinces. Translating this distribution to the military region context, it is clear that in terms of industrial capacity there is a marked difference between military regions. Five of China's thirteen military regions—Nanking, Peking, Shenyang, Wuhan, and Canton—are clearly superior in industrial capacity. All of China's military regions possess some industrial plants within their borders which are capable of producing arms. But only about half clearly have the capacity to produce a wide range of weaponry.

GOVERNMENT–INDUSTRIAL RELATIONSHIP

As the previous general comments on the structure of industry indicate, the operational relationship between the government and industry is intimate. Indeed, so far as the production of weapons is concerned, there is no such thing as nongovernment industry. And whereas source selection, contracting and project monitoring in the United States and other capitalist-based countries are colored by competition among privately owned companies in search of profits, these activities in China take place within a fundamentally different arena.

The highest administrative organ concerned with the production of military equipment is the State Council. This body, formally the executive organ of the National People's Congress, is the state's highest administrative agency. Six offices have been associated with the State Council: Internal Affairs, Agriculture and Forestry, Industry and Communications, Finance, Trade and Foreign Affairs. Donnithorn points out that the State Council's offices are in the position of "over-

---

[8]Philip D. Reichers, "The Electronics Industry of China," in Joint Economic Committee, *People's Republic of China: An Economic Assessment*, p. 93.

[9]*Ibid.*, p. 97.

[10]*Ibid.*, p. 106.

[11]Audrey Donnithorn, *China's Economic System* (New York: Praeger, 1967), p. 145.

lords," each (with the exception of the Office of Foreign Affairs) controlling a group of subordinate ministries. The more than thirty other organs that come directly under the State Council include the Ministry of Defense, State Planning Commission and State Economic Commission. The exact function of the Offices of the State Council are nowhere set forth with much detail, but they are probably the chief policymaking organs, and generally function in a coordinating role in respect to the ministries under them. In the case of military production, however, most interministerial coordination is probably accomplished within either the Premier's office or the Ministry of Defense.

Beneath the State Council level, the ministries concerned with the production of military equipment include the Second Ministry of Machine Building (nuclear weapons), Third Ministry of Machine Building (conventional armaments), Fourth Ministry of Machine Building (communications equipment), Fifth Ministry of Machine Building (artillery), Sixth Ministry of Machine Building (naval shipbuilding), Seventh Ministry of Machine Building (military aircraft), and the Ministry of Defense.

All but the Ministry of Defense are charged with the actual production of military equipment. In contrast, the Defense Ministry probably acts primarily as an interministerial coordinating body and assures that the material produced is properly distributed throughout the People's Liberation Army.

Within the Defense Ministry, the agency most directly concerned with weapons procurement is the General Rear Services Department, which, like that of the Soviet structure after which it is modeled, is the military's foremost logistics agency. The Rear Services Department comprises several subdepartments and bureaus, but their functional identification is not clear. As of 1959, there were at least six subdepartments: medical service, supply, transportation, ordnance, finance and production. By 1971 several other subdepartments had been identified, including Barracks (1961), Petroleum-Oil Lubricants (1967), Equipment (1970) and Enterprises (1971).[12]

Although the production of military equipment in China is strictly government-controlled, this is not to say that source selection and project monitoring there are any easier than elsewhere or that political considerations do not infiltrate these processes. Indeed, these processes are probably viewed as essentially political by China's leaders, who generally appear to have a profound understanding not only of how political concerns and motivation affect industrial production, but also how productive processes can be used to further the leadership's internal and foreign political policies. The intricacies of these relationships are obviously difficult to sort out, but the following factors probably color source selection.

The Role of Weapons Production in the Western Movement of Chinese Industry

Before World War II, modern industry in China was confined largely to the great seaports—Shanghai and Tientsin—and to Japanese-held Manchuria. As late as 1948, only eighteen cities in thirteen provinces (excluding Manchuria) had sufficient manufacturing capacity to be considered even modest industrial centers; ten of China's twenty-six provinces and autonomous regions had no modern industrial complex. Nearly 80% of China's industrial capacity was tied to East and North China.

For a number of strategic and ideological reasons the Communists viewed this geographic concentration of industrial capacity as irrational, and, indeed, a major theme of the first five-year plan was the call for development of new industrial regions and bases to the west. The construction of industrial complexes at T'ai-yuan, Shih-chia-chuang, Loyang, Cheng-chan, Chu-chan, Meng-yang, Lanchow, and Sian and the new iron and steel production complexes at Paot'ou in Inner Mongolia and at Wuhan were all initiated within a context of westward industrial movement.

The effort to move industrial complexes westward was only partially successful as of the early 1970s, and, in retrospect, actually ebbed and flowed a great deal during the preceding twenty years. The initial exuberance of the first five-year plan concerning the westward march of industry was replaced, for example, as early as June 1968 by a retrenchment and shift in investment back toward established industrial complexes in the north and east. And of the nine largest industrial centers presently in China, all but two—Paot'ou and Wuhan—are located in the same areas of modern industry that had existed at the end of World War II.

But the inability of the Chinese to bring about the kind of industrial expansion to the West implied by their early pronouncement was probably due to tactical shifts rather than a general change

[12]Richard E. Gillespie and John Sims, "The General Rear Service Department," in Whitson (ed.), *The Military and Political Power in China in the 1970s*, pp. 194–96.

in orientation. Indeed, considering where they began, the Chinese have done a remarkable job in developing industry outside the traditional centers. It would be difficult to support any argument that they have, in fact, abandoned the commitment to industrial development in the West. And since Chinese industrial output is so closely tied to defense concerns, source selection decisions are probably influenced to some degree by this commitment. Indeed, this commitment may play a more important role in deciding where a given weapons system should be built than cost, labor, or raw material considerations. That is, the Chinese may consciously seek to use weapons production as a means of advancing the westward expansion of industrial capacity by overruling cost considerations, etc., in favor of building weapons in those locations which will best support the longer range concern. The phenomenon is probably roughly analogous to the concern with a real economic impact associated with building major weapons systems in the United States, but whereas geographic concerns affect the source selection process in the United States because of the implication for employment and voting, in China they impinge because of a general commitment within the leadership to shifting industrial capacity westward.

Strategic Considerations

Source selection in China is also affected by the threat of conflict, probably to a much greater extent than in the United States or Soviet Union. This is, of course, due to several factors, among which are the greater threat facing China and the comparatively greater vulnerability of the Chinese weapons production facilities.

There is little doubt that the Chinese have perceived a direct military threat over the last decade or so. In the early and mid-1960s this perception was probably fed by the growing US military presence and activity near China's southern periphery. More recently the perception of direct military threat has been fed and perhaps heightened by the Soviet Union, particularly by the Soviet military buildup along China's northern border which some reports indicate has resulted in the shift of nearly one quarter of the Soviet army to positions from which attacks on China could be launched.[13] This obvious military threat to China is further complicated by the location of China's industry—much of China's industrial capacity is within 300 miles of the Soviet border—and its structure.

The Chinese appear to have an industrial production system with relatively little redundancy. Specialization appears to be a hallmark of the system and several studies of Chinese industry have pointed out that the production of relatively sophisticated end-items is often concentrated in only a few factories. Rhetoric devoted to survival in war aside, the Chinese industrial system is highly susceptible to national disruption and might be nearly immobilized by the destruction of a handful of centers. Several of the centers—Paot'ou and Harbin, for example—are within striking distance of Soviet troops near the border.

Thus, the perception of direct military threat is probably acute within Peking and it is very likely that this anxiety plays some role in source selection. Its most immediate impact is probably two-fold. On the one hand, it probably builds in the desire to develop what the Chinese decision-makers see as their most important weapon systems in areas relatively immune from attack. At the same time, it creates the desire to develop the redundancy or duplication which the Chinese productive system now appears to lack. Both these desires, like that of coloring the selection of those enterprises or factories by the desire to prompt the westward expansion of industry, may work against considerations of short-term costs. But concern with security may also work against the desire to expand industrial capacity in the west, particularly when "westward expansion" is expressed in selecting those areas near the Sino-Soviet border.

Inter-regional Balance

Regionalism has traditionally played an important role in the history of China, for although bound together by a common linguistic and cultural heritage, Chinese institutions continue to reflect the fact that hundreds of millions of Chinese have never traveled or lived more than 100 miles from their home villages. "Warlordism" in China will probably never again reappear, but many qualified observers believe that China's national leaders continue to perceive at least part of their national role as one of expanding China's cultural unity into a true sense of "national" political identification, and by this effort, thwarting the centrifugal forces of regionalism. Indeed, if one assumes that the effort to counteract regionalism does impinge upon decisionmaking in Peking, some insight is gained as to the rationale for the geographic distribution of production resources.

Some comment has already been made regarding the distribution of production facilities in China and the specialization characteristic of the

---

[13]See, for example, the *New York Times*; "Shift in Strategy by Peking is Seen" (July 25, 1972): 1.

industrial system. Translating this into the context of China's military regions, it becomes clear that in terms of industrial capacity, there is significant variation among military regions. In terms of the ability to produce a wide range of military equipment, however, the great specialization apparent in Chinese industry tends to introduce a high degree of equality among the regions.

In terms of industrial capacity, four of China's thirteen military regions—Nanking, Peking, Shenyang and Wuhan—possess nearly 75 percent of the country's total within their borders. While industrial capacity is only an indicator of the regional distribution of weapons production facilities, it is likely that the regional concentration of industrial capacity reflects at least as great a concentration of the capability to produce weapons. This is not to say that the four regions in which capacity is concentrated monopolize weapons production. All of China's military regions possess some plants within their borders that are either now producing arms or ammunition, or, with some modification, could produce armaments. But the distribution of major industrial complexes and the concentration of industrial capacity support the view that relatively few military regions have the capacity to produce a wide range of weaponry. Nanking, Shenyang, and Peking regions come out the best in this respect, having the kind of industrial complexes that could easily be called upon to produce almost the entire spectrum of military equipment. And, as the following table shows, this is in marked contrast to regions such as Sinkiang, Kunming, or Foochow. (See Table 1.)

But weapons production capability probably is not an accurate portrayal of the actual weapons produced in each region. Again, the specialization endemic to the Chinese industrial system plays a role. Even those three or four military regions that appear to have the capacity to produce the entire range of weapons probably do not. And assuming that the same specialization that runs through China is reflected in the production of weapons—that aircraft, tanks or other major items of equipment are produced in only one or two of China's major industrial complexes—the overview suggested does not portray great differences among military regions but one of rough parity. No single military region probably now produces the entire spectrum of weaponry.

The picture gained from all this is one of regional interdependence rather than regional self-sufficiency. The Chinese appear to have consciously developed a national system designed to maintain an equilibrium among military regions, even though some of these regions—Shenyang and Nanking in particular—have the potential to become far superior. Each is actually dependent on production which occurs elsewhere for a complete equipping of the forces stationed within it, suggesting that a concerted effort has been made over the last twenty years to avoid giving any single military region or a minority of regions a monopoly on weapons production. The system places the central decisionmakers in a highly strategic position, for without central control, none of the military regions would be able to equip their forces without extensive re-tooling and capital development.

Assuming that decisionmakers in Peking have consciously sought to build a system which gives the center the balance of power vs. any single region or coalition of regions, it is likely that they would seek to maintain that system in selecting who will build a given weapons system and where. In a sense, Chinese central planners must

Table 1. Industrial Capacity—Weapons Production Capability

Military Region	Industrial Capacity (% of national total)	Equipment Production Capability		
		Transport	Firepower	Communication
Nanking	38	entire range	entire range	entire range
Peking	14	entire range	entire range	entire range
Shenyang	12	entire range	entire range	entire range
Wuhan	7	unknown	entire range	entire range
Canton	7	unknown	entire range	entire range
Chengtu	6	unknown	entire range	entire range
Inner Mongolia	4	entire range	entire range	some components
Foochow	4	unknown	entire range	some components
Lanchow	3.2	unknown	entire range	some components
Tsihan	3	motor vehicle	small arms	some components
Kunming	1	little	most	some components
Sinkiang	1	little	small arms	some components
Tibet	—	little	small arms	some components

balance the political benefit of maintaining the specialization associated with weapons production (which keeps any region from being self-sufficient in terms of weapons production) against the strategic vulnerability of doing so (i.e., in interdependent production system in which the ports are highly specialized, the destruction of only a few factories might destroy the entire system). These decisions must, of course, all take place in the context of "normal" concerns of cost effectiveness, suggesting that the selection of a source for a weapon in China is not easy, despite what appears to be a highly centralized and hierarchical bureaucratic system.

LABOR-MANAGEMENT RELATIONSHIPS

Labor wages and mobility are not determined by market forces in China, but rather by a series of regulations, rules, policies and plans. Indeed, wages, labor welfare, educational and other social benefits, working conditions, hiring, transfers, dismissals, and discipline are all to some extent subservient and determined by the Five-Year Plan. This does not mean that the Chinese system has no unemployment or is as productive as it could be. Richman noted in 1966, for example, that because of the large surplus of unskilled and semiskilled labor, many of the enterprises he inspected were overstaffed and had much disguised unemployment, which, he believed, contributed to low production.[14] On the other hand, Richman and other visitors have argued that without the network of administrative control, the majority of workers would probably receive substantially less pay; and that while the system leads to somewhat higher total labor costs in the short run, it will probably benefit industrial progress over the long time frame.

A fairly consistent antibureaucratic emphasis has been played against the labor management relationship in China, for, with a few exceptions, the Chinese Communists have been very reluctant to develop a clearly perceived bifurcation between managers and workers. They have developed a series of techniques designed specifically to break down barriers of status and communications between the two personnel levels, including the well-publicized requirements that managers perform labor functions on a fairly regular basis and the kind of public criticism meetings which emerged in exaggerated form during the Cultural Revolution. Many of these ef-

forts are ideologically motivated, stemming from the communist underpinnings of the system. But they may have some industrial payoff in the sense that they provide individual workers with the sense of efficacy and personal satisfaction which might otherwise be submerged in the extensive network of state regulations.

It is difficult to determine whether the same labor management relationships run throughout China's defense industries because of the aura of secrecy which surrounds this aspect of the Chinese industrial system. We know, of course, that military officers have been subjected to the same kind of efforts to break down status barriers between them and the men they command, a phenomenon which suggests that the same techniques and relationships that exist in nondefense enterprises probably take place in defense production as well. But there are some hints that defense industries were not subjected to the same degree of turmoil as nondefense enterprises during "worker-management" confrontations of the Cultural Revolution. Nuclear testing, for example, continued through the turmoil of the Cultural Revolution with little if any apparent distraction, suggesting that at least some segments of the defense industrial system have somewhat different labor-managerial relationships.

THE R&D/INDUSTRY RELATIONSHIPS

The research and development structure of China appears closely integrated to the industrial system in general and, in particular, to those segments of Chinese industry which are devoted to the production of weapons. There is, of course, nothing in China which is completely analogous to the private or semi-private R&D institutions in the United States. All research and development is government controlled and directed. This formal R&D structure runs from the research branches of the universities, through special research institutes maintained by the ministries, and into special research and development sections of individual enterprises. But the formal structure is surrounded by an officially prompted bias toward close integration.

Collaboration between research organizations and industrial enterprises is often prescribed by higher authorities and spelled out in the operating plans of the organizations involved. Some observers have suggested that voluntary cooperation also occurs, driven by the initiative and interests of the enterprises and/or research organizations themselves. Richman argues, for example, that there is more cooperation of a vol-

[14]Barry Richman, *Industrial Society in Communist China* (New York: Vintage Books, 1969), p. 376.

untary nature between industrial enterprises in China than in the Soviet Union.[15] But this reflects many of the research techniques and the emphasis on applied sciences stressed by the government. Requirements that scientists and researchers spend periods involved in manual labor or on the assembly line are perhaps the best example of how voluntary cooperation is stimulated by governmental personnel policies.

There may be, however, other factors which result in relatively close integration between Chinese industry and research and development. Richman points to collective risk taking as a contributor to innovation in China and the concomitant R&D/industrial integration. In comparing the Chinese and Soviet industrial systems, he argues that the emphasis on individual responsibility—characteristic of the Soviet system—tends to inhibit innovation. But in China, ". . . innovation activities—including those of a major kind—do not entail as much potential risk, penalties, or losses for individuals as they do in the Soviet Union. . . . This lack of emphasis on individual responsibility or blame for failure in China can hinder industrial programs because irrational, unwarranted and/or unproductive risks are more likely to occur. On the other hand, it does promote a considerable amount of risk type activity that would not otherwise occur."[16]

SOURCES AND PATTERNS OF CONFLICT— INTERFACE AT DEPLOYMENT

Very little is published regarding conflict between cost overruns, performance and reliability underruns, and time-to-completion overruns within China. The history of the Great Leap and its aftermath amply demonstrates that all these phenomena occur in China, and indeed, probably contributed greatly to the general decline of the Chinese economy in the early 1960s. Details are nearly nonexistent regarding the bureaucratic contenders and individuals involved in these conflicts, however, and efforts to outline the pattern of conflict and its resolution require a great deal of guesswork.

Inter-service rivalry probably plays a relatively minor role in cost overruns, etc., not because there is no competition among the various services for a large share of the defense budget, but because Chinese naval and air forces are so over-shadowed by the ground force establishment. Unlike the United States, the Chinese air and naval forces have no statutory independence from the army, and, in terms of the allocation of

defense resources, together probably control less than 25% of the defense budget.

A more logical differentiation might be between members of central planning institutions in Peking and military elites at the region or army level, regardless of service in which they are enrolled. It is logical to assume, for example, that central planners have a perspective somewhat at variance with that of regional or local military elites, a bias which would translate itself into a different view of what kind of problems are most important. Central planners probably tend to believe that cost overruns and time-to-completion overruns are more critical than performance underruns. This is not to say that they are not concerned with quality, but that, as central planners, they must think first of orchestrating the national system to achieve their output goals. Thus, to them, overruns of cost or time are viewed as more dangerous. In contrast, local military elites are concerned much less with assuring that their local commands mesh with a national system than with the quality of their command. As such, they probably attach a higher degree of criticality upon performance and reliability underruns than with costs and completion time problems.

This tension between local and national perspective—by no means unique to the Chinese system—probably focuses on and within the General Rear Service Department, the structural linkage between central production and the field.

The General Rear Services Department provides the primary administrative linkage between the point at which a weapon is produced and its deployment with the operational military unit. Formally charged with assuring the flow of weapons from production centers to operational units and with the repair and reconditioning of materiel, it provides the feedback mechanism for weapons systems evaluations to planning and research and development organizations. The feedback mechanisms of the General Rear Services Department are paralleled by the normal military chain of command and the party hierarchy, but are the most important. As such, it is probably the central arena in which local and national perspectives compete.

This competition may be reflected in the personnel who enter and control the Rear Services Department. If so, a historical case could be made in favor of the national planners as opposed to the local military elites, for, with a few exceptions in the 1954–59 period, high level administrators in the Rear Services Department appear to have come from nationally oriented backgrounds.

---

[15]*Ibid.*, pp. 274–75.
[16]*Ibid.*, p. 339.

THE ACQUISITION OF MILITARY AIRCRAFT IN GREAT BRITAIN AND WEST GERMANY

FRANK GREGORY AND JOHN SIMPSON

The premise of this article is that weapons acquisition is not solely determined by unique national political factors, but that acquisition processes involve common problems, phases and issues that can be compared across national boundaries. Although an eleven-phase process is conceptualized, Great Britain and West Germany are compared in only three phases—program initiation, procurement style, and production. Though starting with a wide gap in their R&D bases, these two countries have developed convergent trends in program initiation and procurement style—culminating in cooperative development of MRCA.

Frank Gregory and John Simpson are Lecturers in Politics at Southampton University, England. Gregory took his M.Sc. degree in International Studies at Southampton in 1968 and Simpson completed his M.Sc. in Economics at University College, London, in 1965. They are co-authors (with G. Williams) of Crisis in Procurement: A Case Study of the TSR-2 *(1969), and several other research monographs.*

INTRODUCTION

Great Britain and West Germany have had very different experiences with their weapons acquisition processes. The British system has undergone a series of evolutionary changes since World War II. In contrast, West Germany did not restart weapons acquisition until the mid-1950s, after the gap of a decade. The different background to the two systems raises the fundamental question of whether any meaningful comparison between national weapons acquisition processes is possible.

In attempting to construct an answer, one basic problem has to be resolved. Are weapons acquisition processes to be seen as dependent variables in relation to their parent political system or viewed as comparable sets of national methods of approaching similar weapons acquisition issues? If one uses the first perspective, the starting point for any cross-national analysis of weapons acquisition processes must be a comparison of the functioning of their political systems. Once this has been done it can form the basis of a comparison of weapons acquisition processes. Using the second perspective, one starts by identifying the common problems, decision stages, issue areas or other points of comparison that appear to be relevant to most weapons acquisition processes, and uses these as a framework to guide and structure comparative analysis. This implies that one cannot meaningfully compare national weapons acquisition processes as such, but one can compare their components. These are related together through the medium of a set of sequential decision points, each one preceding a movement from one component of the weapons acquisition process into the next one. To perform a cross-national analysis using this perspective, it is necessary to identify these components, and relate them together sequentially over time.

The foregoing propositions have not resolved the problem of determining which of the alternative perspectives should be dominant. The answer appears to be dependent upon the focus of the inquiry, and the questions explicitly or implicitly being asked. In practice, as is clear from project studies, such as that of the TSR-2,[1] a complete analysis of how a new weapons system progresses is only possible by applying each perspective to differing decision points in the process. Thus, in routine matters of technical evaluation and decision, such as the initial

---

[1] See J. Simpson, F. Gregory, and G. Williams: *Crisis in Procurement—A Case Study of the TSR-2* (London: R.U.S.I., 1969).

This is an original article written for this volume and the Conference on Comparative Defense Policy held at the Air Force Academy, February 7-9, 1973. Copyright reserved by the author.

determination of a project's cost, time, or performance parameters, the internal operations of the weapons acquisition process are dominant. The action to be taken should it cross any of these boundaries as it progresses usually involves the taking of decisions within the mainstream of a state's political system. Such decisions can often only be explained in terms of the internal workings of that political system at that point in time. In this chapter actual projects are not discussed. The analytical focus is on the components of the weapons acquisition process and the factors operating upon them. As a result the second perspective is here the dominant mode of analysis.

Any attempt to identify categories of phenomena for cross-national comparison often involves some overlap between the categories selected. The components of weapons acquisition processes are no exception to this. Initially, it is possible to identify eleven categories of phenomena for comparative purposes, which are linked together sequentially over time in the following order.

1. *The broad-based process of defence research and component development,* which provides a background for all weapons acquisition decisions.

2. *The process through which the demand for a new weapons project is created.* Inputs into this include the need to replace existing systems, new technological possibilities, the demands of new military tasks, and attempts by commercial concerns to create a market for products they have either already developed or wish to develop.

3. *The process of deciding the specification of the new weapons system.* This involves both deciding the degree to which the system should be optimized on certain roles and carrying out studies to investigate the technical feasibility of the resulting specifications. In addition it may involve performing some component development work. Reviewing the specifications may produce a demand for project redefinition and also active intervention by commercial concerns to promote their own interests.

4. *The overlapping process of costing the project as it becomes more accurately defined,* in order to arrive at figures for the cost-effectiveness of various configurations of the proposed weapons system. This also involves evaluating existing systems to see if they can be adapted to perform the necessary tasks and examining possibilities of cost reduction by combining requirements into multi-purpose weapons systems, or by combining with other states in collaborative projects.

5. *The process of contractor selection.* This may occur through competition, by nomination or

as a by-product of governmental attempts to adjust work loads so as to maintain commercial organizations in being.

6. *The process of the contractor producing a definitive design,* and the resulting cost estimates.

7. *The process of arriving at a decision to proceed to prototype development.* This decision will usually be transferred into the main political process and involve many considerations other than military ones. These include the state of the national economy, likely growth rates for GNP, local levels of unemployment, ideas about defence research spearheading the search for competitive new technologies and pressures by national industries for an opportunity to participate in this search.

8. *The procurement style.* In the case of military aircraft, this has two components. The first is whether research and development activities including prototype production are performed by two separate organizations, as in the USSR,[2] or whether they are integrated together within one state or commercial organization. The second is whether a building-block process of developing new components divorced from particular projects is followed, or whether components are produced initially for a particular weapons system.

9. *The process of selecting the project management and contracting system.* This involves three separate elements.

a. The allocation of responsibility for coordinating and managing the program either to a commercial firm, a governmental agency, a procurement ministry, or to a series of interdepartmental committees.

b. Deciding the type of detailed management techniques to be used, e.g., PERT (Project Evaluation and Review Technique).

c. Deciding the types of contract to be used, i.e., cost plus, fixed price, target price, or incentive contract.

10. *The processes of project review and approval/cancellation.* The former involves the operation of the system used to monitor a project's progress. The latter is concerned with work within the political process which may lead to the cancellation of projects, i.e., cuts in government spending as part of economic policy.

11. *The process of initiating production.* This involves such factors as industrial pressures to maximize the opportunities for domestic production, the rate of production and the consequent unit costs, and the need to maintain continuity of employment.

---

[2]See Arthur Alexander, "Weapons Acquisition in the Soviet Union, U.S. and France," pp. 426–43 of this volume.

It can be seen from this framework that the political process only appears to dominate the weapons acquisition process at two key points: the decision to proceed with a project, and the decision to cancel it. All other decisions can be seen as occurring within the confines of the weapons acquisition process.

On the basis of this framework, it is possible to proceed to examine British and West German experience with the acquisition of military aircraft. In order to keep the analysis within manageable limits however, phases 1 to 4 have been treated together; phases 5, 6, 7, 9, and 10 have been omitted as they are more appropriate to detailed historical case studies of past projects. The analysis therefore breaks down into three sections covering initiation (phases 1–4), procurement style (phase 8) and production (phase 11), and each state will be dealt with separately using this framework.

GREAT BRITAIN

Initiation of Projects

(1) After World War II Britain was the only Western European power to possess a comprehensive industrial capability in the field of military aircraft production, comprising relatively large airframe, engine, and avionic firms. In addition, a number of British government research establishments were conducting basic research related to military aviation products being developed under government contract by industry. Since 1957, however, there has been a tendency to limit expenditure on broad aerospace research and to insist on relating it to areas where eventual production was likely. On the whole, this comprehensive capability still remains in being today, though expertise is lacking in an increasing number of detailed areas.

(2) The major areas of uncertainty surrounding new British military aircraft projects over the last two decades have been the political, technological, and geographical environments within which they were ultimately intended to operate. This resulted in the 1950s in a spate of new projects based on rapidly changing perceptions of these environments. Many of these projects were subsequently cancelled.

During the 1960s the RAF found it necessary to undertake two revaluations of its functions.[3]

Following the 1957 Defence White Paper which questioned the utility of manned aircraft in the missile era, the RAF tried to point out, more explicitly than it had thought necessary in the past, its unique virtues and roles. Then after the RAF's responsibility for providing the strategic nuclear deterrent had terminated, together with many overseas commitments, the RAF had to reconsider its functions and force structure in the light of the stringent financial restrictions imposed by successive defence budgets.

The statements on the Air Estimates of 1961–62 and 1962–63[4] set out the functions of the RAF at the beginning of the decade. The latter stated "The Royal Air Force exists to deploy air power in defence of our national interests and in support of our friends and allies. In particular, it provides:

a. Britain's strategic nuclear striking power

b. The strategic airlift of men and equipment for all three services

c. Long-range striking power against the submarine

d Air defence

e. A major element in the country's tactical nuclear and conventional striking power

f. Reconnaissance both long-range and tactical

g. Army battlefield support

h. Transportation support, especially for the Army."[5]

Both statements found it necessary to spell out, in some detail, the roles of manned aircraft to meet criticisms of their viability. Although at the beginning of the decade Fighter Command still had the role of defending the United Kingdom against the threat of strategic nuclear bombers, the RAF thought ahead to the roles of fighters after this threat receded. It was pointed out that Fighter Command would still be left with the tasks of reconnaissance, the investigation and identification of unidentified aircraft movements, the deterrence or prevention of attempts to jam U.K. radar systems and the provision of aerial defence for overseas operations. Manned aircraft were also claimed to provide the most suitable form of deterrent force for Britain, as the country was not suitable for large-scale missile deployment.[6] It was also pointed out that aircraft were important in maintaining a proper

---

[3]A general background to the development of the RAF since 1945 is provided by the following sources: the annual government White Papers on the Defence and Air Estimates; D. Divine, *Broken Wing*, (U.K.: Hutchinson, 1965); J.W.R. Taylor and P.J.R. Mayer, *Pictorial History of the RAF, Vol. 3, 1945–1969* (London: Geo. Allen, 1970); P. Darby, *British Defence Policy East of Suez, 1947–1968*, (London: Oxford Univ.

Press, 1973); the series of aircraft company histories published by Putnams and articles in *Brassey's*, the *RUSI Journal*, the *RAF Quarterly*, and *Air Power*.

[4]*Statement on the Air Estimates 1961–62*, Cmnd. 1292 (London: HMSO, 1961), pp. 4, 5, & 7; and *Statement on the Air Estimates 1962–63* Cmnd. 1630 (London: HMSO, 1962), pp. 6–8.

[5]Cmnd. 1630, *op. cit.*, p. 6.

[6]*Ibid.*, pp. 6–7.

balance of conventional and nuclear capabilities, and that they alone could provide an accurate means of non-nuclear weapons delivery outside of artillery range.

The subsequent statement on the Air Estimates for 1963–64[7] had to consider the effects of the cancellation of the United States Skybolt air-launched ballistic missile ordered by Britain and the likelihood that Britain would lose permanent overseas bases. Skybolt's cancellation came just as the V-bomber force reached its maximum numerical strength and when the RAF was concurrently considering two possible lines of force development. One concerned improving the *tactical* bomber force of Canberras and later, it was hoped, TSR-2s, by arming them with new bombs, Martel anti-radar and television guided missiles and by developing a tactical nuclear weapon. The second line of development concerned possible applications of STOL technology to meet the problem of operating effectively without fixed bases.

Publication of a specific RAF statement on its military posture ceased in 1965 as a result of the creation of the unified Ministry of Defence. Subsequent Defence White Papers, however, highlighted a number of the RAF's problems. The rising costs of defence equipment and the problem of meeting equipment demands from limited funds were both emphasized.[8] In addition, the high rate of production spending in the early 1960s had limited the money available for developing new equipment, with the result that a major purchase of United States military aircraft was sanctioned in 1965–67 in order to meet the RAF's needs for the late 1960s.[9] At the same time it was recognized that although it was desirable that Britain should retain a comprehensive capability to develop and produce military aircraft, the home market the country could offer for these aircraft was likely to make their unit cost unacceptably high, while the research and development expenditure needed would take up an unacceptably high proportion of the defence budget. The only method of overcoming these problems was seen to be sharing the cost with other countries, via collaborative projects.[10]

In the latter half of the 1960s the RAF lost two roles and assumed a new one. The political decision to withdraw from East of Suez made global operating ability less important. The op-

erational deployment of Britain's Polaris submarines in 1969 ended the RAF's nuclear deterrent role. In contrast, the decision to phase out aircraft carriers meant that the RAF now had to provide fixed wing air support for the Navy. By the end of the 1960s the RAF was mainly a tactical air force with three main tasks, air defence of Britain, long-range maritime patrol and air support of the Fleet, and, particularly, the task of supporting land operations on NATO's central front.[11] As a result, the requirements for military aircraft have become increasingly orientated toward these roles, though in practice it may be another decade before this has fully worked through into operational equipment.

(3 and 4). From 1940 until 1972,[12] the British military aircraft acquisition process involved relationships between three major organizational components. Project definition and costing were closely related to the effectiveness of these linkages. In theory, the Air Staff was responsible for defining the operational requirements of military aircraft, usually after consultation with government research establishments such as the Royal Aircraft Establishment, Farnborough. An intermediary ministry (Aircraft Production, Supply, Aviation Technology, and Aviation Supply in chronological order) was responsible for translating this into hardware. It contracted with commercial firms to do the work, dealt with all the financial aspects of projects, including cost estimating, and was responsible for monitoring and controlling government contracts placed with such firms. It was also responsible, however, for promoting the well-being and health of the air-

[11]See the article by the then Commander in Chief RAF Germany, Air Marshal Sir Christopher Foxley-Norris, "Developments in tactical air operations," *RUSI Journal* 114, no. 655 (Sept. 1969): 5–17.

[12]For description and commentaries on the pre-1972 processes, see W. P. Snyder, *The Politics of British Defence Policy* (Columbus, Ohio: Ohio State University Press, 1964), pp. 143–44; Williams, Simpson, and Gregory, *Case Study of the TSR-2, op. cit.*, and papers 1, 2, and 5–12 in *The Collected Papers on Defence Planning and Weapons Technology* (Dept. of Extra-Mural Studies, Southampton University, 1969). The official reports which give the background to and the details of the current system are: Office of the Minister of Science, "The Report of the Committee on the Management and Control of Research and Development" (London: HMSO, 1961); Ministry of Technology, "The Report of the Steering Group on Development Costs Estimating," vols. 1 and 2 (London: HMSO, 1960); "Second Report of the Select Committee on Science and Technology (Defence Research)," House of Commons Paper No. 213 of Session 1968–69 (London: HMSO, 1968); Ministry of Technology, "The Productivity of the National Aircraft Effort," Report of a Committee Appointed by the Minister of Technology and the President of the SBAC (London: HMSO, 1969), chap. 17; "The Reorganisation of Central Government," Cmnd. 4506 (London: HMSO, 1970); and "Government Organisation for Defence Procurement and Civil Aerospace," Cmnd. 4641 (London: HMSO, 1971).

[7]*Statement on the Air Estimates 1963–64*, Cmnd. 1936 (London: HMSO, 1963), pp. 6–7.

[8]*Statement on the Defence Estimates 1965 Pt.I.*, Cmnd. 1592 (London: HMSO, 1965), p. 6.

[9]*Ibid.*, p. 10.

[10]*Ibid.*

craft industry as a whole. Finally, those firms in the aircraft industry specializing in military aircraft were usually responsible for airframe development, but often had no overall control of a military aircraft project, as the engines and electronics were contracted for separately by the intermediary ministry. Unfortunately, clear communication between these components was often lacking, and therefore the Air Staff often operated without any thought for the financial implications of their actions while the intermediary ministry had no direct control over the details of the O.R. (Operational Requirement). In addition, the intermediary ministry was anxious to spread work evenly around the industry at the expense of the Air Staff's desire to procure technically superior aircraft. Up to the mid-1950s the general approach to military aircraft development was based on the post-war policy planning parameter which assumed peace for ten years. Thus the emphasis was upon extensive theoretical research, the building of a number of specialist research aircraft and the development of limited numbers of prototypes.

With a few exceptions, notably the unsuccessful Swift program, the rapid acceleration of projects financed by the rearmament budgets of the Korean War period led to the production of a satisfactory generation of military aircraft, such as, the Hunter and the V-Bombers (Victor, Valiant, and Vulcan). This suggested that a 'great leap forward' policy, which missed out interim aircraft of the F-86/B-36 type, could be made to work.

This success plus the high rearmament budgets seems to have encouraged the Air Staff in the mid-1950s to plan for a comprehensive reequipment program during the mid-1960s onwards. However, with the cuts in the aircraft research and development programs imposed in 1956–57 and the development of guided missiles, the Air Staff was forced to re-cast its program. The emphasis was placed on obtaining more versatility from fewer types, leading to an interest in multi-role aircraft and in VTOL (vertical takeoff and land), V/STOL (vertical/short takeoff and land), or STOL (short takeoff and land) capabilities.

These changed requirements of the Air Staff coincided with the first major post-war change in the aircraft procurement process. From the mid-1950s, following exhaustive inquiries into the rearmament programs,[13] military aircraft began to be treated as complete weapons systems.

In parallel, disquiet had been expressed over the cost escalations incurred by military aircraft projects and the number of projects initiated but not completed because of escalating costs. This later culminated in the controversy surrounding the costs of the TSR-2,[14] and resulting attempts to set up more detailed and thorough procedures for examining projects before they were allowed to proceed to development, and to increase the accuracy of initial cost estimates.

In 1970 the incoming Conservative government announced its intention of rationalizing the structure of defence procurement and the overlapping military and civil aerospace responsibilities of the Ministry of Technology, the contemporary intermediate ministry.[15] An enquiry was conducted by Derek Rayner, seconded from the commercial firm of Marks & Spencer. Its terms of reference were "To make recommendations, in time for new arrangements to be implemented by 1st April 1972 on:

(a) How best to organize the integration of all defence research and development and procurement activities, under the responsibility of the Secretary of Defence: among the possibilities to be considered should be the establishment of an agency within government.

(b) How best to handle, in the light of (a), the government's relations with the industries concerned, including its responsibilities in support of civil aircraft projects and other civil aerospace activities. The project team should pay particular regard to the need to meet essential defence and civil requirements in the most economical and efficient way."[16]

The Report was issued in April 1971, and it stated: "In essence, the proposals in this report for a new organisation seek to create accountable units of management to handle procurement, to develop and reward the specialist skills which are needed, and to create an atmosphere in which those involved will be motivated to do their utmost to give satisfaction to the user." Reviewing the existing procurement system Rayner made some apt comments on British weapons acquisition problems.[17]

He noted that a government procurement organization has certain inherent problems in the nature of its work which prevent it from operat-

---

[13]See "The Supply of Military Aircraft," Cmnd. 9388 (London: HMSO, 1955) and the Second Report of the Select

Committee on Estimates, "The Supply of Military Aircraft," House of Commons Paper No. 34 of Session 1956–57 (London: HMSO, 1957).

[14]See Williams, Simpson, and Gregory, *Case Study of TSR-2, op. cit.*

[15]Cmnd. 4506, *op. cit.*

[16]*Ibid.*, p. 9.

[17]Cmnd. 4641, *op. cit.*, p. 18.

ing on full commercial principles. For example, a procurement organization is an agency and therefore not its own master, and it cannot escape from the effects of changes in government defence policy.

Rayner concluded that the British defence procurement program had, in general, been characterized by a mismatch between the service requirements and the resources available to meet them. Frequent reductions in the expected allocation of resources to defence had exacerbated this situation. The result was a succession of cancelled projects, reductions in planned purchases of finished equipment, and delays in decisions to proceed with development programs.

The new procurement structure recommended by Rayner and subsequently established has the following major features.

1. A single procurement organization (the Procurement Executive) has been established under a Chief Executive responsible through the Minister of State (Defence Procurement) to the Secretary of State for Defence. This organization is responsible for procurement of all warlike stores. This responsibility was previously diffused within the Ministries of Defence and Aviation Supply.

2. The Chief Executive has responsible to him three Controllers for Sea, Land, and Air Weapons Systems who are also members of their respective Service Boards, a Controller for Guided Weapon and Electronic Systems and a Controller for Research and Development Establishments and Research.

3. The Chief Executive and the Four Systems Controllers are also the Accounting Officers for their respective votes, accountable to the British Parliament for the expenditure incurred by their sections.

4. The Department of Trade and Industry (DTI) has acquired responsibility for government policy toward the aerospace industry and civil aerospace research, development, and production. It can call on the Procurement Executive to give advice on civil programs and, if necessary, execute them.

5. A Ministerial Aerospace Board has been established to oversee collaboration between the DTI and the Procurement Executive and to be the authority for instructions and policy guidance to the latter on civil aerospace matters.

In parallel with these structural changes in the organization of procurement, a detailed blueprint was laid down for the processing of all requirements for new defence projects, including military aircraft. This consisted of six phases.[18]

1. The draft requirement for a new military aircraft would be formulated by the staff of the Assistant Chief of the Air Staff (Operational Requirements), and promulgated as a Staff Target.

2. The Staff Target would be examined by the Ministry of Defence (MoD) (Central) Operational Requirements Committee (ORC). This Committee has responsibility for sponsoring the weapons system concept and operational requirement studies and with examining, harmonizing, and approving new requirements against the background of the overall defence planning parameters.

3. Approval of the Staff Target would lead to a *Feasibility Study* which would involve consultations with the other services, the government R&D establishments, and industry. Preliminary estimates of development, production costs, and time scale would be produced at this stage.

4. The Staff Target would be rewritten in the light of the results of the Feasibility Study as a *Staff Requirement* and reexamined by the ORC.

5. If the ORC accepted the Staff Requirement as valid, it would be submitted to another MoD (Central) committee, the Defence Equipment Policy Committee (DEPC), which would authorize a *Project Definition* (PD) study. This study would normally involve the first commitment of funds to the project. It would have two stages, and include an examination with potential contractors of the areas of technical uncertainty in order to try and draw up a comprehensive cost plan, a time scale for completion, and an estimate of the unit production cost.

6. If, after the PD study, the ORC confirmed that the requirement was still valid, the DEPC would have to consider whether or not the proposed new military aircraft's development should be authorized. A major military aircraft would probably also need the endorsement of the Chiefs of Staff Committee, the Defence Minister, and the Defence and Overseas Policy Committee of the Cabinet.

It is difficult to evaluate the impact of these new organization structures and procedures upon the British weapons acquisition process, as few projects have yet passed through it. Those that have, however, such as the HS1182 advanced jet trainer, appear to have been subjected to much more rigorous attempts to define precisely cost and performance parameters than previously, and have been subjected to more widespread dis-

---

[18]Cmnd. 4641 outlines this process. An invaluable official commentary on it is found in the articles written by Ministry of Defence procurement officials in *Weapons Procurement, Defence Management and International Collaboration.* (London: R.U.S.I. for Defence Studies, 1972), pp. 5–27.

cussions on the trade-offs between costs and performance. However, this aircraft cannot be regarded as an advanced military aircraft. Further, the British policy still decrees that such advanced aircraft will in future be built in collaboration with other European states, and, in such cases, experience suggests that a very different set of procedures to those outlined above are likely to be followed.[19]

Procurement Style

The British experience over the last quarter century provides a comprehensive example of the types of procurement style that are possible. In the decade from 1945 onwards, the British government financed a large number of research aircraft and military prototypes. In addition, a number of companies used their own financial resources to develop potential military aircraft, in the hope that their adoption by the services would allow them to recoup their expenditure and make a profit on the production runs. At the same time, existing military aircraft such the Meteor and Vampire were also going through a process of continuous modification and development. A choice was thus possible between the placing in service of a developed version of existing aircraft or equipping with a completely new type of aircraft. This system was dependent on two factors. One was the relative simplicity of contemporary aircraft which were engine/airframe combinations, with little avionic equipment. As the engines were almost all developed under government contract and supplied free of charge to the airframe firms, this meant that the costs of constructing prototypes or adapting existing airframes were such that companies could fund private venture work. Companies thus had the financial autonomy to ignore government specifications if they chose to. This was a product of their sound financial position, derived from lengthy wartime production runs, and the relative cheapness of new prototype airframes. In addition, there existed a healthy export trade in the immediate postwar period in the early types of jet powered military aircraft, together with a major funding program for civil aircraft prototypes which placed some companies in a position of being able to choose between civil or military contracts.

By 1956–57, however, the situation had changed considerably. As greater speeds and the ability to carry increasing loads of electronic equipment became dominant elements in the development of advanced military aircraft, the cost of building realistic prototypes, as against experimental airframes, escalated alarmingly. It therefore became necessary to make deliberate choices at an early stage between possible lines of development. The previous policy of developing a large number of options, and then choosing one for production was seen as both wasteful in money and skilled manpower and unnecessarily slow. The increased complexity of military aircraft meant that larger design teams became necessary to produce the detailed designs, and this coupled with the decreased number of aircraft projects led to a need to consolidate the airframe and aeroengine industry into larger design and production units. The termination of government contracts for the development of civil aircraft further limited the freedom of maneuver of individual aircraft firms, while the lack of potential home and export orders after 1957 further accelerated the process of contraction and consolidation.

By the late 1960s, therefore, the prototyping method of developing military aircraft had been abandoned. The firms remaining in the industry lacked the financial resources to initiate extensive new development work themselves. The government was attempting to control expenditure on defence technology and was not prepared to finance experimental prototypes. Instead, new advanced military aircraft were to be built as required, using the weapons system concept and assembling prototypes on production jigs. In parallel, very limited development work was allowed on existing types.

In practice, this decision was complicated by three factors. One was that financial limitations tended to favor the adaptation of existing aircraft for new roles, rather than the production of complete new weapons systems. Thus, the Lightning Mk.6, Buccaneer Mk.2, Nimrod and Shackleton AEW aircraft have appeared through this process, while the cancellation of the TSR-2, P1154, and HS681 has led to a situation where an aircraft developed exclusively within the sixteen-year-old weapons system concept has yet to enter service. Second, the one new advanced military aircraft which evolved during this period, the V/STOL Harrier ground attack aircraft, was in existence in prototype form as a product of multinational funding *before* the decision was taken to move to production in 1965. It can thus be claimed to be a product of a prototyping rather than weapons system approach. Finally, the policy decision to collaborate with other European states on the design, development, and pro-

[19]See J. Simpson, and F. Gregory, "West European Collaboration in Weapons Procurement," *Orbis* 16, no. 2 (Summer 1972): 435–61.

duction of advanced aircraft, initiated in 1962, has led to the imminent entry into service of one aircraft, the Sepecat Jaguar, which has employed, so far as the British are concerned, the weapons system approach. The second major Western European project MRCA has also been developed using this system, but will not enter service before the late 1970s.

The British have therefore differed from the French, Russians, and Americans in their procurement style by first using extensively the prototyping method of development, and then abandoning it in favor of a weapons system concept. However, despite this having occurred sixteen years ago, the first aircraft to fully utilize this method has yet to enter service, and to the British, therefore, the method can neither be assessed as a success nor a failure. The limited number of new projects undertaken during this period, and the failure of any of them to enter production, means that it has yet to be fully evaluated.

Production

During World War II, the British aircraft industry evolved into a structure very similar to the current Soviet industry. The established aeroengine and airframe firms operated predominantly as design and development units, with some associated production facilities, but the bulk of production was undertaken by 'shadow factories' mainly managed by automobile firms. As a result, the immediate aftermath of war was relatively painless to the aviation industry, as the major production units could revert back to their pre-war tasks, and the majority of the aircraft firms themselves continue in their existing roles, reinforced by the government policy of financing the production of an extensive range of new prototypes.

Major changes in the structure of the aircraft industry did not occur until the rearmament program of the early 1950s became fully operative. This produced a movement of labor into the production side of the industry at the same time that the design teams were starting work on the next generation of military aircraft. The subcontracting that occurred during this period tended to take place within the industry, with firms producing aircraft designed by competitors, thus contributing to further expansion of production facilities within the industry.

Concurrently the avionics side of the British industry had been striving to develop and produce equipment over a broad front, thus giving Britain a fully comprehensive aircraft design, development, and production capability which industrialists wished to exploit and maintain.

By 1957, however, most of the new aircraft projects had been cancelled, and the rearmament production program curtailed. Although some resources had been redeployed into missile production, this fall in home orders, together with the uncertainties of the civil aircraft program, produced a major problem of industrial policy which successive governments have attempted to resolve. The British aircraft industry was clearly too big for the home market that a sluggish economic growth rate offered, yet it contained experience and expertise that would be of great value to the economy of the country if only it could be used. The industry was seen as a national asset, but one that was very difficult to exploit. The result was a reluctance to reduce the size of the industry to any appreciable extent, including its production facilities, pending attempts to expand exports, or join collaborative projects with other states that involved work sharing. The only conscious attempt to take drastic action to reduce the labor input into the industry occurred through the cancellation of military aircraft projects in 1964–65, yet this produced very little redeployment of labor, despite contemporary statements to the contrary.[20] This reluctance to actively work for reductions in the industry was further reinforced by the slowly increasing British unemployment statistics between 1968 and 1972. These produced political pressures to take all necessary actions to maintain employment within the industry, especially on the production side.

This action took the form of orders for military aircraft, the civil side of the airframe industry having been allowed to contract considerably, unlike the situation in France and Germany. The result has been a drive to increase collaboration with other European states in order to try to expand potential markets and therefore production prospects. This has created tensions within the British aerospace industry, in particular the avionics sector has accused the airframe and aero-engine sector of trying to squeeze it out of collaborative projects in order to produce worksharing arrangements acceptable to other states. Thus from a position where production was not seen as the major function of the aircraft industry in Britain it now dominates the situation.

Accompanying this development has been a change in the relationship between industry and government. In 1957, the government was faced with about twelve airframe design and production units, five engine firms, and a number of

[20]Williams, Gregory, and Simpson, *Case Study of TSR-2, op. cit.*, pp. 55–57.

avionics companies. As a result it was in a position to divide and rule. It now finds itself with only two major airframe firms, one engine firm, and two major avionics groups, and has been making unsuccessful attempts to alter the structure of the industry still further by transforming the two airframe firms into two new firms, one concentrating on aircraft, the other on missiles. These firms are almost totally dependent on government orders for their survival and are in many ways similar to nationalized industries with a commercial management structure grafted onto them. As a result, the power of these firms to persuade government to take their requirements into account in negotiating the work-sharing arrangements of collaborative projects has increased, as the survival of jobs in factories is directly linked to governmental action.

WEST GERMANY

The Initiation of Projects

(1) West Germany had no defence research and development base until it became a member of NATO and rearmament commenced, though some expertise was in existence as a result of aircraft designers working in other countries, such as Spain. In this situation, the decision was taken to pursue a policy of selective innovation within the boundary set by the government decision not to seek national autarky in armaments production. This involved financing specialized research projects, such as those into VTOL aircraft, while at the same time pursuing a two-stage process of license producing complete aircraft, and then, as expertise grew within the industry, designing and producing new aircraft, using mainly components manufactured outside of the state. In addition, the policy decision to attempt to produce all military equipment in collaboration with other NATO states further assisted this growth process. The result is that the German aerospace industry now finds itself with expertise in certain limited areas, but has to rely on licensing and collaborative agreements to obtain components and expertise over a wide field.

(2) Unlike the British experience, the role of the Luftwaffe has remained fairly constant since its rebirth, although emphasis since 1967 has been moving away from battlefield and tactical nuclear operations toward support for conventional warfare.

The post-war German Air Force[21] was de-

signed as a tactical weapon to defend the air space of the Federal Republic and give close support to the ground forces. As Lowenstein and Von Zuhlsdorff point out, a strategic air force was politically unacceptable, because it would convey an offensive and not a defensive aim to the Eastern European states and Russia.

Defence Minister Strauss originally listed the tasks of the German Air Force as:

1. To engage the tactical air force of the enemy.

2. To carry out reconnaissance flights for tactical purposes.

3. To assist in the air defence of European air space.

4. To give close support to ground units.

5. To provide air transport.

Under NATO's pre-Flexible Response strategy of Forward Defence the emphasis was placed upon building up the nuclear component of the Air Force. However, under the strategy of Flexible Response emphasis was shifted to reconnaissance and conventional air support of the ground forces. This was achieved by giving the seven nuclear-armed fighter bomber squadrons a conventional secondary role.

The 1971/72 German Defence White Paper gives an up-to-date picture of the roles of the Air Force, in terms little different from Strauss's formulation. It states that, "The flying combat units must be capable of executing the following types of mission in the seventies: engaging hostile air forces on the ground; air interdiction against enemy reserves in the rear combat zone; battlefield interdiction; air superiority operations; intercept operations; close air support of the ground forces; tactical air reconnaissance and battlefield reconnaissance."[22]

Demand for new weapons projects have been primarily generated by the need to replace the generation of equipment acquired during the rearmament phase. In the case of military aircraft, this has produced a replacement program in which the MRCA is to replace the F-104G for air and battle field interdiction and engagement of enemy air forces on the ground. The RF-4E Phantom is to take over the tactical air reconnaissance role from the RF-104G. The Alpha Jet, a Franco-German project, is to take over the Fiat G-91s battlefield reconnaissance and close air support roles. Lastly, the F-4F Phantom is to

[21]There are few English language sources dealing with the post-war German Air Force. Some general information is

contained in Hubertas Prince von Lowenstein and Volkmar von Zuhlsdorff, *NATO and the Defence of the West* (London: Deutsch, 1963), Ch. 19, pp. 217–30.

[22]*1971–72 German Defence White Paper*, English language version (Bonn: Press and Information Service of the Federal Govt., 1972), pp. 143–44.

replace the F-104G in carrying out air superiority and interceptor missions.

Despite the initiation of the VAK191 and VJ101, V/STOL strike fighter projects in the late 1960s, neither of these projects appears to have generated substantial industrial pressures for production. Rather, the tendency seems to have been for the industry to participate very little in this stage of the procurement process.

(3 & 4) Until the mid-1960s, the equipment procured for the armed forces of the FDR tended to result from political agreements. These related either to a policy of seeking collaboration with other West European states in the production of defence equipment or to the problems of offsetting the exchange costs of US troops in Europe. Only recently has the West German Defence Ministry begun to operate a fully integrated defence planning and armament procurement system. This was inspired by the major reequipment program that was regarded as necessary from 1970 onwards. The 1970 Defence White Paper therefore devoted considerable attention to the problems encountered in the past, and possible methods of overcoming them. It noted that "The arrangements that provide for the interaction between all agencies concerned with development and procurement—the so-called equipment development process—are extremely cumbersome and unwieldy."[23] A Commission was therefore set up by the Federal Defence Ministry to examine methods of improving this process. It was given the following terms of reference:

1. The satisfaction of material requirements will remain organized on uniform lines for all services, broken down by technical categories (principle of equipment-oriented responsibility). Existing approaches to project-oriented organization elements (system managers, project officers) will be expanded for important programs. Duplication of effort will be avoided.

2. The current process of delegating tasks and responsibilities from the Ministry to the subordinate level will be adhered to. This also applies in the case of the Federal Office for Military Technology and Procurement with regard to its subordinate agencies.

3. Although responsibility and control in the armaments field must remain undivided the military personnel responsible for the operation and maintenance of their weapons must have a full share in decisions of fundamental importance.

The equipment development process will be reviewed with this purpose in mind."[24]

The Commission's studies resulted in the promulgation of a Basic Directive on the Reorganisation of Defence Production and Procurement of January 28, 1971. The details of the reorganization and of the Commission's findings were set out in the *Neuordnung des Rüstungsbereiches*. (Framework Edict made by the Minister for the Armaments Sphere).[25]

The reorganization involved both procedures and management. "Under the new procedures, armaments planning has been made an integral part of overall Bundeswehr planning. From the very outset, armaments experts participate in all planning work done by the Forces. This compels the Forces and the armaments sector to collaborate. Weapons and equipment are developed in a sequence of phases. During each phase investigations are made whether the objective, the cost and the time requirement are still in accord. Performance evaluations serve to reduce risks. Permanent study groups in the Service staffs, composed of military personnel, technical experts and economists, formulate the tactical requirements during the first planning phase."[26] In addition, "Planning, development and procurement of complex weapon systems call for a management organisation and for participative work of system managers, project specialists and project officers."[27]

West Germany has thus had similar problems to the United Kingdom in the integration of the activities of the services and the armaments sections within their Ministry of Defence. It differs from the United Kingdom in that all armament procurement activities have always been centralized within that Ministry. Unlike the RAF, however, the Luftwaffe has no single section solely concerned with planning operational requirements, this responsibility being divided between FUL5 (Logistics), FUL6 (Planning) and FUL7 (Procurement and projects). In addition, although the Armaments Department of the Ministry of Defence was the prime organization responsible for procurement, there also existed a subordinate department with similar responsi-

[23] *1970 German Defence White Paper*, English Language version (Bonn: Press and Information Service of the Federal Govt., 1970), p. 155.

[24] *Ibid.*, pp. 155–56.
[25] *Neuordnung des Rüstungsbereiches—Rahwenerlab und Bericht der Organisations Kommission des BMVg zur Neuordnung des Rüstungsbereiches* [Report of the Defence Minister's commission of inquiry into the Armaments Sector] (Bonn: Des Bundesminister der Verteidigung, 1971).
[26] *1971/72 German Defence White Paper, op. cit.*, pp. 139–40.
[27] *Ibid.*

bilities, the Federal Office for Military Technology and Procurement (BWB). The responsibilities of these two organizations were clarified as a result of the reorganization. The BWB is now mainly concerned with initial research and studies of a technical nature on military requirements. Once the budget for the project exceeds DM100,000, however, responsibility passes to the Armaments Department of the Ministry of Defence, with the BWB acting as their contractor. Given the recent nature of these organization innovations, it is difficult to comment on their effectiveness.

Procurement Style

The predominant feature of the military aircraft programs of the Federal Republic has been the lack of a clear connection to date between the process of selective innovation, often involving the building of prototypes as part of a process of selective innovation, and the military aircraft production program. This has been parallelled by both a marked lack of sustained industrial enthusiasm for expanding production facilities, and a pronounced interest in acquiring technological 'spin-offs' from experimental and development work.

This is illustrated by the three major military V/STOL development projects handled by the industry during the last decade, the VJ101, the VAK191B, and the D031. These have received DM1,500 million in funds from the Federal Ministry of Defence. In addition, the Federal Ministry of Finance has provided over DM450 million for the civil A300B and VFW614 projects, as part of a conscious policy of preventing the aviation industry from becoming over-dependent on military orders.

The Federal government also encouraged the emergence of experimental design teams which were not directly tied to a single production facility. These were ERNO (Entwicklungsring Nord), formed by Hamburger Flugzeugbau Gmbh and EWR (Entwicklungsring Sud), formed by Heinkel, Bolkow and Messerschmidt.[28] ERNO worked with Dornier on the development of the D031 VTOL transport and EWR worked on the design of the VJ101 VTOL interceptor. As a result of mergers of the firms within the industry, however, this separation of design and production work no longer exists. These projects were characterized not only by their experimental nature but also by their heavy reliance on external expertise in both the engine and avionics areas. Thus Rolls Royce in Britain has been concerned in the development of engines for these aircraft on both a contract and collaborative basis, while much of the avionics and other specialized components has been imported from either Britain or the United States. However, these projects have enabled knowledge and expertise to be acquired, such that the Federal Republic could enter the MRCA development project as a theoretically equal partner to Britain. This project has been developed along weapons system lines and has resulted in major tensions between the German experience of license-producing United States avionics equipment and the British desire to develop indigenous equipment within their own comprehensive industrial structure. Doubts seem to still exist in some quarters as to whether MRCA will go into production in Germany, thus maintaining the tradition of designing and building experimental aircraft, which are then not produced.

Production

The revival of the German aircraft industry was based upon collaborative production of aircraft. It mainly centred upon the F1046 project, together with the Fiat G91, Breguet Atlantique, and Transall. In these projects, German industry built up a capability of producing components and also assembling aircraft. Thus a significant, if relatively small, production capacity emerged. It proved to be a pressure group of some significance, in that the Federal government felt bound to insist that opportunities for component production be given to German firms in the arrangements for buying both Phantom aircraft and Chinook helicopters from the United States. The rationale for this seems to be more a desire to maintain production expertise in being, than a desire to prevent unemployment occurring, however.

The Federal government has been attempting to reduce the proportion of the industry's workload derived from defence contracts from the current 70–80% to 50–60%.[29] To this end it has funded development of the VFW614 and A300B airbus, in the hope that these projects will have substantial production runs and thus alleviate the problem of providing production work for the industry.

As in the British industry, the last decade has seen a consolidation of the West German aircraft industry into a few major, but still relatively

---

[28] A useful report on EWR is to be found in *Jane's All the World's Aircraft 1962-63*, pp. 62–66.

[29] *Interavia* 4/1972, pp. 328–33.

small, groups. These are three airframe companies, Dornier AG with 7,733 employees, Messerschmidt-Bolkow-Blohm Gmbh (MBB) with 20,000 employees, and VFW-Fokker Gmbh with 20,296 employees; and an engine company, MTU München Gmbh with 5,550 employees.[30] These consolidations may have increased the bargaining power of the firms vis-à-vis the government, but they still remain small in relation to other major German industrial concerns.

The current problem facing the production side of the industry appears to be the reverse of that facing the British. The industry is not large, especially in the electronics and engine area, yet its current development projects, such as the MRCA and ALPHA jet, suggest that if the Federal Republic's share of production is to be directly related to numerical requirements for these aircraft, a major expansion of production facilities will be necessary. Given the buoyant state of the West German economy, however, this could be very difficult to obtain, and there are also doubts whether it is desirable to switch resources from export to defence industries. The problem for West Germany is therefore not how to exploit to the full its existing industry. Rather it is whether it should be allowed to expand to meet expected orders, given the economic costs involved, and the difficulties that could result if it later became necessary to contract the industry.

COMPARISONS AND SUMMARY

Britain and West Germany face the problems of weapons acquisition from very different research and development bases. The British have a very comprehensive capability in the aerospace field, which the Federal Republic lacks. However, the Federal Republic has experienced a consistency in the basic parameters of defence requirements denied to the British. Both states have found themselves dissatisfied with the effectiveness of their procedures for planning and managing weapons acquisition and have recently implemented major revisions. These have been intended to expose development problems before major expenditure has occurred, to attach

more effective financial parameters to projects, and to more closely integrate the activities of the procurement and user services. However, none of these organizational changes has been fully tested due to the time scale of modern defence projects, and it is therefore impossible to pronounce on their success or failure.

It is difficult to make definitive statements about the procurement style of these two states as to date their formal aspirations and their actual behavior have tended to diverge. Having had wide experience with aerodynamic prototyping and experimental aircraft, the British became formally committed to the idea of building aircraft prototypes on production jigs. Yet due to cancellations, the first aircraft produced solely through this system has yet to appear. The Federal Republic is now formally committed to this system also, having previously pursued a parallel system of license building and experimental prototyping. Both states now find themselves hoping to prove the correctness of their formal procurement style through their collaborative activities with MRCA.

The impetus behind British activities in the aircraft field has been a desire to exploit their expertise, and maintain their production potential. The British have thus been initially interested in expanding the market for their aerospace products by exporting and collaborative work-sharing. In contrast, although the Federal government recognises some pressures to keep a limited production capability in being, it now faces the problem of whether to allow it to expand to meet the demands of its own military market.

Faced with similar technological trends, therefore, the two states have found that their perceptions of the necessary changes in their weapons acquisition systems have been very similar in a number of areas. The contrasts between them seem to stem mainly from the legacies of the past. The major point of interest for future comparative analysis may well be their responses to their experience of jointly using the weapons system concept to develop MRCA. This should provide data which may be used to further determine whether it is possible to make a meaningful comparison between weapons acquisition systems independently of their parent political systems.

[30] *Ibid.*

SYSTEM 37 VIGGEN: SCIENCE, TECHNOLOGY, AND THE DOMESTICATION OF GLORY

INGEMAR DORFER

This article is a superb integration of a case study into the general body of theory on weapons acquisition. Dorfer begins with the classic trilogy—quality, time, and cost—combines it with a strategic triad—foreign policy, technology, and politics—and ends with a discussion of uncertainties operative in the Swedish environment. In short, much of the success of the Swedish system can be attributed to three conditions: a foreign policy of neutrality reduces strategic uncertainty; technological conservatism reduces technical uncertainty; and political consensus reduces program uncertainty.

Ingemar Dorfer is a Special Assistant in the Swedish Ministry of Defense. He holds an undergraduate degree from the University of Lund and a Ph.D. in Government from Harvard University. This article has been expanded into book form and published by the Oslo University Press in 1973 under the title, System 37 Viggen: Arms, Technology and the Domestication of Glory.

The technology gap between the United States and Europe has become a fashionable topic of discourse during the last few years.[1] The mismanagement and failure of European weapons systems has attracted the attention of American professors and European opposition leaders alike. The more unusual, then, would seem this story of a weapons system that made it—the Swedish System 37 Viggen.

The story begins in 1958 when SAAB had already successfully developed three generations of postwar military aircraft: J 29 Tunnan, A 32 Lansen, and J 35 Draken. Of these, Lansen had gone into operation in 1956–57 and ought to have been replaced by another strike aircraft. On the other hand, the rising cost of developing aircraft made it important to spread the research and development (R&D) costs over a longer series than the 200 units that would be needed. The principal choice was now between two basically different aircraft. One option was to develop a light strike plane similar to the Fiat G 91 simultaneously produced in Italy. The costs of developing this plane would be quite modest, in fact much less than for J 35 Draken: thus they could be spread over only 200 units. The other option was to go

ahead with AJ 37 Viggen, a much more ambitious program for an aircraft that would have the same capability as the F-4 Phantom currently developed at McDonnell. To bear the projected R&D costs this aircraft would be constructed as a basic flying platform specially equipped for different missions. This model would, in other words, replace both the strike aircraft (A 32 Lansen) and ultimately also the fighters. The R&D costs, estimated at $260 million, could be spread over 800 aircraft.* The third option, to buy aircraft from abroad, was not given serious thought. At this point the Air Board chose Viggen.

This paper, then, is a case study in the development of Viggen. I shall first introduce a

Editor's note: By 1973 the R&D costs on Viggen had grown from $260 million to $320 million for the attack version, and the program had been reduced to about 400 aircraft, plus whatever numbers can be sold abroad. In 1964 the unit cost of each Viggen was estimated to be $1.9 million, but by 1973 that figure had grown to $4.0 million, thus providing incentive to reduce the total number of aircraft in the projected program. From the perspective of Head's diagram of the weapons acquisition process used in the Introduction to this chapter, the "conceptual" phase for Viggen began in 1959, the first prototype flew on February 8, 1967, and the decision to enter the "production" phase for the first 175 aircraft was made on April 5, 1968. The first production aircraft flew on February 23, 1971, and the Swedish Air Force accepted its first aircraft on June 21, 1971. The first Viggen squadron reached an Initial Operational Capability in early 1972, after a thirteen-year development period.

[1] The London Institute for Strategic Studies has even produced six pamphlets on *Defense Technology and the Western Alliance* (April–October 1967).

Reprinted by permission and with minor changes from Public Policy *Vol. 17 (1968): 201–29. This article was written for Harvard's Seminar on Science and Public Policy, and the study was supported by a grant from the Helge Ax:son Johnson Foundation.*

conceptual framework for analysis of the issues at stake. The analysis itself is summarized in the conclusions—what this weapons system tells us about the weapons acquisition process in Sweden, and what that process tells us about the relationship between science, technology, and politics in that country.

THREE AVENUES TO VIGGEN: A CONCEPTUAL FRAMEWORK

In their book *The Weapons Acquisition Process*, Peck and Scherer[2] define three kinds of predictions for the outcome of a weapons program.

1. Quality, or the expected technical performance and reliability of the resulting weapons system.

2. Development time, or the interval between the start of a development effort and the availability of operational weapons.

3. The cost of development.

A large part of the book is devoted to the exploration of the relationships between these three notions. One of the key sentences reads:[3]

It is possible to make tradeoffs among performance, time and resources; that is, a development group can often ensure meeting or exceeding performance goals by expending additional funds or taking more time.

Here we shall use the three notions of quality, time, and cost not for prediction but as a conceptual framework for description and explanation. Sweden is the only country, with the exception of the four great powers, that currently is in the process of developing a major aircraft weapons system. Because Sweden in many respects is unique, we may hope to arrive in the end at something resembling "The Weapons Acquisition Process: Swedish Version." Thus, our task is to find a second set of concepts corresponding to the first set. We have for this purpose chosen foreign policy, technology, and politics. As we shall explore later, foreign policy in Sweden is closely related to the notion of time. The relationship between quality and technology is more obvious. In the case of politics and cost, finally, the politics of Sweden is the politics of distribution. Different sectors of Swedish society are competing for funds, and the government uses the bureaucracy as administrator and distributor.

The relationships between these factors in the weapons acquisition process and those of the political setting help us to investigate the impact of science and technology on politics. That impact can also be defined as the relationship between distribution and innovation. The point of Robert C. Wood's contribution to *Scientists and National Policy-Making* is that the emphasis of the policy-makers' concern has been shifted from distribution to innovation.[4] Thus our last set of concepts should include these two factors. Distribution obviously relates to politics and cost. Innovation relates to technology and quality. The best concept relating to foreign policy and time would be what the economists, especially those concerned with the allocation of resources, call inertia.

TIME—FOREIGN POLICY—INERTIA

Two kinds of inertia are connected with the Swedish air force—that related to the aircraft in the air force and that related to the aircraft constructors at SAAB. The first kind is inherent in all air forces, and the second is the result of Swedish foreign policy.

The notion of time in this case means obsolescence. The 40 squadrons of the air force currently have aircraft whose age ranges from 13 to 0 years. The tradition of using aircraft in the air force,[5] i.e., the strategy, identifies the problem of obsolete aircraft as a replacement problem. The further tradition of neutrality, strengthened during World War II, identifies the problem of obsolete aircraft as a problem of Swedish, i.e., SAAB, aircraft production.

Strategy: The Air Force. The military geography of Scandinavia is an important factor both in Swedish neutrality and in the military strategy which supports this neutrality. After World War II the doctrine of the Swedish air force was built on the experience of the RAF, especially the experience of the Battle of Britain. This doctrine meant an effort to place the fighter squadrons along the Baltic coast to protect Stockholm and the surrounding cities from air bombardment. Like Britain, Sweden has an English Channel; in a military sense Sweden is an island. The only conceivable invasion of Sweden is a sea invasion. Thus, the task of the Swedish strike squadrons has ever since the war been very specific—to sink

[2]Merton J. Peck and Frederick M. Scherer, *The Weapons Acquisition Process: An Economic Analysis* (Boston: Harvard Graduate School of Business Administration, 1962), p. 19.

[3]*Ibid.*, p. 24.

[4]Robert C. Wood, "Scientists and Politics: The Rise of an Apolitical Elite," in Robert Gilpin and Christopher Wright (eds.), *Scientists and National Policy-Making* (New York: Columbia University Press, 1964), pp. 41–72.

[5]As opposed to a mix of aircraft, missiles, and rockets.

an invasion fleet approaching across the Baltic. Of course such an invasion could be combined with a land invasion in the north, but here communications are poor and defense conditions much more favorable. This explains why the main armament of the strike force (A 32 Lansen) is air-to-sea missiles.

In the case of the fighter force a shift in doctrine occurred around 1957. The emphasis was now shifted to a counter-force doctrine, i.e., instead of trying to protect the cities against bombers, the force was to be used against the enemy's support and strike aircraft as well as enemy airlift. The emergence of IRBMs and the increased foreign airlift capability were, of course, the main reasons behind this shift. As a consequence, the last two models of J 35 Draken—D and F—are interceptors rather than fighters.

The second characteristic of the Swedish air force, which makes it unique, is the base system. In peacetime the bulk of the air force is based on the approximately 20 regular air force bases. In the case of war there are a considerably greater number of war bases equipped with the same ground maintenance equipment and supplies. The real innovation, however, is the use of ordinary highways as combat bases. At the highways selected for this purpose, hardened aircraft hangars and taxi runways are being built, supplies and gasoline are stored, communications and radar stations are set up, and so on. Most of these highway bases will go into operation in the early 1970s. In a matter of a few hours the whole air force can be deployed to these dispersed war bases.[6]

The third characteristic of the air force is also a consequence of Swedish neutrality. The command and control system of the air defense, STRIL 60, has a different electronic profile from the NATO battle control system. This means that Soviet countermeasures in the area of electronics are ineffective against Swedish aircraft, as they are directed against the NATO electronic profile. The resulting less vulnerable Swedish electronic system is a windfall profit of neutrality.

All these three factors influence the required capabilities of the Swedish air force.

1. The task of the attack force implies a certain range and weapons load—air-to-sea missiles.

Compared to Viggen, the range of F-4 Phantom is excessively large for these tasks.[7] In the case of missiles, SAAB is at present developing a special air-to-sea missile—robot 04e—tailored specifically to Viggen. To adapt this missile to F-4 Phantom would require special expensive adjustments.

2. The use of reserve bases, including highways, implies both a certain rugged simplicity and the standardization of ground equipment and a maximum landing and take-off distance. All foreign aircraft except F-4 Phantom require a much longer airfield than the 1650 ft. required by Viggen. Even Phantom requires a longer landing distance than Viggen because carrier hooks cannot be used on the Swedish winter highways. The shorter field length required means that Viggen in wartime can operate even from damaged air bases, using stretches of runways.

3. In the case of electronics, all planes bought from abroad have to have Swedish electronics installed.[8] This takes time, and as the recent Swiss experience with Mirage III has shown, it is also very expensive.

Tradition: The Aircraft Industry. During World War II, when Sweden was neutral, she was dependent on her own production of aircraft. Therefore, the capacity of SAAB was developed, culminating in the production of the jet fighter J 29 Tunnan in 1951. During the next decade SAAB developed and produced A 32 Lansen in strike reconnaissance and fighter versions and J 35 Draken A, B, D, and F. So far the record of SAAB has been extremely successful; not one aircraft system has been cancelled. As a result SAAB has, of course, a monopoly in the Swedish military aircraft market, a market that is comparable to the British or French markets.[9]

The foreign policy of Sweden, defined as nonalignment in peace leading to neutrality in war, has to be based on an independent defense capability. For obvious reasons an aircraft industry is one of the prerequisites of such a capability. As there is no market for civil aircraft in Sweden and as an export industry in this field has been ruled out, SAAB is concentrating on military aircraft. Thus the corporation employs at the present time 14,000 persons, of whom 3,200 are scien-

---

[6]Even though some units are on constant alert, this strategy clearly depends on strategic intelligence warnings. There are two possibilities of aggression against Sweden. The overwhelmingly likely case—aggression in connection with a general war—would probably not include a surprise attack. The other option, a limited attack on Sweden, would more probably take the form of a surprise attack. This option is, however, much less likely.

[7]Because of this range, the Phantom requires fewer bases.

[8]Part of the electronics is always imported from abroad. Thus, the autopilot in AJ37 Viggen was developed by Honeywell.

[9]The Royal Swedish Air Force with its 850 combat aircraft is probably the largest air force outside the USSR in Europe. Recent figures for other air forces are: RAF, 825; Poland, 820; France, 675; U.S. air forces in Europe, 700 (tactical); West Germany, 575. These figures refer to combat aircraft and include the naval air forces of Britain, France, and Germany. See *The Military Balance 1967-68* (London: Institute for Strategic Studies, September, 1967).

tists, engineers, and technicians.[10] The key people are, of course, the small group (300 at the most) of scientists and engineers who develop and produce aircraft. In this function they are irreplaceable in Sweden, and if SAAB wants to keep them SAAB has to go on producing airplanes. The group itself, knowing its value, is of course extremely reluctant to stop developing aircraft. Although representing less than 1 percent of all scientists and engineers in the country, in 1963 they spent about 10 percent of all R&D funds.[11]

Thus both the specific strategy and SAAB's specific tradition of making aircraft designed for that strategy reinforce the tendency to build military aircraft in Sweden.

QUALITY—TECHNOLOGY—INNOVATION

Not only major powers live by their wits. States like Japan, the Netherlands, and Sweden also do, if by wits we mean technology and innovation. Over one-third of Sweden's GNP is derived from the export industry. The products of this industry have to compete with the products of all other states, and thus they have to match or surpass them in quality. This is not always easy when "[T]he world is full of large and lusty industries still clad in their government-issue swaddling clothes."[12] In the military field, Sweden is to a much larger extent than other states of the same technological capability (Japan, the Netherlands, Italy, Canada, Belgium, and even Germany) a transformer, an innovator rather than a receiver. The industry has in this area been influenced by the foreign policy; it can also be argued that the foreign policy is based on this industrial capability.

Let us now explore three aspects of this relationship between military technology and Swedish industry. The first aspect is the process of learning by doing, the Swedish insight that you cannot buy the best weapons from abroad in the future if you do not know what you are buying and the seller knows that you do not know. The second aspect focuses on Sweden as an exporter, the spin-off effect of the armament industry. The third concerns Sweden as a transformer of techniques developed abroad (particularly in the United States) and their use in Swedish industry and, indeed, government.

Viggen is of course the focus of all these concerns; the system done for learning, the system from which the spin-offs spin off, the system that attracts American innovations and transforms them, adapts them, to Swedish conditions.

Learning by Doing: Sweden as Future Buyer. The reason that *The Weapons Acquisition Process* is not concerned with this problem is that the United States does not buy major weapons systems from abroad and does not intend to do so in the future. The reason that the *Plowden Report* is quite concerned is that Britain does, and does so more and more.

Until now only the four great powers and Sweden have had military aircraft of the latest generation.[13] The most common modern aircraft in NATO, F-104 G Starfighter, belongs to the generation preceding F-4 Phantom, S 2 Buccaneer, and Mirage IV-A. On the communist side, only the USSR has the light bomber Brewer.[14] Some states in NATO have received F-5 Freedom Fighter, i.e., Norway, Greece, and Turkey, but even if this is an aircraft of the most recent generation, it is a light aircraft with a reduced capacity compared to Phantom. So far only Britain and Australia have been allowed to buy the F 111. We can find several examples of states that have wanted to buy more modern aircraft but have not been allowed to, as well as states that have been allowed to buy them but were unable to handle them.

In the first case, Turkey would have liked to buy Phantom but had to be content with Freedom Fighter.[15] In the second case, Germany bought Starfighter from the United States and Switzerland bought Mirage III from France, both with disastrous consequences.[16]

---

[10]About 12,000 persons are employed in the Swedish aircraft industry. Corresponding figures are: U.S., 630,000; U.K., 260,000; France, 90,000. See *Report of the Committee of Inquiry into the Aircraft Industry*, appointed by the Minister of Aviation under the chairmanship of Lord Plowden, 1964–65 Cmnd. 2853 (London: Her Majesty's Stationery Office, 1965), pp. 10–12. (Hereafter cited as *Plowden Report.*)

[11]Statistics on Swedish R&D are of recent date and still quite hazardous. In 1963, $32 million out of $240 million R&D were spent on Viggen. (*Kungl. Maj:ts proposition nr 136 ar 1964*, p. 9, brought up to date through interviews.) A certain amount of this sum represents, however, trivial development work. I have, therefore, chosen the figure $24 million as the one most comparable to other sums spent on R&D. Strictly speaking, the number of scientists and engineers working on Viggen was only 0.5 percent, but the distinction is, again, a fuzzy one, especially in international comparisons. I have therefore chosen the safer figure of "less than 1 percent." Labor force figures for industries developing and producing System 37 can be found in *Kungl. Maj:ts proposition nr 110 ar 1965*, p. 9.

[12]*Plowden Report*, p. 33.

[13]Last year this tradition was broken. Thus Iran is acquiring F-4 D Phantom; Peru, Mirage M5; and South Africa, Buccaneer S MK 50.

[14]See *The Military Balance 1967–68.*

[15]*Aviation Week*, October 4, 1965, p. 22.

[16]See Robert Rhodes James, *Standardization and Common Production of Weapons in NATO* (London: Institute for Stra-

It is not at all clear that SAAB will venture to develop a major aircraft system to succeed Viggen in the 1980s and 1990s. The modest standards recently adopted by a country as large as Britain preclude any too optimistic predictions in the Swedish case: "one medium-sized combat aircraft at any one time in the 1970s, or share with other countries in developing two such aircraft."[17] If not even Britain can develop her own military aircraft beyond the 1970s, the only option for Sweden would seem to be cooperation with other countries, or purchase. Both forms of acquisition, of course, infringe on a strict neutrality, a neutrality that in this sense has so far been far stricter than the neutrality of India or Egypt, not to mention Switzerland. There is American-Swedish cooperation on the Viggen project, but the project is still nothing like a joint venture. Unless the foreign policy of Sweden is changed, purchase rather than cooperation is bound to be the future solution.

In the case of purchase the position of Sweden would be like that of Germany rather than Turkey, as Sweden would have had an airplane industry making combat aircraft. In fact, it would be even better, because Sweden so far has produced all generations of combat aircraft. The main reason why the German Starfighter program has been so unsuccessful is the fact that Germany for obvious reasons had no experience with aircraft construction between 1945 and 1957. Both as buyers and later as adapters and developers of this weapons system, they were suddenly placed in a technological environment fundamentally different from that of 1945. The result is now an inefficient and extremely expensive air force.

For Switzerland the results have been even more disastrous. In December 1960, 100 Mirage III-S were ordered to be built under license for a cost of $203 million. In 1965 it was obvious that the cost for the 57 aircraft finally purchased would be $274 million. The main reason that this program fared so badly was the necessity to equip the French-built aircraft with entirely new Swiss TARAN electronics. The Swiss had earlier done so with Venom, built in 1951, but they had halted their own P 16 program in 1956. In other words, they tried to skip one generation of military aircraft and failed. As a result the only up-to-date part of the Swiss air force will be two Mirage III fighter squadrons.

The conclusions to be drawn from the German and Swiss experiences are obvious in the Swedish case. If Sweden pursues her neutrality in the future, she will have to make important modifications in all foreign aircraft she buys to adapt them to Swedish conditions, i.e., change the whole electronics system. Furthermore, if she does not show through her own production and knowledge of the technological issues involved that she can handle the most up-to-date aircraft, no state, meaning the United States, is going to sell that aircraft to Sweden. In fact, Australia is the only state currently buying the most up-to-date American combat aircraft. Here the reasons are more obviously political-strategic.

This conclusion has implications even in the case of Swedish export of military aircraft. From an economic point of view, it would seem to be desirable to spread the high R&D costs over longer series, i.e., to enter the export market for military aircraft. Still, Sweden has so far only sold one type abroad—J 29 Tunnan to Austria in 1961, when the model was ten years old. With the exception of 1960, when J 35 Draken competed with Mirage III for the Swiss order, Sweden has not made any effort to enter this market. The main reason is the simple fact that there are very few qualified buyers outside NATO, and within NATO American aircraft have obvious competitive advantages.[18] In retrospect SAAB is far from unhappy over the outcome of the Mirage-Draken competition in the Swiss case. If Switzerland had chosen Draken, SAAB would by now have had their first failure.

Thus the expectation of future purchases of military aircraft from abroad is a very important reason why Sweden is maintaining her aircraft industry as long as possible, especially as Sweden, in contrast to Britain, is able to produce combat aircraft that are cheaper than the American ones.

Spin-off Effects: Sweden as an Exporter. In 1963 the Swedish R&D funds were spent as follows:[19]

One and one-half percent of the GNP was spent on R&D. Corresponding figures the same year were: France, 1.6; Germany, 1.4; Japan, 1.4; and the United States, 3.4 percent.[20] About 53 percent of all R&D was paid by government. One-

tegic Studies, July 1967), pp. 14–16; and "The Mirage III S and the Swiss Air Force," *Interavia* 12 (1965).

[17] *Plowden Report*, p. 26.

[18] In 1968 Sweden sold 46 Draken to Denmark, indicating a new policy for Swedish aircraft exports.

[19] Based on figures in Sven Brohult, "Problems Associated with Swedish Research Policy," *Svenska Handelsbanken Quarterly Review* (1965); and National Central Bureau of Statistics, Stockholm, *Statistical Reports 1965: Research Statistics I. Research and Development in Technology and Natural Sciences in Industry, 1963–1965*, p. 89.

[20] *OECD Observer* 30 (October 1967).

Table 1.

	$ in millions	%
Government, civilian (universities, etc.)	52	22
Space	2	1
Atomic Energy	34*	14
Defense Research Establishment	12	5
Industry: military	44	18
Industry: civilian	96	40
Total	240	100

*Whereof about $17 million was paid by industry.

third of all industrial research was military. Military research, atomic energy, and space absorbed almost 40 percent of all R&D funds. The annual R&D funds spent on Viggen, 1963–67, were about $38 million. The program is, in other words, roughly as large as the civilian Atomic Energy Program. Although part of the $38 million spent annually was spent on relatively trivial development work, the figure is a valid one in comparison with other *industrial* R&D figures. Thus Viggen absorbed 23 percent of all industrial and 73 percent of all industrial military R&D funds. Despite its large share of the R&D funds, System 37 in 1965 counted for only 25 percent of the military output, or 0.64 percent of the industrial production. The military output in all counted for only 2.6 percent of the total industrial production. Less than 1 percent of all Swedish scientists and engineers were employed by the project.[21]

By deduction, we can see that these scientists and engineers each spent more than ten times as much as the average scientist and engineer in Sweden.[22] The whole military industry spent in the early 1960s on the average 13 times as much on R&D as the civilian industry, whereas the military industry excluding System 37 spent on the average four times as much on R&D as the civilian industry. System 37 spent on the average three times as much on R&D as the rest of the military industry, but then the system was, of course, in its R&D phase, whereas the military industry as a whole spanned the whole spectrum from research to production.

Thus it is clear that Viggen occupies an extraordinarily important role in Swedish research

and development; together with the Atomic Energy Program it is by far the most important program. The question is what effect the 23 percent of all industrial research funds spent on System 37 has on the rest of the economy.

On the whole the technological fall-out seems to be just as large from the civilian to the military sector in the case of these industries as vice versa.[23] The most important technological fall-out is probably *within* the military sector, i.e., innovations that are useful for army and navy weapons are made in the development of this aircraft. With the notable exception of BOFORS, these firms are also the main producers of sophisticated weapons systems for the army and navy. In contrast to the American firms,[24] all major Swedish weapons producers are half in and half out of the defense business. Because military and civilian production are mixed in the same firms to a much higher degree than in the United States, technological fall-out *in both directions* would seem to be higher.

Thus about 10 percent of all Swedish R&D funds were used by 200 scientists and engineers in developing System 37. Even at the height of the development stage, these people counted for only 30 percent of all scientists and engineers employed by the firms producing System 37.[25] Because the production of these firms is evenly distributed between military and civilian production, the technological fall-out is considerable. All of these firms are export industries; in the case of LME, 60 percent of the Swedish production is exported. Still, the spin-off effects of the

[21] *Detta är Viggen* (Stockholm: 1964), p. 22.
[22] In 1958 the British aircraft industry spent on the average ten times as much on R&D as the average manufacturing firm. In the United States the comparable figure was 6.5. (*Plowden Report*, p. 7.)

[23] Thus, the digital computer developed by SAAB for Viggen is the fourth generation of computers in Sweden.
[24] Carl Kaysen, "Improving the Efficiency of Military Research and Development," in Carl J. Friedrich and Seymour E. Harris (eds.), *Public Policy*, vol. XII (Cambridge, Mass.: Harvard Graduate School of Public Administration, 1963), p. 231.
[25] See footnote 11.

civilian production seems to be as large as the military spin-off effects. The largest Swedish corporation of all, ASEA, relies almost entirely on civilian orders and export in a branch that is as competitive as those branches represented in the Viggen project—electronics and electrical engineering.

McNamarism: Sweden as an Importer. System 37 has not only caused innovations in the area of Swedish technology; the most important innovations stimulated by the project have been in the area of systems management in its broadest sense. These innovations are all transformations of American ideas brought to the forefront by the Kennedy administration. The reasons that System 37 is the project that has acted as a magnet and catalyst for these innovations are mainly two. First of all, the project is the most expensive weapons project undertaken by Swedish industry, the largest unit ever bought by the government. Secondly, the project was launched at the same time that Robert McNamara took office in the U.S. Defense Department, bringing with him a revolution in defense planning. We shall here explore the two most important areas of innovation caused or stimulated by System 37—systems management and procurement on the one hand and program budgeting on the other. In the area of systems management and procurement, we shall distinguish among the weapons system approach, the planning and progress reporting methods, and finally the contract methods.

The weapons system approach has its origin in the crash program reforms connected with the development of the Atlas missile in 1954.[26] In Sweden earlier aircraft—the J 29, the A 32, and the J 35—had been developed through mutual contracts between the Air Board and the different industries, SAAB, FLYGMOTOR, LME, AGA, and so on. Now, in the case of System 37, the principle of a main contractor was introduced. SAAB was made prime contractor, and with two exceptions all other corporations were made subcontractors under SAAB. The exceptions are FLYGMOTOR, which has a special contract with the Air Board, and AGA, developing the communications radio, which has a special status as side contractor. As a consequence SAAB has formed a special group for supervision called System 37 Central Planning. On the government side this group is matched by System 37 Group, recently strengthened through the transfer of the head of the SAAB group to the chairmanship of the government group. As a re-

sult of the experience with System 37, more Swedish weapons are now developed through the weapons system approach. The most notable example is the navy coast-to-sea and ship-to-ship missile Robot 08, for which SAAB was appointed prime contractor in 1965.

In order to coordinate the progress among SAAB and the subcontractors, a new technique for the solution of systems management problems was needed. In anticipation of the System 37 approach, SAAB had already started experimentation with the PERT system during the fall of 1961. The light aircraft SAAB 105 was the project on which this experiment in planning was first used. Drawing on the experiences of this experiment, SAAB introduced the PERT system for the planning progress reporting and control of System 37 in 1962.[27] All subcontractors are connected through this network, which gives the prime contractor an over-all view of the system progress every two weeks. Later in 1962 the PERT system was introduced also by the Atomic Energy Program and the Missile Bureau of the Air Board.

In the area of incentive system, the large total cost of System 37 has increased the interest in this aspect of the weapons acquisition process. *Flygmaterielberedningen*, appointed in 1964, is the first special investigation committee to oversee the efficient conduct of a weapons system development in Sweden. Simultaneously in 1964, and undoubtedly inspired by the current American interest in cost-effectiveness and incentive studies, a special study of the weapons procurement process in the United States, Canada, and Great Britain was originated in Sweden. On the basis of preliminary conclusions of this report, the contract between SAAB and the Air Board was renegotiated in March 1965. The government was given broader supervisory powers over the project at the same time that SAAB was given greater cost-effectiveness incentives. The study was subsequently published in December 1965,[28] whereupon its author was appointed Under Secretary of Defense.

Program budgeting in the United States has its origin in the RAND Corporation. Even if these

[26]Kaysen, *op. cit.,* pp. 241, 242. The year in which the system approach came into general use was 1953 (*ibid.,* p. 233).

[27]*The USAF PERT Time System Description Manual* was published only in September 1963. See David Novick (ed.), *Program Budgeting* (Cambridge, Mass.: Harvard University Press, 1965), p. 63, n. 5. SAAB was the first European user of the system.

[28]SOU 1965:69 *Om upphandling av försvarsmateriel* (Stockholm, 1965). The author, S-G Olhede, previously had worked for the Scandinavian Airlines System. A parallel study overhauled the organization of the government agencies purchasing military hardware. *SOU 1966:11 Tygförvaltningens centrala organisation* (Stockholm, 1966).

ideas were developed as early as 1954, it was with the appointment of McNamara's team from RAND that the method was first introduced into the Defense Department, beginning with FY 1963.[29] In Sweden the concept of program budgeting was also first developed on the military side, notably in the studies of the Defense Research Establishment. Again, it was System 37 which gave the concept the break-through, however. One of the first tasks of *Flygmaterielberedningen* in 1964 was to order the Defense Research Establishment to carry out studies of the project from the point of view of cost-effectiveness analysis. Within these studies pilot studies on program budgeting of the defense budget were carried out.[30] In fact, as early as the defense budget for FY 1965 (introduced in March 1964), program elements in the air force budget, notably J 35 Draken and System 37, were singled out.[31] As a result the National Bureau of Rationalization started a study of program budgeting in 1965. Aside from the Defense Research Establishment, experiments with program budgeting are currently underway in numerous federal agencies.[32]

Although no formal decision has yet been made about the introduction of program budgeting in the whole federal establishment, the number of pilot studies and the amount of experimentation represents, as usual in Sweden, a *de facto* decision. Thus, it is safe to predict that Sweden soon will follow the American pattern of over-all federal program budgeting established in 1965.

COST—POLITICS—DISTRIBUTION

With two exceptions Sweden has had Social Democratic governments since 1932. The election results are extremely stable. With the exception of the small Communist party, all parties have reached a broad consensus on all major political questions. Thus, the election campaigns center on the allocation of resources; the conservatives want to distribute the resources slightly differently than do the social democrats; the liberals and the agrarians take a position in between. Politics in Sweden has, as it were, almost reached the stage of public administration. The competition for funds is cast in bureaucratic and administrative rather than ideological terms. It would have come as a great surprise to both Lenin and Bernstein that the first socialist country where the state actually is withering away is Sweden. Many of the state's functions have been taken over by the organizations. All Swedes are organized. In charge of this distribution of public funds to the organizations is the bureaucracy. As in France, the civil service is highly paid, has great prestige, and is very professional.

Because distribution forms such an important part of Swedish politics, the annual budget presented to Parliament is the focus of great political interest. The budget has been the instrument for implementing the three great reforms in Swedish politics during the last three decades—the social reforms, labor legislation, and so forth during the 1930s, the policy of high progressive taxes in the 1940s, and the pension reforms of the 1950s. Gradually these reforms, introduced by the social democrats, have become part of the political consensus.[33]

This background on the nature of politics, or rather lack of politics in the traditional sense, in Sweden is necessary for the appreciation of the cost aspect of System 37 Viggen. In a country where the efficient allocation of resources has become a cult, the allocation of such vast resources to so big a project would seem to be a decision requiring the utmost consideration. This, of course, is true only if there are competing sectors of the economy and if these competing sectors actually are aware of their competitive position, and as a consequence of this fact actively compete. As in all competitions, we have to distinguish between the rules of the game and the players. As we shall see, the rules limit to a very large extent the action that the players can take.

Rules: the Budgetary System. About 60 percent of the Swedish R&D funds are allocated through the federal budget, including all R&D funds to the universities. The universities receive their funds under the heading of the Department of Education; System 37, of course, under the

---

[29]Novick, *op. cit.*, p. 87. See also Charles J. Hitch, *Decision-Making for Defense* (Berkeley and Los Angeles: University of California Press, 1965), II, "Planning—Programming—Budgeting."

[30]E.g., Ingemar Stahl, *Kostnadsberäkningar och budgetering* (Stockholm: Planning Section, Swedish Defense Research Establishment, November 1964).

[31]*Kungl. Maj:ts proposition nr 136 ar 1964*, pp. 3, 4.

[32]In January 1966 the Defense Department formed a working group on program budgeting. The defense budget for FY 1968 has been presented in both conventional and program budgeting terms. The present goal is to introduce program defense budgeting fully in FY 1970. (*Försvarsdepartementet*, Stencil, 1967: 2).

[33]For an interpretation of the pension reforms as a holding action, see Seymour Martin Lipset, "Class Structure and Politics," in Stephen R. Graubard (ed.), *A New Europe?* (Boston: Beacon Press, 1963), p. 353. A sophisticated analysis of the battle of the pensions is Björn Molin, "Swedish Party Politics: A Case Study," in *Scandinavian Political Studies 1966: 1* (Helsinki, 1966).

Department of Defense; the Atomic Energy Program under the heading of the Department of Industry.

Thus the defense budget is the key budget for our purpose and needs further consideration. Since 1948 the defense budgets in Sweden have been supplemented by so-called "rolling plans" for equipment and hardware, approved and renewed each year for the coming seven-year period.[34] In the case of the air force this method of planning ahead has been very helpful in the successful development of the three generations of combat aircraft. Through these plans a large proportion of the defense budget is already determined long in advance. The principle of a defense budget sponsored jointly by the four democratic parties was established in 1936 and confirmed during the war in 1942. In 1958 this principle of agreement on a four-year defense budget was supplemented by some innovations cast in terms of the pension reforms. The emerging result is the notion of a "welfare defense."

The keystone in this budgeting system is a so-called kostnadsram, a study carried out by the High Command to explore how much can be achieved at a certain cost. Instead of first determining the goals and then defining the costs, as in the McNamara budgets, this method first defines the cost and then determines what can be achieved at this cost. The habit of first determining the cost derives from the tradition of fixing defense outlays at a rather constant percentage of the GNP—about 5 percent. This kostnadsram is then used by the committee of MP's that is traditionally appointed every four years to work out an agreement on the defense budgets for the coming four-year period. The kostnadsram is supplemented by an elaborate system of price and cost indices worked out every year to calculate the rate of inflation and to estimate a constant price level. Finally, the system has been completed by an annual 2.5 percent increase in funds "for technical development." Thus, the limits of the defense budgets are pretty much fixed in advance. The armed services are restricted to competition for funds that are fixed long beforehand.

Because the R&D budget for System 37 and that for civilian R&D are under two different headings—defense and education—the R&D funds for the respective programs are not seen as competing with each other. Indeed, because System 37 R&D funds are part of the whole sum devoted each year to System 37, which is part of the air force budget, which is part of the defense budget, very few university professors seem to have realized how large a proportion of the research funds actually is spent on System 37. The institutions represented in *Flygmaterielberedningen* are the Departments of Defense, Industry and Finance, and the Defense Research Establishment. No representative for nonmilitary research and development is a member, still less a representative for the universities proper. For the cost of developing Viggen, Sweden could expand the number of institutes of technology from three to eight. This type of argument has never been used publicly.

The second competition influenced by the rules is the narrower competition between the services. Here the air force has had the advantage ever since World War II of being the most glamorous of the services, a very large and powerful organization in proportion to Sweden's total resources. Since that time the air force has received about 45 percent of the defense budget compared to the army's 40 percent and the navy's 15 percent. In terms of equipment and hardware the air force is of course even more predominant; 60 percent compared to 25 percent and 15 percent. As the defense budgets are so little flexible and as they are fixed for such long periods in advance, the optimal budgeting strategy is the art of commitment, or the tactics of burning one's bridges.[35] If a service is able to commit itself to a large, expensive weapons system far enough in advance, the expenses for this weapons system will be included in the rolling seven-year plans, and it will be very difficult for the parliamentary committees to cut any part of *this* percentage of the defense budget. Here the air force has, of course, had the advantage of having large units to commit itself to—the different generations of combat aircraft. In this respect Viggen is no exception; on the contrary, the very size of the project made an early commitment the more attractive. The other services have caught on only recently; the effort of the army in 1960 to go ahead on its own and buy Hawk ground-to-air missiles ended with only one Hawk battalion's being purchased. Now the army has a better project going with battle tank S, developed by BOFORS. The navy, which has fought a losing battle since the air force took over many of its functions with the 1958 defense budget, is now concentrating on the A14 submarine developed jointly by Kockum and the Karlskrona naval shipyard.

[34]SOU 1963:5 *Försvarskostnaderna budgetaren 1963/ 67*, p. 100.

[35]Thomas C. Schelling, "Bargaining Power: The Power to Bind Oneself," *The Strategy of Conflict* (Cambridge, Mass.: Harvard University Press, 1963), pp. 22–28.

The budgetary system is therefore both a great stimulus for the air force to commit itself at an early stage to a project like System 37, and a blinder to comparing R&D budgets on different projects in Sweden. If any institution is against Viggen in Sweden it is not the universities, because they are not aware of any competition.

Players: Institutions. The rules have prevented the potentially most dangerous challenger from entering the game: the universities. In terms of the four broad functions in government and public affairs, it is the scientific function represented by the scientists that has not acted as a check or balance on the other three. The other three functions are the professional, the administrative, and the political.[36] The blurring of these three in Sweden is best personified by the Under Secretary of Defense, Olhede, a professional who on political grounds was appointed administrator. The project that enabled him to combine these three talents was Viggen. For the sake of clarity we can still identify four institutions with the three functions, the armed forces[37] and industry with the professional, the Department of Finance with the administrative, and the government itself with the political function.

As we have already seen, the air force is all for Viggen. The other services cannot do anything about it at this stage, as the project is already well under way and as a cut in the air force budget might create a backlash which would cut into the army and navy budgets also. Instead of fighting Viggen they have tried to find similar big projects to which to commit themselves. In the case of the armed forces, then, System 37 has had a curious spillover effect on budgetary technology.

Industry is also delighted with Viggen. We have already commented on the spin-off effects Viggen may produce in civilian industry. In contrast to the situation in the United States, no part of industry is dissatisfied with the way government has distributed the related projects to different producers. Industry is not dissatisfied because in the Swedish defense industry there are no losers; everyone is a monopolist in his own branch. The alternative to Viggen would clearly be purchase from abroad, and this is not an alternative that Swedish industry favors. In addition to the fall-out effects on technology, there are fall-out effects in terms of prestige and glamor on Swedish technology and industry. Thus, all professionals are for it.

The administrators are the members of *Flygmaterielberedningen*, best symbolized by its representative from the Department of Finance. As we shall see, this is the single Swedish institution that would have any reason to be against Viggen. Even if cost is the focus of all Swedish politics, cost is the specific concern of the Department of Finance. The job of finance is to determine what weapons system that has been declared efficient enough by the military experts is least expensive. The studies of *Flygmaterielberedningen* indicated that Viggen would cost less than F-4 Phantom. The operational costs for Phantom would be 30 percent higher than the same costs for Viggen.[38] In addition, expensive adjustments of Phantom to Swedish conditions would have to be carried out. The cost development of the project is continuously followed, and the initial commitment to produce the whole series of attack, reconnaissance, and fighter versions is now in practice a commitment to produce the attack and reconnaissance versions. If by the time the fighter version is produced there are foreign aircraft of the same quality and competitive prices, the fighter version will be taken under reconsideration.[39]

The government, finally, is concerned with costs, but even more with the other aspects of Viggen. The decision has been a decision supported by all parties; in this sense Viggen is unlikely to cause a cabinet crisis if it fails. Still, the government has now put its prestige, and the prestige of Sweden, behind the project, and it is likely that it will try to carry it through at all reasonable cost. In this area of politics, not the least important aspect in Sweden is the politics of full employment. Any crisis connected with Viggen in the future will be cast in terms of unemployment, not in terms of lost progress in technology. All in all, overwhelming reasons tell the government to support Viggen.

---

[36] Don K. Price, *The Scientific Estate* (Cambridge, Mass.: Belknap Press of Harvard University Press, 1965), p. 135.

[37] As long as Viggen is under development, the military are professionals rather than administrators. In this phase their function is to advise and cooperate with industry on the technical qualities of Viggen, necessary to perform certain military functions. Once Viggen gets into operation, the military become administrators.

[38] *Kungl. Maj:ts proposition nr 110 ar 1965*, p. 14.

[39] In March 1967 the Defense Department committed itself to buy 83 AJ 37 attack aircraft and 17 Sk 37 trainers at a production cost of $210 million. If only 200 Viggens are produced, the total cost will be $685 million—$265 million for R&D, $420 million for production—$3.4 million per unit. Because the R&D costs are "sunk," the comparison price with foreign aircraft is the production price—$2.1 million. (Source: *Kungl. Maj:ts proposition nr 110 ar 1967*, pp. 72–82.) In 1965 the unit cost for F-111 was estimated at $7 million (*Plowden Report*, p. 36).

Thus we have seen that only one institution, the Department of Finance, has any reason at all to seek an alternative to Viggen. The American checks and balances among the scientists, professionals, administrators, and politicians do not exist in this case in Sweden.

TWO CONCLUSIONS: I. THE SWEDISH WEAPONS ACQUISITION PROCESS

Time, Quality, and Cost Reconsidered. We have explored System 37 Viggen in terms of time, quality, and cost. One of the main conclusions of *The Weapons Acquisition Process* is that these three inputs are interchangeable in the United States. The question is whether the same conclusion can be reached in the Swedish case.

As we have seen, the nature of the Swedish polity has a very great influence on these three factors. Time, meaning obsolescence, is seen solely as a replacement problem. Quality is decided on the basis of the resources available rather than in terms of the quality of the potential enemy's weapons; in terms of skilled manpower, including scientists and engineers. Cost, finally, is decided by the budgetary system.

The principle of replacing one-third of the Swedish air force every five years makes quality the least flexible of our three categories. Because all Swedish aircraft developments are top priority programs and because only one aircraft is usually developed at a time, it is simply impossible to switch from one program in progress to another of less quality and cost.[40] The solution is rather to expand the time during which obsolete aircraft are in service, as has been done in the case of A 32 Lansen, and to produce the new aircraft later than originally planned.[41] Thus, in the Swedish context, there is no substitute for quality.

This fact has given the Swedish equivalent of a military crash program a very special meaning. Because all resources are already tied up in the original program, a crash program simply cannot be carried out in Sweden. Thus a Swedish military crash program means the purchase of aircraft from abroad. As we have seen, the regular aircraft production program gives Sweden an advantage in such a contingency—the process of having learned by doing.

Cost is the second inflexible category in the Swedish weapons acquisition process. The notion of a "welfare defense budget" fixes military costs many years in advance. Overruns in cost simply mean that the fixed expenditures of the future are used up earlier than predicted.[42] As a result, time is substituted for cost. This principle of pre-planned costs is of course violated whenever a crash program, i.e., purchase from abroad, is carried out. This violation is always permitted when it can be justified in terms of external danger, and it can always be so justified when crash programs are considered necessary.

Thus time is the only flexible variable of our three, a fact that would seem to have some long-range importance for Swedish foreign policy. Instead of raising the costs for the delivery of a planned number of aircraft of a predetermined quality and at a predetermined date, the date is simply postponed. If the costs for delivering a certain number of aircraft during a certain year are too high, the delivery process is spread out over a longer time period, and the number of aircraft delivered that year is decreased.

Thus changes in Swedish weapons programs are usually changes in time, i.e., first delivery dates, not changes in cost and almost never changes in quality.

Internal and External Uncertainty: Sweden as Suboptimizer. In the American context the distinction between the internal and external uncertainties of a weapons program is a useful one. The internal uncertainties "relate to the possible incidence of unforeseen technical difficulties in the development of a specific weapons system."[43] External uncertainties "relate to factors external to an individual project and yet affecting the outcome and course of that project." External uncertainties are of three kinds:

1. The pace of technological change in weaponry;
2. Changes in strategic requirements;
3. Shifts in government policy.[44]

The over-all determining factor in the Swedish weapons acquisition process is the fact that the Swedish problem is a problem of suboptimization. The question "Defense against what?"[45] is to a very large extent answered by "defense against a foreign aggressor under the circumstances of a balance of power between the Soviet Union and the United States." The Swedish

---

[40]There may, however, be some pressure to slacken the demands on quality for separate units of the weapons system, i.e., armament, leading to imbalance.

[41]The first Viggens go into operation in 1971. The Lansens they replace will by then be 11-15 years old.

[42]One of the risks of the rigid cost limits is that only the R&D costs are covered when the total sum for the program is spent.

[43]Peck and Scherer, *op. cit.*, p. 24.

[44]*Ibid.*

[45]Charles J. Hitch and Roland N. McKean, *The Economics of Defense in the Nuclear Age* (Cambridge, Mass.: Harvard University Press, 1960), chap. 2.

defense makes sense only if it is assumed that the aggressor can devote only a *part* of his resources to the conquest of Sweden. Through a strong Swedish defense the potential enemy will have to increase this part out of proportion to the expected gains, and he will, therefore, refrain.

The problem of suboptimization is relevant both to the internal and the external aspects of a weapons system program in Sweden; in fact, the American distinction is blurred.

To evaluate the nature of uncertainty to the internal (technological) development in Swedish weapons programs, we will find another scheme in *The Weapons Acquisition Process*[46] useful:

Research and Development Steps and Activities

    I. The formation and empirical verification of theories about parameters of the physical world.
    II. The creation and testing of radically new physical concepts, components, devices and techniques.
    III. The identification, modification, and combination of feasible or existing concepts, components, and devices to provide a distinctly new application practical in terms of performance, reliability and cost.
    IV. Relatively minor modifications of existing components, devices and systems to improve performance, increase reliability, reduce cost, and simplify application.

On this scale the United States and the USSR start at Step I; Britain, France, and Sweden at Steps II and III. Italy's Fiat G 91 is a Step III development, whereas the German adaptation of Starfighter belongs to Step IV.

Thus most original risks connected with a weapons program development (Steps I and II) have already been solved before Sweden begins such a program. The programs are, in other words, always within "the state of the art." The internal uncertainties remain, but they are almost all uncertainties of the Step III and Step IV types. The other uncertainties have usually already been solved abroad.

The external uncertainties are also diminished in this Swedish process of suboptimization. The pace of technological change is less important to Sweden than to the United States. As long as the pace of technological change is roughly equal in the two superpowers, the balance on which Swedish foreign policy depends will be maintained, and the Swedish problem remains a

problem of suboptimization: the problem of meeting aggression at the level prescribed by the rules of the game. These rules, dependent on the balance of power, prescribe the level of war for which Sweden is preparing in case of an attack. This is the level of warfare where the Swedish weapons are comparatively most efficient. The external uncertainty of technological change becomes relevant to Sweden only if the change in the East is so much faster than the change in the West that the balance is upset. In this case the Swedish problem moves from the area of suboptimization to the area of optimization, a problem which Sweden cannot handle. So far France is the only state which has attempted to take this step, and it is not entirely clear whether she has succeeded or not. It is entirely clear, however, that if France has succeeded, her success has been dependent on the very balance of power that she rejects.

The second aspect of external uncertainty, change in the strategic requirements, is only the other side of the same coin in Sweden's case. The changes in strategic requirements may be rapid on the top level; the emergence of the ICBMs is the best example. On the lower level these changes are less rapid and less drastic. At the present time these changes on the sublevel which is relevant to Sweden are not important enough or rapid enough to introduce major uncertainty in the ten-year development process of a combat aircraft.

The third external uncertainty, shifts in government policy, is again an unimportant issue in Sweden; unimportant because the government does not change and because defense is not a partisan issue. The only way a project can risk uncertainty is through cost overruns but, as we have seen, then the result is usually overruns in time rather than cancellation.

Thus, the uncertainties connected with weapons projects in the United States are to a very large extent diminished in Sweden, through Sweden's position as a suboptimizer. We have already seen that it is difficult to exchange time, quality, and cost in Swedish weapons developments. But it is not only difficult; it is also much less necessary.

II. SCIENCE AND TECHNOLOGY IN SWEDISH POLITICS: INNOVATIONS IN THE DOMESTICATION OF GLORY

The Swedish "spectrum from truth to power" is the same as the American: the scientists, the professionals, the administrators, and the poli-

[46]Peck and Scherer, *op. cit.*, p. 28.

ticians.[47] Let us see what Viggen has told us about this spectrum in Sweden.

A general remark is necessary as an introduction. In the United States the two most important groups are the "pure" groups, those representing all "truth" and all "power," the scientists and the politicians. The scientists are important because they are at the frontier of knowledge; they are in competition with scientists in other states, especially those in the USSR. If they do not provide new theories and insights for the American engineers to build on, nobody else will, not to the extent that is sufficient for the United States. Like the British industrialists of the nineteenth century, they have only themselves as a guidepost; everyone else defines himself in relation to them.

The politicians are the other most important group. Because their business is to wield power, they wield more power than any other politicians elsewhere. Again, as in the case of the scientists, the power represented by America is the guidepost for other politicians abroad, whose own power is very much influenced by this guidepost. In contrast to their European brethren the American administrators are exactly that: administrators and not wielders of power.

These characteristics of the American spectrum have implications for the Swedish spectrum. Its most significant result is that the scientists and politicians who are most important to Sweden are not inside Sweden but outside. The professionals and the administrators who are most important to Sweden, as a contrast, are clearly Swedes.[48]

The example of Viggen brings out this point. The scientists who made Viggen possible are the scientists outside Sweden who solved the problems connected with Step I (and Step II) on our R&D staircase. Where Sweden comes in, it is the professionals, the engineers, that matter, not the scientists. The politicians who made Viggen possible are, again, the politicians outside Sweden who have decided certain foreign policies which make the neutrality of Sweden possible. The Swedish problem is a suboptimization problem because foreign politicians have decided to maintain a balance of power. For the solution of this suboptimization problem, Viggen is ideal. It would be far less successful as a tool for the solution of a problem posed in terms of total deterrence and defense, independent of the balance of power. The politicians' limited impact on Swedish foreign policy is duplicated by self-imposed limits in Swedish domestic politics. Because there is consensus on so much, there certainly is agreement on defense policy. The power of the politicians is diminished when everyone agrees on the basic principles. The implementation becomes more important, and this, of course, gives the power to the administrators. Thus in defense policy and foreign policy the two middle groups, the professionals and the administrators, have the greatest influence because the two outer groups, the scientists and the politicians, who in the United States define the ground rules, have their ground rules defined in Sweden by their peers abroad.[49] In domestic policy the situation is the same. The engineers are more important than the scientists for the same reasons that we have already outlined. The administrators are more important than the politicians because of the consensus.

The essence of Viggen is the domestication of glory—a tool for defense, not attack, for home consumption, not export, a shining Swedish device that one shows to the outside world only so that others will know that it exists and may be dangerous, not so that they may admire it or try to copy it, like the French *force de dissuasion*. Whereas France wants that force in order to play the game, Sweden wants Viggen in order to be able to continue to stay out of the game.[50] At the same time that Sweden wants to stay out of the game, she wants to transmit rules to the world, based on her domestic experience; rules to obtain consensus, rules so that the game may stop.[51] To create Viggen the engineers and the administrators are better fitted than the scientists and the politicians, whose vulnerable position can be revealed through international comparisons.

This discussion leads to two conclusions about the impact of science and technology on Sweden,

---

[47]Price, *op. cit.*, chap. 5.

[48]This idea can be generalized. In the United States, the scientists and the politicians have the most power. In smaller highly developed states like Sweden, the administrators and professionals do. In less developed states with a tradition of civil service, the administrators have large power, whereas there is a great lack of professionals (India). In the least developed states, again, the power is exclusively with the politicians (the Congo).

[49]Nowhere is this point better shown than in the social sciences, which in Sweden are all too often dedicated to "the concept of conventional wisdom." See John Kenneth Galbraith, *The Affluent Society* (New York: Mentor Books, 1958), p. 19.

[50]"Proliferation probably will not stop with the present fifth nuclear power (China), but this does not mean that it will be unlimited, at least in the foreseeable future. Switzerland and Sweden would use such weapons to protect their neutrality—in other words, they will remain outside the major game." Raymond Aron, "The Anarchical Order of Power," *Daedalus* XCV (Spring 1966): 495.

[51]Note, for instance, the recent creation by the Swedish government of an International Institute for Peace and Conflict Research: SIPRI.

her politics, and her foreign policy. In the United States innovations in politics are introduced by new politicians who come in with new administrations every eight years. In Sweden the government does not change, i.e., the innovations are not introduced by the politicians. The function of new administrations in the United States is in Sweden often performed by new large technological projects, like Viggen. America needed a McNamara to introduce program budgeting in the federal machinery, with all the implications that it will have for politics. Sweden needed Viggen, seen against the background of a McNamara, to do the same. When technique becomes more important than political philosophy, innovation in management carries the promise of political innovation. In the United States new politicians introduce new innovations in politics. In Sweden old administrators introduce the same innovations, cooperating with professionals on new technological projects.

In the case of foreign policy, "objective" developments in science are as important as new policies introduced by new administrations in the United States. The task of Sweden so far has been to suboptimize her defense, a function which has been performed by the engineers rather than the scientists. Here no innovations have taken place; the task of Viggen is precisely to maintain the status quo. We have seen how the lack of checks and balances among the four estates has made it possible for Sweden to devote 10 percent of her R&D resources to a single weapons system. As we have seen, the engineers

are more important than the scientists in Sweden for objective reasons. They are also more important for subjective reasons, because they to a larger extent embody the domestication of glory.[52] Whereas the administrators can introduce innovation in politics, the engineers cannot introduce innovations in foreign policy. In Sweden the administrators have a higher propensity to innovate than the politicians, while the scientists, as everywhere, have a higher propensity to innovate than the professionals (the engineers). In America the scientists and the politicians have power which leads to innovations in both domestic and foreign policy. In Sweden the professionals and the administrators have power which leads to innovations in domestic politics but not in foreign policy.

Thus, the scientists who are able to create innovations in Swedish foreign policy are outside Sweden; only through "objective" scientific discoveries can the international framework be changed, the framework on which Swedish foreign policy is dependent.

Until that happens the two groups best fitted for the domestication of glory, the two inner groups, the professionals and the administrators, will continue to construct that which shows Sweden at her competitive best: weapons designed to maximize the power permitted by the international framework, to protect the values defined by the consensus—weapons like Viggen.

---

[52]Note the parallel of the private firm. Applied research is much more popular than basic research.

THE INDIAN DEFENSE INDUSTRY: TECHNOLOGY AND RESOURCES

WAYNE A. WILCOX

India uses two primary forms of weapons acquisition—direct purchase and license-building, although there has been a definite shift from the former to the latter in recent years. Despite the constraints of the domestic economy, India's stated policy is autarky, and she is moving slowly toward that goal. The two high-priority programs are in nuclear and space technology with the obvious weapons fallout that would result.

Wayne A. Wilcox is Professor and Chairman of the Political Science Department at Columbia University. He is currently on a leave of absence and is Cultural Affairs Officer at the U.S. Embassy in London. His publications include Pakistan: The Consolidation of a Nation *(1963)*; India, Pakistan, and the Rise of China *(1964)*; Asia and United States Policy *(1967); and editor of* Protagonists, Power and the Third World *(1970) and* Asia in World Politics *(1972).*

Arms control policies tailored to less developed countries (LDCs) emphasize the leverage which external powers possess because of the industrial backwardness of most of the new states. Without the transfer of arms, licenses, or plant, most poor countries would be unable to field modern military forces. In the fields of aircraft and missiles, nuclear weapons, and advanced command and control systems only a very few countries possess the essential information, resources, capital, and research and development structures necessary for production. Conventional-weapon arms-limitation policies, therefore, presuppose *arms transfer* controls.

India is, like most LDCs, dependent upon foreign supply of many weapons systems, licenses, and/or crucial components. But unlike many other new states, it possesses a growing indigenous design and production capability in defense industry. Moreover, the pattern of its "dependence" upon external powers shows how difficult it would be for any one of those powers to exercise leverage over fundamental Indian security choices.

Nearly one-fourth of the total sales of all Indian companies are made by foreign-controlled firms[1] and they show higher profits and more rapid growth than Indian private enterprise. They tend to be in technologically sophisticated fields, such as petrochemicals, pharmaceuticals, data processing and office equipment, and communications. These tend to be important in defense industry, and the government of India has made a conscious effort to build equivalent capabilities in the public sector to avoid the problems that might arise from foreign firms having crucial roles to play in national defense choices.

The public sector "dependence" on external support is less visible but quite as real. Hindustan Aeronautics, the state-owned aircraft conglomerate, produces MiG-21s on Soviet license, and has bought technical help from German designers and British engine manufacturers for the HF-24 fighter-bomber. Helicopters are manufactured on French license, and the Vijayanta medium tank on license from Vickers in the United Kingdom. Defense electronics benefit from agreements with the USSR, Britain, the United States, and France. India's nuclear reactors and much of its nuclear information comes from Canada and the United States. The Indian missile program

---

[1] "Control" is a difficult term to operationalize. It is used in Indian parlance to describe firms whose share of the capital, partnership structure, licensed manufacturing processes, or principal marketing operation is heavily influenced by foreign agents. The most helpful source on the subject is Michael Kidron, *Foreign Investments in India* (London: Oxford University Press, 1965).

Reprinted with permission and with minor changes from "Nuclear Weapon Options and the Strategic Environment in South Asia" (Los Angeles: California Arms Control and Foreign Policy Seminar, 1972). This article was written under the auspices of the California Arms Control and Foreign Policy Seminar.

began at the United Nations equatorial launch station in Kerala with US Scout rockets, and is moving forward with French collaboration.

In the case of both the private and the public sector, therefore, India is to a degree dependent upon access to Western and Soviet technology and licensed processes. These Indian efforts are, of course, relatively new in the defense industry field. The previous pattern of Indian defense expenditures was characterized by end-item purchase, especially in the more complex weapons systems field. In the period after 1962 when defense industry was given a high national priority, the Indian military "couldn't wait" and major purchases of Soviet tanks and artillery, aircraft, and naval vessels were made. These purchases were seen as a necessary expedient to build the defense "capital" store, but were seen as an intermediary generation of weapons that would be supplanted with Indian weapons over the next decade.

Almost all Indian defense industry has been slower in meeting production schedules and design specifications than had been hoped. MiG-21 production was so slow as to lead to further purchase of Soviet-built end-item aircraft, and the HF-24 was slow enough in production and "debugging" as to force purchase of large numbers of Soviet SU-7 fighter-bombers. The Indian Navy has attempted the fabrication of two Leander-class frigates in India, and two in the Vickers years in the UK, but the submarine purchases from the USSR were made with no defense industry "back-up" anticipated.

There is less political leverage in this pattern of dependence than might be assumed. Private sector capabilities are limited because firms have to produce in order to satisfy both their share holders and the Indian host government. A politically inspired slowdown would be met by punitive Indian government policy on profit repatriation, import licenses, and perhaps export quotas.

New Delhi has also been careful to spread its technological dependencies quite widely, so that the United States and Britain do not have the ability to stop crucial Indian production processes in the defense field. Since much of the conventional military equipment is of Soviet purchase, and since India has contracted licenses to manufacture such equipment in India, the control that adheres to access to spare parts does not apply, or applies to only part of the arms inventory. Agreements with France and other middle powers allow India to avoid defense production dependence on the superpowers and their close allies. Whatever dependencies do exist, they have a short "half-life" since India is committed to defense production autarky.

The Indian nuclear program shows the pattern quite clearly. The first reactor to go critical and produce power in India was the Tarapur 380 MWe General Electric enriched uranium, heavy water, system bought on concessional terms provided by the U.S. Agency for International Development. It came on stream feeding the Bombay-Gujarat grid in 1969. The second reactor is a Canadian natural uranium, heavy water, system built by Atomic Energy of Canada and located in Rana Pratap Sagar in Rajasthan. This reactor sale was accompanied by Indian demands for access to the Canadian Chalk River design facility, and indigenous Indian design experience in natural uranium reactor design was advanced.

The third Indian reactor is to be of Indian design, utilizing a natural uranium, heavy water, technology, and is to be built in Madras by 1980. The plan calls for 80 percent Indian indigenous materials and construction, presumably to reduce even further the dependence of Indian atomic energy development on foreign controls. Coincident to this plan the Indians have created state corporations for the production of rare earths, uranium and heavy water, and have signed collaborative agreements with France for the development of gas centrifuges and fast breeder reactors. While these are long lead time investments in a rapidly changing technology, they do point toward an Indian capability for a nuclear weapons technology by the end of the decade.

In the last week of May 1970, Dr. Vikram Sarabhai, director of the Indian Atomic Energy Department, "dropped the other shoe" in announcing a ten-year program for nuclear energy and "space." The official announcement noted the following aims:[2]

Augmentation of the facilities for R and D at the Space Science and Technology Centre to be able to build scientific and communication satellites and to environmentally test them; facilities at the Space Science and Technological Centre for the development of inertial guidance systems and on-board miniaturized computers; development at SSTC, TIFR and ECIL and construction of high performance missile tracking radars and PCM communication systems for installation at Shar and at Andamans in the Bay of Bengal for the satellite program; construction of a plant for manufacture of large solid propellant blocks at Shar and a

[2]*Indian and Foreign Review* (June 15, 1970).

facility for static testing of these propellant blocks on the ground and under high altitude simulated conditions; completion of a rocket fabrication facility at Trivandrum for manufacture of large scale rocket castings and hardware for rocket motors including the development of special materials for rocket motor systems; development of in-flight guidance systems for rockets; development in 1973–74 of a "scout" type launcher of four stages, burning solid propellant, capable of putting into orbit a satellite of about 40 Kg payload. This would be followed by development of more advanced rocket systems capable of putting 1,200 Kg payloads into synchronous orbits; fabrication of communication satellites by 1975 capable of providing high quality point-to-point service between metropolitan areas and direct broadcast of television; development of sensors and techniques for remote sensing.

In order to build the present research and development capability to undertake this massive program, the space program of India will have to grow at nearly 100 percent a year for three or four years and its budget grow much faster. In 1967, the Atomic Energy Department had a budget of only about $91 million and about 2,000 scientists, 500 technicians and 8,000 other employees.[3] The most frequently cited price-tag on the ambitious nuclear and space ten-year plan of 1970 was $1.6 billion.

Neither the nuclear power nor space program budget refers to weapons implications or Indian choices in the defense field, but analysts within and outside the country understand that this combination program is directed toward an Indian missile-thermonuclear warhead force by about 1980. Depending upon access to foreign technology, especially that of France, India may therefore have an independence in nuclear defense policy by 1980 which it does not have now. This suggests that arms control policies acceptable to India will be those that do not inhibit its own development of a weapons capability, and yet those which hold some promise of ten-year "insurance" for Indian vulnerabilities.

It is not, of course, simply technology that keeps India from nuclear power status. The Indian economy is weak and the society is poor. The per capita gross national product expressed in U.S. dollars is about 90, lower than Indonesia and much lower than a poor country like South Korea. Moreover, the government accounts for only about 12 percent of the GNP, roughly a third that of industrially developed countries, and therefore must live with smaller budgets for

military research and development. India's foreign exchange gap, seldom lower than half a billion dollars since 1958, is also a formidable constraint.

On the other hand, India's GNP is the ninth largest in the world in absolute terms, and its present armed forces are the fourth largest in the world. The World Bank's studies show that while the ratio between Indian and United States per capita income appears to be 1:30 in monetary terms, the purchasing power in domestic society ratio might be closer to 1:12. For less, therefore, the Indians can buy more goods and services from their economy and therefore their effective budgets may in fact be much larger than their dollar equivalent budgets.

In the study by Emile Benoit and Max Millikan,[4] it was calculated that if the Indian economy continues to grow at about 3.5 percent, and if defense expenditures are maintained at 3.7 percent of the gross domestic product, India could have available a defense budget of about $3 billion by 1980. Even using the World Bank purchasing power multiplier of 2.5, this would appear to be too little for a balanced nuclear-general purpose force, and the large increases in the Indian defense budget after 1969–70 appear to represent a necessary step if India is to meet its self-declared posture. Major economic problems would slow the defense development of the country, but the government appears committed to an increasing defense budget under almost any circumstances. And to the degree that foreign economic assistance aids Indian economic growth, it seems almost sure to indirectly facilitate military development.

The assumption, therefore, that either technological dependence or national poverty will make India amenable to arms control proposals, either in nuclear or general purpose force levels, appears to be in error. Both factors, however, retard Indian strategic weapons development and might be aspects of India's vulnerability that external powers might use to retard India's pace even more. The costs of such pressure, however, in the absence of a global agreement, or the parallel interests of the Indian government, might be quite high. An ultra-nationalist Indian reaction would weaken the influence of foreign governments in other areas of their concern and might lead to widespread nationalization of foreign-owned industry. What leverage exists, therefore, is the leverage to slow rather than to

[3]*Report of the Atomic Energy Department, 1969–70* (New Delhi: 1970).

[4]*The Effect of the Absence of National Defense on Developing Economies*, ACDA/E, 136 (Cambridge, Mass.: MIT Center for International Studies, 1969).

stop defense industry in India, and it lies principally with the USSR. What may be of equal importance is that foreign powers *may* still have the opportunity to exercise some qualitative arms control by facilitating a particular Indian force posture "mix" between strategic and conventional weapons. This is in many ways an imponderable problem, because the nature of Indian security perceptions over the next few years will dictate their defense investment priorities, and India's strategic environment is highly unstable.

WEAPONS ACQUISITION: ISRAEL AND EGYPT

J. C. HUREWITZ

The arms race between Israel and Egypt has developed progressively through four historical periods. In the first (1948-54) neither nation had an industrial base, and there existed a general prohibition against the importation of advanced weapons. The second (1955-60) was characterized by alliance formation—France with Israel and the Soviet Union with Egypt. In the third (1961-67) Israel diversified its sources and began importing some weapons from the United States. The fourth (1967-72) was dominated by massive USSR aid to Egypt and increasing U.S. shipments to Israel. Despite the furor of the Soviet decision to withdraw its advisors and instructors in 1972 a significant trend is developing: Israel is rapidly becoming self-sufficient in weapons production, while Egypt remains heavily dependent on Soviet equipment.

J. C. Hurewitz is Professor of Government and Director of the Middle East Institute, Columbia University. He is the author of many books on the Middle East, including The Struggle for Palestine *(1950),* Diplomacy in the Near and Middle East *(1956), and* Middle East Politics: The Military Dimension *(1969).*

WEAPONS ACQUISITION IN A TWO-TIERED ARMS RACE

Since July 1972 Egypt has dropped out of the arms race with Israel—at least for the time being. We have no way of knowing as yet whether the rivalry has truly ended or if not, how long the interval may last, because the Soviet connection has not been entirely broken. Admittedly, when President Anwar al-Sadat invited Russian military advisers to leave, the Soviet Union responded by withdrawing more men (the instructors as the advisers) and more equipment (the MiG-23s, the MiG-21Js, the Su-11s, and the SA-4s and the SA-6s) than they had been invited to. To many, it appeared that the Soviet-Egyptian alliance had run its course. Yet each side took great pains to assure the other that the basis of their friendship remained intact. Russian naval vessels and personnel did not surrender their privileged use of the Mediterranean ports of Mersa Matruh, Alexandria, and Port Sa'id. Word began to spread in November 1972 that the Soviet Union had sent back to Egypt a number of SA-4 and SA-6 tracked missiles along with instructors. If true, this would confirm that the former arms-transfer arrangements had not been stopped but merely suspended, and that the durability of any new arrangements would clearly depend on mutual satisfaction.

This is an original article written for this volume and the Conference on Comparative Defense Policy held at the Air Force Academy, February 7-9, 1973. Copyright reserved by the author.

Meanwhile, the United States is still fulfilling its latest contracts with Israel for the sale of F-4s and A-4s and a whole range of other equipment, especially electronic and communications devices. Israel's military industry is steadily expanding and growing progressively more sophisticated. Related American firms have been forming local partnerships in Israel, with the government whenever the products are intended largely for military use. Israel's research and development has been expanding at a time of contraction in the United States, and on a small scale Israel has been able to attract engineers and scientists with experience in weapons design and development. But most of the skilled workers have been home-grown engineers, scientists, and technicians, mainly alumni of the Technion (Israel Institute of Technology) at Haifa, which since the early 1950s has been training students for careers in the Ministry of Defense, the armed forces, and the multiplying military industries. In short, as of the start of 1973, the military balance along the Israel-Egyptian ceasefire line—for that matter, in the Arab-Israel zone as a whole—decisively favors Israel.

Still, despite the prevailing optimism in Israel, there is a gnawing sense of anxiety about the future. If the Soviet Union should return to Egypt in strength, once again assuming primary responsibility for its air defense, Israel might lose its commanding lead. Looking somewhat deeper into the future, Israel has reason for apprehension about the monumental sums of floating capital that are likely to accrue to oil-logged Arab states, which may be expected to go to Egypt's aid. Israel's security planners may well fear that the oil-rich Arab governments might attempt to destroy Israel's arms-export markets in Africa, Asia, and even Latin America; purchase the latest weapons systems from major arms producers; and hire Western expatriates to join Arab—including the Egyptian—armed forces for a military showdown. Israel is now largely dependent on one outside supplier, and if that source should run dry, Israel might have nowhere to turn. Accordingly, the pressure for military autarky does not let up, and its progress along with obstinate refusal to withdraw from Sinai keeps Egyptian anxieties alive.

Until a peace settlement is reached, and at the time of writing there are few grounds for assuming that the parties will come to a negotiated understanding in the foreseeable future, the psychological environment which nourishes the spirited Egyptian-Israeli arms rivalry is not likely to change. Similarly, despite the signs of the relaxation of superpower tensions over strategic weapons, of a decline of East-West strains in Europe, and even of a thaw in US relations with China, there are as yet few indications of a superpower détente in the Mediterranean and in the Middle East. There, the lingering Cold War has hardened the special patron-client relations between the USSR and Egypt and between the US and Israel. As we have seen, Egypt has not found it easy to alter the basis of its relations with the Soviet Union. Since July, Egypt has literally gone begging for new arms suppliers; apparently no Western European government has been willing to take on the economic, political, and military liabilities. As part of recurrent efforts at diplomatic mediation in 1969-71 between Egypt and Israel, the United States tried more than once without success to persuade Israel to agree to political concessions by resorting to the tactic of refusing to conclude fresh contracts for the sale of planes. The superpowers manifestly have become as deeply enmeshed as Egypt and Israel in the regional arms race, thus making it a double-tiered race with patron and protégé ranged against patron and protégé.[1]

All big industries in Egypt, including the few that may be labeled military (mostly for the manufacture of spare parts and ammunition and perhaps also light arms) are owned and operated by the government. The government industries are commonly managed by army officers, many inactive, who provide political as well as economic monitoring. But the output for the armed forces is relatively limited, with even more restricted and generally nonproductive experimentation in sophisticated military manufacturing. The problems of source selection and contracting do not arise.

While military industry in Israel is also owned and operated by the government (in a number of instances—particularly in the electronic and communications fields—in partnership with foreign firms, mostly American), the multiplying civilian industries are either private or socialist enterprises or a combination of the two. Military industry, which has flourished since 1967, is run by the Ministry of Defense, which also exclusively manages weapons research and development broadly defined. To the degree possible the scientists, technicians, and employees in research, development, and manufacture are

---

[1]See J. C. Hurewitz, *Middle East Politics: The Military Dimension* (New York: Praeger, for the Council on Foreign Relations, 1969), chaps. 24–25; and J. C. Hurewitz, "Changing Military Perspectives in the Middle East," in *Political Dynamics in the Middle East*, edited by Paul Y. Hammond and Sydney S. Alexander (New York: Elsevier, 1972), especially pp. 85–95.

drawn from the armed forces. The major problem in Israel arises from the constraints of limited resources, human and natural, over which the Ministry of Defense competes with other ministries and with private industry. The budgetary allocations to the Ministry since 1967 have shot up astrononically, much of it going to military infrastructure—such as roads, fortifications, camps, air fields, communications, and anti-guerrilla installations along the ceasefire lines—and administration in the occupied areas as well as to the spiraling investment in weapons and military industry.[2] In fact, in the past two or three years, the continuing steep outlays for the armed forces, including those for weapons and industry, have been slowing down the rate of economic growth.

The only major experiment in innovative military research and development in Egypt took place in the first half of the 1960s, when the government sponsored an ambitious project on local standards for the development of short-range (300 to 500 miles) surface-to-surface missiles and Mach 2 jet planes. The project was undertaken with technicians recruited in Western Europe, and was virtually abandoned as a non-starter even before the war of June 1967, for reasons that I shall explore below. There were unconfirmed reports in 1972 about reviving the project with Soviet or West European help.[3]

In Israel, there is no bidding by industry for research and development of new weapons systems, but simply allocations by the Ministry of Defense to its own subsidiaries. Often, as in the manufacture of TV sets, electronic devices, and computers, there is a lag between the initial production of goods which have value for civilians as well as soldiers and the eventual civilianization of segments of such industries. In brief, with the close cooperation of the armed forces, the Ministry of Defense alone handles system procurement, subject to infrequent veto by the Cabinet for economic reasons and, in the case of a nuclear system, for political reasons as well. The relations between specific military industries and their operational-unit clients are tightly interlocked. Many industrial technicians and workers may actually come from the units in question. In a word, the relations are intimate

and generally positive from the first request for the development of new weapons and weapons systems through deployment after production, with the unit testing the equipment at its several stages of development. In the absence of comparable economic and military organization, such questions do not arise in Egypt.

Problems of labor-management conflict in military industry hardly occur in either state. Egypt imports nearly all its weapons and the government encounters no labor trouble in unloading, storage, transport, or repair, since the armed forces handle all these activities. Owned and managed by the Ministry of Defense, the burgeoning military industry in Israel, numbering perhaps 100 factories or more, lies outside the general range of direct strikes. Still, weapons firms may be indirectly affected by strikes of other government—for example, postal and airport—employees. Similarly irrelevant is the conflict between industry and government on cost or time-to-completion overruns, and performance and reliability underruns. Given the undeveloped military industrial condition, these difficulties do not exist in Egypt. In Israel, when advance estimates prove too low, the problems appear to be resolved within either the Ministry of Defense or the Cabinet.

Ever since becoming an arms protégé of the USSR in the mid-1950s, Egypt has been economically dependent on its supplier for trade, loans, and technical aid. As noted above, Egypt has also been under the strong, but never the inclusive, political influence of the Soviet Union. Even after the dramatic lowering of the Soviet military profile in the second half of 1972, Egypt still leaned heavily, if also uncertainly, on Moscow for political and diplomatic support. No less important since 1967 have been the economic subsidies of the oil-rich Arab states. Moreover, one of the constant checks on Soviet political influence has been the need of Egypt, as leader of the Arab states, to respond to the variable pressures of its Arab neighbors, the Palestine Arabs included.

After the Six Day War Israel, for its part, increased its dependence on private philanthropic remittances and loans (through the sale of bonds) from Jewish communities across the world, especially from the American Jewish community. This has been supplemented, since 1969, by loans and grants from the United States government. Israel's response to political pressures of the United States on issues geographically remote from the Middle East is high, and on issues directly tied to the dispute with the Arab states, medium to low. In sum, neither Egypt nor Israel

---

[2]See, for example, address by Moshe Dayan, the Minister of Defense, at the graduation ceremony of the Command and Staff School, 17 August 1972, in text released by the Information Division of the Ministry of Foreign Affairs, Jerusalem, No. 266, August 20, 1972.

[3]J. C. Hurewitz, *Middle East Politics*, pp. 47–77; "Adventures of an Engine Designer in Egypt," *Flight International* (19 February 1970): 280–81; and *The New York Times* (22 March 1972).

is economically or politically autarkic. The influence of the superpower patrons is nevertheless, circumscribed, yielding highly unstable patterns of arms buildup, although the direction has been steadily, and at times dramatically, upward.

The focus on the Egypt-Israel arms contest distorts the analysis somewhat. But so long as we are aware of the distortion, we need not be distracted by it. We have to keep in the back of our minds that in planning production and in seeking arrangements for procurement, Israel must also take into account arms transfers to other Arab states as well as to Egypt, because it can never know when, as in 1967, it may have to face the combined action of several neighbors. As the challenged party, Israel had to establish and preserve its military superiority to insure its political survival. This anxiety, the propaganda of the Arab states and of the successive and variable components of the Palestine resistance movement, has been nurtured all along by claiming that the Arab military objective is "the restoration of Palestine to its rightful owners."

Egypt, on its side, could also not overlook the flow of arms to other Arab states as well as to Israel, since apart from weapons rivalry with Israel in the postwar years it rarely lost sight of its role as political and military leader in the Arab world. Egypt's disaster in June 1967 gravely undermined its credibility as the Arab states' military leader, and the death of Gamal 'Abd al-Nasir in September 1970 deprived it of political leadership too, since that inherited mantle sat loosely on Anwar al-Sadat's shoulders. Yet even repeated demonstrations of failures—the Six Day War, the limited war of 1969–70, and the crippling effect in 1972 of the removal of Soviet advisers and instructors and the sophisticated hardware that they had manned—did not persuade the Egyptian government to abandon the quest for military superiority through modernization. That urge died hard, since it long antedated the rise of Israel and leadership in the Arab unity movement, going back as it did at least to 1882, when Britain occupied Egypt, and in some respects even to 1841, when the European Concert compelled Mehmed 'Ali to reduce his armed forces to one-tenth their earlier size and to abandon his vibrant military industry. Finally, in Israel's doctrine of military superiority, no self-esteeming Egyptian government could acquiesce, for under its corollary Egypt (together with all other Arab states) would have had to remain forever militarily inferior to its adversary.

Numbers can be misleading. On the surface, with a population at least twelve times that of its rival, Egypt ought to have been able to smother Israel with much larger armed forces and far more hardware. Yet the fact remained that ever since the birth of the state, Israel's citizen army on M-Day plus 2 invariably was able to exceed in size Egypt's fielded regular forces. Nor did Egypt ever develop a meaningful reserves program, so that it never could place confidence in the inactive ranks to shore up the regular forces in time of crisis. While Egypt's inventory of planes and tanks, with the exception of the periods immediately following the wars of 1956 and 1967, constantly overtopped Israel's, such a weapons count by itself tells us nothing. More important was the degree of assimilation of the sophisticated equipment and its serviceability.[4] The main point can be made simply by stating that the Israel Defense Forces (IDF) fully assimilated their imported weapons, almost always upgrading them in the process, and kept them in as workable condition as possible; and by contrast, that the Egyptian Armed Forces (EAF) only imperfectly assimilated the imported sophisticated weapons, rarely if ever adjusted them to local needs, commonly abused them, and failed properly to maintain them. When to this condition are added after 1967 Israel's manifest advance toward military autarky and Egypt's reliance between 1970 and 1972 on direct Soviet participation in the Egyptian air defense, which signified a movement away from military autarky, it became clear that the technological gap between the rivals was widening steadily in Israel's favor.

Still in a very real sense, Egypt was making military progress. It is grossly distortive to measure that development alongside Israel, which moved so far out front that neither the existing Egyptian regime nor any possible successor could hope in the reasonable future to overtake it. Instead, for balanced appreciation, Egypt's achievements had to be evaluated against earlier performance. To explain how such a condition came about is one of the central purposes of the present paper.

THE ORIGINS OF THE RIVALRY

Between Egypt and Israel there could be no race before 1954–55, because both were then nonindustrial states in the military sense. Neither could produce, or at the time even realistically expect to produce the planes,

[4]For the situation in 1956 see Nadav Safran, *From War to War: The Arab-Israeli Confrontation, 1948-1967* (New York: Pegasus, 1969), pp. 210–12.

tanks, and vehicles already in use by its armed forces. The opportunities for weapons procurement, moreover, were regulated by the major Western powers which enjoyed a monopoly of the modern arms market in the Middle East. In the Arab-Israel zone they were not prepared to promote an arms buildup. This, they solemnly affirmed in the Tripartite Declaration of May 25, 1950. In it Britain, France, and the United States laid down explicit rules for purveying military hardware to the Arab states and to Israel, making it clear to boot that they would not tolerate any forcible change of boundaries or armistice lines. The three declarers set up a coordinating committee to regulate the flow of weapons into the area, and proceeded to use the machinery as a form of bribe or coercion for the creation of a collective security system that would bring selected Middle East states into partnership with the three Western powers.

The policy looked relatively harmless and simple at the outset. The Western powers for the most part dispensed obsolete weapons of World War II with the occasional bait of a current model, such as Britain's offer to sell Centurions to Egypt in 1950 as the price for a cooperative settlement of their dispute. The practice of trying to influence decisions of an Egyptian government by proffering or withholding modern items made the politicians under the monarchy and the republic allergic to attempted conditional sales. The signing of the agreement in 1954 for terminating the British military presence liberated Egypt to adopt any policy that it wished for the enlargement and modernization of its armed forces, and the liberation coincided with external opportunities for carrying out such plans. It was, in fact, the creation in 1954–55 of the Baghdad Pact, on Britain's initiative with US encouragement, that paired off the USSR with Egypt and France with Israel.

Egypt and Israel were the regional powers most deeply alienated by the formation of a collective security system with which Egypt had refused to be associated and from which Israel had been deliberately shut out. The Soviet Union viewed the pact as an "aggressive bloc," whose effective operation and further growth it was determined to inhibit. The Soviet Union offered Egypt, and other Arab states, modern hardware without bargaining over classes such as offensive or defensive, strategic or tactical, and without compulsory participation in any alliance. The Soviet-Egyptian arms deal received great notoriety, since the appearance of the USSR as a salesman broke the Western monopoly of the modern weapons market in the Middle East.

By contrast, the French-Israel deal, which had been concluded a year earlier, was initially concealed from the public notice, because France had already been a participant in the Western directorate for managing the arms flow into the region, and also because this was intended as quiet compensation to Israel at a time when the US was taking the first steps to organize the Baghdad Pact through military agreements with Iraq and Pakistan. As one of the signatories of the Tripartite Declaration and one of the sponsors of the nonstarting schemes in 1951–52 for a Western collective security system in partnership with the Middle East states, France took a dim view of its ostentatious exclusion from the plans for the latest scheme and, after Soviet weapons began to pour into Egypt, from the development by the United States and Britain of a counterstrategy to check the growth of Soviet influence in the Arab world.

The Egyptian-Israel competition followed relatively predictable lines. The regional rivals were at first satisfied with weapons declared obsolete or obsolescing by the armed forces of the supplier states, but soon acquired a taste for models in the current inventories, and then moved steadily from the less to the more sophisticated items. As one side passed the other in procuring an important weapon system, the second side made every effort to wheedle out of its patron a matching system and the defense against it.

Before 1955, the arsenals of the IDF and the EAF were lean and comprised essentially rehabilitated relics of World War II with only scattered postwar models discarded by the supplier armed forces, such as the first generation of jet planes. Between 1955 and 1960 the USSR and France continued unloading outmoded hardware, and with it Egypt and Israel were more than pleased, because it generally surpassed in quantity and sometimes also in quality the items in their arsenals before then. The T-34, a medium tank of which Egypt bought 200 copies in its first order, had been the Soviet mainstay in World War II. In vintage, it corresponded to the American M-4 or Sherman, for both went into original production as early as 1941. The Egyptians did not immediately dispose of the medium Centurions (British) or the light AMX-13s (French), so that altogether on the outbreak of the Sinai-Suez War of 1956, they had 430 tanks, including some 30–60 heavy JS-3s. Arrayed against them were Israel's 260 Centurions and 100 AMX-13s. Both sides could also sport troop carriers mounted on half-tracks, tank transporters, and self-propelled assault guns.

The infantry of the two armies, motorized

with jeeps and trucks of most dimensions and purposes, were armed with bazookas, recoilless guns, antitank rifles, and light mortars. Having converted to jets, mostly still subsonic as late as 1960, the two air forces were nevertheless already moving into transonic aircraft. Egypt received before the 1956 war sizable numbers of MiG-15 and MiG-17 fighter-bombers and a handful of Il-28 light bombers. (Later the Soviet Union swiftly more than made good Egypt's losses of planes, tanks, and other equipment.) From France, Israel in turn acquired comparable fighter-bombers (Ouragons and Mystères) and light bombers (Vautours). Radar screens began to take their place in the two air-defense systems. Radio and telephonic equipment united the units with their area commands, and the latter with the supreme command. Egypt also started to accumulate naval power, purchasing 9 submarines and 6 destroyers by 1960. Of these classes of vessels, Israel had invested in only two each, manifestly falling back on air power to repel possible Egyptian naval attack. What Britain and the United States had initiated as cautious enticement into cooperation with the West thus grew into open rivalry in the second half of the 1950s, as the USSR and France removed most barriers to quantity and some also to quality.

In the 1960s before the Six Day War, the Middle East rivals were importing models in their suppliers' active inventories: supersonic fighters, surface-to-air and air-to-air guided missiles, diesel-driven tanks with improved fire-control systems, and in the case of Egypt also missile-firing vessels. While keeping what has been called its "tacit alliance" with France, Israel also sought additional suppliers, so as to enlarge its arms-procurement options. Israel began acquiring military equipment from West Germany as early as 1959, and in the following year the two governments concluded a secret agreement, under which Israel was furnished a wide assortment of used and new hardware ranging from helicopters, submarines, and transport planes to antiaircraft guns and antitank rockets—items manufactured in various West European countries and the United States as well as in West Germany. Furthermore, West Germany absorbed the costs as part of the reparations payments to Israel. In the plans for diversifying the sources of military imports, high priority was given to persuading the United States to abandon its restraints on the direct sale of heavy weapons to Israel. Not until 1962–63 did Israel finally arrange for the purchase from the United States of Hawk antiaircraft missiles. The contract for M-48 tanks was signed

in 1965 and for A-4s in 1966, although delivery of the attack bombers did not begin until two years later.

Meanwhile, by the eve of the Six Day War the Egyptian Air Force included 470 combat planes, of entirely Soviet manufacture, plus Soviet transports, helicopters, and air defense systems.[5] The combat formations of the Israel Air Force at that time comprised 257 planes of exclusively French manufacture or design. For air defense Israel relied on its French Mirage-IIIC and Super-Mystère interceptors and radar system, and two battalions of American surface-to-air Hawk missiles. There were also about 40 American-made transports, and 25 helicopters. In armor for the ground forces, Egypt had also wrested a numerical and qualitative edge over its adversary (in size and modernity). It had 1,010 tanks, almost wholly of Russian manufacture. Israel's estimated 800 tanks were of variable manufacture, and although many were obsolete in the manufacturing countries, all had been modernized and each class standardized by the Israelis, including new guns and new controls. The Egyptian ground forces also had an estimated 150 Soviet self-propelled guns. Israel's 250 self-propelled guns were for the most part put together domestically by mounting howitzers of various sizes on the chassis of obsolete American and French tanks. Two hundred and fifty self-propelled guns were found in the Israel army. Israeli antitank weapons consisted of 106 mm recoilless rifles mounted on jeeps and SS-10 and SS-11 missiles mounted on weapons carriers. Egypt's navy on June 4, 1967 consisted of 8 destroyers, 11 submarines, 12 escort vessels (half of them coastal), 18 missile patrol boats with Styx cruise missiles, 10 minesweepers, and some 50 small patrol boats. Israel still neglected its navy which was composed of 2 destroyers, 1 antiaircraft frigate, 4 submarines, 1 patrol vessel, 3 landing craft, and 14 patrol boats of less than 100 tons each.

AFTERMATH OF 1967

For Egypt, the war of June 1967 ended in four days. By 8 June, Israel had taken possession of the Sinai Peninsula, with the exception of Port Fuad and its immediate vicinity. Egypt lost an estimated 340 combat planes or more than 70

---

[5]Michael Howard and Robert Hunter, "Israel and the Arab World: The Crisis of 1967," *Adelphi Papers*, No. 41 (London: IISS, October 1967), p. 50; Geoffrey Kemp, "Arms & Security: The Egypt-Israel Case," *Adelphi Papers*, No. 52 (London: IISS, October 1968), p. 5, and tables 1–6, pp. 20–27. See also Kemp's paper in this volume, pp. 391–405, for detailed inventories on both sides.

percent of the total, most of them destroyed on the ground in the opening raids by the Israel Air Force on nineteen Egyptian air fields. Also destroyed or captured were some 600 tanks or about 60 percent of the total, along with comparable quantities of vehicles, artillery pieces, and other matériel. The USSR's failure to go to Egypt's aid in the lightning war made it imperative for Moscow to take dramatic action, if it hoped to save its steep investment in Egypt. The Soviet Union immediately began to resupply the denuded Egyptian armed forces. In less than a month nearly 100 planes, mostly MiG-21C/Ds, were flown to Egypt. The pace of rearmament continued brisk throughout the following year, so that by the end of June 1968, the number of combat planes in the Egyptian Air Force had climbed back to 400 or about 85 percent of the total on June 4, 1967. At the time of the Egyptian-Israel ceasefire on June 8, 1967, the EAF had only 30 helicopters or only half the number in its possession four days earlier; by June 1968 their number had increased to 50. Within a year of the disaster, the Soviet government had replaced all the T-54/55s lost in battle.

Meanwhile, for the first time the Soviet Union exacted a political price for the equipment, presumably because Egypt could not afford it, even at the customary generous discounts. Thus as early as the fall of 1967, the Soviet Mediterranean Squadron obtained the right of free access to Alexandria and Port Sa'id, as a deterrent to Israel in the critical phase of Egyptian rearmament. From that date on the Soviet Navy gradually accustomed Egypt and the outside world to its privileged presence at the two Egyptian ports for storage, repair, and replenishment. Starting in May 1968, moreover, the land-based air arm of the Soviet Navy was allowed to use Cairo West airport for regular Tu-16 reconnaissance flights over the Sixth Fleet in the central Mediterranean, as far west as the boot of Italy. Instructively, the Badgers used Egyptian markings. By the end of 1968 the Soviet government had assigned some 3,000 military advisers to the Egyptian Armed Forces.

As victor, Israel felt no immediate pressure to accumulate fresh arms, since its triumph over Egypt (and Jordan and Syria) had been so decisive. Instead, Israel became distracted by the problems of military administration and the assimilation of captured equipment. Still, it did not remain inactive. Israel pressed the US for the delivery of the A-4s; and the first planes arrived in February 1968, only two months after the contractual schedule. The French embargo on arms sales to Israel, introduced on the outbreak of war in June 1967, prevented Israel from taking possession of the 50 Mirage-Vs for which it had paid in full before the Six Day War. To replace them, Israel made a determined effort to persuade the US to sell it 50 F-4s, and between October and December 1968 the negotiations for the sale were consummated. It was agreed that the delivery of the new planes would start in September 1969.

The F-4 Phantom II represented a systemic jump in quality, and the Soviet Air Force had no plane of equal quality. The injection of such an advanced system into the Israel-Egypt area was certain to evoke a joint Soviet-Egyptian response, given the level of Soviet entanglement in Egypt after June 1967 and its thinly disguised use of arms aid as a means of building base facilities on Egyptian territory for the Soviet Navy and naval air arm. The F-4 has a bomb load more than twice that of the Su-7 fighter-bomber, which the Soviet Union began supplying Egypt even before June 1967. With a long combat radius and a top speed exceeding Mach 2.0, the F-4 could be used for interception, escort, bombing, and reconnaissance. It was clear that the Soviet Union was rebuilding the Egyptian Air Force around the MiG-21 for escort and defense and the Su-7 for strike and support. But that combination by itself did not provide adequate defense for Egypt.

It was hard to tell by this time who was setting the pace in the competition. The introduction of such an advanced system as the F-4, it has been argued, presented "a new factor in the Arab-Israel balance of power."[6] That is certainly true. Yet the pressures on Israel at the time were two: the rapid rearmament of Egypt coinciding with the abrupt severance of Israel's French connection; and the rising Soviet military profile in Egypt, starting with the provisional naval rights in the fall of 1967 and followed in the spring of 1968 by the provisional air-reconnaissance rights. The naval presence already served as a deterrent to Israel, coupled as it was with the loss of a destroyer in October 1967, the first victim of a Styx cruise missile. Whichever side was the initiator is basically immaterial. The fact remains that as a result of the irrepressible mutual suspicions, the arms levels were escalating dramatically, this time with the Soviet Union itself weighing in on the military scales on Egypt's side.

Well before the delivery of the first F-4s to Israel, the Soviet Union and Egypt had planned and precipitated a "war of attrition," which it

[6]Kemp, "Arms & Security: The Egypt-Israel Case," p. 7.

was hoped would force Israel to withdraw from Sinai and restore a measure of parity to the diplomatic bargaining between the regional rivals for a settlement of their differences. The concept of an attritional war grew out of Egyptian and Soviet calculations that by keeping the hostilities limited, Egypt might be able to put its massive numerical superiority in population to effective use and to whittle away at Israel's military superiority by hitting it at the most vulnerable point: an extremely limited manpower. With 70,000 to 100,000 Egyptian soldiers deployed for action west of the canal, the Soviet and Egyptian planners must have counted on Israel's committing a comparable number of troops east of the canal, a commitment that Israel could not long afford without serious damage to its economy. In addition, it was expected that Egypt would be able speedily to raise to an intolerable level Israel's casualty rate along the canal. The outer limit of Israeli tolerance might be reached by an average loss of no more than one soldier per day, a goal that Egypt might realistically hope to attain within a reasonably short period. Moreover, the combination of economic and military pressures might be expected to convert Israel into a more pliant diplomatic negotiator.

In rearming Egypt with these ends in view, the Soviet Union gave primary consideration to expanding the armored and artillery units and only secondary consideration to bolstering Egyptian air power. In any case, the expansion of air power was a much slower process at best, because of the longer lead time for training pilots and ground crews. The trends were reflected in the weapons buildup. The overall number of tanks in the EAF in the spring of 1969 reached about 900 or approximately 100 fewer than on June 4, 1967. However, it should be noted that there were qualitative differences. By the end of June 1969 there were approximately 650 T-54/55s in Egypt by contrast to only 500 on the eve of the Six Day War. The restoration of the older and less versatile T-34s lagged, with only 150 in 1969 as contrasted with 350 in 1967. In preparation for the limited war, the Soviet Union also stockpiled heavy artillery and made generous provision for replacement of lost equipment and for the steady flow of ammunition. Egypt launched the war in earnest early in the spring of 1969. Once again, Israel responded in a characteristic way, by developing a strategy that enabled it to use planes as "aerial artillery" for silencing Egyptian guns. Only toward the end of the year did the strategy finally establish Israel's air superiority over the western canal zone, fol-lowing the destruction of many of the Egyptian artillery and SA-2 sites.

The first F-4s reached Israel in September 1969 and, swiftly assimilated, were put into action early in January 1970. With air superiority already assured and the SA-2 network substantially damaged, the new interceptor with almost complete abandon mounted penetration raids into the Delta to the very outskirts of Cairo. The F-4s, using low-flying tactics, evaded the battered SA-2 system, which had been designed to bag high-flying planes. It was now the Soviet Union's turn to make a quantum jump, by assuming joint responsibility with the Egyptian Air Force for Egypt's air defense. The Soviet government decided to supply its protégé not only with improved SA-2 missiles to replace those destroyed but with an SA-3 system designed expressly to shoot down low-flying planes and the Soviet manpower to operate the new system. Also included were ZSU-23-4 four-barrelled 23 mm antiaircraft guns, which until then had not been used outside the Warsaw Pact area. Before starting to install the new SA-3s at the end of February 1970, Moscow had given Washington notice, stating that the new system was essential for the defense of Cairo, Alexandria, and Aswan against the IAF penetration raids.

The associated step, the deployment of a sizable number of the J or most advanced class of the MiG-21 series—having longer radius, higher speed, and better armament than the Cs or the Ds—together with Soviet pilots and ground crews, was taken without advance notice to the US government. The first confirmation that Soviet pilots were flying the new planes came on April 17, 1970, when Israeli pilots overhearing exchanges in Russian in a MiG-21J formation, returned to base rather than challenge the adversary. With the Soviet assumption of primary responsibility for Egypt's air defenses, arms procurement in the Egypt-Israel area suddenly assumed a new face. Without US cooperation, Israel would find it hard to take effective countermeasures, and, for the time being, the United States resisted Israel's requests for immediate delivery of larger numbers of F-4s and A-4s, in part to enable the Department of State to proceed with efforts at diplomatic mediation.

At this point I must stress that the present paper is not concerned with the attritional war or the ceasefire as such but with the consequences of both for arms procurement by Egypt and Israel. I assume therefore that the reader's background on both is sufficient to fill in the detail.

The Soviet intervention in Egypt early in

1970 initially bathed the Egyptians in a feeling of strength and security. Although Israel turned visibly more cautious, the IAF clearly was not running away from the crisis. The unprecedented loss of seven planes between June 30 and the start of the ceasefire on August 7—a rate that Israel could not long sustain without assurances of replacement—was compensated in part by the destruction in the same period of four Soviet-piloted MiG-21Js. Nevertheless Israel was determined to prevent its loss of military superiority over a combined Soviet-Egyptian adversary.

Israel could not consider arms competition with the Soviet Union. But that was not really the name of the game. Rather it was competition with the Soviet Union in Egypt, and its presence there was a matter of concern not to Israel alone but also to the US in the context of the lingering Cold War in the Mediterranean and the Middle East. The Soviet naval and air presence in Egypt constituted a deterrent to Israel in its efforts to compel Egypt by military means to take unpleasant political and diplomatic decisions. The Soviet presence in Egypt also served as a factor in the larger superpower rivalry, which had spilled from the Arab states into the Mediterranean in the 1960s. The use of facilities in Egypt made plausible the Soviet Mediterranean Squadron's challenge of the Sixth Fleet as a military-diplomatic arbiter in the inland sea.

Viewed in this light, the Egyptian-Israel ceasefire of August 7, 1970, which the US had negotiated, aimed at freezing the existing military positions along the canal, the two parties had solemnly undertaken not to seek fresh military advantages. Meanwhile, feverishly laying concrete foundations for the improved SA-2 and the new SA-3 launching pads in the Delta, the Soviet missile crews had penetrated the rim of what was later to become the western standstill zone. "From 8 August," write the authors of *Strategic Survey 1970*,

with scant regard for the terms of the cease-fire, Soviet and UAR personnel proceeded to establish 40–50 new missile sites, most of them within nineteen miles of the Canal and nearly half of them featuring Soviet-manned SA-3 missiles. By the end of October, some 500–600 surface-to-air missile launchers covered the western approaches to the Canal, about 200 of them being within 19 miles of that line. Moreover, the forward sites of the system, carefully spaced 7½ miles apart along the Canal itself in order to give overlapping coverage, also covered an area extending 12 miles into Israel-occupied territory.[7]

The Soviet Union claimed that it was not a party to the standstill agreement and therefore could not be charged with violating it.

Israel, for its part, had agreed to the ceasefire only after receiving explicit assurances from the US that the new arrangement would not result in altering the military balance in Israel's disfavor; in brief, that Israel, in the event of a violation of the ceasefire by the other side, would receive such new weapons systems as would enable it to redress the balance. Israel too violated the ceasefire agreement by shoring the Bar Lev Line along the canal. But it did so only after the Soviet-Egyptian violations and could therefore be upheld as responsive action.

Israel's willingness to engage in the diplomatic discussions with Ambassador Gunner V. Jarring, as the US wished the parties to do, depended on the US willingness to uphold its obligations to Israel in redressing the arms balance. After initial bungling, because of the delayed creation of observation machinery, the US accepted the Israel interpretation. For the first time the United States supplied Israel with a large number of sophisticated electronic devices and ASMs for warning, jamming, and suppressing SAM batteries and, for good measure, agreed to sell Israel small increments of F-4s and A-4s. But it adamantly refused to back Israel's demands for a restoration of the status quo before the ceasefire. As one side effect, Israel's security planners became more convinced than ever of the need to move toward military autarky as rapidly as possible through the further expansion of military industry, a subject that will be examined presently.

Egypt, in the meantime, became steadily more reliant on the USSR. At the start of 1970 there were an estimated 2,500 to 4,000 Soviet instructors and advisers attached to the Egyptian Armed Forces; to these were added by the year's end some 12,000 to 15,000 Soviet military personnel forming the crews for the advanced missiles and for the ground maintenance of the MiG-21Js, plus an estimated 200 pilots. The Soviet Union did not frame new arms transfer policies, but simply loosened the flow of key items into the Egyptian inventory. The fleet of MiG-21C/Ds grew from about 150 in June 1970 to 220 two years later, and of Su-7s from 105 to 120. The two systems became the mainstay of the Egyptian Air Force, corresponding but inferior to the F-4 and the A-4 in the IAF. Responsibility

---

[7] *Strategic Survey, 1970* (London: IISS, 1971), p. 48.

for operating and maintaining the SA-3s in other than the purely Soviet air and naval facilities was progressively transferred to Egyptian personnel in 1971–72, and the size of the Soviet combat technical pool was substantially diminished.

On the other hand, the operation of the MiG-21Js was never handed over to Egyptian pilots or ground crews. Moreover, in 1971, a token number, perhaps as many as a half-dozen, of the new and still not fully tested MiG-23s were deployed in Egypt for reconnaissance experiments, and a squadron or possibly two of Su-11 fighter-bombers wholly for display. Only Soviet personnel were allowed to handle the two classes of aircraft. The Soviet Union also shored up Egypt's air defense with SA-4s (a tracked version of the SA-2) before the end of 1970 and reportedly some SA-6s (the tracked version of the SA-3) in 1971. Both systems, it was suspected, were intended primarily for protecting the six air bases for exclusive Soviet use, and both were wholly operated by Soviet crews. The helicopter fleet, nearly trebled in size from 70 in 1970 to 180 in 1972, included an additional 20 Mi-6 Hooks, each capable of lifting a fully armed paratroop company. Finally, the number of T-54/55 tanks had been enlarged from 950 in 1970 to 1,500 two years later, of the T-34s from 250 to 400, and of armored personnel carriers from 900 to 2,000.

The unfolding arms-transfer program did not satisfy the Egyptian political and military leaders. After all, Egypt framed its arms-acquisition policies, not simply for the defense against further attack, but for the reconquest of Egyptian (and Arab) territory seized by Israel. Yet the classes of weapons systems given to Egypt were clearly inadequate for the desired mission. What the Egyptians wanted was offensive, not defensive, weaponry for a military, not a political, solution to their dispute with Israel. To catch up with, and then to overtake Israel, Egypt would have to beat the adversary at his own game. It does not require much imagination to realize that the Egyptian policymakers, in the final analysis, could be mollified with nothing less than a surface-to-surface missile (SSM) system at least as effective as the MD-660, renamed the Jordan, which was to have a reported radius of 280 miles and was expected momentarily to go into domestic production in Israel; assurances of the early development of an indigenous military industry even more sophisticated than that of Israel; and the guarantee of full military cooperation of the USSR in a renewed war with Israel. Such requests, if they were indeed seriously presented,

the Soviet government could only reject. Any deeper military involvement in Egypt could lead only to the Soviet assumption of responsibility to expel Israel from Sinai, a plan of action that would dictate a much larger Soviet presence than the existing one, which would entail the high risk of confrontation with the US.

In a word, the Russians did not appear either to have faith in the ability of the Egyptian Armed Forces to defeat the IDF in an early encounter or in the ability of the Egyptian government and the Egyptian Armed Forces to develop a military industry that would begin to be competitive with Israel's. This produced the impasse on the Soviet arms-transfer program for Egypt and led to the crisis of July 1972, when Sadat invited the USSR selectively to pull out its advisers and combat personnel and when Brezhnev and Grechko responded by calling back most of the instructors too. As of the time of writing, Egypt has failed to elicit the support of any Western power, which in Egypt can see only liabilities that far exceed the possible political and military advantages of becoming Egypt's arms and military industrial patron. Nor has the Soviet-Egyptian partnership been restored, either on old terms or new.

THE MILITARY INDUSTRIAL DIMENSION

Military industry in Egypt is still relatively modest. It produces light and medium arms and ammunition. As early as 1949 Egypt started to assemble training planes under various European licenses, and apparently on a limited scale continued the activity in later years. Almost all the trainers since 1967 have been imported from the USSR. Also in the final years of the monarchy, the Egyptian government employed a small group of German engineers to try to develop SSMs. Interrupted by the military overturn of King Faruq in 1952, the project was resuscitated by the republican government a year later and then dropped again late in 1956, after the Sinai-Suez War.[8]

When the government in 1958 picked it up once more, the research and development project was transformed into an ambitious program for the manufacture of supersonic jet planes (a trainer and a fighter) as well as SSMs with a range of more than 250 miles and payloads of

[8] Foreign Area Studies of the American University, *Area Handbook for the United Arab Republic* (Egypt) (Washington, D.C.: Government Printing Office, 1970), p. 471.

500 to 2,000 pounds. Recruited for the program were some 500 scientists, engineers, and skilled workers in West Germany (with experience in the production and development of planes and rockets in World War II), Switzerland, Austria, and Spain. Neither the planes nor the missiles ever reached the assembly line, after the early tests, because Egypt's supporting industry could not make the essential components, and these proved impossible to import from the East or the West.

The cost of the two projects reached a peak in 1965, when it was conservatively estimated that Egypt was spending no less than $50 million. The number of European employees diminished to 44 in 1967, and then to 30 by the time that the program was abandoned in mid-1969. Egypt undertook the experiment in the manufacture of sophisticated weaponry, it should be noted, with the cooperation of West Europeans as individuals (but not of their government), which suggested an Egyptian search for release from total dependence on the USSR. Even when Egypt broke off diplomatic relations with West Germany in 1965, President 'Abd al-Nasir did not accept East German offers to replace West German skilled labor on advantageous terms, including payment in soft currency.[9]

The origins of Israel's military industry go back to the mandatory period, when the secret defense force of the Jewish community of Palestine ran underground shops for the salvage of war surplus and the repair of military equipment. The industry expanded steadily in the first two decades of independence but, in retrospect, it was essentially limited before the Six Day War of 1967 to the manufacture of small and medium weapons and components, spare parts and ammunition for heavy equipment. With each import of the light or medium class, Israel procured both the product and the technology, for once its technicians learned how to overhaul a piece of equipment, its military industry also learned how to manufacture a modified, and often improved version. So long as the item in question was in high military demand and could be produced locally, a domestic copy was likely to appear in Israel's arsenal and in its military industrial catalogue for sale abroad, whenever politically and militarily feasible, to help the expanding industry maximize its economies. Nor were the factories wholly imitative. On occasion their own creations, such as the Uzi submachine gun,

became popular even outside of Israel. More than that, Israel's military industry, wherever militarily significant, upgraded automotive equipment and improved the firing power of tanks by adding or substituting larger guns, to say nothing of standardizing the engines and parts of military vehicles and other complex martial machinery of diverse origins.[10]

Military research and development are centered at the Ministry of Defense in the Office of the Chief Scientist, which organizes the scientific and engineering talent throughout the state, including the universities. The office functions through permanent committees for each major type of activity. At the completion of the committee assignment, responsibility for the publication of their findings is handed over to the Ministry's Weapons Development Authority, which sees that the approved new weapons are fed for production into the pertinent existing or newly created industries.

These industries already produce or have on the drawing boards for early production jet fighter-bombers, a wide variety of missiles including an SSM with a range of 280 miles or more, advanced antipersonnel radar, and fast patrol boats with locally manufactured ship-to-ship missiles. In 1966 military industrial output was valued at $100 million; six years later it had quadrupled. Of all the new industries created by the Ministry of Defense in these years, electronics seemed to be expanding most rapidly, from an initial investment of about $16 million in the first year after the war of June 1967 to more than $250 million in the next four years.[11]

Even before the Six Day War the 24mW(th) nuclear research reactor at Dimona was yielding enough plutonium for one bomb a year, with fissile material left over. Israel also later discovered an economical source of uranium as a by-product of its phosphate fertilizer plant at the Dead Sea. Israel has thus been able to stockpile plutonium. Yet evidence is lacking of its having erected a facility to separate the plutonium from the uranium in the fuel rods. According to one close observer, instead of building a separation plant, the Israelis may well have developed a laboratory separation capability. In brief, Israel seems to have assured itself an open option without actually having to produce bombs.[12]

---

[10]See Hurewitz, *Middle East Politics*, pp. 450–51.

[11]See above note 2; and *Government of Israel Yearbook 5730 (1969–70)* (Jerusalem: Keter for the Prime Minister's Office, 1970), pp. 114–18.

[12]Leonard Beaton, "Why Israel Does *Not* Need the Bomb," *The New Middle East* 7 (April 1969): 9–11.

[9]See above, note 3, p. 484.

In the unprecedented enlargement of its military industry, Israel was manifestly seeking to reduce to a minimum its dependence on external sources of supply, and by the start of 1973 had come closest in the Middle East to achieving autarky.

Aerospace Research Center. *International R&D Trends and Policies: An Analysis of Implications for the U.S.* Washington, D.C.: Aerospace Industries Assn. of America, Jan. 1970.

*Alexander, Arthur J. *R&D in Soviet Aviation*, R-589-PR. Santa Monica, Calif.: The RAND Corp., Nov. 1970.

"Arms Across the Channel." *Armed Forces Journal International* 110, no. 9 (May 1973): 56–60.

Armstrong, Richard. "Military-Industrial Complex: Russian Style." *Fortune* 80 (Aug. 1, 1969): 84–87.

*Aspaturian, Vernon V. "The Soviet Military-Industrial Complex—Does It Exist?" *Journal of International Affairs* 26, no. 1 (1972): 1–28.

*Bellany, Ian. "Military Aircraft Procurement and the Small State: The Australian Case." *Proceedings of the Conference on Comparative Defense Policy*, USAF Academy, Colo., Department of Political Science, 1973.

Bellany, Ian, and Richardson, James L. *Australian Defence Procurement*, Canberra Paper #8. Canberra, Australia: Australian National University Press, 1970.

Benecke, Theodor. "Military Technology in West Germany." *Military Review* 47 (Aug. 1967): 41–46.

Bhagavantam, S. "Organization, Management and Progress of Defence Research and Development." *The Indian Journal of Public Administration* 15, no. 3 (July-Sept. 1964): 395–403.

*Bueschel, Richard M. *Communist Chinese Air Power*. New York: Frederick A. Praeger, 1968.

*Calder, Nigel (ed.). *Unless Peace Comes: A Scientific Forecast of New Weapons*. New York: The Viking Press, 1968.

Clemens, Walter C., Jr. "Chinese Nuclear Tests: Trends and Portents." *China Quarterly* (Oct.-Dec. 1967): 111–31.

*Cohen, Stephen. "The Security Policy-Making Process in Operation: Conventional Weapons Systems and Nuclear Weapons Issues." South Asian Inst./E. Asian Inst., Columbia University, *India and Japan: The Emerging Balance of Power in Asia and Opportunities for Arms Control, 1970–75*, ACDA/IR-70. Washington, D.C.: U.S. Arms Control and Disarmament Agency, Apr. 1971, pp. 30–55.

Field, Hugh, and Wilson, Michael. "Sweden's Aircraft Industry." *Flight International* (Dec. 14, 1972): 867–81.

*Frank, Lewis A. "Nasser's Missile Program." *Orbis* 11, no. 3 (Fall 1967): 746–57.

Galloway, Jonathan F. "Multinational Corporations and the Military-Industrial Complex." Mimeo. paper presented to International Studies Association Annual Convention, Dallas, March 14–17, 1972.

Gibert, Stephen P. "Soviet-American Military Aid Competition in the Third World." *Orbis* 13 (Winter 1970): 1117–37.

Gray, Colin. "What is Good for General Motors . . ." *RUSI Journal* (June 1972): 36–42.

Greenwood, A. H. C. "MRCA—The Future System of Military Procurement." *RUSI Journal* 117, no. 3 (Sept. 1972): 3–13.

Greenwood, David. "Economic Constraints and National Defence Efforts." Mimeo. unpublished. Aberdeen, Scotland, N.D.

Guertner, Gary L. "The Political Utility of Military Aid." Mimeo. unpublished, presented to Western Political Science Assn., Portland, Oregon, March 1972.

*Hall, G. R., and Johnson, R. E. *Transfers of United States Aerospace Technology to Japan*, P-3875. Santa Monica, Calif.: The RAND Corp., July 1968.

Head, Richard G. "A Comparative Analysis of European Science Policy: United Kingdom, France, and Germany." Mimeo. unpublished, USAF Academy, Colo., Sept. 1971.

Hewish, Mark. "France's Strategic Missiles." *Flight International* (27 Jan. 1972): 132–37.

*Holloway, David. *Technology, Management and the Soviet Military Establishment*, Adelphi Paper No. 76. London: IISS, April 1971.

Hsieh, Alice Langley. "China's Nuclear-Missile Programme: Regional or Intercontinental?" *China Quarterly* 45 (Jan./Mar. 1971): 85–99.

Hunter, Alex. "Industry and Defence in Australia." Millar, T. B. (ed.), *Australian-New Zealand Defence Co-operation*. Canberra: Australian National University Press, 1968.

Joshua, Wynfred, and Gibert, Stephen P. *Arms for the Third World: Soviet Military and Diplomacy*. Baltimore: The Johns Hopkins Press, 1969.

Kaul, R. "India's Russian Navy." *U.S. Naval Institute Proceedings* 96 (Aug. 1970): 38–45.

*Kemp, Geoffrey. "Arms Traffic and Third World Conflicts." *International Conciliation* 577 (Mar. 1970): entire.

————. "The International Arms Trade: Supplier, Recipient and Arms Control Perspectives." *Political Quarterly* 42 (1971): 376–89.

Kihara, Masao. "The Militarization of the Japanese Economy." *Kyoto University Economic Review* 38 (Oct. 1968): 26–45.

Krieger, F. J. *Soviet Astronautics: 1957–1962*, RM-3595-PR. Santa Monica, Calif.: The RAND Corp., Apr. 1963.

Krylov, Konstantin K. "Soviet Military-Economic Complex." *Military Review* 51 (Nov. 1971): 89–97.

*Leiss, Amelia C., et al. *Arms Transfers to Less Developed Countries*. Vol. III of *Arms Control and Local Conflict*. Cambridge, Mass.: Center for International Studies, MIT, Feb. 1970.

Longrigg, Tony. "Soviet Science and Foreign Policy." *Survey* 17 (Autumn 1971): 30–63.

*= *particularly recommended.*

McLin, Jon. *Rationalizing Defense Production in NATO, Part I & II*, JM-1-68, JM-2-68, Hanover, N.H.: The American Universities Field Staff, Oct. 1968.

Manchester, William. *The Arms of Krupp, 1587–1968.* Boston: Little, Brown, 1968.

"Materiel R&D and Procurement (Sweden)." *Armed Forces Journal International* 110, no. 6 (Feb. 1973): 50–52.

Middleton, Peter. "Germany's Aircraft Industry." *Flight International* (26 Oct 1972): 575–84.

"New Approaches in R&D for the Future (Sweden)." *Armed Forces Journal International* 110, no. 6 (Feb. 1973): 54–55.

Nimitz, Nancy. *Soviet Expenditures on Scientific Research*, RM-3384-PR. Santa Monica, Calif.: The RAND Corp., Jan. 1963.

*Peck, Merton J., and Scherer, Frederic M. *The Weapons Acquisition Process: An Economic Analysis.* Boston: Division of Research, Graduate School of Business Administration, Harvard University, 1962.

*Perry, Robert. *European and U.S. Aircraft Development Strategies*, P-4748. Santa Monica, Calif.: The RAND Corp., Dec. 1971.

Prakash, Ved. "Organization, Management and Progress of Atomic Energy Research in India." *Indian Journal of Public Administration* 15, no. 3 (July-Sept. 1969): 565–75.

*Ra'Anan, Uri. *The USSR Arms the Third World.* Cambridge, Mass.: MIT Press, 1969.

Ramsden, J. M. "France's Aircraft Industry." *Flight International* (9 Nov 1972): 649–56, 662–69.

*Ryan, William L., and Summerlin, Sam. *The China Cloud.* Boston: Little, Brown, 1968.

*Sapolsky, Harvey M. "The Military/Industrial State in Comparative Perspective." *Proceedings of the Conference on Comparative Defense Policy*, USAF Academy, Colo., Department of Political Science, 1973.

*Scheinman, Lawrence. *Atomic Energy Policy in France under the Fourth Republic.* Princeton, N.J.: Princeton University Press, 1965.

*Simpson, John. "The Acquisition of Military Aircraft in Great Britain: A Case History of the TSR-2 Project, 1957–1965." Mimeo. unpublished, University of Southampton, 1973.

*Simpson, John, and Gregory, F. E. C. "West European Collaboration in Weapons Procurement." *Orbis* 16, no. 2 (Summer 1972): 435–61.

Smart, Ian. *Future Conditional: The Prospect for Anglo-French Nuclear Co-operation.* Adelphi Paper No. 78. London: IISS, Aug. 1971.

*Stanley, John, and Pearton, Maurice. *The International Trade in Arms.* New York: Frederick A. Praeger, 1972.

Stewart, Oliver. "The Future of Britain's Aerospace Industry." *Brassey's Annual 1966.* Edited by Moulton et al. New York: Frederick A. Praeger, pp. 227–36.

*Thayer, George. *The War Business.* New York: Avon Books, 1969.

Van Cleave, William R., and Rood, Harold W. "A Technological Comparison of Two Potential Nuclear Powers: India and Japan." *Asian Survey* (July 1967): 482–89.

Vernon, Raymond. *Multi-national Enterprise and National Security.* Adelphi Paper No. 74. London: IISS, January 1971.

Wilding-White, Ted. "Japan's Aircraft Industry." *Flight International* (7 December 1972): 813–23.

*Williams, Geoffrey; Gregory, Frank; and Simpson, John. *Crisis In Procurement: A Case Study of the TSR-2.* London: RUSI, 1969.

*Wolf, Charles, Jr. *Economic Impacts of Military Assistance*, P-4578. Santa Monica, Calif.: The RAND Corporation, February 1971.

Young, Judith H. *The French Strategic Missile Programme.* Adelphi Papers No. 38. London: Institute for Strategic Studies, July 1967.

* = particularly recommended.

PART SIX

THE USE OF FORCE

INTRODUCTION

ANTHONY C. ROGERSON

All the preceding sections—how the military views its role and is viewed, how the defense community is organized, what military doctrine a nation has, what forces it possesses, and how it gets those forces—lead up to the consideration of how nations *actually* use and have used force. This section most closely ties in, of course, with those on Military Doctrine and Force Posture, but there is not necessarily a direct relationship. France has been accused in the past of always preparing to fight the next war with the weapons and tactics of the last, and she is not the only nation to discover that doctrine and force posture do not necessarily relate adequately to the actual needs when force is used. Britain, France, and the United States, for example, have poured the majority of their defense funds and planning since World War II into preparations for major conventional or nuclear wars and yet have actually been involved mainly in counter-guerrilla and irregular warfare. It is, therefore, very important to consider the actual use of force made by various nations to round-off our study of comparative defense policy.

WHY NATIONS USE FORCE

There is a preliminary issue which we should look at before answering the question "How have nations used force?" and that is, "Why do nations use force at all?" This deserves much more inclusive treatment than we can afford here but must at least be touched upon. There are those who believe, for example, that the best use of force would be to renounce it. Such were those in the British Labor Party in the late 1950s and early 1960s who supported unilateral nuclear disarmament on the grounds that this would encourage universal nuclear disarmament.[1] Whether fortunately or unfortunately, such views have not been put into practice. The British Labor Party, having flirted with nuclear disarmament, continued the Polaris submarine development when it came to power in 1964. Whichever of the three images of war one adopts[2]—whether war is caused by man's nature, by the kind of states which exist, or by the international system of states—war is a reality which shows little chance of disappearing and so nations continue to prepare to use, and actually do use, force in their dealings with one another.

THE CHANGING FACE OF WAR

The use of force is determined by political considerations. As Samuel P. Huntington says in his book *Changing Patterns of Military Politics*, "The dominant forces of violence of each age reflects the politics of the age."[3] Thus, he goes on to show that the violence of the seventeenth century reflected the declining power of the Hapsburg Empire and the effect of extreme religious differences; the limited warfare of the eighteenth century was the natural result of the monarchies of the ancient regime; nationalism, liberalism, colonialism and social change produced the characteristic conflicts of the nineteenth century; in the first half of the twentieth century nationalistic rivalries and expansion produced two world wars. What about the second half of the twentieth century? Violence has reflected and will continue to reflect the political changes of our time—the East/West split, the end of colonization and emergence of the Third World, the creation of the State of Israel, the division of the Indian subcontinent, the recurrence of tribal problems in Africa, and

---

[1] See Andrew J. Pierre, *Nuclear Politics* (Oxford: Oxford University Press, 1972), Part 3.

[2] See Kenneth N. Waltz, *Man, the State and War* (New York: Columbia University Press, 1954).

[3] Samuel P. Huntington, "Patterns of Violence in World Politics," in Huntington, (ed.), *Changing Patterns of Military Politics* (New York: Free Press of Glencoe, 1962), p. 46.

Squadron Leader Anthony C. Rogerson (M.A., Oxford) is an RAF Exchange Officer serving as Assistant Professor of Political Science at the USAF Academy. Prior to this, he taught at the RAF College, Cranwell for five years. His special interests are defense studies and political theory.

The views expressed herein are those of the author and do not necessarily reflect the views of the Royal Air Force or the U.K. Ministry of Defence.

social, political and economic stresses in under-developed and developed nations alike—to name but some.

Alastair Buchan brings out the important changes in the use of force over the last century in an interesting way.[4] He postulates observers in 1876, 1906, 1936, and 1951 and reconstructs their view of the likely causes of war in their time. Thus, in 1876 the most serious danger was that of war on land in Central or Western Europe. In 1906 the same danger was there. This time it was complicated by the fear of the costs and the effects of such a war on the eco-nomies and stability of the individual states—there seemed little likelihood, therefore, that it would involve the total mobilization of the par-ticipants' resources. In 1936 a European War was still feared and, following the experience of the First World War, it was expected to be another total conflict—thus the fear of war was sharply deepened, and was reflected in the attempts of men like Neville Chamberlain to avoid it at all costs. Also, the likelihood of the European War growing into a global conflict was all too appar-ent. In 1951 the fear of total, global war was dominant in men's minds, especially in view of the recent victory by the Communists in China and the outbreak of the Korean War in 1950. And yet today, the likelihood of total, global war seems small and the major antagonists in the Cold War are slowly reaching forms of accom-modation with one another. Also, unlike the situation in the other four years considered, the value of territorial conquest has greatly dimin-ished.[5] The prospects for war today look very different from those in the earlier periods.

And yet we have to balance the above with evidence given by Kurt Lang that there is a gen-erally rising trend in the magnitude of war ac-tivity: "From an index based on the number of wars in each century between the twelfth and the twentieth, with each war weighted by its dura-tion, the size of the participating armies, the number of casualties, the number of belligerents and the proportion of combatants among the population, Sorokin[6] infers a generally rising trend in the magnitude of war activity with sig-nificant breaks in the seventeenth century, a period of intense warfare, and in the nineteenth

century, an era of comparative peace."[7] The danger of major war today may have lessened, but this does not mean that the danger of other forms of war is not present—far from it. The changing pattern of war can be seen in the examples in this section of the book. Of the six articles dealing with specific cases of war only two are concerned primarily with the traditional head-on clash between nations over territory.

THE USE OF FORCE

This brings us to a brief survey of the articles in this section. Kenneth Waltz's "Conflict in World Politics" provides a very helpful introduc-tory chapter with his classification of conflicts into four all-inclusive categories. Because we are concerned about how nations have actually used force, most of the conflicts discussed in the other articles in the section fall into his Category B (close association of states: opposition-resolute contention). However, Waltz's article is also im-portant because it brings out alternate ways of conflict resolution and different uses of force, including the deterrent use of force, which, as in the case of the United States and the Soviet Union, produces the situation he classifies as Category A (loose association of states-regres-sion). The whole field of deterrence is an impor-tant aspect of the use of force not considered at length in this section.

Robin Remington's article on the invasion of Czechoslovakia pinpoints what has been the main direct use of force by the Soviet Union: keeping its allies in line. Her comparison of the Czech invasion with the United States' interven-tion in Santo Domingo in 1965 shows that this is a temptation faced by both super-powers in their respective spheres of influence.

The West has long viewed Communist China as a typical, land seeking, expansionist nation, ready and willing to use force in an aggressive fashion. Peter Van Ness makes a good case for this being an incorrect view. China is certainly interested in extending her power, but she has not been, so far, an "expansionist" nation, in the traditional sense.

John Ambler's and Michael Banks's articles bring us to modern guerrilla warfare. France's wars in Indochina and Algeria are classic case studies of the impossibility of winning such wars without political victory. Northern Ireland is unique in many ways, particularly in the under-

---

[4]Alastair Buchan, *War in Modern Society* (London: C. A. Watts, 1966), Chapter 2.

[5]For a treatment of this, see Klaus Knorr, *On the Uses of Military Power in the Nuclear Age* (Princeton, N.J.: Princeton University Press, 1966), pp. 21–34.

[6]P. A. Sorokin, *Social and Cultural Dynamics*, Vol. 3; *Fluctuation of Social Relationships, War and Revolution* (New York: American Book Co., 1937).

[7]Kurt Lang, *Military Institutions and the Sociology of War* (Beverly Hills, Calif.: Sage Publications, 1972), p. 134.

lying causes of conflict, but it nevertheless represents an all-too-likely future use of force—urban guerrilla war.

The last two articles concern more traditional wars—to remind us that these have not disappeared. The India/China War of 1962–65, described by Lorne Kavic, is a typical border-dispute war and is especially interesting in view of India's nonaligned position and its traumatic impact on Indian force posture. Michael Howard and Robert Hunter detail reprisal raids and the Six Day War, showing why Israel won in the latter and the significance of her victory.

FURTHER AREAS FOR STUDY

Many aspects of the use of force have not been touched upon or have hardly been covered in this section. The following are some of the areas which could be studied on a country-by-country basis:

Deterrence.

Internal peace-keeping.

Low-intensity warfare.[8]

Reprisals.

Military aid to the civil community.

United Nations peace-keeping operations.
(These are particularly interesting because of the light they cast on the use of force by such nations as Canada.)

Also, guerrilla warfare, conventional warfare, deterrence, reprisals, military aid to the civil community, etc., can all be studied comparatively. Each requires a volume of its own. Such a comparative study has obviously not been attempted here, but there is room for extensive work in this area. Robert Moss' *Urban Guerrilla Warfare* and *Urban Guerrillas*[9] show the value of such an approach.

---

[8]For an interesting study of this kind of warfare, which includes subversion, insurgency, and peace-keeping, see Frank Kitson, *Low Intensity Operations* (Harrisburg, Pa.: Stackpole Books, 1971).

[9]Robert Moss, *Urban Guerrilla Warfare*, Adelphi Paper No. 79 (London: The International Institute for Strategic Studies, 1971), and *Urban Guerrillas* (London: Temple Smith, 1972).

CONFLICT IN WORLD POLITICS

KENNETH N. WALTZ

Kenneth Waltz's article is built on the premise that there are three different ways in which conflict may be viewed—in terms of each of the units involved, in terms of the interactions of units, or in terms of an actual or postulated organization overarching the units. Taking the third of these, which is usually the appropriate one in cases of international conflict, Professor Waltz classifies conflicts into four main categories based on major differences in the structure of international politics. This classification is extremely valuable in understanding the reasons for nations' potential and actual use of force.

Kenneth N. Waltz is the Ford Professor of Political Science at the University of California at Berkeley. He is the author of Man, the State, and War *(1959) and* Foreign Policy and Democratic Politics *(1967), and has co-edited* The Use of Force *(1971) and* Conflict in World Politics *(1971).*

Wars that shake the world order, or even a regional order, are rare. The systemic unimportance of most wars encourages students to treat wars as events to be understood simply in terms of the attributes and interactions of the contending units. Even so, from the standpoint of the observer, conflict among units cannot be understood without including the organizational perspective.

This statement leads us to the important but difficult question of applying organizational concepts to international relations. Differentiation is a precondition of conflict, and differentiation implies organization, at least in the sense that the different parts stand in a specifiable relation to each other. We can use the term "organization" to cover this pre-institutional condition if we think of an organization simply as a constraint.[1] Because states constrain and limit each other, international relations can be viewed in rudimentary organizational terms. Each state arrives at policies and decides upon actions according to its own internal processes, but its decisions are shaped by the very presence of other states as well as by interactions with them. To make it clear that "organization" need not refer to concrete institutions, and in international relations ordinarily does not refer to them, we shall use the word "structure" and mean by it the relevant environment of states. Sometimes this will be a merely local or regional environment, but more often global structural effects will also come into play. Like a firm operating in a market, a state experiences structural effects whether or not the structure is correctly perceived; and, again like a firm, if the structure is correctly perceived, the strategy of a state can be more intelligently fashioned. Although states are independent, their perceptions of each other and their interactions create a structure to which they tend to adjust. As a consequence of their experience with one another, much of their action becomes habitual.

INTERNATIONAL STRUCTURE AND NATIONAL BEHAVIOR

One may look at conflict in terms of each of the units involved, in terms of the interactions of units, or in terms of an actual or postulated organization that overarches the units. The first perspective is appropriate only when the units are disconnected or near to being so. The second perspective is always insufficient for the reasons given above. The third perspective is ordinarily the appropriate one in cases of international conflict. If conflicts are viewed in terms of the effects of the environment on them and in terms of their effects on the environment, then the classification of conflicts will hinge on major differences in the structure of international politics. The following table sets forth such distinctions, indicates

[1]W. Ross Ashby, *An Introduction to Cybernetics* (New York: Wiley, 1956), p. 131.

Reprinted by permission and with minor changes from Steven L. Spiegel and Kenneth N. Waltz (eds.) Conflict in World Politics *(Cambridge, Mass.: Winthrop Publishers, 1971).*

the modes of behavior typical within the different structures, and distributes the 21 cases examined in *Conflict in World Politics* in an appropriate fashion among categories.[2]

Before taking up each category separately, a few words should be said about the table's right-hand column. It derives from Kurt Singer's profound work on the theory of conflict. He has suggested that in response to situations of conflict:

four and only four basic types of meaningful behavior appear to be possible: renouncing one's objective by staying behind the barrier [regression]; attempting to remove or modify the barrier [integration]; leaving the whole obstructed field [withdrawal]; or resolving to destroy the barrier [resolute contention].

[2]These are the cases examined in Steven L. Spiegel and Kenneth N. Waltz (eds.), *Conflict in World Politics* (Cambridge, Mass.: Winthrop Publishers, 1971), p. 458.

Singer argues persuasively that his classification is complete:

every conflict-solution involves two pairs of opposites, which allow for four and only four combinations: subjective and objective, positive and negative. The subject's attitude may be active or passive; and it may acknowledge the objective incompatibility or repudiate it.[3]

Both regression and withdrawal (*A* and *D*) are passive or negative approaches; both integration and fighting (*C* and *B*) are active or positive. Both in regressing and in fighting (*A* and *B*), the parties accept the presence of an objective incompatibility; both in seeking to integrate and in

[3]Kurt Singer, "The Resolution of Conflict," *Social Research* 6 (1949): 241. See also his "The Meaning of Conflict," *Australasian Journal of Philosophy* 27 (December 1949) and *The Idea of Conflict* (Melbourne: Melbourne University Press, 1949).

	Structure	Typical Modes of Behavior
A.	*Loose association of states*	*Regression*
	US and USSR	
	US and China	
	USSR and China	
	Argentina and Chile	
	India and Pakistan	
	Malaysia, Philippines, Indonesia	
	Somalia, Ethiopia, Kenya	
B.	*Close association of states: Opposition*	*Resolute contention*
	East and West Germany	
	North and South Korea	
	Israel and the Arab Countries	
	South Vietnam	
	Nigeria and Biafra	
	USSR and Czechoslovakia	
	US and Dominican Republic	
	US and Southeast Asia	
C.	*Close association of states: Cooperation*	*Integration*
	France and Germany	
	US and Japan	
	US and Canada	
	Portugal and South Africa	
	Great Britain and France	
	Nuclear proliferation	
D.	*Nonassociation of states*	*Withdrawal*
	For an explanation of this empty category, see p. 508	

trying to withdraw (C and D), they refuse to accept their antagonism. "So long as we cling to the criteria of active and passive, positive and negative attitudes," Singer concludes, "the quadruplet of types can claim completeness and finality."[4]

Singer was writing of conflict in general, from psychic disturbance to war among states. When his categories of conflict are applied to international relations, his claim to completeness is validated. The four types of behavior cover both the strategies of states fending for themselves in an anarchic arena and the strategies of states who try to escape from that arena. A and B represent the traditional view of international politics, with states sometimes maneuvering to avoid war and at other times fighting fiercely. In A and C, states seek to avoid violence either by leaving each other alone or by making cooperative arrangements. In A, states concentrate their attention on their own fates, a tendency that is carried to an extreme in D. In B, C, and D, states seek to alter the organization of their affairs profoundly, though by radically different means in one category as compared to another; and if their aims are realized, international politics is brought to an end within the circle of states involved.

To link behavior with structure requires a careful examination of each category. This examination we now undertake.

LOOSE ASSOCIATION OF STATES: REGRESSION

Domestically, the force of a government is exercised in the name of right and justice; internationally, the force of a state is employed for the stake of its own protection and advantage. Rebels challenge a government's claim to authority; they question the rightfulness and justice of its rule. Wars among states cannot settle questions of authority and justice; they can only determine the allocation of gains and losses among contenders and settle for a time the question of who is the stronger. Domestically and internationally, relations of superordination and subordination are established; but internationally these are relations of strength, not of authority. The power of the strong may deter the weak from asserting their claims, not because the weak recognize a kind of rightfulness of rule on the part of the strong, but simply because it is not sensible to tangle with them. Conversely, the weak may enjoy considerable freedom of action and gain some tangible advantage if they are so far removed in

their capabilities from the strong that the latter are not much bothered by their actions or much concerned by marginal increases in their capabilities.

In the unalloyed anarchy of international relations, each state provides the means for its self-preservation as best it can. Elements of conflict in the competition of states outweigh those of cooperation. When faced with the possibility of cooperative endeavor by which mutual gains may be scored, each state must ask how those gains will be divided. They are compelled to ask not "Will both of us gain?" but "Who will gain more?" If an expected gain is to be divided, say, in the ratio of two to one, one state may use its disproportionate gain to implement a policy intended to damage or destroy the other. Even the prospect of large absolute gains for both parties does not elicit their cooperation so long as each fears how the other will use its increased capabilities. Notice that the impediments to collaboration may not lie in the character and the immediate intention of either party. Instead, the condition of insecurity—at the least, the uncertainty of each about the other's future intentions and actions—works strongly against their cooperation.

The fate of each state depends on its responses to what other states do. Will these responses lead them to integrate their activities in order to improve their well-being, to contend resolutely, or to draw apart and watch each other with wariness and suspicion? The answer depends not only on the extent to which their fates are linked in terms of security but also on how closely they are entangled in other than military ways.

States are closely interdependent if they depend on each other for services and supplies that they cannot easily, if at all, provide for themselves. Out of a condition of mutual dependence is born the desire of each party to control whatever it is dependent upon. In such a condition, states cannot afford simply to leave each other alone. They have strong incentives to make one of two choices: either to use force in order to gain control or to build institutions in order to secure the benefits of cooperation. Their close interdependence leads them either to strive for dominance or to contrive institutions for the regulation of their intertwined affairs. In their daily lives, however, the states of category A are not closely entangled, whether one thinks of entanglement in terms of trade and investment or of cultural exchanges and tourism. Because these states are only loosely connected, they can afford to leave each other alone.

[4]Singer, "The Resolution of Conflict," p. 242.

States of category A accept each other's continued existence, whether or not reluctantly. They seek neither to destroy the structure of their relations nor to change it drastically; rather, they contend for advantage within it. They do not use their political power to create enduring institutions and peaceful patterns of intercourse, but instead to maneuver and manipulate, to threaten and punish. They appear as both antagonists and partners, sometimes skirmishing in a test of wills, sometimes probing to expose weaknesses, sometimes moving toward agreement on specific issues, sometimes simply drawing apart. In the course of their conflicts, they may go to the brink in a sudden flaring of temper or testing of wills and then draw back. The option of drawing back is available, as is the possibility of occasional skirmishing and even of open warfare. But the structure, a loose one, is not broken either when the parties separate and become quiescent or when they confront each other directly. Their confrontations tend to be inconclusive. Their strategies are grounded on the principle that it is better to yield than to risk mutual destruction. The policy dilemma for states in this type of conflict is that both sides are unwilling to resolve differences completely and establish new patterns of coexistence, yet neither side is prepared to destroy the other.

In their relations with each other, the United States and the Soviet Union provide a nearly perfect example of this pattern. Some of their interests coincide: the prevention of nuclear war, the control of other states' weapons, the mutual limitation of defense budgets for the sake of their domestic economies. At the same time, they differ on a number of issues, notably in Europe, southeast Asia, and the Middle East. Neither side is prepared to risk military weakness, but none of their disputes can be pushed to the point of war. Mutual opposition may require rather than preclude the adjustment of differences, and yet first steps toward agreement do not easily lead further. Instead, they mingle with other acts and events that keep the tension quite high. In the United States, for example, the 1963 test-ban treaty was described as possibly a first big step toward wider disarmament agreements. In almost the same breath it was also said that the United States could not lower her guard because the Soviet Union's aims had not changed.[5] Each country appears to the other as the only power in the world that can do it grievous harm, and each must worry about the other's use of this capa-

bility. Their mutual worry limits both the building up of tensions and the abatement of conflict. Incentives to collaborate, and temptations to fight, are limited by the framework of their action. The result is an ebb and flow of tensions as dramatic agreements are made (test ban, nonproliferation treaty) and as specific crises occur (Berlin, Cuba, the Middle East, Vietnam).

In each case within category A, the weaker party has been forced by its weakness to use military force cautiously, to cast about for allies, to resort to ideological warfare, or to readjust its aims. The conflicts between Somalia and Ethiopia/Kenya, and between Pakistan and India, are cases in point. Somalia and Pakistan, both considerably weaker than their adversaries, seek territorial gains at the expense of their neighbors in order to be united with a greater number of their compatriots. Neither of them can destroy its adversary, nor wishes to do so, but their ultimate objectives limit their cooperation. As a consequence, relations between Somalia and Ethiopia/Kenya and between Pakistan and India tend to be dormant when international and domestic conditions prevent the weaker party from pursuing adventurous policies. When the situation is temporarily altered, violence flares up, as in the brief war of 1965 between Pakistan and India and in the sporadic Somali guerrilla campaign that lasted from 1960 to 1967.

More than other cases in this category, Sino-Soviet and Sino-American relations are marked by intense antagonism; but the general patterns are similar. Territorial issues are a major irritant (Taiwan and the Sino-Soviet border area), although these issues are clearly not the sole causes of conflict. As the weaker party, China is unable to press its designs very far against either the United States or the Soviet Union and presents no important military threat to them. The strong parties are not prepared either to use major military force or to work to strengthen their relations with the weak one. Consequently the typical ebb-and-flow pattern prevails: China moves toward the brink over border incidents with the Soviet Union or in response to American actions in east or southeast Asia, while at the same time the Chinese talk sporadically with one of the superpowers in Warsaw or in Peking or Moscow.

In category A, regression is the dominant mode. Adventurous powers are forced to mold their intentions to contingencies, to let present goals await future opportunities, and to draw back from dangerous confrontations. As Singer suggests, regressive strategy represents the approach of a peasant—patient, shrewd, and persistent. This is a strategy of "dropping and

[5]Cf. Kenneth N. Waltz, "The Stability of a Bipolar World," *Daedalus* 93 (Summer 1964): 903–4.

drifting," but the weaker party is "secure in the knowledge that those who yield will . . . conquer in the end."[6] The policies of China, Pakistan, Somalia, Chile, of all of the Malay states, and even of the Soviet Union can often be viewed in these terms.

CLOSE ASSOCIATION OF STATES: RESOLUTE CONTENTION

In category *A*, the opposition of states raises the specter of possible warfare, but because opposition centers on particular issues, compromises and trade-offs can always be attempted. And even when states are fighting, they intermittently bargain and cajole.

In category *B*, the parties contend not simply over the difficult issue of who shall gain or lose. They struggle instead with the calamitous question: Who shall dominate whom? The answer to that question can satisfy only one of the parties. Politics, or political form, becomes the stake around which the conflict revolves. One of the parties in contention, and perhaps both of them, seeks to destroy the structure of their relations by undoing the other regime and, in some cases, by displacing its people. Structural struggles spawn strategies of resolute contention; at least one party decides that he will persist in the struggle even should this mean his own destruction. Bargaining becomes impossible, and the conflict becomes the communication.

As the cases of category *B* suggest, great-power interventions, civil wars, and contention among the dissimilar parts of states that were once united are characteristic instances of this type of struggle. In great-power interventions, conflict is resolved through the adjustment of goals by one party; the weaker state gives way in the face of the threats or the force of the stronger. In civil wars and in the struggle between the parts of a divided state, resolution comes, if it comes at all, through military triumph. Either these conflicts end definitely and abruptly as a result of military action, or they continue in crisis as long as the goal of destruction remains a part of the policy of one of the parties.

The Nigerian civil war was a typical conflict over structure. The conflict could not be resolved through compromise because the conflict involved nothing less than the question of whether one state or two would occupy the area known as Nigeria. As long as Biafra continued to exist, the aims of the federal government were thwarted. The defeat of Biafra transferred Ibo-Nigerian

relations to another framework. In the Arab-Israeli conflict, the Israelis have managed to perpetuate their existence, but they have not managed to alter the aim of their Arab neighbors to destroy Israel. Their intense confrontation has furthered the integration of Israel and has produced some coherence among deeply divided Arab states. Unless at least one side drastically alters its definition of acceptable political arrangements, intense conflict will continue indefinitely.

Conflict within South Vietnam and between the two Germanies and the two Koreas turns on political and ideological differences, in contrast to the strong religious and ethnic divisions in the Middle East. In the German case, the prospect that force will be used to achieve reunification has receded in recent years. The most hopeful possibility in cases of this type is that, as the parties develop separate and viable regimes, the issue politics of category *A* will replace the structural struggles of category *B*. The parties may then discover, as the two Germanies show signs of doing, that they can cooperate on some matters without turning every issue into a test of the legitimacy of regimes. In the Korean case, close kinship has not led to reestablishment of social and economic contacts across a hostile frontier. The very intensity of hostility has promoted the tight political integration of both Koreas, a development that vividly illustrates the maxim that organizations are created by their enemies.[7] The political success of the two Koreas has at once lessened their need for each other and made them capable of vying fiercely for mastery.

At whatever level of intensity, the parties to these conflicts share a dissatisfaction with the status quo. They see their basic goals as being incompatible and define the question between them as being, who shall ultimately prevail?

The three cases of great-power intervention are like the others of this category in that the struggle is over the structure, but different in that the parties are of grossly unequal power. These interventions represent forceful attempts to alter conditions within particular states or regions in order to bring client states into conformity with the superpowers' notions of proper political arrangements. In each instance, the superpower demonstrated concern over the integrity of its alliance system and, more profoundly, betrayed a fear that failure to maintain control in one area would weaken its control and

---

[6]Singer, "The Resolution of Conflict," p. 231.

[7]Kenneth E. Boulding, *Conflict and Defense* (New York: Harper & Row, 1962), p. 162.

lessen the credibility of its commitments elsewhere. In the Dominican Republic and in
Czechoslovakia, solutions were swiftly and decisively achieved in central areas of the superpowers' concerns. In southeast Asia, the United
States sought to reinforce her position at the
periphery of her sphere of interest rather than at
the core. She was unable to change conditions
quickly and was also unwilling to yield. Prolonged conflict resulted. In South Vietnam, the
American problem has not been merely to dissuade a government from taking certain actions
and to compel it to perform others. Instead,
America's self-appointed task has been to promote the establishment of a preferred political
order, an immense undertaking that requires far
more than military means. American aims, if
achieved, would maintain the conditions for continued struggle among the new parts of the old
Indochina. Any major part of Indochina that
achieves strength will want to reunify the whole.
That is the nature of structural struggles. The
might of the superpowers allows them to determine the size and the intensity of such conflicts,
but not always the outcome.

In structural strife, when the conflict is
among unequals the stronger parties face difficult
tasks. They wish to retain control or to maintain
their friends in power, and such ends are difficult
to achieve. In structural strife, when the conflict
is among equals the struggles have continued
interminably.

CLOSE ASSOCIATION OF
STATES: INTEGRATION

What can bring two parties closer together
than to be locked into a prolonged death-grip?
The states of category *B* are closely associated;
they are united in their antagonism. The states of
category *C* are also closely associated, but in cooperative rather than hostile spirit. If states believe that violent conflict would destroy their
common good, they may try to promote closer integration through the establishment of durable
institutions and reliable patterns of behavior.
What makes it possible for trust to replace hostility in the relations of sovereign states so that
they may begin to benefit jointly from peaceful
and cooperative endeavors? This question can
best be answered by considering the change in
the quality of the relations of western European
states that took place after 1945. For centuries
before that date, European great-power politics
tended toward the model of a zero-sum game.
One state viewed another's loss as its own gain
and was constrained to do so by the very condi-

tions of their mutual existence. Faced with the
temptation to cooperate in order to secure joint
benefits, each state became wary and was inclined to draw back. Category *A* described the
condition of their precarious peacetime existence,
a condition that made regression more appropriate than integration. When, on occasion, some
European states did move toward cooperation,
they did so in order to oppose other states more
strongly. The fear that some states would contend
resolutely in a structural struggle for dominance
overwhelmed the possibilities of European integration. European states could not break the alternation from loose association and regressive
behavior to close association and resolute contention as long as each state feared the damaging
blows that other states could strike.

The emergence of the Russian and American
superpowers created a situation that permitted
wider ranging and more effective cooperation
among the states of western Europe. They became consumers of security, to use an expression
common in the days of the League of Nations.
For the first time in modern history, the determinants of war and peace lay outside the arena of
European states, and the means of their preservation were provided by others. These new circumstances made possible the famous "upgrading of the common interest," a phrase which con-
veys the thought that all should work together to
improve everyone's lot rather than being obses-
sively concerned with the precise division of
benefits. Not all impediments to cooperation
were removed, but one important one was—the
fear that the greater advantage of one would be
translated into military force to be used against
the others. Living in the superpowers' shadow,
Britain, France, Germany, and Italy quickly saw
that war among them would be fruitless and soon
began to believe it impossible.

Once the possibility of war among states dis-
appears, all of them can more freely run the risk
of suffering a relative loss. Enterprises can be engaged in that are expected to benefit some parties
more than others, partly in the hope for the latter
that in other activities the balance of benefits will
be reversed and partly in the belief that the overall enterprise itself is valuable. Economic gains
may be granted by one state to another in exchange for expected political advantages, including the benefit of strengthening the structure
of European cooperation. The removal of worries
about security among the states of western
Europe does not mean the termination of conflict; it does produce a change in its content.
Hard bargaining within the EEC (by France over
agricultural policies, for example) indicates that

governments do not lose interest in who will gain more and who will gain less. Conflicts of interest remain, but not the expectation that someone will use force to resolve them.

International conditions permitted western European nations to work to upgrade their common interests. The self-interest of each nation encouraged it to join in, as is evident even in the policy of the most reluctant participant, Great Britain. Mutuality of involvement, and the intertwining of affairs, have drawn these states into common endeavors. They cannot easily, if at all, choose to leave each other alone. Because they cannot, the experience of conflict over interests and over purposes leads to efforts to create an apparatus that will reduce conflict or contain it. Politics—negotiation, log-rolling, compromise—becomes the means of achieving preferred arrangements. To manage conflict, a closer integration of activities is sought. The organization by which integration is to be promoted then becomes the object of struggle. How shall it be constructed, and what shall its purposes be? Once these become the most important questions, international relations begin to look like domestic politics.

Saying this makes it clear that some of the cases placed in category C may belong in category A, or may come to belong there. What placement is appropriate depends on how two questions are answered. Do the parties regard the framework of their relations as being so important that they are willing to compromise on particular military and economic issues in order to preserve and strengthen it? Are the parties free simply to leave each other alone? If the answers are first "yes" and then "no," category C is appropriate.

Contiguity, involvement in each other's affairs, mutual confidence built on common experiences—such factors lessen the possibility and the desirability of turning from cooperation and constructive competition and moving instead toward opposition and sharp contention on issues. The high interdependence of some states, as in the case of western Europe, locks them into a cooperative system, and so may the dependence of one state on another, as in the case of the United States and Canada. The close but asymmetric intermingling of their affairs affords the United States many ways of exerting influence.[8] The

United States does not have to substitute force for persuasion. The imbalance of capabilities makes it unnecessary to do so. Each party, moreover, recognizes that its interests are better served by negotiating differences than by openly quarreling over them.

A state's perception of its own strength affects its definition of interest. In the six cases of category C, three types of weakness have encouraged behavior aimed at strengthening the structure:

1. The parties perceive themselves to be weak in relation to the great powers (West European states).

2. The parties fear potential weakness in relation to adversaries (Portugal and South Africa).

3. A marked difference in capabilities exists between the parties (U.S. and Canada, U.S. and Japan, the superpowers and potential nuclear states).

The nonproliferation treaty nicely shows how, on a particular issue, two countries may try to create a structure distinct from the general structure of their relations. Overall, American-Soviet relations fall into category A. The nonproliferation treaty appears, then, as a case of cooperation on a single issue born out of the desire of duopolists to preserve favored positions, a motivation clearly expressed by William C. Foster in 1965 when he was director of the Arms Control and Disarmament Agency:

When we consider the cost to us of trying to stop the spread of nuclear weapons, we should not lose sight of the fact that widespread nuclear proliferation would mean a substantial erosion in the margin of power which our great wealth and industrial base have long given us relative to much of the rest of the world.[9]

In order to maintain their advantages, strong states may wish to regulate the activities of weak states.

The case of the nonproliferation treaty also shows how different the same structure may look from the standpoint of different states. States that are reluctant to forswear becoming nuclear powers indefinitely will see American-Soviet regulation not as a limited experiment in institution-building but instead as a simple case of contention. Disarmament efforts have been sponsored mainly by the United States and the Soviet Union. Not surprisingly, they have attempted primarily to regulate other people's armaments. "This has resulted," as a Japanese scholar points out, "in formulating regulations governing non-existent armaments—nuclear

---

[8]In 1965, for example, US residents owned 44 percent of the total capital invested in Canadian manufacturing firms. M. Watkins *et al.*, Report of the Task Force on the Structure of Canadian Industry, *Foreign Ownership and the Structure of Canadian Industry* (Ottawa: The Queen's Printer, 1968), pp. 199–200.

[9]William C. Foster, "Arms Control and Disarmament," *Foreign Affairs* 43 (July 1965): 591.

weapons of non-nuclear countries rather than governing existing armaments—nuclear weapons of nuclear powers."[10] Self-interest and common interest do not always diverge; the United States and the Soviet Union have tried to persuade other states to believe that a system of regulation will benefit all. Whether the treaty results in a durable system for effective regulation of course remains to be seen.

NONASSOCIATION OF STATES: WITHDRAWAL

Category *D* is important, and yet it is devoid of cases. The explanation is obvious. "Conflict can occur," as Lewis Coser has said, "only in the interaction between subject and object; it always presupposes a relationship."[11] If effectively pursued, withdrawal strategies eliminate contact. The conflict of the parties may be deeply felt, but if the connection between them is broken, the conflict cannot find violent expression. There is then no case to write about.

In the absence of cases, we can nevertheless say a few words about withdrawal strategies both in aspiration and in reality. The ideal of most anarchists rests on the thought that lessening contacts reduces the possibility of conflict. They have dreamt of small communities of likeminded men living at peace with other such communities because all of them would be nearly self-sufficient and thus little involved in each other's business. The League of Nations' policy of plebiscites, which offered minority ethnic groups the chance to separate themselves from uncongenial nations, was in effect a strategy of preventing conflict by disentangling peoples. National strategies of withdrawal are usually pursued by countries that are especially weak or especially strong. The classic neutralist policies of Switzerland, Sweden, and Belgium, the aspirations of presently underdeveloped countries to remain "unaligned," Britain's traditional aloofness toward continental affairs, American isolationism— all of these fall into the category of withdrawal strategies. The possibility of withdrawing increases with distance. Withdrawal is an option available to the United States in southeast Asia, but not to Israel, Czechoslovakia, Biafra, and North and South Vietnam. The effects of withdrawal strategies are found not in cases of conflict but in instances of conflict resolution, of which more will shortly be said.

---

[10]Hisashi Maeda, "The Nature of Disarmament Problems in the Nuclear Age," unpublished ms. (Honolulu: East-West Center, 1970), p. i.

[11]Lewis Coser, *The Functions of Social Conflict*, p. 59.

SITUATIONS AND STRATEGIES

In each category of the table, a mode of behavior tends to dominate: regression, resolute contention, integration, or withdrawal. Rarely, however, does one of the four modes entirely prevail in the policies adopted by states. Several reasons for the mixture of modes are prominent.

First, the leaders of a state may fully understand the situation they face and may adopt corresponding policies. These leaders may, however, be displeased with the results of their policies and feel inclined to forsake or modify them. The two Koreas and the two Germanies, for example, seek to absorb each other in order to reunify their countries. But through a policy of resolute contention in which the legitimacy of the present structure is denied, a new order is inadvertently created. Each side develops new political, economic, and military ties with a different circle of states. A policy of withdrawal ensues that lessens contact between the two sides and decreases the likelihood of destructive conflict as well. Thus, a policy of resolute contention may foster the opponent's integration into a new order. The desire of the Brandt government to increase contacts with East Germany is based partly on the realization that by resolutely denying the legitimacy of the present structure, the West German government has actually strengthened it.

Second, even if the structure of its relations with others should strongly press a state to adopt a particular strategy, the leaders of the state may fail to understand just what the situation requires. Moreover, the pressures of global and regional structures may push in opposite directions. The complexity of most conflicts makes their placement in one category or another uncertain. We usually find mixed cases, not pure ones. The problem of proper placement becomes still more difficult when the policies of states produce changes, as in the German manner just mentioned, that move a case from one category to another or cause it to fluctuate among them. Even if situation determined strategy uniquely, the difficulties of defining situations precisely would still make for perplexity of choice among strategies.

Third, and most important in practice, the structural factor is only one causal force operating among many. Leaders may well appreciate the strength of the constraints upon them, but they may squirm at the thought of accepting them. China, for example, has pursued a strategy of regression in her actions, but a policy of resolute contention in her many defiant proclamations. The regressive strategy indicates her clear perception of limits; bold statements presumably express the frustrations felt. The vastly superior power of an opponent is a strong argument for adopting strategies of regression or withdrawal. Put starkly, if the superior power presses hard, the weak party should simply surrender. The Dubcek and Balaguer regimes quickly did so; Vietcong and Biafran leaders pursued policies of resolute contention instead. Structural constraints are barriers, but men can try to jump over them. Structure shapes and limits choices; it establishes behavioral tendencies without determining behavior.

RESOLUTION OF CONFLICT

Any one of the four modes of behavior, if formulated in an appropriate strategy and effectively carried through, resolves the conflict: actively, by integrating the parties through common institutions and procedures or by the conquest and absorption of one by the other; passively, by lessening their interactions or by breaking relations completely.

Active resolution seeks to manage conflict, or to end it, by strategies that increase conflict in the short run. The entanglement of states, in their economic affairs, in their physical fears, and in their ideological differences, draws them into conflict and violence. Many of the bitterest and bloodiest wars have been fought by peoples who were closely involved in each other's affairs and who, being most like each other, became obsessed with differences in interests and creeds that outsiders could not even understand.

Strategies of integration seek to promote closer mutual involvement. If successful, such strategies multiply the possibilities of conflict. These strategies are pursued, however, in the expectation that the experience of conflict will itself encourage the parties to seek means of regulation and management. To follow the integrative imperative means not to lessen tensions but to strengthen the order that contains them. The strategy is active and constructive; to the extent that it is successful, it takes the "international" out of international relations by subjecting the interactions of nations to a common control.

The imperative of resolute contention requires that one party struggle to prevail over its opponent, to break his will. The strategy is active, but destructive. The integration of the parties is once again the objective, but here by establishing a relation of dominator and dominated. The victor establishes a new imperium that places once independent states under his own protection and control. However achieved, integration ends international conflict by abolishing international relations.

Not conflict, but the insistence that conflicts be resolved, leads to the use of force. One way to manage a conflict is to refrain from using force in an attempt to resolve it. Using force may produce a settlement to the user's satisfaction; it may help to bring a more adequate organization into being; or it may end in mutual damage and destruction. One may decide to leave the benefits of integration aside in order to avoid risking the calamities of war. Passive modes of resolution avoid this risk. The parties potentially in conflict try to move backward to a looser organization, a simpler order, in which states interact less frequently and in less important ways, gain more autonomy, and become less interdependent. By regression, states reduce their contacts without ending them in the hope that yielding on issues will become easier. The final strategy for the passive resolution of conflict is withdrawal. If states had no relations, they could fight no wars.

As Georg Simmel has said in effect: no conflict, no movement.[12] In individual and in domestic political terms, the modern western mind associates movement with progress. Active strategies draw the parties together. They intensify conflict, and they offer the prospect of increased benefits through the development and management of collective enterprises. But in the relations of states the possibility of promoting progress through conflictive processes carries high costs. In order to evaluate active and passive strategies, we should look at the effects of those processes.

If force may be used by some states to weaken or destroy others, then all states live in fear and are likely to exaggerate the evil intentions and the dangers involved. The possibility that conflict will be conducted by force leads to competition in the arts and the instruments of force. Competition produces a tendency toward the sameness of the competitors, with those who are unable to keep up simply falling by the wayside. Thus Bismarck's startling victories over Austria in 1866 and France in 1870 quickly led the major continental powers (and Japan) to imitate the Prussian military staff system, and the failure of Britain and the United States to follow the pattern simply indicated that they were outside of the immediate arena of competition. Contending states imitate the military innovations contrived by the country of greatest capability and ingenu-

[12]Georg Simmel, *Conflict and the Web of Group Affiliation*, translated by Kurt H. Wolff and Reinhardt Bendix (New York: Free Press, 1955), pp. 14–16.

ity. And so the weapons of major contenders, and even their strategies, begin to look much the same all over the world.

The effects of competition are not confined narrowly to the military realm. Something that might be called socialization to the international political system also occurs. Immediately after their revolution, for example, Bolsheviks appeared on the international scene as the hippies of their day. By his manner of speaking, his dress, and his life style, the hippy dramatically says, "I will not be socialized to *this* system." So the Bolsheviks in the early years of their power preached international revolution and flaunted the conventions of diplomacy. The attitude was well expressed by Trotsky, who, when asked what he would do as foreign minister, replied, "I will issue some revolutionary proclamations to the peoples and then close up the joint."[13] In a competitive arena, however, one party may need the assistance of others. Refusal to play the political game may risk one's own destruction. The pressures of competition were rapidly felt and reflected in the Soviet Union's diplomacy. Thus Lenin, sending foreign minister Chicherin to the Genoa Conference of 1922, bade him farewell with this caution: "Avoid big words."[14] Chicherin, who personified the carefully tailored traditional diplomat rather than the simply uniformed revolutionary, was to refrain from inflammatory rhetoric for the sake of working deals. These he successfully completed with that other pariah power and ideological enemy, Germany.

The close juxtaposition of states promotes their sameness through the disadvantages that arise from a failure to conform to accepted and successful practices. In the Darwinian view, the contending parties are carried to ever higher levels of accomplishment. But in international politics we may well wish that we could forgo some of the movement in exchange for a reduction of conflict through the regression of states. And not only that. One may identify conflict with movement, and movement with progress, and applaud the gradual conformity of states to the patterns set by the most highly developed ones. Or one may view such conformity as a denial of national individuality and deplore the reduction of variety.

It has often been argued that benefits would accrue from passive strategies, not only in terms of the relations of states, but also in terms of those states themselves. Viewed internationally, withdrawal is a negative policy, its imperatives being "do less," "become passive," "acquiesce," "retreat." Viewed internally, the aims of the policy may be positive: to perfect the society, to develop the economy, to strengthen the political order—in short, to become less involved in others' affairs in order to tend to one's own. Plato believed, and he has been echoed by a long line of utopian writers, that only the isolated state could realize its own individuality. Rousseau saw and deplored the homogenization of European culture that was developing from the close interplay of European states and their peoples. American isolationists prized and sought to preserve their nation's detachment from Europe so that a new world could be fashioned free of contamination from the old one. And many now deplore the Coca-Cola-ization of the world. These examples strongly support the argument that only the isolated state can preserve its distinctive personality and have the chance to develop that personality according to its own inner character.

Active strategies promise peace through the more adequate organization of closely interconnected activities. Passive strategies promise peace through lessening the contacts among contenders. Either way, international conflict is ultimately ended only by abolishing international relations. Kant's vision of perpetual peace through a voluntary union of republics competes with Rousseau's utopia of an isolated Corsica. Neither condition is attainable—hence the ubiquity of conflict and the recurrence of war among states.

[13]Leon Trotsky, quoted in Theodore H. Von Laue, "Soviet Diplomacy: G. V. Chicherin, People's Commissar for Foreign Affairs 1918-1930," in Gordon A. Craig and Felix Gilbert (eds.), *The Diplomats 1919-1939*, 1 (New York: Atheneum, 1963), p. 235.

[14]V. I. Lenin, quoted in Barrington Moore Jr., *Soviet Politics: The Dilemma of Power* (Cambridge: Harvard University Press, 1950), p. 204.

CZECHOSLOVAKIA: MULTILATERAL INTERVENTION

ROBIN ALISON REMINGTON

Marx believed that in a communist world there would be peace, since communist states would not war against each other. Ironically, the Soviet Union, since the late 1940s, has only used its force directly against fellow communist states—Czechoslovakia in 1968 being a recent example. Dr. Remington's article describes the process by which the Soviet Union and fellow hard-line satellite allies were led to intervene in Czechoslovakia to protect what they believed to be their own interests and those of communism in general. In an interesting and controversial second part, she compares the Czech invasion with the United States intervention in the Dominican Republic in 1965.

Robin Remington is a Research Associate in Communist Studies at the Massachusetts Institute of Technology: Center for International Studies and a visiting lecturer in Political Science at Yale University. She is the author of The Warsaw Pact: Case Studies in Communist Conflict Resolution *(1971), and has edited* Winter in Prague: Documents on Czechoslovak Communism in Crisis *(1969).*

In August 1968, five members of the Warsaw Treaty Organization (WTO) invaded Czechoslovakia, also a member of the Warsaw Pact. Moscow justified that invasion as an obligation under the Warsaw Treaty. Prague denounced it as a violation, as it was, given any reading of the text. Yet the Warsaw Pact's relationship to the occupation of Czechoslovakia went much deeper than that of a convenient legal cover for the Soviet representative to the United Nations. The invasion marked a sudden break in what had appeared to be the rules of the game within the coalition itself. For throughout 1965–67, Rumania had achieved an increasingly independent foreign policy within the framework of the Warsaw Pact. Allegiance to the Pact provided formal underpinning for a coalition more and more openly subject to the conflicts of interest common to such groupings throughout history. Such allegiance served as the minimum common denominator of coordination for East European Communist states. It was ritualistically essential, and was recognized as such by Rumania and, more recently, by Czechoslovakia.[1]

[1]See Václav Kotyk, "Some Aspects of the History of Relations Among Socialist Countries," *Československý časopis*

DRESDEN

. . . At first the Soviet leadership responded to Czechoslovak developments with an almost patterned version of noninterference in the affairs of fraternal countries. After a quick trip to Prague in December 1967, Brezhnev opted for neutrality on the KSČ internal struggle.[2] There was no public regret at Novotný's passing in Moscow.[3] Nor was there any overt sign that the Prague spring was even a topic for discussion at the March 1968 political consultative committee meeting. . . .

But by the end of March, Soviet anxiety at the possible consequences of liberalization in Prague had ended all but the flimsiest pretense of noninterference in Czechoslovakia's affairs. Not only

historický 4 (1967): in *Czechoslovak Press Survey*, No. 1973, RFE/233 (October 30, 1967): 14.

[2]See V. Mencl and F. Ouředník, "What Happened in January," *Život strany* 16, 17, 18 (August–September 1968) and Document 4 in Robin Alison Remington, ed., *Winter in Prague: Documents on Czechoslovak Communism in Crisis* (Cambridge, Mass.: The MIT Press, 1969).

[3]For a detailed chronology of Soviet and East European reaction to the events following the KSČ CC January Plenum see William F. Robinson, "Czechoslovakia and Its Allies," *Studies in Comparative Communism* 1, nos. 1–2 (July–October, 1968): 141–70.

Reprinted by permission and with minor changes from The Warsaw Pact: Case Studies in Communist Conflict Resolution *(Cambridge, Mass.: The MIT Press, 1971), pp. 94–112, 189–98. Copyright © 1971 by the Massachusetts Institute of Technology. The substance of a portion of this article first appeared as an article "Czechoslovakia and the Warsaw Pact," in the* East European Quarterly 3, *No. 3 (September 1969).*

were there signs that Dubček might be under pressure to stand less closely to Ulbricht with respect to West Germany[4] but how were orthodox Communist regimes to interpret the unheard-of call of censors for an end to censorship?[5]

At Dresden Dubček explained post-January developments in Czechoslovakia. The meeting attempted to define limits of permissible diversity. It was a warning by Moscow and the increasingly jittery East German regime that "special attention" must be paid to West German activity "directed against the interests of East Germany and other socialist countries."[6] The Rumanians, who have consistently opposed meetings devoted to the internal affairs of any socialist country, were not invited—thereby ending Bucharest's veto power apparently exercised at Sofia to prevent any agreement on reorganizing the Warsaw Pact. The Dresden summit unanimously agreed to concrete, if unspecified, measures to strengthen the Warsaw Treaty "in the near future."

... If Prague had doubts about what Dresden meant, the Soviet military newspaper *Krasnaya zvezda*'s statement, attributed to Dubček, that Czechoslovakia was protected from "all upheavals" by its alliance with the Soviet Union and other Warsaw Pact states could have done little to quiet them.[7]

Indeed, Dresden had created uneasy speculation in Czechoslovakia. Dubček felt called upon to explain the "natural" anxiety among Soviet and East European Communist leaders that "anti-socialist" elements should not take advantage of the process of democratization in Prague.[8] Subsequently the youth daily *Mlada fronta* seconded Rumania's objection that Warsaw Pact problems had been discussed at a meeting to which Bucharest had been uninvited.[9] ...

Throughout April the conflict of interest widened. Although the KSČ Action Program[10] assured its allies that the Warsaw Pact was fundamental to the Czechoslovak road to socialism, Moscow and certainly Ulbricht must have found the theory of the necessity for giving support to "realistic" forces within West Germany unpalat-

able, particularly given the marked drop in Czechoslovak anti-West German propaganda and an increasing exchange of high-level visitors with Bonn. Further, the ČSSR Government declaration of April 24 went beyond the Action Program to recognize "democratic" (instead of merely "realistic") trends in the German Federal Republic and favored normalization of relations.[11] The issue of Germany was crucial. Neither the Soviets nor the East Germans could afford to have Czechoslovakia recognize West Germany on other but their terms. Dresden had been called partially to emphasize how seriously Moscow viewed Prague potentially contributing to further isolating Pankow. And by April, Moscow must have wondered whether or not Dubček had gotten the message.

Prague's attitude toward Bonn was not the only problem. By early spring there were pressures for change in Czechoslovak policy toward Israel as well. In Bratislava the attitude toward Israel had become an index of whether one was for or against liberalization. Demands could be heard that the Slovak writer Ladislav Mňačko, who had left Czechoslovakia in protest at the government's anti-Israeli policy following the June 1967 war, be allowed to return home.[12] The Czechoslovak press and radio openly condemned the Polish anti-Zionist campaign following the March student protests at Warsaw University. Not only were letters of protest presented by members of the Czechoslovak Academy of Science to the Polish Embassy but following their dismissal Professors Leszek Kolakowski and Bronislaw Baczko were invited to lecture at Charles University in Prague.[13] On May 6 the Polish Ambassador to Czechoslovakia formally protested against this "anti-Polish" campaign. Tension was building up.

THE MAY–JUNE MANEUVERS

... Dubček flew unexpectedly to Moscow on May 4. He returned, reportedly having reassured Moscow that democratization would not be allowed to turn against socialism in Czechoslovakia, to announce that joint military exercises in individual countries were a part of practical

[4] *Rudé Právo*, March 16, 1968.

[5] Remington, *Winter in Prague*, Document 8, p. 54.

[6] Communiqué of the Dresden Meeting, *Pravda* (March 25, 1968); *CDSP* 20, no. 12 (April 10, 1968): 16–17.

[7] Commentary by Col. V. Alexeyev and Lt. Col. O. Ivanov, *Krasnaya zvezda* (March 30, 1968).

[8] Dubček interview with ČTK, *Pravda* (March 28, 1968); *CDSP* 20, no. 13 (April 17, 1968): 20–21.

[9] Miroslav Pavel, commentary in *Mlada fronta* (April 27, 1968).

[10] Text of the KSČ Action Program is included in Remington, *Winter in Prague*, Document 16, pp. 87–141.

[11] *Rudé Právo* (April 25, 1968).

[12] Gustav Husák referred to a press, radio, and television campaign for the return of Mňačko as early as mid-March, pointing out with apparent annoyance that nothing could be done because at that time the writer had not, in fact, applied to return. Bratislava Domestic Television Service in Slovak, March 20, 1968. Mňačko did return to Czechoslovakia on May 17, 1968.

[13] Robinson, "Czechoslovakia and Its Allies," pp. 144–47.

military cooperation under the Warsaw Pact.[14] Prague had agreed, but so far only in principle.

Despite Dubček's assurances, a meeting of Soviet and other East European leaders (once again minus Rumania) convened in Moscow May 8. Simultaneously, Soviet and Polish troops maneuvered on Czechoslovak borders. The maneuvers, particularly in the context of General Yepishev's rumored remarks about the willingness of the Red Army to do its duty should it be necessary to save socialism in Czechoslovakia,[15] caused serious speculation that invasion was imminent.[16] Prague dismissed such reports as provocation and insisted that the proper Czechoslovak bodies had been informed in advance about routine Warsaw Pact exercises in Southern Poland.

True or not, the fact of these maneuvers did not improve the atmosphere created by Soviet, Polish, and East German press attacks throughout May. Unlike earlier pact maneuvers in Hungary, they were certainly not handled so as to minimize pressure on the Dubček regime,[17] but rather appeared part of a concerted campaign against Prague. On May 8, the former Warsaw Pact Commander I. S. Konev arrived to celebrate Czechoslovakia's liberation day, May 17, Kosygin appeared on May 17 for a ten-day "rest cure" at Karlovy Vary. Simultaneously but separately an eight-man military delegation led by Soviet Defense Minister Grechko and including General Yepishev came for a week's visit. Before this barrage of guests departed, it was agreed that Warsaw Pact staff maneuvers would be held on Czechoslovak territory in June.[18] The question of such maneuvers had become a measure of Prague's good faith, conceivably representing a compromise between Moscow's desire for Warsaw Pact troops on the Czechoslovak-West German border and Prague's distaste for any joint military activity in the country until the political situation was more stable.

Preparations for the June maneuvers coincided with continued political upheaval in Prague. Czechoslovak Defense Minister Martin Dzur announced that small Soviet units had begun entering the country just one day after former President Antonín Novotný had been ousted from the KSČ Central Committee and suspended from party membership.[19] Both Dzur[20] and subsequently Warsaw Pact commander-in-chief Yakubovsky[21] took pains to minimize the number of forces involved. Ostensibly only position-marking and logistic troops would take part. Yet rumors of Soviet demand for tank squads continued, while the press spokesman for the allied command staff exercise, Major-General Josef Čepický, felt called upon to deny reports that Warsaw Pact troops would be permanently stationed in Czechoslovakia.[22]

The tone of Soviet articles explaining the necessity for such joint maneuvers can only have heightened the tension. Emphasis went far beyond combat efficiency. Rather Moscow focused on the uniformity of social and state systems, the common nature of "their Marxist-Leninist world outlook" as the political-ideological foundation for cooperation within the Warsaw Pact. There was consistent and ominous juxtaposition of the issue of strengthening the Warsaw Pact with the CPSU CC April plenum pledge that Soviet Communists remained ready to "do everything necessary" for political, economic, and defensive consolidation of the socialist community.[23] . . .

Nor was Prague's nervousness at the ambiguous circumstances surrounding the planned maneuvers unfounded. For once on Czechoslovak territory Soviet forces were in no hurry to leave. Begun on June 20, the joint exercises officially ended July 1.[24] However, TASS almost immediately rescinded that announcement, and throughout July there was, in fact, no clear indication that Moscow intended Soviet troops to depart.[25]

---

[14] Rudé Právo (May 7, 1968); reprinted in Pravda (May 8, 1968).

[15] Le Monde (May 5, 1968). As Yepishev is head of the main political administration of the Soviet armed forces, such comments from him would hardly be taken lightly. The report caused consternation in Czechoslovakia, Rudé Právo (May 9, 1968). Yepishev did issue a denial but only two weeks later at the airport in Prague.

[16] See The New York Times (May 10, 1968).

[17] Nepszábadság (March 23, 1968) announced that the plans for maneuvers had been approved in 1967, thereby lessening if not eliminating the suspicion that they were timed to coincide with the Dresden meeting. See also Le Monde (March 26, 1968).

[18] ČTK (May 24, 1968); The New York Times (May 25, 1968).

[19] The most detailed and helpful chronology on events within Czechoslovakia is ČSSR: The Road to Democratic Socialism (Facts on Events From January to May 1968) (Prague: Praguepress, 1968).

[20] Dzur interview with Zemědelské noviny (May 31, 1968).

[21] Yakubovsky interview with Rudé Právo correspondent in Moscow, Radio Moscow in Czech to Czechoslovakia, June 17, 1968.

[22] Prague Domestic Service in Czech, June 6, 1968.

[23] The bulk of these commentaries appear in the Soviet military newspaper. See particularly Lt. Col. O. Ivanov, Krasnaya zvezda (June 12, 1968) and Col. K. Sprov, Krasnaya zvezda (June 14, 1968).

[24] Pravda, July 1, 1968. Dzur's interview indicated that the Czechoslovak command was busy creating optimum conditions so that the main-command time objective could be met, Izvestia, June 22, 1968.

[25] Editor's Note: The Czech Press spokesman for the exercises, Josef Cepicky, announced on 1 July that the participating units would begin returning to their permanent stations immediately after the 2 July analysis of results, Prague

PRCHLÍK AND THE WARSAW LETTER

Lieutenant General Václav Prchlík's press interview suggesting basic revisions in the Warsaw Pact along the lines of more rather than less control for East European member states added still another dimension.[26] Head of the KSČ CC military department, the Lt. General said flatly that Soviet representation on the joint command was out of proportion. On a more political level, he attacked "fractionist activities" within the Warsaw Pact that lead to violating principles of sovereignty and noninterference in internal affairs. Prchlík clearly was alluding to the meeting of five pact members in session in Warsaw. For following Ludvík Vaculík's "Two Thousand Word Statement"[27] favoring demonstrations, strikes, and boycotts to force out the remaining Czechoslovak conservatives who misused their power, Prague's dispute with Moscow and the more orthodox East European Communist regimes had escalated into a formal confrontation. . . .

Between July 4 and 6 the leaderships of the Soviet Union, Bulgaria, East Germany, Hungary, and Poland sent letters to the KSČ calling for a multilateral conference to discuss antisocialist activity in Czechoslovakia.[28] The Dubček regime parried by agreeing to bilateral meetings. His suggestion was ignored. Soviet and other East European leaders met in Warsaw as planned. The outcome of that meeting was the famed five-party "Warsaw Letter"—in effect an ultimatum outlining the rationale for invasion. Although not claiming to be an official Warsaw Pact document, the letter justified its interference in Czechoslovak internal affairs, in part, as a common obligation under the Warsaw Pact. The Dubček leadership was accused not only of weakening before demands to abandon "the common coordinated policy" toward West Germany but of tolerating a campaign against Warsaw Pact staff maneuvers on Czechoslovak territory.

Prague's reply answered the charges point by point, citing the Warsaw Treaty staff exercises as "concrete proof" of Czechoslovak faithful fulfillment of commitments. Questions had arisen among the population only after repeated changes of the departure time of allied armies following the end of maneuvers.[29] Moscow's retort did not specifically raise the issue of the Warsaw Pact[30] and had much the general tone of Stalin's reply to Tito in 1948—"We regard your answer incorrect and therefore completely unsatisfactory."[31] . . .

CONFRONTATION: ČIERNÁ-BRATISLAVA

In short circumstances were hardly favorable for the bilateral Soviet-Czechoslovak negotiations to which Dubček had reluctantly agreed.[32] Large-scale Soviet maneuvers along the Czechoslovak-Soviet border coincided with the Čierná talks,[33] while Soviet troops in East Germany were reportedly moving toward Czechoslovakia.[34] After four days of reportedly heated discus-

---

CTK, in English, 1 July 1968. However, throughout the month of July, despite repeated announcements by Prague officials that the Soviet forces would be leaving shortly, the Russian troops stayed on, giving such patently flimsy excuses for their extended stay as the need for equipment repairs and a desire not to interfere with holiday traffic. The last Soviet contingents finally departed Czechoslovak territory on 3 August, the day of the Bratislava meeting discussed below. See the *New York Times* articles on this subject of 10, 12, 14, 15, 16, and 22 July 1968.

[26] Remington, *Winter in Prague*, Document 32.

[27] *Mlada fronta*, June 27, 1968.

[28] The letters were not published. However, they were alluded to in the subsequent Five-Party Warsaw Letter, *Pravda* (July 18, 1968); *CDSP* 20, no. 29 (August 7, 1968): 4–6, and described in Dubček's July 19 speech, *Rudé Právo* (July 20, 1968).

[29] *The New York Times* (July 19, 1968).

[30] "Concerning the Point of View of the CCP Central Committee," *Pravda* (July 22, 1968); *CDSP* 20, no. 29 (August 7, 1968): 10–11.

[31] Robert Bass and Elizabeth Marbury, eds., *The Soviet-Yugoslav Controversy, 1948-1958: A Documentary Record* (New York: Prospect Books, 1959), pp. 6–12. Prague was well aware of the similarities to 1948, openly ranking the Warsaw Letter with the Cominform resolution against Yugoslavia as "one of the darkest aspects of the history of the working class movement," L. Svoboda, "The ČSSR is Not Going to Commit Suicide," *Obrana lidu* (July 27, 1968); Remington, *Winter in Prague*, Document 39.

[32] Originally the Soviets proposed meeting in Moscow, Kiev, or Lviv (*Pravda*, July 20, 1968). However, when the Dubček regime apparently refused to leave Czechoslovakia, practically the entire Soviet Politburo went to the border town of Čierná-nad-Tisu.

[33] *Editor's Note:* Closely following the publication of the Warsaw Letter and the "discovery" of an arms cache of American-made weapons on Czech territory, on 23 July Moscow announced that a new series of massive Soviet troop maneuvers had begun in the Western USSR, covering an 800 mile front from the Baltic to the Black Sea and involving a large-scale call-up of reservists, "Rear Service Exercises," *Izvestia* (24 July 1968). These Rear Service Exercises, codenamed "Niemen," received an unusual amount of publicity in the Soviet media and were reported by their commander, General Maryakhin, to be "the largest exercise ever held by the Soviet Army," Moscow Domestic Service in Russian, 1900 GMT, 28 July 1968. It was also disclosed that major air defense exercises codenamed "Sky Shield" were being conducted in conjunction with the logistics maneuvers near Czechoslovakia's borders, "Exercise 'Sky Shield'," *Krasnaya zvezda* (25 July 1968). On 31 July, the opening day of the Cierna confrontation, Moscow announced that Polish and East German units had joined in the war games, "At the Rear Services Exercises," *Krasnaya zvezda* (31 July 1968). As later events were to demonstrate, the "Niemen" and "Sky Shield" exercises provided the cover for the mobilization and deployment of the logistical and air support utilized in the August invasion.

[34] *Pravda* (July 31, 1968) and *The New York Times* (August 1, 1968).

sion, the other signers of the Warsaw letter were invited to Bratislava where the confrontation continued.

Substantively, the Bratislava statement was a collection of orthodox platitudes that did not so much as refer to what the participants had gone to thrash out—the limits of Czechoslovak domestic reform and foreign policy deviation acceptable to Moscow and other increasingly threatened East European Communist regimes. Rather, the statement committed Prague to a general platform of strengthening the leading role of the Communist party and creating an ever-closer policy coordination within CMEA and the Warsaw Pact. It reiterated the hard line of the CPSU April plenum resolution on West Germany and Israel, pledging the signers to consistently follow "a concerted policy that meets the common interests of the socialist countries" in matters of European affairs. On the nature of the Warsaw Pact, however, the statement was most explicit:

> . . . It serves as an invincible barrier to all who would like to revise the results of the second world war. It reliably defends the gains of socialism and the sovereignty and independence of the fraternal states. . . .
>
> The present situation requires our unremitting efforts to raise the defense capability of every socialist state and the whole socialist commonwealth and to strengthen political and military cooperation in the Warsaw Treaty Organization.[35]

Such a formulation was just one step away from the demand that Warsaw Pact troops be permanently stationed in Czechoslovakia along the border with West Germany.

Rumania, as in the case of Dresden, protested that problems of the Warsaw Pact should not be discussed at meetings to which some member states were uninvited.[36] . . . Not unexpectedly, Bucharest was ignored. Both Moscow and Prague officially hailed the Čierná and Bratislava meetings as a victory for socialist unity.[37]

Yet Prague's diplomatic activity following Bratislava indicates that the Dubček regime had few illusions about the extent of such unity. For a few days overt hostility ceased. During this brief lull, Czechoslovakia worked furiously to consolidate support. Tito arrived in Prague on August 9; a Rumanian delegation headed by President Ceauşescu, August 15. Both leaders were warmly welcomed, in marked contrast to

the reception for Ulbricht, who came for talks in Karlovy Vary. Perhaps more important, the East German visit ended inconclusively with only vague agreement that both sides would continue to oppose the rise of Nazi forces in West Germany.[38] In contrast Tito and the new Czechoslovak-Rumanian Treaty of Friendship, Cooperation, and Mutual Assistance signed during Ceauşescu's visit focused on the principle of noninterference in each other's affairs—a guarantee conspicuously absent from the Bratislava Statement.[39]

Moscow again may have had visions—and with some reason—of a "Communist Little Entente" directed against Soviet hegemony in Eastern Europe. Soviet polemics resumed while Ceauşescu was still in Prague.[40] . . .

Pravda described Czechoslovakia as slipping over the edge of counterrevolution. Hooligans had attacked the Central Committee building; honest, pro-Soviet workers were faced with "frenzied" persecution.[41] The stage was set. Now it was only a matter of time and last-minute political jockeying.[42]

INVASION

The TASS announcement of the occupation of Czechoslovakia avoided any direct mention of the Warsaw Pact, although it maintained that the decision to come to the aid of unidentified party and

---

[35]Bratislava Statement, *Pravda* (August 4, 1968); *CDSP* 20, no. 31 (August 21, 1968): 4–5.

[36]Editorial, *Scînteia* (August 8, 1968).

[37]See Černík interview in *Rudé Právo* (August 2, 1968); Dubček, *Rudé Právo* (August 4, 1968); Zhukov in *Pravda*, August 5 editorial, August 8, 1968 and *Krasnaya Zvezda* editorials August 6 and 8, 1968.

[38]Later candidate member of the SED Politburo and Secretary of the Central Committee, Hermann Axen, accused the Dubček regime of consciously sabotaging the Čierná and Bratislava accords by "fiercely" opposing any formulation relating to the struggle against bourgeois ideology at Karlovy Vary. Hermann Axen, "Proletarischer Internationalismus in unserer Zeit," *Einheit* 10 (September 18, 1968): 1207. *Neues Deutschland* (August 14, 1968); summarized in *Pravda* (August 14, 1968).

[39]*Editor's Note:* On 10 August, the day the "Niemen" exercises were scheduled to conclude—and the date of publication of the KSC draft party statutes—it was announced that yet another set of military maneuvers had begun along Czechoslovakia's borders. This time the maneuvers were described as "Joint Exercises of Communications Troops" and included Soviet, Polish, and East German units, Berlin ADN Domestic Service in German, 2034 GMT, 10 August 1968; "At the Headquarters of the Joint Forces of the Warsaw Pact Countries," *Krasnaya zvezda* (11 August 1968). On 16 August these exercises were extended to Czechoslovakia's southern borders to include Hungarian and Soviet forces there, "Communication of the Hungarian Telegraphic Agency—MII," *Krasnaya zvezda* (17 August 1968). These maneuvers obviously represented the final troop stagings for the invasion of Czechoslovakia. Of the participants in the invasion, only Bulgaria was not publicly identified in these exercises.

[40]Zhukov in *Pravda* (August 16, 1968).

[41]I. Alexandrov, *Pravda* (August 18, 1968); *CDSP* 20, no. 33 (September 4, 1968): 9–10.

[42]Kádár, perhaps still attempting to negotiate a compromise, met with Dubček August 17. See Richard Lowenthal, "The Sparrow in the Cage," *Problems of Communism* 17, no. 6 (November–December 1968): 20–21. On August 19, in a gesture

government leaders in Prague was in "complete accord" with "allied treaties among the fraternal socialist countries."[43] Nor was the alleged appeal for aid addressed to the Warsaw Pact. Rather attacks against Warsaw Pact staff maneuvers in Czechoslovakia were seen as part of a "filthy systematic campaign to weaken friendship with the socialist countries."[44] In sum, Prague's bad attitude toward Warsaw Pact obligations was one reason to intervene; but the WTO was not considered an institutional instrument of intervention. The Soviet editorial entitled "Defense of Socialism is the Highest International Duty" made quite clear, however, that from Moscow's point of view this was a matter of dual responsibility. The defense of socialism in Czechoslovakia was anything but Prague's internal affair. It was the common affair of the socialist commonwealth. It was the CPSU's international duty as Communists, added to obligations under the Warsaw Pact, that had brought Soviet and "allied socialist" troops into Czechoslovakia. Warsaw Pact countries had "a solemn commitment—to stand up in defense of the gains of socialism."[45]

As for the pact as an index of Prague's good faith, the editorial reiterated charges concerning the June maneuvers. Prchlík was attacked. Such attempts to impair the pact became a question for all participants of the Warsaw Treaty Organization, for: "It is impossible to tolerate a breach in this organization. Such a line contradicts the vital interests of all the member countries of the Warsaw Treaty Organization, including the vital interests of the USSR."[46]

Moscow had laid it on the line. The Warsaw Pact was an institutional arrangement for protecting the interests of the socialist commonwealth as defined by the Soviet Union. It was an interpretation that left Rumania no place to go. And one to which Prague could hardly agree.

The Czechoslovak government quickly declared the invasion illegal, demanding immediate withdrawal of all foreign troops and "correct adherence" to the Warsaw Treaty.[47] Rumania, despite Bucharest's exposed position, condemned the use of troops as a "flagrant violation of the

sovereignty of a fraternal socialist country."[48] Ceaușescu further warned that Rumania would not permit any violation of its territory, and reactivated the People's Militia.[49]

Moscow's angry response reiterated and refined the August 22 editorial interpretation of the function of the Warsaw Pact. According to Kudryavtsev:

When the imperialists call the fulfillment of the socialist countries' internationalist duty "intervention," it shows why they are imperialists. But it is strange, to say the least, to hear exactly the same phrases from the mouths of the Rumanian and Yugoslav leaders. Don't they know that the Warsaw Pact was concluded not only to defend the signatory states' national borders and territories? It was concluded in order to defend socialism in response to the creation of the aggressive NATO military bloc, which is openly aimed against the socialist states for the purpose of counteracting communism. And those who now attempt to interpret the Warsaw Pact in narrowly nationalistic terms ('it's none of my business') contribute to the imperialists' frenzied antisocialist campaign. The defense of socialism in Czechoslovakia is not only the internal affair of that country's people but also a problem of defending the positions of world socialism. . . .[50]

Rumors that Soviet troops had moved to Rumanian borders persisted[51] as did reports that the Soviet Ambassador to Bucharest Alexander V. Basov was demanding Warsaw Pact maneuvers on Rumanian territory.[52] Ceaușescu's criticism softened but he did not back down. . . .

---

[48]*Scînteia* (August 22, 1968).

[49]*Ibid.* (August 21, 1968).

[50]V. Kudryavtsev, *Izvestia* (August 25, 1968); *CDSP* 20, no. 35 (September 18, 1968): 7–8.

[51]*Editor's Note:* In an attempt to intimidate the Ceaușescu regime and discourage continued Rumanian expressions of independence, the Kremlin took advantage of the renewed credibility of the use of Soviet military intervention, preceded by Warsaw Pact military maneuvers. In late August Western intelligence reports reported troop shifts within the Soviet Union and movements of Soviet transport aircraft and indications of supply activity designed to bring Soviet and Bulgarian troops near Rumania's borders to a heightened state of readiness, *The New York Times* (1 September 1968). During this time period areas of Soviet Moldavia bordering on Rumania were placed off limits to Western military attachés and journalists (private communication from US embassy official; Paris AFP in English, 0959 GMT, 5 September 1968). Confirming the occurrence of such maneuvers is a Bulgarian announcement that "an operational and tactical exercise was conducted in the eastern part of the country and in the Black Sea area from 20 August to 6 September," Sofia BTA in English, 1906 GMT, 7 September 1968.

[52]*Washington Post* (August 26, 1968); Paul Hoffman, *The New York Times* (August 27, 1968). In response to intelligence reports apparently confirming such rumors, Washington publicly stated that it would view any Soviet military intervention in Yugoslavia or Rumania with the utmost seriousness, *The New York Times* (August 31, 1968) providing a marked contrast to American response to intensive Soviet pressure on Prague at the time of the Čierná meeting, see Tom Wicker in *The New York Times* (August 1, 1968). For an increasingly

---

designed to ensure mixed response from Washington to the imminent invasion, Kosygin informed President Johnson that he was ready for the summit meeting the President had desired and suggested August 21. *The New York Times* (August 23, 1968).

[43]*Pravda* (August 21, 1968).

[44]*Pravda* (August 22, 1968); *CDSP* 20, no. 34 (September 11, 1968): 3–5.

[45]*Pravda* (August 22, 1968); *CDSP, ibid.*, p. 11.

[46]*Ibid.*

[47]"Declaration of the Czechoslovak Government," *Studies in Comparative Communism* 1, nos. 1/2 (July/October 1968): 297.

In fact, notwithstanding Kudryavtsev's vehemence, Czechoslovakia was floundering in a political vacuum. Soviet and East European troops could not find the comrades they had come to assist. The Kádár solution Moscow desired had collapsed when 72-year-old President Svoboda flatly refused to appoint the puppet regime proposed to him by KSČ secretary Alois Indra, who was to have been Prime Minister.[53] Although the Soviet military plan had gone flawlessly, politically the "allied socialist" rescue operation was a fiasco.

Svoboda had flown to Moscow, where progress toward replacing the Dubček regime with pro-Soviet collaborators seemed no greater than in Prague. Soon Dubček (who had been attacked by the August 22 editorial for leading a "right-wing, opportunist, minority" in the KSČ Presidium) and the other arrested leaders joined the negotiations. Thus, since Moscow was unwilling to adopt the Hungarian solution of simply arresting the negotiators,[54] the Soviet leadership ended by restoring to office the Czechoslovak leadership that Soviet troops had invaded Czechoslovakia to replace.

The Soviet-Czechoslovak Communiqué of August 28 euphemistically dismissed the invasion as a "temporary entry of troops" to be withdrawn when the situation "normalized." It reaffirmed the Bratislava commitment to shore up the effectiveness of the Warsaw Pact, one aspect of the strengthening of the defensive might of the socialist commonwealth.[55]

THE BREZHNEV DOCTRINE

Interestingly enough, the subsequent Soviet theoretical justification known as the Brezhnev Doctrine did not mention the Warsaw Pact.

First formulated by S. Kovalev in *Pravda*, it put forth a concept of limited sovereignty within the socialist community.[56] In Kovalev's view, sovereignty among socialist states must not be understood abstractly. Rather, within the socialist commonwealth international law must be subordinated to the laws of class struggle. In short, Moscow reserved the right to intervene militarily or otherwise if developments in any socialist country inflicted damage upon either socialism in that country or the basic interests of other socialist countries. Obviously incompatible with Warsaw Treaty guarantees of independence and noninterference in internal affairs, the logic of this interpretation would restrict the Warsaw Pact to an instrument for political and military coordination among European Communist states.

Emphasis was on consolidation in a world situation threatening the survival of socialism. The idea was hardly new. It echoed the "two-camp theory" outlined by Zhdanov at the founding of the Cominform in 1947, and it implied reimposition of the Soviet hegemony that had reduced East European policy to a gray imitation of Moscow's initiatives until Stalin's death and well into the 1950s. For the invasion of Czechoslovakia left the crux of the matter unambiguous. Moscow, not Prague, had decided that the danger existed. Prior consultation had been limited to those members of the Warsaw Pact that agreed. The threat to Rumania was clear.

Yet, 1968 was not 1947, and the "allied socialist" invasion of Czechoslovakia had left the fading myth of monolithic international Communist unity in shambles.[57] . . .

OCTOBER TREATY

As for Czechoslovakia, the treaty "temporarily" stationing Soviet troops on CSSR territory "for the purpose of safeguarding the security of the countries of the socialist commonwealth against the mounting revanchist ambitions of West German militarist forces" was a logical extension of the Brezhnev Doctrine. Despite the treaty's contention that the presence of such Soviet troops did not violate the sovereignty of Czechoslovakia and would not interfere in the

sharp denunciation of the Rumanian position ridiculing such speculation as Western fabrications, see N. Gribachev, *Pravda* (September 4, 1968).

[53]*Frankfurter Allgemeine Zeitung* (September 23, 1968), and *Der Spiegel* (October 21, 1968): pg. 147. According to the current rewriting of history by the KSČ, "thousands of Communists, individual citizens, and whole collectives of working people" [including members of the Central Committee and the CSSR government] had turned to the "fraternal parties" to prevent a civil war by halting "the frontal onslaught of counter-revolution." "Lesson Drawn from the Crisis the Party and Society after the 13th Congress of the Communist Party of Czechoslovakia," *Rudé Právo* (January 14, 1971). Although he spoke approvingly of this "lesson" in his speech to the CPSU 24th Congress, Brezhnev more modestly referred to an invitation by unidentified party and state leaders. *Pravda* (March 30, 1971).

[54]Paul E. Zinner, *Revolution in Hungary* (New York: Columbia University Press, 1962), p. 317. For a description of the negotiations with the Czechoslovak delegation, see Robert Littell, ed., *The Czech Black Book* (New York: Praeger, 1969).

[55]*Pravda* (August 28, 1968).

[56]*Pravda* (September 26, 1968); *CDSP* 20, no. 39 (October 16, 1968): 10–12. For analysis, see Christian Duevel, "Ideological Acrobatics on Sovereignty," Radio Liberty Research, CRD 361/68 (October 7, 1968).

[57]Kevin Devlin, "The New Crisis in European Communism," *Problems of Communism* 18, no. 6 (November-December 1968): 57.

host country's internal affairs,[58] Moscow was at least as concerned to contain reformers in Prague as militarists in Bonn.

The treaty was harsh. In return for the gradual withdrawal of the majority of Soviet and East European troops occupying the country, the Dubček regime legalized the stationing of an unspecified number of Soviet troops on Czechoslovak territory for an indefinite period of time.[59] It went beyond the similar treaty with Hungary in 1957, for that treaty (as had the one with Poland in 1956) required agreement of the host government for Soviet troop movement outside the area of their stationing. There was no such provision in the Soviet-Czechoslovak Treaty of 1968. Nor was Prague granted any compensation for damages inflicted during the invasion. The Treaty claimed to be in accordance with the Bratislava Statement and the "understanding" reached during bilateral Soviet-Czechoslovak negotiations August 23–26 and October 3–4, 1968. It did not officially derive its authority from the Warsaw Treaty. . . . The crisis had been resolved by a bilateral treaty between Prague and Moscow. However, conflict continued, and the relationship of the Warsaw Pact to "normalization" in Czechoslovakia is an ongoing problem qualitatively different from the role of that alliance at the time of confrontation.

> Politics is a game for and with power is always a struggle in which one side tries to force the other to accept its view of reality and its interpretation of events.
>
> Karel Kosík, "Illusion versus Realism," *Listy*, November 7, 1968

Normalization for Czechoslovakia meant going back, rewriting the history of 1968 to fit the contemporary Soviet view of reality.[60] For once the October Treaty had legitimated Soviet troops remaining in Czechoslovakia, Prague had lost. As Kosík predicted, Moscow prescribed

the formulas of capitulation and it was only a matter of time before those Czechs and Slovaks who wanted to remain within the political elite began to play the game, redefine the situation in Soviet terms, judge the Prague Spring through Soviet eyes, and use the search for "counter-revolutionaries" to secure their own positions. . . .

THE COMPARATIVE FOCUS

It becomes increasingly necessary to reevaluate the steroeotyped images of Communist and non-Communist alliance systems. Traditionally, emphasis has been upon ideology and its imperatives as definitively separating Communist and non-Communist organizations. In large part this interpretation has relied on the nature of Soviet-East European relationships during Stalin's lifetime. Yet from the beginning the OAS, NATO, and the Warsaw Pact followed similar organizational patterns. Both Communist and non-Communist groupings were created in the face of a commonly recognized external threat. And conflicts of interest and attempts to influence the joint organization in line with national policies occur within the Warsaw Pact as well as in non-Communist organizations.

Thus, in my opinion it would be useful to shift the emphasis from ideology (recognizing that ideology itself can serve as an element of power) to power relationships in comparing Communist and non-Communist coalitions. From this perspective a comparative analysis of the Warsaw Pact and the Organization of American States has the most possibilities. For in both the WTO and the OAS a number of significantly less powerful states share membership with one of the most powerful, highly-industrialized nations in the world. As Brzezinski and Huntington have described the interaction process in both coalitions:

This relationship was one of indirect colonialism by means of satellite regimes. Both major powers, in their expansionist phase, had asserted their domination over a contiguous divided and weak region, and imposed upon it their own political supremacy and economic mastery.[61]

Although there may have been significant differences in the pattern of domination, the parallel is sufficient to provide evidence as to what are

---

[58]The incident of the philosophy student Jan Palach who set fire to himself January 16, 1969 partially as a protest at the continued distribution of *Zpravy*, a Soviet occupation news sheet featuring bitter attacks on Czechoslovak reformers, provided a tragic index of how meaningless that pledge was in practice. Not only did circulation of *Zpravy* violate Czechoslovak publishing laws but no such publication appeared in other East European countries where Soviet troops are stationed. See Eric Bourne, *The Christian Science Monitor* (January 23, 1968).

[59]*Pravda* (October 19, 1968); *CDSP* 20, no. 42 (November 6, 1968): 3–4.

[60]For example, a circular distributed to all career officers of the Czechoslovak Army in 1970 asked them to state their reactions to the attempt to proclaim the neutrality of Czechoslovakia and withdraw from the Warsaw Pact, when in fact there had been no such attempt. For an English translation of the circular see *Le Monde* weekly edition, July 15, 1970.

[61]Zbigniew Brzezinski and Samuel P. Huntington, *Political Power: USA/USSR* (New York: The Viking Press, 1967), p. 38. There is an interesting, as yet unpublished, work comparing the two alliances. I am grateful to William Zimmerman for letting me look at his draft manuscript, "Hierarchical Regional Systems and the Politics of System Boundaries."

the relevant questions to ask about regional alliance systems. Is the determining factor ideology or is ideology only one aspect of a relationship largely defined by the power configuration of member states? Is the criterion for behavior tied up with whether these states are Communist or non-Communist, or is it rather a question of whether they are big or small, powerful or weak? One indicator may well be the pattern of response during intra-alliance conflict. And here there is at least some reason to believe that ideological acceptability of governments within the OAS has been as important to the United States as the "correct form of socialist construction" is to the Soviet Union in East Europe. For the US invasion of the Dominican Republic in 1965 had much in common with the Soviet action against Czechoslovakia three years later.

SANTO DOMINGO AND PRAGUE

This is not the place for a detailed recounting of the Dominican crisis.[62] Yet in an analysis of how conflicts are resolved in Communist coalition politics, it is instructive to note how similar instances of intra-alliance strife are dealt with in more ideologically heterogeneous coalitions. . . .

For when stripped to the skeleton of motive, response, and justification, great power "crisis management" in the Dominican Republic in 1965 and in Czechoslovakia in 1968 had a depressing sameness.[63] Both cases involved a conflict of in-

terest between one of the most powerful, highly industrialized countries in the world and a small state within the superpower's sphere of influence. In both, fear of a potentially unacceptable change in the political structure of the small neighbor precipitated invasion. Both superpowers maneuvered to get token participation from other members of the joint defense alliance, although in the case of US intervention the OAS forces were involved only on an ex post facto basis.[64] Both justified resorting to force by a return to blatant cold war clichés. That the rationale behind the decision to act was more complicated than the explanation is not the point. It always is.

Briefly, when the Dominican military junta collapsed in April 1965 beneath the exigencies of the International Monetary Fund austerity program and prolonged drought, the streets filled with people screaming for the return of President Juan Bosch and the constitution of 1963. Within Santo Domingo, two groups sought power—the young officers, headed by Colonel Juan Caamaño, wanted Bosch to return; and the older officers led by General Wessin y Wessin, an extreme rightist, were determined to prevent the former president from setting foot on Dominican soil. Both groups appealed for US support.

At first Washington preferred inaction. The United States had originally supported Bosch when he came to power in February 1963 as the first democratically elected president of the Dominican Republic in over thirty years. However during his few months in office, the US Ambassador John Bartlow Martin became convinced that at best the new president was incompetent and soft on communism, at worst a "deep cover Communist"[65] hiding under nationalism and commitment to social reform. Thus there had been little regret in Washington when Bosch fell in September. The military junta that replaced him was soon controlled by Donald Reid Cabral, a wealthy conservative from a powerful Dominican family, a Yale man with whom the new Ameri-

---

[62]For a carefully researched analysis of the Dominican case, see Jerome Slater, *Intervention and Negotiation: The United States and the Dominican Republic* (New York: Harper and Row, 1970). Other more journalistic, book-length studies are Tad Szulc, *Dominican Diary* (New York: Doubleday and Co., 1965), and Dan Kurzman, *Santo Domingo: Revolt of the Damned* (New York: G. P. Putnam's Sons, 1965). Not surprisingly, much of the material on this topic is polemical. The former US Ambassador to the Dominican Republic who acted as President Johnson's first envoy during the crisis has written his account. John Bartlow Martin, *Overtaken by Events* (New York: Doubleday and Co., 1966). For an official administration version, see "The Dominican Crisis: Correcting some Misconceptions," *State Department Bulletin* (November 8, 1965). The most articulate antiadministration interpretation that, as Slater points out, has come "to be almost unquestioningly accepted by most serious students of American foreign policy" is that of Theodore Draper, "The Dominican Crisis," *Commentary* (December 1965), "U.S. Power and Responsibility—the New Dominican Crisis," *New Leader* (January 31, 1966), "A Case of Political Obscenity," *New Leader* (May 9, 1966), *The Dominican Revolt*, Commentary Report, 1968, and "The Dominican Intervention Reconsidered," *Political Science Quarterly* 86, no. 1 (March 1971): 1–36.

[63]I do not mean to imply that there were not differences between the Dominican crisis of 1965 and Czechoslovakia of 1968. There were differences of which to my mind the most important have been (1) that the United States did not discredit all alternatives on the side of reform in the process of intervention (2) that U.S. forces subsequently withdrew. However,

these are not differences in either motive for intervention, choice of alternative methods for influencing the situation, or subsequent rationalizations.

[64]For a detailed discussion of OAS involvement, see Jerome Slater, "The Limits of Legitimization in International Organizations: The Organization of American States and the Dominican Crisis," *International Organization* 23, no. 1 (Winter 1969): 48–72.

[65]Martin, *Overtaken by Events*, p. 347. One can assume that this assessment grew from Bosch's resistance to Martin's suggestion that the Dominican president eliminate agrarian reform involving land confiscation, close leftist schools, illegally harass or detain Dominicans traveling to Cuba, and imprison or deport both the extreme right and left. *Ibid.*, pp. 487, 510, 562.

can ambassador William Tapley Bennett, Jr., got along smoothly. Bennett himself was out of town when the junta fell, but his telegram to Assistant Secretary of State for Economic Affairs Thomas C. Mann in early April leaves few doubts as to his opinion of the situation: "Little foxes some of them red are chewing at the grapes. . . . A diminution of our effort or failure to act will result in bitter wine."[66]

In short, US policymakers did not want Bosch back, nor did they want to intervene. If possible Wessin y Wessin would pull the chestnuts out of the fire, making the Dominican Republic relatively simple to deal with again. So US diplomats turned a deaf ear to the rebels. They underestimated Caamaño's resistance, the attachment to constitutionalism, and the people's hatred of the corrupt Dominican military.

When it looked as if the constitutionalists might win, however, that was another matter. On May 2, President Johnson himself declared that the revolution had been "taken over and really seized and placed in the hands of a band of Communist conspirators."[67] The American Embassy in Santo Domingo began passing out lists varying from 53 to 70 "known and active" Communists alleged to be working with Caamaño. Ambassador Bennett described sickening but impossible to verify atrocities. Military moves to wipe out Caamaño were made secretly and followed by false explanations. The US troops ostensibly in Santo Domingo only to protect American lives and property were increased to 32,000.

A ratio of one US soldier to every hundred Dominicans can fairly be called overreaction to 53 or even 70 Communists. In Latin America it was taken as a matter of course that these troops had other purposes. As one diplomat said, "you don't need a cannon to kill a fly." Seen in perspective it is hard to challenge the opinion that American marines moved in to support a US-sponsored junta against a vastly more popular constitutionalist movement.

As for Czechoslovakia, the "Prague Spring" was in its most fundamental aspect a program of reform necessitated by Novotný's disastrous economic policies. Although rooted in a desperate need for economic reorganization, the program did not stop at economics. Domestically it at least initiated a partial reordering of institutional relationships. For the Communist party this meant turning the phrase "inner-party democ-

racy" into something more than pious cant; for the writers, an end to censorship; for the Slovaks, a chance to achieve political and economic equality with the Czechs; for nonparty people, a means to some genuine political participation via previously forbidden clubs. The men intent on making these changes in the quality of Czechoslovak political life were dedicated Communists. They did not think of themselves as abandoning communism, but rather as fulfilling its highest ideals.

Throughout Dubček held to what he considered the three essentials of communism: (1) alliance with Moscow via the Warsaw Pact; (2) continuing nationalization of industry; and (3) the leading, if limited, role of the Communist party. Nevertheless as early as the end of March, Soviet anxiety at the possible consequences of democratization in Prague had ended all but the flimsiest pretense of noninterference in Czechoslovak internal affairs. And as the spring progressed it became more and more evident that a significant part of the Soviet leadership did not trust Dubček to hold the line.

Like the United States with respect to Santo Domingo, the USSR would have preferred not to intervene. But Soviet polemicists tried to make clear early in the game that Moscow took its own version of the domino theory with the utmost seriousness.

Subsequently, the famous Warsaw letter sent by the Central Committees of the USSR, GDR, Poland, Hungary, and Bulgaria to Prague was an ultimatum outlining the rationale for invasion. More ominous yet, it specified a concrete program for getting the situation back in hand: complete repression of antisocialist, rightist forces; the banning of political clubs; reimposition of censorship; and reorganization of the KSČ along "fundamental Marxist-Leninist lines." Dubček's defense was brushed aside, and the Soviet press set the stage for invasion with descriptions of hooligans attacking the Czechoslovak Central Committee building and honest workers being subjected to "frenzied persecutions." Moscow claimed that unidentified party and government leaders in Czechoslovakia had requested urgent assistance. However, Soviet and East European troops could not find the object of their search. The comrades they had come to assist did not materialize.

Again as in the case of Santo Domingo, after-the-fact explanations relied heavily on an external Enemy. But Moscow was more ambitious than Washington. The Soviet "White Book" on events in Czechoslovakia drew together conspiracy theories tying the Czech Club of Com-

---

[66]Quoted by Barnard L. Collier in his eyewitness accounts and analysis, *New York Herald Tribune* (May 16, 1965).

[67]Quoted by Slater, *Interventions and Negotiations*, p. 39.

mitted Non-Party Members to anti-Communist activities in West Germany, the British Intelligence Service, and "an international Zionist organization." By comparison Ambassador Bennett's fewer than 100 Communists seemed an unimaginative effort indeed.

The invasion of Santo Domingo and Prague are important not for the sake of academic parallelism. Rather they point to the unpleasant reality that as the political fabric of the cold war wore thin during the 1960s, decisionmakers in Washington and Moscow alike still clung to familiar patterns of hostility as a rationale for forcing their will on other nations. As Slater has succinctly put it:

In 1965 the United States was a prisoner, both at home and abroad, of its own oversimplifications, myths, and outmoded policies, particularly the Monroe Doctrine and its ramifications. Indeed, one of the more revealing aspects of the Dominican crisis was the way in which it highlighted the inflexibility and obsolescence of the operating framework of assumptions of so many U.S. policy makers.[68]

Minus the reference to the Monroe Doctrine, the same could have been said about the Soviet Union in 1968. (And indeed, one could make a case for the idea that despite its more inclusive terminology, the Brezhnev Doctrine was propounded to serve as a socialist version of the Monroe Doctrine in Eastern Europe.)

Both superpowers recognized the need for reform in what it is now fashionable if somewhat misleading to call the "client" state. Both first supported the leader of those reforms, then lost faith in his ability to control the situation at what the superpower considered the minimal acceptable solution. Both acted in the shadow of recent history within its sphere of influence. Lyndon Johnson felt he could not tolerate a "second Cuba." Soviet leaders may well have been equally unwilling to "lose" Czechoslovakia when Khrushchev had "saved" Hungary, or to see Czechoslovakia become "another Yugoslavia" (Gomulka specifically refers to that danger, for example, in his speech defending the Brezhnev Doctrine at the 5th Polish Party Congress in November 1968).

Thus in the case of both the United States and the Soviet Union a sense of threat to the superpower's international credibility combined with fear of intra-alliance problems and domestic reaction (undoubtedly much greater in the Soviet Union but which Slater makes clear was also a consideration in the American decision) led to

military invasion of a small ally in instances where the great power had, in my view, neither legal right nor objective reason to intervene. When the chips were down Washington showed as little respect for the principle of nonintervention as Moscow did for socialist noninterference in internal affairs. That both superpowers organized token multilateralization of their resort to force cannot constitute legitimization—although as a precedent one can hope it might make such interventions more difficult in the future. It only damaged the legitimacy of the regional defense alliance associated with the intervention.[69]

Neither invasion was as disastrous as it might have been had the superpower been met with organized military resistance or prolonged guerrilla warfare. Yet both have had recognizably destructive consequences.[70]

Certainly anti-American nationalism in Latin America did not decrease as a result of the Dominican intervention. Faith that the Alliance for Progress could bring about nonrevolutionary social reform weakened. Castro's scornful description of the OAS as Washington's "Ministry of Colonies" gained credibility in wider circles, while according to Slater, "radical-extremist" if not Communist strength in the Dominican Republic is stronger today than in 1965. Moreover, domestically, that intervention added to the alienation and shame many American students, intellectuals, and ordinary citizens feel as a result of the foreign policy of their government in Vietnam. It deepened the splits in American society, thereby, in my opinion, making the normal operation of internal politics more difficult. . . .

As for Czechoslovakia, the invasion and subsequent Soviet pressure started the KSČ on a path of corruption and decline that there are some signs even Moscow has come to regret. It

[69]Thus although it is an oversimplification of the institutional relationship involved in the invasion of Czechoslovakia, Robert O. Keohane's conclusion that the Warsaw Treaty Organization "might well be labeled an 'Al Capone alliance' in which remaining a faithful ally protects one not against the mythical outside threat but rather against the great-power ally itself, just as, by paying 'protection money' to Capone's gang in Chicago, businessmen protected themselves not against other gangs but against Capone's own thugs" had a point that was made, in equally colorful if somewhat different wording, by Communist parties and states as well as other non-Communist scholars. Robert O. Keohane, "Lilliputians! Dilemmas: Small States in International Politics," *International Organization* 23, no. 2 (1969): 302. It is a point that unfortunately applies to the OAS as well.

[70]Which is not to say that there may not be some positive results also. If a desire to avoid another such intervention helped keep the lid on US interpretations of the 1970 election of Marxist President Allende in Chile, or prevented Moscow from defining striking Polish workers as counterrevolutionaries in December 1970, it is a step in the direction of sanity.

[68]Slater, *Intervention and Negotiation*, p. 201.

split still further the international Communist movement, strained relations among socialist states, and led to the Brezhnev Doctrine which is a return to the philosophy of Soviet diktat that marked Zhdanov's two-camp theory in the late 1940s and the Molotov line on the Warsaw Pact in 1954. It weakened the attraction of the Soviet model for developing countries, strengthened NATO, and at best delayed prospects for détente and arms control. Domestically it led to the almost unheard-of public demonstration in Red Square that, along with the many private conversations with Westerners, testifies to the despair with which the Soviet intellectual community viewed the implications of that invasion for domestic developments in the Soviet Union.

Why?

John Burton has succinctly summarized the stated rationale:

Communism (or Capitalism) is an actual threat to the independence of all non-Communist (or Communist) States because Communism (or Capitalism) as a system is aggressive; it must, therefore, be contained at some point. Social and political change is desirable, but in the process of change, power vacuums occur that play into the hands of local and foreign-inspired minorities. It is therefore necessary to help existing governments to maintain themselves in office if they are generally in support, and meanwhile to persuade them to induce changes. Opposition to all forms of Communism (or Capitalism), whether they be aggressive or not, is a responsibility of the United States (or the Soviets) in its defence of the rest of the world; any weakening of its opposition anywhere would both encourage aggression and discourage resistance to it. The United States and the Soviet Union must oppose the alternative ideology even though there is no direct threat to their territories and even though the nature of the threat were no more than that which arises out of the competition of ideas.[71]

I don't think so. These arguments have lost force even among the decisionmakers who still refer back to them. The United States recognizes differences among Communist states. There is the comparatively good communism of Yugoslavia, or the not too dangerous communism in the USSR or China, or the more dangerous communism of North Korea and North Vietnam, albeit circumscribed in impact. The Soviets recognize realistic forces within capitalism, consider a treaty with the Brandt government in West Germany quite all right, and conduct the SALT negotiations with the Americans.

Is it, as Burton goes on to maintain, a means of avoiding challenges to political and social institutions within a state by identifying those making the challenge with foreign ideologies, i.e., an attempt to avoid the burden of internal change? In part, yes. There is certainly evidence that internal considerations were important. Yet since at the time those decisions were taken neither the US nor the USSR faced an internal crisis that could be called a "what if" factor in the decision to invade, one should be cautious about assuming it tipped the scale. Or there is the provocative notion that such alliances represent human pecking orders in which the superpowers channel aggressions against a smaller ally because it is too dangerous for them to attack one another.[72] However, being unable to make a coherent judgment on that idea given the current state of my knowledge, I would rather say the following.

It is probably correct to say that decisionmakers in Moscow and Washington suffered from faulty analysis, that they acted rashly without understanding the best interests of their nations "in the long run." One can build a case that the Dominican Republic would not have become a Second Cuba or that if it had no vital interest of the United States would have been damaged as badly as it was damaged by the fact of that intervention.[73] And there are persuasive arguments that Czechoslovak "socialism with a human face" would not have abandoned communism, that a more responsive communism might have met some needs in Moscow as well as Prague.

Yet in my view factual refutations are not the point (not when it is still a common, if undemonstrated, assumption that informed observers in Washington considered the Castroite danger the deciding factor in Santo Domingo). For such faulty analysis is not the product of sloppy research. Rather in both superpowers it is a habit of thought, a reflex based on cold war interpretation in which international events are still tallied in terms of a political competition that has little bearing on the internal dynamic of the event. It is a dangerous game in which the question of who "won" or "lost" can all too easily be a self-fulfilling prophecy with domestic factions convinced that their internal political position hangs in the balance.

In this sense there is some truth to the proposition that interventionists in both Moscow and Washington have a reinforcing relationship that

[71]John W. Burton, *Systems, States, Diplomacy and Rules* (Cambridge, Eng.: Cambridge University Press, 1968), pp. 116–17.

[72]Based on Robert Ardrey, *The Territorial Imperative* (London: Collins, The Fontana Library, 1966).

[73]Jerome Slater's *Intervention and Negotiation* has done an admirable job of just that.

goes deeper than their ideological differences. And it becomes difficult not to conclude that at least throughout the 1960s (as the Chinese have stated cryptically if in a different context) what has been important in the operation of Communist and non-Communist coalitions alike is a process whereby: "The time-worn habits of big countries in their relations with small countries continue to make their influence felt in certain ways."[74]

[74]"More on the Historical Experience of the Dictatorship of the Proletariat," *Jen-min Jih-pao* (December 29, 1956), *Current Background*, 433 (January 2, 1957).

IS CHINA AN EXPANSIONIST POWER?

PETER VAN NESS

For a while, after the Communists came to power in China, Western leaders feared that Peking would join in a monolithic Communist expansion throughout the world led by the Soviet Union. Then when the Sino-Soviet split became obvious in the early 1960s, the West feared a Chinese expansionist drive through Southeast Asia—the so called "domino theory." Peter Van Ness shows in this article (published on the eve of the Sino-American detente) that both these fears were probably groundless, and that though China unquestionably seeks greater power and influence in world affairs she is not at the moment an aggressive power in the sense we imagined her to be. The same realization obviously contributed substantially to President Nixon's decision to seek friendlier relations with the People's Republic.

Peter Van Ness is Associate Professor at the Graduate School of International Studies, the University of Denver. He is the author of Revolution and Chinese Foreign Policy: Peking's Support for Wars of National Liberation *(1970).*

Powerful states will seek to expand and enhance their power—this historical truism seems to hold across time and in spite of differing political philosophies. Militant nationalism in the present era only appears to reconfirm the validity of the generalization. Yet, power has been perceived and applied differently by the leaders of powerful states, depending among other things on the domestic dynamic of the state, its relative capabilities as compared with other states, and the ethic—the code of morality or social philosophy—which provides the ideological foundation and legitimacy for political rule. Philosophy may have great impact on political behavior (as analysts of Marxist-Leninist ideology have often demonstrated); and philosophy becomes particularly significant for international relations, I submit, through its influence on perception—how political leaders think, how they view the world, and, perhaps most importantly, how they perceive and evaluate themselves and their own actions.

In presenting an answer to the question posed in the title—is China an expansionist power?—this essay considers "expansionism" to mean a sustained effort to exercise direct control over people and territory beyond a nation's own borders. Most analysts would agree that China unquestionably seeks greater power and influence in world affairs. But, the question remains,

Reprinted with permission and with minor changes from Problems of Communism 20 *(Jan.-Apr. 1971): 68–74.*

do Chinese actions aimed at gaining greater *influence* constitute *expansionism?* My answer is no.

THE HISTORICAL RECORD

China is a revolutionary power. Its ultimate global objectives call for a complete transformation of the existing international system. From its founding in 1949 to the present day, the People's Republic of China, the government of the world's most populous country and third most extensive territory, has verbally assaulted the international status quo, denouncing the major world powers as oppressive regimes and transitory historical relics, and calling at different times for the immediate overthrow of various foreign governments. Also, China's military capabilities are hardly negligible. Peking maintains one of the world's largest standing armies (some three million men) and is rapidly developing both nuclear weapons and a missile delivery capability. A recent example of the advanced state of Chinese rocket technology was the launching last April of the first Chinese earth satellite, sent orbiting around the globe broadcasting "The East Is Red."

Yet, despite Peking's inflammatory rhetoric and its formidable military power, Chinese behavior in foreign affairs has been perhaps surprisingly circumspect. In the twenty-one years since the establishment of the People's Republic, Chinese military units, with the exception of the Korean War, have rarely, and then only briefly, engaged in combat operations beyond or adjacent to China's borders. Let us look at the record.

Chinese military activity over the last two decades can be readily classified into three categories: (1) internal actions—specifically, the re-establishment of China's borders in 1949–50, the suppression of domestic opposition, and the continuance of the civil war with the Nationalists; (2) conflict over disputed territorial boundaries—principally with India and the Soviet Union; and (3) military initiatives taken in support of the defense of neighboring Communist states—namely, North Korea in 1950–53 and North Vietnam in 1965–68.

Fundamental to an understanding of Chinese international behavior is the distinction between internal affairs and foreign relations. Clearly, the periodic military conflicts (especially in 1954 and 1958) with the Chinese Nationalists over the offshore islands, as well as the entire issue of the political future of Taiwan, are internal Chinese affairs—remnants of an uncompleted civil war (in which the United States intervened in June

1950 after the outbreak of the Korean War). Both Chinese governments see this to be the case, and both remain publicly committed to resolving their differences by force. Similarly, the invasion of Tibet by the People's Liberation Army in the autumn of 1950 and the PLA's subsequent suppression of rebellions in that area (particularly in 1959, when the Dalai Lama fled to India) were also operations carried out within boundaries recognized by both Nationalists and Communists as the proper limits of Chinese domain. (Moreover, the region of Tibet has never gained general recognition as an independent country.[1]) To classify these conflicts as international events and to point to them as evidence of an expansionist Chinese foreign policy is to distort and to misunderstand their significance. No matter how repugnant the use of force may be in any context, these events have to do with China's domestic affairs, and are viewed as such by both Chinese governments.

More controversial for purposes of interpretation are armed conflicts arising from disputes over China's territorial boundaries. Analysis of this second category of Chinese military activity principally relates to border conflicts with India and the Soviet Union. In both cases, the location of the border line became an issue after other differences had arisen between China and the two countries, both of which had earlier been friendly with Peking. One possible inference from this fact is that territory *per se* may not have been so important to China as other questions.

With respect to India, relations between Peking and New Delhi began to deteriorate drastically following the 1959 uprising in Tibet and India's decision to provide the rebels with sanctuary and material assistance. Subsequently, military probes were initiated by both sides along the contested border, and finally, in the autumn of 1962, Chinese forces launched an attack into the Northeast Frontier Agency area in Assam and badly defeated the Indian Army. Shortly thereafter, however, the Chinese troops withdrew. Both before and since the 1962 battles, the Chinese have appeared less interested in Assam than in Ladakh to the West, through which they have built a strategically vital highway linking Tibet and Sinkiang. Peking has seemed willing to settle the border dispute by trading concessions regarding Assam for Indian agreement to the status quo in Ladakh.

[1]Arthur Huck, *The Security of China: Chinese Approaches to Problems of War and Strategy* (New York: Columbia University Press, 1970), p. 42.

The story of the Sino-Soviet conflict is well known to readers of this book and does not bear repeating. Suffice it to say that in this case, as in the Sino-Indian dispute, hostilities regarding boundary questions followed the emergence of profound political differences between the two governments. China's particular case is based on a denial of the legitimacy of the so-called "unequal treaties" between China and Russia, which were concluded before Communist governments had come to power in either country.

Analysts differ in their assessments of the relative merits of the Chinese legal position compared with those of India and the Soviet Union regarding their border differences; however, a general conclusion seems to be that there is merit on both sides, and that the Chinese have been no more aggressive in pressing their demands than has the other party.[2] It should be added that during the same period in which conflicts have occurred with India and the USSR, China has signed formal treaties delineating common boundaries with five other neighboring countries (Burma, Nepal, Mongolia, Pakistan, and Afghanistan) and has often made rather generous concessions in the process of negotiating the agreements.[3]

The final category of Chinese military activity—initiatives taken in support of the defense of neighboring Communist states—constitutes the only use of Chinese military units in the history of the People's Republic in combat operations occurring in territory clearly outside China's borders. In both cases, in Korea in 1950–53 and North Vietnam in 1965–68, Chinese troops were used to defend established governments under attack by American-supported offensives arising out of conflicts in the southern half of divided countries (initially begun, respectively, by the North Korean invasion and by the Vietcong insurrection). Both times Peking's intervention was characterized by the prompt withdrawal of Chinese forces as soon as they were no longer required, and no Chinese political control has resulted from the intervention.[4]

Obviously, the extent to which Chinese forces were actually engaged in combat varied greatly in the two cases. With regard to North Vietnam, Chinese troops were presumably requested by Hanoi to relieve Vietnamese forces for combat in the South and to serve as a deterrent to an American invasion of North Vietnam. Apparently, no more than 50,000 Chinese troops at most were ever stationed in North Vietnam, and the vast majority of these were engaged in rebuilding bombed-out railway lines and other facilities, while some played a role in the air defense of the country.[5] In Korea, the situation was very different indeed. Chinese troops intervened in that conflict in the fall of 1950, after United Nations forces—ignoring warnings from Peking—crossed the line which had earlier divided North and South. The existence of the Communist government in Pyongyang was unquestionably at stake as American and South Korean forces sought to unify the country by force, and it was only intervention by the Chinese which prevented this rollback operation from attaining success. Chinese involvement in the Korean War constitutes the most significant case of Chinese military activity since 1949; some 300,000 troops were engaged in combat for almost three years.[6]

Common to all the cases of Chinese military activity having to do with border disputes or assistance to neighboring Communist governments is a pattern of military involvement for limited objectives; cessation of hostilities and withdrawal of troops when these objectives were attained; and virtually no gain for China in terms of expanded territory or political control as a result of its military actions. Indeed, many analysts have inferred an essentially defensive motivation from the various Chinese uses of military force in the international arena.[7]

REVOLUTION

Often allegations of Chinese expansionist designs are most closely associated with Peking's support for foreign revolutions. I have tried to explain the significance of revolution for Chinese foreign relations elsewhere,[8] but here let me re-

[2]See, for example, Robert C. North, *The Foreign Relations of China* (Belmont, Calif.: Dickenson, 1969), pp. 92–94; Gregory Clark, *In Fear of China* (Melbourne: Lansdowne, 1967), especially Ch. V; and Harrison E. Salisbury, *War Between Russia and China* (New York: Bantam, 1970).

[3]Douglas M. Johnston and Hungdah Chiu (eds.), *Agreements of the People's Republic of China 1949–1967: A Calendar* (Cambridge, Mass.: Harvard University Press, 1968).

[4]In fact, North Vietnam and North Korea are presently two of the most independent countries in the Communist world, despite the fact that the Korean government was originally put in power by the Soviet army and was for several years unquestionably a Soviet dependent state.

[5]*The New York Times* (Sept. 3, 1969), p. 1.

[6]Allen S. Whiting, *China Crosses the Yalu: The Decision to Enter the Korean War* (Stanford, Calif.: Stanford University Press, 1969), especially Ch. VII.

[7]See, for example, *ibid.*, Ch. VIII; Clark, *op. cit.*; North, *op. cit.*; and Huck, *op. cit.*

[8]See my *Revolution and Chinese Foreign Policy: Peking's Support for Wars of National Liberation* (Berkeley: University of California Press, 1970).

late support for revolution to the issue of Chinese expansionism.

China, like virtually all major powers, seeks to influence the internal politics of other countries from time to time by providing moral and often material support for individuals and organizations which it favors in those countries. In China's case, many of these organizations are engaged in making revolution against established governments. However, Chinese policy regarding revolutionary movements—as is clear from both public statements and twenty years of history—calls for revolutionaries to rely principally on their own efforts and resources to gain power. The most comprehensive articulation of this concept of self-reliance appears in Lin Piao's variously-interpreted "Long Live the Victory of People's War!"[9] In a discussion of this statement and an analysis of Peking's support for revolutions, Arthur Huck, writing in a study done for the Institute for Strategic Studies, concludes: "Far from being a blueprint for the direct expansion of Chinese influence, it argues that revolution cannot be exported and that the people's forces must be almost entirely self-reliant."[10] In the same vein, a recent empirical study of actual Chinese international behavior in support of revolutions finds that the Chinese have been true to the principle of self-reliance in practice and concludes that Chinese support "is most certainly not a recipe for direct CPR involvement or control of revolutionary movements."[11]

The self-reliance doctrine is apparently derived from a combination of philosophical principle and hard practical experience. The Maoists argue that it is the duty of all peoples to liberate themselves (not to be "liberated" by foreign armies) and that, in fact, reliance on one's own efforts is the only possible way to achieve real self-determination. Similar conclusions have been inferred from the Chinese Communists' own experience and from the revolutionary successes and failures of others. To have any hope of winning power, a revolutionary movement must have the support of the people; foreign armies are hardly likely to help the movement win popular support, and the involvement

of such outside forces in a revolution may drastically distort its purpose. Moreover, history has also shown that successful Communist-led revolutionary movements are virtually impossible to control from abroad after they have attained power (witness the cases of Yugoslavia, North Vietnam, Cuba, and China itself). And even those Communist governments originally placed in power by foreign armies have progressively forged a wider degree of independence from their "liberators" (particularly the regimes in Romania, North Korea, and Czechoslovakia before the Soviet-led invasion).

Over the years, the Chinese have restricted their assistance to foreign revolutionaries primarily to vocal moral support broadcast by the Chinese radio and published in the official press. In some cases, significant material assistance has been rendered and training for combatants provided, either in China or abroad. There have also been stories claiming that Chinese advisors have been discovered working with revolutionaries in the field, but these reports have proven difficult to confirm.[12] In any event, apparently for reasons of both practical politics and moral principle, Peking has consistently refrained from committing Chinese military units to fight on the side of foreign revolutionaries.

If, as the record shows, China has not behaved in a manner indicating expansionist intent, why not? What factors have constrained what might be seen as a natural expansionist tendency on the part of an emergent international power? In my view, the explanation lies partly in the area of comparative economic resources and military capabilities—but perhaps equally in the realm of what might be called moral constraints on international behavior. Let us deal with capabilities first.

After an early period of indecision in 1949 and 1950, the United States adopted a position of unequivocal and adamant opposition to the Poeple's Republic of China following the outbreak of the Korean War in June 1950 and the Chinese intervention in that conflict in October-November. These were the days of a considerably greater solidarity and organizational unity within the Communist world under the authority of Joseph Stalin, and China was seen by most American policymakers as but a single component of a bloc of hostile Communist states. The

---

[9] *Peking Review* (Sept. 3, 1965).

[10] Huck, *op. cit.*, pp. 50–54. Huck also quotes at length from an interview given by Ch'en Yi to an Australian, John Dixon, in which the principle of not using Chinese troops to support foreign revolutions is discussed in detail.

[11] Daniel Lovelace, "People's War and Chinese Foreign Policy: Thailand as a Case Study of Overt Insurgent Support." Ph.D. dissertation, Claremont Graduate School, 1970, especially pp. 215–18.

[12] Reports have been confirmed of Chinese construction troops helping to build roads in Pathet-Lao-held areas of northern Laos. However, the same accounts indicate that the Chinese have not been involved in combat operations. See, for example, *The New York Times*, Sept. 14, 1969, p. 7; Oct. 16, 1969, p. 13; and Dec. 15, 1969, p. 4.

American position formulated on the basis of the Korean conflict has remained the foundation of US policy vis-à-vis China to the present, only superficially modified by recent changes having to do with trade and travel. Military containment has been and continues to be a basic principle of this policy, and a system of military bases has been erected throughout Asia to provide the staging areas to affirm this commitment.

More recently, the world's second super-power, the Soviet Union, has evolved an adversary relationship with China: at first, Moscow withheld support for certain Chinese foreign policy initiatives (in the late 1950s); later it increasingly opposed Peking's policy and actually competed for influence with China in certain areas; and eventually things reached a point of such mutual enmity that each of the two Communist giants, China and the USSR, came to view the other as its most fearsome world enemy.

Hence, virtually since its founding, the Peking government has faced an international situation in which its enemies—first the United States and later both the US and the USSR—were countries which enjoyed a staggering superiority in economic resources and military capabilities. Comparisons with the United States alone are overwhelming. Peking has not published statistics on Chinese economic performance for a decade, but even optimistic estimates of China's present level of GNP would still leave the US with at least a 6-to-1 superiority. Comparative population figures (roughly 200 million Americans and 800 million Chinese) place China at an obviously greater economic disadvantage. Considering military power, the United States holds the advantage in virtually every category, from an immense superiority in nuclear weapons and missile delivery systems,[13] naval and air power, and modern weaponry in general, to a lead even in the comparative number of men under arms (both the US and the USSR have larger standing armies than China's).[14] The addition of the total capabilities of America's allies—not to mention the Soviet Union's power—makes for an extremely intimidating profile of military might arrayed against the People's Republic of China.

Moreover, it is clear that China's principal adversaries are committed to a military containment of Chinese power within China's borders, if not to the overthrow of the Peking government itself. To this end, both the United States and the Soviet Union have separately sought to build diplomatic alliances composed of China's Asian neighbors. Whether for "the defense of the free world" or for "collective security in Asia,"[15] the purpose of these diplomatic initiatives has amounted to the same thing—containment of China.

Confronting this vast array of military might, Peking has chosen to invest its limited resources largely in two kinds of military capability: a nuclear-weapons/missile-delivery system and a large conventional army. Chinese national security strategy is founded on an effort to create as soon as humanly possible a nuclear deterrent to the American and Soviet threat,[16] and in the meantime to organize the defense of Chinese territory on the basis of the Maoist conception of "people's war"—i.e., to draw an invader deep into Chinese territory and destroy him largely through guerrilla tactics. As a result of this strategic conception and these resource-allocation priorities, Peking has invested very little in the modernization and mechanization of the People's Liberation Army. Compared with most conventional armies of the day, the PLA is equipped with little in the way of heavy artillery, tanks, or transport capability; and it includes only a minor air force and almost no navy.

Thus, not only is Peking lacking in comparative military capabilities, but also it has chosen not to invest its scarce resources or to organize its military forces in a manner appropriate for offensive military action. In fact, China today has no real offensive capability in the sense of being able to launch an effective attack on a major power.[17] Should Peking decide to assault a lesser neighboring country, one or the other of the superpowers would very likely intervene.

MAOIST MORALITY

Maoist philosophy and the Chinese conception of proper political action, including the use

---

[15]For a report on the initial response to Moscow's collective security conception, see Hemen Ray's article, "Soviet Diplomacy in Asia," in the March-April 1970 issue of *Problems of Communism*.

[16]For a thoughtful discussion of the question of a Chinese nuclear deterrent, see Huck, *op. cit.*, pp. 75-77. David Mozingo argues that the principal significance of the American ABM is to prevent, or at least to postpone, the establishment of a Chinese nuclear deterrent, hence continuing the credibility of an American first-strike capability against China: *China's Foreign Policy and the Cultural Revolution*, Interim Report, No. 1, Cornell University International Relations of East Asia Project, Ithaca, 1970, p. 60.

[17]See, for example, the analysis by Frank E. Armbruster of the Hudson Institute, "China's Conventional Military Capability," in Tang Tsou (ed.), *China in Crisis: China's Policies in Asia and America's Alternatives* (Chicago: University of Chicago Press, 1968).

---

[13]To date, China has not yet tested an ICBM and has only tested one shorter-range missile/atomic warhead combination.

[14]Huck, *op. cit.*, p. 37.

of military force, make for additional constraints on a possible expansionist design.

One of the most neglected areas in Western studies of communism is the role of morality in Communist political behavior. Many studies have treated "ideology" as a factor, but few have explored the possible moral ramifications of Communist ideology: as a philosophy, as the value foundation for a nation's self-image and world view, as a definition of the good society and proper social behavior, or as a basis for distinguishing right from wrong. This is not surprising because Communists in practice have often subjugated ideal ends to cynical political means, implying by their actions that there were no moral limits to their choice of tactics. Moreover, for the Western analyst, communism has been the enemy; and there is a natural tendency in analyzing one's political adversaries to infuse one's own ideology into the analysis—that is, to confuse analysis with moral denunciations of the enemy, thereby ignoring or at least denigrating the possible influence of some moral code on the actions of the "evil" adversary.

Regarding China, the point is simply that for its leaders, as for other state policymakers, choices for action are not entirely value-free. Policymakers are not as Machiavellian as is often thought; even for veteran manipulators of power, certain choices are to some extent "unthinkable."

The Great Proletarian Cultural Revolution provides an excellent example of the influence of Maoist values on crucially important policy decisions. The Cultural Revolution was not simply a struggle for power, as many analysts would have it; it was also a struggle for the attainment of the Maoist conception of the good society. Moreover, the means—revolution from below—was seen as fundamental to the likelihood of success. Had Mao's objectives simply been to purge some of China's top leaders, presumably the army under the Maoist Lin Piao could have provided sufficient power to do the job. But individual leaders were not the principal target of the Cultural Revolution. Rather, the object of attack was the whole way of life which had been developing in China, characterized by bureaucratization, materialism, self-interest, and an elitist style of party rule. Hence, the purge was indeed directed at leaders responsible for such developments; but, more importantly, Mao's intent was to purge the entire system through a process of challenge from below aimed at virtually every social institution in the country. The means seemed as important to Mao as the ends, and apparently it was his judgment that a less risky

method would not prove sufficient to attain his desired objectives. The risks were great (including the prospect of domestic dissension and production losses, the danger of intervention by foreign enemies in a divided China, and the possibility that profound doubts might be raised about the entire future of party rule); but the stakes were high—the Cultural Revolution was a life-or-death struggle, as Mao saw it, for the ideals of the Chinese Revolution.

Similarly, Maoist thinking conceives of only certain proper means for the attainment of the Chinese international objective of world revolution. Revolution abroad, as in China, must not be imposed from above; and there is certainly no proper role for Chinese or any other foreign military forces in revolutions abroad. To quote Lin Piao, "Revolution, or people's war, in any country is the business of the masses in that country and should be carried out primarily by their own efforts; there is no other way."[18]

The Maoist philosophical commitment to nonintervention by Chinese troops and to the self-reliance of foreign revolutionaries relates directly to Peking's basic view of the world and China's role and influence in it. Daniel Lovelace, in a study of Sino-Thai relations, finds the Maoist conception of influence in international affairs to be largely one based on virtuous example or model effect. Somewhat like their Confucian predecessors, the Maoists seek to exert a moral influence. Lovelace argues that it is self-reliance in each country (i.e., revolutionary success without Chinese involvement or control) which constitutes proof of the universal validity of Maoist doctrine.[19] Hence, one might say that the Maoist philosophical concept of international influence is not of the expansion of Chinese state power, but rather one of the successful diffusion of Maoist political virtue.

From this perspective, for China to invade and seek to control neighboring countries would constitute a flagrant violation of the very principles which Peking has so vigorously propagated. Also, Peking has not been insensitive to

---

[18]"Long Live the Victory of People's War!" loc. cit., p. 19. In the same article, Lin Piao states further: "In order to make a revolution and to fight a people's war and be victorious, it is imperative to adhere to the policy of self-reliance, rely on the strength of the masses in one's own country and prepare to carry on the fight independently even when all material aid from outside is cut off. If one does not operate by one's own efforts, does not independently ponder and solve the problems of the revolution in one's own country and does not rely on the strength of the masses, but leans wholly on foreign aid—even though this be aid from socialist countries which persist in revolution—no victory can be won, or be consolidated even if it is won." Ibid., p. 22.

[19]Lovelace, op. cit. especially pp. 199–201 and pp. 215–18.

world opinion in its search for national dignity and international respect. Policy alternatives which involve actions in violation of principle must appear to Chinese policymakers both personally repugnant and also costly in terms of ideological influence at home and abroad. Thus, Maoist philosophy itself works as a constraint on possible Chinese expansionist tendencies.

THE FUTURE

The future, as always, is not clear. The political outcome of the Cultural Revolution is still in doubt; it is by no means certain that Maoism will prevail in China. Not all of China's leaders in the past have agreed with Mao on questions of principle and strategy. For example, Lo Jui-ch'ing, former PLA Chief of Staff and one of the first major victims of the Cultural Revolution, is said to have favored a much more interventionist foreign policy and the resumption of a close working alliance with the Soviet Union, both of which would have enhanced the possibility of China's implementing an expansionist policy in Asia.[20] Future changes in Chinese leadership may bring men holding such views to power in Peking.

Moreover, there are patterns discernible in the history of Soviet international relations which could possibly provide insights into China's future. In his *The New Class*, Milovan Djilas speaks of two distinct periods in the history of Soviet foreign policy: the first, a "revolutionary" phase, primarily defensive and rather like Chinese foreign policy today; and the second, an "imperialist" phase, aggressive and expansionist, which emerged after the USSR had developed resources and capabilities sufficient to support a more interventionist posture.[21]

Is it inevitable that a more technocratic, less philosophical leadership will come to power in China, which will create the economic and military capabilities essential for vast state power and then use them to support an expansionist policy abroad? No one knows for sure. But it is strange by contrast, I think, that we have taken so long to initiate a meaningful dialogue with the aging visionary in Peking, preoccupied as he is with trying to create his conception of the good society in China, adamantly opposed to reconciliation with the heretics in Moscow, and firmly committed to realizing world revolution only by means of self-reliance.

[20]Donald S. Zagoria, *Vietnam Triangle* (New York: Pegasus, 1967), Ch. III.

[21]Milovan Djilas, *The New Class* (New York: Praeger, 1957), pp. 178–79.

THE ARMY IN NORTHERN IRELAND

MICHAEL BANKS

The reasons for the troubles in Northern Ireland are, of course, unique to that country, but the warfare taking place there is similar to urban guerrilla fighting elsewhere in the world. The study of this European urban guerrilla warfare is thus important, especially in view of the all too probable likelihood of more such warfare throughout the world in the future. Michael Banks, who accompanied infantry patrols on the border and Armagh, assesses military operations in Northern Ireland during the period leading up to the imposition of direct rule by the British government in March 1972. He has also written a brief paragraph on the political origins of the conflict and a postscript especially for the article's inclusion in this book.

Major Banks retired from the British Royal Marines in 1968 to become Defense Advisor to the Liberal Party and Defense Correspondent to the Western Morning News. *His publications include* Commando Climber *(1955),* High Arctic *(1957),* Rakaposhi *(1959), and* Snow Commando *(1961).*

POLITICAL ORIGINS

When Ireland gained her independence from Britain in 1921 the break was not a clean one. Six counties in the north, known as Northern Ireland or Ulster, remained part of the United Kingdom but with a measure of political independence vested in the provincial government at Stormont.

There was gerrymandering in this partition of Ireland which resulted in about one-third of the Ulster population, who were Roman Catholic, finding themselves under the ostensibly permanent rule of the Protestant or Unionist majority. Friction and bitterness were inevitably generated which periodically has spilled over into violence. The most recent, and the most serious, outbreaks started in 1969 and have continued with undiminished intensity.

There have been swift and radical changes, usually for the worse, in the situation in Northern Ireland during the last year and a half. The gunman and the bomber have emerged, automatic fire has been directed at the troops, the Catholic community has, most regrettably, polarized its attitude towards the British Army which it now identifies as the traditional oppressor and enemy. The Army itself was no longer required to act as a buffer between the Catholic and Protestant communities, or even as a para-military anti-riot police force (an unsuitable role it was forced into). Instead it has taken a number of initiatives and has found itself fighting an urban guerrilla warfare campaign reminiscent of its colonial days.

In this article I shall attempt to assess the threat, posed at the moment almost entirely by the IRA, and then describe the way the Army is meeting it. I shall also take a look at some of the new equipment which has been specially developed to meet the specific needs of the conflict in Northern Ireland.

THE IRA

The original IRA, whose memory is much revered by the Republic of Ireland's legitimate Army, were patriots who today would be regarded as freedom fighters. Their aim, an independent Ireland, was nationalistic rather than political. The memory and tradition of these men are now safely enshrined in the pantheon of Irish history. The old IRA bears little relationship to the Official IRA who inherited their name.

The Official IRA is a Marxist-oriented organization whose proclaimed aim is the creation in all Ireland of a united socialist workers' republic. This political aim, obviously, poses almost as much a threat to the Republic of Ireland as it does to Northern Ireland. For this reason the Official IRA is proscribed in the Republic, although attempts to eradicate it have been less than half-hearted, principally on account of the large measure of public sympathy its aims, but not its methods, in Northern Ireland attract.

Although adversity makes for strange bedfellows, it was asking too much for the Catholic/nationalist extremists of the North to make common cause with the Marxists of the Official IRA based in the Republic. Inevitably perhaps a splinter group appeared—the Provisional IRA—which is an organization peculiar to Northern Ireland. Whereas the Officials generally favored political struggle for the attainment of their ends, the Provisionals chose for one of their slogans 'Liberty grows from the barrel of a gun.' They opted for outright violence as the means of unifying Ireland, a patently hollow philosophy and one which has left a trail of blood, misery and bitterness behind it.

When the rift between these two factions of the IRA became irreparable, internecine warfare broke out between them in which an unspecified number of men were killed. An uneasy truce now exists, with the Provisionals very much in the ascendency except in a few small pockets in Belfast.

I want to keep as far away from politics as I can (which is fiendishly difficult when writing about Ireland), but it is worth explaining that the IRA saw very clearly that if the Catholic Civil Rights movement attained its aims of social justice within the Province, which under pressure from London it could well have done, then the IRA would have had the steam taken out of its campaign for the unification of Ireland.

It must therefore be conceded that, using military methods, the IRA has not only taken over the leadership of the Catholics from the Civil Rights leaders but it has also achieved two of its main aims: keeping the question of the unification of Ireland very much a live issue; and the abolition of the Government of Northern Ireland at Stormont.

THE NATURE OF THE THREAT

Until the middle of 1970, the main threat to the troops, who were perforce spread fairly thinly on the ground, was the ability of the Catholics to drum up an enormous crowd at extremely short notice which would then threaten to overwhelm a small or isolated detachment. In mid-1970 the gunman made his appearance and the IRA began to manipulate the crowds which would contain a good proportion of out-and-out troublemakers. The troops were pelted with stones intermingled with petrol or nail bombs, sniped at from behind the crowd, and occasionally subjected to automatic fire.

The Army kept its head and did not overreact against the crowd itself, no doubt to the disappointment of the IRA. Instead the Army took on the IRA in a struggle it had been trained for—a firefight. Although violence was escalated during this period, Army morale was raised. The soldiers at last found themselves doing a military job, fighting the emergent urban guerrillas, and they found it a welcome change from standing in stolid rows being stoned and taunted by hooligans. It was also a time of increasing danger on the streets. One sniper in the Ardoyne killed five men of the Green Howards in skilfully set up ambushes. Usually he would arrange for a disturbance to be staged. On the arrival of an Army patrol he would fire one or two shots from a well-concealed position and then quickly disappear. His 'trade mark' became recognized but he has apparently disappeared from the scene, and it is possible that he himself eventually became a casualty or, perhaps, a detainee.

Naturally the big crowds had little enthusiasm for being caught in the crossfire in this confrontation and disappeared from the streets. It is very probable that the Army came off best in this firefight, as one would expect them to, because the IRA did not choose to sustain the trial of strength.

The IRA then switched to its current campaign of selective terrorism, including the cowardly and cold-blooded abduction and murder of three unarmed young Scottish soldiers who were off-duty and having a drink in a hotel. Public figures and members of the locally enlisted Ulster Defence Regiment became priority IRA targets.

IRA bombing activities also increased in this period, probably because it was found to be less hazardous pastime than shooting it out with the Army. We have all become familiar with press reports of armed terrorists planting bombs, often in crowded shopping areas, and giving bystanders a few minutes warning to move away. The ferocity of the bombing campaign should not be underestimated. The total casualties up to 10 March 1972 were 63 dead and the appalling figure of 1,264 injured. Selective targets, such as the houses of prominent Unionists, have also been either bombed or burnt. Perhaps the most dangerous form of bombing is the Claymore mine, dug into the side of a hedge or placed under a culvert in the road, which is then detonated remotely by electricity when an Army patrol is in the immediate vicinity.

In summary, the threat the Army is counter-ing at the moment includes the hit-and-run sniper, bombs in public places which have to be rendered harmless, the concealed mine in an am-bush position and the threat of abduction and assassination if any of the security forces were to put themselves in a vulnerable position. At the same time the Army must enforce the ban on marches, be they Protestant or Catholic. As events at Londonderry showed, the mixture of a large crowd and a gun-battle between the IRA and the Army can create a tragic situation.

THE ARMY REACTS

The IRA mounted its terrorist campaign in the hope, possibly to be realized sooner than they had imagined, that such disruption would be caused that, in the short term, the UK govern-ment would be forced to abolish Stormont and impose direct rule. In the long term the IRA en-visage public opinion in Britain becoming so an-tagonistic to a continuance of the bloodshed that the British government will be forced to pull out of Ulster and leave the road open to the unifica-tion of Ireland.

In consequence, the operational scene changed considerably in 1971. The Army intensi-fied its intelligence operations in the summer, having first improved its own intelligence organ-ization and, particularly, the co-ordination be-tween the Army and the Police Special Branch. Numerous raids, usually at dawn, were carried out against suspects. Valuable intelligence, often supported by collateral information, began to mount up. The controversial decision was then made to intern suspects under the Special Powers Act of the Stormont government.

During the early hours of 9 August some 300 suspects were rounded up, many of them on in-formation obtained during the recent intelligence raids. About 70 of them were released shortly afterwards. These early arrests have been fol-lowed by many others making a total of about 700 persons who have, at some time or other, been detained.

Detention was followed by the even more con-troversial 'interrogation in depth' of about 40 prime suspects. Modern methods of interrogation first made their appearance during the Korean war when Allied prisoners were broken down mentally or brainwashed. These methods have remained standard practice in Communist coun-tries and it therefore became commonplace in Western armed forces to require troops, princi-pally those most liable to capture, such as air-crew, to undergo Communist-type interrogation

so that they would be mentally prepared and fortified against this modern barbarism should they ever become prisoners of war. It was there-fore a profound shock to the British public to learn that these very same measures had been used in peacetime against mere suspects. Deep interrogation was stopped pending a public in-quiry by Lord Parker into the methods of arrest and interrogation. The Parker Report has now been completed and very stringent regulations have very properly been applied to future methods of interrogation.

The free-for-all deep interrogation was a poli-tical blunder and a departure from the accepted standard of British ethics and justice and it is re-assuring to know that it has been stopped. With internment itself, it was in contravention of the United Nations' concept of human rights.

From the purely military point of view both internment and interrogation proved most pro-ductive. As a result of interrogation, further ar-rests were made and it is safe to say that a con-siderable number of potential murderers are now behind wire. The flood of information the Army and the police extracted enabled them on many occasions to drive up to a specific address and ar-rest the individual they wanted. This accuracy in identifying IRA members must have sent shock waves through the entire membership. No one in the IRA could feel safe any longer. However, success was far from absolute as witness the press conference held in Belfast by Joe Cahill, leader of the Provisionals, a few days after in-ternment had been authorized.

No one imagined that internment would put an end to the IRA, if only for the simple reason that there is an almost inexhaustible supply of youngsters who have been nourished on hatred of the British and who are always ready to offer themselves as recruits. What internment achieved was the disruption of the leadership of the IRA. Evidence for this is, for instance, to be found in the number of bombers who were killed by their own explosives immediately following the internment of known skilled bomb manufac-turers. The number at the time of writing is probably at least 22 and this does not include the 15 people killed in the explosion in McGurk's bar in Belfast which was an accident. An exam-ination of the corpses after this accident indi-cated that some of them were probably leaning over the bomb tinkering with it when it went off.

As a direct result of the affects of internment, the IRA has moved from attacking hard targets toward attacking soft. The armed attacks on mili-tary or police posts have fallen sharply, and IRA efforts have been concentrated on indiscriminate bombings, hit-and-run firing, the remote-controlled Claymore mine and selective assassination, including the attempts in Armagh on the life of the Stormont Home Affairs Junior Minister, Mr. Taylor. Violence spread to England in the notorious and inept bombing of the Airborne Brigade Officers' Mess at Aldershot which killed five women, a gardener and a Roman Catholic Army chaplain.

The Civil Rights movement and the much discussed but so far chimerical Protestant backlash are, at the moment, threats in a lower key which the security forces must watch carefully. It is a valid viewpoint that the Catholic population would have achieved social justice more effectively through a vigorous Civil Rights movement of Gandhi-esque proportions. This would have presented Stormont with a political rather than a military problem. It is, after all, eventually in the arena of politics, albeit under military pressure, that the problem must ultimately be solved. As far as the Protestant backlash is concerned, the Army is uneasily aware of the thousands of weapons 'under Protestant beds' which might be brought out if an unpalatable political solution were forced on them. It is a possibility full of menace. The Army has not forgotten that it first came under heavy fire from Protestant gunmen in the Shankill Road of Belfast in 1969. However, at the time of writing, in the weeks immediately following the imposition of direct rule, all is relatively quiet in the Protestant communities.

ARMY ORGANIZATION AND TACTICS

The rising scale of violence, and particularly the onset of urban guerrilla warfare, has presented a commensurately heavy manpower bill at the Ministry of Defence. The Army strength is now steady around the 15,000 mark with the uncomfortable knowledge that the movement of the manpower graph has, so far, always been upward.

There are grave implications to this heavy manpower requirement: the strategic reserve has been almost completely absorbed and there is a standing requirement for five major units to be detached from BAOR. This latter is particularly unwelcome to the Foreign Office at a time when it is much to our advantage, in the context of entry into the European Common Market, to show ourselves to be good Europeans who are making our full contribution to the security of the Continent.

The forces are commanded by the GOC-in-C Northern Ireland who is also the Director of Operations. Army policy is directly controlled by

the UK government via the Ministry of Defence in Whitehall. Until its abolition, Stormont remained responsible for security within the Province. Military control, within the policy guidelines laid down by Whitehall, devolved upon the Joint Security Committee of Stormont which embodied the proven 'triumvirate' principle for counterinsurgency operations, by which operations are jointly planned by the heads of the civil, police, and military authorities. The Joint Security Committee, which met once a week, included the Home Affairs Minister (a post occupied by the then Prime Minister, Mr. Faulkner), the GOC, and the Chief Constable, together with such other members as were required.

The RN and RAF presence is very small and comes under the operational control of the GOC. The Navy deploys a few minesweepers on coastal patrols under the Senior Naval Officer, Northern Ireland, while the RAF maintains an air base at Aldergrove, Belfast's civil airport. The RAF's most important contributions are the air transport of troops to and from the Province and the provision of troop-carrying helicopters.

Apart from the familiar operational and administrative duties, HQ Northern Ireland, situated at Lisburn, has to wage an all-important propaganda war. In *Brassey's Annual 1971*, Hugh Hanning properly upbraided the Army for not having taken enough steps to protect itself against a weapon just as injurious as the petrol bomb: namely 'calumny.' He went on to assert that the image the Army has been allowed to acquire is now so far from the truth that steps should be taken to set it right.

It would take an advertising campaign of genius to sell the British Army in the Catholic ghettoes, although even here opinion is not completely hardened against the British soldier. The public relations effort at Lisburn has been considerably stepped up, not only by increases in the conventional PR effort feeding the news media, but also by the creation of an Information Policy Cell, a sort of PR think tank, which studies trends in reporting and attempts to keep one step ahead in the propaganda war. The important war of words is now being waged with vigor.

The British Army gets a moderately hostile world press, particularly in the USA. In Ireland itself the news reports are predictably partial while in Britain the media present the Army in no more than a barely fair light. The shooting of thirteen civilians, principally by the 1st Battalion, the Parachute Regiment, on Londonderry's Bloody Sunday gave the Army a damaging press which implied a considerable measure of guilt on the part of the paratroopers. It will stick whether or not this is borne out by the Widgery enquiry, which was immediately set up to investigate the affair.

The peacetime garrison of Northern Ireland was a brigade headquarters with two battalions. There are now three brigades permanently stationed there with headquarters in Londonderry, Lurgan and Lisburn respectively. At the time of writing there are sixteen major units under command of these three brigades, together with a further 4,000 troops at short notice to move to Ulster in anticipation of increased trouble following the imposition of direct rule from the UK.

Until the time of internment, the Army had largely countered trouble as it occurred. Crowds were confronted when they assembled; sniper fire was returned. After internment a more positive policy was pursued. It was decided to hold off in Catholic Londonderry, which was uncomfortably close to the succour of the border anyway; and to maintain no more than necessary patrol activity along the border and in the country towns. A major effort was then concentrated on cleaning up the overridingly important city of Belfast.

The Army moved into Belfast in strength. Foot and vehicle patrols were active in every street, including those in the alleged 'no-go' areas where the Royal Ulster Constabulary had been unable to operate. Many raids and searches of houses, acting on information obtained from detainees, proved fruitful and the IRA was thrown on the defensive. For the first time it was very much the Army that was setting the pace.

Although claims that the IRA had been beaten must be treated with suspicion, there is no doubt that the security situation in Belfast has been greatly improved. It must be acknowledged that the tip-and-run sniper, or the car with a gelignite bomb in the boot, will remain a hazard. But the IRA has moved completely away from hard targets and today the bombers do little more than mingle with the shoppers, plant a bomb in a store, and quickly escape in the crowd. Significantly, night operations, where the IRA and Army meet on rather more equal terms, have declined sharply. The Army can claim considerable credit to have brought increased law and order to Northern Ireland's biggest and economically most important city. A military question at present in abeyance is whether the Army might try to impose the same formula on Londonderry and whether they would achieve the same measure of success in a city which is both politically and geographically far trickier than Belfast.

THE BORDER

The question of the security of the border has become a major problem. The border is 261 miles long and is crossed by a number of major roads and a host of minor roads and lanes. It has always been very much an open frontier, with infrequent customs posts and, of course, no passport formalities required to cross it.

The existence of an open border poses a threat to security because arms, ammunition and explosives can easily be carried across to Northern Ireland from the Republic. Conversely, the Republic offers a safe haven for IRA men on the run. Republic border towns, particularly Dundalk, provide the IRA with convenient safe bases from which to mount raids or ambushes, often carefully prepared, into the North.

It was patently impracticable to control the whole length of the border short of erecting an iron curtain on the Eastern European satellite pattern, which would have been unthinkable. A compromise solution was therefore arrived at whereby most of the minor roads would be cratered thus diverting traffic on to the major roads where it could be watched and, if necessary, searched.

A large number of minor roads were consequently cratered which gave rise to a good deal of small arms fire from the Republic which was not suppressed either by the Irish Army or by their police or Garda. At the same time the watch on the border was intensified using foot patrols, helicopter flights and modern means of surveillance including radar and such innovations as image intensifiers which give enhanced vision at night.

The border is far from sealed, but the increase of patrols, and their unpredictability, has undoubtedly made illegal border crossings a more risky affair. There are many unsatisfactory aspects. For instance in parts of the frontier, concessional routes criss-cross from one side of the border to another. It is expected that free passage will be given on these roads. Again, the customs men go off duty at 5 P.M. and it is then quite open for vehicles to drive across although they run the risk, as they do everywhere in the Province, of a snap check at an Army road block. Finally, smuggling is such a long-established occupation along the border that the IRA do not find it difficult to obtain expert assistance when they need to cross.

I flew in a helicopter border surveillance patrol, called an Eagle flight, mounted by the 1st Battalion, the Devonshire and Dorset Regiment. I found the RAF flying exhilarating in the fast swooping landings to search suspect lorries, and there is no doubt that the sudden appearance of a Wessex helicopter, rapidly disgorging a patrol, must act as a deterrent to any day movement across the border.

THE ULSTER DEFENCE REGIMENT

It may be recalled that soon after the 'B' Special police were disbanded and the Royal Ulster Constabulary disarmed, a new military force, called the Ulster Defence Regiment (UDR) was raised. This force, unlike the police, was to come under the direct control of the Ministry of Defence like any other regiment of the British Army. It was also hoped that it would contain a good percentage of Catholics, again, unlike the police.

The UDR has now been raised and has already recruited over 7,000 of its permitted ceiling strength of 10,000. The number of Catholics coming forward has been disappointing, but it must be borne in mind that joining the UDR is a major decision for a Catholic to make often in an atmosphere where intimidation is rife.

UDR service involves part-time duty, rather along the lines of the Territorial Army. Members are liable to full-time call out and were required for five weeks continuous duty immediately following internment in order to free the Regular Army for other commitments. The UDR is not permitted to take part in crowd control, for obvious reasons. However, their assistance is much appreciated by the Regular Army, particularly in manning road blocks, guarding vulnerable points and in providing local expertise, such as guides to patrols visiting unfamiliar areas.

There is also a Territorial Army in Northern Ireland about 3,000 strong. They have no operational role in the Province but are required for the rapid reinforcement of NATO, in common with other units of the UK Territorial Army.

EQUIPMENT

When the Army moved into Northern Ireland to maintain law and order it was furnished with its normal scale of arms and equipment which are, understandably, designed for conventional warfare. The Army's training was also, of course, directed to that end.

The typical infantryman then found himself cast in the role of policeman with a high-velocity, semi-automatic rifle in his hand, confronted by a stone-throwing crowd. His weapon, like his training, was almost unusable.

Much has been achieved since those early days. The men have adapted quickly to the changing combat situation. New equipment, which had to be specifically designed, was slow to appear but is now widely, if not lavishly, available. It has become a familiar sight to see photographs of troops with bulletproof jackets and tough, transparent plastic shields.

The list of special equipment used, or tried out, by the Army in Northern Ireland is quite impressive and is given in the Appendix.

CONCLUSION

Nobody realizes better than the Army itself that there can be no purely military solution to the communal problems of the Province. Although the eventual solution cannot be seen in military terms, it is nonetheless true that the military situation will have an important impact on the political climate. If the IRA were running rampant, civil war would be one step the nearer. If law and order, of a sort, prevails, the political options are wider and the prospects of communal peace that much the better.

The path of events in Northern Ireland can only increase the soldier's inbred distrust of the politician. After the troubles of 1969, the soldiers held the ring steadfastly and with courage. They gave the politicians that most precious of elements, time, particularly in the crucial year of 1970. The subsequent deterioration of the situation is testimony that the politicans, particularly those at Stormont, failed to appreciate the urgency of the crisis. They squandered the time the soldiers had won for them and the Army has carried the can ever since.

This is a war no one can win. The performance of the IRA has varied between the amateur and the mediocre and they can never win against well-trained, professional troops. Neither can the Army ever win in the sense that it will be able to eliminate an urban guerrilla movement broadly based on a large and sympathetic section of the community.

A fair insight into the current situation was given me by a corporal leading a patrol to whom I spoke one night in Armagh. 'The kids who stoned us this afternoon came over and had a friendly chat this evening,' he said. Other men told me how a number of Catholics, in private and away from the threat of intimidation, could be friendly towards the Army. In other words the situation is not without hope despite the polarized attitudes taken in public.

For nearly three years the Army has stood firm and kept its temper in the face of extreme provocation. After all, there can be few countries in the world where you can hurl rocks at an armed soldier and not get shot for your trouble. The Army has been a model of restraint for which they deserve the very highest credit.

Northern Ireland has not been an entirely negative experience for the British Army. It has had to adapt its tactics and modify its equipment to meet the sort of unrest which is becoming increasingly widespread in the world today. The glare of publicity which has been focused on the Army has contributed significantly in attracting recruits who are now enlisting in greater numbers than for many years. Finally, it has become very much a soldier's war, a fact reflected in the currently high morale. Patrols are usually of section strength which throws heavy responsibility on the corporal and the private. These men have risen splendidly to the occasion and, in the process, have gained invaluable operational experience.

POSTSCRIPT

As this article goes to press a new government in Northern Ireland elected on the system of proportional representation, which is scrupulously fair to minorities, has come into being. This important constitutional improvement, together with other reforms, should help remove some of the basic injustices from which the Catholic minority has suffered. The IRA has no desire to see improved stability in the Province and continues its campaign of urban guerrilla warfare. It is also significant that the Unionist extremists, who resent any power passing to the Catholics, have also resorted to violence. The number of sectarian murders has increased sharply. In Northern Ireland it is going to be a long haul to peace. But where has it not been?

NORTHERN IRELAND—SPECIAL EQUIPMENT

Flak Jacket—A waistcoat made of nylon felt which gives protection against grenades, shell fragments and low-velocity bullets. Weighs 8 lb.

Body Armor—Shaped, bullet-proof plates to protect the torso, thighs and legs. Made of ceramic armor and gives protection against a rifle bullet. Not yet used. Suitable for static patrols and sentries.

Makralon—A tough transparent plastic which can be used as a riot shield through which the soldier can see. It has been known to stop a revolver bullet. Makralon is also used for the windows of trucks.

Baton Round—This is the rubber bullet, fired from a Very's pistol or a riot gun. The bullet is 5¾ in. long with a diameter of 1½ in. It is preferred as an alternative to CS gas because it is more selective in its target.

Stun Gun—This has not been brought into service but is a gun which fires a bag containing ½ lb. of lead shot which can travel 350 ft. and has a 'punch like heavyweight Henry Cooper.'

Explosive Detector—This is a gelignite sniffer which can detect the nitrogen emitted by an explosive even if wrapped in plastic. It can trace clothing, etc., which has been in contact with explosives and acts on the principle of electron capture detection.

Water Cannon—Two high-pressure water cannon are used, principally when CS gas has proved ineffective.

Riot Dye—This can be dispensed by the water cannon or by aerosol and aids the identification of rioters. The colors are yellow, blue, and violet.

Starlight Scope—This is an image intensifier which utilizes available light, usually starlight, and produces an intensified image on a TV-type screen which can be fixed to a weapon and give an accurate enough picture for aimed fire.

Single Point Sights—This is a device to improve night firing in restricted light up to 300 m. Both eyes are kept open, the right eye using an individual light source spot on a green screen.

Foam Barrier—A foam is used which covers a wire obstacle used to separate two crowds. The foam lingers in position and the wire obstacle becomes very difficult to cross.

Handtector—This is an anti-hijacking device which detects small metal objects on the person.

Caltrops—This implement contains four spikes, one of which will always remain vertical. It is used in conjunction with a road block to puncture tyres of vehicles which do not stop.

Vehicles—Many familiar Army vehicles have been much modified for the special conditions of Northern Ireland. Landrovers are fitted with loud-hailers, remote-controlled spotlights, rotating radar, wire cutter against cheese wire stretched across the road, wire mesh over windows, makralon armor covering and extra fire extinguishers for petrol bombs.

A Landrover has been much strengthened and armored for the UDR and is called the Shorland.

The Humber has been armored and is called a Pig.

A four-wheeled tractor has been fitted with a wide armored screen for blocking off streets or for providing cover for advancing troops. It is nicknamed the Paddy Pusher.

A vehicle with a hydraulically elevated armored platform gives visibility over the heads of a crowd.

THE FRENCH EXPERIENCE IN INDOCHINA AND ALGERIA

JOHN STEWARD AMBLER

The true nature of modern war is epitomized in the French experience since 1945. While she has fought only three years of conventional war (in Korea), she has fought sixteen years of unconventional or anti-guerrilla war. Professor Ambler covers three important areas in this article—a general overview of guerrilla warfare and the conditions which lead to its success; a brief description of the French experience in Indochina; and a longer account of the Algerian guerrilla campaign and the French responses to it.

John Steward Ambler is Professor of Political Science at Rice University. He is the author of The French Army in Politics, 1945–62 *(1966) (also in paperback as* Soldiers Against the State, *1968), "The Democratic Union for the Republic" (1968), and* The Government and Politics of France *(1971).*

INTRODUCTION

When the leaders of the January 1960 uprising of European settlers in Algiers were finally brought to trial, one of the paratroop officers who had given them tacit support, Colonel Joseph Broizat, took the stand as a witness and told the court:

... If we, the officers of 1939–1945, who almost led assaults in white gloves and *casoar* [the plumed cap of Saint-Cyr cadets], if we, in short, became interested in the political problem, it was not because of a taste for politicking; it was because of the demands of our professional duty.[1]

[1] Testimony of Broizat in Alain De Sérigny (ed.), *Un Procès* (Paris: La Table Ronde, 1961), p. 29.

The colonel's defense of the army's political ventures in Algiers cannot be dismissed as apologetics pure and simple. As Broizat himself never ceased to explain, from 1946 onward the French Army had been engaged in a new and unorthodox style of war in which military and political questions were inextricably intertwined.

If one is to comprehend the reasons for the French Army's political role in Indochina and especially in Algeria, he must understand something of the rebel foes who forced French officers to question those military values associated with the "Great Mute."

In all modern Western nations clean-cut lines between the political and military realms have been increasingly difficult to trace in this century of total war and cold war. For the officer newly engaged in revolutionary-guerrilla war,

Reprinted by permission with minor changes from The French Army in Politics, 1945–1962 *(Columbus, Ohio: Ohio State University Press, 1966), pp. 149–169. Published by the Mershon Center of the Ohio State University and copyright © 1966 by the Ohio State University Press.*

however, that distinction appears almost irrelevant: down to the level of the squad commander, political and human considerations often must be given priority over tactical military considerations. And no army in the world has as much experience against this style of warfare (or has suffered as serious a politicization from it) as has the French Army.

GUERRILLA WAR

The style of war which the French faced in Indochina and in Algeria belongs to a sizeable category of wars, variously styled "subversive," "brushfire," "unconventional," "irregular," "revolutionary," and (most commonly) "guerrilla." Since 1945 wars of this style have raged in China, Greece, Malaya, the Philippines, and Cuba, in addition to Indochina and Algeria. What are the common and distinguishing features of what will here be called "revolutionary-guerrilla war"?[2] All depend upon the use of guerrilla tactics, especially in the early phases. In this sense, and in their rural or mountainous bases of operation, they are essentially different from the urban revolutions in France in 1789 and in Russia in 1917.[3] But guerrilla forces have often been employed simply as an adjunct to regular armies, or as a means of defense against an invader after the defeat of regular forces (as in Spain in 1803–13 against Napoleon, and in Russia in World War II against Hitler). In the Chinese Communist revolutionary war, and in other similar recent wars, guerrillas were used as a revolutionary offensive weapon which was coupled with intense psychological warfare aimed at subverting the defending regime and building a strong popular revolutionary front.

Revolutionary-guerrilla war of the Communist Chinese style had a number of historical precursors, among them the slave revolt led by Spartacus against the Roman Republic in 73–71 B.C. and, in modern France, the Protestant Camisard rebellion of 1702–4 and the Catholic Vendéen uprising against the revolutionary government after 1793.[4] It was only in the

twentieth century, with the British Colonel T. E. Lawrence and his Arabian guerrillas of World War I, however, that revolutionary-guerrilla war began to be a systematic, self-conscious weapon.[5] Far more important as a mentor to modern rebels was Mao Tse-tung, who combined an excellent comprehension of the age-old rules of guerrilla warfare with an intelligent communist's organizational talent and ideological zeal.[6]

Mao's numerous writings on the subject of revolutionary-guerrilla war return again and again to a central theme: guerrilla war, a tool of the militarily weak, can be successful only if it is also a *people's* war.

Many people think it impossible for guerrillas to exist for long in the enemy's rear. Such a belief reveals lack of comprehension of the relationship that should exist between the people and the troops. The former may be likened to water and the latter to the fish who inhabit it. How may it be said that these two cannot exist together? It is only undisciplined troops who make the people their enemies and who, like the fish out of its native element, cannot live.

. . . .

Because guerrilla warfare basically derives from the masses and is supported by them, it can neither exist nor flourish if it separates itself from their sympathies and cooperation.[7]

Mao's successful pupils in Indochina, Algeria, and Cuba all understood this pre-eminent principle of revolutionary war: the most crucial immediate task is not defeat of the government army (an unrealistic objective in the early years) but development of support from, and control over, the civilian population.[8] Once the "water"

---

[2]Depending upon the criteria of selection, one might also include Indonesia, Cyprus, Kenya, Morocco, Tunisia, etc. In these cases, however, rebellion either lacked the sophisticated political-military organization and development seen in the other examples cited and/or succeeded without need for guerrilla action beyond the terrorist stage.

[3]Some use was made of guerrilla tactics in the American Revolution, especially in the South. But from 1775 onward the Continental Congress and General Washington gave strong priority to the creation of a regular army (Walter Millis, *Arms and Men* [New York: Mentor, 1958], pp. 22–30).

[4]Colonel Gabriel Bonnet, *Les Guerres insurrectionnelles et révolutionnaires* (Paris: Payot, 1958), especially pp. 53–

55, 60–62, and 69–92; Fernand Theibaut, "Par-delà les normes de la guerre conventionnelle . . . les leçons de l'histoire," *RDN* (February 1960): 296–317; Léonard, *L'Armée et ses problèmes au XVIIIe siècle*, chap. 4 ("La Guerre des Camisards, exemple de 'guerre à fond'"); and Colonel André Montagnon, *Une Guerre subversive: La Guerre de Vendée* (Paris: La Colombe, 1959).

[5]T. E. Lawrence, *Seven Pillars of Wisdom* (Garden City, N.Y.: Doubleday, 1935); and Lawrence, "The Evolution of a Revolt," *Army Quarterly* XLI (October 1920) reprinted in his book, *Oriental Assembly* (London: Williams & Norgate, 1939), pp. 103–34.

[6]Mao's principal writings on revolutionary-guerrilla war are to be found in the following: General S. B. Griffith (ed.), *Mao Tse-tung on Guerrilla Warfare* (New York: Praeger, 1961); and Mao Tse-tung, *Selected Works* (New York: International Publishers, 1954), including "Strategic Problems of China's Revolutionary War" (I, 175–253), "Strategic Problems of the Anti-Japanese Guerrilla War" (II, 119–56), "On the Protracted War" (II, 157–243), and "Problems of War and Strategy" (II, 267–281).

[7]Mao Tse-tung, *Mao Tse-tung on Guerrilla Warfare*, pp. 44, 92–93.

[8]General Vo Nguyen Giap, *People's War, People's Army* (Hanoi: Foreign Languages Publishing House, 1961), reprinted

is safe from pollution, the revolutionary-guerrilla movement is virtually assured of eventual victory. The rebels will watch the enemy's every move through millions of civilian eyes and, when outnumbered by enemy troops, will melt unseen into a protective civilian population. Though rebel losses may far outnumber government casualties, as they did in Indochina and in Algeria, a supporting native population produces an inexhaustible supply of replacements. On the other hand, if the rebellion does not succeed in winning over a large portion of the civilian population, it will shrivel and die, as it did in Greece in 1949 and then in Malaya after 1953–54.

Three qualifications are in order with regard to popular support for revolutionary-guerrilla war. First, particularly in the early stages of the war, strong support in certain base areas may be sufficient to launch the movement and eventually to win more general active support, e.g., Fidelist support in Cuba's Oriente Province. Second, the revolutionary movement rarely can hope for the support of the total population, even in an anticolonial war, for inevitably there will be an older native elite fearful of losing all privilege and wealth to the revolution. Third, a revolutionary movement which does not embody an already existing national sentiment, nor one which easily can be aroused by propaganda, usually turns to terrorism on a mass scale in an attempt to coerce "traitors" within the target group to rally to the revolutionary cause. In Kenya, Algeria, and Malaya rebel terrorism struck the indigenous population far more often than it struck European civilians or security forces.[9] Yet the true stakes of revolutionary-guerrilla war remain support from the population, for if the target population cannot be brought to believe that the revolutionary cause is just and right, terrorism may well produce alienation rather than support. Such was the case in Malaya in the early 1950s and in Kenya after the Larbi Massacre in 1953.[10]

The term "guerrilla warfare" alone describes only one of the tactics and one of the phases (albeit the longest one) of revolution on the Chinese Communist model. Though no fixed chronological sequence of phases fits all wars on this model,[11] in very general terms it may be said that a successful revolutionary-guerrilla movement must accomplish the following tasks: (1) develop a political-military organization which eventually extends its control over a majority of the population; (2) organize guerrilla units to harass and eat away at enemy defenses and morale; (3) develop a secure territorial base for training, for escape from pursuing enemy troops, and for the seat of a provisional government (either in a mountainous or remote area where the population is sympathetic, as in Cuba and China, or in a bordering country, as in Vietnam after 1949 and in Algeria); (4) finally, if the enemy's strength and determination are too great to be broken by a long guerrilla war of attrition, develop a regular army and launch a conventional campaign to defeat his armies. The most frequent developmental tendency for a successful revolutionary movement is from an early stage of organization, propaganda, and often terrorism, to expand guerrilla activities, and finally to primary reliance upon a regular revolutionary army.

In the course of a revolutionary-guerrilla war an appeal is usually made for aid from foreign countries, and that aid may be a vital factor in the outcome of the war. Following the Chinese Communist conquest of all of mainland China in 1949, the Vietminh received Chinese war materials, which allowed the development of the large and powerful army that was more than a match for crack French paratroop regiments at Dien Bien Phu in 1954. The process worked in reverse in Greece, where Tito's break with the Cominform in 1948 led to withdrawal of Yugoslav aid and shelter to Greek Communist guerrillas, thus contributing heavily to their defeat a year later.[12] Yet foreign aid or its lack is not necessarily crucial, for guerrillas notoriously supply themselves by disarming prisoners and by raiding enemy depots and arsenals. The Chinese Communists supplied themselves primarily with equipment stolen, captured, and bought from Chiang Kai-shek's troops, and Fidel Castro overthrew the Batista regime without important foreign aid.[13]

in a facsimile edition by Praeger (New York, 1962), pp. 78–79, 124; E. Che Guevara, *Guerrilla Warfare* (New York: Monthly Review Press, 1961), p. 17; *El-Moudjahid* (the official weekly journal of the FLN), No. 46 (July 20, 1959), as quoted in André Mandouze (ed.), *La Révolution algérienne par les textes*, 3rd ed. (Paris: Maspero, 1962), p. 33.

[9]Samuel P. Huntington, "Patterns of Violence in World Politics," in S. P. Huntington (ed.), *Changing Patterns of Military Politics*, p. 25.

[10]Brian Crozier, *The Rebels* (Boston: Beacon Press, 1960), pp. 168, 179.

[11]Colonel Rocolle, "Les Constants de la guerre subversive," *RDN* (February 1958): 245–64.

[12]Colonel J. C. Murray, "The Anti-Bandit War," *Marine Corps Gazette* XXXVIII, nos. 1–5 (January–May 1954), reprinted in Lieutenant Colonel T. N. Greene (ed.), *The Guerrilla—And How to Fight Him* (New York: Praeger, 1962), pp. 65–111; and Jacques Dinfreville, "La Victoire de l'Armée Grecque sur la guérilla communiste," *RDN* (October 1955): 323–33; and *ibid.*, (November 1955): 442–53.

[13]Dickey Chapelle, "How Castro Won," in Lieutenant Colonel T. N. Greene (ed.), *The Guerrilla—And How to Fight Him*, pp. 229–30.

INDOCHINA

The Indochinese and Algerian rebellions occupied the French Army for sixteen years. Each deserves a brief description.

During World War II Ho Chi Minh, alias Nguyen Ai Quoc, founder of the Communist Party of Indochina, succeeded in taking the lead of the newly created League for the Independence of Vietnam, popularly known as the Vietminh.[14] When Japanese troops overthrew the French Vichyite administration in Indochina on March 9, 1945, former schoolteacher Vo Nguyen Giap and his Vietminh guerrillas extended rebel control—first over the Tonkin countryside, and then, following Japanese surrender in August 1945, over the whole of that northernmost province. Free French troops moving in from the south on the heels of the British were able to reestablish control in Hanoi, capital of Tonkin, only after heavy fighting with Vietminh forces. The Vietminh retreated to the countryside, leaving the cities to the French, and strengthened their organizational hold over a population already favorably disposed toward independence.

The war, of course, was then only beginning. The French gradually and painfully learned of the skilful manner in which the Vietminh organized and controlled the Vietnamese population, leaving the French administration, especially outside the larger cities, nothing but a hollow shell cut off from its nominal charges. The Vietminh's chief revolutionary strategist, General Giap, gave clear priority to political over military activities in the early stage of what he termed "armed propaganda" led by Vietminh political-military units.[15] Using non-communist nationalists as well as communists placed in key positions, the Vietminh employed threats along with persuasion in creating a powerful system of "parallel hierarchies," as French military writers have labeled it, composed of an "associational hierarchy" and a "territorial hierarchy."[16] The

Vietminh progressively organized the entire population in its stronghold areas and a large part of the population outside those areas into a series of specialized associations for youth, peasants, non-peasants, women, elderly people, and so forth, according to the natural groupings of the local population. Alongside the associational hierarchy, which rose from village to canton to subprefecture to prefecture to nation, was a territorial hierarchy composed of governing committees for the entire population at each of the same levels, responsible always to the unit above. Alongside these two hierarchies was still a third, this one more selective in composition—the Party. Throughout this overlapping organizational structure, personal responsibility was clearly assigned, and safeguards against disloyalty were multiple and overlapping. A leading French military expert on the Vietminh, Colonel Charles Lacheroy, writes: "We hardly have an example of an agent who lasted over three months in enemy territory."[17]

Though often forced to operate clandestinely, Vietminh territorial committees were capable of administering justice, enforcing decisions through a Vietminh police force, gathering information, and generally undermining effective French control even in areas where French military superiority was undeniable. The Vietminh often succeeded in realizing the full totalitarian possibilities of this system of overlapping structures. The cause of independence became a glorious national mission; its defenders were patriots and its opponents—and often the uncommitted as well—could only be traitors. The pure, hard Vietminh movement dealt violently with "traitors," especially those who collaborated with and informed the French. Vietnamese who were tempted to provide information to French troops when they moved into a village in force could rest assured that the Vietminh would survive any French repression and, when French troops moved on, would claim its revenge.

And so the French controlled the cities and the roads—during daylight hours[18]—while the Vietminh controlled the countryside and built a

---

[14]The best general sources on the Indochinese War are: Philippe Devillers, *Histoire du Viet-Nam de 1940 à 1952* (Paris: Seuil, 1952); Jean Lacouture and Philippe Devillers, *La Fin d'une guerre* (Paris: Seuil, 1960); and Donald Lancaster, *The Emancipation of French Indochina* (London: Oxford University Press, 1961).

[15]Giap, *People's War, People's Army*, pp. 78–79.

[16]The first and foremost French analyst of "parallel hierarchies" is Colonel Charles Lacheroy, who became head of the Service d'Information et d'Action Psychologique in the Ministry of Defense, and later joined the OAS in its futile crusade for French Algeria. See, for example, his articles, "Une Arme du Viet-Minh: Hiérarchies paralléles" (Paris: Section de Documentation Militaire de l'Union Française [hereinafter SDMUF], 1954; mimeo.); "La Campagne d'Indochine, ou une leçon de guerre révolutionnaire," (Paris, SDMUF, 1954; mimeo.), and his lecture, "La Guerre révolutionnaire," in

Centre des Sciences Politiques de l'Institut d'Etudes Juridiques de Nice (ed.), *La Défense nationale* (Paris: Presses Universitaires de France, 1958). See Colonel Nemo, "La Guerre dans le milieu social," *RDN* (May 1956): 605–23; "La Guerre du Viet-Minh," by "un groupe d'officiers," in *RMI*, no. 281 (February–March 1957): 23–39; and Lancaster, *The Emancipation of French Indochina*, pp. 418–28.

[17]*La Défense nationale*, p. 314.

[18]As Lacheroy puts it "Nous exerçons à peu près la 'Royauté du Jour' dans notre zone, mais le Viet y partage très largement avec nous la 'Royauté de la nuit' " ("Une Arme du Viet-Minh: Hiérarchies paralléles," p. 4).

powerful military system composed of local guerrilla and self-defense units, larger regional units, and a powerful regular army. While the Vietminh watched their every move, French forces rarely could decipher the nature and movements of their enemy through the dense screen of popular silence and widespread hostility. As France hesitated to concede independence to a non-communist Vietnamese government, then did so only in form after 1949, the Vietminh built up a political-military machine which, with Chinese Communist military equipment and tens of thousands of bicycle-pushing civilians to carry it, attacked and defeated an important French fortress at Dien Bien Phu. Indigenous troops fighting with the French, soldiers whose morale had never rivaled that of the Vietminh, all but disintegrated as negotiations at Geneva led finally, in July 1954, to an armistice and partition of the country at the seventeenth parallel. Again as in China five years before, a powerful modern army, with air power and armor, had been defeated by a revolutionary enemy equipped initially and primarily only with small arms—and with the loyalty of the civilian population.

ALGERIA

The victory of the National Liberation Front (FLN) in Algeria is even more impressive in some respects, for French interests were greater there. French forces and colonists were more numerous, and FLN military strength, even at its height, considerably less than that of the Vietminh.[19] When a group of impatient young rebels, encouraged by Colonel Nasser of Egypt, broke with the older, factious Algerian nationalist groups in March 1954, and created the embryo of what was to become the FLN and its military twin, the National Liberation Army

(ALN), they benefited from no such power vacuum as Ho Chi Minh enjoyed in 1945. The French government, in fact, saw no reason for serious alarm on November 1, All Saints Day, 1954, when seventy terrorist attacks in Algerian cities, followed by rebel guerrilla raids in the Aurès Mountains, announced the beginning of what was to be a futile eight-year war for France.[20] The obstacles to an FLN victory seemed great indeed. Algeria had been French since the 1830s. Her three departments were considered parts of the French Republic. Over a million Europeans had made their homes on Algerian soil, in contrast to the scant ten to fifteen thousand European residents in Indochina at the outset of the war there.

When the strength of the FLN rebellion grew to serious proportions, the brunt of French defense was no longer left largely to native troops, as it had been in far-off Indochina, where all but some 175,000 men (many of these Africans and Foreign Legionnaires) out of the 500,000 defending troops had been uninspired Indochinese.[21] A French defending army of similar size in Algeria after 1957 was composed largely of draftees from the *métropole*.

Against such a formidable French Army the ALN probably never had more than 30,000 to 40,000 men in arms within Algeria itself, far fewer than the Vietminh's estimated 350,000 troops in 1953.[22] Militarily the French were relatively stronger in Algeria than they had been in Indochina and the rebels considerably weaker. In eight years of war in Algeria, French military forces lost only 9,000 men while killing 141,000 rebels.[23] Though rebel forces were able to re-

---

[19]The Algerian war has already been the subject of an extensive literature. Of particular interest are: Jacques Soustelle, *Aimée et souffrante Algérie* (Paris: Plon, 1956); Germaine Tillion, *L'Algérie en 1957* (Paris: Editions de Minuit, 1957); Serge Bromberger, *Les Rebelles algériens* (Paris: Plon, 1958) (hostile to the FLN); Charles-Henri Favrod, *La Révolution algérienne* (Paris: Plon, 1958) (favorable to the FLN); Mandouze (ed.), *La Révolution algérienne par les textes* (excerpts from FLN documents and publications); Michael Clark, *Algeria in Turmoil* (New York: Praeger, 1959) (a well-documented "French Algeria" viewpoint expressed by a former *New York Times* reporter); R. le Tourneau, *Evolution politique de l'Afrique du Nord Musulmane, 1920–1961* (Paris: Colin, 1962); Roger Trinquier, *La Guerre moderne* (Paris: La Table Ronde, 1961) (pp. 115–21 for a description of the FLN organization); Lucien Poirier, "*Un instrument de guerre révolutionnaire: Le F.L.N.*," *RMI*, no. 289 (December 1957): 7–34, and *ibid.*, no. 290 (January 1958): 69–92; Raymond Aron, *La Tragédie algérienne* (Paris: Plon, 1957); and Aron, *L'Algérie et la république* (Paris: Plon, 1958).

[20]The events of that All Saints Day are described in Clark, *Algeria in Turmoil*, pp. 3–5. See also General C. R. Cherrière, "Les Débuts de l'insurrection algérienne," *RDN* (December 1956): 1450–62. Cherrière was commander of French military forces in Algeria in 1955–56.

[21]Figures are for 1953 (Navarre, *Agonie de l'Indochine*, p. 46).

[22]The Vietminh estimate is by Navarre, *Agonie de l'Indochine*, p. 46. Estimates of FLN guerrilla strength in the Aurès Mountains in the fall of 1954 vary from 350 (Cherrière, *RDN*, p. 1454) to 2,000 (Clark, *Algeria in Turmoil*, p. 122). By March, 1956, French intelligence estimated rebel armed strength at 8,000 regulars and 21,000 auxiliaries (*ibid.*, p. 299). FLN sources claimed as many as 100,000 rebel troops in the fall of 1957, while a Tunisian newspaper close to the FLN, the *Petit Matin*, put the figure at 42,000 (Bromberger, *Les Rebelles*, 248–49). The actual figures, though impossible to determine exactly, were probably between 25,000 and 40,000 in 1957. Completion of an electrified barrier on the Tunisian border in September 1957, thereafter limited ALN access and probably held armed rebel forces within Algeria to about the same limits.

[23]*LM*, March 9, 1962, quoting "official sources." Very likely the figure for rebel casualties includes many Moslems who had little or no connection with the FLN, but who were killed in French raids on rebel villages. See below, pp. 169–70.

plenish their ranks indefinitely and continue a prolonged war of harassment and terrorism, it was not military defeat which forced out the French. In fact, the military operations led by Commander in Chief Maurice Challe in 1959–60 were quite successful against rebel *military* forces. If one looked only at the strength of the rebel army within Algeria, there was some truth to the claim of army Chief of Staff André Zeller in June of 1959: "The victory thus acquired by the military in Algeria is taking a form unknown until now. All that is left is to conclude it politically."[24]

Yet military means proved incapable of breaking the FLN political-military organization and its control over a broadening segment of the population; nor, so long as that organization remained intact, could they halt terrorist attacks and scattered guerrilla raids, despite the considerable success of the French (especially after 1957) in cutting off rebel supplies and reinforcements from abroad and from ALN bases in Tunisia and Morocco.[25] The war came to an end in March 1962, when it had become apparent to De Gaulle and to the majority of Frenchmen that the only alternative to Algerian independence was interminable war.

The FLN owed its victory against apparently strong odds, not so much to foreign aid (as French official and military opinion often held),[26] as to terrorism, political organization, and widespread underlying resentment against the privileged European *colons*. FLN tactics were similar in many respects to those of the Vietminh, although the Algerian rebels, as Arab nationalists, had little love for the Algerian Communist Party, which was predominantly European in composition and initially opposed to Algerian independence.[27]

Since the position of the FLN was much weaker than that of the Vietminh had been at the outset of the war, terrorism played a more important role (probably a necessary one from the rebel point of view) in tightening FLN control over a wavering population.[28] General or systematic terrorism, usually in the form of bomb and grenade explosions in buses, cafés, theaters, and other public places, was designed to pose the "Algerian problem" and to create a climate of fear and lack of confidence in French protection. Shortly the FLN turned as well to selective terrorism aimed at Moslem public officials and, generally, to those Moslems and Europeans who formed a bridge between the two communities. Notes threatening death or mutilation went out to Moslem notables who sat on municipal councils, to shopkeepers who refused to contribute to the FLN, and to many others, even strong Moslem nationalists, who refused to accept FLN authority. For those who did not comply, punishment was immediate, cruel, and widely publicized, as in those cases where the victim was returned to his village alive, but with his nose, lips, ears, or sexual parts savagely cut off.[29] If "treason" was a collective act on the part of a whole village, the FLN on occasion resorted to a general massacre in which women and children were not always spared—for example, in the village of Melouza, where the entire male population of three hundred was slaughtered in

---

[24]"L'Armée de terre liée à la nation," *RDN* (June, 1959): 963. See also General Challe's testimony in *Procès Challe*, p. 26 (". . . En 1960 les rebelles étaient pratiquement défaits . . .").

[25]Arms, probably from Egypt, came into Algeria across the Tunisian border in the early years of the war. Yet a French intelligence report of March 1956, estimated rebel armament to include primarily hunting rifles, which were probably of domestic origin (18,000 hunting rifles as against 3,200 army rifles and 606 small automatic weapons [Clark, *Algeria in Turmoil*, p. 299]). Two ships carrying heavier military equipment intended for the rebels were captured by the French—the Greek ship "Athos" bearing arms from Egypt, in October 1956, and the Yugoslav ship "Slovenija," in January, 1958. In the latter years of the war the ALN maintained regular bases in Tunisia and Morocco.

[26]In regard to foreign responsibility for the war, see, for example, Cherrière, *RDN*, p. 1451; Soustelle, *Aimée et souffrante Algérie*, p. 21; and Déon, *L'Armée d'Algérie et la pacification*, p. 36. With respect to French military disregard for rebel goals and ideology, see Chapter 11 of my *The French Army in Politics* (Columbus, Ohio, Ohio State Univ. Press, 1966).

[27]After the Setif uprising in 1945 the central committee of the Communist Party for North Africa announced: ". . . Il faut tout de suite chatier rapidement et impitoyablement les organisateurs de troubles, passer par les armes les instigateurs de la révolte et les hommes de main, qui ont dirigé l'émeute" (*Liberté* [organ of the Parti Communiste Algérien], May 17, 1945, as quoted by Guy Mollet, *13 Mai 1958, 13 Mai 1962* [Paris: Plon, 1962], p. 140). When again in 1954 the French and Algerian communist parties initially opposed Algerian independence, the FLN condemned them in its Soummam Valley platform of 1956 (Mandouze, *La Révolution algérienne par les textes*, pp. 94–95). On the subject of FLN–Communist Party relations see also *LM*, March 23, 1957; Jean Glories, "Quelques observations sur la révolution algérienne et le communisme," *L'Afrique et l'Asie*, no. 41 (1958): 16–44; ibid., no. 42 (1958): 3–23; and (from a writer closer to the French *guerre révolutionnaire* school) Déon, *L'Armée d'Algérie et la pacification*, pp. 38–52, 178–87, 183–93.

[28]The role of terrorism was more important, I would argue, than suggested by Crozier in *The Rebels*, p. 191. But terrorism alone is hardly capable of establishing community support, as suggested by writers such as Virgil Ney, "Guerrilla War and Modern Strategy," *Orbis* II, no. 1 (Spring 1958): 75; and Colonel Trinquier, *La Guerre moderne*, pp. 40–44.

[29]See Bromberger, *Les Rebelles algériens*, pp. 40, 81; Soustelle, *Aimée et souffrante Algérie*, pp. 23–24, 215–17, 299 (photographs of victims after pp. 88 and 136); and Crozier, *The Rebels*, pp. 170–75.

May 1957, for co-operating, not with the French, but with the rival Algerian National Movement.[30]

In Algeria, as in Indochina, the heart of the rebel movement was not the rebel army but the solid political-administrative organization which again pulled the native population out from under an undermanned French administration. Though somewhat unsystematic in the early stages, the FLN gradually by mid-1956 had extended its organization from mountain strongholds to the whole of Algeria.[31] The official FLN weekly, *El-Moudjahid*, later explained that the fundamental mission of early guerrilla bands was not military activity but "above all the organization of the people and the diffusion of patriotic passwords. These groups organized successful ambushes, lightning attacks, spectacular assaults. But their primary task consisted of setting up the FLN organization."[32] Only then could the ALN be built and supported on this organizational base.

Constructed on a communist-type cellular principle and building from the village or district level up to the six "Willayas" (plus the autonomous zone of Algiers), into which all of Algeria was divided, the FLN organization consisted at most levels of a governing committee of three to five members. At middle and higher levels a political-military chief had the assistance of a political executive, a military executive, an executive for liaison, and another for intelligence. Each of these four executives belonged also to a parallel (and watchdog) system of functional hierarchies, according to their special responsibility.[33] Alongside the territorial and functional hierarchies were, as in Indochina, a number of professional associations, notably the powerful General Union of Algerian Workers formed in February 1956. Though there existed a national liberation army (the ALN), political considerations generally took precedence over military considerations, according to the guiding principle adopted by the rebel congress held in August 1956, in the valley of Soummam. Once the FLN political-military organization was in place, re-

peated military defeats could not destroy the rebel movement.

Underlying much of the effectiveness of FLN terrorism and organization was the vulnerability of Algerian society. An uneven pace of social and economic modernization, coupled with rapid population growth after 1930, had disrupted the traditions and restraints of Arab family and communal life, creating an uprooted and poverty-stricken urban working class, a frustrated educated elite, and a peasantry newly aware of its misery. The French sociologist, Pierre Bourdieu, described the war accurately when he wrote:

Its underlying causes may be found in a bitterly real drama: the overthrow of a vital order and the collapse of a whole world of values.

. . . .

To claim that the war was imposed upon the Algerian people by a handful of ringleaders who resorted to compulsion and trickery is to deny the fact that the struggle was able to draw on strong popular sentiment for its vital strength and purpose, a sentiment inspired by an objective situation.[34]

In Algeria (as in Malaya, for example)[35] rebellion attracted those who had broken with the traditional way but had been refused self-fulfilment within the framework of Western colonial society. The FLN drew strong support from Moslem intellectuals (who were aware of their subordinate social and professional status in a colonial society) and from Moslem youth (who through education, mass media, physical mobility, and especially urbanization were torn from traditional family and communal restraints).

Clearly, one cannot explain the determination, the sacrifice, the fighting spirit of the Algerian rebellion, its hold over Moslem intellectuals and youth, nor the mass of Moslem demonstrators it finally called out on the streets of Algiers in December 1960, without reference to Algerian nationalism, and without mention of the bitterness of an awakening and disoriented native population subordinated socially and economically to a European community only a tenth its size. The failure of French psychological warfare and its theme of "integration" of the two

[30]C. L. Sulzberger, "The Nationalist Strategy of Terror in Algeria," *NYT* (June 5, 1957). One French reserve lieutenant, who favored independence for Algeria, told the writer of finding dozens of Moslem men, women, and children killed and mutilated as the result of a punitive FLN raid in 1958. See the internal FLN directive ordering mass reprisals by burning of villages and massacre of male inhabitants in cases where villagers asked for French protection, in *L'Année politique 1957* (Paris: Presses Universitaires de France, 1958), p. 231.

[31]Poirier, *RMI*, no. 289 (December 1957): 25–26.

[32]No. 53–54, November 1, 1959, as excerpted in Mandouze, *La Révolution algérienne par les textes*, p. 40.

[33]Poirier, *RMI*, no. 290 (January 1958): 72–83.

[34]See Pierre Bourdieu, *The Algerians*, trans. Alan C. M. Ross (Boston: Beacon Press, 1962), pp. 144–45; see also pp. 134–44. This book was originally published in 1958 and revised in 1961 as *Sociologie de l'Algérie* ("Que sais-je" series [Paris: Presses Universitaires de France]).

[35]Lucien Pye, *Guerrilla Communism in Malaya* (Princeton, N.J.: Princeton University Press, 1956), pp. 7, 343–44.

communities is further evidence that not just any goal will do. Lawrence of Arabia once remarked that a rebellion can be made by an active 2 percent of the population, if only—but only if—the bulk of the remaining population is "passively sympathetic" to the rebel cause.[36]

Here, then, was the kind of enemy against which the French Army battled so frustratingly for sixteen years. Shunning the open field of battle, at least in the early stages, this rebel adversary gave clear priority to political organization and control of the population above all purely military objectives. Once having achieved control over the majority of the target population through a blended campaign of propaganda, terrorism, and organization, he could not be rooted out by military action alone.

RESPONSES TO VIETNAM AND ALGERIA

The varied responses of the French Army to such an unorthodox foe are significant in that all of them in some way contributed to the erosion of effective civilian control. What were those responses? Throughout the Indochinese war and in the initial years of the Algerian war, French officers generally failed to understand the nature of the war being waged against them and riposted ineffectually (and worse) with an old-fashioned military attempt at repression. A second type of response was proposed (and occasionally attempted) by numerous military specialists in *la guerre révolutionnaire*, who urged that the French turn back against the rebels their own totalitarian techniques of organization and thought reform. Yet neither the French government nor the majority of French officers were willing to turn the whole of Algeria into a totalitarian state, though most agreed that effective means had to be found to deal, not only with rebel bands, but also with the rebel political-administrative organization. Hence, thirdly, government and army devised other political activities in which military personnel played a leading role, notably "psychological action" and organization and administration at the local and regional levels. Fourthly, once fully involved in the political character of revolutionary-guerrilla war, key French officers became increasingly impatient with the flagging determination of French governments and the French population. It seemed to these officers that, if Algeria were

not to be lost, the army would have to focus its new political and ideological leadership, not only on the Algerians, but on the French government and the metropolitan French population as well.

The civil-military tensions which arose from all of these responses were in good measure the result of the new political demands of revolutionary-guerrilla war and deserve further consideration in that context. Those tensions were also aggravated, however, by the feeble authority of the Fourth Republic, which delegated wide powers and failed to control their exercise. Such was particularly the case with psychological action and military use of torture.

The initial and instinctive reaction of most French officers to colonial rebellion was to call for more troops and more police in order to crush the enemies of France. Colonial uprisings as recent as those in the Algerian city of Sétif on V-E Day in 1945 and in Madagascar in 1947 had been snuffed out quickly with a ruthless campaign of repression which killed several thousand Moslems in the first instance and some thirty thousand Malagache rebels in the second.[37] Yet the French predicament in Indochina after 1946 and in Algeria after 1954 was infinitely more complex than in these and earlier colonial rebellions. Whereas harsh official suppression of revolts at Sétif and in Madagascar had been almost ignored by the French population at home and by the world outside, by the 1950s general and rapid social change in French colonial countries, modern communications, and anticolonialist sympathy both at home and abroad all conspired to publicize colonial revolts and the official reaction to them. Moreover, the enemy was now better organized, more widely dispersed, and skilled in the techniques of revolutionary-guerrilla war.

Like their more aristocratic predecessors of the early eighteenth century against the Camisard rebellion, French officers in Indochina and Algeria soon discovered that against a popular, well-organized, and determined rebellion, a tactic of bloody repression often succeeds only in spreading and intensifying the fire.[38] French

---

[36]T. E. Lawrence, *Oriental Assembly*, p. 134. On the same point see also Griffith, *Mao Tse-tung on Guerrilla Warfare*, p. 43.

[37]Moslem casualties at Sétif have been estimated at figures ranging from 1,300 (by official French sources) to 45,000 (by the FLN); 10,000 is perhaps a reasonable estimate. See Crozier, *The Rebels*, pp. 197–99 (and, with regard to the Madagascar revolt, pp. 199–201); Clark, *Algeria in Turmoil*, pp. 29–38; and Le Tourneau, *Evolution politique de l'Afrique du Nord*, p. 350.

[38]Similar experiences were had by the French in the Vendéen rebellion, by the Germans in Russia and Yugoslavia in World War II, and by the Japanese in China in the late 1930s and early 40s. See Léonard, *L'Armée et ses problèmes au XVIIIe siècle*, pp. 71 and 76 (Camisards); Montagnon, *Une guerre subversive: La Guerre de Vendée*, pp. 16, 116, 120, 122,

troops in Indochina and then in Algeria unthinkingly fell headlong into the trap intended by rebel terrorists to alienate the native population from the French and their army. Upon seeing Frenchmen and their native supporters slaughtered and mutilated by rebel terrorists and guerrillas, who could not be distinguished from the ordinary urban worker or rural peasant and who hid behind a general conspiracy of silence, French soldiers rather naturally came to look upon all natives as rebels until proven otherwise. French reprisals against supposedly rebel villages and summary executions of suspects, practices already rather familiar in Indochina, became commonplace in Algeria.[39]

Given the unorthodox and total character of revolutionary-guerrilla war, it is not surprising that atrocities on both sides usually abound. A French platoon which arrived in an Algerian village to find the gruesomely mutilated bodies of their ambushed comrades not infrequently vented their horrified anger in burning the village and massacring its inhabitants—or by re-

questing an air raid upon the village as a rebel stronghold.[40] In some units (certainly not all) the cycle of terror, reprisal, and increased terror produced an attitude of strong suspicion and hostility with regard to all Moslems. Troops moving into a village often fired at all who ran from them, although many who fled did so only from fear aroused by past reprisals.

Arbitrariness in reprisals and repression was partly the result of the pitiful weakness of French intelligence. Following the 1954 armistice, General Giap is reported to have told French officers, "I won notably because the French were not informed. The French were always an average of a year behind in their evaluation of our strength."[41] The same problem plagued the French in Algeria, where frequent resort to beatings, electric shock, and the "water treatment" (forced ingurgitation or repeated near drowning), in the "interrogation" of suspects often picked up almost at random could not compensate for the absence of a co-operative and sympathetic local native population.

In Algeria those officers who understood the requirements of lasting pacification, particularly those assigned after 1955 to political-military "Specialized Administrative Sections" (SAS), were usually aware that random and uncontrolled brutality was self-defeating rather than "realistic."[42] Hence, despite military objections that "the armed forces are one,"[43] tension developed between most SAS officers, on the one hand, and combat (especially *para*), intelligence, and security-unit officers, on the other. The primary task of the former was to win over the population; that of the latter, to ferret out the rebels and destroy them. One successful commander of an SAS unit, vexed by the brutality of

[39]Instances when suspects were tortured and shot in Indochina were related to the writer in 1956 in Saigon by former French Legionnaires. Napalm air attacks against entire villages in Indochina, ordered as punitive measures, are described by Fall, *Street without Joy*, pp. 104–5, 108, 253–55; Lancaster, *The Emancipation of French Indochina*, p. 224 n. 3; Devillers, *Histoire du Viet-Nam*, pp. 251–52; and Barale, *La IVe République et la guerre*, p. 489. In regard to mass reprisals and summary execution in Algeria, the evidence is weighty. See Dufresnoy, *Des officiers parlent*, pp. 5, 6, 12, 56; Simon, *Contre la torture*, 84–93; Barberot, *Malaventure en Algérie*, 108–16; Servan-Schreiber, *Lieutenant en Algérie*, 13–45, 48, 65, 68–74, 157, 195, 197; J.-M. Darboise, "L'Echec de la pacification," in J.-M. Darboise, M. Heynaud, and J. Martel, *Officiers en Algérie* (Paris: Maspero, 1960), pp. 28–29; R. B. Bruno, "Soldat en Algérie," *Les Temps modernes* XV, no. 171 (June 1960): 1835–36; Pierre Leulliette, *Saint Michel et le dragon: Souvenirs d'un parachutiste* (Paris: Editions de Minuit, 1961), p. 220, and *passim*. A vivid account of French Army arson, massacre, pillage, rape, and torture is found in the work of a former French commando, Benoist Rey. The account is exaggerated and representative of relatively few units, but it is worthy of note (*Les Egorgeurs* ["The Cutthroats"] [Paris: Editions de Minuit, 1961]). A large collection of letters, cables, and petitions from Moslems protesting against French brutality and summary executions is found in Patrick Kessel and Giovanni Pirelli, *Le Peuple algérien et la guerre: Lettres et témoignages, 1954–1962* (Paris: Maspero, 1962), especially pp. 29–31, 36–45, and 299–306. Like the work of Benoist Rey, this collection describes only the most violent aspects of French pacification. For a fictional account of counterterrorism in Algeria see Lartéguy, *Les Centurions*, pp. 294–95. In regard to the generalized and imprecise French concept of the enemy, we have the testimony of Governor-General Jacques Soustelle to the effect that the indiscriminate arrest of supposed Algerian nationalists who had nothing to do with the rebellion of November 1, 1954, only served to feed the rebellion (*Aimée et souffrante Algérie*, p. 28).

[40]In an interview with the writer in April 1963, Reserve Lieutenant J. recalled finding the bodies of French soldiers in 1957 with their sexual organs cut off and stuffed into their mouths. Lartéguy, *Les Centurions*, pp. 294–95, describes a similar incident. Such acts were likely intended as provocations. Mass reprisals are described or mentioned in Servan-Schreiber, *Lieutenant en Algérie*, p. 72; Lieutenant de P. in Dufresnoy, *Des officiers parlent*, p. 12; Darboise, *Officiers en Algérie*, p. 28; Rey, *Les Egorgeurs, passim*, and Lieutenant Philippe Marchat, *RDN*, pp. 1832–33.

[41]Tournoux, *Secrets d'état*, p. 16 n.

[42]In *Malaventure en Algérie*, Colonel Barberot argues convincingly that as the army unknowingly (and often despite contrary intentions) assumed the role of protecting the European minority and its privileges, it destroyed its effectiveness as a pacifying force (pp. 115–17 and *passim*).

[43]See the editorial in *Message*, no. 21 (April 1957), p. 2, for a defense of the unity of the army. In the preceding issue of *Message*, however (no. 20, March 1957: "D'Algérie: Une opinion sur le moral des officiers"), one finds an officer denouncing the use of torture and the army's police role generally (pp. 1–4). The realities and unrealities of army unity are discussed in Chapter 12 of my *French Army in Politics, op. cit.*

and *passim*; Danila Grujic (ed.), *The Liberation Struggle of the Yugoslav Peoples, 1941–1945* (Belgrade, 1961), p. 53; Chalmers Johnson, *Peasant Nationalism and Communist Power* (Stanford, Calif.: Stanford University Press, 1962), pp. 31–70; and Johnson, "Civilian Loyalties and Guerrilla Conflict," *World Politics* XIV, no. 4 (July 1962): 651–52.

troops passing through his sector, reported to his superiors in this manner: "At a time when the population is more and more coming back over to us and when it is important to convince them that French troops are there to protect them, such incidents must absolutely be avoided."[44]

The problem was well stated by another French officer deeply engaged in pacification efforts, an officer said to be none other than Colonel Antoine Argoud, later a key leader in military revolt:

Incapable by their own means of distinguishing rebels from peaceful citizens, they [the forces of order] are forced by lack of information to lead a blind repression, and they amass abuses of justice. Each false *fellagha* struck down is replaced by ten real ones; until the day when our forces, finding before them the totality of the population, will be forced to practice a policy of extermination—an hypothesis excluded by definition—or give up.[45]

Similar sound advice was given the French by Adjoul-Adjoul, a captured rebel leader:

Those people who flee at the sight of French troops because they have learned of or seen with their own eyes summary executions carried out by the troops, or because the fellaghas have forbidden all contact with the French, are so many recruits ready to rejoin the ranks of the outlaws.[46]

Violence and counterviolence increasingly split the Moslem and European communities, throwing more and more of the hesitant into the rebel camp. Moslems continually suspected of being rebels became vitally aware of their alienation from the dominant European community and eventually fulfilled suspicions about them.[47]

The rising cycle of violence and counterviolence had at least two deleterious effects on military morale and, ultimately, on civilian control. Reports of atrocities committed by the French Army made their way to the *métropole*, where many good republicans as well as communists registered disapproval, and politicians and journalists from the extreme Left to the Left-Center launched a series of stinging attacks on the behavior of the nation's army.[48] Within Indochina and Algeria themselves the angry heavy-handedness of many army units tended to cut off the French from the very populations which they would have had to win over if the rebellions were to be crushed. By contributing in this manner to the certainty of French defeat, such tactics had a part in producing that deep sense of frustration and humiliation among officers which played so important a role in the breakdown of civilian control in 1958.[49] If French attempts at military repression of revolutionary-guerrilla war produced some threat to civilian control, more serious civil-military tensions arose after the French Army began to wage a broader and more political counterinsurgency campaign in Algeria.

---

[44]Lieutenant Morin, commander of a subsection near Algiers, as quoted in Barberot, *ibid.*, p. 109.

[45]A "report" of Major "Marcus" (pseudonym), commander of a regiment including a harki, or Moslem, unit (quoted by Servan-Schreiber, *Lieutenant en Algérie,* p. 70). "Marcus" is identified as Argoud by Jacques Fauvet and Jean Planchais in *La Fronde des Généraux,* p. 93. See Argoud's recommendations of 1960 regarding "adapted justice," in Chapter 9 of my *French Army in Politics, op. cit.*

[46]Quoted in Barberot, *Malaventure en Algérie*, p. 113.

[47]See Bourdieu's discussion of the Moslem reaction to being permanent suspects (*The Algerians*, pp. 153–54).

[48]See Chapter 4 and Chapter 9 of my *French Army in Politics, op. cit.*

[49]*Ibid.* Chapter 10.

THE HIMALAYAN CONFLICT, 1962

LORNE J. KAVIC

Neutrality or nonaligment is no guarantee that war will be avoided, as Belgium and Norway discovered in the First and Second World Wars respectively. India relearned the lesson in 1962. Utterly preoccupied with her long-drawn-out enmity with Pakistan, she found herself involved in a major war on a flank where she never seriously expected real danger. Lorne Kavic describes the course of the border war with China and its effect on India's political and military circles.

For a biography of Lorne J. Kavic, see his article "Force Posture: India and Pakistan" in the Force Posture section of this book.

In the autumn of 1960 China pushed a patrol within ten miles of Daulet Beg Oldi, to the south of Karakoram Pass, and in May of the following year the Chinese again pushed forward towards Chushul. Shortly thereafter Chinese troops occupied Dehra Compass, and their establishment of a post on the Chip Chap River 17 miles southeast of Daulet Beg Oldi in the late summer brought them to their 1960 claim line in this quarter. They established other posts at Niagzu and Dambur Guru and occupied Hot Springs.[1]

INDIA'S FORWARD POLICY

In response to these indications of Peking's intention to continue its advances in Ladakh, the Indian government took the monentous decision to challenge the Chinese actions by establishing small and generally isolated outposts in the disputed areas. The objectives of this 'forward policy' were apparently several: to block potential lines of Chinese advance; to undermine Chinese control of the disputed areas through the interposition of Indian posts and patrol activities between Chinese posts; and thereby to threaten Chinese lines of communication and supply.

It is still unclear to whom this policy can be attributed. It was attractive from a political viewpoint and it was practicable from the military viewpoint, although imposing a disproportionate burden upon the existing system of supply and communication. It was apparently based on the

[1]See P. M. Jones, "Passes and Impasses," *Far Eastern Economic Review* (February 28, 1963); 455.

premise that the Chinese had been moving only where there was a vacuum and that they would not challenge Indian posts by force of arms. New Delhi may have hoped that such a modest display of its determination would make Peking amenable to some sort of negotiated settlement.

By April 1961 Indian patrols were probing forward around the long-established Chinese post on the Chip Chap River, setting up perhaps six posts in Ladakh by the end of the year. Several all-year barracks and supply posts were also established in forward areas to permit an Indian presence in the inhospitable area throughout the winter. The developments were viewed with optimism by the Indian Prime Minister. Speaking in the Lok Sabha on 28 November 1961, Nehru declared that "progressively the situation has been changing from the military point of view and we shall continue to take steps to build up these things so that ultimately we may be in a position to take action to recover such territory as is in their possession." He explained that the government regarded Ladakh as of greater immediate importance than NEFA, (North-Eastern Frontier Agency) adding that Longju (evacuated in 1959) would be reoccupied when the time was appropriate. "We cannot take adventurist actions which may lead us in greater military or other difficulties. It is not an easy matter to conduct warfare in these regions. But it may have to be done and therefore we have to prepare for it if necessary." The dispatch of an infantry brigade group to the Congo in March-April 1961 and the operation against Goa in December of the same year, however, suggest that no sharp deteriora-

Reprinted by permission and with minor changes from India's Quest for Security *(Berkeley: University of California Press, 1967), pp. 169–91. Copyright © 1967 by the Regents of the University of California.*

tion of the situation in the Himalayan region was contemplated at that time.

In the spring of 1962, Nehru sanctioned a more provocative policy in Ladakh, involving direct attempts to cut Chinese lines of communications to their forward posts. According to one report, Menon ordered the spring advances in answer to election criticism that he was 'soft' towards China, but he let it be known discreetly that he was more realistic and tougher towards China than was Nehru—being neither optimistic about successful negotiations with China nor under any illusion about Soviet support in the event of a Sino-Indian clash.[2] In the view of another writer, it was Kaul who took the initiative to argue for such action with Nehru on the grounds that the Army needed to maintain its self-respect. "Menon was hamstrung. He could not openly oppose a policy aimed at reclaiming lost Indian territory. Menon's long-standing orders that Indian patrols should not engage the Chinese under any circumstances were revoked. Indian troops were told to hold their ground and open fire if the Chinese sought to dislodge them from any position on Indian soil."[3] The latter version would seem the more accurate; Kaul is known to have favored a tough line against the Chinese, whereas Menon's career and excessively apologetic stand on the issue of Chinese actions in the Himalayas would have rendered problematical his political survival or diplomatic usefulness in the event that China was provoked too far and large-scale conflict ensued.

Several further Indian battalions were shifted into Ladakh to implement the new phase of the 'forward policy'. A number of new posts were established, including one at Spanggur Lake and one on both the north and south shores of Pangong Lake.[4] With a confidence that indicated an increasingly firm attitude on the border question, Nehru claimed in the Lok Sabha on 29 June that India now had the military initiative and that new Indian posts were outflanking and endangering Chinese posts.

CHINESE REACTION

In furtherance of her previous policy and in response to the increasingly forceful Indian pol-

icy, Peking established more posts in the disputed area[5] while the Chinese press warned New Delhi of the possible consequences of its 'aggressive' actions. An editorial in *Jenmin Jihpao* in April hinted at a plot between Nehru, the Dalai Lama, Chiang Kai-shek, and the United States to reinitiate 'interference' in Tibet[6]—presumably by supplying arms to the rebels. The *Peking Review* warned India that, unless it withdrew its 'aggressive posts' and discontinued its provocations, Chinese frontier guards would be 'compelled to defend themselves'.[7] Peking announced that it was resuming 'patrols' in the area between the Karakoram and Kongka passes and would commence patrolling the entire Sino-Indian frontier if India continued to invade and occupy Chinese territory.[8] A Chinese note dated 2 June 1962 warned that her frontier guards would not acquiesce in continuing Indian provocations,[9] and an editorial in *Renmin Ribao* on 9 July warned the Indian government to 'rein in on the brink of the precipice'.[10]

In a show of strength on 10 July, some four hundred Chinese troops encircled an Indian post which had been established a few days before astride the supply line to a forward Chinese post in the Galwan River valley; in accordance with Maoist tactics, a line of retreat was left open for the Indian personnel manning the post. After hurried discussions in New Delhi, the Indian troops were ordered to stand firm and to meet force with force. After several tense days the Chinese detachment withdrew, but Indian and Chinese troops exchanged fire on 16, 19, and 21 July.

In retrospect, this incident in the Galwan River valley appears to have been of great significance. To Peking, it must have indicated that the Indian government was now prepared to risk an armed clash to maintain its positions and that Chinese posts would either have to be abandoned as the supply lines to the individual forward posts were cut, or be secured through offensive action against the Indian forces. From the standpoint of New Delhi, the Chinese withdrawal was seemingly interpreted as confirming the view (hitherto held with less conviction) that China would not risk an open clash but would respect

---

[2] *Foreign Report* (September 20, 1962): 6.

[3] Welles Hangen, *After Nehru, Who?* (London: Rupert Hart-Davis, 1963), p. 258.

[4] A map published in the *Peking Review* on 20 July 1962 (no. 29, p. 15) showed fifteen Indian 'strongpoints' purportedly set up since the spring. It was subsequently charged in the same source (2 November 1962, no. 44, p. 23) that India had set up forty-three 'aggressive strongpoints' in Ladakh between May 1961 and October 1962.

[5] Mrs. Lakshmi Menon, Minister of State for External Affairs, claimed in the Lok Sabha on 3 September 1962 that China had established thirty-four new posts in Ladakh since May 1962. *LSD*, 3rd sess., vol. 8, col. 5531.

[6] Cited, *Peking Review* 17 (27 April 1962): 8–9.

[7] *Ibid.*, no. 18 (4 May 1962): 17.

[8] *Ibid.*

[9] Cited *Peking Review* 24 (June 15, 1962): 9.

[10] Cited, *ibid.*, no. 28 (13 July 1962): 11.

demonstrations of India's determination to maintain its territorial integrity by force of arms, if that was required. Thus emboldened, the Indian authorities decided on an even more resolute course of action in NEFA, where Chinese occupation of Longju remained an open challenge. The scope of the challenge was considerably broadened when Chinese forces seized the Dhola post and Thag La ridge in the Kameng Frontier Division on 8 September. As a former Chief of the Indian Army Staff, General Thimayya, aptly commented in retrospect, "these actions in overrunning our post in Dhola Ridge and in occupying Thag La Ridge must have been with the specific aim of forcing us to react so as to give them a good excuse for launching an attack on us."[11]

New Delhi's response could hardly have been more to Peking's satisfaction, as it could later be argued that it was the 'aggressive' actions of India which necessitated the 'defensive' actions by the so-called Chinese frontier guards. Thus, Nehru stated in London on 10 September that the border dispute could 'develop suddenly into a conflict'.[12] In response to the establishment of another Chinese post ten miles inside the McMahon Line near Tawang on 12 September, troops from the 7th Brigade of India's 4th Infantry Division began to move from Tawang toward the Thag La-Dhola area. There were sporadic clashes between Indian and Chinese forces near Dhola on the night of 20-21 September and at the Che Jao bridge on 29 September. According to one press source, the decision to resort to direct action against the Chinese forces encamped on territory claimed by India was taken on 17 September.[13]

Nehru returned from his overseas trip on 1 October but made no immediate comment on the NEFA situation. On 5 October, however, the Defence Ministry announced that the Chief of the General Staff, Lieutenant-General B. M. Kaul, had been transferred to command of a new corps in NEFA and that he had already left for Tezpur.[14] Despite official efforts to represent the new command as merely a reorganization having no wider significance, its implications were correctly noted by sections of the press. The *Economist* (13 October) expressed the view that the move reflected a government decision "to put

Chinese intentions to the test especially in the McMahon Line Region." The *Times of India* declared on 10 October that the Army was poised for an "all-out effort to expel the Chinese intruders from the Thag La area."

The drift to war quickened as Indian troops made a small probing attack northwest of Dhola on 10 October and it became fairly clear that they were preparing to eject the Chinese from the area. Official and unnecessarily dramatic confirmation of such an intention was given by Nehru in New Delhi on 12 October, when, just before leaving for a visit to Madras and then Ceylon, he declared to the press that the Army had been ordered to eject the Chinese from NEFA.[15] On 15 December Defence Minister Menon stated at Bangalore that the Chinese would be thrown from Indian soil.[16]

A temporary lull in the NEFA skirmishing was broken by an Indian claim on 16 October that their Dhola post had been fired upon. In reply, Peking charged that Indian troops had attacked on 17 October all along the Kechilang River, advancing northwards between Hatung Pass and Pangkangting and towards Sechang Lake.[17] The stage was appropriately set, and a leading Indian daily, the *Hindu*, reported on 19 October that there were elaborate Chinese preparations for an offensive along the borders of Sikkim, Bhutan, and NEFA.

BORDER CONFLICT WITH CHINA

The conflict erupted early on the morning of 20 October at both ends of the Sino-Indian frontier. Indian and Chinese reports differ as to the actual commencement of hostilities, but the preparedness of the Chinese forces was unmistakable. The so-called 'defensive' actions by their 'frontier guards' were delivered in brilliant fashion by large numbers of infantry supported by artillery, mountain guns, mortars, and, on at least one occasion in Ladakh, by tanks.[18]

In Ladakh, Chinese infantry attacked south of the Karakoram Pass at the northwest extremity of the Aksai Chin plateau and in the Pangong Lake area some 100 miles to the southeast. Indian forces were speedily ejected from perhaps eleven posts in the vicinity of Karakoram Pass

---

[11]"Chinese Aggression and After," *International Studies* 5:1, 2 (July-October 1963): 51.

[12]Cited, *The Times* (11 September 1962).

[13]*Times of India* (27 September 1962).

[14]Kaul's new command embraced the area of Uttar Pradesh, Sikkim, Bhutan, and NEFA and reduced Maj.-Gen. Umrao Singh's Eastern Command to the area south of the Brahmaputra River covering Nagaland and the border with East Pakistan.

[15]Cited, *Hindu* (13 October 1962).

[16]Cited, *Daily Telegraph* (15 October 1962).

[17]See *Survey of the Chinese Mainland Press* (SCMP), no. 2839 (16 October 1962): 27; no. 2840 (17 October 1962): 19; no. 2841 (23 October 1962): 23.

[18]The review of developments in the war has been collated from the daily reports of events in the Indian and foreign press and from informed individuals whom the writer interviewed in India.

and from several in the Pangong Lake district but held firm at the vital posts of Daulet Beg Oldi (near the entrance to the pass) and Chushul (immediately south of Pangong Lake and at the head of the vital supply road to Leh). On 27 October other Chinese forces attacked in the vicinity of Demchok (100 miles southeast of Chushul) and quickly overran the Demchok and Jara La posts but were otherwise contained. In one instance, they conceded some ground to a counterattack by elements of the Jammu and Kashmir Militia.

In NEFA, the Chinese forces advanced almost at will despite Indian resistance at several key points. The Tsang Le post on the northern side of the Namka Chu River, the Khinzemane post, and the Indian brigade near Dhola were overrun on the first day, and the Chinese proceeded with a general offensive at both ends of the McMahon Line. In the western sector, Tsang Dar fell on 22 October, Bum La on the 23rd, and Tawang—headquarters of the 7th Infantry Brigade under Brigadier-General J. P. Dalvi—was lost to a three-pronged Chinese divisional assault on the 24th. In the centre, Chinese troops reoccupied the undefended frontier post at Longju (which they had evacuated during the summer because of the outbreak of an epidemic) and captured the Asafila border post 25 miles to the southwest. In the Lohit Frontier Division, a strong Chinese force captured the frontier post at Kibithoo on 22 October and advanced 15 miles down the Lohit Valley to Walong, reaching the vicinity of the town on 25 October. A Chinese offer of negotiations was advanced on 24 October and was rejected by the Indian government as it was undoubtedly expected to be[19]—and a lull set in on the battlefront as both sides prepared for the resumption of the next phase of hostilities.

The Indian Army made desperate efforts to strengthen its defensive positions in NEFA and Ladakh and to prepare against possible Chinese attacks through Sikkim and Bhutan. The measures were in general accordance with the contingency planning prepared in 1961, but their effectiveness was largely destroyed by the rapidity of events. Two brigades were withdrawn from Nagaland and sited at Rangiya (south of Bhutan), and a brigade of four battalions was rushed to defend Walong. The 5th Division from Jullundur-Ferozepore was shifted piecemeal to Mis-

amari (near Tezpur), and three brigades drawn from the 4th and 5th Divisions were hastily deployed into positions astride the Se La-Bomdila-Dirrang Dzong axis, supported by light Stuart tanks from Calcutta and paratroop artillery from Agra. The 17th Division was shifted from Ambala to Goyerkata (in northern Bengal between Bhutan and East Pakistan); two brigades were rushed to Siliguri from Amritsar and Khasali; and the Natu La-Gangtok-Siliguri-Kalimpong axis was further reinforced by two brigades drawn from Calcutta and Ranchi. A divisional organization was formed at Dibrugarh.

In Ladakh, in response to the initial Chinese attacks, a divisional organization was created at Leh, and Chushul was reinforced by air with several battalions of infantry, a battery of 25-pounders, and two troops (normally 32 units) of AMX light tanks which had been detached from the 5th and 17th Divisions. On 4 November the Daulet Beg Oldi post was abandoned as untenable, and its defenders were withdrawn over the 17,500-foot-high Sasar Brangsa Pass to more defensible positions.

India's armored division at Jhansi and the independent armored brigade at Patiala were not disturbed, and events appear to have developed too rapidly for other formations in south and southwest India to be disturbed. The Punjab was thus left almost denuded of combatant formations, suggesting that Army headquarters proceeded on the assumption that Pakistan would not take advantage of India's predicament. The Reserve was activated,[20] and one hundred units of the Territorial Army were embodied; most of the TA personnel were assigned to their previously designated antiaircraft and coastal defence duties, but some were absorbed into technical units of the regular Army.[21]

The adjustments in Ladakh proved adequate to defend the Chushul perimeter against repeated shelling and assault, but the outlying posts at Rezang La and Gurung Hill and four posts in the Spanggur Lake area were overwhelmed by Chinese troops.

The situation in NEFA, however, quickly assumed the proportions of a debacle. Indian troops counterattacked in the Walong area on 13 November and captured a hill feature on a ridge northwest of the town, but were unable to hold it against determined Chinese attacks. With the loss of the vital Otter airstrip, the defending garri-

---

[19]China proposed a mutual withdrawal 20 kilometers behind the line of actual control as of 7 November 1959. For text see *Peking Review* 43 (26 October 1962): 5–6. The Indian government refused to enter into discussions unless Chinese forces withdrew behind the line of actual control as of 8 September 1962.

[20]26,144 JCO's and 110 officers were recalled and 8,989 JCO's and OR's remained with the colors as of 31 December 1962. Ministry of Defence, *Report*, 1963–64, pp. 29–30.
[21]Sixteen units were embodied before the declaration of emergency on 26 October, and a further 84 units thereafter.

son had no choice but to commence a general retirement down the Lohit Valley to a new defensive position about twelve miles distant. The withdrawal on 16 November was made under heavy Chinese fire.

In the Kameng Frontier Division, a force of about six Chinese brigades thrust across the Tawang Chu River near Jang and advanced ten miles to the southeast to attack forward Indian positions at Nurang, eight miles below Se La, on the evening of 17 November. At nightfall, the Indian force withdrew to the main defensive post at Se La which, although a strong physical position, was held by only about five battalions. The defenses were frontally assaulted that same night by perhaps four Chinese brigades while simultaneous attacks were made against Dirrang and Bomdila by a Chinese force which, under cover of a heavy snowfall, had executed an undetected outflanking movement on 16-17 November over a mountain range 20 to 30 miles east of Se La. Both towns fell after some hard fighting in which up to a dozen Stuart tanks were destroyed. The force at Se La abandoned its positions on 18 November in an attempt to break out to the south but was dispersed before a strong Chinese roadblock north of Bomdila. Effective Indian resistance in the Kameng Division thereupon virtually ceased to exist, and Chinese troops swept south a further 30 to 40 miles to the vicinity of Foothills, a small town on the edge of the Assam Plains.

At this point, the Chinese were in possession of all the territory they claimed in Ladakh (Chushul being outside the Chinese claim line), and in NEFA they had advanced to within 40 miles of Tezpur and to within 100 miles of the important Digboi oil fields. Civilians and government officials were fleeing Tezpur, preparations were being made by British officials to evacuate their nationals from the areas north of the Brahmaputra River, and New Delhi seemed almost paralysed by the collapse of the NEFA defences and the fear that the Chinese meant to overrun all of Assam. Lieutenant-General Kaul had been replaced by a 'fighting general', Lieutenant-General Manekshaw, and had been posted to the Punjab, while the Chief of Army Staff, General P. N. Thapar, had gone on indefinite sick leave and the former GOC, Southern Command, J. N. Chaudhuri, had assumed the onerous task of directing the Army through the crisis.[22] The 4th

Division had ceased to exist as a fighting formation, and the badly mauled 5th Division had been withdrawn from the line for reorganization under a new commander. The 2,500 troops in the Lohit Frontier Division were facing a desperate shortage of supplies, nearly 100 miles from the nearest roadhead. Over 10,000 troops were cut off in the Kameng Frontier Division, but in the south of Kameng other Indian forces were hastily constructing new defensive positions north of Foothills. A fairly strong Indian force remained deployed against possible attacks in the Sikkim-Bhutan sector. In Ladakh, the former political deployment in small posts was being readjusted to a more realistic military position astride the highly defensible approaches to Leh.

India's unpreparedness in the military sphere was even more pronounced in the nonmilitary sphere, the confused response of the Prime Minister reflecting his bewilderment at the totally unexpected turn of events.[23] Though apparently not alarmed by the initial attacks, Nehru soon swung to the opposite extreme of acclaiming the Chinese actions as a 'major invasion' in which the fate of Asia and the world was at stake.[24] In an address to a conference of State Information Ministers on 25 October, he drew a parallel with Dunkirk, declaring that the Indian people must respond with the same determination as had the British people in the aftermath of that famous evacuation.[25]

A state of emergency was signed by the President on 25 October and proclaimed the following day. The Defence of India Ordinance of 1962 was promulgated, conferring special powers on the government for the duration of the emergency. Press censorship was invoked and a veil of secrecy was thrown over developments, with the result that both civilian and soldier alike were forced to rely upon Radio Peking for news of the fighting. Chinese nationals and pro-Peking members of the Indian Communist party were hustled into internment camps and jails. A National Defence Fund was established to which the public was invited to donate cash and valuables. Public appeals were also made for warm clothing to correct a shocking shortage which was forcing

---

[22]Both Kaul and Thapar resigned shortly thereafter. According to an authoritative Indian military informant, Nehru had approached President Radhakrishnan with the suggestion that Kaul be appointed to succeed Thapar as COAS but the President had regarded the proposal as 'absurd' in the circumstances.

[23]He confessed in the *Lok Sabha* on 8 November 1962 that the government (i.e., himself) had felt that "this type of aggression was almost a thing of the past."

[24]See, for example, his statement in the *Lok Sabha* on 8 November 1962.

[25]Cited, *Hindu*, 26 October 1962. *Foreign Report* (8 November 1962): 7–8 expressed the view that Nehru's broadcast to the nation on 22 October reflected his fear of alarming the country, while his subsequent swing to the other extreme evidenced his recognition of the need to meet the public mood and the prevailing attitude of the armed forces or be faced with an erosion of his own position.

soldiers to endure unnecessary hardships through exposure and frostbite. The sudden increased demand for blood plasma could not be met from the only two existing plants in the country for freeze-drying of this vital requirement. In the absence of any production mobilization scheme, the sale of new cars, new jeeps, station wagons, trucks, steel products, and corporate stocks were frozen, with a consequent serious and quite unnecessary disorganization of the civilian economy.

The Chinese attacks provoked immediate demands from broad sections of Indian opinion for the removal of the controversial Defence Minister, V. K. Krishna Menon. A strong move developed within the Congress party itself, which crystallized around important persons.[26] Senior members of the party, including the deputy leader, Dr. Harekruchna Mahatab, U. N. Dhebar, Mahavir Tyagi, B. K. P. Singh, and the general secretary of the party, Raghunath Singh, met privately a fortnight before the scheduled session of Parliament and agreed upon the need for Nehru to dismiss Menon and assume the Defence portfolio himself. Dr. Mahatab conveyed the views of the group to the Prime Minister and was received coolly, but the group maintained its pressure. At a meeting of the Executive Committee several days later, Nehru was made completely aware of the strong feeling within the Party over Menon's failure as Defence Minister. The Prime Minister's effort to assume personal blame for the Himalayan situation was not greeted with the usual passive acquiescence. Faced with mounting public clamor and party pressure, Nehru had little choice but to take over the Defence post on 31 October. In an obvious attempt to lessen the significance of the demotion of his intimate friend, Nehru retained Menon in the Cabinet in the newly created post of Minister for Defence Production—but with limited responsibilities relating to inspection and organization of various factories and workshops and the research and development organization.[27]

The demotion, which undoubtedly dealt a deep personal blow to Menon, only appeared to increase his arrogance, as he proceeded to declare at Tezpur that really nothing had changed.[28] Although the claim was probably more of a defensive stratagem than a statement of fact, the remark added to his unpopularity both within and without the Congress party.[29] The next meeting of the Executive Committee, held on the morning of 7 November, was stormy. Members had resorted to the novel (by Indian standards) procedure of collecting signatures to a demand for Menon's complete dismissal from the government, and some of the members even made direct charges.

Nehru made an unsuccessful attempt to convince the members of Menon's sincerity by reading the latter's letter of resignation dated 30 October, and the meeting ended without any indication from the Prime Minister about his subsequent course of action. His attitude was undoubtedly based to some extent on the recognition that he himself was indirectly being attacked.[30] He could not ignore the plain fact, however, that his views could no longer command unquestioning support and that continued refusal on his part to meet the widespread demand (from all but the extreme political Left) for Menon's removal must inevitably weaken his own position and culminate in even more concerted actions leading to direct attacks upon himself. It is believed that he approached the President, Dr. S. S. Radhakrishnan, on the matter and that the latter, although personally friendly to Menon, advised that he would have to be dismissed for the good of the country.[31] Shortly before the general evening meeting of the Congress party on 7 November, Nehru announced in Parliament that he had accepted Menon's resignation: "I feel that Mr. Krishna Menon has done

[26]Details of the developments within the Congress party pertaining to the ouster of Menon are taken from an article in *Thought* (17 November 1962): 6. See also *Hindu* (8 November 1962); *The Times* (8 November 1962); and K. Rangaswami in *Hindu* (9 November 1962).

[27]The *Times of India* (1 November 1962) expressed the view that Nehru had perhaps "unnecessarily halted his journey at a half-way house." In an editorial of the same date, the *New York Times* declared that Menon was still too highly placed and that his removal from the top list of officials "would have been welcome evidence . . . that the Indian Government had completely turned away from the attitude of unrealistic trustfulness toward the Communist world that contributed to the present crisis on India's northern frontier."

[28]The *Hindu* (5 November 1962) reported that "quarters close to Menon" denied that he had made any such statement. In view of Menon's well-known personality traits, however, it is very likely that he did make such a statement.

[29]Commenting on Menon's Tezpur statement, the *Times of India* (3 November 1962) stated: "Perhaps too much importance should not be attached to this characteristic piece of egoism. . . . Yet it needs to be said that a Union Minister capable of audaciously dismissing as nothing changes in a key portfolio which he formerly held invites the severest strictures. It also provokes the question whether the absence of anything resembling regretful admission of past errors does not disqualify him completely from holding a post of any consequence."

[30]As the *Nation* commented on 1 December 1962: "Menon was a scapegoat in one sense. He represented the era of vacillation, of half-heartedness, of uncertainty and confusion and bewilderment. . . . He stood not for Nehru's policies and leadership, but for the lack of them. The politicians' revolt was not against what Nehru had decided, but against what he had not decided—then, and for so many years before."

[31]*Foreign Report* (29 November 1962): 4.

good work but the controversy will not rest until he quits and controversy is bad for the war effort."[32]

The crisis had also led to the establishment of an Emergency Committee of Cabinet and of a variety of other emergency committees within the Defence Ministry. On 6 November, a thirty-member National Defence Council was set up to 'advise' the government on matters directly or indirectly affecting defence. As the crisis deepened, the Cabinet was reorganized in a manner designed to illustrate the government's determination to meet the challenge to the country's territorial integrity and prestige. The youthful and vigorous Chief Minister of Maharashtra, Y. B. Chavan, was appointed to the Defence portfolio on 14 November, and on the same day it was announced that K. Raghuramaiah had been shifted from Minister of State in the Defence Ministry to the post of Minister of Defence Production, that T. T. Krishnamachari, the Minister without Portfolio, had been transferred to the newly created post of Minister for Economic and Defence Co-ordination, and that V. R. P. Rao had replaced O. Pulla Reddy as Defence Secretary.[33] On 15 November retired Major-General Sardanand Singh was appointed to the newly created post of Director-General of Civil Defence.

The situation had, in the meantime, forced the government to appeal for immediate military support from Britain and the United States, the appeal being cloaked in a general appeal for support to all governments excepting Portugal and South Africa. (Relations with the latter country continued to be strained by India's abhorrence of its apartheid policy.) New Delhi sent an urgent request for military supplies to London and Washington on 26 October and received an immediate response from both these governments; the first consignment of British aid arrived in two Royal Air Force Britannias on 29 October, and the first American aid arrived from depots in Western Europe on 1 November. As the NEFA debacle grew, the Indian government on 19 November sent an urgent and specific request for American fighting air support.[34] Washington had not replied to the request when the Chinese announced their unilateral ceasefire.[35]

The surprise Chinese announcement was broadcast over the New China News Agency on 20 November. It declared that China would terminate the conflict at midnight of the following day and on 1 December would commence a withdrawal of her forces to 20 kilometers (12½ miles) north of the McMahon Line and to a similar distance behind the 'line of actual control' in existence in Ladakh as of 7 November 1959. The broadcast stated China's intention to proceed with her withdrawal regardless of the Indian reaction but warned that China reserved the right to strike back in the event that India attempted to reoccupy any of the territory taken by Chinese troops during their advance.[36] The withdrawal appears to have proceeded as planned and was completed in both sectors by about 15 January 1963.[37]

The official Indian reaction to the announcement was to declare that it was a unilateral action and that a precondition to Indian discussions with the Chinese government regarding the border dispute was restoration of the status quo as of 8 September 1962. However, New Delhi had little choice but to respect the Chinese warning against attempts to reoccupy with troops the areas lost to the advancing Chinese.

Immediate attention had necessarily to be given to preparations against renewed fighting in the following spring, with the aid of emergency shipments of military equipment and stores offered, ironically enough, only by the countries of the Western bloc whose approach to the 'Chinese problem' had been subject to such heavy criticisms by the Indian government. The

---

[32]Cited *The Times* (8 November 1962). The *Times of India* (8 November) felt that the removal of Menon was "unquestionably the right one in a democracy" because of his loss of public confidence:

Whenever a Minister, for whatever reason, forfeits the confidence of a substantial part of public opinion that is more than sufficient ground for a resignation and appropriate reshuffle of personnel. The principle of collective cabinet responsibility does not in any way negate the equally valid principle of individual responsibility and it is in relation to this that Mr. Krishna Menon's earlier letter of resignation was most inadequate. Its failure to refer to the military setbacks in NEFA with which Mr. Menon and his Ministry were directly concerned at that time is an astonishing and inexplicable omission.

[33]Reddy was widely considered to be a Menon protégé, but, though this may have contributed to his replacement as such a crucial juncture, it must be noted that his term was completed and that the situation favored a "new look" in a discredited Ministry.

[34]According to an informed British observer on Indian affairs, Nehru made a desperate appeal to Britain and the United States on 19 November for fifteen bomber squadrons to attack the advancing Chinese troops. Michael Edwardes, "Illusion and Reality in India's Foreign Policy," *International Affairs* (January 1965): 52.

[35]According to reports, the Indian Ministry of External Affairs repeated the request on 1 December and Nehru himself repeated it in reply to a query from President Kennedy in early January 1963. See Thomas Brady in *New York Times* (25 January) and (21 February 1963); *Times of India* leader (29 January 1963).

[36]Text of announcement in *Peking Review*, vols. 47 and 48 (30 November 1962): 5–7.

[37]For the timetable of the Chinese withdrawal, see *ibid.*, no. 49 (7 December 1962): 7; no. 50 (14 December 1962): 15; no. 1 (4 January 1963): 26.

Soviet bloc, whose friendship India had so assiduously cultivated, remained studiously noncommittal, and India's nonaligned colleagues chose to treat the issue in accordance with the well-known "Indian approach," from the viewpoint of practical politics that aimed at "reducing tension" rather than at legal or moral niceties.[38]

The brief and limited conflict had exposed many deficiencies in India's defences. The performance of many of the senior Army officers charged with NEFA defences was marked by confusion, uncertainty, and lack of initiative. Kaul had attempted to direct operations from the front instead of from his headquarters, with the result that operations proceeded without coordination; the removal of corps headquarters from Tezpur to Gauhati and then back to Tezpur aggravated an already confused situation. Officers were generally left to their own devices—a situation for which many were not equipped. The commander of the Indian force at Se La made only a half-hearted attempt to break through a Chinese roadblock south of Dirrang Dzong but chose to abandon his roadbound equipment and by-pass the roadblock; the result was that the approximately two brigades comprising his force lost any effectiveness as a fighting formation. The attempt to hold both principal Chinese thrusts as far forward as Se La and Walong in the face of poor logistics disregarded the prudent contingency planning prepared as early as 1961 and enabled the Chinese to destroy two divisions in almost piecemeal fashion. A nervous brigade commander is understood to have contributed to the Bomdila debacle when he effected a disorderly withdrawal of his command (believed to be the 48th Brigade of the 4th Division), thereby exposing two other brigades.

Tactics were too conventional, forces tending to be roadbound both in tactical and logistical movement and unable to cope with the unorthodox procedures so skilfully employed by the Chinese. Officers, many of whom had shown little interest in unorthodox warfare right up to the outbreak of the war, were unable to provide the necessary leadership at company and platoon level and were, furthermore, totally unfamiliar with Chinese tactics, equipment, and capabilities. The troops under their command were deficient in battle training and in training required for operations in the jungles and mountains in which they found themselves, and were also not acclimatized to fight at the heights to which

many of them were exposed. Many of the initial reinforcements for NEFA were Madrassis from the warm tropical south of India. Patrolling was poor, permitting the Chinese to retain the initiative throughout.

There was an overall shortage of equipment; much of what was in existence was obsolete. Although the .303 bolt-action rifle was an effective weapon in the hands of a trained soldier, it was incapable of offsetting Chinese automatics, superior artillery support, and a longer-range mortar. The almost total absence of mines and wire in the forward positions precluded any chance of holding positions against 'human sea' tactics. Stocks of supplies in forward areas were inadequate for augmented forces. The absence of a well-thought-out logistics plan for Himalayan operations prevented the rapid dispatch of stores and equipment from depots to front-line areas.[39] The communications equipment proved almost completely useless under the conditions to which it was subjected, since certain key components generally failed. The extensive shortage of high-altitude clothing caused hundreds of cases of exposure.

The inability of the Army to cope with limited attacks attests to the complacency which affected Indian military preparations in the Himalayan region. Committed to secure the Himalayan frontiers and the Himalayan kingdoms against Chinese attacks, the Indian Army had not been allocated the additional resources to meet its new commitments, nor had the government felt the need to seek some sort of understanding with Pakistan for cooperative action to meet the challenge posed by China. The contingency of war with China was regarded as so remote that New Delhi continued to base military strategy against her weaker neighbor. Her actual planning for the Tibetan frontier allowed for little more than local intrusions, notwithstanding contingency planning against possible divisional attacks which amounted to little more than staff exercises.

The decision to challenge the Chinese in the forward areas of Ladakh in the spring of 1962 and in NEFA in September 1962 was clearly based on the assumption that the Chinese would not risk a major conflict with a country of India's size and international stature merely for the sake of a few square miles of frontier territory. It tended to ignore the fact that Chinese as well as Indian prestige was at stake and that Nehru's public an-

[38] For a discussion of the reaction of the various countries and 'blocs' to India's difficulties, see *International Studies* 5:1, 2 (July-October 1963).

[39] For example, rifles urgently needed in NEFA were reportedly flown to Calcutta from depots elsewhere in India in a matter of hours but then took six days to reach their destinations in the forward areas. See *Times of India* (30 January 1960).

nouncement that he had ordered the Army to clear the Chinese from Indian territory merely ensured that, if only for the sake of prestige, Peking could not passively retire. As a London newspaper expressed it, Nehru's determination may well have been "the accumulated result of affronted pride, reflected in the clamour to do something, and real concern about the possible effect of failure to maintain Indian sovereignty in the north-east frontier."[40] However, his determination revealed itself too late to have the desired effect but in a fashion that ensured the very occurrence that Indian diplomacy had counselled other nations against, placing China in a situation where she could feel that there was no credible recourse but to force of arms.

The extent to which the military (essentially Army) leadership must share the blame for the debacle is difficult to ascertain. Nehru claimed that decisions relating to Himalayan defence "were taken by Government in full consultation with the Chiefs of Staff and other senior Army officers concerned and in the light of their expert advice. This applies particularly to the decision that the Army should not withdraw in October-November 1962 from its forward position in NEFA."[41] He also claimed that his public statement that the Army had been ordered to eject the Chinese was "not my decision alone; it was the viewpoint of the military people too. They wanted to do it. Otherwise I would not have dared to say anything like that."[42] Although some senior officers regarded the 'forward policy' with some concern, in view of the Army's inability to counter any substantial military reaction by China in these forward areas, other high-ranking officers—perhaps even a majority—shared the opinion noted by the *New York Times* writer, A. M. Rosenthal: "Everyone knew it could not happen. Prime Minister Jawaharlal Nehru knew it, his recently dismissed Defence Minister, V. K. Krishna Menon knew it, and even Indian generals knew it. 'We thought it was a sort of game', said one officer of high rank recently. 'They would stick up a post and we would stick up a post and we did not think it would come to much more'."[43]

This smugness did not extend, however, to the proposal apparently advanced by the somewhat impetuous Kaul that the Army eject the Chinese from the Thag La-Dhola area. The proposal was regarded with dismay by more responsible offi-

cers, including Lieutenant-General Sen (GOC, Eastern Command) and the luckless brigadier assigned to effect the dislodgement with a brigade of poorly acclimatized and ill-equipped troops at the end of long and primitive communications with nothing in reserve to provide support. Even Kaul began to doubt the feasibility of the operation after the 10 October clash, which revealed that the Chinese were in the area in far greater strength than was hitherto believed —evidencing poor intelligence up to this point. According to an informed Indian military source, Kaul thereupon returned to New Delhi to stress the need for a far stronger force if the plan was to be carried out. Thapar, the COAS, called in Sen (Kaul's superior in theory although not in practice)[44] for consultations, and the three generals discussed the matter with Defence Minister Menon. The decision as to the course of action in the Thag La-Dhola area in the light of the altered situation was referred to Nehru, who declined to interfere in what he clearly felt to be a 'military' problem. The decision was then taken, in Nehru's presence and with his concurrence, to 'sit tight' until spring, at which time the entire situation could be reviewed. For some unexplained reason, however, probing actions continued and the public remained of the belief that the government was proceeding with its preparations to force the Chinese out of NEFA.[45] It was, in any case, undoubtedly too late to revert to a more prudent policy.

The conflict dispelled any lingering illusions in official Indian circles regarding Chinese inhibitions about employing force against India. It brought into focus a grave threat in a quarter where geography had been regarded as an almost insurmountable barrier to serious attack by land. It confirmed India's dependence upon external help against attack by a major power and the availability of Western military aid in a crisis involving Communist China. It showed that the balance of power thesis did not preclude a limited conflict in which an aggressor could initiate

---

[40] *Daily Telegraph* (15 October 1962).

[41] *LSD*, 3rd sess., vol. 13, col. 1331.

[42] *Ibid.*, 5th sess., vol. 19, col. 2213.

[43] *New York Times* (11 November 1962).

[44] It is understood that Kaul tended to by-pass Sen and deal directly with Thapar and Menon, Thapar himself being a passive bystander to direct dealings between Kaul and Menon and primarily desirous, as one informant stated, 'of finishing his term with the minimum of fuss'. It is also understood that the official enquiry on the NEFA debacle was critical of Sen for not exercising his authority over his subordinate, Kaul, in professional matters.

[45] Such probing actions may well have been decided upon by Menon and Kaul to maintain public belief that the Army was preparing to eject the Chinese—and therefore escape the probable hostile reaction to cessation of all activities by a public which had been led to expect dramatic results. The onset of winter would thereby have enabled both men to ease out of a predicament in which their actions and public statements had placed them.

hostilities and terminate action after achieving the desired objectives—and then resume his pre-conflict military posture without interference. The Chinese advance in NEFA was a reminder that the absence of the necessary strategic depth in the corridor between Bhutan-Sikkim and East Pakistan rendered most problematical any defence of the area against a sustained assault from the north. There had been an unreal obsession with the supposed military threat posed by Muslim Pakistan—the 'historical ghost'—to the detriment of suitable and phased adjustments in defence strategy and foreign policy to accord with the changing geopolitics in the Himalayan region. The result for India was traumatic—militarily, politically, and diplomatically.

THE SIX DAY WAR

MICHAEL HOWARD AND ROBERT HUNTER

While the major powers have assiduously sought to avoid direct conflict since 1945, other nations have not. On three occasions since the Second World War, 1948, 1956, and 1967, the Middle East has erupted into all-out war, and the potential is there for further conflict in the future. Michael Howard and Robert Hunter describe reprisal raids prior to the outbreak of war and then the 1967 Arab/Israeli War in detail, bringing out clearly the way in which Israel achieved her victory, the reasons for her success, and some of the lessons to be learned.

Professor Michael E. Howard is a Fellow of All Souls College, Oxford and the author of The Franco-Prussian War *(1961),* Studies in War and Peace *(1971), and* The British Official History of the Second World War, Military Series: Grand Strategy 1942–3 *(1972).*

Dr. Robert E. Hunter is Senior Fellow at the Overseas Development Council. He is the author of Security in Europe *(second edition 1972),* The Energy "Crisis" and U.S. Foreign Policy *(1973), coeditor of* Development Today: A New Look at United States Relations with the Poor Countries *(1972), and the editor of* The United States and the Developing World: Agenda for Action *(1973).*

REPRISAL RAIDS

The reasons leading to the outbreak of the Six Day War in 1967 are too many and complicated to be dealt with here, but in view of their recent use of similar methods, it is instructing to look briefly at the Israelis' use of reprisals in the months before the war—an unusual, active, compelling use of force characteristic of the Arab-Israeli conflict.

To deal with problems arising out of inter-pretation and implementation of the Armistice Agreements in the Middle East the United Nations had set up a Truce Supervision Organization (UNTSO), which was assisted in its duties by Mixed Armistice Commissions of the appropriate belligerent powers.[1] The Israelis had attended no regular meetings of the Syrian Com-

[1]UNTSO was the successor of the Truce Commission established by the Security Council in April 1948. The Chief of Staff of UNTSO was made chairman of the four Mixed Armistice Commissions.

Excerpted by permission and with minor changes from Israel and the Arab World: The Crisis of 1967 *(London: International Institute of Strategic Studies, October 1967), pp. 13–15, 27–41. Copyright © 1967 the International Institute for Strategic Studies.*

mission since 1951, and had shown considerable reluctance to permit UNTSO observers to investigate some of their activities within the Demilitarized Zone. By 1967, however, mutual complaints had reached a level which made both sides regard the Commission as a useful vehicle for their protests. Each had raids and counter-raids to complain of.[2] In addition, in July 1966, the Israelis had attacked, with artillery and aircraft, the works on the Baniyas water-diversion scheme just across their border; while the Syrians had repeatedly fired on Israelis attempting to cultivate land in the Demilitarized Zone. Predictably the Commission broke up, disagreeably and inconclusively, after only three emergency meetings. But meanwhile two incidents occurred which transcended the normal level of border dispute. The first was the Israeli attack on the Jordanian village of Es Samu on 13 November 1966. The second was the air battle on 7 April 1967, when Israeli aircraft, without loss to themselves, shot down six Syrian MiG fighter aircraft. The repercussions of these events were, as we shall see, to be very considerable indeed.

The Samu raid followed the failure of Israel to get any satisfaction after a complaint to the Security Council about mines laid on her territory by *El Fatah* units. The incident was repeated near the Jordanian frontier; so the Israelis took matters into their own hands with a daylight attack by armour, aircraft, and infantry which did considerable damage to the village and killed eighteen Jordanians.[3] Public opinion even in Israel objected to the violence of this blow against the mildest of their adversaries, and Israel was condemned by the Security Council. But in view of the failure of the Council to condemn the activities of the Syrians, she was naturally unimpressed. 'If Hussein has control of the West Bank and failed to prevent terrorism', asked Yigal Allon, her Minister of Labour, 'why is he entitled to our indulgence? And if he does not exercise control there, what interest have we in preserving his regime? . . . The action at Samu demonstrated to the Powers that Israel is not willing to submit its security to diplomatic bargaining'. In fact the Samu raid precipitated such angry demonstrations in Jordan that Hussein took stern measures to repress his dissident elements; these were seized on by supporters of the Israeli action as further proof of its effectiveness. It had,

they suggested, given Hussein the excuse he needed to show himself master in his own house.

The second incident arose over one of the Israeli attempts to cultivate land in the Demilitarized Zone. Syrian small-arms fire against an Israeli tractor was answered by fire from Israeli forces who somehow happened to be in the neighborhood. Artillery, tanks, and ultimately aircraft joined in, the Israeli aircraft silencing the Syrian gun positions, shooting down six aircraft of the intercepting fighter patrol sent up to meet them, and sweeping on over Damascus in jubilant demonstration of their victory. Even more than the Samu raid, this demonstrated Israel's ability and willingness to react, indeed to overreact, to provocations of the kind which the Syrians had no intention of discontinuing. And like the Samu raid it showed the disunity that still obtained among Israel's principal enemies. Hussein's purge of his activists infuriated the Syrians, who redoubled their attacks on his regime, both in the press and over Damascus Radio. The Jordanians retaliated by jubilantly broadcasting details of the Syrian aircraft forced down over Jordanian territory; and both Syria and Jordan complained loudly of the Egyptian failure to do anything to help them, taunting Nasser—significantly in view of later developments—with sheltering behind the United Nations Emergency Force. Considering that Hussein refused to allow Egyptian units on his territory and that Syria refused Egypt's offer to establish an air base on her soil, they really had little cause for complaint. But Nasser could not stand by indefinitely and watch his allies suffer such humiliating reversals; and more important, neither could the Russians.

Were such humiliations likely to continue? The Israeli government derived no satisfaction from inflicting them, and fully realized the dangers it incurred in doing so: dangers arising not simply from another war fought, like that of 1948, on three fronts against superior forces, but from antagonizing the Great Powers. The Prime Minister, Mr. Levi Eshkol, like David Ben-Gurion before him, believed in the need to retain, almost at any cost, the sympathy of the United States. He was almost as anxious to avoid antagonizing the Soviet Union; and the Soviet Union, he knew, watched with paternal concern over the fortunes of the kaleidoscopic regimes in Damascus.

Yet opinion in Israel would not indefinitely put up with the kind of provocation offered by the *El Fatah* raids.[4] Mr. Eshkol's reputation was one

[2] By October 1966, there were 66,085 complaints outstanding: 35,485 by Israel, and 30,600 by Syria.
[3] The Es Samu attack illustrated the strategic advantage which Syria held over Jordan, *vis-à-vis* Israel. The nature of the terrain meant that Israel could mount reprisal attacks much more easily against Jordan than against Syria.
[4] Between 25 January and 28 March, 1967, the Israeli-Syrian Mixed Armistice Commission received 790 formal Israeli complaints.

for sagacity rather than for decisiveness. He presided over an uneasy coalition delicately responsive to shifts in public opinion—a coalition itself under heavy criticism from the Rafi party founded by Ben-Gurion in 1965, through which such colorful figures as Moshe Dayan, Shimon Peres, and Teddy Kolleck demanded greater drive in government, a more positive foreign policy, and in general a more vigorous and forward-looking 'style'. These demands were attractive to the younger generation of Israelis—'Sabras', born in Israel, justly proud of their achievements, impatient of the older generation of East European immigrants who still so largely dominated the government, less conscious than that generation of Israel's debt to diplomacy and good fortune as well as to her own energy and military force. The last thing Mr Eshkol and his colleagues wanted was a military adventure which would darken the already gloomy economic situation and complicate relations with the Great Powers. But if the Syrians went on with their raids, how was such an adventure to be avoided?

From September 1966 to May 1967 Mr Eshkol and his colleagues—including, a little surprisingly, General Rabin, the Chief of Staff—went on record with a series of increasingly vehement statements threatening Syria with condign punishment if the offensive incidents continued. We have seen how little effect these had as a deterrent to the Syrian government. They may have been more effective in quietening public opinion in Israel itself. What is beyond question is their contribution to the general sense of uneasiness in the Middle East. They came to a climax on 13 May, when Mr Eshkol declared, both in a press conference and in a live broadcast, that Israel would react in her own fashion to the harassing of her borders—"at the place, the time, and in the manner we choose. . . . We shall not recognize the limitations they are trying to impose on our reprisals. If they try to disturb our border, then their border will be disturbed." Furthermore, Israel would react to any attempt to divert the headwaters of the Jordan or to interfere with the freedom of her shipping to the Red Sea. Her armed forces were being overhauled and receiving new equipment, and would be able to fulfil any demands that might be made on them. At the same time General Rabin, speaking to a military audience, was reported as saying that so long as the government continued in power in Damascus the *El Fatah* raids were likely to continue; not an unreasonable appreciation, but one which was seized on by the Arab press and inflated into a threat to overthrow the Ba'athist regime by force.

Mr Eshkol's remarks were unusually strongly worded, but it is doubtful whether Israeli public opinion would have been satisfied with anything less. It was perhaps his domestic audience that he had in mind when he made them: certainly he can hardly have anticipated their effect abroad. The whole Arab world exploded into wrathful activity and the Great Powers suddenly realized that they had on their hands a crisis of major proportions; an imminent conflict between client states to whose survival their own prestige and power were deeply committed.

THE WAR

The crisis ripened, and the war opened at 7:45 on the morning of Monday 5 June, when the Israeli Air Force struck their first blow at the airfields of the UAR.[5] By the end of the week the Israeli armed forces had occupied the Sinai Peninsula, including the eastern bank of the Suez Canal and the western shores of the Tiran Straits; they had conquered the whole West Bank of the Jordan and with it the entire city of Jerusalem; and they had seized the heights from which the Syrian Army had for so long dominated the Upper Jordan Valley. The armies of Egypt and Jordan had been virtually destroyed, and that of Syria routed. There was nothing to stop Israel, if she so wished, from occupying the Suez Canal area, Amman, and Damascus. Military power had not only once again changed the map of the Middle East: it had transformed the pattern of international relations, with consequences which it is still impossible to foresee.

It was only the rapidity of this victory that surprised military specialists in the West. Most of them had assumed that once the war began, superior Israeli training, intelligence, and morale would compensate for any disadvantage in numbers and in strategic position. The total mobilized strength of the Israeli Army was some 275,000 men—and women—organized into 22 infantry brigades, eight armored brigades, and one parachute brigade. In the south, they confronted an Egyptain force in the Sinai Peninsula of about 100,000 men; the total mobilized strength of the Egyptian Army was 240,000 men, of whom about 50,000 were in the Yemen. And in the east, Israel confronted a Jordanian force of 55,000; the Syrian Army, numbering 50,000; and an Iraqi division moving up through Jordan. Time did not permit the engagement of forces promised by other members of the Arab League. All these armies had been provided with up-to-date equip-

[5]Israel time, which is an hour behind Cairo time.

ment by wealthier powers anxious to maintain their influence in the area and find markets for their armament industries. The Israelis had about 800 tanks, including British *Centurions*, American *Super-Shermans*, and M-48 *Pattons*, and French AMX-13s.[6] The Egyptian total was somewhat larger, with a nucleus of Soviet T-54s and T-55s, and many of the older T-34s. They also had a substantial number of tank destroyers. Jordan's 250 tanks were mainly *Pattons* and *Centurions*; the Syrian 400 (only 200 operational) were provided by the Russians; the Iraqis were equipped with both British and Soviet armor. In the air, Syria and Egypt relied on Russian MiG interceptors and fighter-bombers, of which Syria had about 100 and Egypt 400, Egypt possessing also a force of about 80 Tupolev and Ilyushin medium and light bombers which could have done serious damage to Israeli cities. Jordan had almost two dozen British *Hunter* fighter-bombers. The Israeli Air Force was equipped almost completely by the French aircraft industry: *Mirage* III-C and *Super-Mystère* fighters, *Mystère* IV fighter-bombers (about 140 in all), as well as 50 obsolescent *Ouragan* fighter-bombers, 60 *Magister* training aircraft, which could be—and were—used for ground support, and 25 *Vautour* light bombers. If the belligerent powers had been equal in all other respects, Israel would have been quickly crushed.[7]

But they were not equal. In the first place, the military establishments of Israel and of her adversaries reflected the basic difference in the social and economic structure of their societies. The Arab States were still basically agrarian communities with small political and technical élites. Their officer corps, as is usual in developing countries, contained a large proportion of the best-educated and most politically conscious elements in the nation. Many of the officers were skilled professionals, but there appear to have been many others, especially in the Syrian Army, who regarded political fanaticism as a substitute for military expertise and who were concerned more with the army's role in domestic politics than with national defense. Between the officers and their barely literate soldiers a great gap

yawned, betraying the extent to which the Arab revolution remained a middle-class monopoly and showing how little it had as yet affected the peasants from whom the army was still recruited. The Arab soldiers fought with courage but with neither fanaticism nor skill. More important, they had not developed the qualities of intelligence and initiative in their NCOs and junior officers on which the effectiveness of modern armies so largely depends. When plans broke down, as plans invariably do in war, when no orders were available from superior authority, they collapsed; much as the armies of eighteenth-century Europe collapsed before the onslaught of revolutionary France.

Israel, by contrast, was a homogeneous and tightly integrated society, with a high level of general education and a lively realization of the importance of military efficiency to her very survival. She was indeed a garrison state of a kind almost unique in the modern world. Out of a population of 2.75 million, her regular armed forces numbered only some 10,000. The remainder of her standing army, 60,000 strong, consisted of national servicemen who served for two and a half years before being relegated to a reserve from which they were called up for annual training of varying length: two months for officers, five weeks for NCOs, and one month for other ranks. These were minimum periods: the army seldom had difficulty in extending training time if it needed to do so. Not until the age of 45 did this obligation cease, and then the Israeli citizen enrolled in the Civil Defence Force. Service in the technical branches was somewhat longer, and pilots in the Air Force enlisted for a minimum period of five years when they were eighteen years old, and were operational after three years' training. Military units were drawn as far as possible from residents of a single neighborhood, particular members being designated to ensure that mobilization instructions, broadcast in code over the radio, got round to everyone. Test mobilizations were frequent: at any time the reservist might be called out in the middle of the night to report to his unit, and be fully operational by dawn; while vehicles (like horses in Europe before 1914) were as subject to requisition as men.

Finally, the Israeli forces had the great advantage of knowing where they would have to fight. Every yard of their frontiers and the surrounding terrain had been studied from maps, from aerial photographs, and possibly from the reports of clandestine reconnaissance patrols. Terrain conditions were systematically analyzed. Israeli tanks and infantry held exercises over ground as

---

[6] Israel's *Sherman* tanks were relics of the 1940s, while the *Centurions* had long been obsolescent and the *Pattons* were cast-offs from the Bundeswehr. Their excellent performance in this war was unexpected, and was due almost entirely to the high maintenance and training standard of the Israeli Defence Forces.

[7] These figures for armaments are those at present available to the Institute for Strategic Studies. Their accuracy, particularly in relation to the Israeli forces, cannot be guaranteed. Israeli security is excellent, and the precise size of her armed forces remains one of her most closely guarded secrets.

similar as possible to that over which they would have to operate. As a result, when the Sinai campaign began, the Israeli forces showed themselves far more familiar with the conditions of the battlefield than did the Arabs, who had occupied it for so many years.

Full mobilization of the Israeli armed forces produced a quarter of a million men and women: 10 percent of the total population. The strain which this imposed on the economy was obviously considerable, and during the 1967 crisis many Western experts believed that the impossibility of sustaining it for long would force Israel to seek a rapid settlement, whether by capitulation or by war. They exaggerated, much as their predecessors in 1914 had exaggerated in predicting that the strain of mobilization on the European powers would force them to conclude peace within a few weeks. People become very ingenious in wartime, and Israel's small size gave her mobilization arrangements a remarkable degree of flexibility. It certainly suited Israel's policy to have her friends believe that circumstances would compel her, failing their intervention, to force the issue one way or the other, within a few days. Privately, experts in Tel Aviv suggested that the economy even of a fully mobilized Israel would remain viable until the end of the year.

This pattern of military service was very similar to the model created by Prussia in the early nineteenth century; another small country needing to maximize her military resources against her more powerful neighbors. But whereas the Prussian system had resulted in the militarization of society, the Israeli resulted in the civilianization of the army. Israeli troops went about their work with a complete absence of the barrack-square discipline which the forces of other nations consider essential to the maintenance of disciplined obedience. The Israeli Army could do without it, and regarded it as a waste of time. Its units came together to do a particular job, which was examined, discussed, decided upon, and executed in a workmanlike manner. If they fell down on that job, they knew it would mean the end of Israel. Officers maintained their authority not by orthodox discipline but by personal example. Their function was to lead and if necessary to get killed, as many of them did. But if they did get killed, their men knew what to do—and even if they did not, their training and their *esprit de corps* enabled them to keep the initiative. The morale and efficiency of the Israelis was not the product of military indoctrination; it was rooted in their realization that they had escaped massacre once, and were unlikely to get a second chance.

There was another similarity between Israel and Prussia. States surrounded by openly hostile neighbors are strongly tempted to strike first and eliminate one of them, rather than wait until they choose their time to attack concentrically with superior forces. Such preemption is certainly the path of conventional military wisdom, although there may be strong political reasons against it. But Israel's territory was so minute that she could hardly afford to follow the path of political and legal rectitude by allowing her adversaries to strike the first blow and hope to recoup her losses in a counter-attack. Her airfields were too concentrated and vulnerable to a preemptive strike. On the ground she could within a few hours lose Eilat and the Upper Jordan Valley and have her country cut in two. No definition of 'aggression' had yet been devised to suit the circumstances of all States.

At 7:45 A.M. on 5 June, Israeli military authorities announced that Egypt had opened a land and air attack. Egyptian armored forces, they contended, had moved at dawn toward the Negev, and Israeli radar had picked up numerous Egyptian aircraft approaching their borders. Later reports spoke of exceptionally heavy shelling of Israeli outposts from the Gaza Strip. One need neither take these reports at their face value nor dismiss them as complete fabrications. Egyptian air patrols probably were seen on Israeli radar screens. There was certainly shelling from the Gaza Strip. The Israeli command was naturally sensitive to the threat which the Egyptian armored force in Central Sinai posed to Eilat, and its movements that morning may have looked particularly menacing. But it remains very doubtful whether there was anything so unusual about these Egyptian activities as to justify so shattering a riposte. The explanation—and if necessary the justification—for the Israeli offensive must be found in the realm of strategy rather than that of tactics. The decision to launch it was not based entirely on General Gavish's report from Beersheba.

At the moment when the above announcement was being made over Israeli radio stations, Israeli aircraft were opening their attack on nineteen Egyptian airfields in Sinai and the Nile Delta. In the battle to come, complete command of the air was necessary not only to give Israeli forces freedom of movement on the ground—especially in the Sinai Peninsula—but also to free the country of the nagging anxiety about the vulnerability of her cities. The time was well chosen. The Egyptian aircraft had already flown their dawn patrol and were grounded while their pilots had breakfast. They were not lined up in a state of complete unpreparedness wing-to-wing as has sometimes been alleged, but were dispersed at maximum readiness, and sometimes even taxiing for take-off. The Israelis did not even give the Egyptians warning by first attacking their radar stations: they sent their aircraft in low over the sea, or sweeping behind the mountains of the Sinai Peninsula. They probably used electronic deception measures as well. The attacks were so timed as to allow each pilot three passes at his allotted target; then he returned to base, refuelled, and attacked again. With intervals of only ten minutes, attacks against the airfields continued uninterruptedly for three hours. By noon the Egyptian Air Force had lost nearly 300 aircraft, and was of little further use as a fighting force.

The success of this blow was due to two factors alone: intelligence and training. Of the first little can be reliably said, but the results speak for themselves. Among the intelligence services of the world, that of Israel has a high reputation. The effectiveness with which it tapped enemy communications was surprisingly revealed a few days later, when it committed a remarkable breach of security by publishing an intercepted radio-telephone conversation between President Nasser and King Hussein. And the Israeli Air Force had carried out sufficient flights over Egyptian territory over the past few days to have a very exact knowledge of its targets. This knowledge was fed to a group of pilots who had received a gruelling course of training involving a weekly briefing on their targets, a major battle practice every four months, and once a year a full-scale exercise. There had never been any doubt in the minds of the Air Staff that their major function would be a preemptive strike. In the words of General Ezer Weizmann, the creator of the Air Force and its Chief of Staff until 1966, the only place where Israel could be defended was over Cairo. His successor, Brigadier-General Mordecai Hod, brought Weizmann's preparations to completion. He knew that this time, unlike 1956, he could expect no help from the Royal Air Force: but this was a handicap he saw no reason to regret.

Outsiders found it hard to believe that this astonishing and perhaps decisive success did not have some recondite cause, and they interpreted it in predictable ways. American and British commentators looked for a 'secret weapon'—some kind of air-to-ground homing missile which would explain the accuracy with which the Egyptian aircraft were destroyed on the ground. None existed. The only unexpected weapon the Israelis used, and one probably under development by most air forces, was a bomb fitted with retroactive rockets to give it a vertical descent to ensure maximum destruction of runways; a weapon naturally not used against the forward airfields in Sinai, such as El Arish, which the Israelis expected to capture and use themselves. Indeed one of the principal advantages of the Israeli aircraft lay in their comparative *lack* of sophistication, which simplified maintenance and refuelling, making possible the fast turnarounds which enabled pilots to fly six or more sorties in a single day.

This capacity of the Israelis to get the utmost out of their machines and men took their adversaries completely by surprise. It was this that led President Nasser to assert on 9 June, "If we say now that it was a stronger blow than we had expected, we must say at the same time . . . that it was bigger than the potential at his [the enemy's] disposal . . . the enemy was operating with an air force three times stronger than his normal force." This assessment, combined with memories of 1956 and the *a priori* assumption of an 'imperialist-Zionist plot', predisposed the Arabs to believe in Anglo-American intervention.

In fact the reaction in Washington, London, and Moscow to the outbreak of war was one of unanimous consternation. The British feared for their oil supplies; the Russians and Americans dreaded the prospect of escalation to a greater cataclysm still. Mr. Kosygin took the initiative in opening up the 'hot line' from Moscow to Washington with a personal message to President Johnson, in which he is reported as expressing his concern at the turn of events and urging joint action to secure a cease-fire. A cease-fire call from the United Nations was predictable; but in what terms should it be couched? From the beginning the United States and the United Kingdom advocated a cease-fire call without conditions. India, the Soviet Union, and a number of Afro-Asian states held out for a motion condemning Israel and demanding a withdrawal of all her forces to their original positions. They had a case for doing so: the experience of 1948 had shown that cease-fire lines usually harden into frontiers. Had they realized the extent of Israel's initial victories, it is unlikely that they would have prolonged matters as they did; but the delay of the Israeli High Command in issuing a definitive communiqué left them, perhaps designedly, in ignorance. When information about the extent of Egyptian aircraft losses began to leak out during the afternoon of 5 June, the Israeli Army spokesman denounced them as "premature, unclear, and utterly unauthorized." Not until two o'clock the following morning did General

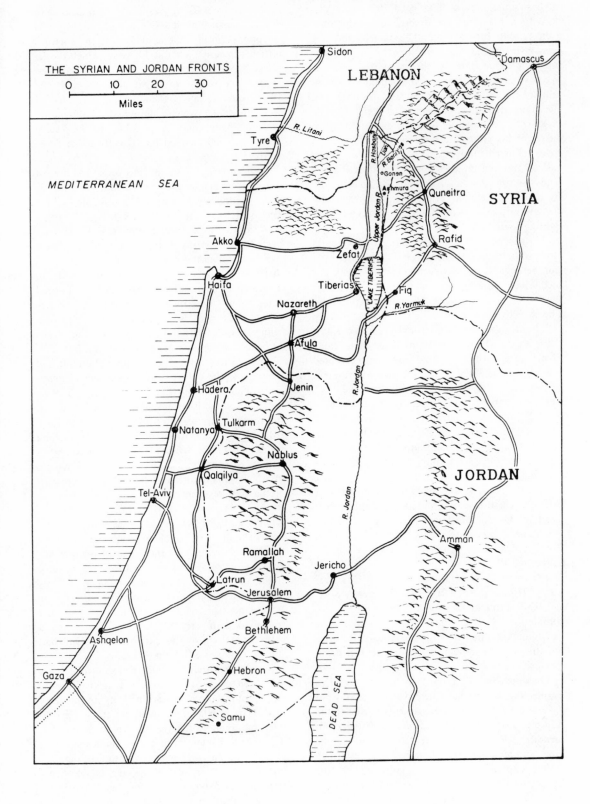

THE SYRIAN AND JORDAN FRONTS

0   10   20   30

Miles

MEDITERRANEAN   SEA

LEBANON

Sidon

Damascus

SYRIA

Tyre

R. Litani

R. Hasbani
R. Banijas
Gonen
Ashmura
Quneitra

Akko

Zefat
Rafid

Haifa

Upper Jordan R.

LAKE TIBERIAS

Tiberias
Fiq
R. Yarmuk

Nazareth

Afula

Hadera
Jenin

R. Jordan

Tulkarm

Natanya

Nablus

Qalqilya

JORDAN

Tel-Aviv

Amman

Ramallah
Jericho

Latrun
Jerusalem

Ashqelon

Bethlehem

Gaza

Hebron

DEAD SEA

Samu

Hod make a statement, and then it was very precise. The Israeli Air Force had destroyed for certain 286 Egyptian, 52 Syrian, 27 Jordanian, and nine Iraqi aircraft, and claimed a further 34 probabilities. They had lost only twenty aircraft themselves.

Even if these figures did not immediately command the credibility they were later shown to deserve, they made it clear that any prolongation of the fighting was likely to be to the Arabs' disadvantage. At the United Nations the Soviet Union reversed its position. On the afternoon of Tuesday 6 June the Security Council unanimously called upon the governments concerned "as a first step to take forthwith all measures for an immediate cease-fire and for a cessation of all military activity in the area."

By that time a great deal had happened in the theater of war. In their broadcasts the Arabs indicated neither surprise nor resentment at the Israeli attack, but rather relief that the expected battle had begun. No Arab nation could now ignore the call to the *jihad*, the Holy War. Lebanon, Syria, Iraq, Kuwait, the Sudan, Algeria, the Yemen, and Jordan all declared war on Israel. Morocco announced the dispatch of troops to the Middle East; Saudi Arabia announced that its troops were entering Jordan; even in moderate Tunisia mobs attacked the embassies of Britain and the United States. Syrian artillery opened fire on Israeli settlements in the Upper Jordan Valley; Syrian aircraft bombed an airfield at Megiddo, attacked a number of villages near Haifa, and claimed to have left the Haifa oil refineries in flames. Iraq claimed, equally without foundation, that her aircraft had raided Tel Aviv. Jordanian artillery did actually begin a spasmodic long-range bombardment of the suburbs of Tel Aviv. At considerably closer range its guns began, at 8:30 A.M., to shell the Jewish quarter of Jerusalem, and soon firing had broken out at many other points on the Israel-Jordan border. There was now military action on three fronts.

The Israeli Air Force reacted against the Syrian and Iraqi air bases, with the results announced by General Hod early next day. Jordan, however, was given a chance. Syria's hostility was accepted as inevitable in Tel Aviv, but it seemed possible that King Hussein might just be able to keep his country out of war. If he did so Israel would be spared a campaign on a second front against an adversary for whose military capacity she had a certain respect. Soon after the Jordanian shelling began, Mr. Eshkol used the UNTSO Headquarters in Jerusalem to pass a message to King Hussein assuring him that if Jordan did not open

serious hostilities Israel would not retaliate. Shortly afterwards he reiterated this assurance, in more general terms, in a statement to the Knesset. King Hussein ignored it. Even if he had known the extent of the damage the UAR Air Force had suffered, it is doubtful whether he could have done anything else. The ink was hardly dry on his pact with the UAR; an Egyptian general was already in command of his armed forces; and his own army commanders were unlikely to have tolerated any hesitation. The shellfire on Jerusalem intensified and extended to the Israeli enclave at Mount Scopus; Jordanian forces occupied UNTSO Headquarters in the old Government House, a vantage point commanding the entire city of Jerusalem; and Jordanian aircraft raided Natanya and the Israeli air base at Kfar Sirkin.

Israel struck back heavily. By midday her air force had finished with the Egyptian airfields and was able to concentrate on the Jordanian bases at Mafraq and Amman, where all Jordan's first-line aircraft were quickly put out of action. On the ground, also, the Israelis swung over to the attack. With so few troops deployed on this front it was essential at least to 'fix' the Jordanian forces until reinforcements could be made available from the main battle in Sinai, and this could be most effectively done by the most ferocious offensive possible. In the words of a senior Israeli military expert, "We were too weak to do anything else." As it was, the Israelis were able, with the one brigade stationed in Jerusalem, an armored brigade of reservists from the coastal plain, a parachute brigade detached from the southern front, and an armored force intended for action against Syria, to drive the Jordanians across the Jordan before operations against Egypt were completed. Even the most optimistic planner would have been unwise to stake much on such an outcome. Its explanation lies almost entirely in Israel's command of the air. On the evening and night of 5 June the Jordanians fought stubbornly and well in the close country and suburbs around Jerusalem and Jenin, inflicting heavy casualties on their assailants. But by Tuesday the 6th movement in daylight was impossible. Israeli aircraft wiped out their convoys and repeatedly attacked their static positions. Israeli armored columns penetrated deeply behind their defenses. By the night of the 6th, the Jordanian Army had collapsed.

The Israeli attacks on Jordan were largely improvised. On the Jerusalem front, while Colonel Amitai's brigade attacked south of the Old City during the afternoon of the 5th and recaptured Government House, the area commander, Brig-

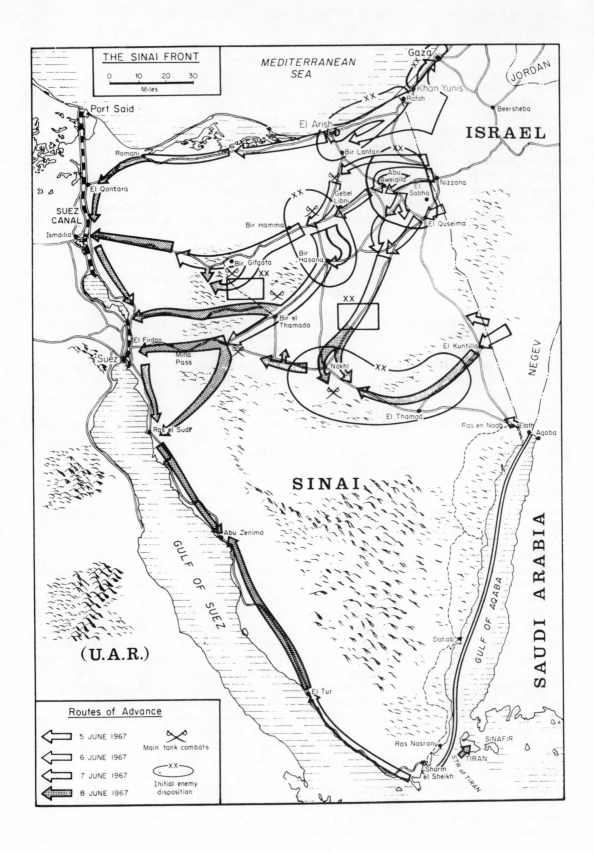

THE SINAI FRONT

0   10   20   30
Miles

MEDITERRANEAN
SEA

Gaza

JORDAN

Khan Yunis
Rafah

Beersheba

El Arish

ISRAEL

Port Said

Romani

Bir Lahfan

Abu
Aweiqila

Nizzana

El Qantara

Gebel
Libni

El Sabha

SUEZ
CANAL

El Quseima

Ismailia

Bir Hamma

Bir Gifgafa

Bir
Hasana

Bir el
Thamada

El Kuntilla

NEGEV

El Firdan

Suez

Mitla
Pass

Nakhl

El Thamad

Ras en Naqb

Elath
Aqaba

Ras el Sudr

SINAI

SAUDI ARABIA

Abu Zenima

GULF OF SUEZ

GULF OF AQABA

(U.A.R.)

El Tur

Dahab

STR. of TIRAN

SINAFIR

Ras Nasrani

TIRAN

Sharm
el Sheikh

Routes of Advance

5 JUNE 1967

Main tank combats

6 JUNE 1967

7 JUNE 1967

8 JUNE 1967

XX

Initial enemy
disposition

adier-General Narkiss, prepared to attack to the north with infantry and armor. His infantry consisted of Colonel Gur's parachute brigade, which had been rushed up from the southern front and most of whose members had never seen the terrain over which they were to fight. Fighting at night in a closely built-up area, against troops defending positions they had been preparing for years, the parachutists had to force their way through to seize the heights which dominated the Old City, from the Sheikh Jarah quarter in the north to the Augusta Victoria Hospital on the Mount of Olives to the east. It was a bloody soldiers' battle in which the Israelis did not have the advantage of surprise and the forces of the Arab Legion opposed to them fought tenaciously. By daybreak on 6 June the Israeli forces had somehow struggled through to Sheikh Jarah and controlled most of the area to the north of the Old City. Meanwhile, to their left, Colonel Ben-Ari's armored force had advanced northward to clear the hills between Jerusalem and Ramallah, frontally attacking heavily fortified positions with excellent fields of fire. By the morning of the 6th it had broken the crust of the Jordanian defenses. In the west, another unit of the brigade had stormed the town of Latrun, which for eighteen years had blocked the road from Jerusalem to Tel Aviv. Both parts of his command converged on Ramallah, and cleared it that night. Next day, Wednesday the 7th, against purely sporadic opposition, Ben-Ari's armor pushed on to Jericho; and later that morning it was on the banks of the Jordan.

Meanwhile in Jerusalem the parachute brigade, fighting throughout the day and night of Tuesday the 6th, had consolidated its hold on the heights to the north-east, while Colonel Amitai's troops cleared the Abu Tor district south of the city in bitter fighting. By the morning of Wednesday the 7th the two Israeli pincers had almost closed round the Old City, and General Dayan ordered them to seize it before the cease-fire agreement reached at the United Nations the previous evening could come into effect. They attacked at 8:30 A.M.; by 2 P.M. the city was in their hands. Dayan himself, Rabin, and Narkiss made their way to the Wailing Wall of the Temple and gazed in silence. The Jews had returned to Jerusalem, after nineteen hundred years.

Meanwhile the rest of the West Bank had fallen into Israeli hands, as a result of the attack launched from the north by the force detached from Brigadier-General Elazar's northern command. Elazar received the order to attack at noon on 5 June, primarily to silence the heavy Jordanian fire on the Israeli positions. The attack which he actually launched at 5 P.M. was rather more ambitious in scope. His objective was the town of Nablus in the very center of the West Bank. He launched his principal attack with a mechanized brigade, supported by tanks, against Jenin, where heavy fighting continued throughout the night. He also launched a feint attack in the Jordan Valley down the right bank of the river, which effectively distracted Jordanian forces from the main thrust. Next day all attempts by the Jordanians to move over the mountain roads, forward or backward, were defeated by the Israeli Air Force, which attacked their convoys with a terrible mixture of high explosive and napalm. By the 7th Jordanian resistance was broken. Elazar's forces joined hands at Nablus with a detachment of Ben-Ari's brigade advancing from the south. Israeli forces stood along the length of the Jordan from Dan to the Dead Sea, while over the bridges poured a stream of terrified Arab refugees, some of them going into exile for the second time in their lives. An Arab population of 900,000, however, including 500,000 Palestinian refugees, remained. It remains to be seen how far the superb success of General Elazar's armored thrust has created for Israel rather more problems than it solved.

While the Israelis were wresting Jerusalem and the West Bank from the Jordanians, the decisive battle of the war was fought in the sands and hills of Sinai. Here the Egyptians had concentrated seven divisions. That in the Gaza Strip, the 20th Division, consisted mainly of the Palestine Liberation Army. The 7th Division lay to the west of it, from the international frontier at Rafah to El Arish. South of the 7th was the 2nd Division, covering the vital road junction at Abu Aweiqila. The 3rd Division was in second line, in the area of Gebel Libni, Bir Hamma, and Bir Hasana. The 6th was stationed in the center of the peninsula on the route from Suez to Eilat, between Nakhl and El Thamad. The principal armored division, the 4th, lay well back, between Bir Gifgafa and Bir el Thamada. Another armored force of something less than divisional strength was said by the Israelis to be moving in Central Sinai in the general direction of Kuntilla—the force which they believed to be threatening the Lower Negev. The 7th and 2nd Divisions were dug into strong positions barring the three roads which led across the Sinai Peninsula to the Canal at El Qantara, Ismailia, and Suez. The Israeli forces had to breach this line and the one behind it held by the 3rd Division, bring the armor to battle, and destroy the fighting force of the Egyptian Army—their first objective. Their second was to seize and hold Sharm-el-Sheikh, where there was a small

Egyptian force; and their third, to provide security for that position, was to clear and occupy the Sinai Peninsula. It was at first an open question whether they should press on to that passage of ill-omen, the Suez Canal.

To achieve these objectives General Gavish had three divisional groups, under Brigadier-Generals Tal, Joffe, and Sharon.[8] Though numerically outnumbered, his forces had an armored strength almost comparable to the Egyptian; and whereas about half the Egyptian tanks were allocated to infantry divisions, the Israeli tank force was concentrated in all-armored units which packed a very considerable punch. The contrast between the two patterns of organization was interesting. The Israeli was that which had brought the Germans their victories in the early years of the Second World War, and which the British had adopted in the Western Desert and, initially, in Normandy. The Egyptians, under Russian tutelage, modelled themselves on the mixed units which were generally adopted in Europe in the latter years of the war, when all-armored units had proved highly vulnerable to resolute infantry armed with antitank weapons. In close country the advantage overwhelmingly lies with mixed units, but in this desert the older formations again proved their worth. It is anyhow doubtful whether the Russians fully appreciated the problems of desert fighting, which they themselves had never had to face. The Egyptians were not trained for the quicksilver mobility of operations without flanks and virtually without supply lines. They sat in ponderous hedgehogs—not unlike the Eighth Army 'Boxes' in front of Tobruk in summer 1942—from which they refused to be drawn. Given their standard of training, this may well have been the wisest course for them to follow.

Gavish attacked at 8:15 A.M. on 5 June. Tal struck in the north against the 7th Division. Sharon, based on Nizzana, attacked the 2nd Division before Abu Aweiqila. Joffe, whose force consisted entirely of reservists (he himself in civil life was head of Israel's Nature Conservancy Board), passed between them, threading his way through sand dunes generally held to be impassable, till at about 4 P.M. he reached the road from Abu Aweiqila to El Arish, where he sat intercepting Egyptian forces moving forward to reinforce their front or, next morning, hurrying rearwards in retreat. Farther south a brigade advanced from Kuntilla, more as a feint to draw Egyptian forces southward than as a serious threat.

Tal attacked in broad daylight, but avoided 7th Division's well-mined front. He divided his forces into two. The brigade on the left wing, like Joffe's force, crossed territory which the Israelis had discovered, by careful tests, to be less impassable than the Egyptians had supposed. They took the Egyptians in the flank, achieving complete surprise, and destroyed, after heavy fighting, a force double their strength. The brigade on the right had a harder time. They had little difficulty in breaking through to the coast at Khan Yunis and cutting off the Palestinians in the Gaza Strip; who were then dealt with by a brigade from General Gavish's reserve. But when they turned west to attack Rafah, they encountered strong prepared positions—fortifications, anti-tank guns, entrenched tanks—manned for the most part by extremely resolute troops. No surprise, no indirect approach was possible. The left-wing brigade, with the divisional reserve, had now come up on their right, and the whole division battered its way grimly forward down the road towards El Arish. By now the air force was available to take part in the ground battle, and air strikes helped to overwhelm the strongest positions.[9] A battalion reached El Arish before midnight; but it was dawn before the last Egyptian stronghold was overcome.

At Abu Aweiqila General Sharon also had a very tough nut to crack: an entrenched position protected by minefields and anti-tank guns, held by four battalions of infantry, six regiments of artillery, and about 90 tanks. He attacked by night—the night of 5 June, which also saw Tal's armor break through to El Arish, Narkiss's parachute troops seize the heights of Sheikh Jarah outside Jerusalem, and Elazar's forces battle their way through Jenin. During the afternoon his infantry and armor closed up to the main Egyptian positions, driving in their outposts.

Flanking forces were sent around the position to north and south, cutting the roads to Quseima, Gebel Libni, and El Arish. Tanks established themselves north-west of the position, with six

---

[8]The largest regular formation in the Israeli Army was the brigade. Larger formations were, like Army Corps in the British Army, created *ad hoc* of whatever combination was suited to the task in hand. Thus General Tal's division contained a preponderance of armor; General Joffe's was entirely armored; General Sharon's was a balanced force of infantry, armor, and parachute troops.

[9]It was afterwards emphasized by General Hod that two-thirds of all sorties flown were 'taking part in the land battle', mostly in striking Egyptian armor and vehicles behind the battle zone. Israeli ground forces had been warned to expect little air cooperation in the earlier phases of operations. But aircraft which could not be used in the main air battle, such as the Fouga *Magister* trainers, were placed at General Gavish's disposal from the very beginning.

artillery regiments on the east, while a parachute battalion was landed by helicopter to attack from the north. At 10:45 P.M. the barrage began, and half an hour later, their objective illuminated by searchlights, the infantry and armor went in to the attack. The battle went on all night. By six o'clock next morning the last resistance had collapsed.

The main Egyptian defences were now shattered. There were still two Egyptian infantry and two armored divisions intact, whereas the Israelis had only two brigades—one in General Joffe's division, one in the south at Kuntilla—which had now been fighting uninterruptedly for twenty-four hours. But the Egyptians now had to conduct a mobile war, of a kind for which they had not been trained, against an enemy who enjoyed complete command of the air and whose morale, always high, was now raised by victory to a pitch of exhilaration at which physical fatigue was almost forgotten. Only these factors can explain the remarkable achievements of the Israeli Defence Force during the next two days.

Much of Tuesday 6 June had to be devoted to consolidation, mopping up, and planning for the next stage. General Gavish's reserve brigade completed the clearing of the Gaza Strip; General Tal's troops smashed the last Egyptian positions south of El Arish at Bir Lahfan, and while a task force set out along the coast road towards the Suez Canal, the rest of his division turned south to make contact with General Joffe's second brigade, which had come up through Abu Aweiqila and was clearing resistance round Gebel Libni. At Gebel Libni, Tal and Joffe laid their plans for the advance. Large Egyptain forces still lay before them, but those forces depended on two roads: one to Ismailia through Bir Hamma and Bir Gifgafa, one to Suez through Bir el Thamada and the Mitla Pass. By a rapid advance these roads could be blocked and the entire Egyptian Army trapped in the desert. Farther south, a thrust by General Sharon could block the retreat of the Egyptian right wing at Nakhl. Speed was essential before the enemy could recover and regroup, and the Israelis wasted no time. The advance began at once and continued through the night.

By the evening of Wednesday 7 June Joffe's leading brigade under Colonel Iska was in position at the eastern end of the Mitla Pass, barring, the road to Suez. Behind them the Pass itself was already blocked by a huge tangle of wrecked vehicles destroyed by the Israeli Air Force. Iska's brigade fought all night against the Egyptian forces bearing down on them, and somehow held their ground until relieved next day by Joffe's

second brigade, which forced its way through the wreckage in the Pass to reach the banks of the Canal at 2 A.M. on the morning of Friday 9 June. Tal and Sharon also successfully blocked their roads; but to reach Bir Gifgafa and Nakhl, respectively, they had to pass through the main forces of the enemy armor. For both this involved thirty-six hours of continuous and confused fighting as the armored forces of both sides streamed in the same direction along the same tracks. Sharon came upon the tanks of an Egyptian armored brigade abandoned intact by their crews. The commander was taken prisoner and explained to his astonished captors that he had been ordered to withdraw but nothing had been said about taking the tanks with him—and that to blow them up would make too much noise. Both at Nakhl and at Gifgafa the Israeli tanks established ambushes which trapped the retreating Egyptians.

Throughout the three days of Tuesday, Wednesday, and Thursday the Israeli Air Force roved the desert at will, where necessary cooperating in the land battle but mainly seeking out and destroying enemy forces wherever they saw them. By Friday morning, when the ceasefire at last came into effect, hardly an Egyptian unit remained intact. The desert was littered with the debris of thousands of vehicles, including over 700 Russian tanks. Egyptian soldiers in tens of thousands, for the most part abandoned by their officers, had cast away arms, equipment, and boots and were hopelessly making their way across the waterless desert in the direction of home. The *jihad* was over. In the course of it, on 7 June, a small force of patrol boats had sailed down the Gulf of Aqaba and, landing unopposed, hoisted the Israeli flag at the Straits of Tiran.

Meanwhile, in New York, Mr. Abba Eban was fighting his country's battles at the Security Council. Although the sympathy of the Western world had not, on the whole, been forfeited by Israel's apparent action in striking the first blow, it was not likely to extend to any blatant violation of a cease-fire resolution by the United Nations. Support from public opinion in the United States, so long as no American involvement was required, was overwhelmingly strong—so strong that Mr. Dean Rusk felt it necessary to soften the statement of one of his officials that the United States was "neutral in thought, word, and deed" by explaining that neutrality was a concept in international law which did not imply indifference. But for Britain, much as she sympathized with the Israeli cause, the prospect of prolonged conflict in the Middle East, with all that this implied for her relations with the Arab world, was intensely disagreeable. The French government, to the fury of most articulate French public opinion, reaffirmed its position of glacial neutrality; while the Soviet Union could only view the humiliation of her clients in the Arab world with alarm and despondency.

The refusal of the Soviet Union to intervene on their behalf, which must have been made clear to the Arab leaders at the very beginning of the conflict, made it the more necessary for her to sponsor their cause at the United Nations; not only to salvage her own reputation with them but to save them from the consequences of their own folly. Dr. Fedorenko found himself in a difficult position. On the one hand he had to get a cease-fire as quickly as possible. On the other he had to read into the record the maximum abuse of Israel's aggression and the iniquity of her supporters in the West. Mr. Eban and Mr. Gideon Raphael, Israel's Permanent Representative at the United Nations, may have consoled themselves for the hours of abuse which they had to endure from Dr. Fedorenko and his Communist and Arab colleagues with the reflection that every hour thus spent was being put to good use by the Israeli High Command.

But it was not in the interests of the Western powers to see the Arabs and their Russian sympathizers reduced to complete despair. Besides, the longer the conflict lasted, the greater was the risk of its spreading. An example of how this might happen occurred on the afternoon of Thursday 8 June, when Israeli aircraft attacked the US Navy vessel USS *Liberty* some 14 nautical miles north of El Arish. The Israelis were able to convince the United States government that the bombing was due to a genuine error of identification, and it seems highly probable that *Liberty*, an electronic intelligence vessel, was monitoring the wireless traffic of both sides. Whatever the facts of the case, this attack led to a reaction in the US Sixth Fleet, whose aircraft flew off to investigate. Realizing that the Russians in their turn might react to this move, a direct explanation was sent over 'the hot line'. The affair in fact was very competently handled; but it must have increased the general anxiety for a cease-fire.

The Security Council, it will be remembered, had already on the afternoon of 6 June called upon the governments concerned "as a first step to take forthwith all measures for an immediate cease-fire and for a cessation of all military activities in the area." Mr. Abba Eban at once informed the Security Council that his country welcomed the cease-fire appeal, but that its im-

plementation "depended on the acceptance and co-operation of the other parties." Syria and Iraq, whose forces were as yet only marginally engaged in the war, rejected the appeal. The UAR remained silent. Only Jordan, whose forces on the West Bank were at their last gasp, responded immediately, but the Israelis were not yet ready to leave her alone. Pointing out that, since the Jordanian Army was under Egyptian command, this decision was of doubtful validity, they continued to fight—in Jerusalem, as we have seen, with redoubled vigor. On 7 June a wrathful Dr. Fedorenko sponsored a more strongly worded motion, adopted unanimously by the Security Council, which "*demand*[*ed*] that the Governments concerned should as a first step cease fire and discontinue all military activities at 20.00 hours GMT on 7 June 1967." This the Israelis accepted. By then the Old City of Jerusalem was securely in their hands.

On the Sinai front, the obstinacy of the UAR government played straight into the hands of Israel. It was not until the evening of Thursday 8 June that their delegate conveyed to the Security Council their acceptance of the cease-fire. By then General Gavish's forces had completed the rout of the Egyptians in Sinai and had only to close up to the Suez Canal. Only Syria now remained.

Up till now the Israeli forces opposite Syria had remained on the defensive, while the Syrians confined themselves to occasional raids in battalion strength and frequent, heavy shelling of the *kibbutzim* in the Jordan Valley below them. It is not clear at what point the Israeli government took the decision to attack Syria, but the decision is not likely to have caused much controversy. Israeli public opinion would have found it difficult to understand or forgive a campaign which, having disposed of Egypt and Jordan, left intact the enemy whose hostility to Israel had been most implacable, whose activities had been directly responsible for the war, and whose forces still dominated one of the most fertile stretches of Israeli land. But the problems of launching an attack were considerable. The Syrian heights above the Upper Jordan Valley are a steep escarpment rising 1,000 feet to the bare plateau which stretches eastwards to Damascus and beyond. The Syrian Army had not only constructed positions from which they could dominate the valley, but also fortified the plateau to a depth of some ten miles with a continuous zone of wire, minefields, trenches, gun emplacements, pillboxes, and tanks. Constructed under Russian direction, it was a masterpiece of defensive fortification, and suitably equipped with artillery, machine-guns, anti-aircraft batteries, and rocket-launchers. Viewing the ground afterwards, it seemed impossible that any army in the world could have taken it, except by a campaign lasting for weeks.

It took the Israelis about twenty-four hours. Their attack was preceded by heavy air attacks which began on the morning of Thursday 8 June and went on all day and all night. There was great pressure to launch the assault that day, before the Syrians could take advantage of the United Nations' demand for a cease-fire, but there were strong reasons against doing so; including the need to bring up forces from other fronts and the value of giving the air barrage time to take effect. As a result the attack was forestalled by a Syrian request for a cease-fire to begin at 3:20 A.M. GMT on Friday 9 June. The Israelis ignored this (as indeed did the Syrian artillery) and attacked at 11:30 that morning. General Elazar struck in the extreme north of the Jordan Valley up the slopes near the Baniyas head waters with a force of infantry, armor, and parachute troops. There was no cover: the way was led by bulldozers carving out tankable tracks under heavy fire. It took three hours and about 700 casualties to gain the crest. At the same time subsidiary attacks were delivered farther down the valley opposite Gonen and Ashmura; and early next morning another mixed force attacked Syria in the far south, tanks and infantry clambering up from the Yarmuk valley, helicopters dropping parachute troops on the escarpment, and moved north-west over the plateau toward Boulmiye and Rafid.

Astonishing as the Israelis' achievement was in getting up onto the escarpment at all, this might have been only the beginning of their task. A considerable part of the Syrian defenses still stretched before them. Yet on Saturday 10 June they had little more to do except advance. After the first few hours of resistance the Syrian troops collapsed and fled. This was not due entirely to the efforts of the Israeli forces; the Syrian government itself took a hand. Early on the Saturday morning Damascus Radio announced the fall of Qnaitra, Syrian Army headquarters and the only major town between the frontier and Damascus. It did so, it has been suggested, in order to strengthen the hand of their representative at the United Nations, who for the past twenty-four hours had been trying to persuade the Security Council to force Israel into accepting the cease-fire. Hearing that their main base had fallen, the Syrian forces panicked. The Israelis were able to walk over positions which might have held them up for weeks. By 2:30 on the afternoon of 10 June

they really were in Qnaitra. Two hours later the cease-fire came into effect.

The third Arab-Israeli War was over. The only prisoners taken by the Israel Defence Force were about 5,500 officers and NCOs. It had inflicted an unknown number of casualties, including perhaps as many as 15,000 killed. It had destroyed or captured 430 combat aircraft and 800 tanks. Its own losses totalled 40 aircraft and just over 3,000 men, of whom 676 were dead. Henceforward there was not likely to be very much difficulty about Israeli rights of passage through the Straits of Tiran.

CONCLUSION

The third Arab-Israeli War is likely to be studied in staff colleges for many years to come. Like the campaigns of the younger Napoleon, the performance of the Israeli Defence Force provided a text-book illustration for all the classical principles of war: speed, surprise, concentration, security, information, the offensive, above all training and morale. Airmen will note with professional approval how the Israeli Air Force was employed, first to gain command of the air by destruction of the enemy air forces, then to take part in the ground battle by interdiction of enemy communications, direct support of ground attacks, and finally pursuit. The flexibility of the administrative and staff system will be examined, and the attention of young officers drawn to the part played by leadership at all levels. Military radicals will observe how the Israelis attained this peak of excellence without the aid of drill-sergeants and the barrack-square. Tacticians will stress the importance they attached, in this as in previous campaigns, to being able to move and fight by night as effectively as they did by day.

Above all it will be seen how Israel observed a principle which appears in few military textbooks but which armed forces neglect at their peril: the Clausewitzian principle of political context, which the British ignored so disastrously in 1956. The Israeli High Command knew that it was not operating in a political vacuum. It worked on the assumption that it would have three days to complete its task before outside pressures compelled a cease-fire. In fact it had four, and needed five. The general disapproval even in the West when Israel ignored the United Nations' cease-fire call and opened her offensive against Syria showed how narrow was the margin on which she had to work. The lesson is clear. So long as there remains a tacit agreement between the super-powers to cooperate in prevent-

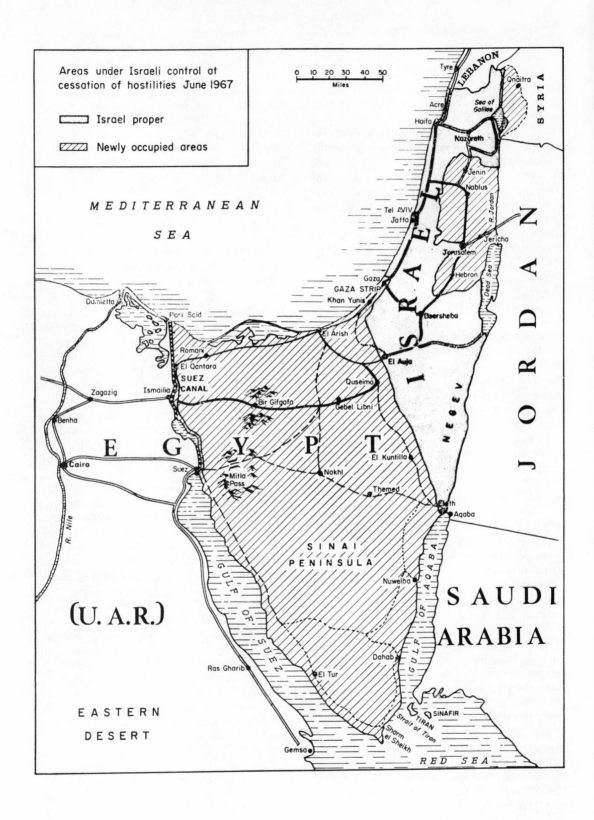

Areas under Israeli control at
cessation of hostilities June 1967

☐ Israel proper

▨ Newly occupied areas

0 10 20 30 40 50
Miles

MEDITERRANEAN

SEA

LEBANON

Tyre

Qnaitra

SYRIA

Acre

Sea of
Galilee

Haifa

Nazareth

Jenin

Nablus

R. Jordan

Tel AVIV

Jaffa

Jericho

Jerusalem

Dead Sea

Hebron

Gaza

GAZA STRIP

Khan Yunis

Beersheba

JORDAN

Damietta

Port Said

El Arish

Romani

El Qantara

El Auja

SUEZ
CANAL

Ismailia

Quseima

Zagazig

Bir Gifgafa

Gebel Libni

NEGEV

Benha

E   G   Y   P   T

El Kuntilla

Cairo

Suez

Nakhl

R. Nile

Mitla
Pass

Themed

Elath

Aqaba

(U.A.R.)

SINAI
PENINSULA

Nuweiba

S A U D I

GULF OF SUEZ

GULF OF AQABA

ARABIA

Dahab

EASTERN

Ras Gharib

El Tur

Strait of Tiran

DESERT

SINAFIR

Sharm
el Sheikh

Gemsa

RED   SEA

ing overt conflicts which threaten international peace and security, a nation using open force to resolve a political problem must do so rapidly, if it is to succeed at all. Once it *has* succeeded, the reluctance of the Great Powers to countenance a second conflict means that it is likely to preserve its gains. The lesson is a sombre one, placing as it does a premium on adventurism and preemption.

Abir, Mordechai, et al. *Conflicts in Africa*. Adelphi Paper No. 93. London: IISS, December 1972.

Allon, Yigal. "The Six Day War." *The Making of Israel's Army*. Bantam Books, pp. 87–106.

Aluko, Olajide. "Ghana and The Nigerian Civil War." *Nigerian Journal of Economic and Social Studies* 12 (November 1970): 341–60.

———. "The Civil War and Nigerian Foreign Policy." *Political Quarterly* 42 (April-June 1971): 177–90.

*Art, Robert J., and Waltz, Kenneth N. (eds.). *The Use of Force*. Boston: Little, Brown, 1971.

Averch, Harvey, and John Kiehler. *Explaining Dissident Success: The Huks in Central Luzon*, P-4753. Santa Monica, Calif.: The RAND Corporation, January 1972.

Azar, Edward E. "Conflict Escalation and Conflict Reduction in an International Crisis: Suez, 1956." *Journal of Conflict Resolution* 16, no. 2 (June 1972): 183–203.

Bayne, E. A. *Economics of a Victor*. New York: American Universities Field Staff, Southwest Asia Series (Israel), vol. 16, no. 2, June 1966.

*Black, Cyril E., and Thornton, Thomas W. *Communism and Revolution*. Princeton, N.J.: Princeton University Press, 1964.

Blechman, Barry. "The Impact of Israel's Reprisals." *Journal of Conflict Resolution* 16, no. 2 (June 1972): 155–81.

Bowett, Derek. "Reprisals Involving Recourse to Armed Force." *American Journal of International Law* 66 (Jan. 1971): 1–36.

*Brown, Neville. "The Nigerian Civil War." *Military Review* (October 1968): 20–31.

*Buchan, Alastair. *War in Modern Society*. New York: Harper & Row, 1968.

*Burns, Arthur Lee, and Heathcote, Nina. *Peace-Keeping by U.N. Forces*. New York: Frederick A. Praeger, 1963.

*Cable, James. *Gunboat Diplomacy*. New York: Frederick A. Praeger, 1971.

*Calder, Angus. *The People's War: Britain, 1939-45*. London: Jonathan Cape, 1969.

Casebook on Insurgency and Revolutionary Warfare. Washington, D.C.: U.S. Dept. of Commerce National Bureau of Standards, 1962, pp. 235–62.

Chalfont, Alun. "The Army and the IRA." *New Statesman* (Apr. 2, 1961), reprinted in *Survival* 13, no. 6 (June 1971): 208–11.

Chick, John D. "Nigeria at War." *Current History* 54, no. 318 (February 1968): 65–71, 212–13.

Cho Soon Sung. "North and South Korea: Stepped Up Aggression and the Search For New Security." *Asian Survey* (January 1969): 29–39.

Churchill, Randolph S., and Churchill, Winston S. *The Six Day War*. London: Penguin Books, 1971.

*Citrin, Jack. *United Nations Peace-Keeping Activities*. Monograph No. 1, 1965–66. Denver: Social Science Foundation, University of Denver, 1966.

Claude, Inis. "UN Use of Military Force." *Journal of Conflict Resolution* 7 (June 1963): 117–29.

Cowley, John. "Australian Military Operations in Vietnam." *RUSI Journal* 113 (Nov. 1968): 310–16.

Crozier, Brian. *The Study of Conflict*. London: Institute for the Study of Conflict, 1970.

Czerwinski, E. J., and Piekalkiewicz, Yaroslaw (eds.). *The Soviet Invasion of Czechoslovakia: Its Effects on Eastern Europe*. New York: Praeger Publishers, 1972.

*Davis, Jack. *Political Violence in Latin America*. Adelphi Paper No. 85. London: The International Institute for Strategic Studies, February 1972.

De La Gorce, Paul-Marie. *The French Army*. New York: George Braziller, 1963.

Dinerstein, H. S. *War and The Soviet Union*. New York: Frederick A. Praeger, 1962.

Dixon, C. Aubrey, and Brunn, Otto Weil. *Communist Guerrilla Warfare*. New York: Frederick A. Praeger, 1957.

Draper, Theodore. *Israel in World Politics: Roots of the Third Arab-Israeli War*. New York: The Viking Press, 1968.

*Dror, Yehezkel. *Crazy States: A Counterconventional Strategic Problem*. Lexington, Mass.: D. C. Heath, 1971.

*Dupree, Louis. *Bangladesh*, Parts I & II. Hanover, N.H.: American University Field Staff, 1972.

Floyd, David. "The Czechoslovak Crisis of 1968." *Brassey's Annual 1969*. Moulton et al. (ed.). New York: Frederick A. Praeger, pp. 33–46.

Forsythe, David P. "UN Peace-keeping and Domestic Instability." *Orbis* 15 (Winter 1972): 1064–84.

Gale, General Sir Richard, GCB, DSO, MC. "Old Problem: New Setting." *RUSI Journal* 117, no. 665 (March 1972): 43–46.

*Galula, David. *Counterinsurgency Warfare*. New York: Frederick A. Praeger, 1964.

Garvey, Jack I. "United Nations Peacekeeping and Host State Consent." *American Journal of International Law* 64 (April 1970): 241–69.

*George, Alexander L. *The Chinese Communist Army in Action*. New York: Columbia University Press, 1967.

Gorlin, Jacques. *Israeli Reprisal Policy and the Limits of U.S. Influence*. Professional Paper No. 22. Washington, D.C.: Center for Naval Analyses, Mar. 23, 1970.

Greene, Fred. "The Indian-Pakistan War and the Asian Power Balance." Mimeo. paper presented at American Political Science Association meeting, Washington, D.C., September 1972.

*Haekkerup, Per. "Scandinavia's Peace-keeping Forces for U.N." *Foreign Affairs* 42 (July 1964): 675–81.

* = Particularly recommended.

*Halperin, Morton H. *Limited War in the Nuclear Age.* New York: John Wiley & Sons, 1963.

*Hanning, Hugh. "Ulster." *Brassey's Annual: 1971.* New York: Praeger Publishers, pp. 147–57.

*Harkabi, Y. *Fedayeen Action and Arab Strategy.* Adelphi Papers No. 53. London: IISS, December 1968.

Harris, H. E. D. "Operation 'Sarsfield': The Irish Army in the Congo, 1960." *Army Quarterly* 83 (Oct. 1961): 62–74.

*Hinton, Harold C. "Conflict on the Ussuri: A Clash of Nationalisms." *Problems of Communism* 20 (Jan.-Apr. 1971): 45–59.

*Hoffman, Stanley. "In Search of a Thread: The UN in the Congo Labyrinth." *International Organization* 16, (Spring 1962): 331–61.

*Horelick, Arnold, and Rush, Myron. *Strategic Power and Soviet Foreign Policy.* Chicago: University of Chicago Press, 1966.

*Howard, Michael, and Hunter, Robert. *Israel and the Arab World: The Crisis of 1967.* Adelphi Paper No. 41. London: IISS, Oct. 1967.

Howe, Russell Warren. "War in Southern Africa." *Foreign Affairs* 48 (October 1969): 150–65.

*Huntington, Samuel. "Patterns of Violence in World Politics." *Patterns of Military Politics.* Edited by Samuel Huntington. New York: The Free Press, 1962, pp. 17–50.

"Intervention in World Politics." *Journal of International Affairs* 22, no. 2 (1968): entire.

James, Allen. *The Politics of Peacekeeping.* New York: Frederick A. Praeger, 1969.

Jenkins, Brian Michael. *Why the North Vietnamese Keep Fighting,* P-4395. Santa Monica, Calif.: The RAND Corporation, August 1970.

———. *The Five Stages of Guerrilla Warfare: Challenge of the 1970's,* P-4670. Santa Monica, Calif.: The RAND Corporation, July 1971.

Jones, David L. "Reprisal, Israeli Style." *Military Review* 50 (August 1970): 91–96.

*Kelly, George A., and Miller, Linda B. *Internal War and International Systems.* Occasional Papers in International Affairs, No. 21, Cambridge, Mass.: Harvard University Center for International Affairs, 1969.

Key, Zachariah. "The UN Force in Korea and Sinai." *International Relations* 2 (April 1961): 168–83.

Kim, Joungwon A. "North Korea's New Offensive." *Foreign Affairs* 48 (October 1969): 166–79.

*Kitson, Frank. *Low Intensity Operations.* Harrisburg, Pa.: Stackpole Books, 1971.

*Knorr, Klaus. *On the Uses of Military Power in the Nuclear Age.* Princeton, N.J.: Princeton University Press, 1966.

Komer, R. W. *The Malayan Emergency in Retrospect: Organization of a Successful Counterinsurgency Effort,* R-957. Santa Monica, Calif.: The RAND Corporation, February 1972.

Laquer, Walter. *The Road to War.* Baltimore, Md.: Penguin Books, 1968.

*Luttwak, Edward. *Coup d'Etat.* New York: Knopf, 1969.

Maier, George. "The Boundary Dispute between Ecuador and Peru." *American Journal of International Law* 63 (Jan. 1969): 28–46.

*Maxwell, Neville. *India's China War.* Garden City, N.Y.: Doubleday, 1972.

*Millar, T. B. "Australia and the War in Vietnam." *Brassey's Annual, 1969.* New York: Frederick A. Praeger, 1969, pp. 226–33.

Morris-Jones, W. H. "Pakistan Post-Mortem and the Roots of Bangladesh." *Political Quarterly* 43 (Apr.-June 1972): 187–200.

*Moss, Robert *Urban Guerrilla Warfare,* Adelphi Paper No. 79. London: IISS, Aug. 1971.

*———. *Urban Guerrillas.* London: Temple Smith Ltd., 1972.

Moulton, J. L. "The Israel-Arab War—June, 1967." *Brassey's Annual, 1967.* New York: Frederick A. Praeger, 1967.

O'Ballance, Edgar. "The India-Pakistan Campaign, 1965." *RUSI Journal* 111, no. 64 (Nov. 66): 330–35.

———. "Israeli Counter-Guerrilla Measures." *RUSI Journal* 117, no. 65 (Mar. 1972): 47–52.

*O'Neill, Bard E. "Israeli Counterinsurgency and the Fedayeen." Mimeo, Air Force Academy, unpublished.

Osanka, Franklin M. (ed.). *Modern Guerrilla Warfare.* New York: Frederick A. Praeger, 1962.

*Paret, Peter, and Shy, John W. *Guerillas in the 1960's.* New York: Frederick A. Praeger, 1962.

*Paul, David W. "Soviet Foreign Policy and the Invasion of Czechoslovakia." *International Studies Quarterly* 15, no. 2 (June 1971): 159–202.

*Quester, George H. *Deterrence before Hiroshima.* New York: John Wiley & Sons, 1966.

*———. *Nuclear Diplomacy.* New York: Dunellen Pub. Co., 1970.

*Remington, Robin Alison. *The Warsaw Pact: Case Studies in Communist Conflict Resolution.* Cambridge, Mass.: MIT Press, 1971.

Reynolds, Robert. "Brazil's Overseas Military Operations." *Military Review* XLVI, no. 11, (Nov. 1966): 85–92.

*Robinson, Thomas W. *The Sino-Soviet Border Dispute: Background, Development, and the March 1969 Clashes,* RM-6171-PR. Santa Monica, Calif.: The RAND Corp., Aug. 1970.

Rosenau, James N. (ed.). *International Aspects of Civil Strife.* Princeton, N.J.: Princeton University Press, 1967.

Schelling, Thomas C. *The Strategy of Conflict.* Cambridge, Mass.: Harvard University Press, 1960.

*———. *Arms and Influence.* New Haven, Conn.: The Yale University Press, 1966.

Schwartz, Walter. "Foreign Powers and the Nigerian War." *Africa Report* 15 (Feb. 1970): 12–14.

*Singer, J. David, and Small, Melvin. *The Wages of War.* New York: John Wiley & Sons, 1972.

*Snyder, Glenn H. *Deterrence and Defense.* Princeton, N.J.: Princeton University Press, 1961.

* = Particularly recommended.

Solomon, David N. "The Soldierly Self and the Peace-Keeping Role: Canadian Officers in Peace-Keeping Forces." Van Doorn, Jacques (ed.)., *Military Profession and Military Regimes.* The Hague: Mouton, 1969.

*Spiegel, Steven L., and Waltz, Kenneth N. (eds.). *Conflict in World Politics.* Cambridge, Mass.: Winthrop Pubs., 1971.

Stegenga, James A. *The United Nations Force in Cyprus.* Columbus, Ohio: Ohio State University Press, 1968.

———. "UN Peacekeeping: The Cyprus Venture." *Journal of Peace Research* 1 (1970): 1–15.

*Thomas, Hugh. *Suez.* New York: Harper & Row, 1967.

*Thompson, Sir Robert. *Defeating Communist Insurgency.* New York: Frederick A. Praeger, 1966.

*———. *Revolutionary War in World Strategy 1945–1969.* New York: Taplinger Pub. Co., 1970.

Tigurd, Pavel. "Czechoslovakia: A Postmortem." *Survey* (Autumn 1969): 133–64.

"United Kingdom's Cross." *Armed Forces Journal International* 110, no. 9 (May 1973): 50–52.

*Vagts, Alfred. *Defense and Diplomacy: The Soldier and the Conduct of Foreign Relations.* New York: Columbia University Press, 1956.

*Werth, Alexander. *Russia at War, 1941–1945.* New York: Avon Books, 1964.

*Whiting, Allen S. *China Crosses the Yalu.* New York: Macmillan, 1960.

*———. "The Use of Force in Foreign Policy by the People's Republic of China." *Annals* 402 (July 1972): 55–66.

Wilson, A. J. "U.N. Peace-Keeping Operations—Some Random Reflections." Moulton et al. (ed.), *Brassey's Annual 1968.* New York: Frederick A. Praeger, pp. 168–76.

Windsor, Philip, and Roberts, Adam. *Czechoslovakia 1968.* New York: Columbia University Press, 1969.

*Wright, Quincy. *A Study of War* (2d ed.). Chicago: University of Chicago Press, 1965.

*Young, Oran R. *The Politics of Force.* Princeton, N.J.: Princeton University Press, 1968.

Young, Peter. "Lessons From the Israel-Arab War of 1967." Moulton et al. (ed.), *Brassey's Annual 1968.* New York: Frederick A. Praeger, pp. 243–51.

*Zelman, Walter A. *Chinese Intervention in the Korean War: A Bilateral Failure of Deterrence,* Security Studies Paper No. 11. Los Angeles: Security Studies Project, UCLA, 1967.

* = Particularly recommended.

CONCLUSION AND BIBLIOGRAPHIC ESSAY

FRANK B. HORTON III

A number of tentative hypotheses about causation in defense policy emerge from the material in this book and a survey of the literature. First we will look at the hypotheses, and follow with a closing word on the literature.

CONCLUSION

Ideally, one would wish to be able to build an empirically falsifiable causal model relating inputs to outputs, and to refine it through a series of tests against available data, in the manner of Hubert Blalock in his *Causal Inferences in Non-experimental Research*.[1] We have by no means gotten that far in this first effort, but we hope that we have at least begun to build the foundation for such an exercise in the future. It might be worthwhile, however, as a heuristic tool, to diagram a very rough causal model that emerges at this point (see Figure 1).

The model suggests a number of tentative hypotheses as elaborations on its framework. First, domestic background affects all the other factors, from the kind of individual recruited into the organizations, to perceptions of the issues, to policy preferences, to choice of action channels and tactics. The focus of this book is on the policy process, and in particular on bureaucratic politics as a causal factor of primary importance in explaining different reactions to similar international situations. Not only is bureaucratic politics a part of domestic background, one that we extract and examine separately, but it is influenced by the other parts. As Michel Crozier makes clear in *The Bureaucratic Phenomenon*,[2] cultural differences can help to explain differences in bureaucratic structure and behavior. As Morton Halperin and others have shown, behavioral differences in bureaucracies can also be explained by differences in their domestic political contexts.[3]

Second, the international environment, while less pervasive in the model than the domestic context, is no less important in explaining defense policy outcomes. Although domestic factors can help to explain differences in approach among states in similar international circumstances, of course international circumstances seldom are the same. Different international circumstances require and produce different outcomes, even among similar states and cultures. In addition, when those international circumstances are similarly compelling, as in Israel today and Switzerland in an earlier era, somewhat similar defense policies result, even in different domestic contexts. Despite the peculiarly Janus-faced nature of defense policy, observed by Samuel Huntington in his article in this book;[4] as Arnold Wolfers has taught us,[5] when one moves from the pole of indifference to the pole of power (as often happens in defense policy), the free play of perceptions, options, and policies to be shaped in the domestic arena is closed off.

But, of course, for most countries, under most circumstances, the national interest does not often emerge as clear and compelling. Both the international and the domestic environments play a part. Most defense issues deal with the international and domestic interests of many organizations and individuals in and outside of the government. They are profoundly affected by the pulling and hauling of these interests in the policy process. The character of every step of that process is crucial: the actors, their interests, their power, the action channels within which the actors choose to attempt to influence policy, their choice of tactics, the character of decisions taken, and the action channels and tactics of implementation, which are often different from but no less important than those used in influencing policy decisions.

---

[1] Hubert Blalock, *Causal Inferences in Non-experimental Research* (Chapel Hill: University of North Carolina Press, 1964).

[2] Michel Crozier, *The Bureaucratic Phenomenon* (Chicago: University of Chicago Press, 1967).

[3] Morton H. Halperin, *Bureaucratic Politics and Foreign Policy* (Washington: The Brookings Institution, forthcoming).

[4] Samuel P. Huntington, "The Two Worlds of Military Policy," pp. 107–12.

[5] Arnold Wolfers, "The Pole of Power and the Pole of Indifference," *Discord and Collaboration* (Baltimore: The Johns Hopkins Press, 1962), pp. 81–102.

The views expressed herein are those of the author and do not necessarily reflect the views of the United States Air Force or the Department of Defense.

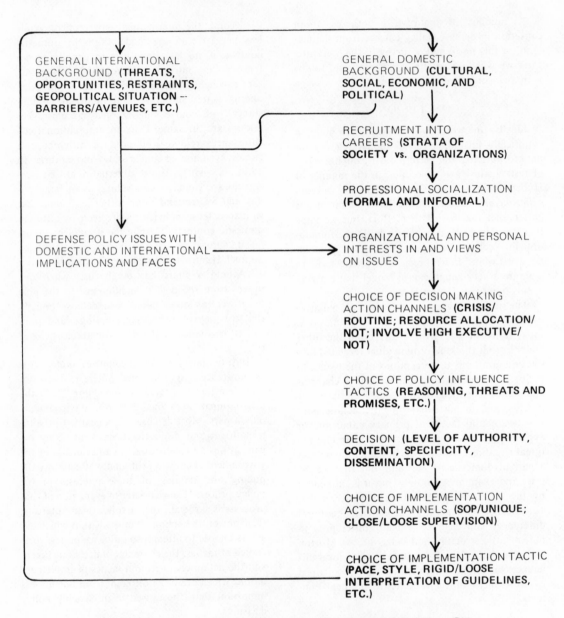

CAUSATION IN COMPARATIVE DEFENSE POLICY

FIGURE 1

While Crozier's point concerning cultural differences in bureaucratic behavior is correct, a few common characteristics stand out. A question was raised in the introduction concerning one crucial sort of bureaucratic behavior, the intervention of the military in politics. In answer, the military always intervenes; differences are a matter of degree. The military is always an actor in the policy process, which, as Roger Hilsman has pointed out, is political.[6] But as to when the military chooses to attempt to control the policy process, the key ingredient seems to be instability in the civilian regime. The threshold for major intervention in politics may be higher for a military organization that has been brought up in a culture and professional socialization process that stress civilian supremacy, but serious instability and chaos will eventually cause nearly any military organization to reach for power. And when they do, they seldom wield it successfully in the long term.

Another common characteristic is that issue areas involving largely routine, day-to-day decisions tend to involve the bureaucracy more, the top decisionmakers less. Organizational routine tends to dominate organizational politics, and both tend to dominate the impact of particular personalities at the top. Such routinized issue areas add up to a large proportion of the totality of defense policy; as such, they cannot be ignored. Policymaking of this sort tends to be resistant to influence from the environments to which it should be responsive. Change is gradual, except for the rare occasion when a top figure takes a serious interest. This sort of decisionmaking characterizes much of the weapons acquisition issue area, many subissues in force posture, a few in the doctrinal area, and a very few—primarily in the area of implementation of larger policy decisions—in the use of force. In Huntington's terms, these tend to be the structural rather than the strategic issues.

Decisions of greater scope are not routinized, and are characterized by the domination of bureaucratic politics and of top personalities over organizational routine. An entirely different set of data would be desirable for making predictions about policy outcomes in issue areas that incorporated decisions of this type. Instead of concentration on organizational SOPs and histories, one would wish to focus on action channels, political histories of the interactions that have taken place within them, and the peculiar predispositions of particular important personalities. Issue areas where this approach would apply would include nearly all of force use, most of military doctrine, many major force posture decisions (in particular the sizing and division of the budget), and a few crucial decisions on weapons acquisition (e.g., to go ahead with full-scale development, to select a source, and to produce, on the more expensive projects). According to Huntington, these issues would tend toward the strategic, but do not exclude the structural.

This is not to say that the nonroutine strategic decisions always precede and provide guidance to the more routine structural decisions. Quite the reverse can be the case, as was demonstrated in the Scheinman piece above.[7] On the question of which comes first, doctrine or force posture, three patterns emerge. The more common one, illustrated by France in the Fourth Republic and the Soviet Union under Stalin, is a series of incremental, routine decisions on force posture taken within the bureaucracy and, at a few crucial points, above it, without the benefit of doctrinal justification. The bureaucracies are concerned with their resources—*new* force posture and weapons acquisition—and their organizational essence—*old* doctrine—and the political leadership is normally not up to challenging this ordering of priorities. This pattern was succeeded in both our historical cases, by a second, less common pattern (in France under De Gaulle and the Soviet Union under Khrushchev) when political leadership saw an opportunity presented by developing force posture, and enforced a major doctrinal change that leap-frogged posture. Such a pattern usually ends after a short period because the goal articulated by the new doctrine is nearly achieved and doctrine and force posture return to routinized processes, as in France, or because the goal is frustrated and then abandoned, with a return to routine, as in the Soviet Union. A third pattern, the least common, is illustrated by Israel, where doctrine and force posture are and remain attuned to each other and to the logic of a day-to-day life-or-death situation. Dire necessity brings and keeps force posture and doctrine together.

The answer to the question of which comes first, force posture or weapons acquisition, also begins to emerge. Two patterns exist. The more common is for force posture to lead weapons acquisition, particularly in times of severe budgetary pressures, as are occurring today in nearly every defense establishment. Ambitious new projects

[6]Roger Hilsman, "Policy-Making in Politics," in James N. Rosenau (ed.), *Foreign Policy and International Politics*, second edition (New York: The Free Press, 1969), pp. 232–38.

[7]Lawrence Sheinman, "The Nuclear Policymaking Process in the Fourth Republic," pp. 140–45.

are being shelved. Changes in weaponry are becoming more conservative than in an earlier postwar era. Yet there are times when the reverse is true, when basic technology provides a new generation of qualitatively different and economically feasible weapons systems, or when an outdated generation of weapons wears out and must be replaced, despite the budget crunch. Either circumstance produces a temporary shift from a quantitative to a qualitative arms race.

One final question from the introduction: What is the relationship of doctrine to force use? As Arnold Horelick observes elsewhere in this volume,[8] doctrine performs a number of functions, only one of which is guidance to forces in actual combat; hence we should not be too surprised to find that doctrine does not always predict accurately the way in which nations actually use their forces. One of the principal reasons for this is the fact that doctrine sometimes fails in the manner warned of by Henry Kissinger—it simply does not anticipate or meet the real challenges.[9] As Squadron Leader Rogerson points out in his section introduction,[10] nations often prepare for the last war, particularly doctrinally, rather than for the next one.

Another important reason for *non sequiturs* between doctrine and force use, nearly as important as the first, is the deterrent function of doctrine. While force posture is a fairly credible signal of intentions, because of the cost involved in producing it, it is a fuzzy signal because it still can be used—or not used—in a number of ways. Official doctrine can serve to strengthen impressions about which way would be chosen; some credibility is retained by official doctrine because of the costs, risks, and difficulties, mainly bureaucratic, of maintaining two sets of doctrine, one for external and one for internal consumption.[11]

Yet some states may be willing to pay the price and struggle with two sets of doctrine. The payoff, especially in the nuclear era, can be great. As George Quester points out in an imaginative essay[12] summarized by Figure 2 below, states with no nuclear weapons, for rational deterrent reasons, even though they know the effects of nuclear weapons, should deemphasize the military and pain-inflicting capacities of nuclear weapons. They should do this in order to partially defuse the deterrent and compellent capacity of those states with nuclear weapons. States with a few nuclear weapons should play up pain-infliction capabilities only, in order to help to equalize the deterrent and compellent effect of their stockpile as compared to others. States on a par with the major nuclear powers should emphasize both qualities of nuclear weapons—reflecting reality as well as their particular rational interests. A state with clear superiority should play up military capabilities only, in a rational attempt to maximize the deterrent and compellent effect of its quantitative advantage.

The last position, and the first and the second (but not the third), are real world cases of "the rationality of irrationality."[13] As Quester points out, both the Soviet Union and China, in their formal announced doctrine, have reflected this rational albeit "unrealistic" doctrinal pattern. Yet it would not be rational for either of them to act in war as if the military or the pain-inflicting capabilities of nuclear weapons were low. Defense becomes at least as important as deterrence. Whether there is a second set of realistic, defensive doctrines in the Soviet Union or China, to be exposed only in wartime, we do not know; they say not. But then, in peacetime, for deterrent purposes, what else could they rationally say?

The questions raised and tentatively answered above could be dealt with in greater detail, and other questions could be raised and addressed, if there were more space here. The editors hope, however, that the reader has been stimulated to further research and analysis.

BIBLIOGRAPHIC ESSAY

If the reader is inclined to look further, there is a fair amount of material available, as indicated by the bibliographies at the end of each of the six sections above. Much of the material, however, is only descriptive, with no attempt, rigorous or otherwise, at explanation. And much of it is centered on a single country, with no attempt at comparative analysis. A great deal remains to be done. But anyone who wishes to do more must, of course, first familiarize himself or herself with the work that is already available.

[8]Arnold Horelick, "Perspectives on the Study of Comparative Military Doctrine," pp. 192–99.

[9]Henry A. Kissinger, "Strategic Doctrine and American Defense Policy," in Kissinger (ed.), *Problems of National Strategy* (New York: Frederick A. Praeger, 1965), p. 9.

[10]See above, pp. 498–500.

[11]See Robert Jervis's unpublished paper, "The Logic and Paradoxes of Signalling in Conflicts," Harvard University, 1967, for an expansion of these ideas.

[12]George H. Quester, "On the Identification of Real and Pretended Communist Military Doctrine," *Journal of Conflict Resolution* 10, no. 2 (June 1966): 172–79.

[13]Many of Thomas C. Schelling's works use this terminology.

	NO NUCLEAR WEAPONS	VERY FEW NUCLEAR WEAPONS	PARITY IN NUCLEAR WEAPONS	SUPERIORITY IN NUCLEAR WEAPONS
MILITARY CAPABILITIES	−	−	+	+
PAIN-INFLICTING CAPABILITIES	−	+	+	−

"+" = PLAY UP CAPABILITIES; "−" = PLAY DOWN

FIGURE 2

There are at least ten major organizations that regularly produce publications in English of considerable interest to the student of comparative defense policy. They are listed with their addresses below:

The Australian National University Center for Strategic and Defence Studies (Canberra Papers) Canberra, A.C.T., 2600, Australia.

The Brookings Institution (U.S. interaction studies, just beginning) 1775 Massachusetts Ave., N.W., Washington, D.C. 20036.

The Institute for Defense Analyses (no longer in the business of comparative defense policy studies, but with several excellent pieces to its credit) 600 Army-Navy Drive, Arlington, Va. 22202.

The International Institute for Strategic Studies (or IISS; see below) 18 Adam St., London WC2 6AL, England.

The International Sociological Association (Military Seminar; see below) c/o Jacques Van Doorn, Department of Sociology, Netherlands Military Academy, Breda, The Netherlands.

The International Studies Association (Military Seminar; see below) 2000 Fifth St. South, Minneapolis, Minn. 55404.

The Inter-University Seminar on Armed Forces and Society (see below) c/o Dept. of Political Science, Loyola Univ. of Chicago, Chicago, Illinois 60611.

The Royal United Services Institute for Defence Studies (or RUSI; see below) Whitehall, London SW1A 2E7, England.

The RAND Corporation (see below) 1700 Main St., Santa Monica, Calif. 90406.

The Stockholm International Peace Research Institute (or SIPRI; see below) 166 Sveavagen, 11346, Stockholm, Sweden.

The IISS is probably the premier institution in the world working in the area, in terms of prestige and the quality and quantity of the work published under its name. The IISS's Adelphi Paper No. 64, *Survey of Strategic Studies* (January 1970), lists the other major strategic institutes worldwide. The annual IISS membership list gives names of significant practitioners and students of comparative defense policy. The IISS, and most of the institutions and individuals it lists, do not stress the military profession or the relationship of the armed forces with society. The institutional and individual membership lists of the Inter-University Seminar and the military seminars of the International Sociological and International Studies Associations, and the seminars themselves, begin to fill this gap. It is interesting to note that the Inter-University Seminar, along with many broader professional societies such as the American Political Science Association, has recently begun to manifest greater interest in the study of comparative defense policy and military institutions, as evidenced in convention panel topics, etc.

For the reader who wants to begin to build a library, the editors would recommend subscriptions to all the IISS publications—the annual *Military Balance* (the most authoritative unclassified accounting of worldwide force postures available), the annual *Strategic Survey* (an authoritative summary of significant strategic events over the past year), the regular Adelphi Papers (monograph-length essays by international experts on a variety of subjects), and the bi-monthly *Survival* (mostly reprints, condensations, and book reviews).

Excellent supplements to *Military Balance* and *Strategic Survey* are the comprehensive bi-annual *Almanac of Military Power*, by T. N. Dupuy and Wendell Blanchard, which covers, for every country in the world, the regional history of the use of force, regional geopolitics, security position, doctrine, structure and process, and alliances, in addition to extensive treatment of force posture; the *SIPRI Yearbook*, which documents large amounts of data relating to arms control and disarmament; the U.S. Arms Control and Disarmament Agency's annual *World Military Expenditures*, containing considerable data on defense budgets; and the very expensive yet indispensable annuals *Jane's All the World's Aircraft, Jane's Fighting Ships,* and *Jane's Weapon Systems*. All the above are listed in the force posture section's bibliography. One other annual of interest, listed under doctrine, is *Brassey's Annual*, a collection of articles of uneven but sometimes excellent quality.

Other organizational publications which should be obtained are those of the RUSI and the RAND Corporation. RUSI's monthly *Journal* has excellent original articles on comparative defense policy by experts, and its special studies are of comparable quality with the IISS's Adelphi Papers. The RAND Corporation has always produced some of the best, most insightful work on Soviet and Chinese defense policies and policy processes available anywhere, to include some truly excellent, mostly classified work by Andrew Marshall (now on the NSC staff) that pioneered the application of organizational process and bureaucratic politics to explaining Soviet defense policy. Marshall's work served as one of the inspirations for this book. RAND's less frequent papers on other countries have become more numerous of late, and have been of uniformly high quality.

A quick review of the books and articles of particular interest from the bibliographies for the six sections is in order. The books treated here are among those indicated in the bibliographies by asterisks as being especially recommended.

In the bibliography on the military profession, which includes books and articles on civil-military relations and the relationship of the military with society, the ground-breaking books by Alfred Vagts (*A History of Militarism*), Samuel Huntington (*The Soldier and the State*), and Morris Janowitz (*The Professional Soldier*) are musts for those who have not read them. They have served as models for much of the work that

has followed, including that in the comparative area. Among the best recent general studies are Bengt Abrahamsson's *Military Professionalism and Political Power*, Morris Janowitz's *The Military and the Political Development of New Nations*, Kurt Lang's *Military Institutions and the Sociology of War*, which contains a lengthy and useful bibliography, and Amos Perlmutter's forthcoming book on military ideology. They are supplemented by a spate of excellent readers, some of them quite expensive, such as Henry Bienen (ed.), *The Military Intervenes* (*not* expensive), which concentrates on developing states; and Morris Janowitz and Jacques van Doorn (eds.), *On Military Ideology* and *On Military Intervention*; Roger Little (ed.), *Handbook of Military Institutions*; Jacques van Doorn (ed.), *Armed Forces and Society*, and his edited *Military Profession and Military Regimes*; M. R. van Gils (ed.), *The Perceived Role of the Military*; and J. N. Wolfe and John Erickson (eds.), *The Armed Services and Society*; all of which concentrate on the developed nations. The reader will note that a large proportion of the above either came out of the Inter-University Seminar and are published by Sage, or are products of the military seminar of the International Sociological Association and are published either by Mouton or Rotterdam, in the Netherlands. A number of individual country studies—the remainder of the books and articles with asterisks—are so noted for their generally applicable insights.

A glance at the relative sizes of bibliographies indicates that much more has been written about the military profession and associated fields than about any of the other five topics covered in this book. The two that have received the least treatment are weapons acquisition and structure and process. Given the somewhat specialized nature of weapons acquisition, the former is not surprising; but the pervasive explanatory power of structure and process makes the latter disappointing. It is in this area that the most work needs to be done. There are certain key writings that provide theoretical underpinnings for the work that remains: Graham Allison's *Essence of Decision*, pulling together the theory of bureaucratic politics with an imaginative and convincing application; Gabriel Almond and G. Bingham Powell's *Comparative Politics: A Developmental Approach*, a landmark study of the functioning of the domestic political system; Michel Crozier's *The Bureaucratic Phenomenon*, demonstrating cultural differences in bureaucratic behavior; Joseph Frankel's *The Making of Foreign Policy*, like many of the works in this section focussing on the related field of comparative foreign policy, but containing insights and approaches applicable to comparative defense policy; Alexander George's *The Operational Code*, expounding on this neglected but promising approach; Morton Halperin's *Bureaucratic Politics and Foreign Policy*, which expands Allison's model of bureaucratic politics; portions of Samuel Huntington's *The Common Defense*; Henry Kissinger's much reprinted "Domestic Structure and Foreign Policy"; Robert Levine's *The Arms Debate*, a unique study of the structure of policy preferences which has general applicability; James N. Rosenau's *The Scientific Study of Foreign Policy*, a collection of essays that spell out Rosenau's formulation of the issue area as an analytical device; T. Alexander Smith's "Toward a Comparative Theory of the Policy Process," which outlines one useful version of issue areas; and the classic work by Richard C. Snyder, H. W. Bruck, and Burton Sapin, *Foreign Policy Decision Making*, listing factors affecting the policy process in nearly *too* great detail. Of the particularly good case studies asterisked in the section bibliography, Michael Brecher's *The Foreign Policy System of Israel* deserves special mention for its excellent and original analytical framework, one applicable to other efforts.

Next to the military profession, more has been written about military doctrine than any other field within comparative defense policy, but most of what has been written, when it attempts any explanation at all, looks only for some *ex post facto* rationale in the external environment. As the papers selected for this book's section on military doctrine make clear, one can fruitfully look further than that. Not much of a general theoretical nature exists. Some of the literature that might have been so classified, such as Schelling's works, will be treated under the topic of the last section, the use of force. The best from the doctrine end-of-section bibliography in the general theoretical vein are: some of Andre Beaufre's work, such as *The Strategy of Action*; Bernard Brodie's *Strategy in the Missile Age*; Alastair Buchan (ed.), *Problems of Modern Strategy*; Edward Meade Earle (ed.), *The Makers of Modern Strategy*; John Erickson (ed.), *The Military-Technical Revolution*; Henry A. Kissinger's commentary and some of the articles in his edited *Problems of National Strategy*; a few articles from *Brassey's Annuals*, and George Quester's article, referred to earlier, "On the Identification of Real and Pretended Communist Military Doctrine," which has broader application than its title implies. Several important national or narrowly comparative works are flagged by the remaining asterisks in the doctrine bibliography.

A great deal has been written in a theoretical vein about force posture and its determinants, but most of it concentrates on one aspect of posture—nuclear weapons—and one category of determinant—the arms race. Other themes are proliferation and recitations of the force mixes of various states. Most of the latter were mentioned above as candidates for the reader's reference library. The better or more significant theoretical or general analytical works include Leonard Beaton's *Must the Bomb Spread?*; Kenneth Boulding's highly imaginative but very abstract *Conflict and Defense*; Hedley Bull's *The Control of the Arms Race*; Abram Chayes's "An Inquiry Into the Workings of Arms Control Agreements," one of the few successful attempts to date to relate an aspect of force posture to bureaucratic politics; Samuel Huntington's original essay on qualitative and quantitative arms races, "Arms Races: Prerequisites and Results"; some of the sections in J. C. Hurewitz's *Middle East Politics*, which critique Huntington and introduce the concept of the two-tiered arms race; Klaus Knorr's two books on the domestic sources of military power, *Military Power and Potential*, and his earlier *The War Potential of Nations*; Martin McGuire's ingenious application of economic interaction models in *Secrecy and the Arms Race*; Lewis Fry Richardson's early work in this vein, *Arms and Insecurity*; Richard N. Rosecrance (ed.), *The Dispersion of Nuclear Weapons*; and Thomas C. Schelling and Morton H. Halperin's *Strategy and Arms Control*, a brilliant and provocative essay linking the two concepts in the title. There are a number of good, workmanlike, but often mostly descriptive, books and essays done on the nuclear and conventional force postures of individual states—as indicated by the asterisks.

Weapons acquisition, as mentioned before, has received relatively little attention as a separate subject in the literature. This is true even of American defense policy. It is primarily the work on American weapons acquisition, however, that provides the theoretical basis for investigations into comparative weapons acquisition, to include the best work done so far on the subject, Ingemar Dorfer's article (above) and new book on System Viggen. The best general material includes the introductory section of Ian Bellany's "Military Aircraft Procurement and the Small State: The Australian Case"; Nigel Calder (ed.), *Unless Peace Comes: A Scientific Forecast of New Weapons*; Geoffrey Kemp, "Arms Traffic and Third World Conflicts"; Amelia Leiss et al., *Arms Transfers to Less Developed Countries*, probably the best book yet available on its subject; Merton J. Peck and Frederic M. Scherer's *The Weapons Acquisition Process: An Economic Analysis*, a major effort and one of the central works in the field; Robert Perry's *European and U.S. Aircraft Development Strategies*; Harvey M. Sapolsky's "The Military/Industrial State in Comparative Perspective," an excellent critique of Arthur Alexander's article in this book; John Stanley and Maurice Pearton, *The International Trade in Arms*; George Thayer, *The War Business*; and Charles Wolf's short but cogent essay, *Economic Impacts of Military Assistance*. If anything, less has been written in the realm of specific country studies in comparative weapons acquisition than in the area of theory. The better of the few that we found are asterisked.

Because the use of force has been treated extensively by students of foreign policy and international politics, a very large literature abounds on the theory of the causes of war and on the decisionmaking processes that precede war. Relatively little has been written, either theoretical or empirical, however, about the other aspects of war raised in the introduction that are interesting and relevant to the study of comparative defense policy. The better theoretical and general treatments of the use of force are Robert J. Art and Kenneth N. Waltz (eds.), *The Use of Force*, which really touches as much on the other topics covered in this book as on the present one; Cyril E. Black and Thomas W. Thornton, *Communism and Revolution*; Alastair Buchan (long director of the IISS), *War in Modern Society*; James Cable, *Gunboat Diplomacy*; Yehezkel Dror, *Crazy States*, a look at deterrence from a different perspective; David Galula's short but important *Counterinsurgency Warfare*; Morton Halperin's *Limited War in the Nuclear Age*, an important work on the structure of modern warfare; Samuel Huntington, "Patterns of Violence in World Politics"; George A. Kelly and Linda B. Miller, *Internal War and International Systems*; Klaus Knorr's *On the Uses of Military Power in the Nuclear Age*; Frank Kitson's *Low Intensity Operations*; Edward Luttwak's imaginative handbook for an all-too-frequent use of force in recent years, *Coup d'Etat*; Robert Moss's excellent comparative studies, mentioned by Squadron Leader Rogerson as an excellent model for others, *Urban Guerrilla Warfare* and *Urban Guerrillas*; Peter Paret and John Shy's *Guerrillas in the 1960's*; George Quester's two books on deterrence, before and after the end of World War II, *Deterrence Before Hiroshima* and *Nuclear Diplomacy*; Thomas Schelling's brilliant and entertaining expositions of limited war, deterrence, and compellence, *The Strategy of Conflict* and *Arms and Influence*; J. David Singer and Melvin Small's recent celebrated quantitative analysis of the causes and results of war, *The Wages of War*; Glenn Snyder's seminal work, *Deterrence and Defense*; Steven L. Spiegel and Kenneth N. Waltz (eds.), *Conflict in World Politics*; Sir Robert Thompson, *Defeating Communist Insurgency*, an influential book by an important adviser on the Vietnam war; Alfred Vagts's *Defense and Diplomacy*, especially the chapters extending deterrence and gunboat diplomacy to the broad history of warfare; Quincy Wright's all-time classic *A Study of War*; and Oran Young's *The Politics of Force*. Many of the case studies the editors found focus on the use of force by the United Nations; Jack Citrin's is particularly good. The good cases on national force use were few and far between—we hope that as attention is drawn to comparative defense policy more will be written.

INDEX